FOOTBALL REGISTER

1985 EDITION

Editors/Football Register
HOWARD BALZER
BARRY SIEGEL

Contributing Editor/Football Register
DAVE SLOAN

President-Chief Executive Officer
RICHARD WATERS

Editor
TOM BARNIDGE

Director of Books and Periodicals
RON SMITH

Published by

The Sporting News

1212 North Lindbergh Boulevard
P.O. Box 56 — St. Louis, MO 63166

Copyright © 1985
The Sporting News Publishing Company
a Times Mirror company

ISBN 0-89204-188-9   ISSN 0071-7258

TABLE
of
CONTENTS

ON THE COVER: Chicago running back Walter Payton became the National Football League's all-time leading rusher last season when he compiled 1,684 yards to bring his career total to 13,309.

Photo by Mitchell B. Reibel

EXPLANATION OF ABBREVIATIONS

AAFC—All America Football Conference. AFL—American Football League. CFL—Canadian Football League. CoFL—Continental Football League. EFL—Eastern Football League. NFL—National Football League. PFLA—Professional Football League of America. USFL—United States Football League. WFL—World Football League.

Att.—Attempts. Avg.—Average. Blk.—Blocked punts. Cmp.—Pass completions. F—Fumbles. FG—Field goals made. FGA—Field goal attempts. G—Games. Gain-Yards gained passing. No.—Number. PC—Passes caught. Pct.—Percentage completed. PI—Passes intercepted. Pts.—Total points scored. TD—Touchdowns. TP—Touchdown passes thrown. XP—Extra points made. XPM—Extra points missed. Yds.—Net yards gained.

Veteran and First-Year Players

*Indicates led league or tied for leadership.

VINCENT STEVEN ABBOTT
(Vince)
Placekicker—Tampa Bay Buccaneers
Born May 31, 1958, at London, England.
Height, 5.11. Weight, 190.
High School—Tsawwassen, Vancouver, Canada, South Delta.
Attended University of Washington and received bachelor of arts degree in accounting
from California State University at Fullerton in 1981.

Signed as free agent by Los Angeles Rams, June 15, 1981.
Released by Los Angeles Rams, August 7, 1981; signed as free agent by San Francisco 49ers, April 20, 1982.
Released by San Francisco 49ers, August 24, 1982; awarded on waivers to Miami Dolphins, August 25, 1982.
Released by Miami Dolphins, August 31, 1982; signed as free agent by Los Angeles Express, November 1, 1982.
Released by Los Angeles Express, February 21, 1984; signed as free agent by Chicago Bears, April 13, 1983.
Released by Chicago Bears, August 21, 1984; signed as free agent by Tampa Bay Buccaneers for 1985, November 9, 1984.

		—————PLACE KICKING—————					
Year	Club	G.	XP.	XPM.	FG.	FGA.	Pts.
1983—Los Angeles USFL...		18	31	3	17	30	82

WALTER AUGUSTUS ABERCROMBIE
Running Back—Pittsburgh Steelers
Born September 26, 1959, at Waco, Tex.
Height, 6.00. Weight, 210.
High School—Waco, Tex., University.
Attended Baylor University.

Selectecd by Pittsburgh in 1st round (12th player selected) of 1982 NFL draft.
On injured reserve with knee injury, September 7 through November 26, 1982; activated, November 27, 1982.

		————RUSHING————				PASS RECEIVING				—TOTAL—		
Year	Club	G.	Att.	Yds.	Avg.	TD.	P.C.	Yds.	Avg.	TD.	TD.	Pts.	F.
1982—Pittsburgh NFL	6	21	100	4.8	2	1	14	14.0	0	2	12	0
1983—Pittsburgh NFL	15	112	446	4.0	4	26	391	15.0	3	7	42	2
1984—Pittsburgh NFL	14	145	610	4.2	1	16	135	8.4	0	1	6	0
Pro Totals—3 Years	35	278	1156	4.2	7	43	540	12.6	3	10	60	2

		KICKOFF RETURNS			
Year	Club	G.	No.	Yds.	Avg.TD.
1982—Pittsburgh NFL	6	7	139	19.9	0
1983—Pittsburgh NFL	15		None		
1984—Pittsburgh NFL	14		None		
Pro Totals—3 Years	35	7	139	19.9	0

Additional pro statistics: Recovered two fumbles, 1982.
Played in AFC Championship Game following 1984 season.

HASSAN ABOULHOSN
Punter—San Francisco 49ers
Born May 15, 1959, at Beirut, Lebanon.
Height, 6.02. Weight, 210.
High School—Temple Hills, Md., Croffland.
Attended Northern Virginia Community College.

Signed as free agent by Washington Redskins, June 10, 1983.
Released by Washington Redskins, July 28, 1983; signed as free agent by Philadelphia Eagles, June 18, 1984.
Released by Philadelphia Eagles, July 25, 1984; signed as free agent by San Francisco 49ers, May 14, 1985.

ROBERT ABRAHAM
Linebacker—Houston Oilers
Born July 13, 1960, at Myrtle Beach, S.C.
Height, 6.01. Weight, 230.
High School—Myrtle Beach, S.C.
Attended North Carolina State University.

Selected by Houston in 3rd round (77th player selected) of 1982 NFL draft.
On injured reserve with broken leg, December 7 through remainder of 1983 season.
Houston NFL, 1982 through 1984.
Games: 1982 (9), 1983 (14), 1984 (16). Total—39.
Pro statistics: Recovered one fumble, 1982; intercepted one pass for no yards, 1983; intercepted one pass for one yard, 1984.

SIDNEY H. ABRAMOWITZ
(Sid)
Offensive Tackle—Seattle Seahawks
Born May 21, 1960, at Culver City, Calif.
Height, 6.06. Weight, 279.
High School—Leavenworth, Kan.
Attended U.S. Air Force Academy and received bachelor of science degree from The University of Tulsa.

Selected by Arizona in 3rd round (36th player selected) of 1983 USFL draft.
Selected by Baltimore in 5th round (113th player selected) of 1983 NFL draft.
Signed by Baltimore Colts, May 25, 1983.
Franchise transferred to Indianapolis, March 31, 1984.
Released by Indianapolis Colts, August 20, 1984; signed as free agent by Seattle Seahawks, October 17, 1984.
Baltimore NFL, 1983; Seattle NFL, 1984.
Games: 1983 (14), 1984 (4). Total—18.

BILL ACKER
Nose Tackle—Buffalo Bills
Born November 7, 1956, at Freer, Tex.
Height, 6.03. Weight, 255.
High School—Freer, Tex.
Received bachelor of science degree in business administration
from University of Texas in 1980.
Brother of Jim Acker, pitcher with Toronto Blue Jays.

Selected by St. Louis in 6th round (142nd player selected) of 1980 NFL draft.
Released by St. Louis Cardinals, October 27, 1981; signed as free agent by Kansas City Chiefs, April 13, 1982.
Released by Kansas City Chiefs, September 6, 1982; re-signed by Chiefs, December 14, 1982.
Released by Kansas City Chiefs, August 29, 1983; awarded on waivers to Cincinnati Bengals, August 30, 1983.
Released by Cincinnati Bengals, September 6, 1983; signed as free agent by Buffalo Bills, September 28, 1983.
Active for 1 game with Cincinnati Bengals in 1983; did not play.
St. Louis NFL, 1980 and 1981; Kansas City NFL, 1982; Cincinnati (0)-Buffalo (11) NFL, 1983; Buffalo NFL, 1984.
Games: 1980 (16), 1981 (8), 1982 (3), 1983 (11), 1984 (15). Total—53.
Pro statistics: Recovered one fumble, 1980.

RICHARD CARL ACKERMAN
(Rick)
Defensive Tackle—Los Angeles Raiders
Born June 16, 1959, at LaGrange, Ill.
Height, 6.04. Weight, 250.
High School—Northbrook, Ill., Glenbard North.
Attended Memphis State University.

Signed as free agent by San Diego Chargers, June 11, 1981.
On injured reserve with neck and elbow injuries, August 25 through entire 1981 season.
Released by San Diego Chargers, November 2, 1984; signed as free agent by Los Angeles Raiders, November 6, 1984.
San Diego NFL, 1982 and 1983; San Diego (9)-Los Angeles Raiders (6) NFL, 1984.
Games: 1982 (9), 1983 (15), 1984 (15). Total—39.
Pro statistics: Recovered two fumbles, 1983.

FREDRICK EARL ACORN
(Fred)
Defensive Back—Tampa Bay Buccaneers
Born March 17, 1961, at Rotan, Tex.
Height, 5.10. Weight, 185.
High School—Rotan, Tex.
Attended University of Texas.

Selected by Houston in 1984 USFL territorial draft.
USFL rights traded with draft choice by Houston Gamblers to Arizona Wranglers for defensive end Cleveland Crosby, February 13, 1984.
Selected by Tampa Bay in 3rd round (57th player selected) of 1984 NFL draft.
Signed by Tampa Bay Buccaneers, July 18, 1984.

		—INTERCEPTIONS—			
Year Club	G.	No.	Yds.	Avg.	TD.
1984—Tampa Bay NFL	16	1	14	14.0	0

JULIUS THOMAS ADAMS
Defensive End—New England Patriots
Born April 26, 1948, at Macon, Ga.
Height, 6.03. Weight, 265.
High School—Macon, Ga., Ballard.
Attended Texas Southern University.

Selected by New England in 2nd round (27th player selected) of 1971 NFL draft.
On injured reserve with fractured shoulder blade, September 8 through remainder of 1978 season.
New England NFL, 1971 through 1984.
Games: 1971 (14), 1972 (11), 1973 (14), 1974 (14), 1975 (9), 1976 (14), 1977 (14), 1978 (1), 1979 (16), 1980 (16), 1981 (16), 1982 (2), 1983 (16), 1984 (16). Total—180.
Pro statistics: Recovered one fumble, 1972, 1973, 1979, 1982 and 1983.

STANLEY EARL ADAMS
(Stan)
Linebacker—Los Angeles Raiders
Born May 22, 1960, at Marion, Ark.
Height, 6.01. Weight, 220.
High School—Marion, Ark.
Attended Memphis State University.

Signed as free agent by Los Angeles Raiders, April 30, 1982.
On injured reserve with sternum injury, September 6 through entire 1982 season.
On injured reserve with knee injury, August 29 through entire 1983 season.
On injured reserve with knee injury, September 28 through remainder of 1984 season.
Los Angeles Raiders NFL, 1984.
Games: 1984 (4).

WILLIS DEAN ADAMS
Wide Receiver—Cleveland Browns
Born August 22, 1956, at Weimar, Tex.
Height, 6.02. Weight, 200.
High School—Schulenburg, Tex.
Attended Navarro Junior College and received bachelor of science degree
in physical education from University of Houston in 1982.

Selected by Cleveland in 1st round (20th player selected) of 1979 NFL draft.
On injured reserve with knee injury, October 22 through remainder of 1981 season.
On inactive list, September 19, 1982.
On injured reserve with knee injury, November 19 through remainder of 1982 season.

| | | ——PASS RECEIVING—— | | | |
Year Club	G.	P.C.	Yds.	Avg.	TD.
1979—Cleveland NFL..............	16	1	6	6.0	0
1980—Cleveland NFL..............	16	8	165	20.6	0
1981—Cleveland NFL..............	7	1	24	24.0	0
1982—Cleveland NFL..............	1		None		
1983—Cleveland NFL..............	16	20	374	18.7	2
1984—Cleveland NFL..............	16	21	261	12.4	0
Pro Totals—6 Years............	72	51	830	16.3	2

Additional pro statistics: Rushed twice for four yards, 1979; fumbled once, 1979, 1983 and 1984; rushed twice for seven yards, 1980; rushed once for two yards and recovered one fumble, 1983.

DAVID IVER AHRENS
Name pronounced AIR-ens.
(Dave)
Linebacker—St. Louis Cardinals
Born December 5, 1958, at Cedar Falls, Iowa.
Height, 6.03. Weight, 230.
High School—Oregon, Wis.
Attended University of Wisconsin.

Selected by St. Louis in 6th round (143rd player selected) of 1981 NFL draft.
St. Louis NFL, 1981 through 1984.
Games: 1981 (16), 1982 (9), 1983 (16), 1984 (16). Total—57.
Pro statistics: Intercepted one pass for 14 yards, 1981; returned one kickoff for five yards and recovered one fumble, 1982; caught one pass for four yards, 1983.

IRA LADOL ALBRIGHT
Fullback-Defensive Tackle—Buffalo Bills
Born January 2, 1959, at Dallas, Tex.
Height, 6.00. Weight, 260.
High School—Dallas, Tex., South Cliff.
Attended Tyler Junior College and Northeastern Oklahoma State University.

Signed by Michigan Panthers, January 24, 1983.
Released by Michigan Panthers, February 27, 1983; re-signed by Panthers, March 1, 1983.
On developmental squad, March 4 through March 13, 1983; activated, March 14, 1983.
On developmental squad, April 21 through May 22, 1983; activated, May 23, 1983.
Selected by Pittsburgh Maulers in 11th round (61st player selected) of USFL expansion draft, September 6, 1983.
On developmental squad, March 29 through April 7, 1984; activated, April 8, 1984.
On developmental squad, April 12 through May 2, 1984; activated, May 3, 1984.
Franchise disbanded, October 25, 1984; not selected in USFL dispersal draft, December 6, 1984.
Signed as free agent by Houston Gamblers, January 21, 1985.
Released by Houston Gamblers, February 11, 1985; signed as free agent by Buffalo Bills, March 20, 1985.
On developmental squad for 6 games with Michigan Panthers in 1983.
On developmental squad for 4 games with Pittsburgh Maulers in 1984.
Michigan USFL, 1983; Pittsburgh USFL, 1984.
Games: 1983 (13), 1984 (14). Total—27.
Pro statistics: Credited with two sacks for six yards and recovered blocked kick in end zone for touchdown, 1983; rushed five times for 15 yards and recovered one fumble, 1984.
Played in USFL Championship Game following 1983 season.

VINCE DENADER ALBRITTON
Safety—Dallas Cowboys
Born July 23, 1962, at Oakland, Calif.
Height, 6.02. Weight, 209.
High School—Oakland, Calif., McClymond.
Attended University of Washington.

Selected by Philadelphia in 16th round (326th player selected) of 1984 USFL draft.
Signed as free agent by Dallas Cowboys, May 3, 1984.
Dallas NFL, 1984.
Games: 1984 (16).
Pro statistics: Recovered two fumbles, 1984.

CHARLES FRED ALEXANDER JR.
Running Back—Cincinnati Bengals
Born July 28, 1957, at Galveston, Tex.
Height, 6.01. Weight, 226.
High School—Galveston, Tex., Ball.
Attended Louisiana State University.
Cousin of Darrin Nelson, running back with Minnesota Vikings; and Kevin Nelson,
running back with Los Angeles Express.

Named as running back on THE SPORTING NEWS College All-America Team, 1978.
Selected by Cincinnati in 1st round (12th player selected) of 1979 NFL draft.

| | | —————RUSHING————— | | | | PASS RECEIVING | | | | —TOTAL— | | |
Year Club	G.	Att.	Yds.	Avg.	TD.	P.C.	Yds.	Avg.	TD.	TD.	Pts.	F.
1979—Cincinnati NFL	16	88	286	3.3	1	11	91	8.3	0	1	6	0
1980—Cincinnati NFL	16	169	702	4.2	2	36	192	5.3	0	2	12	2
1981—Cincinnati NFL	15	98	292	3.0	2	28	262	9.4	1	3	18	0
1982—Cincinnati NFL	9	64	207	3.2	1	14	85	6.1	1	2	12	1
1983—Cincinnati NFL	14	153	523	3.4	3	32	187	5.8	0	3	18	1
1984—Cincinnati NFL	16	132	479	3.6	2	29	203	7.0	0	2	12	2
Pro Totals—6 Years	86	704	2489	3.5	11	150	1020	6.8	2	13	78	6

Additional pro statistics: Recovered one fumble, 1981.
Played in AFC Championship Game following 1981 season.
Played in NFL Championship Game following 1981 season.

DAN LAMARR ALEXANDER
Guard—New York Jets
Born June 17, 1955, at Houston, Tex.
Height, 6.04. Weight, 260.
High School—Houston, Tex., Lamar.
Received degree in law enforcement from Louisiana State University.

Selected by New York Jets in 8th round (200th player selected) of 1977 NFL draft.
New York Jets NFL, 1977 through 1984.
Games: 1977 (14), 1978 (16), 1979 (16), 1980 (16), 1981 (16), 1982 (9), 1983 (16), 1984 (16). Total—119.
Pro statistics: Recovered one fumble, 1978 and 1982.
Played in AFC Championship Game following 1982 season.

LARRY TIMOTHY ALEXANDER
Defensive Tackle—Buffalo Bills
Born November 21, 1959, at Los Angeles, Calif.
Height, 6.02. Weight, 252.
High School—Los Angeles, Calif., Fremont.
Attended Los Angeles Southwest Community College and San Jose State University.

Signed as free agent by San Diego Chargers, July 1, 1982.
Released by San Diego Chargers, August 31, 1982; signed by Oakland Invaders, November 14, 1983.
Released by Oakland Invaders, February 13, 1984; signed as free agent by Hamilton Tiger-Cats, April 27, 1984.
Released by Hamilton Tiger-Cats, June 26, 1984; signed as free agent by Cincinnati Bengals, July 10, 1984.
Released by Cincinnati Bengals, August 13, 1984; signed as free agent by Buffalo Bills, May 10, 1985.

VERNEST RAYNARD ALEXANDER
(Ray)
Wide Receiver—Denver Broncos
Born January 8, 1962, at Miami, Fla.
Height, 6.03. Weight, 177.
High School—Mobile, Ala., John S. Shaw.
Attended Florida A&M University.

Selected by Tampa Bay in 1984 USFL territorial draft.
Signed as free agent by Denver Broncos, May 2, 1984.
Released by Denver Broncos, August 27, 1984; re-signed by Broncos, September 27, 1984.

| | | ——PASS RECEIVING—— | | | |
Year Club	G.	P.C.	Yds.	Avg.	TD.
1984—Denver NFL	8	8	132	16.5	1

RAUL ENRIQUE ALLEGRE
Placekicker—Indianapolis Colts
Born June 15, 1959, at Torreon, Coahuila, Mex.
Height, 5.10. Weight, 165.
High School—Shelton, Wash.
Attended University of Montana and University of Texas.

Signed as free agent by Dallas Cowboys, April 28, 1983.
Traded by Dallas Cowboys to Baltimore Colts for 9th round pick in 1984 draft, August 29, 1983.
Franchise transferred to Indianapolis, March 31, 1984.

		——PLACE KICKING——					
Year	Club	G.	XP.	XPM.	FG.	FGA.	Pts.
1983—Baltimore NFL		16	22	2	30	35	112
1984—Indianapolis NFL		12	14	0	11	18	47
Pro Totals—2 Years		28	36	2	41	53	159

BRIAN G. ALLEN
Wide Receiver—Washington Redskins
Born August 6, 1962, at San Bernardino, Calif.
Height, 6.00. Weight, 180.
High School—Wichita, Kan., Bishop Carroll.
Attended Hutchinson Community College and received degree
in business management from University of Idaho.

Selected by Oklahoma in 15th round (311th player selected) of 1984 USFL draft.
Signed as free agent by Edmonton Eskimos, March 17, 1984.
Released by Edmonton Eskimos, July 7, 1984; signed as free agent by Washington Redskins, July 20, 1984.
On injured reserve with neck injury, August 8 through entire 1984 season.

		——PASS RECEIVING——				
Year	Club	G.	P.C.	Yds.	Avg.	TD.
1984—Edmonton CFL		1	2	10	5.0	0

GARY ALLEN
Running Back—Dallas Cowboys
Born April 23, 1960, at Baldwin Park, Calif.
Height, 5.10. Weight, 179.
High School—Baldwin Park, Calif.
Attended University of Hawaii.
Brother of Doug Allen, rookie wide receiver with New York Jets.

Selected by Houston in 6th round (148th player selected) of 1982 NFL draft.
On commissioner's exempt list, November 19 through November 29, 1982; activated November 30, 1982.
Released by Houston Oilers, August 29, 1983; re-signed by Oilers, August 30, 1983.
Released by Houston Oilers, September 8, 1983; signed as free agent by Dallas Cowboys, September 29, 1983.

			——RUSHING——			PASS RECEIVING				—TOTAL—		
Year	Club	G.	Att.	Yds.	Avg.	TD.	P.C.	Yds.	Avg.	TD.	TD.	Pts.	F.
1982—Houston NFL		7	2	2	1.0	0	2	35	17.5	1	1	6	1
1983—Houston (1)-Dallas (6) NFL		7	1	5	5.0	0		None			1	6	0
1984—Dallas NFL		16		None				None			0	0	2
Pro Totals—3 Years		30	3	7	2.3	0	2	35	17.5	1	2	12	3

			—PUNT RETURNS—				—KICKOFF RET.—			
Year	Club	G.	No.	Yds.	Avg.	TD.	No.	Yds.	Avg.	TD.
1982—Houston NFL		7		None			15	292	19.5	0
1983—Houston (1)-Dallas (6) NFL		7	9	153	17.0	*1	8	178	22.3	0
1984—Dallas NFL		16	54	446	8.3	0	33	666	20.2	0
Pro Totals—3 Years		30	63	599	9.5	1	56	1136	20.3	0

Additional pro statistics: Recovered one fumble, 1984.

LLOYD PATRICK ALLEN
(Known by middle name.)
Cornerback—Houston Oilers
Born August 26, 1961, at Seattle, Wash.
Height, 5.10. Weight, 173.
High School—Seattle, Wash., Garfield.
Attended Utah State University.
Brother of Anthony Allen, wide receiver with Baltimore Stars.

Selected by Washington in 2nd round (27th player selected) of 1984 USFL draft.
Selected by Houston in 4th round (100th player selected) of 1984 NFL draft.
Signed by Houston Oilers, July 18, 1984.

			-INTERCEPTIONS-				—KICKOFF RET.—				—TOTAL—		
Year	Club	G.	No.	Yds.	Avg.	TD.	No.	Yds.	Avg.	TD.	TD.	Pts.	F.
1984—Houston NFL		16	1	2	2.0	0	11	210	19.1	0	0	0	0

MARCUS ALLEN
Running Back—Los Angeles Raiders
Born March 26, 1960, at San Diego, Calif.
Height, 6.02. Weight, 205.
High School—San Diego, Calif., Lincoln.
Attended University of Southern California.
Brother of Damon Allen, rookie quarterback with Edmonton Eskimos.

Named THE SPORTING NEWS NFL Rookie of the Year, 1982.
Heisman Trophy winner, 1981.
Named THE SPORTING NEWS College Player of the Year, 1981.
Named as running back on THE SPORTING NEWS College All-America Team, 1981.
Selected by Los Angeles Raiders in 1st round (10th player selected) of 1982 NFL draft.

			—RUSHING—			PASS RECEIVING				—TOTAL—		
Year Club		G.	Att.	Yds.	Avg. TD.	P.C.	Yds.	Avg.	TD.	TD.	Pts.	F.
1982—Los Angeles Raiders NFL		9	160	697	4.4 *11	38	401	10.6	3	*14	*84	5
1983—Los Angeles Raiders NFL		15	266	1014	3.8 9	68	590	8.7	2	12	72	*14
1984—Los Angeles Raiders NFL		16	275	1168	4.2 13	64	758	11.8	5	*18	108	8
Pro Totals—3 Years		40	701	2879	4.1 33	170	1749	10.3	10	44	264	27

Additional pro statistics: Completed one of four pass attempts for 47 yards and recovered two fumbles, 1982; attempted seven passes with four completions for 111 yards and three touchdowns and recovered two fumbles (including one in end zone for a touchdown), 1983; attempted four passes with one completion for 38 yards and recovered three fumbles, 1984.
Played in AFC Championship Game following 1983 season.
Played in NFL Championship Game following 1983 season.
Played in Pro Bowl (NFL All-Star Game) following 1982 and 1984 seasons.

MARK ALLEN
Tight End—New York Giants
Born April 29, 1960, at Newark, N.J.
Height, 6.04. Weight, 225.
High School—Livingston, N.J.
Attended Montclair State College.

Signed as free agent by Jacksonville Bulls, January 5, 1984.
Released by Jacksonville Bulls, January 12, 1984; signed as free agent by New York Jets, May 4, 1984.
Released by New York Jets, July 23, 1984; signed as free agent by New York Giants, March 21, 1985.

KURT DANIEL ALLERMAN
Linebacker—St. Louis Cardinals
Born August 30, 1955, at Glennridge, N. J.
Height, 6.02. Weight, 232.
High School—Kinnelon, N. J.
Received bachelor of science degree in physical education and recreation from
Penn State University in 1977.

Selected by St. Louis in 3rd round (78th player selected) of 1977 NFL draft.
Released by St. Louis Cardinals, September 2, 1980; signed as free agent by Green Bay Packers, September 24, 1980.
Released by Green Bay Packers, September 6, 1982; claimed on waivers by St. Louis Cardinals, September 8, 1982.
St. Louis NFL, 1977 through 1979 and 1982 through 1984; Green Bay NFL, 1980 and 1981.
Games: 1977 (14), 1978 (15), 1979 (16), 1980 (13), 1981 (16), 1982 (9), 1983 (16), 1984 (16). Total—115.
Pro statistics: Returned two kickoffs for 39 yards, 1977; recovered one fumble for 13 yards, 1978; returned two kickoffs for 16 yards and recovered two fumbles, 1979; recovered one fumble, 1981; returned one kickoff for 11 yards, 1983; recovered one fumble for two yards, 1984.

JOHN MICHAEL ALT
Offensive Tackle—Kansas City Chiefs
Born May 30, 1962, at Stuttgart, West Germany.
Height, 6.07. Weight, 278.
High School—Columbia Heights, Minn.
Attended University of Iowa.

Selected by Oklahoma in 3rd round (46th player selected) of 1984 USFL draft.
Selected by Kansas City in 1st round (21st player selected) of 1984 NFL draft.
Signed by Kansas City Chiefs, July 18, 1984.
Kansas City NFL, 1984.
Games: 1984 (15).

LYLE MARTIN ALZADO
Name pronounced Al-ZAY-doe.
Defensive End—Los Angeles Raiders
Born April 3, 1949, at Brooklyn, N. Y.
Height, 6.03. Weight, 260.
High School—Cedarhurst, N. Y., Lawrence.
Received bachelor of arts degree in special education from Yankton College in 1971.

Named to THE SPORTING NEWS AFC All-Star Team, 1977 and 1978.
Selected by Denver in 4th round (79th player selected) of 1971 NFL draft.

Traded by Denver Broncos to Cleveland Browns for 2nd and 5th round picks in 1980 draft and 3rd round pick in 1981 draft, August 12, 1979.

Traded by Cleveland Browns to Oakland Raiders for 8th round pick in 1982 draft, April 28, 1982.

Franchise transferred to Los Angeles, May 7, 1982.

Denver NFL, 1971 through 1978; Cleveland NFL, 1979 through 1981; Los Angeles Raiders NFL, 1982 through 1984.

Games: 1971 (12), 1972 (14), 1973 (14), 1974 (14), 1975 (14), 1976 (1), 1977 (14), 1978 (16), 1979 (15), 1980 (16), 1981 (15), 1982 (9), 1983 (15), 1984 (16). Total—185.

Pro statistics: Recovered five fumbles for six yards, 1972; recovered one fumble, 1973, 1979, 1981, 1983 and 1984; recovered two fumbles, 1974; recovered three fumbles for 14 yards, 1975; recovered three fumbles for one yard, 1977; credited with one safety, 1978 and 1983; recovered one fumble for seven yards, 1982.

Played in AFC Championship Game following 1977 and 1983 seasons.

Played in NFL Championship Game following 1977 and 1983 seasons.

Played in Pro Bowl (NFL All-Star Game) following 1977 and 1978 seasons.

RICHARD JOHN AMBROSE
(Dick)
Linebacker—Cleveland Browns
Born January 17, 1953, at New Rochelle, N. Y.
Height, 6.00. Weight, 228.
High School—New Rochelle, N. Y., Iona Prep.
Received bachelor of science degree in education research from University of Virginia;
attending law school at Cleveland State University.

Selected by Cleveland in 12th round (290th player selected) of 1975 NFL draft.

On injured reserve with fractured ankle, October 12 through remainder of 1983 season.

On physically unable to perform/reserve with knee injury, August 11 through entire 1984 season.

Cleveland NFL, 1975 through 1983.

Games: 1975 (14), 1976 (10), 1977 (14), 1978 (16), 1979 (15), 1980 (16), 1981 (16), 1982 (9), 1983 (6). Total—116.

Pro statistics: Returned one kickoff for three yards and gained five yards following a lateral on a fumble recovery, 1975; returned one kickoff for 20 yards, 1977; recovered two fumbles, 1977 and 1981; intercepted two passes for 46 yards, 1978; intercepted one pass for no yards, 1979, 1981 and 1982; recovered one fumble for 13 yards, 1979; recovered one fumble, 1975, 1978, 1982 and 1983.

MORTEN ANDERSEN
Placekicker—New Orleans Saints
Born August 19, 1960, at Struer, Denmark.
Height, 6.02. Weight, 206.
High School—Indianapolis, Ind., Davis.
Attended Michigan State University.

Named as placekicker on THE SPORTING NEWS College All-America Team, 1981.

Selected by New Orleans in 4th round (86th player selected) of 1982 NFL draft.

On injured reserve with sprained ankle, September 15 through November 19, 1982; activated, November 20, 1982.

| Year Club | ——PLACE KICKING—— | | | | | |
	G.	XP.	XPM.	FG.	FGA.	Pts.
1982—New Orleans NFL...	8	6	0	2	5	12
1983—New Orleans NFL...	16	37	1	18	23	91
1984—New Orleans NFL...	16	34	0	20	27	94
Pro Totals—3 Years.......	40	77	1	40	55	197

ALFRED ANTHONY ANDERSON
Running Back—Minnesota Vikings
Born August 4, 1961, at Waco, Tex.
Height, 6.01. Weight, 213.
High School—Waco, Tex., Richfield.
Attended Baylor University.

Selected by San Antonio in 1984 USFL territorial draft.

Selected by Minnesota in 3rd round (67th player selected) of 1984 NFL draft.

Signed by Minnesota Vikings, May 18, 1984.

| Year Club | | ——RUSHING—— | | | | PASS RECEIVING | | | | —TOTAL— | | |
	G.	Att.	Yds.	Avg.	TD.	P.C.	Yds.	Avg.	TD.	TD.	Pts.	F.
1984—Minnesota NFL............................	16	201	773	3.8	2	17	102	6.0	1	3	18	8

| Year Club | KICKOFF RETURNS | | | |
	G.	No.	Yds.	Avg.TD.
1984—Minnesota NFL.............	16	30	639	21.3 0

Additional pro statistics: Attempted seven passes with three completions for 95 yards with two touchdowns and one interception and recovered two fumbles, 1984.

BRAD STEWART ANDERSON
Wide Receiver—Chicago Bears
Born January 21, 1961, at Glendale, Ariz.
Height, 6.02. Weight, 196.
High School—Phoenix, Ariz., Alhambra.
Attended Brigham Young University and University of Arizona.

Selected by Arizona in 1984 USFL territorial draft.

Selected by Chicago in 8th round (212th player selected) of 1984 NFL draft.

Signed by Chicago Bears, June 12, 1984.

—PASS RECEIVING—

Year Club	G.	P.C.	Yds.	Avg.	TD.
1984—Chicago NFL	12	3	77	25.7	1

Played in NFC Championship Game following 1984 season.

GARY ALLAN ANDERSON
Placekicker—Pittsburgh Steelers

Born July 16, 1959, at Parys, Orange Free State, South Africa.
Height, 5.11. Weight, 170.
High School—Durban, South Africa, Brettonwood.
Received bachelor of science degree in management and accounting
from Syracuse University in 1982.

Selected by Buffalo in 7th round (171st player selected) of 1982 NFL draft.
Released by Buffalo Bills, September 6, 1982; claimed on waivers by Pittsburgh Steelers, September 7, 1982.

			—PLACE KICKING—			
Year Club	G.	XP.	XPM.	FG.	FGA.	Pts.
1982—Pittsburgh NFL	9	22	0	10	12	52
1983—Pittsburgh NFL	16	38	1	27	31	119
1984—Pittsburgh NFL	16	45	0	24	32	117
Pro Totals—3 Years	41	105	1	61	75	288

Played in AFC Championship Game following 1984 season.
Played in Pro Bowl (NFL All-Star Game) following 1983 season.

KENNETH ALLAN ANDERSON
(Ken)
Quarterback—Cincinnati Bengals

Born February 15, 1949, at Batavia, Ill.
Height, 6.03. Weight, 212.
High School—Batavia, Ill.
Received degree in mathematics from Augustana College and received degree from
Chase Law School at Northern Kentucky University in 1981.

Established NFL records for highest passing efficiency, game (20 or more attempts), 90.91 (20-22), November 10, 1974, against Pittsburgh Steelers; most consecutive seasons leading league in passing (2), 1974 and 1975; most consecutive completions, game (20), January 2, 1983, against Houston Oilers; highest completion percentage, season (70.55), 1982.

Led NFL quarterbacks in passing with 95.9 points in 1974, 94.1 points in 1975, 98.5 points in 1981 and 95.5 points in 1982.

Named THE SPORTING NEWS NFL Player of the Year, 1981.
Named to THE SPORTING NEWS AFC All-Star Team, 1975.
Named to THE SPORTING NEWS NFL All-Star Team, 1981.
Selected by Cincinnati in 3rd round (67th player selected) of 1971 NFL draft.

				—PASSING—						—RUSHING—				—TOTAL—		
Year Club	G.	Att.	Cmp.	Pct.	Gain	T.P.	P.I.	Avg.	Att.	Yds.	Avg.	TD.	TD.	Pts.	F.
1971—Cincinnati NFL	11	131	72	55.0	777	5	4	5.93	22	125	5.7	1	1	6	5
1972—Cincinnati NFL	13	301	171	56.8	1918	7	7	6.37	22	94	4.3	3	3	18	5
1973—Cincinnati NFL	14	329	179	54.4	2428	18	12	7.38	26	97	3.7	0	0	0	5
1974—Cincinnati NFL	13	328	★213	★64.9	★2667	18	10	★8.13	43	314	7.3	2	2	12	3
1975—Cincinnati NFL	13	377	228	60.5	★3169	21	11	8.41	49	188	3.8	2	2	12	4
1976—Cincinnati NFL	14	338	179	53.0	2367	19	14	7.00	31	134	4.3	1	1	6	3
1977—Cincinnati NFL	14	323	166	51.4	2145	11	11	6.64	26	128	4.9	2	2	12	5
1978—Cincinnati NFL	12	319	173	54.2	2219	10	22	6.96	29	167	5.8	1	1	6	8
1979—Cincinnati NFL	15	339	189	55.8	2340	16	10	6.90	28	235	8.4	2	2	12	1
1980—Cincinnati NFL	13	275	166	60.4	1778	6	13	6.47	16	122	7.6	0	0	0	1
1981—Cincinnati NFL	16	479	300	62.6	3754	29	10	7.84	46	320	7.0	1	1	6	5
1982—Cincinnati NFL	9	309	★218	★70.6	2495	12	9	8.07	25	85	3.4	4	4	24	1
1983—Cincinnati NFL	13	297	198	★66.7	2333	12	13	7.86	22	147	6.7	1	1	6	4
1984—Cincinnati NFL	11	275	175	63.6	2107	10	12	7.66	11	64	5.8	0	0	0	1
Pro Totals—14 Years	181	4420	2627	59.4	32497	194	158	7.35	396	2220	5.6	20	20	120	51

Quarterback Rating Points: 1971 (53.4), 1972 (74.1), 1973 (81.5), 1974 (95.9), 1975 (94.1), 1976 (77.0), 1977 (69.8), 1978 (57.8), 1979 (80.9), 1980 (67.1), 1981 (98.5), 1982 (95.5), 1983 (85.6), 1984 (81.0). Total—81.9.

Additional pro statistics: Recovered two fumbles and fumbled five times for minus nine yards, 1971; recovered three fumbles and fumbled five times for minus seven yards, 1973; recovered one fumble, 1974 and 1983; recovered one fumble and fumbled four times for minus four yards, 1975; recovered two fumbles and fumbled five times for minus 13 yards, 1977; recovered three fumbles and fumbled eight times for minus eight yards, 1978; recovered two fumbles, 1980 and 1981; fumbled five times for minus 20 yards, 1981.

Played in AFC Championship Game following 1981 season.
Played in NFL Championship Game following 1981 season.
Played in Pro Bowl (NFL All-Star Game) following 1975, 1981 and 1982 seasons.

—DID YOU KNOW—

That Green Bay's first two plays from scrimmage resulted in Denver scores in an October 15, 1984 contest? Both plays began as fumbles by running backs and ended up as fumble recoveries for touchdowns. In the Packers' next game, October 21 against Seattle, their first offensive play resulted in a 79-yard TD reception by Green Bay's James Lofton.

LAWRENCE ANDREW ANDERSON
(Larry)
Safety—Indianapolis Colts

Born September 25, 1956, at West Monroe, La.
Height, 5.11. Weight, 192.
High School—Monroe, La., Neville.
Received bachelor of science degree in health and physical education
from Louisiana Tech University in 1981.
Cousin of Jerome Barkum, tight end with New York Jets, 1972 through 1983.

Selected by Pittsburgh in 4th round (101st player selected) of 1978 NFL draft.
On injured reserve with knee injury, September 8 through November 14, 1980; activated, November 15, 1980.
Released by Pittsburgh Steelers, September 6, 1982; claimed on waivers by Baltimore Colts, September 8, 1982.
On injured reserve with broken foot, September 28 through November 17, 1983; activated, November 18, 1983.
Franchise transferred to Indianapolis, March 31, 1984.
On injured reserve with ankle injury, October 10 through November 8, 1984; activated, November 9, 1984.

Year Club	G.	No.	Yds.	Avg.	TD.	No.	Yds.	Avg.	TD.	TD.	Pts.	F.
		-PUNT RETURNS-				—KICKOFF RET.—				—TOTAL—		
1978—Pittsburgh NFL	16		None			37	930	25.1	1	1	6	2
1979—Pittsburgh NFL	16		None			34	732	21.5	0	0	0	4
1980—Pittsburgh NFL	4		None			14	379	27.1	0	0	0	0
1981—Pittsburgh NFL	16	20	208	10.4	0	37	825	22.3	0	0	0	0
1982—Baltimore NFL	9	8	54	6.8	0	27	517	19.1	0	0	0	2
1983—Baltimore NFL	9	20	138	6.9	0	18	309	17.2	0	0	0	1
1984—Indianapolis NFL	12	27	182	6.7	0	22	525	23.9	0	0	0	4
Pro Totals—7 Years	82	75	582	7.8	0	189	4217	22.3	1	1	6	13

Additional pro statistics: Intercepted one pass for 19 yards and recovered one fumble, 1979; intercepted one pass for no yards and recovered three fumbles for 41 yards and a touchdown, 1983.
Played in AFC Championship Game following 1978 and 1979 seasons.
Played in NFL Championship Game following 1978 and 1979 seasons.

OTTIS JEROME ANDERSON
(O.J.)
Running Back—St. Louis Cardinals

Born January 19, 1957, at West Palm Beach, Fla.
Height, 6.02. Weight, 220.
High School—West Palm Beach, Fla., Forest Hill.
Attended University of Miami (Fla.).
Step-brother of Mike Taliferro, quarterback at Texas Christian University.

Tied NFL record for most 100-yard games by rookie, season (9), 1979.
Named THE SPORTING NEWS NFL Rookie of the Year, 1979.
Named THE SPORTING NEWS NFC Player of the Year, 1979.
Named to THE SPORTING NEWS NFC All-Star Team, 1979.
Selected by St. Louis in 1st round (8th player selected) of 1979 NFL draft.

Year Club	G.	Att.	Yds.	Avg.	TD.	P.C.	Yds.	Avg.	TD.	TD.	Pts.	F.
		——RUSHING——				PASS RECEIVING				—TOTAL—		
1979—St. Louis NFL	16	331	1605	4.8	8	41	308	7.5	2	10	60	10
1980—St. Louis NFL	16	301	1352	4.5	9	36	308	8.6	0	9	54	5
1981—St. Louis NFL	16	328	1376	4.2	9	51	387	7.6	0	9	54	13
1982—St. Louis NFL	8	145	587	4.0	3	14	106	7.6	0	3	18	2
1983—St. Louis NFL	15	296	1270	4.3	5	54	459	8.5	1	6	36	10
1984—St. Louis NFL	15	289	1174	4.1	6	70	611	8.7	2	8	48	8
Pro Totals—6 Years	86	1690	7364	4.4	40	266	2179	8.2	5	45	270	48

Additional pro statistics: Recovered one fumble, 1979, 1982 and 1984; attempted one pass with no completions, 1979; recovered four fumbles, 1980; recovered three fumbles, 1981 and 1983.
Played in Pro Bowl (NFL All-Star Game) following 1979 and 1980 seasons.

ROGER JOHN ANDERSON
(Known by middle name.)
Linebacker—Green Bay Packers

Born February 14, 1956, at Waukesha, Wis.
Height, 6.03. Weight, 229.
High School—Waukesha, Wis., South.
Received bachelor of arts degree in environmental studies from University
of Michigan in 1978.

Selected by Green Bay in 1st round (26th player selected) of 1978 NFL draft.
On injured reserve with broken arm, December 6 through remainder of 1978 season.
On injured reserve with broken arm, August 28 through October 29, 1979; activated, October 30, 1979.
On injured reserve with broken arm, November 5 through remainder of 1980 season.

Year Club	G.	No.	Yds.	Avg.	TD.	Year Club	G.	No.	Yds.	Avg.	TD.
	——INTERCEPTIONS——						——INTERCEPTIONS——				
1978—Green Bay NFL	13	5	27	5.4	0	1982—Green Bay NFL	9	3	22	7.3	0
1979—Green Bay NFL	7		None			1983—Green Bay NFL	16	5	54	10.8	1
1980—Green Bay NFL	9		None			1984—Green Bay NFL	16	3	24	8.0	0
1981—Green Bay NFL	16	3	12	4.0	0	Pro Totals—7 Years	86	19	139	7.3	1

Additional pro statistics: Recovered one fumble, 1978 through 1980, 1983 and 1984; scored four points, kicking one field goal on one attempt and one extra point on two attempts, 1979; recovered four fumbles for 22 yards, 1981; recovered two fumbles, 1982.

STUART NOEL ANDERSON
Linebacker—Cleveland Browns
Born December 25, 1959, at Mathews, Va.
Height, 6.01. Weight, 224.
High School—Cardinal, Va., Mathews.
Attended University of Virginia.

Selected by Kansas City in 4th round (104th player selected) of 1982 NFL draft.
Released by Kansas City Chiefs, September 6, 1982; signed as free agent by Washington Redskins, December 23, 1982.
On injured reserve with knee injury, January 22, 1983 through remainder of 1982 season playoffs.
USFL rights traded with rights to linebacker Glenn Howard by Washington Federals to Philadelphia Stars for rights to wide receiver Walker Lee and defensive end Ron Estay, October 26, 1982.
Released by Washington Redskins, August 27, 1984; re-signed by Redskins, August 28, 1984.
On injured reserve with groin pull, September 12 through November 21, 1984.
Awarded on procedural waivers to Cleveland Browns, November 23, 1984.
Washington NFL, 1982 and 1983; Washington (2)-Cleveland (4) NFL, 1984.
Games: 1982 (2), 1983 (16), 1984 (6). Total—24.
Pro statistics: Returned one kickoff for seven yards, 1982.
Played in NFC Championship Game following 1983 season.
Played in NFL Championship Game following 1983 season.

JOHN THOMAS ANDREOLI
Linebacker—New England Patriots
Born March 30, 1960, at Jacksonville, N.C.
Height, 6.03. Weight, 232.
High School—Shrewsbury, Mass., St. John's.
Received bachelor of science degree in economics from Holy Cross College.

Signed as free agent by Washington Redskins, May 12, 1982.
Released by Washington Redskins, August 9, 1982.
USFL rights traded with rights to placekicker Brian Snow by Washington Federals to Boston Breakers for rights to placekicker Ron Van Dermeer and defensive back Jim Corcoran, September 9, 1982.
Signed by Boston Breakers, October 12, 1982.
Released by Boston Breakers, February 27, 1983; re-signed by Breakers, May 12, 1983.
On developmental squad, May 20 through May 25, 1983; activated, May 26, 1983.
On developmental squad, June 3 through remainder of 1983 season.
Franchise transferred to New Orleans, October 18, 1983.
Released by New Orleans Breakers, February 23, 1984; signed as free agent by New England Patriots, May 14, 1984.
On injured reserve with elbow injury, July 25 through entire 1984 season.
On developmental squad for 6 games with Boston Breakers in 1983.
Boston USFL, 1983.
Games: 1983 (2).

GEORGE ELDON ANDREWS II
Linebacker—Los Angeles Rams
Born November 28, 1955, at Omaha, Neb.
Height, 6.03. Weight, 221.
High School—Omaha, Neb., Burke
Received bachelor of business administration degree from
University of Nebraska in 1978.

Selected by Los Angeles in 1st round (19th player selected) of 1979 NFL draft.
On injured reserve with knee injury, November 14 through remainder of 1984 season.
Los Angeles Rams NFL, 1979 through 1984.
Games: 1979 (16), 1980 (13), 1981 (15), 1982 (9), 1983 (16), 1984 (11). Total—80.
Pro statistics: Recovered one fumble, 1979, 1980 and 1982; caught one pass for two yards, 1979; intercepted one pass for 22 yards, 1983; recovered four fumbles for nine yards, 1984.
Played in NFC Championship Game following 1979 season.
Played in NFL Championship Game following 1979 season.

THOMAS EDWARD ANDREWS
(Tom)
Offensive Tackle-Center—Chicago Bears
Born January 11, 1962, at Parma, O.
Height, 6.04. Weight, 261.
High School—Parma, O., Padua Franciscian.
Attended University of Louisville.

Selected by Memphis in 6th round (123rd player selected) of 1984 USFL draft.
Selected by Chicago in 4th round (98th player selected) of 1984 NFL draft.
Signed by Chicago Bears, July 2, 1984.
Chicago NFL, 1984.
Games: 1984 (7).
Played in NFC Championship Game following 1984 season.

WILLIAM L. ANDREWS
Running Back—Atlanta Falcons
Born December 25, 1955, at Thomasville, Ga.
Height, 6.00. Weight, 213.
High School—Thomasville, Ga.
Attended Auburn University

Tied NFL record for most seasons, 2,000 yards rushing and receiving combined (2).
Named to THE SPORTING NEWS NFL All-Star Team, 1983.
Selected by Atlanta in 3rd round (79th player selected) of 1979 NFL draft.
On injured reserve with knee injury, August 24 through entire 1984 season.

Year Club	G.	Att.	Yds.	Avg.	TD.	P.C.	Yds.	Avg.	TD.	TD.	Pts.	F.
		——RUSHING——				PASS RECEIVING				—TOTAL—		
1979—Atlanta NFL	15	239	1023	4.3	3	39	309	7.9	2	5	30	5
1980—Atlanta NFL	16	265	1308	4.9	4	51	456	8.9	1	5	30	6
1981—Atlanta NFL	16	289	1301	4.5	10	81	735	9.1	2	12	72	12
1982—Atlanta NFL	9	139	573	4.1	5	42	503	12.0	2	7	42	1
1983—Atlanta NFL	16	331	1567	4.7	7	59	609	10.3	4	11	66	6
Pro Totals—5 Years	72	1263	5772	4.6	29	272	2612	9.6	11	40	240	30

Additional pro statistics: Recovered one fumble, 1979 and 1982; recovered two fumbles, 1980 and 1983; attempted one pass with no completions, 1983.
Played in Pro Bowl (NFL All-Star Game) following 1980 through 1983 seasons.

TYRONE ANTHONY
Running Back—New Orleans Saints
Born March 3, 1962, at Winston-Salem, N.C.
Height, 5.11. Weight, 212.
High School—Clemmons, N.C., West Forsythe.
Attended University of North Carolina.

Selected by Philadelphia in 1984 USFL territorial draft.
Selected by New Orleans in 3rd round (69th player selected) of 1984 NFL draft.
Signed by New Orleans Saints, June 26, 1984.

Year Club	G.	Att.	Yds.	Avg.	TD.	P.C.	Yds.	Avg.	TD.	TD.	Pts.	F.
		——RUSHING——				PASS RECEIVING				—TOTAL—		
1984—New Orleans NFL	15	20	105	5.3	1	12	113	9.4	0	1	6	1

Year Club	G.	No.	Yds.	Avg.	TD.
		KICKOFF RETURNS			
1984—New Orleans NFL	15	22	490	22.3	0

Additional pro statistics: Recovered one fumble, 1984.

HASSON ARBUBAKRR
Name pronounced Ha-SAWH AH-boo-bah-kah.
Defensive End—Minnesota Vikings
Born December 9, 1960, at Newark, N.J.
Height, 6.04. Weight, 250.
High School—Newark, N.J., Weequachic.
Attended Pasadena City College and Texas Tech University.

Selected by Denver in 1983 USFL territorial draft.
Selected by Tampa Bay in 9th round (238th player selected) of 1983 NFL draft.
Signed by Tampa Bay Buccaneers, May 20, 1983.
Released by Tampa Bay Buccaneers, August 27, 1984; signed as free agent by Minnesota Vikings, November 23, 1984.
Tampa Bay NFL, 1983; Minnesota NFL, 1984.
Games: 1983 (16), 1984 (4). Total—20.

DAVID ARCHER
(Dave)
Quarterback—Atlanta Falcons
Born February 15, 1962, at Fayetteville, N.C.
Height, 6.02. Weight, 203.
High School—Soda Springs, Ida.
Attended Snow College and Iowa State University.

Selected by Denver in 9th round (171st player selected) of 1984 USFL draft.
Signed as free agent by Atlanta Falcons, May 2, 1984.

Year Club	G.	Att.	Cmp.	Pct.	Gain	T.P.	P.I.	Avg.	Att.	Yds.	Avg.	TD.	TD.	Pts.	F.
		——PASSING——							——RUSHING——				—TOTAL—		
1984—Atlanta NFL	2	18	11	61.1	181	1	1	10.06	6	38	6.3	0	0	0	1

Quarterback Rating Points: 1984 (90.3).

—DID YOU KNOW—
That Denver's Tony Lilly was a national Punt, Pass and Kick champion as an eighth-grader?

BILLY ARD
Guard—New York Giants
Born March 12, 1959, at East Orange, N.J.
Height, 6.03. Weight, 250.
High School—Watchung, N.J.
Attended Wake Forest University.
Brother of Pat Ard, defensive end at Boston College.

Named as guard on THE SPORTING NEWS College All-America Team, 1980.
Selected by New York Giants in 8th round (221st player selected) of 1981 NFL draft.
On injured reserve with knee injury, December 11 through remainder of 1984 season.
New York Giants NFL, 1981 through 1984.
Games: 1981 (13), 1982 (9), 1983 (16), 1984 (15). Total—53.
Pro statistics: Recovered one fumble, 1981.

CHRIS ALAN ARENDT
Defensive End—Dallas Cowboys
Born May 13, 1961, at Gettysburg, Pa.
Height, 6.05. Weight, 260.
High School—New Oxford, Pa.
Received bachelor of arts degree in history from Duke University in 1983.

Signed as free agent by Denver Broncos, April 28, 1983.
Released by Denver Broncos, August 22, 1983; signed by Jacksonville Bulls, October 6, 1983.
Released by Jacksonville Bulls, January 23, 1984; signed as free agent by Dallas Cowboys, March 22, 1984.
On injured reserve with elbow injury, August 14 through entire 1984 season.

OBED CHUKWUMA ARIRI
Placekicker—Tampa Bay Buccaneers
Born April 7, 1956, at Owerri, Nigeria.
Height, 5.08. Weight, 165.
High School—Owerri, Nigeria, Holy Ghost College.
Received bachelor of science degree in industrial management and economics
from Clemson University in 1980.

Selected by Baltimore in 7th round (178th player selected) of 1981 NFL draft.
Released by Baltimore Colts, August 31, 1981; signed as free agent by Buffalo Bills, April 15, 1982.
Released by Buffalo Bills, August 23, 1982; signed by Washington Federals, October 27, 1982.
Released by Washington Federals, March 28, 1983; signed as free agent by New Jersey Generals, November 17, 1983.
Released by New Jersey Generals, February 13, 1984; signed as free agent by Tampa Bay Buccaneers, April 25, 1984.
Released by Tampa Bay Buccaneers, August 22, 1984; re-signed by Buccaneers, August 28, 1984.

Year Club	——PLACE KICKING——					
	G.	XP.	XPM.	FG.	FGA.	Pts.
1983—Washington USFL...	4	3	2	3	7	12
1984—Tampa Bay NFL	16	38	2	19	26	95
Pro Totals—2 Years.......	20	41	4	22	33	107

ADGER ARMSTRONG
Running Back—Tampa Bay Buccaneers
Born June 21, 1957, at Houston, Tex.
Height, 6.00. Weight, 225.
High School—Houston, Tex., Cyfair and Jersey Village.
Attended Texas A&M University.

Signed as free agent by Dallas Cowboys, May, 1979.
Released by Dallas Cowboys, July 30, 1979; signed as free agent by Houston Oilers, May 23, 1980.
Released by Houston Oilers, September 1, 1980; re-signed by Oilers, September 2, 1980.
On injured reserve with knee injury, September 7 through November 18, 1982; activated, November 19, 1982.
Released by Houston Oilers, August 29, 1983; signed as free agent by Tampa Bay Buccaneers, October 5, 1983.

Year Club		——RUSHING——				PASS RECEIVING				—TOTAL—		
	G.	Att.	Yds.	Avg.	TD.	P.C.	Yds.	Avg.	TD.	TD.	Pts.	F.
1980—Houston NFL.............	16		None				None			0	0	0
1981—Houston NFL.............	16	31	146	4.7	0	29	278	9.6	1	1	6	2
1982—Houston NFL.............	6	8	15	1.9	0	12	75	6.3	0	0	0	0
1983—Tampa Bay NFL.........	11	7	30	4.3	0	15	173	11.5	2	2	12	0
1984—Tampa Bay NFL.........	15	10	34	3.4	2	22	180	8.2	3	5	30	1
Pro Totals—5 Years...........	64	56	225	4.0	2	78	706	9.1	6	8	48	3

Additional pro statistics: Returned three kickoffs for 36 yards, 1981; returned one kickoff for 10 yards, 1983; recovered one fumble, 1983 and 1984.

HARVEY LEE ARMSTRONG
Nose Tackle—Philadelphia Eagles
Born December 29, 1959, at Houston, Tex.
Height, 6.02. Weight, 265.
High School—Houston, Tex., Kashmere.
Attended Southern Methodist University.

Selected by Philadelphia in 7th round (190th player selected) of 1982 NFL draft.

Philadelphia NFL, 1982 through 1984.
Games: 1982 (8), 1983 (16), 1984 (16). Total—40.
Pro statistics: Recovered two fumbles, 1983.

TRON ORTEGA ARMSTRONG
Wide Receiver—New York Jets
Born August 18, 1961, at St. Petersburg, Fla.
Height, 6.02. Weight, 200.
High School—St. Petersburg, Fla., Lakewood.
Attended Eastern Kentucky University.
Cousin of James Lofton, wide receiver with Green Bay Packers.

Selected by Chicago in 3rd round (48th player selected) of 1984 USFL draft.
Selected by New York Jets in 5th round (122nd player selected) of 1984 NFL draft.
Signed by New York Jets, June 6, 1984.
On injured reserve with leg injury, August 1 through entire 1984 season.

JAMES EDWARD ARNOLD
(Jim)
Punter—Kansas City Chiefs
Born January 31, 1961, at Dalton, Ga.
Height, 6.02. Weight, 212.
High School—Dalton, Ga.
Attended Vanderbilt University.

Named as punter on THE SPORTING NEWS College All-America Team, 1982.
Led NFL in punting yards with 4,397 in 1984.
Selected by Kansas City in 5th round (119th player selected) of 1983 NFL draft.

Year Club	G.	No.	Avg.	Blk.
		PUNTING		
1983—Kansas City NFL	16	93	39.9	0
1984—Kansas City NFL	16	*98	*44.9	0
Pro Totals—2 Years	32	191	42.4	0

Additional pro statistics: Rushed once for no yards, recovered two fumbles and fumbled once for minus nine yards, 1984.

WALTER HENSLEE ARNOLD
(Walt)
Tight End—Kansas City Chiefs
Born August 31, 1958, at Galveston, Tex.
Height, 6.03. Weight, 234.
High School—Los Alamos, N. M.
Attended University of New Mexico.

Signed as free agent by Los Angeles Rams, May 29, 1980.
Released by Los Angeles Rams, August 31, 1982; signed as free agent by Houston Oilers, September 7, 1982.
Released by Houston Oilers, August 29, 1983; re-signed by Oilers, September 21, 1983.
Released by Houston Oilers, August 27, 1984; signed as free agent by Washington Redskins, September 5, 1984.
Released by Washington Redskins, October 3, 1984; signed as free agent by Kansas City Chiefs, October 9, 1984.

Year Club	G.	P.C.	Yds.	Avg.	TD.
		PASS RECEIVING			
1980—Los Angeles NFL	16	5	75	15.0	1
1981—Los Angeles NFL	16	20	212	10.6	2
1982—Houston NFL	9		None		
1983—Houston NFL	13	12	137	11.4	1
1984—Wa. (4)-KC (10) NFL	14	11	95	8.6	1
Pro Totals—5 Years	68	48	519	10.8	5

WALKER LEE ASHLEY
(Walker Lee)
Linebacker—Minnesota Vikings
Born July 28, 1960, at Bayonne, N.J.
Height, 6.00. Weight, 231.
High School—Jersey City, N.J., Snyder.
Attended Penn State University.

Selected by Philadelphia in 1983 USFL territorial draft.
Selected by Minnesota in 3rd round (73rd player selected) of 1983 NFL draft.
Signed by Minnesota Vikings, June 16, 1983.
Minnesota NFL, 1983 and 1984.
Games: 1983 (15), 1984 (15). Total—30.

—DID YOU KNOW—

That Miami's Mark Duper and Mark Clayton became the first receivers to accumulate 1,300 yards for the same team in one season? Duper and Clayton had 1,306 and 1,389 yards, respectively, last season.

RICHARD J. ASKEW
(Ricky)
Tight End—New England Patriots
Born February 22, 1961, at Atlus, Okla.
Height, 6.05. Weight, 220.
High School—Euless, Tex., Trinity.
Attended Rice University.

Signed as free agent by New England Patriots, May 21, 1984.
Released by New England Patriots, August 21, 1984; re-signed by Patriots, February 25, 1985.

DANIEL JAMES BARTHOLOMEW AUDICK
(Dan)
Offensive Tackle-Guard—St. Louis Cardinals
Born November 15, 1954, at San Bernardino, Calif.
Height, 6.03. Weight, 253.
High School—Colorado Springs, Colo., Roy J. Wasson.
Received bachelor of business administration degree from University of Hawaii in 1977
and attending San Diego State University for master's degree in business administration.

Selected by Pittsburgh in 4th round (106th player selected) of 1977 NFL draft.
Traded by Pittsburgh Steelers to Cleveland Browns for future considerations, August 17, 1977.
Released by Cleveland Browns, August 30, 1977; signed as free agent by St. Louis Cardinals, November 8, 1977.
Released by St. Louis Cardinals, August 22, 1978; signed as free agent by San Diego Chargers, December 14, 1978.
Traded by San Diego Chargers to San Francisco 49ers for 3rd round pick in 1982 draft, August 17, 1981.
Traded by San Francisco 49ers to St. Louis Cardinals for offensive tackle-guard George Collins, April 21, 1983.
On non-football injury list, November 9 through remainder of 1984 season.
St. Louis NFL, 1977, 1983 and 1984; San Diego NFL, 1978 through 1980; San Francisco NFL, 1981 and 1982.
Games: 1977 (2), 1978 (1), 1979 (16), 1980 (15), 1981 (16), 1982 (7), 1983 (12), 1984 (7). Total—76.
Pro statistics: Recovered two fumbles, 1981.
Played in AFC Championship Game following 1980 season.
Played in NFC Championship Game following 1981 season.
Played in NFL Championship Game following 1981 season.

SCOTT EUGENE AUER
Guard-Offensive Tackle—Kansas City Chiefs
Born October 4, 1961, at Fort Wayne, Ind.
Height, 6.04. Weight, 225.
High School—Fort Wayne, Ind., Elmhurst.
Attended Michigan State University.

Selected by Michigan in 1984 USFL territorial draft.
Selected by Kansas City in 9th round (229th player selected) of 1984 NFL draft.
Signed by Kansas City Chiefs, July 9, 1984.
Kansas City NFL, 1984.
Games: 1984 (16).

LORENZO DOWE AUGHTMAN
(Known by middle name.)
Offensive Lineman—Dallas Cowboys
Born January 28, 1961, at Brewton, Ala.
Height, 6.03. Weight, 258.
High School—Brewton, Ala., T.R. Miller.
Attended Auburn University.

Selected by Birmingham in 1984 USFL territorial draft.
Selected by Dallas in 11th round (304th player selected) of 1984 NFL draft.
Signed by Dallas Cowboys, June 7, 1984.
Dallas NFL, 1984.
Games: 1984 (7).

STEVE PAUL AUGUST
Offensive Tackle—Pittsburgh Steelers
Born September 4, 1954, at Jeannette, Pa.
Height, 6.05. Weight, 258.
High School—Jeannette, Pa.
Received bachelor of science degree in special education from University of Tulsa in 1977.

Selected by Seattle in 1st round (14th player selected) of 1977 NFL draft.
Traded by Seattle Seahawks to Pittsburgh Steelers for 5th round pick in 1985 draft, October 9, 1984.
Seattle NFL, 1977 through 1983; Seattle (6)-Pittsburgh (5) NFL, 1984.
Games: 1977 (6), 1978 (14), 1979 (16), 1980 (16), 1981 (16), 1982 (8), 1983 (15), 1984 (11). Total—102.
Pro statistics: Recovered one fumble, 1978 and 1979; caught one pass for nine yards, 1981.
Played in AFC Championship Game following 1983 and 1984 seasons.

MICHAEL EUGENE AUGUSTYNIAK
(Mike)
Fullback—New York Jets

Born July 17, 1956, at Fort Wayne, Ind.
Height, 5.11. Weight, 226.
High School—Leo, Ind.
Received bachelor of science degree from Purdue University in 1981.

Signed as free agent by New Orleans Saints, May 14, 1980.
Released by New Orleans Saints, August 26, 1980; signed as free agent by New York Jets, February 11, 1981.
On injured reserve with chest injury, November 18 through remainder of 1981 season.
On injured reserve with knee injury, August 27 through entire 1984 season.

Year Club	G.	Att.	Yds.	Avg.	TD.	P.C.	Yds.	Avg.	TD.	TD.	Pts.	F.
		—RUSHING—				PASS RECEIVING				—TOTAL—		
1981—New York Jets NFL	10	85	339	4.0	1	18	144	8.0	0	1	6	3
1982—New York Jets NFL	9	50	178	3.6	4	24	189	7.9	0	4	24	2
1983—New York Jets NFL	8	18	50	2.8	2	10	71	7.1	1	3	18	0
Pro Totals—3 Years	27	153	567	3.7	7	52	404	7.8	1	8	48	5

Additional pro statistics: Recovered two fumbles, 1982.
Played in AFC Championship Game following 1982 season.

CLIFF AUSTIN
Running Back—Atlanta Falcons

Born March 2, 1960, at Atlanta, Ga.
Height, 6.00. Weight, 190.
High School—Avondale Estates, Ga.
Attended Clemson University.

Selected by Washington in 1983 USFL territorial draft.
Selected by New Orleans in 3rd round (66th player selected) of 1983 NFL draft.
Signed by New Orleans Saints, June 21, 1983.
On injured reserve with separated shoulder and hamstring injuries, August 30 through October 7, 1983; activated, October 8, 1983.
Released by New Orleans Saints, August 27, 1984; signed as free agent by Atlanta Falcons, September 4, 1984.

Year Club	G.	Att.	Yds.	Avg.	TD.	P.C.	Yds.	Avg.	TD.	TD.	Pts.	F.
		—RUSHING—				PASS RECEIVING				—TOTAL—		
1983—New Orleans NFL	11	4	16	4.0	0	2	25	12.5	0	0	0	0
1984—Atlanta NFL	15	4	7	1.8	0		None			0	0	0
Pro Totals—2 Years	26	8	23	2.9	0	2	25	12.5	0	0	0	0

Year Club	G.	No.	Yds.	Avg.	TD.
	KICKOFF RETURNS				
1983—New Orleans NFL	11	7	112	16.0	0
1984—Atlanta NFL	15	4	77	19.3	0
Pro Totals—2 Years	26	11	189	17.2	0

ROBERT HAYDEN AVELLINI
(Bob)
Quarterback—New York Jets

Born August 28, 1953, at New York, N. Y.
Height, 6.02. Weight, 210.
High School—New Hyde Park, N. Y., Memorial.
Received bachelor of arts degree in business administration from University of Maryland.

Selected by Chicago in 6th round (135th player selected) of 1975 NFL draft.
Released by Chicago Bears, October 1, 1984; signed as free agent by New York Jets, November 15, 1984.
Active for 16 games with Chicago Bears in 1980; did not play.
Active for 5 games with New York Jets in 1984; did not play.

Year Club	G.	Att.	Cmp.	Pct.	Gain	T.P.	P.I.	Avg.	Att.	Yds.	Avg.	TD.	TD.	Pts.	F.
		—PASSING—							—RUSHING—				—TOTAL—		
1975—Chicago NFL	8	126	67	53.2	942	6	11	7.48	4	—3	—0.8	1	1	6	2
1976—Chicago NFL	14	271	118	43.5	1580	8	15	5.83	18	58	3.2	1	1	6	3
1977—Chicago NFL	14	293	154	52.6	2004	11	18	6.84	37	109	2.9	1	1	6	8
1978—Chicago NFL	13	264	141	53.4	1718	5	16	6.51	34	54	1.6	2	2	12	5
1979—Chicago NFL	7	51	27	52.9	310	2	3	6.08	3	10	3.3	0	0	0	0
1981—Chicago NFL	9	32	15	46.9	185	1	3	5.78	5	2	0.4	0	0	0	0
1982—Chicago NFL	2	20	8	40.0	84	0	0	4.20		None			0	0	0
1983—Chicago NFL	2				None					None			0	0	0
1984—Chi. (4)-N.Y.J. (0) NFL ...	4	53	30	56.6	288	0	3	5.43	3	—5	—1.7	0	0	0	2
Pro Totals—10 Years	73	1110	560	50.5	7111	33	69	6.41	104	225	2.2	5	5	30	20

Quarterback Rating Points: 1975 (57.3), 1976 (49.7), 1977 (61.7), 1978 (54.6), 1979 (59.9), 1981 (36.4), 1982 (52.9), 1984 (48.3). Total—55.1.

Additional pro statistics: Recovered one fumble, 1975; recovered three fumbles and fumbled eight times for minus 17 yards, 1977; fumbled five times for minus 11 yards, 1978.

JOHN MILTON AYERS
Guard—San Francisco 49ers
Born April 4, 1953, at Carrizo Springs, Tex.
Height, 6.05. Weight, 265.
High School—Carrizo Springs, Tex.
Attended University of Texas and West Texas State University.

Selected by San Francisco in 8th round (223rd player selected) of 1976 NFL draft.
On injured reserve entire 1976 season.
On inactive list, September 19, 1982.
San Francisco NFL, 1977 through 1984.
Games: 1977 (14), 1978 (16), 1979 (16), 1980 (16), 1981 (16), 1982 (8), 1983 (16), 1984 (16). Total—118.
Pro statistics: Recovered one fumble, 1978 and 1984.
Played in NFC Championship Game following 1981, 1983 and 1984 seasons.
Played in NFL Championship Game following 1981 and 1984 seasons.

JOE AZELBY
Linebacker—Buffalo Bills
Born March 5, 1962, at New York, N.Y.
Height, 6.01. Weight, 225.
High School—Oradell, N.J., Bergen Catholic.
Received degree in economics from Harvard University in 1984.

Selected by Buffalo in 10th round (263rd player selected) of 1984 NFL draft.
Released by Buffalo Bills, August 27, 1984; re-signed by Bills, September 12, 1984.
Buffalo NFL, 1984.
Games: 1984 (14).
Pro statistics: Recovered one fumble, 1984.

MICHEAL JAMES BAAB
(Mike)
Center—Cleveland Browns
Born December 6, 1959, at Fort Worth, Tex.
Height, 6.04. Weight, 270.
High School—Euless, Tex., Trinity.
Attended Tarrant County Junior College, Austin Community College
and University of Texas.

Selected by Cleveland in 5th round (115th player selected) of 1982 NFL draft.
Cleveland NFL, 1982 through 1984.
Games: 1982 (7), 1983 (15), 1984 (16). Total—38.
Pro statistics: Fumbled once for minus 11 yards, 1984.

STEVEN WILLIAM BAACK
(Steve)
Offensive Tackle—Detroit Lions
Born November 16, 1960, at Ames, Ia.
Height, 6.03. Weight, 260.
High School—John Day, Ore., Grant Union.
Received bachelor of science degree in psychology from University of Oregon in 1984.

Selected by Philadelphia in 9th round (184th player selected) of 1984 USFL draft.
Selected by Detroit in 3rd round (75th player selected) of 1984 NFL draft.
Signed by Detroit Lions, June 20, 1984.
Detroit NFL, 1984.
Games: 1984 (16).

CHRIS BAHR
Placekicker—Los Angeles Raiders
Born February 3, 1953, at State College, Pa.
Height, 5.10. Weight, 170.
High School—State College, Pa., Neshaminy.
Received bachelor of science degree in biology from Penn State University in 1976
and attending Chase Law School at Northern Kentucky University.
Brother of Matt Bahr, placekicker with Cleveland Browns.

Named to THE SPORTING NEWS AFC All-Star Team, 1977.
Named as placekicker on THE SPORTING NEWS College All-America Team, 1975.
Selected by Cincinnati in 2nd round (51st player selected) of 1976 NFL draft.
Released by Cincinnati Bengals, August 26, 1980; signed as free agent by Oakland Raiders, September 1, 1980.
Franchise transferred to Los Angeles, May 7, 1982.
Played with Philadelphia Atoms of North American Soccer League, 1975 (22 games, 11 goals, 2 assists).

Year Club	G.	XP.	XPM.	FG.	FGA.	Pts.	Year Club	G.	XP.	XPM.	FG.	FGA.	Pts.
1976—Cincinnati NFL........	14	39	3	14	27	81	1981—Oakland NFL............	16	27	6	14	24	69
1977—Cincinnati NFL........	14	25	1	19	27	82	1982—L.A. Raiders NFL.....	9	*32	1	10	16	62
1978—Cincinnati NFL........	16	26	3	16	30	74	1983—L.A. Raiders NFL....	16	51	2	21	27	114
1979—Cincinnati NFL........	16	40	2	13	23	79	1984—L.A. Raiders NFL....	16	40	2	20	27	100
1980—Oakland NFL............	16	41	3	19	37	98	Pro Totals—9 Years.......	133	321	23	146	238	759

Additional pro statistics: Punted twice for 44.0 average, 1977; punted four times for 27.0 average, 1978; punted twice for 21.5 average, 1981.
Played in AFC Championship Game following 1980 and 1983 seasons.
Played in NFL Championship Game following 1980 and 1983 seasons.

MATTHEW DAVID BAHR
(Matt)
Placekicker—Cleveland Browns
Born July 6, 1956, at Philadelphia, Pa.
Height, 5.10. Weight, 175.
High School—Langhorne, Pa., Neshaminy.
Received bachelor of science degree in electrical engineering from Penn State University
in 1979; attending Carnegie-Mellon University for master's degree in industrial administration.
Brother of Chris Bahr, placekicker with Los Angeles Raiders.

Selected by Pittsburgh in 6th round (165th player selected) of 1979 NFL draft.
Released by Pittsburgh Steelers, August 31, 1981; signed as free agent by San Francisco 49ers, September 8, 1981.
Traded by San Francisco 49ers to Cleveland Browns for 9th round pick in 1983 draft, October 6, 1981.
Played with Colorado Caribous and Tulsa Roughnecks of North American Soccer League, 1978 (26 games, 3 assists).

		——PLACE KICKING——					
Year	Club	G.	XP.	XPM.	FG.	FGA.	Pts.
1979—Pittsburgh NFL		16	*50	2	18	30	104
1980—Pittsburgh NFL		16	39	3	19	28	96
1981—SF (4)-Cle (11) NFL		15	34	0	15	26	79
1982—Cleveland NFL		9	17	0	7	15	38
1983—Cleveland NFL		16	38	2	21	24	101
1984—Cleveland NFL		16	25	0	24	32	97
Pro Totals—6 Years		88	203	7	104	155	515

Played in AFC Championship Game following 1979 season.
Played in NFL Championship Game following 1979 season.

EDWIN RAYMOND BAILEY
Guard—Seattle Seahawks
Born May 15, 1959, at Savannah, Ga.
Height, 6.04. Weight, 265.
High School—Savannah, Ga., Tompkins.
Attended South Carolina State College.

Selected by Seattle in 5th round (114th player selected) of 1981 NFL draft.
On injured reserve with knee injury, November 10 through December 7, 1984; activated, December 8, 1984.
Seattle NFL, 1981 through 1984.
Games: 1981 (16), 1982 (9), 1983 (16), 1984 (12). Total—53.
Pro statistics: Recovered one fumble, 1982.
Played in AFC Championship Game following 1983 season.

STACEY DWAYNE BAILEY
Wide Receiver—Atlanta Falcons
Born February 10, 1960, at San Rafael, Calif.
Height, 6.00. Weight, 160.
High School—San Rafael, Calif., Terra Linda.
Attended San Jose State University.

Selected by Atlanta in 3rd round (63rd player selected) of 1982 NFL draft.
On inactive list, September 12 and September 19, 1982.

		——PASS RECEIVING——				
Year	Club	G.	P.C.	Yds.	Avg.	TD.
1982—Atlanta NFL		5	2	24	12.0	1
1983—Atlanta NFL		15	55	881	16.0	6
1984—Atlanta NFL		16	67	1138	17.0	6
Pro Totals—3 Years		36	124	2043	16.5	13

Additional pro statistics: Fumbled once, 1982 through 1984; rushed twice for minus five yards and recovered one fumble, 1983.

WILLIAM DONALD BAILEY
(Don)
Center—Indianapolis Colts
Born March 24, 1961, at Miami, Fla.
Height, 6.04. Weight, 257.
High School—Hialeah, Fla., Miami Lakes.
Attended University of Miami (Fla.).

Selected by Tampa Bay in 9th round (108th player selected) of 1983 USFL draft.
Selected by Denver in 11th round (283rd player selected) of 1983 NFL draft.
Signed by Denver Broncos, May 18, 1983.
Released by Denver Broncos, August 22, 1983; signed as free agent by Tampa Bay Buccaneers, October 25, 1983.
On injured reserve with back injury, November 2 through remainder of 1983 season.
Released by Tampa Bay Buccaneers, August 20, 1984; signed as free agent by Indianapolis Colts, October 10, 1984.

Active for 1 game with Tampa Bay Buccaneers in 1983; did not play.
Tampa Bay NFL, 1983; Indianapolis NFL, 1984.
Games: 1984 (10).
Pro statistics: Recovered one fumble and fumbled twice for minus 27 yards, 1984.

WILLIAM ERNEST BAIN
(Bill)
Offensive Tackle—Los Angeles Rams
Born August 9, 1952, at Los Angeles, Calif.
Height, 6.04. Weight, 285.
High School—Santa Fe Springs, Calif., St. Paul.
Attended University of Colorado, San Diego City College and received bachelor of arts degree
in public administration from University of Southern California.

Named as guard on THE SPORTING NEWS College All-America Team, 1974.
Selected by Green Bay in 2nd round (47th player selected) of 1975 NFL draft.
Traded by Green Bay Packers to Denver Broncos for a draft choice, August 31, 1976 (3rd round pick in 1977 draft).
On injured reserve with knee injury entire 1977 season.
Released by Denver Broncos, September 8, 1978; signed as free agent by New York Giants, October 30, 1978.
Released by New York Giants, November 9, 1978; re-signed by Giants, November 15, 1978.
Left New York Giants' camp voluntarily, July 17, 1979; signed as free agent by Washington Redskins, August 1, 1979.
Released by Washington Redskins, August 21, 1979; signed as free agent by Los Angeles Rams, September 28, 1979.
Released by Los Angeles Rams, October 23, 1979; re-signed by Rams, November 20, 1979.
Active for 7 games with New York Giants in 1978; did not play.
Green Bay NFL, 1975; Denver NFL, 1976; New York Giants (0)-Denver (1) NFL, 1978; Los Angeles Rams NFL, 1979 through 1984.
Games: 1975 (14), 1976 (14), 1978 (1), 1979 (8), 1980 (16), 1981 (16), 1982 (9), 1983 (16), 1984 (16). Total—110.
Pro statistics: Returned one kickoff for 10 yards, 1975.
Played in NFC Championship Game following 1979 season.
Played in NFL Championship Game following 1979 season.

CHARLES EDWARD BAKER
(Charlie)
Linebacker—St. Louis Cardinals
Born September 26, 1957, at Mt. Pleasant, Tex.
Height, 6.02. Weight, 234.
High School—Odessa, Tex., Ector.
Attended University of New Mexico.

Selected by St. Louis in 3rd round (81st player selected) of 1980 NFL draft.
On injured reserve with abdominal strain, October 5 through November 8, 1984; activated, November 9, 1984.
St. Louis NFL, 1980 through 1984.
Games: 1980 (16), 1981 (14), 1982 (9), 1983 (16), 1984 (9). Total—64.
Pro statistics: Ran 27 yards with lateral on kickoff return, 1980; recovered one fumble, 1981; recovered two fumbles, 1982.

JAMES ALBERT LONDON BAKER
(Al)
Defensive End—St. Louis Cardinals
Born December 9, 1956, at Jacksonville, Fla.
Height, 6.06. Weight, 270.
High School—Newark, N. J., Weequahic.
Attended Colorado State University.

Named THE SPORTING NEWS NFC Rookie of the Year, 1978.
Selected by Detroit in 2nd round (40th player selected) of 1978 NFL draft.
On reserve-retired list, August 19 through September 10, 1980; activated, September 11, 1980.
On physically unable to perform/active list with groin injury, July 29 through August 30, 1982; activated, August 31, 1982.
Traded by Detroit Lions to St. Louis Cardinals for defensive tackle Mike Dawson and 3rd round pick in 1984 draft, July 18, 1983.
Detroit NFL, 1978 through 1982; St. Louis NFL, 1983 and 1984.
Games: 1978 (16), 1979 (16), 1980 (15), 1981 (11), 1982 (9), 1983 (16), 1984 (15). Total—98.
Pro statistics: Recovered one fumble, 1978 through 1980 and 1982; intercepted one pass for no yards, 1980; intercepted one pass for nine yards, 1981; intercepted two passes for 24 yards and recovered two fumbles, 1983.
Played in Pro Bowl (NFL All-Star Game) following 1978 through 1980 seasons.

JESSE BAKER
Defensive End—Houston Oilers
Born July 10, 1957, at Conyers, Ga.
Height, 6.05. Weight, 272.
High School—Conyers, Ga., Rockdale County.
Attended Jacksonville State University.

Selected by Houston in 2nd round (50th player selected) of 1979 NFL draft.
Houston NFL, 1979 through 1984.
Games: 1979 (16), 1980 (16), 1981 (16), 1982 (9), 1983 (16), 1984 (16). Total—89.
Pro statistics: Recovered one fumble for 20 yards and one touchdown, 1979; recovered one fumble, 1980, 1981 and 1984; recovered one fumble for 56 yards, 1982.
Played in AFC Championship Game following 1979 season.

KEITH LEONARD BAKER
Wide Receiver—San Francisco 49ers
Born June 4, 1957, at Dallas, Tex.
Height, 5.10. Weight, 187.
High School—Dallas, Tex., Franklin D. Roosevelt.
Attended Texas A&M University and Texas Southern University.

Signed as free agent by Montreal Alouettes, April, 1979.
Traded by Montreal Alouettes to Hamilton Tiger-Cats, June, 1981.
Traded by Hamilton Tiger-Cats to Ottawa Rough Riders, September 16, 1984.
Granted free agency, March 1, 1985; signed by San Francisco 49ers, April 10, 1985.

Year Club	G.	Att.	RUSHING Yds.	Avg.	TD.	P.C.	PASS RECEIVING Yds.	Avg.	TD.	TD.	TOTAL Pts.	F.
1979—Montreal CFL	12	3	42	14.0	0	29	571	19.7	5	5	30	0
1980—Montreal CFL	15	4	—20	—5.0	0	51	891	17.5	8	8	48	0
1981—Hamilton CFL	16	3	2	0.7	0	68	1218	17.9	11	11	66	0
1982—Hamilton CFL	16	5	19	3.8	0	80	1282	16.0	8	8	48	0
1983—Hamilton CFL	15	2	10	5.0	0	66	911	13.8	10	10	†62	0
1984—Hamilton (8)-Ottawa (4) CFL	12	2	27	13.5	0	39	623	16.0	5	5	30	1
CFL Totals—6 Years	86	19	80	4.2	0	333	5496	16.5	47	47	284	1

Year Club	G.	PUNT RETURNS No.	Yds.	Avg.	TD.	KICKOFF RET. No.	Yds.	Avg.	TD.
1979—Montreal CFL	12	12	134	11.2	0	5	95	19.0	0
1980—Montreal CFL	15	11	85	7.7	0	3	48	16.0	0
1981—Hamilton CFL	16	9	80	8.9	0			None	
1982—Hamilton CFL	16	10	69	6.9	0	1	26	26.0	0
1983—Hamilton CFL	15	5	21	4.2	0			None	
1984—Hamilton (8)-Ottawa (4) CFL	12	5	18	3.6	0	2	32	16.0	0
CFL Totals—6 Years	86	52	407	7.8	0	11	201	18.3	0

†Includes one 2-point conversion.
Additional CFL statistics: Recovered one fumble, 1979; attempted one pass with no completions, 1979 and 1981; attempted two passes with one completion for 15 yards and a touchdown, 1982; attempted one pass with one interception, 1983.
Played in CFL Championship Game following 1979 season.

RONALD BAKER
(Ron)
Guard—Philadelphia Eagles
Born November 19, 1954, at Gary, Ind.
Height, 6.04. Weight, 270.
High School—Gary, Ind., Emerson.
Attended Indian Hills Junior College and Oklahoma State University.

Selected by Baltimore in 10th round (277th player selected) of 1977 NFL draft.
On injured reserve with ankle injury entire 1977 season.
Traded by Baltimore Colts to Philadelphia Eagles for 8th round pick in 1981 raft, August 26, 1980.
Baltimore NFL, 1978 and 1979; Philadelphia NFL, 1980 through 1984.
Games: 1978 (16), 1979 (16), 1980 (16), 1981 (16), 1982 (9), 1983 (16), 1984 (16). Total—105.
Pro statistics: Returned one kickoff for six yards, 1980; recovered one fumble, 1982 through 1984.
Played in NFC Championship Game following 1980 season.
Played in NFL Championship Game following 1980 season.

BRIAN D. BALDINGER
Center-Guard—Dallas Cowboys
Born January 7, 1959, at Pittsburgh, Pa.
Height, 6.04. Weight, 255.
High School—Massapequa, N.Y.
Attended Nassau Community College and received bachelor of science degree
in psychology from Duke University in 1982.
Brother of Rich Baldinger, offensive tackle-guard with Kansas City Chiefs; and
Gary Baldinger, defensive lineman at Wake Forest University.

Signed as free agent by Dallas Cowboys, April 30, 1982.
On inactive list, September 13 and September 19, 1982.
Dallas NFL, 1982 through 1984.
Games: 1982 (4), 1983 (16), 1984 (16). Total—36.
Played in NFC Championship Game following 1982 season.

RICHARD L. BALDINGER
(Rich)
Offensive Tackle-Guard—Kansas City Chiefs
Born December 31, 1959, at Camp Le Jeune, N.C.
Height, 6.04. Weight, 285.
High School—Massapequa, N.Y.
Attended Wake Forest University.
Brother of Brian Baldinger, center-guard with Dallas Cowboys; and
Gary Baldinger, defensive lineman at Wake Forest University.

Selected by New York Giants in 10th round (270th player selected) of 1982 NFL draft.
On inactive list, September 12, 1982.
Released by New York Giants, August 29, 1983; re-signed by Giants, September 8, 1983.
Released by New York Giants, October 7, 1983; signed as free agent by Kansas City Chiefs, October 26, 1983.
New York Giants NFL, 1982; New York Giants (2)-Kansas City (6) NFL, 1983; Kansas City NFL, 1984.
Games: 1982 (1), 1983 (8), 1984 (14). Total—23.

JOHN KARL BALDISCHWILER
(Known by middle name.)
Offensive Tackle—Indianapolis Colts
Born January 19, 1956, at Okmulgee, Okla.
Height, 6.05. Weight, 267.
High School—Okmulgee, Okla.
Attended University of Oklahoma.

Selected by Miami in 7th round (178th player selected) of 1978 NFL draft.
Traded by Miami Dolphins to Detroit Lions for 10th round pick in 1979 draft, August 28, 1978.
Traded by Detroit Lions to Baltimore Colts for 7th round pick in 1984 draft, July 28, 1983.
Franchise transferred to Indianapolis, March 31, 1984.
Released by Indianapolis Colts after failing physical with neck injury, June 15, 1984; re-signed by Colts, April 1, 1985.
Detroit NFL, 1978 through 1982; Baltimore NFL, 1983.
Games: 1978 (16), 1979 (16), 1980 (16), 1981 (16), 1982 (9), 1983 (14). Total—87.

KEITH MANNING BALDWIN
Defensive End—Cleveland Browns
Born October 13, 1960, at Houston, Tex.
Height, 6.04. Weight, 270.
High School—Houston, Tex., M.B. Smiley.
Attended Texas A&M University.

Selected by Cleveland in 2nd round (31st player selected) of 1982 NFL draft.
Cleveland NFL, 1982 through 1984.
Games: 1982 (9), 1983 (16), 1984 (16). Total—41.

THOMAS BURKE BALDWIN
(Tom)
Defensive Tackle—New York Jets
Born May 13, 1961, at Evergreen Park, Ill.
Height, 6.04. Weight, 270.
High School—Lansing, Ill., Thornton Fractional South.
Attended University of Wisconsin, Thornton Community College and The University of Tulsa.
Brother of Brian Baldwin, pitcher in Los Angeles Dodgers' organization, 1977 through 1979.

Selected by Oklahoma in 1984 USFL territorial draft.
Selected by New York Jets in 9th round (234th player selected) of 1984 NFL draft.
Signed by New York Jets, May 29, 1984.
New York Jets NFL, 1984.
Games: 1984 (16).

QUINTON M. BALLARD
Defensive Tackle—Miami Dolphins
Born November 18, 1960, at Ahoskie, N.C.
Height, 6.03. Weight, 289.
High School—Gatesville, N.C., Gates County.
Attended Elon College
Brother of Joe Ballard, professional boxer.

Signed as free agent by Baltimore Colts, May 10, 1983.
Franchise transferred to Indianapolis, March 31, 1984.
On injured reserve with knee injury, August 27 through September 25, 1984.
Released by Indianapolis Colts, September 26, 1984; signed as free agent by Miami Dolphins, March 29, 1985.
Baltimore NFL, 1983.
Games: 1983 (15).

TED BANKER
Guard-Center—New York Jets
Born February 17, 1961, at Belleville, Ill.
Height, 6.02. Weight, 260.
High School—Belleville, Ill., Althoff.
Attended Southeast Missouri State University.

Signed as free agent by New York Jets, June 20, 1983.
On injured reserve with knee injury, August 12 through entire 1983 season.
New York Jets NFL, 1984.
Games: 1984 (14).
Pro statistics: Returned one kickoff for five yards, 1984.

CARL BANKS
Linebacker—New York Giants
Born February 29, 1962, at Flint, Mich.
Height, 6.04. Weight, 235.
High School—Flint, Mich., Beecher.
Attended Michigan State University.

Named as linebacker on THE SPORTING NEWS College All-America Team, 1983.
Selected by Michigan in 1984 USFL territorial draft.
Selected by New York Giants in 1st round (3rd player selected) of 1984 NFL draft.
Signed by New York Giants, July 12, 1984.
New York Giants NFL, 1984.
Games: 1984 (16).
Pro statistics: Recovered one fumble, 1984.

WILLIAM CHIP BANKS
(Known by middle name.)
Linebacker—Cleveland Browns
Born September 18, 1959, at Ft. Lawton, Okla.
Height, 6.04. Weight, 233.
High School—Augusta, Ga., Lucy Laney.
Attended University of Southern California.

Named as linebacker on THE SPORTING NEWS College All-America Team, 1981.
Selected by Cleveland in 1st round (3rd player selected) of 1982 NFL draft.
Traded with 3rd round pick in 1985 draft and 1st and 6th round picks in 1986 draft by Cleveland Browns to Buffalo Bills for 1st round pick in 1985 supplemental draft, April 9, 1985 (Bills received 1st round pick in 1985 draft from Browns when Banks did not report).

Year Club	G.	No.	Yds.	Avg.	TD.
		—INTERCEPTIONS—			
1982—Cleveland NFL	9	1	14	14.0	0
1983—Cleveland NFL	16	3	95	31.7	1
1984—Cleveland NFL	16	1	8	8.0	0
Pro Totals—3 Years	41	5	117	23.4	1

Additional pro statistics: Recovered one fumble, 1983; recovered three fumbles for 17 yards, 1984.
Played in Pro Bowl (NFL All-Star Game) following 1982 and 1983 seasons.

MARION BARBER
Fullback—New York Jets
Born December 6, 1959, at Fort Lauderdale, Fla.
Height, 6.02. Weight, 224.
High School—Detroit, Mich., Chadsey.
Attended University of Minnesota.

Selected by New York Jets in 2nd round (30th player selected) of 1981 NFL draft.
On injured reserve with concussion, August 17 through entire 1981 season.
On inactive list, September 12 and September 19, 1982.

Year Club	G.	Att.	Yds.	Avg.	TD.	P.C.	Yds.	Avg.	TD.	TD.	Pts.	F.
		—RUSHING—				PASS RECEIVING				—TOTAL—		
1982—New York Jets NFL	6	8	24	3.0	0		None			0	0	0
1983—New York Jets NFL	14	15	77	5.1	1	7	48	6.9	1	2	12	0
1984—New York Jets NFL	14	31	148	4.8	2	10	79	7.9	0	2	12	3
Pro Totals—3 Years	34	54	249	4.6	3	17	127	7.5	1	4	24	3

Additional pro statistics: Returned one kickoff for nine yards and recovered two fumbles, 1983; recovered one fumble, 1984.
Played in AFC Championship Game following 1982 season.

MIKE BARBER
Tight End—Los Angeles Rams
Born June 4, 1953, at Marshall, Tex.
Height, 6.03. Weight, 237.
High School—White Oak, Tex.
Attended Louisiana Tech University.

Selected by Houston in 2nd round (48th player selected) of 1976 NFL draft.
On injured reserve with tendinitis, September 15 through remainder of 1976 season.
Traded with 3rd and 8th round picks in 1982 draft by Houston Oilers to Los Angeles Rams for tight end Lewis Gilbert and 2nd and 3rd round picks in 1982 draft, April 27, 1982.
On injured reserve with knee injury, August 28 through September 28, 1984; activated, September 29, 1984.

Year Club	G.	P.C.	Yds.	Avg.	TD.	Year Club	G.	P.C.	Yds.	Avg.	TD.
	—PASS RECEIVING—						—PASS RECEIVING—				
1976—Houston NFL	1		None			1981—Houston NFL	16	13	190	14.6	1
1977—Houston NFL	13	9	94	10.4	1	1982—L.A. Rams NFL	9	18	166	9.2	1
1978—Houston NFL	16	32	513	16.0	3	1983—L.A. Rams NFL	16	55	657	11.9	3
1979—Houston NFL	15	27	377	14.0	3	1984—L.A. Rams NFL	11	7	42	6.0	0
1980—Houston NFL	16	59	712	12.1	5	Pro Totals—9 Years	113	220	2751	12.5	17

Additional pro statistics: Rushed twice for 14 yards and fumbled four times, 1978; rushed twice for four yards, 1979; fumbled once, 1979, 1983 and 1984; rushed once for one yard and returned one kickoff for 12 yards, 1980; recovered one fumble, 1980 and 1982.

Played in AFC Championship Game following 1978 and 1979 seasons.

LEO BARKER
Linebacker—Cincinnati Bengals
Born November 7, 1959, at Critobal, Panama.
Height, 6.01. Weight, 221.
High School—Cristobal, Panama.
Attended New Mexico State University.

Selected by Arizona in 1984 USFL territorial draft.
Selected by Cincinnati in 7th round (177th player selected) of 1984 NFL draft.
Signed by Cincinnati Bengals, June 26, 1984.
Cincinnati NFL, 1984.
Games: 1984 (16).

DUANE BARNES
Offensive Tackle—New York Jets
Born August 1, 1960 at Pittsburgh, Pa.
Height, 6.05. Weight, 260.
High School—Pittsburgh, Pa., Northgate.
Attended United States Military Academy and West Virginia University.

Selected by Pittsburgh in 1984 USFL territorial draft.
Signed as free agent by Cleveland Browns, May 4, 1984.
Released by Cleveland Browns, August 17, 1984; signed by Pittsburgh Maulers, September 25, 1984.
Franchise disbanded, October 25, 1984; selected by Baltimore Stars in USFL dispersal draft, December 6, 1984.
Released by Baltimore Stars, February 11, 1985; signed as free agent by New York Jets, May 7, 1985.

JEFF BARNES
Linebacker—Los Angeles Raiders
Born March 1, 1955, at Philadelphia, Pa.
Height, 6.02. Weight, 230.
High School—Hayward, Calif.
Attended Chabot College and University of California.

Selected by Oakland in 5th round (139th player selected) of 1977 NFL draft.
Franchise transferred to Los Angeles, May 7, 1982.
Oakland NFL, 1977 through 1981; Los Angeles Raiders NFL, 1982 through 1984.
Games: 1977 (14), 1978 (16), 1979 (16), 1980 (16), 1981 (15), 1982 (9), 1983 (16), 1984 (16). Total—118.
Pro statistics: Recovered two fumbles, 1977; intercepted one pass for eight yards, 1979; recovered one fumble, 1980 and 1984; intercepted one pass for 15 yards, 1984.
Played in AFC Championship Game following 1977, 1980 and 1983 seasons.
Played in NFL Championship Game following 1980 and 1983 seasons.

ROOSEVELT BARNES JR.
Linebacker—Detroit Lions
Born August 3, 1958, at Ft. Wayne, Ind.
Height, 6.02. Weight, 228.
High School—Ft. Wayne, Ind.
Received bachelor's degree in management from Purdue University in 1981.

Selected by Detroit in 10th round (266th player selected) of 1982 NFL draft.
Detroit NFL, 1982 through 1984.
Games: 1982 (9), 1983 (16), 1984 (16). Total—41.
Pro statistics: Recovered one fumble, 1982 and 1983; intercepted two passes for 70 yards, 1983.

ZACHARY EZELL BARNES
(Zach)
Defensive End—San Diego Chargers
Born November 9, 1960, at Dothan, Ala.
Height, 6.05. Weight, 262.
High School—Dothan, Ala.
Received degree in journalism from Alabama State University in 1984.

Selected by Birmingham in 1984 USFL territorial draft.
Selected by San Diego in 9th round (230th player selected) of 1984 NFL draft.
Signed by San Diego Chargers, June 3, 1984.
On injured reserve with ankle injury, August 27 through entire 1984 season.

BUSTER BARNETT
Tight End—Buffalo Bills
Born November 24, 1958, at Brooksville, Miss.
Height, 6.05. Weight, 235.
High School—Macon, Miss., Noxubee.
Received bachelor of science degree from Jackson State University in 1981.

Selected by Buffalo in 11th round (299th player selected) of 1981 NFL draft.

Year Club	PASS RECEIVING				
	G.	P.C.	Yds.	Avg.	TD.
1981—Buffalo NFL	16	4	36	9.0	1
1982—Buffalo NFL	9	4	39	9.8	0
1983—Buffalo NFL	15	10	94	9.4	0
1984—Buffalo NFL	16	8	67	8.4	0
Pro Totals—4 Years	56	26	236	9.1	1

Additional pro statistics: Recovered one fumble, 1984.

DOUGLAS SHIRL BARNETT JR.
(Doug)
Defensive End-Center—Los Angeles Rams
Born April 12, 1960, at Montebello, Calif.
Height, 6.03. Weight, 250.
High School—West Covina, Calif., Edgewood.
Attended Azusa Pacific College.

Selected by Los Angeles Rams in 5th round (118th player selected) of 1982 NFL draft.
On injured reserve with knee injury, August 10 through entire 1984 season.
Los Angeles Rams NFL, 1982 and 1983.
Games: 1982 (9), 1983 (16). Total—25.
Pro statistics: Returned one kickoff for no yards and recovered one fumble, 1983.

WILLIAM PERRY BARNETT
(Bill)
Defensive End—Miami Dolphins
Born May 10, 1956, at St. Paul, Minn.
Height, 6.04. Weight, 260.
High School—Stillwater, Minn.
Received bachelor of arts degree in advertising from University of Nebraska in 1981.

Selected by Miami in 3rd round (75th player selected) of 1980 NFL draft.
On injured reserve with leg injury, September 18 through October 30, 1981; activated, October 31, 1981.
On injured reserve with torn ankle ligaments, December 7 through remainder of 1982 season.
Miami NFL, 1980 through 1984.
Games: 1980 (16), 1981 (9), 1982 (5), 1983 (15), 1984 (16). Total—61.
Pro statistics: Returned one kickoff for seven yards, 1980; recovered one fumble for four yards, 1982.
Played in AFC Championship Game following 1984 season.
Played in NFL Championship Game following 1984 season.

MALCOLM BARNWELL
Wide Receiver—Los Angeles Raiders
Born June 28, 1958, at Charleston, S. C.
Height, 5.11. Weight, 180.
High School—Charleston, S. C., Burke.
Attended Virginia Union University.

Selected by Oakland in 7th round (173rd player selected) of 1980 NFL draft.
On injured reserve with knee injury, August 26 through entire 1980 season.
Franchise transferred to Los Angeles, May 7, 1982.

Year Club		PASS RECEIVING				—KICKOFF RET.—				—TOTAL—		
	G.	P.C.	Yds.	Avg.	TD.	No.	Yds.	Avg.	TD.	TD.	Pts.	F.
1981—Oakland NFL	16	9	190	21.1	1	15	265	17.7	0	1	6	2
1982—Los Angeles Raiders NFL	9	23	387	16.8	0			None		0	0	0
1983—Los Angeles Raiders NFL	16	35	513	14.7	1			None		1	6	0
1984—Los Angeles Raiders NFL	16	45	851	18.9	2			None		2	12	1
Pro Totals—4 Years	57	112	1941	17.3	4	15	265	17.7	0	4	24	3

Additional pro statistics: Rushed twice for 18 yards, 1982; rushed once for 12 yards, 1983; recovered one fumble, 1984.
Played in AFC Championship Game following 1983 season.
Played in NFL Championship Game following 1983 season.

STEVEN JOSEPH BARTKOWSKI
(Steve)
Quarterback—Atlanta Falcons
Born November 12, 1952, at Des Moines, Ia.
Height, 6.04. Weight, 218.
High School—Santa Clara, Calif., Buchser.
Attended University of California at Berkeley.
Son of Roman Bartkowski, former pitcher in Chicago Cubs' organization.

Led NFL quarterbacks in passing with 97.6 points in 1983.
Named NFC Rookie of the Year by THE SPORTING NEWS, 1975.
Selected by Atlanta in 1st round (1st player selected) of 1975 NFL draft.
On injured reserve with knee injury, October 12 through remainder of 1976 season.
On injured reserve with knee injury, November 23 through remainder of 1984 season.

| | | | PASSING | | | | | | | RUSHING | | | | TOTAL | | |
Year	Club	G.	Att.	Cmp.	Pct.	Gain	T.P.	P.I.	Avg.	Att.	Yds.	Avg.	TD.	TD.	Pts.	F.
1975—Atlanta NFL		11	255	115	45.1	1662	13	15	6.52	14	15	1.1	2	2	12	6
1976—Atlanta NFL		5	120	57	47.5	677	2	9	5.64	8	10	1.3	1	1	6	2
1977—Atlanta NFL		8	136	64	47.1	796	5	13	5.85	18	13	0.7	0	0	0	5
1978—Atlanta NFL		14	369	187	50.7	2489	10	18	6.75	33	60	1.8	2	2	12	7
1979—Atlanta NFL		14	380	204	53.7	2505	17	20	6.59	14	36	2.6	2	2	12	4
1980—Atlanta NFL		16	463	257	55.5	3544	*31	16	7.65	25	35	1.4	2	2	12	6
1981—Atlanta NFL		16	533	297	55.7	3829	30	23	7.18	11	2	0.2	0	0	0	4
1982—Atlanta NFL		9	262	166	63.4	1905	8	11	7.27	13	4	0.3	1	1	6	7
1983—Atlanta NFL		14	432	274	63.4	3167	22	5	7.33	16	38	2.4	1	1	6	7
1984—Atlanta NFL		11	269	181	*67.3	2158	11	10	8.02	15	34	2.3	0	0	0	7
Pro Totals—10 Years		118	3219	1802	56.0	22732	149	140	7.06	167	247	1.5	11	11	66	55

Quarterback Rating Points: 1975 (59.3), 1976 (39.6), 1977 (38.5), 1978 (61.1), 1979 (67.2), 1980 (88.0), 1981 (79.2), 1982 (78.1), 1983 (97.6), 1984 (89.7). Total—75.6.

Additional pro statistics: Recovered four fumbles and fumbled six times for minus two yards, 1975; recovered one fumble and fumbled five times for minus one yard, 1977; recovered three fumbles and fumbled seven times for minus nine yards, 1978; fumbled once for minus one yard, 1979; recovered two fumbles, 1980; recovered three fumbles and fumbled four times for minus one yard, 1981; recovered one fumble and fumbled seven times for minus 10 yards, 1982; recovered one fumble, 1983; recovered four fumbles and fumbled seven times for minus 11 yards, 1984.

Played in Pro Bowl (NFL All-Star Game) following 1980 season.

BRIAN DALE BASCHNAGEL

Name pronounced BASH-nay-gull.

Wide Receiver—Chicago Bears

Born January 8, 1954, at Kingston, N. Y.
Height, 5.11. Weight, 184.
High School—Pittsburgh, Pa., North Allegheny.
Received bachelor of science degree in finance from Ohio State University in 1976;
attending Ohio State University for master's degree in finance.

Selected by Chicago in 3rd round (66th player selected) of 1976 NFL draft.
On injured reserve with knee injury, November 21 through remainder of 1977 season.

| | | | PASS RECEIVING | | | | PUNT RETURNS | | | | KICKOFF RET. | | | | TOTAL | | |
Year	Club	G.	P.C.	Yds.	Avg.	TD.	No.	Yds.	Avg.	TD.	No.	Yds.	Avg.	TD.	TD.	Pts.	F.
1976—Chicago NFL		14	13	226	17.4	0	2	2	1.0	0	29	754	26.0	0	0	0	1
1977—Chicago NFL		10	4	50	12.5	0	3	54	18.0	0	23	557	24.2	*1	1	6	1
1978—Chicago NFL		16	2	29	14.5	0	1	2	2.0	0	20	455	22.8	0	0	0	1
1979—Chicago NFL		16	30	452	15.1	2		None			12	260	21.7	0	2	12	0
1980—Chicago NFL		16	28	396	14.1	2		None				None			2	12	0
1981—Chicago NFL		16	34	554	16.3	3		None			2	34	17.0	0	3	18	2
1982—Chicago NFL		9	12	194	16.2	2		None				None			2	12	0
1983—Chicago NFL		16	5	70	14.0	0		None			3	42	14.0	0	0	0	1
1984—Chicago NFL		16	6	53	8.8	0		None				None			0	0	1
Pro Totals—9 Years		129	134	2024	15.1	9	6	58	9.7	0	89	2102	23.6	1	10	60	7

Additional pro statistics: Rushed once for no yards, 1977 and 1984; recovered one fumble for minus nine yards, 1977; attempted one pass with no completions, 1977, 1979 and 1982; recovered two fumbles, 1978, 1981 and 1984; rushed twice for no yards, 1978; recovered one fumble, 1979; rushed once for 10 yards and attempted one pass with one completion for 18 yards, 1981; rushed twice for two yards, 1983; attempted two passes with one completion for seven yards, 1984.

Played in NFC Championship Game following 1984 season.

WILLIAM F. BATES

(Bill)

Safety—Dallas Cowboys

Born June 6, 1961, at Knoxville, Tenn.
Height, 6.01. Weight, 201.
High School—Knoxville, Tenn., Farragut.
Attended University of Tennessee.

Selected by New Jersey in 1983 USFL territorial draft.
Signed as free agent by Dallas Cowboys, April 28, 1983.
On injured reserve with hip injury, September 3 through September 27, 1984; activated, September 28, 1984.
Dallas NFL, 1983 and 1984.
Games: 1983 (16), 1984 (12). Total—28.
Pro statistics: Intercepted one pass for 29 yards, recovered two fumbles and fumbled once, 1983; intercepted one pass for three yards and recovered one fumble, 1984.
Played in Pro Bowl (NFL All-Star Game) following 1984 season.

RALPH KEITH BATTLE

Safety—New York Giants

Born June 15, 1961, at Huntsville, Ala.
Height, 6.02. Weight, 195.
High School—Huntsville, Ala., J.O. Johnson.
Attended Jacksonville State University.

Selected by Memphis in 17th round (337th player selected) of 1984 USFL draft.
Signed as free agent by Cincinnati Bengals, May 20, 1984.
Released by Cincinnati Bengals, August 20, 1984; re-signed by Bengals, August 29, 1984.

Released by Cincinnati Bengals, September 26, 1984; signed as free agent by New York Giants, March 21, 1985.
Cincinnati NFL, 1984.
Games: 1984 (3).

ROBERT GLENN BAUMHOWER
(Bob)
Defensive Tackle—Miami Dolphins
Born August 4, 1955, at Portsmouth, Va.
Height, 6.05. Weight, 265.
High Schools—Palm Beach, Fla., Palm Beach Gardens and Tuscaloosa, Ala.
Attended University of Alabama.

Named to THE SPORTING NEWS AFC All-Star Team, 1979.
Named to THE SPORTING NEWS NFL All-Star Team, 1981.
Selected by Miami in 2nd round (40th player selected) of 1977 NFL draft.
Miami NFL, 1977 through 1984.
Games: 1977 (14), 1978 (16), 1979 (16), 1980 (16), 1981 (16), 1982 (9), 1983 (16), 1984 (15). Total—118.
Pro statistics: Recovered three fumbles, 1977; recovered two fumbles for 13 yards and one touchdown and inter-
cepted one pass for no yards, 1978; recovered one fumble, 1979 and 1983; recovered four fumbles for 14 yards, 1980;
recovered three fumbles for 10 yards, 1981; recovered two fumbles for 23 yards and a touchdown, 1984.
Played in AFC Championship Game following 1982 and 1984 seasons.
Played in NFL Championship Game following 1982 and 1984 seasons.
Played in Pro Bowl (NFL All-Star Game) following 1979 and 1981 through 1983 seasons.
Named to Pro Bowl following 1984 season; replaced due to injury by Joe Klecko.

MARTIN BAYLESS
Safety—Buffalo Bills
Born October 11, 1962, at Dayton, O.
Height, 6.02. Weight, 195.
High School—Dayton, O., Belmont.
Attended Bowling Green State University.

Selected by Memphis in 1st round (20th player selected) of 1984 USFL draft.
Selected by St. Louis in 4th round (101st player selected) of 1984 NFL draft.
Signed by St. Louis Cardinals, July 20, 1984.
Released by St. Louis Cardinals, September 19, 1984; awarded on waivers to Buffalo Bills, September 20, 1984.
St. Louis (3)-Buffalo (13) NFL, 1984.
Games: 1984 (16).

PAT BEACH
Tight End—Indianapolis Colts
Born December 28, 1956, at Grant's Pass, Ore.
Height, 6.04. Weight, 243.
High School—Pullman, Wash.
Attended Washington State University.

Named as tight end on THE SPORTING NEWS College All-America team, 1981.
Selected by Baltimore in 6th round (140th player selected) of 1982 NFL draft.
Franchise transferred to Indianapolis, March 31, 1984.
On non-football injury list with ankle injury, August 10 through August 21, 1984.
On injured reserve with ankle injury, August 22 through entire 1984 season.

		—PASS RECEIVING—				
Year	Club	G.	P.C.	Yds.	Avg.	TD.
1982—Baltimore NFL		9	4	45	11.3	1
1983—Baltimore NFL		16	5	56	11.2	1
Pro Totals—2 Years		25	9	101	11.2	2

Additional pro statistics: Returned one kickoff for no yards, 1983.

THOMAS LYNN BEASLEY
(Tom)
Defensive End—Washington Redskins
Born August 11, 1954, at Bluefield, W. Va.
Height, 6.05. Weight, 248.
High School—Northfork, W. Va.
Attended Virginia Polytechnic Institute.

Selected by Pittsburgh in 3rd round (60th player selected) of 1977 NFL draft.
On injured reserve entire 1977 season.
Released by Pittsburgh Steelers, August 27, 1984; signed as free agent by Washington Redskins, September 19, 1984.
Pittsburgh NFL, 1978 through 1983; Washington NFL, 1984.
Games: 1978 (15), 1979 (13), 1980 (15), 1981 (13), 1982 (7), 1983 (16), 1984 (13). Total—92.
Pro statistics: Recovered one fumble, 1982 and 1984; recovered two fumbles, 1983.
Played in AFC Championship Game following 1978 and 1979 seasons.
Played in NFL Championship Game following 1978 and 1979 seasons.

—DID YOU KNOW—
That the 1984 Bears' 72 quarterback sacks eclipsed the old mark (67) set by the Raiders in 1967?

KURT FRANK BECKER
Guard—Chicago Bears
Born December 22, 1958, at Aurora, Ill.
Height, 6.05. Weight, 270.
High School—Aurora, Ill., East.
Attended University of Michigan.

Selected by Chicago in 6th round (146th player selected) of 1982 NFL draft.
On inactive list, September 12 and September 19, 1982.
Chicago NFL, 1982 through 1984.
Games: 1982 (5), 1983 (16), 1984 (16). Total—37.
Played in NFC Championship Game following 1984 season.

EDWIN JAY BECKMAN
(Ed)
Tight End—Kansas City Chiefs
Born January 2, 1955, at Key West, Fla.
Height, 6.04. Weight, 227.
High School—Miami, Fla., South.
Attended Florida State University.

Signed as free agent by Kansas City Chiefs, May, 1977.

Year Club	G.	P.C.	Yds.	Avg.	TD.	Year Club	G.	P.C.	Yds.	Avg.	TD.
1977—Kansas City NFL	14	1	3	3.0	0	1982—Kansas City NFL	9		None		
1978—Kansas City NFL	16		None			1983—Kansas City NFL	15	13	130	10.0	0
1979—Kansas City NFL	9	2	21	10.5	0	1984—Kansas City NFL	13	7	44	6.3	1
1980—Kansas City NFL	16		None			Pro Totals—8 Years	107	23	198	8.6	1
1981—Kansas City NFL	15		None								

Additional pro statistics: Credited with one safety and returned three kickoffs for 74 yards, 1978; recovered one fumble and returned three kickoffs for 38 yards, 1980; fumbled once, 1983.

JOHN THOMAS BELCHER
(Jack) .
Center—New York Giants
Born April 17, 1961, at Boston, Mass.
Height, 6.04. Weight, 265.
High School—Stoneham, Mass.
Attended Boston College.

Selected by Boston in 1983 USFL territorial draft.
Selected by Los Angeles Rams in 9th round (227th player selected) of 1983 NFL draft.
Signed by Los Angeles Rams, June 3, 1983.
Released by Los Angeles Rams, June 3, 1983; signed by Boston Breakers, September 2, 1983.
Franchise transferred to New Orleans, October 18, 1983.
On developmental squad, March 21 through remainder of 1984 season.
Franchise transferred to Portland, November 13, 1984.
On developmental squad, February 21 through March 10, 1985.
Released by Portland Breakers, March 11, 1985; signed as free agent by New York Giants, March 22, 1985.
On developmental squad for 14 games with New Orleans Breakers in 1984.
On developmental squad for 3 games with Portland Breakers in 1985.
New Orleans USFL, 1984.
Games: 1984 (3).

KEVIN BELCHER
Guard—New York Giants
Born February 23, 1961, at Detroit, Mich.
Height, 6.03. Weight, 276.
High School—Detroit, Mich., Redfore.
Attended University of Texas at El Paso.

Selected by Arizona in 20th round (239th player selected) of 1983 USFL draft.
Selected by New York Giants in 6th round (153rd player selected) of 1983 NFL draft.
Signed by New York Giants, July 7, 1983.
Expected to miss 1985 season due to nerve damage in foot.
New York Giants NFL, 1983 and 1984.
Games: 1983 (16), 1984 (16). Total—32.
Pro statistics: Caught one pass for four yards, 1984.

ANTHONY LOVETT BELK
(Rocky)
Wide Receiver—Los Angeles Raiders
Born June 20, 1960, at Alexandria, Va.
Height, 6.00. Weight, 187.
High School—Alexandria, Va., Fort Hunt.
Attended University of Miami (Fla.).

Selected by Washington in 15th round (172nd player selected) of 1983 USFL draft.

Selected by Cleveland in 7th round (176th player selected) of 1983 NFL draft.
Signed by Cleveland Browns, May 11, 1983.
Released by Cleveland Browns, August 27, 1984; signed as free agent by Los Angeles Raiders for 1985, November 10, 1984.

		—PASS RECEIVING—				
Year	Club	G.	P.C.	Yds.	Avg.	TD.
1983—Cleveland NFL		10	5	141	28.2	2

Additional pro statistics: Rushed once for minus five yards, 1983.

BOBBY LEE BELL JR.
Linebacker—New York Jets

Born February 7, 1962, at St. Paul, Minn.
Height, 6.03. Weight, 217.
High School—Lee's Summit, Mo.
Attended University of Missouri.
Son of Bobby Bell Sr., Hall of Fame linebacker with Kansas City Chiefs, 1963 through 1974.

Selected by Chicago in 3rd round (43rd player selected) of 1984 USFL draft.
Selected by New York Jets in 4th round (91st player selected) of 1984 NFL draft.
Signed by New York Jets, May 29, 1984.
New York Jets NFL, 1984.
Games: 1984 (15).

GERARD ALFRED BELL
(Jerry)
Tight End—Tampa Bay Buccaneers

Born March 7, 1959, at Derby, Conn.
Height, 6.05. Weight, 230.
High School—El Cerrito, Calif.
Received bachelor of science degree in computer information systems
from Arizona State University in 1982.
Selected by Tampa Bay in 3rd round (74th player selected) of 1982 NFL draft.

		—PASS RECEIVING—				
Year	Club	G.	P.C.	Yds.	Avg.	TD.
1982—Tampa Bay NFL		9	1	5	5.0	0
1983—Tampa Bay NFL		16	18	200	11.1	1
1984—Tampa Bay NFL		16	29	397	13.7	4
Pro Totals—3 Years		41	48	602	12.5	5

Additional pro statistics: Recovered one fumble, 1983 and 1984; fumbled once, 1983.

GREG LEON BELL
Running Back—Buffalo Bills

Born August 1, 1962, at Columbus, O.
Height, 5.10. Weight, 210.
High School—Columbus, O., South.
Received bachelor of arts degree in economics from University of Notre Dame in 1984.
Selected by Chicago in 1984 USFL territorial draft.
Selected by Buffalo in 1st round (26th player selected) of 1984 NFL draft.
Signed by Buffalo Bills, July 23, 1984.

		—RUSHING—					PASS RECEIVING				—TOTAL—		
Year	Club	G.	Att.	Yds.	Avg.	TD.	P.C.	Yds.	Avg.	TD.	TD.	Pts.	F.
1984—Buffalo NFL		16	262	1100	4.2	7	34	277	8.1	1	8	48	5

Additional pro statistics: Returned one kickoff for 15 yards and recovered three fumbles, 1984.
Played in Pro Bowl (NFL All-Star Game) following 1984 season.

MARK E. BELL
Tight End—Indianapolis Colts

Born August 30, 1957, at Wichita, Kan.
Height, 6.05. Weight, 246.
High School—Wichita, Kan., Bishop Carroll.
Attended Colorado State University.
Twin brother of Mike Bell, defensive end with Kansas City Chiefs.

Selected by Seattle in 4th round (102nd player selected) of 1979 NFL draft.
On injured reserve with knee injury, September 1 through entire 1981 season.
Released by Seattle Seahawks, August 23, 1983; signed as free agent by Baltimore Colts, October 25, 1983.
Franchise transferred to Indianapolis, March 31, 1984.
Seattle NFL, 1979, 1980 and 1982; Baltimore NFL, 1983; Indianapolis NFL, 1984.
Games: 1979 (16), 1980 (16), 1982 (9), 1983 (7), 1984 (16). Total—64.
Additional pro statistics: Caught two passes for 20 yards, recovered one fumble, 1979 and 1984; fumbled once, 1979; caught one pass for 13 yards, 1980.

MIKE J. BELL
Defensive End—Kansas City Chiefs
Born August 30, 1957, at Wichita, Kan.
Height, 6.04. Weight, 250.
High School—Wichita, Kan., Bishop Carroll.
Attended Colorado State University.
Twin brother of Mark E. Bell, tight end with Indianapolis Colts.

Named as defensive lineman on THE SPORTING NEWS College All-America Team, 1978.
Selected by Kansas City in 1st round (2nd player selected) of 1979 NFL draft.
On injured reserve with knee injury, October 9 through November 16, 1979; activated, November 17, 1979.
On injured reserve with torn bicep, September 20 through remainder of 1980 season.
On injured reserve with groin injury, December 14 through remainder of 1982 season.
On injured reserve with knee injury, December 13 through remainder of 1984 season.
Kansas City NFL, 1979 through 1984.
Games: 1979 (11), 1980 (2), 1981 (16), 1982 (6), 1983 (16), 1984 (15). Total—66.
Pro statistics: Recovered one fumble, 1979, 1981 and 1983; recovered two fumbles and fumbled once, 1984.

RICHARD THOMAS BELL
(Rick)
Running Back—Minnesota Vikings
Born October 18, 1960, at St. Cloud, Minn.
Height, 6.00. Weight, 205.
High School—Cold Spring, Minn., Rocori.
Received bachelor of science degree in business from
St. John's University in 1983.

Signed as free agent by Minnesota Vikings, July 8, 1983.
Released by Minnesota Vikings, August 29, 1983; re-signed by Vikings, September 13, 1983.
Released by Minnesota Vikings, August 21, 1984; re-signed by Vikings, May 10, 1985.
Minnesota NFL, 1983.
Games: 1983 (14).
Pro statistics: Returned one kickoff for 14 yards, 1983.

THEOPOLIS BELL JR.
(Theo)
Wide Receiver—Tampa Bay Buccaneers
Born December 21, 1953, at Bakersfield, Calif.
Height, 6.00. Weight, 190.
High School—Bakersfield, Calif.
Received degree in public management from University of Arizona in 1983.

Selected by Pittsburgh in 4th round (120th player selected) of 1976 NFL draft.
On injured reserve entire 1977 season.
Left Pittsburgh Steelers camp voluntarily and granted roster exemption, August 25 through August 27, 1981.
Released by Pittsburgh Steelers, August 28, 1981; signed as free agent by Tampa Bay Buccaneers, September 2, 1981.
On physically unable to perform/active with strained calf, July 22 through August 7, 1983; activated, August 8, 1983.

Year Club	G.	RUSHING Att.	Yds.	Avg.	TD.	PASS RECEIVING P.C.	Yds.	Avg.	TD.	TOTAL TD.	Pts.	F.
1976—Pittsburgh NFL	14	1	5	5.0	0	3	43	14.3	1	1	6	5
1978—Pittsburgh NFL	16		None				6	53	8.8	1	1	6	0
1979—Pittsburgh NFL	13		None				3	61	20.3	0	0	0	1
1980—Pittsburgh NFL	14		None				29	748	25.8	2	2	12	1
1981—Tampa Bay NFL	16	1	7	7.0	0	21	318	15.1	2	2	12	1
1982—Tampa Bay NFL	9		None				15	203	13.5	0	0	0	0
1983—Tampa Bay NFL	16		None				25	410	16.4	2	2	12	0
1984—Tampa Bay NFL	15		None				22	350	15.9	0	0	0	0
Pro Totals—8 Years	113	2	12	6.0	0	124	2186	17.6	8	8	48	8

Year Club	G.	PUNT RETURNS No.	Yds.	Avg.	TD.
1976—Pittsburgh NFL	14	39	390	10	0
1978—Pittsburgh NFL	16	21	152	7.2	0
1979—Pittsburgh NFL	13	45	378	8.4	0
1980—Pittsburgh NFL	14	34	339	10.0	0
1981—Tampa Bay NFL	16	27	132	4.9	0
1982—Tampa Bay NFL	9	9	62	6.9	0
1983—Tampa Bay NFL	16	10	48	4.8	0
1984—Tampa Bay NFL	15	4	10	2.5	0
Pro Totals—8 Years	113	189	1511	8.0	0

Additional pro statistics: Recovered four fumbles, 1976; recovered one fumble, 1978; recovered two fumbles for 22 yards, 1979; returned three kickoffs for 50 yards, 1980; fumbled once, 1984.
Played in AFC Championship Game following 1976, 1978 and 1979 seasons.
Played in NFL Championship Game following 1978 and 1979 seasons.

—DID YOU KNOW—
That the Seattle Seahawks, who led the NFL in interceptions with 38 in 1984, returned seven for touchdowns?

TODD ANTHONY BELL
Safety—Chicago Bears

Born November 28, 1958, at Middletown, O.
Height, 6.01. Weight, 207.
High School—Middletown, O.
Attended Ohio State University.

Named to THE SPORTING NEWS NFL All-Star Team, 1984.
Selected by Chicago in 4th round (95th player selected) of 1981 NFL draft.

| | | ——INTERCEPTIONS—— | | | |
Year Club	G.	No.	Yds.	Avg.	TD.
1981—Chicago NFL	16	1	92	92.0	1
1982—Chicago NFL	9		None		
1983—Chicago NFL	15		None		
1984—Chicago NFL	16	4	46	11.5	1
Pro Totals—4 Years	56	5	138	27.6	2

Additional pro statistics: Recovered one fumble, 1981; returned one kickoff for 14 yards, 1982; returned two kickoffs for 18 yards and recovered one fumble for 10 yards, 1983; returned two kickoffs for 33 yards and recovered two fumbles for four yards, 1984.
Played in NFC Championship Game following 1984 season.
Played in Pro Bowl (NFL All-Star Game) following 1984 season.

RODNEY CARWELL BELLINGER
Cornerback—Buffalo Bills

Born June 4, 1962, at Miami, Fla.
Height, 5.08. Weight, 181.
High School—Coral Gables, Fla.
Attended University of Miami (Fla).

Selected by Houston in 2nd round (40th player selected) of 1984 USFL draft.
Selected by Buffalo in 3rd round (77th player selected) of 1984 NFL draft.
Signed by Buffalo Bills, July 12, 1984.
On injured reserve with fractured cervical disc, September 13 through October 25, 1984; activated, October 26, 1984.

| | | ——INTERCEPTIONS—— | | | |
Year Club	G.	No.	Yds.	Avg.	TD.
1984—Buffalo NFL	10	1	0	0.0	0

JESSE JAMES BENDROSS
Wide Receiver—San Diego Chargers

Born May 19, 1961, at Hollywood, Fla.
Height, 6.00. Weight, 197.
High School—Miramar, Fla.
Attended Alabama University.

Selected by Birmingham in 1984 USFL territorial draft.
Selected by San Diego in 7th round (174th player selected) of 1984 NFL draft.
Signed by San Diego Chargers, July 12, 1984.

| | | ——PASS RECEIVING—— | | | |
Year Club	G.	P.C.	Yds.	Avg.	TD.
1984—San Diego NFL	16	16	213	13.3	0

Additional pro statistics: Fumbled once, 1984.

ROLF JOACHIM BENIRSCHKE

Name pronounced Ben-ER-shka.

Placekicker—San Diego Chargers

Born February 7, 1955, at Boston, Mass.
Height, 6.01. Weight, 184.
High School—LaJolla, Calif.
Received bachelor of science degree in zoology from University of California at Davis in 1977.

Selected by Oakland in 12th round (334th player selected) of 1977 NFL draft.
Claimed on waivers from Oakland Raiders by San Diego Chargers, September 13, 1977.
On injured reserve with internal disorder, September 29 through remainder of 1979 season.

| | | ——PLACE KICKING—— | | | | |
Year Club	G.	XP.	XPM.	FG.	FGA.	Pts.
1977—San Diego NFL	14	21	3	17	23	72
1978—San Diego NFL	15	37	*6	18	22	91
1979—San Diego NFL	4	12	1	4	4	24
1980—San Diego NFL	16	46	2	24	36	118
1981—San Diego NFL	16	*55	6	19	26	112
1982—San Diego NFL	9	*32	2	16	22	80
1983—San Diego NFL	16	43	2	15	24	88
1984—San Diego NFL	14	41	0	17	26	92
Pro Totals—8 Years	104	287	22	130	183	677

Played in AFC Championship Game following 1980 and 1981 seasons.
Played in Pro Bowl (NFL All-Star Game) following 1982 season.

DAN BENISH
Defensive Tackle—Atlanta Falcons
Born November 21, 1961, at Youngstown, O.
Height, 6.05. Weight, 265.
High School—Hubbard, O.
Attended Clemson University.

Selected by Washington in 1983 USFL territorial draft.
Signed as free agent by Atlanta Falcons, May 3, 1983.
Atlanta NFL, 1983 and 1984.
Games: 1983 (16), 1984 (15). Total—31.

BARRY MARTIN BENNETT
Defensive Tackle-End—New York Jets
Born December 10, 1955, at St. Paul, Minn.
Height, 6.04. Weight, 257.
High School—St. Paul, Minn., North.
Received bachelor of science degree in physical education from Concordia College in 1977.

Selected by New Orleans in 3rd round (60th player selected) of 1978 NFL draft.
On injured reserve with neck injury, October 2 through remainder of 1981 season.
Released by New Orleans Saints, June 24, 1982; signed as free agent by Minnesota Vikings, July 20, 1982.
Released by Minnesota Vikings, September 6, 1982; signed as free agent by New York Jets, September 8, 1982.
On inactive list, September 19, 1982.
New Orleans NFL, 1978 through 1981; New York Jets NFL, 1982 through 1984.
Games: 1978 (16), 1979 (16), 1980 (15), 1981 (3), 1982 (7), 1983 (13), 1984 (15). Total—85.
Pro statistics: Recovered four fumbles for six yards, 1984.
Member of New York Jets for AFC Championship Game following 1982 season; did not play.

BEN BENNETT
Quarterback—Atlanta Falcons
Born May 5, 1962, at Greensboro, N.C.
Height, 6.01. Weight, 195.
High School—Sunnyvale, Calif., Peterson.
Received bachelor of arts degree in history and psychology from Duke University.

Selected by Jacksonville in 1984 USFL territorial draft.
Selected by Atlanta in 6th round (148th player selected) of 1984 NFL draft.
Signed by Jacksonville Bulls, May 5, 1984.
Granted roster exemption, May 5 through May 31, 1984.
On developmental squad, June 1 through June 7, 1984; activated, June 8, 1984.
Released by Jacksonville Bulls, February 7, 1985; signed by Atlanta Falcons, February 26, 1985.
On developmental squad for 1 game with Jacksonville Bulls in 1984.

		—————PASSING—————							—————RUSHING—————				—TOTAL—		
Year	Club	G.	Att.	Cmp.	Pct.	Gain	T.P.	P.I.	Avg.	Att.	Yds.	Avg.	TD.	TD.	Pts.	F.
1984—Jacksonville USFL............		2	13	7	53.8	113	1	0	8.69		None			0	0	0

USFL Quarterback Rating Points: 1984 (108.8).

WOODROW BENNETT JR.
(Woody)
Fullback—Miami Dolphins
Born March 24, 1955, at York, Pa.
Height, 6.02. Weight, 222.
High School—York, Pa., William Penn.
Attended Arizona Western Junior College and University of Miami.

Signed as free agent by Montreal Alouettes, April, 1979.
Released by Montreal Alouettes, June 22, 1979; signed as free agent by New York Jets, July 9, 1979.
Released by New York Jets, November 17, 1980; claimed on waivers by Miami Dolphins, November 18, 1980.
On injured reserve with knee injury, September 22 through remainder of 1981 season.
On physically unable to perform/active list with knee injury, July 22 through August 23, 1982; activated, August 24, 1982.
On injured reserve with knee injury, September 7 through December 30, 1982; activated, December 31, 1982.

		—————RUSHING—————					PASS RECEIVING				—TOTAL—		
Year	Club	G.	Att.	Yds.	Avg.	TD.	P.C.	Yds.	Avg.	TD.	TD.	Pts.	F.
1979—New York Jets NFL..............		15	2	4	2.0	1	1	9	9.0	0	1	6	1
1980—New York Jets (8)-Miami (4) NFL.......		12	46	200	4.3	0	3	26	8.7	1	1	6	2
1981—Miami NFL.................		3	28	104	3.7	0	4	22	5.5	0	0	0	1
1982—Miami NFL.................		1	9	15	1.7	0		None			0	0	0
1983—Miami NFL.................		16	49	197	4.0	2	6	35	5.8	0	2	12	1
1984—Miami NFL.................		16	144	606	4.2	7	6	44	7.3	1	8	48	4
Pro Totals—6 Years..............		63	278	1126	4.1	10	20	136	6.8	2	12	72	9

Additional pro statistics: Returned one kickoff for seven yards, 1979; recovered two fumbles, 1980 and 1984; returned six kickoffs for 88 yards, 1980; recovered one fumble, 1981 and 1983; returned one kickoff for six yards, 1983.
Played in AFC Championship Game following 1982 and 1984 seasons.
Played in NFL Championship Game following 1982 and 1984 seasons.

BRADLEY WILLIAM BENSON
(Brad)
Offensive Tackle—New York Giants
Born November 25, 1955, at Altoona, Pa.
Height, 6.03. Weight, 270.
High School—Altoona, Pa.
Attended Pennsylvania State University.

Selected by New England in 8th round (219th player selected) of 1977 NFL draft.
Released by New England Patriots, September 1, 1977; signed as free agent by New York Giants, November 15, 1977.
On injured reserve with knee injury, August 28 through September 27, 1979; activated, September 28, 1979.
Active for 5 games with New York Giants in 1977; did not play.
New York Giants NFL, 1977 through 1984.
Games: 1978 (16), 1979 (10), 1980 (15), 1981 (11), 1982 (9), 1983 (16), 1984 (16). Total—93.
Pro statistics: Recovered one fumble, 1979.

CHARLES BENSON
Defensive End—Miami Dolphins
Born November 21, 1960, at Houston, Tex.
Height, 6.03. Weight, 267.
High School—Houston, Tex., Aldine.
Attended Baylor University.

Selected by New Jersey in 10th round (118th player selected) of 1983 USFL draft.
Selected by Miami in 3rd round (76th player selected) of 1983 NFL draft.
Signed by Miami Dolphins, July 9, 1983.
On injured reserve with groin injury, August 30 through October 27, 1983; activated, October 28, 1983.
Miami NFL, 1983 and 1984.
Games: 1983 (8), 1984 (16). Total—24.
Played in AFC Championship Game following 1984 season.
Played in NFL Championship Game following 1984 season.

CLIFFORD ANTHONY BENSON
(Cliff)
Tight End—Atlanta Falcons
Born August 28, 1961, at Chicago, Ill.
Height, 6.04. Weight 234.
High School—Palos Heights, Ill., Alan B. Shepard.
Received bachelor of arts degree in social work from Purdue University in 1984.

Selected by Oakland in 1st round (11th player selected) of 1984 USFL draft.
Selected by Atlanta Falcons in 5th round (132nd player selected) of 1984 NFL draft.
Signed by Atlanta Falcons, July 12, 1984.

		——PASS RECEIVING——				
Year	Club	G.	P.C.	Yds.	Avg.	TD.
1984—Atlanta NFL		16	26	244	9.4	0

Additional pro statistics: Rushed three times for eight yards, 1984.

THOMAS CARL BENSON
Linebacker—Atlanta Falcons
Born September 6, 1961, at Ardmore, Okla.
Height, 6.02. Weight, 235.
High School—Ardmore, Okla.
Attended University of Oklahoma.
Cousin of Rich Turner, defensive tackle with Green Bay Packers, 1981 through 1983.

Selected by Oklahoma in 1984 USFL territorial draft.
Selected by Atlanta in 2nd round (36th player selected) of 1984 NFL draft.
Signed by Atlanta Falcons, July 22, 1984.
Atlanta NFL, 1984.
Games: 1984 (16).

RUFUS BESS
Cornerback—Minnesota Vikings
Born September 13, 1956, at Hartsville, S.C.
Height, 5.09. Weight, 185.
High School—Hartsville, S.C., Butler.
Attended South Carolina State College.
Cousin of Rusty Russell, offensive tackle with Philadelphia Eagles.

Signed as free agent by Oakland Raiders, June 1, 1979.
Released by Oakland Raiders, August 18, 1980; claimed on waivers by Buffalo Bills, August 20, 1980.
Released by Buffalo Bills, September 6, 1982; claimed on waivers by Minnesota Vikings, September 7, 1982.
On inactive list, September 12, 1982.

			-INTERCEPTIONS-				-PUNT RETURNS-				—TOTAL—		
Year	Club	G.	No.	Yds.	Avg.	TD.	No.	Yds.	Avg.	TD.	TD.	Pts.	F.
1979—Oakland NFL		16	1	0	0.0	0		None			0	0	0
1980—Buffalo NFL		16		None				None			0	0	0

Year Club	G.	INTERCEPTIONS				-PUNT RETURNS-				—TOTAL—		
		No.	Yds.	Avg.	TD.	No.	Yds.	Avg.	TD.	TD.	Pts.	F.
1981—Buffalo NFL	16	1	12	12.0	0	None				0	0	0
1982—Minnesota NFL	8	None				2	17	8.5	0	0	0	0
1983—Minnesota NFL	14	3	38	12.7	0	21	158	7.5	0	0	0	2
1984—Minnesota NFL	16	3	7	2.3	0	2	9	4.5	0	0	0	1
Pro Totals—6 Years	86	8	57	7.1	0	25	184	7.4	0	0	0	3

Additional pro statistics: Recovered one fumble, 1979; returned one kickoff for six yards and recovered two fumbles for four yards, 1981; returned two kickoffs for 44 yards, 1983; returned three kickoffs for 47 yards and recovered two fumbles, 1984.

GREGORY LEE BEST
(Greg)
Safety—Cleveland Browns
Born January 14, 1960, at New Brighton, Pa.
Height, 5.10. Weight, 185.
High School—Beaver Falls, Pa., Black Hawk.
Received bachelor of science degree in construction science
from Kansas State University in 1983.

Signed as free agent by Pittsburgh Steelers, April 28, 1983.
Released by Pittsburgh Steelers, August 29, 1983; re-signed by Steelers, September 20, 1983.
Released by Pittsburgh Steelers, August 20, 1984; signed as free agent by Cleveland Browns, November 14, 1984.
Pittsburgh NFL, 1983; Cleveland NFL, 1984.
Games: 1983 (13), 1984 (5). Total—18.
Pro statistics: Recovered one fumble for 94 yards and a touchdown, 1983.

DOUGLAS LLOYD BETTERS
(Doug)
Defensive End—Miami Dolphins
Born June 11, 1956, at Lincoln, Neb.
Height, 6.07. Weight, 265.
High School—Arlington Heights, Ill., Arlington.
Attended University of Montana and University of Nevada at Reno.

Named to THE SPORTING NEWS NFL All-Star Team, 1983.
Selected by Miami in 6th round (163rd player selected) of 1978 NFL draft.
Miami NFL, 1978 through 1984.
Games: 1978 (16), 1979 (16), 1980 (16), 1981 (15), 1982 (9), 1983 (16), 1984 (16). Total—104.
Pro statistics: Recovered one fumble, 1980 and 1984; recovered four fumbles, 1983.
Played in AFC Championship Game following 1982 and 1984 seasons.
Played in NFL Championship Game following 1982 and 1984 seasons.
Played in Pro Bowl (NFL All-Star Game) following 1983 season.

STERLING DAVID BIAS
(Moe)
Linebacker—Los Angeles Raiders
Born September 1, 1961, at Los Angeles, Calif.
Height, 6.02. Weight, 225.
High School—Los Angeles, Calif., Manuel Arts.
Attended Pasadena City College and University of Illinois.

Selected by Los Angeles Rams in 12th round (328th player selected) of 1984 NFL draft.
Released by Los Angeles Rams, August 21, 1984.
USFL rights traded with dispersal pick by Los Angeles Express to Birmingham Stallions for rights to offensive tackle Rennie Atkins, December 6, 1984.
Signed as free agent by Los Angeles Raiders, March 12, 1985.

DEAN BIASUCCI
Placekicker—Indianapolis Colts
Born July 25, 1962, at Miramar, Fla.
Height, 6.00. Weight, 188.
High School—Miramar, Fla.
Attended Western Carolina University.

Signed as free agent by Atlanta Falcons, May 16, 1984.
Released by Atlanta Falcons, August 14, 1984; signed as free agent by Indianapolis Colts, September 8, 1984.

	——PLACE KICKING——					
Year Club	G.	XP.	XPM.	FG.	FGA.	Pts.
1984—Indianapolis NFL	15	13	1	3	5	22

CRAIG MARLON BINGHAM
Linebacker—Pittsburgh Steelers
Born September 29, 1959, at Kingston, Jamaica, West Indies.
Height, 6.02. Weight, 220.
High School—Stamford, Conn.
Received bachelor of science degree in speech communications
from Syracuse University in 1982.

Selected by Pittsburgh in 6th round (167th player selected) of 1982 NFL draft.
On injured reserve with dislocated thumb, August 28 through October 4, 1984; activated, October 5, 1984.
Pittsburgh NFL, 1982 through 1984.
Games: 1982 (6), 1983 (12), 1984 (11). Total—29.
Pro statistics: Returned one kickoff for 15 yards, 1983; recovered one fumble, 1984.
Played in AFC Championship Game following 1984 season.

GREGORY RALEIGH BINGHAM
(Gregg)
Linebacker—Houston Oilers
Born March 13, 1951, at Evanston, Ill.
Height, 6.01. Weight, 232.
High School—Chicago, Ill., Gordon Tech.
Attended Purdue University.

Selected by Houston in 4th round (79th player selected) of 1973 NFL draft.
On inactive list, September 12 and September 19, 1982.

Year Club	G.	No.	Yds.	Avg.	TD.
1973—Houston NFL	14	2	22	11.0	0
1974—Houston NFL	14	4	36	9.0	0
1975—Houston NFL	14	4	57	14.3	0
1976—Houston NFL	14	2	18	9.0	0
1977—Houston NFL	14	2	36	18.0	0
1978—Houston NFL	16	None			
1979—Houston NFL	16	3	78	26.0	0
1980—Houston NFL	16	None			
1981—Houston NFL	16	2	20	10.0	0
1982—Houston NFL	7	1	8	8.0	0
1983—Houston NFL	16	1	4	4.0	0
1984—Houston NFL	16	None			
Pro Totals—12 Years	173	21	279	13.3	0

Additional pro statistics: Recovered one fumble, 1974, 1976 and 1981; recovered one fumble for 34 yards and a touchdown and fumbled once, 1977; recovered two fumbles for two yards, 1978; recovered three fumbles, 1979; returned one kickoff for no yards, fumbled once and recovered two fumbles for nine yards, 1980; recovered two fumbles, 1983; recovered one fumble for seven yards, 1984.
Played in AFC Championship Game following 1978 and 1979 seasons.

GUY RICHARD BINGHAM
Offensive Lineman—New York Jets
Born February 25, 1958, at Koizuma Gumma Ken, Japan.
Height, 6.03. Weight, 255.
High School—Aberdeen, Wash., Weatherwax.
Attended University of Montana.

Selected by New York Jets in 10th round of 1980 NFL draft.
On injured reserve with knee injury, September 7 through November 18, 1982; activated, November 19, 1982.
New York Jets NFL, 1980 through 1984.
Games: 1980 (16), 1981 (16), 1982 (7), 1983 (16), 1984 (16). Total—71.
Pro statistics: Returned one kickoff for 19 yards, 1980; recovered one fumble, 1984.
Played in AFC Championship Game following 1982 season.

STEVE L. BIRD
Wide Receiver—Cincinnati Bengals
Born October 20, 1960, at Indianapolis, Ind.
Height, 5.11. Weight, 171.
High School—Corbin, Ky.
Received bachelor of science degree in industrial technology
from Eastern Kentucky University in 1983.
Son of Jerry Bird, forward with New York Knickerbockers, 1958-59; nephew of Roger Bird,
punt returner with Oakland Raiders, 1966 through 1968.

Selected by Washington in 11th round (130th player selected) of 1983 USFL draft.
Selected by St. Louis in 5th round (130th player selected) of 1983 NFL draft.
Signed by St. Louis Cardinals, May 27, 1983.
Released by St. Louis Cardinals, October 24, 1984; signed as free agent by San Diego Chargers, November 2, 1984.
Released by San Diego Chargers, November 7, 1984; signed as free agent by Cincinnati Bengals, March 16, 1985.

Year Club	G.	—PUNT RETURNS—				—KICKOFF RET.—				—TOTAL—		
		No.	Yds.	Avg.	TD.	No.	Yds.	Avg.	TD.	TD.	Pts.	F.
1983—St. Louis NFL	14	14	76	5.4	0	9	194	21.6	0	0	0	1
1984—St. Louis (8)-San Diego (1) NFL	9	6	60	10.0	0	11	205	18.6	0	0	0	1
Pro Totals—2 Years	23	20	136	6.8	0	20	399	20.0	0	0	0	2

Additional pro statistics: Recovered one fumble, 1983.

CARL BIRDSONG
Punter—St. Louis Cardinals
Born January 1, 1959, at Kaufman, Tex.
Height, 6.00. Weight, 192.
High School—Amarillo, Tex.
Received bachelor of science degree in pharmacy
from Southwestern Oklahoma State University in 1983.

Signed as free agent by Buffalo Bills, May 10, 1981.
Released by Buffalo Bills, July 28, 1981; claimed on waivers by St. Louis Cardinals, July 29, 1981.

Year Club	G.	No.	Avg.	Blk.
1981—St. Louis NFL	16	69	41.8	0
1982—St. Louis NFL	9	54	43.8	0
1983—St. Louis NFL	16	85	41.5	0
1984—St. Louis NFL	16	67	38.7	1
Pro Totals—4 Years	57	275	41.3	1

Additional pro statistics: Rushed once for minus two yards, 1981; attempted one pass with one completion for 11 yards, 1983.

Played in Pro Bowl (NFL All-Star Game) following 1983 season.

KEITH BRYAN BISHOP
Guard-Center—Denver Broncos
Born March 10, 1957, at San Diego, Calif.
Height, 6.03. Weight, 265.
High School—Midland, Tex., Robert E. Lee.
Attended University of Nebraska and Baylor University.

Selected by Denver in 6th round (157th player selected) of 1980 NFL draft.
On injured reserve with ankle injury, August 18 through entire 1981 season.
Denver NFL, 1980 and 1982 through 1984.
Games: 1980 (16), 1982 (9), 1983 (16), 1984 (16). Total—57.
Pro statistics: Recovered one fumble, 1982 and 1983.

JAMES BLACK
Running Back—Cleveland Browns
Born April 3, 1962, at Lima, O.
Height, 5.11. Weight, 198.
High School—Dover, O.
Attended University of Akron.

Signed as free agent by Cleveland Browns, June 15, 1984.
Released by Cleveland Browns, August 20, 1984; re-signed by Browns, November 7, 1984.
Released by Cleveland Browns, November 23, 1984; re-signed by Browns, April 3, 1985.
Cleveland NFL, 1984.
Games: 1984 (2).

PETER MICHAEL BLACK
(Mike)
Punter—Detroit Lions
Born January 18, 1961, at Glendale, Calif.
Height, 6.01. Weight, 197.
High School—Glendale, Calif.
Attended Arizona State University.
Nephew of Virgil Carter, quarterback with Chicago Bears, Cincinnati Bengals
and San Diego Chargers, 1968 through 1972, 1975 and 1976.

Selected by Arizona in 1983 USFL territorial draft.
Selected by Detroit in 7th round (181st player selected) of 1983 NFL draft.
Signed by Detroit Lions, June 2, 1983.

Year Club	G.	No.	Avg.	Blk.
1983—Detroit NFL	16	71	41.0	1
1984—Detroit NFL	16	76	41.6	0
Pro Totals—2 Years	32	147	41.3	1

Additional pro statistics: Rushed twice for minus 10 yards, attempted one pass with one interception and fumbled once, 1983; rushed three times for minus six yards and recovered one fumble, 1984.

TODD ALAN BLACKLEDGE
Quarterback—Kansas City Chiefs
Born February 25, 1961, at Canton, O.
Height, 6.03. Weight, 225.
High School—North Canton, O., Hoover.
Received degree in speech communications from Penn State University in 1983.
Son of Ron Blackledge, offensive line coach with Pittsburgh Steelers.

Selected by Kansas City in 1st round (7th player selected) of 1983 NFL draft.
Selected by Philadelphia in 1984 USFL territorial draft.

Year Club	G.	Att.	Cmp.	Pct.	Gain	T.P.	P.I.	Avg.	Att.	Yds.	Avg.	TD.	TD.	Pts.	F.
				PASSING						RUSHING			TOTAL		
1983—Kansas City NFL	4	34	20	58.8	259	3	0	7.62	1	0	0.0	0	0	0	1
1984—Kansas City NFL	11	294	147	50.0	1707	6	11	5.81	18	102	5.7	1	1	6	8
Pro Totals—2 Years	15	328	167	50.9	1966	9	11	5.99	19	102	5.4	1	1	6	9

Quarterback Rating Points: 1983 (112.3), 1984 (59.2). Total—64.3.
Additional pro statistics: Recovered four fumbles and fumbled eight times for minus three yards, 1984.

DONALD KIRK BLACKMON
(Don)
Linebacker—New England Patriots
Born March 14, 1958, at Pompano Beach, Fla.
Height, 6.03. Weight, 235.
High School—Lauderdale Lakes, Fla., Boyd Anderson.
Attended University of Tulsa.
Selected by New England in 4th round (102nd player selected) of 1981 NFL draft.

Year Club	G.	No.	Yds.	Avg.TD.	
1981—New England NFL.......	16		None		
1982—New England NFL.......	9	2	7	3.5	0
1983—New England NFL.......	15	1	39	39.0	0
1984—New England NFL.......	16	1	3	3.0	0
Pro Totals—4 Years............	56	4	49	12.3	0

Additional pro statistics: Recovered two fumbles for 47 yards, 1982.

GLENN ALLEN BLACKWOOD
Safety—Miami Dolphins
Born February 23, 1957, at San Antonio, Tex.
Height, 6.00. Weight, 188.
High School—San Antonio, Tex., Churchill.
Received bachelor of science degree in pre-dental studies from University of Texas in 1979.
Brother of Lyle Blackwood, safety with Miami Dolphins.
Selected by Miami in 8th round (215th player selected) of 1979 NFL draft.
On injured reserve with knee injury, November 19 through remainder of 1979 season.

Year Club	G.	No.	Yds.	Avg.TD.	
1979—Miami NFL	11		None		
1980—Miami NFL	16	3	0	0.0	0
1981—Miami NFL	16	4	124	31.0	0
1982—Miami NFL	9	2	42	21.0	*1
1983—Miami NFL	16	3	0	0.0	0
1984—Miami NFL	16	6	169	28.2	0
Pro Totals—6 Years............	84	18	335	18.6	1

Additional pro statistics: Returned one punt for no yards, 1980; recovered four fumbles, 1980 and 1983; returned two punts for eight yards and recovered one fumble for five yards, 1981; returned two punts for two yards, recovered one fumble, 1982 and 1984; fumbled once, 1982; returned one punt for 10 yards, 1983.
Played in AFC Championship Game following 1982 and 1984 seasons.
Played in NFL Championship Game following 1982 and 1984 seasons.

LYLE V. BLACKWOOD
Safety—Miami Dolphins
Born May 21, 1951, at San Antonio, Tex.
Height, 6.01. Weight, 190.
High School—San Antonio, Tex., Churchill.
Attended Blinn Junior College and Texas Christian University.
Brother of Glenn Blackwood, safety with Miami Dolphins.
Selected by Denver in 9th round (217th player selected) of 1973 NFL draft.
Claimed on waivers from Denver Broncos by Cincinnati Bengals, 1973.
Selected from Cincinnati Bengals by Seattle Seahawks in NFL expansion draft, March 30, 1976.
Claimed on waivers from Seattle Seahawks by Baltimore Colts, August 11, 1977.
Traded by Baltimore Colts to New York Giants for draft pick, July 15, 1977.
Released by New York Giants, August 31, 1981; signed as free agent by Miami Dolphins, September 30, 1981.

Year Club	G.	INTERCEPTIONS No.	Yds.	Avg.	TD.	-PUNT RETURNS- No.	Yds.	Avg.	TD.	—KICKOFF RET.— No.	Yds.	Avg.	TD.	—TOTAL— TD.	Pts.	F.
1973—Cincinnati NFL	7		None			4	12	3.0	0		None			0	0	0
1974—Cincinnati NFL	13		None			10	29	2.9	0	1	17	17.0	0	0	0	0
1975—Cincinnati NFL	14	2	44	22.0	0	23	123	5.3	0		None			0	0	1
1976—Seattle NFL..................	11		None			19	132	6.9	0	9	215	23.8	0	0	0	1
1977—Baltimore NFL	14	*10	163	16.3	0	7	22	3.1	0	1	24	24.0	0	0	0	3
1978—Baltimore NFL	16	4	146	36.5	2	1	2	2.0	0	1	18	18.0	0	2	12	0
1979—Baltimore NFL	16	4	63	15.8	0	4	—1	—0.3	0	3	41	13.7	0	0	0	0
1980—Baltimore NFL	11	1	0	0.0	0		None			2	41	20.5	0	0	0	0
1981—Miami NFL	12	3	12	4.0	0		None				None			0	0	0
1982—Miami NFL	9	2	41	20.5	0		None				None			0	0	0
1983—Miami NFL	16	4	77	19.3	0		None				None			0	0	0
1984—Miami NFL	16	3	29	9.7	0		None				None			0	0	0
Pro Totals—12 Years.....	155	33	575	17.4	2	68	319	4.7	0	17	356	20.9	0	2	12	5

Additional pro statistics: Recovered one fumble, 1975 and 1982; blocked two kicks and caught one pass for eight yards, 1976; recovered four fumbles for four yards, 1977; recovered three fumbles for seven yards, 1978; recovered two fumbles, 1979 and 1984.
Played in AFC Championship Game following 1982 and 1984 seasons.
Played in NFL Championship Game following 1982 and 1984 seasons.

BRIAN TIMOTHY BLADOS
Guard—Cincinnati Bengals
Born January 11, 1962, at Arlington, Va.
Height, 6.04. Weight, 308.
High School—Arlington, Va., Washington Lee.
Attended University of North Carolina.

Selected by Pittsburgh in 1984 USFL territorial draft.
Selected by Cincinnati in 1st round (28th player selected) of 1984 NFL draft.
Signed by Cincinnati Bengals, June 28, 1984.
Cincinnati NFL, 1984.
Games: 1984 (16).

ALBERT MATTHEW BLAIR
(Matt)
Linebacker—Minnesota Vikings
Born September 20, 1950, at Hilo, Hawaii.
Height, 6.05. Weight, 239.
High School—Dayton, O., Colonel White.
Attended Northeastern Oklahoma A&M and received degree in physical education
from Iowa State University.

Named to THE SPORTING NEWS NFC All-Star Team, 1977 and 1978.
Selected by Minnesota in 2nd round (51st player selected) of 1974 NFL draft.
On physically unable to perform/active with knee injury, July 21 through August 20, 1984; activated, August 21, 1984.
On injured reserve with knee injury, August 28 through September 27, 1984; activated, September 28, 1984.

		—INTERCEPTIONS—						—INTERCEPTIONS—			
Year Club	G.	No.	Yds.	Avg.	TD.	Year Club	G.	No.	Yds.	Avg.	TD.
1974—Minnesota NFL	14	1	—3	—3.0	0	1980—Minnesota NFL	14	3	0	0.0	0
1975—Minnesota NFL	14	1	18	18.0	0	1981—Minnesota NFL	16	1	1	1.0	0
1976—Minnesota NFL	14	2	25	12.5	0	1982—Minnesota NFL	9		None		
1977—Minnesota NFL	14	1	18	18.0	0	1983—Minnesota NFL	16	1	0	0.0	0
1978—Minnesota NFL	16	3	28	9.3	0	1984—Minnesota NFL	11		None		
1979—Minnesota NFL	16	3	32	10.7	0	Pro Totals—11 Years	154	16	119	7.4	0

Additional pro statistics: Recovered one fumble for 13 yards, 1974; returned two punts for minus two yards, 1975; fumbled once, 1975 and 1981; recovered five fumbles for eight yards, 1976; returned one kickoff for no yards, 1976 and 1981; recovered two fumbles, 1977, 1981 and 1983; scored one touchdown after blocked kick, 1977; recovered three fumbles for 49 yards and one touchdown (touchdown was 49-yard run with lateral after fumble recovery), 1978; recovered two fumbles for 14 yards, 1979; recovered one fumble, 1980 and 1984.
Played in NFC Championship Game following 1974, 1976 and 1977 seasons.
Played in NFL Championship Game following 1974 and 1976 seasons.
Played in Pro Bowl (NFL All-Star Game) following 1977 through 1982 seasons.

CARL NATHANIEL BLAND
Wide Receiver—Detroit Lions
Born August 17, 1961, at Fluvanna County, Va.
Height, 5.11. Weight, 182.
High School—Richmond, Va., Thomas Jefferson.
Attended Virginia Union University.

Signed as free agent by Detroit Lions, May 3, 1984.
On injured reserve with hamstring injury, August 20 through November 7, 1984; activated after clearing procedural waivers, November 9, 1984.
Detroit NFL, 1984.
Games: 1984 (3).

GERALD BLANTON
(Jerry)
Linebacker—Kansas City Chiefs
Born February 20, 1956, at Toledo, O.
Height, 6.01. Weight, 236.
High School—Toledo, O., Thomas A. Devilbiss.
Attended University of Kentucky.

Selected by Buffalo in 11th round (282nd player selected) of 1978 NFL draft.
Released by Buffalo Bills, August 24, 1978; signed as free agent by Hamilton Tiger-Cats, September 8, 1978.
Released by Hamilton Tiger-Cats, September 15, 1978; signed as free agent by Kansas City Chiefs, December 28, 1978.
On injured reserve with knee injury, September 1 through October 16, 1981; activated, October 17, 1981.
On injured reserve with knee injury, December 15 through remainder of 1981 season.
On injured reserve with ruptured disc in back, August 28 through October 12, 1984; activated, October 13, 1984.
Hamilton CFL, 1978; Kansas City NFL, 1979 through 1984.
Games: 1978 (1), 1979 (16), 1980 (16), 1981 (9), 1982 (9), 1983 (16), 1984 (10). Total NFL—76. Total Pro—77.
Pro statistics: Recovered one fumble, 1979 and 1984; intercepted one pass for 14 yards, 1984.

DENNIS BLIGEN
Fullback—New York Jets
Born March 3, 1962, at New York, N.Y.
Height, 5.11. Weight, 216.
High School—New York, N.Y., Murray Bergtraum.
Attended St. John's University.

Signed as free agent by New York Jets, May 16, 1984.
On injured reserve with fractured thumb, July 31 through October 24, 1984; activated after clearing procedural waivers, October 26, 1984.
Released by New York Jets, November 24, 1984; re-signed by Jets, December 6, 1984.
New York Jets NFL, 1984.
Games: 1984 (1).

DWAINE P. BOARD
Defensive End—San Francisco 49ers
Born November 29, 1956, at Union Hall, Va.
Height, 6.05. Weight, 248.
High School—Rocky Mount, Va., Franklin County.
Received bachelor of science degree in industrial technology from
North Carolina A&T State University in 1979.

Selected by Pittsburgh in 5th round (137th player selected) of 1979 NFL draft.
Released by Pittsburgh Steelers, August 27, 1979; claimed on waivers by San Francisco 49ers, August 28, 1979.
On injured reserve with knee injury, September 23 through remainder of 1980 season.
On injured reserve with knee injury, September 16 through remainder of 1982 season.
San Francisco NFL, 1979 through 1984.
Games: 1979 (16), 1980 (3), 1981 (16), 1982 (1), 1983 (16), 1984 (16). Total—68.
Pro statistics: Recovered five fumbles (including one in end zone for a touchdown), 1983; recovered one fumble, 1984.
Played in NFC Championship Game following 1981, 1983 and 1984 seasons.
Played in NFL Championship Game following 1981 and 1984 seasons.

FREDERICK JEROME BOHANNON
(Fred)
Defensive Back—Tampa Bay Buccaneers
Born May 31, 1958, at Birmingham, Ala.
Height, 6.02. Weight, 205.
High School—Birmingham, Ala., Woodlawn.
Attended Mississippi Valley State University.

Signed as free agent by Toronto Argonauts, April 10, 1982.
Released by Toronto Argonauts, June 20, 1982; signed as free agent by Pittsburgh Steelers, July 15, 1982.
On injured reserve with thigh injury, August 16 through September 4, 1983.
Released by Pittsburgh Steelers, September 5, 1983.
USFL rights traded by Memphis Showboats to Birmingham Stallions for rights to fullback Johnny Davis, December 21, 1983.
Signed by Birmingham Stallions, December 22, 1983.
On developmental squad, April 15 through April 20, 1984; activated, April 21, 1984.
Released by Birmingham Stallions, January 28, 1985; signed as free agent by Tampa Bay Buccaneers, April 18, 1985.
On developmental squad for 1 game with Birmingham Stallions in 1984.

			KICKOFF RETURNS			
Year	Club	G.	No.	Yds.	Avg.	TD.
1982—Pittsburgh USFL		7	14	329	23.5	0
1984—Birmingham USFL		17	3	61	20.3	0
Pro Totals—2 Years		24	17	390	22.9	0

Additional pro statistics: Fumbled three times, 1982; credited with 2½ sacks for 21 yards and recovered two fumbles, 1984.

KIM BOKAMPER
Defensive End—Miami Dolphins
Born September 25, 1954, at San Diego, Calif.
Height, 6.06. Weight, 255.
High School—Milpitas, Calif.
Attended Concordia College, San Jose City College and San Jose State University.

Selected by Miami in 1st round (19th player selected) of 1976 NFL draft.
On injured reserve with knee injury entire 1976 season.
On injured reserve with broken ankle, October 5 through November 1, 1984; activated, November 2, 1984.

		—INTERCEPTIONS—							—INTERCEPTIONS—			
Year	Club	G.	No.	Yds.	Avg.	TD.	Year	Club	G.	No.	Yds.	Avg.	TD.
1977—Miami NFL	14		None			1982—Miami NFL	9	1	1	1.0	0
1978—Miami NFL	16	1	2	2.0	0	1983—Miami NFL	15	2	43	21.5	1
1979—Miami NFL	14	1	3	3.0	0	1984—Miami NFL	11		None		
1980—Miami NFL	16	1	6	6.0	0	Pro Totals—8 Years	111	6	55	9.2	1
1981—Miami NFL	16		None								

Additional pro statistics: Recovered two fumbles for two yards, 1977; credited with one safety, 1978; recovered one fumble and fumbled once, 1983.
Played in AFC Championship Game following 1982 and 1984 seasons.
Played in NFL Championship Game following 1982 and 1984 seasons.
Played in Pro Bowl (NFL All-Star Game) following 1979 season.

RICKEY ALLEN BOLDEN
Tight End—Cleveland Browns
Born September 8, 1961, at Dallas, Tex.
Height, 6.06. Weight, 250.
High School—Dallas, Tex., Hillcrest.
Attended Southern Methodist University.

Selected by Oakland in 4th round (72nd player selected) of 1984 USFL draft.
Selected by Cleveland in 4th round (96th player selected) of 1984 NFL draft.
Signed by Cleveland Browns, May 17, 1984.
On injured reserve with dislocated shoulder, November 21 through remainder of 1984 season.

		——PASS RECEIVING——				
Year	Club	G.	P.C.	Yds.	Avg.	TD.
1984—Cleveland NFL		12	1	19	19.0	0

Additional pro statistics: Fumbled once, 1984.

RUSSELL DEAN BOLINGER
(Russ)
Guard—Los Angeles Rams
Born September 10, 1954, at Wichita, Kan.
Height, 6.05. Weight, 255.
High School—Lompoc, Calif.
Attended University of California at Riverside and California State University at Long Beach.

Selected by Detroit in 3rd round (68th player selected) of 1976 NFL draft.
Traded by Detroit Lions to Los Angeles Rams for 5th round pick in 1983 draft, April 26, 1983.
On injured reserve with knee injury, August 16 through remainder of 1978 season.
Detroit NFL, 1976, 1977 and 1979 through 1982; Los Angeles Rams NFL, 1983 and 1984.
Games: 1976 (12), 1977 (14), 1979 (16), 1980 (16), 1981 (16), 1982 (9), 1983 (16), 1984 (16). Total—115.
Pro statistics: Caught one pass for minus one yard, 1979; recovered one fumble, 1980; recovered two fumbles, 1981.

SCOTT LOUIS BOLZAN
Offensive Tackle—Cleveland Browns
Born July 25, 1962, at Chicago, Ill.
Height, 6.03. Weight, 280.
High School—South Holland, Ill., Thornwood.
Attended Northern Illinois University.

Selected by Chicago in 1984 USFL territorial draft.
Selected by New England in 9th round (238th player selected) of 1984 NFL draft.
Signed by New England Patriots, June 10, 1984.
Released by New England Patriots, August 21, 1984; signed by Chicago Blitz, October 15, 1984.
Franchise disbanded, November 20, 1984.
Selected by Memphis Showboats in USFL dispersal draft, December 6, 1984.
Released by Memphis Showboats, February 11, 1985; re-signed by Showboats, February 22, 1985.
On developmental squad, March 8 through March 15, 1985.
Released by Memphis Showboats, March 16, 1985; signed as free agent by Cleveland Browns, May 6, 1985.
On developmental squad for 1 game with Memphis Showboats in 1985.
Memphis USFL, 1985.
Games: 1985 (2).

ANDREW JOHN BOND
(Known by middle name.)
Tight End—Cleveland Browns
Born March 19, 1961, at Starkville, Miss.
Height, 6.03. Weight, 210.
High School—Valdosta, Ga.
Attended Mississippi State University.

Selected by New Jersey in 1984 USFL territorial draft.
USFL rights traded by New Jersey Generals to Memphis Showboats, January 4, 1984, completing deal in which rights to safety Gary Barbaro were traded by Memphis Showboats to New Jersey Generals for territorial pick in 1984 draft, November 8, 1983.
Signed as free agent by Saskatchewan Roughriders, February 10, 1984.
Selected by Cleveland in 3rd round (77th player selected) of 1984 NFL supplemental draft.
Released by Saskatchewan Roughriders, June 25, 1984; re-signed by Roughriders, July 16, 1984.
On reserve, July 16 through August 11, 1984.
Released by Saskatchewan Roughriders, August 12, 1984; re-signed by Roughriders, March 20, 1985.
Released by Saskatchewan Roughriders, April 29, 1985; signed by Cleveland Browns, May 6, 1985.

MARK BRAXTON BONNER
Offensive Tackle—San Francisco 49ers
Born October 19, 1959, at Sacramento, Calif.
Height, 6.05. Weight, 250.
High School—Sacramento, Calif., Christian Brothers.
Attended Sacramento City College and Oregon State University.

Signed as free agent by Los Angeles Raiders, April 30, 1983.
Released by Los Angeles Raiders, August 16, 1983; signed by Arizona Wranglers, November 6, 1983.
Traded by Arizona Wranglers to Los Angeles Express for future draft pick, January 30, 1984.
Released by Los Angeles Express, February 13, 1984; signed as free agent by San Francisco 49ers, April 10, 1984.
On injured reserve with neck injury, August 13 through entire 1984 season.

JAMIE BOONE
Defensive Back—Cleveland Browns
Born March 6, 1959, at Louisville, Ky.
Height, 6.00. Weight, 205.
High Schools—Red Bank, N.Y., West Point Military Prep and Miami, Fla., Southwest.
Attended University of Miami (Fla.).

Signed by Arizona Wranglers, February 26, 1983.
On developmental squad, March 25 through March 29, 1983.
On injured reserve with knee injury, March 30 through remainder of 1983 season.
Franchise transferred to Chicago, September 30, 1983.
Released by Chicago Blitz, January 30, 1984; signed as free agent by Cleveland Browns, April 3, 1985.
On developmental squad for 1 game with Arizona Wranglers in 1983.
Arizona USFL, 1983.
Games: 1983 (3).
Pro statistics: Returned two punts for 34 yards, 1983.

JON L. BORCHARDT
Guard-Offensive Tackle—Seattle Seahawks
Born August 13, 1957, at Minneapolis, Minn.
Height, 6.05. Weight, 255.
High School—Brooklyn Park, Minn., Park Center.
Received bachelor of science degree in microbiology from Montana State University in 1979.

Selected by Buffalo in 3rd round (62nd player selected) of 1979 NFL draft.
Traded by Buffalo Bills to Seattle Seahawks for draft choice, April 26, 1985.
Buffalo NFL, 1979 through 1984.
Games: 1979 (16), 1980 (16), 1981 (16), 1982 (9), 1983 (16), 1984 (16). Total—89.
Pro statistics: Recovered one fumble, 1981.

MARK STEVEN BORTZ
Guard—Chicago Bears
Born February 12, 1961, at Pardeeville, Wis.
Height, 6.06. Weight, 271.
High School—Pardeeville, Wis.
Attended University of Iowa.

Selected by Los Angeles in 4th round (48th player selected) of 1983 USFL draft.
Selected by Chicago in 8th round (219th player selected) of 1983 NFL draft.
Signed by Chicago Bears, June 2, 1983.
Chicago NFL, 1983 and 1984.
Games: 1983 (16), 1984 (15). Total—31.
Played in NFC Championship Game following 1984 season.

JEFF BOSTIC
Center—Washington Redskins
Born September 18, 1958, at Greensboro, N. C.
Height, 6.02. Weight, 250.
High School—Greensboro, N. C., Benjamin L. Smith.
Attended Clemson University.
Brother of Joe Bostic, guard with St. Louis Cardinals.

Signed as free agent by Philadelphia Eagles, May 20, 1980.
Released by Philadelphia Eagles, August 26, 1980; signed as free agent by Washington Redskins, September 1, 1984.
On injured reserve with knee injury, October 23 through remainder of 1984 season.
Washington NFL, 1980 through 1984.
Games: 1980 (16), 1981 (16), 1982 (9), 1983 (16), 1984 (8). Total—65.
Pro statistics: Recovered one fumble and caught one pass for minus four yards, 1981; recovered three fumbles, 1983; recovered two fumbles, 1984.
Played in NFC Championship Game following 1982 and 1983 seasons.
Played in NFL Championship Game following 1982 and 1983 seasons.
Played in Pro Bowl (NFL All-Star Game) following 1983 season.

JOE EARL BOSTIC JR.
Guard—St. Louis Cardinals
Born April 20, 1957, at Greensboro, N.C.
Height, 6.03. Weight, 265.
High School—Greensboro, N.C., Benjamin L. Smith.
Attended Clemson University.
Brother of Jeff Bostic, center with Washington Redskins.

Selected by St. Louis in 3rd round (64th player selected) of 1979 NFL draft.
St. Louis NFL, 1979 through 1984.
Games: 1979 (16), 1980 (16), 1981 (14), 1982 (8), 1983 (14), 1984 (16). Total—84.
Pro statistics: Recovered one fumble, 1983.

KEITH BOSTIC
Safety—Houston Oilers
Born January 17, 1961, at Ann Arbor, Mich.
Height, 6.01. Weight, 212.
High School—Ann Arbor, Mich., Pioneer.
Attended University of Michigan.

Selected by Michigan in 1983 USFL territorial draft.
Selected by Houston in 2nd round (42nd player selected) of 1983 NFL draft.
Signed by Houston Oilers, June 27, 1983.

| | | —INTERCEPTIONS— | | | |
Year Club	G.	No.	Yds.	Avg.	TD.
1983—Houston NFL	16	2	0	0.0	0
1984—Houston NFL	16		None		
Pro Totals—2 Years	32	2	0	0.0	0

Additional pro statistics: Recovered two fumbles for 25 yards and a touchdown, 1984.

LORENZO BOUIER
Running Back—New York Giants
Born February 27, 1961, at Hartford, Conn.
Height, 6.01. Weight, 205.
High School—Hartford, Conn., Bulkeley.
Attended University of Maine.

Selected by Boston in 10th round (110th player selected) of 1983 USFL draft.
Selected by Dallas in 12th round (331st player selected) of 1983 NFL draft.
Signed by Dallas Cowboys, May 26, 1983.
Released by Dallas Cowboys, July 29, 1983; signed as free agent by Baltimore Colts, August 2, 1983.
Released by Baltimore Colts, August 16, 1983; signed as free agent by New Orleans Breakers, November 12, 1983.
Released by New Orleans Breakers, January 19, 1984; signed as free agent by San Francisco 49ers, April 10, 1984.
Released by San Francisco 49ers, July 19, 1984; signed as free agent by Portland Breakers, January 6, 1985.
Released by Portland Breakers, January 21, 1985; signed as free agent by New York Giants, March 21, 1985.
Played with Connecticut Giants in Atlantic Football League, 1984.

EMIL NICHOLAS BOURES
Offensive Lineman—Pittsburgh Steelers
Born January 29, 1960, at Bridgeport, Pa.
Height, 6.01. Weight, 261.
High School—Norristown, Pa., Bishop Kenrick.
Received bachelor of arts degree in communications from University of Pittsburgh in 1982.

Selected by Pittsburgh in 7th round (182nd player selected) of 1982 NFL draft.
On inactive list, September 13 and September 19, 1982.
On injured reserve with knee injury, November 16 through remainder of 1984 season.
Pittsburgh NFL, 1982 through 1984.
Games: 1982 (5), 1983 (16), 1984 (8). Total—29.
Pro statistics: Fumbled once, 1983.

MATT BOUZA
Wide Receiver—Indianapolis Colts
Born April 8, 1958, at San Jose, Calif.
Height, 6.03. Weight, 211.
High School—Sacramento, Calif., Jesuit.
Attended University of California.

Signed as free agent by San Francisco 49ers, May 8, 1981.
Released by San Francisco 49ers, August 31, 1981; re-signed by 49ers, September 1, 1981.
Released by San Francisco 49ers, September 9, 1981; signed as free agent by Baltimore Colts, May 15, 1982.
On injured reserve with separated shoulder, November 18 through remainder of 1983 season.
Franchise transferred to Indianapolis, March 31, 1984.

| | | —PASS RECEIVING— | | | |
Year Club	G.	P.C.	Yds.	Avg.	TD.
1981—San Francisco NFL	1		None		
1982—Baltimore NFL	9	22	287	13.0	2
1983—Baltimore NFL	11	25	385	15.4	0
1984—Indianapolis NFL	16	22	270	12.3	0
Pro Totals—4 Years	37	69	942	13.7	2

Additional pro statistics: Returned three kickoffs for 31 yards, returned two punts for no yards and recovered one fumble, 1982; fumbled once, 1982 through 1984; returned one kickoff for minus four yards, 1983; returned three punts for 17 yards, 1984.

ALAN MONTEL BOWERS
Running Back—St. Louis Cardinals
Born April 18, 1961, at East St. Louis, Ill.
Height, 6.00. Weight, 206.
High School—East St. Louis, Ill.
Attended Illinois State University.
Spent two years in Navy after first two years of college.

Signed as free agent by St. Louis Cardinals, July 16, 1984.
On injured reserve with broken ankle, August 12 through entire 1984 season.

CHARLES EMANUEL BOWSER
Linebacker—Miami Dolphins
Born October 2, 1959, at Plymouth, N.C.
Height, 6.03. Weight, 232.
High School—Plymouth, N.C.
Received bachelor or arts degree in history from Duke University in 1982.

Selected by Miami in 4th round (108th player selected) of 1982 NFL draft.
Miami NFL, 1982 through 1984.
Games: 1982 (9), 1983 (16), 1984 (15). Total—40.
Pro statistics: Recovered one fumble, 1984.
Played in AFC Championship Game following 1982 and 1984 seasons.
Played in NFL Championship Game following 1982 and 1984 seasons.

WALTER NATHANIEL BOWYER JR.
Name pronounced BOY-er.
(Walt)
Defensive End—Denver Broncos
Born June 29, 1960, at Pittsburgh, Pa.
Height, 6.04. Weight, 252.
High School—Winkinsburg, Pa.
Attended Arizona State University.

Selected by Denver in 10th round (254th player selected) of 1983 NFL draft.
Denver NFL, 1983 and 1984.
Games: 1983 (14), 1984 (16). Total—30.
Pro statistics: Recovered one fumble, 1983 and 1984.

GERARD MARK JOSEPH BOYARSKY
Name pronounced Boy-ARE-ski.
(Jerry)
Nose Tackle—Cincinnati Bengals
Born May 15, 1959, at Scranton, Pa.
Height, 6.03. Weight, 290.
High School—Jermyn, Pa., Lakeland.
Received bachelor of arts degree in political science from University of Pittsburgh in 1981.

Selected by New Orleans in 5th round (128th player selected) of 1981 NFL draft.
On injured reserve with knee injury, September 1 through October 1, 1981; activated, October 2, 1981.
Released by New Orleans Saints, September 6, 1982; signed as free agent by Cincinnati Bengals, December 1, 1982 and 1983.
New Orleans NFL, 1981; Cincinnati NFL, 1982 through 1984.
Games: 1981 (11), 1982 (2), 1983 (15), 1984 (15). Total—43.

BRENT VARNER BOYD
Guard—Minnesota Vikings
Born March 23, 1957, at Downey, Calif.
Height, 6.03. Weight, 275.
High School—La Habra, Calif., Lowell.
Received bachelor of arts degree in sociology from University of California at Los Angeles in 1980,
and attending UCLA for master's degree in business administration.

Selected by Minnesota in 3rd round (68th player selected) of 1980 NFL draft.
On injured reserve with knee injury, September 30 through remainder of 1981 season.
On physically unable to perform/active with knee injury, July 30 through September 1, 1982.
On physically unable to perform/reserve with knee injury, September 2 through November 19, 1982; activated, November 20, 1982.
On injured reserve with fractured fibula, August 27 through entire 1984 season.
Minnesota NFL, 1980 through 1983.
Games: 1980 (16), 1981 (3), 1982 (4), 1983 (16). Total—39.
Pro statistics: Returned one kickoff for 20 yards, 1980.

GREGORY LEE BRACELIN
(Greg)
Linebacker—Indianapolis Colts
Born April 16, 1957, at Lawrence, Kan.
Height, 6.01. Weight, 213.
High School—Richmond, Calif., DeAnza.
Received bachelor of science degree in social science from University of California in 1980.

Selected by Denver in 9th round (243rd player selected) of 1980 NFL draft.
Released by Denver Broncos, August 25, 1981; signed as free agent by Oakland Raiders, August 27, 1981.
Released by Oakland Raiders, September 1, 1981; re-signed by Raiders, September 9, 1981.
Franchise transferred to Los Angeles, May 7, 1982.
Released by Los Angeles Raiders, August 2, 1982; signed as free agent by Baltimore Colts, August 5, 1982.
Franchise transferred to Indianapolis, March 31, 1984.
Denver NFL, 1980; Oakland NFL, 1981; Baltimore NFL, 1982 and 1983; Indianapolis NFL, 1984.
Games: 1980 (12), 1981 (15), 1982 (9), 1983 (16), 1984 (16). Total—68.
Pro statistics: Intercepted one pass for 31 yards and recovered one fumble, 1982; intercepted two passes for 19 yards, 1983.

DONALD CRAIG BRACKEN
(Don)
Punter—Denver Broncos
Born February 16, 1962, at Coalinga, Calif.
Height, 6.01. Weight, 190.
High School—Thermopolis, Wyo., Hot Springs County.
Received bachelor of science degree in physical education from University of Michigan.

Selected by Michigan in 1984 USFL territorial draft.
Signed by Michigan Panthers, January 8, 1984.
Released by Michigan Panthers, February 16, 1984; signed as free agent by Kansas City Chiefs, May 4, 1984.
Released by Kansas City Chiefs, June 1, 1984; signed as free agent by Indianapolis Colts, June 14, 1984.
Released by Indianapolis Colts, August 6, 1984; signed as free agent by Denver Broncos, January 30, 1985.

CARLOS HUMBERTO BRADLEY
Linebacker—San Diego Chargers
Born April 27, 1960, at Philadelphia, Pa.
Height, 6.00. Weight, 226.
High School—Philadelphia, Pa., Germantown.
Received bachelor of science degree in physical education from Wake Forest University in 1981.

Selected by San Diego in 11th round (300th player selected) of 1981 NFL draft.
Released by San Diego Chargers, August 25, 1981; re-signed by Chargers after clearing procedural waivers, October 28, 1981.
On injured reserve with groin injury, December 31 through remainder of 1981 season playoffs.
On injured reserve with sprained ankle, October 9 through December 7, 1984; activated, December 8, 1984.
San Diego NFL, 1981 through 1984.
Games: 1981 (8), 1982 (9), 1983 (16), 1984 (8). Total—41.
Pro statistics: Recovered one fumble, 1983.

ED BRADY
Linebacker—Los Angeles Rams
Born June 17, 1960, at Morris, Ill.
Height, 6.02. Weight, 228.
High School—Morris, Ill.
Attended University of Illinois.

Selected by Chicago in 1984 USFL territorial draft.
Selected by Los Angeles Rams in 8th round (215th player selected) of 1984 NFL draft.
Signed by Los Angeles Rams, July 14, 1984.
Released by Los Angeles Rams, August 27, 1984; re-signed by Rams, August 28, 1984.
Los Angeles Rams NFL, 1984.
Games: 1984 (16).

TODD W. BRAFFORD
Guard—San Francisco 49ers
Born September 2, 1960, at Concord, N.C.
Height, 6.05. Weight, 255.
High School—Fresno, Calif., Hoover.
Received degree in telecommunications from Utah State University.

Signed as free agent by Los Angeles Rams, May 4, 1984.
Released by Los Angeles Rams, August 14, 1984; signed as free agent by San Francisco 49ers, April 16, 1985.

BYRON C. BRAGGS
Defensive End—Tampa Bay Buccaneers
Born October 10, 1959, at Montgomery, Ala.
Height, 6.04. Weight, 270.
High School—Montgomery, Ala., George Washington Carver.
Attended University of Alabama.

Selected by Green Bay in 5th round (117th player selected) of 1981 NFL draft.

Released by Green Bay Packers, August 21, 1984; awarded on waivers to Tampa Bay Buccaneers, August 22, 1984.
Green Bay NFL, 1981 through 1983; Tampa Bay NFL, 1984.
Games: 1981 (16), 1982 (9), 1983 (16), 1984 (14). Total—55.
Pro statistics: Returned one kickoff for no yards, 1981; recovered two fumbles, 1983.

MARK D. BRAMMER
Name pronounced BRAY-mer.
Tight End—Buffalo Bills
Born May 3, 1958, at Traverse City, Mich.
Height, 6.03. Weight, 236.
High School—Traverse City, Mich.
Attended Michigan State University.

Selected by Buffalo in 3rd round (67th player selected) of 1980 NFL draft.
On injured reserve with ankle injury, August 28 through September 28, 1984; activated, September 29, 1984.

		—PASS RECEIVING—			
Year Club	G.	P.C.	Yds.	Avg.	TD.
1980—Buffalo NFL	16	26	283	10.9	4
1981—Buffalo NFL	16	33	365	11.1	2
1982—Buffalo NFL	9	25	225	9.0	2
1983—Buffalo NFL	12	25	215	8.6	2
1984—Buffalo NFL	12	7	49	7.0	0
Pro Totals—5 Years	65	116	1137	9.8	10

Additional pro statistics: Rushed once for eight yards, 1980; rushed twice for 17 yards, recovered one fumble and fumbled three times, 1981; recovered two fumbles, 1982.

CLIFFORD BRANCH
(Cliff)
Wide Receiver—Los Angeles Raiders
Born August 1, 1948, at Houston, Tex.
Height, 5.11. Weight, 170.
High School—Houston, Tex., E. E. Worthing.
Attended Wharton County Junior College and University of Colorado.

Named as wide receiver on THE SPORTING NEWS AFC All-Star Team, 1974 and 1976.
Selected by Oakland in 4th round (98th player selected) of 1972 NFL draft.
Franchise transferred to Los Angeles, May 7, 1982.

		—RUSHING—				PASS RECEIVING				—TOTAL—		
Year Club	G.	Att.	Yds.	Avg.	TD.	P.C.	Yds.	Avg.	TD.	TD.	Pts.	F.
1972—Oakland NFL	14	1	5	5.0	0	3	41	13.7	0	0	0	2
1973—Oakland NFL	13		None			19	290	15.3	3	3	18	0
1974—Oakland NFL	13		None			60	*1092	18.2	*13	13	78	1
1975—Oakland NFL	14	2	18	9.0	0	51	893	17.5	9	9	54	0
1976—Oakland NFL	14	3	12	4.0	0	46	1111	24.2	*12	12	72	0
1977—Oakland NFL	13		None			33	540	16.4	6	6	36	0
1978—Oakland NFL	16		None			49	709	14.5	1	1	6	2
1979—Oakland NFL	14	1	4	4.0	0	59	844	14.3	6	6	36	1
1980—Oakland NFL	16	1	1	1.0	0	44	858	19.5	7	7	42	0
1981—Oakland NFL	16		None			41	635	15.5	1	1	6	0
1982—Los Angeles Raiders NFL	9	2	10	5.0	0	30	575	19.2	4	4	24	0
1983—Los Angeles Raiders NFL	12	1	20	20.0	0	39	696	17.8	5	5	30	0
1984—Los Angeles Raiders NFL	14		None			27	401	14.9	0	0	0	0
Pro Totals—13 Years	178	11	70	6.4	0	501	8685	17.3	67	67	402	6

Additional pro statistics: Returned 12 punts for 21 yards and nine kickoffs for 191 yards, 1972; recovered one fumble, 1974; recovered two fumbles, 1984.
Played in AFC Championship Game following 1973 through 1977, 1980 and 1983 seasons.
Played in NFL Championship Game following 1976, 1980 and 1983 seasons.
Played in Pro Bowl (NFL All-Star Game) following 1974 through 1977 seasons.

SCOT EUGENE BRANTLEY
Linebacker—Tampa Bay Buccaneers
Born February 24, 1958, at Chester, S. C.
Height, 6.01. Weight, 230.
High School—Ocala, Fla., Forest.
Attended University of Florida.

Selected by New York Mets organization in 6th round of free-agent draft, June 8, 1976.
Selected by Tampa Bay in 3rd round (76th player selected) of 1980 NFL draft.

		—INTERCEPTIONS—			
Year Club	G.	No.	Yds.	Avg.	TD.
1980—Tampa Bay NFL	16	1	6	6.0	0
1981—Tampa Bay NFL	16	1	2	2.0	0
1982—Tampa Bay NFL	9		None		
1983—Tampa Bay NFL	16	1	0	0.0	0
1984—Tampa Bay NFL	16	3	55	18.3	0
Pro Totals—5 Years	73	6	63	10.5	0

Additional pro statistics: Returned one kickoff for no yards, 1981; recovered one fumble, 1982; recovered two fumbles, 1984.

RHEUGENE JAMES BRANTON

First name pronounced ROO-jean.

(Gene)
Wide Receiver—Tampa Bay Buccaneers

Born November 23, 1960, at Tampa, Fla.
Height, 6.04. Weight, 210.
High School—Tampa, Fla., King.
Attended Texas Southern University.

Selected by Tampa Bay in 6th round (148th player selected) of 1983 NFL draft.
On injured reserve with knee injury, September 9 through remainder of 1983 season.
On injured reserve with pulled hamstring, August 27 through entire 1984 season.
Tampa Bay NFL, 1983.
Games: 1983 (1).

LARRY BRAZIEL

Name pronounced Bra-ZEAL.

Cornerback—Cleveland Browns

Born September 25, 1954, at Fort Worth, Tex.
Height, 6.00. Weight, 184.
High School—Fort Worth, Tex., Dunbar.
Attended Compton Junior College and University of Southern California.

Selected by Baltimore in 5th round (115th player selected) of 1979 NFL draft.
Released by Baltimore Colts, September 8, 1982; signed as free agent by Cleveland Browns, September 16, 1982.
On inactive list, September 19, 1982.
Released by Cleveland Browns, August 28, 1984; re-signed by Browns, September 19, 1984.

| | | | —INTERCEPTIONS— | | |
Year Club	G.	No.	Yds.	Avg.TD.	
1979—Baltimore NFL	16	4	49	12.3	1
1980—Baltimore NFL	15	2	87	43.5	0
1981—Baltimore NFL	16	3	35	11.7	0
1982—Cleveland NFL.............	6		None		
1983—Cleveland NFL.............	13		None		
1984—Cleveland NFL.............	13		None		
Pro Totals—6 Years...........	79	9	171	19.0	1

Additional pro statistics: Recovered blocked punt in end zone for a touchdown, 1979; recovered one fumble, 1979 and 1981; fumbled once, 1981.

ROBERT LORENZO BRAZILE JR.

Name pronounced Bra-ZEAL.

Linebacker—Houston Oilers

Born February 7, 1953, at Mobile, Ala.
Height, 6.04. Weight, 253.
High School—Mobile, Ala., Vigor.
Attended Jackson State University.
Cousin of Rickey Young, running back with Minnesota Vikings.

Named AFC Rookie of the Year by THE SPORTING NEWS, 1975.
Named to THE SPORTING NEWS AFC All-Star Team, 1976, 1978 and 1979.
Named to THE SPORTING NEWS NFL All-Star Team, 1980.
Selected by Houston in 1st round (6th player selected) of 1975 NFL draft.

| | | | —INTERCEPTIONS— | | |
Year Club	G.	No.	Yds.	Avg.TD.	
1975—Houston NFL................	14		None		
1976—Houston NFL................	14	1	8	8.0	0
1977—Houston NFL................	14	3	40	13.3	0
1978—Houston NFL................	16	1	30	30.0	0
1979—Houston NFL................	16	2	45	22.5	0
1980—Houston NFL................	16	2	38	19.0	0
1981—Houston NFL................	16	2	7	3.5	0
1982—Houston NFL................	9	1	31	31.0	0
1983—Houston NFL................	16		None		
1984—Houston NFL................	16	1	2	2.0	0
Pro Totals—10 Years.........	147	13	201	15.5	0

Additional pro statistics: Recovered five fumbles for 18 yards, 1975; recovered one fumble, 1976, 1982 and 1984; recovered three fumbles, 1979 and 1983.
Played in AFC Championship Game following 1978 and 1979 seasons.
Played in Pro Bowl (NFL All-Star Game) following 1976 through 1982 seasons.

JAMES THOMAS BREECH

(Jim)
Placekicker—Cincinnati Bengals

Born April 11, 1956, at Sacramento, Calif.
Height 5.06. Weight, 161.
High School—Sacramento, Calif.
Attended University of California.

Selected by Detroit in 8th round (206th player selected) of 1978 NFL draft.
Released by Detroit Lions, August 23, 1978; signed as free agent by Oakland Raiders, December 12, 1978.
Released by Oakland Raiders, September 1, 1980; signed as free agent by Cincinnati Bengals, November 25, 1980.
Active for 1 game with Oakland Raiders in 1978; did not play.

Year Club	G.	XP.	XPM.	FG.	FGA.	Pts.
1979—Oakland NFL............	16	41	4	18	27	95
1980—Cincinnati NFL.........	4	11	1	4	7	23
1981—Cincinnati NFL........	16	49	2	22	32	115
1982—Cincinnati NFL........	9	25	1	14	18	67
1983—Cincinnati NFL........	16	39	2	16	23	87
1984—Cincinnati NFL........	16	37	0	22	31	103
Pro Totals—7 Years.......	77	202	10	96	138	490

Additional pro statistics: Punted twice for 33.5 yard average, 1980; fumbled once, 1983.
Played in AFC Championship Game following 1981 season.
Played in NFL Championship Game following 1981 season.

LOUIS EVERETT BREEDEN
Cornerback—Cincinnati Bengals
Born October 26, 1953, at Hamlet, N. C.
Height, 5.11. Weight, 185.
High School—Hamlet., N. C.
Attended Richmond Technical Institute and received bachelor of science degree
from North Carolina Central University in 1977.

Tied NFL record for most yards, interception return (102), vs. San Diego Chargers, November 8, 1981.
Selected by Cincinnati in 7th round (187th player selected) of 1977 NFL draft.
On injured reserve, September 8 through entire 1977 season.
On injured reserve with shoulder injury, November 13 through remainder of 1979 season.

Year Club	G.	No.	Yds.	Avg.	TD.
1978—Cincinnati NFL............	16	3	25	8.3	0
1979—Cincinnati NFL............	10		None		
1980—Cincinnati NFL............	16	7	91	13.0	0
1981—Cincinnati NFL............	16	4	145	*36.3	1
1982—Cincinnati NFL............	6	2	9	4.5	0
1983—Cincinnati NFL............	14	2	47	23.5	0
1984—Cincinnati NFL............	16	4	96	24.0	0
Pro Totals—7 Years............	94	22	413	18.8	1

Additional pro statistics: Recovered one fumble, 1978 and 1983; returned six punts for minus 12 yards, returned one kickoff for 12 yards and fumbled twice, 1978; recovered one fumble for 10 yards, 1981; fumbled once, 1982 and 1984.
Played in AFC Championship Game following 1981 season.
Played in NFL Championship Game following 1981 season.

BRIAN MICHAEL BRENNAN
Wide Receiver—Cleveland Browns
Born February 15, 1962, at Bloomfield, Mich.
Height, 5.09. Weight, 178.
High School—Birmingham, Mich., Brother Rice.
Received bachelor of science degree in finance from Boston College in 1984.

Selected by Denver in 16th round (324th player selected) in 1984 USFL draft.
Selected by Cleveland in 4th round (104th player selected) 1984 NFL draft.
Signed by Cleveland Browns, May 18, 1984.

Year Club	G.	-PASS RECEIVING-				-PUNT RETURNS-				—TOTAL—		
		P.C.	Yds.	Avg.	TD.	No.	Yds.	Avg.	TD.	TD.	Pts.	F.
1984—Cleveland NFL..........................	15	35	455	13.0	3	25	199	8.0	0	3	18	1

HOBY F. J. BRENNER
Tight End—New Orleans Saints
Born June 2, 1959, at Linwood, Calif.
Height, 6.04. Weight, 245.
High School—Fullerton, Calif.
Attended University of Southern California.

Selected by New Orleans in 3rd round (71st player selected) of 1981 NFL draft.
On injured reserve with turf toe, September 1 through October 22, 1981; activated, October 23, 1981.
On injured reserve with knee injury, December 31 through remainder of 1982 season.

Year Club	G.	P.C.	Yds.	Avg.	TD.
1981—New Orleans NFL........	9	7	143	20.4	0
1982—New Orleans NFL........	8	16	171	10.7	0
1983—New Orleans NFL........	16	41	574	14.0	3
1984—New Orleans NFL........	16	28	554	19.8	6
Pro Totals—4 Years............	49	92	1442	15.7	9

Additional pro statistics: Fumbled once, 1981 and 1982; recovered one fumble, 1982.

CHRISTOPHER BREWER
(Chris)
Running Back—Denver Broncos
Born January 23, 1962, at Denver, Colo.
Height, 6.01. Weight, 193.
High School—Denver, Colo., George Washington.
Attended University of Arizona.

Selected by Arizona in 1984 USFL territorial draft.
Selected by Denver in 9th round (245th player selected) of 1984 NFL draft.
Signed by Denver Broncos, May 30, 1984.

		—RUSHING—				PASS RECEIVING				—TOTAL—		
Year Club	G.	Att.	Yds.	Avg.	TD.	P.C.	Yds.	Avg.	TD.	TD.	Pts.	F.
1984—Denver NFL	13	10	28	2.8	0	2	20	10.0	0	0	0	1

Additional pro statistics: Recovered one fumble, 1984.

TIM BREWSTER
Tight End—Philadelphia Eagles
Born October 13, 1960, at Phillipsburg, N.J.
Height, 6.04. Weight, 220.
High School—Phillipsburg, N.J.
Attended Pasadena City College and University of Illinois.

Selected by Chicago in 1984 USFL territorial draft.
Signed as free agent by New York Giants, May 9, 1984.
Released by New York Giants, August 20, 1984; signed as free agent by Philadelphia Eagles, May 8, 1985.

LEON BRIGHT
Running Back—Tampa Bay Buccaneers
Born May 19, 1955, at Starke, Fla.
Height, 5.09. Weight, 192.
High School—Merritt Island, Fla.
Attended Florida State University.

Signed as free agent by British Columbia Lions, March, 1977.
Released by British Columbia Lions, July 3, 1977; re-signed by Lions, July 14, 1977.
On injured list, August 10 through September 10, 1979; activated, September 11, 1979.
On injured list, October 2 through October 11, 1980; activated, October 12, 1980.
Granted free agency, April 1, 1981; signed as free agent by New York Giants, May 28, 1981.
On injured reserve with Achilles tendon injury, August 30 through September 30, 1983; activated, October 1, 1983.
Granted free agency, February 1, 1984.
Rights released by New York Giants, August 27, 1984; signed by Tampa Bay Buccaneers, September 29, 1984.

		—RUSHING—				PASS RECEIVING				—TOTAL—		
Year Club	G.	Att.	Yds.	Avg.	TD.	P.C.	Yds.	Avg.	TD.	TD.	Pts.	F.
1977—British Columbia CFL	15	6	43	7.2	0	45	816	18.1	7	9	54	4
1978—British Columbia CFL	15	4	90	22.5	1	52	781	15.0	2	3	18	0
1979—British Columbia CFL	11	2	7	3.5	0	36	569	15.8	3	5	30	5
1980—British Columbia CFL	15	1	1	1.0	0	13	204	15.7	1	3	18	3
1981—New York Giants NFL	15	51	197	3.9	2	28	291	10.4	0	2	12	3
1982—New York Giants NFL	8	1	5	5.0	0	2	19	9.5	0	0	0	0
1983—New York Giants NFL	7	1	2	2.0	0	2	33	16.5	0	0	0	2
1984—Tampa Bay NFL	12		None				None			0	0	2
NFL Totals—4 Years	42	53	204	3.8	2	32	343	10.7	0	2	12	7
CFL Totals—4 Years	56	13	141	10.8	1	146	2370	16.2	13	20	120	12
Pro Totals—8 Years	98	66	345	5.2	3	178	2713	15.2	13	22	132	19

		—PUNT RETURNS—				—KICKOFF RET.—		
Year Club	G.	No.	Yds.	Avg.	TD.	No.	Yds.	Avg.TD.
1977—British Columbia CFL	15	29	419	*14.4	1	18	596	*33.1 1
1978—British Columbia CFL	15	40	498	*12.5	0	18	425	23.6 0
1979—British Columbia CFL	11	21	319	*15.2	2	27	*820	*30.4 0
1980—British Columbia CFL	15	47	*790	*16.8	1	25	635	25.4 0
1981—New York Giants NFL	15	52	410	7.9	0	25	481	19.2 0
1982—New York Giants NFL	8	*37	*325	8.8	0	4	72	18.0 0
1983—New York Giants NFL	7	17	117	6.9	0	21	475	22.6 0
1984—Tampa Bay NFL	12	23	173	7.5	0	16	303	18.9 0
NFL Totals—4 Years	42	129	1025	7.9	0	66	1331	20.2 0
CFL Totals—4 Years	56	137	2026	14.8	4	88	2476	28.1 1
Pro Totals—8 Years	98	266	3051	11.5	4	154	3807	24.7 1

Additional NFL statistics: Recovered four fumbles, 1981; recovered one fumble, 1984.
Additional CFL statistics: Recovered two fumbles, 1979; intercepted three passes for 94 yards and one touchdown and recovered three fumbles, 1980.

JAMES BRITT
Cornerback—Atlanta Falcons
Born September 12, 1960, at Minden, La.
Height, 6.00. Weight, 185.
High School—Minden, La.
Attended Louisiana State University.

Selected by New Jersey in 14th round (166th player selected) of 1983 USFL draft.
Selected by Atlanta in 2nd round (43rd player selected) of 1983 NFL draft.
Signed by Atlanta Falcons, July 16, 1983.
Atlanta NFL, 1983 and 1984.
Games: 1983 (14), 1984 (16) Total—30.
Pro statistics: Intercepted one pass for 10 yards, 1984.

PETER ANTHONY BROCK
(Pete)
Center—New England Patriots
Born July 14, 1954, at Portland, Ore.
Height, 6.05. Weight, 270.
High School—Beaverton, Ore., Jesuit.
Received bachelor of science degree in biology from University of Colorado in 1976.
Brother of Stan Brock, offensive tackle with New Orleans Saints;
and Willie Brock, center with Detroit Lions, 1978.

Named as center on THE SPORTING NEWS College All-America Team, 1975.
Selected by New England in 1st round (12th player selected) of 1976 NFL draft.
New England NFL, 1976 through 1984.
Games: 1976 (14), 1977 (14), 1978 (15), 1979 (16), 1980 (16), 1981 (16), 1982 (9), 1983 (13), 1984 (12). Total—125.
Pro statistics: Recovered one fumble, 1976, 1980, 1981 and 1982; caught one pass for 6 yards and a touchdown, 1976; fumbled twice, 1979.

RALPH DIETER BROCK
(Known by middle name.)
Quarterback—Los Angeles Rams
Born February 12, 1951, at Birmingham, Ala.
Height, 6.00. Weight, 190.
High School—Birmingham, Ala., Jones Valley.
Attended Auburn University and Jacksonville State University.

Signed as free agent by Winnipeg Blue Bombers, 1974.
On suspended list, August 23 through September 19, 1983.
Traded by Winnipeg Blue Bombers to Hamilton Tiger-Cats for quarterback Tom Clements, September 20, 1983.
Granted free agency, March 1, 1985; signed by Los Angeles Rams, March 29, 1985.

Year Club	G.	Att.	Cmp.	Pct.	Gain	T.P.	P.I.	Avg.	Att.	Yds.	Avg.	TD.	TD.	Pts.	F.
		\-\-\-\-\-\-PASSING\-\-\-\-\-\-							\-\-\-\-\-\-RUSHING\-\-\-\-\-\-				\-TOTAL\-		
1974—Winnipeg CFL	16	27	12	44.4	176	0	2	6.52	2	6	3.0	0	0	0	1
1975—Winnipeg CFL	16	244	116	47.5	1911	11	9	7.83	36	173	4.8	2	2	12	8
1976—Winnipeg CFL	16	402	223	55.5	3101	17	18	7.71	46	72	1.6	2	2	12	7
1977—Winnipeg CFL	16	*418	242	57.9	3063	*23	19	7.33	62	220	3.6	6	6	36	7
1978—Winnipeg CFL	16	*486	*294	60.5	*3755	*23	18	7.73	28	47	1.7	3	3	18	4
1979—Winnipeg CFL	15	354	194	54.8	2383	15	12	6.73	30	97	3.2	1	1	6	2
1980—Winnipeg CFL	16	*514	304	59.1	*4252	*28	12	8.27	43	87	2.0	4	4	24	4
1981—Winnipeg CFL	16	*566	*354	62.5	*4796	*32	15	8.47	35	116	3.3	0	0	0	1
1982—Winnipeg CFL	16	543	314	57.8	4294	28	15	7.91	33	123	3.7	4	4	24	5
1983—Win. (6)-Ham. (6) CFL	12	420	229	54.5	3133	18	15	7.46	27	62	2.3	4	4	24	*10
1984—Hamilton CFL	15	*561	*320	57.0	*3966	15	*23	7.07	48	134	2.8	6	6	36	7
CFL Totals—11 Years	170	4535	2602	57.4	34830	210	158	7.68	390	1137	2.9	32	32	192	56

Additional CFL statistics: Recovered one fumble for 13 yards, 1977; recovered one fumble, 1982.
Played in CFL Championship Game following 1984 season.

STANLEY JAMES BROCK
(Stan)
Offensive Tackle—New Orleans Saints
Born June 8, 1958, at Portland, Ore.
Height, 6.06. Weight, 285.
High School—Beaverton, Ore., Jesuit.
Attended University of Colorado.
Brother of Pete Brock, center with New England Patriots; and
Willie Brock, center with Detroit Lions, 1978.

Named as offensive tackle on THE SPORTING NEWS College All-America Team, 1979.
Selected by New Orleans in 1st round (12th player selected) of 1980 NFL draft.
On injured reserve with knee injury, December 5 through remainder of 1984 season.
New Orleans NFL, 1980 through 1984.
Games: 1980 (16), 1981 (16), 1982 (9), 1983 (16), 1984 (14). Total—71.
Pro statistics: Recovered one fumble, 1980 and 1983; returned two kickoffs for 18 yards and recovered two fumbles, 1981; returned one kickoff for 15 yards, 1983.

MITCHELL EUGENE BROOKINS
Wide Receiver—Buffalo Bills
Born December 10, 1960, at Chicago, Ill.
Height, 5.11. Weight, 196.
High School—Chicago, Ill., Wendell Phillips.
Received bachelor of science degree in business from University of Illinois in 1984.

Selected by Chicago in 1984 USFL territorial draft.
Selected by Buffalo in 4th round (95th player selected) of 1984 NFL draft.
Signed by Buffalo Bills, June 1, 1984.

		——PASS RECEIVING——				
Year	Club	G.	P.C.	Yds.	Avg.	TD.
1984—Buffalo NFL		16	18	318	17.7	1

Additional pro statistics: Rushed twice for 27 yards, 1984.

JAMES ROBERT BROOKS
Running Back—Cincinnati Bengals
Born December 28, 1958, at Warner Robins, Ga.
Height, 5.09. Weight, 177.
High School—Warner Robins, Ga.
Attended Auburn University.
Brother of Joe Brooks, safety at University of South Carolina.

Selected by San Diego in 1st round (24th player selected) of 1981 NFL draft.
Traded by San Diego Chargers to Cincinnati Bengals for running back Pete Johnson, May 29, 1984.

		——RUSHING——				PASS RECEIVING				—TOTAL—		
Year	Club	G.	Att.	Yds.	Avg.	TD.	P.C.	Yds.	Avg.	TD.	TD.	Pts.	F.
1981—San Diego NFL		14	109	525	4.8	3	46	329	7.2	3	6	36	7
1982—San Diego NFL		9	87	430	4.9	6	13	66	5.1	0	6	36	4
1983—San Diego NFL		15	127	516	4.1	3	25	215	8.6	0	3	18	8
1984—Cincinnati NFL		15	103	396	3.8	2	34	268	7.9	2	4	24	4
Pro Totals—4 Years		53	426	1867	4.4	14	118	878	7.4	5	19	114	23

		—PUNT RETURNS—				—KICKOFF RET.—			
Year	Club	G.	No.	Yds.	Avg.	TD.	No.	Yds.	Avg.	TD.
1981—San Diego NFL		14	22	290	13.2	0	40	949	23.7	0
1982—San Diego NFL		9	12	138	11.5	0	*33	*749	22.7	0
1983—San Diego NFL		15	18	137	7.6	0	32	607	19.0	0
1984—Cincinnati NFL		15	None				7	144	20.6	0
Pro Totals—4 Years		53	52	565	10.9	0	112	2449	21.9	0

Additional pro statistics: Recovered two fumbles, 1981; recovered one fumble, 1982; recovered three fumbles, 1983.
Played in AFC Championship Game following 1981 season.

PERRY BROOKS
Defensive Tackle—Washington Redskins
Born December 4, 1954, at Bogalousa, La.
Height, 6.03. Weight, 270.
High School—Angie, La., Wesley Ray.
Received bachelor of science degree in agricultural agronomy from Southern University in 1976.
Brother of Darin Brooks, linebacker at Southern University.

Selected by New England in 7th round (202nd player selected) of 1976 NFL draft.
Released by New England Patriots, August, 1976; signed as free agent by Washington Redskins, March, 1977.
On injured reserve with knee injury, August 30 through entire 1977 season.
On injured reserve with ruptured biceps, August 28 through September 28, 1979; activated, September 29, 1979.
On injured reserve with knee injury, December 8, 1982 through January 21, 1983; activated, January 22, 1983.
Washington NFL, 1978 through 1984.
Games: 1978 (16), 1979 (12), 1980 (12), 1981 (15), 1982 (5), 1983 (16), 1984 (16). Total—92.
Pro statistics: Recovered one fumble, 1979 and 1982; recovered two fumbles, 1981.
Played in NFC Championship Game following 1982 and 1983 seasons.
Played in NFL Championship Game following 1982 and 1983 seasons.

JAMES JAY BROPHY
(Known by middle name.)
Linebacker—Miami Dolphins
Born July 27, 1960, at Akron, O.
Height, 6.03. Weight, 233.
High School—Akron, O., John R. Buchtel.
Attended University of Miami (Fla.).

Selected by Tampa Bay in 4th round (73rd player selected) of 1984 USFL draft.
Selected by Miami in 2nd round (53rd player selected) of 1984 NFL draft.
Signed by Miami Dolphins, May 24, 1984.
Miami NFL, 1984.
Games: 1984 (11).
Played in AFC Championship Game following 1984 season.
Played in NFL Championship Game following 1984 season.

AARON CEDRIC BROWN
Linebacker—Cleveland Browns
Born January 13, 1956, at Warren, O.
Height, 6.02. Weight, 235.
High School—Warren, O., Western Reserve.
Attended Ohio State University.

Selected by Tampa Bay in 10th round of 1978 NFL draft.
On injured reserve with elbow injury, November 17, through December 13, 1979; activated, December 14, 1979.

Released by Tampa Bay Buccaneers, August 24, 1981; signed as free agent by Philadelphia Eagles, January 29, 1982.

Released by Philadelphia Eagles, September 6, 1982; signed as free agent by Winnipeg Blue Bombers, October 4, 1982.

Granted free agency, March 1, 1985; signed by Cleveland Browns, May 6, 1985.

Year Club	G.	No.	Yds.	Avg.	TD.
1978—Tampa Bay NFL	16	1	10	10.0	0
1979—Tampa Bay NFL	12		None		
1980—Tampa Bay NFL	16		None		
1982—Winnipeg CFL	3		None		
1983—Winnipeg CFL	16		None		
1984—Winnipeg CFL	16	4	65	16.3	1
NFL Totals—3 Years	44	1	10	10.0	0
CFL Totals—3 Years	35	4	65	16.3	1
Pro Totals—6 Years	79	5	75	15.0	1

Additional NFL statistics: Recovered one fumble, 1978 and 1980.
Additional CFL statistics: Recovered one fumble, 1983 and 1984; returned one kickoff for nine yards, 1984.
Played in NFC Championship Game following 1979 season.

CEDRIC WALLACE BROWN
First name pronounced SED-rick.
Safety—Tampa Bay Buccaneers
Born May 6, 1954, at Columbus, O.
Height, 6.02. Weight, 200.
High School—Columbus, O., Linden McKinley.
Attended Kent State University.

Selected by Oakland in 12th round (343rd player selected) of 1976 NFL draft.
Released by Oakland Raiders, August, 1976; signed as free agent by Tampa Bay Buccaneers, December 7, 1976.
Traded with future considerations from Tampa Bay Buccaneers to Oakland Raiders for future considerations, May, 1977 (6th and 9th round picks in 1977 draft).
Released by Oakland Raiders, July, 1977; signed as free agent by Tampa Bay Buccaneers, August, 1977.
On injured reserve with ankle injury, October 25 through remainder of 1983 season.
On injured reserve with knee injury, October 30 through remainder of 1984 season.

Year Club	G.	No.	Yds.	Avg.	TD.
1976—Tampa Bay NFL	1		None		
1977—Tampa Bay NFL	14	2	66	33.0	0
1978—Tampa Bay NFL	14	6	110	18.3	0
1979—Tampa Bay NFL	16	3	79	26.3	0
1980—Tampa Bay NFL	13	1	0	0.0	0
1981—Tampa Bay NFL	16	9	215	23.9	2
1982—Tampa Bay NFL	9	3	31	10.3	0
1983—Tampa Bay NFL	8	4	78	19.5	0
1984—Tampa Bay NFL	9	1	14	14.0	0
Pro Totals—9 Years	100	29	593	20.4	2

Additional pro statistics: Recovered one fumble for 24 yards, 1977; fumbled once, 1977, 1978 and 1981; returned two punts for nine yards, 1978; recovered one fumble for five yards, 1979; recovered one fumble for 80 yards and a touchdown, 1980; recovered one fumble, 1981 and 1982.
Played in NFC Championship Game following 1979 season.

CHARLES LEE BROWN
(Bud)
Safety—Miami Dolphins
Born April 19, 1961, at DeKalb, Miss.
Height, 6.00. Weight, 194.
High School—DeKalb, Miss., West Kemper.
Attended University of Southern Mississippi.

Selected by New Orleans in 1984 USFL territorial draft.
Selected by Miami in 11th round (305th player selected) of 1984 NFL draft.
Signed by Miami Dolphins, June 26, 1984.
Released by Miami Dolphins, August 27, 1984; re-signed by Dolphins, August 28, 1984.

Year Club	G.	No.	Yds.	Avg.	TD.
1984—Miami NFL	16	1	53	53.0	0

Played in AFC Championship Game following 1984 season.
Played in NFL Championship Game following 1984 season.

CHARLIE BROWN
Wide Receiver—Washington Redskins
Born October 29, 1957, at Charleston, S.C.
Height, 5.10. Weight, 179.
High School—St. John's Island, S.C.
Attended South Carolina State College.

Selected by Washington in 8th round (201st player selected) of 1981 NFL draft.

On injured reserve with knee injury, September 1 through entire 1981 season.
On injured reserve with stress fracture in leg, October 23 through November 23, 1984; activated, November 24, 1984.

		——PASS RECEIVING——				
Year	Club	G.	P.C.	Yds.	Avg.	TD.
1982—Washington NFL.........		9	32	690	*21.6	8
1983—Washington NFL.........		15	78	1225	15.7	8
1984—Washington NFL.........		9	18	200	11.1	3
Pro Totals—3 Years............		33	128	2115	16.5	19

Additional pro statistics: Recovered one fumble, 1982 and 1983; fumbled once, 1982; rushed four times for 53 yards, 1983.
Played in NFC Championship Game following 1982 and 1983 seasons.
Played in NFL Championship Game following 1982 and 1983 seasons.
Played in Pro Bowl (NFL All-Star Game) following 1982 and 1983 seasons.

CHRISTOPHER DUKE BROWN
(Chris)
Defensive Back—Pittsburgh Steelers
Born April 11, 1962, at Owensboro, Ky.
Height, 6.00. Weight, 195.
High School—Owensboro, Ky., Catholic.
Received bachelor of business administration degree in accounting
from University of Notre Dame in 1984.

Selected by Chicago in 1984 USFL territorial draft.
Selected by Pittsburgh in 6th round (164th player selected) of 1984 NFL draft.
Signed by Pittsburgh Steelers, June 17, 1984.
Pittsburgh NFL, 1984.
Games: 1984 (16).
Pro statistics: Intercepted one pass for 31 yards, returned one kickoff for 11 yards and recovered one fumble, 1984.
Played in AFC Championship Game following 1984 season.

DAVID STEVEN BROWN
(Dave)
Cornerback—Seattle Seahawks
Born January 16, 1953, at Akron, O.
Height, 6.02. Weight, 190.
High School—Akron, O., Garfield.
Received bachelor of arts degree in speech from University of Michigan.

Tied NFL record for most touchdowns scored by interception, game (2), vs. Kansas City Chiefs, November 4, 1984.
Named as safety on THE SPORTING NEWS College All-America Team, 1974.
Selected by Pittsburgh in 1st round (26th player selected) of 1975 NFL draft.
Selected from Pittsburgh Steelers by Seattle Seahawks in NFL expansion draft, March 30, 1976.

		INTERCEPTIONS				PUNT RETURNS			—KICKOFF RET.—				—TOTAL—		
Year	Club	G.	No.	Yds.	Avg.	TD.	No.	Yds.	Avg.	TD.	No.	Yds.	Avg.	TD.	TD.	Pts.	F.
1975—Pittsburgh NFL............		13		None			22	217	9.9	0	6	126	21.0	0	0	0	1
1976—Seattle NFL.................		14	4	70	17.5	0	13	74	5.6	0		None			0	2	0
1977—Seattle NFL.................		14	4	68	17.0	1		None				None			1	6	0
1978—Seattle NFL.................		16	3	44	14.7	0		None				None			0	0	0
1979—Seattle NFL.................		16	5	46	9.2	0		None				None			0	0	0
1980—Seattle NFL.................		16	6	32	5.3	0		None				None			0	0	0
1981—Seattle NFL.................		10	2	2	1.0	0		None				None			0	0	0
1982—Seattle NFL.................		9	1	3	3.0	0		None				None			0	0	0
1983—Seattle NFL.................		16	6	83	13.8	0		None				None			0	0	1
1984—Seattle NFL.................		16	8	179	22.4	*2		None				None			2	12	0
Pro Totals—10 Years.....		140	39	527	13.5	3	35	291	8.3	0	6	126	21.0	0	3	20	2

Additional pro statistics: Scored one safety, 1976; recovered one fumble for eight yards, 1981; recovered two fumbles for 15 yards, 1982; recovered three fumbles, 1983; recovered one fumble, 1984.
Played in AFC Championship Game following 1975 and 1983 seasons.
Played in NFL Championship Game following 1975 season.
Played in Pro Bowl (NFL All-Star Game) following 1984 season.

DONALD COLBY BROWN
(Don)
Offensive Tackle—San Diego Chargers
Born April 2, 1959, at San Jose, Calif.
Height, 6.06. Weight, 262.
High School—San Jose, Calif., Camden.
Received bachelor of arts degree in history from University of Santa Clara in 1982.

Signed as free agent by San Diego Chargers, July 7, 1982.
On injured reserve with back injury, September 6 through entire 1982 season.
Released by San Diego Chargers, August 28, 1984; re-signed by Chargers, April 12, 1985.
San Diego NFL, 1983.
Games: 1983 (13).

GREGORY LEE BROWN
(Greg)
Defensive End—Philadelphia Eagles
Born January 5, 1957, at Washington, D.C.
Height, 6.05. Weight, 260.
High School—Washington, D.C., Woodson.
Attended Kansas State University and Eastern Illinois University.

Signed as free agent by Philadelphia Eagles, May 16, 1981.
Philadelphia NFL, 1981 through 1984.
Games: 1981 (16), 1982 (9), 1983 (16), 1984 (16). Total—57.
Pro statistics: Recovered two fumbles for seven yards and one touchdown, 1981; recovered two fumbles, one for a touchdown, 1982; recovered one fumble, 1984.

GREGORY RAYNARD BROWN
(Greg)
Linebacker—Cleveland Browns
Born December 27, 1961, at Monterey, Calif.
Height, 6.02. Weight, 225.
High School—Woodbridge, Va., Gar-Field.
Attended Univesity of Miami (Fla.)

Signed as free agent by Atlanta Falcons, May 3, 1983.
Released by Atlanta Falcons, July 28, 1983.
USFL rights traded with rights to linebacker Greg Zappala by Birmingham Stallions to Jacksonville Bulls for defensive back Charles Grandjean, November 21, 1984.
Signed by Jacksonville Bulls, November 21, 1984.
Released by Jacksonville Bulls, January 12, 1985; signed as free agent by Cleveland Browns, April 4, 1985.

LARRY BROWN
Offensive Tackle—Pittsburgh Steelers
Born June 16, 1949, at Jacksonville, Fla.
Height, 6.04. Weight, 270.
High School—Starke, Fla., Bradford.
Received degree in education from University of Kansas and attended
Howard University Dental School.

Selected by Pittsburgh in 5th round (106th player selected) of 1971 NFL draft.
On injured reserve with knee and hamstring injuries, October 19 through remainder of 1984 season.

Year Club	—PASS RECEIVING—					Year Club	—PASS RECEIVING—				
	G.	P.C.	Yds.	Avg.	TD.		G.	P.C.	Yds.	Avg.	TD.
1971—Pittsburgh NFL	13	1	3	3.0	1	1979—Pittsburgh NFL	15	1	1	1.0	1
1972—Pittsburgh NFL	9	1	13	13.0	1	1980—Pittsburgh NFL	16		None		
1973—Pittsburgh NFL	14	5	88	17.6	0	1981—Pittsburgh NFL	14		None		
1974—Pittsburgh NFL	14	17	190	11.2	1	1982—Pittsburgh NFL	8		None		
1975—Pittsburgh NFL	14	16	244	15.3	1	1983—Pittsburgh NFL	8		None		
1976—Pittsburgh NFL	13	7	97	13.9	0	1984—Pittsburgh NFL	7		None		
1977—Pittsburgh NFL	14		None			Pro Totals—14 Years	167	48	636	13.3	5
1978—Pittsburgh NFL	8		None								

Additional pro statistics: Recovered one fumble, 1972, 1977, 1979 and 1980; fumbled twice, 1975; recovered four fumbles, 1976.
Played in AFC Championship Game following 1972, 1974 through 1976, 1978 and 1979 seasons.
Played in NFL Championship Game following 1974, 1975, 1978 and 1979 seasons.
Played in Pro Bowl (NFL All-Star Game) following 1982 season.

MARK BROWN
Linebacker—Miami Dolphins
Born July 18, 1961, at New Brunswick, N.J.
Height, 6.02. Weight, 225.
High School—Inglewood, Calif.
Attended Purdue University.

Selected by Boston in 10th round (115th player selected) of 1983 USFL draft.
Selected by Miami in 9th round (250th player selected) of 1983 NFL draft.
Signed by Miami Dolphins, June 15, 1983.
Miami NFL, 1983 and 1984.
Games: 1983 (14), 1984 (16). Total—30.
Pro statistics: Intercepted one pass for no yards, returned one kickoff for no yards and recovered one fumble, 1983.
Played in AFC Championship Game following 1984 season.
Played in NFL Championship Game following 1984 season.

MELVIN ANTHONY BROWN
Cornerback—Minnesota Vikings
Born October 28, 1958, at Biloxi, Miss.
Height, 5.11. Weight, 176.
High School—Biloxi, Miss.
Received degree in law enforcement from University of Mississippi in 1983.

Selected by Birmingham in 1983 USFL territorial draft.
Selected by Minnesota in 10th round (255th player selected) of 1983 NFL draft.

Signed by Minnesota Vikings, June 16, 1983.
On injured reserve with knee injury, August 19 through entire 1983 season.
On injured reserve with knee injury, August 17 through entire 1984 season.

MELVIN LEE BROWN
Wide Receiver—Minnesota Vikings
Born November 29, 1959, at Miami, Fla.
Height, 6.04. Weight, 195.
High School—Miami, Fla., South Dade.
Attended University of North Alabama.

Signed as free agent by Minnesota Vikings, May 2, 1984.
On injured reserve with knee injury, August 8 through entire 1984 season.

RAINAUD FERNANDO BROWN
(Ray)
Defensive End—Indianapolis Colts
Born August 28, 1961, at Rome, Ga.
Height, 6.03. Weight, 255.
High School—Rome, Ga., East Rome.
Attended Clemson University.

Selected by Washington in 1984 USFL territorial draft.
Signed by Washington Federals, January 12, 1984.
Released by Washington Federals, February 6, 1984; signed as free agent by Jacksonville Bulls, February 14, 1984.
Released by Jacksonville Bulls, February 23, 1984; signed as free agent by Dallas Cowboys, May 10, 1984.
Released by Dallas Cowboys, August 27, 1984; signed as free agent by Indianapolis Colts, May 11, 1985.

ROBERT LEE BROWN
Defensive End-Linebacker—Green Bay Packers
Born May 21, 1960, at Edenton, N.C.
Height, 6.02. Weight, 250.
High School—Edenton, N.C., John A. Holmes.
Attended Chowan Junior College and Virginia Polytechnic Institute and State University.

Selected by Green Bay in 4th round (98th player selected) of 1982 NFL draft.
On inactive list, September 20, 1982.
Green Bay NFL, 1982 through 1984.
Games: 1982 (8), 1983 (16), 1984 (16). Total—40.
Pro statistics: Recovered one fumble, 1982; intercepted one pass for five yards and a touchdown, 1984.

RONALD JAMES BROWN
(Ron)
Wide Receiver—Los Angeles Rams
Born March 31, 1961, at Los Angeles, Calif.
Height, 5.11. Weight, 181.
High School—Baldwin Park, Calif.
Attended Arizona State University.
Won gold medal in 4x100 relay during 1984 Olympics.

Selected by Arizona in 1983 USFL territorial draft.
Selected by Cleveland in 2nd round (41st player selected) of 1983 NFL draft.
NFL rights traded by Cleveland Browns to Los Angeles Rams for 2nd round pick in 1984 draft, April 27, 1984.
Signed by Los Angeles Rams, August 16, 1984.

| | | —PASS RECEIVING— | | | |
Year Club	G.	P.C.	Yds.	Avg.	TD.
1984—L.A. Rams NFL	16	23	478	20.8	4

Additional pro statistics: Rushed twice for 25 yards, 1984.

STEVE BROWN
Cornerback—Houston Oilers
Born May 20, 1960, at Sacramento, Calif.
Height, 5.11. Weight, 188.
High School—Sacramento, Calif., C.K. McClatchy.
Attended University of Oregon.

Selected by Arizona in 7th round (74th player selected) of 1983 USFL draft.
Selected by Houston in 3rd round (83rd player selected) of 1983 NFL draft.
Signed by Houston Oilers, June 28, 1983.

| | | -INTERCEPTIONS- | | | | —KICKOFF RET.— | | | | —TOTAL— | | |
Year Club	G.	No.	Yds.	Avg.	TD.	No.	Yds.	Avg.	TD.	TD.	Pts.	F.
1983—Houston NFL	16	1	16	16.0	0	31	795	25.6	*1	1	6	2
1984—Houston NFL	16	1	26	26.0	0	3	17	5.7	0	0	0	1
Pro Totals—2 Years	32	2	42	21.0	0	34	812	23.9	1	1	6	3

Additional pro statistics: Recovered one fumble, 1984.

THEOTIS BROWN JR.
Running Back—Kansas City Chiefs
Born April 20, 1957, at Chicago, Ill.
Height, 6.02. Weight, 225.
High School—Oakland, Calif., Skyline.
Attended University of California at Los Angeles.

Selected by St. Louis in 2nd round (35th player selected) of 1979 NFL draft.
Traded by St. Louis Cardinals to Seattle Seahawks for 4th round picks in 1982 and 1983 drafts, October 13, 1981.
Released by Seattle Seahawks, September 21, 1983; signed as free agent by Kansas City Chiefs, September 24, 1983.
Expected to miss 1985 season due to heart condition.

		——RUSHING——				PASS RECEIVING				—TOTAL—		
Year Club	G.	Att.	Yds.	Avg.	TD.	P.C.	Yds.	Avg.	TD.	TD.	Pts.	F.
1979—St. Louis NFL	16	73	318	4.4	7	25	191	7.6	0	7	42	3
1980—St. Louis NFL	16	40	186	4.7	1	21	290	13.8	1	2	12	2
1981—St. Louis (4)-Seattle (9) NFL	13	156	583	3.7	2	29	328	11.3	0	8	48	8
1982—Seattle NFL	9	53	141	2.7	2	12	95	7.9	0	2	12	3
1983—Seattle(3)-Kansas City(12) NFL	15	130	481	3.7	8	47	418	8.9	2	10	60	4
1984—Kansas City NFL	14	97	337	3.5	4	38	236	6.2	0	4	24	2
Pro Totals—6 Years	83	549	2046	3.7	30	172	1558	9.1	3	33	198	22

Additional pro statistics: Recovered two fumbles, 1979; returned two kickoffs for 26 yards, 1980; recovered three fumbles, 1981; returned two kickoffs for 33 yards, 1982; recovered one fumble, 1982 and 1983; attempted one pass with one completion for 11 yards and returned 15 kickoffs for 301 yards (20.1 avg.), 1983.

THOMAS EDWARD BROWN
(Ted)
Running Back—Minnesota Vikings
Born February 2, 1957, at High Point, N. C.
Height, 5.10. Weight, 210.
High School—High Point, N. C., T. W. Andrews.
Attended North Carolina State University.

Selected by Minnesota in 1st round (16th player selected) of 1979 NFL draft.
On suspended list, December 2 through December 6, 1983; reinstated, December 7, 1983.

		——RUSHING——				PASS RECEIVING				—TOTAL—		
Year Club	G.	Att.	Yds.	Avg.	TD.	P.C.	Yds.	Avg.	TD.	TD.	Pts.	F.
1979—Minnesota NFL	14	130	551	4.2	1	31	197	6.4	0	1	6	6
1980—Minnesota NFL	16	219	912	4.2	8	62	623	10.0	2	10	60	6
1981—Minnesota NFL	16	274	1063	3.9	6	83	694	8.4	2	8	48	3
1982—Minnesota NFL	8	120	515	4.3	1	31	207	6.7	2	3	18	0
1983—Minnesota NFL	10	120	476	4.0	10	41	357	8.7	1	11	66	2
1984—Minnesota NFL	13	98	442	4.5	3	46	349	7.6	3	6	36	2
Pro Totals—6 Years	77	961	3959	4.1	29	294	2427	8.3	10	39	234	19

Additional pro statistics: Returned eight kickoffs for 186 yards (23.3 average) and recovered two fumbles, 1979; recovered three fumbles, 1980 and 1981; attempted one pass with one interception, 1981; recovered one fumble, 1982 and 1983.

JOEY MATTHEW BROWNER
Defensive Back—Minnesota Vikings
Born May 15, 1960, at Warren, O.
Height, 6.02. Weight, 205.
High Schools—Warren, O., Western Reserve; and Atlanta, Ga., Southwest.
Attended University of Southern California.
Brother of Ross Browner, defensive end with Houston Gamblers;
brother of Jim Browner, defensive back with Cincinnati Bengals,
1979 and 1980; and Keith Browner, linebacker with Tampa Bay Buccaneers.

Selected by Los Angeles in 1983 USFL territorial draft.
Selected by Minnesota in 1st round (19th player selected) of 1983 NFL draft.
Signed by Minnesota Vikings, April 30, 1983.

		——INTERCEPTIONS——			
Year Club	G.	No.	Yds.	Avg.	TD.
1983—Minnesota NFL	16	2	0	0.0	0
1984—Minnesota NFL	16	1	20	20.0	0
Pro Totals—2 Years	32	3	20	6.7	0

Additional pro statistics: Recovered four fumbles for four yards and fumbled once, 1983; recovered three fumbles for 63 yards and a touchdown, 1984.

KEITH TELLUS BROWNER
Linebacker—Tampa Bay Buccaneers
Born January 24, 1962, at Warren, O.
Height, 6.05. Weight, 230.
High School—Atlanta, Ga., Southwest.
Attended University of Southern California.
Brother of Ross Browner, defensive end with Houston Gamblers; Jim Browner, defensive back
with Cincinnati Bengals, 1979 and 1980; and Joey Browner, defensive back with Minnesota Vikings.

Selected by Los Angeles in 1984 USFL territorial draft.

Selected by Tampa Bay in 2nd round (30th player selected) of 1984 NFL draft.
Signed by Tampa Bay Buccaneers, May 30, 1984.
Tampa Bay NFL, 1984.
Games: 1984 (16).
Pro statistics: Recovered one fumble, 1984.

NICHOLAS BRUCKNER
(Nick)
Wide Receiver—New York Jets
Born May 19, 1961, at Astoria, N.Y.
Height, 5.11. Weight, 185.
High School—Selden, N.Y., Newfield.
Attended Nassau Community College and Syracuse University.

Signed as free agent by New York Jets, May 20, 1983.
On injured reserve with knee injury, August 10 through November 1, 1983; activated after clearing procedural waivers, November 3, 1983.
Released by New York Jets, August 27, 1984; re-signed by Jets, August 28, 1984.
New York Jets NFL, 1983 and 1984.
Games: 1983 (7), 1984 (16). Total—23.
Pro statistics: Caught one pass for 11 yards, returned two punts for 25 yards, returned one kickoff for 17 yards and recovered one fumble, 1984.

ROBERT LOUIS BRUDZINSKI
(Bob)
Linebacker—Miami Dolphins
Born January 1, 1955, at Fremont, O.
Height, 6.04. Weight, 223.
High School—Fremont, O., Ross.
Received bachelor of science degree in business (marketing) from Ohio State University in 1977.

Named as linebacker on THE SPORTING NEWS College All-America Team, 1976.
Selected by Los Angeles in 1st round (23rd player selected) of 1977 NFL draft.
Granted roster exemption when left camp, September 2, 1980; reinstated, September 6, 1980.
Left camp, November 5, 1980; granted roster exemption, November 6, 1980.
On retired-reserve list, November 12 through remainder of 1980 season.
Traded with 2nd round pick in 1981 draft by Los Angeles Rams to Miami Dolphins for 2nd and 3rd round picks in 1981 draft and 2nd round pick in 1982 draft, April 28, 1981.

Year—Club		G.	No.	Yds.	Avg.	TD.	Year—Club		G.	No.	Yds.	Avg.	TD.
			INTERCEPTIONS							INTERCEPTIONS			
1977—Los Angeles NFL		14	2	24	12.0	0	1982—Miami NFL		9	1	5	5.0	0
1978—Los Angeles NFL		16	1	31	31.0	1	1983—Miami NFL		16		None		
1979—Los Angeles NFL		16	1	26	26.0	1	1984—Miami NFL		16	1	0	0.0	0
1980—Los Angeles NFL		9		None			Pro Totals—8 Years		112	8	121	15.1	1
1981—Miami NFL		16	2	35	17.5	0							

Additional pro statistics: Recovered one fumble for three yards, 1979; recovered one fumble, 1982 and 1983.
Played in NFC Championship Game following 1978 and 1979 seasons.
Played in AFC Championship Game following 1982 and 1984 seasons.
Played in NFL Championship Game following 1979, 1982 and 1984 seasons.

ROBERT ANTHONY BRUER
(Bob)
Tight End—Minnesota Vikings
Born May 22, 1953, at Madison, Wis.
Height, 6.05. Weight, 240.
High School—Montello, Wis.
Received bachelor of science degree in business administration
from Mankato State University in 1975.

Selected by Houston in 9th round (221st player selected) of 1975 NFL draft.
Released by Houston Oilers, August 11, 1975; signed as free agent by Dallas Cowboys, May, 1976.
Released by Dallas Cowboys, August 23, 1976; signed as free agent by Chicago Bears, December 8, 1976.
Released by Chicago Bears, August 27, 1977; signed as free agent by Saskatchewan Roughriders, September 28, 1977.
Granted free agency, April 1, 1979; signed as free agent by San Francisco 49ers, July 18, 1979.
Released by San Francisco 49ers, September 12, 1980; signed as free agent by Minnesota Vikings, September 23, 1980.
On injured reserve with rib injury, December 30 through remainder of 1982 season.
On injured reserve with knee injury, August 27 through entire 1984 season.
Active for 1 game with Chicago Bears in 1976; did not play.

Year—Club		G.	P.C.	Yds.	Avg.	TD.	Year—Club		G.	P.C.	Yds.	Avg.	TD.
			PASS RECEIVING							PASS RECEIVING			
1977—Saskatchewan CFL		4	8	80	10.0	0	1982—Minnesota NFL		8	8	102	12.8	2
1978—Saskatchewan CFL		12	34	491	14.4	2	1983—Minnesota NFL		16	31	315	10.2	2
1979—San Francisco NFL		16	26	254	9.8	1	NFL Totals—6 Years		69	72	709	9.8	8
1980—SF(2)-Min(12) NFL		14		None			CFL Totals—2 Years		16	42	571	13.6	2
1981—Minnesota NFL		15	7	38	5.4	3	Pro Totals—8 Years		85	114	1280	11.2	10

— 56 —

Additional NFL statistics: Returned one kickoff for 20 yards and rushed five times for minus four yards, 1979; fumbled once, 1979 and 1981; returned two kickoffs for 20 yards, 1980.
Additional CFL statistics: Scored two points on one conversion, 1977.

SCOTT LEE BRUNNER
Quarterback—Green Bay Packers
Born March 24, 1957, at Sellersville, Pa.
Height, 6.05. Weight, 200.
High Schools—West Chester, Pa., Henderson and Lawrenceville, N. J.
Received degree from University of Delaware in 1980.
Son of John Brunner, assistant coach with Detroit Lions, Green Bay Packers
and Tampa Bay Buccaneers, 1980 through 1984.

Selected by New York Giants in 6th round (145th player selected) of 1980 NFL draft.
Traded by New York Giants to Denver Broncos for 4th round pick in 1984 draft, April 26, 1984.
On injured reserve with knee injury, August 28 through entire 1984 season.
Traded by Denver Broncos to Green Bay Packers for draft choice, April 26, 1985.

Year	Club	G.	Att.	Cmp.	Pct.	Gain	T.P.	P.I.	Avg.	Att.	Yds.	Avg.	TD.	TD.	Pts.	F.
						PASSING						RUSHING			TOTAL	
1980—N. Y. Giants NFL		6	112	52	46.4	610	4	6	5.45	10	18	1.8	0	0	0	3
1981—N. Y. Giants NFL		16	190	79	41.6	978	5	11	5.15	14	20	1.4	0	0	0	6
1982—N. Y. Giants NFL		9	298	161	54.0	2017	10	9	6.77	19	27	1.4	1	1	6	5
1983—N. Y. Giants NFL		16	386	190	49.2	2516	9	22	6.52	26	64	2.5	0	0	0	8
Pro Totals—4 Years		47	986	482	48.9	6121	28	48	6.21	69	129	1.9	1	1	6	22

Quarterback Rating Points: 1980 (53.0), 1981 (42.7), 1982 (74.1), 1983 (54.3). Total—57.6.
Additional pro statistics: Recovered one fumble, 1980; recovered two fumbles and fumbled six times for minus three yards, 1981; recovered three fumbles and fumbled five times for minus 12 yards, 1982; recovered three fumbles, 1983.

RICHARD GEORGE BRUNOT
(Rick)
Offensive Lineman—Cleveland Browns
Born November 6, 1961, at Meadville, Pa.
Height, 6.04. Weight, 255.
High School—Conneaut, O.
Attended Youngstown State University.
Cousin of Mike Barnes, defensive end with Baltimore Colts, 1973 through 1981.

Signed as free agent by Denver Broncos, May 2, 1984.
On injured reserve, July 13 through July 27, 1984.
Released by Denver Broncos, July 28, 1984; signed as a free agent by Cleveland Browns, May 6, 1985.

RICK DON BRYAN
Defensive Tackle—Atlanta Falcons
Born March 20, 1962, at Tulsa, Okla.
Height, 6.04. Weight, 260.
High School—Coweta, Okla.
Attended University of Oklahoma.

Named as defensive lineman on THE SPORTING NEWS College All-America Team, 1983.
Selected by Oklahoma in 1984 USFL territorial draft.
Selected by Atlanta in 1st round (9th player selected) of 1984 NFL draft.
Signed by Atlanta Falcons, July 20, 1984.
Atlanta NFL, 1984.
Games: 1984 (16).
Pro statistics: Credited with one safety, 1984.

WILLIAM KIRBY BRYAN
(Bill)
Center—Denver Broncos
Born June 21, 1955, at Burlington, N. C.
Height, 6.02. Weight, 258.
High School—Burlington, N. C., Walter Williams.
Received bachelor of arts degree in economics from Duke University in 1977.

Selected by Denver in 4th round (101st player selected) of 1977 NFL draft.
On injured reserve, October 3 through remainder of 1977 season.
Denver NFL, 1978 through 1984.
Games: 1978 (13), 1979 (16), 1980 (16), 1981 (14), 1982 (9), 1983 (16), 1984 (16). Total—100.
Pro statistics: Recovered two fumbles, 1979; recovered one fumble and fumbled twice for minus 20 yards, 1980; fumbled once, 1981 and 1984.

JEFF DWIGHT BRYANT
Defensive End—Seattle Seahawks
Born May 22, 1960, at Atlanta, Ga.
Height, 6.05. Weight, 270.
High School—Decatur, Ga., Gordon.
Attended Clemson University.

Selected by Seattle in 1st round (6th player selected) of 1982 NFL draft.

Seattle NFL, 1982 through 1984.
Games: 1982 (9), 1983 (16), 1984 (16). Total—41.
Pro statistics: Recovered one fumble, 1983; intercepted one pass for one yard, credited with one safety and recovered two fumbles, 1984.
Played in AFC Championship Game following 1983 season.

STEPHEN BRYANT
(Steve)
Wide Receiver—Houston Oilers
Born October 10, 1959, at Los Angeles, Calif.
Height, 6.02. Weight, 197.
High School—Los Angeles, Calif., Washington.
Attended Los Angeles Southwest Junior College and Purdue University.
Selected by Houston in 4th round (94th player selected) of 1982 NFL draft.

		—PASS RECEIVING—				
Year Club	G.	P.C.	Yds.	Avg.	TD.	
1982—Houston NFL	7		None			
1983—Houston NFL	16	16	211	13.2	0	
1984—Houston NFL	14	19	278	14.6	0	
Pro Totals—3 Years	37	35	489	14.0	0	

Additional pro statistics: Recovered one fumble, 1982; attempted one pass with one completion for 24 yards and a touchdown, 1983; fumbled once, 1984.

WARREN BRYANT
Offensive Tackle—Los Angeles Raiders
Born November 11, 1955, at Miami, Fla.
Height, 6.07. Weight, 285.
High School—Miami, Fla., Edison.
Attended University of Kentucky.

Named as offensive tackle on THE SPORTING NEWS College All-America Team, 1976.
Selected by Atlanta in 1st round (6th player selected) of 1977 NFL draft.
On injured reserve with knee injury, November 27 through remainder of 1978 season.
Released by Atlanta Falcons, November 13, 1984; signed as free agent by Los Angeles Raiders, November 15, 1984.
Atlanta NFL, 1977 through 1983; Atlanta (4)-Los Angeles Raiders (5) NFL, 1984.
Games: 1977 (14), 1978 (13), 1979 (16), 1980 (16), 1981 (11), 1982 (9), 1983 (16), 1984 (9). Total—104.
Pro statistics: Recovered one fumble, 1977, 1978 and 1980.

WILLIAM CULLEN BRYANT
(Known by middle name.)
Fullback—Seattle Seahawks
Born May 20, 1951, at Fort Sill, Okla.
Height, 6.01. Weight, 235.
High School—Colorado Springs, Colo., Mitchell.
Received degree from University of Colorado and received master's degree in public administration.

Named cornerback on THE SPORTING NEWS College All-America Team, 1972.
Selected by Los Angeles in 2nd round (31st player selected) of 1973 NFL draft.
Released by Los Angeles Rams, November 26, 1982; signed as free agent by Seattle Seahawks, March 3, 1983.
On injured reserve with back injury, September 28 through October 31, 1984; activated after clearing procedural waivers, November 2, 1984.

		—RUSHING—				PASS RECEIVING				—TOTAL—		
Year Club	G.	Att.	Yds.	Avg.	TD.	P.C.	Yds.	Avg.	TD.	TD.	Pts.	F.
1973—Los Angeles Rams NFL	13		None				None			1	6	0
1974—Los Angeles Rams NFL	14	10	24	2.4	0	2	14	7.0	0	1	6	0
1975—Los Angeles Rams NFL	14	117	467	4.0	2	20	229	11.5	0	2	12	4
1976—Los Angeles Rams NFL	14	21	64	3.0	2	2	28	14.0	0	3	18	2
1977—Los Angeles Rams NFL	14	6	42	7.0	0	4	28	7.0	0	0	0	0
1978—Los Angeles Rams NFL	16	178	658	3.7	7	8	76	9.5	0	7	42	0
1979—Los Angeles Rams NFL	16	177	619	3.5	5	31	227	7.3	0	5	30	2
1980—Los Angeles Rams NFL	16	183	807	4.4	3	53	386	7.3	3	6	36	1
1981—Los Angeles Rams NFL	13	109	436	4.0	1	22	160	7.3	0	1	6	1
1982—Los Angeles Rams NFL	1		None				None			0	0	0
1983—Seattle NFL	10	27	87	3.2	0	3	8	2.7	0	0	0	0
1984—Seattle NFL	9	20	58	2.9	0	3	20	6.7	0	0	0	0
Pro Totals—12 Years	150	848	3262	3.8	20	148	1176	7.9	3	26	156	11

		—PUNT RETURNS—				—KICKOFF RET.—			
Year Club	G.	No.	Yds.	Avg.	TD.	No.	Yds.	Avg.	TD.
1973—Los Angeles Rams NFL	13		None			13	369	28.4	1
1974—Los Angeles Rams NFL	14	17	171	10.1	0	23	617	26.8	*1
1975—Los Angeles Rams NFL	14	2	47	23.5	0	12	280	23.3	0
1976—Los Angeles Rams NFL	14	29	321	11.1	0	16	459	28.7	*1
1977—Los Angeles Rams NFL	14	20	141	7.1	0	2	35	17.5	0
1978—Los Angeles Rams NFL	16	3	27	9.0	0		None		
1979—Los Angeles Rams NFL	16		None				None		
1980—Los Angeles Rams NFL	16		None				None		
1981—Los Angeles Rams NFL	13		None				None		
1982—Los Angeles Rams NFL	1		None				None		

Year Club	G.	—PUNT RETURNS—				—KICKOFF RET.—			
		No.	Yds.	Avg.	TD.	No.	Yds.	Avg.	TD.
1983—Seattle NFL	10			None				None	
1984—Seattle NFL	9	—	—	None		3	53	17.7	0
Pro Totals—12 Years	150	71	707	10.0	0	69	1813	26.3	3

Additional pro statistics: Recovered one fumble, 1973, 1976, 1978, 1979 and 1984; recovered two fumbles, 1975 and 1977.

Played in NFC Championship Game following 1974 through 1976, 1978 and 1979 seasons.
Played in AFC Championship Game following 1983 season.
Played in NFL Championship Game following 1979 season.

BRAD EDWARD BUDDE
Name pronounced Buddy.
Guard—Kansas City Chiefs
Born May 9, 1958, at Detroit, Mich.
Height, 6.04. Weight, 260.
High School—Kansas City, Mo., Rockhurst.
Received bachelor of science degree in public administration from
University of Southern California.
Son of Ed Budde, guard with Kansas City Chiefs, 1963 through 1976;
and brother of John Budde, lineman at Michigan State University.

Named as guard on THE SPORTING NEWS College All-America Team, 1979.
Selected by Kansas City in 1st round (11th player selected) of 1980 NFL draft.
On injured reserve with knee injury, November 23 through remainder of 1983 season.
Kansas City NFL, 1980 through 1984.
Games: 1980 (16), 1981 (16), 1982 (9), 1983 (12), 1984 (16). Total—69.
Pro statistics: Returned three kickoffs for 28 yards, 1980.

MAURY ANTHONY BUFORD
Punter—San Diego Chargers
Born February 18, 1960, at Mount Pleasant, Tex.
Height, 6.01. Weight, 191.
High School—Mount Pleasant, Tex.
Received business degree from Texas Tech University in 1982.
Selected by San Diego in 8th round (215th player selected) of 1982 NFL draft.

Year Club	G.	—PUNTING—		
		No.	Avg.	Blk.
1982—San Diego NFL	9	21	41.3	*2
1983—San Diego NFL	16	63	43.9	0
1984—San Diego NFL	16	66	42.0	0
Pro Totals—3 Years	41	150	42.7	2

Additional pro statistics: Attempted one pass with no completions, 1983.

GLENN BUJNOCH
Guard—Tampa Bay Buccaneers
Born December 20, 1953, at Houston, Tex.
Height, 6.06. Weight, 265.
High School—Houston, Tex., Mt. Carmel.
Received bachelor of arts degree in recreation from Texas A&M University in 1976.

Selected by Cincinnati in 2nd round (38th player selected) of 1976 NFL draft.
On injured reserve with fractured ankle, October 20 through January 9, 1982; activated, January 10, 1982.
Released by Cincinnati Bengals, August 29, 1983; signed as free agent by Tampa Bay Buccaneers, October 19, 1983.
On injured reserve with separated shoulder, August 28 through October 25, 1984; activated, October 26, 1984.
Cincinnati NFL, 1976 through 1982; Tampa Bay NFL, 1983 and 1984.
Games: 1976 (14), 1977 (13), 1978 (16), 1979 (15), 1980 (16), 1981 (6), 1982 (9), 1983 (6), 1984 (8). Total—103.
Pro statistics: Rushed once for four yards and one touchdown, 1977; recovered one fumble, 1978.
Member of Cincinnati Bengals for NFL Championship Game following 1981 season; did not play.

GERALD BULLITT
Linebacker—Washington Redskins
Born December 1, 1960, at Fort Bragg, N.C.
Height, 6.01. Weight, 235.
High School—El Paso, Tex., Andress.
Attended Texas A&M University.

Selected by Houston in 1984 USFL territorial draft.
Signed as free agent by Washington Redskins, May 10, 1984.
On injured reserve with back injury, August 13 through entire 1984 season.

DAN BUNZ
Linebacker—San Francisco 49ers
Born October 7, 1955, at Roseville, Calif.
Height, 6.04. Weight, 225.
High School—Roseville, Calif., Oakmont.
Attended University of California at Riverside and received bachelor of arts degree in sociology
from California State University at Long Beach in 1978.

Selected by San Francisco in 1st round (24th player selected) of 1978 NFL draft.
On injured reserve with groin injury, November 20 through remainder of 1982 season.
On inactive list, September 19, 1982.
On physically unable to perform/active with groin injury, July 22 through August 15, 1983.
On physically unable to perform/reserve with groin injury, August 16 through October 21, 1983; activated, October 22, 1983.
San Francisco NFL, 1978 through 1984.
Games: 1978 (16), 1979 (14), 1980 (16), 1981 (14), 1982 (1), 1983 (9), 1984 (16). Total—86.
Pro statistics: Intercepted one pass for 13 yards and recovered three fumbles for nine yards, 1978; intercepted one pass for two yards, 1979 and 1984; recovered five fumbles for five yards and fumbled once, 1979; recovered three fumbles for 24 yards, 1980; recovered two fumbles, 1981; recovered one fumble, 1983.
Played in NFC Championship Game following 1981, 1983 and 1984 seasons.
Played in NFL Championship Game following 1981 and 1984 seasons.

FERNANZA BURGESS
Safety—New York Jets
Born March 6, 1960, at Miami, Fla.
Height, 6.01. Weight, 210.
High School—Miami, Fla., South Miami.
Attended Morris Brown College.

Signed as free agent by St. Louis Cardinals, May 3, 1983.
On injured reserve with shoulder injury, August 16 through August 22, 1983.
Released by St. Louis Cardinals, August 23, 1983; signed as free agent by Miami Dolphins, May 21, 1984.
Released by Miami Dolphins, August 27, 1984; re-signed by Dolphins, August 28, 1984.
Released by Miami Dolphins, September 28, 1984; signed as free agent by New York Jets, October 3, 1984.
Miami (3)-New York Jets (11) NFL, 1984.
Games: 1984 (14).

GARY BURLEY
Defensive Tackle—Atlanta Falcons
Born December 8, 1952, at Urbancrest, O.
Height, 6.03. Weight, 282.
High School—Grove City, O.
Attended Wharton County Junior College and University of Pittsburgh.

Selected by Cincinnati in 3rd round (55th player selected) of 1975 NFL draft.
Missed entire 1975 season due to ankle injury.
On injured reserve, November 28 through remainder of 1980 season.
On injured reserve with knee injury, December 1 through remainder of 1982 season.
Traded by Cincinnati Bengals to Atlanta Falcons for 7th round pick in 1985 draft, August 23, 1984.
On injured reserve with strained Achilles tendon, September 18 through October 21, 1984; activated, October 22, 1984.
Cincinnati NFL, 1976 through 1983; Atlanta NFL, 1984.
Games: 1976 (14), 1977 (14), 1978 (16), 1979 (16), 1980 (11), 1981 (16), 1982 (4), 1983 (14), 1984 (12). Total—117.
Pro statistics: Recovered two fumbles, 1976 and 1977; credited with one safety, 1978.
Played in AFC Championship Game following 1981 season.
Played in NFL Championship Game following 1981 season.

CLINTON BLANE BURRELL
Safety—Cleveland Browns
Born September 4, 1956, at Franklin, La.
Height, 6.01. Weight, 192.
High School—Franklin, La.
Received bachelor of science degree in business administration
from Louisiana State University in 1979.

Selected by Cleveland in 6th round (151st player selected) of 1979 NFL draft.
On injured reserve with knee injury, September 14 through remainder of 1981 season.
On injured reserve with broken arm, December 6 through remainder of 1983 season.

| | | | ——INTERCEPTIONS—— | | |
Year Club	G.	No.	Yds.	Avg.	TD.
1979—Cleveland NFL	16		None		
1980—Cleveland NFL	15	5	51	10.2	0
1981—Cleveland NFL	2		None		
1982—Cleveland NFL	9	1	14	14.0	*1
1983—Cleveland NFL	12	2	0	0.0	0
1984—Cleveland NFL	13		None		
Pro Totals—6 Years	67	8	65	8.1	1

Additional pro statistics: Recovered one fumble for 11 yards and fumbled once, 1979; recovered four fumbles, 1982; recovered one fumble, 1983.

JAMES E. BURROUGHS
Cornerback—Indianapolis Colts
Born January 21, 1958, at Pahokee, Fla.
Height, 6.01. Weight, 187.
High School—Pahokee, Fla.
Attended Michigan State University.

Named as defensive back on THE SPORTING NEWS College All-America Team, 1981.
Selected by Baltimore in 3rd round (57th player selected) of 1982 NFL draft.
On inactive list, September 12, 1982.
Franchise transferred to Indianapolis, March 31, 1984.
On injured reserve with ankle injury, November 9 through remainder of 1984 season.

Year Club	G.	No.	Yds.	Avg.TD.	
1982—Baltimore NFL	8	1	94	94.0	∗1
1983—Baltimore NFL	16	2	8	4.0	0
1984—Indianapolis NFL	6	3	9	3.0	0
Pro Totals—3 Years............	30	6	111	18.5	1

Additional pro statistics: Recovered one fumble, 1982 and 1983.

LLOYD EARL BURRUSS
Safety—Kansas City Chiefs
Born October 31, 1957, at Charlottesville, Va.
Height, 6.00. Weight, 202.
High School—Charlottesville, Va.
Received bachelor of arts degree in general studies from University of Maryland in 1981.
Selected by Kansas City in 3rd round (78th player selected) of 1981 NFL draft.

Year Club	G.	No.	Yds.	Avg.TD.
1981—Kansas City NFL.........	14	4	75	18.8	1
1982—Kansas City NFL.........	9	1	25	25.0	0
1983—Kansas City NFL.........	12	4	46	11.5	0
1984—Kansas City NFL.........	16	2	16	8.0	0
Pro Totals—4 Years............	51	11	162	14.7	1

Additional pro statistics: Returned five kickoffs for 91 yards, recovered one fumble for four yards and fumbled once, 1981; recovered two fumbles for 26 yards, 1983; recovered one fumble, 1984.

WILLIAM HENRY BURSE
Linebacker—Kansas City Chiefs
Born September 3, 1961, at Christams, Ky.
Height, 6.02. Weight, 232.
High School—Hopkinsville, Ky.
Attended University of Kentucky and Kentucky State University.
Selected by Oakland in 15th round (210th player selected) of 1985 USFL draft.
Signed by Oakland Invaders, January 23, 1985.
Released by Oakland Invaders, February 11, 1985; signed as free agent by Kansas City Chiefs, May 9, 1985.

JIM BURT
Nose Tackle—New York Giants
Born June 7, 1959, at Buffalo, N.Y.
Height, 6.01. Weight, 260.
High School—Orchard Park, N.Y.
Attended University of Miami (Fla.)
Signed as free agent by New York Giants, May 4, 1981.
On injured reserve with back injury, December 24 through remainder of 1982 season.
On injured reserve with back injury, November 2 through remainder of 1983 season.
New York Giants NFL, 1981 through 1984.
Games: 1981 (13), 1982 (4), 1983 (7), 1984 (16). Total—40.
Pro statistics: Recovered one fumble, 1983; recovered two fumbles, 1984.

BLAIR WALTER BUSH
Center—Seattle Seahawks
Born November 25, 1956, at Fort Hood, Tex.
Height, 6.03. Weight, 252.
High School—Palos Verdes, Calif.
Attended University of Washington.
Selected by Cincinnati in 1st round (16th player selected) of 1978 NFL draft.
Traded by Cincinnati Bengals to Seattle Seahawks for 1st round pick in 1985 draft, June 29, 1983.
Cincinnati NFL, 1978 through 1982; Seattle, NFL, 1983 and 1984.
Games: 1978 (16), 1979 (12), 1980 (16), 1981 (16), 1982 (8), 1983 (16), 1984 (16). Total—100.
Pro statistics: Recovered one fumble for 12 yards, 1981.
Played in AFC Championship Game following 1981 and 1983 seasons.
Played in NFL Championship Game following 1981 season.

STEVE RAY BUSICK
Linebacker—Denver Broncos
Born December 10, 1958, at Los Angeles, Calif.
Height, 6.04. Weight, 227.
High School—Temple City, Calif.
Attended University of Southern California.
Selected by Denver in 7th round (181st player selected) of 1981 NFL draft.

Denver NFL, 1981 through 1984.
Games: 1981 (16), 1982 (9), 1983 (16), 1984 (16). Total—57.
Pro statistics: Recovered two fumbles for three yards, 1981; intercepted two passes for 21 yards and recovered one fumble, 1984.

MARK ALLAN BUTKUS
Defensive Tackle—Chicago Bears
Born December 31, 1961, at Chicago, Ill.
Height, 6.04. Weight, 261.
High School—Lansing, Ill., Thornton Fractional South.
Attended University of Illinois.
Nephew of Dick Butkus, Hall of Fame linebacker with Chicago Bears, 1965 through 1973.

Selected by Chicago in 1984 USFL territorial draft.
Selected by Chicago in 11th round (298th player selected) of 1984 NFL draft.
Signed by Chicago Bears, May 17, 1984.
On non-football injury list with knee injury, July 18 through entire 1984 season.

CHARLES WALLACE BUTLER
(Chuck)
Linebacker—Seattle Seahawks
Born December 18, 1961, at New Haven, Conn.
Height, 6.00. Weight, 225.
High School—Oakland, Calif., Bishop O'Dowd.
Attended Boise State University.

Signed as free agent by Seattle Seahawks, May 2, 1984.
On injured reserve with knee injury, August 14 through October 4, 1984; activated after clearing procedural waivers, October 5, 1984.
On injured reserve with back injury, December 1 through remainder of 1984 season.
Seattle NFL, 1984.
Games: 1984 (8).

JERRY O'DELL BUTLER
Wide Receiver—Buffalo Bills
Born October 12, 1957, at Ware Shoals, S.C.
Height, 6.00. Weight, 178.
High School—Ware Shoals, S.C.
Received bachelor of arts degree in recreation and parks administration
from Clemson University in 1980.

Named as wide receiver on THE SPORTING NEWS College All-America Team, 1978.
Named THE SPORTING NEWS AFC Rookie of the Year, 1979.
Selected by Buffalo in 1st round (5th player selected) of 1979 NFL draft.
On did not report list, August 24 through September 2, 1982.
Granted two-game roster exemption, September 3, 1982; activated, September 11, 1982.
On injured reserve with knee injury, November 4 through remainder of 1983 season.
On physically unable to perform/reserve with knee injury, August 14 through entire 1984 season.

| | | ——PASS RECEIVING—— | | | |
Year Club	G.	P.C.	Yds.	Avg.	TD.
1979—Buffalo NFL	13	48	834	17.4	4
1980—Buffalo NFL	16	57	832	14.6	6
1981—Buffalo NFL	16	55	842	15.3	8
1982—Buffalo NFL	7	26	336	12.9	4
1983—Buffalo NFL	9	36	385	10.7	3
Pro Totals—5 Years	61	222	3229	14.5	25

Additional pro statistics: Rushed twice for 13 yards, 1979; fumbled once, 1979 and 1983; rushed once for 18 yards, 1980; rushed once for one yard and fumbled twice, 1981.

JOHN KEITH BUTLER
(Known by middle name.)
Linebacker—Seattle Seahawks
Born May 16, 1956, at Anniston, Ala.
Height, 6.04. Weight, 238.
High School—Huntsville, Ala., Lee.
Attending Memphis State University.

Selected by Seattle in 2nd round (36th player selected) of 1978 NFL draft.
Seattle NFL, 1978 through 1984.
Games: 1978 (16), 1979 (14), 1980 (16), 1981 (16), 1982 (8), 1983 (16), 1984 (16). Total—102.
Pro statistics: Recovered two fumbles, 1978; intercepted one pass for four yards, 1979; intercepted two passes for 11 yards, 1980; intercepted two passes for no yards and fumbled once, 1981; intercepted one pass for no yards, 1983.
Played in AFC Championship Game following 1983 season.

—DID YOU KNOW—
That quarterback Randy Wright, a sixth-round pick in 1984, was the first Packer drafted from the University of Wisconsin since center Ken Bowman in 1964?

RAYMOND LEONARD BUTLER
(Ray)
Wide Receiver—Indianapolis Colts

Born June 28, 1956, at Port Lavaca, Tex.
Height, 6.02. Weight, 195.
High School—Sweeny, Tex.
Attended Wharton County Junior College and received
degree in speech from University of Southern California in 1980.

Selected by Baltimore in 4th round (88th player selected) of 1980 NFL draft.
On injured reserve with broken arm, November 28 through remainder of 1983 season.
Franchise transferred to Indianapolis, March 31, 1984.

		—PASS RECEIVING—			
Year Club	G.	P.C.	Yds.	Avg.	TD.
1980—Baltimore NFL	16	34	574	16.9	2
1981—Baltimore NFL	16	46	832	18.1	9
1982—Baltimore NFL	9	17	268	15.8	2
1983—Baltimore NFL	11	10	207	20.7	3
1984—Indianapolis NFL	16	43	664	15.4	6
Pro Totals—5 Years	68	150	2545	17.0	22

Additional pro statistics: Rushed three times for 10 yards and recovered one fumble, 1982.

ROBERT CALVIN BUTLER
(Bobby)
Cornerback—Atlanta Falcons

Born May 28, 1959, at Boynton Beach, Fla.
Height, 5.11. Weight, 175.
High School—Delray Beach, Fla., Atlantic.
Attended Florida State University.
Cousin of James (Cannonball) Butler, running back with Pittsburgh Steelers,
Atlanta Falcons and St. Louis Cardinals, 1965 through 1972.

Selected by Atlanta in 1st round (25th player selected) of 1981 NFL draft.

		—INTERCEPTIONS—			
Year Club	G.	No.	Yds.	Avg.	TD.
1981—Atlanta NFL	16	5	86	17.2	0
1982—Atlanta NFL	9	2	0	0.0	0
1983—Atlanta NFL	16	4	12	3.0	0
1984—Atlanta NFL	15	2	25	12.5	0
Pro Totals—4 Years	56	13	123	9.5	0

Additional pro statistics: Returned one kickoff for 17 yards and recovered one fumble, 1983; recovered one fumble for 10 yards, 1984.

GREGORY ELLIS BUTTLE
(Greg)
Linebacker—New York Jets

Born June 20, 1954, at Atlantic City, N. J.
Height, 6.03. Weight, 232.
High School—Linwood, N. J., Mainland Regional.
Received bachelor of science degree in liberal arts from Penn State University in 1976.

Named as linebacker on The Sporting News College All-America Team, 1975.
Selected by New York Jets in 3rd round (67th player selected) of 1976 NFL draft.
On injured reserve with knee injury, October 30 through remainder of 1978 season.
On injured reserve with neck injury, November 11 through remainder of 1983 season.

		—INTERCEPTIONS—						—INTERCEPTIONS—			
Year Club	G.	No.	Yds.	Avg.	TD.	Year Club	G.	No.	Yds.	Avg.	TD.
1976—N.Y. Jets NFL	14	2	20	10.0	0	1981—N.Y. Jets NFL	15	2	34	17.0	0
1977—N.Y. Jets NFL	13	2	54	27.0	*1	1982—N.Y. Jets NFL	7	1	9	9.0	0
1978—N.Y. Jets NFL	8	2	34	17.0	0	1983—N.Y. Jets NFL	9	1	17	17.0	0
1979—N.Y. Jets NFL	16	2	27	13.5	0	1984—N.Y. Jets NFL	14	2	5	2.5	0
1980—N.Y. Jets NFL	14	1	15	15.0	0	Pro Totals—9 Years	110	15	215	14.3	1

Additional pro statistics: Recovered two fumbles for 23 yards and one touchdown, fumbled once, and rushed once for 26 yards, 1976; recovered one fumble, 1978 and 1980; credited with one safety and recovered two fumbles, 1981; recovered two fumbles for four yards and a touchdown, 1984.
Played in AFC Championship Game following 1982 season.

DAVID ROY BUTZ
(Dave)
Defensive Tackle—Washington Redskins

Born June 23, 1950, at Lafayette, Ala.
Height, 6.07. Weight, 295.
High School—Park Ridge, Ill., Maine South.
Received bachelor of science degree in physical education from Purdue University in 1973.
Nephew of Earl Butz, former secretary of agriculture.

Named as defensive tackle on The Sporting News College All-America Team, 1972.

Named to THE SPORTING NEWS NFL All-Star Team, 1983.
Selected by St. Louis in 1st round (5th player selected) of 1973 NFL draft.
Played out option with St. Louis Cardinals and signed by Washington Redskins, August 5, 1975; Cardinals received three draft choices (1st round picks in 1977 and 1978 and 2nd round pick in 1979) in exchange for three draft choices (5th and 15th round picks in 1976 and 6th round pick in 1977) as compensation, September 4, 1975.
St. Louis NFL, 1973 and 1974; Washington NFL, 1975 through 1984.
Games: 1973 (12), 1974 (1), 1975 (14), 1976 (14), 1977 (12), 1978 (16), 1979 (15), 1980 (16), 1981 (16), 1982 (9), 1983 (16), 1984 (15). Total—156.
Pro statistics: Returned one kickoff for 23 yards, 1973; recovered one fumble, 1973, 1976 and 1982 through 1984; intercepted one pass for three yards, 1978; intercepted one pass for 26 yards, 1981.
Played in NFC Championship Game following 1982 and 1983 seasons.
Played in NFL Championship Game following 1982 and 1983 seasons.
Played in Pro Bowl (NFL All-Star Game) following 1983 season.

EARNEST ALEXANDER BYNER
Fullback—Cleveland Browns
Born September 15, 1962, at Milledgeville, Ga.
Height, 5.10. Weight, 215.
High School—Milledgeville, Ga., Baldwin.
Attended East Carolina University.

Selected by Cleveland in 10th round (280th player selected) of 1984 NFL draft.

		—RUSHING—				PASS RECEIVING				—TOTAL—		
Year Club	G.	Att.	Yds.	Avg.	TD.	P.C.	Yds.	Avg.	TD.	TD.	Pts.	F.
1984—Cleveland NFL	16	72	426	5.9	2	11	118	10.7	0	3	18	3

		KICKOFF RETURNS			
Year Club	G.	No.	Yds.	Avg.	TD.
1984—Cleveland NFL	16	22	415	18.9	0

Additional pro statistics: Recovered two fumbles for 55 yards and a touchdown, 1984.

DARRYL TERRENCE BYRD
Linebacker—Los Angeles Raiders
Born September 3, 1960, at San Diego, Calif.
Height, 6.01. Weight, 220.
High School—Union City, Calif., James Logan.
Attended Chabot College and University of Illinois.

Selected by Chicago in 1983 USFL territorial draft.
Signed as free agent by Los Angeles Raiders, April 30, 1983.
Released by Los Angeles Raiders, August 29, 1983; re-signed by Raiders, August 30, 1983.
Los Angeles Raiders NFL, 1983 and 1984.
Games: 1983 (16), 1984 (16). Total—32.
Played in AFC Championship Game following 1983 season.
Played in NFL Championship Game following 1983 season.

GILL ARNETTE BYRD
Cornerback—San Diego Chargers
Born February 20, 1961, at San Francisco, Calif.
Height, 5.11. Weight, 201.
High School—San Francisco, Calif., Lowell.
Received degree in business administration and finance
from San Jose State University in 1982.
Nephew of MacArthur Byrd, linebacker with Los Angeles Rams, 1965.

Selected by Oakland in 1983 USFL territorial draft.
Selected by San Diego in 1st round (22nd player selected) of 1983 NFL draft.
Signed by San Diego Chargers, May 20, 1983.
On injured reserve with pulled hamstring, December 12 through remainder of 1984 season.

		—INTERCEPTIONS—			
Year Club	G.	No.	Yds.	Avg.	TD.
1983—San Diego NFL	14	1	0	0.0	0
1984—San Diego NFL	13	4	157	39.3	*2
Pro Totals—2 Years	27	5	157	31.4	2

BRIAN DAVID CABRAL
Original Hawaiian surname is Kealiihaaheo (pronounced Kay-ah-lee-e-ha-hay-o).
Linebacker—Chicago Bears
Born June 23, 1956, at Fort Benning, Ga.
Height, 6.01. Weight, 224.
High School—Honolulu, Hawaii, St. Louis.
Received bachelor of science degree in recreation from University of Colorado.

Selected by Atlanta in 4th round (95th player selected) of 1978 NFL draft.
On injured reserve with knee injury, August 12 through entire 1978 season.
Released by Atlanta Falcons, August 27, 1979; re-signed by Falcons, November 29, 1979.
Traded by Atlanta Falcons to Baltimore Colts for conditional future draft pick, August 14, 1980.
Released by Baltimore Colts, September 1, 1980; signed as free agent by Green Bay Packers, November 5, 1980.
Released by Green Bay Packers, August 17, 1981; signed as free agent by Chicago Bears, August 21, 1981.
Released by Chicago Bears, August 31, 1981; re-signed by Bears, September 1, 1981.

On inactive list, September 12, 1982.
Atlanta NFL, 1979; Green Bay NFL, 1980; Chicago NFL, 1981 through 1984.
Games: 1979 (3), 1980 (7), 1981 (16), 1982 (8), 1983 (16), 1984 (16). Total—66.
Pro statistics: Returned two kickoffs for 11 yards, 1983; caught one pass for seven yards, 1984.
Played in NFC Championship Game following 1984 season.

LYNN DWIGHT CAIN
Running Back—Atlanta Falcons
Born October 16, 1955, at Los Angeles, Calif.
Height, 6.01. Weight, 205.
High School—Los Angeles, Calif., Roosevelt.
Attended East Los Angeles Junior College and received bachelor of arts degree
in speech communication from University of Southern California in 1979.

Selected by Atlanta in 4th round (100th player selected) of 1979 NFL draft.
On injured reserve with knee injury, November 6 through remainder of 1979 season.

Year Club	G.	Att.	Yds.	Avg.	TD.	P.C.	Yds.	Avg.	TD.	TD.	Pts.	F.
1979—Atlanta NFL	10	63	295	4.7	2	15	181	12.1	2	4	24	2
1980—Atlanta NFL	16	235	914	3.9	8	24	223	9.3	1	9	54	6
1981—Atlanta NFL	16	156	542	3.5	4	55	421	7.7	2	6	36	3
1982—Atlanta NFL	9	54	173	3.2	1	13	101	7.8	1	2	12	2
1983—Atlanta NFL	16	19	63	3.3	1	3	24	8.0	0	1	6	1
1984—Atlanta NFL	15	77	276	3.6	3	12	87	7.3	0	3	18	2
Pro Totals—5 Years	82	604	2263	3.7	19	122	1037	8.5	6	25	150	16

Additional pro statistics: Returned seven kickoffs for 149 yards (21.3 average), 1979; recovered two fumbles, 1980 and 1981; returned 11 kickoffs for 200 yards, 1983.

ANTHONY CALDWELL
(Tony)
Linebacker—Los Angeles Raiders
Born April 1, 1961, at Los Angeles, Calif.
Height, 6.01. Weight, 220.
High School—Carson, Calif.
Attended University of Washington.

Selected by Philadelphia in 6th round (65th player selected) of 1983 USFL draft.
Selected by Los Angeles Raiders in 3rd round (82nd player selected) of 1983 NFL draft.
Signed by Los Angeles Raiders, June 10, 1983.
Los Angeles Raiders NFL, 1983 and 1984.
Games: 1983 (16), 1984 (16). Total—32.
Pro statistics: Recovered one fumble, 1983.
Played in AFC Championship Game following 1983 season.
Played in NFL Championship Game following 1983 season.

BRYAN CRAIG CALDWELL
Defensive End—Philadelphia Eagles
Born May 6, 1960, at Oakland, Calif.
Height, 6.04. Weight, 248.
High School—Fountain Valley, Calif.
Attended Mesa Community College and received
degree in special education from Arizona State University in 1983.

Selected by Arizona in 1983 USFL territorial draft.
Selected by Dallas in 3rd round (77th player selected) of 1983 NFL draft.
Signed by Dallas Cowboys, June 28, 1983.
On injured reserve with knee injury, August 16 through entire 1983 season.
Released by Dallas Cowboys, August 27, 1984; signed as free agent by Houston Oilers, September 20, 1984.
Released by Houston Oilers, November 14, 1984; signed as free agent by Philadelphia Eagles, May 8, 1985.
Houston NFL, 1984.
Games: 1984 (8).

KEVIN BRADLEY CALL
Offensive Tackle—Indianapolis Colts
Born November 13, 1961, at Boulder, Colo.
Height, 6.07. Weight, 289.
High School—Boulder, Colo., Fairview.
Attended Colorado State University.

Selected by Denver in 1984 USFL territorial draft.
Selected by Indianapolis in 5th round (130th player selected) of 1984 NFL draft.
Signed by Indianapolis Colts, July 24, 1984.
Indianapolis NFL, 1984.
Games: 1984 (15).

RICHARD JON CAMARILLO
Name pronounced Cama-ree-o.
(Rich)
Punter—New England Patriots
Born November 29, 1959, at Whittier, Calif.
Height, 5.11. Weight, 191.
High School—Pico Rivera, Calif., El Rancho.
Attended Cerritos Junior College and University of Washington.

Named to THE SPORTING NEWS NFL All-Star Team, 1983.
Led NFL in net punting average with 37.1 in 1983.
Signed as free agent by New England Patriots, May 11, 1981.
Released by New England Patriots, August 24, 1981; re-signed by Patriots after clearing procedural waivers, October 20, 1981.
On injured reserve with knee injury, August 28 through November 2, 1984; activated, November 3, 1984.

		—PUNTING—		
Year Club	G.	No.	Avg.	Blk.
1981—New England NFL	9	47	41.7	0
1982—New England NFL	9	49	43.7	0
1983—New England NFL	16	81	44.6	0
1984—New England NFL	7	48	42.1	0
Pro Totals—4 Years	41	225	43.3	0

Additional pro statistics: Recovered one fumble and fumbled once, 1981.
Played in Pro Bowl (NFL All-Star Game) following 1983 season.

GLENN SCOTT CAMERON
Linebacker—Cincinnati Bengals
Born February 21, 1953, at Miami, Fla.
Height, 6.02. Weight, 228.
High School—Coral Gables, Fla.
Received bachelor of science degree in business administration from University of Florida.

Selected by Cincinnati in 1st round (14th player selected) of 1975 NFL draft.
Cincinnati NFL, 1975 through 1984.
Games: 1975 (14), 1976 (14), 1977 (14), 1978 (15), 1979 (15), 1980 (14), 1981 (16), 1982 (9), 1983 (16), 1984 (16). Total—143.
Pro statistics: Recovered one fumble, 1975 and 1980; intercepted three passes for 43 yards, 1980; intercepted one pass for no yards, 1981; recovered one fumble for one yard, 1983; intercepted one pass for 15 yards, 1984.
Played in AFC Championship Game following 1981 season.
Played in NFL Championship Game following 1981 season.

JACK LYNDON CAMERON
Wide Receiver—Chicago Bears
Born November 5, 1961, at Roxboro, N.C.
Height, 6.00. Weight, 182.
High School—Roxboro, N.C., Person.
Attended Winston-Salem State University.

Signed as free agent by Chicago Bears, May 22, 1984.

		PASS RECEIVING				—KICKOFF RET.—				—TOTAL—		
Year Club	G.	P.C.	Yds.	Avg.	TD.	No.	Yds.	Avg.	TD.	TD.	Pts.	F.
1984—Chicago NFL	16	1	13	13.0	0	26	485	18.7	0	0	0	0

Played in NFC Championship Game following 1984 season.

REGGIE LOUIS CAMP
Defensive End—Cleveland Browns
Born February 28, 1961, at San Francisco, Calif.
Height, 6.04. Weight, 264.
High School—Daly City, Calif., Jefferson.
Attended University of California at Berkeley.

Selected by Oakland in 1983 USFL territorial draft.
Selected by Cleveland in 3rd round (68th player selected) of 1983 NFL draft.
Signed by Cleveland Browns, May 31, 1983.
Cleveland NFL, 1983 and 1984.
Games: 1983 (16), 1984 (16). Total—32.
Pro statistics: Recovered one fumble, 1984.

ALLEN DALE CAMPBELL
Linebacker—Tampa Bay Buccaneers
Born April 16, 1963, at Perry, Fla.
Height, 6.05. Weight, 230.
High School—Perry, Fla., Taylor.
Attended Florida State University and Salem College.

Selected by Tampa Bay in 9th round (128th player selected) of 1985 USFL draft.
Signed by Tampa Bay Bandits, January 17, 1985.
Released by Tampa Bay Bandits, January 28, 1985; signed as free agent by Tampa Bay Buccaneers, May 9, 1985.

EARL CHRISTIAN CAMPBELL
Running Back—New Orleans Saints
Born March 29, 1955, at Tyler, Tex.
Height 5.11. Weight, 233.
High School—Tyler, Tex.
Received degree in speech communications from University of Texas in 1980.

Named as running back on THE SPORTING NEWS College All-America Team, 1977.
Named THE SPORTING NEWS College Player of the Year, 1977.
Heisman Trophy winner, 1977.
Established NFL record for most 200-yard games, season (4), 1980.
Tied NFL records for most consecutive games, 200 yards rushing (2), 1980; most consecutive games, 100 yards rushing (7), 1979.
Named THE SPORTING NEWS AFC Rookie and Player of the Year, 1978.
Named to THE SPORTING NEWS AFC All-Star Team, 1978 and 1979.
Named to THE SPORTING NEWS NFL All-Star Team, 1980.
Selected by Houston in 1st round (1st player selected) of 1978 NFL draft.
Traded by Houston Oilers to New Orleans Saints for 1st round pick in 1985 draft, October 9, 1984.

Year Club	G.	Att.	Yds.	Avg.	TD.	P.C.	Yds.	Avg.	TD.	TD.	Pts.	F.
			RUSHING				PASS RECEIVING				TOTAL	
1978—Houston NFL	15	302	*1450	4.8	13	12	48	4.0	0	13	78	9
1979—Houston NFL	16	368	*1697	4.6	*19	16	94	5.9	0	19	114	8
1980—Houston NFL	15	*373	*1934	*5.2	*13	11	47	4.3	0	13	78	4
1981—Houston NFL	16	361	1376	3.8	10	36	156	4.3	0	10	60	10
1982—Houston NFL	9	157	538	3.4	2	18	130	7.2	0	2	12	2
1983—Houston NFL	14	322	1301	4.0	12	19	216	11.4	0	12	72	4
1984—Houston (6)-New Orleans (8) NFL	14	146	468	3.2	4	3	27	9.0	0	4	24	2
Pro Totals—7 Years	99	2029	8764	4.3	73	115	718	6.2	0	73	438	39

Additional pro statistics: Recovered two fumbles, 1978, 1980 and 1981; recovered two fumbles for minus one yard, 1979; attempted two passes with one completion for 57 yards and a touchdown, 1980; attempted one pass with one interception and recovered one fumble, 1982; recovered two fumbles for one yard, 1984.
Played in AFC Championship Game following 1978 and 1979 seasons.
Played in Pro Bowl (NFL All-Star Game) following 1978 through 1983 seasons.

RICHARD DELANO CAMPBELL
(Rich)
Quarterback—Green Bay Packers
Born December 21, 1958, at Miami, Fla.
Height, 6.04. Weight, 219.
High School—San Jose, Calif., Santa Teresa.
Attended University of California.

Selected by Green Bay in 1st round (6th player selected) of 1981 NFL draft.
On inactive list, September 12 and September 20, 1982.

Year Club	G.	Att.	Cmp.	Pct.	Gain	T.P.	P.I.	Avg.	Att.	Yds.	Avg.	TD.	TD.	Pts.	F.
				PASSING							RUSHING			TOTAL	
1981—Green Bay NFL	2	30	15	50.0	168	0	4	5.60			None		0	0	0
1982—Green Bay NFL	1				None						None		0	0	0
1983—Green Bay NFL	1				None						None		0	0	0
1984—Green Bay NFL	3	38	16	42.1	218	3	5	5.74	2	2	1.1	0	0	0	1
Pro Totals—4 Years	7	68	31	45.6	386	3	9	5.68	2	2	1.1	0	0	0	1

Quarterback Rating Points: 1981 (27.5), 1984 (47.8). Total—38.8.

ROBERT SCOTT CAMPBELL
(Known by middle name.)
Quarterback—Pittsburgh Steelers
Born April 15, 1962, at Hershey, Pa.
Height, 6.00. Weight, 201.
High School—Hershey, Pa.
Attended Purdue University.
Son of Ken Campbell, wide receiver with New York Titans of AFL, 1960.

Selected by Philadelphia in 4th round (76th player selected) of 1984 USFL draft.
Selected by Pittsburgh in 7th round (191st player selected) of 1984 NFL draft.
Signed by Pittsburgh Steelers, May 19, 1984.

Year Club	G.	Att.	Cmp.	Pct.	Gain	T.P.	P.I.	Avg.	Att.	Yds.	Avg.	TD.	TD.	Pts.	F.
				PASSING							RUSHING			TOTAL	
1984—Pittsburgh NFL	5	15	8	53.3	109	1	1	7.27	3	—5	—1.7	0	0	0	1

Quarterback Rating Points: 1984 (71.3).
Additional pro statistics: Recovered one fumble, 1984.
Member of Pittsburgh Steelers for AFC Championship Game following 1984 season; did not play.

TODD CAMPBELL
Nose Tackle—New York Jets
Born January 28, 1961, at New Kensington, Pa.
Height, 6.02. Weight, 255.
High School—New Kensington, Pa., Valley.
Attended University of West Virginia.

Signed as free agent by Arizona Wranglers, February 15, 1983.
Released by Arizona Wranglers, March 16, 1983; signed as free agent by Cleveland Browns, May 24, 1983.
Left Cleveland Browns camp voluntarily and released, July 25, 1983; signed as free agent by Miami Dolphins, April 24, 1984.
Released by Miami Dolphins, August 27, 1984; signed as free agent by New York Jets, May 7, 1985.
Arizona USFL, 1983.
Games: 1983 (2).

JOHN RAYMOND CANNON
Defensive End—Tampa Bay Buccaneers
Born July 30, 1960, at Long Branch, N.J.
Height, 6.05. Weight, 260.
High School—Holmdel, N.J.
Received bachelor of business administration degree from
College of William & Mary in 1982.
Brother of Gary Cannon, defensive end at University of Delaware.

Selected by Tampa Bay in 3rd round (83rd player selected) of 1982 NFL draft.
USFL rights traded by Memphis Showboats to Houston Gamblers for rights to defensive end Ray Yakavonis, February 13, 1985.
Tampa Bay NFL, 1982 through 1984.
Games: 1982 (9), 1983 (14), 1984 (16). Total—39.
Pro statistics: Recovered one fumble, 1983 and 1984; intercepted one pass for no yards, 1984.

MARK MAIDA CANNON
Center—Green Bay Packers
Born June 14, 1962, at Whittier, Calif.
Height, 6.03. Weight, 258.
High School—Austin, Tex., S.F. Austin.
Attended University of Texas at Arlington.

Selected by Tampa Bay in 3rd round (62nd player selected) of 1984 USFL draft.
Selected by Green Bay in 11th round (294th player selected) of 1984 NFL draft.
Signed by Green Bay Packers, July 12, 1984.
Green Bay NFL, 1984.
Games: 1984 (16).

WAYNE CAPERS
Wide Receiver—Pittsburgh Steelers
Born May 17, 1961, at Miami, Fla.
Height, 6.02. Weight, 193.
High School—Miami, Fla., South.
Attended Kansas University.

Selected by Pittsburgh in 2nd round (52nd player selected) of 1983 NFL draft.

| | | —PASS RECEIVING— | | | | |
Year Club	G.	P.C.	Yds.	Avg.	TD.
1983—Pittsburgh NFL............	11	10	185	18.5	1
1984—Pittsburgh NFL............	16	7	81	11.6	0
Pro Totals—2 Years............	27	17	266	15.6	1

Additional pro statistics: Rushed once for minus three yards, recovered two fumbles for two yards and fumbled once, 1984.
Played in AFC Championship Game following 1984 season.

BRIAN MILTON CARPENTER
Cornerback—Buffalo Bills
Born November 27, 1960, at Flint, Mich.
Height, 5.10. Weight, 167.
High School—Flint, Mich., Southwestern.
Attended University of Michigan.

Selected by Dallas in 4th round (101st player selected) of 1982 NFL draft.
Released by Dallas Cowboys, September 6, 1982; signed as free agent by New York Giants, September 17, 1982.
Released by New York Giants, August 29, 1983; awarded on waivers to Washington Redskins, August 30, 1983.
Traded by Washington Redskins to Buffalo Bills for 12th round pick in 1985 draft, September 19, 1984.

| | | —INTERCEPTIONS— | | | |
Year Club	G.	No.	Yds.	Avg.	TD.
1982—N.Y. Giants NFL	4		None		
1983—Washington NFL..........	15	1	2	2.0	0
1984—Wa. (3)-Buf. (13) NFL..	16	3	11	3.7	0
Pro Totals—3 Years............	35	4	13	3.3	0

Additional pro statistics: Recovered two fumbles, 1984.
Played in NFC Championship Game following 1983 season.
Played in NFL Championship Game following 1983 season.

DEAN CARPENTER
Placekicker—Cleveland Browns.
Born October 6, 1959, at Chicago, Ill.
Height, 5.10. Weight, 175.
High School—Des Plaines, Ill., Maine West.
Attended University of Chicago.

Signed as free agent by Houston Oilers, July 6, 1983.
Released by Houston Oilers, July 24, 1983; signed by Memphis Showboats, November 12, 1983.
Released by Memphis Showboats, January 23, 1984; signed as free agent by Chicago Bears, April 30, 1984.
Released by Chicago Bears, August 8, 1984; signed as free agent by Cleveland Browns, May 6, 1985.

ROBERT J. CARPENTER JR.
(Rob)
Running Back—New York Giants
Born April 20, 1955, at Lancaster, O.
Height, 6.01. Weight, 230.
High School—Lancaster, O.
Received bachelor of science degree in education from Miami University in 1977.

Selected by Houston in 3rd round (84th player selected) of 1977 NFL draft.
On injured reserve with knee injury, November 14 through remainder of 1978 season.
Traded by Houston Oilers to New York Giants for 3rd round pick in 1982 draft, September 29, 1981.
On did not report list, August 21 through November 28, 1982.
Granted two-game roster exemption, November 29, 1982; activated, December 3, 1982.
On injured reserve with knee injury, November 10 through remainder of 1983 season.

		—RUSHING—				PASS RECEIVING				—TOTAL—		
Year Club	G.	Att.	Yds.	Avg.	TD.	P.C.	Yds.	Avg.	TD.	TD.	Pts.	F.
1977—Houston NFL	11	144	652	4.5	1	23	156	6.8	0	1	6	3
1978—Houston NFL	11	82	348	4.2	5	17	150	8.8	0	5	30	0
1979—Houston NFL	16	92	355	3.9	3	16	116	7.3	1	4	24	3
1980—Houston NFL	15	97	359	3.7	3	43	346	8.0	0	3	18	4
1981—Houston (4)-N.Y. Giants (10) NFL	14	208	822	4.0	5	37	281	7.6	1	6	36	3
1982—New York Giants NFL	5	67	204	3.0	1	7	29	4.1	0	1	6	0
1983—New York Giants NFL	10	170	624	3.7	4	26	258	9.9	2	6	36	2
1984—New York Giants NFL	16	250	795	3.2	7	26	209	8.0	1	8	48	2
Pro Totals—8 Years	98	1110	4159	3.7	29	195	1545	7.9	5	34	204	17

Additional pro statistics: Recovered one fumble, 1977, 1980 and 1984; returned one kickoff for 11 yards, 1978; returned two kickoffs for 34 yards and recovered one fumble for minus two yards, 1979; returned one kickoff for seven yards, 1980.
Played in AFC Championship Game following 1979 season.

ALPHONSO CARREKER
Name pronounced CARE-uh-ker.
Defensive End—Green Bay Packers
Born May 25, 1962, at Columbus, O.
Height, 6.06. Weight, 260.
High School—Columbus, O., Marion Franklin.
Attended Florida State University.

Selected by Tampa Bay in 1984 USFL territorial draft.
Selected by Green Bay in 1st round (12th player selected) of 1984 NFL draft.
Signed by Green Bay Packers, June 20, 1984.
Green Bay NFL, 1984.
Games: 1984 (14).

JAY TIMOTHY CARROLL
Tight End—Tampa Bay Buccaneers
Born November 8, 1961, at Winona, Minn.
Height, 6.04. Weight, 230.
High School—Winona, Minn., Cotter.
Attended University of Minnesota.

Selected by Pittsburgh in 9th round (191st player selected) of 1984 USFL draft.
Selected by Tampa Bay in 7th round (169th player selected) of 1984 NFL draft.
Signed by Tampa Bay Buccaneers, June 21, 1984.

		—PASS RECEIVING—			
Year Club	G.	P.C.	Yds.	Avg.	TD.
1984—Tampa Bay NFL	16	5	50	10.0	1

Additional pro statistics: Recovered one fumble, 1984.

CARLOS A. CARSON
Wide Receiver—Kansas City Chiefs
Born December 28, 1958, at Lake Worth, Fla.
Height, 5.11. Weight, 180.
High School—Lake Worth, Fla., John I. Leonard.
Attended Louisana State University.
Cousin of Darrin Nelson, running back with Minnesota Vikings.

Selected by Kansas City in 5th round (114th player selected) of 1980 NFL draft.
On injured reserve with broken foot, September 23 through December 11, 1981; activated, December 12, 1981.

Year Club	G.	Att.	RUSHING Yds.	Avg.	TD.	PASS RECEIVING P.C.	Yds.	Avg.	TD.	TOTAL TD.	Pts.	F.
1980—Kansas City NFL	16	2	41	20.5	0	5	68	13.6	0	0	0	1
1981—Kansas City NFL	5	1	—1	—1.0	0	7	179	25.6	1	1	6	1
1982—Kansas City NFL	9		None			27	494	18.3	2	2	12	1
1983—Kansas City NFL	16	2	20	10.0	0	80	1351	16.9	7	7	42	2
1984—Kansas City NFL	16	1	—8	—8.0	0	57	1078	18.9	4	4	24	0
Pro Totals—5 Years	62	6	52	8.7	0	176	3170	18.0	14	14	84	5

KICKOFF RETURNS Year Club	G.	No.	Yds.	Avg.	TD.
1980—Kansas City NFL	16	40	917	22.9	0
1981—Kansas City NFL	5	10	227	22.7	0
1982—Kansas City NFL	9		None		
1983—Kansas City NFL	16	1	12	12.0	0
1984—Kansas City NFL	16	1	2	2.0	0
Pro Totals—5 Years	62	52	1158	22.3	0

Additional pro statistics: Recovered one fumble, 1980 and 1981; attempted one pass with one completion for 48 yards and one touchdown, 1983; recovered two fumbles, 1984.
Played in Pro Bowl (NFL All-Star Game) following 1983 season.

HAROLD DONALD CARSON
(Harry)
Linebacker—New York Giants
Born November 26, 1953, at Florence, S. C.
Height, 6.02. Weight, 240.
High School—Florence, S. C., McClenaghan.
Received bachelor of science degree in physical education
from South Carolina State College.

Named to THE SPORTING NEWS NFL All-Star Team, 1984.
Named to THE SPORTING NEWS NFC All-Star Team, 1979.
Selected by New York Giants in 4th round (105th player selected) of 1976 NFL draft.
On injured reserve with knee injury, October 16 through November 13, 1980; activated, November 14, 1980.
On injured reserve, November 24 through remainder of 1980 season.
On injured reserve with knee injury, September 19 through October 28, 1983; activated, October 29, 1983.

Year Club	G.	INTERCEPTIONS No.	Yds.	Avg.	TD.	Year Club	G.	INTERCEPTIONS No.	Yds.	Avg.	TD.
1976—N.Y. Giants NFL	12		None			1981—N.Y. Giants NFL	16		None		
1977—N.Y. Giants NFL	14		None			1982—N.Y. Giants NFL	9	1	6	6.0	0
1978—N.Y. Giants NFL	16	3	86	28.7	0	1983—N.Y. Giants NFL	10		None		
1979—N.Y. Giants NFL	16	3	28	9.3	0	1984—N.Y. Giants NFL	16	1	6	6.0	0
1980—N.Y. Giants NFL	8		None			Pro Totals—9 Years	117	8	126	15.8	0

Additional pro statistics: Recovered one fumble, 1976 through 1978, 1980 and 1984; returned one kickoff for five yards, 1976; recovered three fumbles for 22 yards and one touchdown, 1979; recovered one fumble for two yards, 1981.
Played in Pro Bowl (NFL All-Star Game) following 1978, 1979 and 1981 through 1984 seasons.

MALCOLM DARRYL CARSON
Guard—Miami Dolphins
Born November 1, 1959, at Birmingham, Ala.
Height, 6.02. Weight, 260.
High School—Birmingham, Ala., C.W. Hayes.
Attended University of Tennessee at Chattanooga.

Signed as free agent by Birmingham Stallions, January 16, 1983.
Released by Birmingham Stallions, February 26, 1983; signed as free agent by Memphis Showboats, November 17, 1983.
Released by Memphis Showboats, February 1, 1984; signed as free agent by Minnesota Vikings, June 22, 1984.
Released by Minnesota Vikings, September 5, 1984; signed as free agent by Birmingham Stallions, December 19, 1984.
Released by Birmingham Stallions, January 28, 1985; signed as free agent by Miami Dolphins, April 23, 1985.
Minnesota NFL, 1984.
Games: 1984 (1).

ARCHIE LEE CARTER
Linebacker—Los Angeles Raiders
Born September 15, 1960, at Shreveport, La.
Height, 6.03. Weight, 220.
High School—Los Angeles, Calif., Locke.
Attended Pasadena City College and University of Illinois.

Selected by Chicago in 1984 USFL territorial draft.
Signed as free agent by Seattle Seahawks, May 3, 1984.
Released by Seattle Seahawks, August 14, 1984; signed as free agent by Los Angeles Raiders, March 7, 1985.

DAVID CARTER
Guard-Center—New Orleans Saints
Born November 27, 1953, at Vincennes, Ind.
Height, 6.02. Weight, 275.
High School—Vincennes, Ind., Lincoln.
Attended Western Kentucky University.

Selected by Houston in 6th round (165th player selected) of 1977 NFL draft.
Released by Houston Oilers, October 15, 1984; signed as free agent by New Orleans Saints, October 30, 1984.
Houston NFL, 1977 through 1983; Houston (7)-New Orleans (7) NFL, 1984.
Games: 1977 (14), 1978 (16), 1979 (16), 1980 (16), 1981 (16), 1982 (9), 1983 (16), 1984 (14). Total—117.
Pro statistics: Recovered one fumble, 1977, 1981 and 1982; recovered two fumbles, 1978; fumbled once, 1983.
Played in AFC Championship Game following 1978 and 1979 seasons.

GERALD LOUIS CARTER
Wide Receiver—Tampa Bay Buccaneers
Born June 19, 1957, at Bryan, Tex.
Height, 6.01. Weight, 190.
High School—Bryan, Tex.
Attended Tyler Junior College and Texas A&M University.

Selected by Tampa Bay in 9th round (240th player selected) of 1980 NFL draft
Released by Tampa Bay Buccaneers, August 25, 1980; claimed on procedural waivers by New York Jets, October 23, 1980.
Released by New York Jets, November 17, 1980; signed as free agent by Tampa Bay Buccaneers, December 12, 1980.
Active for 2 games with Tampa Bay Buccaneers in 1980; did not play.

		—PASS RECEIVING—				
Year	Club	G.	P.C.	Yds.	Avg.	TD.
1980—N.Y.J. (3)-T.B. (0) NFL		3			None	
1981—Tampa Bay NFL		16	1	10	10.0	0
1982—Tampa Bay NFL		9	10	140	14.0	0
1983—Tampa Bay NFL		16	48	694	14.5	2
1984—Tampa Bay NFL		16	60	816	13.6	5
Pro Totals—5 Years		60	119	1660	13.9	7

Additional pro statistics: Returned one kickoff for 12 yards, 1980; fumbled once, 1980 and 1984; fumbled three times and rushed once for no yards, 1983; recovered one fumble and rushed once for 16 yards, 1984.

JOSEPH THOMAS CARTER
(Joe)
Running Back—Miami Dolphins
Born June 23, 1962, at Starkville, Miss.
Height, 5.11. Weight, 198.
High School—Starkville, Miss.
Attended University of Alabama.

Selected by Memphis in 5th round (104th player selected) of 1984 USFL draft.
Selected by Miami in 4th round (109th player selected) of 1984 NFL draft.
Signed by Miami Dolphins, July 18, 1984.

		—RUSHING—				PASS RECEIVING			—TOTAL—		
Year	Club	G.	Att.	Yds.	Avg.	TD.	P.C.	Yds.	Avg.	TD.	TD.	Pts.	F.
1984—Miami NFL		13	100	495	5.0	1	8	53	6.6	0	1	6	3

Additional pro statistics: Recovered two fumbles, 1984.
Member of Miami Dolphins for AFC Championship Game following 1984 season; did not play.
Played in NFL Championship Game following 1984 season.

MICHAEL D'ANDREA CARTER
Nose Tackle—San Francisco 49ers
Born October 29, 1960, at Dallas, Tex.
Height, 6.02. Weight, 281.
High School—Dallas, Tex., Thomas Jefferson.
Received bachelor of science degree in sociology from Southern Methodist University in 1984.
Won silver medal in shotput during 1984 Olympics.

Selected by Los Angeles in 10th round (194th player selected) of 1984 USFL draft.
Selected by San Francisco in 5th round (121st player selected) of 1984 NFL draft.
USFL rights traded by Los Angeles Express to New Orleans Breakers for past considerations, June 19, 1984.
Signed by San Francisco 49ers, August 14, 1984.
San Francisco NFL, 1984.
Games: 1984 (16).
Played in NFC Championship Game following 1984 season.
Played in NFL Championship Game following 1984 season.

RUBIN CARTER
Nose Tackle—Denver Broncos
Born December 12, 1952, at Pompano Beach, Fla.
Height, 6.00. Weight, 256.
High School—Ft. Lauderdale, Fla., Stranahan.
Received bachelor of arts degree in business administration from University of Miami (Fla.).

Selected by Denver in 5th round (121st player selected) of 1975 NFL draft.
Denver NFL, 1975 through 1984.
Games: 1975 (14), 1976 (14), 1977 (14), 1978 (16), 1979 (15), 1980 (16), 1981 (16), 1982 (9), 1983 (16), 1984 (15).
Total—145.
Pro statistics: Recovered one fumble, 1976, 1978 and 1981; recovered two fumbles for two yards and one touchdown, 1979; recovered two fumbles, 1980 and 1984; recovered three fumbles, 1983.
Played in AFC Championship Game following 1977 season.
Played in NFL Championship Game following 1977 season.

RUSSELL EDMONDS CARTER JR.
Defensive Back—New York Jets
Born February 10, 1962, at Philadelphia, Pa.
Height, 6.02. Weight, 195.
High School—Ardmore, Pa., Lower Merion.
Attended Southern Methodist University.

Named as defensive back on THE SPORTING NEWS College All-America Team, 1983.
Selected by Denver in 1st round (9th player selected) of 1984 USFL draft.
Selected by New York Jets in 1st round (10th player selected) of 1984 NFL draft.
Signed by New York Jets, May 25, 1984.

		—INTERCEPTIONS—			
Year Club	G.	No.	Yds.	Avg.	TD.
1984—N.Y. Jets NFL	11	4	26	6.5	0

MAURICE CARTHON
Running Back—New York Giants
Born April 24, 1961, at Chicago, Ill.
Height, 6.01. Weight, 225.
High School—Osceola, Ark.
Attended Arkansas State University.

Selected by New Jersey in 8th round (94th player selected) of 1983 USFL draft.
Signed by New Jersey Generals, January 19, 1983.
On developmental squad, June 17 through remainder of 1983 season.
Signed by New York Giants, March 7, 1985, for contract to take effect after being granted free agency after 1985 USFL season.
On developmental squad for 3 games with New Jersey Generals in 1983.

		—RUSHING—				PASS RECEIVING				—TOTAL—		
Year Club	G.	Att.	Yds.	Avg.	TD.	P.C.	Yds.	Avg.	TD.	TD.	Pts.	F.
1983—New Jersey USFL	11	90	334	3.7	3	20	170	8.5	0	3	†24	4
1984—New Jersey USFL	18	238	1042	4.4	11	26	194	7.5	1	12	72	4
Pro Totals—2 Years..................................	29	328	1376	4.2	14	46	364	7.9	1	15	96	8

†Includes three 2-point conversions.
Additional pro statistics: Recovered one fumble, 1984.

BERNARD CARVALHO
Name pronounced Cahr-VAHL-yoh.
(Bernie)
Guard—Miami Dolphins
Born September 29, 1961, at Kapaa, Kauai, Haw.
Height, 6.04. Weight, 255.
High School—Kauai, Haw., Kapaa.
Attended University of Hawaii.

Selected by Oakland in 8th round (156th player selected) of 1984 USFL draft.
Selected by Miami in 7th round (194th player selected) of 1984 NFL draft.
Signed by Miami Dolphins, July 13, 1984.
Released by Miami Dolphins, August 27, 1984; re-signed by Dolphins, March 29, 1985.

MELVIN CARVER
Running Back—Tampa Bay Buccaneers
Born July 14, 1959, at Pensacola, Fla.
Height, 5.11. Weight, 215.
High School—Alameda, Calif., Encinal.
Attended Laney Junior College and University of Nevada at Las Vegas.

Signed as free agent by Tampa Bay Buccaneers, May 3, 1982.
On injured reserve with stress fracture of shin, October 3 through remainder of 1984 season.

		—RUSHING—				PASS RECEIVING				—TOTAL—		
Year Club	G.	Att.	Yds.	Avg.	TD.	P.C.	Yds.	Avg.	TD.	TD.	Pts.	F.
1982—Tampa Bay NFL	9	70	229	3.3	1	4	46	11.5	1	2	12	2
1983—Tampa Bay NFL	16	114	348	3.1	0	32	262	8.2	1	1	6	6
1984—Tampa Bay NFL	5	11	44	4.0	0	3	27	9.0	0	0	0	1
Pro Totals—3 Years...................................	30	195	621	3.2	1	39	335	8.6	2	3	18	9

Year Club	G.	No.	Yds.	Avg.	TD.
1982—Tampa Bay NFL	9	3	62	20.7	0
1983—Tampa Bay NFL	16	2	24	12.0	0
1984—Tampa Bay NFL	5			None	
Pro Totals—3 Years............	30	5	86	17.2	0

Additional pro statistics: Recovered three fumbles, 1982; recovered two fumbles, 1983.

DARIO R. CASARINO
Punter—San Diego Chargers
Born September 30, 1957, at St. Helena, Calif.
Height, 6.07. Weight, 240.
High School—Hollister, Calif.
Received bachelor of arts degree in sociology from University of Washington in 1981.

Signed as free agent by Philadelphia Eagles, June 20, 1981.
Released by Philadelphia Eagles, August 10, 1981; signed as free agent by San Francisco 49ers, April 27, 1982.
Released by San Francisco 49ers, June 18, 1982; signed by Chicago Blitz, February 16, 1983.
Released by Chicago Blitz, February 27, 1983; awarded on waivers to Birmingham Stallions, February 28, 1983.
Released by Birmingham Stallions, March 26, 1983; signed as free agent by Boston Breakers, April 29, 1983.
Franchise transferred to New Orleans, October 18, 1983.
Franchise transferred to Portland, November 13, 1984.
Released by Portland Breakers, February 11, 1985; signed as free agent by San Diego Chargers, April 12, 1985.

		——PUNTING——		
Year Club	G.	No.	Avg.	Blk.
1983—Birm. (3)-Bos. (10) USFL......	13	67	41.5	....
1984—New Orleans USFL................	18	60	40.7	....
Pro Totals—2 Years.....................	31	127	41.1	....

Additional pro statistics: Attempted one pass with no completions, recovered one fumble and fumbled once, 1984.

JEFFREY SCOTT CASE
(Known by middle name.)
Safety—Atlanta Falcons
Born May 17, 1962, at Waynoka, Okla.
Height, 6.00. Weight, 178.
High Schools—Alva, Okla. and Edmond, Okla., Memorial.
Attended Northeastern Oklahoma A&M and University of Oklahoma.

Selected by Oklahoma in 1984 USFL territorial draft.
Selected by Atlanta in 2nd round (32nd player selected) of 1984 NFL draft.
Signed by Atlanta Falcons, July 20, 1984.
Atlanta NFL, 1984.
Games: 1984 (16).
Pro statistics: Credited with one safety, 1984.

DAVID JOHN CASPER
(Dave)
Tight End—Los Angeles Raiders
Born September 26, 1951, at Bemidji, Minn.
Height, 6.04. Weight, 235.
High School—Chilton, Wis.
Received bachelor of arts degree in economics from University of Notre Dame in 1974.

Named to THE SPORTING NEWS AFC All-Star Team, 1976 through 1978.
Selected by Oakland in 2nd round (45th player selected) of 1974 NFL draft.
Traded by Oakland Raiders to Houston Oilers for 1st and 2nd round picks in 1981 draft and 2nd round pick in 1982 draft, October 14, 1980.
Traded with quarterback Archie Manning by Houston Oilers to Minnesota Vikings for 2nd and 4th round picks in 1984 draft, September 20, 1983.
Released by Minnesota Vikings, July 20, 1984; signed as free agent by Los Angeles Raiders, July 25, 1984.
On injured reserve with foot injury, August 31 through November 2, 1984; activated, November 3, 1984.

——PASS RECEIVING——						——PASS RECEIVING——					
Year Club	G.	P.C.	Yds.	Avg.	TD.	Year Club	G.	P.C.	Yds.	Avg.	TD.
1974—Oakland NFL	14	4	26	6.5	3	1980—Oak(6)-Hou(10) NFL....	16	56	796	14.2	4
1975—Oakland NFL	14	5	71	14.2	1	1981—Houston NFL................	16	33	572	17.3	8
1976—Oakland NFL	13	53	691	13.0	10	1982—Houston NFL................	9	36	573	15.9	6
1977—Oakland NFL	14	48	584	12.2	6	1983—Hou.(3)-Min.(10) NFL..	13	20	251	12.6	0
1978—Oakland NFL	16	62	852	13.7	9	1984—L.A. Raiders NFL..........	7	4	29	7.3	2
1979—Oakland NFL................	15	57	771	13.5	3	Pro Totals—11 Years..........	147	378	5216	13.8	52

Additional pro statistics: Recovered two fumbles and rushed once for 5 yards, 1976; fumbled once, 1977 through 1979 and 1982; recovered one fumble in end zone for a touchdown, rushed once for five yards and attempted one pass with no completions, 1978; recovered one fumble, 1979 and 1983; rushed twice for eight yards and fumbled three times, 1980; rushed twice for nine yards, 1982.

Played in AFC Championship Game following 1974 through 1977 seasons.
Played in NFL Championship Game following 1976 season.
Played in Pro Bowl (NFL All-Star Game) following 1976 through 1980 seasons.

RONALD G. CASSIDY
(Ron)
Wide Receiver—Green Bay Packers
Born July 23, 1957, at Ventura, Calif.
Height, 6.00. Weight, 177.
High School—Los Alamitos, Calif.
Attended Fullerton Junior College and Utah State University.

Selected by Green Bay in 8th round (193rd player selected) of 1979 NFL draft.
On injured reserve with ankle injury, August 14 through October 15, 1979; cleared procedural waivers and re-signed, October 17, 1979.
On injured reserve with elbow injury, December 19 through remainder of 1980 season.
On injured reserve with neck injury, August 25 through October 7, 1981; activated after clearing procedural waivers, October 9, 1981.
On injured reserve with shoulder injury, August 31 through entire 1982 season.

Year Club		-PASS RECEIVING-				-PUNT RETURNS-				—TOTAL—		
	G.	P.C.	Yds.	Avg.	TD.	No.	Yds.	Avg.	TD.	TD.	Pts.	F.
1979—Green Bay NFL	8	6	102	17.0	0		None			0	0	0
1980—Green Bay NFL	15	5	109	21.8	0	17	139	8.2	0	0	0	1
1981—Green Bay NFL	11	1	6	6.0	0	2	0	0.0	0	0	0	1
1983—Green Bay NFL	12		None				None			0	0	0
1984—Green Bay NFL	15	2	16	8.0	0		None			0	0	0
Pro Totals—5 Years	61	14	233	16.6	0	19	139	7.3	0	0	0	2

JEREMIAH CASTILLE
Name pronounced Cass-TEEL.
Defensive Back—Tampa Bay Buccaneers
Born January 15, 1961, at Columbus, Ga.
Height, 5.10. Weight, 180.
High School—Phenix City, Ala., Central.
Attended University of Alabama.

Selected by Birmingham in 1983 USFL territorial draft.
Selected by Tampa Bay in 3rd round (72nd player selected) of 1983 NFL draft.
Signed by Tampa Bay Buccaneers, May 18, 1983.

Year Club		——INTERCEPTIONS——			
	G.	No.	Yds.	Avg.	TD.
1983—Tampa Bay NFL	15	1	69	69.0	1
1984—Tampa Bay NFL	16	3	38	12.7	0
Pro Totals—2 Years	31	4	107	26.8	1

Additional pro statistics: Recovered two fumbles for 16 yards, 1984.

CHRIS CASTOR
Wide Receiver—Seattle Seahawks
Born August 13, 1960, at Burlington, N.C.
Height, 6.00. Weight, 170.
High School—Cary, N.C.
Received degree in history from Duke University in 1983.

Selected by Tampa Bay in 5th round (53rd player selected) of 1983 USFL draft.
Selected by Seattle in 5th round (123rd player selected) of 1983 NFL draft.
Signed by Seattle Seahawks, May 27, 1983.

Year Club		——PASS RECEIVING——			
	G.	P.C.	Yds.	Avg.	TD.
1983—Seattle NFL	8		None		
1984—Seattle NFL	15	8	89	11.1	0
Pro Totals—2 Years	23	8	89	11.1	0

Played in AFC Championship Game following 1983 season.

MARK CATANO
Defensive End—Pittsburgh Steelers
Born January 26, 1962, at Yonkers, N.Y.
Height, 6.03. Weight, 265.
High School—Montrose, N.Y., Hendrick Hudson.
Attended Hudson Valley Community College and Valdosta State College.

Selected by Memphis in 12th round (244th player selected) of 1984 USFL draft.
Signed as free agent by Pittsburgh Steelers, May 2, 1984.
Pittsburgh NFL, 1984.
Games: 1984 (16).
Pro statistics: Returned one kickoff for no yards, 1984.
Played in AFC Championship Game following 1984 season.

MATTHEW ANDREW CAVANAUGH
(Matt)
Quarterback—San Francisco 49ers

Born October 27, 1956, at Youngstown, O.
Height, 6.02. Weight, 212.
High School—Youngstown, O., Chaney.
Attended University of Pittsburgh.

Selected by New England in 2nd round (50th player selected) of 1978 NFL draft.
Traded by New England Patriots to San Francisco 49ers for 7th round pick in 1984 draft, 8th round pick in 1985 draft and conditional 7th round pick in 1986 draft, August 10, 1983.
Active for 16 games with New England Patriots in 1978; did not play.

				PASSING						RUSHING				TOTAL	
Year	Club	G.	Att.	Cmp.	Pct.	Gain	T.P.	P.I.	Avg.	Att.	Yds.	Avg.	TD.	TD.	Pts.	F.
1979—New England NFL		13	1	1	100.0	10	0	0	10.00	1	—2	—2.0	0	0	0	0
1980—New England NFL		16	105	63	60.0	885	9	5	8.43	19	97	5.1	0	0	0	1
1981—New England NFL		16	219	115	52.5	1633	5	13	7.46	17	92	5.4	3	3	18	2
1982—New England NFL		7	60	27	45.0	490	5	5	8.17	2	3	1.5	0	0	0	1
1983—San Francisco NFL		5				None				1	8	8.0	0	0	0	0
1984—San Francisco NFL		8	61	33	54.1	449	4	0	7.36	4	—11	—2.8	0	0	0	0
Pro Totals—7 Years		65	446	239	53.6	3467	23	23	7.77	44	187	4.3	3	3	18	4

Quarterback Rating Points: 1979 (108.3), 1980 (95.9), 1981 (60.0), 1982 (66.7), 1984 (99.7). Total—74.8.
Additional pro statistics: Recovered one fumble and fumbled once for minus four yards, 1980; caught one pass for nine yards, 1981.
Played in NFC Championship Game following 1984 season.
Member of San Francisco 49ers for NFC Championship Game following 1983 season; did not play.
Member of San Francisco 49ers for NFL Championship Game following 1984 season; did not play.

FRANK CEPHOUS III
Running Back—New York Giants

Born July 4, 1961, at Philadelphia, Pa.
Height, 5.10. Weight, 205.
High School—Wilmington, Del., Saint Marks.
Attended University of California at Los Angeles.

Selected by San Antonio in 3rd round (45th player selected) of 1984 USFL draft.
Selected by New York Giants in 11th round (283rd player selected) of 1984 NFL draft.
Signed by New York Giants, May 28, 1984.

			RUSHING				PASS RECEIVING				TOTAL	
Year	Club	G.	Att.	Yds.	Avg.	TD.	P.C.	Yds.	Avg.	TD.	TD.	Pts.	F.
1984—New York Giants NFL		16	3	2	0.7	0		None			0	0	0

		KICKOFF RETURNS			
Year	Club	G.	No.	Yds.	Avg.	TD.
1984—N.Y. Giants NFL		16	9	178	19.8	0

JEFF CHADWICK
Wide Receiver—Detroit Lions

Born December 16, 1960, at Detroit, Mich.
Height, 6.03. Weight, 190.
High School—Dearborn, Mich., Divine Child.
Attended Grand Valley State College.

Signed as free agent by Detroit Lions, May 15, 1983.

			PASS RECEIVING			
Year	Club	G.	P.C.	Yds.	Avg.	TD.
1983—Detroit NFL		16	40	617	15.4	4
1984—Detroit NFL		16	37	540	14.6	2
Pro Totals—2 Years		32	77	1157	15.0	6

Additional pro statistics: Rushed once for 12 yards and a touchdown, 1984.

WESLEY SANDY CHANDLER
(Wes)
Wide Receiver—San Diego Chargers

Born August 22, 1956, at New Smyrna Beach, Fla.
Height, 6.00. Weight, 183.
High School—New Smyrna Beach, Fla.
Received degree in speech pathology from University of Florida.

Named as wide receiver on THE SPORTING NEWS College All-America Team, 1977.
Selected by New Orleans in 1st round (3rd player selected) of 1978 NFL draft.
Traded by New Orleans Saints to San Diego Chargers for wide receiver Aundra Thompson and 1st and 3rd round picks in 1982 draft, September 29, 1981.

Year Club	G.	PASS RECEIVING				—PUNT RETURNS—				—KICKOFF RET.—				—TOTAL—		
		P.C.	Yds.	Avg.	TD.	No.	Yds.	Avg.	TD.	No.	Yds.	Avg.	TD.	TD.	Pts.	F.
1978—New Orleans NFL	16	35	472	13.5	2	34	233	6.9	0	32	760	23.8	0	2	12	1
1979—New Orleans NFL	16	65	1069	16.4	6	3	13	4.3	0	7	136	19.4	0	6	36	0
1980—New Orleans NFL	16	65	975	15.0	6	8	36	4.5	0	None				6	36	0
1981—N.O. (4)-S.D. (12) NFL.	16	69	1142	16.6	6	5	79	15.8	0	8	125	15.6	0	6	36	1
1982—San Diego NFL	8	49	*1032	21.1	*9	None				None				9	54	0
1983—San Diego NFL	16	58	845	14.6	5	8	26	3.3	0	None				5	30	3
1984—San Diego NFL	15	52	708	13.6	6	None				None				6	36	0
Pro Totals—7 Years	103	393	6243	15.9	40	58	387	6.7	0	47	1021	21.7	0	40	240	7

Additional pro statistics: Rushed twice for 10 yards, 1978; punted eight times for 31.0 average, 1979; attempted one pass with one completion for 43 yards, rushed once for nine yards and recovered two fumbles, 1980; recovered one fumble for 51 yards, rushed five times for minus one yard and attempted two passes with no completions, 1981; rushed five times for 32 yards, 1982; rushed twice for 25 yards and recovered one fumble, 1983.
Played in AFC Championship Game following 1981 season.
Played in Pro Bowl (NFL All-Star Game) following 1979, 1982 and 1983 seasons.

MICHAEL GEORGE CHAPMAN
(Mike)
Center-Guard—Atlanta Falcons
Born February 10, 1961, at Larado, Tex.
Height, 6.04. Weight, 250.
High School—Austin, Tex., LBJ.
Received bachelor of science degree in communications from University of Texas in 1984.
Signed as free agent by Dallas Cowboys, May 4, 1984.
Released by Dallas Cowboys, August 27, 1984; signed as free agent by Atlanta Falcons, November 13, 1984.
On injured reserve with knee injury, December 11 through remainder of 1984 season.
Atlanta NFL, 1984.
Games: 1984 (4).

MIKE CHARLES
Defensive Tackle—Miami Dolphins
Born September 21, 1962, at Newark, N.J.
Height, 6.04. Weight, 283.
High School—Newark, N.J., Central.
Attended Syracuse University.
Selected by New Jersey in 1983 USFL territorial draft.
Selected by Miami in 2nd round (55th player selected) of 1983 NFL draft.
Signed by Miami Dolphins, July 12, 1983.
On injured reserve with knee injury, November 17 through December 27, 1984; activated, December 28, 1984.
Miami NFL, 1983 and 1984.
Games: 1983 (16), 1984 (10). Total—26.
Pro statistics: Recovered one fumble and credited with one safety, 1983.
Played in AFC Championship Game following 1984 season.
Played in NFL Championship Game following 1984 season.

BARNEY LEWIS CHAVOUS
Name pronounced CHAY-vus.
Defensive End—Denver Broncos
Born March 22, 1951, at Aiken, S. C.
Height, 6.03. Weight, 258.
High School—Aiken, S. C., Schofield.
Received bachelor of science degree in physical education from South Carolina State University in 1973.
Selected by Denver in 2nd round (36th player selected) of 1973 NFL draft.
Denver NFL, 1973 through 1984.
Games: 1973 (14), 1974 (14), 1975 (9), 1976 (13), 1977 (13), 1978 (16), 1979 (16), 1980 (16), 1981 (16), 1982 (9), 1983 (15), 1984 (15). Total—166.
Pro statistics: Recovered two fumbles, 1973 and 1974; recovered one fumble, 1980 and 1981; credited with one safety, 1982; recovered one fumble in end zone for touchdown, 1983.
Played in AFC Championship Game following 1977 season.
Played in NFL Championship Game following 1977 season.

DERON CHERRY
Safety—Kansas City Chiefs
Born September 12, 1959, at Riverside, N.J.
Height, 5.11. Weight, 190.
High School—Palmyra, N.J.
Attended Rutgers University.
Signed as free agent by Kansas City Chiefs, May 4, 1981.
Released by Kansas City Chiefs, August 31, 1981; re-signed by Chiefs, September 23, 1981.
On inactive list, September 19, 1982.
On injured reserve with shoulder separation, December 30 through remainder of 1982 season.

Year Club	G.	No.	Yds.	Avg.	TD.
1981—Kansas City NFL..........	13	1	4	4.0	0
1982—Kansas City NFL..........	7		None		
1983—Kansas City NFL..........	16	7	100	14.3	0
1984—Kansas City NFL..........	16	7	140	20.0	0
Pro Totals—4 Years.............	52	15	244	16.3	0

Additional pro statistics: Returned three kickoffs for 52 yards, 1981; returned one kickoff for 39 yards, 1982; returned two kickoffs for 54 yards, recovered two fumbles for four yards and fumbled twice, 1983; returned one kickoff for no yards, 1984.

Played in Pro Bowl (NFL All-Star Game) following 1983 and 1984 seasons.

JOHN CHESLEY
Tight End—Miami Dolphins
Born July 2, 1962, at Washington, D.C.
Height, 6.05. Weight, 225.
High School—Washington, D.C.
Attended Oklahoma State University.
Brother of Al Chesley, linebacker with Philadelphia Eagles, 1979 through 1982.

Selected by Oklahoma in 1984 USFL territorial draft.
Selected by Miami in 10th round (277th player selected) of 1984 NFL draft.
Signed by Miami Dolphins, July 9, 1984.
Released by Miami Dolphins, August 27, 1984; re-signed by Dolphins, October 19, 1984.
Released by Miami Dolphins, November 2, 1984; re-signed by Dolphins, April 11, 1985.
Miami NFL, 1984.
Games: 1984 (1).

ANTHONY PAUL CHICKILLO
Name pronounced CHI-kill-o.
(Tony)
Nose Tackle—San Diego Chargers
Born July 8, 1960, at Miami, Fla.
Height, 6.03. Weight, 257.
High School—Miami, Fla., Southwest.
Received degree in recreational therapy from University of Miami (Fla.) in 1983.
Son of Nick Chickillo, guard with Chicago Cardinals, 1953.

Selected by New Jersey in 16th round (191st player selected) of 1983 USFL draft.
Selected by Tampa Bay in 5th round (131st player selected) of 1983 NFL draft.
Signed by Tampa Bay Buccaneers, June 6, 1983.
On injured reserve with ankle injury, August 22 through entire 1983 season.
Released by Tampa Bay Buccaneers, August 20, 1984; awarded on waivers to Indianapolis Colts, August 21, 1984.
Released by Indianapolis Colts, August 27, 1984.
USFL rights traded by New Jersey Generals to Orlando Renegades for rights to defensive tackle Charles Cook, October 31, 1984.
Signed as free agent by San Diego Chargers, December 13, 1984.
San Diego NFL, 1984.
Games: 1984 (1).

JEFFREY BRUCE CHRISTENSEN
(Jeff)
Quarterback—Philadelphia Eagles
Born January 8, 1960, at Gibson City, Ill.
Height, 6.03. Weight, 202.
High School—Gibson City, Ill.
Attended Eastern Illinois University.

Selected by New Jersey in 17th round (195th player selected) of 1983 USFL draft.
Selected by Cincinnati in 5th round (137th player selected) of 1983 NFL draft.
Signed by Cincinnati Bengals, June 2, 1983.
Traded by Cincinnati Bengals to Los Angeles Rams for draft choice, July 25, 1984.
Released by Los Angeles Rams, August 15, 1984; signed as free agent by Philadelphia Eagles for 1985, October 23, 1984.
Signed for 1984 season, November 27, 1984.
Active for 3 games with Philadelphia Eagles in 1984; did not play.
Cincinnati NFL, 1983.
Games: 1983 (1).
Pro statistics: Rushed once for minus two yards, 1983.

TODD JAY CHRISTENSEN
Tight End—Los Angeles Raiders
Born August 3, 1956, at Bellefonte, Pa.
Height, 6.03. Weight, 230.
High School—Eugene, Ore., Sheldon.
Attended Brigham Young University.

Named to THE SPORTING NEWS NFL All-Star Team, 1983.
Selected by Dallas in 2nd round (56th player selected) of 1978 NFL draft.

On injured reserve with broken foot, August 28 through entire 1978 season.
Released by Dallas Cowboys, August 27, 1979; claimed on waivers by New York Giants, August 28, 1979.
Released by New York Giants, September 4, 1979; signed as free agent by Oakland Raiders, September 26, 1979.
Franchise transferred to Los Angeles, May 7, 1982.
On did not report list, August 14 through August 22, 1984.
Reported and granted roster exemption, August 23 through August 31, 1984; activated, September 1, 1984.

Year Club	G.	P.C.	Yds.	Avg.	TD.
1979—NYG (1)-Oak (12) NFL	13	None			
1980—Oakland NFL	16	None			
1981—Oakland NFL	16	8	115	14.4	2
1982—L.A. Raiders NFL	9	42	510	12.1	4
1983—L.A. Raiders NFL	16	*92	1247	13.6	12
1984—L.A. Raiders NFL	16	80	1007	12.6	7
Pro Totals—6 Years	86	222	2879	13.0	25

Additional pro statistics: Recovered two fumbles for one yard, 1979; recovered one fumble in end zone for a touchdown and returned one kickoff for 10 yards, 1980; returned four kickoffs for 54 yards and credited with one safety, 1981; recovered one fumble, 1981, 1983 and 1984; rushed once for minus six yards and fumbled three times, 1982; fumbled once, 1983 and 1984.
Played in AFC Championship Game following 1980 and 1983 seasons.
Played in NFL Championship Game following 1980 and 1983 seasons.
Played in Pro Bowl (NFL All-Star Game) following 1983 and 1984 seasons.

JOHN SCOTT CHRISTOPHER
Punter—Chicago Bears
Born December 10, 1960, at Sandusky, O.
Height 6.03. Weight, 200.
High School—Norwalk, O.
Received bachelor of arts degree in geography from Morehead State University in 1983.
Signed as free agent by Cincinnati Bengals, April 28, 1983.
Released by Cincinnati Bengals, August 8, 1983; signed as free agent by Jacksonville Bulls, October 12, 1983.
Released by Jacksonville Bulls, January 30, 1984; signed as free agent by Green Bay Packers, March 27, 1984.
Released by Green Bay Packers, August 20, 1984; signed as free agent by Chicago Bears, March 12, 1985.

SAM CLAPHAN
Name pronounced Clap-in.
Offensive Tackle—San Diego Chargers
Born October 10, 1956, at Tahlequah, Okla.
Height, 6.06. Weight, 282.
High School—Stillwell, Okla.
Received bachelor of science degree in education from University of Oklahoma in 1979.
Selected by Cleveland in 2nd round (47th player selected) of 1979 NFL draft.
On injured reserve with back injury, August 27 through entire 1979 season.
Released by Cleveland Browns, August 26, 1980; signed as free agent by San Diego Chargers, May 1, 1981.
On inactive list, September 12 and September 19, 1982.
San Diego NFL, 1981 through 1984.
Games: 1981 (16), 1982 (2), 1983 (16), 1984 (16). Total—50.
Played in AFC Championship Game following 1981 season.

BRUCE CLARK
Defensive End—New Orleans Saints
Born March 31, 1958, at New Castle, Pa.
Height, 6.03. Weight, 281.
High School—New Castle, Pa.
Attended Penn State University.
Selected by Green Bay in 1st round (4th player selected) of 1980 NFL draft.
Signed by Toronto Argonauts, May 26, 1980.
Granted free agency, March 1, 1982; traded by Green Bay Packers to New Orleans Saints for 1st round pick in 1983 draft, June 10, 1982.
Toronto CFL, 1980 and 1981; New Orleans NFL, 1982 through 1984.
Games: 1980 (16), 1981 (16), 1982 (9), 1983 (15), 1984 (15). Total CFL—32. Total NFL—39. Pro Total—71.
CFL statistics: Intercepted one pass for no yards and recovered four fumbles for six yards, 1980; recovered one fumble, 1981.
NFL statistics: Recovered one fumble, 1983; intercepted one pass for nine yards and recovered two fumbles for five yards, 1984.
Played in Pro Bowl (NFL All-Star Game) following 1984 season.

BRYAN CLARK
Quarterback—Miami Dolphins
Born July 27, 1960, at Redwood City, Calif.
Height, 6.02. Weight, 196.
High School—Los Altos, Calif.
Attended Michigan State University.
Son of Monte Clark, offensive lineman with San Francisco 49ers, Dallas Cowboys and Cleveland Browns, 1959 through 1969; head coach with San Francisco 49ers, 1976, and Detroit Lions, 1978 through 1984.
Selected by San Francisco in 9th round (251st player selected) of 1982 NFL draft.

On inactive list, September 12 and September 19, 1982.
On injured reserve with separated shoulder, August 23 through entire 1983 season.
Released by San Francisco 49ers, September 4, 1984; re-signed by 49ers, September 18, 1984.
Released by San Francisco 49ers, September 29, 1984; signed as free agent by Cincinnati Bengals, December 5, 1984.
Traded by Cincinnati Bengals to Miami Dolphins for draft choice, May 6, 1985.
Active for 7 games with San Francisco 49ers in 1982; did not play.
Active for 2 games with San Francisco 49ers in 1984; did not play.
San Francisco (0)-Cincinnati (1) NFL, 1984.
Games: 1984 (1).

DWIGHT EDWARD CLARK
Wide Receiver—San Francisco 49ers
Born January 1, 1957, at Kinston, N. C.
Height, 6.04. Weight, 215.
High School—Charlotte, N. C., Garinger.
Received bachelor of arts degree in history from Clemson University in 1980.

Selected by San Francisco in 10th round (249th player selected) of 1979 NFL draft.
On injured reserve with knee injury, December 21 through remainder of 1983 season.

| | | | —PASS RECEIVING— | | |
Year Club	G.	P.C.	Yds.	Avg.	TD.
1979—San Francisco NFL	16	18	232	12.9	0
1980—San Francisco NFL	16	82	991	12.1	8
1981—San Francisco NFL	16	85	1105	13.0	4
1982—San Francisco NFL	9	*60	913	15.2	5
1983—San Francisco NFL	16	70	840	12.0	8
1984—San Francisco NFL	16	52	880	16.9	6
Pro Totals—6 Years............	89	367	4961	13.5	31

Additional pro statistics: Recovered one fumble, 1979; fumbled twice, 1980; rushed three times for 32 yards, 1981; attempted one pass with no completions, 1981, 1983 and 1984; fumbled once, 1982; rushed three times for 18 yards, 1983.
Played in NFC Championship Game following 1981 and 1984 seasons.
Played in NFL Championship Game following 1981 and 1984 seasons.
Played in Pro Bowl (NFL All-Star Game) following 1981 and 1982 seasons.

GARY C. CLARK
Wide Receiver—Washington Redskins
Born May 1, 1962, at Radford, Va.
Height, 5.10. Weight, 175.
High School—Dublin, Va., Pulaski County.
Attended James Madison University.

Selected by Jacksonville in 1st round (6th player selected) of 1984 USFL draft.
Signed by Jacksonville Bulls, January 16, 1984.
On developmental squad, May 9 through May 15, 1984; activated, May 16, 1984.
On developmental squad, June 4 through June 11, 1984; activated, June 12, 1984.
Selected by Washington in 2nd round (55th player selected) of 1984 NFL supplemental draft.
On developmental squad, March 17 through March 19, 1985; activated, March 20, 1985.
Released by Jacksonville Bulls, May 1, 1985; signed by Washington Redskins, May 13, 1985.
On developmental squad for 2 games with Jacksonville Bulls in 1984.
On developmental squad for 1 game with Jacksonville Bulls in 1985.

| | | PASS RECEIVING | | | | -PUNT RETURNS- | | | | —KICKOFF RET.— | | | | —TOTAL— | | |
Year Club	G.	P.C.	Yds.	Avg.	TD.	No.	Yds.	Avg.	TD.	No.	Yds.	Avg.	TD.	TD.	Pts.	F.
1984—Jacksonville USFL......	16	56	760	13.6	2	20	84	4.2	0	19	341	18.0	0	2	12	5
1985—Jacksonville USFL......	9	10	61	6.1	1	7	44	6.3	0	3	56	18.7	0	1	6	0
Pro Totals—2 Years.......	25	66	821	12.4	3	27	128	4.7	0	22	397	18.0	0	3	18	5

Additional pro statistics: Rushed twice for nine yards and recovered four fumbles, 1984.

JESSIE L. CLARK
Fullback—Green Bay Packers
Born January 3, 1960, at Thebes, Ark.
Height, 6.00. Weight, 233.
High School—Crossett, Ark.
Attended Louisiana Tech University and received bachelor of arts
degree in criminal justice from University of Arkansas in 1983.
Cousin of Dennis Woodberry, cornerback with Birmingham Stallions.

Selected by Green Bay in 7th round (188th player selected) of 1983 NFL draft.
On injured reserve with muscle tear in elbow, November 16 through remainder of 1984 season.

| | | ——RUSHING—— | | | | PASS RECEIVING | | | | —TOTAL— | | |
Year Club	G.	Att.	Yds.	Avg.	TD.	P.C.	Yds.	Avg.	TD.	TD.	Pts.	F.
1983—Green Bay NFL.............	16	71	328	4.6	0	18	279	15.5	1	1	6	2
1984—Green Bay NFL.............	11	87	375	4.3	4	29	234	8.1	2	6	36	2
Pro Totals—2 Years..................	27	158	703	4.4	4	47	513	10.9	3	7	42	4

Additional pro statistics: Recovered one fumble, 1983.

KELVIN CLARK
Offensive Tackle-Guard—New Orleans Saints
Born January 30, 1956, at Odessa, Tex.
Height, 6.03. Weight, 273.
High School—Odessa, Tex.
Attended University of Nebraska.

Selected by Denver in 1st round (22nd player selected) of 1979 NFL draft.
Traded by Denver Broncos to New Orleans Saints for 4th round pick in 1984 draft, August 30, 1982.
Denver NFL, 1979 through 1981; New Orleans NFL, 1982 through 1984.
Games: 1979 (15), 1980 (14), 1981 (16), 1982 (9), 1983 (16), 1984 (16). Total—86.
Pro statistics: Recovered fumble in end zone for a touchdown, 1983.

MARIO SEAN CLARK
Cornerback—San Francisco 49ers
Born March 29, 1954, at Pasadena, Calif.
Height, 6.02. Weight, 195.
High School—Pasadena, Calif.
Attended University of Oregon.

Selected by Buffalo in 1st round (18th player selected) of 1976 NFL draft.
Granted free agency, February 1, 1984; re-signed by Bills and traded to San Francisco 49ers for 4th round pick in 1985 draft, July 16, 1984.

| | | | —INTERCEPTIONS— | | |
Year Club	G.	No.	Yds.	Avg.	TD.
1976—Buffalo NFL	14	2	21	10.5	0
1977—Buffalo NFL	14	7	151	21.6	0
1978—Buffalo NFL	16	5	29	5.8	0
1979—Buffalo NFL	16	5	95	19.0	0
1980—Buffalo NFL	16	1	0	0.0	0
1981—Buffalo NFL	16	5	142	28.4	0
1982—Buffalo NFL	9		None		
1983—Buffalo NFL	14		None		
1984—San Francisco NFL	11	1	0	0.0	0
Pro Totals—9 Years	126	26	438	16.8	0

Additional pro statistics: Recovered one fumble, 1976, 1982 and 1984; recovered one fumble for three yards, 1977; recovered one fumble for 12 yards, 1979; recovered three fumbles, 1980; recovered two fumbles for five yards, 1981.
Member of San Francisco 49ers for NFC and NFL Championship Game following 1984 season; did not play.

RANDALL BYRON CLARK
(Randy)
Center—St. Louis Cardinals
Born July 26, 1957, at Chicago, Ill.
Height, 6.03. Weight, 254.
High School—Mount Prospect, Ill., Prospect.
Received bachelor of science degree in marketing from Northern Illinois University in 1980.

Selected by Chicago in 8th round (215th player selected) of 1980 NFL draft.
Released by Chicago Bears, August 26, 1980; signed as free agent by St. Louis Cardinals, October 27, 1980.
St. Louis NFL, 1980 through 1984.
Games: 1980 (8), 1981 (16), 1982 (9), 1983 (14), 1984 (16). Total—63.
Pro statistics: Returned two kickoffs for 14 yards, 1980; fumbled once, 1983; recovered two fumbles, 1984.

RANDY CHARLES CLARK
Safety—Pittsburgh Steelers
Born February 18, 1962, at Marshall, Mich.
Height, 6.00. Weight, 204.
High School—Venice, Fla.
Attended University of Florida.

Selected by Tampa Bay in 1984 USFL territorial draft.
Selected by Kansas City in 8th round (202nd player selected) of 1984 NFL draft.
Signed by Kansas City Chiefs, July 12, 1984.
Released by Kansas City Chiefs, August 20, 1984; signed as free agent by Tampa Bay Buccaneers, October 30, 1984.
Released by Tampa Bay Buccaneers, November 12, 1984; signed as free agent by Pittsburgh Steelers, May 9, 1985.

RODERICK PAUL CLARK
(Rod)
Linebacker—St. Louis Cardinals
Born January 14, 1962, at San Marcos, Tex.
Height, 6.02. Weight, 228.
High School—Waller, Tex.
Attended Southwest Texas State University.

Selected by Houston in 1984 USFL territorial draft.
Selected by St. Louis in 6th round (157th player selected) of 1984 NFL draft.
Signed by St. Louis Cardinals, July 5, 1984.
On injured reserve with knee injury, August 21 through entire 1984 season.

STEPHEN SPENCE CLARK
(Steve)
Guard—Miami Dolphins
Born August 2, 1960, at Salt Lake City, Utah.
Height, 6.04. Weight, 255.
High School—Salt Lake City, Utah, Skyline.
Attended University of Utah.

Selected by Miami in 9th round (239th player selected) of 1982 NFL draft.
Released by Miami Dolphins, August 30, 1982; re-signed by Dolphins, December 7, 1982.
Released by Miami Dolphins, August 29, 1983; re-signed by Dolphins, August 30, 1983.
On injured reserve with broken ankle, August 28 through September 27, 1984; activated, September 28, 1984.
Miami NFL, 1982 through 1984.
Games: 1982 (2), 1983 (11), 1984 (12). Total—25.
Pro statistics: Recovered one fumble, 1982.
Played in AFC Championship Game following 1984 season.
Member of Miami Dolphins for AFC Championship Game following 1982 season; did not play.
Played in NFL Championship Game following 1984 season.
Member of Miami Dolphins for NFL Championship Game following 1982 season; did not play.

THOMAS RAY CLARK
Defensive Back—Denver Broncos
Born December 14, 1961, at Birmingham, Ala.
Height, 6.00. Weight, 181.
High School—Birmingham, Ala., Woodlawn.
Attended Troy State University.

Selected by Birmingham in 1985 USFL territorial draft.
Signed as free agent by Birmingham Stallions, January 22, 1985.
Released by Birmingham Stallions, January 28, 1985; signed as free agent by Denver Broncos, March 21, 1985.

KENNETH MAURICE CLARKE
(Ken)
Nose Tackle—Philadelphia Eagles
Born August 28, 1956, at Savannah, Ga.
Height, 6.02. Weight, 255.
High School—Boston, Mass., English.
Received bachelor of science degree in psychology from Syracuse University in 1978.

Signed as free agent by Philadelphia Eagles, May 4, 1978.
Philadelphia NFL, 1978 through 1984.
Games: 1978 (16), 1979 (16), 1980 (16), 1981 (16), 1982 (9), 1983 (16), 1984 (16). Total—105.
Pro statistics: Recovered one fumble, 1978 and 1982; returned one kickoff for no yards and fumbled once, 1980; credited with one safety and returned one kickoff for no yards, 1981; recovered three fumbles for five yards, 1983.
Played in NFC Championship Game following 1980 season.
Played in NFL Championship Game following 1980 season.

RAYMOND DE WAYNE CLAYBORN
(Ray)
Cornerback—New England Patriots
Born January 2, 1955, at Fort Worth, Tex.
Height, 6.00. Weight, 186.
High School—Fort Worth, Tex., Trimble.
Received degree in communications from University of Texas.

Named as cornerback on THE SPORTING NEWS College All-America Team, 1976.
Named to THE SPORTING NEWS NFL All-Star Team, 1983.
Selected by New England in 1st round (16th player selected) of 1977 NFL draft.

Year Club	G.	No.	Yds.	Avg.	TD.	No.	Yds.	Avg.	TD.	TD.	Pts.	F.
			—INTERCEPTIONS—				—KICKOFF RET.—				—TOTAL—	
1977—New England NFL	14		None			28	869	*31.0	*3	3	†20	1
1978—New England NFL	16	4	72	18.0	0	27	636	23.6	0	0	0	0
1979—New England NFL	16	5	56	11.2	0	2	33	16.5	0	0	0	0
1980—New England NFL	16	5	87	17.4	0		None			0	0	0
1981—New England NFL	16	2	39	19.5	0		None			0	0	0
1982—New England NFL	9	1	26	26.0	0		None			0	0	0
1983—New England NFL	16		None				None			0	0	0
1984—New England NFL	16	3	102	34.0	0		None			0	0	0
Pro Totals—8 Years	119	20	382	19.1	0	57	1538	27.0	3	3	20	1

†Includes one safety.
Additional pro statistics: Recovered one fumble, 1978, 1980 and 1982; recovered two fumbles for four yards, 1981.
Played in Pro Bowl (NFL All-Star Game) following 1983 season.

HARVEY CLAYTON
Cornerback—Pittsburgh Steelers
Born April 4, 1961, at Kendall, Fla.
Height, 5.09. Weight, 180.
High School—Miami, Fla., South Dade.
Attended Florida State University.

Selected by Tampa Bay in 1983 USFL territorial draft.
Signed as free agent by Pittsburgh Steelers, May 19, 1983.

Year Club		—INTERCEPTIONS—			
	G.	No.	Yds.	Avg.	TD.
1983—Pittsburgh NFL.............	14	1	70	70.0	1
1984—Pittsburgh NFL.............	14	1	0	0.0	0
Pro Totals—2 Years............	28	2	70	35.0	1

Additional pro statistics: Returned one punt for no yards and recovered one fumble, 1984.
Played in AFC Championship Game following 1984 season.

MARK CLAYTON
Wide Receiver—Miami Dolphins
Born April 8, 1961, at Indianapolis, Ind.
Height, 5.09. Weight, 172.
High School—Indianapolis, Ind., Cathedral.
Attended University of Louisville.
Established NFL record for most touchdown receptions, season (18), 1984.
Selected by Miami in 8th round (223rd player selected) of 1983 NFL draft.

Year Club		-PASS RECEIVING-				-PUNT RETURNS-				—TOTAL—		
	G.	P.C.	Yds.	Avg.	TD.	No.	Yds.	Avg.	TD.	TD.	Pts.	F.
1983—Miami NFL	14	6	114	19.0	1	41	392	9.6	*1	2	12	3
1984—Miami NFL	15	73	1389	19.0	*18	8	79	9.9	0	*18	108	2
Pro Totals—2 Years....................	29	79	1503	19.0	19	49	471	9.6	1	20	120	5

Additional pro statistics: Rushed twice for nine yards, returned one kickoff for 25 yards, attempted one pass with one completion for 48 yards and a touchdown, 1983; recovered one fumble, 1983 and 1984; rushed three times for 35 yards, returned two kickoffs for 15 yards and attempted one pass with one interception, 1984.
Played in AFC Championship Game following 1984 season.
Played in NFL Championship Game following 1984 season.
Played in Pro Bowl (NFL All-Star Game) following 1984 season.

DeCARLOS CLEVELAND
Defensive Lineman—Pittsburgh Steelers
Born July 9, 1961, at Pittsburgh, Pa.
Height, 6.03. Weight, 268.
High School—Wilkinsburg, Pa.
Attended Kent State University.
Signed as free agent by Pittsburgh Steelers, June 26, 1984.
On injured reserve with foot injury, August 14 through entire 1984 season.

KYLE CLIFTON
Linebacker—New York Jets
Born August 23, 1962, at Onley, Tex.
Height, 6.04. Weight, 233.
High School—Bridgeport, Tex.
Attended Texas Christian University.
Selected by Birmingham in 1st round (12th player selected) of 1984 USFL draft.
Selected by New York Jets in 3rd round (64th player selected) of 1984 NFL draft.
Signed by New York Jets, July 12, 1984.
New York Jets NFL, 1984.
Games: 1984 (16).
Pro statistics: Intercepted one pass for no yards and recovered one fumble, 1984.

FREDERICK DEXTOR CLINKSCALE
(Known by middle name.)
Safety—Dallas Cowboys
Born April 13, 1958, at Greenville, S.C.
Height, 5.11. Weight, 190.
High School—Greenville, S.C., J.L. Mann.
Received degree in business administration from South Carolina State College.
Signed as free agent by Dallas Cowboys, May, 1980.
On injured reserved with Achilles tendon injury, August 31 through entire 1981 season.

Year Club		—INTERCEPTIONS—			
	G.	No.	Yds.	Avg.	TD.
1980—Dallas NFL	16		None		
1982—Dallas NFL	9	1	0	0.0	0
1983—Dallas NFL	15	2	68	34.0	1
1984—Dallas NFL	15	3	32	10.7	0
Pro Totals—4 Years............	55	6	100	16.7	1

Additional pro statistics: Recovered one fumble, 1980; recovered four fumbles, 1983; recovered two fumbles, 1984.
Played in NFC Championship Game following 1980 and 1982 seasons.

GARRY WILBERT COBB
Linebacker—Detroit Lions
Born March 16, 1957, at Carthage, N. C.
Height, 6.02. Weight, 227.
High School—Stamford, Conn.
Attended University of Southern California.

Selected by Dallas in 9th round (247th player selected) of 1979 NFL draft.
Released by Dallas Cowboys, August 21, 1979; signed as free agent by Detroit Lions, October 24, 1979.

Year Club	G.	No.	Yds.	Avg.	TD.
1979—Detroit NFL	8		None		
1980—Detroit NFL	16		None		
1981—Detroit NFL	16	3	32	10.7	0
1982—Detroit NFL	6	2	12	6.0	0
1983—Detroit NFL	15	4	19	4.8	0
1984—Detroit NFL	16		None		
Pro Totals—6 Years	77	9	63	7.0	0

Additional pro statistics: Caught one pass for 19 yards and recovered three fumbles, 1981; caught one pass for 25 yards, 1982; recovered two fumbles, 1983.

SHERMAN COCROFT
Safety—Kansas City Chiefs
Born August 29, 1961, at Watsonville, Calif.
Height, 6.02. Weight, 184.
High School—Watsonville, Calif.
Attended Cabrillo College and San Jose State University.

Selected by Oakland in 1984 USFL territorial draft.
Signed as free agent by Seattle Seahawks, May 3, 1984.
Released by Seattle Seahawks, August 21, 1984; signed as free agent by Kansas City Chiefs for 1985, October 15, 1984.

MICHAEL LYNN COFER
(Mike)
Defensive End—Detroit Lions
Born April 7, 1960, at Knoxville, Tenn.
Height, 6.05. Weight, 245.
High School—Knoxville, Tenn., Rule.
Attended University of Tennessee.
Brother of James Cofer, rookie linebacker with Baltimore Stars.

Selected by New Jersey in 1983 USFL territorial draft.
Selected by Detroit in 3rd round (67th player selected) of 1983 NFL draft.
Signed by Detroit Lions, July 1, 1983.
Detroit NFL, 1983 and 1984.
Games: 1983 (16), 1984 (16). Total—32.
Pro statistics: Recovered one fumble, 1983 and 1984.

KEN COFFEY
Safety—Washington Redskins
Born July 11, 1960, at Rantoul, Ill.
Height, 6.00. Weight, 190.
High School—Big Spring, Tex.
Attended Tyler Junior College and Southwest Texas State University.
Brother of Wayne Coffey, wide receiver at Southwest Texas State.

Selected by Washington in 9th round (226th player selected) of 1982 NFL draft.
On injured reserve with blood disorder, August 24 through entire 1982 season.
On injured reserve with dislocated shoulder, August 28 through September 28, 1984; activated, September 29, 1984.

Year Club	G.	No.	Yds.	Avg.	TD.
1983—Washington NFL	13	4	62	15.5	0
1984—Washington NFL	12	1	15	15.0	0
Pro Totals—2 Years	25	5	77	15.4	0

Additional pro statistics: Recovered one fumble, 1983 and 1984; returned one punt for six yards, 1984.
Played in NFC Championship Game following 1983 season.
Played in NFL Championship Game following 1983 season.

PAUL RANDOLPH COFFMAN
Tight End—Green Bay Packers
Born March 26, 1956, at St. Louis, Mo.
Height, 6.03. Weight, 225.
High School—Chase, Kan.
Received degree in milling science from Kansas State University in 1982.

Signed as free agent by Green Bay Packers, May 18, 1978.

| | | | ——PASS RECEIVING—— | | |
Year Club	G.	P.C.	Yds.	Avg.	TD.
1978—Green Bay NFL	16		None		
1979—Green Bay NFL	16	56	711	12.7	4
1980—Green Bay NFL	16	42	496	11.8	3
1981—Green Bay NFL	16	55	687	12.5	4
1982—Green Bay NFL	9	23	287	12.5	2
1983—Green Bay NFL	16	54	814	15.1	11
1984—Green Bay NFL	14	43	562	13.1	9
Pro Totals—7 Years	103	273	3557	13.0	33

Additional pro statistics: Fumbled four times, 1979; rushed once for three yards, 1980; returned three kickoffs for 77 yards, 1981; recovered one fumble, 1981 and 1984; fumbled once, 1981, 1983 and 1984.
Played in Pro Bowl (NFL All-Star Game) following 1982 through 1984 seasons.

CURT COLE
Tight End—Green Bay Packers
Born January 2, 1961, at Austin, Tex.
Height, 6.04. Weight, 230.
High School—Austin, Tex., McCallum.
Attended Texas Tech University.

Selected by Denver in 1984 USFL territorial draft.
Signed as free agent by Green Bay Packers, May 3, 1984.
Released by Green Bay Packers, August 5, 1984; re-signed by Packers, February 15, 1985.

ROBIN COLE
Linebacker—Pittsburgh Steelers
Born September 11, 1955, at Los Angeles, Calif.
Height, 6.02. Weight, 225.
High School—Compton, Calif.
Attended University of New Mexico.
Cousin of Willie Davis, Hall of Fame defensive end with Cleveland Browns and Green Bay Packers, 1958 through 1969.

Selected by Pittsburgh in 1st round (21st player selected) of 1977 NFL draft.
Pittsburgh NFL, 1977 through 1984.
Games: 1977 (8), 1978 (16), 1979 (13), 1980 (14), 1981 (14), 1982 (9), 1983 (16), 1984 (16). Total—106.
Pro statistics: Recovered two fumbles, 1977; recovered one fumble, 1979 and 1981; returned one kickoff for three yards, 1979; intercepted one pass for 34 yards and recovered one fumble for 14 yards, 1980; intercepted one pass for 29 yards, 1981; recovered two fumbles for 20 yards, 1983; intercepted one pass for 12 yards and recovered one fumble for eight yards, 1984.
Played in AFC Championship Game following 1978, 1979 and 1984 seasons.
Played in NFL Championship Game following 1978 and 1979 seasons.
Played in Pro Bowl (NFL All-Star Game) following 1984 season.

GREG COLEMAN
Punter—Minnesota Vikings
Born September 9, 1954, at Jacksonville, Fla.
Height, 6.00. Weight, 185.
High School—Jacksonville, Fla., William M. Raines.
Received degree in criminology from Florida A&M University.
Cousin of Vince Coleman, outfielder with St. Louis Cardinals.

Selected by Cincinnati in 14th round (398th player selected) of 1976 NFL draft.
Released by Cincinnati Bengals, August, 1976; signed as free agent by Cleveland Browns, March, 1977.
Released by Cleveland Browns, August 30, 1978; signed as free agent by Minnesota Vikings, October 20, 1978.

| | | ——PUNTING—— | | |
Year Club	G.	No.	Avg.	Blk.
1977—Cleveland NFL	14	61	39.2	0
1978—Minnesota NFL	9	51	39.0	1
1979—Minnesota NFL	16	90	39.5	1
1980—Minnesota NFL	16	81	38.8	0
1981—Minnesota NFL	15	88	41.4	0
1982—Minnesota NFL	9	*58	41.1	0
1983—Minnesota NFL	16	91	41.5	0
1984—Minnesota NFL	16	82	42.4	0
Pro Totals—8 Years	111	602	40.5	2

Additional pro statistics: Rushed once for minus three yards, 1977; rushed twice for 22 yards, 1978; recovered one fumble, 1981; rushed once for 15 yards, 1982; rushed once for minus nine yards, 1983; rushed twice for 11 yards and attempted one pass with no completions, 1984.

MONTE COLEMAN
Linebacker—Washington Redskins
Born November 4, 1957, at Pine Bluff, Ark.
Height, 6.02. Weight, 230.
High School—Pine Bluff, Ark.
Attended Central Arkansas University.

Selected by Washington in 11th round (289th player selected) of 1979 NFL draft.

On injured reserve with thigh injury, September 16 through October 16, 1983; activated, October 17, 1983.

Year Club	G.	No.	Yds.	Avg.TD.	
1979—Washington NFL..........	16	1	13	13.0	0
1980—Washington NFL..........	16	3	92	30.7	0
1981—Washington NFL..........	12	3	52	17.3	1
1982—Washington NFL..........	8		None		
1983—Washington NFL..........	10		None		
1984—Washington NFL..........	16	1	49	49.0	1
Pro Totals—6 Years...........	78	8	206	25.8	2

Additional pro statistics: Recovered three fumbles, 1979; caught one pass for 12 yards, 1980; recovered two fumbles, 1980 and 1983; recovered one fumble for two yards, 1981; ran 27 yards with lateral on punt return and recovered one fumble, 1984.

Played in NFC Championship Game following 1982 and 1983 seasons.
Played in NFL Championship Game following 1982 and 1983 seasons.

TIMOTHY COLLIER
(Tim)
Cornerback—San Francisco 49ers
Born May 31, 1954, at Dallas, Tex.
Height, 6.00. Weight, 176.
High School—Dallas, Tex., South Oak Cliff.
Attended East Texas State University.

Selected by Kansas City in 9th round (249th player selected) of 1976 NFL draft.
Traded by Kansas City Chiefs to St. Louis Cardinals for 5th round choice in 1980 draft, February 15, 1980.
Released by St. Louis Cardinals, December 8, 1982; signed as free agent by San Francisco 49ers, December 14, 1982.
On injured reserve with Achilles tendon injury, July 29 through entire 1984 season.

Year Club	G.	No.	Yds.	Avg.TD.	
1976—Kansas City NFL	13	2	10	5.0	0
1977—Kansas City NFL	9	2	134	67.0	1
1978—Kansas City NFL..........	15	3	38	12.7	0
1979—Kansas City NFL..........	14	2	45	22.5	0
1980—St. Louis NFL................	12	2	22	11.0	
1981—St. Louis NFL................	14	1	17	17.0	0
1982—St. L. (4)-S.F. (2) NFL..	6		None		
1983—San Francisco NFL	10	3	32	10.7	1
Pro Totals—8 Years	93	15	298	19.9	2

Additional pro statistics: Recovered one fumble, 1976; fumbled once and returned one kickoff for no yards, 1979.
Played in NFC Championship Game following 1983 season.

ANTHONY COLLINS
(Tony)
Running Back—New England Patriots
Born May 27, 1959, at Sanford, Fla.
Height, 5.11. Weight, 212.
High School—Penn Yan, N.Y., Penn Yan Academy.
Attended East Carolina University.
Cousin of Kenny Jackson, wide receiver with Philadelphia Eagles.

Selected by New England in 2nd round (47th player selected) of 1981 NFL draft.

Year Club	G.	RUSHING				PASS RECEIVING				TOTAL		
		Att.	Yds.	Avg.	TD.	P.C.	Yds.	Avg.	TD.	TD.	Pts.	F.
1981—New England NFL...................................	16	204	873	4.3	7	26	232	8.9	0	7	42	8
1982—New England NFL...................................	9	164	632	3.9	1	19	187	9.8	2	3	18	5
1983—New England NFL...................................	16	219	1049	4.8	10	27	257	9.5	0	10	60	10
1984—New England NFL...................................	16	138	550	4.0	5	16	100	6.3	0	5	30	3
Pro Totals—4 Years..................................	57	725	3104	4.3	23	88	776	8.8	2	25	150	26

Year Club	G.	No.	Yds.	Avg.TD.	
		KICKOFF RETURNS			
1981—New England NFL.......	16	39	773	19.8	0
1982—New England NFL.......	9		None		
1983—New England NFL.......	16		None		
1984—New England NFL.......	16	25	544	21.8	0
Pro Totals—4 Years...........	57	64	1317	20.6	0

Additional pro statistics: Returned three punts for 15 yards and attempted one pass with no completions, 1981; recovered two fumbles, 1981 through 1983.
Played in Pro Bowl (NFL All-Star Game) following 1983 season.

DWIGHT DEAN COLLINS
Wide Receiver—Minnesota Vikings
Born August 23, 1961, at Rochester, N.Y.
Height, 6.01. Weight, 208.
High School—Beaver Falls, Pa.
Attended University of Pittsburgh.

Selected by Pittsburgh in 1984 USFL territorial draft.
Selected by Minnesota in 6th round (154th player selected) of 1984 NFL draft.
Signed by Minnesota Vikings, June 2, 1984.

		—PASS RECEIVING—				
Year	Club	G.	P.C.	Yds.	Avg.	TD.
1984—Minnesota NFL		16	11	143	13.0	1

Additional pro statistics: Rushed three times for minus 14 yards, 1984.

GLEN LEON COLLINS
Defensive End—Cincinnati Bengals
Born July 10, 1959, at Jackson, Miss.
Height, 6.06. Weight, 265.
High School—Jackson, Miss., Jim Hill.
Attended Mississippi State University.

Named as defensive tackle on THE SPORTING NEWS College All-America Team, 1981.
Selected by Cincinnati in 1st round (26th player selected) of 1982 NFL draft.
On inactive list, September 19, 1982.
Cincinnati NFL, 1982 through 1984.
Games: 1982 (7), 1983 (16), 1984 (16). Total—39.
Pro statistics: Recovered one fumble, 1983 and 1984.

JIM BRIAN COLLINS
Linebacker—Los Angeles Rams
Born June 11, 1958, at Orange, N.J.
Height, 6.02. Weight, 230.
High School—Mendham, N.J.
Received bachelor of science degree in psychology from Syracuse University in 1981.

Selected by Los Angeles in 2nd round (43rd player selected) of 1981 NFL draft.
On injured reserve with pulled stomach muscle, September 1 through October 2, 1981; activated October 3, 1981.
On injured reserve with knee injury, December 4 through remainder of 1981 season.

		—INTERCEPTIONS—				
Year	Club	G.	No.	Yds.	Avg.	TD.
1981—L.A. Rams NFL		7		None		
1982—L.A. Rams NFL		6		None		
1983—L.A. Rams NFL		16	2	46	23.0	0
1984—L.A. Rams NFL		16	2	43	21.5	0
Pro Totals—4 Years		45	4	89	22.3	0

Additional pro statistics: Recovered one fumble, 1983; recovered two fumbles for 17 yards and fumbled once, 1984.

SCOTT NEAL COLLINS
Linebacker—New York Jets
Born November 10, 1960, at San Diego, Calif.
Height, 6.01. Weight, 230.
High School—Huntington Beach, Calif., Edison.
Attended Orange Coast College and Oregon Tech.

Signed as free agent by New York Jets, May 20, 1984.
On injured reserve with knee injury, July 27 through entire 1984 season.

ANTHONY CRIS COLLINSWORTH
(Known by middle name.)
Wide Receiver—Cincinnati Bengals
Born January 27, 1959, at Dayton, O.
Height, 6.05. Weight, 192.
High School—Titusville, Fla., Astronaut.
Received degree in accounting from University of Florida in 1981.

Selected by Cincinnati in 2nd round (37th player selected) of 1981 NFL draft.
Signed by Tampa Bay Bandits, June 27, 1983, for contract to take effect after being granted free agency, February 1, 1985.
Released by Tampa Bay Bandits, February 18, 1984; re-signed by Bengals, February 21, 1984.

		—PASS RECEIVING—				
Year	Club	G.	P.C.	Yds.	Avg.	TD.
1981—Cincinnati NFL		16	67	1009	15.1	8
1982—Cincinnati NFL		9	49	700	14.3	1
1983—Cincinnati NFL		14	66	1130	17.1	5
1984—Cincinnati NFL		15	64	989	15.5	6
Pro Totals—4 Years		54	246	3828	15.6	20

Additional pro statistics: Recovered one fumble, 1981, 1983 and 1984; fumbled three times, 1981; rushed once for minus 11 yards and fumbled once, 1982; rushed twice for two yards and fumbled twice, 1983; rushed once for seven yards, 1984.
Played in AFC Championship Game following 1981 season.
Played in NFL Championship Game following 1981 season.
Played in Pro Bowl (NFL All-Star Game) following 1981 through 1983 seasons.

JOSEPH CRAIG COLQUITT
(Known by middle name.)
Punter—Pittsburgh Steelers
Born June 9, 1954, at Knoxville, Tenn.
Height, 6.01. Weight, 182.
High School—Knoxville, Tenn., South.
Attended Cleveland State Community College and University of Tennessee.
Nephew of Jimmy Colquitt, rookie punter with New York Giants.

Selected by Pittsburgh in 3rd round (79th player selected) of 1978 NFL draft.
On physically unable to perform/active list with torn Achilles tendon, July 30 through August 23, 1982.
Placed on reserve, August 24 through entire 1982 season.

Year Club	G.	No.	Avg.	Blk.
1978—Pittsburgh NFL	16	66	40.0	0
1979—Pittsburgh NFL	16	68	40.2	0
1980—Pittsburgh NFL	16	61	40.7	0
1981—Pittsburgh NFL	16	84	43.3	0
1983—Pittsburgh NFL	16	80	41.9	0
1984—Pittsburgh NFL	16	70	41.2	0
Pro Totals—6 Years	96	429	41.4	0

Additional pro statistics: Rushed once for 17 yards, fumbled once and recovered one fumble, 1980; rushed once for eight yards, 1981; rushed once for no yards, 1984.
Played in AFC Championship Game following 1978, 1979 and 1984 seasons.
Played in NFL Championship Game following 1978 and 1979 seasons.

JEFFREY COLTER
(Jeff)
Defensive Back—Minnesota Vikings
Born April 23, 1961, at Tucson, Ariz.
Height, 5.10. Weight, 171.
High School—Tucson, Ariz., Amphitheater.
Attended Eastern Arizona Junior College and University of Kansas.

Signed as free agent by Minnesota Vikings, June 21, 1984.
Minnesota NFL, 1984.
Games: 1984 (16).

DARREN COMEAUX
Linebacker—Denver Broncos
Born April 15, 1960, at San Diego, Calif.
Height, 6.01. Weight, 227.
High School—San Diego, Calif.
Attended Arizona State University.

Signed as free agent by Denver Broncos, April 30, 1982.
On injured reserve with broken foot, September 7 through December 15, 1982; activated, December 16, 1982.
Released by Denver Broncos, August 29, 1983; re-signed by Broncos, September 13, 1983.
Denver NFL, 1982 through 1984.
Games: 1982 (3), 1983 (14), 1984 (16). Total—33.
Pro statistics: Intercepted one pass for five yards and recovered one fumble, 1984.

THOMAS JOSEPH CONDON
(Tom)
Guard—Kansas City Chiefs
Born October 26, 1952, at Derby, Conn.
Height, 6.03. Weight, 275.
High School—West Haven, Conn., Notre Dame.
Received bachelor of arts degree in sociology and philosophy from Boston College in 1974.
Attended law school at University of Baltimore and received law degree from
University of Missouri at Kansas City.

Selected by Kansas City in 10th round (250th player selected) of 1974 NFL draft.
On injured reserve with foot injury, December 31 through remainder of 1982 season.
On injured reserve with foot injury, October 26 through November 24, 1983; activated, November 25, 1983.
Kansas City NFL, 1974 through 1984.
Games: 1974 (14), 1975 (9), 1976 (14), 1977 (14), 1978 (16), 1979 (16), 1980 (16), 1981 (16), 1982 (7), 1983 (9), 1984 (16).
Total—147.
Pro statistics: Recovered one fumble, 1977, 1979, 1981 and 1984.

RONNY LAMAR CONE
Fullback—New York Jets
Born April 27, 1961, at Statesboro, Ga.
Height, 6.02. Weight, 225.
High School—Statesboro, Ga.
Received bachelor of science degree in industrial management from Georgia Tech in 1984.

Selected by Jacksonville in 1984 USFL territorial draft.

Selected by New York Jets in 10th round (261st player selected) of 1984 NFL draft.
Signed by New York Jets, May 17, 1984.
On injured reserve with concussion, August 14 through entire 1984 season.

WILLIAM CONTZ
(Bill)
Offensive Tackle—Cleveland Browns
Born December 5, 1961, at Belle Vernon, Pa.
Height, 6.05. Weight, 260.
High School—Belle Vernon, Pa.
Received bachelor of science degree in business logistics
from Penn State University in 1983.

Selected by Philadelphia in 1983 USFL territorial draft.
Selected by Cleveland in 5th round (122nd player selected) of 1983 NFL draft.
Signed by Cleveland Browns, May 31, 1983.
On injured reserve with knee injury, December 12 through remainder of 1984 season.
Cleveland NFL, 1983 and 1984.
Games: 1983 (16), 1984 (15). Total—31.
Pro statistics: Returned one kickoff for three yards, 1983; returned one kickoff for 10 yards, 1984.

JOHNIE EARL COOKS
Linebacker—Indianapolis Colts
Born November 23, 1958, at Leland, Miss.
Height, 6.04. Weight, 243.
High School—Leland, Miss.
Attended Mississippi State University.

Named as linebacker on THE SPORTING NEWS College All-America Team, 1981.
Selected by Baltimore in 1st round (2nd player selected) of 1982 NFL draft.
Franchise transferred to Indianapolis, March 31, 1984.
Baltimore NFL, 1982 and 1983; Indianapolis NFL, 1984.
Games: 1982 (9), 1983 (16), 1984 (16). Total—41.
Pro statistics: Recovered one fumble, 1982; intercepted one pass for 15 yards, recovered two fumbles for 52 yards and a touchdown and fumbled once, 1983.

EVAN COOPER
Cornerback-Kick Returner—Philadelphia Eagles
Born June 28, 1962, at Miami, Fla.
Height, 5.11. Weight, 180.
High School—Miami, Fla., Killian.
Received bachelor of science degree in communications
from University of Michigan in 1984.

Selected by Michigan in 1984 USFL territorial draft.
Selected by Philadelphia in 4th round (88th player selected) of 1984 NFL draft.
Signed by Philadelphia Eagles, June 11, 1984.

| | | —PUNT RETURNS— | | | | —KICKOFF RET.— | | | | —TOTAL— | | |
Year	Club	G.	No.	Yds.	Avg.	TD.	No.	Yds.	Avg.	TD.	TD.	Pts.	F.
1984—Philadelphia NFL		16	40	250	6.3	0	17	299	17.6	0	0	0	0

JAMES ALBERT COOPER
(Jim)
Offensive Tackle—Dallas Cowboys
Born September 28, 1955, at Philadelphia, Pa.
Height, 6.05. Weight, 267.
High School—Philadelphia, Pa., Cardinal Dougherty.
Attended Temple University.

Selected by Dallas in 6th round (164th player selected) of 1977 NFL draft.
On injured reserve with broken ankle, October 20 through remainder of 1984 season.
Dallas NFL, 1977 through 1984.
Games: 1977 (14), 1978 (14), 1979 (15), 1980 (15), 1981 (16), 1982 (9), 1983 (16), 1984 (7). Total—106.
Pro statistics: Recovered one fumble, 1979, 1980 and 1982.
Played in NFC Championship Game following 1977, 1978, and 1980 through 1982 seasons.
Played in NFL Championship Game following 1977 and 1978 seasons.

JOSEPH DONALD COOPER
(Joe)
Placekicker—Houston Oilers
Born October 30, 1960, at Fresno, Calif.
Height, 5.10. Weight, 175.
High School—Fresno, Calif., Bullard.
Received degree in political science from University of California
at Berkeley in 1984; attending San Joaquin College of Law.

Signed as free agent by San Diego Chargers, June 10, 1984.
Released by San Diego Chargers, August 13, 1984; signed as free agent by Houston Oilers, November 12, 1984.

		——PLACE KICKING——					
Year	Club	G.	XP.	XPM.	FG.	FGA.	Pts.
1984—Houston NFL		7	13	0	11	13	46

Additional pro statistics: Rushed once for minus two yards, 1984.

MARION EARL COOPER
(Known by middle name.)
Tight End-Fullback—San Francisco 49ers
Born September 17, 1957, at Giddings, Tex.
Height, 6.02. Weight, 227.
High School—Lexington, Tex., Lincoln.
Received bachelor of science degree in physical education from Rice University in 1981.
Selected by San Francisco in 1st round (13th player selected) of 1980 NFL draft.

			——RUSHING——				PASS RECEIVING				—TOTAL—		
Year	Club	G.	Att.	Yds.	Avg.	TD.	P.C.	Yds.	Avg.	TD.	TD.	Pts.	F.
1980—San Francisco NFL		16	171	720	4.2	5	83	567	6.8	4	9	54	8
1981—San Francisco NFL		16	98	330	3.4	1	51	477	9.4	0	1	6	3
1982—San Francisco NFL		9	24	77	3.2	0	19	153	8.1	1	1	6	1
1983—San Francisco NFL		16		None			15	207	13.8	3	3	18	1
1984—San Francisco NFL		16	3	13	4.3	0	41	459	11.2	4	4	24	0
Pro Totals—5 Years		73	296	1140	3.9	6	209	1863	8.9	12	18	108	13

Additional pro statistics: Recovered three fumbles, 1980; recovered one fumble, 1981 and 1984; returned three kickoffs for 45 yards, 1983; returned one kickoff for no yards, 1984.
Played in NFC Championship Game following 1981, 1983 and 1984 seasons.
Played in NFL Championship Game following 1981 and 1984 seasons.

MARK SAMUEL COOPER
Guard—Denver Broncos
Born February 14, 1960, at Camden, N.J.
Height, 6.05. Weight, 267.
High School—Miami, Fla., Killian.
Received bachelor of arts degree in communications
from University of Miami (Fla.) in 1983.
Selected by New Jersey in 5th round (60th player selected) of 1983 USFL draft.
Selected by Denver in 2nd round (31st player selected) of 1983 NFL draft.
Signed by Denver Broncos, June 26, 1983.
On injured reserve with sprained ankle, December 13 through remainder of 1984 season.
Denver NFL, 1983 and 1984.
Games: 1983 (10), 1984 (15). Total—25.

ANTHONY CORLEY
Running Back—Pittsburgh Steelers
Born August 10, 1960, at Reno, Nev.
Height, 6.00. Weight, 210.
High School—Reno, Nev., Hug.
Attended University of Nevada at Reno.
Selected by Michigan in 7th round (143rd player selected) in 1984 USFL draft.
Signed as free agent by Pittsburgh Steelers, May 22, 1984.

			——RUSHING——				PASS RECEIVING				—TOTAL—		
Year	Club	G.	Att.	Yds.	Avg.	TD.	P.C.	Yds.	Avg.	TD.	TD.	Pts.	F.
1984—Pittsburgh NFL		14	18	89	4.9	0		None			0	0	0

Additional pro statistics: Returned one kickoff for 15 yards and recovered two fumbles, 1984.
Played in AFC Championship Game following 1984 season.

FRED K. CORNWELL
Tight End—Dallas Cowboys
Born August 7, 1961, at Osborne, Kan.
Height, 6.06. Weight, 237.
High School—Canyon Country, Calif., Canyon.
Received bachelor of science degree in civil engineering
from University of California in 1984.
Selected by Los Angeles in 1984 USFL territorial draft.
Selected by Dallas in 3rd round (81st player selected) of 1984 NFL draft.
Signed by Dallas Cowboys, July 8, 1984.

		——PASS RECEIVING——			
Year	Club	G.	P.C.	Yds.	Avg.	TD.
1984—Dallas NFL		14	2	23	11.5	1

—DID YOU KNOW—
That Atlanta's first three selections in the 1984 draft were from Oklahoma? Defensive tackle Rick Bryan was the Falcons' first-round pick while defensive back Scott Case and linebacker Thomas Benson were second-round selections.

DOUGLAS DURANT COSBIE
(Doug)
Tight End—Dallas Cowboys

Born March 27, 1956, at Palo Alto, Calif.
Height, 6.06. Weight, 236.
High School—Mt. View, Calif., St. Francis.
Attended College of the Holy Cross, DeAnza College and received bachelor of science degree
in marketing from University of Santa Clara in 1979.

Selected by Dallas in 3rd round (76th player selected) of 1979 NFL draft.
USFL rights traded by Michigan Panthers to Oakland Invaders for rights to placekicker Wilson Alvarez, September 2, 1982.

		—PASS RECEIVING—			
Year Club	G.	P.C.	Yds.	Avg.	TD.
1979—Dallas NFL	16	5	36	7.2	0
1980—Dallas NFL	16	2	11	5.5	1
1981—Dallas NFL	16	17	225	13.2	5
1982—Dallas NFL	9	30	441	14.7	4
1983—Dallas NFL	16	46	588	12.8	6
1984—Dallas NFL	16	60	789	13.2	4
Pro Totals—6 Years	89	160	2090	13.1	20

Additional pro statistics: Fumbled once, 1979, 1981 and 1984; returned one kickoff for 13 yards and recovered two fumbles, 1980; rushed four times for 33 yards and returned one kickoff for no yards, 1981; rushed once for minus two yards and returned one kickoff for four yards, 1982; returned two kickoffs for 17 yards, 1983.
Played in NFC Championship Game following 1980 through 1982 seasons.
Played in Pro Bowl (NFL All-Star Game) following 1983 and 1984 seasons.

ROCCO CRAIG COSTELLO
(Rocky)
Placekicker—San Diego Chargers

Born October 31, 1961, at Long Beach, Calif.
Height, 5.10. Weight, 163.
High School—La Mirada, Calif., William N. Neff.
Attended Cerritos College and Fresno State University.

Signed as free agent by Denver Broncos, May 2, 1984.
Released by Denver Broncos, August 6, 1984; signed as free agent by San Diego Chargers, May 3, 1985.

JOHN MARK COTNEY
(Known by middle name.)
Safety—Tampa Bay Buccaneers

Born June 26, 1952, at Altus, Okla.
Height, 6.00. Weight, 200.
High School—Altus, Okla.
Attended New Mexico Highlands University and received bachelor of science degree
in physical education from Cameron University.

Selected by Houston in 7th round (171st player selected) of 1975 NFL draft.
Selected from Houston Oilers by Tampa Bay Buccaneers in NFL expansion draft, March 30, 1976.
On injured reserve with knee injury, August 17 through entire 1981 season.
On injured reserve with fractured thumb, September 6 through October 6, 1983; activated, October 7, 1983.

		-INTERCEPTIONS-				-PUNT RETURNS-				—TOTAL—		
Year Club	G.	No.	Yds.	Avg.	TD.	No.	Yds.	Avg.	TD.	TD.	Pts.	F.
1975—Houston NFL	14		None			2	8	4.0	0	0	0	0
1976—Tampa Bay NFL	14	3	25	8.3	0	3	26	8.7	0	0	0	0
1977—Tampa Bay NFL	14	1	0	0.0	0		None			0	0	0
1978—Tampa Bay NFL	16	2	28	14.0	0	5	38	7.6	0	0	0	1
1979—Tampa Bay NFL	16	1	0	0.0	0		None			0	0	0
1980—Tampa Bay NFL	16	3	28	9.3	0		None			0	0	0
1982—Tampa Bay NFL	9		None				None			0	0	0
1983—Tampa Bay NFL	12	2	1	0.5	0		None			0	0	0
1984—Tampa Bay NFL	16	5	123	24.6	0		None			0	0	0
Pro Totals—9 Years	127	17	205	12.1	0	10	72	7.2	0	0	0	1

Additional pro statistics: Returned 10 kickoffs for 189 yards (18.9 average), 1975; recovered one fumble, 1975, 1979 and 1983; recovered two fumbles, 1978; recovered two fumbles for three yards, 1984.
Played in NFC Championship Game following 1979 season.

STEPHEN PAUL COURSON
Name pronounced CORE-sin.
(Steve)
Guard—Tampa Bay Buccaneers

Born October 1, 1955, at Philadelphia, Pa.
Height, 6.01. Weight, 270.
High School—Gettysburg, Pa.
Attended University of South Carolina.

Selected by Pittsburgh in 5th round (125th player selected) of 1977 NFL draft.

On injured reserve entire 1977 season.
On injured reserve with ankle injury, October 15 through December 2, 1980; activated, December 3, 1980.
USFL rights traded by Washington Federals to Houston Gamblers for rights to quarterback Dieter Brock, August 4, 1983.
Traded by Pittsburgh Steelers to Tampa Bay Buccaneers for guard Ray Snell, July 30, 1984.
Pitttsburgh NFL, 1978 through 1983; Tampa Bay NFL, 1984.
Games: 1978 (16), 1979 (16), 1980 (8), 1981 (16), 1982 (8), 1983 (9), 1984 (14). Total—87.
Pro statistics: Recovered one fumble, 1978, 1979 and 1982; recovered two fumbles, 1981.
Played in AFC Championship Game following 1978 and 1979 seasons.
Played in NFL Championship Game following 1978 and 1979 seasons.

MATTHEW CARTER COURTNEY
(Matt)
Defensive End—Kansas City Chiefs
Born December 21, 1961, at Greeley, Colo.
Height, 5.11. Weight, 188.
High School—Arapahoe, Colo.
Attended Idaho State University.

Selected by Jacksonville in 4th round (78th player selected) of 1984 USFL draft.
Signed by Jacksonville Bulls, January 12, 1984.
On developmental squad, June 15 through June 19, 1984; activated, June 20, 1984.
Released by Jacksonville Bulls, October 15, 1984; signed as free agent by Kansas City Chiefs, April 20, 1985.
On developmental squad for 1 game with Jacksonville Bulls in 1984.
Jacksonville USFL, 1984.
Games: 1984 (16).
Pro statistics: Credited with one sack for six yards, intercepted two passes for 14 yards and recovered one fumble, 1984.

TOM COUSINEAU
Linebacker—Cleveland Browns
Born May 16, 1957, at Fairview Park, O.
Height, 6.03. Weight, 225.
High School—Lakewood, O., St. Edwards.
Received degree in marketing from Ohio State University.

Selected by Buffalo in 1st round (1st player selected) of 1979 NFL draft.
Signed by Montreal Alouettes, July 19, 1979.
On reserve list, July 14 through July 27, 1981; activated, July 28, 1981.
On reserve list, August 8 through August 21, 1981; activated, August 22, 1981.
On injured list with elbow injury, August 27 through October 27, 1981; activated, October 28, 1981.
Granted free agency, March 1, 1982; received offer sheet from Houston Oilers, April 19, 1982.
Offer matched by Buffalo Bills and traded to Cleveland Browns for 1st round pick in 1983 draft, 3rd round pick in 1984 draft and 5th round pick in 1985 draft, April 23, 1982.

| | | ——INTERCEPTIONS—— | | | |
Year Club	G.	No.	Yds.	Avg.	TD.
1979—Montreal CFL	14		None		
1980—Montreal CFL	16	1	33	33.0	0
1981—Montreal CFL	4		None		
1982—Cleveland NFL	9	1	6	6.0	0
1983—Cleveland NFL	16	4	47	11.8	0
1984—Cleveland NFL	16	2	9	4.5	0
CFL Totals—3 Years	34	1	33	33.0	0
NFL Totals—3 Years	41	7	62	8.9	0
Pro Totals—6 Years	75	8	95	11.9	0

Additional CFL statistics: Recovered two fumbles, 1979; recovered one fumble, 1980.
Additional NFL statistics: Recovered two fumbles for 14 yards, 1983; recovered two fumbles, 1984.
Played in CFL Championship Game following 1979 season.

JAMES PAUL COVERT
(Jim)
Offensive Tackle—Chicago Bears
Born March 22, 1960, at Conway, Pa.
Height, 6.04. Weight, 283.
High School—Freedom, Pa., Area.
Attended University of Pittsburgh.

Selected by Tampa Bay in 1st round (12th player selected) of 1983 USFL draft.
Selected by Chicago in 1st round (6th player selected) of 1983 NFL draft.
Signed by Chicago Bears, July 20, 1983.
Chicago NFL, 1983 and 1984.
Games: 1983 (16), 1984 (16). Total—32.
Pro statistics: Recovered one fumble, 1983; recovered two fumbles, 1984.
Played in NFC Championship Game following 1984 season.

WILLIAM LAIRD COWHER
(Bill)
Linebacker—Philadelphia Eagles
Born May 8, 1957, at Pittsburgh, Pa.
Height, 6.03. Weight, 230.
High School—Crafton, Pa., Carlynton.
Received bachelor of science degree in education from North Carolina State University in 1979.

Signed as free agent by Philadelphia Eagles, May 8, 1979.
Released by Philadelphia Eagles, August 14, 1979; signed as free agent by Cleveland Browns, February 27, 1980.
On injured reserve with knee injury, August 20 through entire 1981 season.
Traded by Cleveland Browns to Philadelphia Eagles for 9th round pick in 1984 draft, August 21, 1983.
On injured reserve with knee injury, September 25 through remainder of 1984 season.
Cleveland NFL, 1980 and 1982; Philadelphia NFL, 1983 and 1984.
Games: 1980 (16), 1982 (9), 1983 (16), 1984 (4). Total—45.
Pro statistics: Recovered one fumble, 1983.

ARTHUR COX
Tight End—Atlanta Falcons
Born February 5, 1961, at Plant City, Fla.
Height, 6.03. Weight, 255.
High School—Plant City, Fla.
Attended Texas Southern University.

Signed as free agent by Atlanta Falcons, May 4, 1983.

| | | —PASS RECEIVING— | | | |
Year Club	G.	P.C.	Yds.	Avg.	TD.
1983—Atlanta NFL	15	9	83	9.2	1
1984—Atlanta NFL	16	34	329	9.7	3
Pro Totals—2 Years	31	43	412	9.6	4

Additional pro statistics: Fumbled once, 1983 and 1984.

STEVE COX
Punter-Placekicker—Cleveland Browns
Born May 11, 1958, at Shreveport, La.
Height, 6.04. Weight, 195.
High School—Charleston, Ark.
Attended University of Arkansas.

Selected by Cleveland in 5th round (134th player selected) of 1981 NFL draft.
On injured reserve with head injury, August 30 through November 1, 1983; activated, November 2, 1983.

| | | —PUNTING— | | |
Year Club	G.	No.	Avg.	Blk.
1981—Cleveland NFL	16	68	42.4	*2
1982—Cleveland NFL	9	48	39.1	1
1983—Cleveland NFL	7	None		
1984—Cleveland NFL	16	74	43.4	2
Pro Totals—4 Years	48	190	41.9	5

Additional pro statistics: Attempted one field goal and missed, 1981 and 1982; rushed twice for minus 11 yards and recovered one fumble, 1982; successful on only field goal attempt, 1983; made one of three field goal attempts and attempted one pass with one completion for 16 yards, 1984.

ROBERT EDWARD CRABLE
(Bob)
Linebacker—New York Jets
Born September 22, 1959, at Cincinnati, O.
Height, 6.03. Weight, 232.
High School—Cincinnati, O., Moeller.
Received bachelor of science degree in business administration from
University of Notre Dame in 1982.

Named as linebacker on THE SPORTING NEWS College All-America Team, 1980 and 1981.
Selected by New York Jets in 1st round (23rd player selected) of 1982 NFL draft.
On physically unable to perform/active with knee injury, July 14 through August 20, 1984; activated, August 21, 1984.
On injured reserve with knee injury, August 28 through September 27, 1984; activated, September 28, 1984.
On injured reserve with knee injury, November 5 through remainder of 1984 season.
New York Jets NFL, 1982 through 1984.
Games: 1982 (9), 1983 (14), 1984 (5). Total—28.
Pro statistics: Intercepted one pass for no yards, 1983.

ROGER CRAIG
Fullback—San Francisco 49ers
Born July 10, 1960, at Davenport, Ia.
Height, 6.00. Weight, 222.
High School—Davenport, Ia., Central.
Attended University of Nebraska.

Selected by Boston in 1983 USFL territorial draft.
Selected by San Francisco in 2nd round (49th player selected) of 1983 NFL draft.
Signed by San Francisco 49ers, June 13, 1983.

Year Club	G.	—RUSHING—				PASS RECEIVING				—TOTAL—		
		Att.	Yds.	Avg.	TD.	P.C.	Yds.	Avg.	TD.	TD.	Pts.	F.
1983—San Francisco NFL	16	176	725	4.1	8	48	427	8.9	4	12	72	6
1984—San Francisco NFL	16	155	649	4.2	7	71	675	9.5	3	10	60	3
Pro Totals—2 Years	32	331	1374	4.2	15	119	1102	9.3	7	22	132	9

Additional pro statistics: Recovered one fumble, 1983 and 1984.
Played in NFC Championship Game following 1983 and 1984 seasons.
Played in NFL Championship Game following 1984 season.

ROBERT FREDERICK CRAIGHEAD JR.
(Bobby)
Running Back—San Diego Chargers
Born June 7, 1961, at McComb, Miss.
Height, 6.01. Weight, 201.
High School—Monroe, La., River Oaks.
Attended Northeast Louisiana University.

Selected by San Antonio in 9th round (170th player selected) of 1984 USFL draft.
Selected by San Diego in 8th round (219th player selected) of 1984 NFL draft.
Signed by San Diego Chargers, July 12, 1984.
On injured reserve with ankle injury, August 13 through entire 1984 season.

JON D. CRAVER
Linebacker—Cleveland Browns
Born March 24, 1961, at York, Pa.
Height, 6.02. Weight, 241.
High School—Hagerstown, Md., North.
Received bachelor of business administration degree in information systems from
James Madison University in 1983.

Signed as free agent by New England Patriots, May 18, 1983.
Released by New England Patriots, August 16, 1983; awarded on procedural waivers to Houston Oilers, April 6, 1984.
Released by Houston Oilers, August 20, 1984; signed as free agent by Cleveland Browns, April 3, 1985.

LARRY CRAWFORD
Defensive Back—San Diego Chargers
Born December 18, 1959, at Miami, Fla.
Height, 5.11. Weight, 175.
High School—Miami, Fla., Palmetto.
Attended Iowa State University.

Signed as free agent by British Columbia Lions, March 15, 1981.
Granted free agency, March 1, 1985; signed by San Diego Chargers, March 20, 1985.

Year Club	G.	INTERCEPTIONS				-PUNT RETURNS-				—KICKOFF RET.—				—TOTAL—		
		No.	Yds.	Avg.	TD.	No.	Yds.	Avg.	TD.	No.	Yds.	Avg.	TD.	TD.	Pts.	F.
1981—British Columbia CFL.	16	*8	*133	16.6	1	50	551	11.0	0	5	149	29.8	0	1	6	2
1982—British Columbia CFL.	16	4	41	10.3	0	70	691	9.9	0	27	720	26.7	0	0	0	6
1983—British Columbia CFL.	16	*12	172	14.3	2	74	766	10.4	0	6	150	25.0	0	2	12	2
1984—British Columbia CFL.	16	5	165	33.0	0	23	221	9.6	0	5	127	25.4	0	0	0	1
CFL Totals—4 Years	64	29	511	17.6	3	217	2229	10.3	0	43	1146	26.7	0	3	18	11

Additional CFL statistics: Recovered two fumbles, 1981; recovered one fumble, 1982 and 1983; recovered three fumbles for 30 yards, 1984.
Played in CFL Championship Game following 1983 season.

SMILEY LAWRENCE CRESWELL
Defensive End—New England Patriots
Born December 11, 1959, at Monroe, Wash.
Height, 6.04. Weight, 250.
High School—Monroe, Wash.
Attended Columbia Basin Community College and Michigan State University.

Selected by Michigan in 1983 USFL territorial draft.
Selected by New England in 5th round (118th player selected) of 1983 NFL draft.
Signed by New England Patriots, May 16, 1983.
On injured reserve with thumb injury, August 23 through entire 1983 season.
On injured reserve with knee injury, July 25 through entire 1984 season.

NOLAN NEIL CROMWELL
Safety—Los Angeles Rams
Born January 30, 1955, at Smith Center, Kan.
Height, 6.01. Weight, 200.
High School—Ransom, Kan.
Attended University of Kansas.

Named to THE SPORTING NEWS NFL All-Star Team, 1980.

Selected by Los Angeles in 2nd round (31st player selected) of 1977 NFL draft.
On injured reserve with knee injury, November 13 through remainder of 1984 season.

				—INTERCEPTIONS—		
Year	Club	G.	No.	Yds.	Avg.	TD.
1977—L.A. Rams NFL............		14		None		
1978—L.A. Rams NFL............		16	1	31	31.0	0
1979—L.A. Rams NFL............		16	5	109	21.8	0
1980—L.A. Rams NFL............		16	8	140	17.5	1
1981—L.A. Rams NFL............		16	5	94	18.8	0
1982—L.A. Rams NFL............		9	3	33	11.0	0
1983—L.A. Rams NFL............		16	3	76	25.3	1
1984—L.A. Rams NFL............		11	3	54	18.0	1
Pro Totals—8 Years............		114	28	537	19.2	3

Additional pro statistics: Recovered two fumbles for three yards, 1977; returned one punt for eight yards, recovered one fumble in end zone for a touchdown and rushed once for 16 yards and a touchdown, 1978; rushed once for five yards and a touchdown and recovered three fumbles, 1979; scored one point on run for extra point, rushed twice for no yards, attempted one pass with no completions, fumbled twice and recovered one fumble for minus one yard, 1980; rushed once for 17 yards and recovered three fumbles for four yards, 1981; rushed once for 17 yards and a touchdown and recovered one fumble for six yards, 1982; rushed once for no yards and recovered two fumbles, 1983; recovered one fumble, 1984. Total—Rushed eight times for 55 yards and three touchdowns, scored one point on run for extra point, returned one punt for eight yards, recovered 14 fumbles for 12 yards and one touchdown, attempted one pass with no completions and fumbled twice.
Played in NFC Championship Game following 1978 and 1979 seasons.
Played in NFL Championship Game following 1979 season.
Played in Pro Bowl (NFL All-Star Game) following 1980 through 1983 seasons.

PETER JOSEPH CRONAN
Linebacker—Washington Redskins
Born January 13, 1955, at Bourue, Mass.
Height, 6.02. Weight, 238.
High School—Framingham, Mass., Marian.
Received bachelor of science degree in elementary education and sociology from
Boston College in 1977 and attending Boston College for master's degree.

Selected by Seattle in 2nd round (51st player selected) of 1977 NFL draft.
On injured reserve with herniated disc in neck, August 26 through entire 1980 season.
Released by Seattle Seahawks, October 7, 1981; signed as free agent by Washington Redskins, October 12, 1981.
On injured reserve with pulled hamstring, December 23, 1982 through January 21, 1983; activated, January 22, 1983.
On injured reserve with fractured ankle, August 14 through November 25, 1984; activated after clearing procedural waivers, November 27, 1984.
Seattle NFL, 1977 through 1979; Seattle (5)-Washington (10) NFL, 1981; Washington NFL, 1982 through 1984.
Games: 1977 (14), 1978 (15), 1979 (16), 1981 (15), 1982 (7), 1983 (16), 1984 (3). Total—86.
Pro statistics: Recovered three fumbles for eight yards, 1977; intercepted two passes for 15 yards, 1978; recovered two fumbles, 1979; returned three kickoffs for 60 yards, 1981; recovered one fumble, 1981 and 1982; returned one kickoff for 17 yards, 1983.
Played in NFC Championship Game following 1982 and 1983 seasons.
Played in NFL Championship Game following 1982 and 1983 seasons.

JUSTIN ALLEN CROSS
Offensive Tackle—Buffalo Bills
Born April 29, 1959, at Montreal, Quebec, Canada.
Height, 6.06. Weight, 265.
High School—Portsmouth, N.H.
Received bachelor of science degree in biology from Western State (Colo.) College in 1981.

Selected by Buffalo in 10th round (272nd player selected) of 1981 NFL draft.
On injured reserve with back injury, August 29 through entire 1981 season.
On injured reserve with ankle injury, October 22 through remainder of 1984 season.
Buffalo NFL, 1982 through 1984.
Games: 1982 (9), 1983 (15), 1984 (7). Total—31.
Pro statistics: Recovered one fumble, 1983.

RANDALL LAUREAT CROSS
(Randy)
Guard—San Francisco 49ers
Born April 25, 1954, at Brooklyn, N.Y.
Height, 6.03. Weight, 265.
High School—Encino, Calif., Crespi.
Attended University of California at Los Angeles.

Selected by San Francisco in 2nd round (42nd player selected) of 1976 NFL draft.
On injured reserve with ankle injury, November 3 through remainder of 1978 season.
San Francisco NFL, 1976 through 1984.
Games: 1976 (14), 1977 (14), 1978 (9), 1979 (16), 1980 (16), 1981 (16), 1982 (9), 1983 (16), 1984 (16). Total—126.
Pro statistics: Recovered one fumble, 1976 and 1982; fumbled once for minus 37 yards; 1977; fumbled once, 1978; recovered two fumbles, 1979.
Played in NFC Championship Game following 1981, 1983 and 1984 seasons.
Played in NFL Championship Game following 1981 and 1984 seasons.
Played in Pro Bowl (NFL All-Star Game) following 1981, 1982 and 1984 seasons.

DAVID RODNEY CROUDIP
Defensive Back—Los Angeles Rams
Born January 25, 1959, at Indianapolis, Ind.
Height, 5.09. Weight, 183.
High School—Compton, Calif.
Attended Ventura College and San Diego State University.

Selected by Los Angeles in 7th round (78th player selected) of 1983 USFL draft.
Selected by Houston in 18th round (107th player selected) of USFL expansion draft, September 6, 1983.
Released by Houston Gamblers, February 29, 1984; signed as free agent by Los Angeles Rams, April 2, 1984.
Released by Los Angeles Rams, August 27, 1984; re-signed by Rams, August 28, 1984.
Released by Los Angeles Rams, September 19, 1984; re-signed by Rams, September 21, 1984.
Los Angeles USFL, 1983; Houston USFL, 1984; Los Angeles Rams NFL, 1984.
Games: 1983 (18), 1984 USFL (1), 1984 NFL (16). Total USFL—19. Total Pro—35.
Pro statistics: Recovered one fumble, 1983; recovered two fumbles, 1984.

MARLON RAY CROUSE
(Known by middle name.)
Running Back—Green Bay Packers
Born March 16, 1959, at Oakland, Calif.
Height, 6.00. Weight, 200.
High Schools—Alameda, Calif., Encinal, and Berkeley, Calif.
Attended Laney College and University of Nevada at Las Vegas.

Signed as free agent by Kansas City Chiefs, June 8, 1982.
Released by Kansas City Chiefs, August 23, 1982; signed as free agent by Calgary Stampeders, March 15, 1983.
Traded by Calgary Stampeders to Toronto Argonauts, April, 1984.
Released by Toronto Argonauts, June 24, 1984; signed as free agent by Green Bay Packers, July 7, 1984.

Year Club	G.	Att.	Yds.	Avg.	TD.	P.C.	Yds.	Avg.	TD.	TD.	Pts.	F.
1983—Calgary CFL	16	124	703	5.7	9	47	444	9.4	2	11	†68	6
1984—Green Bay NFL	16	53	169	3.2	0	9	93	10.3	1	1	6	0
Pro Totals—2 Years	32	177	872	4.9	9	56	537	9.6	3	12	74	6

†Includes one 2-point conversion.
Additional CFL statistics: Recovered one fumble, 1983.

GEORGE STANLEY CRUMP
Defensive End—New England Patriots
Born July 22, 1959, at Portsmouth, Va.
Height, 6.04. Weight, 260.
High School—Chesapeake, Va., Indian River.
Attended East Carolina University.

Selected by New England in 4th round (85th player selected) of 1982 NFL draft.
On injured reserve with knee injury, September 14 through entire 1983 season.
On physically unable to perform/reserve with knee injury, August 14 through entire 1984 season.
Active for 2 games with New England Patriots in 1983; did not play.
New England NFL, 1982 and 1983.
Games: 1982 (9).
Pro statistics: Credited with one safety, 1982.

DWAYNE CRUTCHFIELD
Fullback—Los Angeles Rams
Born September 30, 1959, at Cincinnati, O.
Height, 6.00. Weight, 245.
High School—Cincinnati, O., North College Hill.
Attended Iowa State University.

Selected by New York Jets in 3rd round (79th player selected) of 1982 NFL draft.
Released by New York Jets, November 18, 1983; awarded on waivers to Houston Oilers, November 21, 1983.
Traded by Houston Oilers to Los Angeles Rams for 6th round pick in 1984 draft, April 9, 1984.

Year Club	G.	Att.	Yds.	Avg.	TD.	P.C.	Yds.	Avg.	TD.	TD.	Pts.	F.
1982—New York Jets NFL	6	22	78	3.5	1		None			1	6	1
1983—N.Y.J. (11)-Hou. (2) NFL	13	140	578	4.1	3	19	133	7.0	0	3	18	2
1984—Los Angeles Rams NFL	15	73	337	4.6	1	2	11	5.5	1	2	12	1
Pro Totals—3 Years	34	235	993	4.2	5	21	144	6.9	1	6	36	4

Additional pro statistics: Returned one kickoff for 20 yards, 1984.
Member of New York Jets for AFC Championship Game following 1982 season; did not play.

ROBERT JOSEPH CRYDER
(Bob)
Offensive Tackle—Seattle Seahawks
Born September 7, 1956, at O'Fallon, Ill.
Height, 6.04. Weight, 282.
High School—O'Fallon, Ill.
Received degree in recreation and park management from University of Alabama in 1978.

Selected by New England in 1st round (18th player selected) of 1978 NFL draft.

On injured reserve with broken wrist, October 6 through remainder of 1978 season.
Traded by New England Patriots to Seattle Seahawks for 3rd round pick in 1985 draft and conditional 2nd round pick in 1986 draft, July 31, 1984.
New England NFL, 1978 through 1983; Seattle NFL, 1984.
Games: 1978 (5), 1979 (16), 1980 (16), 1981 (15), 1982 (9), 1983 (14), 1984 (16). Total—91.
Pro statistics: Recovered one fumble, 1979; recovered three fumbles, 1983.

GEORGE EDWARD CUMBY
Linebacker—Green Bay Packers
Born July 5, 1956, at Gorman, Tex.
Height, 6.00. Weight, 224.
High School—Gorman, Tex.
Attended University of Oklahoma.
Cousin of Kenneth Cumby, linebacker at Oklahoma State University.

Named as linebacker on THE SPORTING NEWS College All-America Team, 1979.
Selected by Green Bay in 1st round (26th player selected) of 1980 NFL draft.
On injured reserve with knee injury, November 5 through remainder of 1980 season.

| | | | —INTERCEPTIONS— | | |
Year Club	G.	No.	Yds.	Avg.	TD.
1980—Green Bay NFL............	9		None		
1981—Green Bay NFL............	16	3	22	7.3	0
1982—Green Bay NFL............	9	1	4	4.0	0
1983—Green Bay NFL............	15		None		
1984—Green Bay NFL............	16	1	7	7.0	0
Pro Totals—5 Years............	65	5	33	6.6	0

Additional pro statistics: Recovered two fumbles for 70 yards, 1981; recovered one fumble, 1982; recovered two fumbles, 1984.

BENNIE LEE CUNNINGHAM JR.
(Bennie)
Tight End—Pittsburgh Steelers
Born December 23, 1954, at Laurens, S. C.
Height, 6.05. Weight, 255.
High School—Seneca, S. C.
Received bachelor of arts degree in secondary education from Clemson University in 1976.
Brother of Howard Cunningham, tight end at South Carolina State College.

Named as tight end on THE SPORTING NEWS College All-America Team, 1975.
Selected by Pittsburgh in 1st round (28th player selected) of 1976 NFL draft.
On injured reserve with hip injury, October 12 through November 30, 1984; activated, December 1, 1984.

| | | | —PASS RECEIVING— | | |
Year Club	G.	P.C.	Yds.	Avg.	TD.
1976—Pittsburgh NFL............	12	5	49	9.8	1
1977—Pittsburgh NFL............	12	20	347	17.4	2
1978—Pittsburgh NFL............	6	16	321	20.1	2
1979—Pittsburgh NFL............	15	36	512	14.2	4
1980—Pittsburgh NFL............	15	18	232	12.9	2
1981—Pittsburgh NFL............	15	41	574	14.0	3
1982—Pittsburgh NFL............	9	21	277	13.2	2
1983—Pittsburgh NFL............	16	35	442	12.6	3
1984—Pittsburgh NFL............	7	4	64	16.0	1
Pro Totals—9 Years..........	107	196	2818	14.4	20

Additional pro statistics: Recovered one fumble, 1976, 1979, 1981 and 1983; fumbled once, 1978; fumbled four times, 1983.
Played in AFC Championship Game following 1976, 1979 and 1984 seasons.
Played in NFL Championship Game following 1979 season.
Member of Pittsburgh Steelers for AFC Championship Game following 1978 season; did not play.
Member of Pittsburgh Steelers for NFL Championship Game following 1978 season; did not play.

AUGUST CURLEY
Linebacker—Detroit Lions
Born January 24, 1960, at Little Rock, Ark.
Height, 6.03. Weight, 226.
High School—Atlanta, Ga., Southwest.
Attended University of Southern California.

Selected by Los Angeles in 1983 USFL territorial draft.
Selected by Detroit in 4th round (94th player selected) of 1983 NFL draft.
Signed by Detroit Lions, June 1, 1983.
On injured reserve with knee injury, November 9 through remainder of 1983 season.
On physically unable to perform/active with knee injury, July 22 through August 19, 1984.
On physically unable to perform/reserve with knee injury, August 20 through October 23, 1984; activated, October 24, 1984.
Detroit NFL, 1983 and 1984.
Games: 1983 (10), 1984 (8). Total—18.
Pro statistics: Returned one kickoff for seven yards, 1983.

WILLIAM CURRAN
Wide Receiver—Atlanta Falcons

Born December 30, 1959, at Inglewood, Calif.
Height, 5.11. Weight, 175.
High School—Encino, Calif., Crespi Carmelite.
Attended University of California at Los Angeles.

Signed as free agent by Atlanta Falcons, May 3, 1982.

Year Club	G.	PASS RECEIVING				–PUNT RETURNS–				–KICKOFF RET.–				–TOTAL–		
		P.C.	Yds.	Avg.	TD.	No.	Yds.	Avg.	TD.	No.	Yds.	Avg.	TD.	TD.	Pts.	F.
1982—Atlanta NFL	7	None				None				None				0	0	0
1983—Atlanta NFL	16	1	15	15.0	0	None				2	26	13.0	0	0	0	1
1984—Atlanta NFL	14	1	7	7.0	0	9	21	2.3	0	11	219	19.9	0	0	0	2
Pro Totals—3 Years	37	2	22	11.0	0	9	21	2.3	0	13	245	18.8	0	0	0	3

Additional pro statistics: Recovered one fumble, 1984.

WILLIAM FRANK CURRIER
(Bill)
Safety—New York Giants

Born January 5, 1955, at Glen Burnie, Md.
Height, 6.00. Weight, 196.
High School—Glen Burnie, Md.
Received bachelor of science degree in physical education from University of South Carolina.

Selected by Houston in 9th round (232nd player selected) of 1977 NFL draft.
Released by Houston Oilers, August 26, 1980; signed as free agent by New England Patriots, September 3, 1980.
Traded by New England Patriots to New York Giants for 11th round pick in 1982 draft, August 31, 1981.
On injured reserve with back injury, August 29 through October 18, 1984; activated, October 19, 1984.

Year Club	G.	INTERCEPTIONS			
		No.	Yds.	Avg.	TD.
1977—Houston NFL	14	2	0	0.0	0
1978—Houston NFL	14	1	8	8.0	0
1979—Houston NFL	16	None			
1980—New England NFL	16	None			
1981—N.Y. Giants NFL	16	3	2	0.7	0
1982—N.Y. Giants NFL	9	1	0	0.0	0
1983—N.Y. Giants NFL	15	2	37	18.5	1
1984—N.Y. Giants NFL	9	1	7	7.0	0
Pro Totals—8 Years	109	10	54	5.4	1

Additional pro statistics: Recovered two fumbles, 1977 and 1978; recovered one fumble, 1979, 1981 and 1983; returned six kickoffs for 98 yards, 1980.
Played in AFC Championship Game following 1978 and 1979 seasons.

CRAIG CURRY
Safety—Tampa Bay Buccaneers

Born July 20, 1961, at Houston, Tex.
Height, 6.00. Weight, 187.
High School—Houston, Tex., Kashmere.
Attended University of Texas.

Selected by San Antonio in 1984 USFL territorial draft.
Selected by Indianapolis in 4th round (93rd player selected) of 1984 NFL draft.
Signed by Indianapolis Colts, May 24, 1984.
Released by Indianapolis Colts, August 20, 1984; signed as free agent by Tampa Bay Buccaneers, November 12, 1984.
Tampa Bay NFL, 1984.
Games: 1984 (5).

GEORGE JESSEL CURRY
(Buddy)
Linebacker—Atlanta Falcons

Born June 4, 1958, at Greenville, N.C.
Height, 6.04. Weight, 228.
High School—Danville, Va., George Washington.
Received bachelor of science degree in business administration from
University of North Carolina in 1980.

Selected by Atlanta in 2nd round (36th player selected) of 1980 NFL draft.
On injured reserve with knee injury, January 7 through remainder of 1982 season playoffs.

Year Club	G.	INTERCEPTIONS			
		No.	Yds.	Avg.	TD.
1980—Atlanta NFL	16	3	13	4.3	0
1981—Atlanta NFL	16	1	35	35.0	1
1982—Atlanta NFL	9	1	0	0.0	0
1983—Atlanta NFL	16	None			
1984—Atlanta NFL	16	None			
Pro Totals—5 Years	73	5	48	9.6	1

Additional pro statistics: Recovered one fumble for 30 yards and a touchdown and fumbled once, 1980; recovered one fumble, 1983; recovered one fumble for four yards, 1984.

ISAAC FISHER CURTIS
Wide Receiver—Cincinnati Bengals

Born October 20, 1950, at Santa Ana, Calif.
Height, 6.01. Weight, 192.
High School—Santa Ana, Calif.
Attended University of California and San Diego State University.

Named to THE SPORTING NEWS AFC All-Star Team, 1974 through 1976.
Selected by Cincinnati in 1st round (15th player selected) of 1973 NFL draft.

| | | —————RUSHING————— | | | | PASS RECEIVING | | | | —TOTAL— | | |
Year Club	G.	Att.	Yds.	Avg.	TD.	P.C.	Yds.	Avg.	TD.	TD.	Pts.	F.
1973—Cincinnati NFL	14	2	—11	—5.5	0	45	843	18.7	9	9	54	0
1974—Cincinnati NFL	14	8	62	7.8	0	30	633	21.1	10	10	60	1
1975—Cincinnati NFL	14	6	—9	—1.5	0	44	934	★21.2	7	7	42	1
1976—Cincinnati NFL	14	3	29	9.7	0	42	771	18.7	6	6	36	1
1977—Cincinnati NFL	8		None			20	338	16.9	2	2	12	0
1978—Cincinnati NFL	16	1	1	1.0	0	47	737	15.7	3	3	18	2
1979—Cincinnati NFL	16	2	—11	—5.5	0	32	605	18.9	8	8	48	1
1980—Cincinnati NFL	15		None			43	610	14.2	3	3	18	0
1981—Cincinnati NFL	15		None			37	609	16.5	2	2	12	1
1982—Cincinnati NFL	9	3	15	5.0	0	23	320	13.9	1	1	6	1
1983—Cincinnati NFL	16		None			42	571	13.6	2	2	12	1
1984—Cincinnati NFL	16		None			12	135	11.3	0	0	0	1
Pro Totals—12 Years	167	25	76	3.0	0	417	7106	17.0	53	53	318	10

Additional pro statistics: Recovered one fumble, 1981.
Played in AFC Championship Game following 1981 season.
Played in NFL Championship Game following 1981 season.
Played in Pro Bowl (NFL All-Star Game) following 1973 through 1976 seasons.

DAVID JOHN D'ADDIO

Name pronounced DAD-ee-oh.

(Dave)
Running Back—Detroit Lions

Born July 13, 1961, at Newark, N.J.
Height, 6.02. Weight, 229.
High School—Union, N.J.
Attended University of Maryland.

Selected by Washington in 1984 USFL territorial draft.
Selected by Detroit in 4th round (106th player selected) of 1984 NFL draft.
Signed by Detroit Lions, July 14, 1984.

| | | ——————RUSHING—————— | | | | PASS RECEIVING | | | | —TOTAL— | | |
Year Club	G.	Att.	Yds.	Avg.	TD.	P.C.	Yds.	Avg.	TD.	TD.	Pts.	F.
1984—Detroit NFL	16	7	46	6.6	0	1	12	12.0	0	0	0	0

Additional pro statistics: Returned one kickoff for no yards, 1984.

DARNELL LEUGTIG DAILEY
Linebacker—Washington Redskins

Born September 8, 1959, at Baltimore, Md.
Height, 6.03. Weight, 238.
High School—Baltimore, Md., Baltimore Polytechnic School of Engineering.
Received bachelor of science degree in general studies from University of Maryland in 1982.
Related to Quintin Dailey, guard with Chicago Bulls.

Selected by St. Louis in 9th round (232nd player selected) of 1982 NFL draft.
On injured reserve with Achilles tendon injury, August 25 through entire 1982 season.
Released by St. Louis Cardinals, August 16, 1983; signed by Washington Federals, September 29, 1983.
On developmental squad, March 24 through May 5, 1984; activated, May 6, 1984.
Franchise transferred to Orlando, October 12, 1984.
Released by Orlando Renegades, January 28, 1985; signed as free agent by Washington Redskins, March 23, 1985.
On developmental squad for 6 games with Washington Federals in 1984.
Washington USFL, 1984.
Games: 1984 (12).

DAVID MERLE DALBY
(Dave)
Center—Los Angeles Raiders

Born October 19, 1950, at Alexandria, Minn.
Height, 6.03. Weight, 255.
High School—Whittier, Calif., La Serna.
Attended University of California at Los Angeles.

Named as center on THE SPORTING NEWS College All-America Team, 1971.
Selected by Oakland in 4th round (100th player selected) of 1972 NFL draft.
Franchise transferred to Los Angeles, May 7, 1982.
Oakland NFL, 1972 through 1981; Los Angeles Raiders, 1982 through 1984.
Games: 1972 (14), 1973 (14), 1974 (14), 1975 (14), 1976 (14), 1977 (14), 1978 (16), 1979 (16), 1980 (16), 1981 (16), 1982 (9), 1983 (16), 1984 (16). Total—189.

Pro statistics: Fumbled once, 1973; recovered one fumble, 1973, 1974, 1978, 1979, 1983 and 1984; caught one pass for one yard, 1979; fumbled once for minus one yard, 1980.
Played in AFC Championship Game following 1973 through 1977, 1980 and 1983 seasons.
Played in NFL Championship Game following 1976, 1980 and 1983 seasons.
Played in Pro Bowl (NFL All-Star Game) following 1977 season.

WILLIAM M. DALTON
Running Back—Detroit Lions
Born February 26, 1961, at Eden, N.C.
Height, 5.10. Weight, 200.
High School—Eden, N.C., Morehead.
Attended Chowan College and West Virginia Institute of Technology.

Signed as free agent by Detroit Lions, June 22, 1984.
Released by Detroit Lions, August 27, 1984; re-signed by Lions, May 14, 1985.

EUGENE DANIEL JR.
Cornerback—Indianapolis Colts
Born May 4, 1961, at Baton Rouge, La.
Height, 6.00. Weight, 179.
High School—Baton Rouge, La., Robert E. Lee.
Attended Louisiana State University.

Selected by New Orleans in 1984 USFL territorial draft.
Selected by Indianapolis in 8th round (205th player selected) of 1984 NFL draft.
Signed by Indianapolis Colts, June 21, 1984.

			—INTERCEPTIONS—		
Year	Club	G.	No.	Yds.	Avg.TD.
1984—Indianapolis NFL		15	6	25	4.2 0

KENNY RAY DANIEL
Defensive Back—New York Giants
Born June 1, 1960, at Martinez, Calif.
Height, 5.10. Weight, 180.
High School—Richmond, Calif., Kennedy.
Attended Contra Costa College and San Jose State University.

Signed as free agent by Washington Redskins, May 24, 1982.
Released by Washington Redskins, August 19, 1982; signed by Oakland Invaders, October 26, 1982.
Signed by New York Giants, March 8, 1984, for contract to take effect after being granted free agency, November 30, 1984.

			—INTERCEPTIONS—		
Year	Club	G.	No.	Yds.	Avg.TD.
1983—Oakland USFL		18	4	51	12.8 0
1984—Oakland USFL		18	6	28	4.7 0
1984—N.Y. Giants NFL		15			None
USFL Totals—2 Years		36	10	79	7.9 0
NFL Totals—1 Year		15	0	0	0.0 0
Pro Totals—3 Years		51	10	79	7.9 0

Additional USFL statistics: Recovered two fumbles for one yards, 1983; recovered two fumbles for 68 yards, 1984.
Additional NFL statistics: Returned one kickoff for 52 yards, 1984.

CALVIN RICHARD DANIELS
Linebacker—Kansas City Chiefs
Born December 26, 1958, at Morehead City, N.C.
Height, 6.03. Weight, 236.
High School—Goldsboro, N.C.
Attended University of North Carolina.

Selected by Kansas City in 2nd round (46th player selected) of 1982 NFL draft.
Kansas City NFL, 1982 through 1984.
Games: 1982 (9), 1983 (16), 1984 (16). Total—41.
Pro statistics: Returned one kickoff for no yards and recovered one fumble, 1983; intercepted two passes for 11 yards and recovered two fumbles, 1984.

GARY DENNIS DANIELSON
Quarterback—Cleveland Browns
Born September 10, 1951, at Detroit, Mich.
Height, 6.02. Weight, 196.
High School—Dearborn, Mich., Divine Child.
Received degree in business from Purdue University.

Signed as free agent by New York Stars (WFL), 1974.
Traded by Charlotte Hornets (WFL) to Chicago Winds (WFL) for future considerations, 1975.
Signed as free agent by Detroit Lions after World Football League folded, 1976.
On injured reserve with knee injury, August 28 through entire 1979 season.
On injured reserve with broken wrist, October 8 through November 24, 1981; activated, November 25, 1981.
USFL rights traded by Michigan Panthers to Arizona Wranglers for 4th round pick in 1984 draft, April 4, 1983.
Traded by Detroit Lions to Cleveland Browns for draft choice, May 1, 1985.

Year Club	G.	Att.	Cmp.	Pct.	Gain	T.P.	P.I.	Avg.	Att.	Yds.	Avg.	TD.	TD.	Pts.	F.
1974—N.Y.-Char. WFL	....	60	28	46.7	305	1	0	5.08	10	51	5.1	3	3	21	....
1975—Chicago WFL	....	15	9	60.0	107	0	2	7.13		None			0	0	....
1976—Detroit NFL	1			None						None			0	0	0
1977—Detroit NFL	13	100	42	42.0	445	1	5	4.45	7	62	8.9	0	0	0	0
1978—Detroit NFL	16	351	199	56.7	2294	18	17	6.54	22	93	4.2	0	0	0	5
1980—Detroit NFL	16	417	244	58.5	3223	13	11	7.73	48	232	4.8	2	2	12	11
1981—Detroit NFL	6	96	56	58.3	784	3	5	8.17	9	23	2.6	2	2	12	2
1982—Detroit NFL	8	197	100	50.8	1343	10	14	6.82	23	92	4.0	0	0	6	6
1983—Detroit NFL	10	113	59	52.2	720	7	4	6.37	6	8	1.3	0	0	0	2
1984—Detroit NFL	15	410	252	61.5	3076	17	15	7.50	41	218	5.3	3	4	24	7
WFL Totals—2 Years	....	75	37	49.3	412	1	2	5.49	10	51	5.1	3	3	21	....
NFL Totals—8 Years	85	1684	952	56.5	11885	69	71	7.06	156	728	4.7	7	8	48	33
Pro Totals—10 Years	....	1759	989	56.2	12297	70	73	6.99	166	779	4.7	10	11	69	....

NFL Quarterback Rating Points: 1977 (38.1), 1978 (73.6), 1980 (82.6), 1981 (73.4), 1982 (60.3), 1983 (78.0), 1984 (83.1). Total—74.8.

Additional pro statistics: Recovered one fumble, 1977, 1982 and 1983; recovered two fumbles and fumbled five times for minus 12 yards, 1978; recovered four fumbles and fumbled 11 times for minus two yards, 1980; fumbled six times for minus 11 yards, 1982; caught one pass for 22 yards and a touchdown, recovered two fumbles and fumbled seven times for minus five yards, 1984.

BYRON DARBY
Defensive End—Philadelphia Eagles
Born June 4, 1960, at Los Angeles, Calif.
Height, 6.04. Weight, 260.
High School—Inglewood, Calif.
Attended University of Southern California.

Selected by Los Angeles in 1983 USFL territorial draft.
Selected by Philadelphia in 5th round (120th player selected) of 1983 NFL draft.
Signed by Philadelphia Eagles, May 25, 1983.
Philadelphia NFL, 1983 and 1984.
Games: 1983 (16), 1984 (16). Total—32.
Pro statistics: Returned two kickoffs for three yards and fumbled once, 1983.

RAMSEY DARDAR
Defensive Tackle—St. Louis Cardinals
Born October 3, 1959, at Cecilia, La.
Height, 6.02. Weight, 264.
High School—Cecilia, La.
Attended Louisiana State University.

Selected by New Jersey in 3rd round (27th player selected) of 1983 USFL draft.
Selected by St. Louis in 3rd round (71st player selected) of 1983 NFL draft.
Signed by St. Louis Cardinals, June 28, 1983.
On injured reserve with knee injury, August 30 through entire 1983 season.
St. Louis NFL, 1984.
Games: 1984 (16).

PHILLIP DARNS
(Phil)
Defensive End—Tampa Bay Buccaneers
Born July 27, 1959, at Tampa, Fla.
Height, 6.03. Weight, 245.
High School—Tampa, Fla., Tampa Bay Tech.
Received bachelor of science degree in criminal justice from
Mississippi Valley State University in 1982.

Signed as free agent by New York Jets, June 2, 1982.
Released by New York Jets, August 30, 1982; signed as free agent by New Jersey Generals, October 22, 1982.
Released by New Jersey Generals, February 20, 1983; signed as free agent by Detroit Lions, May 15, 1983.
On injured reserve with groin injury, August 23 through entire 1983 season.
On physically unable to perform/active with ankle injury, July 22 through August 26, 1984.
Released by Detroit Lions, August 27, 1984; signed as free agent by Tampa Bay Buccaneers, November 6, 1984.
On injured reserve with back injury, December 5 through remainder of 1984 season.
Tampa Bay NFL, 1984.
Games: 1984 (2).

STAN DAVID
Linebacker—Buffalo Bills
Born February 17, 1962, at North Platte, Neb.
Height, 6.03. Weight, 210.
High School—Tucumcari, N.M.
Received degree in mechanical engineering from Texas Tech University in 1984.

Selected by Denver in 1984 USFL territorial draft.
Selected by Buffalo in 7th round (182nd player selected) of 1984 NFL draft.
Signed by Buffalo Bills, July 9, 1984.
Buffalo NFL, 1984.
Games: 1984 (16).
Pro statistics: Returned one kickoff for six yards and ran 36 yards with a blocked punt for a touchdown, 1984.

CHY DAVIDSON
Wide Receiver—New York Jets
Born May 9, 1959, at Queens Village, N.Y.
Height, 5.11. Weight, 175.
High School—Bayside, N.Y.
Received bachelor of arts degree in speech communication from
University of Rhode Island in 1981.

Selected by New England in NFL supplementary draft, June 23, 1981; Patriots forfeited 11th round pick in 1982 draft.

Released by New England Patriots, August 24, 1981; signed as free agent by Washington Redskins, April 2, 1982.
Released by Washington Redskins, September 6, 1982; signed by Washington Federals, January 21, 1983.
Released by Washington Federals, February 26, 1983; signed as free agent by Baltimore Colts, July 1, 1983.
Released by Baltimore Colts, July 25, 1983; signed as free agent by New York Jets, April 9, 1984.
On injured reserve with hip injury, August 14 through November 24, 1984; activated after clearing procedural waivers, November 26, 1984.
New York Jets NFL, 1984.
Games: 1984 (3).
Pro statistics: Returned one kickoff for nine yards, 1984.

BRUCE DAVIS
Wide Receiver—Cleveland Browns
Born February 25, 1963, at Dallas, Tex.
Height, 5.08. Weight, 160.
High School—Dallas, Tex., Franklin D. Roosevelt.
Attended Baylor University.

Selected by San Antonio in 1984 USFL territorial draft.
Selected by Cleveland in 2nd round (50th player selected) of 1984 NFL draft.
Signed by Cleveland Browns, June 6, 1984.

		PASS RECEIVING				—KICKOFF RET.—				—TOTAL—		
Year Club	G.	P.C.	Yds.	Avg.	TD.	No.	Yds.	Avg.	TD.	TD.	Pts.	F.
1984—Cleveland NFL	14	7	119	17.0	2	18	369	20.5	0	2	12	2

Additional pro statistics: Rushed once for six yards, 1984.

BRUCE EDWARD DAVIS
Offensive Tackle—Los Angeles Raiders
Born June 21, 1956, at Rutherfordton, N.C.
Height, 6.06, Weight, 280.
High School—Marbury, Md., Lackey.
Attended University of California at Los Angeles.

Selected by Oakland in 11th round (294th player selected) of 1979 NFL draft.
Franchise transferred to Los Angeles, May 7, 1982.
Oakland NFL, 1979 through 1981; Los Angeles Raiders NFL, 1982 through 1984.
Games: 1979 (12), 1980 (16), 1981 (16), 1982 (9), 1983 (16), 1984 (16). Total—85.
Pro statistics: Recovered one fumble, 1982 and 1983.
Played in AFC Championship Game following 1980 and 1983 seasons.
Played in NFL Championship Game following 1980 and 1983 seasons.

JAMES STEVEN DAVIS
Cornerback—Los Angeles Raiders
Born June 12, 1957, at Los Angeles, Calif.
Height, 6.00. Weight, 190.
High School—Los Angeles, Calif., Crenshaw.
Attended Los Angeles Southwest Junior College and Southern University.

Selected by Oakland in 5th round (118th player selected) of 1981 NFL draft.
On injured reserve, August 25 through entire 1981 season.
Franchise transferred to Los Angeles, May 7, 1982.

		—INTERCEPTIONS—			
Year Club	G.	No.	Yds.	Avg.	TD.
1982—L.A. Raiders NFL	9	2	*107	53.5	*1
1983—L.A. Raiders NFL	16	1	10	10.0	0
1984—L.A. Raiders NFL	15	1	8	8.0	0
Pro Totals—3 Years	40	4	125	31.3	1

Additional pro statistics: Recovered one fumble, 1982 and 1983; recovered two fumbles, 1984.
Played in AFC Championship Game following 1983 season.
Played in NFL Championship Game following 1983 season.

JEFF DAVIS JR.
Cornerback—San Diego Chargers
Born April 20, 1961, at Sanford, Fla.
Height, 6.01. Weight, 190.
High School—Titusville, Fla.
Attended University of South Dakota.

Signed as free agent by Denver Broncos, May 2, 1984.
Released by Denver Broncos, July 20, 1984; signed as free agent by San Diego Chargers, April 12, 1985.

JEFFREY EUGENE DAVIS
(Jeff)
Linebacker—Tampa Bay Buccaneers
Born January 26, 1960, at Greensboro, N.C.
Height, 6.00. Weight, 230.
High School—Greensboro, N.C., Dudley.
Received degree in industrial education from Clemson University in 1984.

Selected by Tampa Bay in 5th round (128th player selected) of 1982 NFL draft.
Tampa Bay NFL, 1982 through 1984.
Games: 1982 (9), 1983 (15), 1984 (16). Total—40.
Pro statistics: Returned one kickoff for no yards and fumbled once, 1982; recovered one fumble, 1982 and 1984; intercepted one pass for no yards, 1984.

JOHNNY LEE DAVIS
Fullback—Cleveland Browns
Born July 17, 1956, at Montgomery, Ala.
Height, 6.01. Weight, 235.
High School—Montgomery, Ala., Sidney Lanier.
Received bachelor of science degree in recreation and park management
from University of Alabama in 1978.

Selected by Tampa Bay in 2nd round (30th player selected) of 1978 NFL draft.
Traded by Tampa Bay Buccaneers to San Francisco 49ers for running back James Owens, August 31, 1981.
Released by San Francisco 49ers, August 30, 1982; signed as free agent by Cleveland Browns, December 2, 1982.
USFL rights traded by Birmingham Stallions to Memphis Showboats for rights to defensive back Fred Bohannon, December 21, 1983.

Year Club	G.	Att.	RUSHING Yds.	Avg.	TD.	PASS RECEIVING P.C.	Yds.	Avg.	TD.	—TOTAL— TD.	Pts.	F.
1978—Tampa Bay NFL	16	97	370	3.8	3	5	13	2.6	0	3	18	2
1979—Tampa Bay NFL	16	59	221	3.7	2	5	57	11.4	0	2	12	0
1980—Tampa Bay NFL	14	39	130	3.3	1	4	17	4.3	0	1	6	1
1981—San Francisco NFL	16	94	297	3.2	7	3	—1	—0.3	0	7	42	1
1982—Cleveland NFL	2	4	3	0.8	1	None				1	6	0
1983—Cleveland NFL	16	13	42	3.2	0	5	20	4.0	0	0	0	0
1984—Cleveland NFL	16	3	15	5.0	1	None				1	6	0
Pro Totals—7 Years	96	309	1078	3.5	15	22	106	4.8	0	15	90	4

Additional pro statistics: Recovered one fumble, 1979; returned one kickoff for no yards, 1981; returned one kickoff for eight yards, 1983.
Played in NFC Championship Game following 1979 and 1981 seasons.
Played in NFL Championship Game following 1981 season.

MICHAEL LEONAR DAVIS
(Mike)
Safety—Los Angeles Raiders
Born April 15, 1956, at Los Angeles, Calif.
Height, 6.03. Weight, 205.
High School—Los Angeles, Calif., Alain Leroy Locke.
Attended East Los Angeles Junior College and received bachelor of science degree
in communications from University of Colorado in 1977.

Selected by Oakland in 2nd round (35th player selected) of 1977 NFL draft.
On injured reserve entire 1977 season.
On injured reserve with knee and ankle injuries, September 23 through November 20, 1981; activated, November 21, 1981.
Franchise transferred to Los Angeles, May 7, 1982.

Year Club	G.	No.	INTERCEPTIONS Yds.	Avg.	TD.
1978—Oakland NFL	16	1	0	0.0	0
1979—Oakland NFL	16	2	22	11.0	0
1980—Oakland NFL	16	3	88	29.3	0
1981—Oakland NFL	7	1	0	0.0	0
1982—L.A. Raiders NFL	9	1	56	56.0	*1
1983—L.A. Raiders NFL	16	1	3	3.0	0
1984—L.A. Raiders NFL	16	2	11	5.5	0
Pro Totals—7 Years	96	11	180	16.4	1

Additional pro statistics: Recovered one fumble, 1978, 1982 and 1984; returned one punt for six yards and recovered three fumbles for 14 yards, 1979; recovered three fumbles for 35 yards, 1980; recovered two fumbles, 1983.
Played in AFC Championship Game following 1980 and 1983 seasons.
Played in NFL Championship Game following 1980 and 1983 seasons.

PRESTON DAVIS
Cornerback—Indianapolis Colts
Born March 10, 1962, at Lubbock, Tex.
Height, 5.11. Weight, 180.
High School—Lubbock, Tex., Estacado.
Attended Baylor University.

Selected by San Antonio in 1984 USFL territorial draft.

Signed as free agent by New England Patriots, July 6, 1984.
Released by New England Patriots, August 27, 1984.
USFL rights traded by San Antonio Gunslingers to Denver Gold for rights to running back James Hadnot, September 5, 1984.
Signed as free agent by Indianapolis Colts, September 18, 1984.

| | | | —INTERCEPTIONS— | | |
Year	Club	G.	No.	Yds.	Avg.	TD.
1984—Indianapolis NFL		12	1	3	3.0	0

RUSSELL ALAN DAVIS
Tight End—Buffalo Bills
Born June 16, 1960 at Harrisburg, Pa.
Height, 6.05. Weight, 230.
High School—Harrisburg, Pa., Central Dauphin East.
Received bachelor of arts degree in communications from
University of Maryland.

Selected by Buffalo in 12th round (322nd player selected) of 1984 NFL draft.
Released by Buffalo Bills, August 28, 1984; re-signed by Bills, May 10, 1985.

WILLIAM HENRY DAVIS JR.
(Billy)
Linebacker—St. Louis Cardinals
Born December 6, 1961, at Alexandria, Va.
Height, 6.04. Weight, 200.
High School—Alexandria, Va., Mt. Vernon.
Attended Clemson University.

Signed as free agent by Denver Broncos, May 2, 1984.
Released by Denver Broncos, July 20, 1984; signed as free agent by St. Louis Cardinals, December 5, 1984.
St. Louis NFL, 1984.
Games: 1984 (1).

JULIUS DAWKINS
Wide Receiver—Buffalo Bills
Born January 4, 1961, at Monessen, Pa.
Height, 6.01. Weight, 196.
High School—Monessen, Pa.
Attended University of Pittsburgh.

Selected by Buffalo in 12th round (320th player selected) of 1983 NFL draft.
On physically unable to perform/active with foot injury, July 18 through July 24, 1983; activated, July 25, 1983.

| | | | —PASS RECEIVING— | | | |
Year	Club	G.	P.C.	Yds.	Avg.	TD.
1983—Buffalo NFL		11	11	123	11.2	1
1984—Buffalo NFL		16	21	295	14.0	2
Pro Totals—2 Years		27	32	418	13.1	3

Additional pro statistics: Recovered one fumble, 1984.

DOUGLAS ARLIN DAWSON
(Doug)
Guard—St. Louis Cardinals
Born December 27, 1961, at Houston, Tex.
Height, 6.03. Weight, 267.
High School—Houston, Tex., Memorial.
Attended University of Texas.

Selected by San Antonio in 1984 USFL territorial draft.
Selected by St. Louis in 2nd round (45th player selected) of 1984 NFL draft.
Signed by St. Louis Cardinals, July 28, 1984.
St. Louis NFL, 1984.
Games: 1984 (15).

JAMES LINWOOD DAWSON
(Lin)
Tight End—New England Patriots
Born June 24, 1959, at Norfolk, Va.
Height, 6.03. Weight, 240.
High School—Kinston, N.C.
Attended North Carolina State University.

Selected by New England in 8th round (212th player selected) of 1981 NFL draft.
On inactive list, September 19, 1982.

| | | —PASS RECEIVING— | | | | |
Year	Club	G.	P.C.	Yds.	Avg.	TD.
1981—New England NFL.......		15	7	126	18.0	0
1982—New England NFL.......		8	13	160	12.3	1
1983—New England NFL.......		13	9	84	9.3	1
1984—New England NFL.......		16	39	427	10.9	4
Pro Totals—4 Years............		52	68	797	11.7	6

Additional pro statistics: Recovered one fumble, 1984.

MICHAEL DAWSON
(Mike)
Nose Tackle-Defensive Tackle—Kansas City Chiefs
Born October 16, 1953, at Dorking, England.
Height, 6.03. Weight, 254.
High School—Tucson, Ariz.
Attended University of Arizona.

Selected by St. Louis in 1st round (22nd player selected) of 1976 NFL draft.
On injured reserve with knee injury, September 30 through remainder of 1980 season.
Traded with 3rd round pick in 1984 draft by St. Louis Cardinals to Detroit Lions for defensive end Al Baker, July 18, 1983.
Granted free agency, February 1, 1984.
Rights released by Detroit Lions, August 21, 1984; signed by Kansas City Chiefs, October 18, 1984.
St. Louis NFL, 1976 through 1982; Detroit NFL, 1983; Kansas City NFL, 1984.
Games: 1976 (13), 1977 (14), 1978 (16), 1979 (16), 1980 (4), 1981 (16), 1982 (9), 1983 (16), 1984 (9). Total—113.
Pro statistics: Recovered two fumbles, 1978 and 1981; intercepted one pass for no yards, 1982.

FREDERICK RUDOLPH DEAN
(Fred)
Defensive End—San Francisco 49ers
Born February 24, 1952, at Arcadia, La.
Height, 6.02. Weight, 236.
High School—Ruston, La.
Attended Louisiana Tech University.

Named to THE SPORTING NEWS AFC All-Star Team, 1979.
Named to THE SPORTING NEWS NFL All-Star Team, 1981.
Selected by San Diego in 2nd round (33rd player selected) of 1975 NFL draft.
On did not report list, August 18 through September 15, 1980; activated, September 16, 1980.
Traded with 1st round pick in 1983 draft by San Diego Chargers to San Francisco 49ers for 1st and 2nd round picks in 1983 draft, October 2, 1981.
Placed on did not report list, August 21 through November 12, 1984.
Reported and granted roster exemption, November 13 through November 15, 1984; activated, November 16, 1984.
San Diego NFL, 1975 through 1980; San Diego (3)-San Francisco (11) NFL, 1981; San Francisco NFL, 1982 through 1984.
Games: 1975 (14), 1976 (14), 1977 (11), 1978 (15), 1979 (13), 1980 (14), 1981 (14), 1982 (9), 1983 (16), 1984 (5). Total—125.
Pro statistics: Recovered four fumbles, 1975; recovered two fumbles for 11 yards and one touchdown and intercepted one pass for 22 yards and one touchdown (tied for league lead in touchdowns on interceptions), 1977; recovered one fumble, 1978, 1980 and 1982; recovered three fumbles for two yards, 1979.
Played in AFC Championship Game following 1980 season.
Played in NFC Championship Game following 1981, 1983 and 1984 seasons.
Played in NFL Championship Game following 1981 and 1984 seasons.
Played in Pro Bowl (NFL All-Star Game) following 1979 through 1981 seasons.
Named to Pro Bowl following 1983 season; replaced due to injury by William Gay.

VERNON DEAN
Cornerback—Washington Redskins
Born May 5, 1959, at Los Angeles, Calif.
Height, 5.11. Weight, 178.
High School—Los Angeles, Calif.
Attended Los Angeles Valley Junior College, U.S. International University
and San Diego State University.

Selected by Washington in 2nd round (49th player selected) of 1982 NFL draft.

| | | —INTERCEPTIONS— | | | | |
Year	Club	G.	No.	Yds.	Avg.	TD.
1982—Washington NFL..........		9	3	62	20.7	0
1983—Washington NFL..........		16	5	54	10.8	0
1984—Washington NFL..........		16	7	114	16.3	*2
Pro Totals—3 Years............		41	15	230	15.3	2

Additional pro statistics: Recovered three fumbles (including one in end zone for a touchdown), 1983; recovered one fumble for six yards, 1984.
Played in NFC Championship Game following 1982 and 1983 seasons.
Played in NFL Championship Game following 1982 and 1983 seasons.

STEVE DeBERG
Quarterback—Tampa Bay Buccaneers
Born January 19, 1954, at Oakland, Calif.
Height, 6.03. Weight, 205.
High School—Anaheim, Calif., Savanna.
Attended Fullerton Junior College and received bachelor of science degree
from San Jose State University in 1980.

Selected by Dallas in 10th round (275th player selected) of 1977 NFL draft.
Claimed on waivers from Dallas Cowboys by San Francisco 49ers, September 12, 1977.
Traded by San Francisco 49ers to Denver Broncos for 4th round pick in 1983 draft, August 31, 1981.
USFL rights traded by Oakland Invaders to Denver Gold for rights to tight end John Thompson and offensive tackle Randy Van Divier, October 7, 1983.
On injured reserve with separated shoulder, November 16 through December 21, 1983; activated, December 22, 1983.
Granted free agency, February 1, 1984; re-signed by Broncos and traded to Tampa Bay Buccaneers for 4th round pick in 1984 draft and 2nd round pick in 1985 draft, April 24, 1984.
Active for 5 games with San Francisco 49ers in 1977; did not play.

Year Club	G.	Att.	Cmp.	Pct.	Gain	T.P.	P.I.	Avg.	Att.	Yds.	Avg.	TD.	TD.	Pts.	F.
1978—San Francisco NFL	12	302	137	45.4	1570	8	22	5.20	15	20	1.3	1	1	6	9
1979—San Francisco NFL	16	*578	*347	60.0	3652	17	21	6.32	17	10	0.6	0	0	0	6
1980—San Francisco NFL	11	321	186	57.9	1998	12	17	6.22	6	4	0.7	0	0	0	4
1981—Denver NFL	14	108	64	59.3	797	6	6	7.38	9	40	4.4	0	0	0	2
1982—Denver NFL	9	223	131	58.7	1405	7	11	6.30	8	27	3.4	1	1	6	4
1983—Denver NFL	10	215	119	55.3	1617	9	7	7.52	13	28	2.2	1	1	6	5
1984—Tampa Bay NFL	16	509	308	60.5	3554	19	18	6.98	28	59	2.1	2	2	12	15
Pro Totals—8 Years	88	2256	1292	57.3	14593	78	102	6.47	96	188	2.0	5	5	30	45

Quarterback Rating Points: 1978 (39.8), 1979 (73.1), 1980 (66.5), 1981 (77.6), 1982 (67.2), 1983 (79.9), 1984 (79.3). Total—69.7.

Additional pro statistics: Recovered two fumbles, 1978 and 1979; fumbled nine times for minus five yards, 1978; fumbled six times for minus 17 yards, 1979; fumbled four times for minus six yards, 1980; recovered two fumbles and fumbled 15 times for minus eight yards, 1984.

CHARLES RAY DeJURNETT
Name pronounced Dee-Scher-NAY.

Nose Tackle—Los Angeles Rams
Born June 17, 1952, at Picayune, Miss.
Height, 6.04. Weight, 260.
High School—Los Angeles, Calif., Crenshaw.
Attended West Los Angeles College and San Jose State University.

Selected by San Diego in 17th round (418th player selected) of 1974 NFL draft.
Signed as free agent by Southern California Sun (WFL), 1974.
Signed by San Diego Chargers after World Football League folded, 1976.
On injured reserve with broken leg, January 10 through remainder of 1980 season playoffs.
On physically unable to perform/active list with leg injury, July 24 through August 16, 1981.
On physically unable to perform/reserve list with leg injury, August 17 through November 4, 1981; transferred to injury reserve November 5 through remainder of 1981 season.
Released by San Diego Chargers, September 6, 1982; signed as free agent by Los Angeles Rams, November 26, 1982.
On injured reserve with pulled groin, September 6 through October 3, 1983; activated, October 4, 1983.
Southern California WFL, 1974 and 1975; San Diego NFL, 1976 through 1980; Los Angeles Rams NFL, 1982 through 1984.
Games: 1974 (20), 1975 (12), 1976 (13), 1977 (11), 1978 (15), 1979 (12), 1980 (15), 1981 (4), 1982 (4), 1983 (10), 1984 (16). Total WFL—32. Total NFL—100. Total Pro—132.
WFL statistics: Intercepted one pass for one yard and recovered one fumble, 1975.
NFL statistics: Recovered one fumble, 1980.

JOSEPH MICHAEL DeLAMIELLEURE
Name pronounced Deh-Lah-meh-LURE.

(Joe)
Guard—Cleveland Browns
Born March 16, 1951, at Detroit, Mich.
Height, 6.03. Weight, 260.
High School—Center Line, Mich., St. Clement.
Received bachelor of science degree in criminal justice from Michigan State University in 1973.
Uncle of Jeff DeLamielleure, safety at Cornell University.

Named to THE SPORTING NEWS AFC All-Star Team, 1975 through 1979.
Named to THE SPORTING NEWS NFL All-Star Team, 1980.
Named as guard on THE SPORTING NEWS College All-America Team, 1972.
Selected by Buffalo in 1st round (26th player selected) of 1973 NFL draft.
On did not report list, August 18 through August 31, 1980.
Traded by Buffalo Bills to Cleveland Browns for 2nd round pick in 1981 draft and 3rd round pick in 1982 draft, September 1, 1980.
Buffalo NFL, 1973 through 1979; Cleveland NFL, 1980 through 1984.
Games: 1973 (14), 1974 (14), 1975 (14), 1976 (14), 1977 (14), 1978 (16), 1979 (16), 1980 (16), 1981 (16), 1982 (9), 1983 (16), 1984 (16). Total—175.
Pro statistics: Recovered one fumble, 1973, 1974, 1977, 1978 and 1984; recovered two fumbles, 1976.
Played in Pro Bowl (NFL All-Star Game) following 1975 through 1980 seasons.

THOMAS DENNING DeLEONE
(Tom)
Center—Cleveland Browns

Born August 13, 1950, at Ravenna, O.
Height, 6.02. Weight, 254.
High School—Kent, O., Kent-Roosevelt.
Received bachelor of science degree in education from Ohio State University.

Named as center on THE SPORTING NEWS College All-America Team, 1971.
Selected by Cincinnati in 5th round (106th player selected) of 1972 NFL draft.
Traded with running back Haskel Stanback by Cincinnati Bengals to Atlanta Falcons for a 3rd round 1975 draft choice, August 21, 1974.
Claimed on waivers from Atlanta Falcons by Houston Oilers, September 17, 1974.
Released by Houston Oilers, September 21, 1974; signed as free agent by Cleveland Browns, September 26, 1974.
On injured reserve with broken ankle, October 29 through remainder of 1981 season.
Cincinnati NFL, 1972 and 1973; Cleveland NFL, 1974 through 1984.
Games: 1972 (13), 1973 (14), 1974 (12), 1975 (14), 1976 (14), 1977 (14), 1978 (16), 1979 (16), 1980 (16), 1981 (8), 1982 (9), 1983 (16), 1984 (15). Total—177.
Pro statistics: Recovered one fumble, 1978; fumbled once, 1983.
Played in Pro Bowl (NFL All-Star Game) following 1979 and 1980 seasons.

ALBERT LOUIS DEL GRECO
(Al)
Placekicker—Green Bay Packers

Born March 2, 1962, at Providence, R. I.
Height, 5.10. Weight, 195.
High School—Coral Gables, Fla.
Attended Auburn University.

Signed as free agent by Miami Dolphins, May 17, 1984.
Released by Miami Dolphins, August 27, 1984; signed as free agent by Green Bay Packers, October 17, 1984.

		———PLACE KICKING———					
Year	Club	G.	XP.	XPM.	FG.	FGA.	Pts.
1984—Green Bay NFL		9	34	0	9	12	61

MICHAEL DELLOCONO
Wide Receiver—New Orleans Saints

Born June 25, 1961, at Baton Rouge, La.
Height, 5.09. Weight, 176.
High School—Baton Rouge, La., Robert E. Lee.
Attended Louisiana Tech University.

Signed as free agent by New Orleans Saints, June 21, 1984.
On injured reserve with back injury, August 27 through entire 1984 season.

TONY LAWRENCE DE LUCA
Nose Tackle—Green Bay Packers

Born November 16, 1960, at Greenwich, Conn.
Height, 6.04. Weight, 250.
High Schools—Greenwich, Conn., and Milford, Conn., Academy.
Attended University of Rhode Island.

Signed as free agent by Los Angeles Rams, May 5, 1984.
Released by Los Angeles Rams, August 21, 1984; awarded on waivers to Green Bay Packers, August 22, 1984.
Released by Green Bay Packers, August 27, 1984; re-signed by Packers, December 12, 1984.
Green Bay NFL, 1984.
Games: 1984 (1).

MARK WESLEY DENNARD
Center—Philadelphia Eagles

Born November 2, 1955, at Bay City, Tex.
Height, 6.01. Weight, 252.
High School—Bay City, Tex.
Received bachelor of arts degree in marketing from Texas A&M University in 1978.

Selected by Miami in 10th round (274th player selected) of 1978 NFL draft.
On injured reserve with broken wrist, August 2 through entire 1978 season.
On injured reserve with calf injury, November 17 through December 17, 1981; activated, December 18, 1981.
On inactive list, September 12, 1982.
On injured reserve with shoulder injury, October 28 through remainder of 1983 season.
Traded by Miami Dolphins to Philadelphia Eagles for 3rd round pick in 1985 draft, March 7, 1984.
Miami NFL, 1979 through 1983; Philadelphia NFL, 1984.
Games: 1979 (16), 1980 (16), 1981 (11), 1982 (8), 1983 (8), 1984 (16). Total—75.
Pro statistics: Recovered one fumble, 1979 and 1980.
Played in AFC Championship Game following 1982 season.
Played in NFL Championship Game following 1982 season.

PRESTON JACKSON DENNARD
Wide Receiver—Buffalo Bills
Born November 28, 1955, at Cordele, Ga.
Height, 6.01. Weight, 183.
High Schools—Phoenix, Ariz., South Mountain and Tempe, Ariz., Marcos de Niza.
Attended University of New Mexico.
Brother of Glenn Dennard, wide receiver at Arizona State University.
Signed as free agent by Los Angeles Rams, May 16, 1978.
Released by Los Angeles Rams, August 22, 1978; re-signed by Rams, September 30, 1978.
Traded by Los Angeles Rams to Buffalo Bills for 5th round pick in 1985 draft, August 1, 1984.

Year Club	G.	P.C.	Yds.	Avg.	TD.
1978—L.A. Rams NFL.............	11	3	35	11.7	0
1979—L.A. Rams NFL.............	15	43	766	17.8	4
1980—L.A. Rams NFL.............	16	36	596	16.6	6
1981—L.A. Rams NFL.............	15	49	821	16.8	4
1982—L.A. Rams NFL.............	9	25	383	15.3	2
1983—L.A. Rams NFL.............	14	33	465	14.1	5
1984—Buffalo NFL..................	16	30	417	13.9	7
Pro Totals—7 Years............	96	219	3483	15.9	28

Additional pro statistics: Rushed four times for 32 yards, 1979; recovered one fumble, 1979 and 1981; fumbled once, 1979, 1981 and 1984; rushed twice for 20 yards and recovered two fumbles, 1980; rushed six times for 29 yards, 1981.
Played in NFC Championship Game following 1978 and 1979 seasons.
Played in NFL Championship Game following 1979 season.

MICHAEL D. DENNIS
(Mike)
Safety-Cornerback—New York Jets
Born June 6, 1958, at Los Angeles, Calif.
Height, 5.10. Weight, 195.
High School—Pasadena, Calif., John Muir.
Attended Pasadena City College and University of Wyoming.
Step-brother of Charles Phillips, safety with Oakland Raiders, 1975 through 1980.
Signed as free agent by New York Giants, June 9, 1980.
On injured reserve with knee injury, December 3 through remainder of 1980 season.
Released by New York Giants, August 27, 1984; awarded on waivers to Kansas City Chiefs, August 28, 1984.
Released by Kansas City Chiefs, August 30, 1984; signed as free agent by San Diego Chargers, October 4, 1984.
Released by San Diego Chargers, October 17, 1984; signed as free agent by New York Jets, November 23, 1984.

Year Club	G.	No.	Yds.	Avg.	TD.
1980—N.Y. Giants NFL	13	5	68	13.6	0
1981—N.Y. Giants NFL	16		None		
1982—N.Y. Giants NFL	9		None		
1983—N.Y. Giants NFL	16	1	0	0.0	0
1984—S.D. (2)-N.Y.J. (4) NFL	6		None		
Pro Totals—5 Years............	60	6	68	11.3	0

Additional pro statistics: Returned three kickoffs for 51 yards and recovered blocked punt in end zone for a touchdown, 1981; returned three kickoffs for 68 yards and recovered one fumble, 1982; returned one kickoff for 54 yards, 1983.

GLENN DENNISON
Tight End—New York Jets
Born November 17, 1961, at Beaver Falls, Pa.
Height, 6.03. Weight, 225.
High School—Beaver Falls, Pa.
Attended University of Miami (Fla.).
Selected by Houston in 3rd round (64th player selected) of 1984 USFL draft.
Selected by New York Jets in 2nd round (39th player selected) of 1984 NFL draft.
Signed by New York Jets, May 29, 1984.

Year Club	G.	P.C.	Yds.	Avg.	TD.
1984—N.Y. Jets NFL	16	16	141	8.8	1

Additional pro statistics: Rushed once for four yards, 1984.

RICK STEVEN DENNISON
Linebacker—Denver Broncos
Born June 22, 1958, at Kalispel, Mont.
Height, 6.03. Weight, 220.
High School—Fort Collins, Colo., Rocky Mountain.
Received bachelor of science degree in civil engineering from Colorado State University in 1980.
Signed as free agent by Buffalo Bills, May 9, 1980.
Released by Buffalo Bills, August 20, 1980; signed as free agent by Denver Broncos, December 29, 1980.
Released by Denver Broncos, August 31, 1981; signed as free agent by Buffalo Bills, February 26, 1982.
Released by Buffalo Bills, August 31, 1982; signed as free agent by Denver Broncos, September 7, 1982.

Denver NFL, 1982 through 1984.
Games: 1982 (9), 1983 (16), 1984 (16). Total—41.
Pro statistics: Returned two kickoffs for 27 yards and recovered one fumble, 1984.

RICHARD LAMAR DENT
Defensive End—Chicago Bears
Born December 13, 1960, at Atlanta, Ga.
Height, 6.05. Weight, 253.
High School—Atlanta, Ga., Murphy.
Attended Tennessee State University.

Selected by Philadelphia in 8th round (89th player selected) of 1983 USFL draft.
Selected by Chicago in 8th round (203rd player selected) of 1983 NFL draft.
Signed by Chicago Bears, May 12, 1983.
Chicago NFL, 1983 and 1984.
Games: 1983 (16), 1984 (16). Total—32.
Pro statistics: Recovered one fumble, 1984.
Played in NFC Championship Game following 1984 season.
Played in Pro Bowl (NFL All-Star Game) following 1984 season.

STEVE LEONARD DeOSSIE
Linebacker—Dallas Cowboys
Born November 22, 1962, at Tacoma, Wash.
Height, 6.02. Weight, 248.
High School—Boston, Mass., Don Bosco Technical.
Received bachelor of science degree in communications from Boston College in 1984.

Selected by New Jersey in 1st round (14th player selected) of 1984 USFL draft.
Selected by Dallas in 4th round (110th player selected) of 1984 NFL draft.
Signed by Dallas Cowboys, May 3, 1984.
Dallas NFL, 1984.
Games: 1984 (16).

WILLIAM HENRY DEVANE JR.
Nose Tackle—Buffalo Bills
Born May 28, 1962, at Jacksonville, N. C.
Height, 6.02. Weight, 275.
High School—Jacksonville, N. C.
Attended Clemson University.

Selected by Miami in 12th round (320th player selected) of 1984 NFL draft.
Released by Miami Dolphins, August 21, 1984; signed as free agent by Buffalo Bills, March 20, 1985.

JOSEPH DEVLIN
(Joe)
Offensive Tackle—Buffalo Bills
Born February 23, 1954 at Phoenixville, Pa.
Height, 6.05. Weight, 250.
High School—Frazer, Pa., Great Valley.
Attended University of Iowa.

Named as guard on THE SPORTING NEWS College All-America Team, 1975.
Selected by Buffalo in 2nd round (52nd player selected) of 1976 NFL draft.
On injured reserve with knee injury, December 13 through remainder of 1978 season.
On injured reserve with broken ankle, August 22 through entire 1983 season.
Buffalo NFL, 1976 through 1982 and 1984.
Games: 1976 (14), 1977 (14), 1978 (14), 1979 (16), 1980 (16), 1981 (16), 1982 (9), 1984 (16). Total—115.
Pro statistics: Recovered one fumble, 1978 and 1982; recovered two fumbles, 1979.

ANTHONY CHARLES DICKERSON
Linebacker—Dallas Cowboys
Born June 9, 1957, at Texas City, Tex.
Height, 6.02. Weight, 219.
High School—Pearland, Tex.
Attended Henderson County Junior College and Southern Methodist University.

Signed as free agent by Calgary Stampeders, April, 1978.
Released by Calgary Stampeders, August 20, 1978; signed as free agent by Toronto Argonauts, September 28, 1978.
Released by Toronto Argonauts, October 6, 1978; signed as free agent by Dallas Cowboys, May 15, 1980.

| | | —INTERCEPTIONS— | | | |
Year Club	G.	No.	Yds.	Avg.	TD.
1978—Cal.(2)-Tor. (1) CFL.....	3	1	0	0.0	0
1980—Dallas NFL	16	2	46	23.0	0
1981—Dallas NFL	16		None		
1982—Dallas NFL	9	1	4	4.0	0
1983—Dallas NFL	16	1	8	8.0	0
1984—Dallas NFL	16	1	0	0.0	0
CFL Totals—1 Year	3	1	0	0.0	0
NFL Totals—5 Years..........	73	5	58	11.6	0
Pro Totals—6 Years...........	76	6	58	9.7	0

Additional CFL statistics: Returned one kickoff for no yards and recovered one fumble, 1978.
Additional NFL statistics: Recovered one fumble, 1980 and 1984; recovered two fumbles, 1981; credited with one safety and recovered three fumbles, 1983.
Played in NFC Championship Game following 1980 through 1982 seasons.

ERIC DEMETRIC DICKERSON
Running Back—Los Angeles Rams
Born September 2, 1960, at Sealy, Tex.
Height, 6.03. Weight, 218.
High School—Sealy, Tex.
Attended Southern Methodist University.
Cousin of Robert Dickerson, running back at University of Texas at El Paso.

Named as running back on THE SPORTING NEWS College All-America Team, 1982.
Named THE SPORTING NEWS NFL Player of the Year, 1983.
Named to THE SPORTING NEWS NFL All-Star Team, 1983 and 1984.
Established NFL records for most yards rushing by rookie (1,808), 1983; most touchdowns rushing by rookie (18), 1983; most yards rushing, season (2,105), 1984; most combined yards, season (2,244), 1984; most games, 100 yards rushing, season (12), 1984.
Selected by Arizona in 1st round (6th player selected) of 1983 USFL draft.
Selected by Los Angeles Rams in 1st round (2nd player selected) of 1983 NFL draft.
Signed by Los Angeles Rams, July 12, 1983.

		——RUSHING——				PASS RECEIVING				—TOTAL—		
Year Club	G.	Att.	Yds.	Avg.	TD.	P.C.	Yds.	Avg.	TD.	TD.	Pts.	F.
1983—Los Angeles Rams NFL	16	*390	*1808	4.6	18	51	404	7.9	2	20	120	13
1984—Los Angeles Rams NFL	16	379	*2105	5.6	*14	21	139	6.6	0	14	84	14
Pro Totals—2 Years	32	769	3913	5.1	32	72	543	7.5	2	34	204	27

Additional pro statistics: Recovered one fumble, 1983; attempted one pass with one interception and recovered four fumbles, 1984.
Played in Pro Bowl (NFL All-Star Game) following 1983 and 1984 seasons.

CLIFFORD LYNN DICKEY
(Known by middle name.)
Quarterback—Green Bay Packers
Born October 19, 1949, at Paola, Kan.
Height, 6.04. Weight, 203.
High School—Osawatomie, Kan.
Received bachelor of science degree in physical education from Kansas State University in 1971.

Selected by Houston in 3rd round (56th player selected) of 1971 NFL draft.
Missed entire season due to hip injury, 1972.
Traded by Houston Oilers to Green Bay Packers for quarterback John Hadl, defensive back Ken Ellis, two draft choices (4th round pick in 1976 and 3rd round pick in 1977) and cash, April 2, 1976.
Placed on physically unable to perform list with broken leg, July 21, 1978; transferred to injured reserve, October 4, 1978.

		——————PASSING——————							——RUSHING——				—TOTAL—		
Year Club	G.	Att.	Cmp.	Pct.	Gain	T.P.	P.I.	Avg.	Att.	Yds.	Avg.	TD.	TD.	Pts.	F.
1971—Houston NFL	6	57	19	33.3	315	0	9	5.53	1	4	4.0	0	0	0	1
1973—Houston NFL	14	120	71	59.2	888	6	10	7.40	6	9	1.5	0	0	†1	5
1974—Houston NFL	14	113	63	55.8	704	2	8	6.23	3	7	2.3	0	0	0	2
1975—Houston NFL	14	4	2	50.0	46	1	4	11.50	1	3	3.0	0	0	0	0
1976—Green Bay NFL	10	243	115	47.3	1465	7	14	6.03	11	19	1.8	1	1	6	7
1977—Green Bay NFL	9	220	113	51.4	1346	5	14	6.12	5	24	4.8	0	0	0	1
1979—Green Bay NFL	5	119	60	50.4	787	5	4	6.61	5	13	2.6	0	0	0	2
1980—Green Bay NFL	16	478	278	58.2	3529	15	25	7.38	19	11	0.6	1	1	6	13
1981—Green Bay NFL	13	354	204	57.6	2593	17	15	7.32	19	6	0.3	0	0	0	8
1982—Green Bay NFL	9	218	124	56.9	1790	12	14	8.21	13	19	1.5	0	0	0	5
1983—Green Bay NFL	16	484	289	59.7	*4458	*32	*29	*9.21	21	12	0.6	3	3	18	9
1984—Green Bay NFL	15	401	237	59.1	3195	25	19	7.97	18	6	0.3	3	3	18	3
Pro Totals—12 Years	141	2811	1575	56.0	21116	126	162	7.51	122	133	1.1	8	8	49	56

Quarterback Rating Points: 1971 (13.3), 1973 (64.3), 1974 (51.0), 1975 (52.1), 1976 (52.1), 1977 (51.4), 1979 (71.5), 1980 (70.0), 1981 (79.1), 1982 (75.4), 1983 (87.3), 1984 (85.6). Total—70.9.
†Scored an extra point.
Additional pro statistics: Recovered three fumbles, 1976 and 1981; recovered one fumble and fumbled twice for minus one yard, 1979; recovered five fumbles and fumbled 13 times for minus seven yards, 1980; fumbled eight times for minus 26 yards, 1981; recovered two fumbles and fumbled five times for minus one yard, 1982; recovered six fumbles, 1983; recovered one fumble and fumbled three times for minus 11 yards, 1984.

CURTIS RAY DICKEY
Running Back—Indianapolis Colts
Born November 27, 1956, at Madisonville, Tex.
Height, 6.00. Weight, 222.
High School—Bryan, Tex.
Attended Texas A&M University.

Selected by Baltimore in 1st round (5th player selected) of 1980 NFL draft.
On inactive list, September 19, 1982.
Franchise transferred to Indianapolis, March 31, 1984.
On injured reserve with knee injury, December 13 through remainder of 1984 season.

Year Club	G.	RUSHING				PASS RECEIVING				TOTAL		
		Att.	Yds.	Avg.	TD.	P.C.	Yds.	Avg.	TD.	TD.	Pts.	F.
1980—Baltimore NFL	15	176	800	4.5	11	25	204	8.2	2	13	78	3
1981—Baltimore NFL	15	164	779	4.8	7	37	419	11.3	3	10	60	8
1982—Baltimore NFL	8	66	232	3.5	1	21	228	10.9	0	1	6	3
1983—Baltimore NFL	16	254	1122	4.4	4	24	483	20.1	3	7	42	9
1984—Indianapolis NFL	10	131	523	4.0	3	14	135	9.6	0	3	18	6
Pro Totals—5 Years	64	791	3456	4.4	26	121	1469	12.1	8	34	204	29

Additional pro statistics: Returned four kickoffs for 86 yards, 1980; recovered one fumble, 1983 and 1984; attempted one pass with one completion for 63 yards and a touchdown, 1984.

CLINT DIDIER
Tight End—Washington Redskins
Born July 14, 1959, at Connell, Wash.
Height, 6.05. Weight, 240.
High School—Connell, Wash.
Attended Columbia Basin Junior College and Portland State University.

Selected by Washington in 12th round (314th player selected) of 1981 NFL draft.
On injured reserve with pulled hamstring, August 18 through entire 1981 season.
On injured reserve with fractured leg, August 28 through September 28, 1984; activated, September 29, 1984.

Year Club	PASS RECEIVING				
	G.	P.C.	Yds.	Avg.	TD.
1982—Washington NFL	8	2	10	5.0	1
1983—Washington NFL	16	9	153	17.0	4
1984—Washington NFL	11	30	350	11.7	5
Pro Totals—3 Years	35	41	513	12.5	10

Additional pro statistics: Recovered one fumble in end zone for a touchdown and fumbled once, 1983.
Played in NFC Championship Game following 1982 and 1983 seasons.
Played in NFL Championship Game following 1982 and 1983 seasons.

SCOTT EDWARD DIERKING
Name pronounced DIR-king.
Running Back—Tampa Bay Buccaneers
Born May 24, 1955, at Great Lakes Naval Base, Ill.
Height, 5.10. Weight, 220.
High School—West Chicago, Ill.
Received bachelor of science degree in economics from Purdue University in 1977.

Selected by New York Jets in 4th round (90th player selected) of 1977 NFL draft.
Traded by New York Jets to Tampa Bay Buccaneers for 5th round pick in 1985 draft, April 17, 1984.
On injured reserve with knee injury, August 28 through October 4, 1984; activated, October 5, 1984.

Year Club	G.	RUSHING				PASS RECEIVING				TOTAL		
		Att.	Yds.	Avg.	TD.	P.C.	Yds.	Avg.	TD.	TD.	Pts.	F.
1977—New York Jets NFL	14	79	315	4.0	0	4	29	7.3	1	1	6	1
1978—New York Jets NFL	15	170	681	4.0	4	19	152	8.0	0	4	24	2
1979—New York Jets NFL	16	186	767	4.1	3	10	121	12.1	0	3	18	1
1980—New York Jets NFL	16	156	567	3.6	6	19	138	7.3	1	7	42	3
1981—New York Jets NFL	16	74	328	4.4	1	26	228	8.8	1	2	12	2
1982—New York Jets NFL	9	38	130	3.4	1	12	80	6.7	1	2	12	2
1983—New York Jets NFL	16	28	113	4.0	3	33	275	8.3	0	3	18	0
1984—Tampa Bay NFL	8	3	14	4.7	0	1	5	5.0	1	1	6	0
Pro Totals—8 Years	110	734	2915	4.0	18	124	1028	8.3	5	23	138	11

Additional pro statistics: Returned six kickoffs for 91 yards, 1977; recovered one fumble, 1978, 1979, 1981 and 1982; attempted one pass with no completions, 1978; fumbled once, 1979; recovered two fumbles, 1980.
Played in AFC Championship Game following 1982 season.

CHRISTIAN JEFFERY DIETERICH
Name pronounced DEE-trick.
(Chris)
Guard—Detroit Lions
Born July 27, 1958, at Freeport, N.Y.
Height, 6.03. Weight, 260.
High School—East Setauket, N.Y., Ward Melville.
Attended North Carolina State University and Suffolk Community College.

Selected by Detroit in 6th round (140th player selected) of 1980 NFL draft.
Released by Detroit Lions, August 26, 1980; re-signed by Lions, October 15, 1980.
On injured reserve with knee injury, November 18 through remainder of 1981 season.
Detroit NFL, 1980 through 1984.
Games: 1980 (8), 1981 (7), 1982 (5), 1983 (16), 1984 (16). Total—52.
Pro statistics: Recovered one fumble, 1980 and 1983.

—DID YOU KNOW—
That the 1984 Miami Dolphins set NFL records for most touchdowns in a season with 70 and most touchdowns passes with 49?

STEPHEN WHITFIELD DILS
(Steve)
Quarterback—Los Angeles Rams

Born December 8, 1955, at Seattle, Wash.
Height, 6.01. Weight, 195.
High School—Vancouver, Wash., Fort Vancouver.
Received bachelor of arts degree in economics from Stanford University in 1979.

Selected by Minnesota in 4th round (97th player selected) of 1979 NFL draft.
Traded by Minnesota Vikings to Los Angeles Rams for 4th round pick in 1985 draft, September 18, 1984.

Year Club	G.	Att.	Cmp.	Pct.	Gain	T.P.	P.I.	Avg.	Att.	Yds.	Avg.	TD.	TD.	Pts.	F.
				—PASSING—						—RUSHING—			—TOTAL—		
1979—Minnesota NFL	1			None							None		0	0	0
1980—Minnesota NFL	16	51	32	62.7	352	3	0	6.90	3	26	8.7	0	0	0	0
1981—Minnesota NFL	2	102	54	52.9	607	1	2	5.95	4	14	3.5	0	0	0	3
1982—Minnesota NFL	9	26	11	42.3	68	0	0	2.62	1	5	5.0	0	0	0	0
1983—Minnesota NFL	16	444	239	53.8	2840	11	16	6.40	16	28	1.8	0	0	0	13
1984—Min. (3)-Rams (7) NFL	10	7	4	57.1	44	1	1	6.29			None		0	0	0
Pro Totals—6 Years	54	630	340	54.0	3911	16	19	6.21	24	73	3.0	0	0	0	16

Quarterback Rating Points: 1980 (102.8), 1981 (66.0), 1982 (49.8), 1983 (66.8), 1984 (75.9). Total—68.8.
Additional pro statistics: Recovered two fumbles. 1981; recovered six fumbles, 1983.

DWAYNE DIXON
Wide Receiver—Tampa Bay Buccaneers

Born August 2, 1962, at Alachua, Fla.
Height, 6.02. Weight, 207.
High School—Alachua, Fla., Santa Fe.
Attended University of Florida.
Brother of Hewritt Dixon, fullback-tight end with Denver Broncos
and Oakland Raiders, 1963 through 1970.

Selected by Tampa Bay in 1984 USFL territorial draft.
Signed as free agent by Kansas City Chiefs, June 20, 1984.
Released by Kansas City Chiefs, August 13, 1984; signed as free agent by Tampa Bay Buccaneers, October 9, 1984.

		—PASS RECEIVING—			
Year Club	G.	P.C.	Yds.	Avg.	TD.
1984—Tampa Bay NFL	10	5	69	13.8	0

HANFORD DIXON
Cornerback—Cleveland Browns

Born December 25, 1958, at Mobile, Ala.
Height, 5.11. Weight, 182.
High School—Theodore, Ala.
Attended University of Southern Mississippi.
Cousin of Lyneal Alston, wide receiver at University of Southern Mississippi.

Named as defensive back on THE SPORTING NEWS College All-America Team, 1980.
Selected by Cleveland in 1st round (22nd player selected) of 1981 NFL draft.

		—INTERCEPTIONS—			
Year Club	G.	No.	Yds.	Avg.	TD.
1981—Cleveland NFL	16		None		
1982—Cleveland NFL	9	4	22	5.5	0
1983—Cleveland NFL	16	3	41	13.7	0
1984—Cleveland NFL	16	5	31	6.2	0
Pro Totals—4 Years	57	12	94	7.8	0

Additional pro statistics: Fumbled once, 1982; recovered one fumble, 1984.

THOMAS MICHAEL DIXON
(Tom)
Offensive Lineman—Pittsburgh Steelers

Born August 21, 1961, at Chicago, Ill.
Height, 6.02. Weight, 247.
High School—Fort Wayne, Ind., Bishop Dwenger.
Attended University of Michigan.

Named as center on THE SPORTING NEWS College All-America Team, 1983.
Selected by Michigan in 1984 USFL territorial draft.
Signed by Michigan Panthers and granted roster exemption, April 20 through June 5, 1984; activated, June 6, 1984.
Selected by Pittsburgh in 2nd round (52nd player selected) of 1984 NFL supplemental draft.
On developmental squad, June 18 through remainder of 1984 season.
Not protected in merger of Oakland Invaders and Michigan Panthers; selected by Oakland Invaders in USFL dispersal draft, December 6, 1984.
Released by Oakland Invaders, January 28, 1985; signed by Pittsburgh Steelers, May 9, 1985.
Active for 1 game with Michigan Panthers in 1984; did not play.
On developmental squad for 1 game with Michigan Panthers in 1984.

ZACHARY DIXON
(Zack)
Running Back—Seattle Seahawks
Born March 5, 1956, at Dorchester, Mass.
Height, 6.01. Weight, 204.
High School—Dorchester, Mass.
Attended Dean Junior College and Temple University.

Selected by Denver in 11th round (297th player selected) of 1979 NFL draft.
Released by Denver Broncos, August 20, 1979; re-signed by Broncos, September 19, 1979.
Released by Denver Broncos, October 26, 1979; signed as free agent by New York Giants, December 1, 1979.
Claimed on waivers from New York Giants by Philadelphia Eagles, May 15, 1980.
On injured reserve with knee injury, October 7 through November 15, 1980.
Released by Philadelphia Eagles, November 16, 1980; signed as free agent by Baltimore Colts, December 19, 1980.
Released by Baltimore Colts, September 14, 1983; signed as free agent by Seattle Seahawks, September 21, 1983.
On injured reserve with knee injury, December 21 through remainder of 1984 season.

		—RUSHING—				PASS RECEIVING				—TOTAL—		
Year Club	G.	Att.	Yds.	Avg.	TD.	P.C.	Yds.	Avg.	TD.	TD.	Pts.	F.
1979—Denver (5)-N.Y.G. (3) NFL	8	3	9	3.0	0		None			0	0	1
1980—Philadelphia (5)-Baltimore (1) NFL	6	2	8	4.0	0	1	5	5.0	0	0	0	0
1981—Baltimore NFL	16	73	285	3.9	0	17	169	9.9	1	1	6	1
1982—Baltimore NFL	9	58	249	4.3	1	20	185	9.3	0	1	6	2
1983—Baltimore (2)-Seattle (13) NFL	15	9	32	3.6	0	1	2	2.0	0	1	6	1
1984—Seattle NFL	13	52	149	2.9	2	2	6	3.0	0	2	12	1
Pro Totals—6 Years	67	197	732	3.7	3	41	367	9.0	1	5	30	6

		KICKOFF RETURNS			
Year Club	G.	No.	Yds.	Avg.	TD.
1979—Den (5)-NYG (3) NFL.	8	3	53	17.7	0
1980—Phil (5)-Bal (1) NFL	6	2	30	15.0	0
1981—Baltimore NFL	16	36	737	20.5	0
1982—Baltimore NFL	9	11	197	17.9	0
1983—Balt. (2)-Sea. (13) NFL	15	*51	*1171	23.0	*1
1984—Seattle NFL	13	25	446	17.8	0
Pro Totals—6 Years	67	128	2634	20.6	1

Additional pro statistics: Recovered one fumble, 1983; returned one punt for five yards, 1984.
Played in AFC Championship Game following 1983 season.

KIRK DODGE
Linebacker—Detroit Lions
Born June 4, 1962, at Whittier, Calif.
Height, 6.01. Weight, 231.
High School—San Francisco, Calif., Lowell.
Attended Fullerton College and University of Nevada at Las Vegas.

Selected by Los Angeles in 6th round (112th player selected) of 1984 USFL draft.
Selected by Atlanta in 7th round (175th player selected) of 1984 NFL draft.
Signed by Atlanta Falcons, June 10, 1984.
Released by Atlanta Falcons, August 26, 1984; signed as free agent by Detroit Lions, October 2, 1984
Detroit NFL, 1984.
Games: 1984 (11).
Pro statistics: Recovered one fumble, 1984.

STEPHEN C. DOIG
(Steve)
Linebacker—Detroit Lions
Born March 28, 1960, at Melrose, Mass.
Height, 6.02. Weight, 242.
High School—North Reading, Mass.
Attended University of New Hampshire.

Selected by Detroit in 3rd round (69th player selected) of 1982 NFL draft.
On injured reserve with ankle injury, October 8 through November 11, 1983; activated, November 12, 1983.
Detroit NFL, 1982 through 1984.
Games: 1982 (9), 1983 (9), 1984 (16). Total—34.

PAUL MATTHEW DOMBROSKI
Cornerback—New England Patriots
Born August 8, 1956, at Sumter, S. C.
Height, 6.00. Weight, 185.
High School—Wahiawa, Hawaii, Lei-Le-Hall.
Attended Linfield College.

Signed as free agent by Kansas City Chiefs, May 10, 1980.
On injured reserve with shoulder injury, October 9 through November 10, 1981; claimed on procedural waivers by New England Patriots, November 12, 1981.
On injured reserve with concussion, September 6 through November 3, 1983; activated, November 4, 1983.
USFL rights traded by Memphis Showboats to Pittsburgh Maulers for rights to defensive back Mark Young, January 30, 1984.

Released by New England Patriots, August 27, 1984; re-signed by Patriots, August 28, 1984.
On injured reserve with knee injury, December 8 through remainder of 1984 season.

Year Club	G.	No.	Yds.	Avg.	TD.
1980—Kansas City NFL..........	16	1	6	6.0	0
1981—K.C.(5)-N.E.(6) NFL......	11		None		
1982—New England NFL.......	9		None		
1983—New England NFL.......	7		None		
1984—New England NFL.......	14	1	23	23.0	0
Pro Totals—5 Years............	57	2	29	14.5	0

——INTERCEPTIONS——

Additional pro statistics: Returned three kickoffs for 66 yards, 1981; returned one kickoff for 19 yards and recovered one fumble, 1982.

JEFF DONALDSON
Safety—Houston Oilers
Born April 19, 1962, at Fort Collins, Colo.
Height, 6.00. Weight, 193.
High School—Fort Collins, Colo.
Attended University of Colorado.

Selected by Denver in 1984 USFL territorial draft.
Selected by Houston in 9th round (228th player selected) of 1984 NFL draft.
Signed by Houston Oilers, July 17, 1984.
Houston NFL, 1984.
Games: 1984 (16).

RAY CANUTE DONALDSON
Center—Indianapolis Colts
Born May 18, 1958, at Rome, Ga.
Height, 6.04. Weight, 269.
High School—Rome, Ga., East.
Attended University of Georgia.
Step-brother of John Tutt, outfielder in Baltimore Orioles' organization.

Selected by Baltimore in 2nd round (32nd player selected) of 1980 NFL draft.
Franchise transferred to Indianapolis, March 31, 1984.
Baltimore NFL, 1980 through 1983; Indianapolis NFL, 1984.
Games: 1980 (16), 1981 (16), 1982 (9), 1983 (16), 1984 (16). Total—73.
Pro statistics: Recovered one fumble, 1981 and 1982; fumbled once, 1983.

DOUG DONLEY
Wide Receiver
Born February 6, 1959, at Cambridge, O.
Height, 6.00. Weight, 178.
High School—Cambridge, O.
Attended Ohio State University.

Selected by Dallas in 2nd round (53rd player selected) of 1981 NFL draft.
Not invited to Dallas Cowboys camp but not officially released, May, 1985.

Year Club	G.	P.C.	Yds.	Avg.	TD.
1981—Dallas NFL	11	3	32	10.7	0
1982—Dallas NFL	6	2	23	11.5	0
1983—Dallas NFL	11	18	370	20.6	2
1984—Dallas NFL	15	32	473	14.8	2
Pro Totals—4 Years............	43	55	898	16.3	4

——PASS RECEIVING——

Additional pro statistics: Returned one punt for three yards, 1981; returned eight kickoffs for 151 yards, one punt for 14 yards and fumbled twice, 1982; returned one punt for one yard, 1983; rushed twice for five yards, 1984.
Played in NFC Championship Game following 1981 and 1982 seasons.

WILLIAM FREDERICK DONNALLEY
(Rick)
Center-Guard—Washington Redskins
Born December 11, 1958, at Wilmington, Del.
Height, 6.02. Weight, 257.
High School—Raleigh, N.C., Sanderson.
Received bachelor of science degree in business administration from
University of North Carolina in 1981.

Selected by Pittsburgh in 3rd round (73rd player selected) of 1981 NFL draft.
On injured reserve with broken hand, August 25 through entire 1981 season.
Traded by Pittsburgh Steelers to Washington Redskins for 5th round pick in 1985 draft, August 20, 1984.
Pittsburgh NFL, 1982 and 1983; Washington NFL, 1984.
Games: 1982 (5), 1983 (16), 1984 (15). Total—36.
Pro statistics: Returned one kickoff for eight yards, 1982; ran two yards with lateral on kickoff return, 1983.

DANIEL E. DOORNINK
(Dan)
Fullback—Seattle Seahawks

Born February 1, 1956, at Yakima, Wash.
Height, 6.03. Weight, 210.
High School—Wapato, Wash.
Received degree from Washington State University; attending
medical school at University of Washington.

Selected by New York Giants in 7th round (174th player selected) of 1978 NFL draft.
Traded by New York Giants to Seattle Seahawks for 7th round pick in 1980 draft, August 21, 1979.

Year Club	G.	Att.	Yds.	Avg.	TD.	P.C.	Yds.	Avg.	TD.	TD.	Pts.	F.
		RUSHING				PASS RECEIVING				TOTAL		
1978—New York Giants NFL	12	60	306	5.1	1	12	66	5.5	0	1	6	2
1979—Seattle NFL	16	152	500	3.3	8	54	432	8.0	1	9	54	6
1980—Seattle NFL	15	100	344	3.4	3	31	237	7.6	2	5	30	2
1981—Seattle NFL	15	65	194	3.0	1	27	350	13.0	4	5	30	3
1982—Seattle NFL	8	45	178	4.0	0	22	176	8.0	0	0	0	2
1983—Seattle NFL	16	40	99	2.5	2	24	328	13.7	2	4	24	1
1984—Seattle NFL	16	57	215	3.8	0	31	365	11.8	2	2	12	0
Pro Totals—7 Years	98	519	1836	3.5	15	201	1954	9.7	11	26	156	16

Additional pro statistics: Returned one kickoff for 13 yards, 1979; recovered one fumble, 1980 through 1983; punted once for 54 yards, 1982.

Played in AFC Championship Game following 1983 season.

KEITH ROBERT DORNEY
Offensive Tackle—Detroit Lions

Born December 3, 1957, at Allentown, Pa.
Height, 6.05. Weight, 265.
High School—Emmaus, Pa.
Received bachelor of science degree in business from Penn State University in 1979.

Named as offensive tackle on THE SPORTING NEWS College All-America Team, 1978.
Selected by Detroit in 1st round (10th player selected) of 1979 NFL draft.
On injured reserve with knee injury, October 15 through December 5, 1980; activated, December 6, 1980.
Detroit NFL, 1979 through 1984.
Games: 1979 (16), 1980 (9), 1981 (16), 1982 (9), 1983 (13), 1984 (16). Total—79.
Pro statistics: Recovered one fumble, 1981.
Played in Pro Bowl (NFL All-Star Game) following 1982 season.

ANTHONY DREW DORSETT

Name pronounced Dor-SETT.

(Tony)
Running Back—Dallas Cowboys

Born April 7, 1954, at Rochester, Pa.
Height, 5.11. Weight, 189.
High School—Aliquippa, Pa., Hopewell.
Attended University of Pittsburgh.

Established NFL record for longest run from scrimmage (99 yards), January 3, 1983, against Minnesota Vikings.
Named THE SPORTING NEWS NFC Rookie of the Year, 1977.
Named to THE SPORTING NEWS NFL All-Star Team, 1981.
Named as running back on THE SPORTING NEWS College All-America Team, 1976.
Named THE SPORTING NEWS College Player of the Year, 1976.
Heisman Trophy winner, 1976.
Selected by Dallas in 1st round (2nd player selected) of 1977 NFL draft.

Year Club	G.	Att.	Yds.	Avg.	TD.	P.C.	Yds.	Avg.	TD.	TD.	Pts.	F.
		RUSHING				PASS RECEIVING				TOTAL		
1977—Dallas NFL	14	208	1007	4.8	12	29	273	9.4	1	13	78	7
1978—Dallas NFL	16	290	1325	4.6	7	37	378	10.2	2	10	60	12
1979—Dallas NFL	14	250	1107	4.4	6	45	375	8.3	1	7	42	9
1980—Dallas NFL	15	278	1185	4.3	11	34	263	7.7	0	11	66	8
1981—Dallas NFL	16	342	1646	4.8	4	32	325	10.2	2	6	36	10
1982—Dallas NFL	9	*177	745	4.2	5	24	179	7.5	0	5	30	6
1983—Dallas NFL	16	289	1321	4.6	8	40	287	7.2	1	9	54	5
1984—Dallas NFL	16	302	1189	3.9	6	51	459	9.0	1	7	42	12
Pro Totals—8 Years	116	2136	9525	4.5	59	292	2539	8.7	8	68	408	69

Additional pro statistics: Attempted one pass with one completion for 34 yards, 1977; recovered four fumbles for 54 yards and one touchdown, 1978; attempted one pass with no completions, 1978, 1980, 1982 and 1983; recovered one fumble, 1979, 1980 and 1982 through 1984; recovered two fumbles, 1981; attempted one pass with one interception, 1984.

Played in NFC Championship Game following 1977, 1978 and 1980 through 1982 seasons.
Played in NFL Championship Game following 1977 and 1978 seasons.
Played in Pro Bowl (NFL All-Star Game) following 1978 and 1981 through 1983 seasons.

—DID YOU KNOW—

That the AFC Central was the only division without a 1,000-yard rusher in 1984? Each of the other five divisions had at least two running backs accomplish the feat.

JOHN DORSEY
Linebacker—Green Bay Packers
Born August 31, 1960, at Leonardtown, Md.
Height, 6.02. Weight, 235.
High School—Leonardtown, Md., Fort Union.
Attended University of Connecticut.

Selected by Philadelphia in 7th round (142nd player selected) of 1984 USFL draft.
Selected by Green Bay in 4th round (99th player selected) of 1984 NFL draft.
Signed by Green Bay Packers, July 12, 1984.
Green Bay NFL, 1984.
Games: 1984 (16).

REGINALD LEE DOSS
(Reggie)
Defensive End—Los Angeles Rams
Born December 7, 1956, at Mobile, Ala.
Height, 6.04. Weight, 263.
High School—San Antonio, Tex., Sam Houston.
Attended Hampton Institute.

Selected by Los Angeles in 7th round (189th player selected) of 1978 NFL draft.
Los Angeles Rams NFL, 1978 through 1984.
Games: 1978 (16), 1979 (16), 1980 (16), 1981 (16), 1982 (9), 1983 (16), 1984 (16). Total—105.
Pro statistics: Recovered one fumble, 1980 through 1984.
Played in NFC Championship Game following 1978 and 1979 seasons.
Played in NFL Championship Game following 1979 season.

MICHAEL REESE DOUGLASS
(Mike)
Linebacker—Green Bay Packers
Born March 15, 1955, at St. Louis, Mo.
Height, 6.00. Weight, 214.
High School—Los Angeles, Calif., Jordan.
Attended Arizona State University, Los Angeles City College and
San Diego State University.

Selected by Green Bay in 5th round (116th player selected) of 1978 NFL draft.
On suspended list, November 30 through December 4, 1983; reinstated, December 5, 1983.

Year Club	G.	No.	Yds.	Avg.	TD.
			—INTERCEPTIONS—		
1978—Green Bay NFL............	16		None		
1979—Green Bay NFL............	16	3	73	24.3	0
1980—Green Bay NFL............	16		None		
1981—Green Bay NFL............	16	3	20	6.7	0
1982—Green Bay NFL............	9	2	55	27.5	0
1983—Green Bay NFL............	15		None		
1984—Green Bay NFL............	16		None		
Pro Totals—7 Years............	104	8	148	18.5	0

Additional pro statistics: Recovered two fumbles, 1978, 1980 and 1984; recovered three fumbles, 1981; recovered one fumble for six yards, 1982; recovered four fumbles for 57 yards and two touchdowns, 1983.

DONALD M. DOW
(Don)
Offensive Tackle—San Francisco 49ers
Born August 15, 1960, at Seattle, Wash.
Height, 6.06. Weight, 280.
High School—Bainbridge Island, Wash.
Received bachelor of arts degree in sociology from University of Washington.

Selected by Philadelphia in 10th round (113th player selected) of 1983 USFL draft.
Selected by Seattle in 12th round (317th player selected) of 1983 NFL draft.
Signed by Seattle Seahawks, May 9, 1983.
Released by Seattle Seahawks, August 16, 1983; signed by Philadelphia Stars, October 21, 1983.
Released injured by Philadelphia Stars, January 30, 1984; signed as free agent by San Francisco 49ers, May 10, 1984.
On injured reserve with pinched nerve in neck, August 21 through entire 1984 season.

MICHAEL LYNN DOWNS
(Mike)
Safety—Dallas Cowboys
Born June 9, 1959, at Dallas, Tex.
Height, 6.03. Weight, 195.
High School—Dallas, Tex., South Oak Cliff.
Received degree in business and political science from Rice University in 1981.

Signed as free agent by Dallas Cowboys, May, 1981.

Year Club	—INTERCEPTIONS—				
	G.	No.	Yds.	Avg.	TD.
1981—Dallas NFL	15	7	81	11.6	0
1982—Dallas NFL	9	1	22	22.0	0
1983—Dallas NFL	16	4	80	20.0	0
1984—Dallas NFL	16	7	126	18.0	1
Pro Totals—4 Years...........	56	19	309	16.3	1

Additional pro statistics: Recovered one fumble, 1981; recovered three fumbles for 87 yards and one touchdown, 1982; recovered two fumbles for 10 yards and a touchdown, 1983; recovered two fumbles for 28 yards, 1984.

Played in NFC Championship Game following 1981 and 1982 seasons.

DAVID DRECHSLER
(Dave)
Guard—Green Bay Packers

Born July 18, 1960, at Cleveland, N.C.
Height, 6.03. Weight, 264.
High School—Mount Ulla, N.C., West Rowan.
Received degree in business from University of North Carolina in 1982.

Selected by Philadelphia in 1983 USFL territorial draft.
Selected by Green Bay in 2nd round (48th player selected) of 1983 NFL draft.
Signed by Green Bay Packers, July 8, 1983.
Green Bay NFL, 1983 and 1984.
Games: 1983 (16), 1984 (16). Total—32.
Pro statistics: Returned one kickoff for one yard, 1983.

CHRIS DRESSEL
Tight End—Houston Oilers

Born February 7, 1961, at Placentia, Calif.
Height, 6.04. Weight, 238.
High School—Placentia, Calif., El Dorado.
Attended Stanford University.

Selected by Oakland in 1983 USFL territorial draft.
Selected by Houston in 3rd round (69th player selected) of 1983 NFL draft.
Signed by Houston Oilers, June 22, 1983.

Year Club	—PASS RECEIVING—				
	G.	P.C.	Yds.	Avg.	TD.
1983—Houston NFL...............	16	32	316	9.9	4
1984—Houston NFL...............	16	40	378	9.5	2
Pro Totals—2 Years...........	32	72	694	9.6	6

Additional pro statistics: Returned four kickoffs for 40 yards and rushed once for three yards, 1983; fumbled once, 1984.

KENNY WAYNE DUCKETT
Wide Receiver—New Orleans Saints

Born October 1, 1959, at Winston-Salem, N.C.
Height, 6.00. Weight, 182.
High School—Winston-Salem, N.C., Reynolds.
Attended Wake Forest University.

Selected by New Orleans in 3rd round (68th player selected) of 1982 NFL draft.
On non-football injury list with diabetes, November 19 through remainder of 1984 season.

Year Club		PASS RECEIVING				—KICKOFF RET.—				—TOTAL—		
	G.	P.C.	Yds.	Avg.	TD.	No.	Yds.	Avg.	TD.	TD.	Pts.	F.
1982—New Orleans NFL..............	7	12	196	16.3	2	2	39	19.5	0	2	12	0
1983—New Orleans NFL..............	14	19	283	14.9	2	33	719	21.8	0	2	12	1
1984—New Orleans NFL..............	11	3	24	8.0	0	29	580	20.0	0	0	0	0
Pro Totals—3 Years..................	32	34	503	14.8	4	62	1299	21.0	0	4	24	1

Additional pro statistics: Rushed twice for minus 16 yards, 1983; rushed once for minus three yards, 1984.

BOBBY RAY DUCKWORTH
Wide Receiver—San Diego Chargers

Born November 27, 1958, at Crossett, Ark.
Height, 6.03. Weight, 197.
High School—Hamburg, Ark.
Attended University of Arkansas.

Selected by San Diego in 6th round (162nd player selected) of 1981 NFL draft.
On non-football injury list with toe injury, August 5 through entire 1981 season.
On inactive list, September 12 and September 19, 1982.

Year Club	—PASS RECEIVING—				
	G.	P.C.	Yds.	Avg.	TD.
1982—San Diego NFL	5	2	77	38.5	0
1983—San Diego NFL	16	20	422	21.1	5
1984—San Diego NFL	16	25	715	28.6	4
Pro Totals—3 Years...........	37	47	1214	25.8	9

Additional pro statistics: Fumbled once, 1984.

MARK DAVID DUDA
Defensive Tackle—St. Louis Cardinals
Born February 4, 1961, at Wilkes Barre, Pa.
Height, 6.03. Weight, 263.
High School—Plymouth, Pa., Wyoming Valley West.
Attended University of Maryland.

Selected by Washington in 1983 USFL territorial draft.
Selected by St. Louis in 4th round (96th player selected) of 1983 NFL draft.
Signed by St. Louis Cardinals, May 9, 1983.
On injured reserve with dislocated kneecap, November 6 through remainder of 1984 season.
St. Louis NFL, 1983 and 1984.
Games: 1983 (14), 1984 (8). Total—22.
Pro statistics: Returned one kickoff for 12 yards and recovered two fumbles, 1983; recovered one fumble, 1984.

DAVID RUSSELL DUERSON
(Dave)
Safety—Chicago Bears
Born November 28, 1960, at Muncie, Ind.
Height, 6.00. Weight, 202.
High School—Muncie, Ind., Northside.
Received bachelor of arts degree in economics from University of Notre Dame in 1983.
Cousin of Allen Leavell, guard with Houston Rockets.

Selected by Chicago in 1983 USFL territorial draft.
Selected by Chicago in 3rd round (64th player selected) of 1983 NFL draft.
Signed by Chicago Bears, June 25, 1983.

		KICKOFF RETURNS				
Year Club	G.	No.	Yds.	Avg.	TD.	
1983—Chicago NFL	16	3	66	22.0	0	
1984—Chicago NFL	16	4	95	23.8	0	
Pro Totals—2 Years	32	7	161	23.0	0	

Additional pro statistics: Intercepted one pass for nine yards and returned one punt for four yards, 1984.
Played in NFC Championship Game following 1984 season.

DONALD DUFEK
(Don)
Safety—Seattle Seahawks
Born April 28, 1954, at Ann Arbor, Mich.
Height, 6.00. Weight, 195.
High School—Grand Rapids, Mich., Pioneer.
Received bachelor of arts degree in speech from University of Michigan in 1976.
Brother of Joe Dufek, quarterback with Buffalo Bills.

Selected by Detroit Red Wings in 6th round of 1974 NHL draft.
Selected by Seattle in 5th round (126th player selected) of 1976 NFL draft.
On injured reserve with knee injury, August 16 through entire 1978 season.
On injured reserve with broken leg, November 28 through remainder of 1979 season.
Released by Seattle Seahawks, August 26, 1980; re-signed by Seahawks after clearing procedural waivers, October 30, 1980.
Released by Seattle Seahawks, August 25, 1981; re-signed by Seahawks, September 2, 1981.
Released by Seattle Seahawks, August 29, 1983; re-signed by Seahawks, September 14, 1983.
On injured reserve with knee injury, October 10 through November 8, 1984; activated after clearing procedural waivers, November 10, 1984.
Seattle NFL, 1976, 1977 and 1979 through 1984.
Games: 1976 (14), 1977 (13), 1979 (13), 1980 (8), 1981 (15), 1982 (9), 1983 (14), 1984 (9). Total—95.
Pro statistics: Returned nine kickoffs for 177 yards, 1976; returned one kickoff for 21 yards and intercepted two passes for 26 yards, 1977; returned three kickoffs for 45 yards, 1981; intercepted one pass for 16 yards, 1982; recovered one fumble, 1983 and 1984.
Played in AFC Championship Game following 1983 season.

JOE DUFEK
Quarterback—Buffalo Bills
Born August 23, 1961, at Ann Arbor, Mich.
Height, 6.04. Weight, 215.
High School—Kent, O., Roosevelt.
Attended Yale University.
Brother of Don Dufek, safety with Seattle Seahawks.

Signed as free agent by Seattle Seahawks, May 21, 1983.
Released by Seattle Seahawks, July 18, 1983; awarded on waivers to Buffalo Bills, July 20, 1983.

		PASSING							RUSHING				TOTAL		
Year Club	G.	Att.	Cmp.	Pct.	Gain	T.P.	P.I.	Avg.	Att.	Yds.	Avg.	TD.	TD.	Pts.	F.
1983—Buffalo NFL	5				None						None		0	0	0
1984—Buffalo NFL	5	150	74	49.3	829	4	8	5.53	9	22	2.4	1	1	6	1
Pro Totals—2 Years	10	150	74	49.3	829	4	8	5.53	9	22	2.4	1	1	6	1

Quarterback Rating Points: 1984 (52.9).

DAN DUFOUR
Guard-Center—Atlanta Falcons
Born October 18, 1960, at Lynn, Mass.
Height, 6.05. Weight, 280.
High School—Lynn, Mass., Classical.
Attended University of California at Los Angeles.

Selected by Boston in 7th round (83rd player selected) of 1983 USFL draft.
Signed as free agent by Atlanta Falcons, May 3, 1983.
On injured reserve with groin injury, September 4 through November 9, 1984; activated, November 10, 1984.
Atlanta NFL, 1983 and 1984.
Games: 1983 (16), 1984 (6). Total—22.
Played in AFC Championship Game following 1983 season.

ADAM JOSEPH DUHE JR.
Name pronounced DU-ay.
(A. J.)
Linebacker—Miami Dolphins
Born November 27, 1955, at New Orleans, La.
Height, 6.04. Weight, 240.
High School—Reserve, La., Leon Goudchaux.
Received bachelor of arts degree in general studies from Louisiana State University in 1978.

Named THE SPORTING NEWS AFC Rookie of the Year, 1977.
Selected by Miami in 1st round (13th player selected) of 1977 NFL draft.
On physically unable to perform/active with knee injury, July 19 through August 20, 1984; activated, August 21, 1984.
On injured reserve with knee injury, August 28 through September 27, 1984; activated, September 28, 1984.
Miami NFL, 1977 through 1984.
Games: 1977 (14), 1978 (13), 1979 (13), 1980 (16), 1981 (16), 1982 (9), 1983 (15), 1984 (12). Total—108.
Pro statistics: Recovered two fumbles, 1977; recovered two fumbles for 75 yards and credited with one safety, 1978; intercepted one pass for 11 yards, 1981; recovered one fumble, 1981 and 1983; intercepted one pass for no yards, 1982; intercepted one pass for seven yards and returned one kickoff for no yards, 1984.
Played in AFC Championship Game following 1982 and 1984 seasons.
Played in NFL Championship Game following 1982 and 1984 seasons.
Played in Pro Bowl (NFL All-Star Game) following 1984 season.

CLYDE LEWIS DUNCAN
Wide Receiver—St. Louis Cardinals
Born February 5, 1961, at Oxon Hill, Md.
Height, 6.01. Weight, 192.
High School—Oxon Hill, Md.
Received degree in political science from University of Tennessee in 1984.

Selected by Memphis in 1984 USFL territorial draft.
Selected by St. Louis in 1st round (17th player selected) of 1984 NFL draft.
Signed by St. Louis Cardinals, September 10, 1984.
Granted roster exemption, September 10 through September 20, 1984; activated, September 21, 1984.
On injured reserve with dislocated shoulder, October 19 through November 22, 1984; activated, November 23, 1984.
St. Louis NFL, 1984.
Games: 1984 (8).

GARY EDWARD DUNN
Nose Tackle—Pittsburgh Steelers
Born August 24, 1953, at Coral Gables, Fla.
Height, 6.03. Weight, 265.
High School—Coral Gables, Fla.
Received bachelor of business administration degree from University of Miami (Fla.) in 1976.

Selected by Pittsburgh in 6th round (159th player selected) of 1976 NFL draft.
On injured reserve entire 1977 season.
Pittsburgh NFL, 1976 and 1978 through 1984.
Games: 1976 (5), 1978 (16), 1979 (16), 1980 (16), 1981 (16), 1982 (9), 1983 (13), 1984 (16). Total—107.
Pro statistics: Recovered one fumble, 1978; recovered two fumbles, 1979; recovered one fumble for one yard, 1981.
Played in AFC Championship Game following 1978, 1979 and 1984 seasons.
Played in NFL Championship Game following 1978 and 1979 seasons.

PATRICK NEIL DUNSMORE
(Pat)
Tight End—Chicago Bears
Born October 2, 1959, at Duluth, Minn.
Height, 6.03. Weight, 237.
High School—Ankeny, Ia.
Received degree in physical education from Drake University in 1983.

Selected by Chicago in 11th round (126th player selected) of 1983 USFL draft.
Selected by Chicago in 4th round (107th player selected) of 1983 NFL draft.
Signed by Chicago Bears, June 25, 1983.
On injured reserve with groin injury, August 28 through September 27, 1984; activated, September 28, 1984.

		—PASS RECEIVING—				
Year	Club	G.	P.C.	Yds.	Avg.	TD.
1983—Chicago NFL		16	8	102	12.8	0
1984—Chicago NFL		12	9	106	11.8	1
Pro Totals—2 Years		28	17	208	12.2	1

Played in NFC Championship Game following 1984 season.

MARK SUPER DUPER
(Given name at birth was Mark Kirby Dupas.)
Wide Receiver—Miami Dolphins
Born January 25, 1959, at Pineville, La.
Height, 5.09. Weight, 187.
High School—Moreauville, La.
Attended Northwestern (La.) State University.

Selected by Miami in 2nd round (52nd player selected) of 1982 NFL draft.
On inactive list, September 12 and September 19, 1982.

		—PASS RECEIVING—				
Year	Club	G.	P.C.	Yds.	Avg.	TD.
1982—Miami NFL		2		None		
1983—Miami NFL		16	51	1003	19.7	10
1984—Miami NFL		16	71	1306	18.4	8
Pro Totals—3 Years		34	122	2309	18.9	18

Additional pro statistics: Recovered one fumble, 1984.
Played in AFC Championship Game following 1984 season.
Played in NFL Championship Game following 1984 season.
Member of Miami Dolphins for AFC and NFL Championship Game following 1982 season; did not play.
Played in Pro Bowl (NFL All-Star Game) following 1983 and 1984 seasons.

JOHN OWEN DUTTON
Defensive Tackle—Dallas Cowboys
Born February 6, 1951, at Rapid City, S. D.
Height, 6.07. Weight, 267.
High School—Rapid City, S. D.
Attended University of Nebraska.

Named to THE SPORTING NEWS AFC All-Star Team, 1975 and 1976.
Named as defensive tackle on THE SPORTING NEWS College All-America Team, 1973.
Selected by Baltimore in 1st round (5th player selected) of 1974 NFL draft.
Placed on retired reserve list by Baltimore Colts, August 21, 1979.
Traded by Baltimore Colts to Dallas Cowboys for 1st and 2nd round picks in 1980 draft, October 9, 1979; activated, October 22, 1979.
Baltimore NFL, 1974 through 1978; Dallas NFL, 1979 through 1984.
Games: 1974 (14), 1975 (14), 1976 (14), 1977 (12), 1978 (14), 1979 (8), 1980 (16), 1981 (16), 1982 (9), 1983 (16), 1984 (16). Total—149.
Pro statistics: Recovered one fumble, 1974, 1975, 1977 and 1983; recovered three fumbles for 10 yards, 1978; intercepted one pass for 38 yards and a touchdown and recovered two fumbles, 1980; credited with one safety, 1981 and 1984.
Played in NFC Championship Game following 1980 and 1982 seasons.
Member of Dallas Cowboys for NFC Championship Game following 1981 season; did not play.
Played in Pro Bowl (NFL All-Star Game) following 1975 through 1977 seasons.

KENNY EASLEY
Safety—Seattle Seahawks
Born January 15, 1959, at Chesapeake, Va.
Height, 6.03. Weight, 206.
High School—Chesapeake, Va., Oscar Smith.
Attended University of California at Los Angeles.
Cousin of Walt Easley, running back with San Francisco 49ers, Chicago Blitz
and Pittsburgh Maulers, 1981 through 1984.

Named to THE SPORTING NEWS NFL All-Star Team, 1984.
Named as defensive back on THE SPORTING NEWS College All-America Team, 1978 through 1980.
Selected by Chicago Bulls in 10th round of 1981 NBA draft.
Selected by Seattle in 1st round (4th player selected) of 1981 NFL draft.

		-INTERCEPTIONS-				-PUNT RETURNS-				—TOTAL—		
Year	Club	G.	No.	Yds.	Avg.	TD.	No.	Yds.	Avg.	TD.	TD.	Pts.	F.
1981—Seattle NFL		14	3	155	51.7	1		None			1	6	0
1982—Seattle NFL		8	4	48	12.0	0	1	15	15.0	0	0	0	0
1983—Seattle NFL		16	7	106	15.1	0	1	6	6.0	0	0	0	0
1984—Seattle NFL		16	*10	126	12.6	*2	16	194	12.1	0	2	12	0
Pro Totals—4 Years		54	24	435	18.1	3	18	215	11.9	0	3	18	0

Additional pro statistics: Recovered four fumbles for 25 yards, 1981; recovered one fumble, 1982 and 1984; recovered three fumbles for 29 yards, 1983.
Played in AFC Championship Game following 1983 season.
Played in Pro Bowl (NFL All-Star Game) following 1982 through 1984 seasons.

BO EASON
Safety—Houston Oilers

Born March 10, 1961, at Walnut Grove, Calif.
Height, 6.02. Weight, 200.
High School—Walnut Grove, Calif., Delta.
Attended University of California at Davis.
Brother of Tony Eason, quarterback with New England Patriots.

Selected by Oakland in 1st round (18th player selected) of 1984 USFL draft.
Selected by Houston in 2nd round (54th player selected) of 1984 NFL draft.
Signed by Houston Oilers, July 22, 1984.
On injured reserve with knee injury, October 25 through November 23, 1984; activated, November 24, 1984.
Houston NFL, 1984.
Games: 1984 (10).
Pro statistics: Intercepted one pass for 20 yards and recovered one fumble, 1984.

CHARLES CARROLL EASON IV
(Tony)
Quarterback—New England Patriots

Born October 8, 1959, at Blythe, Calif.
Height, 6.04. Weight, 212.
High School—Clarksburg, Calif., Delta.
Attended American River College and received bachelor of science degree
in physical education from University of Illinois in 1983.
Brother of Bo Eason, safety with Houston Oilers.

Selected by Chicago in 1983 USFL territorial draft.
USFL rights traded with running back Calvin Murray and 1st round pick in 1983 draft by Chicago Blitz to Arizona Wranglers for rights to placekicker Frank Corral and 1st round pick in 1983 draft, January 4, 1983.
Selected by New England in 1st round (15th player selected) of 1983 NFL draft.
Signed by New England Patriots, June 2, 1983.

| | | |—PASSING—| | | | | | |—RUSHING—| | | |—TOTAL—| |
Year Club	G.	Att.	Cmp.	Pct.	Gain	T.P.	P.I.	Avg.	Att.	Yds.	Avg.	TD.	TD.	Pts.	F.
1983—New England NFL	16	95	46	48.4	557	1	5	5.86	19	39	2.1	0	0	0	5
1984—New England NFL	16	431	259	60.1	3228	23	8	7.49	40	154	3.9	5	5	30	7
Pro Totals—2 Years	32	526	305	58.0	3785	24	13	7.20	59	193	3.3	5	5	30	12

Quarterback Rating Points: 1983 (48.4), 1984 (93.4). Total—85.3.
Additional pro statistics: Recovered one fumble, 1983; recovered two fumbles and fumbled seven times for minus five yards, 1984.

BRAD M. EDELMAN
Guard—New Orleans Saints

Born September 3, 1960, at Jacksonville, Fla.
Height, 6.06. Weight, 265.
High School—Creve Coeur, Mo., Parkway North.
Attended University of Missouri.

Named as center on THE SPORTING NEWS College All-America Team, 1981.
Selected by New Orleans on 2nd round (30th player selected) of 1982 NFL draft.
On injured reserve with knee injury, October 9 through November 18, 1984; activated, November 19, 1984.
New Orleans NFL, 1982 through 1984.
Games: 1982 (9), 1983 (16), 1984 (11). Total—36.

EDDIE EDWARDS
Defensive End—Cincinnati Bengals

Born April 25, 1954, at Sumter, S. C.
Height, 6.05. Weight, 256.
High School—Fort Pierce, Fla., Fort Pierce Central.
Attended Arizona Western College and University of Miami.

Selected by Cincinnati in 1st round (3rd player selected) of 1977 NFL draft.
Cincinnati NFL, 1977 through 1984.
Games: 1977 (12), 1978, (16), 1979 (14), 1980 (16), 1981 (14), 1982 (9), 1983 (16), 1984 (16). Total—113.
Pro statistics: Recovered one fumble for three yards, 1977; recovered two fumbles, 1978 and 1979; intercepted one pass for two yards, 1978; recovered one fumble, 1980 through 1983; recovered three fumbles for minus two yards, 1984.
Played in AFC Championship Game following 1981 season.
Played in NFL Championship Game following 1981 season.

HERMAN LEE EDWARDS
Cornerback—Philadelphia Eagles

Born April 27, 1954, at Fort Monmouth, N. J.
Height, 6.00. Weight, 190.
High School—Monterey, Calif.
Attended Monterey Peninsula College, University of California and received bachelor of science degree
in criminal justice from San Diego State University in 1976.

Signed as free agent by Philadelphia Eagles, May, 1977.

Year	Club			—INTERCEPTIONS—			
		G.	No.	Yds.	Avg.	TD.	
1977—Philadelphia NFL		14	6	9	1.5	0	
1978—Philadelphia NFL		16	7	59	8.4	0	
1979—Philadelphia NFL		16	3	6	2.0	0	
1980—Philadelphia NFL		16	3	12	4.0	0	
1981—Philadelphia NFL		16	3	1	0.3	0	
1982—Philadelphia NFL		9	5	3	0.6	0	
1983—Philadelphia NFL		16	1	0	0.0	0	
1984—Philadelphia NFL		16	2	0	0.0	0	
Pro Totals—8 Years		119	30	90	3.0	0	

Additional pro statistics: Recovered two fumbles and fumbled once, 1977; recovered one fumble for 26 yards and a touchdown and fumbled once, 1978; recovered one fumble, 1979; recovered one fumble for four yards, 1981.
Played in NFC Championship Game following 1980 season.
Played in NFL Championship Game following 1980 season.

RICHARD RANDOLPH EDWARDS
(Randy)
Defensive End—Seattle Seahawks
Born March 9, 1961, at Marietta, Ga.
Height, 6.04. Weight, 255.
High School—Marietta, Ga., Wheeler.
Attended University of Alabama.

Selected by Birmingham in 1984 USFL territorial draft.
Signed as free agent by Seattle Seahawks, May 2, 1984.
Seattle NFL, 1984.
Games: 1984 (13).

STANLEY EDWARDS
(Stan)
Running Back—Houston Oilers
Born May 20, 1960, at Detroit, Mich.
Height, 6.00. Weight, 210.
High School—Detroit, Mich., Kettering.
Attended University of Michigan.

Selected by Houston in 3rd round (72nd player selected) of 1982 NFL draft.
On injured reserve with dislocated shoulder, September 7 through November 18, 1982; activated, November 19, 1982.
Released by Houston Oilers, August 27, 1984; re-signed by Oilers, September 12, 1984.

			—RUSHING—				PASS RECEIVING				—TOTAL—		
Year	Club	G.	Att.	Yds.	Avg.	TD.	P.C.	Yds.	Avg.	TD.	TD.	Pts.	F.
1982—Houston NFL		7	15	58	3.9	0	9	53	5.9	0	0	0	0
1983—Houston NFL		14	16	40	2.5	0	9	79	8.8	1	1	6	0
1984—Houston NFL		14	60	267	4.5	1	20	151	7.6	0	1	6	2
Pro Totals—3 Years		35	91	365	4.0	1	38	283	7.4	1	2	12	2

RON EGLOFF
Tight End—San Diego Chargers
Born October 3, 1955, at Garden City, Mich.
Height, 6.05. Weight, 227.
High School—Plymouth, Mich.
Attended University of Wisconsin.

Signed as free agent by Denver Broncos, May, 1977.
On injured reserve with pulled hamstring, October 24 through remainder of 1978 season.
Released by Denver Broncos, August 20, 1984; signed as free agent by San Diego Chargers, September 12, 1984.
Released by San Diego Chargers, October 12, 1984; re-signed by Chargers, October 23, 1984.

Year	Club		—PASS RECEIVING—				
		G.	P.C.	Yds.	Avg.	TD.	
1977—Denver NFL		13	2	27	13.5	0	
1978—Denver NFL		8	4	33	8.3	1	
1979—Denver NFL		15	5	70	14.0	0	
1980—Denver NFL		16	6	85	14.2	0	
1981—Denver NFL		16	17	231	13.6	1	
1982—Denver NFL		9	10	96	9.6	0	
1983—Denver NFL		16	20	205	10.3	2	
1984—San Diego NFL		12	11	92	8.4	0	
Pro Totals—8 Years		105	75	839	11.2	4	

Additional pro statistics: Recovered one fumble, 1977; returned one kickoff for no yards, 1979; returned one kickoff for seven yards, recovered one fumble for six yards and fumbled twice, 1981; returned two kickoffs for 20 yards, 1984.
Played in AFC Championship Game following 1977 season.
Played in NFL Championship Game following 1977 season.

CHARLES KALEV EHIN

(Middle name is an Estonian name meaning Atlas, or great person.)

(Chuck)
Defensive End—San Diego Chargers

Born July 1, 1961, at Marysville, Calif.
Height, 6.04. Weight, 260.
High School—Layton, Utah.
Attended Brigham Young University.

Selected by Chicago in 17th round (198th player selected) of 1983 USFL draft.
Selected by San Diego in 12th round (329th player selected) of 1983 NFL draft.
Signed by San Diego Chargers, June 6, 1983.
San Diego NFL, 1983 and 1984.
Games: 1983 (9), 1984 (16). Total—25.
Pro statistics: Recovered one fumble, 1984.

ANDERSON ERIK EKERN

Name pronounced EH-kern.

(Andy)
Offensive Tackle—Indianapolis Colts

Born July 26, 1961, at Columbia, Mo.
Height, 6.06. Weight, 265.
High School—Mexico, Mo.
Received bachelor of science degree in agricultural economics from
University of Missouri in 1983.
Cousin of Carl Ekern, linebacker with Los Angeles Rams.

Selected by New England in 12th round (326th player selected) of 1983 NFL draft.
On injured reserve with knee injury, August 29 through entire 1983 season.
Released by New England Patriots, August 27, 1984; awarded on waivers to Indianapolis Colts, August 28, 1984.
On injured reserve with broken wrist, September 10 through remainder of 1984 season.
Indianapolis NFL, 1984.
Games: 1984 (2).

CARL FREDERICK EKERN

Name pronounced EH-kern.

Linebacker—Los Angeles Rams

Born May 27, 1954, at Richland, Wash.
Height, 6.03. Weight, 222.
High School—Sunnyvale, Calif., Fremont.
Received bachelor of business administration degree from San Jose State University and attending
California State University at Long Beach for master's degree in business administration.
Cousin of Andy Ekern, offensive tackle with Indianapolis Colts.

Selected by Los Angeles in 5th round (128th player selected) of 1976 NFL draft.
On injured reserve with knee injury, August 20 through entire 1979 season.
On injured reserve with knee injury, November 23 through remainder of 1982 season.
Los Angeles Rams NFL, 1976 through 1978 and 1980 through 1984.
Games: 1976 (14), 1977 (14), 1978 (16), 1980 (15), 1981 (16), 1982 (3), 1983 (16), 1984 (16). Total—110.
Pro statistics: Returned one kickoff for eight yards, 1977; intercepted one pass for nine yards, 1982; intercepted one pass for one yard and recovered two fumbles, 1983; recovered one fumble, 1984.
Played in NFC Championship Game following 1976 and 1978 seasons.

HOMER CARY ELIAS
Guard—Detroit Lions

Born May 1, 1955, at Fort Benning, Ga.
Height, 6.02. Weight, 255.
High School—Seale, Ala., Mount Olive.
Attended Tennessee State University.
Related to Oliver Davis, safety with Oakland Invaders.

Selected by Detroit in 4th round (107th player selected) of 1978 NFL draft.
Detroit NFL, 1978 through 1984.
Games: 1978 (16), 1979 (15), 1980 (14), 1981 (16), 1982 (9), 1983 (14), 1984 (12). Total—96.
Pro statistics: Recovered two fumbles, 1978 and 1981; recovered one fumble, 1983.

JIM A. ELIOPULOS
Linebacker—New York Jets

Born April 18, 1959, at Dearborn, Mich.
Height, 6.02. Weight, 230.
High School—Cheyenne, Wyo., Central.
Attended Westminster College and University of Wyoming.

Selected by Dallas in 3rd round (81st player selected) of 1982 NFL draft.
On injured reserve with knee injury, September 6 through entire 1982 season.
Released by Dallas Cowboys, August 22, 1983; awarded on waivers to St. Louis Cardinals, August 23, 1983.
Released by St. Louis Cardinals, September 28, 1983; signed as free agent by New York Jets, October 19, 1983.
Released by New York Jets, August 27, 1984; re-signed by Jets, October 3, 1984.
St. Louis (4)-New York Jets (8) NFL, 1983; New York Jets NFL, 1984.

Games: 1983 (12), 1984 (11). Total—23.
Pro statistics: Recovered one fumble, 1983.

WILLIAM ELKO
(Bill)
Nose Tackle—San Diego Chargers
Born December 28, 1959, at New York, N.Y.
Height, 6.05. Weight, 277.
High School—Windber, Pa.
Attended Arizona State University and Louisiana State University.
Nephew of Frank Kush, head coach with Arizona Outlaws.

Selected by Tampa Bay in 18th round (205th player selected) of 1983 USFL draft.
Selected by San Diego in 7th round (192nd player selected) of 1983 NFL draft.
Signed by San Diego Chargers, July 11, 1983.
San Diego NFL, 1983 and 1984.
Games: 1983 (11), 1984 (15). Total—26.
Pro statistics: Recovered one fumble, 1983.

HENRY ELLARD
Wide Receiver—Los Angeles Rams
Born July 21, 1961, at Fresno, Calif.
Height, 5.11. Weight, 170.
High School—Fresno, Calif., Hoover.
Attended Fresno State University.

Named to THE SPORTING NEWS NFL All-Star Team, 1984.
Selected by Oakland in 1983 USFL territorial draft.
Selected by Los Angeles Rams in 2nd round (32nd player selected) of 1983 NFL draft.
Signed by Los Angeles Rams, July 22, 1983.

		PASS RECEIVING				-PUNT RETURNS-				—KICKOFF RET.—				—TOTAL—		
Year	Club	G.	P.C.	Yds.	Avg. TD.	No.	Yds.	Avg.	TD.	No.	Yds.	Avg.	TD.	TD.	Pts.	F.
1983—L.A. Rams NFL		12	16	268	16.8	0	16	217	*13.6	*1	15	314	20.9	0	1	6	2
1984—L.A. Rams NFL		16	34	622	18.3	6	30	403	13.4	*2	2	24	12.0	0	8	48	4
Pro Totals—2 Years		28	50	890	17.8	6	46	620	13.5	3	17	338	19.9	0	9	54	6

Additional pro statistics: Rushed three times for seven yards, 1983; recovered two fumbles, 1983 and 1984; rushed three times for minus five yards, 1984.
Played in Pro Bowl (NFL All-Star Game) following 1984 season.

ANTHONY ROBERT ELLIOTT
(Tony)
Nose Tackle—New Orleans Saints
Born April 23, 1959, at New York, N.Y.
Height, 6.02. Weight, 280.
High School—Bridgeport, Conn., Harding.
Attended University of Wisconsin and North Texas State University.

Selected by New Orleans in 5th round (114th player selected) of 1982 NFL draft.
On reserve/non-football injury, November 11 through December 8, 1983; activated, December 9, 1983.
Released by New Orleans Saints, July 12, 1984; re-signed by Saints, October 26, 1984.
Granted roster exemption, October 26 through November 23, 1984; activated, November 24, 1984.
New Orleans NFL, 1982 through 1984.
Games: 1982 (9), 1983 (12), 1984 (4). Total—25.
Pro statistics: Recovered one fumble, 1982.

GERRY LYNN ELLIS
First name pronounced Gary.
Fullback—Green Bay Packers
Born November 12, 1957, at Columbia, Mo.
Height, 5.11. Weight, 225.
High School—Columbia, Mo., Hickman.
Attended Fort Scott Junior College and University of Missouri.

Selected by Los Angeles in 7th round (192nd player selected) of 1980 NFL draft.
Released by Los Angeles Rams, September 1, 1980; signed as free agent by Green Bay Packers, September 10, 1980.

		——RUSHING——				PASS RECEIVING				—TOTAL—		
Year	Club	G.	Att.	Yds.	Avg. TD.	P.C.	Yds.	Avg. TD.		TD.	Pts.	F.
1980—Green Bay NFL		15	126	545	4.3	5	48	496	10.3	3	8	48	7
1981—Green Bay NFL		15	196	860	4.4	4	65	499	7.7	3	7	42	5
1982—Green Bay NFL		9	62	228	3.7	1	18	140	7.8	0	1	6	6
1983—Green Bay NFL		15	141	696	4.9	4	52	603	11.6	2	6	36	7
1984—Green Bay NFL		16	123	581	4.7	4	36	312	8.7	2	6	36	2
Pro Totals—5 Years		70	648	2910	4.5	18	219	2050	9.4	10	28	168	27

Additional pro statistics: Recovered five fumbles, 1980; attempted two passes with one completion for 23 yards 1981; recovered one fumble, 1981 and 1983; attempted five passes with two completions for 31 yards and one touchdown and one interception, 1983; attempted four passes with one completion for 17 yards, 1984.

KERWIN RAY ELLIS

(Known by middle name.)

Safety—Philadelphia Eagles

Born April 27, 1959, at Canton, O.
Height, 6.01. Weight, 192.
High School—Canton, O., McKinley.
Attended Ohio State University.

Selected by Philadelphia in 12th round (331st player selected) of 1981 NFL draft.

		—INTERCEPTIONS—				
Year	Club	G.	No.	Yds.	Avg.	TD.
1981—Philadelphia NFL	....	16		None		
1982—Philadelphia NFL	....	9		None		
1983—Philadelphia NFL	....	16	1	18	18.0	0
1984—Philadelphia NFL	....	16	7	119	17.0	0
Pro Totals—4 Years	....	57	8	137	17.1	0

Additional pro statistics: Recovered one fumble, 1981, 1983 and 1984; returned seven kickoffs for 119 yards, 1983; returned two kickoffs for 25 yards and fumbled once, 1984.

RIKI MORGAN ELLISON

(Formerly known as Riki Gray.)

Linebacker—San Francisco 49ers

Born August 15, 1960, at Christchurch, New Zealand.
Height, 6.02. Weight, 220.
High School—Tucson, Ariz., Amphitheater.
Received bachelor of arts degree in international relations, certificate of defense and strategic studies
and physical education from University of Southern California in 1983; and attending
University of Southern California for master's degree in international relations and foreign policy.

Selected by Los Angeles in 1983 USFL territorial draft.
Selected by San Francisco in 5th round (117th player selected) of 1983 NFL draft.
Signed by San Francisco 49ers, June 1, 1983.
San Francisco NFL, 1983 and 1984.
Games: 1983 (16), 1984 (16). Total—32.
Played in NFC Championship Game following 1983 and 1984 seasons.
Played in NFL Championship Game following 1984 season.

NEIL ELSHIRE

Defensive End—Minnesota Vikings

Born March 8, 1958, at Salem, Ore.
Height, 6.06. Weight, 260.
High School—Albany, Ore., South.
Attended University of Oregon.

Signed as free agent by Washington Redskins, May 1, 1981.
On injured reserve with knee injury, August 17 through October 14, 1981; claimed on procedural waivers by Minnesota Vikings, October 16, 1981.
On injured reserve with knee injury, December 8 through remainder of 1982 season.
On injured reserve with knee injury, August 28 through September 27, 1984; activated, September 28, 1984.
Minnesota NFL, 1981 through 1984.
Games: 1981 (4), 1982 (5), 1983 (16), 1984 (12). Total—37.
Pro statistics: Returned one kickoff for seven yards, 1982; recovered three fumbles, 1983; recovered one fumble, 1984.

JOHN ALBERT ELWAY

Quarterback—Denver Broncos

Born June 28, 1960, at Port Angeles, Wash.
Height, 6.04. Weight, 202.
High School—Granada Hills, Calif.
Received bachelor of arts degree in economics from Stanford University in 1983.
Son of Jack Elway, head football coach at Stanford University.

Named as quarterback on THE SPORTING NEWS College All-America Team, 1980 and 1982.
Selected by Oakland in 1983 USFL territorial draft.
Selected by Baltimore in 1st round (1st player selected) of 1983 NFL draft.
Rights traded by Baltimore Colts to Denver Broncos for quarterback Mark Herrmann, rights to offensive lineman Chris Hinton and 1st round pick in 1984 draft, May 2, 1983.
Signed by Denver Broncos, May 2, 1983.

		—PASSING—							—RUSHING—				—TOTAL—		
Year	Club	G.	Att.	Cmp.	Pct.	Gain	T.P.	P.I.	Avg.	Att.	Yds.	Avg.	TD.	TD.	Pts.	F.
1983—Denver NFL	....	11	259	123	47.5	1663	7	14	6.42	28	146	5.2	1	1	6	6
1984—Denver NFL	....	15	380	214	56.3	2598	18	15	6.84	56	237	4.2	1	1	6	14
Pro Totals—2 Years	....	26	639	337	52.7	4261	25	29	6.67	84	383	4.6	2	2	12	20

Quarterback Rating Points: 1983 (54.9), 1984 (76.8). Total—68.1.
Additional pro statistics: Recovered three fumbles, 1983; recovered five fumbles and fumbled 14 times for minus 10 yards, 1984.

Year	Club	League	Pos.	G.	AB.	R.	H.	2B.	3B.	HR.	RBI.	B.A.	PO.	A.	E.	F.A.
1982—Oneonta		NYP	OF	42	151	26	48	6	2	4	25	.318	69	8	0	1.000

Selected by Kansas City Royals' organization in 18th round of free-agent draft, June 5, 1979.
Selected by New York Yankees' organization in 2nd round of free-agent draft, June 8, 1981.

DARRYL ALAN EMERSON
Wide Receiver—Buffalo Bills
Born December 15, 1960, at Buffalo, N. Y.
Height, 6.00. Weight, 190.
High School—Buffalo, N.Y., Grover Cleveland.
Attended Michigan State University, Ventura College and University of Maryland.

Signed as free agent by Buffalo Bills, June 28, 1984.
Released by Buffalo Bills, August 14, 1984; re-signed by Bills, May 10, 1985.

LOWELL DOUGLAS ENGLISH
(Doug)
Defensive Tackle—Detroit Lions
Born August 25, 1953, at Dallas, Tex.
Height, 6.05. Weight, 258.
High School—Dallas, Tex., Bryan Adams.
Received bachelor of social and behavioral science degree from University of Texas.

Selected by Detroit in 2nd round (38th player selected) of 1975 NFL draft.
On reserve-retired list entire 1980 season.
Reinstated, June 29, 1981.
Detroit NFL, 1975 through 1979 and 1981 through 1984.
Games: 1975 (14), 1976 (7), 1977 (14), 1978 (14), 1979 (16), 1981 (16), 1982 (9), 1983 (15), 1984 (16). Total—121.
Pro statistics: Recovered one fumble, 1976, 1977, 1982 and 1984; credited with one safety, 1977 and 1979; recovered two fumbles, 1979; recovered three fumbles for 20 yards, 1981; credited with two safeties, 1983.
Played in Pro Bowl (NFL All-Star Game) following 1978 and 1981 through 1983 seasons.

PHILLIP EARL EPPS
(Phil)
Wide Receiver—Green Bay Packers
Born November 11, 1959, at Atlanta, Tex.
Height, 5.10. Weight, 155.
High School—Atlanta, Tex.
Attended Texas Christian University.
Cousin of Cedric Mack, wide receiver with St. Louis Cardinals.

Selected by Green Bay in 12th round (321st player selected) of 1982 NFL draft.
USFL rights traded with future draft picks by San Antonio Gunslingers to Philadelphia Stars for rights to running back Billy Campfield, March 5, 1984.

			PASS RECEIVING				-PUNT RETURNS-				—KICKOFF RET.—				—TOTAL—		
Year	Club	G.	P.C.	Yds.	Avg.	TD.	No.	Yds.	Avg.	TD.	No.	Yds.	Avg.	TD.	TD.	Pts.	F.
1982—Green Bay NFL		9	10	226	22.6	2	20	150	7.5	0	None				2	12	1
1983—Green Bay NFL		16	18	313	17.4	0	36	324	9.0	*1	None				1	6	2
1984—Green Bay NFL		16	26	435	16.7	3	29	199	6.9	0	12	232	19.3	0	3	18	1
Pro Totals—3 Years		41	54	974	18.0	5	85	673	7.9	1	12	232	19.3	0	6	36	4

Additional pro statistics: Recovered one fumble, 1984.

RICH ERENBERG
Running Back—Pittsburgh Steelers
Born April 17, 1962, at Chappaqua, N.Y.
Height, 5.10. Weight, 200.
High School—Chappaqua, N.Y., Horace Greeley.
Attended Colgate University.

Selected by New Jersey in 1984 USFL territorial draft.
Selected by Pittsburgh in 9th round (247th player selected) of 1984 NFL draft.
Signed by Pittsburgh Steelers, June 16, 1984.

			RUSHING				PASS RECEIVING				—TOTAL—		
Year	Club	G.	Att.	Yds.	Avg.	TD.	P.C.	Yds.	Avg.	TD.	TD.	Pts.	F.
1984—Pittsburgh NFL		16	115	405	3.5	2	38	358	9.4	1	3	18	3

				KICKOFF RETURNS			
Year	Club	G.	No.	Yds.	Avg.	TD.
1984—Pittsburgh NFL		16	28	575	20.5	0

Additional pro statistics: Recovered three fumbles, 1984.
Played in AFC Championship Game following 1984 season.

RUSSELL ALLEN ERXLEBEN

Name pronounced ERKS-lay-ben.

Punter—Los Angeles Rams

Born January 13, 1957, at Seguin, Tex.
Height, 6.04. Weight, 219.
High School—Seguin, Tex.
Received degree in business and finance from University of Texas.

Named as punter on THE SPORTING NEWS College All-America Team, 1977 and 1978.
Selected by New Orleans in 1st round (11th player selected) of 1979 NFL draft.
On injured reserve with leg injury, September 13 through remainder of 1979 season.
Released by New Orleans Saints, August 27, 1984; signed as free agent by Los Angeles Rams, January 30, 1985.

Year Club	G.	No.	—PUNTING— Avg.	Blk.	XP.	XPM.	PLACE KICKING—— FG.	FGA.	Pts.
1979—New Orleans NFL	1	4	37.0	0	4	0	2	2	10
1980—New Orleans NFL	16	89	39.3	0	2	0	2	5	8
1981—New Orleans NFL	16	66	40.5	0			None		
1982—New Orleans NFL	9	46	43.0	0	1	0	0	1	1
1983—New Orleans NFL	16	74	41.0	0			None		
Pro Totals—5 Years	58	279	40.6	0	7	0	4	8	19

Additional pro statistics: Attempted one pass with one interception, 1979; attempted one pass with no completions, 1980; rushed twice for 10 yards and fumbled once, 1981; attempted two passes with one completion for 39 yards and a touchdown, 1982; rushed twice for minus nine yards and attempted one pass with one completion for 24 yards, 1983.

NORMAN JULIUS ESIASON

(Boomer)

Quarterback—Cincinnati Bengals

Born April 17, 1961, at West Islip, N.Y.
Height, 6.04. Weight, 210.
High School—Islip Terrace, N.Y., East Islip.
Attended University of Maryland.

Selected by Washington in 1984 USFL territorial draft.
Selected by Cincinnati in 2nd round (38th player selected) of 1984 NFL draft.
Signed by Cincinnati Bengals, June 19, 1984.

Year Club	G.	Att.	Cmp.	Pct.	—PASSING— Gain	T.P.	P.I.	Avg.	Att.	RUSHING— Yds.	Avg.	TD.	—TOTAL— TD.	Pts.	F.
1984—Cincinnati NFL	10	102	51	50.0	530	3	3	5.20	19	63	3.3	2	2	12	4

Quarterback Rating Points: 1984 (62.9).
Additional pro statistics: Recovered two fumbles and fumbled four times for minus two yards, 1984.

RONALD ARDEN ESSINK

(Ron)

Offensive Tackle—Seattle Seahawks

Born July 30, 1958, at Zeeland, Mich.
Height, 6.06. Weight, 275.
High School—Zeeland, Mich.
Attended Grand Valley State College.

Selected by Seattle in 10th round (265th player selected) of 1980 NFL draft.
On inactive list, September 12 and September 19, 1982.
Seattle NFL, 1980 through 1984.
Games: 1980 (16), 1981 (16), 1982 (7), 1983 (16), 1984 (16). Total—71.
Pro statistics: Caught one pass for two yards and a touchdown, 1980; recovered one fumble, 1980 and 1983.
Played in AFC Championship Game following 1983 season.

LEON EVANS

Defensive End—Philadelphia Eagles

Born October 12, 1961, at Silver Spring, Md.
Height, 6.06. Weight, 270.
High School—Silver Spring, Md., Montgomery Blair.
Attended University of Miami (Fla.).

Signed as free agent by Washington Redskins, July 15, 1983.
Released by Washington Redskins, August 21, 1983; signed as free agent by Philadelphia Eagles, February 15, 1984.
On injured reserve with knee injury, August 27 through entire 1984 season.

MAJOR DONEL EVERETT

Fullback—Philadelphia Eagles

Born January 4, 1960, at New Hebron, Miss.
Height, 5.11. Weight, 215.
High School—New Hebron, Miss.
Attended Mississippi College.

Selected by Birmingham in 13th round (149th player selected) of 1983 NFL draft.
Signed by Birmingham Stallions, January 21, 1983.
Released by Birmingham Stallions, February 7, 1983; signed as free agent by Philadelphia Eagles, May 12, 1983.

Year Club		RUSHING				PASS RECEIVING				—TOTAL—		
	G.	Att.	Yds.	Avg.	TD.	P.C.	Yds.	Avg.	TD.	TD.	Pts.	F.
1983—Philadelphia NFL	16	5	7	1.4	0	2	18	9.0	0	0	0	0
1984—Philadelphia NFL	16			None				None		0	0	0
Pro Totals—2 Years..................................	32	5	7	1.4	0	2	18	9.0	0	0	0	0

		KICKOFF RETURNS			
Year Club	G.	No.	Yds.	Avg.	TD.
1983—Philadelphia NFL	16	14	275	19.6	0
1984—Philadelphia NFL	16	3	40	13.3	0
Pro Totals—2 Years............	32	17	315	18.5	0

Additional pro statistics: Recovered one fumble, 1983.

ROBERT ALAN FADA
(Rob)
Guard—Chicago Bears
Born May 7, 1961, at Fairborn, O.
Height, 6.02. Weight, 272.
High School—Fairborn, O., Parks Hills.
Received degree in pre-medicine from University of Pittsburgh in 1983.

Selected by Arizona in 4th round (47th player selected) of 1983 USFL draft.
Selected by Chicago in 9th round (230th player selected) of 1983 NFL draft.
Signed by Chicago Bears, June 10, 1983.
On injured reserve with knee injury, September 21 through November 11, 1983; activated, November 12, 1983.
Chicago NFL, 1983 and 1984.
Games: 1983 (5), 1984 (13). Total—18.
Played in NFC Championship Game following 1984 season.

JAMES JOHN FAHNHORST
(Jim)
Linebacker—San Francisco 49ers
Born November 8, 1958, at St. Cloud, Minn.
Height, 6.04. Weight, 235.
High School—St. Cloud, Minn., Technical.
Attended University of Minnesota.
Brother of Keith Fahnhorst, offensive tackle with San Francisco 49ers.

Selected by Minnesota in 4th round (92nd player selected) of 1982 NFL draft.
Signed by Chicago Blitz, August 16, 1982.
USFL rights subsequently traded by Los Angeles Express to Chicago Blitz for rights to tight end Mike Sherrod and wide receiver Kris Haines and 6th, 7th and 8th round picks in 1983 draft, November 2, 1982.
Franchise transferred to Arizona, September 30, 1983.
Signed by San Francisco 49ers, June 13, 1984; Minnesota Vikings did not exercise right of first refusal, June 28, 1984.
On injured reserve with knee injury, December 5 through remainder of 1984 season.
Chicago USFL, 1983; Arizona USFL, 1984; San Francisco NFL, 1984.
Games: 1983 (18), 1984 USFL (18), 1984 NFL (14). Total USFL—36. Total Pro—50.
USFL statistics: Intercepted one pass for 19 yards, recovered three fumbles for six yards and credited with one sack for nine yards, 1983; intercepted one pass for no yards, credited with one sack for seven yards and recovered one fumble, 1984.
NFL statistics: Intercepted two passes for nine yards, 1984.
Played in USFL Championship Game following 1984 season.

KEITH VICTOR FAHNHORST
Offensive Tackle—San Francisco 49ers
Born February 6, 1952, at St. Cloud, Minn.
Height, 6.06. Weight, 273.
High School—St. Cloud, Minn., Tech.
Received degree in psychology from University of Minnesota.
Brother of Jim Fahnhorst, linebacker with San Francisco 49ers.

Selected by San Francisco in 2nd round (35th player selected) of 1974 NFL draft.
San Francisco NFL, 1974 through 1984.
Games: 1974 (14), 1975 (14), 1976 (13), 1977 (14), 1978 (15), 1979 (16), 1980 (16), 1981 (16), 1982 (9), 1983 (16), 1984 (15). Total—158.
Pro statistics: Recovered two fumbles, 1974 and 1981; caught one pass for one yard and returned one kickoff for 13 yards, 1975; recovered one fumble, 1975, 1977, 1978 and 1983.
Played in NFC Championship Game following 1981, 1983 and 1984 seasons.
Played in NFL Championship Game following 1981 and 1984 seasons.
Played in Pro Bowl (NFL All-Star Game) following 1984 season.

PAUL JAY FAIRCHILD
Guard—New England Patriots
Born August 14, 1961, at Carroll, Ia.
Height, 6.04. Weight, 270.
High School—Glidden, Ia., Ralston.
Attended Ellsworth Junior College and received bachelor of
general science degree in liberal arts from University of Kansas in 1984.

Selected by Houston in 6th round (124th player selected) of 1984 USFL draft.
Selected by New England in 5th round (124th player selected) of 1984 NFL draft.
Signed by New England Patriots, June 18, 1984.
New England NFL, 1984.
Games: 1984 (7).

MICHAEL LaVERN FANNING
(Mike)
Defensive Tackle—Seattle Seahawks
Born February 2, 1953, at Mt. Clemens, Mich.
Height, 6.06. Weight, 255.
High School—Tulsa, Okla., Edison.
Received bachelor of arts degree from University of Notre Dame in 1975.

Named as defensive tackle on THE SPORTING NEWS College All-America Team, 1974.
Selected by Los Angeles in 1st round (9th player selected) of 1975 NFL draft.
Traded by Los Angeles Rams to Detroit Lions for 5th round pick in 1984 draft, April 26, 1983.
Released by Detroit Lions, February 1, 1984; signed as free agent by Seattle Seahawks, April 13, 1984.
On physically unable to perform with pulled calf muscle, July 19 through July 24, 1984; activated, July 25, 1984.
Los Angeles NFL, 1975 through 1982; Detroit NFL, 1983; Seattle NFL, 1984.
Games: 1975 (8), 1976 (14), 1977 (14), 1978 (16), 1979 (16), 1980 (15), 1981 (16), 1982 (8), 1983 (14), 1984 (16). Total—137.
Pro statistics: Recovered one fumble for three yards, 1976; recovered one fumble, 1979 through 1981; credited with one safety, 1983.
Played in NFC Championship Game following 1975, 1976, 1978 and 1979 seasons.
Played in NFL Championship Game following 1979 season.

KEN MARK FANTETTI
Linebacker—Detroit Lions
Born April 7, 1957, at Toledo, Ore.
Height, 6.02. Weight, 232.
High School—Gresham, Ore.
Attended University of Wyoming.

Selected by Detroit in 2nd round (37th player selected) of 1979 NFL draft.
Placed on did not report list, August 20 through August 27, 1984.
Reported and granted roster exemption, August 28 through September 7, 1984; activated, September 8, 1984.
Detroit NFL, 1979 through 1984.
Games: 1979 (16), 1980 (16), 1981 (16), 1982 (9), 1983 (16), 1984 (14). Total—87.
Pro statistics: Returned two kickoffs for 18 yards, 1979; intercepted one pass for 10 yards, 1980; intercepted two passes for 18 yards, 1981; recovered one fumble, 1981 and 1983; intercepted two passes for no yards, 1983; intercepted one pass for one yard, 1984.

JOHN HOWARD FARLEY
Running Back—Cincinnati Bengals
Born August 11, 1961, at Stockton, Calif.
Height, 5.10. Weight, 202.
High School—Stockton, Calif., A.A. Stagg.
Attended California State University at Sacramento.

Selected by New Orleans in 7th round (139th player selected) of 1984 USFL draft.
Selected by Cincinnati in 4th round (92nd player selected) of 1984 NFL draft.
Signed by Cincinnati Bengals, June 25, 1984.

		—RUSHING—				PASS RECEIVING				—TOTAL—		
Year Club	G.	Att.	Yds.	Avg.	TD.	P.C.	Yds.	Avg.	TD.	TD.	Pts.	F.
1984—Cincinnati NFL	13	7	11	1.6	0	2	11	5.5	0	0	0	1

		KICKOFF RETURNS		
Year Club	G.	No.	Yds.	Avg.TD.
1984—Cincinnati NFL	13	6	93	15.5 0

Additional pro statistics: Recovered one fumble, 1984.

GEORGE FARMER III
Wide Receiver—Los Angeles Rams
Born December 5, 1958, at Los Angeles, Calif.
Height, 5.10. Weight, 175.
High School—Gardena, Calif.
Attended Santa Monica City College and Southern University.

Selected by Los Angeles in 9th round (248th player selected) of 1980 NFL draft.
On injured reserve, August 18 through entire 1980 season.
On injured reserve with knee injury, August 18 through entire 1981 season.

		—PASS RECEIVING—			
Year Club	G.	P.C.	Yds.	Avg.	TD.
1982—L.A. Rams NFL	8	17	344	20.2	2
1983—L.A. Rams NFL	16	40	556	13.9	5
1984—L.A. Rams NFL	14	7	75	10.7	0
Pro Totals—3 Years	38	64	975	15.2	7

Additional pro statistics: Recovered one fumble, 1982; rushed once for minus nine yards, 1983.

SEAN WARD FARRELL
Guard-Offensive Tackle—Tampa Bay Buccaneers
Born May 25, 1960, at Southampton, N.Y.
Height, 6.03. Weight, 260.
High School—Westhampton Beach, N.Y.
Received bachelor of arts degree in general arts and sciences from Penn State University in 1982.

Named to THE SPORTING NEWS NFL All-Star Team, 1984.
Named as guard on THE SPORTING NEWS College All-America Team, 1981.
Selected by Tampa Bay in 1st round (17th player selected) of 1982 NFL draft.
Tampa Bay NFL, 1982 through 1984.
Games: 1982 (9), 1983 (10), 1984 (15). Total—34.
Pro statistics: Recovered one fumble, 1983; recovered two fumbles, 1984.

PAUL V. FARREN
Guard-Offensive Tackle—Cleveland Browns
Born December 24, 1960, at Weymouth, Mass.
Height, 6.05. Weight, 260.
High School—Cohasset, Mass.
Received bachelor of science degree in marketing finance from Boston University in 1983.

Selected by Boston in 1983 USFL territorial draft.
Selected by Cleveland in 12th round (316th player selected) of 1983 NFL draft.
Signed by Cleveland Browns, May 31, 1983.
Cleveland NFL, 1983 and 1984.
Games: 1983 (16), 1984 (15). Total—31.
Pro statistics: Recovered one fumble, 1984.

CHRISTOPHER ALAN FAULKNER
(Chris)
Tight End—Los Angeles Rams
Born April 13, 1960, at Tipton, Ind.
Height, 6.04. Weight, 257.
High School—Arcadia, Ind., Hamilton Heights.
Attended University of Florida.

Selected by Tampa Bay in 1983 USFL territorial draft.
Selected by Dallas in 4th round (108th player selected) of 1983 NFL draft.
Signed by Dallas Cowboys, July 10, 1983.
Released by Dallas Cowboys, August 22, 1983; signed as free agent by Los Angeles Rams, January 31, 1984.
On non-football injury list, November 26 through remainder of 1984 season.
Los Angeles Rams NFL, 1984.
Games: 1984 (8).
Pro statistics: Caught one pass for six yards, 1984.

RON EDWARD FAUROT
Name pronounced Fa-ROW.
Defensive Tackle-Defensive End—New York Jets
Born January 27, 1962, at Wichita, Kan.
Height, 6.07. Weight, 262.
High School—Hurst, Tex., L.D. Bell.
Received bachelor of science degree in business administration
from University of Arkansas in 1984.

Selected by Oklahoma in 1st round (2nd player selected) of 1984 USFL draft.
Selected by New York Jets in 1st round (15th player selected) of 1984 NFL draft.
Signed by New York Jets, May 31, 1984.
New York Jets NFL, 1984.
Games: 1984 (15).
Pro statistics: Recovered one fumble, 1984.

IVY RICKY FEACHER
(Known by middle name.)
Wide Receiver—Cleveland Browns
Born February 11, 1954, at Crystal River, Fla.
Height, 5.10. Weight, 180.
High School—Brooksville, Fla., Hernando.
Attended Mississippi Valley State University.
Cousin of Curtis Bunche, defensive end with Tampa Bay Bandits and Chicago Blitz, 1983 and 1984.

Selected by New England in 10th round (270th player selected) of 1976 NFL draft.
Released by New England Patriots, September 27, 1976; signed as free agent by Cleveland Browns, October 5, 1976.

| | | PUNT RETURNS | | | —KICKOFF RET.— | | | | —TOTAL— | | |
Year Club	G.	No.	Yds.	Avg.	TD.	No.	Yds.	Avg.	TD.	TD.	Pts.	F.
1976—N.E. (3)-Clev. (10) NFL	13	13	142	10.9	0	24	551	23.0	0	0	0	3
1977—Cleveland NFL	14	2	15	7.5	0	11	219	19.9	0	0	0	2
1978—Cleveland NFL	16		None				None			0	0	0
1979—Cleveland NFL	16		None			2	51	25.5	0	1	6	1
1980—Cleveland NFL	16		None				None			4	24	0

Year Club	G.	No.	Yds.	Avg.	TD.	No.	Yds.	Avg.	TD.	TD.	Pts.	F.
		-PUNT RETURNS-				-KICKOFF RET.-				-TOTAL-		
1981—Cleveland NFL	16	None				None				3	18	0
1982—Cleveland NFL	9	None				None				3	18	0
1983—Cleveland NFL	9	None				None				3	18	1
1984—Cleveland NFL	16	None				None				1	6	0
Pro Totals—9 Years	125	15	157	10.5	0	37	821	22.2	0	15	90	7

Year Club	G.	P.C.	Yds.	Avg.	TD.
		——PASS RECEIVING——			
1976—NE(3)-Clv.(10) NFL	13	None			
1977—Cleveland NFL	14	None			
1978—Cleveland NFL	16	4	76	19.0	0
1979—Cleveland NFL	16	7	103	14.7	1
1980—Cleveland NFL	16	10	244	24.4	4
1981—Cleveland NFL	16	29	654	22.6	3
1982—Cleveland NFL	9	28	408	14.6	3
1983—Cleveland NFL	9	13	217	16.7	3
1984—Cleveland NFL	16	22	382	17.4	1
Pro Totals—9 Years	125	113	2084	18.4	15

Additional pro statistics: Recovered two fumbles, 1976; recovered one fumble, 1977 through 1980; rushed once for minus one yard, 1979 and 1981.

GRANT EARL FEASEL
Center—Minnesota Vikings
Born June 28, 1960, at Barstow, Calif.
Height, 6.08. Weight, 267.
High School—Barstow, Calif.
Received bachelor of science degree in biology from Abilene Christian University in 1983.
Brother of Greg Feasel, offensive tackle with Denver Gold.

Selected by Baltimore in 6th round (161st player selected) of 1983 NFL draft.
Franchise transferred to Indianapolis, March 31, 1984.
Released by Indianapolis Colts, October 10, 1984; signed as free agent by Minnesota Vikings, October 17, 1984.
Baltimore NFL, 1983; Indianapolis (6)-Minnesota (9) NFL, 1984.
Games: 1983 (11), 1984 (15). Total—26.

GERRY FEEHERY
Center—Philadelphia Eagles
Born March 9, 1960, at Philadelphia, Pa.
Height, 6.02. Weight, 268.
High School—Springfield, Pa., Cardinal O'Hara.
Received bachelor of science degree in marketing from Syracuse University.

Selected by New Jersey in 1983 USFL territorial draft.
Signed as free agent by Philadelphia Eagles, May 4, 1983.
On injured reserve with knee injury, November 4 through remainder of 1983 season.
Philadelphia NFL, 1983 and 1984.
Games: 1983 (2), 1984 (6). Total—8.

RONALD LEE FELLOWS
(Ron)
Cornerback—Dallas Cowboys
Born November 7, 1958, at South Bend, Ind.
Height, 6.00. Weight, 174.
High School—South Bend, Ind., Washington.
Attended Butler (Kan.) County Community College and University of Missouri.

Selected by Dallas in 7th round (173rd player selected) of 1981 NFL draft.

Year Club	G.	No.	Yds.	Avg.	TD.	No.	Yds.	Avg.	TD.	TD.	Pts.	F.
		-PUNT RETURNS-				-KICKOFF RET.-				-TOTAL-		
1981—Dallas NFL	16	11	44	4.0	0	8	170	21.3	0	0	0	0
1982—Dallas NFL	9	25	189	7.6	0	16	359	22.4	0	0	0	3
1983—Dallas NFL	16	10	75	7.5	0	43	855	19.9	0	2	12	4
1984—Dallas NFL	16	None				6	94	15.7	0	0	0	3
Pro Totals—4 Years	57	46	308	6.7	0	73	1478	20.2	0	2	12	10

Year Club	G.	No.	Yds.	Avg.	TD.
		——INTERCEPTIONS——			
1981—Dallas NFL	16	None			
1982—Dallas NFL	9	None			
1983—Dallas NFL	16	5	139	27.8	1
1984—Dallas NFL	16	3	3	1.0	0
Pro Totals—4 Years	57	8	142	17.8	1

Additional pro statistics: Recovered one fumble, 1982; returned blocked field goal attempt 62 yards for a touchdown and recovered three fumbles, 1983; recovered one fumble for 12 yards, 1984.
Played in NFC Championship Game following 1981 and 1982 seasons.

JOHN GARY FENCIK
(Known by middle name.)
Safety—Chicago Bears
Born June 11, 1954, at Chicago, Ill.
Height, 6.01. Weight 197.
High School—Barrington, Ill.
Received bachelor of arts degree in history from Yale University; attending
Northwestern University for master's degree in management.

Named to THE SPORTING NEWS NFC All-Star Team, 1979.
Named to THE SPORTING NEWS NFL All-Star Team, 1981.
Selected by Miami in 10th round (281st player selected) of 1976 NFL draft.
Released by Miami Dolphins, September 6, 1976; signed as free agent by Chicago Bears, September 15, 1976.

| | | | —INTERCEPTIONS— | | | |
Year	Club	G.	No.	Yds.	Avg.	TD.
1976—Chicago NFL		13		None		
1977—Chicago NFL		14	4	33	8.3	0
1978—Chicago NFL		16	4	77	19.3	0
1979—Chicago NFL		14	6	31	5.2	0
1980—Chicago NFL		15	1	8	8.0	0
1981—Chicago NFL		16	6	121	20.2	1
1982—Chicago NFL		9	2	2	1.0	0
1983—Chicago NFL		7	2	34	17.0	0
1984—Chicago NFL		16	5	102	20.4	0
Pro Totals—9 Years		120	30	408	13.6	1

Additional pro statistics: Recovered one fumble, 1976, 1981, 1983 and 1984; recovered two fumbles for 13 yards, 1978; recovered two fumbles, 1979; recovered three fumbles for 52 yards, 1980; fumbled once, 1984.
Played in NFC Championship Game following 1984 season.
Played in Pro Bowl (NFL All-Star Game) following 1980 and 1981 seasons.

JOE CARLTON FERGUSON JR.
Quarterback—Detroit Lions
Born April 23, 1950, at Alvin, Tex.
Height, 6.01. Weight, 195.
High School—Shreveport, La., Woodlawn.
Received bachelor of science degree in physical education from
University of Arkansas in 1973.

Established NFL record for fewest passes intercepted among qualifiers, season (1), 1976.
Tied NFL records for most fumbles and most own fumbles recovered, game (4), September 18, 1977, against Miami Dolphins.
Selected by Buffalo in 3rd round (57th player selected) of 1973 NFL draft.
Traded by Buffalo Bills to Detroit Lions for 1986 draft choice, April 30, 1985.

| | | | —PASSING— | | | | | | —RUSHING— | | | | —TOTAL— | | |
Year	Club	G.	Att.	Cmp.	Pct.	Gain	T.P.	P.I.	Avg.	Att.	Yds.	Avg.	TD.	TD.	Pts.	F.
1973—Buffalo NFL		14	164	73	44.5	939	4	10	5.73	48	147	3.1	2	2	12	7
1974—Buffalo NFL		14	232	119	51.3	1588	12	12	6.84	54	111	2.1	2	2	12	*14
1975—Buffalo NFL		14	321	169	52.6	2426	*25	17	7.56	23	82	3.6	1	1	6	4
1976—Buffalo NFL		7	151	74	49.0	1086	9	1	7.19	18	81	4.5	0	0	0	2
1977—Buffalo NFL		14	*457	221	48.4	*2803	12	*24	6.13	41	279	6.8	2	2	12	12
1978—Buffalo NFL		16	330	175	53.0	2136	16	15	6.47	27	76	2.8	0	0	0	5
1979—Buffalo NFL		16	458	238	52.0	3572	14	15	7.80	22	68	3.1	1	1	6	5
1980—Buffalo NFL		16	439	251	57.2	2805	20	18	6.39	31	65	2.1	0	0	0	9
1981—Buffalo NFL		16	498	252	50.6	3652	24	20	7.33	20	29	1.5	1	1	6	2
1982—Buffalo NFL		9	264	144	54.5	1597	7	*16	6.05	16	46	2.9	1	2	12	5
1983—Buffalo NFL		16	508	281	55.3	2995	26	25	5.90	20	88	4.4	0	0	0	3
1984—Buffalo NFL		12	344	191	55.5	1991	12	17	5.79	19	102	5.4	0	0	0	8
Pro Totals—12 Years		164	4166	2188	52.5	27590	181	190	6.62	339	1174	3.5	10	11	66	76

Quarterback Rating Points: 1973 (45.6), 1974 (69.0), 1975 (81.3), 1976 (90.0), 1977 (54.6), 1978 (70.5), 1979 (74.5), 1980 (74.6), 1981 (74.1), 1982 (56.3), 1983 (69.3), 1984 (63.5). Total—68.6.
Additional pro statistics: Recovered four fumbles, fumbled seven times for minus three yards and caught one pass for minus three yards, 1973; recovered five fumbles and fumbled 14 times for minus 13 yards, 1974; recovered three fumbles, 1975, 1978, 1979 and 1983; fumbled four times for minus one yard, 1975; recovered seven fumbles and fumbled 12 times for minus seven yards, 1977; fumbled five times for minus three yards and caught one pass for minus six yards, 1978; recovered one fumble and fumbled nine times for minus 12 yards, 1980; recovered two fumbles, one for a touchdown and fumbled five times for minus 10 yards, 1982; recovered two fumbles and fumbled eight times for minus 26 yards, 1984.

KEITH TYRONE FERGUSON
Defensive End—San Diego Chargers
Born April 3, 1959, at Miami, Fla.
Height, 6.05. Weight, 255.
High School—Miami, Fla., Edison.
Attended Ohio State University.

Selected by San Diego in 5th round (131st player selected) of 1981 NFL draft.
San Diego NFL, 1981 through 1984.
Games: 1981 (16), 1982 (9), 1983 (16), 1984 (16). Total—57.
Pro statistics: Recovered one fumble, 1982 and 1984; recovered two fumbles, 1983.
Played in AFC Championship Game following 1981 season.

VASQUERO DIAZ FERGUSON
(Vagas)
Running Back—Tampa Bay Buccaneers
Born March 6, 1957, at Richmond, Ind.
Height, 6.00. Weight, 180.
High School—Richmond, Ind.
Received bachelor of arts degree in economics from University of Notre Dame in 1980.
Cousin of Lamar Lundy, defensive end with Los Angeles Rams, 1957 through 1969.

Selected by New England in 1st round (25th player selected) of 1980 NFL draft.
On commissioner's exempt list, November 20 through November 29, 1982.
On injured reserve with pulled hamstring, November 30 through remainder of 1982 season.
Released by New England Patriots, August 29, 1983; signed as free agent by Houston Oilers, September 8, 1983.
Released by Houston Oilers, September 29, 1983; signed as free agent by Cleveland Browns, October 12, 1983.
Released by Cleveland Browns, November 2, 1983; signed by Chicago Blitz, December 20, 1983.
Franchise disbanded, November 20, 1984; not selected in USFL dispersal draft, December 6, 1984.
Signed as free agent by Tampa Bay Buccaneers, February 28, 1985.

			——RUSHING——				PASS RECEIVING				—TOTAL—		
Year	Club	G.	Att.	Yds.	Avg.	TD.	P.C.	Yds.	Avg.	TD.	TD.	Pts.	F.
1980—New England NFL		16	211	818	3.9	2	22	173	7.9	0	2	12	3
1981—New England NFL		13	78	340	4.4	3	4	39	9.8	0	3	18	1
1982—New England NFL		2	1	5	5.0	0		None			0	0	0
1983—Hou. (1)-Cle. (1) NFL		2		None				None			0	0	0
1984—Chicago USFL		18	113	499	4.4	3	10	120	12.0	1	4	24	2
NFL Totals—4 Years		33	290	1163	4.0	5	26	212	8.2	0	5	30	4
USFL Totals—1 Year		18	113	499	4.4	3	10	120	12.0	1	4	24	2
Pro Totals—5 Years		51	403	1662	4.1	8	36	332	9.2	1	9	54	6

Additional NFL statistics: Recovered one fumble, 1981; returned two kickoffs for 36 yards, 1983.
Additional USFL statistics: Recovered one fumble, 1984.

VINCE FERRAGAMO
Quarterback—Los Angeles Rams
Born April 24, 1954, at Torrance, Calif.
Height, 6.03. Weight, 212.
High School—Wilmington, Calif., Banning.
Attended University of California, received bachelor of science degree in pre-med from
University of Nebraska in 1977 and attends Creighton University medical school.

Selected by Los Angeles in 4th round (91st player selected) of 1977 NFL draft.
Granted free agency, February 2, 1981; signed by Montreal Alouettes, April 27, 1981.
On reserve list, October 15 through remainder of 1981 season.
Released by Montreal Concordes, June 5, 1982; re-signed by Los Angeles Rams, July 7, 1982.

			——PASSING——							——RUSHING——				—TOTAL—		
Year	Club	G.	Att.	Cmp.	Pct.	Gain	T.P.	P.I.	Avg.	Att.	Yds.	Avg.	TD.	TD.	Pts.	F.
1977—L.A. Rams NFL		3	15	9	60.0	83	2	0	5.53	1	0	0.0	0	0	0	0
1978—L.A. Rams NFL		9	20	7	35.0	114	0	2	5.70	2	10	5.0	0	0	0	0
1979—L.A. Rams NFL		8	110	53	48.2	778	5	10	7.07	3	—2	—0.7	0	0	0	2
1980—L.A. Rams NFL		16	404	240	59.4	3199	30	19	7.92	15	34	2.3	1	1	6	4
1981—Montreal CFL		13	342	175	51.2	2182	7	*25	6.38	15	57	3.8	0	0	0	5
1982—L.A. Rams NFL		7	209	118	56.5	1609	9	9	7.70	4	3	0.8	1	1	6	1
1983—L.A. Rams NFL		16	464	274	59.1	3276	22	23	7.06	22	17	0.8	0	0	0	8
1984—L.A. Rams NFL		3	66	29	43.9	317	2	8	4.80	4	0	0.0	0	0	0	0
CFL Total—1 Year		13	342	175	51.2	2182	7	25	6.38	15	57	3.8	0	0	0	5
NFL Totals—7 Years		62	1288	730	56.7	9376	70	71	7.28	51	62	1.2	2	2	12	15
Pro Totals—8 Years		75	1630	905	55.5	11558	77	96	7.09	66	119	1.8	2	2	12	20

NFL Quarterback Rating Points: 1977 (114.7), 1978 (15.4), 1979 (48.8), 1980 (89.7), 1982 (77.7), 1983 (75.9), 1984 (29.2). Total—74.8.
Additional NFL statistics: Recovered one fumble, 1979; recovered two fumbles, 1980 and 1983.
Additional CFL statistics: Recovered one fumble, 1981.
Played in NFC Championship Game following 1978 and 1979 seasons.
Played in NFL Championship Game following 1979 season.

RONALD LEE FERRARI
(Ron)
Linebacker—San Francisco 49ers
Born July 30, 1959, at Springfield, Ill.
Height, 6.00. Weight, 212.
High School—Moweaqua, Ill.
Attended Lake Land College and received bachelor of science degree in agricultural economics
from University of Illinois in 1982.

Selected by San Francisco in 7th round (195th player selected) of 1982 NFL draft.
On injured reserve with knee injury, November 12 through remainder of 1984 season.
San Francisco NFL, 1982 through 1984.
Games: 1982 (9), 1983 (16), 1984 (11). Total—36.
Pro statistics: Returned two kickoffs for 19 yards, 1982.
Played in NFC Championship Game following 1983 season.

EARL THOMAS FERRELL
Running Back—St. Louis Cardinals
Born March 27, 1958, at Halifax, Va.
Height, 6.00. Weight, 215.
High School—South Boston, Va., Halifax County.
Attended East Tennessee State University.
Uncle of David Ferrell, rookie linebacker with St. Louis Cardinals.

Selected by St. Louis in 5th round (125th player selected) of 1982 NFL draft.

			—RUSHING—			PASS RECEIVING				—TOTAL—		
Year	Club	G.	Att.	Yds.	Avg.	TD.	P.C.	Yds.	Avg.	TD.	TD.	Pts.	F.
1982—St. Louis NFL		9		None				None			0	0	0
1983—St. Louis NFL		16	7	53	7.6	1		None			1	6	2
1984—St. Louis NFL		16	41	190	4.6	1	26	218	8.4	1	2	12	3
Pro Totals—3 Years		41	48	243	5.1	2	26	218	8.4	1	3	18	5

			—PUNT RETURNS—				—KICKOFF RET.—			
Year	Club	G.	No.	Yds.	Avg.	TD.	No.	Yds.	Avg.	TD.
1982—St. Louis NFL		9	1	6	6.0	0	4	88	22.0	0
1983—St. Louis NFL		16	1	17	17.0	0	13	257	19.8	0
1984—St. Louis NFL		16		None			1	0	0.0	0
Pro Totals—3 Years		41	2	23	11.5	0	18	345	19.2	0

ALFRED FIELDS
(Jitter)
Cornerback—New Orleans Saints
Born August 16, 1962, at Dallas, Tex.
Height, 5.08. Weight, 188.
High School—Dallas, Tex., H. Grady Spruce.
Attended University of Texas.

Selected by San Antonio in 1984 USFL territorial draft.
Selected by New Orleans in 5th round (123rd player selected) of 1984 NFL draft.
Signed by New Orleans Saints, June 23, 1984.

			—PUNT RETURNS—				—KICKOFF RET.—				—TOTAL—		
Year	Club	G.	No.	Yds.	Avg.	TD.	No.	Yds.	Avg.	TD.	TD.	Pts.	F.
1984—New Orleans NFL		13	27	236	8.7	0	19	356	18.7	0	0	0	2

Additional pro statistics: Recovered one fumble, 1984.

JOSEPH CHARLES FIELDS JR.
(Joe)
Center—New York Jets
Born November 14, 1953, at Woodbury, N. J.
Height, 6.02. Weight, 253.
High School—Gloucester City, N. J., Catholic.
Attended University of Rutgers at Camden and received bachelor of science degree
in accounting from Widener College.

Selected by New York Jets in 14th round (349th player selected) of 1975 NFL draft.
New York Jets NFL, 1975 through 1984.
Games: 1975 (14), 1976 (14), 1977 (14), 1978 (16), 1979 (15), 1980 (13), 1981 (16), 1982 (9), 1983 (12), 1984 (16).
Total—139.
Pro statistics: Fumbled once for minus 21 yards and recovered one fumble for four yards, 1975; fumbled once for minus 14 yards, 1976; recovered one fumble, 1977, 1980 and 1984; fumbled once for minus 15 yards, 1981.
Played in AFC Championship Game following 1982 season.
Played in Pro Bowl (NFL All-Star Game) following 1981 and 1982 seasons.

DAVID M. FINZER
Punter—Chicago Bears
Born February 3, 1959, at Chicago, Ill.
Height, 6.00. Weight, 195.
High School—Wilmette, Ill., Loyola Academy.
Attended University of Illinois and DePauw University.

Signed as free agent by Dallas Cowboys, April 30, 1982.
Released by Dallas Cowboys, August 31, 1982; signed as free agent by Chicago Bears, April 7, 1983.
Released by Chicago Bears, August 16, 1983; signed by Chicago Blitz, November 7, 1983.
Released by Chicago Blitz, January 30, 1984; signed as free agent by San Diego Chargers, May 20, 1984.
Traded by San Diego Chargers to Chicago Bears for 12th round pick in 1985 draft, August 15, 1984.

		—PUNTING—		
Year	Club	G.	No.	Avg.	Blk.
1984—Chicago NFL		16	83	40.1	2

Additional pro statistics: Rushed twice for no yards, 1984.
Played in NFC Championship Game following 1984 season.

JEFFREY MICHAEL FISHER
(Jeff)
Safety—Chicago Bears
Born February 25, 1958, at Culver City, Calif.
Height, 5.11. Weight, 188.
High School—Woodland Hills, Calif., Taft.
Received bachelor of science degree in public administration
from University of Southern California in 1981.

Selected by Chicago in 7th round (177th player selected) of 1981 NFL draft.
On injured reserve with broken leg, October 24 through remainder of 1983 season.

Year Club	G.	INTERCEPTIONS				—PUNT RETURNS—				—KICKOFF RET.—				—TOTAL—		
		No.	Yds.	Avg.	TD.	No.	Yds.	Avg.	TD.	No.	Yds.	Avg.	TD.	TD.	Pts.	F.
1981—Chicago NFL	16	2	3	1.5	0	43	509	11.8	1	7	102	14.6	0	1	6	3
1982—Chicago NFL	9	3	19	6.3	0	7	53	7.6	0	7	102	14.6	0	0	0	2
1983—Chicago NFL	8			None		13	71	5.5	0			None		0	0	0
1984—Chicago NFL	16			None		*57	492	8.6	0			None		0	0	4
Pro Totals—4 Years	49	5	22	4.4	0	120	1125	9.4	1	14	204	14.6	0	1	6	5

Additional pro statistics: Recovered one fumble, 1981 and 1984.
Played in NFC Championship Game following 1984 season.

RODERICK FISHER
Cornerback—Los Angeles Rams
Born November 23, 1961, at Dallas, Tex.
Height, 5.10. Weight, 190.
High School—Dallas, Tex., South Oak Cliff.
Attended Oklahoma State University.

Selected by Oklahoma in 1984 USFL territorial draft.
Selected by Los Angeles Rams in 12th round (309th player selected) of 1984 NFL draft.
Signed by Los Angeles Rams, July 14, 1984.
On injured reserve with pulled hamstring, August 27 through entire 1984 season.

JOHN W. FITZPATRICK
Offensive Lineman—Dallas Cowboys
Born June 6, 1961, at Chicago, Ill.
Height, 6.03. Weight, 285.
High School—Greencastle, Ind.
Attended University of Wyoming and received bachelor of arts degree
in criminal law from Purdue University in 1984.

Signed as free agent by Dallas Cowboys, May 3, 1984.
On injured reserve with knee injury, August 13 through entire 1984 season.

ALLEN EDWARD FLEMING
Wide Receiver—San Francisco 49ers
Born September 10, 1962, at San Francisco, Calif.
Height, 5.11. Weight, 175.
High School—Vallejo, Calif., Hogan.
Attended University of California at Davis.

Signed as free agent by San Francisco 49ers, May 10, 1984.
On injured reserve with knee injury, August 27 through entire 1984 season.

TOM FLICK
Quarterback—Cleveland Browns
Born August 30, 1958, at Patuxent River, Md.
Height, 6.03. Weight, 190.
High School—Bellevue, Wash.
Attended University of Washington.

Selected by Washington in 4th round (90th player selected) of 1981 NFL draft.
Traded by Washington Redskins to New England Patriots for quarterback Tom Owen, August 25, 1982.
On inactive list, September 12 and September 19, 1982.
On injured reserve with elbow injury, August 16 through September 28, 1983.
Released by New England Patriots, September 29, 1983; signed as free agent by Cleveland Browns, January 3, 1984.

Year Club	G.	PASSING							RUSHING				TOTAL		
		Att.	Cmp.	Pct.	Gain	T.P.	P.I.	Avg.	Att.	Yds.	Avg.	TD.	TD.	Pts.	F.
1981—Washington NFL	6	27	13	48.1	143	0	2	5.30			None		0	0	2
1982—New England NFL	3	5	0	0.0	0	0	0	0.00			None		0	0	0
1984—Cleveland NFL	1	1	1	100.0	2	0	0	2.00			None		0	0	1
Pro Totals—3 Years	10	33	14	42.4	145	0	2	4.39	0	0	0.0	0	0	0	3

Quarterback Rating Points: 1981 (33.4), 1982 (0.0), 1984 (79.2). Total—30.3.
Additional pro statistics: Recovered one fumble, 1981.

SAM T. FLORES
Placekicker—Miami Dolphins
Born November 8, 1961, at Miami, Fla.
Height, 6.00. Weight, 185.
High School—Uniondale, N.Y.
Attended Nassau Community College and C.W. Post College.

Signed as free agent by Cleveland Browns, May 19, 1984.

Released by Cleveland Browns after failing physical with back injury, July 14, 1984; signed as free agent by Miami Dolphins, April 24, 1985.

LARRY DARNELL FLOWERS
Safety—New York Giants
Born April 19, 1958, at Temple, Tex.
Height, 6.01. Weight, 195.
High School—Temple, Tex.
Attended Texas Tech University.

Selected by Tampa Bay in 4th round (102nd player selected) of 1980 NFL draft.

Released by Tampa Bay Buccaneers, August 6, 1980; claimed on waivers by New York Giants, August 8, 1980.

On injured reserve with concussion, August 26 through entire 1980 season.

Released by New York Giants, September 8, 1982; re-signed by Giants, November 23, 1982.

New York Giants NFL, 1981 through 1984.

Games: 1981 (16), 1982 (6), 1983 (14), 1984 (16). Total—52.

Pro statistics: Intercepted one pass for nine yards, 1981; recovered one fumble, 1981 and 1983; intercepted one pass for 19 yards, 1983.

GEORGE FLOYD JR.
Defensive Back—New York Jets
Born December 21, 1960, at Tampa, Fla.
Height, 5.11. Weight, 190.
High School—Brooksville, Fla., Hernando.
Received bachelor of arts degree in physical education from
Eastern Kentucky University in 1982.

Selected by New York Jets in 4th round (107th player selected) of 1982 NFL draft.

On inactive list, September 12, 1982.

On injured reserve with knee injury, August 29 through entire 1983 season.

On injured reserve with knee injury, August 27 through October 24, 1984; activated after clearing procedural waivers, October 26, 1984.

New York Jets NFL, 1982 and 1984.

Games: 1982 (7), 1984 (8). Total—15.

Played in AFC Championship Game following 1982 season.

THOMAS J. FLYNN
(Tom)
Safety—Green Bay Packers
Born March 24, 1962, at Verona, Pa.
Height, 6.00. Weight, 195.
High School—Pittsburgh, Pa., Penn Hills.
Attended University of Pittsburgh.

Selected by Pittsburgh in 1984 USFL territorial draft.

Selected by Green Bay in 5th round (126th player selected) of 1984 NFL draft.

Signed by Green Bay Packers, July 1, 1984.

		—INTERCEPTIONS—				—PUNT RETURNS—				—TOTAL—		
Year Club	G.	No.	Yds.	Avg.	TD.	No.	Yds.	Avg.	TD.	TD.	Pts.	F.
1984—Green Bay NFL	16	9	106	11.8	0	15	128	8.5	0	0	0	1

Additional pro statistics: Recovered three fumbles for three yards, 1984.

BRAD FOJTIK
Defensive End—Kansas City Chiefs
Born September 17, 1961, at Auburndale, Fla.
Height, 6.05. Weight, 250.
High School—Lakeland, Fla., Santa Fe Catholic.
Attended Florida State University.

Signed as free agent by Seattle Seahawks, May 29, 1984.

Released by Seattle Seahawks, August 27, 1984; signed as free agent by Kansas City Chiefs for 1985, October 15, 1984.

STEPHEN JAMES FOLEY
(Steve)
Safety—Denver Broncos
Born November 11, 1953, at New Orleans, La.
Height, 6.02. Weight, 190.
High School—New Orleans, La., Jesuit.
Received degree in business administration from Tulane University.

Selected by Denver in 8th round (199th player selected) of 1975 NFL draft.
Signed as free agent by Jacksonville Express (WFL), 1975.
Signed by Denver Broncos after World Football League folded, May 1976.
On injured reserve with fractured arm, September 14 through remainder of 1982 season.

		—INTERCEPTIONS—						—INTERCEPTIONS—			
Year Club	G.	No.	Yds.	Avg.	TD.	Year Club	G.	No.	Yds.	Avg.	TD.
1975—Jacksonville WFL	10	1	30	30.0	0	1982—Denver NFL	1	None			
1976—Denver NFL	14	4	95	23.8	0	1983—Denver NFL	14	5	28	5.6	0
1977—Denver NFL	13	3	22	7.3	0	1984—Denver NFL	16	6	97	16.2	1
1978—Denver NFL	16	6	84	14.0	0	WFL Totals—1 Year	10	1	30	30.0	0
1979—Denver NFL	16	6	14	2.3	0	NFL Totals—9 Years	122	39	536	13.7	1
1980—Denver NFL	16	4	115	*28.8	0	Pro Totals—10 Years	132	40	566	14.2	1
1981—Denver NFL	16	5	81	16.2	0						

Additional WFL statistics: Returned one punt for two yards, 1975.
Additional NFL statistics: Fumbled once, 1976, 1979 and 1983; rushed once for 14 yards, 1978; recovered one fumble, 1981 and 1983; recovered two fumbles for 22 yards and a touchdown, 1984.
Played in AFC Championship Game following 1977 season.
Played in NFL Championship Game following 1977 season.

DEWEY FORTE
Defensive Tackle—San Diego Chargers
Born October 31, 1961, at Lakeland, Fla.
Height, 6.05. Weight, 270.
High School—Lakeland, Fla., Kathleen.
Attended Bethune-Cookman College.

Selected by Tampa Bay in 1984 USFL territorial draft.
USFL rights traded with rights to defensive tackle Lee Williams by Tampa Bay Bandits to Los Angeles Express for draft choice, March 2, 1984.
Signed by Los Angeles Express, March 6, 1984.
Granted roster exemption, March 6 through March 15, 1984; activated, March 16, 1984.
On developmental squad, March 16 through March 29, 1984; activated, March 30, 1984.
On developmental squad, April 28 through May 3, 1984; activated, May 4, 1984.
Selected by Miami in 2nd round (53rd player selected) of 1984 NFL supplemental draft.
NFL rights traded with 2nd round pick in 1985 draft by Miami Dolphins to San Diego Chargers for running back Pete Johnson, September 22, 1984.
Released by Los Angeles Express, October 20, 1984; signed by San Diego Chargers for 1985, October 24, 1984.
On developmental squad for 3 games with Los Angeles Express in 1984.
Los Angeles USFL, 1984.
Games: 1984 (13).
Pro statistics: Credited with three sacks for 22 yards, 1984.

JEROME FOSTER
Defensive End—Houston Oilers
Born July 25, 1960, at Detroit, Mich.
Height, 6.02. Weight, 263.
High School—Detroit, Mich., Kettering.
Attended Ohio State University.

Selected by Oakland in 5th round (55th player selected) of 1983 USFL draft.
Selected by Houston in 5th round (139th player selected) of 1983 NFL draft.
Signed by Houston Oilers, June 22, 1983.
On injured reserve with knee injury, September 20 through November 9, 1984; activated, November 10, 1984.
Houston NFL, 1983 and 1984.
Games: 1983 (16), 1984 (9). Total—25.

ROY ALLEN FOSTER
Guard-Offensive Tackle—Miami Dolphins
Born May 24, 1960, at Los Angeles, Calif.
Height, 6.04. Weight, 272.
High Schools—Woodland Hills, Calif., Taft and Shawnee Mission, Kan., West.
Attended University of Southern California.

Named as guard on THE SPORTING NEWS College All-America Team, 1981.
Selected by Miami in 1st round (24th player selected) of 1982 NFL draft.
Miami NFL, 1982 through 1984.
Games: 1982 (9), 1983 (16), 1984 (16). Total—41.
Pro statistics: Recovered one fumble, 1984.
Played in AFC Championship Game following 1982 and 1984 seasons.
Played in NFL Championship Game following 1982 and 1984 seasons.

ELBERT FOULES
Cornerback—Philadelphia Eagles
Born July 4, 1961, at Greenville, Miss.
Height, 5.11. Weight, 185.
High School—Greenville, Miss.
Attended Alcorn State University.
Cousin of Wilbert Montgomery, running back with Philadelphia Eagles.

Signed as free agent by Philadelphia Eagles, May 12, 1983.

		—INTERCEPTIONS—				
Year	Club	G.	No.	Yds.	Avg.	TD.
1983—Philadelphia NFL		16	1	0	0.0	0
1984—Philadelphia NFL		16	4	27	6.8	0
Pro Totals—2 Years............		32	5	27	5.4	0

Additional pro statistics: Returned one punt for seven yards, 1983.

JOHN CHARLES FOURCADE
Quarterback—New York Giants
Born October 11, 1960, at Gretna, La.
Height, 6.01. Weight, 200.
High School—Marrero, La., Archbishop Shaw.
Attended University of Mississippi.

Signed as free agent by Toronto Argonauts, May 5, 1982.
Traded by Toronto Argonauts to British Columbia Lions, May 20, 1982.
Released by British Columbia Lions, July 4, 1982; re-signed by Lions, July 8, 1982.
Released by British Columbia Lions, June 30, 1983; signed by Birmingham Stallions, October 10, 1983.
Released by Birmingham Stallions, February 13, 1984; signed as free agent by Memphis Showboats, May 31, 1984.
On developmental squad, May 31 through remainder of 1984 season.
Released by Memphis Showboats, January 23, 1985; signed as free agent by New York Giants, May 3, 1985.
On developmental squad for 4 games with Memphis Showboats in 1984.

			—PASSING—						—RUSHING—			—TOTAL—		
Year	Club	G.	Att.	Cmp.	Pct.	Gain	T.P.	P.I.	Avg.	Att.	Yds.	Avg.	TD.	TD. Pts. F.
1982—British Columbia CFL.....		4	14	5	35.7	55	0	3	3.93	2	37	18.5	0	0 0 0

DANIEL FRANCIS FOUTS
(Dan)
Quarterback—San Diego Chargers
Born June 10, 1951, at San Francisco, Calif.
Height, 6.03. Weight, 205.
High School—San Francisco, Calif., St. Ignatius Prep.
Received bachelor of science degree in political science from University
of Oregon in 1973. Attended University of California at San Diego.

Established NFL records for most 300-yard passing games, career (35); most passes attempted, season (609), 1981.
Tied NFL record for most consecutive games, 400 yards passing (2), 1984.
Named THE SPORTING NEWS NFL Player of the Year, 1979.
Named THE SPORTING NEWS AFC Player of the Year, 1979.
Named to THE SPORTING NEWS AFC All-Star Team, 1979.
Selected by San Diego in 3rd round (64th player selected) of 1973 NFL draft.
On injured reserve with knee and groin injuries, December 8 through remainder of 1984 season.

			—PASSING—							—RUSHING—			—TOTAL—		
Year	Club	G.	Att.	Cmp.	Pct.	Gain	T.P.	P.I.	Avg.	Att.	Yds.	Avg.	TD.	TD.	Pts. F.
1973—San Diego NFL		10	194	87	44.8	1126	6	13	5.80	7	32	4.6	0	0	0 2
1974—San Diego NFL		11	237	115	48.5	1732	8	13	7.31	19	63	3.3	1	1	6 4
1975—San Diego NFL		10	195	106	54.4	1396	2	10	7.16	23	170	7.4	2	2	12 3
1976—San Diego NFL		14	359	208	57.9	2535	14	15	7.06	18	65	3.6	0	0	0 8
1977—San Diego NFL		4	109	69	63.3	869	4	6	7.97	6	13	2.2	0	0	0 4
1978—San Diego NFL		15	381	224	58.8	2999	24	20	7.87	20	43	2.2	2	2	12 10
1979—San Diego NFL		16	530	332	*62.6	*4082	24	24	7.70	26	49	1.9	2	2	12 13
1980—San Diego NFL		16	*589	*348	59.1	*4715	30	24	8.01	23	15	0.7	2	2	12 11
1981—San Diego NFL		16	*609	*360	59.1	*4802	*33	17	7.89	22	56	2.5	0	0	0 9
1982—San Diego NFL		9	330	204	61.8	*2883	*17	11	*8.74	9	8	0.9	1	1	6 2
1983—San Diego NFL		10	340	215	63.2	2975	20	15	8.75	12	—5	—0.4	1	1	6 5
1984—San Diego NFL		13	507	317	62.5	3740	19	17	7.38	12	—29	—2.4	0	0	0 8
Pro Totals—12 Years.........		144	4380	2585	59.0	33854	201	185	7.73	197	480	2.4	11	11	66 79

Quarterback Rating Points: 1973 (46.0), 1974 (61.4), 1975 (59.3), 1976 (75.3), 1977 (77.5), 1978 (83.2), 1979 (82.6), 1980 (84.6), 1981 (90.6), 1982 (93.6), 1983 (92.5), 1984 (83.4). Total—81.3.
Additional pro statistics: Recovered one fumble, 1973, 1975 and 1984; recovered four fumbles, 1976; recovered three fumbles, 1978, 1980 and 1982; fumbled 10 times for minus four yards, 1978; recovered six fumbles and fumbled 13 times for minus 20 yards, 1979; fumbled 11 times for minus five yards, 1980; recovered two fumbles and fumbled nine times for minus 22 yards, 1981; recovered two fumbles, 1983; caught one pass for no yards, 1984.
Played in AFC Championship Game following 1980 and 1981 seasons.
Played in Pro Bowl (NFL All-Star Game) following 1979 through 1983 seasons.

AMOS EMANUEL FOWLER
Center—Detroit Lions
Born February 11, 1956, at Pensacola, Fla.
Height, 6.03. Weight, 253.
High School—Fort Walton Beach, Fla.
Attended University of Southern Mississippi.

Selected by Detroit in 5th round (121st player selected) of 1978 NFL draft.
Placed on did not report list, August 20 through September 4, 1984.
Reported and granted roster exemption, September 5 through September 7, 1984; activated, September 8, 1984.
Detroit NFL, 1978 through 1984.
Games: 1978 (16), 1979 (12), 1980 (13), 1981 (16), 1982 (9), 1983 (16), 1984 (15). Total—97.
Pro statistics: Recovered one fumble, 1978 and 1980; recovered two fumbles for minus 10 yards, 1981; recovered two fumbles, 1982.

BOBBY LANE FOWLER
Tight End—New Orleans Saints
Born September 11, 1960, at Temple, Tex.
Height, 6.02. Weight, 230.
High School—Angleton, Tex.
Attended University of Texas-El Paso and Louisiana Tech University.

Signed as free agent by New Orleans Saints, June 20, 1984.
Released by New Orleans Saints, August 27, 1984; re-signed by Saints, May 9, 1985.

DELBERT FOWLER
Linebacker—Green Bay Packers
Born May 4, 1958, at Cleveland, O.
Height, 6.02. Weight, 214.
High School—Cleveland, O., Glenville.
Attended University of West Virginia.

Selected by Houston in 5th round (133rd player selected) of 1981 NFL draft.
On injured reserve with sprained shoulder, August 24 through entire 1981 season.
Released by Houston Oilers, September 6, 1982; signed as free agent by Montreal Concordes, September 20, 1982.
Traded by Montreal Concordes to Winnipeg Blue Bombers for linebacker Ken Ciancone, July 1, 1984.
Granted free agency, March 1, 1985; signed by Green Bay Packers, May 5, 1985.
Montreal CFL, 1982 and 1983; Winnipeg CFL, 1984.
Games: 1982 (7), 1983 (16), 1984 (15). Total—38.
CFL statistics: Recovered one fumble, 1982 through 1984.

STEVEN TODD FOWLER
(Known by middle name.)
Running Back—Dallas Cowboys
Born June 9, 1962, at Van, Tex.
Height, 6.03. Weight, 218.
High School—Van, Tex.
Attended Henderson County Junior College and Stephen F. Austin State Univesity

Selected by Houston in 16th round (329th player selected) of 1984 USFL draft.
Signed by Houston Gamblers, January 20, 1984.
Selected by Dallas in 1st round (25th player selected) of 1984 NFL supplemental draft.
Signed by Dallas Cowboys, September 24, 1984, for contract to take effect after being granted free agency after 1985 USFL season.

Year Club			—RUSHING—				PASS RECEIVING				—TOTAL—		
		G.	Att.	Yds.	Avg.	TD.	P.C.	Yds.	Avg.	TD.	TD.	Pts.	F.
1984—Houston USFL		18	170	1003	5.9	11	24	301	12.5	2	13	78	4

Additional pro statistics: Recovered four fumbles, 1984.

DENNIS JAMES FOWLKES
Linebacker—Minnesota Vikings
Born March 11, 1961, at Columbus, O.
Height, 6.02. Weight, 236.
High School—Columbus, O., East.
Attended West Virginia University.

Selected by Washington in 10th round (117th player selected) of 1983 USFL draft.
Signed as free agent by Pittsburgh Steelers, May 5, 1983.
On injured reserve with concussion, August 23, 1983 through September 4, 1983.
Released by Pittsburgh Steelers, September 5, 1983; signed as free agent by Minnesota Vikings, October 6, 1983.
Minnesota NFL, 1983 and 1984.
Games: 1983 (11), 1984 (14). Total—25.
Pro statistics: Recovered two fumbles for five yards, 1983.

TIM FOX
Safety—San Diego Chargers
Born November 1, 1953, at Canton, O.
Height, 5.11. Weight, 186.
High School—Canton, O., Glenwood.
Received bachelor of arts degree in communications from Ohio State University in 1976.

Named as safety on THE SPORTING NEWS College All-America Team, 1975.
Selected by New England in 1st round (21st player selected) of 1976 NFL draft.
Traded by New England Patriots to San Diego Chargers for 2nd round pick in 1982 draft and 3rd round pick in 1983 draft, April 27, 1982.
On inactive list, September 12, 1982.
On injured reserve with fractured ankle, October 1 through October 30, 1983; activated, October 31, 1983.
On physically unable to perform/active with ankle injury, July 21 through August 20, 1984; activated, August 21, 1984.
On injured reserve with ankle injury, August 28 through September 27, 1984; activated, September 28, 1984.

		——INTERCEPTIONS——			
Year Club	G.	No.	Yds.	Avg.	TD.
1976—New England NFL	13	3	67	22.3	0
1977—New England NFL	14	3	39	13.0	0
1978—New England NFL.......	16	2	10	5.0	0
1979—New England NFL.......	16	2	38	19.0	0
1980—New England NFL.......	16	4	41	10.3	0
1981—New England NFL.......	16	3	20	6.7	0
1982—San Diego NFL	7	4	103	25.8	0
1983—San Diego NFL	12	2	14	7.0	0
1984—San Diego NFL	11	1	36	36.0	0
Pro Totals—9 Years...........	121	24	368	15.3	0

Additional pro statistics: Recovered four fumbles for 11 yards, 1976; recovered one fumble, 1977, 1978 and 1984; credited with one safety, 1978; recovered one fumble for four yards, 1979; fumbled once, 1982.

Played in Pro Bowl (NFL All-Star Game) following 1980 season.

FREDERICK DOUGLAS FRANCE JR.
(Doug)
Offensive Tackle—Houston Oilers
Born April 26, 1953, at Dayton, O.
Height, 6.05. Weight, 266.
High School—Dayton, O., Colonel White.
Attended Ohio State University

Named to THE SPORTING NEWS NFC All-Star Team, 1978.
Selected by Los Angeles in 1st round (20th player selected) of 1975 NFL draft.
On injured reserve with torn rotor cuff, October 27 through remainder of 1981 season.
On reserve/retired list, July 15, 1982 through July 12, 1983.
Traded by Los Angeles Rams to Houston Oilers for 10th round pick in 1984 draft, July 13, 1983.
On injured reserve with shoulder injury, August 9 through entire 1984 season.
Los Angeles NFL, 1975 through 1981; Houston NFL, 1983.
Games: 1975 (14), 1976 (14), 1977 (13), 1978 (16), 1979 (16), 1980 (16), 1981 (8), 1983 (13). Total—110.
Pro statistics: Recovered one fumble, 1979 and 1983.
Played in NFC Championship Game following 1975, 1976, 1978 and 1979 seasons.
Played in NFL Championship Game following 1979 season.
Played in Pro Bowl (NFL All-Star Game) following 1977 and 1978 seasons.

RUSSELL ROSS FRANCIS
(Russ)
Tight End—San Francisco 49ers
Born April 3, 1953, at Seattle, Wash.
Height, 6.06. Weight, 242.
High Schools—Kailua, Oahu, Hawaii; and Pleasant Hill, Ore.
Attended University of Oregon.
Son of Ed Francis, part-time scout with New England Patriots;
and uncle of Jon Francis, tight end at Boise State University.

Selected by Kansas City Royals in 9th round of free-agent draft, June 5, 1974.
Selected by New England in 1st round (16th player selected) of 1975 NFL draft.
On did not report list, August 18 through entire 1981 season.
Traded with 2nd round pick in 1982 draft by New England Patriots to San Francisco 49ers for 1st, 4th and two 2nd round picks in 1982 draft, April 27, 1982.
On injured reserve with neck injury, October 23 through December 6, 1984; activated, December 7, 1984.

		——PASS RECEIVING——						——PASS RECEIVING——			
Year Club	G.	P.C.	Yds.	Avg.	TD.	Year Club	G.	P.C.	Yds.	Avg.	TD.
1975—New England NFL	14	35	636	18.2	4	1980—New England NFL.......	15	41	664	16.2	8
1976—New England NFL......	13	26	367	14.1	4	1982—San Francisco NFL	9	23	278	12.1	2
1977—New England NFL	10	16	229	14.3	4	1983—San Francisco NFL	16	33	357	10.8	4
1978—New England NFL.......	15	39	543	13.9	4	1984—San Francisco NFL	10	23	285	12.4	2
1979—New England NFL.......	12	39	557	14.3	5	Pro Totals—9 Years	114	275	3857	14.0	36

Additional pro statistics: Fumbled once, 1975, 1976, 1978 and 1984; rushed twice for 12 yards and recovered one fumble, 1976 and 1978; recovered one fumble for three yards, 1977; attempted one pass with one completion for 45 yards, 1982; fumbled twice, 1982 and 1983; recovered two fumbles, 1984.

Played in NFC Championship Game following 1983 and 1984 seasons.
Played in NFL Championship Game following 1984 season.
Played in Pro Bowl (NFL All-Star Game) following 1976 and 1977 seasons.
Named to play in Pro Bowl following 1978 season; replaced due to injury by Riley Odoms.

JOHN E. FRANK
Tight End—San Francisco 49ers
Born April 17, 1962, at Pittsburgh, Pa.
Height, 6.03. Weight, 225.
High School—Pittsburgh, Pa., Mount Lebanon.
Received bachelor of arts degree in pre-med
from Ohio State University in 1984.

Selected by New Jersey in 1984 USFL territorial draft.
USFL rights traded with rights to guard Joe Lukens by New Jersey Generals to Pittsburgh Maulers for cornerback Kerry Justin, November 15, 1983.

Selected by San Francisco in 2nd round (56th player selected) of 1984 NFL draft.
Signed by San Francisco 49ers, July 16, 1984.

Year Club		—PASS RECEIVING—				
	G.	P.C.	Yds.	Avg.	TD.	
1984—San Francisco NFL	15	7	60	8.6	1	

Played in NFC Championship Game following 1984 season.
Member of San Francisco 49ers for NFL Championship Game following 1984 season; did not play.

ANDRA BERNARD FRANKLIN
Fullback—Miami Dolphins
Born August 22, 1959, at Anniston, Ala.
Height, 5.10. Weight, 228.
High School—Anniston, Ala.
Attended University of Nebraska.

Selected by Miami in 2nd round (56th player selected) of 1981 NFL draft.
On injured reserve with knee injury, September 10 through remainder of 1984 season.

Year Club		——RUSHING——				PASS RECEIVING				—TOTAL—		
	G.	Att.	Yds.	Avg.	TD.	P.C.	Yds.	Avg.	TD.	TD.	Pts.	F.
1981—Miami NFL	16	201	711	3.5	7	3	6	2.0	1	8	48	5
1982—Miami NFL	9	*177	701	4.0	7	3	9	3.0	0	7	42	3
1983—Miami NFL	15	224	746	3.3	8		None			8	48	6
1984—Miami NFL	2	20	74	3.7	0		None			0	0	0
Pro Totals—4 Years	42	622	2232	3.6	22	6	15	2.5	1	23	138	14

Additional pro statistics: Recovered one fumble, 1981 and 1983.
Played in AFC Championship Game following 1982 season.
Played in NFL Championship Game following 1982 season.
Played in Pro Bowl (NFL All-Star Game) following 1982 season.

ANTHONY RAY FRANKLIN
(Tony)
Placekicker—New England Patriots
Born November 18, 1956, at Big Spring, Tex.
Height, 5.08. Weight, 182.
High School—Fort Worth, Tex., Arlington Heights.
Attended Texas A&M University.

Selected by Philadelphia in 3rd round (74th player selected) of 1979 NFL draft.
Traded by Philadelphia Eagles to New England Patriots for 6th round pick in 1985 draft, February 21, 1984.

Year Club		——PLACE KICKING——				
	G.	XP.	XPM.	FG.	FGA.	Pts.
1979—Philadelphia NFL ...	16	36	3	23	31	105
1980—Philadelphia NFL ...	16	48	0	16	31	96
1981—Philadelphia NFL ...	16	41	2	20	31	101
1982—Philadelphia NFL ...	9	23	2	6	9	41
1983—Philadelphia NFL ...	16	24	3	15	26	69
1984—New England NFL..	16	42	0	22	28	108
Pro Totals—6 Years	89	214	10	102	156	520

Additional pro statistics: Punted once for 32 yards, 1979; punted once for 13 yards, 1981.
Played in NFC Championship Game following 1980 season.
Played in NFL Championship Game following 1980 season.

BYRON PAUL FRANKLIN
Wide Receiver—Buffalo Bills
Born September 3, 1958, at Florence, Ala.
Height, 6.01. Weight, 179.
High School—Sheffield, Ala.
Attended Auburn University.

Selected by Buffalo in 2nd round (50th player selected) of 1981 NFL draft.
On injured reserve with sciatic nerve injury, September 6 through entire 1982 season.

Year Club		PASS RECEIVING				-PUNT RETURNS-				—KICKOFF RET.—				—TOTAL—		
	G.	P.C.	Yds.	Avg.	TD.	No.	Yds.	Avg.	TD.	No.	Yds.	Avg.	TD.	TD.	Pts.	F.
1981—Buffalo NFL	13	2	29	14.5	0	5	45	9.0	0	21	436	20.8	0	0	0	2
1983—Buffalo NFL	15	30	452	15.1	4		None				None			4	24	0
1984—Buffalo NFL	16	69	862	12.5	4		None				None			4	24	4
Pro Totals—3 Years	44	101	1343	13.3	8	5	45	9.0	0	21	436	20.8	0	8	48	6

Additional pro statistics: Rushed once for minus 11 yards, 1981; rushed once for three yards, 1983; rushed once for minus seven yards, 1984.

—DID YOU KNOW—
That the scoring leaders for each NFC team were placekickers, while three AFC teams were led by non-placekickers? The three non-kickers were Greg Bell of Buffalo, Marcus Allen of the Los Angeles Raiders and Miami's Mark Clayton.

ELVIS FRANKS
Defensive End—Cleveland Browns
Born July 9, 1957, at Doucette, Tex.
Height, 6.04. Weight, 265.
High School—Woodville, Tex., Kirby.
Attended Morgan State University.

Selected by Cleveland in 5th round (116th player selected) of 1980 NFL draft.
Cleveland NFL, 1980 through 1984.
Games: 1980 (16), 1981 (16), 1982 (9), 1983 (16), 1984 (16). Total—73.
Pro statistics: Recovered one fumble, 1980 and 1983; recovered one fumble for three yards, 1982.

GUY SHELTON FRAZIER
Linebacker—Cincinnati Bengals
Born July 20, 1959, at Detroit, Mich.
Height, 6.02. Weight, 221.
High School—Detroit, Mich., Cass Tech.
Attended University of Wyoming.

Selected by Cincinnati in 4th round (93rd player selected) of 1981 NFL draft.
On injured reserve with broken hand, October 10 through November 16, 1983; activated, November 17, 1983.
Cincinnati NFL, 1981 through 1984.
Games: 1981 (16), 1982 (9), 1983 (10), 1984 (16). Total—51.
Played in AFC Championship Game following 1981 season.
Played in NFL Championship Game following 1981 season.

LESLIE A. FRAZIER
Cornerback—Chicago Bears
Born April 3, 1959, at Columbus, Miss.
Height, 6.00. Weight, 189.
High School—Columbus, Miss., Lee.
Attended Alcorn State University.

Signed as free agent by Chicago Bears, July 18, 1981.

| | | -INTERCEPTIONS- | | | | —KICKOFF RET.— | | | | —TOTAL— | | |
Year Club	G.	No.	Yds.	Avg.	TD.	No.	Yds.	Avg.	TD.	TD.	Pts.	F.
1981—Chicago NFL	13		None			6	77	12.8	0	0	0	0
1982—Chicago NFL	9		None			2	0	0.0	0	0	0	0
1983—Chicago NFL	16	7	135	19.3	1		None			1	6	0
1984—Chicago NFL	11	5	89	17.8	0		None			0	0	0
Pro Totals—4 Years	49	12	224	18.7	1	8	77	9.6	0	1	6	0

Additional pro statistics: Recovered one fumble for seven yards, 1982; recovered one fumble for three yards, 1983.
Played in NFC Championship Game following 1984 season.

ANDREW BRIAN FREDERICK
(Andy)
Offensive Tackle—Chicago Bears
Born July 25, 1954, at Oak Park, Ill.
Height, 6.06. Weight, 265.
High School—Westchester, Ill., St. Joseph
Received bachelor of science degree in business from University of New Mexico in 1977.

Selected by Dallas in 5th round (137th player selected) of 1977 NFL draft.
Released by Dallas Cowboys, August 21, 1979; re-signed by Cowboys, August 31, 1979.
Released by Dallas Cowboys, September 6, 1982; claimed on waivers by Cleveland Browns, September 7, 1982.
On inactive list, September 12, 1982.
Traded by Cleveland Browns to Chicago Bears for past consideration, April 28, 1983 (Bears had acquired offensive lineman Gerry Sullivan from Browns in 1982 for 6th round pick in 1983 but Sullivan retired three days after reporting).
Released by Chicago Bears, August 29, 1983; re-signed by Bears, August 30, 1983.
Dallas NFL, 1977 through 1981; Cleveland NFL, 1982; Chicago NFL, 1983 and 1984.
Games: 1977 (14), 1978 (16), 1979 (16), 1980 (16), 1981 (16), 1982 (7), 1983 (16), 1984 (16). Total—117.
Pro statistics: Recovered one fumble, 1978.
Played in NFC Championship Game following 1977, 1978, 1980 and 1984 seasons.
Member of Dallas Cowboys for NFC Championship Game following 1981 season; did not play.
Played in NFL Championship Game following 1977 and 1978 seasons.

MICHAEL JOSEPH FREEMAN
(Mike)
Guard—Denver Broncos
Born October 13, 1961, at Mt. Holly, N.J.
Height, 6.03. Weight, 249.
High Schools—Tucson, Ariz., Sahuaro and Fountain Valley, Calif.
Attended University of Arizona.
Nephew of Bob Freeman, defensive back with Cleveland Browns, Green Bay Packers,
Philadelphia Eagles and Washington Redskins, 1957 through 1962.

Signed as free agent by Denver Broncos, May 2, 1984.
Denver NFL, 1984.
Games: 1984 (9).

REESE BRYAN FREEMAN
Defensive Tackle—San Francisco 49ers
Born April 5, 1962, at Omaha, Neb.
Height, 6.03. Weight, 245.
High School—Omaha, Neb., Central.
Attended University of Northern Colorado.

Selected by New Jersey in 15th round (298th player selected) of 1984 USFL draft.
Signed by New Jersey Generals, January 7, 1984.
Released by New Jersey Generals, January 20, 1984; signed as free agent by Dallas Cowboys, May 3, 1984.
Released by Dallas Cowboys, July 23, 1984; signed as free agent by San Antonio Gunslingers, November 28, 1984.
Released by San Antonio Gunslingers, January 28, 1985; signed as free agent by San Francisco 49ers, May 14, 1985.

STEVEN JAY FREEMAN
(Steve)
Safety—Buffalo Bills
Born May 8, 1953, at Lamesa, Tex.
Height, 5.11. Weight, 185.
High School—Memphis, Tenn., Whitehaven.
Attended Mississippi State University.

Named to THE SPORTING NEWS NFL All-Star Team, 1983.
Selected by New England in 5th round (117th player selected) of 1975 NFL draft.
Claimed on waivers from New England Patriots by Buffalo Bills, August 21, 1975.

| | | | —INTERCEPTIONS— | | |
Year Club	G.	No.	Yds.	Avg.	TD.
1975—Buffalo NFL	14	2	44	22.0	1
1976—Buffalo NFL	14		None		
1977—Buffalo NFL	14	1	4	4.0	0
1978—Buffalo NFL	16		None		
1979—Buffalo NFL	16	3	62	20.7	1
1980—Buffalo NFL	16	7	107	15.3	1
1981—Buffalo NFL	16		None		
1982—Buffalo NFL	9	3	27	9.0	0
1983—Buffalo NFL	16	3	40	13.3	0
1984—Buffalo NFL	15	3	45	15.0	0
Pro Totals—10 Years	146	22	329	15.0	3

Additional pro statistics: Recovered one fumble, 1975, 1976, 1982 and 1984; recovered two fumbles, 1979; returned one kickoff for no yards, 1981; recovered two fumbles for 31 yards, 1983.

WILLIAM JASPER FRIZZELL
Defensive Back—Detroit Lions
Born September 8, 1962, at Greenville, N.C.
Height, 6.03. Weight, 198.
High School—Greenville, N.C., J.H. Rose.
Attended North Carolina Central University.

Selected by Detroit in 10th round (259th player selected) of 1984 NFL draft.
Detroit NFL, 1984.
Games: 1984 (16).

IRVING DALE FRYAR
Wide Receiver-Kickoff Returner—New England Patriots
Born September 28, 1962, at Mount Holly, N.J.
Height, 6.00. Weight, 200.
High School—Mount Holly, N.J., Rancocas Valley Regional.
Attended University of Nebraska.

Named as wide receiver on THE SPORTING NEWS College All-America Team, 1983.
Selected by Chicago in 1st round (3rd player selected) of 1984 USFL draft.
Signed by New England Patriots, April 11, 1984.
Selected officially by New England in 1st round (1st player selected) of 1984 NFL draft.

| | | —RUSHING— | | | | PASS RECEIVING | | | | —TOTAL— | | |
Year Club	G.	Att.	Yds.	Avg.	TD.	P.C.	Yds.	Avg.	TD.	TD.	Pts.	F.
1984—New England NFL	14	2	—11	—5.5	0	11	164	14.9	1	1	6	4

| | | —PUNT RETURNS— | | | | —KICKOFF RET.— | | |
Year Club	G.	No.	Yds.	Avg.	TD.	No.	Yds.	Avg.	TD.
1984—New England NFL	14	36	347	9.6	0	5	95	19.0	0

Additional pro statistics: Recovered one fumble, 1984.

DAVID FRYE
(Dave)
Linebacker—Atlanta Falcons
Born June 21, 1961, at Cincinnati, O.
Height, 6.02. Weight, 213.
High School—Cincinnati, O., Woodward.
Attended Santa Ana College and Purdue University.

Signed as free agent by Atlanta Falcons, May 9, 1983.
Atlanta NFL, 1983 and 1984.
Games: 1983 (16), 1984 (16). Total—32.
Pro statistics: Recovered two fumbles, 1983 and 1984.

JEFFERY AVERY FULLER
(Jeff)
Safety—San Francisco 49ers
Born August 8, 1962, at Dallas, Tex.
Height, 6.02. Weight, 216.
High School—Dallas, Tex., Franklin D. Roosevelt.
Attended Texas A&M University.

Selected by Houston in 1984 USFL territorial draft.
Selected by San Francisco in 5th round (139th player selected) of 1984 NFL draft.
Signed by San Francisco 49ers, May 29, 1984.
San Francisco NFL, 1984.
Games: 1984 (13).
Pro statistics: Intercepted one pass for 38 yards, 1984.
Played in NFC Championship Game following 1984 season.
Played in NFL Championship Game following 1984 season.

STEPHEN RAY FULLER
(Steve)
Quarterback—Chicago Bears
Born January 5, 1957, at Enid, Okla.
Height, 6.04. Weight, 198.
High School—Spartanburg, S.C.
Received degree from Clemson University.

Selected by Kansas City in 1st round (23rd player selected) of 1979 NFL draft.
On injured reserve with knee injury, December 18 through remainder of 1980 season.
Traded by Kansas City Chiefs to Los Angeles Rams for cornerback Lucious Smith and 5th round pick in 1985 draft, August 19, 1983.
Traded by Los Angeles Rams to Chicago Bears for 11th round pick in 1984 draft and 6th round pick in 1985 draft, April 30, 1984.
On injured reserve with separated shoulder, August 28 through October 5, 1984; activated, October 6, 1984.
Active for 16 games with Los Angeles Rams in 1983; did not play.

Year Club	G.	Att.	Cmp.	Pct.	Gain	T.P.	P.I.	Avg.	Att.	Yds.	Avg.	TD.	TD.	Pts.	F.
				PASSING						RUSHING				TOTAL	
1979—Kansas City NFL	16	270	146	54.1	1484	6	14	5.50	50	264	5.3	1	1	6	6
1980—Kansas City NFL	14	320	193	60.3	2250	10	12	7.03	60	274	4.6	4	4	24	*16
1981—Kansas City NFL	13	134	77	57.5	934	3	4	6.97	19	118	6.2	0	0	0	4
1982—Kansas City NFL	9	93	49	52.7	665	3	2	7.15	10	56	5.6	0	0	0	3
1984—Chicago NFL	6	78	53	67.9	595	3	0	7.63	15	89	5.9	1	1	6	0
Pro Totals—6 Years	58	895	518	57.9	5928	25	32	6.62	154	801	5.2	6	6	36	29

Quarterback Rating Points: 1979 (55.8), 1980 (76.1), 1981 (73.9), 1982 (77.3), 1984 (103.3). Total—72.3.
Additional pro statistics: Recovered three fumbles and fumbled six times for minus four yards, 1979; recovered seven fumbles and fumbled 16 times for minus 43 yards, 1980; recovered one fumble and fumbled four times for minus six yards, 1981; recovered two fumbles, 1982.
Played in NFC Championship Game following 1984 season.

DAN B. FULTON
(Danny)
Wide Receiver—San Francisco 49ers
Born September 2, 1956, at Memphis, Tenn.
Height, 6.02. Weight, 186.
High School—Omaha, Neb., Tech.
Attended University of Nebraska and University of Nebraska at Omaha.

Selected by Buffalo in 3rd round (65th player selected) of 1978 NFL draft.
On injured reserve with foot injury, August 31 through entire 1978 season.
Released by Buffalo Bills, September 1, 1980; signed as free agent by Cleveland Browns, January 8, 1981.
Released by Cleveland Browns, August 29, 1983; signed by Chicago Blitz, May 5, 1984.
On developmental squad, May 5 through May 13, 1984.
Released by Chicago Blitz, May 14, 1984; signed as free agent by San Francisco 49ers, May 17, 1984.
On injured reserve with shoulder injury, August 13 through entire 1984 season.
On developmental squad for 2 games with Chicago Blitz in 1984.

Year Club	G.	P.C.	Yds.	Avg.	TD.
		PASS RECEIVING			
1979—Buffalo NFL	6	2	34	17.0	0
1981—Cleveland NFL	5	2	38	19.0	0
1982—Cleveland NFL	9	1	9	9.0	0
Pro Totals—3 Years	20	5	81	16.2	0

DERRICK TYRONE GAFFNEY
Wide Receiver—New York Jets

Born May 24, 1955, at Jacksonville, Fla.
Height, 6.01. Weight, 182.
High School—Jacksonville, Fla., Raines.
Received degree in public relations from University of Florida in 1978.

Selected by New York Jets in 8th round (197th player selected) of 1978 NFL draft.
On injured reserve with bruised quadricep, November 26 through remainder of 1984 season.

| | | | —PASS RECEIVING— | | | |
Year	Club	G.	P.C.	Yds.	Avg.	TD.
1978—N.Y. Jets NFL		16	38	691	18.2	3
1979—N.Y. Jets NFL		16	32	534	16.7	1
1980—N.Y. Jets NFL		13	24	397	16.5	2
1981—N.Y. Jets NFL		16	14	246	17.6	0
1982—N.Y. Jets NFL		9	11	207	18.8	1
1983—N.Y. Jets NFL		16	17	243	14.3	0
1984—N.Y. Jets NFL		12	19	285	15.0	0
Pro Totals—7 Years		98	155	2603	16.8	7

Additional pro statistics: Rushed twice for minus two yards, 1978; returned one kickoff for six yards and recovered one fumble, 1984.

Played in AFC Championship Game following 1982 season.

GREGORY SCOTT GAINES
(Greg)
Linebacker—Seattle Seahawks

Born October 16, 1958, at Martinsville, Va.
Height, 6.03. Weight, 220.
High School—Hermitage, Tenn., DuPont.
Attended University of Tennessee.
Nephew of Ray Oldham, safety with Baltimore Colts, Pittsburgh Steelers,
New York Giants and Detroit Lions, 1973 through 1982.

Signed as free agent by Seattle Seahawks, May 6, 1981.
On injured reserve with knee injury, October 28 through remainder of 1981 season.
On injured reserve with knee injury, August 31 through entire 1982 season.
Seattle NFL, 1981, 1983 and 1984.
Games: 1981 (8), 1983 (16), 1984 (16). Total—40.
Pro statistics: Recovered one fumble, 1981; recovered four fumbles, 1983; intercepted one pass for 18 yards, 1984.
Played in AFC Championship Game following 1983 season.

BLANE GAISON
Safety—Atlanta Falcons

Born May 13, 1958, At Kaneohe, Hawaii.
Height, 6.01. Weight, 188.
High School—Pearl City, Hawaii, Kamehameha.
Attended University of Hawaii.

Signed as free agent by Atlanta Falcons, June, 1981.
Atlanta NFL, 1981 through 1984.
Games: 1981 (14), 1982 (9), 1983 (16), 1984 (15). Total—54.
Pro statistics: Intercepted one pass for no yards, 1981 and 1982; returned three kickoffs for 43 yards, 1981; recovered one fumble, 1981 and 1984; returned two kickoffs for 14 yards, 1982; recovered one fumble for 64 yards and a touchdown, 1983; returned one kickoff for 15 yards, 1984.

HOWARD LEE GAJAN JR.

Name pronounced Guy-jawn.

(Hokie)
Running Back—New Orleans Saints

Born September 6, 1959, at Baton Rouge, La.
Height, 5.11. Weight, 225.
High School—Baker, La.
Attended Louisiana State University.

Selected by New Orleans in 10th round (249th player selected) of 1981 NFL draft.
On injured reserve with head injuries suffered in car accident, August 18 through entire 1981 season.
Released by New Orleans Saints, September 6, 1982; re-signed by Saints, September 7, 1982.

| | | | —RUSHING— | | | | PASS RECEIVING | | | | —TOTAL— | | |
Year	Club	G.	Att.	Yds.	Avg.	TD.	P.C.	Yds.	Avg.	TD.	TD.	Pts.	F.
1982—New Orleans NFL		9	19	77	4.1	0	3	10	3.3	0	0	0	0
1983—New Orleans NFL		16	81	415	5.1	4	17	130	7.6	0	4	24	3
1984—New Orleans NFL		14	102	615	*6.0	5	35	288	8.2	2	7	42	0
Pro Totals—3 Years		39	202	1107	5.5	9	55	428	7.8	2	11	66	3

Additional pro statistics: Returned one kickoff for 18 yards, 1982; recovered one fumble, 1982 and 1983; attempted one pass with no completions, 1983; attempted one pass with one completion for 34 yards and a touchdown, 1984.

ANTHONY GALBREATH

Name pronounced GALL-breath.

(Tony)
Running Back—New York Giants

Born January 29, 1954, at Fulton, Mo.
Height, 6.00. Weight, 228.
High School—Fulton, Mo.
Attended Centerville Community College and University of Missouri.

Selected by New Orleans in 2nd round (32nd player selected) of 1976 NFL draft.
On injured reserve with knee injury, December 16 through remainder of 1979 season.
Traded by New Orleans Saints to Minnesota Vikings for 3rd round pick in 1982 draft, August 31, 1981.
On inactive list, September 19, 1982.
Traded by Minnesota Vikings to New York Giants for linebacker Brad Van Pelt, July 12, 1984.

| | | —RUSHING— | | | | PASS RECEIVING | | | | —TOTAL— | | |
Year Club	G.	Att.	Yds.	Avg.	TD.	P.C.	Yds.	Avg.	TD.	TD.	Pts.	F.
1976—New Orleans NFL	14	136	570	4.2	7	54	420	7.8	1	8	48	7
1977—New Orleans NFL	14	168	644	3.8	3	41	265	6.5	0	3	18	3
1978—New Orleans NFL	16	186	635	3.4	5	74	582	7.9	2	7	42	6
1979—New Orleans NFL	15	189	708	3.7	9	58	484	8.3	1	10	67	5
1980—New Orleans NFL	16	81	308	3.8	3	57	470	8.2	2	5	30	3
1981—Minnesota NFL	14	42	198	4.7	2	18	144	8.0	0	2	12	2
1982—Minnesota NFL	8	39	116	3.0	1	17	153	9.0	0	1	6	1
1983—Minnesota NFL	13	113	474	4.2	4	45	348	7.7	2	6	36	4
1984—New York Giants NFL	16	22	97	4.4	0	37	357	9.6	0	0	0	0
Pro Totals—9 Years	126	976	3750	3.8	34	401	3223	8.0	8	42	259	31

Additional pro statistics: Recovered one fumble, 1976 and 1979; returned 20 kickoffs for 399 yards and returned two punts for eight yards, 1976; recovered two fumbles for one yard, 1978; made one of two extra points and two of three field goals for seven points and attempted three passes with two completions for 70 yards and one interception, 1979; recovered two fumbles, 1980 and 1983; returned six kickoffs for 86 yards and attempted two passes with no completions, 1980; returned one kickoff for 16 yards, 1981; attempted one pass with one completion for 13 yards, 1984.

JIM PATRICK GALLERY
Placekicker—Buffalo Bills

Born September 15, 1961, at Morton, Minn.
Height, 6.01. Weight, 202.
High School—Morton, Minn.
Attended University of Minnesota.

Selected by Tampa Bay in 10th round (254th player selected) of 1984 NFL draft.
NFL rights released by Tampa Bay Buccaneers, July 5, 1984; signed as free agent by Buffalo Bills, July 9, 1984.
Released by Buffalo Bills, August 14, 1984; re-signed by Bills, May 10, 1985.

RUSSELL ALVIN GALLON
Defensive Tackle-Defensive End—Denver Broncos

Born July 14, 1962, at Tampa, Fla.
Height, 6.07. Weight, 260.
High School—Tampa, Fla., Thomas Jefferson Comprehensive.
Attended University of Florida.

Brother of Ricky Gallon, third round selection (51st player selected) of Buffalo Braves in 1978 NBA draft.

Selected by Tampa Bay in 1985 USFL territorial draft.
Signed by Tampa Bay Bandits, December 20, 1984.
Released by Tampa Bay Bandits, February 11, 1985; signed as free agent by Denver Broncos, March 21, 1985.

DAVID LAWRENCE GALLOWAY
Defensive Tackle—St. Louis Cardinals

Born February 16, 1959, at Tampa, Fla.
Height, 6.03. Weight, 277.
High School—Brandon, Fla.
Attended University of Florida.

Selected by St. Louis in 2nd round (38th player selected) of 1982 NFL draft.
On injured reserve with dislocated shoulder, September 8 through November 30, 1982; activated, December 1, 1982.
St. Louis NFL, 1982 through 1984.
Games: 1982 (5), 1983 (16), 1984 (14). Total—35.
Pro statistics: Intercepted one pass for 17 yards, credited with one safety and recovered one fumble, 1983.

DUANE KEITH GALLOWAY
Cornerback—Detroit Lions

Born November 7, 1961, at Los Angeles, Calif.
Height, 5.09. Weight 185.
High School—Los Angeles, Calif., Crenshaw.
Attended Santa Monica City College and Arizona State University.

Selected by Los Angeles in 19th round (217th player selected) of 1983 USFL draft.
Signed by Los Angeles Express, January 26, 1983.
Released by Los Angeles Express, February 20, 1983; signed as free agent by Saskatchewan Roughriders, March 15, 1983.

Released by Saskatchewan Roughriders, June 28, 1983; re-signed by Roughriders, July 27, 1983.
Released by Saskatchewan Roughriders, September 11, 1983; signed as free agent by Indianapolis Colts, May 15, 1984.
On injured reserve with thigh injury, August 13 through September 17, 1984.
Released by Indianapolis Colts, September 18, 1984; signed as free agent by Detroit Lions, May 9, 1985.
Saskatchewan CFL, 1983.
Games: 1983 (6).

MICHAEL GAMBRELL
(Mike)
Center—Cleveland Browns
Born July 24, 1962, at Lake Charles, La.
Height, 6.05. Weight, 257.
High School—Slidell, La.
Attended Louisiana State University.

Signed as free agent by Cleveland Browns, June 17, 1984.
Released by Cleveland Browns, August 27, 1984; re-signed by Browns after clearing procedural waivers, March 3, 1985.

GEFF GANDY
Linebacker—Indianapolis Colts
Born May 1, 1960, at Dallas, Tex.
Height, 6.01. Weight, 228.
High School—San Antonio, Tex., Winston Churchill.
Attended Baylor University.

Selected by Washington in 10th round (279th player selected) of 1983 NFL draft.
On injured reserve with knee injury, August 29 through entire 1983 season.
Released by Washington Redskins, August 21, 1984; signed as free agent by Indianapolis Colts, April 27, 1985.

EDGAR I. GARCIA
(Eddie)
Placekicker—Miami Dolphins
Born April 15, 1960, at New Orleans, La.
Height, 5.08. Weight, 178.
High School—Dallas, Tex., Woodrow Wilson.
Received bachelor of business administration degree from
Southern Methodist University in 1982.

Selected by Green Bay in 10th round (264th player selected) of 1982 NFL draft.
On inactive list, September 12, 1982.
On injured reserve with pulled groin, September 15 through remainder of 1982 season.
On injured reserve with pulled hamstring, October 17 through November 12, 1984.
Released by Green Bay Packers, November 13, 1984; signed as free agent by Miami Dolphins, March 20, 1985.

				—PLACE KICKING—			
Year	Club	G.	XP.	XPM.	FG.	FGA.	Pts.
1983—Green Bay NFL		12		None			
1984—Green Bay NFL		7	14	1	3	9	23
Pro Totals—2 Years		19	14	1	3	9	23

FRANK GARCIA
Punter—Tampa Bay Buccaneers
Born June 5, 1957, at Tucson, Ariz.
Height, 6.00. Weight, 200.
High School—Tucson, Ariz., Salpointe.
Attended Arizona State University, received bachelor of science degree
in secondary education from University of Arizona and
attending Arizona for master's degree in special education.

Signed as free agent by Atlanta Falcons, May 5, 1979.
Released by Atlanta Falcons, July 26, 1979; signed as free agent by San Diego Chargers, June, 1980.
Released by San Diego Chargers, July 28, 1980; signed as free agent by Green Bay Packers, March 11, 1981.
Released by Green Bay Packers, August 17, 1981; signed as free agent by Tampa Bay Buccaneers, August 21, 1981.
Released by Tampa Bay Buccaneers, August 24, 1981; signed as free agent by Seattle Seahawks, December 16, 1981.
Released by Seattle Seahawks, August 31, 1982; signed as free agent by Chicago Blitz, March 19, 1983.
On developmental squad, April 10, 1983.
Released by Chicago Blitz, April 11, 1983; signed as free agent by Tampa Bay Buccaneers, May 11, 1983.
On developmental squad for 1 game with Chicago Blitz in 1983.

			—PUNTING—		
Year	Club	G.	No.	Avg.	Blk.
1981—Seattle NFL		1	2	37.0	0
1983—Chicago USFL		3	18	37.5	0
1983—Tampa Bay NFL		16	*95	42.2	1
1984—Tampa Bay NFL		16	68	41.9	0
NFL Totals—3 Years		33	165	42.0	1
USFL Totals—1 Year		3	18	37.5	0
Pro Totals—4 Years		36	183	41.6	1

Additional pro statistics: Attempted one pass with no completions, 1984.

ELLIS PENISTON GARDNER
Offensive Lineman—Indianapolis Colts
Born September 16, 1961, at Chattanooga, Tenn.
Height, 6.05. Weight, 250.
High School—Chattanooga, Tenn., McCallie.
Attended Georgia Tech.

Selected by Kansas City in 6th round (146th player selected) of 1983 NFL draft.
Released by Kansas City Chiefs, August 13, 1984; awarded on waivers to Houston Oilers, August 14, 1984.
Released by Houston Oilers, August 27, 1984; re-signed by Oilers, August 28, 1984.
Released by Houston Oilers, September 5, 1984; signed as free agent by Indianapolis Colts, September 12, 1984.
On injured reserve with back injury, November 14 through remainder of 1984 season.
Active for 1 game with Houston Oilers in 1984; did not play.
Kansas City NFL, 1983; Houston (0)-Indianapolis (9) NFL, 1984.
Games: 1983 (8), 1984 (9). Total—17.

SCOTT AARON GARNETT
Nose Tackle—Denver Broncos
Born December 3, 1962, at Harrisburg, Pa.
Height, 6.02. Weight, 271.
High School—Pasadena, Calif., John Muir.
Attended University of Washington.

Selected by Washington in 4th round (66th player selected) of 1984 USFL draft.
Selected by Denver in 8th round (218th player selected) of 1984 NFL draft.
Signed by Denver Broncos, May 15, 1984.
Denver NFL, 1984.
Games: 1984 (16).
Pro statistics: Recovered one fumble, 1984.

ALVIN LYNN GARRETT
Wide Receiver
Born October 1, 1956, at Mineral Wells, Tex.
Height, 5.07. Weight, 185.
High School—Mineral Wells, Tex.
Attended Angelo State University.

Selected by San Diego in 9th round (237th player selected) of 1979 NFL draft.
Released by San Diego Chargers, August 27, 1979; signed as free agent by New York Giants, March 1, 1980.
On injured reserve with fractured ribs, December 19 through remainder of 1980 season.
Released by New York Giants, August 31, 1981; re-signed by Giants, September 1, 1981.
Released by New York Giants, November 17, 1981; claimed on waivers by Washington Redskins, November 18, 1981.
On injured reserve with ankle injury, September 19 through remainder of 1984 season.
Granted free agency, February 1, 1985; signing rights released by Washington Redskins, May 16, 1985.

| | | —RUSHING— | | | PASS RECEIVING | | | | —TOTAL— | | |
Year Club	G.	Att.	Yds.	Avg. TD.	P.C.	Yds.	Avg. TD.		TD.	Pts.	F.
1980—New York Giants NFL	15	9	31	3.4 0	5	69	13.8	1	1	6	5
1981—N.Y. Giants (9)-Washington (4) NFL...	13	1	2	2.0 0		None			0	0	1
1982—Washington NFL	9		None		1	6	6.0	0	0	0	0
1983—Washington NFL	15	2	0	0.0 0	25	332	13.3	1	1	6	0
1984—Washington NFL	3		None		1	5	5.0	0	0	0	0
Pro Totals—5 Years	55	12	33	2.8 0	32	412	12.9	2	2	12	6

| | | —PUNT RETURNS— | | | —KICKOFF RET.— | | |
Year Club	G.	No.	Yds.	Avg. TD.	No.	Yds.	Avg.TD.
1980—New York Giants NFL	15	35	287	8.2 0	28	527	18.8 0
1981—New York Giants (9)-Washington (4) NFL	13	8	57	7.1 0	18	401	22.3 0
1982—Washington NFL	9		None		2	35	17.5 0
1983—Washington NFL	15		None		2	50	25.0 0
1984—Washington NFL	3		None			None	
Pro Totals—5 Years	55	43	344	8.0 0	50	1013	20.3 0

Additional pro statistics: Recovered three fumbles, 1980.
Played in NFC Championship Game following 1982 and 1983 seasons.
Played in NFL Championship Game following 1982 and 1983 seasons.

GREGG DAVID GARRITY
Wide Receiver—Philadelphia Eagles
Born November 24, 1960, at Pittsburgh, Pa.
Height, 5.10. Weight, 171.
High School—Wexford, Pa., North Allegheny.
Received bachelor of science degree in industrial arts education
from Penn State University in 1983.

Selected by Philadelphia in 1983 USFL territorial draft.
Selected by Pittsburgh in 5th round (140th player selected) of 1983 NFL draft.
Signed by Pittsburgh Steelers, May 20, 1983.
Released by Pittsburgh Steelers, October 23, 1984; awarded on waivers to Philadelphia Eagles, October 24, 1984.

		—PASS RECEIVING—			
Year Club	G.	P.C.	Yds.	Avg.	TD.
1983—Pittsburgh NFL.............	15	19	279	14.7	1
1984—Pitt. (6)-Phi. (4) NFL...	10	2	22	11.0	0
Pro Totals—2 Years...........	25	21	301	14.3	1

Additional pro statistics: Recovered one fumble and fumbled once, 1983.

ARNOLD P. GARRON
Safety—New England Patriots
Born April 15, 1962, at Berwyn, Ill.
Height, 6.01. Weight, 195.
High School—Framingham, Mass., South.
Received bachelor of science degree in hotel management from University of New Hampshire in 1984.
Son of Larry Garron, running back with Boston Patriots, 1960 through 1968.

Selected by Denver in 7th round (130th player selected) of 1984 USFL draft.
Signed as free agent by Washington Redskins, May 11, 1984.
Released by Washington Redskins, July 31, 1984.
USFL rights traded by Denver Gold to Chicago Blitz for past considerations, October 11, 1984.
Signed as free agent by New England Patriots, February 25, 1985.

KEITH JERROLD GARY
Defensive End—Pittsburgh Steelers
Born September 14, 1959, at Bethesda, Md.
Height, 6.03. Weight, 260.
High School—Fairfax, Va., Chantilly.
Attended Ferrum Junior College and University of Oklahoma.

Selected by Pittsburgh in 1st round (17th player selected) of 1981 NFL draft.
Signed by Montreal Alouettes, July 7, 1981.
On reserve, August 30 through September 4, 1982.
On injured list, September 5 through remainder of 1982 season.
Granted free agency, March 11, 1983; signed by Pittsburgh Steelers, April 15, 1983.
Montreal CFL, 1981 and 1982; Pittsburgh NFL, 1983 and 1984.
Games: 1981 (13), 1982 (7), 1983 (16), 1984 (16). Total CFL—20. Total NFL—32. Total Pro—52.
CFL statistics: Recovered one fumble for 20 yards, 1982.
NFL statistics: Recovered two fumbles for 17 yards, 1983; recovered one fumble for six yards, 1984.
Played in AFC Championship Game following 1984 season.

RUSSELL CRAIG GARY
Safety—New Orleans Saints
Born July 31, 1959, at Minneapolis, Minn.
Height, 5.11. Weight, 195.
High School—Minneapolis, Minn., Central.
Attended University of Nebraska.

Selected by New Orleans in 2nd round (29th player selected) of 1981 NFL draft.

		—INTERCEPTIONS—			
Year Club	G.	No.	Yds.	Avg.	TD.
1981—New Orleans NFL........	14	1	0	0.0	0
1982—New Orleans NFL........	9	2	25	12.5	0
1983—New Orleans NFL........	14	3	70	23.3	0
1984—New Orleans NFL........	16			None	
Pro Totals—4 Years............	53	6	95	15.8	0

Additional pro statistics: Recovered two fumbles, 1982; fumbled once, 1983; recovered one fumble for five yards, 1984.

MARCUS D. GASTINEAU
Name pronounced GAS-tin-oh.
(Mark)
Defensive End—New York Jets
Born November 20, 1956, at Ardmore, Okla.
Height, 6.05. Weight, 265.
High School—Springerville, Ariz., Round Valley.
Attended Eastern Arizona Junior College, Arizona State University and
East Central (Okla.) University

Named to THE SPORTING NEWS NFL All-Star Team, 1984.
Selected by New York Jets in 2nd round (41st player selected) of 1979 NFL draft.
New York Jets NFL, 1979 through 1984.
Games: 1979 (16), 1980 (16), 1981 (16), 1982 (9), 1983 (16), 1984 (16). Total—89.
Pro statistics: Recovered two fumbles, 1981; recovered two fumbles (including one in end zone for a touchdown),
1983; recovered one fumble in end zone for a touchdown, 1984.
Played in AFC Championship Game following 1982 season.
Played in Pro Bowl (NFL All-Star Game) following 1981 through 1984 seasons.

WILLIE JAMES GAULT
Wide Receiver—Chicago Bears

Born September 5, 1960, at Griffin, Ga.
Height, 6.00. Weight, 178.
High School—Griffin, Ga.
Attended University of Tennessee.

Selected by New Jersey in 1983 USFL territorial draft.
Selected by Chicago in 1st round (18th player selected) of 1983 NFL draft.
Signed by Chicago Bears, August 16, 1983.

| | | —RUSHING— | | | | PASS RECEIVING | | | | —TOTAL— | | |
Year Club	G.	Att.	Yds.	Avg.	TD.	P.C.	Yds.	Avg.	TD.	TD.	Pts.	F.
1983—Chicago NFL	16	4	31	7.8	0	40	836	20.9	8	8	48	1
1984—Chicago NFL	16		None			34	587	17.3	6	6	36	1
Pro Totals—2 Years	32	4	31	7.8	0	74	1423	19.2	14	14	84	2

| | | —PUNT RETURNS— | | | | —KICKOFF RET.— | | | |
Year Club	G.	No.	Yds.	Avg.	TD.	No.	Yds.	Avg.	TD.
1983—Chicago NFL	16	9	60	6.7	0	13	276	21.2	0
1984—Chicago NFL	16		None			1	12	12.0	0
Pro Totals—2 Years	32	9	60	6.7	0	14	288	20.6	0

Additional pro statistics: Recovered one fumble, 1983.
Played in NFC Championship Game following 1984 season.

STAN GAY
Defensive Back—Atlanta Falcons

Born December 6, 1960, at Tuskegee, Ala.
Height, 5.10. Weight, 180.
High School—Tuskegee Institute, Ala. Logan Hall.
Attended University of Alabama.

Signed as free agent by Atlanta Falcons, May 2, 1984.
On injured reserve, August 21 through entire 1984 season.

WILLIAM H. GAY
(Bill)
Defensive Lineman—Detroit Lions

Born May 28, 1955, at San Francisco, Calif.
Height, 6.05. Weight, 255.
High School—San Diego, Calif., Herbert Hoover.
Attended San Diego City College and University of Southern California.
Related to Dwight McDonald, wide receiver with San Diego Chargers, 1975 through 1978.

Selected by Denver in 2nd round (55th player selected) of 1978 NFL draft.
Traded by Denver Broncos to Detroit Lions for defensive back Charlie West and 6th round pick in 1979 draft, August 14, 1978.
Detroit NFL, 1978 through 1984.
Games: 1978 (16), 1979 (15), 1980 (16), 1981 (16), 1982 (9), 1983 (15), 1984 (16). Total—103.
Pro statistics: Recovered one fumble, 1978, 1981 and 1982; returned one kickoff for no yards, recovered one fumble in end zone for a touchdown and fumbled once, 1979; intercepted one pass for seven yards, 1982; recovered one fumble for 11 yards, 1983; recovered two fumbles for 30 yards, 1984.
Played in Pro Bowl (NFL All-Star Game) following 1983 season.

SHAUN LaNARD GAYLE
Defensive Back—Chicago Bears

Born March 8, 1962, at Newport News, Va.
Height, 5.11. Weight, 195.
High School—Hampton, Va., Bethel.
Received bachelor of science degree in education from Ohio State University in 1984

Selected by Michigan in 14th round (288th player selected) of 1984 USFL draft.
Selected by Chicago in 10th round (271st player selected) of 1984 NFL draft.
Signed by Chicago Bears, June 21, 1984.
On injured reserve with broken ankle, December 12 through remainder of 1984 season.
Chicago NFL, 1984.
Games: 1984 (15).
Pro statistics: Intercepted one pass for minus one yard, 1984.

JAMES GEATHERS
Defensive End—New Orleans Saints

Born June 26, 1960, at Georgetown, S.C.
Height, 6.07. Weight, 267.
High School—Georgetown, S.C., Choppee.
Attended Wichita State University.
Brother of Robert Geathers, defensive end with Boston Breakers, 1983.

Selected by Oklahoma in 1984 USFL territorial draft.
Selected by New Orleans in 2nd round (42nd player selected) of 1984 NFL draft.
Signed by New Orleans Saints, May 30, 1984.
New Orleans NFL, 1984.
Games: 1984 (16).

DENNIS GENTRY
Running Back—Chicago Bears
Born February 10, 1959, at Lubbock, Tex.
Height, 5.08. Weight, 184.
High School—Lubbock, Tex., Dunbar.
Attended Baylor University.

Selected by Chicago in 4th round (89th player selected) of 1982 NFL draft.

		—RUSHING—				PASS RECEIVING				—TOTAL—		
Year	Club	G.	Att.	Yds.	Avg.	TD.	P.C.	Yds.	Avg.	TD.	TD.	Pts.	F.
1982—Chicago NFL		9	4	21	5.3	0	1	9	9.0	0	0	0	4
1983—Chicago NFL		15	16	65	4.1	0	2	8	4.0	0	0	0	1
1984—Chicago NFL		16	21	79	3.8	1	4	29	7.3	0	1	6	0
Pro Totals—3 Years		40	41	165	4.0	1	7	46	6.6	0	1	6	5

			—PUNT RETURNS—				—KICKOFF RET.—			
Year	Club	G.	No.	Yds.	Avg.	TD.	No.	Yds.	Avg.	TD.
1982—Chicago NFL		9	17	89	5.2	0	9	161	17.9	0
1983—Chicago NFL		15			None		7	130	18.6	0
1984—Chicago NFL		16			None		11	209	19.0	0
Pro Totals—3 Years		40	17	89	5.2	0	27	500	18.5	0

Additional pro statistics: Recovered one fumble, 1982.
Played in NFC Championship Game following 1984 season.

RALPH GIACOMARRO
Punter—Atlanta Falcons
Born January 17, 1961, at Passaic, N.J.
Height, 6.01. Weight, 190.
High School—Saddle Brook, N.J.
Attended Penn State University.

Selected by Philadelphia in 1983 USFL territorial draft.
Selected by Atlanta in 10th round (268th player selected) of 1983 NFL draft.
Signed by Atlanta Falcons, July 15, 1983.

			—PUNTING—		
Year	Club	G.	No.	Avg.	Blk.
1983—Atlanta NFL		16	70	40.3	1
1984—Atlanta NFL		16	68	42.0	2
Pro Totals—2 Years		32	138	41.1	3

Additional pro statistics: Rushed twice for 13 yards and attempted one pass with one completion for 23 yards, 1983; recovered one fumble and fumbled once, 1983 and 1984; rushed once for no yards, 1984.

ERNEST GERARD GIBSON
Defensive Back—New England Patriots
Born October 3, 1961, at Jacksonville, Fla.
Height, 5.10. Weight, 185.
High School—Jacksonville, Fla., Bishop Kenny.
Received bachelor of arts degree in political science from Furman University in 1984.

Selected by Memphis in 3rd round (44th player selected) of 1984 USFL draft.
USFL rights traded by Memphis Showboats to Birmingham Stallions for rights to quarterback Walter Lewis, January 16, 1984.
Selected by New England in 6th round (151st player selected) of 1984 NFL draft.
Signed by New England Patriots, June 6, 1984.

			—INTERCEPTIONS—		
Year	Club	G.	No.	Yds.	Avg.	TD.
1984—New England NFL		15	2	4	2.0	0

Additional pro statistics: Returned one punt for three yards and recovered one fumble, 1984.

JON WILLIAM GIESLER
Name pronounced Geese-ler.
Offensive Tackle—Miami Dolphins
Born December 23, 1956, at Toledo, O.
Height, 6.05. Weight, 260.
High School—Elmore, O., Woodmore.
Received bachelor of science degree in education from University of Michigan in 1979.

Selected by Miami in 1st round (24th player selected) of 1979 NFL draft.
On injured reserve with shoulder injury, September 2 through October 9, 1980; activated, October 10, 1980.
Miami NFL, 1979 through 1984.
Games: 1979 (16), 1980 (10), 1981 (16), 1982 (9), 1983 (16), 1984 (16). Total—83.
Pro statistics: Recovered one fumble, 1981.
Played in AFC Championship Game following 1982 and 1984 seasons.
Played in NFL Championship Game following 1982 and 1984 seasons.

JIMMIE GILES JR.
Tight End—Tampa Bay Buccaneers
Born November 8, 1954, at Natchez, Miss.
Height, 6.03. Weight, 240.
High School—Greenville, Miss.
Received bachelor of science degree in business administration from Alcorn State University in 1977.
Related to Sammy White, wide receiver with Minnesota Vikings.

Selected by Houston in 3rd round (70th player selected) of 1977 NFL draft.
Traded with four draft choices (1st and 2nd round in 1978 and 3rd and 5th round in 1979) by Houston Oilers to Tampa Bay Buccaneers for 1st round pick in 1978 draft, April 24, 1978.
On reserve/did not report, August 16 through August 26, 1983.
Reinstated and granted roster exemption, August 27 through September 1, 1983; activated, September 2, 1983.

Year Club	G.	P.C.	Yds.	Avg.	TD.
1977—Houston NFL	14	17	147	8.6	0
1978—Tampa Bay NFL	16	23	324	14.1	2
1979—Tampa Bay NFL	16	40	579	14.5	7
1980—Tampa Bay NFL	16	33	602	18.2	4
1981—Tampa Bay NFL	16	45	786	17.5	6
1982—Tampa Bay NFL	9	28	499	17.8	3
1983—Tampa Bay NFL	11	25	349	14.0	1
1984—Tampa Bay NFL	14	24	310	12.9	2
Pro Totals—8 Years	112	235	3596	15.3	25

Additional pro statistics: Rushed once for minus 10 yards, 1977; returned five kickoffs for 60 yards, rushed once for minus one yard, 1978; fumbled once, 1978 and 1983; rushed twice for seven yards, 1979; recovered one fumble, 1979, 1980 and 1982; fumbled twice, 1980 and 1982; rushed once for one yard, 1982.
Played in NFC Championship Game following 1979 season.
Played in Pro Bowl (NFL All-Star Game) following 1980 through 1982 seasons.

RECORD AS BASEBALL PLAYER

Selected by Los Angeles Dodgers' organization in 12th round of free-agent draft, June 8, 1976.
Placed on restricted list, July 14, 1977.

Year Club	League	Pos.	G.	AB.	R.	H.	2B.	3B.	HR.	RBI.	B.A.	PO.	A.	E.	F.A.
1976—Bellingham	Northw.	O-1-3	29	51	4	4	0	0	0	0	.078	16	5	2	.913

FERNANDARS GILLESPIE
(Scoop)
Running Back—Pittsburgh Steelers
Born February 26, 1962, at St. Louis, Mo.
Height, 5.10. Weight, 185.
High School—St. Louis, Mo., Southwest.
Received bachelor of arts degree in communications and business from
William Jewell College in 1984.

Selected by Pittsburgh in 12th round (332nd player selected) of 1984 NFL draft.
Released by Pittsburgh Steelers, August 27, 1984; re-signed by Steelers, September 11, 1984.

		—RUSHING—				PASS RECEIVING				—TOTAL—		
Year Club	G.	Att.	Yds.	Avg.	TD.	P.C.	Yds.	Avg.	TD.	TD.	Pts.	F.
1984—Pittsburgh NFL	14	7	18	2.6	0	1	12	12.0	0	0	0	1

Additional pro statistics: Returned one kickoff for 12 yards and recovered two fumbles, 1984.
Played in AFC Championship Game following 1984 season.

REGINALD GIPSON
Running Back—Buffalo Bills
Born July 27, 1960, at Birmingham, Ala.
Height, 6.02. Weight, 205.
High School—Brighton, Ala.
Attended Alabama A&M University.

Selected by Oakland in 13th round (151st player selected) of 1983 USFL draft.
Selected by Seattle in 6th round (150th player selected) of 1983 NFL draft.
Signed by Seattle Seahawks, June 15, 1983.
Released by Seattle Seahawks, August 29, 1983; signed as free agent by Buffalo Bills, March 27, 1984.
On injured reserve with back injury, August 14 through entire 1984 season.

ANDREW GISSINGER III
Center-Offensive Tackle—San Diego Chargers
Born July 4, 1959, at Barberton, O.
Height, 6.05. Weight, 282.
High School—Parma, O., Valley Forge.
Attended Syracuse University.

Selected by San Diego in 6th round (141st player selected) of 1981 NFL draft.
On injured reserve with back injury, August 31 through entire 1981 season.
San Diego NFL, 1982 through 1984.
Games: 1982 (9), 1983 (16), 1984 (16). Total—41.
Pro statistics: Returned one kickoff for no yards, 1982; caught one pass for three yards, 1984.

NESBY LEE GLASGOW
Safety—Indianapolis Colts
Born April 15, 1957, at Los Angeles, Calif.
Height, 5.10. Weight, 180.
High School—Gardena, Calif.
Attended University of Washington.

Tied NFL record for most combined kick returns, game (12), September 2, 1979, vs. Denver Broncos.
Selected by Baltimore in 8th round (207th player selected) of 1979 NFL draft.
Franchise transferred to Indianapolis, March 31, 1984.

Year Club	G.	INTERCEPTIONS				—PUNT RETURNS—				—KICKOFF RET.—				—TOTAL—		
		No.	Yds.	Avg.	TD.	No.	Yds.	Avg.	TD.	No.	Yds.	Avg.	TD.	TD.	Pts.	F.
1979—Baltimore NFL	16	1	—1	—1.0	0	44	352	8.0	1	50	1126	22.5	0	1	6	8
1980—Baltimore NFL	16	4	65	16.3	0	23	187	8.1	0	33	743	22.5	0	0	0	5
1981—Baltimore NFL	14	2	35	17.5	0	None				1	35	35.0	0	0	0	0
1982—Baltimore NFL	9	None				4	24	6.0	0	None				0	0	0
1983—Baltimore NFL	16	3	35	11.7	0	1	9	9.0	0	None				0	0	0
1984—Indianapolis NFL	16	1	8	8.0	0	7	79	11.3	0	None				0	0	1
Pro Totals—6 Years	87	11	142	12.9	0	79	651	8.2	1	84	1904	22.7	0	1	6	14

Additional pro statistics: Recovered two fumbles, 1979 through 1981; recovered one fumble, 1984.

CLYDE M. GLOVER
Defensive End—Kansas City Chiefs
Born July 16, 1960, at New Orleans, La.
Height, 6.06. Weight, 266.
High School—Las Vegas, Nev., Sunset.
Attended Walla Walla Community College and Fresno State University.

Selected by Oakland in 1984 USFL territorial draft.
Signed as free agent by New England Patriots, May 14, 1984.
Released by New England Patriots, August 21, 1984; signed as free agent by Kansas City Chiefs for 1985, October 15, 1984.

CHRISTOPHER JAMES GODFREY
(Chris)
Guard—New York Giants
Born May 17, 1958, at Detroit, Mich.
Height, 6.03. Weight, 265.
High Schools—Detroit, Mich., De LaSalle and Miami, Fla., Lake.
Received bachelor of science degree in business from University of Michigan in 1980.

Signed as free agent by Washington Redskins, May 20, 1980.
Released by Washington Redskins, August 26, 1980; signed as free agent by New York Jets, September 23, 1980.
On physically unable to perform/active list with knee injury, July 17 through August 10, 1981.
Released by New York Jets, August 11, 1981; claimed on waivers by Green Bay Packers, August 13, 1981.
On injured reserve with knee injury, August 31 through entire 1981 season.
Released by Green Bay Packers, August 30, 1982; signed by Michigan Panthers, January 24, 1983.
Signed by New York Giants, April 28, 1984, to contract to take effect after being granted free agency, November 30, 1984.
On developmental squad, May 13 through May 19, 1984; activated, May 20, 1984.
On developmental squad, June 2 through remainder of 1984 season.
On developmental squad for 5 games with Michigan Panthers in 1984.
New York Jets NFL, 1980; Michigan Panthers USFL, 1983 and 1984; New York Giants NFL, 1984.
Games: 1980 (6), 1983 (18), 1984 USFL (13), 1984 NFL (10). Total NFL—16. Total USFL—31. Total Pro—47.
Pro statistics: Recovered two fumbles, 1983.
Played in USFL Championship Game following 1983 season.

MIKE DAVID GOEDECKER
Linebacker—Cleveland Browns
Born August 25, 1959, at Rochester, Pa.
Height, 6.01. Weight, 225.
High School—Rochester, Pa.
Received bachelor of science degree in physical education from University of Miami (Fla.).

Signed as free agent by San Diego Chargers, May 25, 1982.
Released by San Diego Chargers, July 29, 1982; signed by Tampa Bay Bandits, January 21, 1983.
On developmental squad, March 4 through March 12, 1983; activated, March 13, 1983.
On developmental squad, April 18 through April 21, 1983; activated, April 22, 1983.
Selected by Jacksonville Bulls in 6th round (32nd player selected) of USFL expansion draft, September 6, 1983.
Released injured by Jacksonville Bulls, January 30, 1984; signed as free agent by Orlando Renegades, November 16, 1984.
Released by Orlando Renegades, January 28, 1985; signed as free agent by Cleveland Browns, May 6, 1985.
On developmental squad for 2 games with Tampa Bay Bandits in 1983.
Played with Virginia Hunters in American Football Association, 1981.
Tampa Bay USFL, 1983.
Games: 1983 (16).
Pro statistics: Credited with three sacks for 32 yards, returned one kickoff for no yards, scored two 2-point conversions and intercepted one pass for seven yards, 1983.

DERREL GLEN GOFOURTH
Guard—San Diego Chargers
Born March 20, 1955, at Little Parsons, Kan.
Height, 6.03. Weight, 260.
High School—Parsons, Kan.
Attended Oklahoma State University.

Selected by Green Bay in 7th round (172nd player selected) of 1977 NFL draft.
On injured reserve with knee injury, December 17 through remainder of 1981 season.
Traded by Green Bay Packers to San Diego Chargers for 12th round pick in 1984 draft, July 28, 1983.
Green Bay NFL, 1977 through 1982; San Diego NFL, 1983 and 1984.
Games: 1977 (14), 1978 (16), 1979 (16), 1980 (16), 1981 (15), 1982 (9), 1983 (15), 1984 (16). Total—117.
Pro statistics: Returned one kickoff for 13 yards, 1977; recovered one fumble, 1981 and 1982; returned one kickoff for no yards, 1984.

TIMOTHY GEORGE GOLDEN
(Tim)
Linebacker—New England Patriots
Born November 15, 1959, at Pahokee, Fla.
Height, 6.01. Weight, 220.
High School—Lauderdale Lakes, Fla., Boyd H. Anderson.
Attended University of Florida.

Signed as free agent by New England Patriots, May 22, 1981.
Left New England Patriots camp voluntarily and placed on left-camp retired list, July 22, 1981; reinstated, April 15, 1982.
Released by New England Patriots, August 27, 1984; re-signed by Patriots, September 5, 1984.
New England NFL, 1982 through 1984.
Games: 1982 (9), 1983 (16), 1984 (15). Total—40.
Pro statistics: Returned one kickoff for 10 yards and recovered two fumbles, 1983; recovered one fumble, 1984.

ROBERT PERRY GOLIC
Name pronounced Go-lick.
(Bob)
Nose Tackle—Cleveland Browns
Born October 26, 1957, at Cleveland, O.
Height, 6.02. Weight, 260.
High School—Cleveland, O., St. Joseph.
Received bachelor of business administration degree in management from
University of Notre Dame in 1979.
Son of Louis Golic, former player with Montreal Alouettes, Hamilton Tiger-Cats and Saskatchewan
Roughriders; and brother of Mike Golic, rookie defensive end with Houston Oilers.

Selected by New England in 2nd round (52nd player selected) of 1979 NFL draft.
On injured reserve with shoulder injury, August 28 through December 14, 1979; activated, December 15, 1979.
Released by New England Patriots, August 31, 1982; signed as free agent by Cleveland Browns, September 2, 1982.
On inactive list, September 12, 1982.
New England NFL, 1979 through 1982; Cleveland NFL, 1983 and 1984.
Games: 1979 (1), 1980 (16), 1981 (16), 1982 (6), 1983 (16), 1984 (15). Total—70.
Pro statistics: Recovered one fumble, 1981; intercepted one pass for seven yards and a touchdown, 1983; recovered one fumble for 18 yards, 1984.

CONRAD GOODE
Offensive Tackle—New York Giants
Born January 19, 1962, at St. Louis, Mo.
Height, 6.06. Weight, 285.
High School—Creve Coeur, Mo., Parkway Central.
Attended University of Missouri.
Stepson of Irv Goode, guard-center with St. Louis Cardinals, Buffalo Bills and
Miami Dolphins, 1962 through 1974.

Selected by Oklahoma in 1st round (22nd player selected) of 1984 USFL draft.
Selected by New York Giants in 4th round (87th player selected) of 1984 NFL draft.
Signed by New York Giants, June 8, 1984.
New York Giants NFL, 1984.
Games: 1984 (8).

JOHN TIMOTHY GOODE
Tight End—St. Louis Cardinals
Born November 5, 1962, at Cleveland Heights, O.
Height, 6.02. Weight, 222.
High School—Cleveland, O., Benedictine.
Attended Youngstown State University.

Selected by Oklahoma in 5th round (85th player selected) of 1984 USFL draft.
Selected by St. Louis in 5th round (136th player selected) of 1984 NFL draft.
Signed by St. Louis Cardinals, July 19, 1984.

		—————PASS RECEIVING—————				
Year Club		G.	P.C.	Yds.	Avg.	TD.
1984—St. Louis NFL.................		16	3	23	7.7	0

EUGENE GOODLOW
Wide Receiver—New Orleans Saints
Born December 19, 1958, at St. Louis, Mo.
Height, 6.02. Weight, 181.
High School—Rochester, N.Y., McQuaid Jesuit.
Attended Kansas State University.

Signed by Winnipeg Blue Bombers, September 22, 1980.
Selected by New Orleans in 3rd round (66th player selected) of 1982 NFL draft.
On injured list with neck injury, August 20 through remainder of 1982 season.
Granted free agency, March 1, 1983; signed by New Orleans Saints, March 2, 1983.
On injured reserve with pulled hamstring, October 5 through November 18, 1984; activated, November 19, 1984.

		—PASS RECEIVING—			
Year Club	G.	P.C.	Yds.	Avg.	TD.
1980—Winnipeg CFL..............	5	17	206	12.1	1
1981—Winnipeg CFL..............	16	∗100	1494	14.9	4
1982—Winnipeg CFL..............	6	30	515	17.2	8
1983—New Orleans NFL........	16	41	487	11.9	2
1984—New Orleans NFL........	10	22	281	12.8	3
CFL Totals—3 Years	27	147	2215	15.1	13
NFL Totals—2 Years..........	26	63	768	12.2	5
Pro Totals—5 Years............	53	210	2983	14.2	18

Additional CFL statistics: Returned three punts for 22 yards, two kickoffs for 38 yards and fumbled once, 1980; returned four kickoffs for 72 yards and recovered two fumbles, 1981.
Additional NFL statistics: Rushed once for three yards, 1983; rushed once for five yards, 1984.

DON CHARLES GOODMAN
Running Back—New York Giants
Born April 23, 1959, at Los Angeles, Calif.
Height, 5.11. Weight, 220.
High School—Los Angeles, Calif., Crenshaw.
Attended University of Cincinnati.

Signed as free agent by Washington Redskins, May 2, 1984.
Released by Washington Redskins, August 27, 1984; signed as free agent by New York Giants, March 21, 1985.

JOHN RICHARD GOODMAN
Defensive End—Pittsburgh Steelers
Born November 21, 1958, at Oklahoma City, Okla.
Height, 6.06. Weight, 255.
High School—Richardson, Tex., L. V. Berkner.
Attended University of Oklahoma.

Selected by Pittsburgh in 2nd round (56th player selected) of 1980 NFL draft.
On injured reserve with knee injury, September 2 through entire 1980 season.
Pittsburgh NFL, 1981 through 1984.
Games: 1981 (15), 1982 (9), 1983 (14), 1984 (14). Total—52.
Played in AFC Championship Game following 1984 season.

D. SCOTT GORDON
(Known by middle name.)
Guard—Houston Oilers
Born September 23, 1960, at Palo Alto, Calif.
Height, 6.04. Weight, 265.
High School—Maple Valley, Wash., Tahoma.
Attended Walla Walla Community College and University of Santa Clara.

Signed as free agent by Houston Oilers, July 5, 1984.
Released by Houston Oilers, August 14, 1984; re-signed by Oilers, April 3, 1985.

RUSSELL CRAIG GRAHAM
(Russ)
Offensive Tackle—Pittsburgh Steelers
Born May 5, 1961, at Borger, Tex.
Height, 6.02. Weight, 245.
Attended Oklahoma State University.

Selected by Michigan in 10th round (111th player selected) of 1983 USFL draft.
Signed by Michigan Panthers, January 12, 1983.
On developmental squad, April 21 through April 26, 1983.
Released by Michigan Panthers, April 27, 1983; signed as free agent by Pittsburgh Steelers, May 10, 1983.
Released by Pittsburgh Steelers after not reporting, July 15, 1983; re-signed by Steelers, June 15, 1984.
On injured reserve with knee injury, August 27 through entire 1984 season.
Michigan USFL, 1983.
Games: 1983 (4).

WILLIAM ROGER GRAHAM
Safety—Detroit Lions
Born September 27, 1959, at Silsbee, Tex.
Height, 5.11. Weight, 190.
High School—Silsbee, Tex.
Attended University of Texas.

Selected by Detroit in 5th round (127th player selected) of 1982 NFL draft.
On injured reserve with broken foot, September 7 through November 19, 1982; activated, November 20, 1982.

Year Club	G.	No.	Yds.	Avg.	TD.
		—INTERCEPTIONS—			
1982—Detroit NFL	7	None			
1983—Detroit NFL	14	None			
1984—Detroit NFL	14	3	22	7.3	0
Pro Totals—3 Years	35	3	22	7.3	0

Additional pro statistics: Recovered three fumbles, 1983; recovered two fumbles, 1984.

NORMAN LANCE GRANGER
(Norm)
Running Back—Dallas Cowboys
Born September 14, 1961, at Newark, N.J.
Height, 5.09. Weight, 220.
High School—Newark, N.J., Barringer.
Attended University of Iowa.

Selected by Oklahoma in 2nd round (37th player selected) of 1984 USFL draft.
Selected by Dallas in 5th round (137th player selected) of 1984 NFL draft.
Signed by Dallas Cowboys, May 16, 1984.
Dallas NFL, 1984.
Games: 1984 (15).
Pro statistics: Returned two kickoffs for six yards and recovered one fumble, 1984.

DARRYL GRANT
Defensive Tackle—Washington Redskins
Born November 22, 1959, at San Antonio, Tex.
Height, 6.01. Weight, 275.
High School—San Antonio, Tex., Highlands.
Attended Rice University.

Selected by Washington in 9th round (231st player selected) of 1981 NFL draft.
Washington NFL, 1981 through 1984.
Games: 1981 (15), 1982 (9), 1983 (16), 1984 (15). Total—55.
Pro statistics: Returned one kickoff for 20 yards, 1981; recovered two fumbles, 1983; recovered four fumbles for 22 yards and a touchdown, 1984.
Played in NFC Championship Game following 1982 and 1983 seasons.
Played in NFL Championship Game following 1982 and 1983 seasons.

OTIS GRANT
Wide Receiver—Los Angeles Rams
Born August 13, 1961, at Atlanta, Ga.
Height, 6.03. Weight, 197.
High School—Atlanta, Ga., Carver.
Attended Michigan State University.

Selected by Michigan in 1983 USFL territorial draft.
Selected by Los Angeles Rams in 5th round (134th player selected) of 1983 NFL draft.
Signed by Los Angeles Rams, June 28, 1983.
On non-football injury list, December 7 through remainder of 1984 season.
Selected by Pittsburgh Pirates' organization in 6th round of free-agent draft, June 6, 1979.

Year Club	G.	P.C.	Yds.	Avg.	TD.
		—PASS RECEIVING—			
1983—L.A. Rams NFL	16	12	221	18.4	1
1984—L.A. Rams NFL	14	9	64	7.1	0
Pro Totals—2 Years	30	21	285	13.6	1

Additional pro statistics: Rushed twice for minus 10 yards, recovered one fumble and fumbled once, 1983.

WILFRED L. GRANT
(Will)
Center—Buffalo Bills
Born March 7, 1954, at Boston, Mass.
Height, 6.04. Weight, 255.
High School—Braintree, Mass., Thayer Academy.
Attended Idaho State University and University of Kentucky.

Selected by Buffalo in 10th round (255th player selected) of 1978 NFL draft.
Buffalo NFL, 1978 through 1984.
Games: 1978 (16), 1979 (16), 1980 (16), 1981 (16), 1982 (9), 1983 (16), 1984 (16). Total—105.
Pro statistics: Recovered one fumble, 1980 and 1981.

MARSHARNE DeWAYNE GRAVES
Offensive Tackle—Denver Broncos
Born July 8, 1962, at Memphis, Tenn.
Height, 6.03. Weight, 272.
High School—San Francisco, Calif., Lincoln.
Attended University of Arizona.

Selected by Arizona in 1984 USFL territorial draft.
Signed as free agent by Denver Broncos, May 2, 1984.
Released by Denver Broncos, August 27, 1984; re-signed by Broncos for 1985, October 9, 1984.
Signed for 1984 season, November 5, 1984.
Denver NFL, 1984.
Games: 1984 (1).

EARNEST GRAY
Wide Receiver—New York Giants
Born March 2, 1957, at Greenwood, Miss.
Height, 6.03. Weight, 195.
High School—Greenwood, Miss.
Attended Memphis State University.

Selected by New York Giants in 2nd round (36th player selected) of 1979 NFL draft.
On injured reserve with broken hand, November 17 through December 13, 1984; activated, December 14, 1984.

| | | | —PASS RECEIVING— | | |
Year Club	G.	P.C.	Yds.	Avg.	TD.
1979—N.Y. Giants NFL	16	28	537	19.2	4
1980—N.Y. Giants NFL	16	52	777	14.9	10
1981—N.Y. Giants NFL	16	22	360	16.4	2
1982—N.Y. Giants NFL	9	25	426	17.0	4
1983—N.Y. Giants NFL	16	78	1139	14.6	5
1984—N.Y. Giants NFL	12	38	529	13.9	2
Pro Totals—6 Years............	85	243	3768	15.5	27

Additional pro statistics: Rushed twice for two yards and returned one kickoff for no yards, 1979; fumbled once, 1979 through 1981; recovered one fumble, 1980.

JOHNNIE LEE GRAY
Safety
Born December 18, 1953, at Lake Charles, La.
Height, 5.11. Weight, 202.
High School—Lompoc, Calif.
Attended Allan Hancock College and California State University at Fullerton.

Signed as free agent by Green Bay Packers, 1975.
On injured reserve with knee injury, November 4 through remainder of 1981 season.
On injured reserve with torn quadricep, August 30 through December 14, 1984; activated, December 15, 1984.
Released by Green Bay Packers, April 3, 1985.
Active for 1 game with Green Bay Packers in 1984; did not play.

| | | INTERCEPTIONS | | | | PUNT RETURNS | | | | —TOTAL— | | |
Year Club	G.	No.	Yds.	Avg.	TD.	No.	Yds.	Avg.	TD.	TD.	Pts.	F.
1975—Green Bay NFL	14	1	7	7.0	0	1	27	27.0	0	0	0	0
1976—Green Bay NFL	14	4	101	25.2	1	37	307	8.3	0	1	6	0
1977—Green Bay NFL	14	1	12	12.0	0	10	68	6.8	0	0	0	0
1978—Green Bay NFL	16	3	66	22.0	0	11	95	8.6	0	0	0	1
1979—Green Bay NFL	16	5	66	13.2	0	13	61	4.7	0	0	0	3
1980—Green Bay NFL	16	5	54	10.8	0	4	41	10.3	0	0	0	0
1981—Green Bay NFL	9		None			1	0	0.0	0	0	0	0
1982—Green Bay NFL	9	1	21	21.0	0	6	48	8.0	0	0	0	0
1983—Green Bay NFL	16	2	5	2.5	0	2	9	4.5	0	0	0	2
Pro Totals—10 Years.................	124	22	332	15.1	1	85	656	7.7	0	1	6	6

Additional pro statistics: Recovered four fumbles, 1975, 1976 and 1979; returned one kickoff for 23 yards, 1976; recovered two fumbles, 1977 and 1978; returned five kickoffs for 63 yards and recovered four fumbles for 30 yards, 1980; returned two kickoffs for 24 yards, 1981; recovered one fumble, 1981 and 1983; returned two kickoffs for 29 yards, 1982; returned 11 kickoffs for 178 yards, 1983.

KEVIN GRAY
Safety—Chicago Bears
Born September 11, 1957, at Chicago, Ill.
Height, 5.11. Weight, 179.
High School—Chicago, Ill., Hyde Park.
Attended Kennedy-King College and Eastern Illinois University.

Signed as free agent by New Orleans Saints, May 6, 1982.
Released by New Orleans Saints, August 29, 1983; signed by Jacksonville Bulls, November 15, 1983.
On developmental squad, March 23 through April 5, 1984; activated, April 6, 1984.
Released by Jacksonville Bulls, February 26, 1985; signed as free agent by Chicago Bears, May 8, 1985.
On developmental squad for 2 games with Jacksonville Bulls in 1984.
New Orleans NFL, 1982; Jacksonville USFL, 1984 and 1985.
Games: 1982 (8), 1984 (15), 1985 (1). Total USFL—16. Total Pro—24.
Pro statistics: Intercepted three passes for two yards, returned one kickoff for 14 yards and recovered one fumble, 1984.

DONALD GRECO
(Don)
Guard—Detroit Lions
Born April 1, 1959, at St. Louis, Mo.
Height, 6.03. Weight, 265.
High School—St. Louis, Mo., Riverview Gardens.
Attended Western Illinois University.

Selected by Detroit in 3rd round (72nd player selected) of 1981 NFL draft.
On injured reserve with pinched nerve, August 31 through entire 1981 season.
Detroit NFL, 1982 through 1984.
Games: 1982 (9), 1983 (12), 1984 (16). Total—37.
Pro statistics: Recovered one fumble, 1983 and 1984.

BOYCE K. GREEN
Running Back—Cleveland Browns
Born June 24, 1960, at Beaufort, S.C.
Height, 5.11. Weight, 215.
High School—Beaufort, S.C.
Received bachelor of science degree from Carson-Newman College in 1984.

Selected by Cleveland in 11th round (288th player selected) of 1983 NFL draft.

Year Club	G.	—RUSHING— Att.	Yds.	Avg.	TD.	PASS RECEIVING P.C.	Yds.	Avg.	TD.	—TOTAL— TD.	Pts.	F.
1983—Cleveland NFL	13	104	497	4.8	3	25	167	6.7	1	4	24	4
1984—Cleveland NFL	16	202	673	3.3	0	12	124	10.3	1	1	6	3
Pro Totals—2 Years	29	306	1170	3.8	3	37	291	7.9	2	5	30	7

Year Club	G.	KICKOFF RETURNS No.	Yds.	Avg.	TD.
1983—Cleveland NFL	13	17	350	20.6	0
1984—Cleveland NFL	16		None		
Pro Totals—2 Years	29	17	350	20.6	0

Additional pro statistics: Recovered two fumbles, 1984.

CLEVELAND CARL GREEN
Offensive Tackle—Miami Dolphins
Born September 11, 1957, at Bolton, Miss.
Height, 6.03. Weight, 262.
High School—Utica, Miss., Hinds County.
Attended Southern University.

Signed as free agent by Miami Dolphins, May, 1979.
On injured reserve with broken hand, October 10 through November 6, 1980; activated, November 7, 1980.
On inactive list, September 19, 1982.
Miami NFL, 1979 through 1984.
Games: 1979 (16), 1980 (12), 1981 (6), 1982 (3), 1983 (16), 1984 (16). Total—69.
Pro statistics: Recovered one fumble, 1980.
Played in AFC Championship Game following 1982 and 1984 seasons.
Played in NFL Championship Game following 1982 and 1984 seasons.

CURTIS GREEN
Defensive Lineman—Detroit Lions
Born June 3, 1958, at Quincy, Fla.
Height, 6.03. Weight, 258.
High School—Quincy, Fla., James A. Shanks.
Attended Alabama State University.

Selected by Detroit in 2nd round (46th player selected) of 1981 NFL draft.
On inactive list, September 19, 1982.
Detroit NFL, 1981 through 1984.
Games: 1981 (14), 1982 (7), 1983 (16), 1984 (16). Total—53.
Pro statistics: Recovered one fumble, 1981.

DARRELL GREEN
Cornerback—Washington Redskins
Born February 15, 1960, at Houston, Tex.
Height, 5.08. Weight, 170.
High School—Houston, Tex., Jesse Jones.
Attended Texas A&I University.

Selected by Denver in 10th round (112th player selected) of 1983 USFL draft.
Selected by Washington in 1st round (28th player selected) of 1983 NFL draft.
Signed by Washington Redskins, June 10, 1983.

Year Club	G.	—INTERCEPTIONS— No.	Yds.	Avg.	TD.
1983—Washington NFL	16	2	7	3.5	0
1984—Washington NFL	16	5	91	18.2	1
Pro Totals—2 Years	32	7	98	14.0	1

Additional pro statistics: Returned four punts for 29 yards, recovered one fumble and fumbled once, 1983; returned two punts for 13 yards, 1984.
Played in NFC Championship Game following 1983 season.
Played in NFL Championship Game following 1983 season.
Played in Pro Bowl (NFL All-Star Game) following 1984 season.

GARY F. GREEN
Cornerback—Los Angeles Rams
Born October 22, 1955, at San Antonio, Tex.
Height, 5.11. Weight, 191.
High School—San Antonio, Tex., Sam Houston.
Received bachelor of science degree in physical education from Baylor University in 1977.
Cousin of David Hill, tight end with Los Angeles Rams; and Jim Hill, defensive back with San Diego Chargers, Green Bay Packers and Cleveland Browns, 1969 through 1975.
Named as cornerback on THE SPORTING NEWS College All-America Team, 1976.
Selected by Kansas City in 1st round (10th player selected) of 1977 NFL draft.
Traded by Kansas City Chiefs to Los Angeles Rams for 1st and 5th round picks in 1984 draft, May 1, 1984.

		—INTERCEPTIONS—				-PUNT RETURNS-				—TOTAL—		
Year Club	G.	No.	Yds.	Avg.	TD.	No.	Yds.	Avg.	TD.	TD.	Pts.	F.
1977—Kansas City NFL	11	3	19	6.3	0	14	115	8.2	0	0	0	3
1978—Kansas City NFL	16	1	0	0.0	0	1	6	6.0	0	0	0	0
1979—Kansas City NFL	16	5	148	29.6	0		None			0	0	0
1980—Kansas City NFL	16	2	25	12.5	0		None			0	0	1
1981—Kansas City NFL	16	5	37	7.4	0		None			0	0	0
1982—Kansas City NFL	9	2	42	21.0	*1		None			1	6	0
1983—Kansas City NFL	16	6	59	9.8	0		None			0	0	0
1984—Los Angeles Rams NFL	16	3	88	29.3	0		None			0	0	0
Pro Totals—8 Years	116	27	418	15.5	1	15	121	8.1	0	1	6	4

Additional pro statistics: Recovered two fumbles, 1977 through 1979 and 1983; returned one kickoff for 27 yards, 1978; recovered one fumble, 1981 and 1984; recovered one fumble for 18 yards, 1982.
Played in Pro Bowl (NFL All-Star Game) following 1981 through 1983 seasons.

HUGH DONELL GREEN
Linebacker—Tampa Bay Buccaneers
Born July 27, 1959, at Natchez, Miss.
Height, 6.02. Weight, 225.
High School—Natchez, Miss., North.
Attended University of Pittsburgh.
Named THE SPORTING NEWS College Player of the Year, 1980.
Named as defensive end on THE SPORTING NEWS College All-America Team, 1979 and 1980.
Named to THE SPORTING NEWS NFL All-Star Team, 1983.
Selected by Tampa Bay in 1st round (7th player selected) of 1981 NFL draft.
On non-football injury list with eye and wrist injury, November 1 through November 29, 1984; activated, November 30, 1984.

		——INTERCEPTIONS——			
Year Club	G.	No.	Yds.	Avg.	TD.
1981—Tampa Bay NFL	16	2	56	28.0	0
1982—Tampa Bay NFL	9	1	31	31.0	0
1983—Tampa Bay NFL	16	2	54	27.0	*2
1984—Tampa Bay NFL	8		None		
Pro Totals—4 Years	49	5	141	28.2	2

Additional pro statistics: Recovered one fumble, 1981; recovered two fumbles for 11 yards and fumbled once, 1983.
Played in Pro Bowl (NFL All-Star Game) following 1982 and 1983 seasons.

JACOB CARL GREEN
Defensive End—Seattle Seahawks
Born January 21, 1957, at Pasadena, Tex.
Height, 6.03. Weight, 255.
High School—Houston, Tex., Kashmere.
Attended Texas A&M University.
Cousin of George Small, defensive tackle with New York Giants and Calgary Stampeders, 1980 through 1983.
Named to THE SPORTING NEWS NFL All-Star Team, 1984.
Selected by Seattle in 1st round (10th player selected) of 1980 NFL draft.
Seattle NFL, 1980 through 1984.
Games: 1980 (14), 1981 (16), 1982 (9), 1983 (16), 1984 (16). Total—71.
Pro statistics: Recovered one fumble, 1981; intercepted one pass for 73 yards and a touchdown and recovered two fumbles, 1983; recovered four fumbles, 1984.
Played in AFC Championship Game following 1983 season.

LAWRENCE GREEN
Linebacker—New York Giants
Born May 15, 1962, at Florence, Ala.
Height, 6.02. Weight, 230.
High School—Florence, Ala., Bradshaw.
Attended University of Tennessee-Chattanooga.
Selected by Washington in 7th round (135th player selected) of 1984 USFL draft.

Selected by New York Giants in 12th round (311th player selected) of 1984 NFL draft.
Signed by New York Giants, June 5, 1984.
On injured reserve with hamstring injury, August 28 through entire 1984 season.

MICHAEL JAMES GREEN
(Mike)
Linebacker—San Diego Chargers
Born June 29, 1961, at Port Arthur, Tex.
Height, 6.00. Weight, 226.
High School—Port Arthur, Tex., Lincoln.
Attended Oklahoma State University.

Selected by Michigan in 15th round (178th player selected) of 1983 USFL draft.
Selected by San Diego in 9th round (245th player selected) of 1983 NFL draft.
Signed by San Diego Chargers, May 26, 1983.
San Diego NFL, 1983 and 1984.
Games: 1983 (16), 1984 (16). Total—32.
Pro statistics: Intercepted one pass for three yards, 1983; recovered one fumble, 1984.

ROY GREEN
Wide Receiver—St. Louis Cardinals
Born June 30, 1957, at Magnolia, Ark.
Height, 6.00. Weight, 195.
High School—Magnolia, Ark.
Attended Henderson State University

Tied NFL record for longest kickoff return, game (106 yards), against Dallas Cowboys, October 21, 1979.
Named to THE SPORTING NEWS NFC All-Star Team, 1979.
Named to THE SPORTING NEWS NFL All-Star Team, 1983 and 1984.
Selected by St. Louis in 4th round (89th player selected) of 1979 NFL draft.
On injured reserve with knee injury, December 15 through remainder of 1980 season.

		INTERCEPTIONS			–PUNT RETURNS–			—KICKOFF RET.—				—TOTAL—		
Year Club	G.	No.	Yds.	Avg. TD.	No.	Yds.	Avg. TD.	No.	Yds.	Avg. TD.		TD.	Pts.	F.
1979—St. Louis NFL	16		None		8	42	5.3	0	41	1005	24.5	*1	1	6	4
1980—St. Louis NFL	15	1	10	10.0	0	16	168	10.5	1	32	745	23.3	0	1	6	2
1981—St. Louis NFL	16	3	44	14.7	0		None		8	135	16.9	0	5	30	2
1982—St. Louis NFL	9		None		3	20	6.7	0		None			3	18	1
1983—St. Louis NFL	16		None			None		1	14	14.0	0	14	84	3
1984—St. Louis NFL	16		None			None		1	18	18.0	0	12	72	1
Pro Totals—6 Years	88	4	54	13.5	0	27	230	8.5	1	83	1917	23.1	1	36	216	13

		——PASS RECEIVING——			
Year Club	G.	P.C.	Yds.	Avg. TD.	
1979—St. Louis NFL	16	1	15	15.0	0
1980—St. Louis NFL	15		None		
1981—St. Louis NFL	16	33	708	21.5	4
1982—St. Louis NFL	9	32	453	14.2	3
1983—St. Louis NFL	16	78	1227	15.7	*14
1984—St. Louis NFL	16	78	*1555	19.9	12
Pro Totals—6 Years	88	222	3958	17.8	33

Additional pro statistics: Recovered two fumbles, 1979; rushed three times for 60 yards and one touchdown, 1981; rushed six times for eight yards, attempted one pass with no completions and recovered one fumble for two yards, 1982; rushed four times for 49 yards and recovered one fumble, 1983; rushed once for minus 10 yards, 1984.
Played in Pro Bowl (NFL All-Star Game) following 1983 and 1984 seasons.

KEN GREENE
Safety—San Diego Chargers
Born May 8, 1956, at Lewiston, Ida.
Height, 6.02. Weight, 196.
High School—Omak, Wash.
Received bachelor of science degree in physical education from
Washington State University in 1978.

Selected by St. Louis in 1st round (19th player selected) of 1978 NFL draft.
On injured reserve with knee injury, October 22 through November 20, 1980; activated, November 21, 1980.
On injured reserve with separated shoulder, December 16 through remainder of 1981 season.
Traded by St. Louis Cardinals to San Diego Chargers for 3rd and 8th round picks in 1984 draft, May 2, 1983.

		——INTERCEPTIONS——			
Year Club	G.	No.	Yds.	Avg. TD.	
1978—St. Louis NFL	16		None		
1979—St. Louis NFL	16	3	37	12.3	0
1980—St. Louis NFL	12	4	41	10.3	0
1981—St. Louis NFL	15	7	111	15.9	0
1982—St. Louis NFL	8	1	2	2.0	0
1983—San Diego NFL	16		None		
1984—San Diego NFL	15		None		
Pro Totals—7 Years	98	15	191	12.7	0

Additional pro statistics: Recovered one fumble, 1980 and 1981 through 1983; recovered two fumbles, 1984.

MARCELLUS L. GREENE
Cornerback—Minnesota Vikings
Born December 12, 1957, at Indianapolis, Ind.
Height, 6.00. Weight, 185.
High School—Indianapolis, Ind., Shortridge.
Attended University of Arizona.

Signed by Toronto Argonauts, April 15, 1981.
Selected by Los Angeles Rams in 11th round (296th player selected) of 1981 NFL draft.
Traded by Toronto Argonauts to Saskatchewan Roughriders for quarterback Joe Barnes, June 25, 1982.
Traded with defensive end Lyle Woznesensky by Saskatchewan Roughriders to Toronto Argonauts for 1st round pick in 1984 draft, June 25, 1983.
Granted free agency, March 1, 1984; signed by Los Angeles Rams, March 5, 1984.
Released by Los Angeles Rams, August 27, 1984; awarded on waivers to Minnesota Vikings, August 28, 1984.

Year Club	G.	INTERCEPTIONS No.	Yds.	Avg.	TD.	-PUNT RETURNS- No.	Yds.	Avg.	TD.	—KICKOFF RET.— No.	Yds.	Avg.	TD.	—TOTAL— TD.	Pts.	F.
1981—Toronto CFL	13	4	51	12.8	0	1	4	4.0	0	3	47	15.7	0	0	0	0
1982—Saskatchewan CFL	16	2	0	0.0	0	None				None				0	0	0
1983—Toronto CFL	12	2	0	0.0	0	12	84	7.0	0	14	292	20.9	0	0	0	0
1984—Minnesota NFL	14	None				None				None				0	0	0
CFL Totals—3 Years	41	8	51	6.4	0	13	88	6.8	0	17	339	19.9	0	0	0	0
NFL Totals—1 Year	14	0	0	0.0	0	0	0	0.0	0	0	0	0.0	0	0	0	0
Pro Totals—4 Years	55	8	51	6.4	0	13	88	6.8	0	17	339	19.9	0	0	0	0

Additional pro statistics: Recovered one fumble for 11 yards, 1982; recovered one fumble, 1983.

CURTIS WILLIAM GREER
Defensive End—St. Louis Cardinals
Born November 10, 1957, at Detroit, Mich.
Height, 6.04. Weight, 258.
High School—Detroit, Mich., Cass Tech.
Received bachelor of science degree in speech communication
from University of Michigan in 1979.

Selected by St. Louis in 1st round (6th player selected) of 1980 NFL draft.
On injured reserve with concussion, September 9 through October 9, 1980; activated, October 10, 1980.
On injured reserve with broken thumb, December 15 through remainder of 1980 season.
St. Louis NFL, 1980 through 1984.
Games: 1980 (11), 1981 (16), 1982 (9), 1983 (16), 1984 (16). Total—68.
Pro statistics: Recovered four fumbles for two yards, 1981; recovered three fumbles, 1982; recovered one fumble for five yards, 1983.

ROBERT LEE GREGOR
(Bob)
Safety—San Diego Chargers
Born February 10, 1957, at Riverside, Calif.
Height, 6.02. Weight, 190.
High School—Danville, Calif., Monte Vista.
Received degree in business management from Washington State University in 1980.

Selected by San Diego in 4th round (108th player selected) of 1980 NFL draft.
On injured reserve, August 26 through entire 1980 season.
On injured reserve with dislocated elbow, November 24 through December 30, 1982; activated, December 31, 1982.
On injured reserve with knee injury, November 12 through remainder of 1983 season.
On injured reserve with ankle injury, October 17 through remainder of 1984 season.

Year Club	G.	INTERCEPTIONS No.	Yds.	Avg.	TD.
1981—San Diego NFL	14	2	11	5.5	0
1982—San Diego NFL	4	1	6	6.0	0
1983—San Diego NFL	5	None			
1984—San Diego NFL	7	1	12	12.0	0
Pro Totals—4 Years	30	4	29	7.3	0

Additional pro statistics: Returned three kickoffs for 47 yards, 1981.
Played in AFC Championship Game following 1981 season.

JAMES VICTOR GRIFFIN
Safety—Cincinnati Bengals
Born September 7, 1961, at Camilla, Ga.
Height, 6.02. Weight, 197.
High School—Camilla, Ga., Mitchell.
Attended Middle Tennessee State University.

Selected by Cincinnati in 7th round (193rd player selected) of 1983 NFL draft.

Year Club	G.	INTERCEPTIONS No.	Yds.	Avg.	TD.
1983—Cincinnati NFL	16	1	41	41.0	1
1984—Cincinnati NFL	16	1	57	57.0	1
Pro Totals—2 Years	32	2	98	49.0	2

Additional pro statistics: Recovered two fumbles, 1984.

JEFF GRIFFIN
Cornerback—St. Louis Cardinals
Born July 19, 1958, at Carson, Calif.
Height, 6.00. Weight, 185.
High School—Wilmington, Calif., Banning.
Attended University of Utah.

Selected by St. Louis in 3rd round (61st player selected) of 1981 NFL draft.
On injured reserve with broken arm, August 30 through October 3, 1983; activated, October 4, 1983.
On injured reserve with broken arm, October 27 through remainder of 1983 season.
On injured reserve with broken arm, August 28 through October 18, 1984; activated, October 19, 1984.

		—INTERCEPTIONS—			
Year Club	G.	No.	Yds.	Avg.	TD.
1981—St. Louis NFL	16	1	4	4.0	0
1982—St. Louis NFL	8	1	8	8.0	0
1983—St. Louis NFL	3			None	
1984—St. Louis NFL	8	2	0	0.0	0
Pro Totals—4 Years	35	4	12	3.0	0

Additional pro statistics: Returned two kickoffs for 34 yards, 1981; returned one kickoff for 12 yards, 1982.

KEITH GRIFFIN
Running Back—Washington Redskins
Born October 26, 1961, at Columbus, O.
Height, 5.08. Weight, 185.
High School—Columbus, O., Eastmoor.
Attended University of Miami (Fla.).
Brother of Archie Griffin, running back with Cincinnati Bengals and Jacksonville Bulls,
1976 through 1982 and 1984; and Ray Griffin, defensive back with Cincinnati Bengals, 1978 through 1984.

Selected by Oklahoma in 11th round (212th player selected) of 1984 USFL draft.
Selected by Washington in 10th round (279th player selected) of 1984 NFL draft.
Signed by Washington Redskins, July 13, 1984.

		—RUSHING—				PASS RECEIVING				—TOTAL—		
Year Club	G.	Att.	Yds.	Avg.	TD.	P.C.	Yds.	Avg.	TD.	TD.	Pts.	F.
1984—Washington NFL	16	97	408	4.2	0	8	43	5.4	0	0	0	7

		KICKOFF RETURNS			
Year Club	G.	No.	Yds.	Avg.	TD.
1984—Washington NFL	16	9	164	18.2	0

RAYMOND GRIFFIN
(Ray)
Cornerback
Born June 29, 1956, at Columbus, O.
Height, 5.10. Weight, 186.
High School—Columbus, O., Eastmoor.
Attended Ohio State University.
Brother of Archie Griffin, running back with Cincinnati Bengals and Jacksonville Bulls,
1976 through 1982 and 1984; and Keith Griffin, running back with Washington Redskins.

Named as safety on The Sporting News College All-America Team, 1977.
Selected by Cincinnati in 2nd round (35th player selected) of 1978 NFL draft.
On injured reserve with dislocated shoulder, September 22 through October 29, 1981; activated, October 30, 1981.
On injured reserve with knee injury, August 29 through September 30, 1984; activated, October 1, 1984.
Released by Cincinnati Bengals, May 17, 1985.

		-INTERCEPTIONS-				—KICKOFF RET.—				—TOTAL—		
Year Club	G.	No.	Yds.	Avg.	TD.	No.	Yds.	Avg.	TD.	TD.	Pts.	F.
1978—Cincinnati NFL	15			None		37	787	21.3	0	0	0	0
1979—Cincinnati NFL	12	4	167	41.8	1	1	15	15.0	0	1	6	0
1980—Cincinnati NFL	16	2	80	40.0	*2			None		2	12	0
1981—Cincinnati NFL	8			None		2	31	15.5	0	0	0	0
1982—Cincinnati NFL	9	1	21	21.0	0			None		0	0	0
1983—Cincinnati NFL	16	2	24	12.0	0			None		0	0	0
1984—Cincinnati NFL	12	2	13	6.5	0			None		0	0	0
Pro Totals—7 Years	88	11	305	27.7	3	40	833	20.8	0	3	18	0

Additional pro statistics: Recovered one fumble, 1978, 1979, 1981 and 1984; recovered two fumbles for 14 yards, 1980; recovered two fumbles for 13 yards, 1983.
Played in AFC Championship Game following 1981 season.
Played in NFL Championship Game following 1981 season.

ANTHONY GRIGGS
Linebacker—Philadelphia Eagles
Born February 12, 1960, at Lawton, Okla.
Height, 6.03. Weight, 230.
High School—Willingboro, N.J., John F. Kennedy.
Attended Villanova University and Ohio State University.
Cousin of Billy Griggs, tight end with New York Jets.

Selected by Philadelphia in 4th round (104th player selected) of 1982 NFL draft.

Year Club		——INTERCEPTIONS——			
Year Club	G.	No.	Yds.	Avg.	TD.
1982—Philadelphia NFL	9			None	
1983—Philadelphia NFL	16	3	61	20.3	0
1984—Philadelphia NFL	16			None	
Pro Totals—3 Years............	41	3	61	20.3	0

Additional pro statistics: Recovered one fumble, 1982.

WILLIAM EDWARD GRIGGS
(Billy)
Tight End—New York Jets
Born August 4, 1962, at Camden, N.J.
Height, 6.03. Weight, 230.
High School—Pennsauken, N.J.
Received bachelor of arts degree in sociology from University of Virginia in 1984.
Cousin of Anthony Griggs, linebacker with Philadelphia Eagles.

Selected by New York Jets in 8th round (203rd player selected) of 1984 NFL draft.
On injured reserve with ankle injury, August 14 through entire 1984 season.

RANDALL COLLINS GRIMES
(Randy)
Offensive Lineman—Tampa Bay Buccaneers
Born July 20, 1960, at Tyler, Tex.
Height, 6.04. Weight, 260.
High School—Tyler, Tex., Robert E. Lee.
Attended Baylor University.

Selected by New Jersey in 6th round (70th player selected) of 1983 USFL draft.
Selected by Tampa Bay in 2nd round (45th player selected) of 1983 NFL draft.
Signed by Tampa Bay Buccaneers, June 6, 1983.
Tampa Bay NFL, 1983 and 1984.
Games: 1983 (15), 1984 (10). Total—25.
Pro statistics: Recovered one fumble, 1983.

RUSS GRIMM
Guard—Washington Redskins
Born May 2, 1959, at Scottsdale, Pa.
Height, 6.03. Weight, 275.
High School—Southmoreland, Pa.
Attended University of Pittsburgh.

Selected by Washington in 3rd round (69th player selected) of 1981 NFL draft.
Washington NFL, 1981 through 1984.
Games: 1981 (14), 1982 (9), 1983 (16), 1984 (16). Total—55.
Pro statistics: Recovered one fumble, 1981 and 1982; recovered two fumbles, 1984.
Played in NFC Championship Game following 1982 and 1983 seasons.
Played in NFL Championship Game following 1982 and 1983 seasons.
Played in Pro Bowl (NFL All-Star Game) following 1983 and 1984 seasons.

JOHN GLENN GRIMSLEY
Linebacker—Houston Oilers
Born February 25, 1962, at Canton, O.
Height, 6.02. Weight, 232.
High School—Canton, O., McKinley.
Attended University of Kentucky.

Selected by Denver in 3rd round (59th player selected) of 1984 USFL draft.
Selected by Houston in 6th round (141st player selected) of 1984 NFL draft.
Signed by Houston Oilers, July 7, 1984.
Houston NFL, 1984.
Games: 1984 (16).

STEVEN JAMES GROGAN
(Steve)
Quarterback—New England Patriots
Born July 24, 1953, at San Antonio, Tex.
Height, 6.04. Weight, 210.
High School—Ottawa, Kan.
Received bachelor of science degree in physical education from Kansas State University in 1975.

Selected by New England in 5th round (116th player selected) of 1975 NFL draft.

Year Club	G.	——PASSING——							——RUSHING——				—TOTAL—		
Year Club	G.	Att.	Cmp.	Pct.	Gain	T.P.	P.I.	Avg.	Att.	Yds.	Avg.	TD.	TD.	Pts.	F.
1975—New England NFL...........	13	274	139	50.7	1976	11	18	7.21	30	110	3.7	3	3	18	6
1976—New England NFL...........	14	302	145	48.0	1903	18	20	6.30	60	397	6.6	12	13	78	6
1977—New England NFL...........	14	305	160	52.5	2162	17	21	7.09	61	324	5.3	1	1	6	7
1978—New England NFL...........	16	362	181	50.0	2824	15	23	7.80	81	539	*6.7	5	5	30	9

Year	Club	G.	Att.	Cmp.	Pct.	Gain	T.P.	P.I.	Avg.	Att.	Yds.	Avg.	TD.	TD.	Pts.	F.
						PASSING					RUSHING			TOTAL		
1979—New England NFL............		16	423	206	48.7	3286	*28	20	7.77	64	368	5.8	2	2	12	12
1980—New England NFL............		12	306	175	57.2	2475	18	22	*8.09	30	112	3.7	1	1	6	4
1981—New England NFL............		8	216	117	54.2	1859	7	16	*8.61	12	49	4.1	2	2	12	5
1982—New England NFL............		6	122	66	54.1	930	7	4	7.62	9	42	4.7	1	1	6	2
1983—New England NFL............		12	303	168	55.4	2411	15	12	7.96	23	108	4.7	2	2	12	4
1984—New England NFL............		3	68	32	47.1	444	3	6	6.53	7	12	1.7	0	0	0	4
Pro Totals—10 Years.........		114	2681	1389	51.8	20270	139	162	7.56	377	2061	5.5	29	30	180	59

Quarterback Rating Points: 1975 (60.2), 1976 (60.8), 1977 (65.3), 1978 (63.3), 1979 (77.5), 1980 (73.1), 1981 (63.0), 1982 (84.2), 1983 (81.4), 1984 (46.4). Total—69.1.

Additional pro statistics: Recovered four fumbles and fumbled six times for minus 12 yards, 1975; recovered four fumbles and one touchdown and fumbled six times for minus 18 yards, 1976; recovered two fumbles and fumbled seven times for minus 41 yards, 1977; recovered two fumbles and fumbled nine times for minus 24 yards, 1978; recovered four fumbles and fumbled 12 times for minus 12 yards, 1979; recovered one fumble and fumbled four times for minus 10 yards, 1980; recovered two fumbles, caught two passes for 27 yards and fumbled five times for minus eight yards, 1981; recovered one fumble 1982 and 1983; caught one pass for minus eight yards, 1983; recovered two fumbles and fumbled four times for minus three yards, 1984.

ELOIS GROOMS

First name pronounced Eh-LOYS.

Defensive Tackle—St. Louis Cardinals

Born May 20, 1953, at Tompkinsville, Ky.
Height, 6.04. Weight, 250.
High School—Tompkinsville, Ky.
Received bachelor of science degree in health and physical education
from Tennessee Tech University in 1975.

Selected by New Orleans in 3rd round (63rd player selected) of 1975 NFL draft.
Traded by New Orleans Saints to St. Louis Cardinals for 3rd round pick in 1983 draft, August 3, 1982.
New Orleans NFL, 1975 through 1981; St. Louis NFL, 1982 through 1984.
Games: 1975 (10), 1976 (11), 1977 (14), 1978 (16), 1979 (16), 1980 (16), 1981 (16), 1982 (9), 1983 (11), 1984 (11). Total—130.

Pro statistics: Recovered two fumbles, 1977 and 1979; caught one pass for three yards and one touchdown, 1977; recovered one fumble, 1978, 1980 and 1982; intercepted one pass for minus two yards and credited with one safety, 1979; intercepted one pass for 37 yards, 1980; recovered one fumble for 20 yards, 1981; intercepted one pass for 10 yards and recovered one fumble for 40 yards and a touchdown, 1983.

ALFRED E. GROSS

(Al)

Safety—Cleveland Browns

Born January 4, 1961, at Stockton, Calif.
Height, 6.03. Weight, 186.
High School—Stockton, Calif., Franklin.
Attended University of Arizona.

Selected by Arizona in 1983 USFL territorial draft.
Selected by Dallas in 9th round (246th player selected) of 1983 NFL draft.
Signed by Dallas Cowboys, June 20, 1983.
Released by Dallas Cowboys, August 2, 1983; awarded on waivers to Cleveland Browns, August 4, 1983.

Year	Club	G.	No.	Yds.	Avg.	TD.
				INTERCEPTIONS		
1983—Cleveland NFL..............		16	1	18	18.0	0
1984—Cleveland NFL..............		16	5	103	20.6	0
Pro Totals—2 Years...........		32	6	121	20.2	0

Additional pro statistics: Recovered one fumble for four yards, 1983; recovered two fumbles for 28 yards, 1984.

JAMES DUANE GROSS

(J. D.)

Linebacker—Indianapolis Colts

Born November 7, 1961, at Landover, Md.
Height, 6.00. Weight, 233.
High School—Hyattsville, Md., Northwestern.
Attended University of Maryland.

Signed as free agent by Washington Redskins, May 4, 1984.
Released by Washington Redskins, July 23, 1984.
USFL rights traded by Orlando Renegades to New Jersey Generals for past considerations, January 21, 1985.
Signed by New Jersey Generals, January 22, 1985.
Released by New Jersey Generals, January 28, 1985; signed as free agent by Indianapolis Colts, May 6, 1985.

JEFFREY EUGENE GROTH

(Jeff)

Wide Receiver—New Orleans Saints

Born July 2, 1957, at Mankato, Minn.
Height, 5.10. Weight, 182.
High School—Chagrin Falls, O.
Received degree in business administration from Bowling Green State University.

Selected by Miami in 8th round (206th player selected) of 1979 NFL draft.
Released by Miami Dolphins, August 27, 1979; re-signed by Dolphins, August 28, 1979.
Released by Miami Dolphins, September 29, 1979; re-signed by Dolphins, October 2, 1979.
Released by Miami Dolphins, October 13, 1979; claimed on waivers by Houston Oilers, October 16, 1979.
Released by Houston Oilers, August 31, 1981; signed as free agent by New Orleans Saints, September 9, 1981.
Selected by Chicago Cubs' organization in 9th round of free-agent draft, June 5, 1978.
Selected by Atlanta Braves' organization in 32nd round of free-agent draft, June 5, 1979.
Selected by Texas Rangers' organization in secondary phase of free-agent draft, January 8, 1980.

| Year Club | G. | PASS RECEIVING | | | | -PUNT RETURNS- | | | | -KICKOFF RET.- | | | | -TOTAL- | | |
		P.C.	Yds.	Avg.	TD.	No.	Yds.	Avg.	TD.	No.	Yds.	Avg.	TD.	TD.	Pts.	F.
1979—Mia. (4)-Hou. (6) NFL .	10	1	6	6.0	0			None		1	21	21.0	0	0	0	0
1980—Houston NFL	16	4	57	11.8	0	1	0	0.0	0	12	216	18.0	0	0	0	2
1981—New Orleans NFL	15	20	380	19.0	1	37	436	11.8	0	3	50	16.7	0	1	6	0
1982—New Orleans NFL	9	30	383	12.8	1	21	144	6.9	0			None		1	6	1
1983—New Orleans NFL	16	49	585	11.9	1	39	275	7.1	0			None		1	6	3
1984—New Orleans NFL	16	33	487	14.8	0	6	32	5.3	0			None		0	0	0
Pro Totals—6 Years	82	137	1888	13.8	3	104	887	8.5	0	16	287	17.9	0	3	18	6

Additional pro statistics: Recovered one fumble, 1980 and 1982; rushed twice for 27 yards, 1981; rushed once for one yard, 1982; rushed once for 15 yards and recovered two fumbles, 1983.
Played in AFC Championship Game following 1979 season.

MICHAEL ANTHONY GUENDLING
(Mike)
Linebacker—San Diego Chargers
Born June 18, 1962, at Chicago, Ill.
Height, 6.03. Weight, 241.
High School—Arlington Heights, Ill., St. Viator.
Attended Northwestern University.

Selected by Philadelphia in 13th round (266th player selected) of 1983 USFL draft.
Selected by San Diego in 2nd round (33rd player selected) of 1984 NFL draft.
Signed by San Diego Chargers, June 15, 1984.
On injured reserve with knee injury, July 21 through entire 1984 season.

DAVID RUSTON GUILBEAU
(Rusty)
Linebacker—New York Jets
Born November 20, 1958, at Opalousas, Fla.
Height, 6.04. Weight, 237.
High School—Sunset, La.
Attended McNeese State University.

Selected by St. Louis in 3rd round (73rd player selected) of 1982 NFL draft.
Released by St. Louis Cardinals, September 6, 1982; signed as free agent by New York Jets, November 23, 1982.
New York Jets NFL, 1982 through 1984.
Games: 1982 (4), 1983 (16), 1984 (16). Total—36.
Played in AFC Championship Game following 1982 season.

MICHAEL DONALD GUMAN
(Mike)
Running Back—Los Angeles Rams
Born April 21, 1958, at Allentown, Pa.
Height, 6.02. Weight, 218.
High School—Bethlehem, Pa., Catholic.
Received bachelor of science degree in marketing from Penn State University in 1980.

Selected by Los Angeles in 6th round (154th player selected) of 1980 NFL draft.

| Year Club | G. | RUSHING | | | | PASS RECEIVING | | | | TOTAL | | |
		Att.	Yds.	Avg.	TD.	P.C.	Yds.	Avg.	TD.	TD.	Pts.	F.
1980—Los Angeles Rams NFL	16	100	410	4.1	4	14	131	9.4	0	4	24	4
1981—Los Angeles Rams NFL	16	115	433	3.8	4	18	130	7.2	0	4	24	2
1982—Los Angeles Rams NFL	9	69	266	3.9	2	31	310	10.0	0	2	12	3
1983—Los Angeles Rams NFL	16	7	42	6.0	0	34	347	10.2	4	4	24	0
1984—Los Angeles Rams NFL	16	1	2	2.0	0	19	161	8.5	0	1	6	0
Pro Totals—5 Years	73	292	1153	3.9	10	116	1079	9.3	4	15	90	9

Additional pro statistics: Attempted one pass with one completion for 31 yards and a touchdown, returned two punts for six yards and returned two kickoffs for 25 yards, 1980; attempted one pass with one completion for seven yards and a touchdown and returned one kickoff for 10 yards, 1981; attempted one pass with one interception and returned eight kickoffs for 102 yards, 1982; returned two kickoffs for 30 yards, 1983; returned one kickoff for 43 yards and a touchdown and recovered one fumble, 1984.

CARLTON WILLIE GUNN
Defensive End—Tampa Bay Buccaneers
Born August 12, 1960, at Tampa, Fla.
Height, 6.02. Weight, 305.
High School—Tampa, Fla., Robinson.
Attended University of Tennessee and Carson-Newman College.

Selected by Memphis in 8th round (158th player selected) of 1984 USFL draft.
Signed by Memphis Showboats, January 17, 1984.
On developmental squad, February 24 through March 10, 1984; activated, March 11, 1984.
On developmental squad, March 25 through April 24, 1984; activated, April 25, 1984.
Released by Memphis Showboats, February 11, 1985; signed as free agent by Tampa Bay Buccaneers, April 12, 1985.
On developmental squad for 7 games with Memphis Showboats in 1984.
Memphis USFL, 1984.
Games: 1984 (11).
Pro statistics: Intercepted one pass for no yards and credited with 1½ sacks for 3½ yards, 1984.

MICHEAL WAYNE GUNTER
Running Back—Kansas City Chiefs
Born February 18, 1961, at Gladewater, Tex.
Height, 5.11. Weight, 205.
High School—Gladewater, Tex.
Attended University of Tulsa.

Selected by Oklahoma in 1984 USFL territorial draft.
Selected by Tampa Bay in 4th round (107th player selected) of 1984 NFL draft.
Signed by Tampa Bay Buccaneers, May 25, 1984.
Released by Tampa Bay Buccaneers, August 20, 1984; awarded on waivers to Indianapolis Colts, August 21, 1984.
Released by Indianapolis Colts, August 27, 1984; signed as free agent by Kansas City Chiefs, October 16, 1984.

		—RUSHING—				PASS RECEIVING			—TOTAL—		
Year Club	G.	Att.	Yds.	Avg.	TD.	P.C.	Yds.	Avg. TD.	TD.	Pts.	F.
1984—Kansas City NFL	4	15	12	0.8	0	None			0	0	0

JAMES JOEL GUSTAFSON
(Jim)
Wide Receiver—Minnesota Vikings
Born March 16, 1961, at Minneapolis, Minn.
Height, 6.01. Weight, 180.
High School—Bloomington, Minn., Lincoln.
Received degree in finance from St. Thomas College in 1983.

Signed as free agent by Cincinnati Bengals, April 28, 1983.
Released by Cincinnati Bengals, August 29, 1983; signed as free agent by Minnesota Vikings, March 3, 1984.
Released by Minnesota Vikings, August 13, 1984; re-signed by Vikings, April 21, 1985.

KEITH EDWIN GUTHRIE
Nose Tackle—San Diego Chargers
Born August 17, 1962, at Tyler, Tex.
Height, 6.03. Weight, 267.
High School—Tyler, Tex., John Tyler.
Attended Texas A&M University.

Selected by Houston in 1984 USFL territorial draft.
Selected by San Diego in 6th round (144th player selected) of 1984 NFL draft.
Signed by San Diego Chargers, June 10, 1984.
On injured reserve with chipped tailbone, August 28 through September 27, 1984; activated, September 28, 1984.
San Diego NFL, 1984.
Games: 1984 (11).

WILLIAM RAY GUY
(Known by middle name.)
Punter—Los Angeles Raiders
Born December 22, 1949, at Swainsboro, Ga.
Height, 6.03. Weight, 195.
High School—Thomson, Ga.
Attended University of Southern Mississippi.

Named as punter on THE SPORTING NEWS College All-America Team, 1972.
Named to THE SPORTING NEWS AFC All-Star Team, 1973 through 1978.
Selected by Oakland in 1st round (23rd player selected) of 1973 NFL draft.
Franchise transferred to Los Angeles, May 7, 1982.
Selected by Cincinnati Reds' organization in 14th round of free-agent draft, June 5, 1969.
Selected by Houston Astros' organization in secondary phase of free-agent draft, June 8, 1971.
Selected by Atlanta Braves' organization in 17th round of free-agent draft, June 6, 1972.
Selected by Cincinnati Reds' organization in secondary phase of free-agent draft, January 10, 1973.

	—PUNTING—						—PUNTING—		
Year Club	G.	No.	Avg.	Blk.	Year Club	G.	No.	Avg.	Blk.
1973—Oakland NFL	14	69	45.3	0	1980—Oakland NFL	16	71	43.6	0
1974—Oakland NFL	14	74	*42.2	0	1981—Oakland NFL	16	96	43.7	0
1975—Oakland NFL	14	68	*43.8	0	1982—Los Angeles Raiders NFL	9	47	39.1	0
1976—Oakland NFL	14	67	41.6	0	1983—Los Angeles Raiders NFL	16	78	42.8	0
1977—Oakland NFL	14	59	*43.3	0	1984—Los Angeles Raiders NFL	16	91	41.9	0
1978—Oakland NFL	16	81	42.7	*2	Pro Totals—12 Years	175	870	42.8	3
1979—Oakland NFL	16	69	42.6	1					

Additional pro statistics: Rushed once for 21 yards, 1973; fumbled once for seven yard loss and attempted one pass

— 165 —

with one interception, 1974; attempted one pass with one completion for 22 yards, 1975; fumbled once for 14 yard loss, 1976; rushed once for no yards and kicked one extra point after touchdown, 1976; recovered one fumble, 1976 and 1980; rushed three times for 38 yards and attempted one pass with one completion for 32 yards, 1980; fumbled once, 1981; rushed two times for minus three yards, 1982; rushed twice for minus 13 yards, 1983.

Played in AFC Championship Game following 1973 through 1977, 1980 and 1983 seasons.
Played in NFL Championship Game following 1976, 1980 and 1983 seasons.
Played in Pro Bowl (NFL All-Star Game) following 1973 through 1978 and 1980 seasons.

MICHAEL HADDIX
Running Back—Philadelphia Eagles
Born December 27, 1961, at Tippah County, Miss.
Height, 6.02. Weight, 225.
High School—Walnut, Miss.
Attended Mississippi State University.

Selected by Denver in 2nd round (16th player selected) of 1983 USFL draft.
Selected by Philadelphia in 1st round (8th player selected) of 1983 NFL draft.
Signed by Philadelphia Eagles, May 13, 1983.

| | | ——RUSHING—— | | | | PASS RECEIVING | | | | —TOTAL— | | |
Year Club	G.	Att.	Yds.	Avg.	TD.	P.C.	Yds.	Avg.	TD.	TD.	Pts.	F.
1983—Philadelphia NFL	14	91	220	2.4	2	23	254	11.0	0	2	12	4
1984—Philadelphia NFL	14	48	130	2.7	1	33	231	7.0	0	1	6	2
Pro Totals—2 Years	28	139	350	2.5	3	56	485	8.7	0	3	18	6

Additional pro statistics: Returned three kickoffs for 51 yards, 1983.

RICKEY GABRIEL HAGOOD
Defensive Tackle—Los Angeles Raiders
Born April 24, 1961, at Easley, S.C.
Height, 6.02. Weight, 295.
High School—Easley, S.C., Wren.
Attended University of South Carolina.
Brother of Kent Hagood, fullback at University of South Carolina.

Selected by Washington in 1984 USFL territorial draft.
Selected by Seattle in 4th round (86th player selected) of 1984 NFL draft.
Signed by Seattle Seahawks, July 9, 1984.
Released by Seattle Seahawks, August 27, 1984; awarded on waivers to San Diego Chargers, August 28, 1984.
Released by San Diego Chargers, September 12, 1984.
USFL rights traded by Orlando Renegades to Tampa Bay Bandits for running back Homes Johnson, November 21, 1984.
Signed as free agent by Los Angeles Raiders, March 10, 1985.

JOHN YANCY HAINES
Defensive Tackle—Minnesota Vikings
Born December 16, 1961, at Fort Worth, Tex.
Height, 6.06. Weight, 260.
High School—Fort Worth, Tex., Arlington Heights.
Attended University of Texas.

Selected by San Antonio in 1984 USFL territorial draft.
Selected by Minnesota in 7th round (180th player selected) of 1984 NFL draft.
Signed by Minnesota Vikings, June 26, 1984.
On physically unable to perform/reserve with knee injury, August 8 through October 23, 1984; activated, October 24, 1984.
Minnesota NFL, 1984.
Games: 1984 (8).
Pro statistics: Recovered one fumble for six yards, 1984.

CARL BLAKE HAIRSTON
Defensive End—Cleveland Browns
Born December 15, 1952, at Martinsville, Va.
Height, 6.04. Weight, 260.
High School—Martinsville, Va.
Attended University of Maryland (Eastern Shore).

Selected by Philadelphia in 7th round (191st player selected) of 1976 NFL draft.
Traded by Philadelphia Eagles to Cleveland Browns for 9th round pick in 1985 draft, February 9, 1984.
Philadelphia NFL, 1976 through 1983; Cleveland NFL, 1984.
Games: 1976 (14), 1977 (14), 1978 (16), 1979 (15), 1980 (16), 1981 (16), 1982 (9), 1983 (16), 1984 (16). Total—132.
Pro statistics: Recovered one fumble, 1977, 1980 and 1981; intercepted one pass for no yards, 1980; recovered two fumbles for 24 yards, 1982; recovered two fumbles, 1983.
Played in NFC Championship Game following 1980 season.
Played in NFL Championship Game following 1980 season.

—DID YOU KNOW—

That the Rams' Eric Dickerson, who accumulated an NFL record 2,105 rushing yards in 1984, outrushed all but seven teams in the NFL?

ALI HAJI-SHEIKH
Placekicker—New York Giants
Born January 11, 1961, at Ann Arbor, Mich.
Height, 6.00. Weight, 172.
High School—Arlington, Tex.
Attended University of Michigan.

Established NFL record for most field goals, season (35), 1983.
Named to THE SPORTING NEWS NFL All-Star Team, 1983.
Selected by Michigan in 1983 USFL territorial draft.
Selected by New York Giants in 9th round (237th player selected) of 1983 NFL draft.
Signed by New York Giants, June 13, 1983.

		——PLACE KICKING——					
Year	Club	G.	XP.	XPM.	FG.	FGA.	Pts.
1983—N.Y. Giants NFL		16	22	1	*35	42	127
1984—N.Y. Giants NFL		16	32	3	17	33	83
Pro Totals—2 Years.......		32	54	4	52	75	210

Additional pro statistics: Had only attempted punt blocked, 1984.
Played in Pro Bowl (NFL All-Star Game) following 1983 season.

DARRYL HALEY
Offensive Tackle—New England Patriots
Born February 16, 1961, at Los Angeles, Calif.
Height, 6.04. Weight, 275.
High School—Los Angeles, Calif., Alin Leroy Locke.
Attended University of Utah.
Cousin of Darrell Jackson, pitcher with Minnesota Twins, 1978 through 1982.

Selected by New England in 2nd round (55th player selected) of 1982 NFL draft.
New England NFL, 1982 through 1984.
Games: 1982 (9), 1983 (16), 1984 (16). Total—41.

ALVIN HALL
Defensive Back—Detroit Lions
Born August 12, 1958, at Dayton, O.
Height, 5.10. Weight, 184.
High School—Dayton, O., Fairview.
Attended Miami (O.) University.

Signed as free agent by Cleveland Browns, May 7, 1980.
Released by Cleveland Browns, August 20, 1980; signed as free agent by Detroit Lions, May 8, 1981.

			-INTERCEPTIONS-			—KICKOFF RET.—				—TOTAL—		
Year	Club	G.	No.	Yds.	Avg.	TD.	No.	Yds.	Avg.	TD.	TD. Pts.	F.
1981—Detroit NFL..		16	1	60	60.0	1	25	525	21.0	0	1 6	1
1982—Detroit NFL..		9	1	2	2.0	0	16	426	26.6	*1	1 6	1
1983—Detroit NFL..		16	2	18	9.0	0	23	492	21.4	0	0 0	1
1984—Detroit NFL..		16	2	64	32.0	0	19	385	20.3	0	0 0	3
Pro Totals—4 Years...................................		57	6	144	24.0	1	83	1828	22.0	1	2 12	6

Additional pro statistics: Recovered one fumble, 1982 and 1984; returned eight punts for 109 yards and recovered two fumbles, 1983; returned seven punts for 30 yards, 1984.

RONALD DAVID HALLSTROM
(Ron)
Offensive Tackle-Guard—Green Bay Packers
Born June 11, 1959, at Holden, Mass.
Height, 6.06. Weight, 283.
High School—Moline, Ill.
Attended Iowa Central Junior College and University of Iowa.

Selected by Green Bay in 1st round (22nd player selected) of 1982 NFL draft.
On inactive list, September 12 and September 20, 1982.
Green Bay NFL, 1982 through 1984.
Games: 1982 (6), 1983 (16), 1984 (16). Total—38.
Pro statistics: Recovered two fumbles for one yard, 1984.

HARRY E. HAMILTON
Safety—New York Jets
Born November 29, 1962, at Jamaica, N.Y.
Height, 6.00. Weight, 193.
High School—Nanticoke, Pa., John S. Fine.
Received bachelor of arts degree in pre-law and liberal arts from Penn State University in 1984.
Brother of Lance Hamilton, defensive back; and Darren Hamilton,
wide receiver, both at Penn State University.

Selected by Philadelphia in 1984 USFL territorial draft.
Selected by New York Jets in 7th round (176th player selected) of 1984 NFL draft.
Signed by New York Jets, May 29, 1984.
On injured reserve with knee injury, October 22 through remainder of 1984 season.
New York Jets NFL, 1984.
Games: 1984 (8).

STEVEN HAMILTON
(Steve)
Defensive End—Washington Redskins
Born September 28, 1961, at Niagara Falls, N.Y.
Height, 6.04. Weight, 253.
High School—Williamsville, N.Y., East
Attended Fork Union Military Academy and East Carolina University.

Selected by Michigan in 4th round (79th player selected) of 1984 USFL draft.
Selected by Washington in 2nd round (55th player selected) of 1984 NFL draft.
Signed by Washington Redskins, June 5, 1984.
On injured reserve with fractured ankle, August 20 through entire 1984 season.

WAYMON RAY HAMILTON
Running Back—Cleveland Browns
Born May 31, 1961, at Brawley, Calif.
Height, 5.11. Weight, 224.
High School—Calipatria, Calif.
Attended Brigham Young University.

Selected by Washington in 10th round (196th player selected) of 1984 USFL draft.
Signed by Washington Federals, January 18, 1984.
Released with knee injury by Washington Federals, February 13, 1984; re-signed by Federals, March 21, 1984.
On developmental squad, March 21 through April 12, 1984; activated, April 13, 1984.
On developmental squad, April 20 through remainder of 1984 season.
Franchise transferred to Orlando, October 12, 1984.
Released by Orlando Renegades, January 18, 1985; signed as free agent by Cleveland Browns, May 6, 1985.
On developmental squad for 13 games with Washington Federals in 1984.
Washington USFL, 1984.
Games: 1984 (1).

WES HAMILTON
Guard—Minnesota Vikings
Born April 24, 1953, at Texas City, Tex.
Height, 6.03. Weight, 270.
High School—Flossmoor, Ill., Homewood-Flossmoor.
Received bachelor of science degree in education from University of Tulsa in 1976.

Selected by Minnesota in 3rd round (85th player selected) of 1976 NFL draft.
On injured reserve with knee injury, August 28 through October 5, 1984; activated, October 6, 1984.
Minnesota NFL, 1976 through 1984.
Games: 1976 (13), 1977 (14), 1978 (16), 1979 (16), 1980 (13), 1981 (16), 1982 (9), 1983 (15), 1984 (4). Total—116.
Pro statistics: Recovered one fumble, 1979.
Played in NFC Championship Game following 1977 season.

BOB HAMM
Defensive End—Kansas City Chiefs
Born April 24, 1959, at Kansas City, Mo.
Height, 6.04. Weight, 263.
High School—Mountain View, Calif., St. Francis.
Attended University of Nevada at Reno.

Signed as free agent by Kansas City Chiefs, May 9, 1983.
On injured reserve with knee injury, August 28 through September 27, 1984; activated, September 28, 1984.
Released by Kansas City Chiefs, August 29, 1983; awarded on waivers to Houston Oilers, August 30, 1983.
Traded with 1986 draft choice by Houston Oilers to Kansas City Chiefs for 5th and 6th round picks in 1985 draft, April 30, 1985.
Houston NFL, 1983 and 1984.
Games: 1983 (16), 1984 (12). Total—28.
Pro statistics: Recovered one fumble, 1984.

DANIEL OLIVER HAMPTON
(Dan)
Defensive Lineman—Chicago Bears
Born September 19, 1957, at Oklahoma City, Okla.
Height, 6.05. Weight, 270.
High School—Jacksonville, Ark.
Attended University of Arkansas.

Named to THE SPORTING NEWS NFL All-Star Team, 1984.
Selected by Chicago in 1st round (4th player selected) of 1979 NFL draft.
Chicago NFL, 1979 through 1984.
Games: 1979 (16), 1980 (16), 1981 (16), 1982 (9), 1983 (11), 1984 (15). Total—83.
Pro statistics: Recovered two fumbles, 1979; recovered three fumbles, 1984.
Played in NFC Championship Game following 1984 season.
Played in Pro Bowl (NFL All-Star Game) following 1980, 1982 and 1984 seasons.

ANTHONY DUANE HANCOCK
Wide Receiver—Kansas City Chiefs
Born June 10, 1960, at Cleveland, O.
Height, 6.00. Weight, 200.
High School—Cleveland, O., John Hay.
Attended University of Tennessee.
Cousin of Von Mansfield, safety with Michigan Panthers.

Selected by Kansas City in 1st round (11th player selected) of 1982 NFL draft.

| | | PASS RECEIVING | | | | –PUNT RETURNS– | | | | —KICKOFF RET.— | | | | —TOTAL— | | |
Year Club	G.	P.C.	Yds.	Avg.	TD.	No.	Yds.	Avg.	TD.	No.	Yds.	Avg.	TD.	TD.	Pts.	F.
1982—Kansas City NFL	9	7	116	16.6	1	12	103	8.6	0	27	609	22.6	0	1	6	1
1983—Kansas City NFL	16	37	584	15.8	1	14	81	5.8	0	29	515	17.8	0	1	6	2
1984—Kansas City NFL	14	10	217	21.7	1	3	14	4.7	0	2	32	16.0	0	1	6	1
Pro Totals—3 Years	39	54	917	17.0	3	29	198	6.8	0	58	1156	19.9	0	3	18	4

Additional pro statistics: Recovered one fumble, 1984.

DUAN EDWARD HANKS
Wide Receiver—Miami Dolphins
Born July 28, 1961, at Detroit, Mich.
Height, 6.00. Weight, 180.
High School—Detroit, Mich., Cass Tech.
Attended Stephen F. Austin State University.

Selected by Philadelphia in 14th round (283rd player selected) of 1984 USFL draft.
Signed by Philadelphia Stars, January 27, 1984.
On injured reserve, February 20 through February 23, 1984.
Released by Philadelphia Stars, February 24, 1984.
Selected by Miami in 3rd round (82nd player selected) of 1984 NFL supplemental draft.
Signed by Miami Dolphins, July 5, 1984.
On injured reserve with shoulder injury, August 1 through September 11, 1984.
Released by Miami Dolphins, September 12, 1984; re-signed by Baltimore Stars, October 26, 1984.
Released by Baltimore Stars, February 11, 1985; re-signed by Dolphins, April 20, 1985.

CHARLES ALVIN HANNAH
(Charley)
Offensive Tackle—Los Angeles Raiders
Born July 26, 1955, at Albertville, Ala.
Height, 6.05. Weight, 260.
High School—Chattanooga, Tenn., Baylor.
Attended University of Alabama.
Son of Herb Hannah, tackle with New York Giants, 1951, and brother
of John Hannah, guard with New England Patriots.

Selected by Tampa Bay in 3rd round (56th player selected) of 1977 NFL draft.
On injured reserve, November 14 through remainder of 1977 season.
On injured reserve with knee injury, December 7 through December 26, 1979; activated, December 27, 1979.
Traded by Tampa Bay Buccaneers to Los Angeles Raiders for defensive end Dave Browning and 4th round pick in 1984 draft, July 18, 1983.
Tampa Bay NFL, 1977 through 1982; Los Angeles Raiders NFL, 1983 and 1984.
Games: 1977 (9), 1978 (16), 1979 (14), 1980 (16), 1981 (15), 1982 (7), 1983 (16), 1984 (15). Total—108.
Pro statistics: Recovered one fumble for eight yards and fumbled once for minus 32 yards, 1978; attempted one pass with no completions, 1980.
Played in NFC Championship Game following 1979 season.
Played in AFC Championship Game following 1983 season.
Played in NFL Championship Game following 1983 season.

JOHN ALLEN HANNAH
Guard—New England Patriots
Born April 4, 1951, at Canton, Ga.
Height, 6.03. Weight, 265.
High Schools—Chattanooga, Tenn., Baylor and Albertville, Tenn.
Attended University of Alabama.
Son of Herb Hannah, tackle with New York Giants, 1951, and brother of
Charley Hannah, offensive tackle with Los Angeles Raiders.

Named to THE SPORTING NEWS AFC All-Star Team, 1974, 1976, 1978 and 1979.
Named to THE SPORTING NEWS NFL All-Star Team, 1980, 1981 and 1984.
Named as center on THE SPORTING NEWS College All-America Team, 1972.
Selected by New England in 1st round (4th player selected) of 1973 NFL draft.
New England NFL, 1973 through 1984.
Games: 1973 (13), 1974 (14), 1975 (14), 1976 (14), 1977 (11), 1978 (16), 1979 (16), 1980 (16), 1981 (16), 1982 (8), 1983 (16), 1984 (15). Total—169.
Pro statistics: Recovered one fumble, 1973 and 1979; returned one kickoff for no yards, 1973; recovered one fumble in end zone for a touchdown, 1974; recovered two fumbles, 1978 and 1981; recovered three fumbles, 1983.
Played in Pro Bowl (NFL All-Star Game) following 1976, 1978 through 1982 and 1984 seasons.
Named to Pro Bowl following 1983 season; replaced due to injury by Bob Kuechenberg.

THOMAS HANNON
(Tom)
Safety—Minnesota Vikings
Born March 5, 1955, at Massillon, O.
Height, 5.11. Weight, 184.
High School—Massillon, O., Washington.
Received degree in physical education and community planning from Michigan State University.
Selected by Minnesota in 3rd round (83rd player selected) of 1977 NFL draft.

Year Club	G.	No.	Yds.	Avg.TD.	Year Club	G.	No.	Yds.	Avg.TD.
1977—Minnesota NFL	12			None	1982—Minnesota NFL	9			None
1978—Minnesota NFL	16	2	0	0.0 0	1983—Minnesota NFL	16			None
1979—Minnesota NFL	16	4	85	21.3 0	1984—Minnesota NFL	16	1	0	0.0 0
1980—Minnesota NFL	16	4	89	22.3 1	Pro Totals—8 Years	117	15	202	13.5 1
1981—Minnesota NFL	16	4	28	7.0 0					

Additional pro statistics: Recovered three fumbles, 1978 and 1979; recovered two fumbles, 1980 and 1982; fumbled once, 1980; recovered one fumble for 31 yards and credited with two safeties, 1981; recovered two fumbles for 17 yards, 1983.
Played in NFC Championship Game following 1977 season.

BRIAN HANSEN
Punter—New Orleans Saints
Born October 26, 1960, at Hawarden, Ia.
Height, 6.03. Weight, 218.
High School—Hawarden, Ia., West Sioux Community.
Attended Sioux Falls College.
Selected by New Orleans in 9th round (237th player selected) of 1984 NFL draft.

Year Club	G.	No.	Avg.	Blk.
1984—New Orleans NFL	16	69	43.8	1

Additional pro statistics: Rushed twice for minus 27 yards, 1984.
Played in Pro Bowl (NFL All-Star Game) following 1984 season.

CHARLES EDWARD HARBISON
Defensive Back—Buffalo Bills
Born October 27, 1959, at Gaston County, N.C.
Height, 6.01. Weight, 185.
High School—Boiling Springs, N.C., Crest.
Attended Gardner-Webb College.
Signed as free agent by Buffalo Bills, May 1, 1982.
Released by Buffalo Bills, August 9, 1982; signed by Boston Breakers, November 16, 1982.
Franchise transferred to New Orleans, October 18, 1983.
On developmental squad, April 7 through April 13, 1984; activated, April 14, 1984.
Franchise transferred to Portland, November 13, 1984.
Released by Portland Breakers, February 18, 1985; signed as free agent by Buffalo Bills, March 22, 1985.
On developmental squad for 1 game with New Orleans Breakers in 1984.

Year Club	G.	No.	Yds.	Avg.TD.
1983—Boston USFL	18	2	66	33.0 0
1984—New Orleans USFL	17	1	0	0.0 0
Pro Totals—2 Years	35	3	66	22.0 0

Additional pro statistics: Recovered three fumbles for one yard, credited with two sacks for 13 yards and returned two kickoffs for 18 yards, 1983; recovered two fumbles, 1984.

MICHAEL HARDEN
(Mike)
Safety—Denver Broncos
Born February 16, 1958, at Memphis, Tenn.
Height, 6.01. Weight, 190.
High School—Detroit, Mich., Central.
Received bachelor of arts degree in social studies from University of Michigan in 1980.
Selected by Denver in 5th round (131st player selected) of 1980 NFL draft.
On injured reserve with knee injury, December 16 through remainder of 1982 season.

Year Club	G.	—INTERCEPTIONS— No.	Yds.	Avg.	TD.	—KICKOFF RET.— No.	Yds.	Avg.	TD.	—TOTAL— TD.	Pts.	F.
1980—Denver NFL	16		None			12	214	17.8	0	0	0	1
1981—Denver NFL	16	2	34	17.0	0	11	178	16.2	0	0	0	0
1982—Denver NFL	5	2	3	1.5	0		None			0	0	0
1983—Denver NFL	15	4	127	31.8	0	1	9	9.0	0	0	0	0
1984—Denver NFL	16	6	79	13.2	1	1	4	4.0	0	1	6	1
Pro Totals—5 Years	68	14	243	17.4	1	25	405	16.2	0	1	6	2

Additional pro statistics: Returned two punts for 36 yards and recovered one fumble, 1981; recovered one fumble for 13 yards, 1982; recovered three fumbles, 1983; recovered two fumbles, 1984.

GREG HARDING
Safety—New Orleans Saints
Born July 31, 1960, at New Orleans, La.
Height, 6.02. Weight, 197.
High School—Houma, La., Terrebonne.
Attended Nicholls State University.

Signed as free agent by Houston Gamblers, September 6, 1983.
Released by Houston Gamblers, January 30, 1984; signed as free agent by New Orleans Saints, May 2, 1984.
On injured reserve with knee injury, August 14 through November 28, 1984; activated after clearing procedural waivers, November 30, 1984.
New Orleans NFL, 1984.
Games: 1984 (3).

WILLIAM DAVID HARDISON
(Dee)
Defensive End—New York Giants
Born May 2, 1956, at Jacksonville, N. C.
Height, 6.04. Weight, 274.
High School—Newton Grove, N. C., Hobbton.
Attended University of North Carolina.

Selected by Buffalo in 2nd round (32nd player selected) of 1978 NFL draft.
Released by Buffalo Bills, August 25, 1981; signed as free agent by New York Giants, December 8, 1981.
On injured reserve with hip injury, November 30 through December 30, 1982; activated, December 31, 1982.
Active for 2 games with New York Giants in 1981; did not play.
Buffalo NFL, 1978 through 1980; New York Giants NFL, 1981 through 1984.
Games: 1978 (16), 1979 (16), 1980 (16), 1982 (5), 1983 (16), 1984 (15). Total—84.
Pro statistics: Recovered one fumble, 1983.

ANDRE HARDY
Running Back-Kick Returner—Philadelphia Eagles
Born November 28, 1961, at San Diego, Calif.
Height, 6.01. Weight, 233.
High School—San Diego, Calif., Herbert Hoover.
Attended San Diego City College, Weber State College and received
bachelor of science degree in communications from St. Mary's College (Cal.) in 1984.

Selected by San Antonio in 5th round (86th player selected) of 1984 USFL draft.
Selected by Philadelphia in 5th round (116th player selected) of 1984 NFL draft.
Signed by Philadelphia Eagles, May 31, 1984.

		—RUSHING—				PASS RECEIVING				—TOTAL—		
Year Club	G.	Att.	Yds.	Avg.	TD.	P.C.	Yds.	Avg.	TD.	TD.	Pts.	F.
1984—Philadelphia NFL	6	14	41	2.9	0	2	22	11.0	0	0	0	0

Additional pro statistics: Returned one kickoff for 20 yards, 1984.

BRUCE ALAN HARDY
Tight End—Miami Dolphins
Born June 1, 1956, at Murray, Utah.
Height, 6.05. Weight, 232.
High School—Copperton, Utah, Bingham.
Received bachelor of science degree in business administration
from Arizona State University.

Selected by Miami in 9th round (247th player selected) of 1978 NFL draft.

		—PASS RECEIVING—			
Year Club	G.	P.C.	Yds.	Avg.	TD.
1978—Miami NFL	16	4	32	8.0	2
1979—Miami NFL	16	30	386	12.9	3
1980—Miami NFL	16	19	159	8.4	2
1981—Miami NFL	16	15	174	11.6	0
1982—Miami NFL	9	12	66	5.5	2
1983—Miami NFL	15	22	202	9.2	0
1984—Miami NFL	16	28	257	9.2	5
Pro Totals—7 Years	104	130	1276	9.8	14

Additional pro statistics: Returned two kickoffs for 27 yards, 1978; attempted one pass with no completions, 1979; fumbled once, 1980 and 1981; rushed once for two yards, 1983.
Played in AFC Championship Game following 1982 and 1984 seasons.
Played in NFL Championship Game following 1982 and 1984 seasons.

LARRY HARDY
Tight End—New Orleans Saints
Born July 9, 1956, at Mendenhall, Miss.
Height, 6.03. Weight, 246.
High School—Mendenhall, Miss.
Attended Jackson State University.
Brother of Edgar Hardy, guard with San Francisco 49ers, 1973; and Bertha Hardy, former player with
New Orleans Pride of the Women's Professional Basketball League.

Selected by New Orleans in 12th round (309th player selected) of 1978 NFL draft.
On injured reserve with thigh injury, October 28 through remainder of 1983 season.
On injured reserve with thigh injury, August 27 through November 6, 1984; activated after clearing procedural waivers, November 8, 1984.

		—PASS RECEIVING—			
Year Club	G.	P.C.	Yds.	Avg.	TD.
1978—New Orleans NFL........	16	5	131	26.2	1
1979—New Orleans NFL........	16	1	3	3.0	1
1980—New Orleans NFL........	16	13	197	15.2	0
1981—New Orleans NFL........	16	23	275	12.0	1
1982—New Orleans NFL........	9	8	67	8.4	1
1983—New Orleans NFL........	6	2	29	14.5	0
1984—New Orleans NFL........	6	4	50	12.5	1
Pro Totals—7 Years............	85	56	752	13.4	5

Additional pro statistics: Returned two kickoffs for three yards, 1978; recovered two fumbles and fumbled twice, 1981; fumbled once, 1982.

JAMES HARGROVE
(Jim)
Running Back—Buffalo Bills
Born November 13, 1957, at Newton Grove, N.C.
Height, 6.02. Weight, 228.
High School—Smithfield, N.C., Smithfield-Selma.
Attended Wake Forest University.

Signed as free agent by Cincinnati Bengals, May 5, 1981.
Released by Cincinnati Bengals, September 6, 1982; signed by Denver Gold, December 7, 1982.
Traded by Denver Gold to Michigan Panthers for linebacker Joe Stevens, February 27, 1983.
On developmental squad, March 11 through March 17, 1983.
Traded by Michigan Panthers to Boston Breakers for draft pick, March 18, 1983.
On reserve/left squad, May 28 through remainder of 1983 season.
Franchise transferred to New Orleans, October 18, 1983.
Released by New Orleans Breakers, February 29, 1984; signed as free agent by Buffalo Bills, May 10, 1985.
On developmental squad for 1 game with Michigan Panthers in 1983.
Active for 1 game with Michigan Panthers in 1983; did not play.
Active for 1 game with New Orleans Breakers in 1984; did not play.

		—RUSHING—				PASS RECEIVING				—TOTAL—		
Year Club	G.	Att.	Yds.	Avg.	TD.	P.C.	Yds.	Avg.	TD.	TD.	Pts.	F.
1981—Cincinnati NFL	15	16	66	4.1	1	1	0	0.0	0	1	6	1

Played in AFC Championship Game following 1981 season.
Played in NFL Championship Game following 1981 season.

DERRICK TODD HARMON
Running Back—San Francisco 49ers
Born April 26, 1963, at New York, N.Y.
Height, 5.10. Weight, 202.
High School—Queens, N.Y., Bayside.
Attended bachelor of science degree in engineering physics from Cornell University in 1984.

Selected by Oklahoma in 17th round (335th player selected) of 1984 USFL draft.
Selected by San Francisco in 9th round (248th player selected) of 1984 NFL draft.
Signed by San Francisco 49ers, May 4, 1984.

		—RUSHING—				PASS RECEIVING				—TOTAL—		
Year Club	G.	Att.	Yds.	Avg.	TD.	P.C.	Yds.	Avg.	TD.	TD.	Pts.	F.
1984—San Francisco NFL	16	39	192	4.9	1	1	2	2.0	0	1	6	1

		KICKOFF RETURNS		
Year Club	G.	No.	Yds.	Avg.TD.
1984—San Francisco NFL	16	13	357	27.5 0

Additional pro statistics: Attempted two passes with no completions and recovered two fumbles, 1984.
Played in NFC Championship Game following 1984 season.
Played in NFL Championship Game following 1984 season.

BRUCE S. HARPER
Running Back—New York Jets
Born June 20, 1955, at Englewood, N. J.
Height, 5.08. Weight, 177.
High School—Englewood, N. J., Dwight Morrow.
Attended Kutztown State College and attending Bergen County Community College.

Signed as free agent by New York Jets, May, 1977.
On injured reserve with knee injury, October 3 through remainder of 1984 season.

		—RUSHING—				PASS RECEIVING				—TOTAL—		
Year Club	G.	Att.	Yds.	Avg.	TD.	P.C.	Yds.	Avg.	TD.	TD.	Pts.	F.
1977—New York Jets NFL	14	44	198	4.5	0	21	209	10.0	1	1	6	7
1978—New York Jets NFL	16	58	303	5.2	2	13	196	15.1	2	5	30	3
1979—New York Jets NFL	16	65	282	4.3	0	17	250	14.7	2	2	12	6
1980—New York Jets NFL	15	45	126	2.8	0	50	634	12.7	3	3	18	2

Year Club	G.	Att.	RUSHING Yds.	Avg.	TD.	P.C.	PASS RECEIVING Yds.	Avg.	TD.	TD.	—TOTAL— Pts.	F.
1981—New York Jets NFL	16	81	393	4.9	4	52	459	8.8	1	5	30	7
1982—New York Jets NFL	9	20	125	6.3	0	14	177	12.6	1	1	6	1
1983—New York Jets NFL	9	51	354	6.9	1	48	413	8.6	2	3	18	1
1984—New York Jets NFL	4	10	48	4.8	1	5	71	14.2	0	1	6	0
Pro Totals—8 Years	99	374	1829	4.9	8	220	2409	11.0	12	21	126	27

Year Club	G.	No.	—PUNT RETURNS— Yds.	Avg.	TD.	No.	—KICKOFF RET.— Yds.	Avg.	TD.
1977—New York Jets NFL	14	34	425	12.5	0	*42	*1035	24.6	0
1978—New York Jets NFL	16	30	378	12.6	1	*55	*1280	23.3	0
1979—New York Jets NFL	16	33	290	8.8	0	*55	*1158	21.1	0
1980—New York Jets NFL	15	28	242	8.6	0	49	1070	21.8	0
1981—New York Jets NFL	16	35	265	7.6	0	23	480	20.9	0
1982—New York Jets NFL	9	23	184	8.0	0	18	368	20.4	0
1983—New York Jets NFL	9		None			1	16	16.0	0
1984—New York Jets NFL	4		None				None		
Pro Totals—8 Years	99	183	1784	9.7	1	243	5407	22.3	0

Additional pro statistics: Attempted one pass with no completions, 1977; recovered two fumbles, 1977, 1979 and 1981; recovered one fumble, 1978 and 1982; recovered three fumbles, 1980.
Played in AFC Championship Game following 1982 season.

DENNIS WAYNE HARRAH
Guard—Los Angeles Rams
Born March 9, 1953, at Charleston, W. Va.
Height, 6.05. Weight, 270.
High School—Charleston, W. Va., Stonewall Jackson.
Attended University of Miami (Fla.).

Named as offensive tackle on THE SPORTING NEWS College All-America Team, 1974.
Selected by Los Angeles in 1st round (11th player selected) of 1975 NFL draft.
On injured reserve with knee injury, November 8 through remainder of 1977 season.
On did not report list, August 19 through September 7, 1980; activated, September 8, 1980.
Los Angeles Rams NFL, 1975 through 1984.
Games: 1975 (14), 1976 (14), 1977 (8), 1978 (15), 1979 (13), 1980 (15), 1981 (15), 1982 (9), 1983 (15), 1984 (16).
Total—134.
Pro statistics: Recovered one fumble, 1982.
Played in NFC Championship Game following 1975, 1976, 1978 and 1979 seasons.
Played in NFL Championship Game following 1979 season.
Played in Pro Bowl (NFL All-Star Game) following 1978 through 1980 seasons.

WILLARD RACE HARRELL
Running Back—St. Louis Cardinals
Born September 16, 1952, at Stockton, Calif.
Height, 5.08. Weight, 182.
High School—Stockton, Calif., Edison.
Received bachelor of arts degree in physical education from University of the Pacific in 1975.

Selected by Green Bay in 3rd round (58th player selected) of 1975 NFL draft.
Released by Green Bay Packers, August 30, 1978; signed as free agent by St. Louis Cardinals, September 12, 1978.
On injured reserve with neck injury, December 15 through remainder of 1979 season.
On inactive list, September 12 and September 19, 1982.

Year Club	G.	Att.	RUSHING Yds.	Avg.	TD.	P.C.	PASS RECEIVING Yds.	Avg.	TD.	TD.	—TOTAL— Pts.	F.
1975—Green Bay NFL	14	121	359	3.0	1	34	261	7.7	2	3	18	11
1976—Green Bay NFL	13	130	435	3.3	3	17	201	11.8	1	4	24	9
1977—Green Bay NFL	13	60	140	2.3	1	19	194	10.2	0	2	12	3
1978—St. Louis NFL	13	35	134	3.8	0	3	5	1.7	0	1	6	4
1979—St. Louis NFL	14	19	100	5.3	0	3	33	11.0	0	0	0	5
1980—St. Louis NFL	16	42	170	4.0	3	9	52	5.8	0	3	18	3
1981—St. Louis NFL	16	5	6	1.2	1	14	131	9.4	1	2	12	0
1982—St. Louis NFL	7	4	14	3.5	0	11	127	11.5	0	0	0	0
1983—St. Louis NFL	14	4	13	3.3	0	3	25	8.3	0	0	0	1
1984—St. Louis NFL	16	9	20	2.2	1	14	106	7.6	0	1	6	0
Pro Totals—10 Years	136	429	1391	3.2	10	127	1135	8.9	4	16	96	36

Year Club	G.	Att.	Cmp.	PASSING Pct.	Gain	T.P.	P.I.	Avg.	No.	—PUNT RET.— Yds.	Avg.	TD.	No.	—KICKOFF RET.— Yds.	Avg.	TD.
1975—Green Bay NFL	14	5	3	60.0	61	3	0	12.20	21	136	6.5	0	3	78	26.0	0
1976—Green Bay NFL	13	4	1	25.0	40	1	1	10.00	3	−7	−2.3	0		None		
1977—Green Bay NFL	13	1	1	100.0	33	0	0	33.00	28	253	9.0	1	3	48	16.0	0
1978—St. Louis NFL	13			None					21	196	9.3	1	19	389	20.5	0
1979—St. Louis NFL	14	1	0	0.0	0	0	0	0.00	32	205	6.4	0	22	497	22.6	0
1980—St. Louis NFL	16			None					11	31	2.8	0	19	348	18.3	0
1981—St. Louis NFL	16			None					1	8	8.0	0	7	118	16.9	0
1982—St. Louis NFL	7	1	1	100.0	10	0	0	10.00	1	1	1.0	0	8	150	18.8	0
1983—St. Louis NFL	14			None					5	31	6.2	0	3	62	20.7	0
1984—St. Louis NFL	16			None						None			13	231	17.8	0
Pro Totals—10 Years	136	12	6	50.0	144	4	1	12.00	123	854	6.9	2	97	1921	19.8	0

Additional pro statistics: Recovered three fumbles, 1975, 1978 and 1979; recovered two fumbles, 1980; recovered one fumble for two yards, 1981.

PERRY DONELL HARRINGTON
Running Back—St. Louis Cardinals
Born May 13, 1958, at Bentonia, Miss.
Height, 5.11. Weight, 210.
High School—Jackson, Miss., Lanier.
Received bachelor of science degree in finance from Jackson State University in 1980.

Selected by Philadelphia in 2nd round (53rd player selected) of 1980 NFL draft.
On injured reserve with broken leg, September 28 through remainder of 1981 season.
Granted free agency, February 1, 1984; re-signed by Eagles and traded to Cleveland Browns for conditional pick in 1985 draft, July 23, 1984.
Released by Cleveland Browns, August 27, 1984; signed as free agent by St. Louis Cardinals, November 8, 1984.

		——RUSHING——				PASS RECEIVING				—TOTAL—		
Year Club	G.	Att.	Yds.	Avg.	TD.	P.C.	Yds.	Avg.	TD.	TD.	Pts.	F.
1980—Philadelphia NFL	14	32	166	5.2	1	3	24	8.0	0	1	6	1
1981—Philadelphia NFL	4	34	140	4.1	2	9	27	3.0	0	2	12	1
1982—Philadelphia NFL	9	56	231	4.1	1	13	74	5.7	0	1	6	2
1983—Philadelphia NFL	15	23	98	4.3	1	1	19	19.0	0	1	6	1
1984—St. Louis NFL	6	3	6	2.0	0			None		0	0	0
Pro Totals—5 Years	48	148	641	4.3	5	26	144	5.5	0	5	30	5

		KICKOFF RETURNS			
Year Club	G.	No.	Yds.	Avg.	TD.
1980—Philadelphia NFL	14	6	104	17.3	0
1981—Philadelphia NFL	4		None		
1982—Philadelphia NFL	9		None		
1983—Philadelphia NFL	15	4	79	19.8	0
1984—St. Louis NFL	6		None		
Pro Totals—5 Years	48	10	183	18.3	0

Played in NFC Championship Game following 1980 season.
Played in NFL Championship Game following 1980 season.

ALFRED CARL HARRIS
(Al)
Linebacker—Chicago Bears
Born December 31, 1956, at Bangor, Me.
Height, 6.05. Weight, 250.
High School—Wahiawa, Hawaii, Leilehua.
Attended Arizona State University.
Cousin of Ricky Bell, running back with Tampa Bay Buccaneers and
San Diego Chargers, 1977 through 1982.

Named as defensive lineman on THE SPORTING NEWS College All-America Team, 1978.
Selected by Chicago in 1st round (9th player selected) of 1979 NFL draft.
On injured reserve with knee injury, August 28 through October 25, 1979; activated, October 26, 1979.
On inactive list, September 19, 1982.
Chicago NFL, 1979 through 1984.
Games: 1979 (4), 1980 (16), 1981 (16), 1982 (8), 1983 (13), 1984 (16). Total—73.
Pro statistics: Caught one pass for 18 yards, intercepted one pass for 44 yards and a touchdown and recovered three fumbles for five yards, 1981; recovered two fumbles, 1983; intercepted one pass for 34 yards, 1984.
Played in NFC Championship Game following 1984 season.

BOB HARRIS
Linebacker—St. Louis Cardinals
Born November 11, 1960, at Everett, Wash.
Height, 6.02. Weight, 215.
High School—Decatur, Ga., Cedar Grove.
Attended Auburn University.

Selected by Birmingham in 1983 USFL territorial draft.
Selected by St. Louis in 8th round (211th player selected) of 1983 NFL draft.
Signed by St. Louis Cardinals, June 7, 1983.
On injured reserve with knee injury, November 9 through remainder of 1983 season.

		—INTERCEPTIONS—			
Year Club	G.	No.	Yds.	Avg.	TD.
1983—St. Louis NFL	8	3	10	3.3	0
1984—St. Louis NFL	16		None		
Pro Totals—2 Years	24	3	10	3.3	0

CLINTON CLAY HARRIS
(Clint)
Safety—New York Giants
Born August 19, 1962, at Norfolk, Va.
Height, 6.00. Weight, 205.
High School—Chesapeake, Va., Great Bridge.
Attended East Carolina University.

Selected by Washington in 6th round (109th player selected) of 1984 USFL draft.
Selected by New York Giants in 5th round (115th player selected) of 1984 NFL draft.

Signed by New York Giants, June 3, 1984.
On injured reserve with knee injury, August 27 through entire 1984 season.

DURIEL LaDON HARRIS JR.
Wide Receiver—Dallas Cowboys
Born November 27, 1954, at Port Arthur, Tex.
Height, 5.11. Weight, 176.
High School—Port Arthur, Tex., Austin.
Attended New Mexico State University.
Son of Duriel Harris, assistant coach at Tulane University, 1983 and 1984.

Selected by Miami in 3rd round (80th player selected) of 1976 NFL draft.
Traded by Miami Dolphins to Cleveland Browns for 4th round pick in 1985 draft, March 27, 1984.
Released by Cleveland Browns, November 12, 1984; awarded on waivers to Dallas Cowboys, November 13, 1984.

		PASS RECEIVING				–PUNT RETURNS–				—KICKOFF RET.—				—TOTAL—		
Year Club	G.	P.C.	Yds.	Avg.	TD.	No.	Yds.	Avg.	TD.	No.	Yds.	Avg.	TD.	TD.	Pts.	F.
1976—Miami NFL	12	22	372	16.9	1	9	79	8.7	0	17	559	*32.9	0	1	6	1
1977—Miami NFL	14	34	601	17.7	5		None			4	91	22.8	0	5	30	0
1978—Miami NFL	16	45	654	14.5	3		None			29	657	22.7	0	3	18	0
1979—Miami NFL	15	42	798	19.0	3		None				None			3	18	0
1980—Miami NFL	12	33	583	17.7	2		None			5	89	17.8	0	2	12	1
1981—Miami NFL	15	53	911	17.2	2		None			1	20	20.0	0	2	12	0
1982—Miami NFL	9	22	331	15.0	1		None				None			1	6	0
1983—Miami NFL	12	15	260	17.3	1		None				None			1	6	0
1984—Cle.(11)-Dal.(5) NFL	16	33	521	15.8	2	9	73	8.1	0		None			2	12	0
Pro Totals—9 Years	121	299	5031	16.8	20	18	152	8.4	0	56	1416	25.3	0	20	120	2

Additional pro statistics: Rushed once for 20 yards, 1979; rushed once for 13 yards, 1982; rushed once for no yards, 1983.
Played in AFC Championship Game following 1982 season.
Played in NFL Championship Game following 1982 season.

ERIC WAYNE HARRIS
Cornerback—Los Angeles Rams
Born August 11, 1955, at Memphis, Tenn.
Height, 6.03. Weight, 202.
High School—Memphis, Tenn., Hamilton.
Attended Memphis State University.

Selected by Kansas City in 4th round (104th player selected) of 1977 NFL draft.
Signed by Toronto Argonauts, April, 1977.
Granted free agency, April 15, 1980; given offer sheet by New Orleans Saints, April 26, 1980.
Offer matched by Kansas City Chiefs, April 28, 1980; signed by Chiefs, May 16, 1980.
Traded by Kansas City Chiefs to Los Angeles Rams for running back Jewerl Thomas, August 19, 1983.
On injured reserve with ankle injury, November 2 through December 7, 1984; activated, December 8, 1984.

		——INTERCEPTIONS——			
Year Club	G.	No.	Yds.	Avg.	TD.
1977—Toronto CFL	16	7	166	23.7	1
1978—Toronto CFL	16	3	27	9.0	0
1979—Toronto CFL	16	3	12	4.0	0
1980—Kansas City NFL	15	7	54	7.7	0
1981—Kansas City NFL	16	7	109	15.6	0
1982—Kansas City NFL	8	3	66	22.0	*1
1983—L.A. Rams NFL	16	4	100	25.0	0
1984—L.A. Rams NFL	7		None		
CFL Totals—3 Years	48	13	205	15.8	1
NFL Totals—5 Years	62	21	329	15.7	1
Pro Totals—8 Years	110	34	534	15.7	2

Additional CFL statistics: Returned three punts for no yards and recovered four fumbles for two yards, 1977; fumbled once, 1977 and 1978; returned one kickoff for no yards and recovered two fumbles for 12 yards, 1978; recovered two fumbles, 1979.
Additional NFL statistics: Recovered two fumbles for 20 yards, 1981; recovered one fumble, 1983 and 1984.

GEORGE WASHINGTON HARRIS JR.
(Weedy)
Linebacker—Green Bay Packers
Born December 2, 1960, at Waco, Tex.
Height, 6.02. Weight, 223.
High School—Waco, Tex., Richfield.
Attended University of Houston.

Selected by Boston in 4th round (38th player selected) of 1983 USFL draft.
Selected by Denver in 5th round (116th player selected) of 1983 NFL draft.
Signed by Denver Broncos, May 13, 1983.
On injured reserve with knee injury, August 30 through entire 1983 season.
Released by Denver Broncos, August 27, 1984; signed as free agent by Green Bay Packers, February 15, 1985.

JOHN EDWARD HARRIS
Safety—Seattle Seahawks

Born June 13, 1956, at Fort Benning, Ga.
Height, 6.02. Weight, 200.
High School—Miami, Fla., Jackson.
Received bachelor of science degree in political science from Arizona State University in 1978.

Selected by Seattle in 7th round (173rd player selected) of 1978 NFL draft.
On did not report list, August 31 through September 1, 1982; activated and granted two-game roster exemption, September 2, 1982.
Activated, September 10, 1982.

		—INTERCEPTIONS—						—INTERCEPTIONS—			
Year Club	G.	No.	Yds.	Avg.TD.		Year Club	G.	No.	Yds.	Avg.TD.	
1978—Seattle NFL	16	4	65	16.3	0	1982—Seattle NFL	9	4	33	8.3	0
1979—Seattle NFL	14	2	30	15.0	0	1983—Seattle NFL	16	2	15	7.5	0
1980—Seattle NFL	16	6	28	4.7	0	1984—Seattle NFL	16	6	79	13.2	0
1981—Seattle NFL	16	10	155	15.5	2	Pro Totals—7 Years	103	34	405	11.9	2

Additional pro statistics: Returned five punts for 58 yards, 1978; fumbled once, 1978, 1979 and 1981; returned eight punts for 70 yards and returned one kickoff for 21 yards, 1979; recovered one fumble, 1979, 1980 and 1984; recovered three fumbles, 1981; returned two punts for 27 yards and recovered three fumbles for 62 yards, 1983; returned one kickoff for seven yards, 1984.
Played in AFC Championship Game following 1983 season.

JOHN LEE HARRIS
Defensive End—Miami Dolphins

Born August 3, 1960, at Demopolis, Ala.
Height, 6.04. Weight, 250.
High School—Demopolis, Ala.
Attended Alabama A&M University and Mississippi Valley State University.

Signed as free agent by Oakland Invaders, January 26, 1983.
Released by Oakland Invaders, February 16, 1983; signed as free agent by Miami Dolphins, May 5, 1984.
Left Miami Dolphins camp voluntarily and released, July 30, 1984; re-signed by Dolphins, March 29, 1985.

LEOTIS HARRIS
Guard—Green Bay Packers

Born June 28, 1955, at Little Rock, Ark.
Height, 6.01. Weight, 265.
High School—Little Rock, Ark., Hall.
Attended University of Arkansas.

Selected by Green Bay in 6th round (144th player selected) of 1978 NFL draft.
On injured reserve with knee injury, October 10 through remainder of 1983 season.
On physically unable to perform/active with knee injury, July 19 through August 20, 1984.
On physically unable to perform/reserve with knee injury, August 21 through entire 1984 season.
Green Bay NFL, 1978 through 1983.
Games: 1978 (13), 1979 (15), 1980 (16), 1981 (16), 1982 (9), 1983 (5). Total—74.
Pro statistics: Recovered one fumble, 1979, 1980 and 1981.

MICHAEL LEE HARRIS
(M.L.)
Tight End—Cincinnati Bengals

Born January 16, 1954, at Columbus, O.
Height, 6.05. Weight, 238.
High School—Columbus, O., North.
Attended University of Tampa and Kansas State University

Signed by Hamilton Tiger-Cats, April, 1976.
Granted free agency, April, 1978; signed by Toronto Argonauts, May, 1978 (Argonauts sent linebacker Ray Nettles to Tiger-Cats as compensation).
Granted free agency, April 1, 1980; signed as free agent by Cincinnati Bengals, April 30, 1980.
On injured reserve with broken thumb, October 29 through November 27, 1980; activated, November 28, 1980.
On injured reserve with knee injury, November 28 through remainder of 1983 season.

		—RUSHING—				PASS RECEIVING				—TOTAL—		
Year Club	G.	Att.	Yds.	Avg.	TD.	P.C.	Yds.	Avg.	TD.	TD.	Pts.	F.
1976—Hamilton CFL	11	5	—1	—0.2	1	24	550	22.9	3	4	24	2
1977—Hamilton CFL	16	4	12	3.0	2	43	771	17.9	6	8	48	1
1978—Toronto CFL	12	5	16	3.2	0	32	496	15.5	3	3	18	0
1979—Toronto CFL	12	3	13	4.3	0	46	530	11.5	1	1	6	1
1980—Cincinnati NFL	12	1	0	0.0	0	10	137	13.7	0	0	0	0
1981—Cincinnati NFL	15			None		13	181	13.9	2	2	12	1
1982—Cincinnati NFL	9	2	—3	—1.5	0	10	103	10.3	3	3	18	0
1983—Cincinnati NFL	12			None		8	66	8.3	2	2	12	0
1984—Cincinnati NFL	16	1	—2	—2.0	0	48	759	15.8	2	2	12	2
CFL Totals—4 Years	51	17	40	2.4	3	145	2347	16.2	13	16	96	4
NFL Totals—5 Years	64	3	—5	—1.7	0	89	1246	14.0	9	9	54	3
Pro Totals—9 Years	115	20	35	1.8	3	234	3593	15.4	22	25	150	7

Additional CFL statistics: Returned three kickoffs for 51 yards, 1976; recovered one fumble, 1976 and 1977; returned one kickoff for 20 yards, 1978.

Additional NFL statistics: Recovered two fumbles for three yards, 1981; returned one kickoff for 12 yards and recovered one fumble, 1984.

Played in AFC Championship Game following 1981 season.

Played in NFL Championship Game following 1981 season.

NEIL ANTHONY HARRIS
Defensive Back—Indianapolis Colts
Born February 12, 1962, at Kansas City, Kan.
Height, 6.00. Weight, 195.
High School—Kansas City, Kan., J.C. Harmon.
Attended University of Nebraska.

Selected by Portland in 13th round (179th player selected) of 1985 USFL draft.

Signed by Portland Breakers, January 23, 1985.

Released by Portland Breakers, February 18, 1985; signed as free agent by Indianapolis Colts, May 11, 1985.

ROY ELLIOTT HARRIS
Defensive Tackle—Atlanta Falcons
Born March 26, 1961, at Winter Garden, Fla.
Height, 6.02. Weight, 266.
High School—Winter Garden, Fla., West Orange.
Attended University of Florida.

Selected by Tampa Bay in 1984 USFL territorial draft.

Signed as free agent by Atlanta Falcons, May 2, 1984.

Atlanta NFL, 1984.

Games: 1984 (15).

Pro statistics: Recovered one fumble, 1984.

TIM ALLEN HARRIS
Running Back—Houston Oilers
Born June 15, 1961, at Compton, Calif.
Height, 5.09. Weight, 206.
High School—Compton, Calif.
Attended Washington State University.

Selected by Los Angeles in 16th round (192nd player selected) of 1983 USFL draft.

Signed as free agent by Pittsburgh Steelers, May 1, 1983.

Released by Pittsburgh Steelers, August 29, 1983; re-signed by Steelers, August 30, 1983.

Released by Pittsburgh Steelers, August 6, 1984.

USFL rights traded by Los Angeles Express to Pittsburgh Maulers for rights to linebackers Carky and Marky Alexander, September 7, 1984.

Signed as free agent by Houston Oilers, April 3, 1985.

| | | | KICKOFF RETURNS | | |
Year Club	G.	No.	Yds.	Avg.	TD.
1983—Pittsburgh NFL............	14	18	289	16.1	0

Additional pro statistics: Rushed twice for 15 yards, returned three punts for 12 yards, recovered one fumble and fumbled twice, 1983.

DENNIS HARRISON
Defensive End—Philadelphia Eagles
Born July 31, 1956, at Cleveland, O.
Height, 6.08. Weight, 280.
High School—Murfreesboro, Tenn., Riverdale.
Received bachelor of science degree in education from Vanderbilt University in 1978.

Selected by Philadelphia in 4th round (92nd player selected) of 1978 draft.

On injured reserve with knee injury, August 28 through September 28, 1979; activated, September 29, 1979.

Philadelphia NFL, 1978 through 1984.

Games: 1978 (16), 1979 (12), 1980 (15), 1981 (13), 1982 (9), 1983 (16), 1984 (16). Total—97.

Pro statistics: Intercepted one pass for 12 yards, 1978; recovered three fumbles, 1981; recovered one fumble, 1982 and 1984; recovered one fumble for 16 yards, 1983.

Played in NFC Championship Game following 1980 season.

Played in NFL Championship Game following 1980 season.

Played in Pro Bowl (NFL All-Star Game) following 1982 season.

MARCK HARRISON
Running Back—Cleveland Browns
Born April 20, 1961, at Columbus, O.
Height, 5.08. Weight, 195.
High School—Columbus, O., Eastmoor.
Attended University of Wisconsin.

Selected by Jacksonville in 1985 USFL territorial draft.

USFL rights traded with rights to center Dan Turk and tight end Ken Whisenhunt by Jacksonville Bulls to Tampa Bay Bandits for rights to running back Cedric Jones, placekicker Bobby Raymond and defensive back Eric Riley, January 3, 1985.

USFL rights traded by Tampa Bay Bandits to Orlando Renegades for draft choice, March 7, 1985.

Signed by Orlando Renegades and granted roster exemption, March 7 through March 13, 1985; activated, March 14, 1985.

On developmental squad, April 12 through April 17, 1985; activated, April 18, 1985.

Released by Orlando Renegades, April 24, 1985; signed as free agent by Cleveland Browns, May 6, 1985.

On developmental squad for 1 game with Orlando Renegades in 1985.

Year Club		—RUSHING—				PASS RECEIVING				—TOTAL—		
	G.	Att.	Yds.	Avg.	TD.	P.C.	Yds.	Avg.	TD.	TD.	Pts.	F.
1985—Orlando USFL	3	3	5	1.7	0	1	5	5.0	0	0	0	0

Additional pro statistics: Returned one kickoff for nine yards, 1985.

MICHAEL ALBERT HARTENSTINE
Name pronounced Heart-In-Stine.
(Mike)
Defensive End—Chicago Bears
Born July 27, 1953, at Bethlehem, Pa.
Height, 6.03. Weight, 258.
High School—Bethlehem, Pa., Liberty.
Attended Penn State University.

Selected by Chicago in 2nd round (31st player selected) of 1975 NFL draft.

Chicago NFL, 1975 through 1984.

Games: 1975 (14), 1976 (14), 1977 (14), 1978 (16), 1979 (16), 1980 (16), 1981 (16), 1982 (9), 1983 (16), 1984 (16). Total—147.

Pro statistics: Scored a safety and recovered two fumbles for five yards, 1975; recovered three fumbles for 3 yards and scored one touchdown on a 12 yard lateral, 1976; recovered three fumbles, 1977; recovered three fumbles for 10 yards, 1978; recovered one fumble, 1979; recovered one fumble for four yards, 1981; recovered one fumble for 10 yards and a touchdown, 1983; recovered two fumbles, 1984.

Played in NFC Championship Game following 1984 season.

PERRY EDMUND HARTNETT
Guard—Buffalo Bills
Born April 28, 1960, at Galveston, Tex.
Height, 6.05. Weight, 275.
High School—Galveston, Tex., Adidas.
Attended Southern Methodist University.

Selected by Chicago in 5th round (116th player selected) of 1982 NFL draft.

Released by Chicago Bears, August 29, 1983; re-signed by Bears, September 21, 1983.

USFL rights traded by San Antonio Gunslingers to Chicago Blitz for defensive back Ricky Harr, October 27, 1983.

Released by Chicago Bears, November 12, 1983; signed by Chicago Blitz, November 21, 1983.

On developmental squad, April 19 through April 27, 1984; activated, April 28, 1984.

Franchise disbanded, November 20, 1984.

Selected by Baltimore Stars in USFL dispersal draft, December 6, 1984.

On developmental squad for 1 game with Chicago Blitz in 1984.

Released by Baltimore Stars, February 18, 1985; signed as free agent by Buffalo Bills, May 10, 1985.

Chicago NFL, 1982 and 1983; Chicago USFL, 1984.

Games: 1982 (9), 1983 (2), 1984 (16). Total NFL—11. Total Pro—27.

CARTER HARTWIG
Safety—Houston Oilers
Born February 27, 1956, at Culver City, Calif.
Height, 6.00. Weight, 203.
High School—Fresno, Calif., Central Union.
Received bachelor of science degree in public administration from University of Southern California.

Selected by Houston in 8th round (214th player selected) of 1979 NFL draft.

On injured reserve with pulled hamstring, December 6 through remainder of 1984 season.

Year Club		-INTERCEPTIONS-				—KICKOFF RET.—				—TOTAL—		
	G.	No.	Yds.	Avg.	TD.	No.	Yds.	Avg.	TD.	TD.	Pts.	F.
1979—Houston NFL	16	2	24	12.0	0	13	238	18.3	0	0	0	0
1980—Houston NFL	15	1	0	0.0	0	None				0	0	0
1981—Houston NFL	16	3	78	26.0	0	None				0	0	0
1982—Houston NFL	9	None				None				0	0	0
1983—Houston NFL	16	None				None				0	0	0
1984—Houston NFL	14	3	23	7.7	0	None				0	0	0
Pro Totals—6 Years	86	9	125	13.9	0	13	238	18.3	0	0	0	0

Additional pro statistics: Recovered three fumbles for one yard, 1979; recovered one fumble, 1981 and 1984; recovered two fumbles, 1983.

Played in AFC Championship Game following 1979 season.

JOHN DANIEL HARTY
Defensive Tackle—San Francisco 49ers
Born December 17, 1958, at Sioux City, Iowa.
Height, 6.04. Weight, 263.
High School—Sioux City, Iowa, Heelan.
Attended University of Iowa.

Selected by San Francisco in 2nd round (36th player selected) of 1981 NFL draft.

On injured reserve with foot injury, November 23 through remainder of 1983 season.

On physically unable to perform/active with fractured foot, July 19 through August 12, 1984.
On physically unable to perform/reserve with fractured foot, August 13 through entire 1984 season.
San Francisco NFL, 1981 through 1983.
Games: 1981 (14), 1982 (9), 1983 (5). Total—28.
Played in NFC Championship Game following 1981 season.
Played in NFL Championship Game following 1981 season.

MAURICE HARVEY
Safety—Tampa Bay Buccaneers
Born January 14, 1956, at Cincinnati, O.
Height, 5.09. Weight, 187.
High School—Cincinnati, O., Princeton.
Received bachelor of science degree in physical education from Ball State University in 1978
and attending Ball State for master's degree in coaching.

Selected by Oakland in 4th round (86th player selected) of 1978 NFL draft.
Claimed on waivers from Oakland Raiders by Denver Broncos, August 29, 1978.
On injured reserve with knee injury, August 28 through entire 1979 season.
Released by Denver Broncos, August 11, 1981; claimed on waivers by Green Bay Packers, August 13, 1981.
Released by Green Bay Packers, September 30, 1983; signed as free agent by Detroit Lions, October 5, 1983.
Released by Detroit Lions, August 27, 1984; signed as free agent by Tampa Bay Buccaneers, September 4, 1984.

| | | —INTERCEPTIONS— | | | |
Year Club	G.	No.	Yds.	Avg.	TD.
1978—Denver NFL	16		None		
1980—Denver NFL	15	1	18	18.0	0
1981—Green Bay NFL	16	6	217	36.2	0
1982—Green Bay NFL	9	2	32	16.0	0
1983—G.B. (4)-Det. (9) NFL ..	13		None		
1984—Tampa Bay NFL	15		None		
Pro Totals—6 Years	84	9	267	29.7	0

Additional pro statistics: Recovered three fumbles and fumbled once, 1981; recovered three fumbles for 25 yards and one touchdown, 1982.

JAMES DONALD HASLETT
(Jim)
Linebacker—Buffalo Bills
Born December 9, 1955, at Pittsburgh, Pa.
Height, 6.03. Weight, 232.
High School—Pittsburgh, Pa., Avalon.
Attended Indiana (Pa.) University.
Brother of Jon Haslett, rookie linebacker with Buffalo Bills; and
cousin of Hal Stringert, defensive back with The Hawaiians (WFL)
and San Diego Chargers, 1974 through 1980.

Selected by Buffalo in 2nd round (51st player selected) of 1979 NFL draft.
On injured reserve with back injury, September 13 through November 17, 1983; activated, November 18, 1983.

| | | —INTERCEPTIONS— | | | |
Year Club	G.	No.	Yds.	Avg.	TD.
1979—Buffalo NFL	16	2	15	7.5	0
1980—Buffalo NFL	16	2	30	15.0	0
1981—Buffalo NFL	16		None		
1982—Buffalo NFL	6		None		
1983—Buffalo NFL	5		None		
1984—Buffalo NFL	15		None		
Pro Totals—6 Years	74	4	45	11.3	0

Additional pro statistics: Recovered two fumbles, 1979; recovered one fumble, 1980 through 1982; caught one pass for four yards, 1982; recovered three fumbles for 10 yards, 1984.

DONALD WILLIAM HASSELBECK
(Don)
Tight End—New York Giants
Born April 1, 1955, at Cincinnati, O.
Height, 6.07. Weight, 245.
High School—Cincinnati, O., LaSalle.
Attended University of Colorado.

Named as tight end on THE SPORTING NEWS College All-America Team, 1976.
Selected by New England in 2nd round (52nd player selected) of 1977 NFL draft.
Granted roster exemption, August 18, 1981; activated August 29, 1981.
On injured reserve with knee injury, December 11 through remainder of 1981 season.
Traded by New England Patriots to Los Angeles Raiders for tight end Derrick Ramsey, September 13, 1983.
Released by Los Angeles Raiders, August 27, 1984; awarded on waivers to Minnesota Vikings, August 28, 1984.
Granted free agency after not receiving qualifying offer, February 1, 1985; signed by New York Giants, May 21, 1985.

			—PASS RECEIVING—		
Year Club	G.	P.C.	Yds.	Avg.	TD.
1977—New England NFL.......	14	9	76	8.4	4
1978—New England NFL.......	16	7	107	15.3	0
1979—New England NFL.......	16	13	158	12.2	0
1980—New England NFL.......	16	8	130	16.3	4
1981—New England NFL.......	14	46	808	17.6	6
1982—New England NFL.......	9	15	158	10.5	1
1983—N.E. (1)-Rai. (14) NFL.	15	3	24	8.0	2
1984—Minnesota NFL.............	16	1	10	10.0	0
Pro Totals—8 Years........	116	102	1471	14.4	17

Additional pro statistics: Fumbled once, 1979; returned one kickoff for seven yards and fumbled twice, 1981; recovered one fumble, 1984.

Played in AFC Championship Game following 1983 season.

Played in NFL Championship Game following 1983 season.

STEVE F. HATHAWAY
Linebacker—Indianapolis Colts
Born April 26, 1962, at Beaver, Pa.
Height, 6.04. Weight, 238.
High School—Beaver, Pa.
Attended West Virginia University.

Selected by Pittsburgh in 1984 USFL territorial draft.

Selected by Indianapolis in 12th round (317th player selected) of 1984 NFL draft.

Signed by Indianapolis Colts, May 24, 1984.

On injured reserve with knee injury, October 20 through remainder of 1984 season.

Indianapolis NFL, 1984.

Games: 1984 (6).

Pro statistics: Returned one kickoff for two yards and recovered one fumble, 1984.

FRANK HAWKINS
Running Back—Los Angeles Raiders
Born July 3, 1959, at Las Vegas, Nev.
Height, 5.09. Weight, 210.
High School—Las Vegas, Nev., Western.
Received degree in criminal justice from University of Nevada at Reno in 1981.
Cousin of Larry Heater, running back with New York Giants, 1980 through 1983.

Selected by Oakland in 10th round (276th player selected) of 1981 NFL draft.

Released by Oakland Raiders, August 25, 1981; re-signed by Raiders, September 23, 1981.

Franchise transferred to Los Angeles, May 7, 1982.

		—RUSHING—				PASS RECEIVING				—TOTAL—		
Year Club	G.	Att.	Yds.	Avg.	TD.	P.C.	Yds.	Avg.	TD.	TD.	Pts.	F.
1981—Oakland NFL..	13	40	165	4.1	0	10	109	10.9	0	0	0	1
1982—Los Angeles Raiders NFL	9	27	54	2.0	2	7	35	5.0	1	3	18	1
1983—Los Angeles Raiders NFL	16	110	526	4.8	6	20	150	7.5	2	8	48	2
1984—Los Angeles Raiders NFL	16	108	376	3.5	3	7	51	7.3	0	3	18	3
Pro Totals—4 Years.........	54	285	1121	3.9	11	44	345	7.8	3	14	84	7

Additional pro statistics: Recovered one fumble, 1981, 1983 and 1984; returned one kickoff for seven yards, 1981.

Played in AFC Championship Game following 1983 season.

Played in NFL Championship Game following 1983 season.

JIM PATRICK HAWN
Guard—San Diego Chargers
Born May 6, 1961, at Dunlap, Ia.
Height, 6.04. Weight, 273.
High School—Placentia, Calif., El Dorado.
Attended Arizona State University.

Signed as free agent by Baltimore Colts, May 25, 1983.

On injured reserve with hernia, August 16 through September 26, 1983.

Released by Baltimore Colts, September 27, 1983; signed as free agent by San Diego Chargers, May 20, 1984.

On injured reserve with neck injury, August 27 through entire 1984 season.

STEVE HAWORTH
Safety—Atlanta Falcons
Born September 16, 1961, at Manila, Philippines.
Height, 6.00. Weight, 190.
High School—Durant, Okla.
Attended University of Oklahoma.

Selected by New Jersey in 1983 USFL territorial draft.

Selected by Houston in 6th round (142nd player selected) of 1983 NFL draft.

Signed by Houston Oilers, June 22, 1983.

Released by Houston Oilers, August 22, 1983; signed as free agent by Atlanta Falcons, October 6, 1983.

On injured reserve with hamstring injury, August 28 through October 23, 1984; activated, October 24, 1984.

On non-football injury list, December 1 through remainder of 1984 season.

Atlanta NFL, 1983 and 1984.

Games: 1983 (11), 1984 (5). Total—16.

GREGORY DALE HAWTHORNE
(Greg)
Tight End—New England Patriots
Born September 5, 1956, at Fort Worth, Tex.
Height, 6.03. Weight, 225.
High School—Fort Worth, Tex., Poly.
Attended Baylor University.

Selected by Pittsburgh in 1st round (28th player selected) of 1979 NFL draft.
Traded by Pittsburgh Steelers to New England Patriots for 9th round pick in 1985 draft, August 21, 1984.

Year Club	G.	—RUSHING— Att.	Yds.	Avg.	TD.	PASS RECEIVING P.C.	Yds.	Avg.	TD.	—TOTAL— TD.	Pts.	F.
1979—Pittsburgh NFL	15	28	123	4.4	1	8	47	5.9	0	1	6	2
1980—Pittsburgh NFL	15	63	226	3.6	4	12	158	13.2	0	4	24	6
1981—Pittsburgh NFL	10	25	58	2.3	2	4	23	5.8	0	2	12	1
1982—Pittsburgh NFL	9	15	68	4.5	0	12	182	15.2	3	3	18	0
1983—Pittsburgh NFL	10	5	47	9.4	0	19	300	15.8	0	0	0	0
1984—New England NFL	14			None		7	127	18.1	0	0	0	0
Pro Totals—6 Years	73	136	522	3.8	7	62	837	13.5	3	10	60	9

Year Club	G.	KICKOFF RETURNS No.	Yds.	Avg.	TD.
1979—Pittsburgh NFL	15	2	46	23.0	0
1980—Pittsburgh NFL	15	9	169	18.8	0
1981—Pittsburgh NFL	10	7	138	19.7	0
1982—Pittsburgh NFL	9			None	
1983—Pittsburgh NFL	10			None	
1984—New England NFL	14	1	14	14.0	0
Pro Totals—6 Years	73	19	367	19.3	0

Additional pro statistics: Recovered one fumble, 1979 and 1983; recovered three fumbles, 1980.
Played in AFC Championship Game following 1979 season.
Played in NFL Championship Game following 1979 season.

GARY HAYES
Defensive Back—Green Bay Packers
Born August 19, 1957, at Tuscon, Ariz.
Height, 5.10. Weight, 180.
High School—El Cerrito, Calif.
Attended Fresno State University.

Signed as free agent by St. Louis Cardinals, May 29, 1980.
Released by St. Louis Cardinals, August 26, 1980; signed as free agent by Edmonton Eskimos, February 15, 1981.
USFL rights traded by Oakland Invaders to Los Angeles Express for rights to defensive end Chris Lindstrom and cornerback Jeff Allen, September 27, 1983.
Granted free agency, March 1, 1984; signed by Green Bay Packers, March 21, 1984.

Year Club	G.	INTERCEPTIONS No.	Yds.	Avg.	TD.	–PUNT RETURNS– No.	Yds.	Avg.	TD.	—KICKOFF RET.— No.	Yds.	Avg.	TD.	—TOTAL— TD.	Pts.	F.
1981—Edmonton CFL	15	2	39	19.5	0	71	601	8.5	0	9	209	23.2	0	0	0	2
1982—Edmonton CFL	16	2	27	13.5	0	*100	818	8.2	0	5	95	19.0	0	0	0	2
1983—Edmonton CFL	16	1	34	34.0	0	61	380	6.2	0	13	269	20.7	0	0	0	2
1984—Green Bay NFL	16			None		4	24	6.0	0			None		0	0	0
CFL Totals—3 Years	47	5	100	20.0	0	232	1799	7.8	0	27	573	21.2	0	0	0	6
NFL Totals—1 Year	16	0	0	0.0	0	4	24	6.0	0	0	0	0.0	0	0	0	0
Pro Totals—4 Years	63	5	100	20.0	0	236	1823	7.7	0	27	573	21.2	0	0	0	6

Additional pro statistics: Recovered one fumble, 1983.
Played in CFL Championship Game following 1981 and 1982 seasons.

JEFFREY HAYES
(Jeff)
Punter—Washington Redskins
Born August 19, 1959, at Elkin, N.C.
Height, 5.11. Weight, 175.
High School—Elkin, N.C.
Attended University of North Carolina.

Signed as free agent by Washington Redskins, May 24, 1982.

Year Club	G.	—PUNTING— No.	Avg.	Blk.
1982—Washington NFL	9	51	38.0	1
1983—Washington NFL	16	72	38.8	0
1984—Washington NFL	16	72	39.4	1
Pro Totals—3 Years	41	195	38.8	2

Additional pro statistics: Rushed twice for 63 yards, 1983; rushed twice for 13 yards, recovered one fumble and fumbled twice, 1984.
Played in NFC Championship Game following 1982 and 1983 seasons.
Played in NFL Championship Game following 1982 and 1983 seasons.

JOE HAYES
Wide Receiver-Kick Returner—Philadelphia Eagles
Born September 15, 1960, at Dallas, Tex.
Height, 5.09. Weight, 185.
High School—Dallas, Tex., South Oak Cliff.
Attended Texas A&I University and Central State University (Okla.).

Selected by Washington in 14th round (274th player selected) of 1984 USFL draft.
Selected by Philadelphia in 7th round (172nd player selected) of 1984 NFL draft.
Signed by Philadelphia Eagles, May 25, 1984.
On injured reserve with sprained ankle, November 24 through remainder of 1984 season.

		KICKOFF RETURNS				
Year	Club	G.	No.	Yds.	Avg.	TD.
1984—Philadelphia NFL		12	22	441	20.0	0

Additional pro statistics: Recovered one fumble and fumbled twice, 1984.

LESTER HAYES
Cornerback—Los Angeles Raiders
Born January 22, 1955, at Houston, Tex.
Height, 6.00. Weight, 200.
High School—Houston, Tex., Wheatley.
Attended Texas A&M University.

Named to THE SPORTING NEWS NFL All-Star Team, 1980 and 1981.
Named as safety on THE SPORTING NEWS College All-America Team, 1976.
Selected by Oakland in 5th round (126th player selected) of 1977 NFL draft.
Franchise transferred to Los Angeles, May 7, 1982.

			INTERCEPTIONS				—KICKOFF RET.—				—TOTAL—		
Year	Club	G.	No.	Yds.	Avg.	TD.	No.	Yds.	Avg.	TD.	TD.	Pts.	F.
1977—Oakland NFL		14	1	27	27.0	0	3	57	19.0	0	0	0	1
1978—Oakland NFL		16	4	86	21.5	0		None			0	0	0
1979—Oakland NFL		16	7	100	14.3	*2		None			2	12	0
1980—Oakland NFL		16	*13	*273	21.0	1	1	0	0.0	0	1	6	0
1981—Oakland NFL		16	3	0	0.0	0		None			0	0	0
1982—Los Angeles Raiders NFL		9	2	0	0.0	0		None			0	0	0
1983—Los Angeles Raiders NFL		16	2	49	24.5	0		None			0	0	0
1984—Los Angeles Raiders NFL		16	1	3	3.0	0		None			0	0	0
Pro Totals—8 Years		119	33	538	16.3	3	4	57	14.3	0	3	18	1

Additional pro statistics: Recovered two fumbles for minus three yards, 1977; recovered two fumbles, 1980.
Played in AFC Championship Game following 1977, 1980 and 1983 seasons.
Played in NFL Championship Game following 1980 and 1983 seasons.
Played in Pro Bowl (NFL All-Star Game) following 1980 through 1984 seasons.

JAMES HAYNES
Linebacker—New Orleans Saints
Born August 9, 1960, at Tallulah, La.
Height, 6.02. Weight, 227.
High School—Tallulah, La.
Attended Mississippi Valley State University.

Signed as free agent by New Orleans Saints, June 20, 1984.
On injured reserve with rotator cuff injury, August 27 through October 4, 1984; activated after clearing procedural waivers, October 5, 1984.
New Orleans NFL, 1984.
Games: 1984 (10).

LOUIS JULES HAYNES
Linebacker—Washington Redskins
Born January 17, 1960, at New Orleans, La.
Height, 6.00. Weight, 227.
High School—New Orleans, La., Oliver Perry Walker.
Attended Bishop College and North Texas State University.

Selected by Kansas City in 4th round (100th player selected) of 1982 NFL draft.
On inactive list, September 12 and September 19, 1982.
On injured reserve with knee injury, October 3 through remainder of 1983 season.
Released by Kansas City Chiefs, August 15, 1984; signed as free agent by Washington Redskins, May 16, 1985.
Kansas City NFL, 1982 and 1983.
Games: 1982 (6), 1983 (5). Total—11.
Pro statistics: Recovered one fumble, 1982 and 1983.

MARK HAYNES
Cornerback—New York Giants
Born November 6, 1958, at Kansas City, Kan.
Height, 5.11. Weight, 198.
High School—Kansas City, Kan., Harmon.
Attended University of Colorado.

Selected by New York Giants in 1st round (8th player selected) of 1980 NFL draft.

Left camp voluntarily and granted roster exemption, August 21 through August 27, 1984; returned and activated, August 28, 1984.

On injured reserve with knee injury, December 14 through remainder of 1984 season.

		—INTERCEPTIONS—			
Year Club	G.	No.	Yds.	Avg.	TD.
1980—N.Y. Giants NFL	15	1	6	6.0	0
1981—N.Y. Giants NFL	16	1	9	9.0	0
1982—N.Y. Giants NFL	9	1	0	0.0	0
1983—N.Y. Giants NFL	15	3	18	6.0	0
1984—N.Y. Giants NFL	15	7	90	12.9	0
Pro Totals—5 Years............	70	13	123	9.5	0

Additional pro statistics: Returned two kickoffs for 40 yards, 1980; recovered one fumble, 1981; recovered two fumbles for four yards, 1983; recovered two fumbles for 12 yards, 1984.

Played in Pro Bowl (NFL All-Star Game) following 1982 and 1983 seasons.

Named to Pro Bowl following 1984 season; replaced due to injury by Eric Wright.

MICHAEL JAMES HAYNES
(Mike)
Cornerback—Los Angeles Raiders

Born July 1, 1953, at Denison, Tex.
Height, 6.02. Weight, 190.
High School—Los Angeles, Calif., John Marshall.
Attending Arizona State University.
Brother of Reggie Haynes, tight end with Washington Redskins, 1978.

Named to THE SPORTING NEWS NFL All-Star Team, 1984.
Named to THE SPORTING NEWS AFC All-Star Team, 1976, 1978 and 1979.
Named by THE SPORTING NEWS as AFC Rookie of the Year, 1976.
Named as defensive back on THE SPORTING NEWS College All-America Team, 1975.
Selected by New England in 1st round (5th player selected) of 1976 NFL draft.
On did not report list, September 1 through September 22, 1980.
Granted roster exemption, September 23 through September 28, 1980; activated, September 29, 1980.
On injured reserve with collapsed lung, November 6 through December 10, 1981; activated, December 11, 1981.
Granted free agency, February 1, 1983; signed by Los Angeles Raiders, November 2, 1983 (Haynes had sued NFL when trade to Raiders was voided because it was after trading deadline).
Contract awarded to Raiders in settlement, November 10, 1983, with Patriots receiving 1st round pick in 1984 draft and 2nd round pick in 1985 draft and Raiders receiving 7th round pick in 1985 draft.
Granted roster exemption, November 10, 1983; activated, November 18, 1983.

		INTERCEPTIONS				PUNT RETURNS				—TOTAL—		
Year Club	G.	No.	Yds.	Avg.	TD.	No.	Yds.	Avg.	TD.	TD.	Pts.	F.
1976—New England NFL..............................	14	8	90	11.3	0	45	608	13.5	2	2	12	3
1977—New England NFL..............................	14	5	54	10.8	0	24	200	8.3	0	0	0	4
1978—New England NFL..............................	16	6	123	20.5	1	14	183	13.1	0	1	6	1
1979—New England NFL..............................	16	3	66	22.0	0	5	16	3.2	0	0	0	1
1980—New England NFL..............................	13	1	31	31.0	0	17	140	8.2	0	1	6	2
1981—New England NFL..............................	8	1	3	3.0	0	6	12	2.0	0	0	0	0
1982—New England NFL..............................	9	4	26	6.5	0	None				0	0	0
1983—Los Angeles Raiders NFL	5	1	0	0.0	0	None				0	0	0
1984—Los Angeles Raiders NFL	16	6	*220	36.7	1	None				1	6	0
Pro Totals—9 Years......................	111	35	613	17.5	2	111	1159	10.4	2	5	30	11

Additional pro statistics: Recovered three fumbles, 1976 and 1979; recovered two fumbles, 1977; ran 65 yards with blocked field goal for a touchdown and recovered three fumbles for six yards, 1980.

Played in AFC Championship Game following 1983 season.
Played in NFL Championship Game following 1983 season.
Played in Pro Bowl (NFL All-Star Game) following 1976 through 1980 and 1982 seasons.
Member of Pro Bowl following 1984 season; did not play.

ANDREW ROOSEVELT HEADEN
(Andy)
Linebacker—New York Giants

Born July 8, 1960, at Asheboro, N.C.
Height, 6.05. Weight, 230.
High School—Asheboro, N.C., Eastern Randolph.
Attended Clemson University.

Selected by Washington in 1983 USFL territorial draft.
Selected by New York Giants in 8th round (205th player selected) of 1983 NFL draft.
Signed by New York Giants, June 13, 1983.
On injured reserve with sprained foot, October 10 through November 16, 1984; activated, November 17, 1984.
New York Giants NFL, 1983 and 1984.
Games: 1983 (16), 1984 (11). Total—27.
Pro statistics: Intercepted one pass for four yards and recovered one fumble for 81 yards and a touchdown, 1984.

HERMAN WILLIE HEARD JR.
Running Back—Kansas City Chiefs

Born November 24, 1961, at Denver, Colo.
Height, 5.10. Weight, 184.
High School—Denver, Colo., South.
Attended Fort Lewis College and University of Southern Colorado.

Selected by Kansas City in 3rd round (61st player selected) of 1984 NFL draft.

Year Club		G.	Att.	RUSHING Yds.	Avg.	TD.	PASS RECEIVING P.C.	Yds.	Avg.	TD.	TOTAL TD.	Pts.	F.
1984—Kansas City NFL		16	165	684	4.1	4	25	223	8.9	0	4	24	5

Additional pro statistics: Recovered three fumbles, 1984.

JOHNNY LYNDELL HECTOR
Running Back—New York Jets
Born November 26, 1960, at Lafayette, La.
Height, 5.11. Weight, 197.
High School—New Iberia, La.
Attended Texas A&M University.
Selected by Chicago in 2nd round (19th player selected) of 1983 USFL draft.
Selected by New York Jets in 2nd round (51st player selected) of 1983 NFL draft.
Signed by New York Jets, June 9, 1983.

Year Club		G.	Att.	RUSHING Yds.	Avg.	TD.	PASS RECEIVING P.C.	Yds.	Avg.	TD.	TOTAL TD.	Pts.	F.
1983—New York Jets NFL		10	16	85	5.3	0	5	61	12.2	1	1	6	2
1984—New York Jets NFL		13	124	531	4.3	1	20	182	9.1	0	1	6	2
Pro Totals—2 Years		23	140	616	4.4	1	25	243	9.7	1	2	12	4

Year Club		G.	KICKOFF RETURNS No.	Yds.	Avg.	TD.
1983—New York Jets NFL		10	14	274	19.6	0
1984—New York Jets NFL		13		None		
Pro Totals—2 Years		23	14	274	19.6	0

VICTOR HEFLIN
Cornerback—St. Louis Cardinals
Born July 7, 1960, at Springfield, Mass.
Height, 6.00. Weight, 184.
High School—Dayton, O., Wayne.
Attended Delaware State College.
Brother of Vince Heflin, wide receiver with Miami Dolphins.
Selected by Denver in 6th round (143rd player selected) of 1983 NFL draft.
Released by Denver Broncos, August 23, 1983; signed as free agent by St. Louis Cardinals, October 27, 1983.
St. Louis NFL, 1983 and 1984.
Games: 1983 (8), 1984 (16). Total—24.
Pro statistics: Intercepted one pass for 19 yards, 1984.

VINCE HEFLIN
Wide Receiver—Miami Dolphins
Born July 7, 1959, at Dayton, Ohio.
Height, 6.00. Weight, 185.
High School—Dayton, Ohio, Wayne.
Attended Central State (O.) University.
Brother of Victor Heflin, cornerback with St. Louis Cardinals.
Signed as free agent by Miami Dolphins, July 1, 1982.
Released by Miami Dolphins, August 29, 1983; re-signed by Dolphins, September 6, 1983.

Year Club		G.	PUNT RETURNS No.	Yds.	Avg.	TD.	KICKOFF RET. No.	Yds.	Avg.	TD.	TOTAL TD.	Pts.	F.
1982—Miami NFL		6		None			2	49	24.5	0	0	0	0
1983—Miami NFL		14	1	19	19.0	0	1	27	27.0	0	0	0	0
1984—Miami NFL		16	6	76	12.7	0	9	130	14.4	0	0	0	1
Pro Totals—3 Years		36	7	95	13.6	0	12	206	17.2	0	0	0	1

Played in AFC Championship Game following 1982 and 1984 seasons.
Played in NFL Championship Game following 1982 and 1984 seasons.

MICHAEL WILLIAM HEGMAN
(Mike)
Linebacker—Dallas Cowboys
Born January 17, 1953, at Memphis, Tenn.
Height, 6.01. Weight, 225.
High School—Memphis, Tenn., Northside.
Attended Alabama A&M University and Tennessee State University.
Selected by Dallas in 7th round (173rd player selected) of 1975 NFL draft.
On injured reserve with broken arm, September 8 through October 14, 1981; activated, October 15, 1981.
Did not play in 1975.
Dallas NFL, 1976 through 1984.
Games: 1976 (14), 1977 (14), 1978 (16), 1979 (16), 1980 (16), 1981 (11), 1982 (9), 1983 (16), 1984 (16). Total—128.
Pro statistics: Recovered one fumble, 1976, 1977 and 1984; intercepted one pass for no yards, 1977; recovered two fumbles, 1978; intercepted two passes for two yards and recovered one fumble in end zone for a touchdown, 1980; recovered one fumble for nine yards and a touchdown, 1983; intercepted three passes for three yards, 1984.

Played in NFC Championship Game following 1977, 1978, 1981 and 1982 seasons.
Member of Dallas Cowboys for NFC Championship Game following 1980 season; did not play.
Played in NFL Championship Game following 1977 and 1978 seasons.

RONALD RAMON HELLER
(Ron)
Offensive Tackle—Tampa Bay Buccaneers
Born August 25, 1962, at East Meadow, N.Y.
Height, 6.06. Weight, 270.
High School—Farming Dale, N.Y.
Received bachelor of science degree in administration of justice
from Penn State University in 1984.

Selected by Philadelphia in 1984 USFL territorial draft.
Selected by Tampa Bay in 4th round (112th player selected) of 1984 NFL draft.
Signed by Tampa Bay Buccaneers, June 6, 1984.
Tampa Bay NFL, 1984.
Games: 1984 (14).

REUBEN STANLEY HENDERSON
Cornerback—San Diego Chargers
Born October 3, 1958, at Santa Monica, Calif.
Height, 6.00. Weight, 196.
High School—Fontana, Calif.
Attended Oklahoma State University and San Diego State University.

Selected by Chicago in 6th round (150th player selected) of 1981 NFL draft.
Traded by Chicago Bears to San Diego Chargers for 4th and 8th round picks in 1983 draft, April 20, 1983.
On injured reserve with groin injury, November 2 through December 2, 1984; activated, December 3, 1984.

| | | —INTERCEPTIONS— | | | |
Year Club	G.	No.	Yds.	Avg.	TD.
1981—Chicago NFL	16	4	84	21.0	0
1982—Chicago NFL	5		None		
1983—San Diego NFL	14		None		
1984—San Diego NFL	12		None		
Pro Totals—4 Years	47	4	84	21.0	0

Additional pro statistics: Recovered one fumble, 1981; returned one punt for no yards and fumbled once, 1984.

WYATT M. HENDERSON
Wide Receiver—Indianapolis Colts
Born November 10, 1956, at Bakersfield, Calif.
Height, 5.10. Weight, 180.
High School—Los Angeles, Calif., Fairfax.
Attended Los Angeles Valley Junior College and received
bachelor of arts degree from Fresno State University.

Signed as free agent by Los Angeles Rams, May 5, 1980.
Released by Los Angeles Rams, August 18, 1980; signed as free agent by San Diego Chargers, February 12, 1981.
On injured reserve with ankle injury, December 31 through remainder of 1981 season playoffs.
Released by San Diego Chargers, August 26, 1982; signed by Oakland Invaders, November 9, 1982.
Selected by Jacksonville Bulls in 9th round (53rd player selected) of USFL expansion draft, September 6, 1983.
Released by Jacksonville Bulls, February 18, 1985; signed as free agent by Indianapolis Colts, May 11, 1985.

| | | —RUSHING— | | | | PASS RECEIVING | | | | —TOTAL— | | |
Year Club	G.	Att.	Yds.	Avg.	TD.	P.C.	Yds.	Avg.	TD.	TD.	Pts.	F.
1981—San Diego NFL	15		None				None			0	0	0
1983—Oakland USFL	18	5	59	11.8	0	54	801	14.8	9	9	54	1
1984—Jacksonville USFL	17		None			14	213	15.2	1	1	6	0
NFL Totals—1 Year	15		None				None			0	0	0
USFL Totals—2 Years	35	5	59	11.8	0	68	1014	14.9	10	10	60	1
Pro Totals—3 Years	50	5	59	11.8	0	68	1014	14.9	10	10	60	1

Additional pro statistics: Recovered one fumble, 1983.

BERNARD HENRY
Wide Receiver—Indianapolis Colts
Born April 9, 1960, at Los Angeles, Calif.
Height, 6.01. Weight, 179.
High School—Los Angeles, Calif., John C. Fremont.
Attended Arizona State University.

Signed as free agent by Baltimore Colts, May 5, 1982.
Released by Baltimore Colts, August 29, 1983; re-signed by Colts, August 30, 1983.
Franchise transferred to Indianapolis, March 31, 1984.

| | | —PASS RECEIVING— | | | |
Year Club	G.	P.C.	Yds.	Avg.	TD.
1982—Baltimore NFL	6	7	110	15.7	0
1983—Baltimore NFL	15	30	416	13.9	4
1984—Indianapolis NFL	14	11	139	12.6	2
Pro Totals—3 Years	35	48	665	13.9	6

LUTHER HENSON
Nose Tackle—New England Patriots
Born March 25, 1959, at Sandusky, O.
Height, 6.00. Weight, 275.
High School—Sandusky, O.
Attended Ohio State University.

Signed as free agent by Cincinnati Bengals, May 3, 1981.
Released by Cincinnati Bengals, August 31, 1981; signed as free agent by New England Patriots, March 10, 1982.
On inactive list, September 19, 1982.
On injured reserve with knee injury, September 28 through remainder of 1983 season.
Released by New England Patriots, August 27, 1984; re-signed by Patriots, October 17, 1984.
New England NFL, 1982 through 1984.
Games: 1982 (8), 1983 (4), 1984 (9). Total—21.

MATTHEW BERNARD HERKENHOFF
(Matt)
Offensive Tackle—Kansas City Chiefs
Born April 12, 1951, at Melrose, Minn.
Height, 6.04. Weight, 272.
High School—Melrose, Minn.
Attended University of Minnesota.

Selected by Kansas City in 4th round (94th player selected) of 1974 NFL draft.
Selected by New York in 9th round of 1974 WFL draft.
Contract breached by Charlotte Hornets (WFL) and signed by Kansas City Chiefs, June, 1975.
Missed entire 1975 season due to leg injuries.
On injured reserve with knee injury, October 2 through remainder of 1979 season.
On injured reserve with knee injury, December 9 through remainder of 1980 season.
New York-Charlotte WFL, 1974; Kansas City NFL, 1976 through 1984.
Games: 1974 (?), 1976 (14), 1977 (14), 1978 (16), 1979 (5), 1980 (14), 1981 (16), 1982 (9), 1983 (12), 1984 (15). Total NFL—115.
Pro statistics: Recovered one fumble, 1976 and 1981.

DOUG HERMANN
Defensive End—Washington Redskins
Born January 1, 1961, at Custer, S.D.
Height, 6.04. Weight, 275.
High School—Custer, S.D.
Attended University of Nebraska.

Selected by Memphis in 11th round (210th player selected) of 1984 USFL draft.
Signed as free agent by Washington Redskins, May 10, 1984.
On injured reserve with back injury, August 13 through entire 1984 season.

MATT HERNANDEZ
Offensive Tackle—Minnesota Vikings
Born October 16, 1961, at Detroit, Mich.
Height, 6.06. Weight, 260.
High School—East Detroit, Mich.
Attended Purdue University.

Selected by Chicago in 15th round (174th player selected) of 1983 USFL draft.
Selected by Seattle in 8th round (210th player selected) of 1983 NFL draft.
Signed by Seattle Seahawks, May 6, 1983.
Released by Seattle Seahawks, August 27, 1984; signed as free agent by Minnesota Vikings, September 12, 1984.
Seattle NFL, 1983; Minnesota NFL, 1984.
Games: 1983 (8), 1984 (13). Total—21.
Played in AFC Championship Game following 1983 season.

MARK DONALD HERRMANN
Quarterback—San Diego Chargers
Born January 8, 1959, at Cincinnati, O.
Height, 6.04. Weight, 206.
High School—Carmel, Ind.
Received bachelor of science degree in business
management from Purdue University in 1981.

Selected by Denver in 4th round (98th player selected) of 1981 NFL draft.
On inactive list, September 19, 1982.
Traded with rights to offensive tackle Chris Hinton and 1st round pick in 1984 draft by Denver Broncos to Baltimore Colts for rights to quarterback John Elway, May 2, 1983.
On injured reserve with broken collarbone, August 30 through October 27, 1983; activated, October 28, 1983.
Franchise transferred to Indianapolis, March 31, 1984.
On injured reserve with broken thumb, August 28 through October 19, 1984; activated, October 20, 1984.
Granted free agency, February 1, 1985; re-signed by Colts and traded to San Diego Chargers for draft choice, March 27, 1985.
Active for 16 games with Denver Broncos in 1981; did not play.

Year Club	G.	Att.	Cmp.	Pct.	Gain	T.P.	P.I.	Avg.	Att.	Yds.	Avg.	TD.	TD.	Pts.	F.
				PASSING						RUSHING				TOTAL	
1982—Denver NFL	2	60	32	53.3	421	1	4	7.02	3	7	2.3	1	1	6	1
1983—Baltimore NFL	2	36	18	50.0	256	0	3	7.11	1	0	0.0	0	0	0	2
1984—Indianapolis NFL	3	56	29	51.8	352	1	6	6.29		None			0	0	0
Pro Totals—4 Years	7	152	79	52.0	1029	2	13	6.77	4	7	1.8	1	1	6	3

Quarterback Rating Points: 1982 (53.5), 1983 (38.7), 1984 (37.8). Total—42.1.
Additional pro statistics: Recovered one fumble, 1983.

RONALD HESTER
(Ron)
Linebacker—Miami Dolphins
Born May 26, 1959, at Atlanta, Ga.
Height, 6.02. Weight, 222.
High School—Umatilla, Fla.
Received bachelor of science degree in physical education from
Florida State University in 1982.

Selected by Miami in 6th round (164th player selected) of 1982 NFL draft.
On injured reserve with knee injury, August 30 through entire 1983 season.
On physically unable to perform/active with knee injury, July 19 through August 20, 1984.
On physically unable to perform/reserve with knee injury, August 21 through entire 1984 season.
Miami NFL, 1982.
Games: 1982 (9).
Pro statistics: Recovered one fumble, 1982.
Played in AFC Championship Game following 1982 season.
Played in NFL Championship Game following 1982 season.

ROBERT TODD HEWKO
(Bob)
Quarterback—Dallas Cowboys
Born June 8, 1960, at Abington, Pa.
Height, 6.03. Weight, 195.
High School—William Grove, Pa., Upper Moreland.
Received bachelor of science degree in public relations from University of Florida in 1983.

Signed as free agent by Tampa Bay Buccaneers, April 28, 1983.
On injured reserve with knee injury, October 7 through remainder of 1983 season.
Released by Tampa Bay Buccaneers, July 5, 1984.
USFL rights traded by Houston Gamblers to Washington Federals for draft choice, July 5, 1984.
Signed as free agent by Dallas Cowboys, January 10, 1985.
Tampa Bay NFL, 1983.
Games: 1983 (2).

DWIGHT HICKS
Safety—San Francisco 49ers
Born April 5, 1956, at Mount Holly, N. J.
Height, 6.01. Weight, 192.
High School—Pennsauken, N. J.
Attended University of Michigan.
Brother of Ivan Hicks, defensive back at University of Michigan; and Jason Hicks,
quarterback/defensive back at University of Miami (Fla.).

Selected by Detroit in 6th round (150th player selected) of 1978 NFL draft.
Released by Detroit Lions, August 15, 1978; signed as free agent by Toronto Argonauts, September 16, 1978.
Released by Toronto Argonauts, October 14, 1978; signed as free agent by Philadelphia Eagles, December 28, 1978.
Released by Philadelphia Eagles, August 28, 1979; signed as free agent by San Francisco 49ers, October 24, 1979.

Year Club	G.	No.	Yds.	Avg.	TD.	No.	Yds.	Avg.	TD.	TD.	Pts.	F.
		INTERCEPTIONS				PUNT RETURNS				TOTAL		
1978—Toronto CFL	3	2	0	0.0	0	6	60	10.0	0	0	0	0
1979—San Francisco NFL	8	5	57	11.4	0	13	120	9.2	0	0	0	0
1980—San Francisco NFL	16	4	73	18.3	0	12	58	4.8	0	0	0	0
1981—San Francisco NFL	16	9	*239	26.6	1	19	171	9.0	0	2	12	1
1982—San Francisco NFL	9	3	5	1.7	0	10	54	5.4	0	0	0	0
1983—San Francisco NFL	15	2	102	51.0	*2		None			2	12	0
1984—San Francisco NFL	16	3	42	14.0	0		None			0	0	1
CFL Totals—1 Year	3	2	0	0.0	0	6	60	10.0	0	0	0	0
NFL Totals—6 Years	80	26	518	19.9	3	54	403	7.5	0	4	24	2
Pro Totals—7 Years	83	28	518	18.5	3	60	463	7.7	0	4	24	2

Additional pro statistics: Returned two kickoffs for 36 yards and recovered one fumble for two yards, 1979; recovered two fumbles, 1980; returned one kickoff for 22 yards, recovered four fumbles for 80 yards and a touchdown and fumbled once, 1981; recovered two fumbles for five yards, 1983; recovered three fumbles for six yards, 1984.
Played in NFC Championship Game following 1981, 1983 and 1984 seasons.
Played in NFL Championship Game following 1981 and 1984 seasons.
Played in Pro Bowl (NFL All-Star Game) following 1981 through 1984 seasons.

MARK HICKS
Linebacker—Seattle Seahawks

Born November 7, 1960, at Los Angeles, Calif.
Height, 6.02. Weight, 225.
High School—Los Angeles, Calif., Washington.
Attended Arizona State University.

Selected by Arizona in 1983 USFL territorial draft.
Signed as free agent by Seattle Seahawks, April 28, 1983.
On injured reserve with neck and shoulder injuries, August 29 through October 5, 1983; activated after clearing procedural waivers, October 7, 1983.
On non-football injury/active with knee injury, July 14 through August 13, 1984.
On non-football injury/reserve with knee injury, August 14 through entire 1984 season.
Seattle NFL, 1983.
Games: 1983 (10).
Played AFC Championship Game following 1983 season.

MARK BRYAN HICKS
(Known by middle name.)
Safety—Cincinnati Bengals

Born January 24, 1957, at Lake Charles, La.
Height, 6.00. Weight, 192.
High School—Lake Charles, La., St. Louis.
Received bachelor of science degree in biology from McNeese State University in 1979.

Selected by Cincinnati in 5th round (113th player selected) of 1980 NFL draft.
On injured reserve with shoulder injury, August 31 through entire 1983 season.
On injured reserve with fractured arm, August 27 through entire 1984 season.

Year Club	G.	No.	Yds.	Avg.	TD.
1980—Cincinnati NFL	16	1	8	8.0	0
1981—Cincinnati NFL	16		None		
1982—Cincinnati NFL	7		None		
Pro Totals—3 Years	39	1	8	8.0	0

Additional pro statistics: Recovered one fumble and returned five kickoffs for 87 yards, 1980; returned one punt for four yards and recovered two fumbles for three yards, 1981.
Played in AFC Championship Game following 1981 season.
Played in NFL Championship Game following 1981 season.

JAY WALTER HILGENBERG
Center—Chicago Bears

Born March 21, 1959, at Iowa City, Ia.
Height, 6.03. Weight, 255.
High School—Iowa City, Ia., City.
Attended University of Iowa.
Brother of Joel Hilgenberg, center-guard with New Orleans Saints; and nephew of Wally Hilgenberg,
linebacker with Detroit Lions and Minnesota Vikings, 1964 through 1979.

Signed as free agent by Chicago Bears, May 8, 1981.
Chicago NFL, 1981 through 1984.
Games: 1981 (16), 1982 (9), 1983 (16), 1984 (16). Total—57.
Pro statistics: Recovered one fumble for five yards, 1982; recovered one fumble, 1983.
Played in NFC Championship Game following 1984 season.

JOEL HILGENBERG
Center-Guard—New Orleans Saints

Born July 10, 1962, at Iowa City, Ia.
Height, 6.03. Weight, 253.
High School—Iowa City, Ia., City.
Attended University of Iowa.
Brother of Jay Hilgenberg, center with Chicago Bears; and nephew of Wally Hilgenberg,
linebacker with Detroit Lions and Minnesota Vikings, 1964 through 1979.

Selected by Washington in 6th round (109th player selected) of 1984 USFL draft.
USFL rights traded with 1st round pick in 1985 draft by Washington Federals to Birmingham Stallions for quarterback Reggie Collier, January 12, 1984.
Selected by New Orleans in 4th round (97th player selected) of 1984 NFL draft.
Signed by New Orleans Saints, July 24, 1984.
On injured reserve with dislocated elbow, October 30 through December 6, 1984; activated, December 7, 1984.
New Orleans NFL, 1984.
Games: 1984 (10).

—DID YOU KNOW—

That although punter-placekicker Steve Cox has only been successful on two of his six field goal attempts in his four-year NFL career, those two successes rank among the six longest field goals in NFL history? In 1983 Cox connected from 58 yards away in his only attempt while his only successful field goal in 1984 was from 60 yards.

ANDREW HILL
(Drew)
Wide Receiver—Los Angeles Rams
Born October 5, 1956, at Newman, Ga.
Height, 5.09. Weight, 170.
High School—Newman, Ga.
Received bachelor of arts degree in industrial management from Georgia Tech in 1981.

Established NFL record for most kickoff returns, season (60), 1981.
Selected by Los Angeles in 12th round (328th player selected) of 1979 NFL draft.
On injured reserve with back injury, August 24 through entire 1983 season.

Year Club	G.	PASS RECEIVING				—KICKOFF RET.—				—TOTAL—		
		P.C.	Yds.	Avg.	TD.	No.	Yds.	Avg.	TD.	TD.	Pts.	F.
1979—Los Angeles Rams NFL	16	4	94	23.5	1	40	803	20.1	0	1	6	2
1980—Los Angeles Rams NFL	16	19	416	21.9	2	43	880	20.5	*1	3	18	2
1981—Los Angeles Rams NFL	16	16	355	22.2	3	*60	1170	19.5	0	3	18	1
1982—Los Angeles Rams NFL	9	7	92	13.1	0	2	42	21.0	0	0	0	0
1984—Los Angeles Rams NFL	16	14	390	27.9	4	26	543	20.9	0	4	24	0
Pro Totals—5 Years	73	60	1347	22.5	10	171	3438	20.1	1	11	66	5

Additional pro statistics: Returned one punt for no yards, 1979; recovered one fumble and rushed once for four yards, 1980; rushed once for 14 yards, returned two punts for 22 yards and recovered one fumble, 1981.
Played in NFC Championship Game following 1979 season.
Played in NFL Championship Game following 1979 season.

DAVID HILL
Tight End—Los Angeles Rams
Born January 1, 1954, at San Antonio, Tex.
Height, 6.02. Weight, 240.
High School—San Antonio, Tex., Highlands.
Attended Texas A&I University.
Brother of Jim Hill, defensive back with San Diego Chargers, Green Bay Packers and Cleveland Browns, 1969 through 1975; cousin of Gary Green, cornerback back with Los Angeles Rams.

Selected by Detroit in 2nd round (46th player selected) of 1976 NFL draft.
Traded by Detroit Lions to Los Angeles Rams for cornerback Rod Perry and 3rd round pick in 1984 draft, August 19, 1983.

Year Club	G.	RUSHING				PASS RECEIVING				—TOTAL—		
		Att.	Yds.	Avg.	TD.	P.C.	Yds.	Avg.	TD.	TD.	Pts.	F.
1976—Detroit NFL	14		None			19	249	13.1	5	5	30	2
1977—Detroit NFL	14	4	10	2.5	0	32	465	14.5	2	2	12	1
1978—Detroit NFL	16	3	12	4.0	0	53	633	11.9	4	4	24	1
1979—Detroit NFL	16	1	15	15.0	0	47	569	12.1	3	3	18	1
1980—Detroit NFL	16		None			39	424	10.9	1	1	6	1
1981—Detroit NFL	15		None			33	462	14.0	4	4	24	1
1982—Detroit NFL	9		None			22	252	11.5	4	4	24	0
1983—Los Angeles Rams NFL	16		None			28	280	10.0	2	2	12	1
1984—Los Angeles Rams NFL	16		None			31	300	9.7	1	1	6	2
Pro Totals—9 Years	132	8	37	4.6	0	304	3634	12.0	26	26	156	10

Additional pro statistics: Attempted one pass which was intercepted, 1976; recovered one fumble, 1976 through 1979, 1983 and 1984; attempted one pass with no completions, 1977.
Played in Pro Bowl (NFL All-Star Game) following 1979 season.

EDDIE WAYNE HILL
Running Back—Miami Dolphins
Born May 13, 1957, at Nashville, Tenn.
Height, 6.02. Weight, 206.
High School—Nashville, Tenn., Hillsboro.
Attended Memphis State University.

Selected by Los Angeles in 2nd round (54th player selected) of 1979 NFL draft.
On injured reserve with shoulder separation, October 22 through remainder of 1980 season.
Traded by Los Angeles Rams to Miami Dolphins for 4th round pick in 1983 draft, July 22, 1981.
On injured reserve with ankle injury, September 13 through October 23, 1981; activated, October 24, 1981.

Year Club	G.	RUSHING				PASS RECEIVING				—TOTAL—		
		Att.	Yds.	Avg.	TD.	P.C.	Yds.	Avg.	TD.	TD.	Pts.	F.
1979—Los Angeles NFL	16	29	114	3.9	1	4	36	9.0	0	2	12	4
1980—Los Angeles NFL	7	39	120	3.1	0	4	29	7.3	0	0	0	2
1981—Miami NFL	11	37	146	3.9	1	12	73	6.1	1	2	12	2
1982—Miami NFL	9	13	51	3.9	0	6	33	5.5	0	0	0	2
1983—Miami NFL	16	2	12	6.0	0		None			0	0	0
1984—Miami NFL	16		None				None			0	0	0
Pro Totals—6 Years	75	120	443	3.7	2	26	171	6.6	2	4	24	10

Year Club	G.	KICKOFF RETURNS				Year Club	G.	KICKOFF RETURNS			
		No.	Yds.	Avg.TD.				No.	Yds.	Avg.TD.	
1979—Los Angeles NFL	16	15	305	20.3	0	1983—Miami NFL	16		None		
1980—Los Angeles NFL	7		None			1984—Miami NFL	16	1	14	14.0	0
1981—Miami NFL	11	1	11	11.0	0	Pro Totals—6 Years	75	17	330	19.4	0
1982—Miami NFL	9		None								

Additional pro statistics: Recovered four fumbles, 1979; attemped one pass with one completion for 14 yards, 1981; attempted one pass with no completions, 1982; recovered one fumble, 1983.
Played in NFC Championship Game following 1979 season.
Played in AFC Championship Game following 1982 and 1984 seasons.
Played in NFL Championship Game following 1979, 1982 and 1984 seasons.

GREG HILL
Cornerback—Kansas City Chiefs
Born February 12, 1961, at Orange, Tex.
Height, 6.01. Weight, 189.
High School—West Orange, Tex., Stark.
Attended Oklahoma State University.

Selected by Philadelphia in 3rd round (32nd player selected) of 1983 USFL draft.
Selected by Houston in 4th round (86th player selected) of 1983 NFL draft.
Signed by Houston Oilers, June 25, 1983.
Released by Houston Oilers, August 27, 1984; awarded on waivers to Kansas City Chiefs, August 28, 1984.

		—INTERCEPTIONS—			
Year Club	G.	No.	Yds.	Avg.TD.	
1983—Houston NFL	14		None		
1984—Kansas City NFL	15	2	—1	—0.5	0
Pro Totals—2 Years	29	2	—1	0.5	0

Additional pro statistics: Fumbled once, 1984.

JOHN STARK HILL
Center
Born April 16, 1950, at East Orange, N. J.
Height, 6.02. Weight, 264.
High School—Somerset, N. J., Franklin.
Received bachelor of science degree in industrial engineering
from Lehigh University in 1972.

Selected by New York Giants in 6th round (132nd player selected) of 1972 NFL draft.
Claimed on waivers from New York Giants by New Orleans Saints, September 19, 1975.
Released by New Orleans Saints, April 3, 1985.
New York Giants NFL, 1972 through 1974; New Orleans NFL, 1975 through 1984.
Games: 1972 (14), 1973 (12), 1974 (12), 1975 (14), 1976 (14), 1977 (14), 1978 (16), 1979 (16), 1980 (15), 1981 (13), 1982 (9), 1983 (16), 1984 (11). Total—176.
Pro statistics: Fumbled once and recovered one fumble for minus 13 yards, 1973; recovered one fumble for one yard, 1975; recovered one fumble, 1977 and 1980.

KENNY HILL
Safety—New York Giants
Born July 25, 1958, at Oak Grove, La.
Height, 6.00. Weight, 195.
High School—Oak Grove, La.
Received bachelor of science degree in molecular physics from Yale University in 1980.

Selected by Oakland in 8th round (194th player selected) of 1980 NFL draft.
On injured reserve with hip pointer, August 26 through entire 1980 season.
On injured reserve with pulled hamstring, August 31 through October 18, 1981; activated after clearing procedural waivers, October 20, 1981.
Franchise transferred to Los Angeles, May 7, 1982.
Traded by Los Angeles Raiders to New York Giants for 7th round pick in 1985 draft, August 27, 1984.
Oakland NFL, 1981; Los Angeles Raiders NFL, 1982 and 1983; New York Giants NFL, 1984.
Games: 1981 (9), 1982 (9), 1983 (16), 1984 (12). Total—46.
Pro statistics: Returned one kickoff for 21 yards, 1981; returned two kickoffs for 20 yards and fumbled once, 1982; returned one kickoff for 27 yards, 1984.
Played in AFC Championship Game following 1983 season.
Played in NFL Championship Game following 1983 season.

KENT ANGELO HILL
Guard—Los Angeles Rams
Born March 7, 1957, at Americus, Ga.
Height, 6.05. Weight, 260.
High School—Americus, Ga.
Received bachelor of science degree in industrial management from Georgia Tech in 1979.

Named to THE SPORTING NEWS NFL All-Star Team, 1983.
Selected by Los Angeles in 1st round (26th player selected) of 1979 NFL draft.
Los Angeles Rams NFL, 1979 through 1984.
Games: 1979 (16), 1980 (16), 1981 (16), 1982 (9), 1983 (16), 1984 (16). Total—89.
Pro statistics: Recovered two fumbles, 1982.
Played in NFC Championship Game following 1979 season.
Played in NFL Championship Game following 1979 season.
Played in Pro Bowl (NFL All-Star Game) following 1980 and 1982 through 1984 seasons.

LEROY ANTHONY HILL JR.
(Tony)
Wide Receiver—Dallas Cowboys

Born June 23, 1956, at San Diego, Calif.
Height, 6.02. Weight, 198.
High School—Long Beach, Calif., Long Beach Polytechnic.
Received bachelor of science degree in political science from Stanford University in 1977.

Selected by Dallas in 3rd round (62nd player selected) of 1977 NFL draft.
On injured reserve with shoulder separation, September 6 through October 12, 1984; activated, October 13, 1984.

Year Club	G.	PASS RECEIVING				PUNT RETURNS				—KICKOFF RET.—				—TOTAL—		
		P.C.	Yds.	Avg.	TD.	No.	Yds.	Avg.	TD.	No.	Yds.	Avg.	TD.	TD.	Pts.	F.
1977—Dallas NFL	14	2	21	10.5	0	10	124	12.4	0	3	64	21.3	0	0	0	0
1978—Dallas NFL	16	46	823	17.9	6	11	101	9.2	0	None				6	36	1
1979—Dallas NFL	16	60	1062	17.7	10	6	43	7.2	0	1	32	32.0	0	10	60	1
1980—Dallas NFL	16	60	1055	17.6	8	None				None				8	48	0
1981—Dallas NFL	16	46	953	20.7	4	None				None				4	24	1
1982—Dallas NFL	9	35	526	15.0	1	None				None				1	6	0
1983—Dallas NFL	12	49	801	16.3	7	None				None				7	42	1
1984—Dallas NFL	11	58	864	14.9	5	None				None				5	30	0
Pro Totals—8 Years	110	356	6105	17.1	41	27	268	9.9	0	4	96	24.0	0	41	246	4

Additional pro statistics: Rushed three times for 17 yards and attempted one pass with no completions, 1978; rushed twice for 18 yards, 1979; rushed four times for 27 yards, 1980; rushed once for minus three yards, 1981; rushed once for 22 yards, 1982; rushed once for two yards, 1983; rushed once for seven yards, 1984.
Played in NFC Championship Game following 1977, 1978 and 1980 through 1982 seasons.
Played in NFL Championship Game following 1977 and 1978 seasons.
Played in Pro Bowl (NFL All-Star Game) following 1978 and 1979 seasons.

RODRICK HILL
(Rod)
Cornerback—Buffalo Bills

Born March 14, 1959, at Detroit, Mich.
Height, 6.00. Weight, 193.
High School—Detroit, Mich., M.L. King.
Attended Kentucky State University.

Selected by Dallas in 1st round (25th player selected) of 1982 NFL draft.
Traded with 5th round pick in 1985 draft by Dallas Cowboys to Buffalo Bills for 5th round pick in 1985 draft and conditional 1986 draft choice, August 23, 1984.
On injured reserve with fractured ankle, September 12 through remainder of 1984 season.

Year Club	G.	INTERCEPTIONS				-PUNT RETURNS-				—KICKOFF RET.—				—TOTAL—		
		No.	Yds.	Avg.	TD.	No.	Yds.	Avg.	TD.	No.	Yds.	Avg.	TD.	TD.	Pts.	F.
1982—Dallas NFL	9	None				4	39	9.8	0	None				0	0	1
1983—Dallas NFL	14	2	12	6.0	0	30	232	7.7	0	14	243	17.4	0	0	0	2
1984—Buffalo NFL	2	None				None				None				0	0	0
Pro Totals—3 Years	25	2	12	6.0	0	34	271	8.0	0	14	243	17.4	0	0	0	3

Additional pro statistics: Recovered three fumbles, 1982; recovered two fumbles, 1983.
Played in NFC Championship Game following 1982 season.

TROY J. HILL
Defensive Back—Cleveland Browns

Born February 18, 1962, at South River, N.J.
Height, 5.11. Weight, 180.
High School—South River, N.J.
Attended University of Pittsburgh.
Brother-in-law of Drew Pearson, wide receiver with
Dallas Cowboys, 1973 through 1983.

Selected by Pittsburgh in 1984 USFL territorial draft.
Signed by Pittsburgh Maulers, May 4, 1984.
Granted roster exemption, May 4, 1984; activated, May 9, 1984.
Franchise disbanded, October 25, 1984.
Selected by Baltimore Stars in USFL dispersal draft, December 6, 1984.
Released by Baltimore Stars, January 28, 1985; signed as free agent by Cleveland Browns, May 6, 1985.

		KICKOFF RETURNS		
Year Club	G.	No.	Yds.	Avg.TD.
1984—Pittsburgh USFL	7	7	141	20.1 0

Additional pro statistics: Credited with one sack for 11 yards, recovered one fumble and fumbled once, 1984.

JOSEPH LIONEL HINES
(Joe)
Linebacker—Tampa Bay Buccaneers

Born February 14, 1960, at Newark, N.J.
Height, 6.00. Weight, 225.
High School—Newark, N.J., Weequahic.
Attended Pasadena City College and Texas Christian University.

Selected by Denver in 17th round (201st player selected) of 1983 USFL draft.
Signed as free agent by Washington Redskins, June 1, 1983.
Released by Washington Redskins, July 26, 1983.
USFL rights traded with rights to defensive tackle Ruben Vaughan by Denver Gold to Washington Federals for rights to defensive back Steve Trimble, October 6, 1983.
Signed by Washington Federals, November 3, 1983.
Franchise transferred to Orlando, October 12, 1984.
Released by Orlando Renegades, January 23, 1985; signed as free agent by Tampa Bay Buccaneers, April 18, 1985.
Washington USFL, 1984.
Games: 1984 (18).
Pro statistics: Credited with eight sacks for 76 yards, intercepted two passes for three yards, returned one kickoff for nine yards and recovered four fumbles, 1984.

BRYAN E. HINKLE
Linebacker—Pittsburgh Steelers
Born June 4, 1959, at Long Beach, Calif.
Height, 6.01. Weight, 220.
High School—Silverdale, Wash., Central Kitsap.
Attended University of Oregon.

Selected by Pittsburgh in 6th round (156th player selected) of 1981 NFL draft.
On injured reserve with ankle injury and concussion, August 31 through entire 1981 season.
On injured reserve with torn quadricep, January 7 through remainder of 1982 season playoffs.

			—INTERCEPTIONS—			
Year	Club	G.	No.	Yds.	Avg.	TD.
1982—Pittsburgh NFL		9	None			
1983—Pittsburgh NFL		16	1	14	14.0	1
1984—Pittsburgh NFL		15	3	77	25.7	0
Pro Totals—3 Years		40	4	91	22.8	1

Additional pro statistics: Recovered two fumbles for four yards, 1983; recovered two fumbles for 21 yards and a touchdown, 1984.
Played in AFC Championship Game following 1984 season.

CHRISTOPHER JERROD HINTON
(Chris)
Guard-Offensive Tackle—Indianapolis Colts
Born July 31, 1961, at Chicago, Ill.
Height, 6.04. Weight, 280.
High School—Chicago, Ill., Wendell Phillips.
Attended Northwestern University.

Named as offensive tackle on THE SPORTING NEWS All-America Team, 1982.
Selected by Chicago in 1983 USFL territorial draft.
Selected by Denver in 1st round (4th player selected) of 1983 NFL draft.
Rights traded with quarterback Mark Herrmann, and 1st round pick in 1984 draft by Denver Broncos to Baltimore Colts for rights to quarterback John Elway, May 2, 1983.
Signed by Baltimore Colts, May 12, 1983.
Franchise transferred to Indianapolis, March 31, 1984.
On injured reserve with fractured fibula, October 8 through remainder of 1984 season.
Baltimore NFL, 1983; Indianapolis NFL, 1984.
Games: 1983 (16), 1984 (6). Total—22.
Pro statistics: Recovered one fumble, 1983.
Played in Pro Bowl (NFL All-Star Game) following 1983 season.

ERIC ELLSWORTH HIPPLE
Quarterback—Detroit Lions
Born September 16, 1957, at Lubbock, Tex.
Height, 6.02. Weight, 196.
High School—Downey, Calif., Warren.
Received bachelor of science degree in business administration from
Utah State University in 1980.

Selected by Detroit in 4th round (85th player selected) of 1980 NFL draft.
On injured reserve with knee injury, October 18 through December 13, 1984; activated, December 14, 1984.

			—————PASSING—————						—RUSHING—				—TOTAL—		
Year	Club	G.	Att.	Cmp.	Pct.	Gain	T.P.	P.I.	Avg.	Att.	Yds.	Avg.	TD.	TD.	Pts.	F.
1980—Detroit NFL		15	None							None				0	0	0
1981—Detroit NFL		16	279	140	50.2	2358	14	15	8.45	41	168	4.1	7	7	42	*14
1982—Detroit NFL		9	86	36	41.9	411	2	4	4.78	10	57	5.7	0	0	0	1
1983—Detroit NFL		16	387	204	52.7	2577	12	18	6.66	41	171	4.2	3	3	18	12
1984—Detroit NFL		8	38	16	42.1	246	1	1	6.47	2	3	1.5	0	0	0	0
Pro Totals—5 Years		64	790	396	50.1	5592	29	38	7.08	94	399	4.2	10	10	60	27

Quarterback Rating Points: 1981 (73.3), 1982 (66.9), 1983 (64.7), 1984 (62.0). Total—65.7.
Additional pro statistics: Recovered four fumbles and fumbled 14 times for minus 10 yards; recovered six fumbles, 1983.

TERRELL LEE HOAGE
(Terry)
Safety—New Orleans Saints
Born April 11, 1962, at Ames, Iowa.
Height, 6.03. Weight, 199.
High School—Huntsville, Tex.
Attended University of Georgia.

Named as defensive back on THE SPORTING NEWS College All-America Team, 1983.
Selected by Jacksonville in 1984 USFL territorial draft.
Selected by New Orleans in 3rd round (68th player selected) of 1984 NFL draft.
Signed by New Orleans Saints, July 25, 1984.
New Orleans NFL, 1984.
Games: 1984 (14).
Pro statistics: Recovered one fumble, 1984.

FLOYD HODGE
Wide Receiver—Atlanta Falcons
Born July 18, 1959, at Compton, Calif.
Height, 6.00. Weight, 195.
High School—Los Angeles, Calif., Centennial.
Attended Los Angeles Valley College and University of Utah.

Signed as free agent by Atlanta Falcons, May 5, 1981.
On injured reserve with knee injury, August 18 through entire 1981 season.

		—PASS RECEIVING—			
Year Club	G.	P.C.	Yds.	Avg.	TD.
1982—Atlanta NFL	9	14	160	11.4	0
1983—Atlanta NFL	12	25	280	11.2	4
1984—Atlanta NFL	12	24	234	9.8	0
Pro Totals—3 Years	33	63	674	10.7	4

Additional pro statistics: Rushed twice for 11 yards and returned one kickoff for 23 yards, 1982; attempted two passes with one completion for 28 yards and one interception, 1983; rushed twice for 17 yards and fumbled once, 1984.

GARY E. HOFFMAN
Offensive Tackle—Green Bay Packers
Born September 28, 1961, at Sacramento, Calif.
Height, 6.07. Weight, 282.
High School—Sacramento, Calif., Christian Brothers.
Received degree in science from University of Santa Clara.

Selected by San Antonio in 9th round (189th player selected) of 1984 USFL draft.
Selected by Green Bay in 10th round (267th player selected) of 1984 NFL draft.
Signed by Green Bay Packers, June 6, 1984.
On injured reserve with eye injury, August 27 through December 14, 1984; activated after clearing procedural waivers, December 15, 1984.
Green Bay NFL, 1984.
Games: 1984 (1).

GARY KEITH HOGEBOOM
Name pronounced HOAG-ih-boom.
Quarterback—Dallas Cowboys
Born August 21, 1958, at Grand Rapids, Mich.
Height, 6.04. Weight, 199.
High School—Grand Rapids, Mich., Northview.
Attended Central Michigan University.

Selected by Dallas in 5th round (133rd player selected) of 1980 NFL draft.

Year Club	G.	—————PASSING—————							—RUSHING—				—TOTAL—		
		Att.	Cmp.	Pct.	Gain	T.P.	P.I.	Avg.	Att.	Yds.	Avg.	TD.	TD.	Pts.	F.
1980—Dallas NFL	2	None							None				0	0	0
1981—Dallas NFL	1	None							None				0	0	0
1982—Dallas NFL	4	8	3	37.5	45	0	1	5.63	3	0	0.0	0	0	0	2
1983—Dallas NFL	6	17	11	64.7	161	1	1	9.47	6	—10	—1.7	0	0	0	0
1984—Dallas NFL	16	367	195	53.1	2366	7	14	6.45	15	19	1.3	0	0	0	8
Pro Totals—5 Years	29	392	209	53.3	2572	8	16	6.56	24	9	0.4	0	0	0	10

Quarterback Rating Points: 1982 (17.2), 1983 (90.6), 1984 (63.7). Total—63.4.
Additional pro statistics: Recovered four fumbles and fumbled eight times for minus three yards, 1984.
Member of Dallas Cowboys for NFC Championship Game following 1980 and 1981 seasons; did not play.
Played in NFC Championship Game following 1982 season.

WILLIAM BENJAMIN HOGGARD
(Dee Dee)
Cornerback—Cleveland Browns
Born May 20, 1961, at Windsor, N.C.
Height, 6.00. Weight, 188.
High School—Windsor, N.C., Bertie.
Attended North Carolina State University.

Selected by Washington in 12th round (141st player selected) of 1983 USFL draft.
Signed as free agent by Washington Redskins, April 28, 1983.
Released by Washington Redskins, July 30, 1983; signed by Washington Federals, October 21, 1983.
On developmental squad, March 2 through March 6, 1984.
Released by Washington Federals, March 7, 1984; signed by Cleveland Browns, May 6, 1985.
On developmental squad for 1 game with Washington Federals in 1984.
Washington USFL, 1984.
Games: 1984 (1).

ERIC W. HOLLE
Defensive Lineman—Kansas City Chiefs
Born December 5, 1960, at Houston, Tex.
Height, 6.04. Weight, 250.
High School—Austin, Tex., LBJ.
Attended University of Texas.

Selected by San Antonio in 1984 USFL territorial draft.
Selected by Kansas City in 5th round (117th player selected) of 1984 NFL draft.
Signed by Kansas City Chiefs, July 12, 1984.
Kansas City NFL, 1984.
Games: 1984 (16).
Pro statistics: Recovered one fumble for two yards, 1984.

BRIAN DOUGLASS HOLLOWAY
Offensive Tackle—New England Patriots
Born July 25, 1959, at Omaha, Neb.
Height, 6.07. Weight, 288.
High School—Potomac, Md., Winston Churchill.
Received bachelor of arts degree in economics from Stanford University in 1981.

Selected by New England in 1st round (19th player selected) of 1981 NFL draft.
New England NFL, 1981 through 1984.
Games: 1981 (16), 1982 (9), 1983 (16), 1984 (16). Total—57.
Pro statistics: Recovered one fumble, 1981.
Played in Pro Bowl (NFL All-Star Game) following 1983 and 1984 seasons.

ROBERT HOLLY
(Bob)
Quarterback—Atlanta Falcons
Born June 1, 1960, at Clifton, N.J.
Height, 6.02. Weight, 205.
High School—Clifton, N.J.
Received bachelor of arts degree in history from Princeton University.

Selected by Washington in 11th round (291st player selected) of 1982 NFL draft.
Traded by Washington Redskins to Philadelphia Eagles for 7th round pick in 1985 draft, August 14, 1984.
Released by Philadelphia Eagles, August 27, 1984; re-signed by Eagles, August 28, 1984.
Released by Philadelphia Eagles, October 16, 1984; signed as free agent by Atlanta Falcons, November 23, 1984.
Active for 9 games with Washington Redskins in 1982; did not play.
Active for 7 games with Philadelphia Eagles in 1984; did not play.
Active for 4 games with Atlanta Falcons in 1984; did not play.

| | | | | —————PASSING————— | | | | | ——RUSHING—— | | | —TOTAL— | | |
Year	Club	G.	Att.	Cmp.	Pct.	Gain	T.P.	P.I.	Avg.	Att.	Yds.	Avg.	TD.	TD.	Pts.	F.
1983—Washington NFL		5	1	1	100.0	5	0	0	5.00	4	13	3.3	0	0	0	2

Quarterback Rating Points: 1983 (87.5).
Member of Washington Redskins for NFC Championship Game following 1982 and 1983 seasons; did not play.
Member of Washington Redskins for NFL Championship Game following 1982 and 1983 seasons; did not play.

RODNEY A. HOLMAN
Tight End—Cincinnati Bengals
Born April 20, 1960, at Ypsilanti, Mich.
Height, 6.03. Weight, 232.
High School—Ypsilanti, Mich.
Received degree from Tulane University in 1981.
Cousin of Preston Pearson, running back with Baltimore Colts,
Pittsburgh Steelers and Dallas Cowboys, 1967 through 1980.

Selected by Cincinnati in 3rd round (82nd player selected) of 1982 NFL draft.

| | | ——PASS RECEIVING—— | | | |
Year	Club	G.	P.C.	Yds.	Avg.	TD.
1982—Cincinnati NFL		9	3	18	6.0	1
1983—Cincinnati NFL		16	2	15	7.5	0
1984—Cincinnati NFL		16	21	239	11.4	1
Pro Totals—3 Years		41	26	272	10.5	2

Additional pro statistics: Recovered one fumble and fumbled once, 1984.

TOM HOLMOE
Defensive Back—San Francisco 49ers
Born March 7, 1960, at Los Angeles, Calif.
Height, 6.02. Weight, 180.
High School—La Crescenta, Calif., Valley.
Attended Brigham Young University.

Selected by Boston in 9th round (102nd player selected) of 1983 USFL draft.
Selected by San Francisco in 4th round (90th player selected) of 1983 NFL draft.
Signed by San Francisco 49ers, July 16, 1983.
San Francisco NFL, 1983 and 1984.
Games: 1983 (16), 1984 (16). Total—32.
Pro statistics: Recovered one fumble, 1983.
Played in NFC Championship Game following 1983 and 1984 seasons.
Played in NFL Championship Game following 1984 season.

PETER JOSEPH HOLOHAN
(Pete)
Tight End—San Diego Chargers
Born July 25, 1959, at Albany, N.Y.
Height, 6.04. Weight, 249.
High School—Liverpool, N.Y.
Attended University of Notre Dame.

Selected by San Diego in 7th round (189th player selected) of 1981 NFL draft.
Left San Diego Chargers voluntarily and placed on left-camp retired list; October 28, 1981; reinstated, April 30, 1982.

USFL rights traded with wide receiver Neil Balholm, defensive end Bill Purifoy, tight end Mike Hirn and linebacker Orlando Flanagan by Chicago Blitz to Denver Gold for center Glenn Hyde and defensive end Larry White, December 28, 1983.

Year Club	G.	P.C.	Yds.	Avg.	TD.
		—PASS RECEIVING—			
1981—San Diego NFL	7	1	14	14.0	0
1982—San Diego NFL	9		None		
1983—San Diego NFL	16	23	272	11.8	2
1984—San Diego NFL	15	56	734	13.1	1
Pro Totals—4 Years	47	80	1020	12.8	3

Additional pro statistics: Recovered one fumble, 1982; attempted one pass with no completions, 1983; attempted two passes with one completion for 25 yards and a touchdown and recovered two fumbles for 19 yards, 1984.

MICHAEL HOLSTON
(Mike)
Wide Receiver—Houston Oilers
Born January 8, 1958, at Seat Pleasant, Md.
Height, 6.03. Weight, 188.
High School—Blandensburg, Md.
Attended Hagerstown Junior College and Morgan State University.

Selected by Houston in 3rd round (79th player selected) of 1981 NFL draft.

Year Club	G.	P.C.	Yds.	Avg.	TD.
		—PASS RECEIVING—			
1981—Houston NFL	16	27	427	15.8	2
1982—Houston NFL	9	5	116	23.2	1
1983—Houston NFL	16	14	205	14.6	0
1984—Houston NFL	16	22	287	13.0	1
Pro Totals—4 Years	57	68	1035	15.2	4

Additional pro statistics: Recovered one fumble, 1983 and 1984.

HARRY THOMPSON HOLT III
Tight End—Cleveland Browns
Born December 29, 1957, at Harlingen, Tex.
Height, 6.04. Weight, 230.
High Schools—Harlingen, Tex. and Tucson, Ariz., Sunnyside.
Attended University of Arizona.

Signed as free agent by British Columbia Lions, September 13, 1978.
Released by British Columbia Lions, September 14, 1978; re-signed by Lions, September 21, 1978.
On injured list, November 2 through remainder of 1978 season.
On injured list, November 1 through remainder of 1979 season.
On injured list, October 19 through remainder of 1980 season.
Placed on retired list, June 20 through July 12, 1981.
Activated and placed on reserve, July 13 through July 20, 1981; activated, July 21, 1981.
On reserve, August 20 through September 1, 1981; activated, September 2, 1981.
On reserve, September 9 through September 28, 1981; activated, September 29, 1981.
On reserve, October 21 through October 27, 1981; activated, October 28, 1981.
On reserve, August 30 through September 10, 1982; activated, September 11, 1982.
On reserve, October 3 through October 29, 1982; activated, October 30, 1982.
On injured list, October 30 through remainder of 1982 season.

Granted free agency, March 1, 1983.

USFL rights traded with wide receiver Jerome Stelly and future draft picks by Chicago Blitz to Michigan Panthers for center Tom Piette, April 28, 1983.

Signed by Cleveland Browns, May 19, 1983.

On injured reserve with rib injury, October 6 through November 1, 1984; activated, November 2, 1984.

			—RUSHING—			PASS RECEIVING				—TOTAL—		
Year Club	G.	Att.	Yds.	Avg.	TD.	P.C.	Yds.	Avg.	TD.	TD.	Pts.	F.
1978—British Columbia CFL	7	27	107	4.0	1	14	201	14.4	1	2	12	2
1979—British Columbia CFL	15	7	51	7.3	1	32	560	17.5	2	3	18	1
1980—British Columbia CFL	14	12	103	8.6	0	38	648	17.1	5	6	36	2
1981—British Columbia CFL	8	3	4	1.3	0	18	367	20.4	2	2	12	0
1982—British Columbia CFL	10	4	21	5.3	0	35	588	16.8	4	4	24	0
1983—Cleveland NFL	15	3	8	2.7	0	29	420	14.5	3	3	18	1
1984—Cleveland NFL	12	1	12	12.0	0	20	261	13.1	0	0	0	0
CFL Totals—5 Years	54	53	286	5.4	2	137	2364	17.3	14	17	102	5
NFL Totals—2 Years	27	4	20	5.0	0	49	681	13.9	3	3	18	1
Pro Totals—7 Years	81	57	306	5.4	2	186	3045	16.4	17	20	120	6

		—PUNT RETURNS—			
Year Club	G.	No.	Yds.	Avg.	TD.
1978—British Columbia CFL	7	6	62	10.3	0
1979—British Columbia CFL	15		None		
1980—British Columbia CFL	14	21	258	12.3	1
1981—British Columbia CFL	8		None		
1982—British Columbia CFL	10	1	5	5.0	0
1983—Cleveland NFL	15		None		
1984—Cleveland NFL	12		None		
CFL Totals—5 Years	54	28	325	11.6	1
NFL Totals—2 Years	27		None		
Pro Totals—7 Years	81	28	325	11.6	1

Additional CFL statistics: Returned five kickoffs for 127 yards (25.4-yard average, 1978; recovered one fumble, 1979, 1980 and 1982; attempted one pass with no completions, 1982.

Additional NFL statistics: Recovered one fumble, 1983; returned one kickoff for one yard, 1984.

JOHN STEPHANIE HOLT
Cornerback—Tampa Bay Buccaneers
Born May 14, 1959, at Lawton, Okla.
Height, 5.11. Weight, 180.
High School—Enid, Okla.
Attended West Texas State University.

Selected by Tampa Bay in 4th round (89th player selected) of 1981 NFL draft.

USFL rights traded with rights to defensive end Clenzie Pierson by Denver Gold to Houston Gamblers for rights to center George Yarno, September 23, 1983.

		-INTERCEPTIONS-				-PUNT RETURNS-				—TOTAL—		
Year Club	G.	No.	Yds.	Avg.	TD.	No.	Yds.	Avg.	TD.	TD.	Pts.	F.
1981—Tampa Bay NFL	16	1	13	13.0	0	9	100	11.1	0	0	0	1
1982—Tampa Bay NFL	9		None			16	81	5.1	0	0	0	2
1983—Tampa Bay NFL	16	3	43	14.3	0	5	43	8.6	0	0	0	1
1984—Tampa Bay NFL	15	1	25	25.0	0	6	17	2.8	0	0	0	0
Pro Totals—4 Years	56	5	81	16.2	0	36	241	6.7	0	0	0	4

		KICKOFF RETURNS			
Year Club	G.	No.	Yds.	Avg.	TD.
1981—Tampa Bay NFL	16	11	274	24.9	0
1982—Tampa Bay NFL	9		None		
1983—Tampa Bay NFL	16		None		
1984—Tampa Bay NFL	15		None		
Pro Totals—4 Years	56	11	274	24.9	0

Additional pro statistics: Recovered one fumble, 1982 through 1984.

—DID YOU KNOW—

That in the game (vs. New Orleans on October 7, 1984) in which Chicago's Walter Payton broke Jim Brown's all-time career rushing record, Payton also broke Brown's record for most 100-yard rushing games in a career? And that in the game (vs. Houston on December 9, 1984) in which Los Angeles' Eric Dickerson broke O.J. Simpson's single-season rushing record, Dickerson also broke Simpson's record (shared with Earl Campbell) for most 100-yard rushing games in a season? He set the record with 12.

ESTUS HOOD III
Cornerback—Green Bay Packers
Born November 14, 1955, at Hattiesburg, Miss.
Height, 5.11. Weight, 189.
High School—Kankakee, Ill., Eastridge.
Attended Illinois State University.
Selected by Green Bay in 3rd round (62nd player selected) of 1978 NFL draft.

			—INTERCEPTIONS—			
Year	Club	G.	No.	Yds.	Avg.	TD.
1978—Green Bay NFL.............		16	3	18	6.0	0
1979—Green Bay NFL.............		16	2	8	4.0	0
1980—Green Bay NFL.............		15	1	0	0.0	0
1981—Green Bay NFL.............		16	3	59	19.7	1
1982—Green Bay NFL.............		9	1	0	0.0	0
1983—Green Bay NFL.............		16	None			
1984—Green Bay NFL.............		16	1	8	8.0	0
Pro Totals—7 Years.............		104	11	93	8.5	1

Additional pro statistics: Returned three kickoffs for 74 yards, 1978; recovered one fumble, 1978 and 1980; returned one punt for no yards, 1983.

WINFORD D. HOOD
Guard—Denver Broncos
Born March 29, 1962, at Atlanta, Ga.
Height, 6.03. Weight, 262.
High School—Atlanta, Ga., Therrell.
Attended University of Georgia.
Selected by Jacksonville in 1984 USFL territorial draft.
Selected by Denver in 8th round (207th player selected) of 1984 NFL draft.
Signed by Denver Broncos, May 21, 1984.
Denver NFL, 1984.
Games: 1984 (16).

MELVIN CHARLES HOOVER
Wide Receiver—Philadelphia Eagles
Born September 21, 1959, at Charlotte, N.C.
Height, 6.00. Weight, 185.
High School—North Mecklenburg, N.C.
Attended Arizona State University.
Selected by New York Giants in 6th round (145th player selected) of 1981 NFL draft.
Released by New York Giants, August 18, 1981; claimed on waivers by Green Bay Packers, August 20, 1981.
Released by Green Bay Packers, August 24, 1981; signed as free agent by Toronto Argonauts, September 6, 1981.
Released by Toronto Argonauts, September 14, 1981; signed as free agent by Philadelphia Eagles, March 6, 1982.
Released by Philadelphia Eagles, August 29, 1983; re-signed by Eagles, August 30, 1983.

			—RUSHING—				PASS RECEIVING				—TOTAL—		
Year	Club	G.	Att.	Yds.	Avg.	TD.	P.C.	Yds.	Avg.	TD.	TD.	Pts.	F.
1982—Philadelphia NFL		7	1	5	5.0	0	None				0	0	0
1983—Philadelphia NFL		11	None				10	221	22.1	0	0	0	3
1984—Philadelphia NFL		12	None				6	143	23.8	2	2	12	0
Pro Totals—3 Years.....................		30	1	5	5.0	0	16	364	22.8	2	2	12	3

			—PUNT RETURNS—				—KICKOFF RET.—		
Year	Club	G.	No.	Yds.	Avg.	TD.	No.	Yds.	Avg. TD.
1982—Philadelphia NFL		7	None				7	113	16.1 0
1983—Philadelphia NFL		11	7	44	6.3	0	None		
1984—Philadelphia NFL		12	None				None		
Pro Totals—3 Years...		30	7	44	6.3	0	7	113	16.1 0

THOMAS HOPKINS
Offensive Tackle—Dallas Cowboys
Born January 13, 1960, at Butler, Ala.
Height, 6.06. Weight, 260.
High School—Butler, Ala., Choctaw County.
Received bachelor of arts degree in telecommunications
from Alabama A&M University in 1983.
Selected by Boston in 17th round (203rd player selected) of 1983 USFL draft.
Selected by Cleveland in 10th round (262nd player selected) of 1983 NFL draft.
Signed by Cleveland Browns, May 11, 1983.
Released by Cleveland Browns, August 27, 1984; signed as free agent by Dallas Cowboys, March 10, 1985.
Cleveland NFL, 1983.
Games: 1983 (2).

WES HOPKINS
Safety—Philadelphia Eagles

Born September 26, 1961, at Birmingham, Ala.
Height, 6.01. Weight, 210.
High School—Birmingham, Ala., John Carroll.
Attended Southern Methodist University.

Selected by New Jersey in 4th round (46th player selected) of 1983 USFL draft.
Selected by Philadelphia in 2nd round (35th player selected) of 1983 NFL draft.
Signed by Philadelphia Eagles, May 26, 1983.

		—INTERCEPTIONS—			
Year Club	G.	No.	Yds.	Avg.	TD.
1983—Philadelphia NFL	14	None			
1984—Philadelphia NFL	16	5	107	21.4	0
Pro Totals—2 Years............	30	5	107	21.4	0

Additional pro statistics: Recovered three fumbles, 1984.

MICHAEL HORAN
(Mike)
Punter—Philadelphia Eagles

Born February 1, 1959, at Orange, Calif.
Height, 5.11. Weight, 190.
High School—Fullerton, Calif., Sunny Hills.
Attended California State University at Long Beach.

Selected by Atlanta in 9th round (235th player selected) of 1982 NFL draft.
Released by Atlanta Falcons, September 4, 1982; signed as free agent by Green Bay Packers, March 15, 1983.
Released by Green Bay Packers after failing physical, May 6, 1983; signed as free agent by Buffalo Bills, May 25, 1983.
Released by Buffalo Bills, August 22, 1983; signed as free agent by Philadelphia Eagles, May 7, 1984.

		—PUNTING—		
Year Club	G.	No.	Avg.	Blk.
1984—Philadelphia NFL	16	92	42.2	0

TOM HORNOF
Guard—Washington Redskins

Born July 13, 1961, at Evanston, Ill.
Height, 6.04. Weight, 270.
High School—Creve Coeur, Mo., DeSmet.
Attended University of Missouri.

Selected by Houston in 14th round (290th player selected) of 1984 USFL draft.
Signed as free agent by Washington Redskins, May 2, 1984.
On injured reserve with back injury, July 31 through entire 1984 season.

RAYMOND ANTHONY HORTON
(Ray)
Cornerback—Cincinnati Bengals

Born April 12, 1960, at Tacoma, Wash.
Height, 5.11. Weight, 190.
High School—Tacoma, Wash., Mt. Tahoma.
Received bachelor of arts degree in sociology from University of Washington in 1983.

Selected by Los Angeles in 3rd round (25th player selected) of 1983 USFL draft.
Selected by Cincinnati in 2nd round (53rd player selected) of 1983 NFL draft.
Signed by Cincinnati Bengals, May 21, 1983.

		INTERCEPTIONS				-PUNT RETURNS-				—KICKOFF RET.—				—TOTAL—		
Year Club	G.	No.	Yds.	Avg.	TD.	No.	Yds.	Avg.	TD.	No.	Yds.	Avg.	TD.	TD.	Pts.	F.
1983—Cincinnati NFL............	16	5	121	24.2	1	1	10	10.0	0	5	128	25.6	0	1	6	1
1984—Cincinnati NFL............	15	3	48	16.0	1	2	—1	—0.5	0		None			1	6	0
Pro Totals—2 Years.......	31	8	169	21.1	2	3	9	3.0	0	5	128	25.6	0	2	12	1

Additional pro statistics: Recovered one fumble, 1983 and 1984.

JEFF HOSTETLER
Quarterback—New York Giants

Born April 22, 1961, at Hollsopple, Pa.
Height, 6.03. Weight, 212.
High School—Johnstown, Pa., Conemaugh Valley.
Attended West Virginia University.

Selected by Pittsburgh in 1984 USFL territorial draft.
Selected by New York Giants in 3rd round (59th player selected) of 1984 NFL draft.
USFL rights traded with rights to cornerback Dwayne Woodruff by Pittsburgh Maulers to Arizona Wranglers for draft choice, May 2, 1984.
Signed by New York Giants, June 12, 1984.
Active for 16 games with New York Giants in 1984; did not play.

JAMES HUSEN HOUGH
(Jim)
Guard—Minnesota Vikings

Born August 4, 1956, at Lynwood, Calif.
Height, 6.02. Weight, 268.
High School—La Mirada, Calif.
Attended Utah State University.

Selected by Minnesota in 4th round (100th player selected) of 1978 NFL draft.
On injured reserve with knee injury, September 24 through October 23, 1980; activated, October 24, 1980.
On injured reserve with knee injury, December 11 through remainder of 1980 season.
On injured reserve with knee injury, October 31 through remainder of 1984 season.
Minnesota NFL, 1978 through 1984.
Games: 1978 (15), 1979 (16), 1980 (10), 1981 (16), 1982 (9), 1983 (16), 1984 (9). Total—91.
Pro statistics: Recovered one fumble, 1979 and 1982.

KEVIN NATHANIEL HOUSE
Wide Receiver—Tampa Bay Buccaneers

Born December 20, 1957, at St. Louis, Mo.
Height, 6.01. Weight, 180.
High School—University City, Mo.
Attended Southern Illinois University.

Selected by Tampa Bay in 2nd round (49th player selected) of 1980 NFL draft.
Selected by St. Louis (baseball) Cardinals' organization in 26th round of free-agent draft, June 5, 1979.
Selected by Chicago White Sox' organization in 20th round of free-agent draft, June 3, 1980.

| | | ——PASS RECEIVING—— | | | |
Year Club	G.	P.C.	Yds.	Avg.	TD.
1980—Tampa Bay NFL	14	24	531	22.1	5
1981—Tampa Bay NFL	16	56	1176	21.0	9
1982—Tampa Bay NFL	9	28	438	15.6	2
1983—Tampa Bay NFL	16	47	769	16.4	5
1984—Tampa Bay NFL	16	76	1005	13.2	5
Pro Totals—5 Years............	71	231	3919	17.0	26

Additional pro statistics: Rushed once for 32 yards, 1980; fumbled once, 1980 and 1982; rushed twice for nine yards, attempted one pass with no completions and fumbled twice, 1981; rushed once for minus one yard, 1982; rushed once for minus four yards, 1983; recovered one fumble, 1984.

CARL DELANO HOWARD
Cornerback—Dallas Cowboys

Born September 20, 1961, at Newark, N.J.
Height, 6.02. Weight, 188.
High Schools—Irvington, N.J., Technical.
Attended Rutgers University.

Selected by New Jersey in 1984 USFL territorial draft.
Signed as free agent by Dallas Cowboys, May 3, 1984.
On injured reserve with knee injury, November 20 through remainder of 1984 season.
Dallas NFL, 1984.
Games: 1984 (10).

JAMES THOMAS HOWARD
(Known by middle name.)
Linebacker—St. Louis Cardinals

Born August 18, 1954, at Lubbock, Tex.
Height, 6.02. Weight, 215.
High School—Lubbock, Tex., Dunbar.
Attended Texas Tech University.

Selected by Kansas City in 3rd round (67th player selected) of 1977 NFL draft.
On injured reserve with separated shoulder, December 9 through remainder of 1981 season.
Granted free agency, February 1, 1984.
Placed on did not report list, August 20 through August 31, 1984.
Traded by Kansas City Chiefs to St. Louis Cardinals for 7th round pick in 1985 draft and granted roster exemption, September 1, 1984; activated, September 6, 1984.

| | | ——INTERCEPTIONS—— | | | |
Year Club	G.	No.	Yds.	Avg.	TD.
1977—Kansas City NFL..........	13	1	0	0.0	0
1978—Kansas City NFL..........	16	1	0	0.0	0
1979—Kansas City NFL..........	16	1	19	19.0	0
1980—Kansas City NFL..........	16		None		
1981—Kansas City NFL..........	9		None		
1982—Kansas City NFL..........	9	2	10	5.0	0
1983—Kansas City NFL..........	16		None		
1984—St. Louis NFL................	15	2	—4	—2.0	0
Pro Totals—8 Years............	110	7	25	3.6	0

Additional pro statistics: Recovered one fumble, 1978 and 1982; recovered three fumbles for 18 yards and one touchdown, 1980; recovered two fumbles for 65 yards and one touchdown, 1981; recovered one fumble for 29 yards and a touchdown, 1984.

PAUL EUGENE HOWARD
Guard—Denver Broncos

Born September 12, 1950, at San Jose, Calif.
Height, 6.03. Weight, 260.
High School—Central Valley, Calif.
Attended Brigham Young University.

Selected by Denver in 3rd round (54th player selected) of 1973 NFL draft.
Missed entire 1976 season due to injury.
Denver NFL, 1973 through 1975 and 1977 through 1984.
Games: 1973 (14), 1974 (14), 1975 (14), 1977 (14), 1978 (13), 1979 (16), 1980 (14), 1981 (16), 1982 (9), 1983 (16), 1984 (16).
Total—156.
Pro statistics: Recovered one fumble, 1975 and 1977.
Played in AFC Championship Game following 1977 season.
Played in NFL Championship Game following 1977 season.

BOBBY GLEN HOWE
(Known by middle name.)
Offensive Tackle—Pittsburgh Steelers

Born October 18, 1961, at New Albany, Miss.
Height, 6.06. Weight, 280.
High School—New Albany, Miss., W.P. Daniel.
Attended University of Southern Mississippi.

Selected by New Orleans in 1984 USFL territorial draft.
Selected by Atlanta in 9th round (233rd player selected) of 1984 NFL draft.
Signed by Atlanta Falcons, June 4, 1984.
Released by Atlanta Falcons, August 26, 1984; signed as free agent by Pittsburgh Steelers, May 9, 1985.

LEROY HOWELL
Defensive End—Buffalo Bills

Born November 4, 1962, at Columbus, S.C.
Height, 6.04. Weight, 235.
High School—Columbus, S.C., Richland Northeast.
Attended Appalachian State University.

Selected by New Orleans in 7th round (133rd player selected) of 1984 USFL draft.
Selected by Buffalo in 9th round (236th player selected) of 1984 NFL draft.
Signed by Buffalo Bills, July 9, 1984.
On injured reserve with knee injury, August 28 through December 13, 1984; activated, December 14, 1984.
Active for 1 game with Buffalo Bills in 1984; did not play.

PAT GERRAD HOWELL
Guard—Houston Oilers

Born March 12, 1957, at Fresno, Calif.
Height, 6.06. Weight, 265.
High School—Fresno, Calif.
Received bachelor of arts degree in speech communication from
University of Southern California in 1979.

Named as guard on THE SPORTING NEWS College All-America Team, 1978.
Selected by Atlanta in 2nd round (49th player selected) of 1979 NFL draft.
Released by Atlanta Falcons, September 14, 1983; signed as free agent by Houston Oilers, October 19, 1983.
Atlanta NFL, 1979 through 1982; Atlanta (2)-Houston (7) NFL, 1983; Houston NFL, 1984.
Games: 1979 (15), 1980 (5), 1981 (16), 1982 (9), 1983 (9), 1984 (11). Total—65.

HARLAN CHARLES HUCKLEBY
Running Back—Green Bay Packers

Born December 30, 1957, at Detroit, Mich.
Height, 6.01. Weight, 201.
High School—Detroit, Mich., Cass Tech.
Attended University of Michigan.

Selected by New Orleans in 5th round (120th player selected) of 1979 NFL draft.
Released by New Orleans Saints, August 27, 1979; signed as free agent by Saskatchewan Roughriders, September 2, 1979.
Released by Saskatchewan Roughriders, June 25, 1980; signed as free agent by Green Bay Packers, July 17, 1980.

| | | —RUSHING— | | | PASS RECEIVING | | | | —TOTAL— | | |
Year Club	G.	Att.	Yds.	Avg.	TD.	P.C.	Yds.	Avg.	TD.	TD.	Pts.	F.
1979—Saskatchewan CFL	8	58	259	4.5	1	10	37	3.7	0	1	6	1
1980—Green Bay NFL	16	6	11	1.8	1	3	11	3.7	0	1	6	0
1981—Green Bay NFL	16	139	381	2.7	5	27	221	8.2	3	8	48	3
1982—Green Bay NFL	9	4	19	4.8	0		None			0	0	0
1983—Green Bay NFL	16	50	182	3.6	4	10	87	8.7	0	4	24	4
1984—Green Bay NFL	16	35	145	4.1	0	8	65	8.1	0	0	0	1
NFL Totals—5 Years	73	234	738	3.2	10	48	384	8.0	3	13	78	8
CFL Total—1 Year	8	58	259	4.5	1	10	37	3.7	0	1	6	1
Pro Totals—6 Years	81	292	997	3.4	11	58	421	7.3	3	14	84	9

Year Club	G.	No.	Yds.	Avg.	TD.
1979—Saskatchewan CFL......	8	11	212	19.3	0
1980—Green Bay NFL............	16	3	59	19.7	0
1981—Green Bay NFL............	16	7	134	19.1	0
1982—Green Bay NFL............	9	5	89	17.8	0
1983—Green Bay NFL............	16	41	757	18.5	0
1984—Green Bay NFL............	16	14	261	18.6	0
NFL Totals—5 Years........	73	70	1300	18.6	0
CFL Total—1 Year..............	8	11	212	19.3	0
Pro Totals—6 Years...........	81	81	1512	18.7	0

Additional CFL statistics: Recovered one fumble, 1979.
Additional NFL statistics: Recovered one fumble, 1983 and 1984.

KENNETH WAYNE HUFF
(Ken)
Guard—Washington Redskins
Born February 21, 1953, at Hutchinson, Kan.
Height, 6.04. Weight, 265.
High Schools—Deerfield, Mass., Deerfield Academy and Coronado, Calif.
Received bachelor of arts degree in psychology from University of North Carolina.

Named as guard on THE SPORTING NEWS College All-America Team, 1974.
Selected by Baltimore in 1st round (3rd player selected) of 1975 NFL draft.
Granted free agency, February 1, 1983; Colts withdrew offer August 23, 1983 and signed by Washington Redskins, August 25, 1983.
Baltimore NFL, 1975 through 1982; Washington NFL, 1983 and 1984.
Games: 1975 (9), 1976 (8), 1977 (14), 1978 (16), 1979 (14), 1980 (16), 1981 (16), 1982 (9), 1983 (13), 1984 (15). Total—130.
Pro statistics: Returned one kickoff for 15 yards, 1977; recovered one fumble, 1980; caught one pass for minus one yard, 1981; recovered three fumbles, 1984.
Member of Washington Redskins for NFC Championship Game following 1983 season; did not play.
Played in NFL Championship Game following 1983 season.

TIM HUFFMAN
Offensive Tackle—Green Bay Packers
Born August 31, 1959, at Canton, O.
Height, 6.05. Weight, 282.
High School—Dallas, Tex., Thomas Jefferson.
Attended University of Notre Dame.
Brother of Dave Huffman, center-guard with Memphis Showboats.

Selected by Green Bay in 9th round (227th player selected) of 1981 NFL draft.
On injured reserve with foot injury, September 1 through September 28, 1981; activated, September 29, 1981.
On injured reserve with ankle injury, November 13 through remainder of 1981 season.
Green Bay NFL, 1981 through 1984.
Games: 1981 (6), 1982 (9), 1983 (15), 1984 (16). Total—46.

DAVID A. HUGHES
Fullback—Seattle Seahawks
Born June 1, 1959, at Honolulu, Hawaii.
Height, 6.00. Weight, 220.
High School—Pearl City, Hawaii, Kamehameha.
Attended Boise State University.

Selected by Seattle in 2nd round (31st player selected) of 1981 NFL draft.

Year Club	G.	—RUSHING— Att.	Yds.	Avg.	TD.	PASS RECEIVING P.C.	Yds.	Avg.	TD.	—TOTAL— TD.	Pts.	F.
1981—Seattle NFL........	16	47	135	2.9	0	35	263	7.5	2	2	12	4
1982—Seattle NFL........	9	30	106	3.5	0	11	98	8.9	1	1	6	0
1983—Seattle NFL........	16	83	313	3.8	1	10	100	10.0	1	2	12	2
1984—Seattle NFL........	16	94	327	3.5	1	22	121	5.5	1	2	12	4
Pro Totals—4 Years....	57	254	881	3.5	2	78	582	7.5	5	7	42	10

Year Club	G.	KICKOFF RETURNS No.	Yds.	Avg.	TD.
1981—Seattle NFL..................	16		None		
1982—Seattle NFL..................	9	1	17	17.0	0
1983—Seattle NFL..................	16	12	282	23.5	0
1984—Seattle NFL..................	16	17	348	20.5	0
Pro Totals—4 Years...........	57	30	647	21.6	0

Additional pro statistics: Recovered one fumble, 1981; recovered three fumbles, 1984.
Played in AFC Championship Game following 1983 season.

—DID YOU KNOW—
That Tampa Bay's James Wilder was the only running back in the NFL to rank within the top 10 in both rushing and pass receptions in 1984?

MICHAEL HUMISTON
(Mike)
Linebacker—Indianapolis Colts
Born January 8, 1959, at Oceanside, Calif.
Height, 6.03. Weight, 238.
High School—Anderson, Calif., Union.
Attended Shasta Junior College and Weber State College.

Signed as free agent by Buffalo Bills, May 10, 1981.
Released by Buffalo Bills, September 6, 1982; signed as free agent by Baltimore Colts, September 15, 1982.
On injured reserve with ankle injury, August 30 through entire 1983 season.
Franchise transferred to Indianapolis, March 31, 1984.
Buffalo NFL, 1981; Baltimore NFL, 1982; Indianapolis NFL, 1984.
Games: 1981 (16), 1982 (7), 1984 (16). Total—39.
Pro statistics: Recovered one fumble, 1981; credited with one safety and recovered two fumbles, 1984.

DAVID HENRY HUMM
Quarterback—Los Angeles Raiders
Born April 2, 1952, at Las Vegas, Nev.
Height, 6.02. Weight, 194.
High School—Las Vegas, Nev., Bishop Gorman.
Attended University of Nebraska.

Named as quarterback on THE SPORTING NEWS College All-America Team, 1974.
Selected by Oakland in 5th round (128th player selected) of 1975 NFL draft.
Released by Oakland Raiders, August 19, 1980; claimed on waivers by Buffalo Bills, August 21, 1980.
Released by Buffalo Bills, August 31, 1981; signed as free agent by Baltimore Colts, November 25, 1981.
Released by Baltimore Colts, June 9, 1983; signed by Los Angeles Raiders, July 26, 1983.
Released by Los Angeles Raiders, August 29, 1983; re-signed by Raiders, November 7, 1983.
Released by Los Angeles Raiders, August 27, 1984; re-signed by Raiders, October 10, 1984.
On injured reserve with knee injury, November 5 through remainder of 1984 season.

Year Club	G.	Att.	Cmp.	Pct.	Gain	T.P.	P.I.	Avg.	Att.	Yds.	Avg.	TD.	TD.	Pts.	F.
				PASSING						RUSHING			TOTAL		
1975—Oakland NFL	7	38	18	47.4	246	3	2	6.47	7	21	3.0	0	0	0	3
1976—Oakland NFL	14	5	3	60.0	41	0	0	8.20	None				0	0	0
1977—Oakland NFL	14			None					None				0	0	0
1978—Oakland NFL	16	26	14	53.8	151	0	1	5.81	5	—4	—0.8	0	0	0	1
1979—Oakland NFL	16			None					None				0	0	0
1980—Buffalo NFL	16	14	4	28.6	39	0	1	2.79	1	5	5.0	0	0	0	1
1981—Baltimore NFL	1	24	7	29.2	90	0	2	3.75	None				0	0	0
1982—Baltimore NFL	2	23	13	56.5	130	0	1	5.65	None				0	0	0
1983—L.A. Raiders NFL	6			None					1	—1	—1.0	0	0	0	0
1984—L.A. Raiders NFL	3	7	4	57.1	56	0	1	8.00	2	7	3.5	0	0	0	2
Pro Totals—10 Years	95	137	63	46.0	753	3	8	5.50	16	28	1.8	0	0	0	7

Quarterback Rating Points: 1975 (72.8), 1976 (86.3), 1978 (55.3), 1980 (10.0), 1981 (8.1), 1982 (54.8), 1984 (43.5). Total—46.5.
Additional pro statistics: Recovered one fumble, 1978 and 1984.
Played in AFC Championship Game following 1976, 1977 and 1983 seasons.
Member of Oakland Raiders for AFC Championship Game following 1975 season; did not play.
Played in NFL Championship Game following 1976 and 1983 seasons.

ROBERT CHARLES HUMPHERY
(Bobby)
Wide Receiver—New York Jets
Born August 23, 1961, at Lubbock, Tex.
Height, 5.10. Weight, 170.
High School—Lubbock, Tex., Estacado.
Attended New Mexico State University.

Named to THE SPORTING NEWS NFL All-Star Team, 1984.
Selected by New York Jets in 9th round (247th player selected) of 1983 NFL draft.
On injured reserve with broken finger, August 1 through entire 1983 season.

Year Club	G.	P.C.	Yds.	Avg.	TD.	No.	Yds.	Avg.	TD.	TD.	Pts.	F.
		PASS RECEIVING				KICKOFF RET.				TOTAL		
1984—New York Jets NFL	16	14	206	14.7	1	22	675	*30.7	*1	2	12	2

Additional pro statistics: Recovered two fumbles, 1984.

DONNIE HUMPHREY
Defensive End—Green Bay Packers
Born April 20, 1961, at Huntsville, Ala.
Height, 6.03. Weight, 275.
High School—Huntsville, Ala., J.O. Johnson.
Attended Auburn University.

Selected by Birmingham in 1984 USFL territorial draft.
Selected by Green Bay in 3rd round (72nd player selected) of 1984 NFL draft.
Signed by Green Bay Packers, July 12, 1984.
Green Bay NFL, 1984.
Games: 1984 (16).

STEFAN GOVAN HUMPHRIES
Guard—Chicago Bears
Born January 20, 1962, at Fort Lauderdale, Fla.
Height, 6.04. Weight, 265.
High School—Fort Lauderdale, Fla., St. Thomas Aquinas.
Received bachelor of science degree in engineering science
from University of Michigan in 1984.

Named as guard on THE SPORTING NEWS College All-America Team, 1983.
Selected by Michigan in 1984 USFL territorial draft.
Selected by Chicago in 3rd round (71st player selected) of 1984 NFL draft.
Signed by Chicago Bears, July 2, 1984.
On injured reserve with knee injury, December 5 through remainder of 1984 season.
Chicago NFL, 1984.
Games: 1984 (9).

RICKY CARDELL HUNLEY
Linebacker—Denver Broncos
Born November 11, 1961, at Petersburg, Va.
Height, 6.02. Weight, 238.
High School—Petersburg, Va.
Received degree in business from University of Arizona in 1984.
Brother of Lamonte Hunley, rookie linebacker with Indianapolis Colts.

Selected by Arizona in 1984 USFL territorial draft.
Selected by Cincinnati in 1st round (7th player selected) in 1984 NFL draft.
NFL rights traded by Cincinnati Bengals to Denver Broncos for 1st and 3rd round picks in 1986 draft and 5th round pick in 1987 draft, October 9, 1984.
Signed by Denver Broncos, October 16, 1984.
Granted roster exemption, October 16 though October 25, 1984; activated, October 26, 1984.
Selected by Pittsburgh Pirates' organization in 26th round of free-agent draft, June 3, 1980.
Denver NFL, 1984.
Games: 1984 (8).

BYRON RAY HUNT
Linebacker—New York Giants
Born December 17, 1958, at Longview, Tex.
Height, 6.05. Weight, 242.
High School—Longview, Tex., White Oak.
Attended Southern Methodist University.
Brother of Sam Hunt, defensive end with New England Patriots
and Green Bay Packers, 1974 through 1980.

Selected by New York Giants in 9th round (224th player selected) of 1981 NFL draft.

| | | | —INTERCEPTIONS— | | |
Year Club	G.	No.	Yds.	Avg.	TD.
1981—N.Y. Giants NFL	16	1	7	7.0	0
1982—N.Y. Giants NFL	9		None		
1983—N.Y. Giants NFL	16		None		
1984—N.Y. Giants NFL	13	1	14	14.0	0
Pro Totals—4 Years............	54	2	21	10.5	0

Additional pro statistics: Recovered two fumbles, 1984.

DARYL LYNN HUNT
Linebacker—Houston Oilers
Born November 3, 1956, at Odessa, Tex.
Height, 6.03. Weight, 243.
High School—Odessa, Tex., Permian.
Attended University of Oklahoma.

Selected by Houston in 6th round (143rd player selected) of 1979 NFL draft.
On injured reserve with knee injury, August 28 through November 12, 1984; activated after clearing procedural waivers, November 14, 1984.
Houston NFL, 1979 through 1984.
Games: 1979 (16), 1980 (16), 1981 (16), 1982 (9), 1983 (16), 1984 (5). Total—78.
Pro statistics: Recovered one fumble, 1979 and 1980; returned three kickoffs for 19 yards, 1981; returned one kickoff for 12 yards, 1983.
Played in AFC Championship Game following 1979 season.

JOHN STEPHEN HUNT
Guard—Dallas Cowboys
Born November 6, 1962, at Orlando, Fla.
Height, 6.04. Weight, 253.
High School—Orlando, Fla., Edgewater.
Attended University of Florida.

Selected by Tampa Bay in 1984 USFL territorial draft.
Selected by Dallas in 9th round (232nd player selected) of 1984 NFL draft.
Signed by Dallas Cowboys, May 11, 1984.
On injured reserve with back injury, September 28 through November 16, 1984; activated, November 17, 1984.
Dallas NFL, 1984.
Games: 1984 (2).

DANIEL LEWIS HUNTER
Cornerback—Denver Broncos

Born September 1, 1962, at Arkadelphia, Ark.
Height, 5.11. Weight, 167.
High School—Arkadelphia, Ark.
Attended Henderson State University.

Signed as free agent by Los Angeles Express, January 13, 1984.
Released by Los Angeles Express, February 22, 1984; signed as free agent by Dallas Cowboys, May 10, 1984.
Released by Dallas Cowboys, August 13, 1984; signed as free agent by Denver Broncos, February 27, 1985.

JIMMY L. HUNTER
Linebacker—New York Jets

Born April 10, 1960, at Birmingham, Ala.
Height, 6.02. Weight, 225.
High School—Tampa, Fla., Hillsborough.
Attended Indiana University.

Signed as free agent by New York Jets, May 4, 1983.
On injured reserve with knee injury, August 29 through entire 1983 season.
Released by New York Jets, August 20, 1984.
USFL rights traded by Jacksonville Bulls to Birmingham Stallions for rights to defensive back Derrick Franklin, October 4, 1984.
Signed by Birmingham Stallions, November 27, 1984.
Released by Birmingham Stallions, January 28, 1985; re-signed by New York Jets, May 7, 1985.

TONY WAYNE HUNTER
Tight End—Buffalo Bills

Born May 22, 1960, at Cincinnati, O.
Height, 6.04. Weight, 235.
High School—Cincinnati, O., Moeller.
Received bachelor of science degree in economics from University of Notre Dame in 1984.

Selected by Chicago in 1983 USFL territorial draft.
Selected by Buffalo in 1st round (12th player selected) of 1983 NFL draft.
Signed by Buffalo Bills, June 17, 1983.
On injured reserve with back injury, September 29 through October 25, 1984; activated, October 26, 1984.

Year Club	G.	P.C.	Yds.	Avg.	TD.
1983—Buffalo NFL	13	36	402	11.2	3
1984—Buffalo NFL	11	33	331	10.0	2
Pro Totals—2 Years	24	69	733	10.6	5

Additional pro statistics: Rushed twice for 28 yards, 1983; recovered one fumble and fumbled once, 1983 and 1984; rushed once for six yards, 1984.

ANTHONY LaRUE HUTCHISON
Running Back—Chicago Bears

Born February 4, 1961, at Houston, Tex.
Height, 5.10. Weight, 186.
High School—Converse, Tex., Judson.
Attended Texas Tech University.

Selected by Denver in 1983 USFL territorial draft.
Selected by Chicago in 10th round (256th player selected) of 1983 NFL draft.
Signed by Chicago Bears, May 12, 1983.

Year Club	G.	Att.	Yds.	Avg.	TD.	P.C.	Yds.	Avg.	TD.	TD.	Pts.	F.
1983—Chicago NFL	16	6	13	2.2	1	None				1	6	1
1984—Chicago NFL	12	14	39	2.8	1	1	7	7.0	0	1	6	0
Pro Totals—2 Years	28	20	52	2.6	2	1	7	7.0	0	2	12	1

Year Club	G.	No.	Yds.	Avg.	TD.
1983—Chicago NFL	16	17	259	15.2	0
1984—Chicago NFL	12		None		
Pro Totals—2 Years	28	17	259	15.2	0

Played in NFC Championship Game following 1984 season.

GLENN THATCHER HYDE
Center-Guard—Denver Broncos

Born March 14, 1951, at Boston, Mass.
Height, 6.03. Weight, 252.
High School—Lexington, Mass.
Received bachelor of science degree in physical education and health from University of Pittsburgh in 1974.

Signed as free agent by Atlanta Falcons, 1974.
Traded by Atlanta Falcons to Washington Redskins for a 1976 8th round draft choice, March 10, 1975.

Released by Washington Redskins, September 5, 1975; signed as free agent by Charlotte Hornets (WFL), September, 1975.
Signed as free agent by New England Patriots after World Football League folded, 1976.
Played in World Football League with Chicago Fire, 1974.
Released by New England Patriots, September 6, 1976; signed as free agent by Denver Broncos, September 28, 1976.
Released by Denver Broncos, August 29, 1978; re-signed by Broncos, September 8, 1978.
Traded by Denver Broncos to Baltimore Colts for 8th round pick in 1983 draft, September 6, 1982.
Released by Baltimore Colts, December 7, 1982.
USFL rights traded by Washington Federals to Denver Gold for a 1984 draft pick, December 14, 1982.
Signed by Denver Gold, December 20, 1982.
On developmental squad, May 22 through May 24, 1983; activated, May 25, 1983.
Traded with defensive end Larry White by Denver Gold to Chicago Blitz for wide receiver Neil Balholm, tight end Mike Hirn, defensive end Bill Purifoy, linebacker Orlando Flanagan and rights to tight end Peter Holohan, December 28, 1983.
Franchise disbanded, November 20, 1984; not selected in USFL dispersal draft, December 6, 1984.
Signed as free agent by Denver Broncos, December 13, 1984.
Granted free agency, February 1, 1985 when not tendered qualifying offer; re-signed by Broncos, April 9, 1985.
On developmental squad for 1 game with Denver Gold in 1983.
Active for 1 game with Denver Broncos in 1984; did not play.
Chicago WFL, 1974; Charlotte WFL, 1975; Denver NFL, 1976 through 1981 and 1984; Baltimore NFL, 1982; Denver USFL, 1983; Chicago USFL, 1984.
Games: 1974 (?), 1975 (1), 1976 (11), 1977 (14), 1978 (15), 1979 (16), 1980 (16), 1981 (16), 1982 (5), 1983 (17), 1984 USFL (18). Total NFL—93. Total USFL—35. Total Pro—128.
Pro statistics: Returned one kickoff for 15 yards, 1977.
Played in AFC Championship Game following 1977 season.
Played in NFL Championship Game following 1977 season.

COACHING RECORD
Player-coach, Denver USFL, June 2 through remainder of 1983 season.

TUNCH ALI ILKIN
Name pronounced TOON-ch ILL-kin.
Offensive Tackle—Pittsburgh Steelers
Born September 23, 1957, at Istanbul, Turkey
Height, 6.03. Weight, 255.
High School—Highland Park, Ill.
Received bachelor of science degree in broadcasting from Indiana State University in 1980.
Selected by Pittsburgh in 6th round (165th player selected) of 1980 NFL draft.
Released by Pittsburgh Steelers, August 25, 1980; re-signed by Steelers, October 15, 1983.
On injured reserve with shoulder injury, August 30 through September 29, 1983; activated, September 30, 1983.
Pittsburgh NFL, 1980 through 1984.
Games: 1980 (10), 1981 (16), 1982 (8), 1983 (11), 1984 (16). Total—61.
Pro statistics: Recovered one fumble, 1981 and 1983.
Played in AFC Championship Game following 1984 season.

BRIAN DeWAYNE INGRAM
Linebacker—New England Patriots
Born October 31, 1959, at Memphis, Tenn.
Height, 6.04. Weight, 235.
High School—Memphis, Tenn., Hamilton.
Attended University of Tennessee.
Selected by New England in 4th round (111th player selected) of 1982 NFL draft.
On inactive list, September 12, 1982.
On injured reserve with knee injury, September 28 through remainder of 1983 season.
New England NFL, 1982 through 1984.
Games: 1982 (8), 1983 (4), 1984 (12). Total—24.

LeROY IRVIN JR.
Cornerback—Los Angeles Rams
Born September 15, 1957, at Fort Dix, N.J.
Height, 5.11. Weight, 184.
High School—Augusta, Ga., Glenn Hills.
Attended University of Kansas.
Established NFL record for most punt return yards, game (207), against Atlanta Falcons, October 11, 1981.
Tied NFL record for most touchdowns, punt returns, game (2), against Atlanta Falcons, October 11, 1981.
Named to THE SPORTING NEWS NFL All-Star Team, 1981.
Selected by Los Angeles in 3rd round (70th player selected) of 1980 NFL draft.

Year Club	G.	-INTERCEPTIONS-				-PUNT RETURNS-				—TOTAL—		
		No.	Yds.	Avg.	TD.	No.	Yds.	Avg.	TD.	TD.	Pts.	F.
1980—Los Angeles Rams NFL	16	2	80	40.0	0	42	296	7.0	0	0	0	5
1981—Los Angeles Rams NFL	16	3	18	6.0	0	46	*615	*13.4	*3	3	18	3
1982—Los Angeles Rams NFL	9		None			22	242	11.0	1	1	6	4
1983—Los Angeles Rams NFL	15	4	42	10.5	0	25	212	8.5	0	0	0	4
1984—Los Angeles Rams NFL	16	5	166	33.2	*2	9	83	9.2	0	2	12	0
Pro Totals—5 Years	72	14	306	21.9	2	144	1448	10.1	4	6	36	16

Additional pro statistics: Returned one kickoff for five yards and recovered three fumbles, 1980; recovered three fumbles for 14 yards, 1981; recovered two fumbles, 1982 and 1983; returned one kickoff for 22 yards, 1983; returned two kickoffs for 33 yards, 1984.

TIM IRWIN
Offensive Tackle—Minnesota Vikings
Born December 13, 1956, at Knoxville, Tenn.
Height, 6.07. Weight, 285.
High School—Knoxville, Tenn., Central.
Received degree from University of Tennessee in 1981.

Selected by Minnesota in 3rd round (74th player selected) of 1981 NFL draft.
Minnesota NFL, 1981 through 1984.
Games: 1981 (7), 1982 (9), 1983 (16), 1984 (16). Total—48.
Pro statistics: Recovered one fumble, 1983; recovered one fumble for two yards, 1984.

EDDIE LEE IVERY
(Eddie Lee)
Running Back—Green Bay Packers
Born July 30, 1957, at McDuffie, Ga.
Height, 6.00. Weight, 210.
High School—Thomson, Ga.
Attended Georgia Tech.

Selected by Green Bay in 1st round (15th player selected) of 1979 NFL draft.
On injured reserve with knee injury, September 5 through remainder of 1979 NFL season.
On injured reserve with knee injury, September 8 through remainder of 1981 season.
On reserve/non-football injury with drug problems, October 28 through remainder of 1983 season.
On injured reserve with knee injury, August 29 through October 5, 1984; activated, October 6, 1984.

Year Club	G.	Att.	Yds.	Avg.	TD.	P.C.	Yds.	Avg.	TD.	TD.	Pts.	F.
1979—Green Bay NFL	1	3	24	8.0	0		None			0	0	1
1980—Green Bay NFL	16	202	831	4.1	3	50	481	9.6	1	4	24	3
1981—Green Bay NFL	1	14	72	5.1	1	2	10	5.0	0	1	6	0
1982—Green Bay NFL	9	127	453	3.6	9	16	186	11.6	1	10	60	2
1983—Green Bay NFL	8	86	340	4.0	2	16	139	8.7	1	3	18	1
1984—Green Bay NFL	10	99	552	5.6	6	19	141	7.4	1	7	42	1
Pro Totals—6 Years	45	531	2272	4.3	21	103	957	9.3	4	25	150	8

Additional pro statistics: Recovered two fumbles, 1980; attempted one pass with no completions, 1982; returned one kickoff for 17 yards and attempted two passes with two completions for 50 yards, 1983.

ALFRED JACKSON
Wide Receiver—Atlanta Falcons
Born August 3, 1955, at Cameron, Tex.
Height, 6.00. Weight, 190.
High School—Caldwell, Tex.
Received bachelor of science degree in history from University of Texas.

Selected by Atlanta in 7th round (167th player selected) of 1978 NFL draft.
On injured reserve with broken collarbone, October 1 through remainder of 1983 season.

Year Club	G.	P.C.	Yds.	Avg.	TD.	No.	Yds.	Avg.	TD.	No.	Yds.	Avg.	TD.	TD.	Pts.	F.
1978—Atlanta NFL	15	26	526	20.2	2	11	89	8.1	0	11	225	20.5	0	2	12	3
1979—Atlanta NFL	12	11	156	14.2	0		None			1	20	20.0	0	0	0	0
1980—Atlanta NFL	16	23	412	17.9	7		None			3	70	23.3	0	7	42	0
1981—Atlanta NFL	16	37	604	16.3	6		None				None			7	42	0
1982—Atlanta NFL	9	26	361	13.9	1		None				None			1	6	0
1983—Atlanta NFL	4	13	220	16.9	3		None				None			3	18	0
1984—Atlanta NFL	16	52	731	14.1	2		None				None			2	12	0
Pro Totals—7 Years	88	188	3010	16.0	21	11	89	8.1	0	15	315	21.0	0	22	132	3

Additional pro statistics: Rushed twice for five yards and recovered one fumble in end zone for touchdown, 1981; rushed once for four yards, 1982; recovered one fumble, 1984.

BILLY THURMAN JACKSON
Running Back—Kansas City Chiefs
Born September 13, 1959, at Phenix City, Ala.
Height, 5.10. Weight, 215.
High School—Phenix City, Ala., Central.
Attended University of Alabama.

Selected by Kansas City in 7th round (180th player selected) of 1981 NFL draft.

Year Club	G.	Att.	Yds.	Avg.	TD.	P.C.	Yds.	Avg.	TD.	TD.	Pts.	F.
1981—Kansas City NFL	16	111	398	3.6	10	6	31	5.2	1	11	66	1
1982—Kansas City NFL	9	86	243	2.8	3	5	41	8.2	0	3	18	1
1983—Kansas City NFL	16	152	499	3.3	2	32	243	7.6	0	2	12	3
1984—Kansas City NFL	16	50	225	4.5	1	15	101	6.7	1	2	12	2
Pro Totals—4 Years	57	399	1365	3.4	16	58	416	7.2	2	18	108	7

Additional pro statistics: Returned three kickoffs for 60 yards, 1981; recovered two fumbles, 1983; recovered one fumble, 1984.

CHARLES MELVIN JACKSON
Linebacker—New York Jets

Born March 22, 1955, at Los Angeles, Calif.
Height, 6.02. Weight, 222.
High School—Berkeley, Calif.
Attended University of Washington.
Cousin of Odell Jones, pitcher in Baltimore Orioles' organization.

Selected by Denver in 9th round (241st player selected) of 1977 NFL draft.
On injured reserve, August 30 through 1977 season.
Released by Denver Broncos, August 29, 1978; claimed on waivers by Kansas City Chiefs, August 30, 1978.
On injured reserve with rib injury, November 2 through November 29, 1979; activated, November 30, 1979.
Granted free agency, February 2, 1981; signed as free agent by Edmonton Eskimos, May 4, 1981.
Released by Edmonton Eskimos, June 29, 1981; signed as free agent by Kansas City Chiefs, July 4, 1981.
Left Kansas City Chiefs voluntarily and granted roster exemption, October 3 through October 9, 1984.
Placed on reserve/left squad, October 10 through remainder of 1984 season.
Traded by Kansas City Chiefs to New York Jets for 7th round pick in 1985 draft, April 25, 1985.
Kansas City NFL, 1978 through 1984.
Games: 1978 (16), 1979 (12), 1980 (16), 1981 (14), 1982 (9), 1983 (15), 1984 (4). Total—86.
Pro statistics: Recovered one fumble, 1979; recovered three fumbles for 33 yards, 1981; recovered two fumbles for four yards, 1982; recovered four fumbles for 47 yards and a touchdown, 1983; intercepted one pass for 16 yards, 1984.

EARNEST JACKSON
Running Back—San Diego Chargers

Born December 18, 1959, at Needville, Tex.
Height, 5.10. Weight, 208.
High School—Rosenburg, Tex., Lamar.
Attended Texas A&M University.

Selected by Oakland in 9th round (103rd player selected) of 1983 USFL draft.
USFL rights traded by Oakland Invaders to Michigan Panthers for 8th round pick in 1984 draft, March 24, 1983.
Selected by San Diego in 8th round (202nd player selected) of 1983 NFL draft.
Signed by San Diego Chargers, July 11, 1983.

		—RUSHING—				PASS RECEIVING				—TOTAL—		
Year Club	G.	Att.	Yds.	Avg.	TD.	P.C.	Yds.	Avg.	TD.	TD.	Pts.	F.
1983—San Diego NFL	12	11	39	3.5	0	5	42	8.4	0	0	0	1
1984—San Diego NFL	16	296	1179	4.0	8	39	222	5.7	1	9	54	3
Pro Totals—2 Years	28	307	1218	4.0	8	44	264	6.0	1	9	54	4

		KICKOFF RETURNS			
Year Club	G.	No.	Yds.	Avg.	TD.
1983—San Diego NFL	12	11	201	18.3	0
1984—San Diego NFL	16	1	10	10.0	0
Pro Totals—2 Years	28	12	211	17.6	0

Additional pro statistics: Recovered one fumble, 1983; recovered two fumbles, 1984.
Played in Pro Bowl (NFL All-Star Game) following 1984 season.

JEFFERY PAUL JACKSON
(Jeff)
Linebacker—Atlanta Falcons

Born October 9, 1961, at Shreveport, Ga.
Height, 6.01. Weight, 228.
High School—Griffin, Ga.
Attended Auburn University.

Selected by Birmingham in 1984 USFL territorial draft.
Selected by Atlanta in 8th round (206th player selected) of 1984 NFL draft.
Signed by Atlanta Falcons, June 10, 1984.
Atlanta NFL, 1984.
Games: 1984 (16).
Pro statistics: Intercepted one pass for 35 yards and a touchdown and recovered one fumble, 1984.

KENNY JACKSON
Wide Receiver—Philadelphia Eagles

Born February 15, 1962, at Neptune, N.J.
Height, 6.00. Weight, 180.
High School—South River, N.J.
Attended Penn State University.
Cousin of Tony Collins, running back with New England Patriots.

Selected by Philadelphia in 1984 USFL territorial draft.
Selected by Philadelphia in 1st round (4th player selected) of 1984 NFL draft.
Signed by Philadelphia Eagles, May 1, 1984.
On injured reserve with separated shoulder, October 22 through November 22, 1984; activated, November 23, 1984.

		—PASS RECEIVING—			
Year Club	G.	P.C.	Yds.	Avg.	TD.
1984—Philadelphia NFL	11	26	398	15.3	1

MICHAEL ANTHONY JACKSON
Linebacker—Seattle Seahawks

Born July 15, 1957, at Pasco, Wash.
Height, 6.01. Weight, 220.
High School—Pasco, Wash.
Attended University of Washington.

Selected by Seattle in 3rd round (57th player selected) of 1979 NFL draft.
On suspended list, December 26, 1982.
On injured reserve with knee injury, October 19 through November 25, 1983; activated, November 26, 1983.
On injured reserve with knee injury, October 5 through November 11, 1984; activated, November 12, 1984.

			—INTERCEPTIONS—		
Year Club	G.	No.	Yds.	Avg.	TD.
1979—Seattle NFL	15		None		
1980—Seattle NFL	15	2	9	4.5	0
1981—Seattle NFL	16	2	51	25.5	0
1982—Seattle NFL	8	2	29	14.5	0
1983—Seattle NFL	11		None		
1984—Seattle NFL	8		None		
Pro Totals—6 Years	73	6	89	14.8	0

Additional pro statistics: Recovered one fumble, 1979, 1982 and 1983; recovered two fumbles, 1980 and 1981.
Played in AFC Championship Game following 1983 season.

RICKEY ANDERSON JACKSON
Linebacker—New Orleans Saints

Born March 20, 1958, at Pahokee, Fla.
Height, 6.02. Weight, 236.
High School—Pahokee, Fla.
Attended University of Pittsburgh.

Selected by New Orleans in 2nd round (51st player selected) of 1981 NFL draft.
New Orleans NFL, 1981 through 1984.
Games: 1981 (16), 1982 (9), 1983 (16), 1984 (16). Total—57.
Pro statistics: Recovered one fumble, 1981; intercepted one pass for 32 yards and recovered two fumbles, 1982; intercepted one pass for no yards and recovered two fumbles for minus two yards, 1983; fumbled once, 1983 and 1984; recovered four fumbles for four yards and intercepted one pass for 14 yards, 1984.
Played in Pro Bowl (NFL All-Star Game) following 1983 and 1984 seasons.

ROBERT CHARLES JACKSON
(Bobby)
Cornerback—New York Jets

Born December 23, 1956, at Albany, Ga.
Height, 5.10. Weight, 180.
High School—Albany, Ga.
Received degree in criminology from Florida State University.
Cousin of Alfred Jenkins, wide receiver with Birmingham Express (WFL)
and Atlanta Falcons, 1974 through 1983.

Selected by New York Jets in 6th round (140th player selected) of 1978 NFL draft.
On injured reserve with broken arm, November 17 through December 25, 1981; activated, December 26, 1981.
On injured reserve with pulled hamstring, October 3 through remainder of 1984 season.

			—INTERCEPTIONS—		
Year Club	G.	No.	Yds.	Avg.	TD.
1978—New York Jets NFL	16	5	26	5.2	0
1979—New York Jets NFL	16	4	63	15.8	1
1980—New York Jets NFL	15	1	7	7.0	0
1981—New York Jets NFL	9		None		
1982—New York Jets NFL	9	5	84	16.8	*1
1983—New York Jets NFL	15	2	8	4.0	0
1984—New York Jets NFL	3		None		
Pro Totals—7 Years	83	17	188	11.1	2

Additional pro statistics: Recovered one fumble, 1978; recovered two fumbles for 80 yards and returned a blocked field goal 95 yards for a touchdown, 1982.
Played in AFC Championship Game following 1982 season.

ROBERT E. JACKSON
(Bob)
Guard—Cleveland Browns

Born April 1, 1953, at Charlotte, N. C.
Height, 6.05. Weight, 260.
High School—Huntersville, N. C., North Mecklenberg.
Attended Duke University.

Signed as free agent by Cleveland Browns, 1975.
Cleveland NFL, 1975 through 1984.
Games: 1975 (14), 1976 (14), 1977 (14), 1978 (16), 1979 (16), 1980 (14), 1981 (16), 1982 (9), 1983 (16), 1984 (16).
Total—145.

Pro statistics: Recovered one fumble, 1975 and 1984; recovered two fumbles for three yards, 1976; returned one kickoff for 21 yards and recovered two fumbles, 1977; returned one kickoff for 19 yards, 1978; returned one kickoff for 18 yards, 1979; returned one kickoff for no yards, 1980.

ROBERT MICHAEL JACKSON
Safety—Cincinnati Bengals
Born October 21, 1958, at Grand Rapids, Mich.
Height, 5.10. Weight, 186.
High School—Allendale, Mich.
Attended Central Michigan University.

Selected by Cincinnati in 11th round (285th player selected) of 1981 NFL draft.
On injured reserve with knee injury, August 10 through entire 1981 season.

| | | | —INTERCEPTIONS— | | |
Year Club	G.	No.	Yds.	Avg.	TD.
1982—Cincinnati NFL	9		None		
1983—Cincinnati NFL	16	2	21	10.5	0
1984—Cincinnati NFL	16	4	32	8.0	1
Pro Totals—3 Years	41	6	53	8.8	1

Additional pro statistics: Recovered one fumble, 1982; recovered three fumbles, 1984.

ROGER JACKSON
Defensive Back—Denver Broncos
Born February 28, 1959, at Macon, Ga.
Height, 6.00. Weight, 186.
High School—Macon, Ga., Central.
Received bachelor of science degree in physical education from
Bethune-Cookman College in 1982.

Signed as free agent by Denver Broncos, May 6, 1982.
Released by Denver Broncos, August 27, 1984; re-signed by Broncos, August 28, 1984.

| | | | —INTERCEPTIONS— | | |
Year Club	G.	No.	Yds.	Avg.	TD.
1982—Denver NFL	9		None		
1983—Denver NFL	16	1	15	15.0	0
1984—Denver NFL	16	1	23	23.0	0
Pro Totals—3 Years	41	2	38	19.0	0

Additional pro statistics: Recovered one fumble 1982; fumbled once, 1983.

TERENCE LEON JACKSON
(Terry)
Cornerback—Seattle Seahawks
Born December 9, 1955, at Sherman, Tex.
Height, 5.11. Weight, 197.
High School—San Diego, Calif., St. Augustine's.
Attended San Diego City College, San Diego State University and attending
Bergen County Community College.
Brother of Monte Jackson, cornerback with Los Angeles Rams and
Oakland-Los Angeles Raiders, 1975 through 1983.

Selected by New York Giants in 5th round (120th player selected) of 1978 NFL draft.
On injured reserve with dislocated shoulder, October 29 through remainder of 1980 season.
On inactive list, September 20, 1982.
Traded by New York Giants to Seattle Seahawks for 6th round pick in 1985 draft, March 12, 1984.

| | | | —INTERCEPTIONS— | | |
Year Club	G.	No.	Yds.	Avg.	TD.
1978—N.Y. Giants NFL	15	7	115	16.4	1
1979—N.Y. Giants NFL	16	3	10	3.3	0
1980—N.Y. Giants NFL	8	1	5	5.0	0
1981—N.Y. Giants NFL	16	3	57	19.0	1
1982—N.Y. Giants NFL	8	4	75	18.8	0
1983—N.Y. Giants NFL	12	6	20	3.3	0
1984—Seattle NFL	16	4	78	19.5	1
Pro Totals—7 Years	91	28	360	12.9	3

Additional pro statistics: Returned four punts for one yard, 1978; recovered one fumble, 1978 and 1981; ran 47 yards with blocked punt for a touchdown, returned one punt for five yards and recovered one fumble for minus two yards, 1979; recovered three fumbles for 11 yards, 1980; returned two punts for 22 yards, 1981; recovered one fumble for 35 yards and a touchdown, 1983.

THOMAS JACKSON
(Tom)
Linebacker—Denver Broncos
Born April 4, 1951, at Cleveland, O.
Height, 5.11. Weight, 220.
High School—Cleveland, O., John Adams.
Attended University of Louisville.

Named to THE SPORTING NEWS AFC All-Star Team, 1977.
Selected by Denver in 4th round (88th player selected) of 1973 NFL draft.

Year Club	G.	No.	Yds.	Avg.	TD.	Year Club	G.	No.	Yds.	Avg.	TD.
1973—Denver NFL	8			None		1980—Denver NFL	16			None	
1974—Denver NFL	13	1	39	39.0	0	1981—Denver NFL	16			None	
1975—Denver NFL	14	2	0	0.0	0	1982—Denver NFL	9	1	8	8.0	0
1976—Denver NFL	14	7	136	19.4	1	1983—Denver NFL	15	1	0	0.0	0
1977—Denver NFL	13	4	95	23.8	*1	1984—Denver NFL	16			None	
1978—Denver NFL	16	3	28	9.3	1	Pro Totals—12 Years	163	20	340	17.0	3
1979—Denver NFL	13	1	34	34.0	0						

Additional pro statistics: Fumbled once and recovered two fumbles, 1976; fumbled once, 1977; recovered two fumbles for 70 yards, 1979; recovered one fumble, 1981 and 1984; returned one kickoff for two yards and recovered two fumbles for 34 yards, 1983.
Played in AFC Championship Game following 1977 season.
Played in NFL Championship Game following 1977 season.
Played in Pro Bowl (NFL All-Star Game) following 1977 through 1979 seasons.

JOE JACOBY
Offensive Tackle—Washington Redskins

Born July 6, 1959, at Louisville, Ky.
Height, 6.07. Weight, 305.
High School—Louisville, Ky., Western.
Attended University of Louisville.

Named to THE SPORTING NEWS NFL All-Star Team, 1983 and 1984.
Signed as free agent by Washington Redskins, May 1, 1981.
Washington NFL, 1981 through 1984.
Games: 1981 (14), 1982 (9), 1983 (16), 1984 (16). Total—55.
Pro statistics: Recovered one fumble, 1981 and 1982; recovered fumble in end zone for a touchdown, 1984.
Played in NFC Championship Game following 1982 and 1983 seasons.
Played in NFL Championship Game following 1982 and 1983 seasons.
Played in Pro Bowl (NFL All-Star Game) following 1983 and 1984 seasons.

JESSE CRAIG JAMES
(Known by middle name.)
Running Back—New England Patriots.

Born January 2, 1961, at Jacksonville, Tex.
Height, 6.00. Weight, 215.
High School—Houston, Tex., Stratford.
Attended Southern Methodist University.
Brother of Chris James, third baseman in Philadelphia Phillies' organization.

Selected by Washington in 1st round (4th player selected) of 1983 USFL draft.
Signed by Washington Federals, January 12, 1983.
Selected by New England in 7th round (187th player selected) of 1983 NFL draft.
On developmental squad, March 19 through April 14, 1983; activated, April 15, 1983.
On developmental squad, March 9 through April 11, 1984.
Released with knee injury by Washington Federals, April 12, 1984; signed by New England Patriots, April 20, 1984.
On developmental squad for 4 games with Washington Federals in 1983.
On developmental squad for 5 games with Washington Federals in 1984.

		—RUSHING—				PASS RECEIVING				—TOTAL—		
Year Club	G.	Att.	Yds.	Avg.	TD.	P.C.	Yds.	Avg.	TD.	TD.	Pts.	F.
1983—Washington USFL	14	202	823	4.1	4	40	342	8.6	2	6	36	6
1984—Washington USFL	2	16	61	3.8	0	1	13	13.0	0	0	0	0
1984—New England NFL	15	160	790	4.9	1	22	159	7.2	0	1	6	4
USFL Totals—2 Years	16	218	884	4.1	4	41	355	8.7	2	6	36	6
NFL Totals—1 Year	15	160	790	4.9	1	22	159	7.2	0	1	6	4
Pro Totals—3 Years	31	378	1674	4.4	5	63	514	8.2	2	7	42	10

JOHN WILBUR JAMES JR.
Punter—Houston Oilers

Born January 21, 1949, at Panama City, Fla.
Height, 6.03. Weight, 196.
High School—Gainesville, Fla.
Received bachelor of arts degree in economics from University of Florida.
Uncle of Louis Berry, punter at Florida State University.

Established NFL record for most punts, season (109), 1978; most punts, career (1,083).
Named to THE SPORTING NEWS NFC All-Star Team, 1975 through 1977.
Led NFL punters in yards with 4,349 in 1977 and 4,227 in 1978.
Signed as free agent by Atlanta Falcons, 1972.
Released by Atlanta Falcons, September 6, 1982; signed as free agent by Detroit Lions, September 10, 1982.
Released by Detroit Lions, November 20, 1982; signed as free agent by Houston Oilers, December 3, 1982.

Year	Club		G.	No.	Avg.	Blk.	Year	Club		G.	No.	Avg.	Blk.
		PUNTING							**PUNTING**				
1972	Atlanta NFL		14	61	42.8	0	1979	Atlanta NFL		16	83	39.7	1
1973	Atlanta NFL		14	63	42.6	0	1980	Atlanta NFL		16	79	39.1	0
1974	Atlanta NFL		14	*96	40.5	1	1981	Atlanta NFL		16	87	40.7	1
1975	Atlanta NFL		14	89	41.5	1	1982	Det. (2)-Hou. (5) NFL		7	43	40.5	0
1976	Atlanta NFL		14	*101	42.1	0	1983	Houston NFL		16	79	39.7	1
1977	Atlanta NFL		14	*105	41.4	0	1984	Houston NFL		16	88	39.6	0
1978	Atlanta NFL		16	*109	38.8	1		Pro Totals—13 Years		187	1083	40.6	6

Additional pro statistics: Attempted one pass with one completion for 25 yards, 1975; recovered one fumble, 1976 and 1979; attempted one pass with no completions, 1977, 1980 and 1981; attempted one pass with one completion for 20 yards, 1979; rushed once for no yards, 1979 and 1983; rushed once for 13 yards, 1980; rushed once for minus seven yards, 1981; attempted one pass with one completion for seven yards, 1983.

Played in Pro Bowl (NFL All-Star Game) following 1975 through 1977 seasons.

LIONEL JAMES
Kick Returner-Running Back—San Diego Chargers
Born May 25, 1962, at Albany, Ga.
Height, 5.06. Weight, 172.
High School—Albany, Ga., Dougherty.
Attended Auburn University.

Selected by Birmingham in 1984 USFL territorial draft.
Selected by San Diego in 5th round (118th player selected) of 1984 NFL draft.
Signed by San Diego Chargers, June 8, 1984.

Year	Club		G.	Att.	Yds.	Avg.	TD.	P.C.	Yds.	Avg.	TD.	TD.	Pts.	F.
				RUSHING				**PASS RECEIVING**				**TOTAL**		
1984	San Diego NFL		16	25	115	4.6	0	23	206	9.0	0	1	6	9

Year	Club		G.	No.	Yds.	Avg.	TD.	No.	Yds.	Avg.TD.
				PUNT RETURNS				**KICKOFF RET.**		
1984	San Diego NFL		16	30	208	6.9	1	*43	*959	22.3	0

Additional pro statistics: Attempted two passes with no completions and one interception and recovered four fumbles, 1984.

ROLAND ORLANDO JAMES
Safety—New England Patriots
Born February 18, 1958, at Xenia, O.
Height, 6.02. Weight, 191.
High School—Jamestown, O., Greenview.
Attended University of Tennessee.

Named as cornerback on THE SPORTING NEWS College All-America Team, 1979.
Selected by New England in 1st round (14th player selected) of 1980 NFL draft.
On injured reserve with knee injury, January 6, 1983 through remainder of 1982 season playoffs.

Year	Club		G.	No.	Yds.	Avg.	TD.	No.	Yds.	Avg.	TD.	TD.	Pts.	F.
				INTERCEPTIONS				**PUNT RETURNS**				**TOTAL**		
1980	New England NFL		16	4	32	8.0	0	33	331	10.0	1	1	6	2
1981	New England NFL		16	2	29	14.5	0	7	56	8.0	0	0	0	1
1982	New England NFL		7	3	12	4.0	0		None			0	0	1
1983	New England NFL		16	5	99	19.8	0		None			0	0	0
1984	New England NFL		15	2	14	7.0	0		None			0	0	0
	Pro Totals—5 Years		70	16	186	11.6	0	40	387	9.7	1	1	6	4

Additional pro statistics: Recovered one fumble, 1980, 1981 and 1984; recovered four fumbles, 1983; credited with one safety, 1984.

RONNIE NATHANIEL JAMES
Fullback—Los Angeles Raiders
Born January 2, 1961, at Los Angeles, Calif.
Height, 6.02. Weight, 230.
High School—Houston, Tex., Jack Yates.
Attended Texas A&M University and Grambling State University.

Signed as free agent by Los Angeles Express, March 28, 1984.
On developmental squad, March 28 through May 10, 1984; activated, May 11, 1984.
On developmental squad, June 9 through remainder of 1984 season.
Released by Los Angeles Express, January 11, 1985; signed as free agent by Los Angeles Raiders, February 21, 1985.
On developmental squad for 9 games with Los Angeles Express in 1984.
Los Angeles USFL, 1984.
Games: 1984 (5).
Pro statistics: Returned one kickoff for seven yards, 1984.

VICTOR CEDRICK JAMES
Wide Receiver—New York Giants
Born February 6, 1961, at Los Angeles, Calif.
Height, 6.00. Weight, 190.
High School—Los Angeles, Calif., Fremont.
Attended Los Angeles Valley Junior College and University of Colorado.

Selected by Buffalo in 10th round (272nd player selected) of 1982 NFL draft.
Released by Buffalo Bills, August 2, 1982; signed by Denver Gold, Sepember 29, 1982.
Released by Denver Gold, February 20, 1984; signed as free agent by Chicago Blitz, March 14, 1984.
On developmental squad, March 14 through March 23, 1984; activated, March 24, 1984.
Franchise disbanded, November 20, 1984; signed as free agent by New York Giants, May 14, 1985.
On developmental squad for 1 game with Chicago Blitz in 1984.

Year Club		PASS RECEIVING				—KICKOFF RET.—				—TOTAL—		
	G.	P.C.	Yds.	Avg.	TD.	No.	Yds.	Avg.	TD.	TD.	Pts.	F.
1983—Denver USFL	18	25	348	13.9	4	4	51	12.8	0	4	24	0
1984—Chicago USFL	14	3	27	9.0	1	18	394	21.9	0	1	6	2
Pro Totals—2 Years	32	28	375	13.4	5	22	445	20.2	0	5	30	2

Additional pro statistics: Recovered two fumbles for minus two yards and rushed three times for 25 yards, 1983; recovered two fumbles, 1984.

JOHN MICHAEL JANATA
Offensive Tackle—Tampa Bay Buccaneers
Born April 10, 1961, at Chicago, Ill.
Height, 6.07. Weight, 255.
High School—Las Vegas, Nev., Bonanza.
Attended Antelope Valley College and University of Illinois.

Signed as free agent by Chicago Bears, May 4, 1983.
Released by Chicago Bears, August 27, 1984; signed as free agent by Tampa Bay Buccaneers, February 17, 1985.
Chicago NFL, 1983.
Games: 1983 (15).
Pro statistics: Returned one kickoff for two yards and recovered one fumble, 1983.

FREDERICK MURRAY JARMAN
(Known by middle name.)
Wide Receiver—Denver Broncos
Born January 26, 1961, at Birmingham, Ala.
Height, 6.05. Weight, 210.
High School—Boca Raton, Fla., St. Andrew's.
Attended Clemson University (did not play college football).

Selected by Denver in 12th round (326th player selected) of 1984 NFL draft.
Selected by Phoenix in 3rd round (59th player selected) of 1984 NBA draft.
Signed by Phoenix Suns, August 17, 1984.
Placed on suspended list after choosing not to report, October 8, 1984.
Signed by Denver Broncos, January 20, 1985.

RONALD VINCENT JAWORSKI
(Ron)
Quarterback—Philadelphia Eagles
Born March 23, 1951, at Lackawanna, N. Y.
Height, 6.02. Weight, 196.
High School—Lackawanna, N. Y.
Attended Youngstown State University.

Selected by Los Angeles in 2nd round (37th player selected) of 1973 NFL draft.
Member of Los Angeles Rams' taxi squad, 1973.
Traded by Los Angeles Rams to Philadelphia Eagles for tight end Charle Young, March 10, 1977.
On injured reserve with broken fibula, November 27 through remainder of 1984 season.

Year Club		PASSING						RUSHING				—TOTAL—		
	G.	Att.	Cmp.	Pct.	Gain	T.P.	P.I.	Avg.	Att.	Yds.	Avg.	TD.	TD.	Pts.	F.
1974—Los Angeles NFL	5	24	10	41.7	144	0	1	6.00	7	34	4.9	1	1	6	1
1975—Los Angeles NFL	14	48	24	50.0	302	0	2	6.29	12	33	2.8	2	2	12	1
1976—Los Angeles NFL	5	52	20	28.5	273	1	2	5.25	2	15	7.5	1	1	6	0
1977—Philadelphia NFL	14	346	166	48.0	2183	18	21	6.31	40	127	3.2	5	5	30	6
1978—Philadelphia NFL	16	398	206	51.8	2487	16	16	6.25	30	79	2.6	0	0	0	7
1979—Philadelphia NFL	16	374	190	50.8	2669	18	12	7.14	43	119	2.8	2	2	12	12
1980—Philadelphia NFL	16	451	257	57.0	3529	27	12	7.82	27	95	3.5	1	1	6	6
1981—Philadelphia NFL	16	461	250	54.2	3095	23	20	6.71	22	128	5.8	0	0	0	3
1982—Philadelphia NFL	9	286	167	58.4	2076	12	12	7.26	10	9	0.9	0	0	0	9
1983—Philadelphia NFL	16	446	235	52.7	3315	20	18	7.43	25	129	5.2	1	1	6	11
1984—Philadelphia NFL	13	427	234	54.8	2754	16	14	6.45	5	18	3.6	1	1	6	5
Pro Totals—11 Years	140	3313	1759	53.1	22827	151	133	6.89	223	786	3.5	14	14	84	61

Quarterback Rating Points: 1974 (44.3), 1975 (52.5), 1976 (22.8), 1977 (60.3), 1978 (68.0), 1979 (76.8), 1980 (90.9), 1981 (74.0), 1982 (77.5), 1983 (75.1), 1984 (73.5). Total—73.7.
Additional pro statistics: Recovered two fumbles and fumbled once for minus three yards, 1975; recovered three fumbles and fumbled six times for minus four yards, 1977; recovered three fumbles and fumbled seven times for minus one yard, 1978; recovered five fumbles and fumbled 12 times for minus 23 yards, 1979; recovered four fumbles, 1980 and 1983; recovered three fumbles and fumbled three times for minus three years, 1981; recovered four fumbles and fumbled nine times for minus 11 yards, 1982; recovered two fumbles, 1984.
Played in NFC Championship Game following 1975 and 1980 seasons.
Member of Los Angeles Rams for NFC Championship Game following 1974 and 1976 seasons; did not play.
Played in NFL Championship Game following 1980 season.
Played in Pro Bowl (NFL All-Star Game) following 1980 season.

JAMES WILSON JEFFCOAT
(Jim)
Defensive End—Dallas Cowboys

Born April 1, 1961, at Long Branch, N.J.
Height, 6.05. Weight, 257.
High School—Matawan, N.J., Regional.
Received bachelor of arts degree in communications
from Arizona State University in 1983.

Selected by Arizona in 1983 USFL territorial draft.
Selected by Dallas in 1st round (23rd player selected) of 1983 NFL draft.
Signed by Dallas Cowboys, May 24, 1983.
Dallas NFL, 1983 and 1984.
Games: 1983 (16), 1984 (16). Total—32.
Pro statistics: Recovered fumble in end zone for a touchdown, 1984.

JOHN LARRY JEFFERSON
Wide Receiver—Green Bay Packers

Born February 3, 1956, at Dallas, Tex.
Height, 6.01. Weight, 204.
High School—Dallas, Tex., Roosevelt.
Attended Arizona State University.

Named to THE SPORTING NEWS AFC All-Star Team, 1979.
Named to THE SPORTING NEWS NFL All-Star Team, 1980.
Selected by San Diego in 1st round (14th player selected) of 1978 NFL draft.
On did not report list, August 17 through September 16, 1981.
Traded with 1st round pick in 1982 draft by San Diego Chargers to Green Bay Packers for wide receiver Aundra Thompson, 1st round picks in 1982 and 1983 drafts and 2nd round picks in 1982 and 1984 drafts, September 17, 1981.

		—PASS RECEIVING—			
Year Club	G.	P.C.	Yds.	Avg.	TD.
1978—San Diego NFL	14	56	1001	17.9	*13
1979—San Diego NFL	15	61	1090	17.9	10
1980—San Diego NFL	16	82	*1340	16.3	*13
1981—Green Bay NFL	13	39	632	16.2	4
1982—Green Bay NFL	8	27	452	16.7	0
1983—Green Bay NFL	16	57	830	14.6	7
1984—Green Bay NFL	13	26	339	13.0	0
Pro Totals—7 Years	95	348	5684	16.3	47

Additional pro statistics: Rushed once for seven yards and recovered one fumble, 1978; rushed once for 16 yards and returned one kickoff for no yards, 1980; rushed twice for 22 yards and returned one kickoff for three yards, 1981; rushed two times for 16 yards, 1982; fumbled once, 1983.
Played in AFC Championship Game following 1980 season.
Played in Pro Bowl (NFL All-Star Game) following 1978 through 1980 and 1982 seasons.

THOMAS JOHN JELESKY
(Tom)
Offensive Tackle—Philadelphia Eagles

Born October 4, 1960, at Merrillville, Ind.
Height, 6.06. Weight, 290.
High School—Merrillville, Ind.
Attended Purdue University.

Signed as free agent by Philadelphia Eagles, December 14, 1983.
Selected by Denver in 14th round (277th player selected) of 1984 USFL draft.
On injured reserve with knee injury, August 27 through entire 1984 season.
Active for 1 game with Philadelphia Eagles in 1983; did not play.

KENNETH WALTON JENKINS
(Ken)
Running Back-Safety—Detroit Lions

Born May 8, 1959, at Washington, D.C.
Height, 5.08. Weight, 183.
High School—Bethesda, Md., Landon.
Attended Bucknell University.

Signed as free agent by Philadelphia Eagles, May 8, 1982.
On injured reserve with broken toe, September 6 through entire 1982 season.
Released by Philadelphia Eagles, August 29, 1983; signed as free agent by Detroit Lions, September 29, 1983.

		—RUSHING—				PASS RECEIVING				—TOTAL—		
Year Club	G.	Att.	Yds.	Avg.	TD.	P.C.	Yds.	Avg.	TD.	TD.	Pts.	F.
1983—Detroit NFL	12	None				None				0	0	2
1984—Detroit NFL	14	78	358	4.6	1	21	246	11.7	0	1	6	0
Pro Totals—2 Years	26	78	358	4.6	1	21	246	11.7	0	1	6	2

Year Club	G.	—PUNT RETURNS—				—KICKOFF RET.—			
		No.	Yds.	Avg.	TD.	No.	Yds.	Avg.TD.	
1983—Detroit NFL	12	23	230	10.0	0	22	459	20.9	0
1984—Detroit NFL	14	1	1	1.0	0	18	396	22.0	0
Pro Totals—2 Years	26	24	231	9.6	0	40	855	21.4	0

Additional pro statistics: Recovered one fumble, 1983 and 1984; attempted one pass with no completions, 1984.

RONALD NORMAN JENKINS
(Ron)
Wide Receiver—Dallas Cowboys
Born February 28, 1961, at Denver, Colo.
Height, 5.11. Weight, 166.
High School—Rohnert Park, Rancho Cotate.
Attended Santa Rosa Junior College and Colorado State University.

Signed as free agent by Dallas Cowboys, May 3, 1984.
On injured reserve with hepatitis, August 10 through entire 1984 season.

DAVID TUTHILL JENNINGS
(Dave)
Punter—New York Giants
Born June 8, 1952, at New York, N. Y.
Height, 6.04. Weight, 205.
High School—Garden City, N. Y.
Received bachelor of arts degree in economics from St. Lawrence University in 1974.
Cousin of Carlton Fisk, catcher with Chicago White Sox.

Named to THE SPORTING NEWS NFC All-Star Team, 1979.
Named to THE SPORTING NEWS NFL All-Star Team, 1980.
Led NFL punters in yards with 4,445 in 1979 and 4,211 in 1980.
Signed as free agent by Houston Oilers, 1974.
Released by Houston Oilers and signed as free agent by New York Giants, July, 1974.

Year Club	G.	—PUNTING—		
		No.	Avg.	Blk.
1974—New York Giants NFL	14	68	39.8	*2
1975—New York Giants NFL	14	76	40.9	0
1976—New York Giants NFL	14	74	41.3	3
1977—New York Giants NFL	14	100	39.9	0
1978—New York Giants NFL	16	95	42.1	0
1979—New York Giants NFL	16	*104	42.7	0
1980—New York Giants NFL	16	94	*44.8	0
1981—New York Giants NFL	16	97	43.3	0
1982—New York Giants NFL	9	49	42.8	0
1983—New York Giants NFL	16	84	40.3	1
1984—New York Giants NFL	16	90	40.0	*3
Pro Totals—11 Years	161	931	41.6	9

Additional pro statistics: Rushed once for no yards, recovered two fumbles, fumbled once for minus 13 yards and attempted one pass with one completion for minus one yard, 1978; rushed twice for 11 yards and attempted two passes with two completions for 48 yards, 1979; attempted one pass with no completions, 1983.
Played in Pro Bowl (NFL All-Star Game) following 1978 through 1980 and 1982 seasons.

STANFORD JAMISON JENNINGS
Running Back—Cincinnati Bengals
Born March 12, 1962, at Summerville, S.C.
Height, 6.01. Weight, 205.
High School—Summerville, S.C.
Attended Furman University.

Selected by Michigan in 1st round (17th player selected) of 1984 USFL draft.
Selected by Cincinnati in 3rd round (65th player selected) of 1984 NFL draft.
Signed by Cincinnati Bengals, July 2, 1984.

Year Club	G.	—RUSHING—				PASS RECEIVING				—TOTAL—		
		Att.	Yds.	Avg.	TD.	P.C.	Yds.	Avg.	TD.	TD.	Pts.	F.
1984—Cincinnati NFL	15	79	379	4.8	2	35	346	9.9	3	5	30	3

Year Club	G.	KICKOFF RETURNS		
		No.	Yds.	Avg.TD.
1984—Cincinnati NFL	15	22	452	20.5 0

Additional pro statistics: Recovered two fumbles, 1984.

DERRICK JENSEN
Tight End—Los Angeles Raiders
Born April 27, 1956, at Waukegan, Ill.
Height, 6.01. Weight, 215.
High Schools—Waukegan, Ill. and Osawatomie, Kan.
Attended University of Texas at Arlington.

Selected by Oakland in 3rd round (57th player selected) of 1978 NFL draft.
On injured reserve, August 29 through entire 1978 season.
Franchise transferred to Los Angeles, May 7, 1982.

| Year Club | G. | —RUSHING— | | | | PASS RECEIVING | | | | —TOTAL— | | |
		Att.	Yds.	Avg.	TD.	P.C.	Yds.	Avg.	TD.	TD.	Pts.	F.
1979—Oakland NFL	16	73	251	3.4	0	7	23	3.3	1	1	6	6
1980—Oakland NFL	16	14	30	2.1	0	7	87	12.4	0	1	6	1
1981—Oakland NFL	16	117	456	3.9	4	28	271	9.7	0	4	24	0
1982—Los Angeles Raiders NFL	9		None				None			0	0	0
1983—Los Angeles Raiders NFL	16	1	5	5.0	0	1	2	2.0	1	1	6	1
1984—Los Angeles Raiders NFL	16	3	3	1.0	1	1	1	1.0	1	2	12	0
Pro Totals—6 Years	89	208	745	3.6	5	44	384	8.7	3	9	54	8

Additional pro statistics: Recovered three fumbles, 1979, returned one kickoff for no yards, 1979 and 1983; returned one kickoff for 33 yards and a touchdown, 1980; recovered one fumble, 1981; returned one kickoff for 27 yards, 1982; returned one kickoff for 11 yards, 1984.
Played in AFC Championship Game following 1980 and 1983 seasons.
Played in NFL Championship Game following 1980 and 1983 seasons.

JAMES CHRISTOPHER JENSEN
(Jim)
Wide Receiver—Miami Dolphins
Born November 14, 1958, at Abington, Pa.
Height, 6.04. Weight, 215.
High School—Doylestown, Pa., Central Bucks.
Received bachelor of science degree in special education from Boston University in 1981.

Selected by Miami in 11th round (291st player selected) of 1981 NFL draft.
On inactive list, September 12 and September 19, 1982.

| Year Club | G. | —PASS RECEIVING— | | | |
		P.C.	Yds.	Avg.	TD.
1981—Miami NFL	16		None		
1982—Miami NFL	6		None		
1983—Miami NFL	16		None		
1984—Miami NFL	16	13	139	10.7	2
Pro Totals—4 Years	54	13	139	10.7	2

Additional pro statistics: Attempted one pass with no completions, 1982; attempted one pass with one completion for 35 yards and a touchdown, 1984.
Played in AFC Championship Game following 1982 and 1984 seasons.
Played in NFL Championship Game following 1982 and 1984 seasons.

RUSSELL D. JENSEN
(Russ)
Quarterback—Los Angeles Raiders
Born July 13, 1961, at La Mirada, Calif.
Height, 6.02. Weight, 220.
High School—La Mirada, Calif.
Attended San Francisco State University and California Lutheran College.

Selected by Los Angeles in 1983 USFL territorial draft.
Signed by Los Angeles Express, January 20, 1983.
On developmental squad, March 4 through July 1, 1983; activated, July 2, 1983.
On developmental squad, February 24 through June 21, 1984; activated, June 22, 1984.
On developmental squad, February 24 through February 27, 1985.
Left Los Angeles Express voluntarily and granted roster exemption, February 28 through March 3, 1985.
Released by Los Angeles Express, March 4, 1985; signed as free agent by Los Angeles Raiders, March 20, 1985.
On developmental squad for 17 games with Los Angeles Express in 1983.
On developmental squad for 17 games with Los Angeles Express in 1984.
On developmental squad for 1 game with Los Angeles Express in 1985.

| Year Club | G. | —PASSING— | | | | | | | —RUSHING— | | | | —TOTAL— | | |
		Att.	Cmp.	Pct.	Gain	T.P.	P.I.	Avg.	Att.	Yds.	Avg.	TD.	TD.	Pts.	F.
1984—Los Angeles USFL	1	6	2	33.3	33	0	1	5.50		None			0	0	0

Quarterback Rating Points: 1984 (13.2).

MARK DARRELL JERUE
Linebacker—Los Angeles Rams
Born January 15, 1960, at Seattle, Wash.
Height, 6.03. Weight, 229.
High School—Mercer Island, Wash.
Attended University of Washington.

Selected by New York Jets in 5th round (135th player selected) of 1982 NFL draft.
On injured reserve with heart irregularity, August 24 through entire 1982 season.
Released by New York Jets, August 29, 1983; awarded on waivers to Baltimore Colts, August 30, 1983.
Traded by Baltimore Colts to Los Angeles Rams for quarterback Mark Reed, August 30, 1983.
USFL rights traded with rights to running back Ted McKnight and 1st and 5th round picks in 1984 draft by Jacksonville Bulls to Oakland Invaders for rights to quarterback Turk Schonert, October 24, 1983.
Los Angeles Rams NFL, 1983 and 1984.
Games: 1983 (16), 1984 (16). Total—32.

GARY MICHAEL JETER
Defensive End—Los Angeles Rams
Born January 24, 1955, at Weirton, W. Va.
Height, 6.04. Weight, 260.
High School—Cleveland, O., Cathedral Latin.
Attended University of Southern California.
Nephew of Bob Jeter, back with Green Bay Packers and Chicago Bears, 1963 through 1973;
and Tony Jeter, end with Pittsburgh Steelers, 1966 and 1968.

Selected by New York Giants in 1st round (5th player selected) of 1977 NFL draft.
On injured reserve with knee injury, December 8 through remainder of 1978 season.
On injured reserve with knee injury, September 1 through October 1, 1981; activated, October 2, 1981.
On inactive list, September 20, 1982.
On injured reserve with knee injury, November 24 through December 23, 1982; activated, December 24, 1982.
Traded by New York Giants to Los Angeles Rams for 3rd and 6th round picks in 1983 draft, April 13, 1983.
On injured reserve with herniated disc, August 28 through November 8, 1984; activated, November 9, 1984.
New York Giants NFL, 1977 through 1982; Los Angeles Rams NFL, 1983 and 1984.
Games: 1977 (14), 1978 (13), 1979 (16), 1980 (16), 1981 (12), 1982 (4), 1983 (16), 1984 (5). Total—96.
Pro statistics: Recovered one fumble, 1978 and 1979; recovered three fumbles for seven yards, 1980.

PAUL V. JOHNS
Wide Receiver—Seattle Seahawks
Born November 14, 1958, at Waco, Tex.
Height, 5.11. Weight, 170.
High School—Wichita Falls, Tex., S.H. Rider.
Attended Tyler Junior College and University of Tulsa.
Brother of Freeman Johns, wide receiver with Los Angeles Rams
and Saskatchewan Roughriders, 1976 through 1979.

Signed as free agent by Seattle Seahawks, April 30, 1981.
On injured reserve with ruptured disc in neck, September 28 through remainder on 1984 season.
Expected to miss 1985 season.

		PASS RECEIVING				-PUNT RETURNS-				—KICKOFF RET.—				—TOTAL—		
Year	Club	G.	P.C.	Yds.	Avg.	TD.	No.	Yds.	Avg.	TD.	No.	Yds.	Avg.	TD.	TD.	Pts.	F.
1981—Seattle NFL		16	8	131	16.4	1	16	177	11.1	0	5	81	16.2	0	1	6	1
1982—Seattle NFL		9	15	234	15.6	1	19	210	11.1	0	3	57	19.0	0	1	6	2
1983—Seattle NFL		11	34	486	14.3	4	28	316	11.3	*1		None			5	30	1
1984—Seattle NFL		4	17	207	12.2	1	11	140	12.7	1		None			2	12	2
Pro Totals—4 Years		40	74	1058	14.3	7	74	843	11.4	2	8	138	17.3	0	9	54	6

Additional pro statistics: Rushed once for minus one yard, 1982; rushed twice for 12 yards and recovered two fumbles, 1983.
Played in AFC Championship Game following 1983 season.

BOBBY JOHNSON
Wide Receiver—New York Giants
Born December 14, 1961, at East St. Louis, Ill.
Height, 5.11. Weight, 171.
High School—East St. Louis, Ill., Assumption.
Attended Independence Junior College and Kansas University.

Selected by Philadelphia in 3rd round (65th player selected) of 1984 USFL draft.
Signed by Philadelphia Stars, February 7, 1984.
Released by Philadelphia Stars, February 20, 1984; signed as free agent by New York Giants, May 16, 1984.

		——PASS RECEIVING——				
Year	Club	G.	P.C.	Yds.	Avg.	TD.
1984—N.Y. Giants NFL		16	48	795	16.6	7

BOBBY CHARLES JOHNSON
Safety—New Orleans Saints
Born September 1, 1960, at La Grange, Tex.
Height, 6.00. Weight, 186.
High School—La Grange, Tex.
Attended University of Texas.
Brother of Johnnie Johnson, safety with Los Angeles Rams.

Signed as free agent by Dallas Cowboys, May 4, 1982.
Released by Dallas Cowboys, September 6, 1982; signed as free agent by New Orleans Saints, June 27, 1983.
Released by New Orleans Saints, August 29, 1983; re-signed by Saints, August 30, 1983.

		——INTERCEPTIONS——				
Year	Club	G.	No.	Yds.	Avg.	TD.
1983—New Orleans NFL		16	2	80	40.0	1
1984—New Orleans NFL		16	1	7	7.0	0
Pro Totals—2 Years		32	3	87	29.0	1

Additional pro statistics: Recovered one fumble and fumbled once, 1983.

CECIL ELLORD JOHNSON
Linebacker—Tampa Bay Buccaneers
Born August 19, 1955, at Miami, Fla.
Height, 6.02. Weight, 235.
High School—Miami, Fla., Jackson.
Received bachelor of arts degree in sociology from University of Pittsburgh.
Brother of Robert Johnson, drummer with K.C. and the Sunshine Band.

Signed as free agent by Tampa Bay Buccaneers, May, 1977.
On injured reserve with foot and back injuries, October 5 through remainder of 1983 season.
On injured reserve with knee injury, October 26 through remainder of 1984 season.

Year Club	G.	No.	Yds.	Avg.	TD.	Year Club	G.	No.	Yds.	Avg.	TD.
1977—Tampa Bay NFL	13	1	0	0.0	0	1982—Tampa Bay NFL	9	None			
1978—Tampa Bay NFL	13	2	5	2.5	0	1983—Tampa Bay NFL	5	None			
1979—Tampa Bay NFL	15		None			1984—Tampa Bay NFL	8	None			
1980—Tampa Bay NFL	16		None			Pro Totals—8 Years	95	8	89	11.1	0
1981—Tampa Bay NFL	16	5	84	16.8	0						

Additional pro statistics: Fumbled once, 1977 and 1981; recovered four fumbles, 1977 and 1979; recovered two fumbles, 1978.
Played in NFC Championship Game following 1979 season.

CHARLES JOHNSON
(Charlie)
Nose Tackle—Minnesota Vikings
Born January 17, 1952, at West Columbia, Tex.
Height, 6.03. Weight, 282.
High School—Columbia, Tex.
Attended Tyler Junior College and University of Colorado.
Spent two years in Army, including tour in Vietnam, before entering junior college.

Named to THE SPORTING NEWS NFC All-Star Team, 1979.
Selected by Philadelphia in 7th round (175th player selected) of 1977 NFL draft.
On injured reserve, December 6 through remainder of 1977 season.
Traded by Philadelphia Eagles to Minnesota Vikings for 2nd round pick in 1983 draft, August 19, 1982.
Philadelphia NFL, 1977 through 1981; Minnesota NFL, 1982 through 1984.
Games: 1977 (12), 1978 (16), 1979 (16), 1980 (16), 1981 (16), 1982 (9), 1983 (16), 1984 (16). Total—117.
Pro statistics: Recovered two fumbles, 1977 and 1981; recovered one fumble, 1978; recovered two fumbles for minus one yard, 1979; intercepted three passes for nine yards, 1980; intercepted one pass for no yards, 1981; recovered one fumble for 44 yards and a touchdown, 1982; intercepted one pass for two yards and recovered one fumble for 50 yards and a touchdown, 1983.
Played in NFC Championship Game following 1980 season.
Played in NFL Championship Game following 1980 season.
Played in Pro Bowl (NFL All-Star Game) following 1979 through 1981 seasons.

DANIEL JEROME JOHNSON
(Dan)
Tight End—Miami Dolphins
Born May 17, 1960, at Minneapolis, Minn.
Height, 6.03. Weight, 240.
High School—New Hope, Minn., Cooper.
Attended Golden Valley Lutheran Junior College and Iowa State University.

Selected by Miami in 7th round (170th player selected) of 1982 NFL draft.
On injured reserve with shin splints, September 6 through entire 1982 season.

		—PASS RECEIVING—				
Year Club	G.	P.C.	Yds.	Avg.	TD.	
1983—Miami NFL	16	24	189	7.9	4	
1984—Miami NFL	16	34	426	12.5	3	
Pro Totals—2 Years	32	58	615	10.6	7	

Additional pro statistics: Fumbled once, 1983.
Played in AFC Championship Game following 1984 season.
Played in NFL Championship Game following 1984 season.

DEMETRIOUS JOHNSON
Defensive Back—Detroit Lions
Born July 21, 1961, at St. Louis, Mo.
Height, 5.11. Weight, 190.
High School—St. Louis, Mo., McKinley.
Attended University of Missouri.

Selected by Denver in 1st round (9th player selected) of 1983 USFL draft.
Selected by Detroit in 5th round (115th player selected) of 1983 NFL draft.
Signed by Detroit Lions, June 1, 1983.
Detroit NFL, 1983 and 1984.
Games: 1983 (14), 1984 (16). Total—30.
Pro statistics: Recovered one fumble, 1983 and 1984; returned one punt for no yards, 1984.

DENNIS CRAIG JOHNSON
Linebacker—Minnesota Vikings
Born June 19, 1958, at Flint, Mich.
Height, 6.03. Weight, 235.
High School—Flint, Mich., Northwestern.
Attended University of Southern California.

Named as linebacker on THE SPORTING NEWS College All-America Team, 1979.
Selected by Minnesota in 4th round (92nd player selected) of 1980 NFL draft.
On injured reserve with knee injury, September 2 through October 3, 1980; activated, October 4, 1980.
Minnesota NFL, 1980 through 1984.
Games: 1980 (12), 1981 (16), 1982 (9), 1983 (16), 1984 (16). Total—69.
Pro statistics: Recovered one fumble, 1980 and 1984; recovered two fumbles, 1982.

EDDIE JOHNSON
Linebacker—Cleveland Browns
Born February 3, 1959, at Albany, Ga.
Height, 6.01. Weight, 215.
High School—Albany, Ga., Daughtery.
Attended University of Louisville.

Selected by Cleveland in 7th round (187th player selected) of 1981 NFL draft.
Cleveland NFL, 1981 through 1984.
Games: 1981 (16), 1982 (9), 1983 (16), 1984 (16). Total—57.
Pro statistics: Returned one kickoff for seven yards and recovered one fumble, 1981; intercepted two passes for three yards, 1984.

EZRA RAY JOHNSON
Defensive End—Green Bay Packers
Born October 2, 1955, at Shreveport, La.
Height, 6.04. Weight, 259.
High School—Shreveport, La., Green Oaks.
Attended Morris Brown College.

Selected by Green Bay in 1st round (28th player selected) of 1977 NFL draft.
On injured reserve with knee injury, December 14 through remainder of 1984 season.
Green Bay NFL, 1977 through 1984.
Games: 1977 (14), 1978 (16), 1979 (11), 1980 (15), 1981 (16), 1982 (9), 1983 (16), 1984 (13). Total—110.
Pro statistics: Recovered one fumble, 1977; recovered two fumbles and returned one kickoff for 14 yards, 1978; recovered two fumbles, 1983.
Played in Pro Bowl (NFL All-Star Game) following 1978 season.

GARY LYNN JOHNSON
Defensive Tackle—San Francisco 49ers
Born August 31, 1952, at Shreveport, La.
Height, 6.02. Weight, 251.
High School—Bossier City, La., Mitchell.
Attended Grambling State University.

Named to THE SPORTING NEWS NFL All-Star Team, 1980.
Selected by San Diego in 1st round (8th player selected) of 1975 NFL draft.
Traded by San Diego Chargers to San Francisco 49ers for 5th and 11th picks in 1986 draft, September 28, 1984.
San Diego NFL, 1975 through 1983; San Diego (4)-San Francisco (12) NFL, 1984.
Games: 1975 (14), 1976 (14), 1977 (14), 1978 (15), 1979 (16), 1980 (16), 1981 (16), 1982 (9), 1983 (16), 1984 (16). Total—146.
Pro statistics: Recovered one fumble, 1975, 1977 and 1981; intercepted one pass for 52 yards and a touchdown, 1978; recovered two fumbles for 36 yards and fumbled once, 1979; recovered three fumbles, 1980; intercepted one pass for 41 yards and a touchdown, 1981; credited with one safety, 1982 and 1984; recovered two fumbles, 1983; recovered three fumbles for 36 yards and a touchdown, 1984.
Played in AFC Championship Game following 1980 and 1981 seasons.
Played in NFC Championship Game following 1984 season.
Played in NFL Championship Game following 1984 season.
Played in Pro Bowl (NFL All-Star Game) following 1979 through 1982 seasons.

JOHNNIE JOHNSON JR.
Safety—Los Angeles Rams
Born October 8, 1956, at La Grange, Tex.
Height, 6.01. Weight, 183.
High School—La Grange, Tex.
Attended University of Texas.
Brother of Bobby Johnson, safety with New Orleans Saints.

Named as safety on THE SPORTING NEWS College All-America Team, 1980.
Selected by Los Angeles in 1st round (17th player selected) of 1980 NFL draft.
On injured reserve with broken ankle, August 28 through October 16, 1984; activated, October 17, 1984.

Year Club	G.	No.	Yds.	Avg.TD.	Year Club	G.	No.	Yds.	Avg.TD.
1980—L.A. Rams NFL	16	3	102	34.0 1	1983—L.A. Rams NFL	16	4	115	28.8 *2
1981—L.A. Rams NFL	16		None		1984—L.A. Rams NFL	9	2	21	10.5 0
1982—L.A. Rams NFL	9	1	7	7.0 0	Pro Totals—5 Years	66	10	245	24.5 3

Additional pro statistics: Returned one punt for three yards, 1980 and 1984; recovered five fumbles for 16 yards, 1980; returned one punt for 39 yards and recovered five fumbles for five yards, 1981; recovered two fumbles for nine yards, 1982; returned 14 punts for 109 yards, recovered two fumbles for four yards and fumbled once, 1983.

KENNETH EUGENE JOHNSON
(Ken)
Defensive End—Buffalo Bills

Born March 25, 1955, at Nashville, Tenn.
Height, 6.05. Weight, 253.
High School—Nashville, Tenn., Stratford.
Attended Knoxville College.

Selected by Buffalo in 4th round (83rd player selected) of 1979 NFL draft.
On injured reserve with ankle injury, August 28 through November 28, 1979; activated, November 29, 1979.
Buffalo NFL, 1979 through 1984.
Games: 1979 (3), 1980 (16), 1981 (16), 1982 (6), 1983 (16), 1984 (16). Total—73.
Pro statistics: Credited with one safety, 1980; recovered one fumble, 1983 and 1984.

KENNETH RAY JOHNSON
(Kenny)
Cornerback—Atlanta Falcons

Born January 7, 1958, at Columbia, Miss.
Height, 5.11. Weight, 176.
High School—Moss Point, Miss.
Attended Mississippi State University.

Selected by Atlanta in 5th round (137th player selected) of 1980 NFL draft.
Tied NFL record for most touchdowns scored by interception, game (2), against Green Bay Packers, November 27, 1983.

			INTERCEPTIONS			–PUNT RETURNS–			—KICKOFF RET.—				—TOTAL—		
Year	Club	G.	No.	Yds.	Avg. TD.	No.	Yds.	Avg. TD.	No.	Yds.	Avg. TD.		TD.	Pts.	F.
1980—Atlanta NFL		16	4	49	12.3	0	23	281	12.2	0	None			0	0	2
1981—Atlanta NFL		16	3	35	11.7	0	4	6	1.5	0	None			2	12	1
1982—Atlanta NFL		9	2	30	15.0	0	None			None				0	0	0
1983—Atlanta NFL		16	2	57	28.5	*2	None			11	224	20.4	0	2	12	1
1984—Atlanta NFL		16	5	75	15.0	0	10	79	7.9	0	19	359	18.9	0	0	0	2
Pro Totals—5 Years		73	16	246	15.4	2	37	366	9.9	0	30	583	19.4	0	4	24	6

Additional pro statistics: Recovered four fumbles for seven yards, 1980; recovered two fumbles for 55 yards and two touchdowns, 1981; recovered one fumble, 1983.

LAWRENCE WENDELL JOHNSON
Cornerback—Buffalo Bills

Born September 11, 1957, at Gary, Ind.
Height, 5.11. Weight, 204.
High School—Gary, Ind., Roosevelt.
Attended University of Wisconsin.

Named as cornerback on THE SPORTING NEWS College All-America Team, 1978.
Selected by Cleveland in 2nd round (40th player selected) of 1979 NFL draft.
On injured reserve with shoulder injury, September 17 through remainder of 1980 season.
On injured reserve with knee injury, December 29 through remainder of 1982 season.
Traded by Cleveland Browns to Buffalo Bills for draft choice, October 9, 1984.

		——INTERCEPTIONS——			
Year	Club	G.	No.	Yds.	Avg.TD.
1979—Cleveland NFL		16		None	
1980—Cleveland NFL		2	1	3	3.0	0
1981—Cleveland NFL		16		None	
1982—Cleveland NFL		8	4	17	4.3	0
1983—Cleveland NFL		16	2	0	0.0	0
1984—Cle. (6)-Buf. (10) NFL		16	1	0	0.0	0
Pro Totals—6 Years		74	8	20	2.5	0

Additional pro statistics: Recovered one fumble, 1980 and 1982.

MICHAEL McCOLLY JOHNSON
(Butch)
Wide Receiver—Denver Broncos

Born May 28, 1954, at Los Angeles, Calif.
Height, 6.01. Weight, 191.
High School—Los Angeles, Calif., Dorsey.
Attended University of California at Riverside.
Brother-in-law of singer-songwriter Bill Withers;
cousin of former Massachusetts Senator Edward Brooke.

Tied NFL record for most punt returns, game (9), against Buffalo Bills, November 15, 1976.
Selected by Dallas in 3rd round (87th player selected) of 1976 NFL draft.
On injured reserve with broken finger, August 29 through October 4, 1979; activated, October 5, 1979.
Traded with 2nd round pick in 1984 draft by Dallas Cowboys to Houston Oilers for wide receiver Mike Renfro, 2nd round pick in 1984 draft and 5th round pick in 1985 draft, April 13, 1984.
Traded by Houston Oilers to Denver Broncos for 3rd round pick in 1985 draft, August 20, 1984.

Year Club	G.	PASS RECEIVING P.C. Yds. Avg. TD.				-PUNT RETURNS- No. Yds. Avg. TD.				—KICKOFF RET.— No. Yds. Avg. TD.				—TOTAL— TD. Pts. F.		
1976—Dallas NFL	14	5	84	16.8	2	45	489	10.9	0	28	693	24.8	0	2	12	5
1977—Dallas NFL	14	12	135	11.3	1	50	423	8.5	0	22	536	24.4	0	1	6	4
1978—Dallas NFL	16	12	155	12.9	0	51	401	7.9	0	29	603	20.8	0	0	0	5
1979—Dallas NFL	11	6	105	17.5	1		None				None			1	6	0
1980—Dallas NFL	16	19	263	13.8	4		None				None			4	24	0
1981—Dallas NFL	16	25	552	22.1	5		None				None			5	30	0
1982—Dallas NFL	9	12	269	22.4	3		None				None			3	18	0
1983—Dallas NFL	16	41	561	13.7	3		None				None			3	18	0
1984—Denver NFL	16	42	587	14.0	6		None				None			6	36	1
Pro Totals—9 Years	128	174	2711	15.6	25	146	1313	9.0	0	79	1832	23.2	0	25	150	15

Additional pro statistics: Recovered two fumbles, 1976 and 1977; rushed once for minus three yards, 1977; recovered one fumble, 1978; rushed once for 13 yards, 1979; rushed once for nine yards, 1982; rushed once for no yards, 1983; rushed once for three yards, 1984.

Played in NFC Championship Game following 1977, 1978 and 1980 through 1982 seasons.
Played in NFL Championship Game following 1977 and 1978 seasons.

MIKE JOHNSON
Defensive End—Houston Oilers
Born April 24, 1962, at Chicago, Ill.
Height, 6.05, Weight, 253.
High School—Chicago, Ill., South Shore.
Attended Arizona Western College and University of Illinois.

Selected by Chicago in 1984 USFL territorial draft.
Selected by Houston in 9th round (228th player selected) of 1984 NFL draft.
Signed by Houston Oilers, July 7, 1984.
Houston NFL, 1984.
Games: 1984 (16).
Pro statistics: Recovered one fumble, 1984.

NATHANIEL JOHNSON
(Nate)
Wide Receiver—Cleveland Browns
Born May 12, 1957, at St. Petersburg, Fla.
Height, 5.11. Weight, 192.
High School—St. Petersburg, Fla., Dixie Hollins.
Attended Mott Community College and received bachelor of arts degree
in sociology from Hillsdale College in 1980.

Selected by Pittsburgh in 7th round (193rd player selected) of 1980 NFL draft.
Released by Pittsburgh Steelers, August 25, 1980; signed as free agent by New York Giants, September 2, 1980.
Released by New York Giants, July 20, 1981; awarded on waivers to Baltimore Colts, July 22, 1981.
Released by Baltimore Colts, August 25, 1981; signed as free agent by Winnipeg Blue Bombers, March 12, 1982.
Traded with quarterback Nickie Hall and defensive lineman Jason Riley by Winnipeg Blue Bombers to Saskatchewan Roughriders for quarterback John Hufnagel and defensive lineman J.C. Pelusi, October 1, 1983.
Traded by Saskatchewan Roughriders to Calgary Stampeders for defensive back Lepoleon Ingram, June 11, 1984.
Released by Calgary Stampeders, August 20, 1984; signed as free agent by Cleveland Browns, February 21, 1985.

Year Club	G.	PASS RECEIVING P.C. Yds. Avg. TD.				-PUNT RETURNS- No. Yds. Avg. TD.				—KICKOFF RET.— No. Yds. Avg. TD.				—TOTAL— TD. Pts. F.		
1980—N.Y. Giants NFL	16		None				None			5	89	17.8	0	0	0	0
1982—Winnipeg CFL	13	24	368	15.3	4	17	171	10.1	0	22	587	26.7	0	4	24	1
1983—Winn (7)-Sas (4) CFL	11	19	365	19.2	3	13	158	12.2	0	16	459	28.7	0	3	18	2
1984—Calgary CFL	7	21	270	12.9	3	27	211	7.8	0	11	194	17.6	0	3	18	2
NFL Totals—1 Year	16	0	0	0.0	0	0	0	0.0	0	5	89	17.8	0	0	0	0
CFL Totals—3 Years	31	64	1003	15.7	10	57	540	9.5	0	49	1240	25.3	0	10	60	5
Pro Totals—4 Years	47	64	1003	15.7	10	57	540	9.5	0	54	1329	24.6	0	10	60	5

Additional CFL statistics: Rushed once for 11 yards, 1984.

NORM JOHNSON
Placekicker—Seattle Seahawks
Born May 31, 1960, at Inglewood, Calif.
Height, 6.02. Weight, 193.
High School—Garden Grove, Calif., Pacifica.
Attended University of California at Los Angeles.
Brother of Mitchell Johnson, lineman at University of California at Los Angeles.

Named to THE SPORTING NEWS NFL All-Star Team, 1984.
Signed as free agent by Seattle Seahawks, May 4, 1982.

Year Club	——PLACE KICKING—— G. XP. XPM. FG. FGA. Pts.					
1982—Seattle NFL	9	13	1	10	14	43
1983—Seattle NFL	16	49	1	18	25	103
1984—Seattle NFL	16	50	1	20	24	110
Pro Totals—3 Years	41	112	3	48	63	256

Additional pro statistics: Attempted one pass with one completion for 27 yards, 1982.
Played in AFC Championship Game following 1983 season.
Played in Pro Bowl (NFL All-Star Game) following 1984 season.

PETE JOHNSON
Fullback—Miami Dolphins
Born March 2, 1954, at Peach County, Ga.
Height, 6.00. Weight, 250.
High Schools—Peach County, Ga. and Long Beach, N. Y.
Attended Ohio State University.

Selected by Cincinnati in 2nd round (49th player selected) of 1977 NFL draft.
On suspended list for drug use, July 25 through September 25, 1983; reinstated, September 26, 1983.
On reserve/non-football injury list with calf injury, September 26 through October 9, 1983; activated, October 10, 1983.
Traded by Cincinnati Bengals to San Diego Chargers for running back James Brooks, May 29, 1984.
Traded by San Diego Chargers to Miami Dolphins for 2nd round pick in 1985 draft and NFL rights to defensive tackle Dewey Forte, September 22, 1984.

		—RUSHING—				PASS RECEIVING				—TOTAL—		
Year Club	G.	Att.	Yds.	Avg.	TD.	P.C.	Yds.	Avg.	TD.	TD.	Pts.	F.
1977—Cincinnati NFL	14	153	585	3.8	4	5	49	9.8	0	4	24	1
1978—Cincinnati NFL	16	180	762	4.2	7	31	236	7.6	0	7	42	4
1979—Cincinnati NFL	16	243	865	3.6	14	24	154	6.4	1	15	90	6
1980—Cincinnati NFL	12	186	747	4.0	6	21	172	8.2	1	7	42	2
1981—Cincinnati NFL	16	274	1077	3.9	12	46	320	7.0	4	16	96	4
1982—Cincinnati NFL	9	156	622	4.0	7	31	267	8.6	0	7	42	1
1983—Cincinnati NFL	11	210	763	3.6	14	15	129	8.6	0	14	84	2
1984—San Diego (3)-Miami (13) NFL	16	87	205	2.4	12	2	7	3.5	0	12	72	1
Pro Totals—8 Years	110	1489	5626	3.8	76	175	1334	7.6	6	82	492	21

Additional pro statistics: Returned one kickoff for 11 yards, 1977; recovered one fumble, 1977 and 1979 through 1983; recovered two fumbles for minus two yards, 1978; recovered two fumbles, 1984.
Played in AFC Championship Game following 1981 and 1984 seasons.
Played in NFL Championship Game following 1981 season.
Member of Miami Dolphins for NFL Championship Game following 1984 season; did not play.

RANDY S. JOHNSON
Running Back—Buffalo Bills
Born April 11, 1960, at Dallas, Tex.
Height, 5.11. Weight, 205.
High School—Dallas, Tex., Thomas Jefferson.
Attended University of Texas at Arlington.

Selected by Arizona in 9th round (183rd player selected) of 1984 USFL draft.
Signed by Arizona Wranglers, January 14, 1984.
On developmental squad, February 24 through May 10, 1984; activated, May 11, 1984.
Not protected in merger of Arizona Wranglers and Oklahoma Outlaws; selected by Orlando Renegades in USFL dispersal draft, December 6, 1984.
Released by Orlando Renegades, March 13, 1985; signed as free agent by Buffalo Bills, May 10, 1985.
On developmental squad for 11 games with Arizona Wranglers in 1984.

		—RUSHING—				PASS RECEIVING				—TOTAL—		
Year Club	G.	Att.	Yds.	Avg.	TD.	P.C.	Yds.	Avg.	TD.	TD.	Pts.	F.
1984—Arizona USFL	7	13	53	4.1	0	None				0	0	0
1985—Orlando USFL	3	6	19	3.2	0	3	29	9.7	0	0	0	0
Pro Totals—2 Years	10	19	72	3.8	0	3	29	9.7	0	0	0	0

Played in USFL Championship Game following 1984 season.

ROBERT LEE JOHNSON
(Bobby)
Running Back—Los Angeles Raiders
Born September 30, 1962, at Monterey, Calif.
Height, 6.02. Weight, 195.
High School—Monterey, Calif.
Attended Monterey Peninsula College and San Jose State University.

Selected by Oakland in 1984 USFL territorial draft.
Selected by Kansas City in 11th round (285th player selected) of 1984 NFL draft.
Signed by Kansas City Chiefs, July 9, 1984.
On injured reserve with foot injury, August 13 through October 9, 1984.
Released by Kansas City Chiefs, October 10, 1984; signed as free agent by Los Angeles Raiders, February 19, 1985.

RON JOHNSON
Safety—Pittsburgh Steelers
Born June 8, 1956, at Detroit, Mich.
Height, 5.11. Weight, 195.
High School—Detroit, Mich., Northwestern.
Attended Eastern Michigan University.

Selected by Pittsburgh in 1st round (22nd player selected) of 1978 NFL draft.

	—INTERCEPTIONS—						—INTERCEPTIONS—			
Year Club	G.	No.	Yds.	Avg.TD.		Year Club	G.	No.	Yds.	Avg.TD.
1978—Pittsburgh NFL	16	4	24	6.0	0	1982—Pittsburgh NFL	9	2	5	2.5	0
1979—Pittsburgh NFL	11	1	20	20.0	0	1983—Pittsburgh NFL	12	3	84	28.0	1
1980—Pittsburgh NFL	16	1	19	19.0	0	1984—Pittsburgh NFL	15			None	
1981—Pittsburgh NFL	12	2	8	4.0	0	Pro Totals—7 Years	91	13	160	12.3	1

Additional pro statistics: Recovered one fumble, 1978 and 1979; recovered one fumble for five yards, 1983.
Played in AFC Championship Game following 1978, 1979 and 1984 seasons.
Played in NFL Championship Game following 1978 and 1979 seasons.

WILLIAM ARTHUR JOHNSON
(Billy White Shoes)
Wide Receiver—Atlanta Falcons
Born January 21, 1952, at Bouthwyn, Pa.
Height, 5.09. Weight, 177.
High School—Boothwyn, Pa., Chichester.
Attended Widener College.

Tied NFL record for most touchdowns, combined returns, season (4), 1975.
Named to THE SPORTING NEWS NFL All-Star Team, 1983.
Selected by Houston in 15th round (365th player selected) of 1974 NFL draft.
On injured reserve with knee injury, November 10 through remainder of 1978 season.
On injured reserve with knee injury, September 11 through remainder of 1979 season.
Granted free agency, February 2, 1981; signed by Montreal Alouettes, May 19, 1981.
Released by Montreal Concordes, April 15, 1982; signed as free agent by Atlanta Falcons, July 20, 1982.
On injured reserve with knee injury, October 9 through remainder of 1984 season.
Played for Philadelphia Athletics of American Professional Slo-Pitch Softball League, 1978.

| | | —RUSHING— | | | PASS RECEIVING | | | | —TOTAL— | | |
Year Club	G.	Att.	Yds.	Avg. TD.	P.C.	Yds.	Avg.	TD.	TD.	Pts.	F.
1974—Houston NFL	14	5	82	16.4 1	29	388	13.4	2	3	18	1
1975—Houston NFL	14	5	17	3.4 0	37	393	10.6	1	5	30	5
1976—Houston NFL	14	6	6	1.0 0	47	495	10.5	4	4	24	3
1977—Houston NFL	14	6	102	17.0 1	20	412	20.6	3	7	42	2
1978—Houston NFL	5		None		1	10	10.0	0	0	0	0
1979—Houston NFL	2		None		6	108	18.0	1	1	6	0
1980—Houston NFL	16	2	1	0.5 0	31	343	11.1	2	2	12	1
1981—Montreal CFL	16	1	—9	—9.0 0	65	1060	16.3	5	5	30	3
1982—Atlanta NFL	9		None		2	11	5.5	0	0	0	1
1983—Atlanta NFL	16	15	83	5.5 0	64	709	11.1	4	5	30	4
1984—Atlanta NFL	6	3	8	2.7 0	24	371	15.5	3	3	18	1
NFL Totals—10 Years	110	42	299	7.1 2	261	3240	12.4	20	30	180	18
CFL Total—1 Year	16	1	—9	—9.0 0	65	1060	16.3	5	5	30	3
Pro Totals—11 Years	126	43	290	6.7 2	326	4300	13.2	25	35	210	21

| | | —PUNT RETURNS— | | | | —KICKOFF RET.— | | |
Year Club	G.	No.	Yds.	Avg.	TD.	No.	Yds.	Avg.TD.
1974—Houston NFL	14	30	409	13.6	0	29	785	27.1 0
1975—Houston NFL	14	40	612	*15.3	*3	33	798	24.2 *1
1976—Houston NFL	14	38	403	10.6	0	26	579	22.3 0
1977—Houston NFL	14	35	539	*15.4	*2	25	630	25.2 1
1978—Houston NFL	5	8	60	7.5	0	4	73	18.3 0
1979—Houston NFL	2	4	17	4.3	0	4	37	9.3 0
1980—Houston NFL	16		None				None	
1981—Montreal CFL	16	59	597	10.1	0		None	
1982—Atlanta NFL	9	24	273	11.4	0		None	
1983—Atlanta NFL	16	46	489	10.6	*1		None	
1984—Atlanta NFL	6	15	152	10.1	0	2	39	19.5 0
NFL Totals—10 Years	110	240	2954	12.3	6	123	2941	23.9 2
CFL Total—1 Year	16	59	597	10.1	0	0	0	0.0 0
Pro Totals—11 Years	126	299	3551	11.9	6	123	2941	23.9 2

Additional pro statistics: Recovered one fumble, 1975 and 1976; attempted one pass with no completions and recovered two fumbles, 1983.
Played in Pro Bowl (NFL All-Star Game) following 1975, 1977 and 1983 seasons.

MICHAEL JOHNSTON
(Mike)
Placekicker—Buffalo Bills
Born September 20, 1961, at Rochester, N.Y.
Height, 5.11. Weight, 184.
High School—Rochester, N.Y., Cardinal Mooney.
Attended University of Notre Dame.

Signed as free agent by Dallas Cowboys, May 3, 1984.
Released by Dallas Cowboys, July 29, 1984; signed as free agent by Buffalo Bills, May 10, 1985.

CHARLES JOINER JR.
(Charlie)
Wide Receiver—San Diego Chargers
Born October 14, 1947, at Many, La.
Height, 5.11. Weight, 180.
High School—Lake Charles, La., W. O. Boston.
Received bachelor of science degree in business administration from
Grambling College in 1969.
Cousin of Tom Woodland, defensive tackle with New Jersey Generals.

Established NFL record for most pass receptions, career (657).
Selected by Houston AFL in 4th round (93rd player selected) of 1969 AFL-NFL draft.
Traded with linebacker Ron Pritchard by Houston Oilers to Cincinnati Bengals for running backs Fred Willis and Paul Robinson, October 25, 1972.
Traded by Cincinnati Bengals to San Diego Chargers for defensive end Coy Bacon, April 2, 1976.

		RUSHING				PASS RECEIVING				TOTAL		
Year Club	G.	Att.	Yds.	Avg.	TD.	P.C.	Yds.	Avg.	TD.	TD.	Pts.	F.
1969—Houston AFL	7		None			7	77	11.0	0	0	0	0
1970—Houston NFL	9		None			28	416	14.9	3	3	18	0
1971—Houston NFL	14		None			31	681	22.0	7	7	42	1
1972—Houston (6)-Cin. (6) NFL	12	3	14	4.7	0	24	439	18.3	2	2	12	2
1973—Cincinnati NFL	5		None			13	214	16.5	0	0	0	1
1974—Cincinnati NFL	14	4	20	5.0	0	24	390	16.3	1	1	6	3
1975—Cincinnati NFL	14		None			37	726	19.6	5	5	30	1
1976—San Diego NFL	14		None			50	1056	20.1	7	7	42	0
1977—San Diego NFL	14		None			35	542	15.5	6	6	36	1
1978—San Diego NFL	16		None			33	607	18.4	1	1	6	2
1979—San Diego NFL	16	1	—12	—12.0	0	72	1008	14.0	4	4	24	1
1980—San Diego NFL	16		None			71	1132	15.9	4	4	24	3
1981—San Diego NFL	16		None			70	1188	17.0	7	7	42	2
1982—San Diego NFL	9		None			36	545	15.1	0	0	0	1
1983—San Diego NFL	16		None			65	960	14.8	3	3	18	2
1984—San Diego NFL	16		None			61	793	13.0	6	6	36	0
Pro Totals—16 Years	208	8	22	2.8	0	657	10774	16.4	56	56	336	20

	KICKOFF RETURNS						KICKOFF RETURNS			
Year Club	G.	No.	Yds.	Avg.	TD.	Year Club	G.	No.	Yds.	Avg. TD.
1969—Houston AFL	7	3	73	24.3	0	1978—San Diego NFL	16		None	
1970—Houston NFL	9		None			1979—San Diego NFL	16		None	
1971—Houston NFL	14	1	25	25.0	0	1980—San Diego NFL	16		None	
1972—Hou.(6)-Cin.(6) NFL	12	5	88	17.6	0	1981—San Diego NFL	16		None	
1973—Cincinnati NFL	5		None			1982—San Diego NFL	9		None	
1974—Cincinnati NFL	14		None			1983—San Diego NFL	16		None	
1975—Cincinnati NFL	14		None			1984—San Diego NFL	16		None	
1976—San Diego NFL	14		None			Pro Totals—16 Years	208	10	194	19.4 0
1977—San Diego NFL	14	1	8	8.0	0					

Additional pro statistics: Recovered one fumble, 1975 and 1976.
Played in AFC Championship Game following 1980 and 1981 seasons.
Played in Pro Bowl (NFL All-Star Game) following 1976, 1979 and 1980 seasons.

TIM JOINER
Linebacker—Houston Oilers
Born January 7, 1961, at Los Angeles, Calif.
Height, 6.04. Weight, 248.
High School—Baton Rouge, La., Catholic.
Attended Louisiana State University.

Selected by Arizona in 10th round (119th player selected) of 1983 USFL draft.
Selected by Houston in 3rd round (58th player selected) of 1983 NFL draft.
Signed by Houston Oilers, July 12, 1983.
On injured reserve with knee injury, August 28 through October 4, 1984; activated, October 5, 1984.
Houston NFL, 1983 and 1984.
Games: 1983 (15), 1984 (11). Total—26.
Pro statistics: Recovered one fumble, 1984.

KENNETH CLAY JOLLY
(Ken)
Linebacker—Kansas City Chiefs
Born February 28, 1962, at Dallas, Tex.
Height, 6.02. Weight, 220.
High School—Dallas, Tex., Bryan Adams.
Attended Mid-America Nazarene.

Signed as free agent by Kansas City Chiefs, May 22, 1984.
Kansas City NFL, 1984.
Games: 1984 (16).

ANTHONY JONES
Tight End—Washington Redskins
Born May 16, 1960, at Baltimore, Md.
Height, 6.03. Weight, 248.
High School—Baltimore, Md., Patterson.
Attended University of Maryland (Eastern Shore) and Wichita State University.

Selected by Oklahoma in 1984 USFL territorial draft.
Selected by Washington in 11th round (306th player selected) of 1984 NFL draft.
Signed by Washington Redskins, June 21, 1984.
On injured reserve with neck injury, December 21 through remainder of 1984 season.

		PASS RECEIVING			
Year Club	G.	P.C.	Yds.	Avg.	TD.
1984—Washington NFL	16	1	6	6.0	0

ANTHONY LEVINE JONES
(A. J.)
Running Back—Los Angeles Rams

Born May 30, 1959, at Youngstown, O.
Height, 6.01. Weight, 202.
High School—Youngstown, O., North.
Attended University of Texas.
Brother of Mike Jones, running back with Oakland Invaders.

Selected by Los Angeles Rams in 8th round (202nd player selected) of 1982 NFL draft.
On inactive list, September 12 and September 19, 1982.
On injured reserve with chest injury, November 2 through December 13, 1983; activated, December 14, 1983.
On injured reserve with pulled groin, November 30 through remainder of 1984 season.
Los Angeles Rams NFL, 1982 through 1984.
Games: 1982 (6), 1983 (9), 1984 (13). Total—28.
Pro statistics: Recovered one fumble, 1984.

BRODERICK JONES
(Ricky)
Linebacker

Born March 9, 1955, at Birmingham, Ala.
Height, 6.02. Weight, 230.
High School—Birmingham, Ala., Woodlawn.
Attended Tuskegee Institute.

Signed as free agent by Cleveland Browns, May, 1977.
Released by Cleveland Browns, September 1, 1980; signed as free agent by Baltimore Colts, September 23, 1980.
On injured reserve, December 19 through remainder of 1980 season.
Franchise transferred to Indianapolis, March 31, 1984.
On injured reserve with knee injury, August 28 through entire 1984 season.
Granted free agency, February 1, 1985; signing rights released by Indianapolis Colts, May 10, 1985.
Cleveland NFL, 1977 through 1979; Baltimore NFL, 1980 through 1983.
Games: 1977 (3), 1978 (15), 1979 (16), 1980 (12), 1981 (16), 1982 (9), 1983 (16). Total—87.
Pro statistics: Recovered one fumble, 1978 and 1981; recovered two fumbles, 1980.

CEDRIC JONES
Running Back—Atlanta Falcons

Born February 18, 1963, at Valdosta, Ga.
Height, 5.09. Weight, 187.
High School—Valdosta, Ga., Lowndes.
Attended Florida State University.

Selected by Tampa Bay in 1985 USFL territorial draft.
USFL rights traded with rights to placekicker Bobby Raymond and defensive back Eric Riley by Tampa Bay Bandits to Jacksonville Bulls for rights to running back Marck Harrison, center Dan Turk and tight end Ken Whisenhunt, January 3, 1985.
Signed by Jacksonville Bulls, January 19, 1985.
On developmental squad, February 21 through March 5, 1985.
Released by Jacksonville Bulls, March 6, 1985; signed as free agent by Atlanta Falcons, May 2, 1985.
On developmental squad for 2 games with Jacksonville Bulls in 1985.

CEDRIC DECORRUS JONES
Wide Receiver—New England Patriots

Born June 1, 1960, at Norfolk, Va.
Height, 6.00. Weight, 184.
High School—Weldon, N.C.
Received bachelor of arts degree in history and political science from
Duke University in 1982.

Selected by New England in 3rd round (56th player selected) of 1982 NFL draft.
On inactive list, September 19, 1982.

Year Club		—PASS RECEIVING—			
	G.	P.C.	Yds.	Avg.	TD.
1982—New England NFL.......	2	1	5	5.0	0
1983—New England NFL.......	15	20	323	16.2	1
1984—New England NFL.......	14	19	244	12.8	2
Pro Totals—3 Years...........	31	40	572	14.3	3

Additional pro statistics: Returned four kickoffs for 63 yards, 1983; fumbled once, 1983 and 1984; returned one kickoff for 20 yards and recovered fumble in end zone for a touchdown, 1984.

DARYLL KEITH JONES
Defensive Back—Green Bay Packers

Born March 23, 1962, at Columbia, Ga.
Height, 6.00. Weight, 190.
High School—Columbus, Ga., Carver.
Attended University of Georgia.

Selected by Jacksonville in 1984 USFL territorial draft.
Selected by Green Bay in 7th round (181st player selected) of 1984 NFL draft.

Signed by Green Bay Packers, June 6, 1984.
Green Bay NFL, 1984.
Games: 1984 (16).
Pro statistics: Returned one kickoff for 19 yards and recovered three fumbles, 1984.

DAVID J. JONES
Center—Detroit Lions
Born October 25, 1961, at Taipei, Taiwan.
Height, 6.03. Weight, 266.
High School—Austin, Tex., David Crockett.
Attended University of Texas.

Selected by Houston in 1984 USFL territorial draft.
Selected by Detroit in 8th round (214th player selected) of 1984 NFL draft.
Signed by Detroit Lions, June 4, 1984.
On injured reserve with pulled hamstring, September 8 through October 12, 1984; activated, October 13, 1984.
On injured reserve with back injury, December 14 through remainder of 1984 season.
Detroit NFL, 1984.
Games: 1984 (10).

DEMETRIUS L. JONES
Safety—Denver Broncos
Born September 12, 1961, at Detroit, Mich.
Height, 6.00. Weight, 181.
High School—Detroit, Mich., Henry Ford.
Received bachelor of business administration degree in finance
from Western Michigan University.

Selected by Michigan in 1984 USFL territorial draft.
Signed by Michigan Panthers, January 9, 1984.
Released by Michigan Panthers, January 23, 1984; signed as free agent by Denver Broncos, May 2, 1984.
On injured reserve with broken leg, July 19 through entire 1984 season.

DON MICHAEL JONES
Wide Receiver—San Francisco 49ers
Born October 13, 1960, at Los Angeles, Calif.
Height, 6.02. Weight, 200.
High School—Nacogdoches, Tex.
Received bachelor of arts degree in political science from Texas A&M University.

Selected by Houston in 1984 USFL territorial draft.
Selected by Cleveland in 9th round (227th player selected) of 1984 NFL draft.
Signed by Cleveland Browns, June 26, 1984.
Released by Cleveland Browns, August 15, 1984; signed as free agent by San Francisco 49ers, April 16, 1985.

DWIGHT SEAN JONES
(Known by middle name.)
Defensive End—Los Angeles Raiders
Born December 19, 1962, at Kingston, Jamaica.
Height, 6.07. Weight, 265.
High School—Montclair, N.J., Kimberly Academy.
Attended Northeastern University.
Brother of Max Jones, linebacker with Birmingham Stallions, 1984.

Selected by Washington in 5th round (91st player selected) of 1984 USFL draft.
Selected by Los Angeles Raiders in 2nd round (51st player selected) of 1984 NFL draft.
Signed by Los Angeles Raiders, July 12, 1984.
Los Angeles Raiders NFL, 1984.
Games: 1984 (16).

E.J. JONES
Running Back—Kansas City Chiefs
Born February 1, 1962, at Chicago, Ill.
Height, 5.11. Weight, 212.
High School—Chicago, Ill., Vocational.
Attended Kansas University.

Signed as free agent by Kansas City Chiefs, May 2, 1984.
Released by Kansas City Chiefs, August 13, 1984; re-signed by Chiefs for 1985, October 15, 1984.

EDWARD LEE JONES
(Too Tall)
Defensive End—Dallas Cowboys
Born February 23, 1951, at Jackson, Tenn.
Height, 6.09. Weight, 287.
High School—Jackson, Tenn., Central-Merry.
Attended Tennessee State University.

Named as defensive end on THE SPORTING NEWS College All-America Team, 1973.

Placed on retired reserve, June 19, 1979.
Selected by Dallas in 1st round (1st player selected) of 1974 NFL draft.
Dallas NFL, 1974 through 1978 and 1980 through 1984.
Games: 1974 (14), 1975 (14), 1976 (14), 1977 (14), 1978 (16), 1980 (16), 1981 (16), 1982 (9), 1983 (16), 1984 (16). Total—145.
Pro statistics: Intercepted one pass for two yards, 1975; recovered one fumble, 1975, 1976 and 1982; recovered three fumbles, 1980 and 1981; intercepted one pass for no yards, 1982; intercepted one pass for 12 yards, 1983; recovered two fumbles, 1983 and 1984.
Played in NFC Championship Game following 1975, 1977, 1978 and 1980 through 1982 seasons.
Played in NFL Championship Game following 1975, 1977 and 1978 seasons.
Played in Pro Bowl (NFL All-Star Game) following 1981 through 1983 seasons.

GORDON JONES
Wide Receiver—Los Angeles Raiders
Born July 25, 1957, at Buffalo, N. Y.
Height, 6.00. Weight, 190.
High School—N. Versailles, Pa., East Allegheny.
Attended University of Pittsburgh.

Selected by Tampa Bay in 2nd round (34th player selected) of 1979 NFL draft.
Released by Tampa Bay Buccaneers, August 29, 1983; signed as free agent by Los Angeles Rams, September 8, 1983.
On injured reserve with broken foot, November 21 through remainder of 1983 season.
Released by Los Angeles Rams, September 4, 1984; signed as free agent by Los Angeles Raiders, March 15, 1985.
Active for 1 game with Los Angeles Rams in 1984; did not play.

| | | —PASS RECEIVING— | | | |
Year Club	G.	P.C.	Yds.	Avg.	TD.
1979—Tampa Bay NFL	12	4	80	20.0	1
1980—Tampa Bay NFL	16	48	669	13.9	5
1981—Tampa Bay NFL	13	20	276	13.8	1
1982—Tampa Bay NFL	9	14	205	14.6	1
1983—L.A. Rams NFL	11	11	172	15.6	0
Pro Totals—6 Years	61	97	1402	14.5	8

Additional pro statistics: Rushed once for 12 years, 1979; rushed once for minus 10 yards, 1980; fumbled once, 1980 and 1982.
Played in NFC Championship Game following 1979 season.

GREG JONES
Running Back—Washington Redskins
Born August 1, 1960, at Milwaukee, Wis.
Height, 5.11. Weight, 180.
High School—Milwaukee, Wis., Messmer.
Attended Alcorn State University.

Signed as free agent by Washington Redskins, April 28, 1983.
Released by Washington Redskins, August 29, 1983; signed as free agent by Washington Federals, December 8, 1983.
On developmental squad, April 20 through April 25, 1984.
On injured reserve with knee injury, April 26 through May 18, 1984.
Released by Washington Federals, May 19, 1984; signed as free agent by Washington Redskins, May 27, 1984.
On non-football injury list with knee injury, July 13 through entire 1984 season.
On developmental squad for 1 game with Washington Federals in 1984.
Washington USFL, 1984.
Games: 1984 (8).

JAMES JONES
Fullback—Detroit Lions
Born March 21, 1961, at Pompano Beach, Fla.
Height, 6.02. Weight, 228.
High School—Pompano Beach, Fla., Ely.
Attended University of Florida.

Selected by Tampa Bay in 1983 USFL territorial draft.
Selected by Detroit in 1st round (13th player selected) of 1983 NFL draft.
Signed by Detroit Lions, May 12, 1983.

| | | —RUSHING— | | | | PASS RECEIVING | | | | —TOTAL— | | |
Year Club	G.	Att.	Yds.	Avg.	TD.	P.C.	Yds.	Avg.	TD.	TD.	Pts.	F.
1983—Detroit NFL	14	135	475	3.5	6	46	467	10.2	1	7	42	4
1984—Detroit NFL	16	137	532	3.9	3	77	662	8.6	5	8	48	6
Pro Totals—2 Years	30	272	1007	3.7	9	123	1129	9.2	6	15	90	10

Additional pro statistics: Recovered one fumble and attempted two passes with no completions, 1983; attempted five passes with three completions for 62 yards and a touchdown and recovered three fumbles, 1984.

JAMES JONES JR.
Running Back—Dallas Cowboys
Born December 6, 1958, at Vicksburg, Miss.
Height, 5.10. Weight, 189.
High School—Vicksburg, Miss.
Attended Mississippi State University.

Selected by Dallas in 3rd round (80th player selected) of 1980 NFL draft.
On injured reserve with knee injury, August 30 through entire 1983 season.
On physically unable to perform/active with knee injury, July 19 through August 20, 1984.
On physically unable to perform/reserve with knee injury, August 21 through October 19, 1984; activated, October 20, 1984.

			—RUSHING—			PASS RECEIVING				—TOTAL—		
Year	Club	G.	Att.	Yds.	Avg.	TD.	P.C.	Yds.	Avg.	TD.	TD.	Pts.	F.
1980—Dallas NFL		16	41	135	3.3	0	5	39	7.8	0	0	0	5
1981—Dallas NFL		16	34	183	5.4	1	6	37	6.2	0	1	6	4
1982—Dallas NFL		5		None				None			0	0	0
1984—Dallas NFL		9	8	13	1.6	0	7	57	8.1	1	1	6	0
Pro Totals—4 Years		46	83	331	4.0	1	18	133	7.4	1	2	12	9

			—PUNT RETURNS—				—KICKOFF RET.—			
Year	Club	G.	No.	Yds.	Avg.	TD.	No.	Yds.	Avg.	TD.
1980—Dallas NFL		16	54	548	10.1	0	32	720	22.5	0
1981—Dallas NFL		16	33	188	5.7	0	27	517	19.1	0
1982—Dallas NFL		5		None			2	46	23.0	0
1984—Dallas NFL		9		None				None		
Pro Totals—4 Years		46	87	736	8.5	0	61	1283	21.0	0

Additional pro statistics: Recovered two fumbles, 1981.
Played in NFC Championship Game following 1980 and 1981 seasons.
Member of Dallas Cowboys for NFC Championship Game following 1982 season; did not play.

JOHNNY JONES
(Lam)
Wide Receiver—New York Jets

Born April 4, 1958, at Lawton, Okla.
Height, 5.11. Weight, 180.
High School—Lampasas, Tex.
Attended University of Texas.

Named as wide receiver on THE SPORTING NEWS College All-America Team, 1979.
Selected by New York Jets in 1st round (2nd player selected) of 1980 NFL draft.
On injured reserve with broken collarbone, August 28 through October 25, 1984; activated, October 26, 1984.

			—RUSHING—			PASS RECEIVING				—TOTAL—		
Year	Club	G.	Att.	Yds.	Avg.	TD.	P.C.	Yds.	Avg.	TD.	TD.	Pts.	F.
1980—New York Jets NFL		16	2	5	2.5	0	25	482	19.3	3	3	18	1
1981—New York Jets NFL		15	2	0	0.0	0	20	342	17.1	3	3	18	2
1982—New York Jets NFL		8	1	2	2.0	0	18	294	16.3	2	2	12	0
1983—New York Jets NFL		14	4	10	2.5	0	43	734	17.1	4	4	24	2
1984—New York Jets NFL		8		None			32	470	14.7	1	1	6	1
Pro Totals—5 Years		61	9	17	1.9	0	138	2322	16.8	13	13	78	6

Additional pro statistics: Returned four kickoffs for 67 yards, 1980; recovered one fumble, 1980 and 1982; returned one kickoff for six yards and recovered two fumbles, 1981.
Played in AFC Championship Game following 1982 season.

KENNETH EUGENE JONES
(Ken)
Offensive Tackle—Buffalo Bills

Born December 1, 1952, at St. Louis, Mo.
Height, 6.05. Weight, 260.
High School—Bridgeton, Mo., Pattonville.
Attended Arkansas State University.

Named as guard on THE SPORTING NEWS College All-America Team, 1975.
Selected by Buffalo in 2nd round (45th player selected) of 1976 NFL draft.
Buffalo NFL, 1976 through 1984.
Games: 1976 (12), 1977 (14), 1978 (16), 1979 (16), 1980 (16), 1981 (15), 1982 (9), 1983 (16), 1984 (16). Total—130.
Pro statistics: Recovered two fumbles, 1976 and 1981; recovered one fumble, 1978 through 1980 and 1983.

MICHAEL ANTHONY JONES
(Mike)
Wide Receiver—Minnesota Vikings

Born April 14, 1960, at Chattanooga, Tenn.
Height, 5.11. Weight, 176.
High School—Chattanooga, Tenn., Riverside.
Attended Tennessee State University.

Selected by Minnesota in 6th round (159th player selected) of 1983 NFL draft.

			—PASS RECEIVING—			
Year	Club	G.	P.C.	Yds.	Avg.	TD.
1983—Minnesota NFL		16	6	95	15.8	0
1984—Minnesota NFL		16	38	591	15.6	1
Pro Totals—2 Years		32	44	686	15.6	1

Additional pro statistics: Rushed once for nine yards and returned two kickoffs for 31 yards, 1983; rushed four times for 45 yards, recovered two fumbles and fumbled once, 1984.

ROBBIE JONES
Linebacker—New York Giants
Born December 25, 1959, at Demopolis, Ala.
Height, 6.02. Weight, 230.
High School—Demopolis, Ala.
Attended University of Alabama.

Selected by Birmingham in 1983 USFL territorial draft.
Selected by New York Giants in 12th round (309th player selected) of 1983 NFL draft.
Signed by New York Giants, July 6, 1983.
On injured reserve with abrasion to spinal cord, August 22 through entire 1983 season.
New York Giants NFL, 1984.
Games: 1984 (16).

ROBERT E. JONES
(Bobby)
Wide Receiver—Buffalo Bills
Born July 12, 1955, at Sharon, Pa.
Height, 5.11. Weight, 185.
High School—Brookfield, O.
Attended Youngstown State University and Millikin University.
Cousin of Carl Furillo, outfielder with Brooklyn and Los Angeles Dodgers, 1946 through 1960.

Signed as free agent by New York Jets, May 11, 1978.
On injured reserve with knee injury, September 5 through October 12, 1979; activated, October 13, 1979.
Traded by New York Jets to Cleveland Browns for 8th round pick in 1984 draft, July 27, 1983.
Did not report, July 19, 1984.
Released by Cleveland Browns, July 23, 1984; signed by Portland Breakers, January 23, 1985.
Released by Portland Breakers, January 28, 1985; signed as free agent by Buffalo Bills, May 10, 1985.
Played with Sharon Old Express and Shenango Valley Blasters of Mid-Atlantic Football League, 1976 and 1977.

| | | ——PASS RECEIVING—— | | | |
Year Club	G.	P.C.	Yds.	Avg.	TD.
1978—N.Y. Jets NFL	16	1	18	18.0	0
1979—N.Y. Jets NFL	10	19	379	19.9	1
1980—N.Y. Jets NFL	15	14	193	13.8	0
1981—N.Y. Jets NFL	16	16	239	14.9	1
1982—N.Y. Jets NFL	9	3	32	10.7	0
1983—Cleveland NFL	15	36	507	14.1	4
Pro Totals—6 Years	81	89	1368	15.4	6

Additional pro statistics: Recovered one fumble, 1978; rushed once for four yards, returned seven kickoffs for 140 yards and fumbled twice, 1979; returned two kickoffs for 50 yards and returned one punt for no yards, 1980; recovered one fumble for 61 yards and a touchdown and returned one punt for one yard, 1981; rushed once for 19 yards, 1983.
Played in AFC Championship Game following 1982 season.

RULON KENT JONES
Defensive End—Denver Broncos
Born March 25, 1958, at Salt Lake City, Utah.
Height, 6.06. Weight, 260.
High School—Ogden, Utah, Weber.
Attended Utah State University.

Named as defensive tackle on THE SPORTING NEWS College All-America Team, 1979.
Selected by Denver in 2nd round (42nd player selected) of 1980 NFL draft.
On injured reserve with knee injury, September 21 through October 20, 1983; activated, October 21, 1983.
Denver NFL, 1980 through 1984.
Games: 1980 (16), 1981 (16), 1982 (9), 1983 (12), 1984 (16). Total—69.
Pro statistics: Credited with one safety, 1980 and 1983; recovered one fumble, 1980 and 1981; recovered two fumbles for four yards, 1983; recovered two fumbles for five yards and a touchdown, 1984.

TERRY WAYNE JONES
Defensive Tackle—Green Bay Packers
Born November 8, 1956, at Sandersville, Ga.
Height, 6.02. Weight, 253.
High School—Sandersville, Ga., Washington County.
Attended University of Alabama.

Selected by Green Bay in 11th round (287th player selected) of 1978 NFL draft.
On injured reserve with knee injury, September 12 through October 11, 1979; activated, October 12, 1979.
Released by Green Bay Packers, September 1, 1980; re-signed by Packers, September 5, 1980.
On injured reserve with Achilles tendon injury, September 6 through remainder of 1983 season.
Green Bay NFL, 1978 through 1984.
Games: 1978 (16), 1979 (12), 1980 (15), 1981 (16), 1982 (9), 1983 (1), 1984 (16). Total—85.
Pro statistics: Recovered one fumble, 1979, 1980 and 1984; recovered two fumbles, 1981.

WILLIE LORENZO JONES
Defensive End—Cleveland Browns
Born November 22, 1957, at Dublin, Ga.
Height, 6.04. Weight, 245.
High School—Homestead, Fla., South Dade.
Attended Florida State University.

Selected by Oakland in 2nd round (42nd player selected) of 1979 NFL draft.
On non-football injury list with personal problems, August 31 through September 25, 1981; activated, September 26, 1981.
On non-football injury list with personal problems, November 27 through remainder of 1981 season.
Franchise transferred to Los Angeles, May 7, 1982.
On injured reserve with knee injury, September 6 through entire 1982 season.
Released by Los Angeles Raiders, July 27, 1983; signed as free agent by Saskatchewan Roughriders, March 20, 1984.
Released by Saskatchewan Roughriders, August 19, 1984; signed as free agent by Cleveland Browns, December 18, 1984.
Oakland NFL, 1979 through 1981; Saskatchewan CFL, 1984.
Games: 1979 (16), 1980 (16), 1981 (8), 1984 (1). Total NFL—40. Total Pro—41.
Pro statistics: Recovered two fumbles for 11 yards and a touchdown, 1980; recovered one fumble for nine yards and a touchdown, 1981.
Played in AFC Championship Game following 1980 season.
Played in NFL Championship Game following 1980 season.

CURTIS WAYNE JORDAN
Safety—Washington Redskins
Born January 25, 1954, at Lubbock, Tex.
Height, 6.02. Weight, 205.
High School—Lubbock, Tex., Monterey.
Received degree in advertising and public relations from Texas Tech University.

Selected by Tampa Bay in 6th round (158th player selected) of 1976 NFL draft.
On injured reserve with broken collarbone, August 17 through December 9, 1981; claimed on procedural waivers by Washington Redskins, December 11, 1981.

| | | —INTERCEPTIONS— | | | | | | —INTERCEPTIONS— | | |
Year Club	G.	No.	Yds.	Avg.TD.		Year Club	G.	No.	Yds.	Avg.TD.
1976—Tampa Bay NFL	11	2	10	5.0	0	1981—Washington NFL	2	None			
1977—Tampa Bay NFL	12	1	0	0.0	0	1982—Washington NFL	9	None			
1978—Tampa Bay NFL	16	3	23	7.7	0	1983—Washington NFL	15	1	20	20.0	0
1979—Tampa Bay NFL	16	None				1984—Washington NFL	16	2	18	9.0	0
1980—Tampa Bay NFL	16	None				Pro Totals—9 Years	113	9	71	7.9	0

Additional pro statistics: Recovered one fumble, 1976, 1977, 1979 and 1980; returned one kickoff for no yards, 1980; recovered blocked punt in end zone for a touchdown, 1982; recovered two fumbles for 20 yards, 1983; recovered one fumble for 29 yards and a touchdown, 1984.
Played in NFC Championship Game following 1979, 1982 and 1983 seasons.
Played in NFL Championship Game following 1982 and 1983 seasons.

DAVID JORDAN
Guard—New York Giants
Born July 14, 1962, at Birmingham, Ala.
Height, 6.06. Weight, 276.
High School—Vestavia Hills, Ala.
Attended Auburn University.

Selected by Birmingham in 1984 USFL territorial draft.
Selected by New York Giants in 10th round (255th player selected) of 1984 NFL draft.
Signed by New York Giants, June 3, 1984.
New York Giants NFL, 1984.
Games: 1984 (14).

DONALD RAY JORDAN
Fullback—Chicago Bears
Born February 9, 1962, at Houston, Tex.
Height, 6.00. Weight, 210.
High School—Houston, Tex. James Madison.
Attended University of Houston.

Selected by San Antonio in 1984 USFL territorial draft.
Selected by Chicago in 12th round (330th player selected) of 1984 NFL draft.
Signed by Chicago Bears, June 15, 1984.
On injured reserve with knee injury, December 15 through remainder of 1984 season.

| | | —RUSHING— | | | | PASS RECEIVING | | | | —TOTAL— | | |
Year Club	G.	Att.	Yds.	Avg.	TD.	P.C.	Yds.	Avg.	TD.	TD.	Pts.	F.
1984—Chicago NFL	13	11	70	6.4	0	1	6	6.0	0	0	0	1

Additional pro statistics: Returned five kickoffs for 62 yards and recovered three fumbles, 1984.

—DID YOU KNOW—

That on November 4, 1984, in a game between San Francisco and Cincinnati, both head coaches were former quarterback coaches for the opposing teams? Sam Wyche, head coach of the Bengals, formerly was the quarterback coach for the 49ers and Joe Montana, while the 49ers' Bill Walsh once served as quarterback coach for the Bengals and Ken Anderson.

KENT W. JORDAN
Tight End—Houston Oilers
Born October 29, 1959, at Berkeley, Calif.
Height, 6.07. Weight, 250.
High School—Piedmont, Calif.
Attended Cabrillo Junior College and received bachelor of arts degree
from St. Mary's (Calif.) College.

Selected by Los Angeles Raiders in 9th round (249th player selected) of 1983 NFL draft.
On reserve/non-football injury list with back injury, August 1 through enitre 1983 season.
Released by Los Angeles Raiders, August 21, 1984; signed as free agent by Houston Oilers, May 6, 1985.

SHELBY LEWIS JORDAN
Offensive Tackle—Los Angeles Raiders
Born January 23, 1952, at East St. Louis, Ill.
Height, 6.07. Weight, 285.
High School—East St. Louis, Ill.
Received degree from Washington (Mo.) University and attending
Bryant College for master's degree in marketing.

Selected by Houston in 7th round (157th player selected) of 1973 NFL draft.
Released by Houston Oilers, 1973; signed as free agent by New England Patroits, April 2, 1974.
Missed entire 1974 and 1976 seasons due to injury.
On reserve/did not report, August 16 through August 28, 1983; reinstated, August 29, 1983.
Granted roster exemption, August 29 through September 5, 1983.
Traded by New England Patriots to Los Angeles Raiders for 4th round pick in 1985 draft, September 6, 1983.
Granted roster exemption, September 6 through September 19, 1983; activated, September 20, 1983.
On injured reserve with knee injury, November 15 through remainder of 1984 season.
New England NFL, 1975 and 1977 through 1982; Los Angeles Raiders NFL, 1983 and 1984.
Games: 1975 (14), 1977 (10), 1978 (16), 1979 (14), 1980 (16), 1981 (16), 1982 (9), 1983 (13), 1984 (11). Total—119.
Pro statistics: Recovered two fumbles for 12 yards, 1975; recovered one fumble, 1979.
Played in AFC Championship Game following 1983 season.
Played in NFL Championship Game following 1983 season.

STEVEN RUSSELL JORDAN
(Steve)
Tight End—Minnesota Vikings
Born January 10, 1961, at Phoenix, Ariz.
Height, 6.03. Weight, 230.
High School—Phoenix, Ariz., South Mountain.
Received bachelor of science degree in civil engineering from Brown University in 1982.

Selected by Minnesota in 7th round (179th player selected) of 1982 NFL draft.

| | | |—PASS RECEIVING—| | | |
Year	Club	G.	P.C.	Yds.	Avg.	TD.
1982—Minnesota NFL		9	3	42	14.0	0
1983—Minnesota NFL		13	15	212	14.1	2
1984—Minnesota NFL		14	38	414	10.9	2
Pro Totals—3 Years		36	56	668	11.9	4

Additional pro statistics: Rushed once for four yards and a touchdown and recovered one fumble, 1984.

RANDALL PHILLIP JOSTES
(Randy)
Defensive Tackle—Tampa Bay Buccaneers
Born August 15, 1961, at Lincoln, Neb.
Height, 6.05. Weight, 262.
High School—Omaha, Neb., Ralston.
Attended University of Missouri.

Selected by Arizona in 6th round (71st player selected) of 1983 USFL draft.
Signed by Arizona Wranglers, February 2, 1983.
On injured reserve with pinched nerve from beginning of season through May 6, 1983; activated, May 7, 1983.
Franchise transferred to Chicago, September 30, 1983.
On developmental squad, May 18 through May 24, 1984; activated, May 25, 1984.
Franchise disbanded, November 20, 1984; not selected in USFL dispersal draft, December 6, 1984.
Signed as free agent by Tampa Bay Buccaneers, February 17, 1985.
On developmental squad for 1 game with Chicago Blitz in 1984.
Arizona USFL, 1983; Chicago USFL, 1984.
Games: 1983 (9), 1984 (17). Total—26.
Pro statistics: Credited with one sack for three yards and recovered one fumble, 1983; credited with 2½ sacks for 16½ yards, returned one kickoff for no yards and recovered two fumbles, 1984.

JAMES ALLEN JOYCE
(Jim)
Defensive End—Denver Broncos
Born September 12, 1961, at Cumberland, Md.
Height, 6.04. Weight, 240.
High School—Gaithersburg, Md.
Received degree in general studies from University of Maryland in 1984.

Selected as free agent by Denver Broncos, May 2, 1984.
On injured reserve with shoulder injury, August 13 through entire 1984 season.

WILLIE JOYNER
Running Back—Houston Oilers
Born April 2, 1962, at Brooklyn, N.Y.
Height, 5.10. Weight, 200.
High School—Brooklyn, N.Y., Lafayette.
Attended University of Maryland.

Selected by Washington in 1984 USFL territorial draft.
Selected by Houston in 7th round (170th player selected) of 1984 NFL draft.
Signed by Houston Oilers, July 18, 1984.

| | | —RUSHING— | | | PASS RECEIVING | | | —TOTAL— | | |
Year Club	G.	Att.	Yds.	Avg. TD.	P.C. Yds.	Avg. TD.		TD.	Pts.	F.
1984—Houston NFL	10	14	22	1.6 0	None			0	0	0

| | | KICKOFF RETURNS | | |
Year Club	G.	No.	Yds.	Avg.TD.
1984—Houston NFL	10	3	57	19.0 0

WILLIAM THADIUS JUDSON
Cornerback—Miami Dolphins
Born March 26, 1959, at Detroit, Mich.
Height, 6.01. Weight, 187.
High School—Atlanta, Ga., Sylvan Hills.
Received bachelor of science degree in business administration
from South Carolina State College in 1981.

Selected by Miami in 8th round (208th player selected) of 1981 NFL draft.
On injured reserve with hamstring injury, August 31 through entire 1981 season.

| | | —INTERCEPTIONS— | | |
Year Club	G.	No.	Yds.	Avg.TD.
1982—Miami NFL	9		None	
1983—Miami NFL	16	6	60	10.0 0
1984—Miami NFL	16	4	121	30.3 1
Pro Totals—3 Years	41	10	181	18.1 1

Additional pro statistics: Recovered two fumbles for 37 yards, 1984.
Played in AFC Championship Game following 1982 and 1984 seasons.
Played in NFL Championship Game following 1982 and 1984 seasons.

ESTER JAMES JUNIOR III
(E.J.)
Linebacker—St. Louis Cardinals
Born December 8, 1959, at Sallsburg, N.C.
Height, 6.03. Weight, 235.
High School—Nashville, Tenn., Maplewood.
Attended University of Alabama.

Named as defensive end on THE SPORTING NEWS College All-America Team, 1980.
Selected by St. Louis in 1st round (5th player selected) of 1981 NFL draft.
On suspended list for drug use, July 25 through September 25, 1983; reinstated, September 26, 1983.

| | | —INTERCEPTIONS— | | |
Year Club	G.	No.	Yds.	Avg.TD.
1981—St. Louis NFL	16	1	5	5.0 0
1982—St. Louis NFL	9		None	
1983—St. Louis NFL	12	3	27	9.0 0
1984—St. Louis NFL	16	1	18	18.0 0
Pro Totals—4 Years	53	5	50	10.0 0

Additional pro statistics: Recovered one fumble, 1982; recovered one fumble for one yard, 1983.
Played in Pro Bowl (NFL All-Star Game) following 1984 season.

ABNER KIRK JUNKIN
(Trey)
Linebacker—Los Angeles Raiders
Born January 23, 1961, at Conway, Ark.
Height, 6.02. Weight, 221.
High School—North Little Rock, Ark., Northeast.
Attended Louisiana Tech University.

Selected by Buffalo in 4th round (93rd player selected) of 1983 NFL draft.
Released by Buffalo Bills, September 12, 1984; signed as free agent by Washington Redskins, September 25, 1984.
Granted free agency after not receiving qualifying offer, February 1, 1985; signed by Los Angeles Raiders, March 10, 1985.
Buffalo NFL, 1983; Buffalo (2)-Washington (12) NFL, 1984.
Games: 1983 (16), 1984 (14). Total—30.
Pro statistics: Recovered one fumble, 1983 and 1984.

VYTO KAB
Tight End—Philadelphia Eagles
Born December 23, 1959, at Albany, Ga.
Height, 6.05. Weight, 240.
High School—Wayne, N.J., DePaul.
Attended Penn State University.

Selected by Philadelphia in 3rd round (78th player selected) of 1982 NFL draft.
On injured reserve with ankle injury, December 14 through remainder of 1983 season.

Year Club		—PASS RECEIVING—			
	G.	P.C.	Yds.	Avg.	TD.
1982—Philadelphia NFL	9	4	35	8.8	1
1983—Philadelphia NFL	14	18	195	10.8	1
1984—Philadelphia NFL	16	9	102	11.3	3
Pro Totals—3 Years............	39	31	332	10.7	5

MARK KEVIN KAFENTZIS
Safety—Indianapolis Colts
Born June 30, 1958, at Richland, Wash.
Height, 5.10. Weight, 200.
High School—Richland, Wash., Columbia.
Attended Columbia Basin Junior College and received degree in marketing from University of Hawaii.

Selected by Cleveland in 8th round (199th player selected) of 1982 NFL draft.
Released by Cleveland Browns, August 29, 1983; signed as free agent by Baltimore Colts, September 6, 1983.
Franchise transferred to Indianapolis, March 31, 1984.
Cleveland NFL, 1982; Baltimore NFL, 1983; Indianapolis NFL, 1984.
Games: 1982 (9), 1983 (15), 1984 (16). Total—40.
Pro statistics: Intercepted one pass for 59 yards and a touchdown, returned five kickoffs for 69 yards and fumbled once, 1984.

JOHN FREDERICK KAISER
Linebacker—Seattle Seahawks
Born June 6, 1962, at Oconomowoc, Wis.
Height, 6.03. Weight, 221.
High School—Hartland, Wis., Arrowhead.
Attended College of the Sequoias and University of Arizona.
Cousin of Billy McCool, pitcher with Cincinnati Reds, San Diego Padres
and St. Louis Cardinals, 1964 through 1970.

Selected by Arizona in 1984 USFL territorial draft.
Selected by Seattle in 6th round (162nd player selected) of 1984 NFL draft.
Signed by Seattle Seahawks, June 15, 1984.
Seattle NFL, 1984.
Games: 1984 (16).

JOHN KAMANA
Running Back—Los Angeles Rams
Born December 3, 1961, at Honolulu, Haw.
Height, 6.02. Weight, 215.
High School—Honolulu, Haw., Punahoa.
Attended University of Southern California.

Signed as free agent by Los Angeles Rams, May 4, 1984.
On injured reserve with groin injury, August 27 through November 27, 1984; activated after clearing procedural waivers, November 28, 1984.
Los Angeles Rams NFL, 1984.
Games: 1984 (3).

RICHARD JAMES KANE
(Rick)
Running Back
Born November 12, 1954, at Lincoln, Neb.
Height, 6.00. Weight, 200.
High School—Pleasanton, Calif., Amador Valley.
Attended University of Oregon and San Jose State University.

Selected by Detroit in 3rd round (69th player selected) of 1977 NFL draft.
On inactive list, September 12 and September 19, 1982.
On reserve/did not report, August 16 through August 28, 1983; activated, August 29, 1983.
Released by Detroit Lions, August 28, 1984; signed as free agent by Washington Redskins, September 4, 1984.
Released by Washington Redskins, November 28, 1984; re-signed by Redskins, December 21, 1984.
Released by Washington Redskins, May 16, 1985.

Year Club		—RUSHING—				PASS RECEIVING				—TOTAL—		
	G.	Att.	Yds.	Avg.	TD.	P.C.	Yds.	Avg.	TD.	TD.	Pts.	F.
1977—Detroit NFL...............	14	124	421	3.4	4	18	186	10.3	0	4	24	10
1978—Detroit NFL...............	15	44	153	3.5	2	16	161	10.1	0	2	12	1
1979—Detroit NFL...............	16	94	332	3.5	4	9	104	11.6	1	5	30	4
1980—Detroit NFL...............	16	31	125	4.0	0	5	26	5.2	0	0	0	3

Year Club	G.	Att.	Yds.	Avg.	TD.	P.C.	Yds.	Avg.	TD.	TD.	Pts.	F.
		—RUSHING—				PASS RECEIVING				—TOTAL—		
1981—Detroit NFL	16	77	332	4.3	2	18	187	10.4	1	3	18	2
1982—Detroit NFL	6	7	17	2.4	0	3	25	8.3	0	0	0	0
1983—Detroit NFL	14	4	19	4.8	0	2	15	7.5	0	0	0	0
1984—Washington NFL	12	17	43	2.5	0	1	7	7.0	0	0	0	3
Pro Totals—8 Years	109	398	1442	3.6	12	72	711	9.9	2	14	84	23

KICKOFF RETURNS

Year Club	G.	No.	Yds.	Avg.TD.	Year Club	G.	No.	Yds.	Avg.TD.
1977—Detroit NFL	14	16	376	23.5 0	1982—Detroit NFL	6	1	19	19.0 0
1978—Detroit NFL	15	8	156	19.5 0	1983—Detroit NFL	14		None	
1979—Detroit NFL	16	13	281	21.6 0	1984—Washington NFL	12	3	43	14.3 0
1980—Detroit NFL	16	23	495	21.5 0	Pro Totals—8 Years	109	64	1370	21.4 0
1981—Detroit NFL	16		None						

Additional pro statistics: Returned one punt for 13 yards and recovered three fumbles, 1977; recovered two fumbles, 1979.

KURT KAPISCHKE
Offensive Tackle—Green Bay Packers
Born March 14, 1962, at Wiesbaden, Germany.
Height, 6.05. Weight, 256.
High School—Antioch, Ill.
Received bachelor of arts degree in business administration from Augustana College (Ill.).
Selected by Michigan in 17th round (349th player selected) of 1984 USFL draft.
Signed by Michigan Panthers, January 10, 1984.
Released by Michigan Panthers, February 13, 1984; signed as free agent by Dallas Cowboys, May 10, 1984.
Released by Dallas Cowboys, August 13, 1984; signed as free agent by Green Bay Packers, February 15, 1985.

KENNETH SCOTT KAPLAN
(Ken)
Offensive Tackle—Tampa Bay Buccaneers
Born January 12, 1960, at Boston, Mass.
Height, 6.05. Weight, 270.
High School—Brockton, Mass.
Attended University of New Hampshire.
Selected by Tampa Bay in 6th round (158th player selected) of 1983 NFL draft.
On injured reserve with back injury, August 29 through entire 1983 season.
Tampa Bay NFL, 1984.
Games: 1984 (16).

RICHARD JOHN KARLIS
(Rich)
Placekicker—Denver Broncos
Born May 23, 1959, at Salem, O.
Height, 6.00. Weight, 180.
High School—Salem, O.
Attended University of Cincinnati.
Signed as free agent by Houston Oilers, June 5, 1981.
Released by Houston Oilers, July 31, 1981; signed as free agent by Denver Broncos, June 4, 1982.

Year Club	G.	XP.	XPM.	FG.	FGA.	Pts.
		—PLACE KICKING—				
1982—Denver NFL	9	15	1	11	13	48
1983—Denver NFL	16	33	1	21	25	96
1984—Denver NFL	16	38	3	21	28	101
Pro Totals—3 Years	41	86	5	53	66	245

KANI KAUAHI
Center—Seattle Seahawks
Born September 6, 1959, at Kekaha, Hawaii.
Height, 6.02. Weight, 260.
High School—Honolulu, Hawaii, Kamehameha.
Attended Arizona State University and University of Hawaii.
Signed as free agent by Seattle Seahawks, April 30, 1982.
Seattle NFL, 1982 through 1984.
Games: 1982 (2), 1983 (10), 1984 (16). Total—28.
Pro statistics: Recovered two fumbles, 1984.
Member of Seattle Seahawks for AFC Championship Game following 1983 season; did not play.

MEL KAUFMAN
Linebacker—Washington Redskins
Born February 24, 1958, at Los Angeles, Calif.
Height, 6.02. Weight, 218.
High School—Santa Monica, Calif.
Attended California Poly State University at San Luis Obispo.

Signed as free agent by Washington Redskins, May 6, 1981.
On injured reserve with shoulder injury, November 19 through remainder of 1981 season.

Year Club		G.	No.	Yds.	Avg.	TD.
1981—Washington NFL		11	2	25	12.5	0
1982—Washington NFL		9		None		
1983—Washington NFL		16	2	93	46.5	1
1984—Washington NFL		15		None		
Pro Totals—4 Years		51	4	118	29.5	1

Additional pro statistics: Recovered one fumble, 1982 and 1984; recovered one fumble for 30 yards and a touchdown, 1983.
Played in NFC Championship Game following 1982 and 1983 seasons.
Played in NFL Championship Game following 1982 and 1983 seasons.

CLARENCE HUBERT KAY
Tight End—Denver Broncos
Born July 30, 1961, at Seneca, S.C.
Height, 6.02. Weight, 237.
High School—Seneca, S.C.
Attended University of Georgia.

Selected by Jacksonville in 1984 USFL territorial draft.
Selected by Denver in 7th round (186th player selected) of 1984 NFL draft.
Signed by Denver Broncos, May 17, 1984.

		—PASS RECEIVING—				
Year Club		G.	P.C.	Yds.	Avg.	TD.
1984—Denver NFL		16	16	136	8.5	3

Additional pro statistics: Fumbled once, 1984.

WILLIAM HENRY KAY
(Bill)
Cornerback—San Diego Chargers
Born January 10, 1960, at Detroit, Mich.
Height, 6.01. Weight, 190.
High School—Maywood, Ill., Proviso East.
Attended Purdue University.

Selected by Houston in 6th round (159th player selected) of 1981 NFL draft.
Released by Houston Oilers, August 27, 1984; awarded on waivers to St. Louis Cardinals, August 28, 1984.
Released by St. Louis Cardinals, November 8, 1984; signed as free agent by San Diego Chargers, November 14, 1984.

		—INTERCEPTIONS—				
Year Club		G.	No.	Yds.	Avg.	TD.
1981—Houston NFL		16	2	47	23.5	0
1982—Houston NFL		9		None		
1983—Houston NFL		16	2	31	15.5	0
1984—St.L. (10)-S.D. (5) NFL.		15		None		
Pro Totals—4 Years		56	4	78	19.5	0

TIM ALLYNN KEARSE
Wide Receiver—San Diego Chargers
Born October 24, 1959, at York, Pa.
Height, 5.10. Weight, 193.
High School—York, Pa.
Attended San Jose State University.

Selected by Oakland in 1983 USFL territorial draft.
Selected by San Diego in 11th round (303rd player selected) of 1983 NFL draft.
Signed with British Columbia Lions, June 1, 1983.
Traded with defensive back Ken Hinton by British Columbia Lions to Saskatchewan Roughriders for draft pick, August 28, 1983.
Released by Saskatchewan Roughriders, April 29, 1985; signed by San Diego Chargers, May 7, 1985.

Year Club	G.	-PASS RECEIVING-				-PUNT RETURNS-				—TOTAL—		
		P.C.	Yds.	Avg.	TD.	No.	Yds.	Avg.	TD.	TD.	Pts.	F.
1983—B.C. (1)-Sask. (6) CFL	7	9	144	16.0	1	15	201	13.4	1	2	12	0
1984—Saskatchewan CFL	8	19	240	12.6	0	11	125	11.4	1	1	6	3
Pro Totals—2 Years	15	28	384	13.7	1	26	326	12.5	2	3	18	3

Additional CFL statistics: Returned one kickoff for 24 yards, 1983; rushed once for five yards and ran for seven yards with lateral on kickoff return, 1984.

CHRISTOPHER PAUL KEATING
(Chris)
Linebacker—Buffalo Bills
Born October 12, 1957, at Boston, Mass.
Height, 6.02. Weight, 233.
High School—Cohasset, Mass., Archbishop Williams.
Received bachelor of business administration degree in marketing
from University of Maine in 1979.

Signed as free agent by Buffalo Bills, May 27, 1979.
Released by Buffalo Bills, August 27, 1979; re-signed by Bills, August 28, 1979.
On injured reserve with knee injury, December 18 through remainder of 1980 season.
On injured reserve with torn hamstring, August 25 through November 4, 1981; activated after clearing procedural waivers, November 6, 1981.
On injured reserve with ankle injury, December 11 through remainder of 1981 season.
Released by Buffalo Bills, September 6, 1982; re-signed by Bills, September 7, 1982.
Buffalo NFL, 1979 through 1984.
Games: 1979 (16), 1980 (15), 1981 (2), 1982 (9), 1983 (16), 1984 (16). Total—74.
Pro statistics: Returned one kickoff for 14 yards, 1979; returned three kickoffs for 38 yards, 1980; recovered one fumble, 1980 and 1983; intercepted one pass for 14 yards and returned one kickoff for nine yards, 1982; intercepted two passes for 20 yards, 1983; recovered one fumble for 34 yards and a touchdown, 1984.

BOBBY KEMP
Safety—Cincinnati Bengals
Born May 29, 1959, at Oakland, Calif.
Height, 6.00. Weight, 191.
High School—North Miami Beach, Fla.
Attended Taft Junior College and California State University at Fullerton.

Selected by Cincinnati in 8th round (202nd player selected) of 1981 NFL draft.
On injured reserve with dislocated shoulder, August 28 through October 12, 1984; activated, October 13, 1984.

		—INTERCEPTIONS—			
Year Club	G.	No.	Yds.	Avg.	TD.
1981—Cincinnati NFL	16		None		
1982—Cincinnati NFL	9	1	0	0.0	0
1983—Cincinnati NFL	16	3	26	8.7	0
1984—Cincinnati NFL	10	4	27	6.8	0
Pro Totals—4 Years	51	8	53	6.6	0

Additional pro statistics: Returned one kickoff for no yards, 1981; recovered one fumble, 1983 and 1984; fumbled once, 1984.
Played in AFC Championship Game following 1981 season.
Played in NFL Championship Game following 1981 season.

JEFFREY ALLAN KEMP
(Jeff)
Quarterback—Los Angeles Rams
Born July 11, 1959, at Santa Ana, Calif.
Height, 6.01. Weight, 201.
High School—Potomac, Md., Winston Churchill.
Received bachelor of arts degree in economics from Dartmouth College in 1981;
and attending Pepperdine University for master's in business administration.
Son of Jack Kemp, quarterback with Pittsburgh Steelers, Los Angeles and San Diego Chargers
and Buffalo Bills, 1957, 1960 through 1967 and 1969; currently Republican Congressman from New York.
Signed as free agent by Los Angeles Rams, May 11, 1981.
Released by Los Angeles Rams, August 31, 1981; re-signed by Rams, September 1, 1981.
On injured reserve with back injury, October 3 through December 1, 1981; activated, December 2, 1981.
On inactive list, September 12 and September 19, 1982.
Active for 7 games with Los Angeles Rams in 1982; did not play.

		—————PASSING—————							—RUSHING—				—TOTAL—		
Year Club	G.	Att.	Cmp.	Pct.	Gain	T.P.	P.I.	Avg.	Att.	Yds.	Avg.	TD.	TD.	Pts.	F.
1981—L.A. Rams NFL	1	6	2	33.3	25	0	1	4.17	2	9	4.5	0	0	0	0
1983—L.A. Rams NFL	4	25	12	48.0	135	1	0	5.40	3	—2	—0.7	0	0	0	2
1984—L.A. Rams NFL	14	284	143	50.4	2021	13	7	7.12	34	153	4.5	1	1	6	8
Pro Totals—4 Years	19	315	157	49.8	2181	14	8	6.92	39	160	4.1	1	1	6	10

Quarterback Rating Points: 1981 (7.6), 1983 (77.9), 1984 (78.7). Total—76.7.
Additional pro statistics: Recovered three fumbles and fumbled eight times for minus 16 yards, 1984.

FLORIAN GERARD KEMPF
Placekicker—Houston Oilers
Born May 25, 1956, at Philadelphia, Pa.
Height, 5.09. Weight, 170.
High School—Philadelphia, Pa., Cardinal Dougherty.
Received bachelor of arts degree in international relations
and German from University of Pennsylvania in 1978.
Signed as free agent by New England Patriots, May 10, 1981.
Released by New England Patriots, August 18, 1981; signed as free agent by Houston Oilers, February 20, 1982.
On injured reserve with back injury, November 24 through remainder of 1984 season.

		—————PLACE KICKING—————				
Year Club	G.	XP.	XPM.	FG.	FGA.	Pts.
1982—Houston NFL	9	16	2	4	6	28
1983—Houston NFL	16	33	1	17	21	84
1984—Houston NFL	9	14	0	4	6	26
Pro Totals—3 Years	34	63	3	25	33	138

Additional pro statistics: Caught one pass for seven yards, 1983.

MICHAEL LEE KENN
(Mike)
Offensive Tackle—Atlanta Falcons
Born February 9, 1956, at Evanston, Ill.
Height, 6.07. Weight, 266.
High School—Evanston, Ill.
Received bachelor of arts degree in general studies from University of Michigan in 1978.

Named to THE SPORTING NEWS NFL All-Star Team, 1980.
Selected by Atlanta in 1st round (13th player selected) of 1978 NFL draft.
Atlanta NFL, 1978 through 1984.
Games: 1978 (16), 1979 (16), 1980 (16), 1981 (16), 1982 (9), 1983 (16), 1984 (14). Total—103.
Pro statistics: Recovered two fumbles, 1978 and 1979; recovered three fumbles, 1980; recovered one fumble, 1981 through 1983.
Played in Pro Bowl (NFL All-Star Game) following 1980 through 1984 seasons.

ALLAN STEPHEN KENNEDY
Offensive Tackle—San Francisco 49ers
Born January 8, 1958, at Vancouver, British Columbia.
Height, 6.07. Weight, 275.
High School—Woodland Hills, Calif., El Camino Real.
Received bachelor of arts degree in criminal justice from Washington State University.

Selected by Washington in 10th round (267th player selected) of 1981 NFL draft.
Released by Washington Redskins, August 24, 1981; signed as free agent by San Francisco 49ers, September 9, 1981.
On injured reserve with broken finger, September 10 through December 3, 1981; activated, December 4, 1981.
On injured reserve with ankle injury, September 7 through entire 1982 season.
San Francisco NFL, 1981, 1983 and 1984.
Games: 1981 (3), 1983 (16), 1984 (15). Total—34.
Played in NFC Championship Game following 1981, 1983 and 1984 seasons.
Played in NFL Championship Game following 1981 and 1984 seasons.

MICHAEL SCOTT KENNEDY
(Mike)
Safety—Houston Oilers
Born February 26, 1959, at Toledo, O.
Height, 6.00. Weight, 195.
High School—Toledo, O., St. Francis DeSales.
Attended University of Toledo.

Signed as free agent by Atlanta Falcons, April 30, 1982.
Released by Atlanta Falcons, September 4, 1982; signed as free agent by Birmingham Stallions, January 26, 1983.
Released by Birmingham Stallions, February 20, 1983; signed as free agent by Buffalo Bills, May 12, 1983.
Released by Buffalo Bills, August 30, 1983; re-signed by Bills, September 28, 1983.
Released by Buffalo Bills, August 27, 1984; signed as free agent by Houston Oilers, August 30, 1984.
On non-football injury list with knee injury, October 18 through November 22, 1984; activated, November 23, 1984.

| | | | —INTERCEPTIONS— | | | |
Year	Club	G.	No.	Yds.	Avg.	TD.
1983—Buffalo NFL		12	1	22	22.0	1
1984—Houston NFL		11		None		
Pro Totals—2 Years		23	1	22	22.0	1

Additional pro statistics: Recovered one fumble, 1983.

LONNIE KENNELL
Defensive Tackle—Tampa Bay Buccaneers
Born February 8, 1961, at Crescent City, Fla.
Height, 6.02. Weight, 248.
High School—Crescent City, Fla.
Attended Wichita State University.

Signed as free agent by Pittsburgh Maulers, May 4, 1983.
Released by Pittsburgh Maulers, August 29, 1983; signed as free agent by Oklahoma Outlaws, February 16, 1984.
Released by Oklahoma Outlaws, February 20, 1984; signed as free agent by Birmingham Stallions, March 14, 1984.
On developmental squad, March 26 and March 27, 1984.
On reserve/retired list, March 28 through May 28, 1984.
Released by Birmingham Stallions, May 29, 1984; signed as free agent by Indianapolis Colts, June 15, 1984.
Released by Indianapolis Colts, August 27, 1984; signed as free agent by Tampa Bay Buccaneers, February 17, 1985.
On developmental squad for 1 game with Birmingham Stallions in 1984.
Birmingham USFL, 1984.
Games: 1984 (1).

STEVEN FAUCETTE KENNEY
(Steve)
Guard—Philadelphia Eagles
Born December 26, 1955, at Wilmington, N. C.
Height, 6.04. Weight, 270.
High School—Raleigh, N. C., Sanderson.
Attended Clemson University.

Signed as free agent by Philadelphia Eagles, May 14, 1979.
On injured reserve with knee injury, August 21 through entire 1979 season.
Philadelphia NFL, 1980 through 1984.
Games: 1980 (15), 1981 (13), 1982 (9), 1983 (16), 1984 (11). Total—64.
Pro statistics: Recovered two fumbles, 1981; recovered one fumble, 1982.
Played in NFC Championship Game following 1980 season.
Played in NFL Championship Game following 1980 season.

WILLIAM PATRICK KENNEY
(Bill)
Quarterback—Kansas City Chiefs
Born January 20, 1955, at San Francisco, Calif.
Height, 6.04. Weight, 211.
High School—San Clemente, Calif.
Attended Arizona State University, Saddleback Community College and received bachelor of science degree
in business management from University of Northern Colorado in 1978.
Son of Charles Kenney, guard with San Francisco 49ers, 1947.

Selected by Miami in 12th round (333rd player selected) of 1978 NFL draft.
Traded by Miami Dolphins to Washington Redskins for 6th round pick in 1979 draft, August 1, 1978.
Released by Washington Redskins, August 21, 1978; signed as free agent by Kansas City Chiefs, January 19, 1979.
On injured reserve with broken thumb, August 28 through October 5, 1984; activated, October 6, 1984.
Active for 16 games with Kansas City Chiefs in 1979; did not play.

		PASSING							RUSHING				TOTAL		
Year Club	G.	Att.	Cmp.	Pct.	Gain	T.P.	P.I.	Avg.	Att.	Yds.	Avg.	TD.	TD.	Pts.	F.
1980—Kansas City NFL.............	3	69	37	53.6	542	5	2	7.86	8	8	1.0	0	0	0	1
1981—Kansas City NFL.............	13	274	147	53.6	1983	9	16	7.24	24	89	3.7	1	1	6	4
1982—Kansas City NFL.............	7	169	95	56.2	1192	7	6	7.05	13	40	3.1	0	0	0	3
1983—Kansas City NFL.............	16	*603	*346	57.4	4348	24	18	7.21	23	59	2.6	3	3	18	7
1984—Kansas City NFL.............	9	282	151	53.5	2098	15	10	7.44	9	—8	—0.9	0	0	0	8
Pro Totals—6 Years..........	48	1397	776	55.5	10163	60	52	7.27	77	188	2.4	4	4	24	23

Quarterback Rating Points: 1980 (91.4), 1981 (63.8), 1982 (77.0), 1983 (80.8), 1984 (80.7). Total—77.6.
Additional pro statistics: Fumbled once for minus six yards, 1980; fumbled four times for minus two yards, 1981;
recovered two fumbles, 1982; caught one pass for no yards and recovered four fumbles, 1983; recovered three fumbles
and fumbled eight times for minus 34 yards, 1984.
Played in Pro Bowl (NFL All-Star Game) following 1983 season.

DON EMIT KERN III
Tight End—Cincinnati Bengals
Born August 25, 1962, at Los Gatos, Calif.
Height, 6.04. Weight, 225.
High School—Saratoga, Calif.
Attended West Valley College and Arizona State University.

Selected by Arizona in 1984 USFL territorial draft.
Selected by Cincinnati in 6th round (150th player selected) of 1984 NFL draft.
Signed by Cincinnati Bengals, June 11, 1984.

		PASS RECEIVING			
Year Club	G.	P.C.	Yds.	Avg.	TD.
1984—Cincinnati NFL	16	2	14	7.0	0

MICHAEL JOSEPH KERRIGAN
(Mike)
Quarterback—New England Patriots
Born April 27, 1960, at Chicago, Ill.
Height, 6.03. Weight, 205.
High School—Chicago, Ill., Mt. Carmel.
Attended Northwestern University.

Signed as free agent by New England Patriots, May 7, 1982.
On injured reserve with concussion, September 6 through entire 1982 season.
Released by New England Patriots, August 27, 1984; re-signed by Patriots, September 27, 1984.
Released by New England Patriots, October 20, 1984; re-signed by Patriots, November 7, 1984.

		PASSING							RUSHING				TOTAL		
Year Club	G.	Att.	Cmp.	Pct.	Gain	T.P.	P.I.	Avg.	Att.	Yds.	Avg.	TD.	TD.	Pts.	F.
1983—New England NFL...........	1	14	6	42.9	72	0	1	5.14	1	14	14.0	0	0	0	0
1984—New England NFL...........	1	1	1	100.0	13	0	0	13.00		None			0	0	0
Pro Totals—2 Years..........	2	15	7	46.7	85	0	1	5.67	1	14	14.0	0	0	0	0

Quarterback Rating Points: 1983 (29.5), 1984 (118.8). Total—36.7.

TYRONE KEYS
Defensive End—Chicago Bears
Born October 24, 1959, at Brookhaven, Miss.
Height, 6.07. Weight, 267.
High School—Jackson, Miss., Callaway.
Attended Mississippi State University.

Selected by New York Jets in 5th round (113th player selected) of 1981 NFL draft.
Signed as free agent by British Columbia Lions, May 20, 1981.
On reserve list, July 12 through July 18, 1981; activated, July 19, 1981.
On reserve list, July 25 through August 2, 1981; activated, August 3, 1981.
On reserve list, August 16 through September 12, 1981; activated, September 13, 1981.
On reserve list, September 21 through remainder of 1981 season.
On reserve list, July 2 through July 17, 1982; activated, July 18, 1982.
On reserve list, August 15 through August 31, 1982; activated, September 1, 1982.
On reserve list, September 12 through September 18, 1982; activated, September 19, 1982.
On reserve list, October 17 through October 23, 1982; activated, October 24, 1982.
Traded by British Columbia Lions to Toronto Argonauts, April 15, 1983.
Released by Toronto Argonauts, July 2, 1983.
NFL rights traded by New York Jets to Chicago Bears for 5th round pick in 1985 draft, July 13, 1983.
Signed by Chicago Bears, July 10, 1983.
British Columbia CFL, 1981 and 1982; Chicago NFL, 1983 and 1984.
Games: 1981 (5), 1982 (10), 1983 (14), 1984 (15). Total CFL—15. Total NFL—29. Total Pro—44.
Played in NFC Championship Game following 1984 season.

KEITH DARRYL KIDD
Wide Receiver—Minnesota Vikings
Born September 10, 1962, at Crossett, Ark.
Height, 6.01. Weight, 198.
High School—Crossett, Ark.
Attended University of Arkansas.

Selected by Washington in 2nd round (31st player selected) of 1984 USFL draft.
Selected by Minnesota in 9th round (235th player selected) of 1984 NFL draft.
Signed by Minnesota Vikings, August 1, 1984.
On physically unable to perform/reserve with knee injury, August 8 through entire 1984 season.

MAX JOHN KIDD
(Known by middle name.)
Punter—Buffalo Bills
Born August 22, 1961, at Springfield, Ill.
Height, 6.03. Weight, 201.
High School—Findlay, O.
Received bachelor of science degree in industrial engineering and
management science from Northwestern University in 1984.

Selected by Chicago in 1984 USFL territorial draft.
Selected by Buffalo in 5th round (128th player selected) of 1984 NFL draft.
Signed by Buffalo Bills, June 1, 1984.

		——PUNTING——		
Year	Club	G.	No.	Avg. Blk.
1984—Buffalo NFL		16	88	42.0 2

BLAIR ARMSTRONG KIEL
Quarterback—Tampa Bay Buccaneers
Born November 29, 1961, at Columbus, Ind.
Height, 6.00. Weight, 200.
High School—Columbus, Ind., East.
Received degree in marketing from University of Notre Dame in 1984.

Selected by Chicago in 1984 USFL territorial draft.
Selected by Tampa Bay in 11th round (281st player selected) of 1984 NFL draft.
Signed by Tampa Bay Buccaneers, June 5, 1984.
On non-football injury list with ulcerative colitis, November 13 through remainder of 1984 season.

			————————PASSING————————							——RUSHING——			—TOTAL—		
Year	Club	G.	Att.	Cmp.	Pct.	Gain	T.P.	P.I.	Avg.	Att.	Yds.	Avg. TD.	TD.	Pts.	F.
1984—Tampa Bay NFL		10	None							None			0	0	0

JEFF C. KIEWEL
Guard—Atlanta Falcons
Born September 27, 1960, at Phoenix, Ariz.
Height, 6.04. Weight, 254.
High School—Tucson, Ariz., Sabino.
Attended University of Arizona.

Selected by Arizona in 1983 USFL territorial draft.
Signed by Arizona Wranglers, February 26, 1983.
On developmental squad, May 28 through June 3, 1983; activated, June 4, 1983.
On developmental squad, February 24 through entire 1984 season.
Not protected in merger of Arizona Wranglers and Oklahoma Outlaws; selected by Houston Gamblers in USFL
dispersal draft, December 6, 1984.
Released by Houston Gamblers, February 18, 1985; re-signed by Gamblers, February 19, 1985.
On developmental squad, February 21 through February 25, 1985.
Contract voided by USFL, February 26, 1985; signed as free agent by Atlanta Falcons, March 16, 1985.
On developmental squad for 1 game with Arizona Wranglers in 1983.
On developmental squad for 18 games with Arizona Wranglers in 1984.

On developmental squad for 1 game with Houston Gamblers in 1985.
Arizona USFL, 1983.
Games: 1983 (16).
On developmental squad for USFL Championship Game following 1984 season.

BRUCE MICHAEL KIMBALL
Guard—Washington Redskins
Born August 19, 1959, at Beverly, Mass.
Height, 6.02. Weight, 260.
High School—Byfield, Mass., Triton.
Attended Bridgeton (Mass.) Academy Prep School and received bachelor of science degree
in physical education from University of Massachusetts in 1979.

Selected by Pittsburgh in 7th round (192nd player selected) of 1979 NFL draft.
Released by Pittsburgh Steelers, August 20, 1979; signed as free agent by Toronto Argonauts, September 6, 1979.
On injured reserve, September 22 through remainder of 1980 season.
Granted free agency, March 1, 1981; signed as free agent by New York Giants, March 27, 1981.
On injured reserve with knee injury, July 24 through entire 1981 season.
On injured reserve with fractured leg, September 13 through remainder of 1982 season.
Released by New York Giants, August 15, 1983; signed as free agent by Washington Redskins, August 25, 1983.
Released by Washington Redskins, August 27, 1984; re-signed by Redskins, October 23, 1984.
Toronto CFL, 1979 and 1980; New York Giants NFL, 1982; Washington NFL, 1983 and 1984.
Games: 1979 (8), 1980 (11), 1982 (1), 1983 (16), 1984 (8). Total CFL—19. Total NFL—25. Total Pro—44.
Pro statistics: Recovered two fumbles, 1980.
Played in NFC Championship Game following 1983 season.
Played in NFL Championship Game following 1983 season.

JON JOSEPH KIMMEL
Linebacker—Philadelphia Eagles
Born July 21, 1960, at Binghamton, N.Y.
Height, 6.04. Weight, 240.
High School—Conklin, N.Y., Susquehanna Valley.
Received bachelor of arts degree in geology from Colgate University.

Signed by Arizona Wranglers, January 20, 1983.
On developmental squad, May 15 through May 21, 1983; activated, May 22, 1983.
Franchise transferred to Chicago, September 30, 1983.
Traded by Chicago Blitz to Denver Gold for quarterback Ron Reeves, March 21, 1984.
On developmental squad, March 21 through March 30, 1984; activated, March 31, 1984.
Signed by Philadelphia Eagles for 1985, October 22, 1984 (contract to take effect after granting free agency,
November 30, 1984).
On developmental squad for 1 game with Arizona Wranglers in 1983.
On developmental squad for 1 game with Denver Gold in 1984.
Arizona USFL, 1983; Chicago (4)-Denver (12) USFL, 1984.
Games: 1983 (17), 1984 (16). Total—33.
Pro statistics: Credited with one sack for nine yards and recovered three fumbles, 1983; returned one punt for no
yards and fumbled once, 1984.

TERRY KINARD
Safety—New York Giants
Born November 24, 1959, at Bitburg, West Germany.
Height, 6.01. Weight, 200.
High School—Sumter, S.C.
Attended Clemson University.

Named as defensive back on THE SPORTING NEWS College All-America Team, 1982.
Selected by Washington in 1983 USFL territorial draft.
Selected by New York Giants in 1st round (10th player selected) of 1983 NFL draft.
Signed by New York Giants, May 17, 1983.

Year Club	G.	No.	——INTERCEPTIONS—— Yds.	Avg.	TD.
1983—New York Giants NFL	16	3	49	16.3	0
1984—New York Giants NFL	15	2	29	14.5	0
Pro Totals—2 Years............	31	5	78	15.6	0

Additional pro statistics: Recovered one fumble for 10 yards, 1983; returned one punt for no yards, recovered one
fumble and fumbled once, 1984.

ANGELO TYRONE KING
Linebacker—Detroit Lions
Born February 10, 1958, at Columbia, S.C.
Height, 6.01. Weight, 222.
High School—Columbia, S.C.
Attended South Carolina State College.

Signed as free agent by Dallas Cowboys, May, 1981.
Released by Dallas Cowboys, August 25, 1981; re-signed by Cowboys, September 8, 1981.
Traded by Dallas Cowboys to Detroit Lions for 1986 draft choice, August 27, 1984.
Dallas NFL, 1981 through 1983; Detroit NFL, 1984.
Games: 1981 (15), 1982 (9), 1983 (16), 1984 (16). Total—56.
Pro statistics: Recovered two fumbles, 1981.
Played in NFC Championship Game following 1981 and 1982 seasons.

GORDON DAVID KING
Offensive Tackle—New York Giants
Born February 3, 1956, at Madison, Wis.
Height, 6.06. Weight, 275.
High School—Fair Oaks, Calif., Bella Vista.
Received bachelor of arts degree in communications/psychology from
Stanford University in 1978.

Named as offensive tackle on THE SPORTING NEWS College All-America Team, 1977.
Selected by New York Giants in 1st round (10th player selected) of 1978 NFL draft.
On injured reserve with ankle injury, November 29 through remainder of 1978 season.
On injured reserve with dislocated elbow, August 29 through October 18, 1979; activated, October 19, 1979.
On injured reserve with broken arm, December 6 through remainder of 1983 season.
On physically unable to perform/reserve with broken arm, July 19 through entire 1984 season.
New York Giants NFL, 1978 through 1983.
Games: 1978 (11), 1979 (7), 1980 (12), 1981 (16), 1982 (9), 1983 (14). Total—69.
Pro statistics: Recovered one fumble, 1979, 1981 and 1982.

KENNETH L. KING
(Kenny)
Running Back—Los Angeles Raiders
Born March 7, 1957, at Clarendon, Tex.
Height, 5.11. Weight, 205.
High School—Clarendon, Tex.
Attended University of Oklahoma.

Selected by Houston in 3rd round (72nd player selected) of 1979 NFL draft.
On injured reserve with rib injury, November 21 through remainder of 1979 season.
Traded by Houston Oilers to Oakland Raiders for safety Jack Tatum and 7th round picks in 1980 and 1981 draft, April 30, 1980.
On injured reserve with bruised sternum, December 21 through remainder of 1981 season.
Franchise transferred to Los Angeles, May 7, 1982.

Year Club	G.	Att.	Yds.	Avg.	TD.	P.C.	Yds.	Avg.	TD.	TD.	Pts.	F.
1979—Houston NFL	12	3	9	3.0	0	None				0	0	0
1980—Oakland NFL	15	172	761	4.4	4	22	145	6.6	0	4	24	6
1981—Oakland NFL	14	170	828	4.9	0	27	216	8.0	0	0	0	10
1982—Los Angeles Raiders NFL	9	69	264	3.8	2	9	57	6.3	0	2	12	1
1983—Los Angeles Raiders NFL	15	82	294	3.6	1	14	149	10.6	1	2	12	1
1984—Los Angeles Raiders NFL	16	67	254	3.8	0	14	99	7.1	0	0	0	3
Pro Totals—6 Years	81	563	2410	4.3	7	86	666	7.7	1	8	48	21

Additional pro statistics: Returned one kickoff for 17 yards, 1979; recovered two fumbles, 1981; recovered one fumble, 1984.
Played in AFC Championship Game following 1980 and 1983 seasons.
Played in NFL Championship Game following 1980 and 1983 seasons.
Named to play in Pro Bowl (NFL All-Star Game) following 1980 season; replaced due to injury by Franco Harris.

LINDEN KEITH KING
Linebacker—San Diego Chargers
Born June 28, 1955, at Memphis, Tenn.
Height, 6.04. Weight, 250.
High School—Colorado Springs, Colo., Air Academy.
Attended Colorado State University.

Selected by San Diego in 3rd round (77th player selected) of 1977 NFL draft.
On injured reserve, September 12 through 1977 season.
On injured reserve with ankle injury, November 5, 1980, through January 9, 1981; activated, January 10, 1981.
San Diego NFL, 1978 through 1984.
Games: 1978 (14), 1979 (16), 1980 (5), 1981 (16), 1982 (9), 1983 (16), 1984 (16). Total—92.
Pro statistics: Intercepted one pass for three yards and recovered one fumble for 14 yards, 1978; recovered two fumbles, 1979, 1983 and 1984; intercepted one pass for 28 yards, 1981; recovered one fumble, 1982; intercepted one pass for 19 yards, 1983; intercepted two passes for 52 yards and fumbled once, 1984.
Played in AFC Championship Game following 1980 and 1981 seasons.

REGGIE KINLAW
Defensive Tackle—Los Angeles Raiders
Born January 9, 1957, at Miami, Fla.
Height, 6.02. Weight, 245.
High School—Miami, Fla., Springs.
Attended University of Oklahoma.
Brother of Marcus Kinlaw, offensive lineman at University of Miami (Fla.); and
cousin of Dan Driessen, first baseman with Montreal Expos.

Selected by Oakland in 12th round (320th player selected) of 1979 NFL draft.
On injured reserve with knee injury, September 9 through remainder of 1981 season.
Franchise transferred to Los Angeles, May 7, 1982.
Oakland NFL, 1979 through 1981; Los Angeles Raiders NFL, 1982 through 1984.
Games: 1979 (16), 1980 (14), 1981 (1), 1982 (9), 1983 (16), 1984 (13). Total—69.
Pro statistics: Recovered one fumble, 1982.
Played in AFC Championship Game following 1980 and 1983 seasons.
Played in NFL Championship Game following 1980 and 1983 seasons.

LARRY D. KINNEBREW
Running Back—Cincinnati Bengals
Born June 11, 1959, at Rome, Ga.
Height, 6.01. Weight, 252.
High School—Rome, Ga., East.
Attended Tennessee State University.
Selected by Cincinnati in 6th round (165th player selected) of 1983 NFL draft.

Year	Club	G.	Att.	Yds.	Avg.	TD.	P.C.	Yds.	Avg.	TD.	TD.	Pts.	F.
				RUSHING				PASS RECEIVING				TOTAL	
1983—Cincinnati NFL		16	39	156	4.0	3	2	4	2.0	0	3	18	3
1984—Cincinnati NFL		16	154	623	4.0	9	19	159	8.4	1	10	60	4
Pro Totals—2 Years		32	193	779	4.0	12	21	163	7.8	1	13	78	7

Additional pro statistics: Recovered one fumble, 1983; returned one kickoff for seven yards, 1984.

MARK STEVEN KIRCHNER
Offensive Tackle—Indianapolis Colts
Born October 19, 1959, at Pasadena, Tex.
Height, 6.03. Weight, 261.
High School—Deer Park, Tex.
Received degree in finance from Baylor University in 1982.
Selected by Denver in 4th round (40th player selected) of 1983 USFL draft.
Selected by Pittsburgh in 7th round (191st player selected) of 1983 NFL draft.
Signed by Pittsburgh Steelers, June 16, 1983.
Released by Pittsburgh Steelers, August 29, 1983; re-signed by Steelers, August 30, 1983.
Released by Pittsburgh Steelers, September 30, 1983; awarded on waivers to Kansas City Chiefs, October 3, 1983.
Released by Kansas City Chiefs, August 20, 1984; signed as free agent by Indianapolis Colts, September 12, 1984.
Pittsburgh (3)-Kansas City (5) NFL, 1983; Indianapolis NFL, 1984.
Games: 1983 (8), 1984 (11). Total—19.

SYD KITSON
Guard—Dallas Cowboys
Born September 27, 1958, at Orange, N.J.
Height, 6.04. Weight, 264.
High School—New Providence, N.J.
Attended Wake Forest University.
Selected by Green Bay in 3rd round (61st player selected) of 1980 NFL draft.
On injured reserve with neck injury, October 14 through November 12, 1981; activated, November 13, 1981.
On injured reserve with neck and shoulder injuries, September 7 through entire 1982 season.
Released by Green Bay Packers, October 23, 1984; signed as free agent by Dallas Cowboys, November 28, 1984.
Green Bay NFL, 1980, 1981 and 1983; Green Bay (8)-Dallas (1) NFL, 1984.
Games: 1980 (14), 1981 (11), 1983 (16), 1984 (9). Total—50.
Pro statistics: Caught one pass for nine yards and returned one kickoff for no yards, 1983.

JOSEPH EDWARD KLECKO
(Joe)
Defensive End-Defensive Tackle—New York Jets
Born October 15, 1953, at Chester, Pa.
Height, 6.03. Weight, 263.
High School—Chester, Pa., St. James.
Received bachelor of arts degree in history from Temple University in 1977.
Named to THE SPORTING NEWS NFL All-Star Team, 1981.
Selected by New York Jets in 6th round (144th player selected) of 1977 NFL draft.
On injured reserve with knee injury, November 26, 1982 through January 4, 1983; activated, January 5, 1983.
Played semi-pro football with Ridley Township Green Knights, 1971 and 1972.
New York Jets NFL, 1977 through 1984.
Games: 1977 (13), 1978 (16), 1979 (16), 1980 (15), 1981 (16), 1982 (2), 1983 (16), 1984 (12). Total—106.
Pro statistics: Recovered one fumble, 1978 and 1983; recovered two fumbles, 1981 and 1984.
Played in AFC Championship Game following 1982 season.
Played in Pro Bowl (NFL All-Star Game) following 1981, 1983 and 1984 seasons.

VICTOR K. KLEVER
(Rocky)
Tight End—New York Jets
Born July 10, 1959, at Portland, Ore.
Height, 6.03. Weight, 225.
High School—Anchorage, Alaska, West.
Received degree in business management from University of Montana in 1982.
Selected by New York Jets in 9th round (247th player selected) of 1982 NFL draft.
On injured reserve with broken hand, August 24 through entire 1982 season.
Released by New York Jets, August 29, 1983; re-signed by Jets after clearing procedural waivers, November 3, 1983.

		—PASS RECEIVING—				
Year Club	G.	P.C.	Yds.	Avg.	TD.	
1983—New York Jets NFL....	5		None			
1984—New York Jets NFL....	16	3	29	9.7	1	
Pro Totals—2 Years............	21	3	29	9.7	1	

DAVID JOHN KLUG
(Dave)
Linebacker—Houston Oilers
Born May 17, 1958, at Litchfield, Minn.
Height, 6.04. Weight, 230.
High School—Litchfield, Minn.
Received bachelor of arts degree from Concordia College in 1980.

Selected by Kansas City in 4th round (94th player selected) of 1980 NFL draft.
On non-football injury list with ankle injury suffered before draft, October 15 through entire 1980 season.
On injured reserve with knee injury, September 16 through remainder of 1983 season.
On physically unable to perform/reserve with knee injury, August 21 through October 22, 1984.
Released by Kansas City Chiefs, October 23, 1984; signed as free agent by Houston Oilers, April 3, 1985.
Kansas City NFL, 1981 through 1983.
Games: 1981 (15), 1982 (9), 1983 (1). Total—25.
Pro statistics: Recovered blocked punt in end zone for a touchdown, 1982.

GREGORY MICHAEL KOCH
Name pronounced Cook.
(Greg)
Offensive Tackle—Green Bay Packers
Born June 14, 1955, at Bethesda, Md.
Height, 6.04. Weight, 276.
High School—Houston, Tex., Spring Woods.
Attended University of Arkansas.

Selected by Green Bay in 2nd round (39th player selected) of 1977 NFL draft.
Green Bay NFL, 1977 through 1984.
Games: 1977 (14), 1978 (16), 1979 (16), 1980 (16), 1981 (16), 1982 (9), 1983 (15), 1984 (15). Total—117.

PETER ALAN KOCH
(Pete)
Defensive End—Cincinnati Bengals
Born January 23, 1962, at Nassau County, N.Y.
Height, 6.06. Weight, 265.
High School—New Hyde Park, N.Y., Memorial.
Attended University of Maryland.
Brother of Larry Koch, pitcher in St. Louis Cardinals' organization, 1967, 1968, 1970 and 1971.

Selected by Washington in 1984 USFL territorial draft.
Selected by Cincinnati in 1st round (16th player selected) of 1984 NFL draft.
Signed by Cincinnati Bengals, July 30, 1984.
Cincinnati NFL, 1984.
Games: 1984 (16).

MATTHEW JOSEPH KOFLER
(Matt)
Quarterback—Buffalo Bills
Born August 30, 1959, at Longview, Wash.
Height, 6.03. Weight, 192.
High School—San Diego, Calif., Patrick Henry.
Attended San Diego Mesa Junior College and San Diego State University.
Son of Otto Kofler, assistant coach at Stanford University.

Selected by Buffalo in 2nd round (48th player selected) of 1982 NFL draft.
On inactive list, September 12 and September 19, 1982.

		—————PASSING—————								—RUSHING—				—TOTAL—		
Year Club	G.	Att.	Cmp.	Pct.	Gain	T.P.	P.I.	Avg.	Att.	Yds.	Avg.	TD.	TD.	Pts.	F.
1982—Buffalo NFL.....................	4			None					2	21	10.5	0	0	0	0
1983—Buffalo NFL.....................	16	61	35	57.4	440	4	3	7.21	4	25	6.3	0	0	0	0
1984—Buffalo NFL.....................	16	93	33	35.5	432	2	5	4.65	10	80	8.0	0	0	0	1
Pro Totals—3 Years..........	36	154	68	44.2	872	6	8	5.66	16	126	7.9	0	0	0	1

Quarterback Rating Points: 1983 (81.3), 1984 (35.8). Total—53.8.
Additional pro statistics: Recovered one fumble, 1984.

—DID YOU KNOW—
That in Seattle's 45-0 victory over Kansas City on November 4, 1984, the Seahawks scored four touchdowns on interception returns of 58 yards or more?

ROBERT HENRY KOHRS
(Bob)
Linebacker-Defensive End—Pittsburgh Steelers
Born November 8, 1958, at Phoenix, Ariz.
Height, 6.03. Weight, 235.
High School—Phoenix, Ariz., Brophy Prep.
Attended Arizona State University.

Selected by Pittsburgh in 2nd round (35th player selected) of 1980 NFL draft.
On injured reserve with broken foot, September 1 through entire 1980 season.
On injured reserve with knee injury, November 4 through remainder of 1983 season.
On physically unable to perform/reserve with knee injury, August 21 through October 11, 1984; activated, October 12, 1984.
Pittsburgh NFL, 1981 through 1984.
Games: 1981 (16), 1982 (9), 1983 (9), 1984 (10). Total—44.
Pro statistics: Recovered one fumble, 1981 through 1983; returned one kickoff for six yards and credited with one safety, 1983.
Played in AFC Championship Game following 1984 season.

CHRISTOPHER JAMES KOLODZIEJSKI
Name pronounced Ko-la-JESS-skee.
(Chris)
Tight End—Pittsburgh Steelers
Born January 5, 1961, at Augsburg, Germany.
Height, 6.03. Weight, 231.
High School—Santa Monica, Calif.
Received bachelor of science degree in finance from University of Wyoming in 1984.

Selected by Denver in 1984 USFL territorial draft.
Selected by Pittsburgh in 2nd round (52nd player selected) of 1984 NFL draft.
Signed by Pittsburgh Steelers, July 20, 1984.
On injured reserve with knee injury, October 15 through remainder of 1984 season.

		—PASS RECEIVING—				
Year	Club	G.	P.C.	Yds.	Avg.	TD.
1984—Pittsburgh NFL.............		7	5	59	11.8	0

WILLIAM JEFFREY KOMLO
(Jeff)
Quarterback—Seattle Seahawks
Born July 30, 1956, at Cleverly, Md.
Height, 6.02. Weight, 200.
High School—Hyattsville, Md., DeMatha.
Attended University of Delaware and attending Villanova University.
Brother of Drew Komlo, quarterback at University of Delaware.

Selected by Detroit in 9th round (231st player selected) of 1979 NFL draft.
Released by Detroit Lions, September 6, 1982; claimed on waivers by Atlanta Falcons, September 7, 1982.
On inactive list, September 12 and September 19, 1982.
Released by Atlanta Falcons, August 22, 1983; signed as free agent by Tampa Bay Buccaneers, October 7, 1983.
On injured reserve with elbow injury, August 20 through entire 1984 season.
Granted free agency after not receiving qualifying offer, February 1, 1985; signed by Seattle Seahawks, February 28, 1985.
Active for 7 games with Atlanta Falcons in 1982; did not play.

		—————PASSING—————							—RUSHING—				—TOTAL—		
Year	Club	G.	Att.	Cmp.	Pct.	Gain	T.P.	P.I.	Avg.	Att.	Yds.	Avg.	TD.	TD.	Pts.	F.
1979—Detroit NFL......................		16	368	183	49.7	2238	11	23	6.08	30	107	3.6	2	2	12	11
1980—Detroit NFL......................		4	4	2	50.0	26	0	1	6.50		None			0	0	0
1981—Detroit NFL......................		3	57	29	50.9	290	1	3	5.09	6	3	0.5	0	0	0	2
1983—Tampa Bay NFL		2	8	4	50.0	49	0	1	6.13	2	11	5.5	0	0	0	2
Pro Totals—5 Years...........		25	437	218	49.9	2603	12	28	5.96	38	121	3.2	2	2	12	15

Quarterback Rating Points: 1979 (52.6), 1980 (31.3), 1981 (49.6), 1983 (29.7). Total—50.8.
Additional pro statistics: Recovered six fumbles and fumbled 11 times for minus 22 yards, 1979; recovered two fumbles, 1981.

STEVE KORTE
Center—New Orleans Saints
Born January 15, 1960, at Denver, Colo.
Height, 6.02. Weight, 272.
High School—Littleton, Colo., Arapahoe.
Attended University of Arkansas.

Named as guard on THE SPORTING NEWS College All-America Team, 1982.
Selected by Birmingham in 2nd round (20th player selected) of 1983 USFL draft.
Selected by New Orleans in 2nd round (38th player selected) of 1983 NFL draft.
Signed by New Orleans Saints, June 20, 1983.
USFL rights traded by Birmingham Stallions to Memphis Showboats for offensive tackle Phil McKinnely, January 22, 1985.

New Orleans NFL, 1983 and 1984.
Games: 1983 (16), 1984 (15). Total—31.
Pro statistics: Recovered one fumble in end zone for a touchdown, 1983; recovered one fumble, 1984.

JIM KOVACH
Name pronounced KOE-vawch.
Linebacker—New Orleans Saints
Born May 1, 1956, at Parma Heights, O.
Height, 6.02. Weight, 239.
High School—Parma Heights, O., Valley Forge.
Received bachelor of science degree in pre-med from University of Kentucky
in 1979; attending medical school at University of Kentucky.

Selected by New Orleans in 4th round (93rd player selected) of 1979 NFL draft.
On injured reserve with dislocated shoulder, December 3 through remainder of 1980 season.
New Orleans NFL, 1979 through 1984.
Games: 1979 (16), 1980 (11), 1981 (15), 1982 (8), 1983 (16), 1984 (15). Total—81.
Pro statistics: Returned one kickoff for 10 yards, 1979; intercepted one pass for no yards, 1980; intercepted one pass for 13 yards, 1981; recovered one fumble, 1981 and 1982; intercepted one pass for 16 yards, 1984.

GARY STUART KOWALSKI
Offensive Tackle—Los Angeles Rams
Born July 2, 1960, at New Haven, Conn.
Height, 6.05. Weight, 250.
High School—Clinton, Conn., Morgan.
Attended Boston College.

Selected by Boston in 1983 USFL territorial draft.
Selected by Los Angeles Rams in 6th round (144th player selected) of 1983 NFL draft.
Signed by Los Angeles Rams, June 3, 1983.
On injured reserve with knee injury, August 28 through entire 1984 season.
Los Angeles Rams NFL, 1983.
Games: 1983 (15).

BRUCE KOZERSKI
Offensive Tackle-Center—Cincinnati Bengals
Born April 2, 1962, at Plains, Pa.
Height, 6.04. Weight, 275.
High School—Wilkes-Barre, Pa., James M. Coughlin.
Attended Holy Cross College.

Selected by Houston in 12th round (245th player selected) of 1984 USFL draft.
Selected by Cincinnati in 9th round (231st player selected) of 1984 NFL draft.
Signed by Cincinnati Bengals, June 10, 1984.
Cincinnati NFL, 1984.
Games: 1984 (16).

MICHAEL JOHN KOZLOWSKI
(Mike)
Safety—Miami Dolphins
Born February 24, 1956, at Newark, N. J.
Height, 6.00. Weight, 198.
High School—Encinitas, Calif., San Dieguito.
Attended San Diego State University (on volleyball scholarship), Brigham Young University,
Mira Costa Junior College and University of Colorado.
Brother of Glen Kozlowski, wide receiver at Brigham Young University.

Selected by Miami in 10th round (272nd player selected) of 1979 NFL draft.
On injured reserve with ankle injury, August 30 through entire 1980 season.
Tied NFL record for most touchdowns scored by interception, game (2), against New York Jets, December 16, 1983.

Year Club	G.	INTERCEPTIONS				-PUNT RETURNS-				—KICKOFF RET.—				—TOTAL—		
		No.	Yds.	Avg.	TD.	No.	Yds.	Avg.	TD.	No.	Yds.	Avg.	TD.	TD.	Pts.	F.
1979—Miami NFL	16		None			3	21	7.0	0	4	85	21.3	0	0	0	0
1981—Miami NFL	14	3	37	12.3	0	1	9	9.0	0	1	40	40.0	0	1	6	0
1982—Miami NFL	9	1	36	36.0	0		None			1	10	10.0	0	0	0	0
1983—Miami NFL	16	2	73	36.5	*2	2	10	6.0	0	4	50	12.5	0	2	12	2
1984—Miami NFL	16	1	26	26.0	0	4	41	10.3	0	2	23	11.5	0	0	0	0
Pro Totals—5 Years	71	7	172	24.6	2	10	81	8.1	0	12	208	17.3	0	3	18	2

Additional pro statistics: Recovered one fumble, 1979 and 1983; recovered one fumble for 25 yards and a touchdown, 1981; recovered two fumbles for 30 yards, 1982.
Played in AFC Championship Game following 1982 and 1984 seasons.
Played in NFL Championship Game following 1982 and 1984 seasons.

—DID YOU KNOW—

That San Francisco placed nine players on the 1984 NFC Pro Bowl squad while the Raiders had eight on the AFC squad?

THOMAS KRAMER
(Tommy)
Quarterback—Minnesota Vikings
Born March 7, 1955, at San Antonio, Tex.
Height, 6.02. Weight, 200.
High School—San Antonio, Tex., Robert E. Lee.
Received bachelor of business administration degree from Rice University.
Selected by Minnesota in 1st round (27th player selected) of 1977 NFL draft.
On injured reserve with knee injury, September 20 through remainder of 1983 season.

					—PASSING—					—RUSHING—			—TOTAL—		
Year	Club	G.	Att.	Cmp.	Pct.	Gain	T.P.	P.I.	Avg.	Att.	Yds.	Avg.	TD.	TD.	Pts.	F.
1977—Minnesota NFL		6	57	30	52.6	425	5	4	7.46	10	3	0.3	0	0	0	3
1978—Minnesota NFL		4	16	5	31.3	50	0	1	3.13	1	10	10.0	0	0	0	0
1979—Minnesota NFL		16	566	315	55.7	3397	23	24	6.00	32	138	4.3	1	1	6	9
1980—Minnesota NFL		15	522	299	57.3	3582	19	23	6.86	31	115	3.7	1	1	6	2
1981—Minnesota NFL		14	593	322	54.3	3912	26	24	6.60	10	13	1.3	0	0	0	8
1982—Minnesota NFL		9	308	176	57.1	2037	15	12	6.61	21	77	3.7	3	3	18	3
1983—Minnesota NFL		3	82	55	67.1	550	3	4	6.71	8	3	0.4	0	0	0	2
1984—Minnesota NFL		9	236	124	52.5	1678	9	10	7.11	15	9	0.6	0	1	6	10
Pro Totals—8 Years		76	2380	1326	55.7	15631	100	102	6.57	128	368	2.9	5	6	36	37

Quarterback Rating Points: 1977 (77.2), 1978 (15.0), 1979 (69.7), 1980 (72.1), 1981 (72.8), 1982 (77.3), 1983 (77.8), 1984 (70.6). Total—72.0.

Additional pro statistics: Fumbled three times for minus three yards, 1977; ran three yards with lateral on pass reception and fumbled nine times for minus six yards, 1979; recovered two fumbles, 1979 and 1980; recovered three fumbles, 1981; recovered one fumble and fumbled three times for minus 21 yards, 1982; recovered one fumble, 1983; caught one pass for 20 yards and a touchdown, recovered three fumbles and fumbled 10 times for minus five yards, 1984.

Member of Minnesota Vikings for NFC Championship Game following 1977 season; did not play.

BARRY RICHARD KRAUSS
Linebacker—Indianapolis Colts
Born March 17, 1957, at Pompano Beach, Fla.
Height, 6.03. Weight, 247.
High School—Pompano Beach, Fla.
Received bachelor of science degree in education from University of Alabama.
Named as linebacker on THE SPORTING NEWS College All-America Team, 1978.
Selected by Baltimore in 1st round (6th player selected) of 1979 NFL draft.
Franchise transferred to Indianapolis, March 31, 1984.
Baltimore NFL, 1979 through 1983; Indianapolis NFL, 1984.
Games: 1979 (15), 1980 (16), 1981 (16), 1982 (9), 1983 (16), 1984 (16). Total—88.
Pro statistics: Recovered two fumbles, 1979, 1981 and 1983; recovered one fumble, 1980; intercepted one pass for 10 yards, 1981; caught one pass for five yards and a touchdown, 1982; rushed once for minus one yard, 1983; intercepted three passes for 20 yards, recovered two fumbles for minus five yards and fumbled once, 1984.

RICH KRAYNAK
Linebacker—Philadelphia Eagles
Born January 20, 1961, at Phoenixville, Pa.
Height, 6.01. Weight, 221.
High School—Phoenixville, Pa.
Attended University of Pittsburgh.
Selected by Philadelphia in 8th round (93rd player selected) of 1983 USFL draft.
Selected by Philadelphia in 8th round (201st player selected) of 1983 NFL draft.
Signed by Philadelphia Eagles, May 25, 1983.
Philadelphia NFL, 1983 and 1984.
Games: 1983 (16), 1984 (14). Total—30.
Pro statistics: Recovered one fumble, 1983; returned blocked punt eight yards for a touchdown, 1984.

STEVE KENNETH KREIDER
Wide Receiver—Cincinnati Bengals
Born May 12, 1958, at Reading, Pa.
Height, 6.03. Weight, 192.
High School—Leesport, Pa., Schuylkill Valley.
Received bachelor of science degree in electrical engineering from Lehigh University in 1979
and received master's degree in electrical engineering from Lehigh.
Selected by Cincinnati in 6th round (139th player selected) of 1979 NFL draft.

		—PASS RECEIVING—			
Year	Club	G.	P.C.	Yds.	Avg.	TD.
1979—Cincinnati NFL	15	3	20	6.7	0
1980—Cincinnati NFL	16	17	272	16.0	0
1981—Cincinnati NFL	16	37	520	14.1	5
1982—Cincinnati NFL	9	16	230	14.4	1
1983—Cincinnati NFL	16	42	554	13.2	1
1984—Cincinnati NFL	16	20	243	12.2	1
Pro Totals—6 Years	88	135	1839	13.6	8

Additional pro statistics: Fumbled once, 1979, 1980 and 1984; rushed twice for no yards, 1979; returned one kickoff

for 19 yards and recovered one fumble, 1980; attempted one pass with no completions, 1980 and 1983; rushed once for 21 yards, attempted three passes with one completion for 13 yards and fumbled twice, 1981; scored extra point on run, 1982; rushed once for two yards, 1983.
Played in AFC Championship Game following 1981 season.
Played in NFL Championship Game following 1981 season.

JAMES KENDALL KREMER
Name pronounced Kramer.
(Ken)
Nose Tackle—Kansas City Chiefs
Born July 16, 1957, at Hammond, Ind.
Height, 6.04. Weight, 260.
High School—Lansing, Ill., Thornton South.
Attended Ball State University.

Selected by Kansas City in 7th round (167th player selected) of 1979 NFL draft.
Kansas City NFL, 1979 through 1984.
Games: 1979 (16), 1980 (14), 1981 (16), 1982 (9), 1983 (16), 1984 (16). Total—87.
Pro statistics: Recovered one fumble, 1980 and 1983; recovered two fumbles, 1981; intercepted one pass for one yard, 1984.

MITCH KRENK
Tight End—Chicago Bears
Born November 19, 1959, at Crete, Neb.
Height, 6.02. Weight, 225.
High School—Nebraska City, Neb.
Attended University of Nebraska.

Selected by Boston in 1983 USFL territorial draft.
Signed as free agent by Seattle Seahawks, April 28, 1983.
Released by Seattle Seahawks, August 29, 1983; signed as free agent by Dallas Cowboys, March 3, 1984.
Released by Dallas Cowboys, August 27, 1984; awarded on waivers to Chicago Bears, August 28, 1984.
On injured reserve with neck injury, September 28 through November 8, 1984; activated, November 9, 1984.

		—PASS RECEIVING—				
Year	Club	G.	P.C.	Yds.	Avg.	TD.
1984—Chicago NFL		8	2	31	15.5	0

Played in NFC Championship Game following 1984 season.

DAVID M. KRIEG
Name pronounced Craig.
(Dave)
Quarterback—Seattle Seahawks
Born October 20, 1958, at Iola, Wis.
Height, 6.01. Weight, 185.
High School—Schofield, Wis., D.C. Everest.
Received bachelor of science degree in marketing management from Milton College in 1980.

Signed as free agent by Seattle Seahawks, May 6, 1980.

		—————PASSING—————							—RUSHING—				—TOTAL—		
Year	Club	G.	Att.	Cmp.	Pct.	Gain	T.P.	P.I.	Avg.	Att.	Yds.	Avg.	TD.	TD.	Pts.	F.
1980—Seattle NFL		1	2	0	0.0	0	0	0	0.00	None				0	0	0
1981—Seattle NFL		7	112	64	57.1	843	7	5	7.53	11	56	5.1	1	1	6	4
1982—Seattle NFL		3	78	49	62.8	501	2	2	6.42	6	−3	−0.5	0	0	0	5
1983—Seattle NFL		9	243	147	60.5	2139	18	11	8.80	16	55	3.4	2	2	12	10
1984—Seattle NFL		16	480	276	57.5	3671	32	*24	7.65	46	186	4.0	3	3	18	11
Pro Totals—5 Years		36	915	536	58.6	7154	59	42	7.82	79	294	3.7	6	6	36	30

Quarterback Rating Points: 1980 (0.0), 1981 (83.3), 1982 (79.0), 1983 (95.0), 1984 (83.3). Total—85.7.
Additional pro statistics: Recovered one fumble and fumbled twice for minus 14 yards, 1982; caught one pass for 11 yards and recovered two fumbles, 1983; recovered three fumbles and fumbled 11 times for minus 24 yards, 1984.
Played in AFC Championship Game following 1983 season.
Played in Pro Bowl (NFL All-Star Game) following 1984 season.

TIMOTHY A. KRUMRIE
Name pronounced KRUM-RYG.
(Tim)
Nose Tackle—Cincinnati Bengals
Born May 20, 1960, at Eau Claire, Wis.
Height, 6.02. Weight, 262.
High School—Mondovi, Wis.
Attended University of Wisconsin.

Selected by Tampa Bay in 7th round (84th player selected) of 1983 USFL draft.
Selected by Cincinnati in 10th round (276th player selected) of 1983 NFL draft.
Signed by Cincinnati Bengals, May 19, 1983.
Cincinnati NFL, 1983 and 1984.
Games: 1983 (16), 1984 (16). Total—32.
Pro statistics: Recovered one fumble, 1983; recovered one fumble for eight yards, 1984.

GARY WAYNE KUBIAK
Quarterback—Denver Broncos
Born August 15, 1961, at Houston, Tex.
Height, 6.00. Weight, 192.
High School—Houston, Tex., Saint Pius X.
Attended Texas A&M University.
Selected by Denver in 8th round (197th player selected) of 1983 NFL draft.

			PASSING							RUSHING				TOTAL	
Year	Club	G.	Att.	Cmp.	Pct.	Gain	T.P.	P.I.	Avg.	Att.	Yds.	Avg.	TD.	TD.	Pts.	F.
1983—Denver NFL		4	22	12	54.5	186	1	1	8.45	4	17	4.3	1	1	6	0
1984—Denver NFL		7	75	44	58.7	440	4	1	5.87	9	27	3.0	1	1	6	1
Pro Totals—2 Years		11	97	56	57.7	626	5	2	6.45	13	44	3.4	2	2	12	1

Quarterback Rating Points: 1983 (78.9), 1984 (87.6). Total—85.6.
Additional pro statistics: Caught one pass for 20 yards, 1984.

LARRY KUBIN
Linebacker—Washington Redskins
Born February 26, 1959, at Union, N.J.
Height, 6.02. Weight, 238.
High School—Union, N.J.
Received bachelor of arts degree in philosophy from Penn State University in 1980.
Selected by Washington in 6th round (148th player selected) of 1981 NFL draft.
On injured reserve with knee injury, September 1 through entire 1981 season.
Washington NFL, 1982 through 1984.
Games: 1982 (9), 1983 (12), 1984 (16). Total—37.
Pro statistics: Recovered one fumble, 1982.
Played in NFC Championship Game following 1982 and 1983 seasons.
Played in NFL Championship Game following 1982 and 1983 seasons.

ROD RANDLE KUSH
Safety—Buffalo Bills
Born December 29, 1956, at Omaha, Neb.
Height, 6.00. Weight, 188.
High School—Omaha, Neb., Harry A. Burke.
Received bachelor of science degree in criminal justice from
University of Nebraska at Omaha in 1979.
Selected by Buffalo in 5th round (114th player selected) of 1979 NFL draft.
On injured reserve with foot injury, August 22 through entire 1979 season.
On injured reserve with knee injury, October 8 through remainder of 1980 season.
On injured reserve with knee injury, October 12 through remainder of 1983 season.

			INTERCEPTIONS			
Year	Club	G.	No.	Yds.	Avg.	TD.
1980—Buffalo NFL	5		None			
1981—Buffalo NFL	16	1	19	19.0	0	
1982—Buffalo NFL	9		None			
1983—Buffalo NFL	4		None			
1984—Buffalo NFL	16	1	15	15.0	0	
Pro Totals—5 Years	50	2	34	17.0	0	

Additional pro statistics: Recovered five fumbles, 1980; rushed once for minus six yards and recovered three fumbles for five yards, 1981; fumbled once, 1981 and 1984; recovered one fumble, 1984.

FULTON GERALD KUYKENDALL
Linebacker—Atlanta Falcons
Born June 10, 1953, at Coronado, Calif.
Height, 6.04. Weight, 228.
High School—Vallejo, Calif., St. Patrick's.
Received bachelor of science degree in kinesiology from University of California at Los Angeles.
Selected by Atlanta in 6th round (132nd player selected) of 1975 NFL draft.
On injured reserve with back injury, October 26 through remainder of 1976 season.
On injured reserve with broken arm, October 18 through remainder of 1977 season.
On injured reserve with shoulder injury, September 29 through November 13, 1980; activated, November 14, 1980.
Atlanta NFL, 1975 through 1984.
Games: 1975 (14), 1976 (7), 1977 (5), 1978 (16), 1979 (16), 1980 (10), 1981 (16), 1982 (9), 1983 (14), 1984 (16). Total—123.
Pro statistics: Recovered two fumbles, 1975; recovered one fumble, 1976, 1978, 1979, 1981 and 1983; intercepted one pass for 20 yards and a touchdown, 1981; intercepted two passes for 22 yards, 1982; recovered two fumbles for nine yards, 1984.

ERIC HENRY LAAKSO
Name pronounced LAX-o.
Offensive Tackle—Miami Dolphins
Born November 29, 1956, at New York, N.Y.
Height, 6.04. Weight, 260.
High School—Danielson, Conn., Killingly.
Received bachelor of science degree in geology from Tulane University in 1978.

Named to The Sporting News NFL All-Star Team, 1983.
Selected by Miami in 4th round (106th player selected) of 1978 NFL draft.
On injured reserve with leg injury, August 28 through October 12, 1979; activated, October 13, 1979.
On injured reserve with knee injury, September 25 through remainder of 1984 season.
Miami NFL, 1978 through 1984.
Games: 1978 (16), 1979 (10), 1980 (16), 1981 (16), 1982 (9), 1983 (15), 1984 (4). Total—86.
Pro statistics: Recovered one fumble, 1981.
Played in AFC Championship Game following 1982 season.
Played in NFL Championship Game following 1982 season.

KENNETH WAYNE LACY
(Ken)
Running Back—Kansas City Chiefs
Born November 1, 1960, at Waco, Tex.
Height, 6.00. Weight, 220.
High School—Dallas, Tex., Kimball.
Attended The University of Tulsa.

Selected by Michigan in 6th round (69th player selected) of 1983 USFL draft.
Signed by Michigan Panthers, February 2, 1983.
On developmental squad from beginning of season through March 10, 1983; activated, March 11, 1983.
On developmental squad, March 11 through April 6, 1984; activated, April 7, 1984.
Signed by Kansas City Chiefs, April 9, 1984, for contract to take effect after being granted free agency, November 30, 1984.
On developmental squad for 1 game with Michigan Panthers in 1983.
On developmental squad for 4 games with Michigan Panthers in 1984.

			—RUSHING—				PASS RECEIVING				—TOTAL—		
Year	Club	G.	Att.	Yds.	Avg.	TD.	P.C.	Yds.	Avg.	TD.	TD.	Pts.	F.
1983—Michigan USFL		17	232	1180	5.1	6	40	433	10.8	2	8	48	10
1984—Michigan USFL		14	134	548	4.1	2	28	280	10.0	1	3	18	3
1984—Kansas City NFL		15	46	165	3.6	2	13	87	6.7	2	4	24	2
USFL Totals—2 Years		31	366	1728	4.7	8	68	713	10.5	3	11	66	13
NFL Totals—1 Year		15	46	165	3.6	2	13	87	6.7	2	4	24	2
Pro Totals—3 Years		46	412	1893	4.6	10	81	800	9.9	5	15	90	15

Additional pro statistics: Recovered one fumble and attempted and completed one pass for 38 yards and a touchdown, 1983.
Played in USFL Championship Game following 1983 season.

DAVID WALTER LAFARY
Name pronounced La-FARR-ee.
(Dave)
Offensive Tackle—New Orleans Saints
Born January 13, 1955, at Cincinnati, O.
Height, 6.07. Weight, 285.
High School—Cincinnati, O., LaSalle.
Received degree in health and physical education from Purdue University.

Selected by New Orleans in 5th round (118th player selected) of 1977 NFL draft.
On injured reserve with broken ankle, September 3 through remainder of 1984 season.
New Orleans NFL, 1977 through 1983.
Games: 1977 (10), 1978 (15), 1979 (16), 1980 (15), 1981 (16), 1982 (9), 1983 (16), 1984 (1). Total—98.
Pro statistics: Caught one pass for five yards, 1981; recovered one fumble, 1981 and 1983.

GREG LaFLEUR
Tight End—St. Louis Cardinals
Born September 16, 1958, at Lafayette, La.
Height, 6.04. Weight, 236.
High School—Ville Platt, La.
Received bachelor of arts degree in sociology from Louisiana State University in 1981.

Selected by Philadelphia in 3rd round (82nd player selected) of 1981 NFL draft.
Released by Philadelphia Eagles, August 31, 1981; claimed on waivers by St. Louis Cardinals, September 1, 1981.

		—PASS RECEIVING—				
Year	Club	G.	P.C.	Yds.	Avg.	TD.
1981—St. Louis NFL		16	14	190	13.6	2
1982—St. Louis NFL		9	5	67	13.4	1
1983—St. Louis NFL		16	12	99	8.3	0
1984—St. Louis NFL		16	17	198	11.6	0
Pro Totals—4 Years		57	48	554	11.5	3

Additional pro statistics: Fumbled three times, 1983.

JOHN HAROLD LAMBERT
(Jack)
Linebacker—Pittsburgh Steelers
Born July 8, 1952, at Mantua, O.
Height, 6.04. Weight, 220.
High School—Mantua, O., Crestwood.
Attended Kent State University.

Named to THE SPORTING NEWS NFL All-Star Team, 1981 and 1983.
Named to THE SPORTING NEWS AFC All-Star Team, 1975, 1976, 1978 and 1979.
Selected by Pittsburgh in 2nd round (46th player selected) of 1974 NFL draft.
On inactive list, September 13, 1982.
On injured reserve with dislocated toe, December 6 through January 3, 1984; activated, January 4, 1984.

Year Club	G.	No.	Yds.	Avg.	TD.	Year Club	G.	No.	Yds.	Avg.	TD.
		INTERCEPTIONS						INTERCEPTIONS			
1974—Pittsburgh NFL	14	2	19	9.5	0	1980—Pittsburgh NFL	14	2	1	0.5	0
1975—Pittsburgh NFL	14	2	35	17.5	0	1981—Pittsburgh NFL	16	6	76	12.7	0
1976—Pittsburgh NFL	14	2	32	16.0	0	1982—Pittsburgh NFL	8	1	6	6.0	0
1977—Pittsburgh NFL	11	1	5	5.0	0	1983—Pittsburgh NFL	15	2	—1	—0.5	0
1978—Pittsburgh NFL	16	4	41	10.3	0	1984—Pittsburgh NFL	8		None		
1979—Pittsburgh NFL	16	6	29	4.8	0	Pro Totals—11 Years	146	28	243	8.7	0

Additional pro statistics: Fumbled once and recovered one fumble for 11 yards, 1974; recovered one fumble for 21 yards, 1975; recovered eight fumbles for 36 yards, 1976; recovered two fumbles, 1978 and 1983; recovered two fumbles for 38 yards, 1981; recovered one fumble for one yard, 1982.
Played in AFC Championship Game following 1974 through 1976, 1978, 1979 and 1984 seasons.
Played in NFL Championship Game following 1974, 1975, 1978 and 1979 seasons.
Played in Pro Bowl (NFL All-Star Game) following 1975 through 1983 seasons.

MICHAEL GEDDIE LANDRUM
(Mike)
Tight End—Atlanta Falcons
Born November 6, 1961, at Laurel, Miss.
Height, 6.02. Weight, 235.
High School—Columbia, Miss.
Attended University of Southern Mississippi.

Selected by Birmingham in 10th round (195th player selected) of 1984 USFL draft.
Signed by Birmingham Stallions, January 9, 1984.
Released by Birmingham Stallions, January 26, 1984; signed as free agent by Atlanta Falcons, May 2, 1984.

Year Club	G.	P.C.	Yds.	Avg.	TD.
		PASS RECEIVING			
1984—Atlanta NFL	15	6	66	11.0	0

Additional pro statistics: Recovered one fumble, 1984.

RONALD PAUL LANDRY
(Ron)
Fullback—Miami Dolphins
Born July 8, 1962, at Jennings, La.
Height, 6.02. Weight, 225.
High School—Jennings, La.
Attended McNeese State University.

Selected by Pittsburgh in 7th round (131st player selected) of 1984 USFL draft.
USFL rights traded with draft pick by Pittsburgh Maulers to New Orleans Breakers for offensive tackle Keith Jones, February 10, 1984.
Selected by Miami in 8th round (221st player selected) of 1984 NFL draft.
Signed by Miami Dolphins, July 9, 1984.
On injured reserve with knee injury, August 21 through entire 1984 season.

ERIC LANE
Running Back—Seattle Seahawks
Born January 6, 1959, at Oakland, Calif.
Height, 6.00. Weight, 195.
High School—Hayward, Calif.
Attended Chabot Junior College and Brigham Young University.
Nephew of MacArthur Lane, running back with St. Louis Cardinals,
Green Bay Packers and Kansas City Chiefs, 1968 through 1978.

Selected by Seattle in 8th round (196th player selected) of 1981 NFL draft.

Year Club	G.	Att.	Yds.	Avg.	TD.	P.C.	Yds.	Avg.	TD.	TD.	Pts.	F.
		RUSHING				PASS RECEIVING				TOTAL		
1981—Seattle NFL	14	8	22	2.8	0	7	58	8.3	0	0	0	0
1982—Seattle NFL	9		None				None			0	0	1
1983—Seattle NFL	16	3	1	0.3	0	2	9	4.5	0	0	0	2
1984—Seattle NFL	15	80	299	3.7	4	11	101	9.2	1	5	30	1
Pro Totals—4 Years	54	91	322	3.5	4	20	168	8.4	1	5	30	4

Year Club	G.	No.	Yds.	Avg.	TD.
		KICKOFF RETURNS			
1981—Seattle NFL	14	10	208	20.8	0
1982—Seattle NFL	9	11	172	15.6	0
1983—Seattle NFL	16	4	58	14.5	0
1984—Seattle NFL	15		None		
Pro Totals—4 Years	54	25	438	17.5	0

Additional pro statistics: Recovered one fumble, 1981 through 1983; attempted one pass with no completions, 1982; recovered three fumbles, 1984.
Played in AFC Championship Game following 1983 season.

PAUL JOHN LANE JR.
(Skip)
Defensive Back—Kansas City Chiefs
Born January 30, 1960, at Norwalk, Conn.
Height, 6.01. Weight, 205.
High School—Westport, Conn., Staples.
Attended University of Mississippi.

Signed as free agent by Memphis Showboats, January 7, 1984.
Released by Memphis Showboats, February 8, 1984; signed as free agent by New York Jets, May 20, 1984.
Released by New York Jets, August 20, 1984; signed as free agent by Ottawa Rough Riders, September 4, 1984.
Released by Ottawa Rough Riders, September 19, 1984; signed as free agent by New York Jets, November 7, 1984.
Released by New York Jets, November 30, 1984; signed as free agent by Kansas City Chiefs, December 10, 1984.
Ottawa CFL, 1984; New York Jets (3)-Kansas City (1) NFL, 1984.
Games: 1984 CFL (1), 1984 NFL (4). Total Pro—5.

GENE ERIC LANG
Running Back—Denver Broncos
Born March 15, 1962, at Pass Christian, Miss.
Height, 5.10. Weight, 196.
High School—Pass Christian, Miss.
Attended Louisiana State University.

Selected by Denver in 11th round (298th player selected of 1984 NFL draft.

		------RUSHING------				PASS RECEIVING				—TOTAL—		
Year Club	G.	Att.	Yds.	Avg.	TD.	P.C.	Yds.	Avg.	TD.	TD.	Pts.	F.
1984—Denver NFL	16	8	42	5.3	2	4	24	6.0	1	3	18	0

		KICKOFF RETURNS		
Year Club	G.	No.	Yds.	Avg.TD.
1984—Denver NFL	16	19	404	21.3 0

Additional pro statistics: Recovered one fumble for six yards, 1984.

MARK EDWARD LANG
Linebacker—Kansas City Chiefs
Born June 27, 1961, at Monahans, Tex.
Height, 6.02. Weight, 235.
High School—Iraan, Tex.
Attended University of Texas.

Selected by San Antonio in 1984 USFL territorial draft.
Selected by Kansas City in 12th round (314th player selected) of 1984 NFL draft.
Signed by Kansas City Chiefs, June 20, 1984.
On injured reserve with knee injury, August 27 through entire 1984 season.

KENNETH WAYNE LANIER
(Ken)
Offensive Tackle—Denver Broncos
Born July 8, 1959, at Columbus, O.
Height, 6.03. Weight, 269.
High School—Columbus, O., Marion Franklin.
Received degree in industrial arts from Florida State University in 1981.

Selected by Denver in 5th round (125th player selected) of 1981 NFL draft.
Denver NFL, 1981 through 1984.
Games: 1981 (8), 1982 (9), 1983 (16), 1984 (16). Total—49.
Pro statistics: Recovered one fumble, 1982 and 1984.

PAUL JAY LANKFORD
Cornerback—Miami Dolphins
Born June 15, 1958, at New York, N.Y.
Height, 6.02. Weight, 182.
High School—Farmingdale, N.Y.
Received bachelor of science degree in health planning and administration
from Penn State University in 1982.

Selected by Miami in 3rd round (80th player selected) of 1982 NFL draft.
On inactive list, September 12 and September 19, 1982.

		——INTERCEPTIONS——		
Year Club	G.	No.	Yds.	Avg.TD.
1982—Miami NFL	7	None		
1983—Miami NFL	16	1	10	10.0 0
1984—Miami NFL	16	3	25	8.3 0
Pro Totals—3 Years	39	4	35	8.8 0

Additional pro statistics: Recovered one fumble, 1984.
Played in AFC Championship Game following 1982 and 1984 seasons.
Played in NFL Championship Game following 1982 and 1984 seasons.

MIKE LANSFORD
Placekicker—Los Angeles Rams

Born July 20, 1958, at Monterrey Park, Calif.
Height, 6.00. Weight, 183.
High School—Arcadia, Calif.
Attended Pasadena City College and University of Washington.

Selected by New York Giants in 12th round (312th player selected) of 1980 NFL draft.
Released by New York Giants, August 3, 1980; claimed on waivers by San Francisco 49ers, August 5, 1980.
Released by San Francisco 49ers, August 18, 1980; signed as free agent by Oakland Raiders, June, 1981.
Released by Oakland Raiders, August 18, 1981; signed as free agent by Los Angeles Rams, July 1, 1982.
On injured reserve with knee injury, August 24 through November 23, 1983; activated after clearing procedural waivers, November 25, 1983.

		——PLACE KICKING——					
Year Club	G.	XP.	XPM.	FG.	FGA.	Pts.
1982—L.A. Rams NFL........	9	23	1	9	15	50
1983—L.A. Rams NFL........	4	9	0	6	9	27
1984—L.A. Rams NFL........	16	37	1	25	33	112
Pro Totals—3 Years.......	29	69	2	40	57	189

STEVE M. LARGENT
Wide Receiver—Seattle Seahawks

Born September 28, 1954, at Tulsa, Okla.
Height, 5.11. Weight 184.
High School—Oklahoma City, Okla., Putnam.
Received bachelor of science degree in biology from University of Tulsa in 1976.

Named to THE SPORTING NEWS NFL All-Star Team, 1983.
Named to THE SPORTING NEWS AFC All-Star Team, 1978.
Selected by Houston in 4th round (117th player selected) of 1976 NFL draft.
Traded by Houston Oilers to Seattle Seahawks for 8th round pick in 1977 draft, August 26, 1976.
On injured reserve with broken wrist, December 16 through remainder of 1979 season.

		PASS RECEIVING				PUNT RETURNS				—KICKOFF RET.—				—TOTAL—		
Year Club	G.	P.C.	Yds.	Avg.	TD.	No.	Yds.	Avg.	TD.	No.	Yds.	Avg.	TD.	TD.	Pts.	F.
1976—Seattle NFL..................	14	54	705	13.0	4	4	36	9.0	0	8	156	19.5	0	4	24	2
1977—Seattle NFL..................	14	33	643	19.5	10	4	32	8.0	0		None			10	60	0
1978—Seattle NFL..................	16	71	1168	16.5	8		None				None			8	48	0
1979—Seattle NFL..................	15	66	1237	18.7	9		None				None			9	54	0
1980—Seattle NFL..................	16	66	1064	16.1	6		None				None			6	36	1
1981—Seattle NFL..................	16	75	1224	16.3	9		None				None			10	60	2
1982—Seattle NFL..................	8	34	493	14.5	3		None				None			3	18	0
1983—Seattle NFL..................	15	72	1074	14.9	11		None				None			11	66	3
1984—Seattle NFL..................	16	74	1164	15.7	12		None				None			12	72	1
Pro Totals—9 Years.......	130	545	8772	16.1	72	8	68	8.5	0	8	156	19.5	0	73	438	9

Additional pro statistics: Rushed four times for minus 14 yards, 1976; recovered one fumble, 1978; rushed once for two yards and recovered two fumbles, 1980; rushed six times for 47 yards and one touchdown and attempted one pass with no completions, 1981; rushed once for eight yards, 1982; attempted one pass with one completion for 11 yards, 1983; rushed twice for 10 yards, 1984.
Played in AFC Championship Game following 1983 season.
Played in Pro Bowl (NFL All-Star Game) following 1978, 1981 and 1984 seasons.
Named in Pro Bowl following 1979 season; replaced due to wrist injury.

ANTHONY DONALD LASTER
(Known by middle name.)
Offensive Tackle—Detroit Lions

Born December 13, 1958, at Albany, Ga.
Height, 6.04. Weight, 278.
High School—Dougherty, Ga.
Attended Tennessee State University.

Selected by Washington in 12th round (309th player selected) of 1982 NFL draft.
On inactive list, September 19, 1982.
On injured reserve with sprained neck, August 30 through entire 1983 season.
Released by Washington Redskins, August 27, 1984; signed as free agent by Detroit Lions, September 4, 1984.
Washington NFL, 1982; Detroit NFL, 1984.
Games: 1982 (8), 1984 (14). Total—22.
Played in NFC Championship Game following 1982 season.
Played in NFL Championship Game following 1982 season.

ALBERT LATIMER
(Al)
Safety—Detroit Lions

Born October 14, 1957, at Winter Park, Fla.
Height, 5.11. Weight, 177.
High School—Altamonte Springs, Fla., Lyman.
Attended Ferrum Junior College and Clemson University.

Signed as free agent by Philadelphia Eagles, May 8, 1979.
On injured reserve with knee injury, November 28 through remainder of 1979 season.

On injured reserve with knee injury, August 19 through October 6, 1980.
Released by Philadelphia Eagles, October 7, 1980; signed as free agent by San Francisco 49ers, October 29, 1980.
Released by San Francisco 49ers, November 8, 1980; signed as free agent by Winnipeg Blue Bombers, May, 1981.
Released by Winnipeg Blue Bombers, June 30, 1981; signed as free agent by Detroit Lions, July 5, 1982.
On injured reserve with pulled hamstring, August 30 through November 29, 1982; activated after clearing procedural waivers, December 1, 1982.
On injured reserve with knee injury, October 27 through remainder of 1983 season.
Active for 1 game with San Francisco 49ers in 1980; did not play.
Philadelphia NFL, 1979; San Francisco NFL, 1980; Detroit NFL, 1982 through 1984.
Games: 1979 (13), 1982 (4), 1983 (8), 1984 (15). Total—40.
Pro statistics: Returned one kickoff for 18 yards, 1979; intercepted one pass for no yards, 1983; recovered one fumble, 1984.

HUGH BRANDON LAUFENBERG
(Babe)
Quarterback—Washington Redskins
Born December 5, 1959, at Burbank, Calif.
Height, 6.02. Weight, 195.
High School—Encino, Calif., Crespi Carmelite.
Attended Stanford University, University of Missouri,
Los Angeles Pierce College and Indiana University.

Selected by Chicago in 20th round (235th player selected) of 1983 USFL draft.
Selected by Washington in 6th round (168th player selected) of 1983 NFL draft.
Signed by Washington Redskins, June 17, 1983.
On injured reserve with rotator cuff injury, August 27 through entire 1984 season.
Active for 16 games with Washington Redskins in 1983; did not play.
Member of Washington Redskins for NFC and NFL Championship Game following 1983 season; did not play.

JAMES DAVID LAUGHLIN
(Jim)
Linebacker—Los Angeles Rams
Born July 5, 1958, at Euclid, O.
Height, 6.01. Weight, 222.
High School—Lyndhurst, O., Charles F. Brush.
Received bachelor of science degree in business administration from Ohio State University in 1980.

Selected by Atlanta in 4th round (91st player selected) of 1980 NFL draft.
Released by Atlanta Falcons, August 28, 1983; signed as free agent by Green Bay Packers, September 6, 1983.
Released by Green Bay Packers, August 27, 1984; signed as free agent by Los Angeles Rams, November 30, 1984.

| | | | —INTERCEPTIONS— | | |
Year Club	G.	No.	Yds.	Avg.	TD.
1980—Atlanta NFL	16	1	7	7.0	0
1981—Atlanta NFL	14		None		
1982—Atlanta NFL	9		None		
1983—Green Bay NFL	15	1	22	22.0	0
1984—L.A. Rams NFL	3		None		
Pro Totals—5 Years	57	2	29	14.5	0

Additional pro statistics: Recovered one fumble, 1981; returned one kickoff for 10 yards, 1982.

HENRY LAWRENCE
Offensive Tackle—Los Angeles Raiders
Born September 26, 1951, at Danville, Pa.
Height, 6.04. Weight, 275.
High Schools—Palmetto, Fla., Lincoln; Bradenton, Fla., Manatee; and Wyoming, N. Y., Central.
Received bachelor of science degree in political science from Florida A&M University in 1974.

Selected by Oakland in 1st round (19th player selected) of 1974 NFL draft.
Franchise transferred to Los Angeles, May 7, 1982.
Oakland NFL, 1974 through 1981; Los Angeles Raiders NFL, 1982 through 1984.
Games: 1974 (14), 1975 (14), 1976 (8), 1977 (14), 1978 (16), 1979 (16), 1980 (16), 1981 (16), 1982 (9), 1983 (16), 1984 (16).
Total—155.
Pro statistics: Recovered one fumble, 1975, 1977 through 1979 and 1982; recovered two fumbles, 1980 and 1981.
Played in AFC Championship Game following 1974 through 1977, 1980 and 1983 seasons.
Played in NFL Championship Game following 1976, 1980 and 1983 seasons.
Played in Pro Bowl (NFL All- Star Game) following 1983 and 1984 seasons.

PATRICK JOSEPH LEAHY
(Pat)
Placekicker—New York Jets
Born March 19, 1951, at St. Louis, Mo.
Height, 6.00. Weight, 189.
High School—St. Louis, Mo., Augustinian Academy.
Received degree in marketing from St. Louis University
(did not play college football).

Named to THE SPORTING NEWS AFC All-Star Team, 1978.
Signed as free agent by St. Louis Cardinals, 1974.
Released by St. Louis Cardinals and signed as free agent by New York Jets, November 8, 1974.
On injured reserve with knee injury, October 13 through remainder of 1979 season.

Year Club	—PLACE KICKING— G. XP. XPM. FG. FGA. Pts.						Year Club	—PLACE KICKING— G. XP. XPM. FG. FGA. Pts.					
1974—N.Y. Jets NFL	6	18	1	6	11	36	1980—N.Y. Jets NFL	16	36	0	14	22	78
1975—N.Y. Jets NFL	14	27	3	13	21	66	1981—N.Y. Jets NFL	16	38	1	25	36	113
1976—N.Y. Jets NFL	14	16	4	11	16	49	1982—N.Y. Jets NFL	9	26	*5	11	17	59
1977—N.Y. Jets NFL	14	18	3	15	25	63	1983—N.Y. Jets NFL	16	36	1	16	24	84
1978—N.Y. Jets NFL	16	41	1	22	30	107	1984—N.Y. Jets NFL	16	38	1	17	24	89
1979—N.Y. Jets NFL	6	12	3	8	13	36	Pro Totals—11 Years	143	306	23	158	239	780

Additional pro statistics: Recovered one fumble, 1975.
Played in AFC Championship Game following 1982 season.

CARL LEE III
Defensive Back—Minnesota Vikings
Born February 6, 1961, at South Charleston, W. Va.
Height, 5.11. Weight, 185.
High School—South Charleston, W. Va.
Attended Marshall University.

Selected by Minnesota in 7th round (186th player selected) of 1983 NFL draft.

Year Club	—INTERCEPTIONS— G. No. Yds. Avg.TD.				
1983—Minnesota NFL	16	1	31	31.0	0
1984—Minnesota NFL	16	1	0	0.0	0
Pro Totals—2 Years	32	2	31	15.5	0

Additional pro statistics: Recovered one fumble, 1984.

KEITH LAMAR LEE
Defensive Back—New England Patriots
Born December 22, 1957, at San Antonio, Tex.
Height, 5.11. Weight, 193.
High School—Los Angeles, Calif., Gardena.
Attended Santa Monica City College and Colorado State University.

Selected by Buffalo in 5th round (129th player selected) of 1980 NFL draft.
On injured reserve with knee injury, August 21 through entire 1980 season.
Released by Buffalo Bills, August 25, 1981; signed as free agent by New England Patriots, August 28, 1981.
New England NFL, 1981 through 1984.
Games: 1981 (15), 1982 (9), 1983 (15), 1984 (15). Total—54.
Pro statistics: Returned two kickoffs for 20 yards and intercepted one pass for no yards, 1981; returned one kickoff for 14 yards, 1982; returned four kickoffs for 40 yards, returned one punt for no yards, recovered two fumbles and fumbled once, 1983; returned three kickoffs for 43 yards, 1984.

LARRY DWAYNE LEE
Guard—Detroit Lions
Born September 10, 1959, at Dayton, O.
Height, 6.02. Weight, 260.
High School—Dayton, O., Roth.
Attended University of California at Los Angeles.
Cousin of Rick Porter, running back with Memphis Showboats.

Selected by Detroit in 5th round (129th player selected) of 1981 NFL draft.
Detroit NFL, 1981 through 1984.
Games: 1981 (16), 1982 (9), 1983 (16), 1984 (15). Total—56.
Pro statistics: Returned one kickoff for no yards, 1981; returned one kickoff for 14 yards, 1982; returned one kickoff for 11 yards, 1983; recovered one fumble and fumbled twice for minus 24 yards, 1984.

MARK ANTHONY LEE
Cornerback—Green Bay Packers
Born March 20, 1958, at Hanford, Calif.
Height, 5.11. Weight, 187.
High School—Hanford, Calif.
Attended University of Washington.

Selected by Green Bay in 2nd round (34th player selected) of 1980 NFL draft.

Year Club	G.	INTERCEPTIONS No. Yds. Avg. TD.				-PUNT RETURNS- No. Yds. Avg. TD.				—KICKOFF RET.— No. Yds. Avg. TD.				—TOTAL— TD. Pts. F.		
1980—Green Bay NFL	15	None				5	32	6.4	0	30	589	19.6	0	0	0	1
1981—Green Bay NFL	16	6	50	8.3	0	20	187	9.4	1	14	270	19.3	0	1	6	0
1982—Green Bay NFL	9	1	40	40.0	0	None				None				0	0	0
1983—Green Bay NFL	16	4	23	5.8	0	1	—4	—4.0	0	1	0	0	0	0	0	1
1984—Green Bay NFL	16	3	33	11.0	0	None				None				0	0	0
Pro Totals—5 Years	72	14	146	10.4	0	26	215	8.3	1	45	859	19.1	0	1	6	2

Additional pro statistics: Recovered one fumble, 1981; recovered one fumble for 15 yards, 1983; recovered two fumbles, 1984.

RONALD VAN LEE
(Ronnie)
Guard—Miami Dolphins
Born December 24, 1956, at Pine Bluff, Ark.
Height, 6.04. Weight, 265.
High School—Tyler, Tex.
Attended Baylor University.

Selected by Miami in 3rd round (65th player selected) of 1979 NFL draft.
Released by Miami Dolphins, August 29, 1983; signed as free agent by Atlanta Falcons, September 14, 1983.
Traded with 6th round pick in 1985 draft by Atlanta Falcons to Miami Dolphins for cornerback Gerald Small, August 26, 1984.

Year Club	G.	P.C.	Yds.	Avg.	TD.
1979—Miami NFL	16	2	14	7.0	0
1980—Miami NFL	16	7	83	11.9	2
1981—Miami NFL	16	14	64	4.6	1
1982—Miami NFL	9	2	6	3.0	0
1983—Atlanta NFL	14		None		
1984—Miami NFL	16		None		
Pro Totals—6 Years	87	25	167	6.7	3

Played in AFC Championship Game following 1982 and 1984 seasons.
Played in NFL Championship Game following 1982 and 1984 seasons.

DAVID JOHN LEVENICK
(Dave)
Linebacker—Atlanta Falcons
Born May 28, 1959, at Milwaukee, Wis.
Height, 6.03. Weight, 220.
High School—Grafton, Wis.
Attended University of Wisconsin.

Selected by Atlanta in 12th round (315th player selected) of 1982 NFL draft.
On injured reserve with knee injury, September 8 through entire 1982 season.
Released by Atlanta Falcons, August 27, 1984; re-signed by Falcons, August 28, 1984.
On injured reserve with hamstring injury, September 4 through October 23, 1984; activated, October 24, 1984.
Atlanta NFL, 1983 and 1984.
Games: 1983 (16), 1984 (8). Total—24.

ALBERT RAY LEWIS
Cornerback—Kansas City Chiefs
Born October 6, 1960, at Mansfield, La.
Height, 6.02. Weight, 190.
High School—Mansfield, La., DeSoto.
Attended Grambling State University.

Selected by Philadelphia in 15th round (175th player selected) of 1983 USFL draft.
Selected by Kansas City in 3rd round (61st player selected) of 1983 NFL draft.
Signed by Kansas City Chiefs, May 19, 1983.
On injured reserve with knee injury, December 10 through remainder of 1984 season.

Year Club	G.	No.	Yds.	Avg.	TD.
1983—Kansas City NFL	16	4	42	10.5	0
1984—Kansas City NFL	15	4	57	14.3	0
Pro Totals—2 Years	31	8	99	12.4	0

Additional pro statistics: Recovered two fumbles, 1983.

CLIFF LEWIS
Linebacker—Green Bay Packers
Born November 9, 1959, at Bewton, Ala.
Height, 6.01. Weight, 224.
High School—Fort Walton Beach, Fla.
Attended University of Southern Mississippi.
Cousin of Walter Lewis, quarterback with Memphis Showboats.

Selected by Green Bay in 12th round (311th player selected) of 1981 NFL draft.
Green Bay NFL, 1981 through 1984.
Games: 1981 (16), 1982 (9), 1983 (16), 1984 (16). Total—57.
Pro statistics: Returned one kickoff for four yards, 1982; returned one punt for no yards, 1983.

DARRYL LEWIS
Tight End—Cleveland Browns
Born April 16, 1961, at Mt. Pleasant, Tex.
Height, 6.06. Weight, 227.
High School—Daingerfield, Tex.
Attended University of Texas at Arlington.
Brother of Gary Lewis, tight end with Green Bay Packers.

Selected by New England in 5th round (128th player selected) of 1983 NFL draft.
On injured reserve with knee injury, August 16 through entire 1983 season.
Released by New England Patriots, August 21, 1984; signed as free agent by Cleveland Browns, November 21, 1984.
Cleveland NFL, 1984.
Games: 1984 (2).

DAVID WAYNE LEWIS
Tight End—Detroit Lions
Born June 8, 1961, at Portland, Ore.
Height, 6.03. Weight, 235.
High School—Portland, Ore., U.S. Grant.
Received bachelor of science degree in political science
from University of California at Berkeley in 1984.

Selected by Oakland in 1984 USFL territorial draft.
Selected by Detroit in 1st round (20th player selected) of 1984 NFL draft.
Signed by Detroit Lions, July 19, 1984.

		——PASS RECEIVING——			
Year	Club	G.	P.C.	Yds.	Avg. TD.
1984—Detroit NFL...................		16	16	236	14.8 3

Additional pro statistics: Recovered two fumbles and fumbled twice, 1984.

GARY LEWIS
Nose Tackle—New Orleans Saints
Born January 14, 1961, at Oklahoma City, Okla.
Height, 6.03. Weight, 260.
High School—Oklahoma City, Okla., Millwood.
Attended Oklahoma State University.

Selected by Birmingham in 3rd round (29th player selected) of 1983 USFL draft.
Selected by New Orleans in 4th round (98th player selected) of 1983 NFL draft.
Signed by New Orleans Saints, June 6, 1983.
On injured reserve with knee injury, August 30 through November 11, 1983; activated, November 12, 1983.
On non-football injury list with Beck's disease (cyst on chest), August 27 through entire 1984 season.
New Orleans NFL, 1983.
Games: 1983 (6).

GARY WAYNE LEWIS
Tight End—Green Bay Packers
Born December 30, 1958, at Mt. Pleasant, Tex.
Height, 6.05. Weight, 234.
High School—Dangerfield, Tex.
Attended University of Texas at Arlington.
Brother of Darryl Lewis, tight end with Cleveland Browns.

Selected by Green Bay in 2nd round (35th player selected) of 1981 NFL draft.
Signed by Chicago Blitz, November 15, 1983, for contract to take effect after being granted free agency, February 1, 1984.
Signed by Green Bay Packers, September 10, 1984.
Granted roster exemption, September 10 through September 14, 1984; activated, September 15, 1984.
On non-football injury list with blood clots in lungs, October 6 through remainder of 1984 season.

		——PASS RECEIVING——				
Year	Club	G.	P.C.	Yds.	Avg.	TD.
1981—Green Bay NFL............		16	3	31	10.3	0
1982—Green Bay NFL............		9	3	21	7.0	0
1983—Green Bay NFL............		16	11	204	18.5	1
1984—Chicago USFL		17	33	415	12.6	1
1984—Green Bay NFL............		3	4	29	7.3	0
NFL Totals—4 Years..........		44	21	285	13.6	1
USFL Totals—1 Year..........		17	33	415	12.6	1
Pro Totals—5 Years............		61	54	700	13.0	2

Additional NFL statistics: Rushed four times for 16 yards and a touchdown and recovered one fumble, 1983.
Additional USFL statistics: Scored one 2-point conversion and recovered one fumble, 1984.

LEO LEWIS JR.
Wide Receiver—Minnesota Vikings
Born September 17, 1956, at Columbia, Mo.
Height, 5.08. Weight, 170.
High School—Columbia, Mo., Hickman.
Attended University of Missouri.
Son of Leo Lewis, running back with Winnipeg Blue Bombers, 1955 through 1966;
brother of Marc Lewis, wide receiver with Denver Gold.

Signed as free agent by St. Louis Cardinals, May 21, 1979.
On injured reserve with ankle injury, August 21 through November 15, 1979.
Released by St. Louis Cardinals, November 16, 1979; signed as free agent by Calgary Stampeders, March, 1980.
Released by Calgary Stampeders, August 7, 1980; signed as free agent by Hamilton Tiger-Cats, August 13, 1980.
Released by Hamilton Tiger-Cats, August 20, 1980; signed as free agent by Minnesota Vikings, May 10, 1981.
Released by Minnesota Vikings, August 25, 1981; re-signed after clearing procedural waivers, November 11, 1981.

Year Club	G.	Att.	Yds.	Avg.	TD.	P.C.	Yds.	Avg.	TD.	TD.	Pts.	F.
		—RUSHING—				PASS RECEIVING				—TOTAL—		
1980—Calgary (5)-Hamilton (1) CFL	6	1	62	62.0	1	8	91	11.4	1	2	12	0
1981—Minnesota NFL	4	1	16	16.0	0	2	58	29.0	0	0	0	0
1982—Minnesota NFL	9			None		8	150	18.8	3	3	18	0
1983—Minnesota NFL	14	1	2	2.0	0	12	127	10.6	0	0	0	0
1984—Minnesota NFL	16	2	11	5.5	0	47	830	17.7	4	4	24	1
NFL Totals—4 Years	43	4	29	7.3	0	69	1165	16.9	7	7	42	1
CFL Total—1 Year	6	1	62	62.0	1	8	91	11.4	1	2	12	0
Pro Totals—5 Years	49	5	91	18.2	1	77	1256	16.3	8	9	54	1

Year Club	G.	No.	Yds.	Avg.	TD.	No.	Yds.	Avg.	TD.
		—PUNT RETURNS—				—KICKOFF RET.—			
1980—Calgary (5)-Hamilton (1) CFL	6	22	163	7.4	0	15	345	23.0	0
1981—Minnesota NFL	4		None				None		
1982—Minnesota NFL	9		None				None		
1983—Minnesota NFL	14	3	52	17.3	0	1	25	25.0	0
1984—Minnesota NFL	16	4	31	7.8	0	1	31	31.0	0
NFL Totals—4 Years	43	7	83	11.9	0	2	56	28.0	0
CFL Total—1 Year	6	22	163	7.4	0	15	345	23.0	0
Pro Totals—5 Years	49	29	246	8.5	0	17	401	23.6	0

Additional pro statistics: Recovered three fumbles, 1984.

REGINALD ANTHONY LEWIS
(Reggie)
Defensive End—New Orleans Saints
Born January 20, 1954, at New Orleans, La.
Height, 6.02. Weight, 251.
High School—Los Angeles, Calif., Crenshaw.
Attended University of Oregon and San Diego State University.

Selected by San Francisco in 16th round (443rd player selected) of 1976 NFL draft.
Signed by British Columbia Lions, April, 1976.
Released by British Columbia Lions, June 26, 1976; signed by San Francisco 49ers, March, 1977.
Released by San Francisco 49ers, August 24, 1977; signed as free agent by Calgary Stampeders, September 2, 1977.
On reserve list, July 30 through August 13, 1981; activated, August 14, 1981.
Traded by Calgary Stampeders to Toronto Argonauts for linebacker Danny Bass, October 1, 1981.
Granted free agency, March 1, 1982; signed as free agent by New Orleans Saints, April 16, 1982.
Calgary CFL, 1977 through 1980; Calgary (8)-Toronto (4) CFL, 1981; New Orleans NFL, 1982 through 1984.
Games: 1977 (9), 1978 (16), 1979 (16), 1980 (16), 1981 (12), 1982 (9), 1983 (12), 1984 (13). Total CFL—69. Total NFL—34. Total Pro—103.
CFL statistics: Recovered three fumbles for five yards, 1978; recovered four fumbles for 19 yards and one touchdown, 1979; recovered one fumble, 1980.
NFL statistics: Intercepted one pass for 27 yards and a touchdown, 1983.

RODNEY EARL LEWIS
Cornerback—New Orleans Saints
Born April 2, 1959, at Minneapolis, Minn.
Height, 5.11. Weight, 188.
High School—Minneapolis, Minn., Central.
Attended University of Nebraska.

Named as defensive back on THE SPORTING NEWS College All-America Team, 1981.
Selected by New Orleans in 3rd round (58th player selected) of 1982 NFL draft.
On injured reserve with knee injury, September 17 through remainder of 1983 season.

Year Club	G.	No.	Yds.	Avg.	TD.
		—INTERCEPTIONS—			
1982—New Orleans NFL	9	1	12	12.0	0
1983—New Orleans NFL	2		None		
1984—New Orleans NFL	16		None		
Pro Totals—3 Years	27	1	12	12.0	0

Additional pro statistics: Recovered one fumble, 1983.

TIMOTHY JAY LEWIS
(Tim)
Defensive Back—Green Bay Packers
Born December 18, 1961, at Quakertown, Pa.
Height, 5.11. Weight, 191.
High School—Perkasie, Pa., Pennridge.
Received bachelor of arts degree in economics from University of Pittsburgh in 1983.
Brother of Will Lewis, cornerback with Houston Gamblers; cousin of Robb Riddick,
running back with Buffalo Bills; cousin of Alan Page, defensive tackle with
Minnesota Vikings and Chicago Bears, 1967 through 1981.

Selected by Washington in 2nd round (21st player selected) of 1983 USFL draft.
Selected by Green Bay in 1st round (11th player selected) of 1983 NFL draft.
Signed by Green Bay Packers, July 21, 1983.

Year Club	G.	No.	-INTERCEPTIONS- Yds.	Avg.	TD.	No.	—KICKOFF RET.— Yds.	Avg.	TD.	TD.	—TOTAL— Pts.	F.
1983—Green Bay NFL	16	5	111	22.2	0	20	358	17.9	0	0	0	3
1984—Green Bay NFL	16	7	151	21.6	1		None			1	6	0
Pro Totals—2 Years	32	12	262	21.8	1	20	358	17.9	0	1	6	3

Additional pro statistics: Recovered one fumble, 1983.

TODD LIEBENSTEIN
Defensive End—Washington Redskins
Born January 9, 1960, at Las Vegas, Nev.
Height, 6.06. Weight, 255.
High School—Las Vegas, Nev., Valley.
Attended University of Nevada at Las Vegas.

Selected by Washington in 4th round (99th player selected) of 1982 NFL draft.
On non-football injury list with bacterial infection, September 11 through remainder of 1984 season.
Washington NFL, 1982 through 1984.
Games: 1982 (9), 1983 (15), 1984 (1). Total—25.
Pro statistics: Recovered two fumbles for five yards, 1983.
Played in NFC Championship Game following 1982 and 1983 seasons.
Played in NFL Championship Game following 1982 and 1983 seasons.

GEORGE VINCENT LILJA
Offensive Tackle—Cleveland Browns
Born March 3, 1958, at Evergreen Park, Ill.
Height, 6.04. Weight, 262.
High School—Orland Park, Ill., Carl Sandburg.
Received bachelor of arts degree in general studies from University of Michigan in 1981.

Selected by Los Angeles in 4th round (104th player selected) of 1981 NFL draft.
On injured reserve with ankle injury, August 31 through entire 1981 season.
Released by Los Angeles Rams, September 8, 1983; signed as free agent by New York Jets, September 27, 1983.
Released by New York Jets, November 15, 1984; signed as free agent by Cleveland Browns, November 21, 1984.
Active for 1 game with Los Angeles Rams in 1983; did not play.
Los Angeles Rams NFL, 1982; Los Angeles Rams (0)-New York Jets (1) NFL, 1983; New York Jets (3)-Cleveland (4) NFL, 1984.
Games: 1982 (9), 1983 (1), 1984 (7). Total—17.

ROBERT ANTHONEY LILLY
(Tony)
Safety—Denver Broncos
Born February 15, 1962, at Alexandria, Va.
Height, 6.00. Weight, 199.
High School—Woodbridge, Va.
Attended University of Florida.

Selected by Tampa Bay in 1984 USFL territorial draft.
Selected by Denver in 3rd round (78th player selected) of 1984 NFL draft.
Signed by Denver Broncos, May 23, 1984.
Denver NFL, 1984.
Games: 1984 (13).
Pro statistics: Intercepted one pass for five yards, recovered one fumble for three yards and fumbled once, 1984.

DAVID ALAN LINDSTROM
(Dave)
Defensive End—Kansas City Chiefs
Born November 16, 1954, at Cambridge, Mass.
Height, 6.06. Weight, 255.
High School—Weymouth, Mass., South.
Attended Boston University.
Brother of Chris Lindstrom, defensive tackle with Tampa Bay Buccaneers.

Selected by San Diego in 6th round (146th player selected) of 1977 NFL draft.
On injured reserve, September 12 through 1977 season.
Released by San Diego Chargers, August 28, 1978; claimed on waivers by Kansas City Chiefs, August 30, 1978.
On injured reserve with knee injury, November 30 through remainder of 1979 season.
Kansas City NFL, 1978 through 1984.
Games: 1978 (16), 1979 (13), 1980 (16), 1981 (16), 1982 (9), 1983 (16), 1984 (16). Total—102.
Pro statistics: Recovered one fumble, 1980; returned one kickoff for one yard, 1982; returned one kickoff for no yards, 1983.

ADAM JAMES LINGNER
Center-Guard—Kansas City Chiefs
Born November 2, 1960, at Indianapolis, Ill.
Height, 6.04. Weight, 250.
High School—Rock Island, Ill.,Alleman.
Attended University of Illinois.

Selected by Chicago in 1983 USFL territorial draft.

Selected by Kansas City in 9th round (231st player selected) of 1983 NFL draft.
Signed by Kansas City Chiefs, June 1, 1983.
Kansas City NFL, 1983 and 1984.
Games: 1983 (16), 1984 (16). Total—32.

RONNIE LEON LIPPETT
Cornerback—New England Patriots
Born December 10, 1960, at Melborne, Fla.
Height, 5.11. Weight, 180.
High School—Sebring, Fla.
Attended University of Miami (Fla.).
Selected by New England in 8th round (214th player selected) of 1983 NFL draft.

		—INTERCEPTIONS—			
Year Club	G.	No.	Yds.	Avg.	TD.
1983—New England NFL.......	16	None			
1984—New England NFL.......	16	3	23	7.7	0
Pro Totals—2 Years............	32	3	23	7.7	0

Additional pro statistics: Recovered one fumble, 1983 and 1984; fumbled once, 1984.

LOUIS LIPPS
Wide Receiver—Pittsburgh Steelers
Born August 9, 1962, at New Orleans, La.
Height, 5.10. Weight, 190.
High School—Reverse, La., East St. John's.
Attended University of Southern Mississippi.
Named THE SPORTING NEWS NFL Rookie of the Year, 1984.
Selected by Arizona in 8th round (155th player selected) of 1984 USFL draft.
Selected by Pittsburgh in 1st round (23rd player selected) of 1984 NFL draft.
Signed by Pittsburgh Steelers, May 19, 1984.

		—RUSHING—				PASS RECEIVING				—TOTAL—		
Year Club	G.	Att.	Yds.	Avg.	TD.	P.C.	Yds.	Avg.	TD.	TD.	Pts.	F.
1984—Pittsburgh NFL..	14	3	71	23.7	1	45	860	19.1	9	11	66	8

		—PUNT RETURNS—			
Year Club	G.	No.	Yds.	Avg.	TD.
1984—Pittsburgh NFL..............	14	53	*656	12.4	1

Additional pro statistics: Recovered two fumbles, 1984.
Played in AFC Championship Game following 1984 season.
Played in Pro Bowl (NFL All-Star Game) following 1984 season.

RUSSELL JOHN LISCH
(Rusty)
Quarterback—Chicago Bears
Born December 21, 1956, at Belleville, Ill.
Height, 6.03. Weight, 215.
High School—Belleville, Ill., West.
Received degree in architectural engineering from University of Notre Dame in 1980.
Selected by St. Louis in 4th round (89th player selected) of 1980 NFL draft.
Released by St. Louis Cardinals, August 27, 1984; awarded on waivers to Chicago Bears, August 28, 1984.

		—PASSING—							—RUSHING—				—TOTAL—		
Year Club	G.	Att.	Cmp.	Pct.	Gain	T.P.	P.I.	Avg.	Att.	Yds.	Avg.	TD.	TD.	Pts.	F.
1980—St. Louis NFL....................	2	17	6	35.3	68	0	3	4.00		None			0	0	0
1981—St. Louis NFL....................	9			None						None			0	0	0
1982—St. Louis NFL....................	8			None						None			0	0	0
1983—St. Louis NFL....................	4	13	6	46.2	66	1	2	5.08	2	9	4.5	0	0	0	1
1984—Chicago NFL....................	7	85	43	50.6	413	0	6	4.86	18	121	6.7	0	0	0	5
Pro Totals—5 Years...........	30	115	55	47.8	547	1	11	4.76	20	130	6.5	0	0	0	6

Quarterback Rating Points: 1980 (8.6), 1983 (47.8), 1984 (35.1). Total—25.2.
Additional pro statistics: Recovered one fumble and fumbled five times for minus six yards, 1984.
Member of Chicago Bears for NFC Championship Game following 1984 season; did not play.

DAVID LITTLE
(Dave)
Tight End—Kansas City Chiefs
Born April 18, 1961, at Selma, Calif.
Height, 6.02. Weight, 239.
High School—Fresno, Calif., Roosevelt.
Attended Middle Tennessee State University.
Signed as free agent by Memphis Showboats, January 11, 1984.
Released by Memphis Showboats, February 20, 1984; signed as free agent by Kansas City Chiefs, June 21, 1984.
On injured reserve with knee injury, November 6 through remainder of 1984 season.

		—PASS RECEIVING—			
Year Club	G.	P.C.	Yds.	Avg.	TD.
1984—Kansas City NFL..........	10	1	13	13.0	0

DAVID LAMAR LITTLE
Linebacker—Pittsburgh Steelers
Born January 3, 1959, at Miami, Fla.
Height, 6.01. Weight, 220.
High School—Miami, Fla., Jackson.
Attended University of Florida.
Brother of Larry Little, guard with San Diego Chargers
and Miami Dolphins, 1967 through 1980; currently head coach at Bethune-Cookman College.

Selected by Pittsburgh in 7th round (183rd player selected) of 1981 NFL draft.
Pittsburgh NFL, 1981 through 1984.
Games: 1981 (16), 1982 (9), 1983 (16), 1984 (16). Total—57.
Pro statistics: Recovered one fumble, 1981; recovered one fumble for two yards, 1982.
Played in AFC Championship Game following 1984 season.

EUGENE LOCKHART JR.
Linebacker—Dallas Cowboys
Born March 8, 1961, at Crockett, Tex.
Height, 6.02. Weight, 233.
High School—Crockett, Tex.
Received bachelor of arts degree in marketing from University of Houston in 1983.

Selected by Houston in 1984 USFL territorial draft.
Selected by Dallas in 6th round (152nd player selected) of 1984 NFL draft.
Signed by Dallas Cowboys, May 8, 1984.
Dallas NFL, 1984.
Games: 1984 (15).
Pro statistics: Intercepted one pass for 32 yards and recovered one fumble, 1984.

CHARLES DUANE LOEWEN
Name pronounced LAY-vin.
(Chuck)
Guard-Offensive Tackle—San Diego Chargers
Born January 23, 1957, at Mountain Lake, Minn.
Height, 6.04. Weight, 264.
High School—Mountain Lake, Minn.
Received bachelor of science degree in commercial economics and agricultural business
from South Dakota State University; received master's degree in business administration
from Arizona State University.

Selected by San Diego in 7th round (175th player selected) of 1980 NFL draft.
On injured reserve with ankle injury, September 22 through November 15, 1981; activated, November 16, 1981.
On injured reserve with back injury, August 16 through entire 1983 season.
San Diego NFL, 1980 through 1982 and 1984.
Games: 1980 (16), 1981 (9), 1982 (9), 1984 (13). Total—47.
Played in AFC Championship Game following 1980 and 1981 seasons.

JAMES DAVID LOFTON
Wide Receiver—Green Bay Packers
Born July 5, 1956, at Fort Ord, Calif.
Height, 6.03. Weight, 197.
High School—Los Angeles, Calif., Washington.
Received bachelor of science degree in industrial engineering from
Stanford University in 1978.
Cousin of Kevin Bass, outfielder with Houston Astros;
and cousin of Tron Armstrong, wide receiver with New York Jets.

Named to THE SPORTING NEWS NFL All-Star Team, 1980 and 1981.
Selected by Green Bay in 1st round (6th player selected) of 1978 NFL draft.

		—RUSHING—				PASS RECEIVING				—TOTAL—		
Year Club	G.	Att.	Yds.	Avg.	TD.	P.C.	Yds.	Avg.	TD.	TD.	Pts.	F.
1978—Green Bay NFL	16	3	13	4.3	0	46	818	17.8	6	6	36	2
1979—Green Bay NFL	15	1	—1	—1.0	0	54	968	17.9	4	4	24	5
1980—Green Bay NFL	16			None		71	1226	17.3	4	4	24	0
1981—Green Bay NFL	16			None		71	1294	18.2	8	8	48	0
1982—Green Bay NFL	9	4	101	25.3	1	35	696	19.9	4	5	30	0
1983—Green Bay NFL	16	9	36	4.0	0	58	1300	★22.4	8	8	48	0
1984—Green Bay NFL	16	10	82	8.2	0	62	1361	★22.0	7	7	42	1
Pro Totals—7 Years	104	27	231	8.6	1	397	7663	19.3	41	42	252	8

Additional pro statistics: Returned one kickoff for no yards and attempted two passes with no completions, 1978; attempted one pass with no completions, 1979; recovered one fumble, 1981; attempted one pass with one completion for 43 yards, 1982.
Played in Pro Bowl (NFL All-Star Game) following 1978 and 1980 through 1984 seasons.

—DID YOU KNOW—
That the Los Angeles Rams scored an NFL-record three safeties in a 33-12 win over the New York Giants on September 30, 1984? All three came in the third quarter.

DAVID LOGAN
Nose Tackle—Tampa Bay Buccaneers
Born October 25, 1956, at Pittsburgh, Pa.
Height, 6.02. Weight, 250.
High School—East Liberty, Pa., Peabody.
Received bachelor of arts and science degree in urban and black studies from
University of Pittsburgh in 1979.
Related to Bill Cartwright, center with New York Knicks.

Named to THE SPORTING NEWS NFL All-Star Team, 1984.
Selected by Tampa Bay in 12th round (307th player selected) of 1979 NFL draft.
On injured reserve with knee injury, August 28 through November 16, 1979; activated, November 17, 1979.
On injured reserve with back injury, December 27 through remainder of 1979 playoffs.
Tampa Bay NFL, 1979 through 1984.
Games: 1979 (5), 1980 (16), 1981 (16), 1982 (9), 1983 (16), 1984 (16). Total—78.
Pro statistics: Recovered one fumble for 60 yards and a touchdown, 1980; recovered one fumble for 21 yards and a touchdown, 1981; recovered one fumble for 54 yards and a touchdown, 1983; intercepted one pass for 27 yards and a touchdown, 1984.

NEIL VINCENT LOMAX
Quarterback—St. Louis Cardinals
Born February 17, 1959, at Portland, Ore.
Height, 6.03. Weight, 215.
High School—Lake Oswego, Ore.
Attended Portland State University.

Selected by St. Louis in 2nd round (33rd player selected) of 1981 NFL draft.

Year Club	G.	Att.	Cmp.	Pct.	Gain	T.P.	P.I.	Avg.	Att.	Yds.	Avg.	TD.	TD.	Pts.	F.
1981—St. Louis NFL	14	236	119	50.4	1575	4	10	6.67	19	104	5.5	2	2	12	6
1982—St. Louis NFL	9	205	109	53.2	1367	5	6	6.67	28	119	4.3	1	1	6	8
1983—St. Louis NFL	13	354	209	59.0	2636	24	11	7.45	27	127	4.7	2	2	12	9
1984—St. Louis NFL	16	560	345	61.6	4614	28	16	8.24	35	184	5.3	3	3	18	11
Pro Totals—4 Years	52	1355	782	57.7	10192	61	43	7.52	109	534	4.9	8	8	48	34

Quarterback Rating Points: 1981 (60.1), 1982 (70.1), 1983 (92.0), 1984 (92.5). Total—83.2.
Additional pro statistics: Caught one pass for 10 yards, recovered one fumble and fumbled eight times for minus one yard, 1982; recovered three fumbles, 1983; recovered two fumbles and fumbled 11 times for minus five yards, 1984.
Played in Pro Bowl (NFL All-Star Game) following 1984 season.

HOWARD M. LONG
(Howie)
Defensive End—Los Angeles Raiders
Born January 6, 1960, at Somerville, Mass.
Height, 6.05. Weight, 265.
High School—Milford, Mass.
Received degree in communications from Villanova University in 1981.

Named to THE SPORTING NEWS NFL All-Star Team, 1983.
Selected by Oakland in 2nd round (48th player selected) of 1981 NFL draft.
Franchise transferred to Los Angeles, May 7, 1982.
Left Los Angeles Raiders camp voluntarily, July 30 through August 2, 1984; returned, August 3, 1984.
Oakland NFL, 1981; Los Angeles Raiders NFL, 1982 through 1984.
Games: 1981 (16), 1982 (9), 1983 (16), 1984 (16). Total—57.
Pro statistics: Recovered two fumbles, 1983; recovered two fumbles for four yards, 1984.
Played in AFC Championship Game following 1983 season.
Played in NFL Championship Game following 1983 season.
Played in Pro Bowl (NFL All-Star Game) following 1983 and 1984 seasons.

TERRY LUTHER LONG
Guard—Pittsburgh Steelers
Born July 21, 1959, at Columbia, S.C.
Height, 5.11. Weight, 272.
High School—Columbia, S.C., Eau Claire.
Attended East Carolina University.
Spent two years in Army before entering college.

Selected by Washington in 4th round (76th player selected) of 1984 USFL draft.
Selected by Pittsburgh in 4th round (111th player selected) of 1984 NFL draft.
Signed by Pittsburgh Steelers, July 10, 1984.
Pittsburgh NFL, 1984.
Games: 1984 (12).
Pro statistics: Returned one punt for no yards and fumbled once, 1984.
Played in AFC Championship Game following 1984 season.

—DID YOU KNOW—
That only three teams have not made the playoffs during the 1980s? Kansas City, Baltimore-Indianapolis and New Orleans hold claim to that distinction.

RONALD MANDEL LOTT
(Ronnie)
Defensive Back—San Francisco 49ers
Born May 8, 1959, at Albuquerque, N.M.
Height, 6.00. Weight, 199.
High School—Rialto, Calif., Eisenhower.
Received bachelor of science degree in public administration
from University of Southern California in 1981.

Named as defensive back on THE SPORTING NEWS College All-America Team, 1980.
Named to THE SPORTING NEWS NFL All-Star Team, 1981.
Selected by San Francisco in 1st round (8th player selected) of 1981 NFL draft.

Year	Club	G.	No.	Yds.	Avg.	TD.
1981—San Francisco NFL		16	7	117	16.7	*3
1982—San Francisco NFL		9	2	95	47.5	*1
1983—San Francisco NFL		15	4	22	5.5	0
1984—San Francisco NFL		12	4	26	6.5	0
Pro Totals—4 Years............		52	17	260	15.3	4

Additional pro statistics: Returned seven kickoffs for 111 yards, recovered two fumbles and fumbled once, 1981; recovered one fumble, 1983.
Played in NFC Championship Game following 1981, 1983 and 1984 seasons.
Played in NFL Championship Game following 1981 and 1984 seasons.
Played in Pro Bowl (NFL All-Star Game) following 1981 through 1984 seasons.

RANDY LOVE
Running Back—St. Louis Cardinals
Born September 30, 1956, at Garland, Tex.
Height, 6.01. Weight, 205.
High School—Garland, Tex.
Attended University of Houston.

Selected by New England in 8th round (216th player selected) of 1979 NFL draft.
Released by New England Patriots, August 16, 1979; signed as free agent by St. Louis Cardinals, November 15, 1979.

Year	Club	G.	Att.	Yds.	Avg.	TD.	P.C.	Yds.	Avg.	TD.	TD.	Pts.	F.
1979—St. Louis NFL...............		4		None				None			0	0	0
1980—St. Louis NFL...............		16	1	3	3.0	0		None			0	0	3
1981—St. Louis NFL...............		16	3	11	3.7	0		None			0	0	0
1982—St. Louis NFL...............		9		None				None			0	0	1
1983—St. Louis NFL...............		16	35	103	2.9	2	6	58	9.7	1	3	18	4
1984—St. Louis NFL...............		16	25	90	3.6	1	7	33	4.7	1	2	12	1
Pro Totals—6 Years..................		77	64	207	3.2	3	13	91	7.0	2	5	30	9

Additional pro statistics: Returned three kickoffs for 46 yards, 1980 and 1981; recovered two fumbles, 1980 and 1981; returned four kickoffs for 69 yards, 1982; recovered one fumble, 1982 and 1983; returned three kickoffs for 71 yards, 1983; returned one kickoff for one yard, 1984.

WOODROW LOWE
Linebacker—San Diego Chargers
Born June 9, 1954, at Columbus, Ga.
Height, 6.00. Weight, 219.
High School—Phenix City, Ala.
Attended University of Alabama.

Selected by San Diego in 5th round (131st player selected) of 1976 NFL draft.

Year	Club	G.	No.	Yds.	Avg.	TD.
1976—San Diego NFL.............		14	1	8	8.0	0
1977—San Diego NFL.............		14	1	28	28.0	0
1978—San Diego NFL.............		16	1	16	16.0	0
1979—San Diego NFL.............		16	5	150	*30.0	*2
1980—San Diego NFL.............		16	3	72	24.0	1
1981—San Diego NFL.............		16	3	0	0.0	0
1982—San Diego NFL.............		9	1	2	2.0	0
1983—San Diego NFL.............		16		None		
1984—San Diego NFL.............		15	3	61	20.3	1
Pro Totals—9 Years.........		132	18	337	18.7	4

Additional pro statistics: Recovered two fumbles, 1976; recovered one fumble, 1978, 1980 and 1983; recovered one fumble for two yards, 1979; fumbled once, 1984.
Played in AFC Championship Game following 1980 and 1981 seasons.

DOMINIC GERALD LOWERY
(Nick)
Placekicker—Kansas City Chiefs
Born May 27, 1956, at Munich, Germany
Height, 6.04. Weight, 189.
High School—Washington, D. C., St. Albans.
Received bachelor of arts degree in government from Dartmouth College in 1978.

Established NFL record for highest field goal percentage, career (74.7).
Signed as free agent by New York Jets, May 17, 1978.
Released by New York Jets, August 21, 1978; signed as free agent by New England Patriots, September 19, 1978.
Released by New England Patriots, October 6, 1978; signed as free agent by Cincinnati Bengals, July 2, 1979.
Released by Cincinnati Bengals, August 13, 1979; signed as free agent by Washington Redskins, August 18, 1979.
Released by Washington Redskins, August 20, 1979; re-signed by Redskins, August 25, 1979.
Released by Washington Redskins, August 27, 1979; signed as free agent by Kansas City Chiefs, February 16, 1980.

			——PLACE KICKING——				
Year	Club	G.	XP.	XPM.	FG.	FGA.	Pts.
1978—New Eng. NFL		2	7	0	0	1	7
1980—Kansas City NFL		16	37	0	20	26	97
1981—Kansas City NFL		16	37	1	26	36	115
1982—Kansas City NFL		9	17	0	19	*24	74
1983—Kansas City NFL		16	44	1	24	30	116
1984—Kansas City NFL		16	35	0	23	33	104
Pro Totals—6 Years		75	177	2	112	150	513

Additional pro statistics: Recovered one fumble, 1981.
Played in Pro Bowl (NFL All-Star Game) following 1981 season.

OLIVER LUCK
Quarterback—Houston Oilers
Born April 5, 1960, at Cleveland, O.
Height, 6.02. Weight, 193.
High School—Cleveland, O., St. Ignacius.
Received bachelor of arts degree in history from West Virginia University in 1982.

Selected by Houston in 2nd round (44th player selected) of 1982 NFL draft.
Active for 9 games with Houston Oilers in 1982; did not play.

			——————PASSING——————							——RUSHING——				—TOTAL—		
Year	Club	G.	Att.	Cmp.	Pct.	Gain	T.P.	P.I.	Avg.	Att.	Yds.	Avg.	TD.	TD.	Pts.	F.
1983—Houston NFL		7	217	124	57.1	1375	8	13	6.34	17	55	3.2	0	0	0	5
1984—Houston NFL		4	36	22	61.1	256	2	1	7.11	10	75	7.5	1	1	6	2
Pro Totals—3 Years		11	253	146	57.7	1631	10	14	6.45	27	130	4.8	1	1	6	7

Quarterback Rating Points: 1983 (63.4), 1984 (89.6). Total—67.5.
Additional pro statistics: Recovered one fumble, 1983; recovered two fumbles, 1984.

MICHAEL CHRISTOPHER WILBERT LUCKHURST
(Mick)
Placekicker—Atlanta Falcons
Born March 31, 1958, at Redbourn, England.
Height, 6.02. Weight, 180.
High School—Redbourn, England, St. Columbus College.
Attended St. Cloud State University and University of California.
Husband of Terri Moody Luckhurst, professional golfer.

Signed as free agent by Atlanta Falcons, May 5, 1981.

			——PLACE KICKING——				
Year	Club	G.	XP.	XPM.	FG.	FGA.	Pts.
1981—Atlanta NFL		16	51	0	21	33	114
1982—Atlanta NFL		9	21	1	10	14	51
1983—Atlanta NFL		16	43	2	17	22	94
1984—Atlanta NFL		16	31	0	20	27	91
Pro Totals—4 Years		57	146	3	68	96	350

DAVID GRAHAM LUTZ
Offensive Tackle—Kansas City Chiefs
Born December 30, 1959, at Monroe, N.C.
Height, 6.05. Weight, 285.
High School—Wadesboro, N.C., Bowman.
Attended Georgia Tech.

Selected by Oakland in 3rd round (31st player selected) of 1983 USFL draft.
Selected by Kansas City in 2nd round (34th player selected) of 1983 NFL draft.
Signed by Kansas City Chiefs, June 1, 1983.
On injured reserve with knee injury, September 4 through November 8, 1984; activated, November 9, 1984.
Kansas City NFL, 1983 and 1984.
Games: 1983 (16), 1984 (7). Total—23.

ALLEN LYDAY
Defensive Back—Houston Oilers
Born September 16, 1960, at Wichita, Kan.
Height, 5.10. Weight, 186.
High School—Wichita, Kan., South.
Attended Texas Southern University and University of Nebraska.

Selected by Boston in 1983 USFL territorial draft.
Signed as free agent by Kansas City Chiefs, April 28, 1983.

Released by Kansas City Chiefs, August 29, 1983; signed by New Orleans Breakers, November 7, 1983.
Released by New Orleans Breakers, January 27, 1984; awarded on procedural waivers to Houston Oilers, April 6, 1984.
Released by Houston Oilers, August 20, 1984; re-signed by Oilers after clearing procedural waivers, October 25, 1984.
On injured reserve with knee injury, November 21 through remainder of 1984 season.
Houston NFL, 1984.
Games: 1984 (4).
Pro statistics: Intercepted one pass for 12 yards, 1984.

ROBERT LYLES
Linebacker—Houston Oilers
Born March 21, 1961, at Los Angeles, Calif.
Height, 6.01. Weight, 223.
High School—Los Angeles, Calif., Belmont.
Attended Texas Christian University.

Selected by Houston in 5th round (114th player selected) of 1984 NFL draft.
On injured reserve with knee injury, September 25 through December 6, 1984; activated, December 7, 1984.
Houston NFL, 1984.
Games: 1984 (6).

THOMAS FRANK LYNCH
(Tom)
Guard—Buffalo Bills
Born May 24, 1955, at Chicago, Ill.
Height, 6.05. Weight, 250.
High School—Whitman, Mass., Whitman-Hanson.
Received bachelor of business administration degree in marketing from Boston College in 1977.

Selected by Seattle in 2nd round (30th player selected) of 1977 NFL draft.
Placed on did not report list, August 18 through October 12, 1981.
Traded by Seattle Seahawks to Buffalo Bills for 3rd round pick in 1982 draft, October 13, 1981.
Granted two-game exemption, October 13, 1981; activated, October 17, 1981.
Seattle NFL, 1977 through 1980; Buffalo NFL, 1981 through 1984.
Games: 1977 (14), 1978 (16), 1979 (15), 1980 (16), 1981 (5), 1982 (8), 1983 (15), 1984 (16). Total—105.

JOHNNY ROSS LYNN
Defensive Back—New York Jets
Born December 19, 1956, at Los Angeles, Calif.
Height, 6.00. Weight, 198.
High School—Pasadena, Calif., John Muir.
Attended University of California at Los Angeles.

Selected by New York Jets in 4th round (98th player selected) of 1979 NFL draft.
On injured reserve with knee injury, September 1 through entire 1980 season.
USFL rights traded by Washington Federals to Los Angeles Express for rights to quarterback Vince Evans, November 11, 1983.
Signed by Los Angeles Express, November 21, 1983, for contract to take effect after being granted free agency, February 1, 1984.
Re-signed by New York Jets after exercising buyout option in contract with Los Angeles Express, February, 1984.

| | | —INTERCEPTIONS— | | | |
Year Club	G.	No.	Yds.	Avg.	TD.
1979—N.Y. Jets NFL	16	2	46	23.0	0
1981—N.Y. Jets NFL	13	3	76	25.3	0
1982—N.Y. Jets NFL	8	1	3	3.0	0
1983—N.Y. Jets NFL	16	3	70	23.3	1
1984—N.Y. Jets NFL	14	2	16	8.0	0
Pro Totals—5 Years	67	11	211	19.2	1

Additional pro statistics: Recovered blocked punt in end zone for a touchdown and recovered two fumbles, 1979; recovered one fumble, 1982; ran two yards with lateral on fumble recovery, 1984.
Played in AFC Championship Game following 1982 season.

MARTY LYONS
Defensive Tackle—New York Jets
Born January 15, at Tokoma Park, Md.
Height, 6.05. Weight, 269.
High School—St. Petersburg, Fla., Catholic.
Attended University of Alabama.

Named as defensive lineman on THE SPORTING NEWS College All-America Team, 1978.
Selected by New York Jets in 1st round (14th player selected) of 1979 NFL draft.
New York Jets NFL, 1979 through 1984.
Games: 1979 (16), 1980 (16), 1981 (12), 1982 (7), 1983 (16), 1984 (13). Total—80.
Pro statistics: Recovered three fumbles, 1979; recovered one fumble, 1981; recovered one fumble for 10 yards, 1982.
Played in AFC Championship Game following 1982 season.

WILLIAM THOMAS MAAS
(Bill)
Nose Tackle—Kansas City Chiefs
Born March 2, 1962, at Newton Square, Pa.
Height, 6.04. Weight, 265.
High School—Newton Square, Pa., Marple Newtown.
Attended University of Pittsburgh.
Brother-in-law of Dan Marino, quarterback with Miami Dolphins.

Selected by Pittsburgh in 1984 USFL territorial draft.
Selected by Kansas City in 1st round (5th player selected) of 1984 NFL draft.
Signed by Kansas City Chiefs, July 13, 1984.
Kansas City NFL, 1984.
Games: 1984 (14).

DONALD MATTHEW MACEK
Name pronounced MAY-sick.
(Don)
Center—San Diego Chargers
Born July 21, 1954, at Manchester, N. H.
Height, 6.02. Weight, 260.
High School—Manchester, N. H., Central.
Received bachelor of science degree in marketing from Boston College and
attending National University for master's degree in marketing.

Selected by San Diego in 2nd round (31st player selected) of 1976 NFL draft.
On injured reserve with neck injury, December 7 through remainder of 1979 season.
Left San Diego Chargers camp voluntarily, August 7 through August 21, 1984; returned, August 22, 1984.
San Diego NFL, 1976 through 1984.
Games: 1976 (14), 1977 (14), 1978 (14), 1979 (10), 1980 (16), 1981 (15), 1982 (9), 1983 (11), 1984 (13). Total—116.
Pro statistics: Recovered one fumble, 1976, 1977, 1980, 1981 and 1983; returned one kickoff for six yards, 1978;
fumbled once, 1978 and 1982; fumbled twice for minus 23 yards, 1980.
Played in AFC Championship Game following 1980 and 1981 seasons.

MICHAEL BRUCE MACHUREK
(Mike)
Quarterback—Detroit Lions
Born July 22, 1960, at Las Vegas, Nev.
Height, 6.01. Weight, 205.
High School—San Diego, Calif., Madison.
Attended San Diego Community College and Idaho State University.

Selected by Detroit in 6th round (154th player selected) of 1982 NFL draft.
Released by Detroit Lions, September 6, 1982; re-signed by Lions, September 7, 1982.
On inactive list, September 12 and 19, 1982.
On commissioner's exempt list, November 20 through November 29, 1982; activated, November 30, 1982.
On physically unable to perform/active with cancer surgery, July 21 through August 7, 1983; activated, August 8, 1983.
Active for 5 games with Detroit Lions in 1982; did not play.
Active for 16 games with Detroit Lions in 1983; did not play.

Year Club		G.	Att.	Cmp.	Pct.	Gain	T.P.	P.I.	Avg.	Att.	Yds.	Avg.	TD.	TD.	Pts.	F.
				—PASSING—						—RUSHING—				—TOTAL—		
1984—Detroit NFL		4	43	14	32.6	193	0	6	4.49	1	9	9.0	0	0	0	0

Quarterback Rating Points: 1984 (8.3).

CEDRIC MANUEL MACK
Wide Receiver—St. Louis Cardinals
Born September 14, 1960, at Freeport, Tex.
Height, 6.00. Weight, 190.
High School—Freeport, Tex., Brazosport.
Attended Baylor University.
Cousin of Phillip Epps, wide receiver with Green Bay Packers.

Selected by Oakland in 12th round (138th player selected) of 1983 USFL draft.
Selected by St. Louis in 2nd round (44th player selected) of 1983 NFL draft.
Signed by St. Louis Cardinals, July 11, 1983.
On injured reserve with dislocated shoulder, September 28 through October 25, 1984; activated, October 26, 1984.
Selected by New York Yankees' organization in 22nd round of free-agent draft, June 5, 1979.

Year Club	G.	No.	Yds.	Avg.	TD.	P.C.	Yds.	Avg.	TD.	TD.	Pts.	F.
		—INTERCEPTIONS—				—PASS RECEIVING—				—TOTAL—		
1983—St. Louis NFL	16	3	25	8.3	0	None				0	0	0
1984—St. Louis NFL	12	None				5	61	12.2	0	0	0	0
Pro Totals—2 Years	28	3	25	8.3	0	5	61	12.2	0	0	0	0

KEVIN MACK
Running Back—Cleveland Browns
Born August 9, 1962, at Kings Mountain, N.C.
Height, 6.01. Weight, 200.
High School—Kings Mountain, N.C.
Attended Clemson University.

Selected by Washington in 1984 USFL territorial draft.
Rights traded with rights to defensive tackle James Robinson by Washington Federals to Los Angeles Express for draft choices, March 16, 1984.
Signed by Los Angeles Express, March 16, 1984.
Granted roster exemption, March 16, 1984; activated, March 23, 1984.
On developmental squad, March 30 through April 6, 1984; activated, April 7, 1984.
On developmental squad, April 28 through May 10, 1984; activated, May 11, 1984.
Selected by Cleveland in 1st round (11th player selected) of 1984 NFL supplemental draft.
Released by Los Angeles Express, January 31, 1985; signed by Cleveland Browns, February 1, 1985.
On developmental squad for 3 games with Los Angeles Express in 1984.

| | | —RUSHING— | | | | PASS RECEIVING | | | | —TOTAL— | | |
Year Club	G.	Att.	Yds.	Avg.	TD.	P.C.	Yds.	Avg.	TD.	TD.	Pts.	F.
1984—Los Angeles USFL	12	73	330	4.5	4	6	38	6.3	0	4	24	3

Additional USFL statistics: Returned three kickoffs for 20 yards and recovered four fumbles, 1984.

KYLE ERICKSON MACKEY
Quarterback—St. Louis Cardinals
Born March 2, 1962, at Alpine, Tex.
Height, 6.02. Weight, 220.
High School—Alpine, Tex.
Attended East Texas State University.
Son of Dee Mackey, tight end with San Francisco 49ers, Baltimore Colts
and New York Jets, 1960 through 1965.

Selected by Washington in 11th round (215th player selected) of 1984 USFL draft.
Selected by St. Louis in 11th round (296th player selected) of 1984 NFL draft.
Signed by St. Louis Cardinals, July 16, 1984.
Active for 16 games with St. Louis Cardinals in 1984; did not play.

L.E. MADISON
Linebacker—Pittsburgh Steelers
Born July 15, 1962, at Topeka, Kan.
Height, 6.01. Weight, 225.
High School—Manhattan, Kan.
Attended Kansas State University.

Selected by Washington in 11th round (220th player selected) of 1984 USFL draft.
Signed as free agent by Pittsburgh Steelers, May 22, 1984.
On injured reserve with knee injury, August 27 through entire 1984 season.

FRANK MAGWOOD
Wide Receiver—New York Giants
Born July 7, 1961, at Charleston, S.C.
Height, 6.00. Weight, 188.
High School—John's Island, S.C., St. John's.
Attended Clemson University.

Selected by Washington in 1983 USFL territorial draft.
Selected by New York Giants in 12th round (318th player selected) of 1983 NFL draft.
Signed by New York Giants, June 13, 1983.
On injured reserve with dislocated shoulder, August 22 through entire 1983 season.
On injured reserve with knee injury, August 13 through entire 1984 season.

STEVEN KENNETH MAIDLOW
(Steve)
Linebacker—Cincinnati Bengals
Born June 6, 1960, at Lansing, Mich.
Height, 6.02. Weight, 234.
High School—East Lansing, Mich.
Attended Michigan State University.

Selected by Michigan in 1983 USFL territorial draft.
Selected by Cincinnati in 4th round (109th player selected) of 1983 NFL draft.
Signed by Cincinnati Bengals, May 19, 1983.
Cincinnati NFL, 1983 and 1984.
Games: 1983 (16), 1984 (16). Total—32.

RYDELL MALANCON

Name pronounced Mah-LOHN-SOHN.

Linebacker—Atlanta Falcons

Born January 10, 1962, at New Orleans, La.
Height, 6.01. Weight, 219.
High School—St. James, La.
Attended Louisiana State University.

Selected by New Orleans in 1984 USFL territorial draft.
Selected by Atlanta in 4th round (94th player selected) of 1984 NFL draft.
Signed by Atlanta Falcons, July 15, 1984.
On injured reserved with ankle injury, September 28 through November 30, 1984; activated, December 1, 1984.
Atlanta NFL, 1984.
Games: 1984 (7).
Pro statistics: Returned one kickoff for no yards, 1984.

RICK LEROY MALLORY

Offensive Lineman—Tampa Bay Buccaneers

Born October 21, 1960, at Seattle, Wash.
Height, 6.02. Weight, 265.
High School—Renton, Wash., Lindbergh.
Attended University of Washington.

Selected by Arizona in 11th round (221st player selected) of 1984 USFL draft.
Selected by Tampa Bay in 9th round (225th player selected) of 1984 NFL draft.
Signed by Tampa Bay Buccaneers, June 21, 1984.
On injured reserve with ankle injury, August 27 through entire 1984 season.

MARK M. MALONE

Quarterback—Pittsburgh Steelers

Born November 22, 1958, at El Cajon, Calif.
Height, 6.04. Weight, 218.
High School—El Cajon, Calif., Valley.
Attended Arizona State University.

Selected by Pittsburgh in 1st round (28th player selected) of 1980 NFL draft.
On physically unable to perform/active with knee injury, July 29 through August 23, 1982.
On reserve, August 24 through December 13, 1982; activated, December 14, 1982.
Active for 3 games with Pittsburgh Steelers in 1982; did not play.

Year Club	G.	Att.	Cmp.	Pct.	Gain	T.P.	P.I.	Avg.	Att.	Yds.	Avg.	TD.	TD.	Pts.	F.
					PASSING					RUSHING				TOTAL	
1980—Pittsburgh NFL	1				None					None			0	0	0
1981—Pittsburgh NFL	8	88	45	51.1	553	3	5	6.28	16	68	4.3	2	3	18	2
1983—Pittsburgh NFL	2	20	9	45.0	124	1	2	6.20			None		0	0	0
1984—Pittsburgh NFL	13	272	147	54.0	2137	16	17	7.86	25	42	1.7	3	3	18	4
Pro Totals—5 Years	24	380	201	52.9	2814	20	24	7.41	41	110	2.7	5	6	36	6

Quarterback Rating Points: 1981 (58.4), 1983 (42.5), 1984 (73.4). Total—68.5.
Additional pro statistics: Caught one pass for 90 yards and a touchdown and returned one kickoff for three yards, 1981; recovered one fumble, 1983; recovered two fumbles, 1984.
Played in AFC Championship Game following 1984 season.

WILLIAM H. MANDLEY

(Pete)

Wide Receiver—Detroit Lions

Born July 29, 1961, at Mesa, Ariz.
Height, 5.10. Weight, 191.
High School—Mesa, Ariz., Westwood.
Attended Northern Arizona University.

Selected by Arizona in 1984 USFL territorial draft.
Selected by Detroit in 2nd round (47th player selected) of 1984 NFL draft.
Signed by Detroit Lions, July 10, 1984.

Year Club	G.	P.C.	Yds.	Avg.	TD.	No.	Yds.	Avg.	TD.	No.	Yds.	Avg.	TD.	TD.	Pts.	F.
		PASS RECEIVING				-PUNT RETURNS-				KICKOFF RET.				TOTAL		
1984—Detroit NFL	15	3	38	12.7	0	2	0	0.0	0	22	390	17.7	0	0	0	2

Additional pro statistics: Recovered two fumbles, 1984.

DINO M. MANGIERO

Name pronounced Man-gee-air-oh.

Nose Tackle—Seattle Seahawks

Born December 29, 1958, at New York, N. Y.
Height, 6.02. Weight, 270.
High School—Staten Island, N. Y., Curtis.
Received bachelor of science degree in physical education from Rutgers University in 1980.

Signed as free agent by Kansas City Chiefs, May, 1980.
Released by Kansas City Chiefs, August 26, 1980; re-signed by Chiefs, September 3, 1980.
On injured reserve with knee injury, August 11 through October 19, 1981; activated after clearing procedural waivers, October 21, 1981.

On injured reserve with hand injury, September 6 through November 22, 1982; re-signed after clearing procedural waivers, November 24, 1982.

Released by Kansas City Chiefs, August 27, 1984; awarded on waivers to Seattle Seahawks, August 28, 1984.

Kansas City NFL, 1980 through 1983; Seattle NFL, 1984.

Game: 1980 (16), 1981 (9), 1982 (6), 1983 (16), 1984 (15). Total—62.

Pro statistics: Intercepted one pass for no yards and recovered one fumble, 1980; returned one kickoff for eight yards, 1982; recovered one fumble for 32 yards, 1983.

DEXTER MANLEY
Defensive End—Washington Redskins
Born July 2, 1959, at Houston, Tex.
Height, 6.03. Weight, 253.
High School—Houston, Tex., Yates.
Attended Oklahoma State University.

Selected by Washington in 5th round (119th player selected) of 1981 NFL draft.

Washington NFL, 1981 through 1984.

Games: 1981 (16), 1982 (9), 1983 (16), 1984 (15). Total—56.

Pro statistics: Intercepted one pass for minus two yards and recovered three fumbles for three yards, 1982; intercepted one pass for one yard, 1983; recovered one fumble, 1984.

Played in NFC Championship Game following 1982 and 1983 seasons.

Played in NFL Championship Game following 1982 and 1983 seasons.

CHARLES MANN
Defensive End—Washington Redskins
Born April 12, 1961, at Sacramento, Calif.
Height, 6.06. Weight, 260.
High School—Sacramento, Calif., Valley.
Attended University of Nevada at Reno.

Selected by Oakland in 18th round (210th player selected) of 1983 USFL draft.

Selected by Washington in 3rd round (84th player selected) of 1983 NFL draft.

Signed by Washington Redskins, May 9, 1983.

Washington NFL, 1983 and 1984.

Games: 1983 (16), 1984 (16). Total—32.

Pro statistics: Credited with one safety, 1983; recovered one fumble, 1984.

Played in NFC Championship Game following 1983 season.

Played in NFL Championship Game following 1983 season.

ELISHA ARCHIE MANNING III
(Known by middle name.)
Quarterback—Minnesota Vikings
Born May 19, 1949, at Cleveland, Miss.
Height, 6.03. Weight, 211.
High School—Drew, Miss.
Received bachelor of public administration degree from University of Mississippi in 1971.

Named THE SPORTING NEWS NFC Player of the Year, 1978.

Named to THE SPORTING NEWS NFC All-Star Team, 1978.

Selected by New Orleans in 1st round (2nd player selected) of 1971 NFL draft.

Traded by New Orleans Saints to Houston Oilers for offensive tackle Leon Gray, September 17, 1982.

Traded with tight end Dave Casper by Houston Oilers to Minnesota Vikings for 2nd and 4th round picks in 1984 draft, September 20, 1983.

On reserve/non-football injury list with Graves disease (thyroid), December 5 through remainder of 1983 season.

Active for 5 games in 1976, did not play (bothered by shoulder injury).

| | | | | PASSING | | | | | | RUSHING | | | | TOTAL | |
Year Club	G.	Att.	Cmp.	Pct.	Gain	T.P.	P.I.	Avg.	Att.	Yds.	Avg.	TD.	TD.	Pts.	F.
1971—New Orleans NFL	12	177	86	48.6	1164	6	9	6.58	33	172	5.2	4	4	24	7
1972—New Orleans NFL	14	*448	*230	51.3	2781	18	21	6.21	63	351	5.6	2	2	12	9
1973—New Orleans NFL	13	267	140	52.4	1642	10	21	6.15	63	293	4.7	2	2	12	9
1974—New Orleans NFL	11	261	134	51.3	1429	6	16	5.48	28	204	7.3	1	1	6	4
1975—New Orleans NFL	13	338	159	47.0	1683	7	20	4.98	33	186	5.6	1	1	6	7
1977—New Orleans NFL	10	205	113	55.1	1284	8	9	6.26	39	270	6.9	5	5	30	5
1978—New Orleans NFL	16	471	291	61.8	3416	17	16	7.25	38	202	5.3	1	1	6	8
1979—New Orleans NFL	16	420	252	60.0	3169	15	20	7.55	35	186	5.3	2	2	12	4
1980—New Orleans NFL	16	509	309	60.7	3716	23	20	7.30	23	166	7.2	0	0	0	6
1981—New Orleans NFL	12	232	134	57.8	1447	5	11	6.24	2	28	14.0	0	0	0	3
1982—N.O. (1)-Hou. (6) NFL	7	132	67	50.8	880	6	8	6.67	13	85	6.5	0	0	0	5
1983—Hou. (3)-Minn. (2) NFL	5	88	44	50.0	755	2	8	8.58	3	12	4.0	0	0	0	2
1984—Minnesota NFL	6	94	52	55.3	545	2	3	5.80	11	42	3.8	0	0	0	4
Pro Totals—14 Years	151	3642	2011	55.2	23911	125	173	6.57	384	2197	5.7	18	18	108	73

Quarterback Rating Points: 1971 (60.1), 1972 (64.5), 1973 (65.0), 1974 (40.9), 1975 (44.4), 1977 (68.8), 1978 (81.6), 1979 (75.6), 1980 (81.8), 1981 (64.0), 1982 (61.8), 1983 (49.2), 1984 (66.1). Total—66.8.

Additional pro statistics: Caught one pass for minus seven yards, recovered three fumbles and fumbled seven times for minus two yards, 1971; recovered four fumbles, 1972; recovered two fumbles and fumbled nine times for minus 15 yards, 1973; recovered one fumble, 1975 and 1977; recovered four fumbles and fumbled eight times for minus 26 yards, 1978; recovered two fumbles and fumbled four times for minus four yards, 1979; recovered two fumbles and fumbled six times for minus three yards, 1980; recovered one fumble and fumbled five times for minus four yards, 1982; recovered two fumbles, 1983 and 1984.

Played in Pro Bowl (NFL All-Star Game) following 1978 and 1979 seasons.

WADE RONALD ARTHUR MANNING
Wide Receiver—Denver Broncos

Born July 25, 1955, at Meadville, Pa.
Height, 5.11. Weight, 190.
High School—Shaker Heights, O.
Received bachelor of science degree in education from Ohio State University
in 1978 (did not play college football).
Related to Anthony D. Manning, outfielder in Cleveland Indians'
organization, 1971 through 1976.

Signed as free agent by Dallas Cowboys, May, 1979.
On injured reserve with knee injury, October 5 through November 20, 1979; activated, November 21, 1979.
Traded by Dallas Cowboys to Buffalo Bills for future considerations, September 1, 1980; returned to Cowboys after failing physical, September 2, 1980.
On injured reserve with knee injury, September 3 through entire 1980 season.
Traded by Dallas Cowboys to Buffalo Bills for 8th round pick in 1982 draft, August 18, 1981.
Traded by Buffalo Bills to Denver Broncos for 8th round pick in 1982 draft, August 24, 1981.
Released by Denver Broncos, August 29, 1983; signed by Denver Gold, October 4, 1983.
Released by Denver Gold, February 13, 1984; signed as free agent by Cleveland Browns, March 1, 1984.
Released by Cleveland Browns, August 20, 1984; signed as free agent by Denver Broncos, February 12, 1985.

		PASS RECEIVING				-PUNT RETURNS-				—KICKOFF RET.—				—TOTAL—		
Year Club	G.	P.C.	Yds.	Avg.	TD.	No.	Yds.	Avg.	TD.	No.	Yds.	Avg.	TD.	TD.	Pts.	F.
1979—Dallas NFL	9		None			10	55	5.5	0	7	145	20.7	0	0	0	1
1981—Denver NFL	16	3	49	16.3	0	41	378	9.2	0	26	514	19.8	0	0	0	3
1982—Denver NFL	9	3	46	15.3	0			None		15	346	23.1	0	0	0	0
Pro Totals—3 Years	34	6	95	15.8	0	51	433	8.5	0	48	1005	20.9	0	0	0	4

BRISON MANOR JR.
Defensive End—Denver Broncos

Born August 10, 1952, at Bridgeton, N. J.
Height, 6.04. Weight, 248.
High School—Bridgeton, N. J.
Attended Pratt Junior College and University of Arkansas.

Selected by New York Jets in 15th round (380th player selected) of 1975 NFL draft.
Released by New York Jets, September 9, 1975; signed as free agent by Denver Broncos, March 26, 1976.
On injured reserve entire 1976 season.
Traded by Denver Broncos to Tampa Bay Buccaneers for draft choice, August 13, 1984.
Released by Tampa Bay Buccaneers, November 6, 1984; signed as free agent by Denver Broncos, November 13, 1984.
Denver NFL, 1977 through 1983; Tampa Bay (6)-Denver (5) NFL, 1984.
Games: 1977 (13), 1978 (14), 1979 (16), 1980 (16), 1981 (16), 1982 (9), 1983 (16), 1984 (11). Total—111.
Pro statistics: Recovered one fumble, 1979 and 1983; recovered one fumble for five yards, 1980; intercepted one pass for 16 yards, 1981.
Played in AFC Championship Game following 1977 season.
Played in NFL Championship Game following 1977 season.

LIONEL MANUEL JR.
Wide Receiver—New York Giants

Born April 13, 1962, at Rancho Cucamonga, Calif.
Height, 5.11. Weight, 175.
High School—La Puente, Calif., Bassett.
Attended Citrus College and University of The Pacific.

Selected by Los Angeles in 1984 USFL territorial draft.
Selected by New York Giants in 7th round (171st player selected) of 1984 NFL draft.
Signed by New York Giants, June 4, 1984.

		-PASS RECEIVING-				-PUNT RETURNS-				—TOTAL—		
Year Club	G.	P.C.	Yds.	Avg.	TD.	No.	Yds.	Avg.	TD.	TD.	Pts.	F.
1984—New York Giants NFL	16	33	619	18.8	4	8	62	7.8	0	4	24	2

Additional pro statistics: Rushed three times for two yards, 1984.

KENNETH MARGERUM
(Ken)
Wide Receiver—Chicago Bears

Born October 5, 1958, at Fountain Valley, Calif.
Height, 6.00. Weight, 180.
High School—Fountain Valley, Calif.
Attended Stanford University.

Named as wide receiver on THE SPORTING NEWS College All-America Team, 1979.
Selected by Chicago in 3rd round (67th player selected) of 1981 NFL draft.
On physically unable to perform/reserve with knee injury, July 20 through entire 1984 season.

		—PASS RECEIVING—			
Year Club	G.	P.C.	Yds.	Avg.	TD.
1981—Chicago NFL	16	39	584	15.0	1
1982—Chicago NFL	9	14	207	14.8	3
1983—Chicago NFL	15	21	336	16.0	2
Pro Totals—3 Years	40	74	1127	15.2	6

Additional pro statistics: Rushed once for 11 yards and recovered one fumble, 1981; fumbled once, 1982 and 1983; rushed once for seven yards, 1983.

DANIEL CONSTANTINE MARINO
(Dan)
Quarterback—Miami Dolphins
Born September 15, 1961, at Pittsburgh, Pa.
Height, 6.04. Weight, 214.
High School—Pittsburgh, Pa., Central Catholic.
Received bachelor of science degree in communications from University of Pittsburgh.
Brother-in-law of Bill Maas, nose tackle with Kansas City Chiefs.

Named THE SPORTING NEWS NFL Player of the Year, 1984.
Named to THE SPORTING NEWS NFL All-Star Team, 1984.
Named THE SPORTING NEWS NFL Rookie of the Year, 1983.
Named as quarterback on THE SPORTING NEWS College All-America Team, 1981.
Established NFL records for completion percentage by rookie (58.45), 1983; most touchdowns passing, season (48), 1984; most passing yards gained, season (5,084), 1984; most passes completed, season (362), 1984; most games, 300 yards passing, season (9), 1984; most games, 400 yards passing, season (4), 1984.
Tied NFL record for most consecutive games, 400 yards passing (2), 1984.
Led NFL quarterbacks in passing with 108.9 points in 1984.
Selected by Los Angeles in 1st round (1st player selected) of 1983 USFL draft.
Selected by Miami in 1st round (27th player selected) of 1983 NFL draft.
Signed by Miami Dolphins, July 9, 1983.
Selected by Kansas City Royals' organization in 4th round of free-agent draft, June 5, 1979.

		—————PASSING—————							————RUSHING————				—TOTAL—		
Year Club	G.	Att.	Cmp.	Pct.	Gain	T.P.	P.I.	Avg.	Att.	Yds.	Avg.	TD.	TD.	Pts.	F.
1983—Miami NFL	11	296	173	58.4	2210	20	6	7.47	28	45	1.6	2	2	12	5
1984—Miami NFL	16	*564	*362	64.2	*5084	*48	17	*9.01	28	—7	—0.3	0	0	0	6
Pro Totals—2 Years	27	860	535	62.2	7294	68	23	8.48	56	38	0.7	2	2	12	11

Quarterback Rating Points: 1983 (96.0), 1984 (108.9). Total—104.3.
Additional pro statistics: Recovered two fumbles, 1983; recovered two fumbles and fumbled six times for minus three yards, 1984.
Played in AFC Championship Game following 1984 season.
Played in NFL Championship Game following 1984 season.
Played in Pro Bowl (NFL All-Star Game) following 1984 season.
Named to Pro Bowl (NFL All-Star Game) following 1983 season; replaced due to injury by Bill Kenney.

FRED D. MARION
Safety—New England Patriots
Born January 2, 1959, at Gainesville, Fla.
Height, 6.02. Weight, 191.
High School—Gainesville, Fla., Buchholz.
Attended University of Miami (Fla.).
Brother of Frank Marion, linebacker with Memphis Southmen (WFL) and New York Giants, 1975 and 1977 through 1983.

Selected by New England in 5th round (112th player selected) of 1982 NFL draft.

		—INTERCEPTIONS—			
Year Club	G.	No.	Yds.	Avg.	TD.
1982—New England NFL	9		None		
1983—New England NFL	16	2	4	2.0	0
1984—New England NFL	16	2	39	19.5	0
Pro Totals—3 Years	41	4	43	10.8	0

Additional pro statistics: Recovered one fumble, 1982 and 1984.

CURT MARSH
Guard-Center—Los Angeles Raiders
Born August 25, 1959, at Tacoma, Wash.
Height, 6.05. Weight, 270.
High School—Snohomish, Wash.
Attended University of Washington.

Selected by Oakland in 1st round (23rd player selected) of 1981 NFL draft.
On injured reserve with rib injury, September 2 through October 9, 1981; activated, October 10, 1981.
Franchise transferred to Los Angeles, May 7, 1982.
On injured reserve with back injury, August 30 through entire 1983 season.
Oakland NFL, 1981; Los Angeles Raiders NFL, 1982 and 1984.
Games: 1981 (11), 1982 (9), 1984 (16). Total—36.
Pro statistics: Recovered one fumble, 1981.

DOUG MARSH
Tight End—St. Louis Cardinals
Born June 18, 1958, at Akron, O.
Height, 6.03. Weight, 240.
High School—Akron, O., Central.
Attended University of Michigan.

Selected by St. Louis in 2nd round (33rd player selected) of 1980 NFL draft.
On injured reserve with knee injury, September 1 through October 1, 1981; activated, October 2, 1981.
On injured reserve with dislocated hip, October 28 through remainder of 1981 season.

Year Club	G.	P.C.	Yds.	Avg.	TD.
1980—St. Louis NFL	16	22	269	12.2	4
1981—St. Louis NFL	4	6	80	13.3	1
1982—St. Louis NFL	8	5	83	16.6	0
1983—St. Louis NFL	16	32	421	13.2	8
1984—St. Louis NFL	16	39	608	15.6	5
Pro Totals—5 Years	60	104	1461	14.0	18

Additional pro statistics: Fumbled once, 1980, 1981 and 1983; rushed once for minus five yards, 1984.

DAVID MARSHALL
Linebacker—Cleveland Browns
Born January 3, 1961, at Cleveland, O.
Height, 6.03. Weight, 220.
High School—Cleveland, O., Benedictine.
Attended Eastern Michigan University.

Selected by Michigan in 1984 USFL territorial draft.
Signed as free agent by Cleveland Browns, June 18, 1984.
Cleveland NFL, 1984.
Games: 1984 (16).

HENRY H. MARSHALL
Wide Receiver—Kansas City Chiefs
Born August 9, 1954, at Broxton, Ga.
Height, 6.02. Weight, 220.
High School—Dalzell, S.C., Hillcrest.
Attended University of Missouri.

Selected by Kansas City in 3rd round (79th player selected) of 1976 NFL draft.
On injured reserve with knee injury, November 25 through remainder of 1981 season.
On injured reserve with broken arm, December 7 through remainder of 1983 season.

Year Club	G.	Att.	Yds.	Avg.	TD.	P.C.	Yds.	Avg.	TD.	TD.	Pts.	F.
		RUSHING				PASS RECEIVING				TOTAL		
1976—Kansas City NFL	14	5	101	20.2	1	28	443	15.8	2	3	18	1
1977—Kansas City NFL	14	7	11	1.6	0	23	445	19.3	4	4	24	2
1978—Kansas City NFL	16	1	—5	—5.0	0	26	433	16.7	2	2	12	0
1979—Kansas City NFL	16	2	34	17.0	1	21	332	15.8	1	2	12	0
1980—Kansas City NFL	16	3	22	7.3	0	47	799	17.0	6	6	36	0
1981—Kansas City NFL	12	3	69	23.0	0	38	620	16.3	4	4	24	2
1982—Kansas City NFL	9	3	25	8.3	0	40	549	13.7	3	3	18	0
1983—Kansas City NFL	13		None			50	788	15.8	6	6	36	0
1984—Kansas City NFL	16		None			62	912	14.7	4	4	24	2
Pro Totals—9 Years	126	24	257	10.7	2	335	5321	15.9	32	34	204	7

Additional pro statistics: Returned one kickoff for no yards, 1976; returned six punts for 51 yards, 1978; attempted one pass with one interception, 1981; attempted one pass with no completions, 1982.

LEONARD MARSHALL
Defensive End—New York Giants
Born October 22, 1961, at Franklin, La.
Height, 6.03. Weight, 285.
High School—Franklin, La.
Attended Louisiana State University.

Brother of Chris Marshall, linebacker at Tulane University; and related
to Eddie Robinson, head coach at Grambling State University; Ernie Ladd,
defensive lineman with San Diego Chargers, Houston Oilers and Kansas City Chiefs,
1961 through 1968; and Warren Wells, wide receiver with Detroit Lions and Oakland
Raiders, 1964 and 1967 through 1970.

Selected by Tampa Bay in 10th round (109th player selected) of 1983 USFL draft.
Selected by New York Giants in 2nd round (37th player selected) of 1983 NFL draft.
Signed by New York Giants, June 13, 1983.
New York Giants NFL, 1983 and 1984.
Games: 1983 (14), 1984 (16). Total—30.
Pro statistics: Credited with one safety, 1983.

WILBER BUDDYHIA MARSHALL
Linebacker—Chicago Bears
Born April 18, 1962, at Titusville, Fla.
Height, 6.01. Weight, 225.
High School—Titusville, Fla., Astronaut.
Attended University of Florida.

Selected by Tampa Bay in 1984 USFL territorial draft. .
Selected by Chicago in 1st round (11th player selected) of 1984 NFL draft.
Signed by Chicago Bears, June 19, 1984.
Chicago NFL, 1984.
Games: 1984 (15).
Played in NFC Championship Game following 1984 season.

CHARLES MARTIN
Defensive Tackle—Green Bay Packers
Born August 31, 1958, at Canton, Ga.
Height, 6.05. Weight, 275.
High School—Canton, Ga., Cherokee.
Attended Livingston University.

Selected by Birmingham in 15th round (173rd player selected) of 1983 USFL draft.
Signed by Birmingham Stallions, January 22, 1983.
On developmental squad, March 26 through April 9, 1983; activated, April 10, 1983.
On developmental squad, June 17 through July 1, 1983; activated, July 2, 1983.
Released by Birmingham Stallions, February 13, 1984; signed as free agent by Green Bay Packers, July 7, 1984.
On developmental squad for 4 games with Birmingham Stallions in 1983.
Birmingham USFL, 1983; Green Bay NFL, 1984.
Games: 1983 (14), 1984 (16). Total—30.
Pro statistics: Recovered one fumble, 1983.

CHRISTOPHER MARTIN
(Chris)
Linebacker—Minnesota Vikings
Born December 19, 1960, at Huntsville, Ala.
Height, 6.02. Weight, 230.
High School—Huntsville, Ala., J. O. Johnson.
Attended Auburn University.

Selected by Birmingham in 1983 USFL territorial draft.
Signed as free agent by New Orleans Saints, May 5, 1983.
On injured reserve with ankle injury, December 17 through remainder of 1983 season.
Released by New Orleans Saints, August 27, 1984; awarded on waivers to Minnesota Vikings, August 28, 1984.
New Orleans NFL, 1983; Minnesota NFL, 1984.
Games: 1983 (15), 1984 (16). Total—31.
Pro statistics: Recovered one fumble for eight yards and a touchdown, 1984.

DOUG MARTIN
Defensive End—Minnesota Vikings
Born May 22, 1957, at Fairfield, Calif.
Height, 6.03. Weight, 255.
High School—Fairfield, Calif., Armijo.
Attended University of Washington.
Brother of George Martin, defensive end with New York Giants.

Selected by Minnesota in 1st round (9th player selected) of 1980 NFL draft.
Placed on did not report list, August 15, 1980; activated, September 13, 1980.
Granted free agency, February 1, 1984.
Placed on did not report list, August 14 through August 17, 1984; re-signed by Vikings, August 18, 1984.
Granted roster exemption, August 21 through August 31, 1984; activated, September 1, 1984.
Minnesota NFL, 1980 through 1984.
Games: 1980 (11), 1981 (16), 1982 (9), 1983 (16), 1984 (13). Total—65.
Pro statistics: Recovered one fumble, 1981; intercepted one pass for no yards, 1982; recovered two fumbles, 1983.

GEORGE DWIGHT MARTIN
Defensive End—New York Giants
Born February 16, 1953, at Greenville, S. C.
Height, 6.04. Weight, 255.
High School—Fairfield, Calif., Armijo.
Attended University of Oregon.
Brother of Doug Martin, defensive end with Minnesota Vikings.

Selected by New York Giants in 11th round (262nd player selected) of 1975 NFL draft.
New York Giants NFL, 1975 through 1984.
Games: 1975 (14), 1976 (14), 1977 (10), 1978 (16), 1979 (16), 1980 (16), 1981 (16), 1982 (9), 1983 (14), 1984 (16). Total—141.
Pro statistics: Recovered two fumbles, 1976; intercepted one pass for 30 yards and one touchdown, 1977; recovered one fumble, 1977, 1980 and 1984; ran 83 yards with blocked field goal for a touchdown, 1978; recovered three fumbles, 1979; caught one pass for four yards and a touchdown, 1980; recovered three fumbles for 28 yards and two touchdowns, 1981.

MICHAEL MARTIN
(Mike)
Wide Receiver—Cincinnati Bengals

Born November 18, 1960, at Washington, D.C.
Height, 5.10. Weight, 186.
High School—Washington, D.C., Eastern.
Attended University of Illinois.

Selected by Chicago in 1983 USFL territorial draft.
Selected by Cincinnati in 8th round (221st player selected) of 1983 NFL draft.
Signed by Cincinnati Bengals, May 19, 1983.
On injured reserve with broken fibula, November 17 through remainder of 1983 season.

			PASS RECEIVING				–PUNT RETURNS–				—KICKOFF RET.—				—TOTAL—		
Year	Club	G.	P.C.	Yds.	Avg.	TD.	No.	Yds.	Avg.	TD.	No.	Yds.	Avg.	TD.	TD.	Pts.	F.
1983—Cincinnati NFL		10	2	22	11.0	0	23	227	9.9	0	1	19	19.0	0	0	0	2
1984—Cincinnati NFL		15	11	164	14.9	0	24	376	★15.7	0	19	386	20.3	0	0	0	4
Pro Totals—2 Years		25	13	186	14.3	0	47	603	12.8	0	20	405	20.3	0	0	0	6

Additional pro statistics: Rushed twice for 21 yards, 1983; rushed once for three yards and recovered two fumbles, 1984.

ROBBIE L. MARTIN
Wide Receiver-Safety—Detroit Lions

Born December 3, 1958, at Los Angeles, Calif.
Height, 5.08. Weight, 177.
High School—Villa Park, Calif.
Attended California Poly State University at San Luis Obispo.

Selected by Pittsburgh in 4th round (100th player selected) of 1981 NFL draft.
Released by Pittsburgh Steelers, August 24, 1981; claimed on waivers by Detroit Lions, August 26, 1981.
On injured reserve with knee injury, September 13 through October 28, 1983; activated, October 29, 1983.

			–PUNT RETURNS–				—KICKOFF RET.—				—TOTAL—		
Year	Club	G.	No.	Yds.	Avg.	TD.	No.	Yds.	Avg.	TD.	TD.	Pts.	F.
1981—Detroit NFL		16	52	450	8.7	1	25	509	20.4	0	1	6	3
1982—Detroit NFL		9	26	275	10.6	0	16	268	16.8	0	0	0	3
1983—Detroit NFL		10	15	183	12.2	★1	8	140	17.5	0	1	6	3
1984—Detroit NFL		14	25	210	8.4	0	10	144	14.4	0	0	0	5
Pro Totals—4 Years		49	118	1118	9.5	2	59	1061	18.0	0	2	12	14

Additional pro statistics: Recovered two fumbles, 1981; caught one pass for 18 yards, 1982; recovered one fumble, 1982 and 1983; rushed once for 14 yards, caught one pass for nine yards and recovered four fumbles, 1984.

ROD MARTIN
Linebacker—Los Angeles Raiders

Born April 7, 1954, at Welch, W. Va.
Height, 6.02. Weight, 220.
High School—Los Angeles, Calif., Hamilton.
Attended Los Angeles City College and University of Southern California.
Brother of Ricky Martin, wide receiver with Oakland Invaders.

Named to THE SPORTING NEWS NFL All-Star Team, 1983.
Selected by Oakland in 12th round (317th player selected) of 1977 NFL draft.
Traded with defensive back Steve Jackson by Oakland Raiders to San Francisco 49ers for future considerations, August 30, 1977.
Released by San Francisco 49ers, September 14, 1977; signed as free agent by Oakland Raiders, November 7, 1977.
Franchise transferred to Los Angeles, May 7, 1982.

			—INTERCEPTIONS—							—INTERCEPTIONS—			
Year	Club	G.	No.	Yds.	Avg.TD.		Year	Club	G.	No.	Yds.	Avg.TD.
1977—Oakland NFL		1			None		1982—L.A. Raiders NFL		9	3	60	20.0 ★1
1978—Oakland NFL		15			None		1983—L.A. Raiders NFL		16	4	81	20.3 ★2
1979—Oakland NFL		16			None		1984—L.A. Raiders NFL		16	2	31	15.5 1
1980—Oakland NFL		16	2	15	7.5 0		Pro Totals—8 Years		105	12	194	16.2 4
1981—Oakland NFL		16	1	7	7.0 0							

Additional pro statistics: Recovered one fumble, 1979; recovered two fumbles for 42 yards and a touchdown, 1980; recovered three fumbles, 1981; returned one kickoff for no yards, 1983; recovered one fumble for 77 yards and a touchdown and credited with one safety, 1984.
Played in AFC Championship Game following 1977, 1980 and 1983 seasons.
Played in NFL Championship Game following 1980 and 1983 seasons.
Played in Pro Bowl (NFL All-Star Team) following 1983 and 1984 seasons.

—DID YOU KNOW—

That tight ends with the last name of Hardy caught touchdown passes in consecutive Monday night games? Larry Hardy of New Orleans caught one touchdown pass in the Saints' 27-24 victory over Pittsburgh on November 19 while Bruce Hardy of Miami caught two scoring passes in the Dolphins' 28-17 win against the Jets on November 26.

EUGENE RAYMOND MARVE
Linebacker—Buffalo Bills
Born August 14, 1960, at Flint, Mich.
Height, 6.02. Weight, 230.
High School—Flint, Mich., Northern.
Attended Saginaw Valley State College.

Selected by Buffalo in 3rd round (59th player selected) of 1982 NFL draft.
Buffalo NFL, 1982 through 1984.
Games: 1982 (9), 1983 (16), 1984 (16). Total—41.
Pro statistics: Intercepted one pass for no yards and recovered one fumble, 1982; recovered three fumbles, 1984.

MICKEY MARVIN
Guard—Los Angeles Raiders
Born October 5, 1955, at Hendersonville, N.C.
Height, 6.04. Weight, 260.
High School—Hendersonville, N.C., Brevard.
Attended University of Tennessee.

Selected by Oakland in 4th round (112th player selected) of 1977 NFL draft.
On injured reserve with knee injury, September 12 through December 6, 1979; activated, December 7, 1979.
Franchise transferred to Los Angeles, May 7, 1982.
Oakland NFL, 1977 through 1981; Los Angeles Raiders NFL, 1982 through 1984.
Games: 1977 (8), 1978 (14), 1979 (2), 1980 (16), 1981 (16), 1982 (9), 1983 (14), 1984 (9). Total—88.
Pro statistics: Recovered one fumble, 1978, 1980, 1981 and 1984.
Played in AFC Championship Game following 1977, 1980 and 1983 seasons.
Played in NFL Championship Game following 1980 and 1983 seasons.

ANTHONY CHARLES MASSAGLI
(Tony)
Placekicker—Miami Dolphins
Born March 14, 1961, at Los Angeles, Calif.
Height, 5.09. Weight, 174.
High School—Alto Loma, Calif.
Attended Claremont McKenna-Harvey Mudd-Scripps College,
California State Poly University (Pomona) and Boise State University.

Signed as free agent by Los Angeles Rams, May 12, 1984.
Released by Los Angeles Rams, August 14, 1984.
USFL rights traded by Los Angeles Express to Oakland Invaders for past considerations, January 18, 1985.
Signed by Oakland Invaders, January 25, 1985.
Released by Oakland Invaders, January 28, 1985; signed as free agent by Miami Dolphins, April 11, 1985.

CHRISTOPHER DWAYNE MASSEY
(Known by middle name.)
Offensive Tackle—Miami Dolphins
Born September 29, 1961, at Jackson, Miss.
Height, 6.05. Weight, 267.
High School—Jackson, Miss., Wingfield.
Received bachelor of science degree in sociology from University of Southern Mississippi.

Selected by Pittsburgh in 10th round (202nd player selected) of 1984 USFL draft.
Signed as free agent by Dallas Cowboys, May 3, 1984.
On injured reserve, August 13 through October 8, 1984.
Released by Dallas Cowboys, October 9, 1984; signed as free agent by Miami Dolphins, March 29, 1985.

BRUCE MARTIN MATHISON
Quarterback—San Diego Chargers
Born April 25, 1959, at Superior, Wis.
Height, 6.03. Weight, 203.
High School—Superior, Wis.
Attended University of Nebraska.

Selected by Boston in 1983 USFL territorial draft.
Selected by San Diego in 10th round (272nd player selected) of 1983 NFL draft.
Signed by San Diego Chargers, May 26, 1983.

					PASSING						RUSHING			TOTAL	
Year Club	G.	Att.	Cmp.	Pct.	Gain	T.P.	P.I.	Avg.	Att.	Yds.	Avg.	TD.	TD.	Pts.	F.
1983—San Diego NFL	1	5	3	60.0	41	0	1	8.20	1	0	0.0	0	0	0	1
1984—San Diego NFL	2				None						None		0	0	0
Pro Total—2 Years	3	5	3	60.0	41	0	1	8.20	1	0	0.0	0	0	0	1

ALLAMA MATTHEWS
Tight End—Atlanta Falcons
Born August 24, 1961, at Jacksonville, Fla.
Height, 6.02. Weight, 230.
High School—Jacksonville, Fla., Andrew Jackson.
Attended Vanderbilt University.

Selected by Philadelphia in 12th round (137th player selected) of 1983 USFL draft.
Selected by Atlanta in 12th round (322nd player selected) of 1983 NFL draft.
Signed by Atlanta Falcons, May 16, 1983.
On injured reserve with neck injury, October 9 through remainder of 1984 season.

				—PASS RECEIVING—		
Year	Club	G.	P.C.	Yds.	Avg.	TD.
1983—Atlanta NFL		15	3	37	12.3	0
1984—Atlanta NFL		6	1	7	7.0	0
Pro Totals—2 Years		21	4	44	11.0	0

Additional pro statistics: Recovered one fumble, 1983; returned one kickoff for three yards, 1984.

BRUCE MATTHEWS
Offensive Tackle-Center—Houston Oilers
Born August 8, 1961, at Arcadia, Calif.
Height, 6.04. Weight, 280.
High School—Arcadia, Calif.
Received degree in industrial engineering from University of Southern California in 1983.
Son of Clay Matthews Sr., end with San Francisco 49ers, 1950 and 1953 through 1955;
brother of Clay Matthews Jr., linebacker with Cleveland Browns.
Named as guard on The Sporting News College All-America Team, 1982.
Selected by Los Angeles in 1983 USFL territorial draft.
Selected by Houston in 1st round (9th player selected) of 1983 NFL draft.
Signed by Houston Oilers, July 24, 1983.
Houston NFL, 1983 and 1984.
Games: 1983 (16); 1984 (16). Total—32.

WILLIAM CLAY MATTHEWS JR.
(Known by middle name.)
Linebacker—Cleveland Browns
Born March 15, 1956, at Palo Alto, Calif.
Height, 6.02. Weight, 235.
High Schools—Arcadia, Calif. and Winnetka, Ill., New Trier East.
Received bachelor of science degree in business administration from
University of Southern California in 1978; attending Southern Cal for master's in business administration.
Son of Clay Matthews Sr., end with San Francisco 49ers, 1950 and 1953 through 1955;
brother of Bruce Matthews, offensive tackle-center with Houston Oilers.
Named to The Sporting News NFL All-Star Team, 1984.
Named as linebacker on The Sporting News College All-America Team, 1977.
Selected by Cleveland in 1st round (12th player selected) of 1978 NFL draft.
On injured reserve with broken ankle, September 16 through December 30, 1982; activated, December 31, 1982.

				—INTERCEPTIONS—		
Year	Club	G.	No.	Yds.	Avg.	TD.
1978—Cleveland NFL		15	1	5	5.0	0
1979—Cleveland NFL		16	1	30	30.0	0
1980—Cleveland NFL		14	1	6	6.0	0
1981—Cleveland NFL		16	2	14	7.0	0
1982—Cleveland NFL		2		None		
1983—Cleveland NFL		16		None		
1984—Cleveland NFL		16		None		
Pro Totals—7 Years		95	5	55	11.0	0

Additional pro statistics: Recovered two fumbles, 1979; recovered one fumble, 1980 and 1984; recovered two fumbles for 16 yards, 1981.

NEIL JOHN MAUNE
Guard—Philadelphia Eagles
Born November 4, 1960, at Washington, Mo.
Height, 6.04. Weight, 249.
High School—Washington, Mo., St. Francis Borgia.
Received bachelor of arts degree in government from University of Notre Dame in 1984.
Selected by Chicago in 1984 USFL territorial draft.
Selected by Dallas in 9th round (249th player selected) of 1984 NFL draft.
Signed by Dallas Cowboys, July 3, 1984.
Released by Dallas Cowboys, August 13, 1984; signed as free agent by Philadelphia Eagles for 1985, November 9, 1984.

RICHARD DOMINIC MAUTI
Name pronounced MAW-tee.
(Rich)
Wide Receiver—Washington Redskins
Born May 25, 1954, at Hollis Place, N. Y.
Height, 6.00. Weight, 195.
High School—East Meadow, N. Y.
Attended Nassau Community College and Pennsylvania State University.
Signed as free agent by New Orleans Saints, 1977.

On injured reserve with broken arm, November 3 through remainder of 1980 season.
On injured reserve with broken collarbone, August 25 through entire 1981 season.
Released by New Orleans Saints, August 20, 1984; signed as free agent by Washington Redskins, August 22, 1984.
Released by Washington Redskins, August 27, 1984; re-signed by Redskins, August 28, 1984.

Year	Club	G.	PASS RECEIVING				PUNT RETURNS				—KICKOFF RET.—				—TOTAL—		
			P.C.	Yds.	Avg.	TD.	No.	Yds.	Avg.	TD.	No.	Yds.	Avg.	TD.	TD.	Pts.	F.
1977—New Orleans NFL		14	4	71	17.8	0	37	281	7.6	0	27	609	22.6	0	0	0	2
1978—New Orleans NFL		16	8	69	8.6	2		None			17	388	22.8	0	2	12	0
1979—New Orleans NFL		15	2	64	32.0	0	27	218	8.1	0	36	801	22.3	0	0	0	3
1980—New Orleans NFL		9	1	10	10.0	0	11	111	10.1	0	31	798	25.7	0	0	0	0
1982—New Orleans NFL		9	4	70	17.5	0		None			5	93	18.6	0	0	0	0
1983—New Orleans NFL		16	2	30	15.0	0		None			8	147	18.4	0	0	0	0
1984—Washington NFL		16		None			1	2	2.0	0	1	16	16.0	0	0	0	0
Pro Totals—7 Years		95	21	314	15.0	2	76	612	8.1	0	125	2852	22.8	0	2	12	5

Additional pro statistics: Recovered one fumble, 1978 and 1979; rushed once for two yards, 1980.

VERNON MAXWELL
Linebacker—Indianapolis Colts
Born October 25, 1961, at Birmingham, Ala.
Height, 6.02. Weight, 238.
High School—Los Angeles, Calif., Verbum Dei.
Attended Arizona State University.

Named as linebacker on The Sporting News College All-America Team, 1982.
Selected by Arizona in 1983 USFL territorial draft.
Selected by Baltimore in 2nd round (29th player selected) of 1983 USFL draft.
Signed by Baltimore Colts, July 21, 1983.
Franchise transferred to Indianapolis, March 31, 1984.
Baltimore NFL, 1983; Indianapolis NFL, 1984.
Games: 1983 (16), 1984 (16). Total—32.
Pro statistics: Intercepted one pass for 31 yards, 1983; recovered two fumbles, 1983 and 1984.

DEAN CURTIS MAY
Quarterback—Philadelphia Eagles
Born May 26, 1962, at Orlando, Fla.
Height, 6.05. Weight, 220.
High Schools—Louisville, Ky., Trinity, and Tampa, Fla., Chamberlain.
Attended University of Louisville.

Selected by Chicago in 9th round (175th player selected) of 1984 USFL draft.
Selected by Miami in 5th round (138th player selected) of 1984 NFL draft.
Signed by Miami Dolphins, July 11, 1984.
Released by Miami Dolphins, August 27, 1984; signed as free agent by Philadelphia Eagles, October 16, 1984.
Philadelphia NFL, 1984.
Games: 1984 (2).
Pro statistics: Attempted one pass with one completion for 33 yards, 1984.

MARK MAY
Offensive Tackle-Guard—Washington Redskins
Born November 2, 1959, at Oneonta, N.Y.
Height, 6.06. Weight, 295.
High School—Oneonta, N.Y.
Attended University of Pittsburgh.

Outland Trophy winner, 1980.
Named as offensive tackle on The Sporting News College All-America Team, 1980.
Selected by Washington in 1st round (20th player selected) of 1981 NFL draft.
Washington NFL, 1981 through 1984.
Games: 1981 (16), 1982 (9), 1983 (15), 1984 (16). Total—56.
Pro statistics: Recovered one fumble, 1983.
Played in NFC Championship Game following 1982 and 1983 seasons.
Played in NFL Championship Game following 1982 and 1983 seasons.

STAFFORD EARL MAYS
Defensive End—St. Louis Cardinals
Born March 13, 1958, at Lawrence, Kan.
Height, 6.02. Weight, 250.
High School—Tacoma, Wash., Lincoln.
Attended Mt. Hood Junior College and University of Washington.

Selected by St. Louis in 9th round (225th player selected) of 1980 NFL draft.
St. Louis NFL, 1980 through 1984.
Games: 1980 (16), 1981 (16), 1982 (8), 1983 (16), 1984 (16). Total—72.
Pro statistics: Recovered one fumble, 1981 and 1982; recovered two fumbles, 1983.

KEN McALISTER
Linebacker—Kansas City Chiefs
Born April 15, 1960, at Oakland, Calif.
Height, 6.05. Weight, 220.
High School—Oakland, Calif.
Attended University of San Francisco (did not play college football).

Signed as free agent by Seattle Seahawks, April 30, 1982.

Released by Seattle Seahawks, September 14, 1983; signed as free agent by San Francisco 49ers, November 23, 1983.

Released by San Francisco 49ers, December 30, 1983; signed as free agent by Kansas City Chiefs, February 1, 1984.

Seattle NFL, 1982; Seattle (2)-San Francisco (4) NFL, 1983; Kansas City NFL, 1984.

Games: 1982 (9), 1983 (6), 1984 (15). Total—30.

Pro statistics: Returned two kickoffs for 41 yards and recovered one fumble, 1982; returned three kickoffs for 59 yards, 1983; intercepted two passes for 33 yards and recovered one fumble, 1984.

JOE SHEPARD McCALL
Running Back—Los Angeles Raiders
Born February 17, 1962, at Miami, Fla.
Height, 5.11. Weight, 195.
High School—Miami, Fla., Jackson.
Received bachelor of science degree in speech and communications
from University of Pittsburgh in 1984.

Selected by Pittsburgh in 1984 USFL territorial draft.
Selected by Los Angeles Raiders in 3rd round (84th player selected) of 1984 NFL draft.
Signed by Los Angeles Raiders, June 12, 1984.
On injured reserve with knee injury, October 3 through remainder of 1984 season.

		—RUSHING—				PASS RECEIVING				—TOTAL—		
Year Club	G.	Att.	Yds.	Avg.	TD.	P.C.	Yds.	Avg.	TD.	TD.	Pts.	F.
1984—Los Angeles Raiders NFL	3	1	3	3.0	0		None			0	0	0

REESE McCALL
Tight End—Detroit Lions
Born June 16, 1956, at Bessemer, Ala.
Height, 6.06. Weight, 245.
High School—Bessemer, Ala., Jess Lanier.
Received bachelor of science degree in physical education from
Auburn University in 1978.

Selected by Baltimore in 1st round (25th player selected) of 1978 NFL draft.
On inactive list, September 12 and September 19, 1982.
On reserve/did not report, August 14 through August 17, 1983.
Traded by Baltimore Colts to Tampa Bay Buccaneers for future draft pick, August 18, 1983.
Released by Tampa Bay Buccaneers, August 29, 1983; awarded on waivers to Detroit Lions, August 30, 1983.

		—PASS RECEIVING—			
Year Club	G.	P.C.	Yds.	Avg.	TD.
1978—Baltimore NFL	16	11	160	14.5	1
1979—Baltimore NFL	14	37	536	14.5	4
1980—Baltimore NFL	16	18	322	17.9	5
1981—Baltimore NFL	16	21	314	15.0	2
1982—Baltimore NFL	7	2	6	3.0	0
1983—Detroit NFL	16	1	6	6.0	0
1984—Detroit NFL	16	3	15	5.0	0
Pro Totals—7 Years	101	93	1359	14.6	12

Additional pro statistics: Returned one punt for 37 yards and ran five yards with blocked punt for a touchdown, 1978; recovered one fumble, 1978 and 1980; fumbled once, 1978 through 1980; recovered two fumbles, 1979.

LAURENCE ANTHONY McCARREN
(Larry)
Center—Green Bay Packers
Born November 9, 1951, at Park Forest, Ill.
Height, 6.03. Weight, 248.
High School—Park Forest, Ill.
Attended University of Illinois.

Selected by Green Bay in 12th round (308th player selected) of 1973 NFL draft.
On injured reserve with neck injury, December 15 through remainder of 1984 season.
Green Bay NFL, 1973 through 1984.
Games: 1973 (5), 1974 (14), 1975 (14), 1976 (14), 1977 (14), 1978 (16), 1979 (16), 1980 (16), 1981 (16), 1982 (9), 1983 (16), 1984 (12). Total—162.
Pro statistics: Recovered one fumble and fumbled once for minus 28 yards, 1980; fumbled once, 1981.
Played in Pro Bowl (NFL All-Star Game) following 1982 and 1983 seasons.

MICHAEL ANTHONY McCLEARN
(Mike)
Offensive Tackle—Washington Redskins
Born January 7, 1961, at Newburgh, N.Y.
Height, 6.04. Weight, 274.
High School—Montgomery, N.Y., Valley Central.
Attended Temple University.

Selected by Philadelphia in 1983 USFL territorial draft.
Selected by Cleveland in 8th round (209th player selected) of 1983 NFL draft.
Signed by Cleveland Browns, May 11, 1983.

Released by Cleveland Browns, August 16, 1983; signed by Philadelphia Stars, September 19, 1983.
On developmental squad, February 24 through March 9, 1984; activated, March 10, 1984.
On developmental squad, April 28 through May 11, 1984; activated, May 12, 1984.
On developmental squad, May 18 through June 1, 1984; activated, June 2, 1984.
On developmental squad, June 21 through remainder of 1984 season.
Franchise transferred to Baltimore, November 1, 1984.
Released injured by Baltimore Stars, February 18, 1985; signed as free agent by Washington Redskins, March 6, 1985.
On developmental squad for 7 games with Philadelphia Stars in 1984.
Philadelphia USFL, 1984.
Games: 1984 (9).
Played in USFL Championship Game following 1984 season.

MIKE McCLOSKEY
Tight End—Houston Oilers
Born February 2, 1961, at Philadelphia, Pa.
Height, 6.05. Weight, 246.
High School—Philadelphia, Pa., Father Judge.
Attended Penn State University.

Selected by Philadelphia in 1983 USFL territorial draft.
Selected by Houston in 4th round (88th player selected) of 1983 NFL draft.
Signed by Houston Oilers, June 22, 1983.

Year Club	G.	P.C.	Yds.	Avg.	TD.
1983—Houston NFL	16	16	137	8.6	1
1984—Houston NFL	15	9	152	16.9	1
Pro Totals—2 Years	31	25	289	11.6	2

Additional pro statistics: Returned one kickoff for 11 yards, 1983.

MILT McCOLL
Linebacker—San Francisco 49ers
Born August 28, 1959, at Oak Park, Ill.
Height, 6.06. Weight, 230.
High School—Covina, Calif., South Hills.
Attended Stanford University and studied at Stanford's overseas campus at Cliveden, England, 1980;
and currently attending medical school at Stanford University.
Son of Bill McColl, end with Chicago Bears, 1952 through 1959.

Signed as free agent by San Francisco 49ers, July 1, 1981.
On injured reserve with pulled hamstring, October 22 through November 17, 1983; activated, November 18, 1983.
San Francisco NFL, 1981 through 1984.
Games: 1981 (16), 1982 (9), 1983 (12), 1984 (16). Total—53.
Pro statistics: Intercepted one pass for 22 yards, 1981.
Played in NFC Championship Game following 1981 and 1984 seasons.
Member of San Francisco 49ers for NFC Championship Game following 1983 season; did not play.
Played in NFL Championship Game following 1981 and 1984 seasons.

PHIL McCONKEY
Wide Receiver—New York Giants
Born February 24, 1957, at Buffalo, N.Y.
Height, 5.10. Weight, 165.
High School—Buffalo, N.Y., Caniaius.
Attended U.S. Naval Academy.

Signed as free agent by New York Giants, May 6, 1983.
On military reserve, August 29 through entire 1983 season.
On injured reserve with broken ribs, November 26 through remainder of 1984 season.

	PASS RECEIVING				–PUNT RETURNS–				—KICKOFF RET.—				—TOTAL—		
Year Club	G.	P.C.	Yds.	Avg.	TD.	No.	Yds.	Avg.	TD.	No.	Yds.	Avg.	TD.	TD.	Pts.	F.
1984—N.Y. Giants NFL	13	8	154	19.3	0	46	306	6.7	0	28	541	19.3	0	1	6	2

Additional pro statistics: Recovered kickoff in end zone for a touchdown and recovered one fumble, 1984.

GLENN BRIAN McCORMICK
Center—Cleveland Browns
Born January 28, 1960, at San Diego, Calif.
Height, 6.05. Weight, 251.
High School—San Diego, Calif., Patrick Henry.
Attended Mesa Junior College and University of Arizona.

Selected by Arizona in 1983 USFL territorial draft.
Signed by Arizona Wranglers, January 30, 1983.
Franchise transferred to Chicago, September 30, 1983.
Traded by Chicago Blitz to San Antonio Gunslingers for 8th round pick in 1985 draft, February 13, 1984.
On developmental squad, April 13 through April 17, 1984.
Released by San Antonio Gunslingers, April 18, 1984; signed as free agent by Cleveland Browns, May 6, 1985.
On developmental squad for 1 game with San Antonio Gunslingers in 1984.
Arizona USFL, 1983; San Antonio USFL, 1984.
Games: 1983 (17), 1984 (4). Total—21.

MICHAEL CHARLES McCOY
(Mike)
Defensive Back—Green Bay Packers
Born August 16, 1953, at West Memphis, Ark.
Height, 5.11. Weight, 190.
High School—West Memphis, Ark.
Attended West Los Angeles Junior College and University of Colorado.

Selected by Green Bay in 3rd round (72nd player selected) of 1976 NFL draft.
On injured reserve with knee injury, November 1 through remainder of 1983 season.
On injured reserve with knee injury, August 14 through entire 1984 season.

| | | -INTERCEPTIONS- | | | | —KICKOFF RET.— | | | | —TOTAL— | | |
Year Club	G.	No.	Yds.	Avg.	TD.	No.	Yds.	Avg.	TD.	TD.	Pts.	F.
1976—Green Bay NFL	14		None			18	457	25.4	0	0	0	1
1977—Green Bay NFL	14		None				None			0	0	0
1978—Green Bay NFL	16	3	34	11.3	0		None			0	0	2
1979—Green Bay NFL	16	3	60	20.0	0	11	248	22.5	0	0	0	1
1980—Green Bay NFL	16	1	0	0.0	0	14	261	18.6	0	0	0	1
1981—Green Bay NFL	16	2	20	10.0	0	11	221	20.1	0	0	0	1
1982—Green Bay NFL	9		None				None			0	0	0
1983—Green Bay NFL	9		None				None			0	0	0
Pro Totals—8 Years	110	9	114	12.7	0	54	1187	22.0	0	0	0	6

Additional pro statistics: Returned four punts for two yards, 1977; recovered one fumble, 1978, 1981 and 1982; recovered two fumbles, 1979.

LeCHARLS McDANIEL
Cornerback—New York Giants
Born October 15, 1958, at Ft. Bragg, N.C.
Height, 5.09. Weight, 169.
High School—Seaside, Calif.
Attended California Poly State University at San Luis Obispo.
Cousin of Orlando McDaniel, wide receiver with Denver Broncos, 1982.

Signed as free agent by Washington Redskins, May 6, 1981.
Released by Washington Redskins, September 9, 1981; re-signed by Redskins after clearing procedural waivers, November 11, 1981.
Released by Washington Redskins, November 21, 1981; re-signed by Redskins, November 25, 1981.
Released by Washington Redskins, September 6, 1982; re-signed by Redskins, September 15, 1982.
Released by Washington Redskins, August 21, 1983; signed as free agent by New York Giants, October 20, 1983.
On injured reserve with knee injury, August 13 through October 8, 1984; activated after clearing procedural waivers, October 10, 1984.
Released by New York Giants, October 19, 1984; re-signed by Giants, December 11, 1984.
Active for 2 games with New York Giants in 1984; did not play.
Washington NFL, 1981 and 1982; New York Giants NFL, 1983 and 1984.
Games: 1981 (6), 1982 (8), 1983 (9). Total—23.
Pro statistics: Intercepted one pass for seven yards, 1982.
Played in NFC Championship Game following 1982 season.
Played in NFL Championship Game following 1982 season.

JAMES McDONALD
Tight End—Los Angeles Rams
Born March 29, 1961, at Long Beach, Calif.
Height, 6.05. Weight, 240.
High School—Long Beach, Calif., Polytechnic.
Attended University of Southern California.

Signed as free agent by Los Angeles Rams, May 20, 1983.

| | | ——PASS RECEIVING—— | | | |
Year Club	G.	P.C.	Yds.	Avg.	TD.
1983—L.A. Rams NFL	16	1	1	1.0	1
1984—L.A. Rams NFL	16	4	55	13.8	0
Pro Totals—2 Years	32	5	56	11.2	1

MIKE McDONALD
Linebacker—Los Angeles Rams
Born June 22, 1958, at North Hollywood, Calif.
Height, 6.01. Weight, 235.
High School—Burbank, Calif., John Burroughs.
Attended University of Southern California.

Signed as free agent by Los Angeles Rams, December 21, 1983.
Released by Los Angeles Rams, August 27, 1984; re-signed by Rams, August 28, 1984.
Los Angeles Rams NFL, 1984.
Games: 1984 (16).

COACHING RECORD
Graduate assistant coach at University of Southern California, 1980 and 1981.
Assistant coach at Burroughs (Calif.) High School, 1982 and 1983.

PAUL McDONALD
Quarterback—Cleveland Browns
Born February 23, 1958, at Montebello, Calif.
Height, 6.02. Weight, 185.
High School—La Puente, Calif., Bishop Amat.
Received degree from University of Southern California and
attending Case Western Reserve for master's degree in business.
Selected by Cleveland in 4th round (109th player selected) of 1980 NFL draft.

Year Club	G.	Att.	Cmp.	Pct.	Gain	T.P.	P.I.	Avg.	Att.	Yds.	Avg.	TD.	TD.	Pts.	F.
1980—Cleveland NFL	15				None				3	2	0.7	0	0	0	2
1981—Cleveland NFL	12	57	35	61.4	463	4	2	8.12	2	0	0.0	0	0	0	4
1982—Cleveland NFL	9	149	73	49.0	993	5	8	6.66	7	—13	—1.9	0	0	0	3
1983—Cleveland NFL	16	68	32	47.1	341	1	4	5.01	3	17	5.7	0	0	0	1
1984—Cleveland NFL	16	493	271	55.0	3472	14	23	7.04	22	4	0.2	1	1	6	16
Pro Totals—5 Years	68	767	411	53.6	5269	24	37	6.87	37	10	0.3	1	1	6	26

Quarterback Rating Points: 1981 (95.8), 1982 (59.5), 1983 (42.6), 1984 (67.3). Total—65.7.
Additional pro statistics: Fumbled twice for minus nine yards, 1980; recovered one fumble, 1983; caught one pass for minus four yards, recovered five fumbles and fumbled 16 times for minus five yards, 1984.

REGINALD LEE McELROY
(Reggie)
Offensive Tackle-Guard—New York Jets
Born March 4, 1960, at Beaumont, Tex.
Height, 6.06. Weight, 270.
High School—Beaumont, Tex., Charlton Pollard.
Attended West Texas State University.

Selected by New York Jets in 2nd round (51st player selected) of 1982 NFL draft.
On injured reserve with knee injury, August 24 through entire 1982 season.
New York Jets NFL, 1983 and 1984.
Games: 1983 (16), 1984 (16). Total—32.
Pro statistics: Returned one kickoff for seven yards, 1983.

VANN WILLIAM McELROY
Safety—Los Angeles Raiders
Born January 13, 1960, at Birmingham, Ala.
Height, 6.02. Weight, 190.
High School—Uvalde, Tex.
Received bachelor of business administration degree in marketing management
from Baylor University in 1983.

Selected by Los Angeles Raiders in 3rd round (64th player selected) of 1982 NFL draft.
On inactive list, September 12 and September 19, 1982.

Year Club	G.	No.	Yds.	Avg.	TD.
1982—L.A. Raiders NFL	7		None		
1983—L.A. Raiders NFL	16	8	68	8.5	0
1984—L.A. Raiders NFL	16	4	42	10.5	0
Pro Totals—3 Years	39	12	110	9.2	0

Additional pro statistics: Intercepted one pass for no yards, 1982; recovered three fumbles for five yards, 1983; recovered four fumbles for 12 yards, 1984.
Played in AFC Championship Game following 1983 season.
Played in NFL Championship Game following 1983 season.
Played in Pro Bowl (NFL All-Star Game) following 1983 and 1984 seasons.

PAUL McFADDEN
Placekicker—Philadelphia Eagles
Born September 24, 1961, at Cleveland, O.
Height, 5.11. Weight, 155.
High School—Euclid, O.
Received bachelor of science degree in general administration
from Youngstown State University in 1984.

Selected by Chicago in 9th round (174th player selected) of 1984 USFL draft.
Selected by Philadelphia in 12th round (312th player selected) of 1984 NFL draft.
Signed by Philadelphia Eagles, July 15, 1984.

Year Club	G.	XP.	XPM.	FG.	FGA.	Pts.
1984—Philadelphia NFL	16	26	1	*30	*37	116

ANTHONY EUGENE McGEE
(Tony)
Defensive End—Washington Redskins
Born January 18, 1949, at Battle Creek, Mich.
Height, 6.03. Weight, 250.
High School—Battle Creek, Mich.
Attended University of Wyoming and Bishop College.

Selected by Chicago in 3rd round (64th player selected) of 1971 NFL draft.
Traded by Chicago Bears to New England Patriots for two draft choices (8th round pick in 1975 and 3rd round pick in 1976), September 10, 1974.
Traded by New England Patriots to Washington Redskins for 9th round pick in 1984 draft, September 2, 1982.
Chicago NFL, 1971 through 1973; New England NFL, 1974 through 1981; Washington NFL, 1982 through 1984.
Games: 1971 (14), 1972 (14), 1973 (14), 1974 (14), 1975 (13), 1976 (14), 1977 (14), 1978 (16), 1979 (16), 1980 (16), 1981 (16), 1982 (9), 1983 (16), 1984 (16). Total—202.
Pro statistics: Recovered three fumbles, 1971; recovered four fumbles, 1973; recovered one fumble for eight yards, 1977; recovered one fumble, 1978 and 1981; recovered two fumbles, 1983.
Played in NFC Championship Game following 1982 and 1983 seasons.
Played in NFL Championship Game following 1982 and 1983 seasons.

BUFORD LAMAR McGEE
Running Back—San Diego Chargers
Born August 16, 1960, at Durant, Miss.
Height, 6.00. Weight, 206.
High School—Durant, Miss.
Received bachelor of science degree in business from University of Mississippi in 1984.
Selected by Birmingham in 1984 USFL territorial draft.
Selected by San Diego in 11th round (286th player selected) of 1984 NFL draft.
Signed by San Diego Chargers, June 2, 1984.

Year Club	G.	Att.	Yds.	Avg.	TD.	P.C.	Yds.	Avg.	TD.	TD.	Pts.	F.
		—RUSHING—				PASS RECEIVING				—TOTAL—		
1984—San Diego NFL	16	67	226	3.4	4	9	76	8.4	2	6	36	1

Year Club	G.	No.	Yds.	Avg.	TD.
	KICKOFF RETURNS				
1984—San Diego NFL	16	14	315	22.5	0

Additional pro statistics: Recovered one fumble, 1984.

EDWARD HOYT McGILL
(Eddie)
Tight End—St. Louis Cardinals
Born July 5, 1960, at Asheville, N.C.
Height, 6.06. Weight, 240.
High School—Enka, N.C.
Attended Western Carolina University.
Selected by St. Louis in 10th round (259th player selected) of 1982 NFL draft.
On injured reserve with broken collarbone, September 13 through December 16, 1983; activated, December 17, 1983.
On injured reserve with knee injury, August 28 through remainder of 1984 season.
St. Louis NFL, 1982 and 1983.
Games: 1982 (9), 1983 (2). Total—11.
Pro statistics: Caught one pass for 11 yards, 1983.

MARK ALLEN McGRATH
Wide Receiver—Washington Redskins
Born December 17, 1957, at San Diego, Calif.
Height, 5.11. Weight, 175.
High School—Seattle, Wash., Shorecrest.
Attended Montana State University.
Signed as free agent by Seattle Seahawks, May 5, 1980.
On injured reserve with knee injury, August 19 through entire 1980 season.
On injured reserve with broken hand, October 13 through remainder of 1981 season.
Released by Seattle Seahawks, September 6, 1982; signed as free agent by Washington Redskins, April 5, 1983.
On injured reserve with separated shoulder, September 8 through December 15, 1983; activated, December 16, 1983.
Released by Washington Redskins, August 22, 1984; re-signed by Redskins, September 19, 1984.

Year Club	G.	P.C.	Yds.	Avg.	TD.
		—PASS RECEIVING—			
1981—Seattle NFL	6	4	47	11.8	0
1983—Washington NFL	2	1	6	6.0	0
1984—Washington NFL	13	10	118	11.8	1
Pro Totals—3 Years	21	15	171	11.4	1

Member of Washington Redskins for NFC and NFL Championship Game following 1983 season; did not play.

LAWRENCE McGREW
(Larry)
Linebacker—New England Patriots
Born July 23, 1957, at Berkeley, Calif.
Height, 6.05. Weight, 233.
High School—Berkeley, Calif.
Attended Contra Costa Junior College and received degree in speech communications from University of Southern California in 1980.

Selected by New England in 2nd round (45th player selected) of 1980 NFL draft.
On injured reserve with knee and elbow injuries, December 19 through remainder of 1980 season.
On injured reserve with knee injury, August 31 through entire 1981 season.
New England NFL, 1980 and 1982 through 1984.
Games: 1980 (11), 1982 (8), 1983 (16), 1984 (16). Total—51.
Pro statistics: Intercepted one pass for three yards and recovered one fumble, 1983.

CURTIS McGRIFF
Defensive End—New York Giants
Born May 17, 1958, at Donaldsonville, Ga.
Height, 6.05. Weight, 276.
High School—Cottonwood, Ala.
Attended University of Alabama.

Signed as free agent by New York Giants, June 9, 1980.
On injured reserve with knee injury, December 1 through remainder of 1980 season.
On injured reserve with knee injury, December 8 through remainder of 1981 season.
On injured reserve with knee injury, October 26 through remainder of 1983 season.
New York Giants NFL, 1980 through 1984.
Games: 1980 (13), 1981 (14), 1982 (9), 1983 (8), 1984 (16). Total—60.

PAT McINALLY
Punter—Cincinnati Bengals
Born May 7, 1953, at Villa Park, Calif.
Height, 6.06. Weight, 212.
High School—Villa Park, Calif.
Received degree from Harvard University.

Named to THE SPORTING NEWS NFL All-Star Team, 1981.
Selected by Cincinnati in 5th round (120th player selected) of 1975 NFL draft.
Missed entire 1975 season due to leg injury.

		—PASS RECEIVING—					—PUNTING—			
Year Club	G.	P.C.	Yds.	Avg.TD.	Year Club		G.	No.	Avg.	Blk.
1976—Cincinnati NFL	14		None		1976—Cincinnati NFL		14	76	39.5	0
1977—Cincinnati NFL	14	17	258	15.2	3	1977—Cincinnati NFL	14	67	41.8	1
1978—Cincinnati NFL	16	15	189	12.6	0	1978—Cincinnati NFL	16	91	*43.1	0
1979—Cincinnati NFL	16	1	24	24.0	0	1979—Cincinnati NFL	16	89	41.3	2
1980—Cincinnati NFL	16	18	269	14.9	2	1980—Cincinnati NFL	16	83	40.8	*2
1981—Cincinnati NFL	16	6	68	11.3	0	1981—Cincinnati NFL	16	72	*45.4	1
1982—Cincinnati NFL	9		None		1982—Cincinnati NFL		9	31	38.7	0
1983—Cincinnati NFL	16		None		1983—Cincinnati NFL		16	67	41.9	*2
1984—Cincinnati NFL	16		None		1984—Cincinnati NFL		16	67	42.3	0
Pro Totals—9 Years	133	57	808	14.2	5	Pro Totals—9 Years	133	643	41.8	8

Additional pro statistics: Recovered two fumbles, fumbled once, rushed once for four yards and attempted one pass with one completion for four yards, 1977; rushed once for 18 yards, 1979; rushed once for no yards, recovered one fumble and fumbled twice, 1980; rushed once for minus 27 yards, 1981; attempted two passes with two completions for 77 yards, 1984.
Played in AFC Championship Game following 1981 season.
Played in NFL Championship Game following 1981 season.
Played in Pro Bowl (NFL All-Star Game) following 1981 season.

GUY MAURICE McINTYRE
Guard—San Francisco 49ers
Born Feburary 17, 1961, at Thomasville, Ga.
Height, 6.03. Weight, 271.
High School—Thomasville, Ga.
Attended University of Georgia.

Selected by Jacksonville in 1984 USFL territorial draft.
Selected by San Francisco in 3rd round (73rd player selected) of 1984 NFL draft.
Signed by San Francisco 49ers, May 8, 1984.
San Francisco NFL, 1984.
Games: 1984 (15).
Pro statistics: Returned one kickoff for no yards, 1984.
Played in NFC Championship Game following 1984 season.
Played in NFL Championship Game following 1984 season.

RICK E. McIVOR
Quarterback—St. Louis Cardinals
Born September 26, 1960, at Fort Davis, Tex.
Height, 6.04. Weight, 210.
High School—Fort Stockton, Tex.
Attended University of Texas.

Selected by Houston in 1984 USFL territorial draft.
Selected by St. Louis in 3rd round (80th player selected) of 1984 NFL draft.
Signed by St. Louis Cardinals, July 16, 1984.

		—————PASSING—————							—RUSHING—				—TOTAL—		
Year Club	G.	Att.	Cmp.	Pct.	Gain	T.P.	P.I.	Avg.	Att.	Yds.	Avg.	TD.	TD.	Pts.	F.
1984—St. Louis NFL	4	4	0	0.0	0	0	0	0.00	3	5	1.7	0	0	0	0

Quarterback Rating Points: 1984 (39.6).

KIRK ERICSON McJUNKIN
Guard-Offensive Tackle—Pittsburgh Steelers
Born March 15, 1961, at Dallas, Tex.
Height, 6.03. Weight, 250.
High School—Dallas, Tex., Lake Highlands.
Received bachelor of business administration degree in finance
from University of Texas in 1984.

Selected by San Antonio in 1984 USFL territorial draft.
Selected by Pittsburgh in 10th round (276th player selected) of 1984 NFL draft.
Signed by Pittsburgh Steelers, June 11, 1984.
On injured reserve with knee injury, August 14 through entire 1984 season.

REGINALD McKENZIE
(Reggie)
Guard—Seattle Seahawks
Born July 27, 1950, at Detroit, Mich.
Height, 6.05. Weight, 255.
High School—Highland Park, Mich.
Received bachelor of science degree in physical education from University
of Michigan in 1972.

Named as guard on THE SPORTING NEWS College All-America Team, 1971.
Named to THE SPORTING NEWS AFC All-Star Team, 1973 and 1974.
Selected by Buffalo in 2nd round (27th player selected) of 1972 NFL draft.
On injured reserve with knee injury, October 15 through remainder of 1981 season.
Traded by Buffalo Bills to Seattle Seahawks for 12th round pick in 1985 draft, June 28, 1983.
Buffalo NFL, 1972 through 1982; Seattle NFL, 1983 and 1984.
Games: 1972 (14), 1973 (14), 1974 (14), 1975 (14), 1976 (14), 1977 (14), 1978 (16), 1979 (16), 1980 (16), 1981 (6), 1982 (9), 1983 (14), 1984 (10). Total—171.
Pro statistics: Returned one kickoff for 15 yards, 1975; recovered one fumble, 1976 through 1978; recovered one fumble for 30 yards and fumbled once, 1980.
Member of Seattle Seahawks for AFC Championship Game following 1983 season; did not play.

ODIS McKINNEY JR.
Safety—Los Angeles Raiders
Born May 19, 1957, at Detroit, Mich.
Height, 6.02. Weight, 190.
High School—Reseda, Calif.
Attended Los Angeles Valley Junior College and University of Colorado.

Selected by New York Giants in 2nd round (37th player selected) of 1978 NFL draft.
Traded by New York Giants to Oakland Raiders for 8th round pick in 1981 draft, May 26, 1980.
Franchise transferred to Los Angeles, May 7, 1982.

		—INTERCEPTIONS—			
Year Club	G.	No.	Yds.	Avg.	TD.
1978—N.Y. Giants NFL	14	1	11	11.0	0
1979—N.Y. Giants NFL	15	1	25	25.0	0
1980—Oakland NFL	16	3	22	7.3	0
1981—Oakland NFL	16	3	38	12.7	0
1982—L.A. Raiders NFL	9		None		
1983—L.A. Raiders NFL	16	1	0	0.0	0
1984—L.A. Raiders NFL	16	1	0	0.0	0
Pro Totals—7 Years	102	10	96	9.6	0

Additional pro statistics: Recovered one fumble, 1978, 1979, 1981 and 1984; fumbled once, 1979, 1980 and 1984; recovered one fumble for four yards and returned one punt for no yards, 1980; returned one kickoff for no yards, 1984.
Played in AFC Championship Game following 1980 and 1983 seasons.
Played in NFL Championship Game following 1980 and 1983 seasons.

DENNIS LEWIS McKINNON
Wide Receiver—Chicago Bears
Born August 22, 1961, at Quitman, Ga.
Height, 6.02. Weight, 185.
High School—Miami, Fla., South Miami Senior.
Received bachelor of arts degree in criminology from Florida State University in 1983.

Signed as free agent by Chicago Bears, May 4, 1983.

		PASS RECEIVING				-PUNT RETURNS-				—KICKOFF RET.—				—TOTAL—		
Year Club	G.	P.C.	Yds.	Avg.	TD.	No.	Yds.	Avg.	TD.	No.	Yds.	Avg.	TD.	TD.	Pts.	F.
1983—Chicago NFL	16	20	326	16.3	4	34	316	9.3	*1	2	42	21.0	0	5	30	2
1984—Chicago NFL	12	29	431	14.9	3	5	62	12.4	0			None		3	18	1
Pro Totals—2 Years	28	49	757	15.4	7	39	378	9.7	1	2	42	21.0	0	8	48	3

Additional pro statistics: Recovered one fumble, 1983; rushed twice for 12 yards, 1984.
Played in NFC Championship Game following 1984 season.

—DID YOU KNOW—
That NFC Central teams won only three of 18 contests with AFC teams in 1984?

DENNIS N. McKNIGHT
Center-Guard—San Diego Chargers
Born September 12, 1959, at Dallas, Tex.
Height, 6.03. Weight, 273.
High School—Staten Island, N.Y., Wagner.
Received degree from Drake University in 1981.

Signed as free agent by Cleveland Browns, May 3, 1981.
Released by Cleveland Browns, August 18, 1981; signed as free agent by San Diego Chargers, March 30, 1982.
On inactive list, September 12 and September 19, 1982.
San Diego NFL, 1982 through 1984.
Games: 1982 (7), 1983 (16), 1984 (16). Total—39.
Pro statistics: Recovered two fumbles, 1983 and 1984.

JOE McLAUGHLIN
Linebacker—New York Giants
Born July 1, 1957, at Stoneham, Mass.
Height, 6.01. Weight, 235.
High School—Stoneham, Mass.
Attended University of Massachusetts.
Brother of Mike McLaughlin, center with Portland Breakers.

Signed as free agent by New York Giants, June, 1979.
Released by New York Giants, August 15, 1979; claimed on procedural waivers by Green Bay Packers, November 28, 1979.
Released by Green Bay Packers, May, 1980; signed as free agent by Buffalo Bills, July, 1980.
Released by Buffalo Bills, August 26, 1980; signed as free agent by New York Giants, October 31, 1980.
On inactive list, September 12, 1982.
On injured reserve with knee injury, November 18 through remainder of 1983 season.
Green Bay NFL, 1979; New York Giants NFL, 1980 through 1984.
Games: 1979 (3), 1980 (8), 1981 (16), 1982 (8), 1983 (7), 1984 (16). Total—58.
Pro statistics: Returned two kickoffs for 27 yards and fumbled once, 1980; returned two kickoffs for nine yards, 1981; returned one kickoff for 14 yards, 1982; returned one kickoff for eight yards, 1983; returned two kickoffs for 18 yards and recovered one fumble, 1984.

DANA McLEMORE
Kick Returner-Cornerback—San Francisco 49ers
Born July 1, 1960, at Los Angeles, Calif.
Height, 5.10. Weight, 183.
High School—Los Angeles, Calif., Venice.
Attended University of Hawaii.

Selected by San Francisco in 10th round (269th player selected) of 1982 NFL draft.
On inactive list, September 12, 1982.

Year Club	G.	No.	—PUNT RETURNS— Yds.	Avg.	TD.	No.	—KICKOFF RET.— Yds.	Avg.	TD.	TD.	—TOTAL— Pts.	F.
1982—San Francisco NFL	8	7	156	22.3	1	16	353	22.1	0	1	6	0
1983—San Francisco NFL	14	31	331	10.7	*1	30	576	19.2	0	1	6	0
1984—San Francisco NFL	16	45	521	11.6	1	3	80	26.7	0	2	12	1
Pro Totals—3 Years	38	83	1008	12.1	3	49	1009	20.6	0	4	24	1

Additional pro statistics: Intercepted two passes for 54 yards and a touchdown, 1984.
Played in NFC Championship Game following 1983 and 1984 seasons.
Played in NFL Championship Game following 1984 season.

MICHAEL JAMES McLEOD
(Mike)
Defensive Back—Green Bay Packers
Born May 4, 1958, at Bozeman, Mont.
Height, 6.00. Weight, 180.
High School—Cheyenne, Wyo., East.
Received bachelor of science degree in political science degree from Montana State University and received degree in law from University of Alberta.

Signed as free agent by Edmonton Eskimos, March 15, 1980.
On injured list, June 23 through August 13, 1980; activated, August 14, 1980.
Released by Edmonton Eskimos, August 27, 1980; signed as free agent by Green Bay Packers, September 25, 1984.

Year Club	G.	No.	INTERCEPTIONS Yds.	Avg.	TD.	No.	—PUNT RETURNS— Yds.	Avg.	TD.	No.	—KICKOFF RET.— Yds.	Avg.	TD.	TD.	—TOTAL— Pts.	F.
1980—Edmonton CFL	6	1	21	21.0	0	15	97	6.5	0		None			0	0	0
1981—Edmonton CFL	16	5	31	6.2	0		None			1	25	25.0	0	0	0	0
1982—Edmonton CFL	16	1	22	22.0	0	5	58	11.6	0	1	0	0.0	0	0	0	0
1983—Edmonton CFL	16	4	52	13.0	0		None				None			0	0	0
1984—Edmonton CFL	7	1	0	0.0	0	11	145	13.2	0		None			0	0	1
1984—Green Bay NFL	12	1	0	0.0	0		None				None			0	0	0
CFL Totals—5 Years	61	12	126	10.5	0	31	300	9.7	0	2	25	12.5	0	0	0	1
NFL Totals—1 Year	12	1	0	0.0	0	0	0	0.0	0	0	0	0.0	0	0	0	0
Pro Totals—6 Years	73	13	126	9.7	0	31	300	9.7	0	2	25	12.5	0	0	0	1

Additional CFL statistics: Recovered two fumbles, 1981; recovered one fumble for two yards, 1983.
Additional NFL statistics: Recovered one fumble, 1984.
Played in CFL Championship Game following 1980 through 1982 seasons.

JAMES ROBERT McMAHON
(Jim)
Quarterback—Chicago Bears
Born August 21, 1959, at Jersey City, N.J.
Height, 6.00. Weight, 187.
High School—Roy, Utah.
Attended Brigham Young University.

Selected by Chicago in 1st round (5th player selected) of 1982 NFL draft.
On injured reserve with lacerated kidney, November 9 through remainder of 1984 season.

		—————PASSING—————								—RUSHING—				—TOTAL—		
Year	Club	G.	Att.	Cmp.	Pct.	Gain	T.P.	P.I.	Avg.	Att.	Yds.	Avg.	TD.	TD.	Pts.	F.
1982—Chicago NFL		8	210	120	57.1	1501	9	7	7.15	24	105	4.4	1	1	6	1
1983—Chicago NFL		14	295	175	59.3	2184	12	13	7.40	55	307	5.6	2	3	18	4
1984—Chicago NFL		9	143	85	59.4	1146	8	2	8.01	39	276	7.1	2	2	12	1
Pro Totals—3 Years		31	648	380	58.6	4831	29	22	7.46	118	688	5.8	5	6	36	6

Quarterback Rating Points: 1982 (80.1), 1983 (77.6), 1984 (97.8). Total—82.8.
Additional pro statistics: Punted once for 59 yards, 1982; caught one pass for 18 yards and a touchdown, punted once for 36 yards and recovered three fumbles, 1983; caught one pass for 42 yards, 1984.

STEVE DOUGLAS McMICHAEL
Defensive Tackle—Chicago Bears
Born October 17, 1957, at Houston, Tex.
Height, 6.02. Weight, 260.
High School—Freer, Tex.
Attended University of Texas.

Selected by New England in 3rd round (73rd player selected) of 1980 NFL draft.
On injured reserve with back injury, November 3 through remainder of 1980 season.
Released by New England Patriots, August 24, 1981; signed as free agent by Chicago Bears, October 15, 1981.
New England NFL, 1980; Chicago NFL, 1981 through 1984.
Games: 1980 (6), 1981 (10), 1982 (9), 1983 (16), 1984 (16). Total—57.
Pro statistics: Recovered one fumble, 1981; recovered one fumble for 64 yards, 1982; recovered two fumbles, 1983.
Played in NFC Championship Game following 1984 season.

LEWIS LORANDO McMILLAN
(Randy)
Fullback—Indianapolis Colts
Born December 17, 1958, at Havre de Grace, Md.
Height, 6.00. Weight, 212.
High School—Belair, Md., North Hartford.
Attended Hartford Community College and University of Pittsburgh.

Selected by Baltimore in 1st round (12th player selected) of 1981 NFL draft.
Franchise transferred to Indianapolis, March 31, 1984.

		——————RUSHING——————				PASS RECEIVING				—TOTAL—		
Year	Club	G.	Att.	Yds.	Avg.	TD.	P.C.	Yds.	Avg.	TD.	TD.	Pts.	F.
1981—Baltimore NFL		16	149	597	4.0	3	50	466	9.3	1	4	24	1
1982—Baltimore NFL		9	101	305	3.0	1	15	90	6.0	0	1	6	1
1983—Baltimore NFL		16	198	802	4.1	5	24	195	8.1	1	6	36	5
1984—Indianapolis NFL		16	163	705	4.3	5	19	201	10.6	0	5	30	1
Pro Totals—4 Years		57	611	2409	3.9	14	108	952	8.8	2	16	96	8

Additional pro statistics: Recovered one fumble, 1982; recovered three fumbles, 1983.

SEAN McNANIE
Defensive End—Buffalo Bills
Born September 9, 1961, at Mundelein, Ill.
Height, 6.05. Weight, 252.
High School—Mundelein, Ill.
Attended Arizona State University and San Diego State University.

Selected by Oakland in 2nd round (30th player selected) of 1984 USFL draft.
Selected by Buffalo in 3rd round (79th player selected) of 1984 NFL draft.
Signed by Buffalo Bills, June 1, 1984.
Buffalo NFL, 1984.
Games: 1984 (15).

DONALD McNEAL
(Don)
Cornerback—Miami Dolphins
Born May 6, 1958, at Atmore, Ala.
Height, 5.11. Weight, 192.
High School—Atmore, Ala., Escambia County.
Attended University of Alabama.

Named as cornerback on THE SPORTING NEWS College All-America Team, 1979.
Selected by Miami in 1st round (21st player selected) of 1980 NFL draft.
On injured reserve with wrist injury, December 11 through remainder of 1980 season.

On injured reserve with Achilles tendon injury, August 29 through entire 1983 season.

Year Club		G.	No.	Yds.	Avg.TD.	
1980—Miami NFL		13	5	17	3.4	0
1981—Miami NFL		12		None		
1982—Miami NFL		9	4	42	10.5	*1
1984—Miami NFL		11	3	41	13.7	1
Pro Totals—4 Years		45	12	100	8.3	2

Additional pro statistics: Recovered one fumble, 1980 and 1981; recovered two fumbles for five yards, 1984.
Played in AFC Championship Game following 1982 and 1984 seasons.
Played in NFL Championship Game following 1982 and 1984 seasons.

FREEMAN McNEIL
Running Back—New York Jets

Born April 22, 1959, at Jackson, Miss.
Height, 5.11. Weight, 212.
High School—Wilmington, Calif., Banning.
Attended University of California at Los Angeles.

Selected by New York Jets in 1st round (3rd player selected) of 1981 NFL draft.
On injured reserve with foot injury, October 10 through November 13, 1981; activated, November 14, 1981.
On injured reserve with separated shoulder, September 27 through November 10, 1983; activated, November 11, 1983.
On injured reserve with broken ribs, December 6 through remainder of 1984 season.

Year Club		G.	Att.	Yds.	Avg.	TD.	P.C.	Yds.	Avg.	TD.	TD.	Pts.	F.
				RUSHING			PASS RECEIVING				TOTAL		
1981—New York Jets NFL		11	137	623	4.5	2	18	171	9.5	1	3	18	5
1982—New York Jets NFL		9	151	*786	*5.2	6	16	187	11.7	1	7	42	7
1983—New York Jets NFL		9	160	654	4.1	1	21	172	8.2	3	4	24	4
1984—New York Jets NFL		12	229	1070	4.7	5	25	294	11.8	1	6	36	4
Pro Totals—4 Years		41	677	3133	4.6	14	80	824	10.3	6	20	120	20

Additional pro statistics: Attempted one pass with one completion for five yards and a touchdown, 1983; recovered one fumble, 1983 and 1984.
Played in AFC Championship Game following 1982 season.
Played in Pro Bowl (NFL All-Star Game) following 1982 season.
Named to Pro Bowl following 1984 season; replaced due to injury by Greg Bell.

FREDERICK ARNOLD McNEILL
(Fred)
Linebacker—Minnesota Vikings

Born May 6, 1952, at Durham, N. C.
Height, 6.02. Weight, 225.
High School—Baldwin Park, Calif.
Received degree in economics from University of California at Los Angeles;
attending William Mitchell Law School.
Brother of Rod McNeill, running back with New Orleans Saints and
Tampa Bay Buccaneers, 1974 through 1976.

Named as defensive end on THE SPORTING NEWS College All-America Team, 1973.
Selected by Minnesota in 1st round (17th player selected) of 1974 NFL draft.

Year Club		G.	No.	Yds.	Avg.TD.	Year Club		G.	No.	Yds.	Avg.TD.
	INTERCEPTIONS						INTERCEPTIONS				
1974—Minnesota NFL		14		None		1980—Minnesota NFL		16		None	
1975—Minnesota NFL		14	1	0	0.0 0	1981—Minnesota NFL		16	2	26	13.0 0
1976—Minnesota NFL		13		None		1982—Minnesota NFL		9		None	
1977—Minnesota NFL		14	1	0	0.0 0	1983—Minnesota NFL		16		None	
1978—Minnesota NFL		16	2	1	0.5 0	1984—Minnesota NFL		13	1	0	0.0 0
1979—Minnesota NFL		16		None		Pro Totals—11 Years		157	7	27	3.9 0

Additional pro statistics: Recovered one fumble, 1974, 1975, 1977 and 1979; fumbled once, 1976; recovered six fumbles for 39 yards and ran 16 yards with blocked punt for a touchdown, 1978; recovered three fumbles, 1980; recovered one fumble for 11 yards, 1981; recovered two fumbles, 1984.
Played in NFC Championship Game following 1974, 1976 and 1977 seasons.
Played in NFL Championship Game following 1974 and 1976 seasons.

BRUCE EDWARD McNORTON
Cornerback—Detroit Lions

Born February 28, 1959, at Daytona Beach, Fla.
Height, 5.11. Weight, 175.
High School—Daytona Beach, Fla., Spruce Creek.
Received bachelor of arts degree in social work from Georgetown (Ky.) College in 1982.

Selected by Detroit in 4th round (96th player selected) of 1982 NFL draft.
On injured reserve with knuckle injury, September 10 through December 10, 1982; activated, December 11, 1982.

Year Club		G.	No.	Yds.	Avg.TD.	
			INTERCEPTIONS			
1982—Detroit NFL		4		None		
1983—Detroit NFL		16	7	30	4.3	0
1984—Detroit NFL		16	2	0	0.0	0
Pro Totals—3 Years		36	9	30	3.3	0

MILES GREGORY McPHERSON
Defensive Back—San Diego Chargers
Born March 30, 1960, at Queens, N.Y.
Height, 5.11. Weight, 191.
High School—Malverne, N.Y.
Attended University of New Haven.

Selected by Los Angeles Rams in 10th round (256th player selected) of 1982 NFL draft.
Released by Los Angeles Rams, September 6, 1982; signed as free agent by San Diego Chargers, November 24, 1982.
On injured reserve with broken collarbone, December 12 through remainder of 1983 season.
On injured reserve with knee injury, September 28 through November 9, 1984; actiivated, November 10, 1984.
San Diego NFL, 1982 through 1984.
Games: 1982 (6), 1983 (11), 1984 (9). Total—26.
Pro statistics: Intercepted one pass for no yards, returned five kickoffs for 77 yards and fumbled once, 1983; recovered one fumble, 1984.

DAN McQUAID
Offensive Tackle—Los Angeles Rams
Born October 4, 1960, at Cortland, Calif.
Height, 6.07. Weight, 255.
High School—Clarksburg, Calif., Delta.
Attended University of Nevada at Las Vegas.

Selected by New Jersey in 16th round (318th player selected) of 1984 USFL draft.
Signed as free agent by Los Angeles Rams, May 4, 1984.
On injured reserve with back injury, August 21 through entire 1984 season.

ANTHONY McSWAIN
(Chuck)
Running Back—Dallas Cowboys
Born February 21, 1961, at Rutherford, N.C.
Height, 6.00. Weight, 191.
High School—Forest City, N.C., Chase.
Attended Clemson University.
Brother of Rod McSwain, cornerback with New England Patriots.

Selected by Washington in 1983 USFL territorial draft.
Selected by Dallas in 5th round (135th player selected) of 1983 NFL draft.
Signed by Dallas Cowboys, May 26, 1983.
On injured reserve with torn tendon in finger, September 26 through remainder of 1983 season.

| | | | KICKOFF RETURNS | | | |
Year	Club	G.	No.	Yds.	Avg.	TD.
1983—Dallas NFL		1	1	17	17.0	0
1984—Dallas NFL		15	20	403	20.2	0
Pro Totals—2 Years		16	21	420	20.0	0

Additional pro statistics: Fumbled twice, 1984.

RODNEY McSWAIN
(Rod)
Cornerback—New England Patriots
Born January 28, 1962, at Caroleen, N.C.
Height, 6.01. Weight, 198.
High School—Forest City, N.C., Chase.
Attended Clemson University.
Brother of Chuck McSwain, running back with Dallas Cowboys.

Selected by Washington in 1984 USFL territorial draft.
Selected by Atlanta in 3rd round (63rd player selected) of 1984 NFL draft.
Signed by Atlanta Falcons, May 16, 1984.
Traded by Atlanta Falcons to New England Patriots for 8th round pick in 1985 draft, August 27, 1984.
New England NFL, 1984.
Games: 1984 (15).
Pro statistics: Recovered one fumble, 1984.

MICHAEL LEE MEADE
(Mike)
Fullback—Detroit Lions
Born February 12, 1960, at Dover, Del.
Height, 5.10. Weight, 224.
High School—Dover, Del.
Received bachelor of science degree in business management
from Penn State University in 1982.

Selected by Green Bay in 5th round (126th player selected) of 1982 NFL draft.
On injured reserve with broken leg, November 24 through remainder of 1982 season.
Released by Green Bay Packers, August 27, 1984; awarded on waivers to Detroit Lions, August 28, 1984.

Year Club	G.	RUSHING Att. Yds. Avg. TD.	PASS RECEIVING P.C. Yds. Avg. TD.	TOTAL TD. Pts. F.
1982—Green Bay NFL	2	14 42 3.0 0	3 —5 —1.7 0	0 0 0
1983—Green Bay NFL	16	55 201 3.7 1	16 110 6.9 2	3 18 2
1984—Detroit NFL	15	None	None	0 0 1
Pro Totals—3 Years	33	69 243 3.5 1	19 105 5.5 2	3 18 3

Additional pro statistics: Returned two kickoffs for 31 yards, 1982; recovered one fumble, 1983; returned four kickoffs for 32 yards, 1984.

DARRYL SCOTT MEADOWS
Safety—Houston Oilers
Born February 15, 1961, at Cincinnati, O.
Height, 6.01. Weight, 199.
High School—Cincinnati, O., LaSalle.
Attended University of Toledo.

Signed as free agent by Houston Oilers, June 2, 1983.
Released by Houston Oilers, August 29, 1983; re-signed by Oilers, September 2, 1983.
Released by Houston Oilers, October 2, 1984; re-signed by Oilers, October 12, 1984.
Houston NFL, 1983 and 1984.
Games: 1983 (16), 1984 (13). Total—29.

JOHNNY MEADS
Linebacker—Houston Oilers
Born June 25, 1961, at Labadieville, La.
Height, 6.02. Weight, 225.
High School—Napoleonville, La., Assumption.
Attended Nicholls State University.

Selected by New Orleans in 3rd round (55th player selected) of 1984 USFL draft.
Selected by Houston in 3rd round (58th player selected) of 1984 NFL draft.
Signed by Houston Oilers, July 17, 1984.
Houston NFL, 1984.
Games: 1984 (16).

KARL BERNARD MECKLENBURG
Defensive End-Linebacker—Denver Broncos
Born September 1, 1960, at Seattle, Wash.
Height, 6.03. Weight, 250.
High School—Edina, Minn., West.
Attended Augustana College (S.D.) and received bachelor of
science degree in biology from University of Minnesota in 1983.

Selected by Chicago in 21st round (246th player selected) of 1983 USFL draft.
Selected by Denver in 12th round (310th player selected) of 1983 NFL draft.
Signed by Denver Broncos, May 14, 1983.

Year Club	G.	INTERCEPTIONS No. Yds. Avg.TD.
1983—Denver NFL	16	None
1984—Denver NFL	16	2 105 52.5 0
Pro Totals—2 Years	32	2 105 52.5 0

Additional pro statistics: Recovered one fumble, 1984.

LANCE ALAN MEHL
Name pronounced Mell.
Linebacker—New York Jets
Born February 14, 1958, at Bellaire, O.
Height, 6.03. Weight, 235.
High School—Bellaire, O.
Received bachelor of science degree in industrial arts education from
Pennsylvania State University in 1980.

Selected by New York Jets in 3rd round (69th player selected) of 1980 NFL draft.

Year Club	G.	INTERCEPTIONS No. Yds. Avg.TD.
1980—New York Jets NFL	14	None
1981—New York Jets NFL	15	3 17 5.7 0
1982—New York Jets NFL	9	2 38 19.0 0
1983—New York Jets NFL	16	7 57 8.1 1
1984—New York Jets NFL	16	None
Pro Totals—5 Years	70	12 112 9.3 1

Additional pro statistics: Recovered one fumble, 1981 through 1984.
Played in AFC Championship Game following 1982 season.

—DID YOU KNOW—

That for the second straight season in 1984, the AFC and NFC tied in interconference victories, 26-26?

GREGORY PAUL MEISNER
(Greg)
Nose Tackle—Los Angeles Rams
Born April 23, 1959, at New Kensington, Pa.
Height, 6.03. Weight, 265.
High School—New Kensington, Pa., Valley.
Received bachelor of arts degree in psychology from University of Pittsburgh in 1981.

Selected by Los Angeles in 3rd round (63rd player selected) of 1981 NFL draft.
On non-football injury list with head injuries suffered in bar fight, August 18 through October 23, 1981; activated, October 24, 1981.
On injured reserve with knee injury, December 16 through remainder of 1982 season.
Los Angeles Rams NFL, 1981 through 1984.
Games: 1981 (9), 1982 (6), 1983 (16), 1984 (16). Total—47.
Pro statistics: Returned one kickoff for 17 yards, 1981; recovered one fumble, 1984.

GUIDO A. MERKENS
Quarterback-Wide Receiver—New Orleans Saints
Born August 14, 1955, at San Antonio, Tex.
Height, 6.01. Weight, 195.
High School—San Antonio, Tex., Edison.
Received bachelor of science degree in physical education from
Sam Houston State University in 1976.

Signed as free agent by Houston Oilers, June, 1978.
Released by Houston Oilers, August 29, 1978; re-signed by Oilers, September 22, 1978.
On injured reserve with knee injury, August 26 through November 12, 1980; re-signed after clearing procedural waivers, November 14, 1980.
Released by Houston Oilers, December 13, 1980; signed as free agent by New Orleans Saints, December 15, 1980.

| | | -PASS RECEIVING- | | | | -PUNT RETURNS- | | | | —TOTAL— | | |
Year Club	G.	P.C.	Yds.	Avg.	TD.	No.	Yds.	Avg.	TD.	TD.	Pts.	F.
1978—Houston NFL	12	1	6	6.0	0	13	132	10.2	0	0	0	3
1979—Houston NFL	16	3	44	14.7	1	2	6	3.0	0	1	6	1
1980—Houston (3)-N. Orl. (1) NFL	4		None				None			0	0	
1981—New Orleans NFL	16	29	458	15.8	1	1	—12	—12.0	0	1	6	1
1982—New Orleans NFL	9		None				None			0	0	1
1983—New Orleans NFL	16		None				None			0	0	
1984—New Orleans NFL	16		None				None			0	0	0
Pro Totals—7 Years	89	33	508	15.4	2	16	126	7.9	0	2	12	6

| | | —————PASSING————— | | | | | | | |
Year Club	G.	Att.	Cmp.	Pct.	Gain	T.P.	P.I.	Avg.
1978—Houston NFL	12			None				
1979—Houston NFL	16			None				
1980—Houston (3)-New Orleans (1) NFL	4			None				
1981—New Orleans NFL	16	2	1	50.0	20	0	0	10.00
1982—New Orleans NFL	9	49	18	36.7	186	1	2	3.80
1983—New Orleans NFL	16			None				
1984—New Orleans NFL	16			None				
Pro Totals—7 Years	89	51	19	37.3	206	1	2	4.04

Quarterback Rating Points: 1981 (85.4), 1982 (38.1). Total—40.4.
Additional pro statistics: Returned two kickoffs for 22 yards, 1979; recovered one fumble, 1979 and 1980; returned two kickoffs for 38 yards, rushed twice for minus one yard and recovered three fumbles, 1981; rushed nine times for 30 yards, 1982; rushed once for 16 yards and punted four times for a 36.0 average, 1983.
Played in AFC Championship Game following 1978 and 1979 seasons.

RICHARD CASEY MERRILL
(Known by middle name.)
Defensive End—New York Giants
Born July 16, 1957, at Oakland, Calif.
Height, 6.04. Weight, 260.
High School—Danville, Calif., Monte Vista.
Received bachelor of arts degree in history from University of California at Davis in 1979.

Selected by Cincinnati in 5th round (113th player selected) of 1979 NFL draft.
Released by Cincinnati Bengals, August 27, 1979; signed as free agent by Green Bay Packers, September 11, 1979.
On injured reserve with knee injury, December 12 through remainder of 1979 season.
Released by Green Bay Packers, October 5, 1983; signed as free agent by New York Giants, October 13, 1983.
Green Bay NFL, 1979 through 1982; Green Bay (5)-New York Giants (10) NFL, 1983; New York Giants NFL, 1984.
Games: 1979 (13), 1980 (16), 1981 (16), 1982 (9), 1983 (15), 1984 (16). Total—85.
Pro statistics: Recovered one fumble, 1980; recovered three fumbles, 1981.

SAM MERRIMAN
Linebacker—Seattle Seahawks
Born May 5, 1961, at Tucson, Ariz.
Height, 6.03. Weight, 225.
High School—Tucson, Ariz., Amphitheater.
Attended University of Idaho.

Selected by Arizona in 12th round (143rd player selected) of 1983 USFL draft.
Selected by Seattle in 7th round (177th player selected) of 1983 NFL draft.
Signed by Seattle Seahawks, May 22, 1983.
Seattle NFL, 1983 and 1984.
Games: 1983 (16), 1984 (16). Total—32.
Pro statistics: Recovered one fumble, 1983.
Played in AFC Championship Game following 1983 season.

MICHAEL LAMAR MERRIWEATHER
(Mike)
Linebacker—Pittsburgh Steelers
Born November 26, 1960, at Albans, N.Y.
Height, 6.02. Weight, 215.
High School—Vallejo, Calif.
Received bachelor of arts degree in history from University of the Pacific in 1982.
Selected by Pittsburgh in 3rd round (70th player selected) of 1982 NFL draft.

Year Club	G.	No.	Yds.	Avg.	TD.
			—INTERCEPTIONS—		
1982—Pittsburgh NFL	9		None		
1983—Pittsburgh NFL	16	3	55	18.3	1
1984—Pittsburgh NFL	16	2	9	4.5	0
Pro Totals—3 Years	41	5	64	12.8	1

Additional pro statistics: Returned one punt for three yards, 1982; recovered two fumbles, 1983; recovered one fumble, 1984.
Played in AFC Championship Game following 1984 season.
Played in Pro Bowl (NFL All-Star Game) following 1984 season.

PETER HENRY METZELAARS
(Pete)
Tight End—Seattle Seahawks
Born May 24, 1960, at Three Rivers, Mich.
Height, 6.07. Weight, 240.
High School—Portage, Mich., Central.
Received bachelor of science degree in economics from Wabash College in 1982.
Selected by Seattle in 3rd round (75th player selected) of 1982 NFL draft.
On injured reserve with knee injury, October 17 through November 30, 1984; activated, December 1, 1984.

Year Club	G.	P.C.	Yds.	Avg.	TD.
			—PASS RECEIVING—		
1982—Seattle NFL	9	15	152	10.1	0
1983—Seattle NFL	16	7	72	10.3	1
1984—Seattle NFL	9	5	80	16.0	0
Pro Totals—3 Years	34	27	304	11.3	1

Additional pro statistics: Recovered one fumble and fumbled twice, 1982; returned one kickoff for no yards, 1983; fumbled once, 1984.
Played in AFC Championship Game following 1983 season.

ROBERT ANTHONY MICHO
(Bob)
Tight End—San Diego Chargers
Born March 7, 1962, at Omaha, Neb.
Height, 6.03. Weight, 227.
High School—Austin, Tex., L.C. Anderson.
Attended University of Texas.
Selected by Houston in 1984 USFL territorial draft.
Selected by Denver in 10th round (272nd player selected) of 1984 NFL draft.
Signed by Denver Broncos, May 12, 1984.
On injured reserve with toe injury, August 13 through November 7, 1984.
Awarded on procedural waivers to San Diego Chargers, November 9, 1984.
San Diego NFL, 1984.
Games: 1984 (6).

FRANK MIDDLETON
Running Back—Indianapolis Colts
Born October 28, 1960, at Savannah, Ga.
Heightt, 5.11. Weight, 201.
High School—Savannah, Ga., Sol C. Johnson.
Attended Florida A&M University.
Selected by Tampa Bay in 1983 USFL territorial draft.
Signed as free agent by Seattle Seahawks, April 28, 1983.
Released by Seattle Seahawks, July 25, 1983; signed as free agent by Tampa Bay Bandits, September 30, 1983.
Released by Tampa Bay Bandits, January 17, 1984; signed as free agent by Indianapolis Colts, June 21, 1984.

Year Club		—RUSHING—				—KICKOFF RET.—				—TOTAL—		
	G.	Att.	Yds.	Avg.	TD.	No.	Yds.	Avg.	TD.	TD.	Pts.	F.
1984—Indianapolis NFL	16	92	275	3.0	1	15	112	7.5	1	2	12	2

Additional pro statistics: Returned one kickoff for 11 yards and recovered two fumbles, 1984.

BRYAN MILLARD
Offensive Tackle—Seattle Seahawks
Born December 2, 1960, at Sioux City, Iowa.
Height, 6.05. Weight, 282.
High School—Dumas, Tex.
Attended University of Texas.

Selected by New Jersey in 12th round (142nd player selected) of 1983 USFL draft.
Signed by New Jersey Generals, February 4, 1983.
On injured reserve with knee injury, April 18 through remainder of 1983 season.
On developmental squad, May 6 through May 10, 1984; activated, May 11, 1984.
Granted free agency, July 15, 1984; signed as free agent by Seattle Seahawks, July 31, 1984.
On injured reserve with knee injury, December 8 through remainder of 1984 season.
On developmental squad for 1 game with New Jersey Generals in 1984.
New Jersey USFL, 1983 and 1984; Seattle NFL, 1984.
Games: 1983 (7), 1984 USFL (17), 1984 NFL (14). Total USFL—24. Total Pro—38.

MATT G. MILLEN
Linebacker—Los Angeles Raiders
Born March 12, 1958, at Hokendauqua, Pa.
Height, 6.02. Weight, 250.
High School—Whitehall, Pa.
Received bachelor of business administration degree in marketing from
Pennsylvania State University in 1980.
Nephew of Andy Tomasic, back with Pittsburgh Steelers, 1942 and 1946 and
pitcher with New York Giants, 1949.

Selected by Oakland in 2nd round (43rd player selected) of 1980 NFL draft.
Franchise transferred to Los Angeles, May 7, 1982.

Year Club	G.	—INTERCEPTIONS—			
		No.	Yds.	Avg.	TD.
1980—Oakland NFL	16	2	17	8.5	0
1981—Oakland NFL	16			None	
1982—L.A. Raiders NFL	9	3	77	25.7	0
1983—L.A. Raiders NFL	16	1	14	14.0	0
1984—L.A. Raiders NFL	16			None	
Pro Totals—5 Years	73	6	108	18.0	0

Additional pro statistics: Recovered one fumble, 1981; returned one kickoff for 13 yards and recovered two fumbles, 1982; returned two kickoffs for 19 yards, 1983.
Played in AFC Championship Game following 1980 and 1983 seasons.
Played in NFL Championship Game following 1980 and 1983 seasons.

BRETT MILLER
Offensive Tackle—Atlanta Falcons
Born October 2, 1958 at Lynwood, Calif.
Height, 6.07. Weight, 285.
High School—Glendale, Calif.
Attended Glendale Community College and University of Iowa.

Selected by Washington in 5th round (57th player selected) of 1983 USFL draft.
Selected by Atlanta in 5th round (129th player selected) of 1983 NFL draft.
Signed by Atlanta Falcons, May 25, 1983.
Atlanta NFL, 1983 and 1984.
Games: 1983 (16), 1984 (15). Total—31.

JUNIOR MILLER
Tight End—New Orleans Saints
Born November 26, 1957, at Midland, Tex.
Height, 6.04. Weight, 240.
High School—Midland, Tex., Robert E. Lee.
Attended University of Nebraska.

Named as tight end on THE SPORTING NEWS College All-America Team, 1979.
Selected by Atlanta in 1st round (7th player selected) of 1980 NFL draft.
Placed on did not report list, August 14 through August 19, 1984.
Reported and granted roster exemption, August 20 through August 23, 1984; activated, August 24, 1984.
Traded by Atlanta Falcons to New Orleans Saints for 6th round pick in 1985 draft, August 26, 1984.

Year Club	G.	—PASS RECEIVING—		
		P.C.	Yds.	Avg.	TD.
1980—Atlanta NFL	16	46	584	12.7	9
1981—Atlanta NFL	16	32	398	12.4	3
1982—Atlanta NFL	9	20	221	11.1	1
1983—Atlanta NFL	15	16	125	7.8	0
1984—New Orleans NFL	15	8	81	10.1	1
Pro Totals—5 Years	71	122	1409	11.5	14

Additional pro statistics: Rushed twice for minus two yards and fumbled twice, 1980; recovered one fumble, 1982; fumbled once, 1982 and 1983; rushed once for two yards, 1983.
Played in Pro Bowl (NFL All-Star Game) following 1980 and 1981 seasons.

KENNETH EDWARD MILLER
(Ken)
Defensive Back—Chicago Bears
Born June 24, 1958, at Pine Bluff, Ark.
Height, 6.00. Weight, 182.
High School—Flint, Mich., Beecher.
Attended Eastern Michigan University.

Selected by Dallas in 7th round (191st player selected) of 1981 NFL draft.
Released by Dallas Cowboys, August 25, 1981; signed as free agent by Montreal Alouettes, September 8, 1981.
Released by Montreal Alouettes, September 27, 1981; re-signed by Alouettes, October 18, 1981.
Franchise renamed Concordes, 1982.
Traded by Montreal Concordes to Ottawa Rough Riders, March 25, 1983.
Granted free agency, March 1, 1985; signed by Chicago Bears, May 3, 1985.

Year Club	G.	No.	Yds.	Avg.	TD.
1981—Montreal CFL..............	3	None			
1982—Montreal CFL..............	12	None			
1983—Ottawa CFL	16	2	0	0.0	0
1984—Ottawa CFL	15	4	35	8.8	0
CFL Totals—4 Years	46	6	35	5.8	0

Additional CFL statistics: Recovered two fumbles for 12 yards, 1982; recovered two fumbles, 1984.

SHAWN MILLER
Nose Tackle—Los Angeles Rams
Born March 14, 1961, at Ogden, Utah.
Height, 6.04. Weight, 255.
High School—Ogden, Utah, Weber.
Attended Utah State University.

Signed as free agent by Los Angeles Rams, May 5, 1984.
Released by Los Angeles Rams, August 27, 1984; re-signed by Rams, August 28, 1984.
On injured reserve with back injury, November 9 through remainder of 1984 season.
Los Angeles Rams NFL, 1984.
Games: 1984 (8).

JIM MILLS
Offensive Tackle—Indianapolis Colts
Born September 23, 1961, at Vancouver, B.C., Can.
Height, 6.09. Weight, 281.
High School—Richmond, B.C., Can.
Attended University of Hawaii.

Selected by Los Angeles in 6th round (67th player selected) of 1983 USFL draft.
Selected by Baltimore in 9th round (225th player selected) of 1983 NFL draft.
Signed by Baltimore Colts, May 25, 1983.
On injured reserve with knee injury, October 25 through remainder of 1983 season.
Franchise transferred to Indianapolis, March 31, 1984.
Baltimore NFL, 1983; Indianapolis NFL, 1984.
Games: 1983 (7), 1984 (14). Total—21.

RICHARD MILOT
(Rich)
Linebacker—Washington Redskins
Born May 28, 1957, at Coraopolis, Pa.
Height, 6.04. Weight, 237.
High School—Coraopolis, Pa., Moon.
Received bachelor of business administration degree in marketing from
Pennsylvania State University in 1979.

Selected by Washington in 7th round (182nd player selected) of 1979 NFL draft.
On injured reserve with knee injury, October 20 through November 20, 1981; activated, November 21, 1981.

Year Club	G.	No.	Yds.	Avg.	TD.
1979—Washington NFL..........	14	None			
1980—Washington NFL..........	16	4	—8	—2.0	0
1981—Washington NFL..........	11	None			
1982—Washington NFL..........	9	None			
1983—Washington NFL..........	16	2	20	10.0	0
1984—Washington NFL..........	14	3	42	14.0	0
Pro Totals—6 Years...........	80	9	54	6.0	0

Additional pro statistics: Recovered one fumble, 1980; recovered one fumble for 18 yards and fumbled once, 1981.
Played in NFC Championship Game following 1982 and 1983 seasons.
Played in NFL Championship Game following 1982 and 1983 seasons.

FRANKY LyDALE MINNIFIELD
(Frank)
Cornerback—Cleveland Browns

Born January 1, 1960, at Lexington, Ky.
Height, 5.09. Weight, 180.
High School—Lexington, Ky., Henry Clay.
Attended University of Louisville.
Related to Dirk Minniefield, second round selection of Dallas Mavericks in 1983 NBA draft.

Selected by Chicago in 3rd round (30th player selected) of 1983 USFL draft.
Signed by Chicago Blitz, January 28, 1983.
On injured reserve with knee injury, March 8 through remainder of 1983 season.
Franchise transferred to Arizona, September 30, 1983.
On developmental squad, March 4 through March 21, 1984; activated, March 22, 1984.
On developmental squad, April 27 through May 6, 1984; activated, May 7, 1984.
Signed by Cleveland Browns, May 20, 1984.
Released by Arizona Wranglers, August 23, 1984.
Cleveland Browns contract approved by NFL, August 25, 1984.
Granted roster exemption, August 25 through August 30, 1984; activated, August 31, 1984.
On developmental squad for 3 games with Arizona Wranglers in 1984.

Year Club	G.	No.	Yds.	Avg.	TD.
1983—Chicago USFL	1	None			
1984—Arizona USFL	15	4	74	18.5	1
1984—Cleveland NFL	15	1	26	26.0	0
USFL Totals—2 Years	16	4	74	18.5	1
NFL Totals—1 Year	15	1	26	26.0	0
Pro Totals—3 Years	31	5	100	20.6	1

Additional USFL statistics: Recovered two fumbles for minus six yards, 1984.
Additional NFL statistics: Recovered two fumbles for 10 yards, 1984.
Played in USFL Championship Game following 1984 season.

CEDRIC ALWYN MINTER
Running Back—New York Jets

Born November 13, 1958, at Charleston, S.C.
Height, 5.10. Weight, 200.
High School—Boise, Idaho, Borah.
Attended Boise State University.

Signed as free agent by Toronto Argonauts, March, 1981.
Granted free agency, March 1, 1984; signed by New York Jets, April 26, 1984.
On injured reserve with pulled quadricep, October 26 through November 23, 1984; activated, November 24, 1984.

Year Club		RUSHING				PASS RECEIVING				TOTAL		
	G.	Att.	Yds.	Avg.	TD.	P.C.	Yds.	Avg.	TD.	TD.	Pts.	F.
1981—Toronto CFL	15	182	815	4.5	3	28	371	13.3	0	3	22	2
1982—Toronto CFL	16	120	563	4.7	7	61	828	13.6	5	12	76	1
1983—Toronto CFL	14	107	599	5.6	5	38	444	11.7	3	8	48	1
1984—New York Jets NFL	8	34	136	4.0	1	10	109	10.9	1	2	12	1
CFL Totals—3 Years	45	409	1977	4.8	15	127	1643	12.9	8	23	146	4
NFL Totals—1 Year	8	34	136	4.0	1	10	109	10.9	1	2	12	1
Pro Totals—4 Years	53	443	2113	4.8	16	137	1752	12.8	9	25	158	5

Year Club		PUNT RETURNS				KICKOFF RET.			
	G.	No.	Yds.	Avg.	TD.	No.	Yds.	Avg.	TD.
1981—Toronto CFL	15	3	41	13.7	0	11	266	22.0	0
1982—Toronto CFL	16	3	42	14.0	0	12	227	18.9	0
1983—Toronto CFL	14	None				None			
1984—New York Jets NFL	8	4	44	11.0	0	10	224	22.4	0
CFL Totals—3 Years	45	6	83	13.8	0	23	493	21.4	0
NFL Totals—1 Year	8	4	44	11.0	0	10	224	22.4	0
Pro Totals—4 Years	53	10	127	12.7	0	33	717	21.7	0

Additional pro statistics: Attempted one pass with one completion for 22 yards and a touchdown and recovered two fumbles, 1981; attempted one pass with no completions, 1982.
Played in CFL Championship Game following 1982 and 1983 seasons.

DEAN MARTIN MIRALDI
Offensive Tackle-Guard—Philadelphia Eagles

Born April 8, 1958, at Culver City, Calif.
Height, 6.05. Weight, 285.
High School—Rosemead, Calif.
Attended California State University at Long Beach and University of Utah.

Selected by Philadelphia in 2nd round (55th player selected) of 1981 NFL draft.
On injured reserve with pulled hamstring, September 1 through entire 1981 season.
On inactive list, September 12 and September 19, 1982.
On injured reserve with knee injury, November 19 through December 23, 1982; activated, December 24, 1982.
Philadelphia NFL, 1982 through 1984.
Games: 1982 (1), 1983 (13), 1984 (16). Total—30.

JOHN C. MISKO
Punter—Los Angeles Rams
Born October 1, 1954, at Highland Park, Mich.
Height, 6.05. Weight, 207.
High School—Porterville, Calif.
Attended Porterville Junior College and Oregon State University.

Signed as free agent by Buffalo Bills, June, 1980.
Released by Buffalo Bills, August 26, 1980; claimed on procedural waivers by New York Jets, February 19, 1981.
Released by New York Jets, August 25, 1981; signed as free agent by Los Angeles Rams, March 15, 1982.
Released by Los Angeles Rams, September 6, 1982; re-signed by Rams, September 7, 1982.

		——PUNTING——			
Year Club		G.	No.	Avg.	Blk.
1982—L.A. Rams NFL		9	45	43.6	1
1983—L.A. Rams NFL		16	82	40.3	1
1984—L.A. Rams NFL		16	74	38.7	0
Pro Totals—3 Years		41	201	40.4	2

LEONARD BOYD MITCHELL
Offensive Tackle—Philadelphia Eagles
Born October 12, 1958, at Houston, Tex.
Height, 6.07. Weight, 285.
High School—Houston, Tex., Booker T. Washington.
Attended University of Houston.

Named as defensive tackle on THE SPORTING NEWS College All-America Team, 1980.
Selected by Philadelphia in 1st round (27th player selected) of 1981 NFL draft.
Philadelphia NFL, 1981 through 1984.
Games: 1981 (16), 1982 (9), 1983 (10), 1984 (16). Total—51.

LYVONIA ALBERT MITCHELL
(Stump)
Running Back—St. Louis Cardinals
Born March 15, 1959, at St. Mary's, Ga.
Height, 5.09. Weight, 188.
High School—St. Mary's, Ga., Camden County.
Attended The Citadel.

Established NFL record for most yards, combined kick returns, season (1,737), 1981.
Selected by St. Louis in 9th round (226th player selected) of 1981 NFL draft.

		——RUSHING——				PASS RECEIVING				—TOTAL—		
Year Club		G.	Att.	Yds.	Avg.	TD.	P.C.	Yds.	Avg.	TD.	TD.	Pts.	F.
1981—St. Louis NFL		16	31	175	5.6	0	6	35	5.8	1	2	12	3
1982—St. Louis NFL		9	39	189	4.8	1	11	149	13.5	0	1	6	3
1983—St. Louis NFL		15	68	373	5.5	3	7	54	7.7	0	3	18	5
1984—St. Louis NFL		16	81	434	5.4	9	26	318	12.2	2	11	66	6
Pro Totals—4 Years		56	219	1171	5.3	13	50	556	11.1	3	17	102	17

		—PUNT RETURNS—				—KICKOFF RET.—			
Year Club		G.	No.	Yds.	Avg.	TD.	No.	Yds.	Avg.	TD.
1981—St. Louis NFL		16	42	445	10.6	1	55	*1292	23.5	0
1982—St. Louis NFL		9	27	165	6.1	0	16	364	22.8	0
1983—St. Louis NFL		15	38	337	8.9	0	36	778	21.6	0
1984—St. Louis NFL		16	38	333	8.8	0	35	804	23.0	0
Pro Totals—4 Years		56	145	1280	8.8	1	142	3238	22.8	0

Additional pro statistics: Recovered one fumble, 1982 and 1983; recovered two fumbles and attempted one pass with one completion for 20 yards, 1984.

ART MONK
Wide Receiver—Washington Redskins
Born December 5, 1957, at White Plains, N.Y.
Height, 6.03. Weight, 209.
High School—White Plains, N.Y.
Attended Syracuse University.

Established NFL record for most pass receptions, season (106), 1984.
Named to THE SPORTING NEWS NFL All-Star Team, 1984.
Selected by Washington in 1st round (18th player selected) of 1980 NFL draft.
On injured reserve with broken foot, January 7, 1983 through remainder of 1982 season playoffs.
On injured reserve with knee injury, September 2 through September 29, 1983; activated, September 30, 1983.

		——RUSHING——				PASS RECEIVING				—TOTAL—		
Year Club		G.	Att.	Yds.	Avg.	TD.	P.C.	Yds.	Avg.	TD.	TD.	Pts.	F.
1980—Washington NFL		16		None			58	797	13.7	3	3	18	0
1981—Washington NFL		16	1	—5	—5.0	0	56	894	16.0	6	6	36	0
1982—Washington NFL		9	7	21	3.0	0	35	447	12.8	1	1	6	3
1983—Washington NFL		12	3	—19	—6.3	0	47	746	15.9	5	5	30	0
1984—Washington NFL		16	2	18	9.0	0	*106	1372	12.9	7	7	42	0
Pro Totals—5 Years		69	13	15	1.2	0	302	4256	14.1	22	22	132	3

Additional pro statistics: Returned one kickoff for 10 yards, 1980; attempted one pass with one completion for 46 yards, 1983; fumbled once, 1984.

Played in NFC Championship Game following 1983 season.
Played in NFL Championship Game following 1983 season.
Played in Pro Bowl (NFL All-Star Game) following 1984 season.

CARL MONROE
Running Back-Kick Returner—San Francisco 49ers
Born February 20, 1960, at Pittsburgh, Pa.
Height, 5.08. Weight, 166.
High School—San Jose, Calif., William C. Overfelt.
Attended Gavilan College and University of Utah.

Selected by Philadelphia in 23rd round (272nd player selected) of 1983 USFL draft.
Signed as free agent by San Francisco 49ers, April 28, 1983.
Released by San Francisco 49ers, August 29, 1983; re-signed by 49ers, September 1, 1983.
On injured reserve with broken foot, October 4 through December 29, 1983; activated, December 30, 1983.

		—RUSHING—				PASS RECEIVING				—TOTAL—		
Year Club	G.	Att.	Yds.	Avg.	TD.	P.C.	Yds.	Avg.	TD.	TD.	Pts.	F.
1983—San Francisco NFL	5	10	23	2.3	0	2	61	30.5	0	0	0	0
1984—San Francisco NFL	16	3	13	4.3	0	11	139	12.6	1	1	6	2
Pro Totals—2 Years	21	13	36	2.8	0	13	200	15.4	1	1	6	2

		KICKOFF RETURNS		
Year Club	G.	No.	Yds.	Avg. TD.
1983—San Francisco NFL	5	8	152	19.0 0
1984—San Francisco NFL	16	27	561	20.8 0
Pro Totals—2 Years	21	35	713	20.4 0

Played in NFC Championship Game following 1983 and 1984 seasons.
Played in NFL Championship Game following 1984 season.

JOSEPH C. MONTANA
(Joe)
Quarterback—San Francisco 49ers
Born June 11, 1956, at Monongahela, Pa.
Height, 6.02. Weight, 195.
High School—Monongahela, Pa., Ringgold.
Received bachelor of business administration degree in marketing from
University of Notre Dame in 1978.

Established NFL records for highest passer rating, career (92.7); highest completion percentage, career (63.7); lowest interception percentage, career (2.60); most consecutive 300-yard games, season (5), 1982.
Selected by San Francisco in 3rd round (82nd player selected) of 1979 NFL draft.

		—PASSING—							—RUSHING—				—TOTAL—		
Year Club	G.	Att.	Cmp.	Pct.	Gain	T.P.	P.I.	Avg.	Att.	Yds.	Avg.	TD.	TD.	Pts.	F.
1979—San Francisco NFL	16	23	13	56.5	96	1	0	4.17	3	22	7.3	0	0	0	1
1980—San Francisco NFL	15	273	176	*64.5	1795	15	9	6.58	32	77	2.4	2	2	12	4
1981—San Francisco NFL	16	488	311	*63.7	3565	19	12	7.31	25	95	3.8	2	2	12	2
1982—San Francisco NFL	9	*346	213	61.6	2613	*17	11	7.55	30	118	3.9	1	1	6	4
1983—San Francisco NFL	16	515	332	64.5	3910	26	12	7.59	61	284	4.7	2	2	12	3
1984—San Francisco NFL	16	432	279	64.6	3630	28	10	8.40	39	118	3.0	2	2	12	4
Pro Totals—6 Years	88	2077	1324	63.7	15609	106	54	7.52	190	714	3.8	9	9	54	18

Quarterback Rating Points: 1979 (80.9), 1980 (87.8), 1981 (88.2), 1982 (87.9), 1983 (94.6), 1984 (102.9). Total—92.7.
Additional pro statistics: Recovered one fumble, 1979 and 1980; recovered two fumbles and fumbled four times for minus two yards, 1982; recovered two fumbles and fumbled four times for minus three yards, 1984.
Played in NFC Championship Game following 1981, 1983 and 1984 seasons.
Played in NFL Championship Game following 1981 and 1984 seasons.
Played in Pro Bowl (NFL All-Star Game) following 1981, 1983 and 1984 seasons.

BLANCHARD MONTGOMERY III
Linebacker—San Francisco 49ers
Born February 17, 1961, at Los Angeles, Calif.
Height, 6.02. Weight, 236.
High School—Granada Hills, Calif.
Attended University of California at Los Angeles.

Selected by Arizona in 5th round (52nd player selected) of 1983 USFL draft.
Selected by San Francisco in 3rd round (59th player selected) of 1983 NFL draft.
Signed by San Francisco 49ers, May 17, 1983.
On injured reserve with neck injury, November 17 through remainder of 1983 season.
San Francisco NFL, 1983 and 1984.
Games: 1983 (11), 1984 (16). Total—27.
Pro statistics: Recovered one fumble, 1984.
Played in NFC Championship Game following 1984 season.
Played in NFL Championship Game following 1984 season.

CLEOTHA MONTGOMERY
(Cle)
Wide Receiver—Los Angeles Raiders
Born July 1, 1956, at Greenville, Miss.
Height, 5.08. Weight, 180.
High School—Greenville, Miss.
Attended Abilene Christian University.
Brother of Wilbert Montgomery, running back with Philadelphia Eagles.

Signed as free agent by Washington Redskins, May, 1978.
Released by Washington Redskins, July 17, 1978; signed as free agent by Denver Broncos, May, 1980.
Released by Denver Broncos, August 26, 1980; signed as free agent by Cincinnati Bengals, September 19, 1980.
Released by Cincinnati Bengals, September 1, 1981; signed as free agent by Cleveland Browns, September 10, 1981.
Released by Cleveland Browns, October 9, 1981; signed as free agent by Oakland Raiders, December 16, 1981.
Franchise transferred to Los Angeles, May 7, 1982.
Released by Los Angeles Raiders, September 6, 1982; re-signed by Raiders, September 7, 1982.

		-PUNT RETURNS-				—KICKOFF RET.—				—TOTAL—		
Year Club	G.	No.	Yds.	Avg.	TD.	No.	Yds.	Avg.	TD.	TD.	Pts.	F.
1980—Cincinnati NFL	14	31	223	7.2	0	44	843	19.2	0	0	0	3
1981—Cleveland (4)-Oakland (1) NFL	5	17	121	7.1	0	17	382	22.5	0	0	0	2
1982—Los Angeles Raiders NFL	9		None			17	312	18.4	0	0	0	0
1983—Los Angeles Raiders NFL	14		None			21	464	22.1	0	0	0	1
1984—Los Angeles Raiders NFL	16	14	194	13.9	1	26	555	21.3	0	1	6	1
Pro Totals—5 Years	58	62	538	8.7	1	125	2556	20.4	0	1	6	7

Additional pro statistics: Rushed once for 12 yards and recovered two fumbles, 1980; recovered one fumble, 1981 and 1984; recovered two fumbles, 1982; rushed twice for seven yards and caught two passes for 29 yards, 1983; rushed once for one yard, 1984.

Played in AFC Championship Game following 1983 season.
Played in NFL Championship Game following 1983 season.

WILBERT MONTGOMERY
Running Back—Philadelphia Eagles
Born September 16, 1954, at Greenville, Miss.
Height, 5.10. Weight, 195.
High School—Greenville, Miss.
Attended Jackson State University and Abilene Christian University.
Brother of Cle Montgomery, wide receiver with Los Angeles Raiders.

Selected by Philadelphia in 6th round (154th player selected) of 1977 NFL draft.

		——RUSHING——				PASS RECEIVING				—TOTAL—		
Year Club	G.	Att.	Yds.	Avg.	TD.	P.C.	Yds.	Avg.	TD.	TD.	Pts.	F.
1977—Philadelphia NFL	14	45	183	4.1	2	3	18	6.0	0	3	18	4
1978—Philadelphia NFL	14	259	1220	4.7	9	34	195	5.7	1	10	60	6
1979—Philadelphia NFL	16	338	1512	4.5	9	41	494	12.0	5	14	84*14
1980—Philadelphia NFL	12	193	778	4.0	8	50	407	8.1	2	10	60	3
1981—Philadelphia NFL	15	286	1402	4.9	8	49	521	10.6	2	10	60	6
1982—Philadelphia NFL	8	114	515	4.5	7	20	258	12.9	2	9	54	3
1983—Philadelphia NFL	5	29	139	4.8	0	9	53	5.9	0	0	0	1
1984—Philadelphia NFL	16	201	789	3.9	2	60	501	8.4	0	2	12	5
Pro Totals—8 Years	100	1465	6538	4.5	45	266	2447	9.2	12	58	348	42

		KICKOFF RETURNS						KICKOFF RETURNS			
Year Club	G.	No.	Yds.	Avg.TD.		Year Club	G.	No.	Yds.	Avg.TD.	
1977—Philadelphia NFL	14	23	619	*26.9 1		1982—Philadelphia NFL	8	1	12	12.0 0	
1978—Philadelphia NFL	14	6	154	25.7 0		1983—Philadelphia NFL	5		None		
1979—Philadelphia NFL	16	1	6	6.0 0		1984—Philadelphia NFL	16		None		
1980—Philadelphia NFL	12	1	23	23.0 0		Pro Totals—8 Years	100	32	814	25.4 1	
1981—Philadelphia NFL	15		None								

Additional pro statistics: Recovered two fumbles, 1979, 1981 and 1982; recovered one fumble, 1980 and 1984; attempted one pass with no completions, 1980; attempted two passes with no completions, 1984.
Played in NFC Championship Game following 1980 season.
Played in NFL Championship Game following 1980 season.
Played in Pro Bowl (NFL All-Star Game) following 1978 and 1979 seasons.

MAX MONTOYA JR.
Guard—Cincinnati Bengals
Born May 12, 1956, at Montebello, Calif.
Height, 6.05. Weight, 275.
High School—La Puente, Calif.
Attended Mt. San Jacinto Junior College and University of California at Los Angeles.

Selected by Cincinnati in 7th round (168th player selected) of 1979 NFL draft.
Cincinnati NFL, 1979 through 1984.
Games: 1979 (11), 1980 (16), 1981 (16), 1982 (9), 1983 (16), 1984 (16). Total—84.
Pro statistics: Recovered one fumble, 1981.
Played in AFC Championship Game following 1981 season.
Played in NFL Championship Game following 1981 season.

WARREN MOON
Quarterback—Houston Oilers
Born November 18, 1956, at Los Angeles, Calif.
Height, 6.03. Weight, 210.
High School—Los Angeles, Calif., Hamilton.
Attended University of Washington.

Tied NFL record for most fumbles, season (17), 1984.
Signed as free agent by Edmonton Eskimos, March, 1978.
USFL rights traded by Memphis Showboats to Los Angeles Express for future draft pick, August 30, 1983.
Granted free agency, March 1, 1984; signed by Houston Oilers, March 1, 1984.

| | | | | | PASSING | | | | | RUSHING | | | | TOTAL | |
Year	Club	G.	Att.	Cmp.	Pct.	Gain	T.P.	P.I.	Avg.	Att.	Yds.	Avg.	TD.	TD.	Pts.	F.
1978—Edmonton CFL		15	173	89	51.4	1112	5	7	6.43	30	114	3.8	1	1	6	1
1979—Edmonton CFL		16	274	149	54.4	2382	20	12	8.69	56	150	2.7	2	2	12	1
1980—Edmonton CFL		16	331	181	54.7	3127	25	11	9.45	55	352	6.4	3	3	18	0
1981—Edmonton CFL		15	378	237	62.7	3959	27	12	10.47	50	298	6.0	3	3	18	1
1982—Edmonton CFL		16	562	333	59.3	5000	36	16	8.90	54	259	4.8	4	4	24	1
1983—Edmonton CFL		16	664	380	57.2	5648	31	19	8.51	85	527	6.2	3	3	18	7
1984—Houston NFL		16	450	259	57.6	3338	12	14	7.42	58	211	3.6	1	1	6	*17
CFL Totals—6 Years		94	2382	1369	57.5	21228	144	77	8.91	330	1700	5.2	16	16	96	11
NFL Totals—1 Year		16	450	259	57.6	3338	12	14	7.42	58	211	3.6	1	1	6	17
Pro Totals—7 Years		110	2832	1628	57.5	24566	156	91	8.67	388	1911	4.9	17	17	102	28

Quarterback Rating Points: 1984 (76.9).
Additional CFL statistics: Recovered one fumble, 1982.
Additional NFL statistics: Recovered seven fumbles and fumbled 17 times for minus one yard, 1984.
Played in CFL Championship Game following 1978 through 1982 seasons.

ALVIN MOORE
Running Back—Indianapolis Colts
Born May 3, 1959, at Randolph , Ariz.
Height, 6.00. Weight, 194.
High School—Coolidge, Ariz.
Attended Arizona State University.
Related to Lee Roy Selmon, defensive end with Tampa Bay Buccaneers; and Dewey Selmon,
linebacker with Tampa Bay Buccaneers and San Diego Chargers, 1976 through 1982.

Selected by Arizona in 1983 USFL territorial draft.
Selected by Baltimore in 7th round (169th player selected) of 1983 NFL draft.
Signed by Baltimore Colts, May 22, 1983.
Franchise transferred to Indianapolis, March 31, 1984.

| | | | | RUSHING | | | PASS RECEIVING | | | | TOTAL | |
Year	Club	G.	Att.	Yds.	Avg.	TD.	P.C.	Yds.	Avg.	TD.	TD.	Pts.	F.
1983—Baltimore NFL		15	57	205	3.6	1	6	38	6.3	0	1	6	0
1984—Indianapolis NFL		13	38	127	3.3	2	9	52	5.8	0	2	12	3
Pro Totals—2 Years		28	95	332	3.5	3	15	90	6.0	0	3	18	3

Additional pro statistics: Returned two kickoffs for 40 yards, 1983; attempted one pass with no completions and returned two kickoffs for 19 yards, 1984.

BOOKER THOMAS MOORE
Fullback—Buffalo Bills
Born June 23, 1959, at Flint, Mich.
Height, 5.11. Weight, 224.
High School—Flint, Mich., Southwestern.
Attended Pennsylvania State University.

Selected by Buffalo in 1st round (28th player selected) of 1981 NFL draft.
On non-football injury list with Guillian Barre syndrome, August 18 through entire 1981 season.

| | | | | RUSHING | | | PASS RECEIVING | | | | TOTAL | |
Year	Club	G.	Att.	Yds.	Avg.	TD.	P.C.	Yds.	Avg.	TD.	TD.	Pts.	F.
1982—Buffalo NFL		5	16	38	2.4	0	1	8	8.0	0	0	0	2
1983—Buffalo NFL		15	60	275	4.6	0	34	199	5.9	1	1	6	1
1984—Buffalo NFL		15	24	84	3.5	0	33	172	5.2	0	0	0	4
Pro Totals—3 Years		35	100	397	4.0	0	68	379	5.6	1	1	6	7

Additional pro statistics: Recovered one fumble, 1983 and 1984.

DERLAND PAUL MOORE
Nose Tackle—New Orleans Saints
Born October 7, 1951, at Malden, Mo.
Height, 6.04. Weight, 273.
High School—Poplar Bluff, Mo.
Attended University of Oklahoma.

Selected by New Orleans in 2nd round (29th player selected) of 1973 NFL draft.
On injured reserve with knee injury, November 29 through remainder of 1977 season.
On injured reserve with knee and ankle injuries, November 27 through remainder of 1984 season.
New Orleans NFL, 1973 through 1984.

Games: 1973 (13), 1974 (14), 1975 (14), 1976 (14), 1977 (10), 1978 (15), 1979 (15), 1980 (16), 1981 (16), 1982 (9), 1983 (16), 1984 (12). Total—164.

Pro statistics: Recovered one fumble, 1973, 1980, 1981 and 1982; intercepted one pass for no yards and returned one kickoff for 14 yards, 1973; recovered two fumbles, 1977; recovered one fumble for six yards, 1978.

E. BLAKE MOORE
(Known by middle name.)
Center-Guard—Green Bay Packers
Born May 18, 1958, at Durham, N.C.
Height, 6.05. Weight, 272.
High School—Chattanooga, Tenn., Baylor.
Received bachelor of arts degree from The College of Wooster in 1980.

Signed as free agent by Cincinnati Bengals, May 1, 1980.
Released by Cincinnati Bengals, August 27, 1984; signed as free agent by Green Bay Packers, September 18, 1984.
Cincinnati NFL, 1980 through 1983; Green Bay NFL, 1984.
Games: 1980 (16), 1981 (14), 1982 (4), 1983 (16), 1984 (11). Total—61.
Pro statistics: Caught one pass for three yards and a touchdown, 1984.
Played in AFC Championship Game following 1981 season.
Played in NFL Championship Game following 1981 season.

JEFFERY D. MOORE
(Jeff)
Running Back—Washington Redskins
Born August 20, 1956, at Kosciusko, Miss.
Height, 6.00. Weight, 196.
High School—Kosciusko, Miss.
Attended Jackson State University.

Selected by Seattle in 12th round (319th player selected) of 1979 NFL draft.
Released by Seattle Seahawks, September 15, 1981; signed as free agent by San Francisco 49ers, April 27, 1982.
Released by San Francisco 49ers, August 26, 1984; signed as free agent by Washington Redskins, October 17, 1984.
On injured reserve with hamstring injury, December 29 through remainder of 1984 season.

| | | —RUSHING— | | | | PASS RECEIVING | | | | —TOTAL— | | |
Year Club	G.	Att.	Yds.	Avg.	TD.	P.C.	Yds.	Avg.	TD.	TD.	Pts.	F.
1979—Seattle NFL	16	44	168	3.8	2	14	128	9.1	0	2	12	5
1980—Seattle NFL	14	60	202	3.4	0	25	231	9.2	0	0	0	4
1981—Seattle NFL	2	1	15	15.0	0	3	18	6.0	0	0	0	0
1982—San Francisco NFL	9	85	281	3.3	4	37	405	10.9	4	8	48	4
1983—San Francisco NFL	15	15	43	2.9	1	19	206	10.8	0	1	6	0
1984—Washington NFL	7	3	13	4.3	0	17	115	6.8	2	2	12	1
Pro Totals—6 Years	63	208	722	3.5	7	115	1103	9.6	6	13	78	14

| | | —PUNT RETURNS— | | | | —KICKOFF RET.— | | |
Year Club	G.	No.	Yds.	Avg.	TD.	No.	Yds.	Avg.	TD.
1979—Seattle NFL	16	10	90	9.0	0	31	641	20.7	0
1980—Seattle NFL	14		None			1	11	11.0	0
1981—Seattle NFL	2		None				None		
1982—San Francisco NFL	9		None			1	15	15.0	0
1983—San Francisco NFL	15		None			7	117	16.7	0
1984—Washington NFL	7		None				None		
Pro Totals—6 Years	63	10	90	9.0	0	40	784	19.6	0

Additional pro statistics: Recovered one fumble, 1979; recovered two fumbles, 1980.
Played in NFC Championship Game following 1983 season.

MALCOLM G. MOORE
Wide Receiver—Dallas Cowboys
Born June 24, 1961, at San Fernando, Calif.
Height, 6.05. Weight, 205.
High School—San Fernando, Calif.
Attended University of Southern California.

Selected by Los Angeles in 1984 USFL territorial draft.
Signed by Los Angeles Express, January 19, 1984.
Selected by Dallas in 2nd round (54th player selected) of 1984 NFL supplemental draft.
Released by Los Angeles Express, February 11, 1985; signed by Dallas Cowboys, March 20, 1985.

| | —PASS RECEIVING— | | | |
Year Club	G.	P.C.	Yds.	Avg.	TD.
1984—Los Angeles USFL	17	31	354	11.4	0

Additional pro statistics: Fumbled once, 1984.

NATHANIEL MOORE
(Nat)
Wide Receiver—Miami Dolphins
Born September 19, 1951, at Tallahassee, Fla.
Height, 5.09. Weight, 188.
High School—Miami, Fla., Edison.
Attended Tennessee-Martin College, Miami-Dade (South) Community College and University of Florida.
Cousin of Ken Johnson, running back with New York Giants, 1979.

Named to THE SPORTING NEWS AFC All-Star Team, 1977.
Selected by Jacksonville Sharks in 5th round of 1974 WFL draft.
Selected by Miami in 3rd round (78th player selected) of 1974 NFL draft.
On physically unable to perform/active with knee injury, July 30 through August 23, 1982; activated, August 24, 1982.

Year Club	G.	—RUSHING—				PASS RECEIVING				—TOTAL—		
		Att.	Yds.	Avg.	TD.	P.C.	Yds.	Avg.	TD.	TD.	Pts.	F.
1974—Miami NFL	13	3	16	5.3	0	37	605	16.4	2	2	12	1
1975—Miami NFL	14	8	69	8.6	0	40	705	17.6	4	4	24	1
1976—Miami NFL	9	4	36	9.0	0	33	625	18.9	4	4	24	1
1977—Miami NFL	14	14	89	6.4	1	52	765	14.7	*12	*13	78	0
1978—Miami NFL	16	4	−3	−0.8	0	48	645	13.4	10	10	60	1
1979—Miami NFL	16	3	22	7.3	0	48	840	17.5	6	6	36	1
1980—Miami NFL	16	1	3	3.0	0	47	564	12.0	7	7	42	1
1981—Miami NFL	13	1	3	3.0	0	26	452	17.4	2	2	12	0
1982—Miami NFL	9		None			8	82	10.3	1	1	6	0
1983—Miami NFL	16		None			39	558	14.3	6	6	36	1
1984—Miami NFL	16	1	3	3.0	0	43	573	13.3	6	6	36	2
Pro Totals—11 Years	152	39	238	6.1	1	421	6414	15.2	60	61	366	9

Year Club	G.	—PUNT RETURNS—				—KICKOFF RET.—			
		No.	Yds.	Avg.	TD.	No.	Yds.	Avg.	TD.
1974—Miami NFL	13	9	136	15.1	0	22	587	26.7	0
1975—Miami NFL	14	8	80	10.0	0	9	243	27.0	0
1976—Miami NFL	9	8	72	9.0	0	2	28	14.0	0
1977—Miami NFL	14		None				None		
1978—Miami NFL	16	1	11	11.0	0		None		
1979—Miami NFL	16		None				None		
1980—Miami NFL	16		None				None		
1981—Miami NFL	13		None				None		
1982—Miami NFL	9		None				None		
1983—Miami NFL	16		None				None		
1984—Miami NFL	16		None				None		
Pro Totals—11 Years	152	26	299	11.5	0	33	858	26.0	0

Additional pro statistics: Completed one pass for 31 yards, 1974; recovered one fumble, 1974, 1975, 1977 and 1980; attempted one pass with no completions, 1980.
Played in AFC Championship Game following 1982 and 1984 seasons.
Played in NFL Championship Game following 1982 and 1984 seasons.
Played in Pro Bowl (NFL All-Star Game) following 1977 season.

STEPHEN ELLIOTT MOORE
(Steve)
Offensive Tackle—New England Patriots
Born October 1, 1960, at Memphis, Tenn.
Height, 6.04. Weight, 285.
High School—Memphis, Tenn., Fairley.
Attended Tennessee State University.
Brother of Jeffrey B. Moore, wide receiver with Los Angeles Rams, 1980 and 1981.

Selected by Birmingham in 4th round (37th player selected) of 1983 USFL draft.
Selected by New England in 3rd round (80th player selected) of 1983 NFL draft.
Signed by New England Patriots, May 25, 1983.
New England NFL, 1983 and 1984.
Games: 1983 (4), 1984 (16). Total—20.

EMERY MATTHEW MOOREHEAD
Wide Receiver—Chicago Bears
Born March 22, 1954, at Evanston, Ill.
Height, 6.02. Weight, 225.
High School—Evanston, Ill.
Received bachelor of arts degree in communications from University of Colorado in 1977.

Selected by New York Giants in 6th round (153rd player selected) of 1977 NFL draft.
On injured reserve with bruised kidney, November 27 through remainder of 1979 season.
Traded by New York Giants to Denver Broncos for 8th round pick in 1981 draft, May 23, 1980.
Released by Denver Broncos, September 1, 1980; re-signed by Broncos, September 2, 1980.
Released by Denver Broncos, August 3, 1981; claimed on waivers by Chicago Bears, August 4, 1981.
Released by Chicago Bears, August 29, 1981; re-signed by Bears after clearing procedural waivers, October 21, 1981.

Year Club	G.	—RUSHING—				PASS RECEIVING				—TOTAL—		
		Att.	Yds.	Avg.	TD.	P.C.	Yds.	Avg.	TD.	TD.	Pts.	F.
1977—New York Giants NFL	13	1	5	5.0	0	12	143	11.9	1	1	6	0
1978—New York Giants NFL	10		None			3	45	15.0	0	0	0	0
1979—New York Giants NFL	13	36	95	2.6	0	9	62	6.9	0	0	0	0
1980—Denver NFL	16	2	7	3.5	0		None			0	0	0
1981—Chicago NFL	9		None				None			0	0	0
1982—Chicago NFL	9	2	3	1.5	0	30	363	12.1	5	5	30	0
1983—Chicago NFL	16	5	6	1.2	0	42	597	14.2	3	3	18	0
1984—Chicago NFL	16	1	−2	−2.0	0	29	497	17.1	1	1	6	0
Pro Totals—8 Years	102	47	114	2.4	0	125	1707	13.7	10	10	60	0

Additional pro statistics: Returned four punts for 65 yards (16.3 average), 1977; returned two punts for 52 yards (26.0 average), 1978; returned one kickoff for 16 yards, 1979; returned one kickoff for 18 yards, 1980; returned 23 kickoffs for 476 yards (20.7 average), 1981.
Played in NFC Championship Game following 1984 season.

ERIC MORAN
Offensive Tackle—Houston Oilers
Born June 10, 1960, at Spokane, Wash.
Height, 6.05. Weight, 280.
High School—Pleasanton, Calif., Foothill.
Attended University of Washington.
Son of Jim Moran, defensive tackle with New York Giants, 1964 through 1967;
and brother of Rich Moran, rookie guard with Green Bay Packers.

Selected by Oakland in 16th round (186th player selected) of 1983 USFL draft.
Selected by Dallas in 10th round (273rd player selected) of 1983 NFL draft.
USFL rights traded by Oakland Invaders to Los Angeles Express for rights to defensive tackle Brian Douglas and linebacker Randy McClanahan, May 2, 1983.
Signed by Los Angeles Express, June 9, 1983.
Released injured by Los Angeles Express, February 15, 1984; signed by Dallas Cowboys, April 27, 1984.
Released by Dallas Cowboys, August 27, 1984; signed as free agent by Houston Oilers, September 5, 1984.
Los Angeles USFL, 1983; Houston NFL, 1984.
Games: 1983 (3), 1984 (8). Total—11.

MICHAEL KARL MORGAN
(Known by middle name.)
Nose Tackle—Tampa Bay Buccaneers
Born February 23, 1961, at Houma, La.
Height, 6.01. Weight, 255.
High School—Houma, La., Vandebilt Catholic.
Attended University of California at Los Angeles.

Selected by Arizona in 21st round (242nd player selected) of 1983 USFL draft.
Signed as free agent by Saskatchewan Roughriders, May 2, 1983.
Released by Saskatchewan Roughriders, June 26, 1984; signed as free agent by Tampa Bay Buccaneers, July 10, 1984.
Released by Tampa Bay Buccaneers, August 27, 1984; re-signed by Buccaneers, September 5, 1984.
Released by Tampa Bay Buccaneers, October 19, 1984; re-signed by Buccaneers, October 26, 1984.
Saskatchewan CFL, 1983; Tampa Bay NFL, 1984.
Games: 1983 (16), 1984 (13). Total—29.
Pro statistics: Recovered one fumble, 1983.

STANLEY DOUGLAS MORGAN
Wide Receiver—New England Patriots
Born February 17, 1955, at Easley, S. C.
Height, 5.11. Weight, 181.
High School—Easley, S. C.
Received bachelor of science degree in education from University of Tennessee in 1979.

Selected by New England in 1st round (25th player selected) of 1977 NFL draft.

Year Club	G.	Att.	Yds.	Avg.	TD.	P.C.	Yds.	Avg.	TD.	TD.	Pts.	F.
		RUSHING				PASS RECEIVING				TOTAL		
1977—New England NFL	14	1	10	10.0	0	21	443	*21.1	3	3	18	0
1978—New England NFL	16	2	11	5.5	0	34	820	24.1	5	5	30	6
1979—New England NFL	16	7	39	5.6	0	44	1002	*22.8	*12	13	78	1
1980—New England NFL	16	4	36	9.0	0	45	991	*22.0	6	6	36	0
1981—New England NFL	13	2	21	10.5	0	44	1029	*23.4	6	6	36	2
1982—New England NFL	9	2	3	1.5	0	28	584	20.9	3	3	18	0
1983—New England NFL	16	1	13	13.0	0	58	863	14.9	2	2	12	5
1984—New England NFL	13			None		38	709	18.7	5	5	30	0
Pro Totals—8 Years	113	19	133	7.0	0	312	6441	20.6	42	43	258	14

Year Club	G.	No.	Yds.	Avg.	TD.
		PUNT RETURNS			
1977—New England NFL	14	16	220	13.8	0
1978—New England NFL	16	32	335	10.5	0
1979—New England NFL	16	29	289	10.0	1
1980—New England NFL	16		None		
1981—New England NFL	13	15	116	7.7	0
1982—New England NFL	9		None		
1983—New England NFL	16		None		
1984—New England NFL	13		None		
Pro Totals—8 Years	113	92	960	10.4	1

Additional pro statistics: Returned one kickoff for 17 yards, 1978; returned one kickoff for 12 yards, 1979; recovered one fumble for three yards, 1980; recovered two fumbles, 1981 and 1983.
Played in Pro Bowl (NFL All-Star Game) following 1979 and 1980 seasons.

LARRY MORIARTY
Running Back—Houston Oilers
Born April 24, 1958, at Santa Barbara, Calif.
Height, 6.01. Weight, 228.
High School—Santa Barbara, Calif., Dos Pueblos.
Attended Santa Barbara City Junior College and University of Notre Dame.
Cousin of Pat Moriarty, running back with Cleveland Browns, 1979; and Tom Moriarty,
safety with Atlanta Falcons, Pittsburgh Steelers, Michigan Panthers and
Pittsburgh Maulers, 1977 through 1981, 1983 and 1984.

Selected by Chicago in 1983 USFL territorial draft.
Selected by Houston in 5th round (114th player selected) of 1983 NFL draft.
Signed by Houston Oilers, July 14, 1983.

		—RUSHING—				PASS RECEIVING				—TOTAL—		
Year Club	G.	Att.	Yds.	Avg.	TD.	P.C.	Yds.	Avg.	TD.	TD.	Pts.	F.
1983—Houston NFL	16	65	321	4.9	3	4	32	8.0	0	3	18	1
1984—Houston NFL	14	189	785	4.2	6	31	206	6.6	1	7	42	5
Pro Totals—2 Years	30	254	1106	4.4	9	35	238	6.8	1	10	60	6

Additional pro statistics: Returned two kickoffs for 25 yards and recovered one fumble, 1983; attempted one pass with one completion for 16 yards and recovered two fumbles, 1984.

MICHAEL HENRY MOROSKI
(Mike)
Quarterback—Atlanta Falcons
Born September 4, 1957, at Bakersfield, Calif.
Height, 6.04. Weight, 200.
High School—Novato, Calif.
Received bachelor of arts degree in agricultural economics from University of California at Davis.

Selected by Atlanta in 6th round (154th player selected) of 1979 draft.
On injured reserve with broken collarbone, September 14 through December 18, 1981; activated, December 19, 1981.
USFL rights traded by Los Angeles Express to Denver Gold for rights to wide receiver Billy Waddy, January 21, 1984.

		—————PASSING—————							—RUSHING—				—TOTAL—		
Year Club	G.	Att.	Cmp.	Pct.	Gain	T.P.	P.I.	Avg.	Att.	Yds.	Avg.	TD.	TD.	Pts.	F.
1979—Atlanta NFL	2	15	8	53.3	97	0	0	6.47	3	31	10.3	1	1	6	1
1980—Atlanta NFL	3	3	2	66.7	24	0	0	8.00		None			0	0	0
1981—Atlanta NFL	3	26	12	46.2	132	0	1	5.08	3	17	5.7	0	0	0	0
1982—Atlanta NFL	9	13	10	76.9	87	1	0	6.69		None			0	0	0
1983—Atlanta NFL	16	70	45	64.3	575	2	4	8.21	2	12	6.0	0	0	0	2
1984—Atlanta NFL	16	191	102	53.4	1207	2	9	6.32	21	98	4.7	0	0	0	6
Pro Totals—6 Years	49	318	179	56.3	2122	5	14	6.67	29	158	5.4	1	1	6	9

Quarterback Rating Points: 1979 (73.5), 1980 (91.0), 1981 (45.9), 1982 (119.7), 1983 (75.6), 1984 (56.8). Total—63.8.
Additional pro statistics: Recovered two fumbles, 1984.

JOE MORRIS
Running Back—New York Giants
Born September 15, 1960, at Fort Bragg, N.C.
Height, 5.07. Weight, 195.
High Schools—Southern Pines, N.C. and Ayer, Mass.
Attended Syracuse University.
Brother of Jamie Morris, wide receiver at University of Michigan.

Selected by New York Giants in 2nd round (45th player selected) of 1982 NFL draft.

		—RUSHING—				PASS RECEIVING				—TOTAL—		
Year Club	G.	Att.	Yds.	Avg.	TD.	P.C.	Yds.	Avg.	TD.	TD.	Pts.	F.
1982—New York Giants NFL	5	15	48	3.2	1	8	34	4.3	0	1	6	1
1983—New York Giants NFL	15	35	145	4.1	0	2	1	0.5	1	1	6	2
1984—New York Giants NFL	16	133	510	3.8	4	12	124	10.3	0	4	24	1
Pro Totals—3 Years	36	183	703	3.8	5	22	159	7.2	1	6	36	4

		KICKOFF RETURNS		
Year Club	G.	No.	Yds.	Avg.TD.
1982—New York Giants NFL	5		None	
1983—New York Giants NFL	15	14	255	18.2 0
1984—New York Giants NFL	16	6	69	11.5 0
Pro Totals—3 Years	36	20	324	16.2 0

Additional pro statistics: Recovered one fumble, 1982 and 1983.

RANDALL MORRIS
Running Back—Seattle Seahawks
Born April 22, 1961, at Anniston, Ala.
Height, 6.00. Weight, 190.
High School—Long Beach, Calif., Polytechnic.
Attended University of Tennessee.
Brother of Thomas Morris, safety with Detroit Lions.

Selected by Memphis in 1984 USFL territorial draft.
Selected by Seattle in 10th round (270th player selected) of 1984 NFL draft.
Signed by Seattle Seahawks, May 18, 1984.
On injured reserve with neck injury, August 28 through September 27, 1984; activated, September 28, 1984.

Year Club		G.	Att.	Yds.	—RUSHING— Avg.	TD.	P.C.	Yds.	PASS RECEIVING Avg.	TD.	TD.	—TOTAL— Pts.	F.
1984—Seattle NFL		10	58	189	3.3	0	9	61	6.8	0	0	0	2

Year Club	G.	No.	KICKOFF RETURNS Yds.	Avg.TD.
1984—Seattle NFL	10	8	153	19.1 0

Additional pro statistics: Recovered one fumble, 1984.

WAYNE LEE MORRIS
Running Back—San Diego Chargers
Born May 3, 1954, at Dallas, Tex.
Height, 6.00. Weight, 210.
High School—Dallas, Tex., South Oak Cliff.
Attended Southern Methodist University.

Selected by St. Louis in 5th round (141st player selected) of 1976 NFL draft.
On injured reserve with knee injury, December 1 through remainder of 1978 season.
On injured reserve with ankle injury, December 17 through remainder of 1983 season.
Placed on did not report list, August 21 through October 3, 1984.
Released by St. Louis Cardinals, October 4, 1984; signed as free agent by San Diego Chargers, October 9, 1984.

Year Club	G.	Att.	Yds.	—RUSHING— Avg.	TD.	P.C.	Yds.	PASS RECEIVING Avg.	TD.	TD.	—TOTAL— Pts.	F.
1976—St. Louis NFL	14	64	292	4.6	3	8	75	9.4	1	4	24	4
1977—St. Louis NFL	12	165	661	4.0	8	24	222	9.3	1	9	54	5
1978—St. Louis NFL	13	174	631	3.6	1	33	298	9.0	1	2	12	1
1979—St. Louis NFL	15	106	387	3.7	8	35	237	6.8	1	9	54	2
1980—St. Louis NFL	16	117	456	3.9	6	15	110	7.3	1	7	42	0
1981—St. Louis NFL	16	109	417	3.8	5	19	165	8.7	0	5	30	0
1982—St. Louis NFL	9	84	274	3.3	2	4	19	4.8	0	4	24	1
1983—St. Louis NFL	15	75	257	3.4	2	14	55	3.9	0	2	12	2
1984—San Diego NFL	10	5	12	2.4	1	5	20	4.0	0	1	6	0
Pro Totals—9 Years	120	899	3387	3.8	38	157	1201	7.6	5	43	258	15

Year Club	G.	No.	KICKOFF RETURNS Yds.	Avg.TD.	Year Club	G.	No.	KICKOFF RETURNS Yds.	Avg.TD.
1976—St. Louis NFL	14	9	181	20.1 0	1981—St. Louis NFL	16		None	
1977—St. Louis NFL	12	2	39	19.5 0	1982—St. Louis NFL	9	1	14	14.0 0
1978—St. Louis NFL	13	3	66	22.0 0	1983—St. Louis NFL	15		None	
1979—St. Louis NFL	15		None		1984—San Diego NFL	10		None	
1980—St. Louis NFL	16		None		Pro Totals—9 Years	120	15	300	20.0 0

Additional pro statistics: Recovered one fumble, 1976, 1979 and 1984.

GUY WALKER MORRISS
Center—New England Patriots
Born May 13, 1951, at Colorado City, Tex.
Height, 6.04. Weight, 270.
High School—Arlington, Tex., Sam Houston.
Received bachelor of science degree in physical education from Texas Christian University in 1973.

Selected by Philadelphia in 2nd round (28th player selected) of 1973 NFL draft.
Released by Philadelphia Eagles, March 5, 1984; signed as free agent by New England Patriots, July 31, 1984.
Philadelphia NFL, 1973 through 1983; New England NFL, 1984.
Games: 1973 (14), 1974 (14), 1975 (14), 1976 (14), 1977 (13), 1978 (16), 1979 (16), 1980 (16), 1981 (16), 1982 (9), 1983 (16), 1984 (16). Total—174.
Pro statistics: Recovered one fumble, 1973; fumbled twice and recovered two fumbles for minus 10 yards, 1974; fumbled twice and recovered one fumble, 1975; fumbled once, 1977 and 1983; fumbled twice for minus eight yards, 1981.
Played in NFC Championship Game following 1980 season.
Played in NFL Championship Game following 1980 season.

MICHAEL DA'MOND MORTON
Kick Returner-Running Back—Tampa Bay Buccaneers
Born February 6, 1960, at Birmingham, Ala.
Height, 5.08. Weight, 180.
High School—Inglewood, Calif.
Attended University of Nevada at Las Vegas.

Selected by Tampa Bay in 12th round (325th player selected) of 1982 NFL draft.

Year Club	G.	Att.	Yds.	—RUSHING— Avg.	TD.	P.C.	Yds.	PASS RECEIVING Avg.	TD.	TD.	—TOTAL— Pts.	F.
1982—Tampa Bay NFL	9	2	3	1.5	0	1	5	5.0	0	0	0	1
1983—Tampa Bay NFL	16	13	28	2.2	0	1	9	9.0	0	0	0	5
1984—Tampa Bay NFL	16	16	27	1.7	0		None			0	0	3
Pro Totals—3 Years	41	31	58	1.9	0	2	14	7.0	0	0	0	9

Year Club	KICKOFF RETURNS				
	G.	No.	Yds.	Avg.	TD.
1982—Tampa Bay NFL	9	21	361	17.2	0
1983—Tampa Bay NFL	16	30	689	23.0	0
1984—Tampa Bay NFL	16	38	835	22.0	0
Pro Totals—3 Years............	41	89	1885	21.2	0

Additional pro statistics: Recovered one fumble, 1982; recovered two fumbles, 1983 and 1984.

DONALD HOWARD MOSEBAR
(Don)
Guard-Offensive Tackle—Los Angeles Raiders
Born September 11, 1961, at Yakima, Calif.
Height, 6.06. Weight, 265.
High School—Visalia, Calif., Mount Whitney.
Attended University of Southern California.

Selected by Los Angeles in 1983 USFL territorial draft.
Selected by Los Angeles Raiders in 1st round (26th player selected) of 1983 NFL draft.
Signed by Los Angeles Raiders, August 29, 1983.
Granted roster exemption, August 29, 1983; activated, September 9, 1983.
On injured reserve with back injury, November 8 through remainder of 1984 season.
Los Angeles Raiders NFL, 1983 and 1984.
Games: 1983 (14), 1984 (10). Total—24.
Played in AFC Championship Game following 1983 season.
Played in NFL Championship Game following 1983 season.

MARK DeWAYNE MOSELEY
Placekicker—Washington Redskins
Born March 12, 1948, at Lanesville, Tex.
Height, 6.00. Weight, 205.
High School—Livingston, Tex.
Attended Texas A&M University and Stephen F. Austin College.

Established NFL records for most consecutive field goals (23), 1981-82; highest field goal percentage, season (95.24), 1982; most points scored by kicker, season (161), 1983.
Named to THE SPORTING NEWS NFC All-Star Team, 1979.
Named THE SPORTING NEWS NFL Player of the Year, 1982.
Selected by Philadelphia in 14th round (346th player selected) of 1970 NFL draft.
Placed on waivers by Philadelphia Eagles and signed by Houston Oilers as free agent, September 13, 1971.
Released by Houston Oilers, 1973; signed as free agent by Washington Redskins, February 1, 1974.

Year Club	PLACE KICKING						Year Club	PLACE KICKING					
	G.	XP.	XPM.	FG.	FGA.	Pts.		G.	XP.	XPM.	FG.	FGA.	Pts.
1970—Philadelphia NFL ...	14	25	3	14	25	67	1979—Washington NFL.....	16	39	0	★25	★33	114
1971—Houston NFL............	12	25	2	16	26	73	1980—Washington NFL.....	16	27	3	18	33	81
1972—Houston NFL...........	1	2	0	1	2	5	1981—Washington NFL.....	16	38	4	19	30	95
1974—Washington NFL.....	13	27	2	17	30	81	1982—Washington NFL.....	9	16	3	★20	21	76
1975—Washington NFL.....	14	37	2	16	25	85	1983—Washington NFL.....	16	★62	1	33	★47	★161
1976—Washington NFL.....	14	31	1	★22	34	97	1984—Washington NFL.....	16	48	3	24	31	120
1977—Washington NFL.....	14	19	0	★21	★37	82	Pro Totals—14 Years.....	187	426	25	266	404	1224
1978—Washington NFL.....	16	30	1	19	30	87							

Additional pro statistics: Punted 10 times for 35.0 average and recovered one fumble, 1970.
Played in NFC Championship Game following 1982 and 1983 seasons.
Played in NFL Championship Game following 1982 and 1983 seasons.
Played in Pro Bowl (NFL All-Star Game) following 1979 and 1982 seasons.

MICHAEL GENE MOSLEY
(Mike)
Wide Receiver—Buffalo Bills
Born June 30, 1958, at Hillsboro, Tex.
Height, 6.01. Weight, 186.
High School—Humble, Tex.
Attended Texas A&M University.

Selected by Buffalo in 3rd round (76th player selected) of 1981 NFL draft.
On injured reserve with pulled hamstring, August 18 through entire 1981 season.
On injured reserve with knee injury, November 18 through remainder of 1983 season.
On injured reserve with knee injury, August 28 through November 16, 1984; activated, November 17, 1984.

Year Club		PASS RECEIVING				PUNT RETURNS				KICKOFF RET.				TOTAL		
	G.	P.C.	Yds.	Avg.	TD.	No.	Yds.	Avg.	TD.	No.	Yds.	Avg.	TD.	TD.	Pts.	F.
1982—Buffalo NFL.................	9	9	96	10.7	0	11	61	5.5	0	18	487	★27.1	0	0	0	3
1983—Buffalo NFL.................	7	14	180	12.9	3		None			9	236	26.2	0	3	18	1
1984—Buffalo NFL.................	4	4	38	9.5	0		None				None			0	0	0
Pro Totals—3 Years........	20	27	314	11.6	3	11	61	5.5	0	27	723	26.8	0	3	18	4

Additional pro statistics: Recovered two fumbles, 1982; attempted one pass with no completions, 1984.

MARTIN MOSS
Defensive Tackle—Detroit Lions
Born December 6, 1958, at San Diego, Calif.
Height, 6.04. Weight, 252.
High School—San Diego, Calif., Lincoln.
Received bachelor of arts degree in sociology from
University of California at Los Angeles in 1982.

Selected by Detroit in 8th round (208th player selected) of 1982 NFL draft.
Detroit NFL, 1982 through 1984.
Games: 1982 (5), 1983 (15), 1984 (16). Total—36.

WALTER STEPHEN MOTT
(Steve)
Center—Detroit Lions
Born March 24, 1961, at New Orleans, La.
Height, 6.03. Weight, 260.
High School—Marrero, La., Archbishop Shaw.
Attended University of Alabama.

Selected by Birmingham in 1983 USFL territorial draft.
Selected by Detroit in 5th round (121st player selected) of 1983 NFL draft.
Signed by Detroit Lions, June 1, 1983.
On physically unable to perform/active with knee injury, July 22 through August 8, 1984; activated, August 9, 1984.
On injured reserve with dislocated ankle, October 8 through remainder of 1984 season.
Detroit NFL, 1983 and 1984.
Games: 1983 (13), 1984 (6). Total—19.
Pro statistics: Fumbled once, 1983.

ZEKE MOWATT
Tight End—New York Giants
Born March 5, 1961, at Wauchula, Fla.
Height, 6.03. Weight, 238.
High School—Wauchula, Fla., Hardee County.
Attended Florida State University.

Selected by Tampa Bay in 1983 USFL territorial draft.
Signed as free agent by New York Giants, June 1, 1983.

Year Club	G.	P.C.	Yds.	Avg.	TD.
1983—New York Giants NFL	16	21	280	13.3	1
1984—New York Giants NFL	16	48	698	14.5	6
Pro Totals—2 Years............	32	69	978	14.2	7

PAUL STEWART MOYER
Safety—Seattle Seahawks
Born July 26, 1961, at Villa Park, Calif.
Height, 6.01. Weight, 201.
High School—Villa Park, Calif.
Attended Fullerton College and Arizona State University.

Signed as free agent by Seattle Seahawks, April 28, 1983.

Year Club	G.	No.	Yds.	Avg.	TD.
1983—Seattle NFL....................	16	1	19	19.0	1
1984—Seattle NFL....................	16		None		
Pro Totals—2 Years............	32	1	19	19.0	1

Additional pro statistics: Recovered three fumbles, 1983.
Played in AFC Championship Game following 1983 season.

CALVIN SALEEM MUHAMMAD
(Formerly known as Calvin Vincent Rainey.)
Wide Receiver—Washington Redskins
Born December 10, 1958, at Jacksonville, Fla.
Height, 5.11. Weight, 190.
High School—Jacksonville, Fla., William M. Raines.
Attended Texas Southern University.

Signed by Toronto Argonauts, April 10, 1980.
Selected by Oakland in 12th round (322nd player selected) of 1980 NFL draft.
On injured list, July 8 through entire 1980 season.
Released by Toronto Argonauts, June 29, 1981; signed by Oakland Raiders, July, 1981.
On injured reserve with knee injury, August 15 through entire 1981 season.
Franchise transferred to Los Angeles, May 7, 1982.
On injured reserve with dislocated shoulder, August 28 through October 2, 1984; activated, October 3, 1984.
Traded by Los Angeles Raiders to Washington Redskins for 4th round pick in 1985 draft, October 3, 1984.

Year Club	G.	P.C.	Yds.	Avg.	TD.
1982—L.A. Raiders NFL........	8	3	92	30.7	1
1983—L.A. Raiders NFL........	15	13	252	19.4	2
1984—Washington NFL..........	10	42	729	17.4	4
Pro Totals—3 Years............	33	58	1073	18.5	7

Above the table: ——PASS RECEIVING——

Additional pro statistics: Fumbled twice, 1983; recovered two fumbles and fumbled once, 1984.
Played in AFC Championship Game following 1983 season.
Played in NFL Championship Game following 1983 season.

MIKE MULARKEY
Tight End—Minnesota Vikings
Born November 19, 1961, at Miami, Fla.
Height, 6.04. Weight, 233.
High School—Fort Lauderdale, Fla., Northeast.
Attended University of Florida.

Selected by Tampa Bay in 1983 USFL territorial draft.
Selected by San Francisco in 9th round (229th player selected) of 1983 NFL draft.
Signed by San Francisco 49ers, June 1, 1983.
Released by San Francisco 49ers, August 29, 1983; awarded on waivers to Minnesota Vikings, August 30, 1983.
On injured reserve with ankle injury, September 30 through remainder of 1983 season.

Year Club	G.	P.C.	Yds.	Avg.	TD.
1983—Minnesota NFL............	3		None		
1984—Minnesota NFL............	16	14	134	9.6	2
Pro Totals—2 Years...........	19	14	134	9.6	2

Above the table: ——PASS RECEIVING——

Additional pro statistics: Recovered one fumble and fumbled once, 1984.

THOMAS FRANCIS MULLADY
Name pronounced MULL-i-dee.
(Tom)
Tight End—New York Giants
Born January 30, 1957, at Dayton, O.
Height, 6.03. Weight, 232.
High School—Chattanooga, Tenn., McCallie.
Received bachelor of arts degree in business administration from
Southwestern at Memphis in 1979.

Selected by Buffalo in 7th round (170th player selected) of 1979 NFL draft.
Released by Buffalo Bills, August 13, 1979; signed as free agent by New York Giants, November 27, 1979.

Year Club	G.	P.C.	Yds.	Avg.	TD.
1979—New York Giants NFL	2		None		
1980—New York Giants NFL	16	28	391	14.0	2
1981—New York Giants NFL	16	14	136	9.7	1
1982—New York Giants NFL	9	27	287	10.6	0
1983—New York Giants NFL	16	13	184	14.2	1
1984—New York Giants NFL	16	2	35	17.5	0
Pro Totals—6 Years............	75	84	1033	12.3	4

Above the table: ——PASS RECEIVING——

Additional pro statistics: Fumbled once, 1981 and 1982; recovered one fumble, 1983.

MARK ALAN MULLANEY
Defensive End—Minnesota Vikings
Born April 30, 1953, at Denver, Colo.
Height, 6.06. Weight, 245.
High School—Denver, Colo., George Washington.
Attended Colorado State University.

Selected by Minnesota in 1st round (25th player selected) of 1975 NFL draft.
On injured reserve with broken collarbone, September 30 through December 4, 1983; activated, December 5, 1983.
On injured reserve with nerve damage in neck, November 23 through remainder of 1984 season.
Minnesota NFL, 1975 through 1984.
Games: 1975 (14), 1976 (12), 1977 (14), 1978 (15), 1979 (16), 1980 (16), 1981 (15), 1982 (9), 1983 (7), 1984 (7). Total—125.
Pro statistics: Recovered two fumbles for three yards, 1976; recovered one fumble, 1978, 1980, 1981 and 1983.
Played in NFC Championship Game following 1976 and 1977 seasons.
Played in NFL Championship Game following 1976 season.

DAVLIN MULLEN
Cornerback—New York Jets
Born February 17, 1960, at McKeesport, Pa.
Height, 6.01. Weight, 177.
High School—Clairton, Pa.
Attended Western Kentucky University.

Selected by New York Jets in 8th round (217th player selected) of 1983 NFL draft.

Year Club	G.	INTERCEPTIONS No. Yds. Avg. TD.	-PUNT RETURNS- No. Yds. Avg. TD.	-KICKOFF RET.- No. Yds. Avg. TD.	-TOTAL- TD. Pts. F.
1983—New York Jets NFL....	11	None	2 13 6.5 0	3 57 19.0 0	0 0 1
1984—New York Jets NFL....	15	1 25 25.0 0	1 8 8.0 0	2 34 17.0 0	0 0 0
Pro Totals—2 Years.......	26	1 25 25.0 0	3 21 7.0 0	5 91 18.2 0	0 0 1

ERIC MULLINS
Wide Receiver—Houston Oilers
Born July 30, 1962, at Houston, Tex.
Height, 5.11. Weight, 181.
High School—Houston, Tex., Strake Jesuit Preparatory.
Attended Stanford University.
Selected by Houston in 6th round (161st player selected) of 1984 NFL draft.

Year Club	——PASS RECEIVING—— G. P.C. Yds. Avg. TD.
1984—Houston NFL.................	14 6 85 14.2 1

Additional pro statistics: Rushed once for no yards, 1984.

MIKE MUNCHAK
Guard—Houston Oilers
Born May 3, 1960, at Scranton, Pa.
Height, 6.03. Weight, 286.
High School—Scranton, Pa., Central.
Received bachelor of business administration degree from Penn State University in 1982.
Selected by Houston in 1st round (8th player selected) of 1982 NFL draft.
On injured reserve with broken ankle, November 24 through December 23, 1982; activated, December 24, 1982.
Houston NFL, 1982 through 1984.
Games: 1982 (4), 1983 (16), 1984 (16). Total—36.
Played in Pro Bowl (NFL All-Star Game) following 1984 season.

HARRY VANCE MUNCIE
(Chuck)
Running Back—San Diego Chargers
Born March 17, 1953, at Uniontown, Pa.
Height, 6.03. Weight, 228.
High School—Uniontown, Pa.
Attended Arizona Western College and received bachelor of science degree
in criminology from University of California.
Brother of Bill Munsey, running back with British Columbia Lions (CFL) for six years;
and Nelson Munsey, defensive back with Baltimore Colts and Minnesota Vikings, 1972 through 1978.
Named running back on THE SPORTING NEWS College All-America Team, 1975.
Selected by New Orleans in 1st round (3rd player selected) of 1976 NFL draft.
Traded by New Orleans Saints to San Diego Chargers for 2nd round pick in 1981 draft, October 7, 1980.
Traded by San Diego Chargers to Miami Dolphins for 2nd round pick in 1985 draft, September 10, 1984 (deal voided after failing physical, September 14, 1984).
On non-football injury list with drug problems, September 15 through remainder of 1984 season.

Year Club	G.	——RUSHING—— Att. Yds. Avg. TD.	PASS RECEIVING P.C. Yds. Avg. TD.	—TOTAL— TD. Pts. F.
1976—New Orleans NFL.................................	12	149 659 4.4 2	31 272 8.8 0	2 12 6
1977—New Orleans NFL.................................	14	201 811 4.0 6	21 248 11.8 1	7 42 3
1978—New Orleans NFL.................................	13	160 557 3.5 7	26 233 9.0 0	7 42 7
1979—New Orleans NFL.................................	16	238 1198 5.0 11	40 308 7.7 0	11 66 8
1980—N. Orl. (4)-S. Diego (11) NFL	15	175 827 4.7 6	31 259 8.4 0	6 36 11
1981—San Diego NFL	15	251 1144 4.6 *19	43 362 8.4 0	*19 114 9
1982—San Diego NFL	9	138 569 4.1 8	25 207 8.3 1	9 54 4
1983—San Diego NFL	15	235 886 3.8 12	42 396 9.4 1	13 78 5
1984—San Diego NFL	1	14 51 3.6 0	4 38 9.5 0	0 0 1
Pro Totals—9 Years...................	110	1561 6702 4.3 71	263 2323 8.8 3	74 444 57

Year Club	G.	KICKOFF RETURNS No. Yds. Avg.TD.	Year Club	G.	KICKOFF RETURNS No. Yds. Avg.TD.
1976—New Orleans NFL........	12	3 69 23.0 0	1981—San Diego NFL	15	None
1977—New Orleans NFL........	14	1 19 19.0 0	1982—San Diego NFL	9	None
1978—New Orleans NFL........	13	None	1983—San Diego NFL	15	None
1979—New Orleans NFL........	16	None	1984—San Diego NFL	1	None
1980—NO(4)-SD(11)NFL........	15	16 344 21.5 0	Pro Totals—9 Years	110	20 432 21.6 0

Additional pro statistics: Recovered one fumble, 1976, 1978, 1982 and 1983; attempted one pass with no completions, 1978; attempted two passes with one completion for 40 yards and a touchdown and recovered two fumbles, 1979; attempted one pass with one completion for three yards and a touchdown and recovered four fumbles, 1981; attempted three passes with two completions for 83 yards and two touchdowns, 1982.
Played in AFC Championship Game following 1980 and 1981 seasons.
Played in Pro Bowl (NFL All-Star Game) following 1979, 1981 and 1982 seasons.

MICHAEL ANTHONY MUNOZ

(Known by middle name.)

Offensive Tackle—Cincinnati Bengals

Born August 19, 1958, at Ontario, Calif.
Height, 6.06. Weight, 278.
High School—Ontario, Calif., Chaffey.
Received bachelor of science degree in public administration from
University of Southern California in 1980.

Named to THE SPORTING NEWS NFL All-Star Team, 1981 and 1984.
Selected by Cincinnati in 1st round (3rd player selected) of 1980 NFL draft.
Cincinnati NFL, 1980 through 1984.
Games: 1980 (16), 1981 (16), 1982 (9), 1983 (16), 1984 (16). Total—73.
Pro statistics: Caught one pass for minus six yards, 1980; caught one pass for one yard and a touchdown and recovered one fumble, 1984.
Played in AFC Championship Game following 1981 season.
Played in NFL Championship Game following 1981 season.
Played in Pro Bowl (NFL All-Star Game) following 1981, 1983 and 1984 seasons.

MARK HODGE MURPHY

Safety—Washington Redskins

Born July 13, 1955, at Fulton, N. Y.
Height, 6.04. Weight, 210.
High School—Williamsville, N. Y., Clarence Central.
Received bachelor of arts degree in economics from Colgate University in 1977 and
attending American University for master's degree.

Named to THE SPORTING NEWS NFL All-Star Team, 1983.
Signed as free agent by Washington Redskins, May, 1977.
On injured reserve with knee injury, September 25 through November 16, 1984; activated, November 17, 1984.

| | | —INTERCEPTIONS— | | | |
Year Club	G.	No.	Yds.	Avg.	TD.
1977—Washington NFL..........	14		None		
1978—Washington NFL..........	16		None		
1979—Washington NFL..........	16	3	29	9.7	0
1980—Washington NFL..........	16	6	58	9.7	0
1981—Washington NFL..........	16	7	68	9.7	0
1982—Washington NFL..........	9	2	0	0.0	0
1983—Washington NFL..........	15	*9	127	14.1	0
1984—Washington NFL..........	7		None		
Pro Totals—8 Years..........	109	27	282	10.4	0

Additional pro statistics: Returned three kickoffs for 44 yards, 1977; caught one pass for 13 yards, 1978; recovered two fumbles for 22 yards, 1979; recovered one fumble and fumbled once, 1980; recovered three fumbles, 1981.
Played in NFC Championship Game following 1982 and 1983 seasons.
Played in NFL Championship Game following 1982 and 1983 seasons.
Played in Pro Bowl (NFL All-Star Game) following 1983 season.

MARK STEVEN MURPHY

Safety—Green Bay Packers

Born April 22, 1958, at Canton, O.
Height, 6.02. Weight, 199.
High School—Canton, O., Glen Oaks.
Received bachelor of science degree in business administration from West Liberty State College.

Signed as free agent by Green Bay Packers, April 25, 1980.
On injured reserve with broken hand, August 14 through December 17, 1980; activated after clearing procedural waivers, December 19, 1980.

| | | —INTERCEPTIONS— | | | |
Year Club	G.	No.	Yds.	Avg.	TD.
1980—Green Bay NFL............	1		None		
1981—Green Bay NFL............	16	3	57	19.0	0
1982—Green Bay NFL............	9		None		
1983—Green Bay NFL............	16		None		
1984—Green Bay NFL............	16	1	4	4.0	0
Pro Totals—5 Years............	58	4	61	15.3	0

Additional pro statistics: Recovered two fumbles, 1981; recovered one fumble, 1983; recovered one fumble for two yards and fumbled once, 1984.

EDWARD PETER MURRAY

(Ed)

Placekicker—Detroit Lions

Born August 29, 1956, at Halifax, Nova Scotia.
Height, 5.10. Weight, 175.
High School—Victoria, British Columbia, Spectrum.
Received bachelor of science degree in physical education from Tulane University in 1980.
Cousin of Mike Rogers, center with New York Rangers of NHL.

Selected by Detroit in 7th round (166th player selected) of 1980 NFL draft.

On suspended list, September 10 through November 19, 1982; reinstated, November 20, 1982.

		——PLACE KICKING——					
Year	Club	G.	XP.	XPM.	FG.	FGA.	Pts.
1980—Detroit NFL..............		16	35	1	*27	*42	116
1981—Detroit NFL..............		16	46	0	25	35	*121
1982—Detroit NFL..............		7	16	0	11	12	49
1983—Detroit NFL..............		16	38	0	25	32	113
1984—Detroit NFL..............		16	31	0	20	27	91
Pro Totals—5 Years.......		71	166	1	108	148	490

Played in Pro Bowl (NFL All-Star Game) following 1980 season.

WILBUR LEE MYERS
Safety—Denver Broncos

Born August 17, 1961, at Bassfield, Miss.
Height, 5.11. Weight, 195.
High School—Bassfield, Miss.
Received bachelor of business administration degree
from Delta State University in 1983.

Signed as free agent by Denver Broncos, April 28, 1983.
On injured reserve with knee injury, August 27 through entire 1984 season.
Denver NFL, 1983.
Games: 1983 (16).

JESSE JAMES MYLES
Running Back—Denver Broncos

Born September 28, 1960, at New Orleans, La.
Height, 5.10. Weight, 210.
High School—Gray, La., H.L. Bourgeois.
Attended Louisiana State University.

Signed as free agent by Denver Broncos, April 28, 1983.
Released by Denver Broncos, August 29, 1983; re-signed by Broncos, August 30, 1983.
Released by Denver Broncos, August 27, 1984; re-signed by Broncos, August 28, 1984.
On injured reserve with fractured shoulder blade, September 5 through November 9, 1984; activated, November 10, 1984.

			——RUSHING——				PASS RECEIVING				—TOTAL—		
Year	Club	G.	Att.	Yds.	Avg.	TD.	P.C.	Yds.	Avg.	TD.	TD.	Pts.	F.
1983—Denver NFL		16	8	52	6.5	0	7	119	17.0	1	1	6	0
1984—Denver NFL		7	5	7	1.4	0	2	22	11.0	0	0	0	0
Pro Totals—2 Years....................		23	13	59	4.5	0	9	141	15.7	1	1	6	0

JOSEPH ANDREW NASH
(Joe)
Nose Tackle—Seattle Seahawks

Born October 11, 1960, at Boston, Mass.
Height, 6.03. Weight, 250.
High School—Dorchester, Mass., Boston College High.
Received bachelor of arts degree in sociology from Boston College in 1982.

Signed as free agent by Seattle Seahawks, April 30, 1982.
On inactive list, September 12 and September 19, 1982.
Seattle NFL, 1982 through 1984.
Games: 1982 (7), 1983 (16), 1984 (16). Total—39.
Pro statistics: Recovered three fumbles (including one in end zone for a touchdown), 1984.
Played in AFC Championship Game following 1983 season.
Played in Pro Bowl (NFL All-Star Game) following 1984 season.

TONY CURTIS NATHAN
Running Back—Miami Dolphins

Born December 14, 1956, at Birmingham, Ala.
Height, 6.00. Weight, 206.
High School—Birmingham, Ala., Woodlawn.
Attended University of Alabama.

Named to THE SPORTING NEWS AFC All-Star Team, 1979.
Selected by Miami in 3rd round (61st player selected) of 1979 NFL draft.

			——RUSHING——				PASS RECEIVING				—TOTAL—		
Year	Club	G.	Att.	Yds.	Avg.	TD.	P.C.	Yds.	Avg.	TD.	TD.	Pts.	F.
1979—Miami NFL		16	16	68	4.3	0	17	213	12.5	2	3	18	8
1980—Miami NFL		16	60	327	5.5	1	57	588	10.3	5	6	36	9
1981—Miami NFL		13	147	782	*5.3	5	50	452	9.0	3	8	48	2
1982—Miami NFL		8	66	233	3.5	1	16	114	7.1	0	1	6	2
1983—Miami NFL		16	151	685	4.5	3	52	461	8.9	1	4	24	2
1984—Miami NFL		16	118	558	4.7	1	61	579	9.5	2	3	18	3
Pro Totals—6 Years....................		85	558	2653	4.8	11	253	2407	9.5	13	25	150	26

Year Club	G.	No.	Yds.	Avg.	TD.	No.	Yds.	Avg.	TD.
			—PUNT RETURNS—				—KICKOFF RET.—		
1979—Miami NFL	16	28	306	10.9	1	45	1016	22.6	0
1980—Miami NFL	16	23	178	7.7	0	5	102	20.4	0
1981—Miami NFL	13		None				None		
1982—Miami NFL	8		None				None		
1983—Miami NFL	16		None				None		
1984—Miami NFL	16		None				None		
Pro Totals—6 Years	85	51	484	9.5	1	50	1118	22.4	0

Additional pro statistics: Recovered one fumble, 1980 and 1984; attempted one pass with no completions, 1980; recovered two fumbles and attempted one pass with no completions, 1981; attempted two passes with one completion for 15 yards and one touchdown, 1982; attempted four passes with three completions for 46 yards and returned three kickoffs for 15 yards, 1983.

Played in AFC Championship Game following 1982 and 1984 seasons.

Played in NFL Championship Game following 1982 and 1984 seasons.

ROBERT NEAL
(Speedy)
Fullback—Buffalo Bills
Born August 26, 1962, at Key West, Fla.
Height, 6.02. Weight, 254.
High School—Key West, Fla.
Attended University of Miami (Fla.).

Selected by Tampa Bay in 4th round (77th player selected) of 1984 USFL draft.
Selected by Buffalo in 3rd round (82nd player selected) of 1984 NFL draft.
Signed by Buffalo Bills, July 19, 1984.

Year Club	G.	Att.	Yds.	Avg.	TD.	P.C.	Yds.	Avg.	TD.	TD.	Pts.	F.
			——RUSHING——				PASS RECEIVING				—TOTAL—	
1984—Buffalo NFL	12	49	175	3.6	1	9	76	8.4	0	1	6	0

RENALDO NEHEMIAH
Wide Receiver—San Francisco 49ers
Born March 24, 1959, at Newark, N.J.
Height, 6.01. Weight, 183.
High School—Scotch Plains, N.J., Fanwood.
Attended University of Maryland.

Signed as free agent by San Francisco 49ers, April 16, 1982.

Year Club	G.	P.C.	Yds.	Avg.	TD.
		—PASS RECEIVING—			
1982—San Francisco NFL	8	8	161	20.1	1
1983—San Francisco NFL	16	17	236	13.9	1
1984—San Francisco NFL	16	18	357	19.8	2
Pro Totals—3 Years	40	43	754	17.5	4

Additional pro statistics: Rushed once for minus one yard, 1982; fumbled once, 1983.
Played in NFC Championship Game following 1983 and 1984 seasons.
Played in NFL Championship Game following 1984 season.

BILL NEILL
Defensive Tackle
Born March 15, 1959, at Norristown, Pa.
Height, 6.04. Weight, 267.
High School—Collegeville, Pa., Perkiomen Valley.
Attended University of Pittsburgh.

Selected by New York Giants in 5th round (115th player selected) of 1981 NFL draft.
On inactive list, September 12, 1982.
On injured reserve with knee injury, September 8 through remainder of 1983 season.
Released by New York Giants, August 27, 1984; signed as free agent by Green Bay Packers, August 28, 1984.
Released by Green Bay Packers, May 22, 1985.
New York Giants NFL, 1981 through 1983; Green Bay NFL, 1984.
Games: 1981 (16), 1982 (7), 1983 (1), 1984 (16). Total—40.
Pro statistics: Recovered one fumble, 1981.

MICHAEL NELMS
(Mike)
Kick Returner-Wide Receiver—Washington Redskins
Born April 8, 1955, at Fort Worth, Tex.
Height, 6.01. Weight, 202.
High School—Fort Worth, Tex., O. D. Wyatt.
Attended Tarrant Junior College, Sam Houston State University and Baylor University.

Named to THE SPORTING NEWS NFL All-Star Team, 1981.
Selected by Buffalo in 7th round (170th player selected) of 1977 NFL draft.
Released by Buffalo Bills, August 27, 1977; signed as free agent by Hamilton Tiger-Cats, September 3, 1977.
On injured list, September 8 through October 14, 1977.
Released by Hamilton Tiger-Cats, October 15, 1977; signed as free agent by Ottawa Rough Riders, October 21, 1977.

Granted free agency, April 1, 1980; signed as free agent by Washington Redskins, April 23, 1980.
On injured reserve with knee injury, December 16 through remainder of 1983 season.

Year Club	G.	INTERCEPTIONS				–PUNT RETURNS–				—KICKOFF RET.—				—TOTAL—		
		No.	Yds.	Avg.	TD.	No.	Yds.	Avg.	TD.	No.	Yds.	Avg.	TD.	TD.	Pts.	F.
1977—Ham.(2)-Ot.(3) CFL.....	5	3	86	28.7	0	17	188	11.1	0	5	100	20.0	0	0	0	0
1978—Ottawa CFL	16	6	110	18.3	1	49	408	8.3	0	8	191	23.9	0	1	6	4
1979—Ottawa CFL	15	*10	124	12.4	0	*106	*1155	10.9	2	3	71	23.7	0	2	12	1
1980—Washington NFL.........	16		None			48	487	10.1	0	38	810	21.3	0	0	0	1
1981—Washington NFL.........	16	1	3	3.0	0	45	492	10.9	2	37	1099	*29.7	0	2	12	2
1982—Washington NFL.........	8		None			32	252	7.9	0	23	557	24.2	0	0	0	3
1983—Washington NFL.........	12		None			38	289	7.6	0	35	802	22.9	0	0	0	0
1984—Washington NFL.........	16		None			49	428	8.7	0	42	860	20.5	0	0	0	1
CFL Totals—3 Years	36	19	320	16.8	1	172	1751	10.2	2	16	362	22.6	0	3	18	5
NFL Totals—5 Years.....	68	1	3	3.0	0	212	1948	9.2	2	175	4128	23.6	0	2	12	7
Pro Totals—8 Years.......	104	20	323	16.2	1	384	3699	9.6	4	191	4490	23.5	0	5	30	12

Additional pro statistics: Recovered one fumble, 1978; recovered one fumble for six yards, 1979.
Played in NFC Championship Game following 1982 season.
Played in NFL Championship Game following 1982 season.
Played in Pro Bowl (NFL All-Star Game) following 1980 through 1982 seasons.

CHARLES LaVERNE NELSON
(Chuck)
Placekicker—Buffalo Bills
Born February 23, 1960, at Seattle, Wash.
Height, 5.11. Weight, 175.
High School—Everett, Wash.
Attended University of Washington.

Named as placekicker on THE SPORTING NEWS College All-America Team, 1982.
Selected by Chicago in 23rd round (270th player selected) of 1983 USFL draft.
Selected by Los Angeles Rams in 4th round (87th player selected) of 1983 NFL draft.
Signed by Los Angeles Rams, July 13, 1983.
Released by Los Angeles Rams, August 27, 1984; signed as free agent by Buffalo Bills, October 30, 1984.

Year Club	G.	XP.	XPM.	FG.	FGA.	Pts.
			—PLACE KICKING—			
1983—L. A. Rams NFL	12	33	*4	5	11	48
1984—Buffalo NFL..............	7	14	0	3	5	23
Pro Totals—2 Years.......	19	47	4	8	16	71

Additional pro statistics: Recovered one fumble, 1983.

CURTIS SHANE NELSON
(Known by middle name.)
Linebacker—San Diego Chargers
Born May 25, 1955, at Mathis, Tex.
Height, 6.01. Weight, 225.
High School—Mathis, Tex.
Attended Blinn Junior College and Baylor University.

Signed as free agent by Buffalo Bills, June, 1977.
On injured reserve with knee injury, November 6 through December 10, 1981; activated, December 11, 1981.
On injured reserve with knee injury, December 18 through remainder of 1981 season.
On injured reserve with knee injury, September 14 through remainder of 1982 season.
Released by Buffalo Bills after failing physical, August 30, 1983; signed as free agent by San Diego Chargers, February 26, 1985.

Year Club	G.	No.	Yds.	Avg.	TD.
		—INTERCEPTIONS—			
1977—Buffalo NFL..................	14		None		
1978—Buffalo NFL..................	16	3	69	23.0	0
1979—Buffalo NFL..................	16	1	13	13.0	0
1980—Buffalo NFL..................	16		None		
1981—Buffalo NFL..................	10		None		
1982—Buffalo NFL..................	1		None		
Pro Totals—6 Years...........	73	4	82	20.5	0

Additional pro statistics: Recovered two fumbles, 1977 and 1980; recovered one fumble, 1978 and 1979.

COACHING RECORD
Assistant freshman coach at Cornell University, 1984.

DARRELL NELSON
Tight End—Pittsburgh Steelers
Born October 27, 1961, at Memphis, Tenn.
Height, 6.02. Weight, 235.
High School—Memphis, Tenn., Mitchell.
Attended Memphis State University.

Selected by Memphis in 1984 USFL territorial draft.
Signed as free agent by Pittsburgh Steelers, June 15, 1984.

Released by Pittsburgh Steelers, August 27, 1984; re-signed by Steelers, August 28, 1984.
On injured reserve with knee injury, September 11 through October 18, 1984; activated, October 19, 1984.

			—PASS RECEIVING—			
Year	Club	G.	P.C.	Yds.	Avg.	TD.
1984—Pittsburgh NFL		11	2	31	15.5	0

Played in AFC Championship Game following 1984 season.

DARRIN MILO NELSON
Running Back—Minnesota Vikings
Born January 2, 1959, at Sacramento, Calif.
Height, 5.09. Weight, 185.
High School—Downey, Calif., Pius X.
Received bachelor of science degree in urban and environmental planning
from Stanford University in 1981.
Brother of Kevin Nelson, running back with Los Angeles Express;
cousin of Ozzie Newsome, tight end with Cleveland Browns; and
Carlos Carson, wide receiver with Kansas City Chiefs.
Selected by Minnesota in 1st round (7th player selected) of 1982 NFL draft.

			—RUSHING—				PASS RECEIVING				—TOTAL—		
Year	Club	G.	Att.	Yds.	Avg.	TD.	P.C.	Yds.	Avg.	TD.	TD.	Pts.	F.
1982—Minnesota NFL		7	44	136	3.1	0	9	100	11.1	0	0	0	2
1983—Minnesota NFL		15	154	642	4.2	1	51	618	12.1	0	1	6	5
1984—Minnesota NFL		15	80	406	5.1	3	27	162	6.0	1	4	24	4
Pro Totals—3 Years		37	278	1184	4.3	4	87	880	10.1	1	5	30	11

			—PUNT RETURNS—				—KICKOFF RET.—			
Year	Club	G.	No.	Yds.	Avg.	TD.	No.	Yds.	Avg.	TD.
1982—Minnesota NFL		7		None			6	132	22.0	0
1983—Minnesota NFL		15		None			18	445	24.7	0
1984—Minnesota NFL		15	23	180	7.8	0	39	891	22.8	0
Pro Totals—3 Years		37	23	180	7.8	0	63	1468	23.3	0

Additional pro statistics: Recovered one fumble, 1983; recovered three fumbles, 1984.

DAVID NELSON
Running Back—Miami Dolphins
Born November 23, 1963, at Miami, Fla.
Height, 6.01. Weight, 220.
High School—North Miami Beach, Fla.
Attended Taft Junior College and Heidelberg College.
Signed as free agent by Miami Dolphins, May 2, 1984.
Released by Miami Dolphins, August 21, 1984; signed as free agent by Minnesota Vikings, August 24, 1984.
Released by Minnesota Vikings, September 12, 1984.
USFL rights traded by Denver Gold to Jacksonville Bulls for linebacker Fernando Jackson, October 12, 1984.
Signed by Jacksonville Bulls, October 12, 1984.
Released by Jacksonville Bulls, February 11, 1985; signed as free agent by Miami Dolphins, April 11, 1985.
Minnesota NFL, 1984.
Games: 1984 (2).
Pro statistics: Rushed once for three yards and returned one kickoff for no yards, 1984.

DERRIE L. NELSON
Linebacker—San Diego Chargers
Born February 8, 1958, at York, Neb.
Height, 6.01. Weight, 234.
High School—Fairmont, Neb.
Attended University of Nebraska.
Nephew of Bob Cerv, outfielder-first baseman with New York Yankees,
Kansas City A's and Houston Colt .45s, 1951 through 1962;
and cousin of Eric Swanson, wide receiver at University of Tennessee.
Selected by Dallas in 4th round (108th player selected) of 1981 NFL draft.
Released by Dallas Cowboys, August 14, 1981; signed as free agent by Cleveland Browns, August 21, 1981.
Released by Cleveland Browns, August 24, 1981; signed as free agent by San Diego Chargers, March 30, 1982.
On injured reserve with hip pointer, August 31 through entire 1982 season.
On injured reserve with finger nerve injury, August 20 through November 7, 1984; activated after clearing procedural waivers, November 9, 1984.
San Diego NFL, 1983 and 1984.
Games: 1983 (15), 1984 (6). Total—21.
Pro statistics: Ran 21 yards with blocked punt for a touchdown, 1983.

EDMUND CLAU-VON NELSON
Nose Tackle-Defensive End—Pittsburgh Steelers
Born April 30, 1960, at Live Oak, Fla.
Height, 6.03. Weight, 270.
High School—Tampa, Fla., C. Leon King.
Attended Auburn University.
Selected by Pittsburgh in 7th round (172nd player selected) of 1982 NFL draft.
Pittsburgh NFL, 1982 through 1984.

Games: 1982 (8), 1983 (16), 1984 (16). Total—40.
Pro statistics: Recovered one fumble, 1982.
Played in AFC Championship Game following 1984 season.

KARL NELSON
Offensive Tackle—New York Giants
Born June 14, 1960, at DeKalb, Ill.
Height, 6.06. Weight, 285.
High School—DeKalb, Ill.
Attended Iowa State University.

Selected by Tampa Bay in 4th round (44th player selected) of 1983 USFL draft.
Selected by New York Giants in 3rd round (70th player selected) of 1983 NFL draft.
Signed by New York Giants, June 13, 1983.
On injured reserve with foot injury, August 23 through entire 1983 season.
New York Giants NFL, 1984.
Games: 1984 (16).

LEE MARTIN NELSON
Safety—St. Louis Cardinals
Born January 30, 1954, at Kissimmee, Fla.
Height, 5.10. Weight, 185.
High School—Melbourne, Fla.
Attended Pensacola Junior College and Florida State University.

Selected by St. Louis in 15th round (420th player selected) of 1976 NFL draft.
On injured reserve, November 22 through remainder of 1977 season.

| | | —INTERCEPTIONS— | | | | —KICKOFF RET.— | | | | —TOTAL— | | |
Year	Club	G.	No.	Yds.	Avg.	TD.	No.	Yds.	Avg.	TD.	TD.	Pts.	F.
1976—St. Louis NFL		14		None			1	43	43.0	0	0	0	0
1977—St. Louis NFL		10	4	37	9.3	0	3	68	22.7	0	0	0	0
1978—St. Louis NFL		16	1	—3	—3.0	0	3	58	19.3	0	0	0	0
1979—St. Louis NFL		16		None				None			0	0	0
1980—St. Louis NFL		16		None			1	29	29.0	0	0	0	0
1981—St. Louis NFL		15		None				None			0	0	0
1982—St. Louis NFL		8	1	7	7.0	0		None			0	0	0
1983—St. Louis NFL		16	1	8	8.0	0		None			0	0	0
1984—St. Louis NFL		16		None				None			0	0	0
Pro Totals—9 Years		128	7	49	7.0	0	8	198	24.8	0	0	0	0

Additional pro statistics: Recovered one fumble, 1976, 1979 and 1980; returned one punt for four yards, 1977; returned four punts for 88 yards, 1979; returned one punt for five yards, 1980; recovered two fumbles, 1981; recovered four fumbles for 36 yards and a touchdown, 1983.

ROBERT LEE NELSON
(Bob)
Linebacker—Los Angeles Raiders
Born June 30, 1953, at Stillwater, Minn.
Height, 6.04. Weight, 235.
High School—Stillwater, Minn.
Received bachelor of science degree in education from University of Nebraska.

Selected by Buffalo in 2nd round (42nd player selected) of 1975 NFL draft.
Missed most of 1975 season due to leg injury (on active roster for 3 games but did not play).
Played out option with Buffalo Bills; signed as free agent by Oakland Raiders, March, 1978.
On injured reserve, August 11 through entire 1978 season.
Released by Oakland Raiders, August 21, 1979; signed as free agent by San Francisco 49ers, November 2, 1979.
On injured reserve with broken arm, November 14 through remainder of 1979 season.
Released by San Francisco 49ers after failing physical, July 19, 1980; signed as free agent by Oakland Raiders, July 25, 1980.
On injured reserve with shoulder injury, October 8 through November 26, 1980; activated, November 27, 1980.
On injured reserve with knee injury, August 25 through entire 1981 season.
Franchise transferred to Los Angeles, May 7, 1982.
On injured reserve with knee injury, November 23 through remainder of 1984 season.
Buffalo NFL, 1976 and 1977; San Francisco NFL, 1979; Oakland NFL, 1980; Los Angeles Raiders NFL, 1982 through 1984.
Games: 1976 (14), 1977 (11), 1979 (1), 1980 (9), 1982 (9), 1983 (16), 1984 (12). Total—72.
Pro statistics: Recovered one fumble, 1976 and 1983; returned one kickoff for 10 yards, 1977; intercepted one pass for no yards, 1980.
Played in AFC Championship Game following 1980 and 1983 seasons.
Played in NFL Championship Game following 1980 and 1983 seasons.

STEVEN LEE NELSON
(Steve)
Linebacker—New England Patriots
Born April 26, 1951, at Farmington, Minn.
Height, 6.02. Weight, 230.
High School—Anoka, Minn.
Attended Augsburg College and received bachelor of science degree in education
from North Dakota State University in 1974.

Named to THE SPORTING NEWS NFL All-Star Team, 1980.
Selected by New England in 2nd round (34th player selected) of 1974 NFL draft.
On injured reserve with knee injury, November 16 through remainder of 1976 season.
On injured reserve with separated shoulder, October 2 through October 30, 1981; activated, October 31, 1981.
On injured reserve with broken thumb, September 28 through November 24, 1983; activated, November 25, 1983.

Year Club	G.	No.	Yds.	Avg.TD.		Year Club	G.	No.	Yds.	Avg.TD.
			—INTERCEPTIONS—						—INTERCEPTIONS—	
1974—New England NFL	11		None			1980—New England NFL	16	3	37	12.3 0
1975—New England NFL	14	2	8	4.0 0		1981—New England NFL	12	1	9	9.0 0
1976—New England NFL	10	2	32	16.0 0		1982—New England NFL	9		None	
1977—New England NFL	13		None			1983—New England NFL	8	1	6	6.0 0
1978—New England NFL	14	5	104	20.8 0		1984—New England NFL	16	1	0	0.0 0
1979—New England NFL	15	1	18	18.0 0		Pro Totals—11 Years	138	16	214	13.4 0

Additional pro statistics: Recovered one fumble, 1974, 1977, 1979, 1980 and 1983; recovered three fumbles, 1976; recovered four fumbles, 1978.
Played in Pro Bowl (NFL All-Star Game) following 1980 and 1984 seasons.

EDWARD KENNETH NEWMAN
(Ed)
Guard—Miami Dolphins
Born June 4, 1951, at Woodbury, N. Y.
Height, 6.02. Weight, 255.
High School—Syosset, N. Y.
Attended Florida Atlantic University and received bachelor of science degree
in psychology from Duke University.

Selected by Miami in 6th round (156th player selected) of 1973 NFL draft.
On injured reserve with knee injury, November 23 through remainder of 1978 season.
On injured reserve with knee injury, December 31 through remainder of 1982 season.
Miami NFL, 1973 through 1984.
Games: 1973 (11), 1974 (14), 1975 (14), 1976 (14), 1977 (14), 1978 (12), 1979 (16), 1980 (16), 1981 (16), 1982 (8), 1983 (16), 1984 (16). Total—167.
Pro statistics: Recovered one fumble, 1974, 1976 and 1978; recovered two fumbles, 1980.
Played in AFC Championship Game following 1973 and 1984 seasons.
Played in NFL Championship Game following 1973 and 1984 seasons.
Played in Pro Bowl (NFL All-Star Game) following 1981, 1983 and 1984 seasons.
Named to Pro Bowl following 1982 season; replaced due to injury by Bob Kuechenberg.

OZZIE NEWSOME
Tight End—Cleveland Browns
Born March 15, 1956, at Muscle Shoals, Ala.
Height, 6.02. Weight, 232.
High School—Leighton, Ala., Colbert County.
Attended University of Alabama.
Cousin of Darrin Nelson, running back with Minnesota Vikings, and Kevin Nelson,
running back with Los Angeles Express.

Named to THE SPORTING NEWS NFL All-Star Team, 1984.
Named to THE SPORTING NEWS AFC All-Star Team, 1979.
Named as wide receiver on THE SPORTING NEWS College All-America Team, 1977.
Selected by Cleveland in 1st round (23rd player selected) of 1978 NFL draft.

Year Club	G.	P.C.	Yds.	Avg.	TD.
		—PASS RECEIVING—			
1978—Cleveland NFL	16	38	589	15.5	2
1979—Cleveland NFL	16	55	781	14.2	9
1980—Cleveland NFL	16	51	594	11.6	3
1981—Cleveland NFL	16	69	1002	14.5	6
1982—Cleveland NFL	8	49	633	12.9	3
1983—Cleveland NFL	16	89	970	10.9	6
1984—Cleveland NFL	16	89	1001	11.2	5
Pro Totals—7 Years	104	440	5570	12.7	34

Additional pro statistics: Returned two punts for 29 yards, rushed 13 times for 96 yards and two touchdowns and fumbled once, 1978; rushed once for six yards, 1979; rushed twice for 13 yards and fumbled twice, 1980; rushed twice for 20 yards, 1981.
Played in Pro Bowl (NFL All-Star Game) following 1981 and 1984 seasons.

TIMOTHY ARTHUR NEWSOME
(Timmy)
Fullback—Dallas Cowboys
Born May 17, 1958, at Ahoskie, N. C.
Height, 6.01. Weight, 235.
High School—Ahoskie, N. C.
Received bachelor of arts degree in business administration from
Winston-Salem State University in 1980.

Selected by Dallas in 6th round (162nd player selected) of 1980 NFL draft.

Year Club	G.	Att.	RUSHING Yds.	Avg.	TD.	PASS RECEIVING P.C.	Yds.	Avg.	TD.	TOTAL TD.	Pts.	F.
1980—Dallas NFL	16	25	79	3.2	2	4	43	10.8	0	2	12	0
1981—Dallas NFL	15	13	38	2.9	0		None			0	0	1
1982—Dallas NFL	9	15	98	6.5	1	6	118	19.7	1	2	12	1
1983—Dallas NFL	16	44	185	4.2	2	18	250	13.9	4	6	36	0
1984—Dallas NFL	15	66	268	4.1	5	26	263	10.1	0	5	30	3
Pro Totals—5 Years	71	163	668	4.1	10	54	674	12.5	5	15	90	5

Year Club	G.	KICKOFF RETURNS No.	Yds.	Avg.	TD.
1980—Dallas NFL	16	12	293	24.4	0
1981—Dallas NFL	15	12	228	19.0	0
1982—Dallas NFL	9	5	74	14.8	0
1983—Dallas NFL	16	1	28	28.0	0
1984—Dallas NFL	15		None		
Pro Totals—5 Years	71	30	623	20.8	0

Additional pro statistics: Recovered two fumbles, 1980; recovered one fumble, 1982.
Played in NFC Championship Game following 1980 through 1982 seasons.

VINCENT KARL NEWSOME
(Vince)
Safety—Los Angeles Rams

Born January 22, 1961, at Braintree, Wash.
Height, 6.01. Weight, 179.
High School—Vacaville, Calif.
Attended University of Washington.

Selected by Oakland in 4th round (42nd player selected) of 1983 USFL draft.
Selected by Los Angeles Rams in 4th round (97th player selected) of 1983 NFL draft.
Signed by Los Angeles Rams, May 22, 1983.
Los Angeles Rams NFL, 1983 and 1984.
Games: 1983 (16), 1984 (16). Total—32.
Pro statistics: Intercepted one pass for 31 yards, 1984.

MARK NICHOLS
Wide Receiver—Detroit Lions

Born October 29, 1959, at Bakersfield, Calif.
Height, 6.02. Weight, 208.
High School—Bakersfield, Calif.
Attended Bakersfield Junior College and San Jose State University.

Selected by Detroit in 1st round (16th player selected) of 1981 NFL draft.
On injured reserve with broken foot, December 25 through remainder of 1982 season.

Year Club	G.	PASS RECEIVING P.C.	Yds.	Avg.	TD.
1981—Detroit NFL	12	10	222	22.2	1
1982—Detroit NFL	7	8	146	18.3	2
1983—Detroit NFL	16	29	437	15.1	1
1984—Detroit NFL	15	34	744	21.9	1
Pro Totals—4 Years	50	81	1549	19.1	5

Additional pro statistics: Rushed three times for 50 yards, returned four kickoffs for 74 yards and fumbled once, 1981; rushed once for three yards, 1982; rushed once for 13 yards and fumbled twice, 1983; rushed three times for 27 yards and recovered one fumble, 1984.

SCOTT STEPHEN NICOLAS
Linebacker—Cleveland Browns

Born August 7, 1960, at Wichita Falls, Tex.
Height, 6.03. Weight, 226.
High School—Clearwater, Fla.
Received bachelor of business administration degree in marketing
from University of Miami (Fla.) in 1982.

Selected by Cleveland in 12th round (310th player selected) of 1982 NFL draft.
Cleveland NFL, 1982 through 1984.
Games: 1982 (9), 1983 (16), 1984 (16). Total—41.
Pro statistics: Returned two kickoffs for 16 yards and fumbled once for minus 14 yards, 1982; returned two kickoffs for 29 yards, 1983; recovered one fumble and returned one kickoff for 12 yards, 1984.

JEFFRY ALLEN NIXON
(Jeff)
Safety—Buffalo Bills

Born October 13, 1956, at Fursten Feldbruck, Germany.
Height, 6.03. Weight, 190.
High School—Woodbridge, Va., Gar-Field.
Received bachelor of arts degree in physical education from University of Richmond in 1979.
Maternally related to composer Johann Sebastian Bach.

Selected by Buffalo in 4th round (87th player selected) of 1979 NFL draft.
On injured reserve with knee injury, October 8 through December 5, 1980; activated, December 6, 1980.
On physically unable to perform/reserve with knee injury, July 15 through entire 1983 season.
On injured reserve with knee injury, August 14 through entire 1984 season.

| | | | —INTERCEPTIONS— | | | |
Year	Club	G.	No.	Yds.	Avg.	TD.
1979—Buffalo NFL		16	6	81	13.5	0
1980—Buffalo NFL		7	5	81	16.2	1
1981—Buffalo NFL		13		None		
1982—Buffalo NFL		7		None		
Pro Totals—4 Years		43	11	162	14.7	1

Additional pro statistics: Recovered one fumble, 1980.

FALANIKO NOGA
First name pronounced Fah-lah-NEE-koh.
Linebacker—St. Louis Cardinals
Born March 2, 1962, at American Samoa.
Height, 6.01. Weight, 230.
High School—Honolulu, Haw., Farrington.
Attended University of Hawaii.

Selected by Oakland in 10th round (192nd player selected) of 1984 USFL draft.
Selected by St. Louis in 8th round (201st player selected) of 1984 NFL draft.
Signed by St. Louis Cardinals, July 16, 1984.
St. Louis NFL, 1984.
Games: 1984 (16).
Pro statistics: Recovered one fumble, 1984.

KEITH NORD
Safety—Minnesota Vikings
Born March 13, 1957, at Minneapolis, Minn.
Height, 6.00. Weight, 195.
High School—Minneapolis, Minn., Minnetonka.
Received degree in marketing from St. Cloud State University in
1979; and attending University of Minnesota for master's degree.

Signed as free agent by Minnesota Vikings, May 26, 1979.
On injured reserve with torn Achilles tendon, September 20 through remainder of 1983 season.
On physically unable to perform/reserve with Achilles tendon injury, August 8 through entire 1984 season.
Minnesota NFL, 1979 through 1983.
Games: 1979 (16), 1980 (16), 1981 (16), 1982 (9), 1983 (3). Total—60.
Pro statistics: Returned three punts for 11 yards, 1979; recovered one fumble, 1979, 1981 and 1982; fumbled once, 1979; returned one kickoff for 70 yards and a touchdown and recovered three fumbles, 1980; returned 14 kickoffs for 229 yards and fumbled twice, 1981; returned three kickoffs for 43 yards, 1982; intercepted one pass for no yards, 1983.

CHRIS NORMAN
Punter—Denver Broncos
Born May 25, 1962, at Albany, Ga.
Height, 6.02. Weight, 198.
High School—Albany, Ga., Dougherty.
Attended University of South Carolina.

Signed as free agent by Denver Broncos, May 2, 1984.

| | | | —PUNTING— | | |
Year	Club	G.	No.	Avg.	Blk.
1984—Denver NFL		16	96	40.1	0

Additional pro statistics: Recovered one fumble and fumbled once, 1984.

TIM NORMAN
Guard—Chicago Bears
Born July 10, 1959, at Winfield, Ill.
Height, 6.06. Weight, 270.
High School—West Chicago, Ill.
Attended University of Illinois.

Signed as free agent by Washington Redskins, May 12, 1982.
Released by Washington Redskins, July 26, 1982; signed by Chicago Blitz, November 30, 1982.
Selected by San Antonio Gunslingers in 1st round (4th player selected) of USFL expansion draft, September 6, 1983.
Granted free agency, November 1, 1983.
USFL rights traded with rights to defensive end Tyrone Howard and draft pick by San Antonio Gunslingers to Arizona Wranglers for rights to quarterback Brad Wright and defensive backs James Bell and Mark Allen, November 22, 1983.
Signed as free agent by Chicago Bears, December 9, 1983.
On injured reserve with knee injury, August 27 through entire 1984 season.
Chicago USFL, 1983; Chicago NFL, 1983.
Games: 1983 USFL (17), 1983 NFL (1). Total Pro—18.

TOMMY NORMAN
Wide Receiver—Atlanta Falcons
Born October 25, 1961, at Greenville, Miss.
Height, 5.11. Weight, 174.
High School—Greenville, Miss.
Attended Jackson State University.

Selected by Los Angeles in 9th round (178th player selected) of 1984 USFL draft.
Selected by Atlanta in 11th round (287th player selected) of 1984 NFL draft.
Signed by Los Angeles Express, May 3, 1984.
Granted roster exemption, May 3 through remainder of 1984 season.
Released by Los Angeles Express, February 18, 1985; signed as free agent by Atlanta Falcons, March 22, 1985.

ULYSSES NORRIS JR.
Tight End—Buffalo Bills
Born January 15, 1957, at Monticello, Ga.
Height, 6.04. Weight, 232.
High School—Monticello, Ga.
Received bachelor of science degree in physical education from University of Georgia in 1979.

Selected by Detroit in 4th round (88th player selected) of 1979 NFL draft.
On injured reserve with appendicitis, September 19 through October 18, 1981; activated, October 19, 1981.
Released by Detroit Lions, August 27, 1984; signed as free agent by Buffalo Bills, August 28, 1984.

		—PASS RECEIVING—			
Year Club	G.	P.C.	Yds.	Avg.	TD.
1979—Detroit NFL	16	4	43	10.8	1
1980—Detroit NFL	16		None		
1981—Detroit NFL	12	8	132	16.5	0
1982—Detroit NFL	9	3	51	17.0	0
1983—Detroit NFL	15	26	291	11.2	7
1984—Buffalo NFL	14		None		
Pro Totals—6 Years	82	41	517	12.6	8

Additional pro statistics: Recovered one fumble, 1980 and 1983; returned one kickoff for no yards, 1983.

TERENCE JOHN NUGENT
(Terry)
Quarterback—Cleveland Browns
Born December 5, 1961, at Merced, Calif.
Height, 6.04. Weight, 218.
High School—Elk Grove, Calif.
Attended Colorado State University.

Selected by Denver in 1984 USFL territorial draft.
Selected by Cleveland in 6th round (158th player selected) of 1984 NFL draft.
Signed by Cleveland Browns, June 14, 1984.
Active for 16 games with Cleveland Browns in 1984; did not play.

VICTOR HUGO OATIS
Wide Receiver—Cleveland Browns
Born January 6, 1959, at Monroe, La.
Height, 6.00. Weight, 177.
High School—Winnsboro, La.
Received degree in drafting technology from Northwestern (La.) State University.

Selected by Philadelphia in 19th round (224th player selected) of 1983 USFL draft.
Selected by Philadelphia in 6th round (147th player selected) of 1983 NFL draft.
Signed by Philadelphia Eagles, May 13, 1983.
Released by Philadelphia Eagles, August 22, 1983; awarded on waivers to Baltimore Colts, August 24, 1983.
Franchise transferred to Indianapolis, March 31, 1984.
On injured reserve with thigh injury, August 27 through entire 1984 season.
Traded by Indianapolis Colts to Cleveland Browns for draft choice, May 16, 1985.

		—PASS RECEIVING—			
Year Club	G.	P.C.	Yds.	Avg.	TD.
1983—Baltimore NFL	9	6	93	15.5	0

RONNIE ALEXANDER O'BARD
Cornerback—San Diego Chargers
Born June 11, 1958, at San Diego, Calif.
Height, 5.10. Weight, 185.
High School—Spring Valley, Calif., Monte Vista.
Attended University of Idaho, Grossmont College and Brigham Young University.

Signed as free agent by San Diego Chargers, May 20, 1984.
Released on injured waivers with dislocated thumb, August 27, 1984; signed as free agent by Arizona Outlaws, November 29, 1984.
Released by Arizona Outlaws, January 19, 1985; signed as free agent by San Diego Chargers, April 26, 1985.
Played for San Diego Sharks in California Football League, 1982 and 1983.

KENNETH JOHN O'BRIEN JR.
(Ken)
Quarterback—New York Jets

Born November 27, 1960, at Long Island, N.Y.
Height, 6.04. Weight, 210.
High School—Sacramento, Calif., Jesuit.
Attended California State University at Sacramento and received degree in
political science from University of California at Davis in 1983.

Selected by Oakland in 6th round (66th player selected) of 1983 USFL draft.
Selected by New York Jets in 1st round (24th player selected) of 1983 NFL draft.
Signed by New York Jets, July 21, 1983.
Active for 16 games with New York Jets in 1983; did not play.

					PASSING						RUSHING				TOTAL	
Year	Club	G.	Att.	Cmp.	Pct.	Gain	T.P.	P.I.	Avg.	Att.	Yds.	Avg.	TD.	TD.	Pts.	F.
1984—N.Y. Jets NFL		10	203	116	57.1	1402	6	7	6.91	16	29	1.8	0	0	0	4

Quarterback Rating Points: 1984 (74.0).
Additional pro statistics: Recovered two fumbles, 1984.

MICHAEL LOUIS OBROVAC
(Mike)
Offensive Tackle—Cincinnati Bengals

Born October 11, 1955, at Canton, O.
Height, 6.06. Weight, 275.
High School—Canton, O., McKinley.
Attended Bowling Green State University.

Signed as free agent by Toronto Argonauts, April, 1978.
Released by Toronto Argonauts, June 15, 1978; re-signed by Argonauts, March, 1979.
On injured list, July 6 through September 12, 1980; activated, September 12, 1980.
Granted free agency, March 1, 1981; signed as free agent by Cincinnati Bengals, March 10, 1981.
Left Cincinnati Bengals camp voluntarily, August 13, 1981; returned, August 23, 1981.
On injured reserve with knee injury, October 9 through December 8, 1981; activated, December 9, 1981.
On injured reserve with knee injury, August 28 through entire 1984 season.
Toronto CFL, 1979 and 1980; Cincinnati, NFL, 1981 through 1983.
Games: 1979 (16), 1980 (7), 1981 (6), 1982 (9), 1983 (10). Total CFL—23. Total NFL—25. Total Pro—48.
Played in AFC Championship Game following 1981 season.
Played in NFL Championship Game following 1981 season.

CLIFTON ODOM
(Cliff)
Linebacker—Indianapolis Colts

Born August 15, 1958, at Beaumont, Tex.
Height, 6.02. Weight, 233.
High School—Beaumont, Tex., French.
Attended University of Texas at Arlington.

Selected by Cleveland in 3rd round (72nd player selected) of 1980 NFL draft.
On injured reserve with knee injury, November 3 through remainder of 1980 season.
Released by Cleveland Browns, August 18, 1981; signed as free agent by Oakland Raiders, March 1, 1982.
Franchise transferred to Los Angeles, May 7, 1982.
Released by Los Angeles Raiders, August 10, 1982; signed as free agent by Baltimore Colts, August 12, 1982.
Released by Baltimore Colts, September 6, 1982; re-signed by Colts, September 7, 1982.
Franchise transferred to Indianapolis, March 31, 1984.
Cleveland NFL, 1980; Baltimore NFL, 1982 and 1983; Indianapolis NFL, 1984.
Games: 1980 (8), 1982 (8), 1983 (15), 1984 (16). Total—47.
Pro statistics: Recovered one fumble, 1984.

CORNELIUS JOSEPH O'DONOGHUE
(Neil)
Placekicker—St. Louis Cardinals

Born June 18, 1953, at Dublin, Ireland.
Height, 6.06. Weight, 210.
High School—Dublin, Ireland.
Attended St. Bernard College and Auburn University.

Named as placekicker on THE SPORTING NEWS College All-America Team, 1976.
Selected by Buffalo in 5th round (127th player selected) of 1977 NFL draft.
Released by Buffalo Bills, October 18, 1977; signed as free agent by Tampa Bay Buccaneers, January 26, 1978.
Released by Tampa Bay Buccaneers, August 31, 1980; signed as free agent by St. Louis Cardinals, October 16, 1980.

		PLACE KICKING							PLACE KICKING				
Year	Club	G.	XP.	XPM.	FG.	FGA.	Pts.	Year	Club	G.	XP.	XPM.	FG.	FGA.	Pts.
1977—Buffalo NFL	5	4	1	2	6	10	1982—St. Louis NFL	8	15	1	8	13	39
1978—Tampa Bay NFL	15	25	4	13	23	64	1983—St. Louis NFL	16	45	2	15	28	90
1979—Tampa Bay NFL	16	30	5	11	19	63	1984—St. Louis NFL	16	48	3	23	35	117
1980—St. Louis NFL	10	18	0	11	15	51	Pro Totals—8 Years	102	221	17	102	171	527
1981—St. Louis NFL	16	36	1	19	32	93							

Additional pro statistics: Recovered one fumble, 1979, 1981 and 1983.
Played in NFC Championship Game following 1979 season.

MARK OGREN
Linebacker—New York Jets
Born November 16, 1961, at Duluth, Minn.
Height, 6.03. Weight, 219.
High School—Port Wing, Wis., South Shore.
Received degree in business administration and finance from
University of Minnesota at Duluth in 1984.

Signed as free agent by New York Jets, May 20, 1984.
On injured reserve with knee injury, August 7 through entire 1984 season.

HUBERT OLIVER
(Hubie)
Fullback—Philadelphia Eagles
Born November 12, 1957, at Elyria, O.
Height, 5.10. Weight, 212.
High School—Elyria, O.
Attended University of Arizona.

Selected by Philadelphia in 10th round (275th player selected) of 1981 NFL draft.
On injured reserve with knee injury, September 7 through December 9, 1982; activated, December 10, 1982.
On injured reserve with knee injury, December 22 through remainder of 1982 season.
Active for 2 games with Philadelphia Eagles in 1982; did not play.

Year Club	G.	—RUSHING— Att.	Yds.	Avg.	TD.	PASS RECEIVING P.C.	Yds.	Avg.	TD.	—TOTAL— TD.	Pts.	F.
1981—Philadelphia NFL	13	75	329	4.4	1	10	37	3.7	0	1	6	1
1983—Philadelphia NFL	16	121	434	3.6	1	49	421	8.6	2	3	18	5
1984—Philadelphia NFL	16	72	263	3.7	0	32	142	4.4	0	0	0	0
Pro Totals—4 Years	45	268	1026	3.8	2	91	600	6.6	2	4	24	6

Additional pro statistics: Recovered two fumbles, 1983; recovered one fumble, 1984.

NEAL OLKEWICZ
Linebacker—Washington Redskins
Born January 30, 1957, at Phoenixville, Pa.
Height, 6.00. Weight, 233.
High School—Phoenixville, Pa.
Received bachelor of arts degree in law enforcement from University of Maryland in 1979.

Signed as free agent by Washington Redskins, May 7, 1979.
On injured reserve with knee injury, December 10 through remainder of 1981 season.

Year Club	G.	—INTERCEPTIONS— No.	Yds.	Avg.	TD.
1979—Washington NFL	16	1	4	4.0	0
1980—Washington NFL	12		None		
1981—Washington NFL	14	2	22	11.0	1
1982—Washington NFL	9		None		
1983—Washington NFL	16	1	14	14.0	0
1984—Washington NFL	16		None		
Pro Totals—6 Years	83	4	40	10.0	1

Additional pro statistics: Recovered one fumble, 1980; recovered three fumbles, 1982; recovered two fumbles, 1983 and 1984.
Played in NFC Championship Game following 1982 and 1983 seasons.
Played in NFL Championship Game following 1982 and 1983 seasons.

JAMES HENRY OSBORNE
(Jim)
Defensive Tackle—Chicago Bears
Born September 7, 1949, at Sylvania, Ga.
Height, 6.03. Weight, 259.
High School—Fort Lauderdale, Fla., Dillard.
Received bachelor of arts degree in accounting from Southern University.

Selected by Chicago in 7th round (182nd player selected) of 1972 NFL draft.
Chicago NFL, 1972 through 1984.
Games: 1972 (14), 1973 (14), 1974 (14), 1975 (12), 1976 (14), 1977 (13), 1978 (15), 1979 (16), 1980 (16), 1981 (16), 1982 (9), 1983 (16), 1984 (15). Total—184.
Pro statistics: Recovered two fumbles, 1972 and 1980; fumbled once and returned one kickoff for no yards, 1973; recovered one fumble, 1973, 1979 and 1983; returned one kickoff for no yards, 1975; recovered two fumbles for seven yards, 1981; credited with one safety, 1982.
Played in NFC Championship Game following 1984 season.

VINCENT LEE OSBY
(Vince)
Linebacker—San Diego Chargers
Born July 8, 1961, at Los Angeles, Calif.
Height, 6.00. Weight, 222.
High School—Lynwood, Calif.
Attended Pasadena City College and University of Illinois.

Signed as free agent by San Diego Chargers, May 20, 1984.
Released by San Diego Chargers, August 27, 1984; re-signed by Chargers, August 28, 1984.
San Diego NFL, 1984.
Games: 1984 (16).

STANLEY EUGENE OSIECKI
(Sandy)
Quarterback—Kansas City Chiefs
Born May 18, 1960, at Ansonia, Conn.
Height, 6.05. Weight, 202.
High School—Ansonia, Conn.
Attended Arizona State University.

Selected by Arizona in 1984 USFL territorial draft.
Signed by Arizona Wranglers, January 8, 1984.
Released by Arizona Wranglers, February 13, 1984; signed as free agent by Kansas City Chiefs, May 4, 1984.

Year Club	G.	Att.	Cmp.	Pct.	Gain	T.P.	P.I.	Avg.	Att.	Yds.	Avg.	TD.	TD.	Pts.	F.
				PASSING						RUSHING				TOTAL	
1984—Kansas City NFL	4	17	7	41.2	64	0	1	3.76	1	−2	−2.0	0	0	0	0

Quarterback Rating Points: 1984 (27.6).

LOUIS BYRON OUBRE III
Name pronounced OO-bray.
Guard—New Orleans Saints
Born May 15, 1958, at New Orleans, La.
Height, 6.04. Weight, 270.
High School—New Orleans, La., St. Augustine.
Attended University of Oklahoma.

Selected by New Orleans in 5th round (112th player selected) of 1981 NFL draft.
On injured reserve with shoulder separation, August 5 through entire 1981 season.
New Orleans NFL, 1982 through 1984.
Games: 1982 (9), 1983 (16), 1984 (12). Total—37.

DENNIS RAY OWENS
Nose Tackle—New England Patriots
Born February 27, 1960, at Clinton, N.C.
Height, 6.01. Weight, 258.
High School—Clinton, N.C.
Attended North Carolina State University.

Signed as free agent by New England Patriots, May 13, 1982.
New England NFL, 1982 through 1984.
Games: 1982 (9), 1983 (16), 1984 (16). Total—41.
Pro statistics: Recovered one fumble, 1982 and 1984; recovered one fumble for four yards, 1983.

JAMES E. OWENS
Running Back—Tampa Bay Buccaneers
Born July 5, 1955, at Sacramento, Calif.
Height, 5.11. Weight, 200.
High School—Sacramento, Calif., Norte del Rio.
Attended University of California at Los Angeles.

Selected by San Francisco in 2nd round (29th player selected) of 1979 NFL draft.
Traded by San Francisco 49ers to Tampa Bay Buccaneers for running back Johnny Davis, August 31, 1981.
On injured reserve with knee injury, September 26 through remainder of 1984 season.

Year Club	G.	Att.	Yds.	Avg.	TD.	P.C.	Yds.	Avg.	TD.	TD.	Pts.	F.
			RUSHING				PASS RECEIVING				TOTAL	
1979—San Francisco NFL	16	7	33	4.7	0	10	121	12.1	0	1	6	4
1980—San Francisco NFL	14		None			9	133	14.8	0	1	6	3
1981—Tampa Bay NFL	16	91	406	4.5	3	12	145	12.1	0	3	18	1
1982—Tampa Bay NFL	8	76	238	3.1	0	8	42	5.3	1	1	6	2
1983—Tampa Bay NFL	12	96	266	2.8	5	15	81	5.4	1	6	36	0
1984—Tampa Bay NFL	4	1	1	1.0	0	2	13	6.5	1	1	6	0
Pro Totals—6 Years	70	271	944	3.5	8	56	535	9.6	3	13	78	10

Year Club	KICKOFF RETURNS				
	G.	No.	Yds.	Avg.	TD.
1979—San Francisco NFL	16	41	1002	24.4	*1
1980—San Francisco NFL	14	31	726	23.4	*1
1981—Tampa Bay NFL	16	24	473	19.7	0
1982—Tampa Bay NFL	8	3	52	17.3	0
1983—Tampa Bay NFL	12	20	380	19.0	0
1984—Tampa Bay NFL	4	8	168	21.0	0
Pro Totals—6 Years...........	70	127	2801	22.1	2

Additional pro statistics: Recovered three fumbles, 1980; recovered one fumble, 1981 and 1983.

MEL OWENS
Linebacker—Los Angeles Rams
Born December 7, 1958, at Detroit, Mich.
Height, 6.02. Weight, 224.
High School—DeKalb, Ill.
Received bachelor of arts degree in literature from University of Michigan in 1981.

Selected by Los Angeles in 1st round (9th player selected) of 1981 NFL draft.
Los Angeles Rams NFL, 1981 through 1984.
Games: 1981 (16), 1982 (7), 1983 (16), 1984 (16). Total—55.
Pro statistics: Recovered two fumbles, 1983 and 1984; intercepted one pass for minus four yards, 1984.

GARY A. PADJEN
Linebacker—Indianapolis Colts
Born July 2, 1958, at Salt Lake City, Utah.
Height, 6.02. Weight, 241.
High School—Kearns, Utah.
Received degree in general business from Arizona State University.

Signed as free agent by Dallas Cowboys, May, 1980.
Released by Dallas Cowboys, August 25, 1980; signed as free agent by Washington Redskins, April 6, 1981.
Released by Washington Redskins, August 10, 1981; signed as free agent by Baltimore Colts, March 15, 1982.
On inactive list, September 19, 1982.
Franchise transferred to Indianapolis, March 31, 1984.
Baltimore NFL, 1982 and 1983; Indianapolis NFL, 1984.
Games: 1982 (8), 1983 (16), 1984 (16). Total—40.
Pro statistics: Recovered one fumble, 1983; returned one punt for no yards and fumbled once, 1984.

MIKE JOHN PAGEL
Quarterback—Indianapolis Colts
Born September 13, 1960, at Douglas, Ariz.
Height, 6.02. Weight, 201.
High School—Phoenix, Ariz., Washington.
Attended Arizona State University.
Brother of Karl Pagel, outfielder-first baseman with Chicago Cubs and Cleveland Indians, 1978, 1979 and 1981 through 1983; and minor league coach, Cleveland Indians' organization, 1984.

Selected by Baltimore in 4th round (84th player selected) of 1982 NFL draft.
Franchise transferred to Indianapolis, March 31, 1984.

Year Club		PASSING							RUSHING				TOTAL		
	G.	Att.	Cmp.	Pct.	Gain	T.P.	P.I.	Avg.	Att.	Yds.	Avg.	TD.	TD.	Pts.	F.
1982—Baltimore NFL	9	221	111	50.2	1281	5	7	5.80	19	82	4.3	1	1	6	9
1983—Baltimore NFL	15	328	163	49.7	2353	12	17	7.17	54	441	8.2	0	0	0	4
1984—Indianapolis NFL	11	212	114	53.8	1426	8	8	6.73	26	149	5.7	1	1	6	4
Pro Totals—3 Years..........	35	761	388	51.0	5060	25	32	6.65	99	672	6.8	2	2	12	17

Quarterback Rating Points: 1982 (62.4), 1983 (64.0), 1984 (71.8). Total—65.8.
Additional pro statistics: Recovered three fumbles and fumbled nine times for minus four yards, 1982; recovered one fumble, 1984.

ANTHONY R. PAIGE
(Tony)
Fullback—New York Jets
Born October 14, 1962, at Washington, D.C.
Height, 5.10. Weight, 230.
High School—Hyattsville, Md., DeMatha Catholic.
Attended Virginia Tech.

Selected by Pittsburgh in 1984 USFL territorial draft.
Selected by New York Jets in 6th round (149th player selected) of 1984 NFL draft.
Signed by New York Jets, May 29, 1984.

Year Club		RUSHING				PASS RECEIVING				TOTAL		
	G.	Att.	Yds.	Avg.	TD.	P.C.	Yds.	Avg.	TD.	TD.	Pts.	F.
1984—New York Jets NFL	16	35	130	3.7	7	6	31	5.2	1	8	48	1

Additional pro statistics: Returned three kickoffs for seven yards, 1984.

STEPHONE PAIGE
Wide Receiver—Kansas City Chiefs
Born October 15, 1961, at Long Beach, Calif.
Height, 6.01. Weight, 180.
High School—Long Beach, Calif., Polytechnic.
Attended Saddleback College and Fresno State University.

Selected by Oakland in 1983 USFL territorial draft.
Signed as free agent by Kansas City Chiefs, May 9, 1983.

Year Club	G.	PASS RECEIVING				—KICKOFF RET.—				—TOTAL—		
		P.C.	Yds.	Avg.	TD.	No.	Yds.	Avg.	TD.	TD.	Pts.	F.
1983—Kansas City NFL	16	30	528	17.6	6		None			6	36	1
1984—Kansas City NFL	16	30	541	18.0	4	27	544	20.1	0	4	24	0
Pro Totals—2 Years	32	60	1069	17.8	10	27	544	20.1	0	10	60	1

Additional pro statistics: Recovered one fumble, 1983; rushed three times for 19 yards, 1984.

JEFFREY FRANKLIN PAINE
(Jeff)
Linebacker—Kansas City Chiefs
Born August 19, 1961, at Garland, Tex.
Height, 6.02. Weight, 224.
High School—Richardson, Tex.
Attended Texas A&M University.

Selected by San Antonio in 1984 USFL territorial draft.
Selected by Kansas City in 5th round (134th player selected) of 1984 NFL draft.
Signed by Kansas City Chiefs, July 9, 1984.
Kansas City NFL, 1984.
Games: 1984 (14).

IRVIN LEE PANKEY
(Irv)
Offensive Tackle—Los Angeles Rams
Born February 15, 1958, at Aberdeen, Md.
Height, 6.04. Weight, 267.
High School—Aberdeen, Md.
Attended Pennsylvania State University.

Selected by Los Angeles in 2nd round (50th player selected) of 1980 NFL draft.
On injured reserve with torn Achilles tendon, August 16 through entire 1983 season.
Los Angeles Rams NFL, 1980 through 1984.
Games: 1980 (16), 1981 (13), 1982 (9), 1984 (16). Total—54.
Pro statistics: Recovered two fumbles and returned one kickoff for no yards, 1981.

WILLIAM PARIS
(Bubba)
Offensive Tackle—San Francisco 49ers
Born October 6, 1960, at Louisville, Ky.
Height, 6.06. Weight, 293.
High School—Louisville, Ky., DeSales.
Received degree from University of Michigan in 1982.

Selected by San Francisco in 2nd round (29th player selected) of 1982 NFL draft.
On injured reserve with knee injury, September 6 through entire 1982 season.
San Francisco NFL, 1983 and 1984.
Games: 1983 (16), 1984 (16). Total—32.
Pro statistics: Recovered one fumble, 1984.
Played in NFC Championship Game following 1983 and 1984 seasons.
Played in NFL Championship Game following 1984 season.

ANDREW JAMES PARKER
(Andy)
Tight End—Los Angeles Raiders
Born September 8, 1961, at Redlands, Calif.
Height, 6.05. Weight, 235.
High Schools—Dana Point, Calif., Dana Hills and Encinitas, Calif., San Dieguito.
Received bachelor of science degree in physical education
from University of Utah in 1984.

Selected by Philadelphia in 5th round (100th player selected) of 1984 USFL draft.
Selected by Los Angeles Raiders in 5th round (127th player selected) of 1984 NFL draft.
Signed by Los Angeles Raiders, June 19, 1984.
On injured reserve with back injury, November 3 through remainder of 1984 season.
Los Angeles Raiders NFL, 1984.
Games: 1984 (9).

KERRY PARKER
Cornerback—Kansas City Chiefs
Born October 3, 1955, at New Orleans, La.
Height, 6.01. Weight, 200.
High School—New Orleans, La., Carver.
Attended Grambling State University.

Signed as free agent by Oakland Raiders, May 15, 1979.
On injured reserve with knee injury, August 21 through entire 1979 season.
Released by Oakland Raiders, September 1, 1980; signed as free agent by British Columbia Lions, October 26, 1980.
Granted free agency, March 1, 1984; signed by Kansas City Chiefs, March 19, 1984.

| | | —INTERCEPTIONS— | | | |
Year Club	G.	No.	Yds.	Avg.	TD.
1980—British Columbia CFL.	1		None		
1981—British Columbia CFL.	12	2	0	0.0	0
1982—British Columbia CFL.	16	3	37	12.3	0
1983—British Columbia CFL.	16	6	86	14.3	1
1984—Kansas City NFL..........	15		None		
CFL Totals—4 Years	45	11	123	11.2	1
NFL Totals—1 Year............	15	0	0	0.0	0
Pro Totals—5 Years............	60	11	123	11.2	1

Additional pro statistics: Recovered one fumble, 1982; recovered two fumbles for 36 yards and a touchdown and returned one punt for 18 yards, 1983.

STEVEN R. PARKER
(Steve)
Defensive End—Indianapolis Colts
Born September 21, 1959, at Evanston, Ill.
Height, 6.03. Weight, 262.
High School—Evanston, Ill., Evanston Township.
Attended East Tennessee State University,
received degree in psychology from Eastern Illinois University and received master's degree
in international marketing from Northwestern University.

Signed as free agent by Hamilton Tiger-Cats, September 27, 1981.
Released by Hamilton Tiger-Cats, July 18, 1982; signed as free agent by Baltimore Colts, May 25, 1983.
Franchise transferred to Indianapolis, March 31, 1984.
On injured reserve with knee injury, November 28 through remainder of 1984 season.
Hamilton CFL, 1981 and 1982; Baltimore NFL, 1983; Indianapolis NFL, 1984.
Games: 1981 (4), 1982 (2), 1983 (16), 1984 (9). Total CFL—6. Total NFL—25. Total Pro—31.
Pro statistics: Recovered three fumbles, 1983.

RICK PARROS
Running Back—Denver Broncos
Born June 14, 1958, at Brooklyn, N. Y.
Height, 5.11. Weight, 200.
High School—Salt Lake City, Utah, Granite.
Attended Utah State University.

Selected by Denver in 4th round (107th player selected) of 1980 NFL draft.
On injured reserve with knee injury, July 25 through entire 1980 season.
On injured reserve with neck injury, October 28 through remainder of 1983 season.

| | | —RUSHING— | | | | PASS RECEIVING | | | | —TOTAL— | | |
Year Club	G.	Att.	Yds.	Avg.	TD.	P.C.	Yds.	Avg.	TD.	TD.	Pts.	F.
1981—Denver NFL	16	176	749	4.3	2	25	216	8.6	1	3	18	6
1982—Denver NFL	9	77	277	3.6	1	37	259	7.0	2	3	18	3
1983—Denver NFL	6	30	96	3.2	1	12	126	10.5	2	3	18	3
1984—Denver NFL	15	46	208	4.5	2	6	25	4.2	0	2	12	0
Pro Totals—4 Years....................	46	329	1330	4.0	6	80	626	7.8	5	11	66	12

Additional pro statistics: Recovered one fumble, 1981 and 1983.

ELVIS PATTERSON
Defensive Back—New York Giants
Born October 21, 1960, at Bryan, Tex.
Height, 5.11. Weight, 188.
High School—Houston, Tex., Jack Yates.
Attended University of Kansas.

Selected by Jacksonville in 10th round (207th player selected) of 1984 USFL draft.
Signed as free agent by New York Giants, May 3, 1984.
New York Giants NFL, 1984.
Games: 1984 (15).

—DID YOU KNOW—

That in a 35-10 loss at Pittsburgh on October 28, 1984, the Atlanta Falcons scored their only points on a field goal as time expired in the first half and a touchdown as the game ended?

WHITNEY PAUL
Linebacker—New Orleans Saints
Born October 8, 1953, at Galveston, Tex.
Height, 6.03. Weight, 215.
High School—Galveston, Tex., Ball.
Attended University of Colorado.

Selected by Kansas City in 10th round (277th player selected) of 1976 NFL draft.
Traded by Kansas City Chiefs to New Orleans Saints for 7th round pick in 1983 draft, July 31, 1982.

Year Club	G.	—INTERCEPTIONS— No.	Yds.	Avg.TD.	Year Club	G.	—INTERCEPTIONS— No.	Yds.	Avg.TD.
1976—Kansas City NFL	14	None			1981—Kansas City NFL	15	2	30	15.0 0
1977—Kansas City NFL	14	1	6	6.0 0	1982—New Orleans NFL	9	1	14	14.0 0
1978—Kansas City NFL	16	3	21	7.0 0	1983—New Orleans NFL	16	2	3	1.5 0
1979—Kansas City NFL	15	1	28	28.0 0	1984—New Orleans NFL	16	None		
1980—Kansas City NFL	12	1	0	0.0 0	Pro Totals—9 Years	127	11	102	9.3 0

Additional pro statistics: Recovered one fumble, 1976; recovered two fumbles, 1977; returned one kickoff for no yards, recovered one fumble and fumbled once, 1978; recovered three fumbles, 1979; recovered two fumbles for 32 yards and a touchdown, 1980; recovered one fumble for 47 yards and a touchdown, 1981.

JIMMY C. PAYNE
Defensive Tackle—Buffalo Bills
Born February 9, 1960, at Athens, Ga.
Height, 6.04. Weight, 270.
High School—Athens, Ga., Cedar Shoals.
Attended University of Georgia.

Selected by Tampa Bay in 2nd round (13th player selected) of 1983 USFL draft.
Selected by Buffalo in 4th round (112th player selected) of 1983 NFL draft.
Signed by Buffalo Bills, May 17, 1983.
On injured reserve with knee and ankle injuries, August 30 through entire 1983 season.
On injured reserve with knee injury, August 8 through entire 1984 season.

WALTER JERRY PAYTON
Running Back—Chicago Bears
Born July 25, 1954, at Columbia, Miss.
Height, 5.10. Weight, 202.
High School—Columbia, Miss.
Received bachelor of arts degree in communications and special education from Jackson State University.
Brother of Eddie Payton, kick returner with Cleveland Browns, Detroit Lions, Kansas City Chiefs,
Toronto Argonauts and Minnesota Vikings, 1977 through 1982; nephew of Rickey Young,
running back with Minnesota Vikings.

Established NFL records for most yards gained, rushing, game (275), November 20, 1977, against Minnesota Vikings; most rushing yards, career (13,309); most rushing attempts, career (3,047); most combined yards, career (17,304); most combined attempts, career (3,457); most consecutive combined 2,000-yard seasons (2), 1983 and 1984; most games, 100 yards rushing, career (63).
Tied NFL record for most seasons, 1,000 yards rushing (8).
Named NFC Player of the Year by THE SPORTING NEWS, 1976 and 1977.
Named to THE SPORTING NEWS NFL All-Star Team, 1980 and 1984.
Named to THE SPORTING NEWS NFC All-Star Team, 1976 through 1979.
Selected by Chicago in 1st round (4th player selected) of 1975 NFL draft.
USFL rights traded by Birmingham Stallions to Chicago Blitz for rights to quarterback Phil Kessel and a draft pick, January 23, 1984.

Year Club	G.	—RUSHING— Att.	Yds.	Avg.	TD.	PASS RECEIVING P.C.	Yds.	Avg.	TD.	—TOTAL— TD.	Pts.	F.
1975—Chicago NFL	13	196	679	3.5	7	33	213	6.5	0	7	42	9
1976—Chicago NFL	14	*311	1390	4.5	13	15	149	14.9	0	13	78	10
1977—Chicago NFL	14	*339	*1852	*5.5	*14	27	269	10.0	2	*16	96	11
1978—Chicago NFL	16	*333	1395	4.2	11	50	480	9.6	0	11	66	5
1979—Chicago NFL	16	*369	1610	4.4	14	31	313	10.1	2	16	96	7
1980—Chicago NFL	16	317	1460	4.6	6	46	367	8.0	1	7	42	5
1981—Chicago NFL	16	339	1222	3.6	6	41	379	9.2	2	8	48	9
1982—Chicago NFL	9	148	596	4.0	1	32	311	9.7	0	1	6	3
1983—Chicago NFL	16	314	1421	4.5	6	53	607	11.5	2	8	48	5
1984—Chicago NFL	16	381	1684	4.4	11	45	368	8.2	0	11	66	5
Pro Totals—10 Years	146	3047	13309	4.4	89	373	3456	9.3	9	98	588	69

Year Club	G.	—PASSING— Att.	Cmp.	Pct.	Gain	T.P.	P.I.	Avg.	—KICKOFF RET.— No.	Yds.	Avg.	TD.
1975—Chicago NFL	13	1	0	00.0	0	0	1	0.00	14	444	*31.7	0
1976—Chicago NFL	14			None					1	0	0.0	0
1977—Chicago NFL	14			None					2	95	47.5	0
1978—Chicago NFL	16			None						None		
1979—Chicago NFL	16	1	1	100.0	54	1	0	54.00		None		
1980—Chicago NFL	16	3	0	00.0	0	0	0	0.00		None		
1981—Chicago NFL	16	2	0	00.0	0	0	0	0.00		None		
1982—Chicago NFL	9	3	1	33.3	39	1	0	13.00		None		
1983—Chicago NFL	16	6	3	50.0	95	3	2	15.83		None		
1984—Chicago NFL	16	8	3	37.5	47	2	1	5.88		None		
Pro Totals—10 Years	146	24	8	33.3	235	7	4	9.79	17	539	31.7	0

Additional pro statistics: Punted once for 39 yards, 1975; recovered one fumble, 1975, 1982 and 1984; recovered five fumbles, 1977; recovered two fumbles, 1978, 1979 and 1983; recovered three fumbles, 1980 and 1981.
Played in NFC Championship Game following 1984 season.
Played in Pro Bowl (NFL All-Star Game) following 1976 through 1980, 1983 and 1984 seasons.

WAYNE LAMAR PEACE
Quarterback—Cincinnati Bengals
Born November 3, 1961, at Gainesville, Fla.
Height, 6.02. Weight, 215.
High School—Lakeland, Fla.
Attended University of Florida.

Selected by Tampa Bay in 1984 USFL territorial draft.
Signed by Tampa Bay Bandits, February 7, 1984.
Selected by Cincinnati in 1st round (7th player selected) of 1984 NFL supplemental draft.
Traded by Tampa Bay Bandits to Portland Breakers for two draft choices, February 6, 1985.
Left Portland Breakers voluntarily, February 8, 1985 (rights reverted to Tampa Bay Bandits).
Released by Tampa Bay Bandits, February 15, 1985; signed by Cincinnati Bengals, February 21, 1985.

Year Club	G.	Att.	Cmp.	Pct.	Gain	T.P.	P.I.	Avg.	Att.	Yds.	Avg.	TD.	TD.	Pts.	F.
				PASSING						RUSHING				TOTAL	
1984—Tampa Bay USFL	8	43	18	41.9	215	1	4	5.00	6	35	5.8	0	0	0	1

Quarterback Rating Points: 1984 (26.8).

JEFFREY KENNARD PEGUES
(Jeff)
Linebacker—Washington Redskins
Born January 19, 1962, at Laurinburg, N.C.
Height, 6.02. Weight, 236.
High School—Laurinburg, N.C., Scotland.
Attended East Carolina University.

Selected by Washington in 5th round (125th player selected) of 1984 NFL draft.
On injured reserve with shoulder injury, August 27 through entire 1984 season.

SCOTT JOHN PELLUER
Linebacker—New Orleans Saints
Born April 26, 1959, at Yakima, Wash.
Height, 6.02. Weight, 227.
High School—Bellevue, Wash., Interlake.
Attended Washington State University.
Brother of Steve Pelluer, quarterback with Dallas Cowboys.

Selected by Dallas in 4th round (91st player selected) of 1981 NFL draft.
Released by Dallas Cowboys, August 31, 1981; claimed on waivers by New Orleans Saints, September 1, 1981.
On inactive list, September 12, 1982.
New Orleans NFL, 1981 through 1984.
Games: 1981 (16), 1982 (6), 1983 (16), 1984 (16). Total—54.
Pro statistics: Recovered one fumble, 1981.

STEVEN CARL PELLUER
(Steve)
Quarterback—Dallas Cowboys
Born July 29, 1962, at Yakima, Wash.
Height, 6.04. Weight, 210.
High School—Bellevue, Wash., Interlake.
Attended University of Washington.
Brother of Scott Pelluer, linebacker with New Orleans Saints.

Selected by Oakland in 6th round (110th player selected) of 1984 USFL draft.
Selected by Dallas in 5th round (113th player selected) of 1984 NFL draft.
Signed by Dallas Cowboys, July 7, 1984.
Dallas NFL, 1984.
Games: 1984 (1).

GEORGE EVANS PEOPLES
Fullback—Tampa Bay Buccaneers
Born August 25, 1960, at Tampa, Fla.
Height, 6.00. Weight, 215.
High School—Tampa, Fla., King.
Attended Auburn University.

Selected by Dallas in 8th round (216th player selected) of 1982 NFL draft.
Released by Dallas Cowboys, August 29, 1983; awarded on waivers to New England Patriots, August 30, 1983.
Released by New England Patriots, August 27, 1984; signed as free agent by Tampa Bay Buccaneers, November 6, 1984.

Year Club	G.	Att.	—RUSHING— Yds. Avg. TD.			PASS RECEIVING P.C. Yds. Avg. TD.				—TOTAL— TD. Pts. F.		
1982—Dallas NFL	8	7	22	3.1	0	None				0	0	0
1983—New England NFL	16		None			None				0	0	0
1984—Tampa Bay NFL	6	1	2	2.0	0	None				0	0	0
Pro Totals—3 Years	30	8	24	3.0	0	0	0	0.0	0	0	0	0

Additional pro statistics: Recovered one fumble, 1982 and 1983.
Played in NFC Championship Game following 1982 season.

EDWARD JOSEPH PEROT
Name pronounced Pay-row.
(Pete)
Guard
Born April 28, 1957, at Natchitoches, La.
Height, 6.02. Weight, 261.
High School—Natchitoches, La., St. Mary's.
Attended Northwestern Louisiana State University.

Selected by Philadelphia in 2nd round (48th player selected) of 1979 NFL draft.
On injured reserve with shoulder injury, August 29 through entire 1983 season.
Granted free agency, February 1, 1985; signing rights released by Philadelphia Eagles, May 7, 1985.
Philadelphia NFL, 1979 through 1982 and 1984.
Games: 1979 (14), 1980 (16), 1981 (16), 1982 (9), 1984 (12). Total—67.
Played in NFC Championship Game following 1980 season.
Played in NFL Championship Game following 1980 season.

JESSE BENNETT PERRIN
(Benny)
Safety—St. Louis Cardinals
Born October 20, 1959, at Orange County, Calif.
Height, 6.02. Weight, 175.
High School—Decatur, Ala.
Attended University of Alabama.

Selected by St. Louis in 3rd round (65th player selected) of 1982 NFL draft.

Year Club	G.	No.	—INTERCEPTIONS— Yds. Avg.TD.		
1982—St. Louis NFL	9	1	35	35.0	0
1983—St. Louis NFL	16	4	50	12.5	0
1984—St. Louis NFL	16	4	22	5.5	0
Pro Totals—3 Years	41	9	107	11.9	0

Additional pro statistics: Recovered two fumbles for 32 yards and a touchdown, attempted one pass with one completion for four yards and rushed once for no yards, 1983; attempted one pass with one completion for no yards and recovered two fumbles for 16 yards, 1984.

ANTHONY LEMONT PETERS
(Tony)
Safety—Washington Redskins
Born April 28, 1953, at Oklahoma City, Okla.
Height, 6.01. Weight, 190.
High School—Pauls Valley, Okla.
Attended Northeastern Oklahoma A&M and University of Oklahoma.

Selected by Cleveland in 4th round (82nd player selected) of 1975 NFL draft.
Left Cleveland Browns' camp in contract dispute, August 1, 1979.
Traded by Cleveland Browns to Washington Redskins for 5th round pick in 1980 draft and 4th and 10th round picks in 1981 draft, August 17, 1979.
Suspended indefinitely, September 2, 1983, with drug charges pending.
Suspended November 18, 1983 for remainder of 1983 season; reinstated, May 15, 1984.
On injured reserve with abdominal strain, November 17 through remainder of 1984 season.

Year Club	G.	No.	—INTERCEPTIONS— Yds. Avg.TD.		
1975—Cleveland NFL	14	1	0	0.0	0
1976—Cleveland NFL	14		None		
1977—Cleveland NFL	14	2	29	14.5	0
1978—Cleveland NFL	16	2	7	3.5	0
1979—Washington NFL	16	1	—4	—4.0	0
1980—Washington NFL	16	4	59	14.8	0
1981—Washington NFL	16	3	0	0.0	0
1982—Washington NFL	9	1	14	14.0	0
1984—Washington NFL	8		None		
Pro Totals—9 Years	123	14	105	7.5	0

Additional pro statistics: Recovered one fumble for 10 yards, 1975; returned one punt for no yards, 1979; fumbled once, 1979 and 1980; returned one kickoff for five yards, 1981; recovered one fumble, 1981, 1982 and 1984.
Played in NFC Championship Game following 1982 season.
Played in NFL Championship Game following 1982 season.
Played in Pro Bowl (NFL All-Star Game) following 1982 season.

KURT DAVID PETERSEN
Guard—Dallas Cowboys
Born June 17, 1957, at St. Louis, Mo.
Height, 6.04. Weight, 268.
High School—St. Louis, Mo., Lutheran North.
Received bachelor of science degree in industrial
education from University of Missouri in 1980.

Selected by Dallas in 4th round (105th player selected) of 1980 NFL draft.
Dallas NFL, 1980 through 1984.
Games: 1980 (16), 1981 (16), 1982 (9), 1983 (14), 1984 (13). Total—68.
Pro statistics: Recovered one fumble, 1980; recovered two fumbles for three yards, 1981; recovered two fumbles, 1982.
Played in NFC Championship Game following 1980 through 1982 seasons.

THEODORE HANS PETERSEN III
(Ted)
Offensive Tackle
Born February 7, 1955, at Kankakee, Ill.
Height, 6.05. Weight, 253.
High School—Momence, Ill.
Received bachelor of science degree in health and physical education from
Eastern Illinois University in 1977.

Selected by Pittsburgh in 4th round (93rd player selected) of 1977 NFL draft.
On physically unable to perform/reserve with hip tumor, August 5 through October 15, 1981; activated, October 16, 1981.
On injured reserve with hip injury, October 31 through remainder of 1981 season.
On inactive list, September 13 and September 19, 1982.
On injured reserve with ankle injury, December 3 through remainder of 1983 season.
Released by Pittsburgh Steelers, August 14, 1984; signed as free agent by Cleveland Browns, August 29, 1984.
Released by Cleveland Browns, November 7, 1984; signed as free agent by Indianapolis Colts, November 14, 1984.
Granted free agency, February 1, 1985; signing rights released by Indianapolis Colts, May 10, 1985.
Pittsburgh NFL, 1977 through 1983; Cleveland (4)-Indianapolis (5) NFL, 1984.
Games: 1977 (14), 1978 (15), 1979 (16), 1980 (16), 1981 (2), 1982 (7), 1983 (13), 1984 (9). Total—92.
Pro statistics: Recovered one fumble, 1980 and 1984; recovered two fumbles, 1983.
Played in AFC Championship Game following 1978 and 1979 seasons.
Played in NFL Championship Game following 1978 and 1979 seasons.

KIRK DOUGLAS PHILLIPS
Wide Receiver—Dallas Cowboys
Born July 31, 1960, at Poteau, Okla.
Height, 6.01. Weight, 202.
High School—Spiro, Okla.
Attended The University of Tulsa.
Cousin of Rod Shoate, linebacker with New England Patriots, New Jersey Generals and Memphis Showboats,
1975 and 1977 through 1981, 1983 and 1984.

Signed as free agent by Dallas Cowboys, April 28, 1983.
On injured reserve with thumb injury, August 16 through entire 1983 season.

			—PASS RECEIVING—			
Year Club		G.	P.C.	Yds.	Avg.	TD.
1984—Dallas NFL		8	1	6	6.0	0

BILL PICKEL
Name pronounced Pick-ELL.
Defensive Lineman—Los Angeles Raiders
Born November 5, 1959, at Queens, N.Y.
Height, 6.05. Weight, 255.
High Schools—Milford, Conn., and Brooklyn, N.Y., St. Francis.
Attended Rutgers University.
Brother of George Pickel, defensive tackle at Rutgers University.

Selected by New Jersey in 1983 USFL territorial draft.
Selected by Los Angeles Raiders in 2nd round (54th player selected) of 1983 NFL draft.
Signed by Los Angeles Raiders, May 26, 1983.
Los Angeles Raiders NFL, 1983 and 1984.
Games: 1983 (16), 1984 (16). Total—32.
Pro statistics: Recovered one fumble, 1983.
Played in AFC Championship Game following 1983 season.
Played in NFL Championship Game following 1983 season.

CLAY FLOYD PICKERING
Wide Receiver—Cincinnati Bengals
Born June 2, 1961, at Jacksonville, Fla.
Height, 6.05. Weight, 215.
High School—Akron, O., Archbishop.
Attended University of Maine.

Signed as free agent by Cincinnati Bengals, May 20, 1984.
Released by Cincinnati Bengals, August 27, 1984; re-signed by Bengals, August 28, 1984.
On injured reserve with pulled hamstring, September 21 through remainder of 1984 season.
Cincinnati NFL, 1984.
Games: 1984 (3).

LAWRENCE D. PILLERS
Defensive Lineman—San Francisco 49ers
Born November 4, 1952, at Hazelhurst, Miss.
Height, 6.04. Weight, 250.
High School—Hazelhurst, Miss.
Received degree from Alcorn State University in 1976.
Brother-in-law of Dave Washington, linebacker with Denver Broncos, Buffalo Bills,
San Francisco 49ers and Detroit Lions, 1970 through 1979.

Selected by New York Jets in 11th round (296th player selected) of 1976 NFL draft.
Released by New York Jets, September 23, 1980; claimed on waivers by San Francisco 49ers, September 25, 1980.
New York Jets NFL, 1976 through 1979; New York Jets (3)-San Francisco (13) NFL, 1980; San Francisco NFL, 1981 through 1984.
Games: 1976 (14), 1977 (13), 1978 (16), 1979 (16), 1980 (16), 1981 (14), 1982 (9), 1983 (16), 1984 (16). Total—130.
Pro statistics: Recovered two fumbles, 1976 and 1978; recovered one fumble, 1977, 1979, 1982 and 1984; intercepted one pass for 16 yards, 1983.
Played in NFC Championship Game following 1981, 1983 and 1984 seasons.
Played in NFL Championship Game following 1981 and 1984 seasons.

JOSEPH ANTHONY PISARCIK
Name pronounced Pis-AR-chick.
(Joe)
Quarterback—Philadelphia Eagles
Born July 2, 1952, at Kingston, Pa.
Height, 6.04. Weight, 220.
High School—Kingston, Pa., Central Catholic.
Attended New Mexico State University.

Signed as free agent by Calgary Stampeders, 1974.
Signed as free agent by New York Giants, May, 1977.
On injured reserve with shoulder injury, October 16 through remainder of 1979 season.
Traded by New York Giants to Philadelphia Eagles for 6th round pick in 1981 draft, April 22, 1980.

Year Club	G.	Att.	Cmp.	Pct.	Gain	T.P.	P.I.	Avg.	Att.	Yds.	Avg.	TD.	TD.	Pts.	F.
1974—Calgary CFL	16	168	87	51.7	1087	3	5	6.47	16	63	3.9	0	0	0	1
1975—Calgary CFL	16	320	181	56.5	2252	18	15	7.04	30	92	3.1	3	3	18	1
1976—Calgary CFL	11	163	96	58.8	1128	2	9	6.92	22	56	2.5	1	1	6	2
1977—N.Y. Giants NFL	13	241	103	42.7	1346	4	14	5.59	27	57	2.1	2	2	12	6
1978—N.Y. Giants NFL	15	301	143	47.5	2096	12	23	6.96	17	68	4.0	1	1	6	2
1979—N.Y. Giants NFL	4	108	43	39.8	537	2	6	4.97	1	6	6.0	0	0	0	1
1980—Philadelphia NFL	9	22	15	68.2	187	0	0	8.50	3	—3	—1.0	0	0	0	1
1981—Philadelphia NFL	7	15	8	53.3	154	2	2	10.27	7	1	0.1	0	0	0	0
1982—Philadelphia NFL	1	1	1	100.0	24	0	0	24.00			None		0	0	0
1983—Philadelphia NFL	5	34	16	47.1	172	1	0	5.06	3	—1	—0.3	0	0	0	1
1984—Philadelphia NFL	7	176	96	54.5	1036	3	3	5.89	7	19	2.7	2	2	12	4
CFL Totals—3 Years	43	651	364	55.9	4467	23	29	6.86	68	211	3.1	4	4	24	4
NFL Totals—8 Years	61	898	425	47.3	5552	24	48	6.18	65	147	2.3	5	5	30	15
Pro Totals—11 Years	104	1549	789	50.9	10019	47	77	6.47	133	358	2.7	9	9	54	19

NFL Quarterback Rating Points: 1977 (42.5), 1978 (52.3), 1979 (39.0), 1980 (94.3), 1981 (89.3), 1982 (118.8), 1983 (72.2), 1984 (70.6). Total—54.2.
Additional pro statistics: Recovered two fumbles, 1977; recovered one fumble and fumbled twice for minus three yards, 1978; recovered one fumble, 1983.
Member of Philadelphia Eagles for NFC Championship Game following 1980 season; did not play.
Member of Philadelphia Eagles for NFL Championship Game following 1980 season; did not play.

DANNY RAY PITTMAN
Wide Receiver—St. Louis Cardinals
Born April 3, 1958, at Memphis, Tenn.
Height, 6.02. Weight, 205.
High School—Pasadena, Calif., John Muir.
Attended Pasadena City College and University of Wyoming.

Selected by New York Giants in 4th round (90th player selected) of 1980 NFL draft.
On injured reserve with broken jaw, September 9 through November 5, 1981; activated, November 6, 1981.
Released by New York Giants, October 29, 1983; awarded on waivers to St. Louis Cardinals, November 1, 1983.
On injured reserve with stress fracture in leg, August 27 through October 10, 1984; activated after clearing procedural waivers, October 12, 1984.

Year	Club	G.	P.C.	PASS RECEIVING Yds.	Avg.	TD.	—KICKOFF RET.— No.	Yds.	Avg.	TD.	—TOTAL— TD.	Pts.	F.
1980—New York Giants NFL		11	25	308	12.3	0	2	41	20.5	0	0	0	1
1981—New York Giants NFL		8	1	8	8.0	0	10	194	19.4	0	0	0	2
1982—New York Giants NFL		8	1	21	21.0	0	5	117	23.4	0	0	0	0
1983—N.Y.G. (8)-St.L. (4) NFL		12	9	175	19.4	1	6	107	17.8	0	1	6	0
1984—St. Louis NFL		10	10	145	14.5	0	14	319	22.8	0	0	0	1
Pro Totals—5 Years		49	46	657	14.3	1	37	778	21.0	0	1	6	4

Additional pro statistics: Rushed once for minus seven yards, 1980; returned one punt for 13 yards, 1981; recovered one fumble, 1981 and 1984; returned six punts for 40 yards, 1982; returned four punts for 10 yards, 1984.

MIKE PITTS
Defensive End—Atlanta Falcons
Born September 25, 1960, at Baltimore, Md.
Height, 6.05. Weight, 270.
High School—Baltimore, Md., Polytechnic.
Attended University of Alabama.
Cousin of Rick Porter, running back with Memphis Showboats.

Named as defensive end on THE SPORTING NEWS College All-America Team, 1982.
Selected by Birmingham in 1983 USFL territorial draft.
Selected by Atlanta in 1st round (16th player selected) of 1983 NFL draft.
Signed by Atlanta Falcons, July 16, 1983.
On injured reserve with knee injury, December 6 through remainder of 1984 season.
Atlanta NFL, 1983 and 1984.
Games: 1983 (16), 1984 (14). Total—30.
Pro statistics: Recovered one fumble for 26 yards, 1983; recovered two fumbles, 1984.

MICHAEL RICORDO PLEASANT
Wide Receiver—Los Angeles Rams
Born August 16, 1955, at Muskogee, Okla.
Height, 6.02. Weight, 193.
High School—Muskogee, Okla.
Received degree in special education and physical education
from University of Oklahoma in 1978.

Signed as free agent by Oakland Raiders, May 10, 1981.
Released by Oakland Raiders, August 13, 1981; signed as free agent by Los Angeles Rams, July 1, 1982.
Released by Los Angeles Rams, August 31, 1982; signed as free agent by San Diego Chargers, April 20, 1983.
On injured reserve with pulled hamstring, August 27 through entire 1983 season.
Released by San Diego Chargers, August 14, 1984; signed as free agent by Los Angeles Rams for 1985, November 13, 1984.
Signed for 1984 season, November 14, 1984.
Los Angeles Rams NFL, 1984.
Games: 1984 (5).
Pro statistics: Returned two kickoffs for 48 yards, 1984.

ARTHUR SCOTT PLUNKETT
(Art)
Offensive Tackle—St. Louis Cardinals
Born March 8, 1959, at Chicago, Ill.
Height, 6.07. Weight, 262.
High Schools—Arlington Heights, Ill., Arlington and Salt Lake City, Utah, Skyline.
Attended University of Nevada at Las Vegas.

Selected by Los Angeles in 8th round (216th player selected) of 1981 NFL draft.
On injured reserve with back injury, August 24 through October 26, 1981; claimed on procedural waivers by St. Louis Cardinals, October 28, 1981.
St. Louis NFL, 1981 through 1984.
Games: 1981 (8), 1982 (9), 1983 (16), 1984 (16). Total—49.

JAMES WILLIAM PLUNKETT JR.
(Jim)
Quarterback—Los Angeles Raiders
Born December 5, 1947, at San Jose, Calif.
Height, 6.02. Weight, 220.
High Schools—San Jose, Calif., Overfeldt and James Lick.
Attended Stanford University.

Heisman Trophy winner, 1970.
Named THE SPORTING NEWS College Football Player of the Year, 1970.
Named as quarterback on THE SPORTING NEWS College All-America Team, 1970.
Named THE SPORTING NEWS AFC Rookie of the Year, 1971.
Selected by New England in 1st round (1st player selected) of 1971 NFL draft.
Traded by New England Patriots to San Francisco 49ers for quarterback Tom Owen and four draft choices (two 1st round selections in 1976 plus 1st and 2nd round picks in 1977), April 5, 1976.
Released by San Francisco 49ers, August 28, 1978; signed as free agent by Oakland Raiders, September 12, 1978.
Franchise transferred to Los Angeles, May 7, 1982.
On injured reserve with pulled abdominal muscle, October 13 through November 11, 1984; activated, November 12, 1984.

Active for 14 games with Oakland Raiders in 1978; did not play.

Year Club	G.	Att.	Cmp.	Pct.	Gain	T.P.	P.I.	Avg.	Att.	Yds.	Avg.	TD.	TD.	Pts.	F.
			PASSING							RUSHING			TOTAL		
1971—New England NFL..........	14	328	158	48.2	2158	19	16	6.58	45	210	4.7	0	0	0	6
1972—New England NFL..........	14	355	169	47.6	2196	8	25	6.19	36	230	6.4	1	1	6	6
1973—New England NFL..........	14	376	193	51.3	2550	13	17	6.78	44	209	4.8	5	5	30	6
1974—New England NFL..........	14	352	173	49.1	2457	19	22	6.98	30	161	5.4	2	2	12	4
1975—New England NFL..........	5	92	36	39.1	571	3	7	6.21	4	7	1.8	1	1	6	2
1976—San Francisco NFL..........	12	243	126	51.9	1592	13	16	6.55	19	95	5.0	0	0	0	1
1977—San Francisco NFL..........	14	248	128	51.6	1693	9	14	6.83	28	71	2.5	1	1	6	2
1979—Oakland NFL....................	4	15	7	46.7	89	1	1	5.93	3	18	6.0	0	0	0	0
1980—Oakland NFL....................	13	320	165	51.6	2299	18	16	7.18	28	141	5.0	2	2	12	9
1981—Oakland NFL....................	9	179	94	52.5	1045	4	9	5.84	12	38	3.2	1	1	6	3
1982—L.A. Raiders NFL.............	9	261	152	58.2	2035	14	15	7.80	15	6	0.4	0	0	0	4
1983—L.A. Raiders NFL.............	14	379	230	60.7	2935	20	18	7.74	26	78	3.0	0	0	0	7
1984—L.A. Raiders NFL.............	8	198	108	54.5	1473	6	10	7.44	16	14	0.9	1	1	6	2
Pro Totals—14 Years	144	3346	1739	52.0	23093	147	186	6.90	306	1278	4.2	14	14	84	52

Quarterback Rating Points: 1971 (68.6), 1972 (46.1), 1973 (66.0), 1974 (63.8), 1975 (39.9), 1976 (62.8), 1977 (62.2), 1979 (60.1), 1980 (72.8), 1981 (56.7), 1982 (77.3), 1983 (82.7), 1984 (67.6). Total—65.5.

Additional pro statistics: Recovered one fumble, 1972 through 1974, 1981, 1982 and 1984; recovered two fumbles, 1977 and 1980; fumbled three times for minus six yards, 1981; fumbled four times for minus seven yards, 1982; recovered three fumbles, 1983.

Played in AFC Championship Game following 1980 and 1983 seasons.

Played in NFL Championship Game following 1980 and 1983 seasons.

JOHNNIE EDWARD POE
Cornerback—New Orleans Saints

Born August 29, 1959, at St. Louis, Mo.

Height, 6.01. Weight, 190.

High School—East St. Louis, Ill., Lincoln.

Attended University of Missouri.

Selected by New Orleans in 6th round (144th player selected) of 1981 NFL draft.

Year Club	G.	No.	Yds.	Avg.	TD.
		INTERCEPTIONS			
1981—New Orleans NFL........	15	1	0	0.0	0
1982—New Orleans NFL........	9		None		
1983—New Orleans NFL........	16	7	146	20.9	1
1984—New Orleans NFL........	16	1	16	16.0	0
Pro Totals—4 Years............	56	9	162	18.0	1

Additional pro statistics: Recovered one fumble for 10 yards and returned one punt for two yards, 1981; recovered one fumble, 1982; recovered two fumbles, 1983.

FRANK POLLARD
Running Back—Pittsburgh Steelers

Born June 15, 1957, at Clifton, Tex.

Height, 5.10. Weight, 218.

High School—Meridian, Tex.

Attended Baylor University.

Selected by Pittsburgh in 11th round (305th player selected) of 1980 NFL draft.

Year Club	G.	Att.	Yds.	Avg.	TD.	P.C.	Yds.	Avg.	TD.	TD.	Pts.	F.
		RUSHING				PASS RECEIVING				TOTAL		
1980—Pittsburgh NFL..............	16	4	16	4.0	0		None			0	0	5
1981—Pittsburgh NFL..............	14	123	570	4.6	2	19	156	8.2	0	2	12	5
1982—Pittsburgh NFL..............	9	62	238	3.8	2	6	39	6.5	0	2	12	3
1983—Pittsburgh NFL..............	16	135	608	4.5	4	16	127	7.9	0	4	24	5
1984—Pittsburgh NFL..............	15	213	851	4.0	6	21	186	8.9	0	6	36	9
Pro Totals—5 Years..................	70	537	2283	4.3	14	62	508	8.2	0	14	84	23

Year Club	G.	No.	Yds.	Avg.	TD.
		KICKOFF RETURNS			
1980—Pittsburgh NFL.............	16	22	494	22.5	0
1981—Pittsburgh NFL.............	14		None		
1982—Pittsburgh NFL.............	9		None		
1983—Pittsburgh NFL.............	16		None		
1984—Pittsburgh NFL.............	15		None		
Pro Totals—5 Years............	70	22	494	22.5	0

Additional pro statistics: Returned one punt for five yards, 1980; recovered one fumble, 1983; recovered two fumbles, 1984.

Played in AFC Championship Game following 1984 season.

—DID YOU KNOW—

That in the 49ers' 23-17 win over the Bengals on November 4, 1984, the first downs accumulated by each team was equal to the points those teams scored in Super Bowl XVI? That score was San Francisco 26, Cincinnati 21.

NATHAN POOLE
Running Back—Seattle Seahawks

Born December 17, 1956, at Alexander City, Ala.
Height, 5.09. Weight, 212.
High School—Alexander City, Ala., Benjamin Russell.
Attended University of Louisville.

Selected by Cincinnati in 10th round (250th player selected) of 1979 NFL draft.
Released by Cincinnati Bengals, August 10, 1981; signed as free agent by Toronto Argonauts, August 18, 1981.
Released by Toronto Argonauts, August 29, 1981; signed as free agent by Denver Broncos, April 16, 1982.
Released by Denver Broncos, August 20, 1984; signed by Chicago Blitz, October 27, 1984.
Franchise disbanded, November 20, 1984; signed as free agent by Seattle Seahawks, May 8, 1985.

Year Club	G.	Att.	Yds.	Avg.	TD.	P.C.	Yds.	Avg.	TD.	TD.	Pts.	F.
			RUSHING				PASS RECEIVING				—TOTAL—	
1979—Cincinnati NFL	16	1	—3	—3.0	0	1	—10	—10.0	0	0	0	2
1980—Cincinnati NFL	16	5	6	1.2	0	2	—4	—2.0	0	0	0	1
1981—Toronto CFL	1	6	33	5.5	0	1	4	4.0	0	0	0	0
1982—Denver NFL	9	7	36	5.1	0			None		0	0	0
1983—Denver NFL	16	81	246	3.0	4	20	184	9.2	0	4	24	1
NFL Totals—4 Years	57	94	285	3.0	4	23	170	7.4	0	4	24	4
CFL Total—1 Year	1	6	33	5.5	0	1	4	4.0	0	0	0	0
Pro Totals—5 Years	58	100	318	3.2	4	24	174	7.3	0	4	24	4

Year Club	G.	No.	Yds.	Avg.	TD.
		KICKOFF RETURNS			
1979—Cincinnati NFL	16	7	128	18.3	0
1980—Cincinnati NFL	16	1	8	8.0	0
1981—Toronto CFL	1		None		
1982—Denver NFL	9	1	0	0.0	0
1983—Denver NFL	16		None		
NFL Totals—4 Years	57	9	136	15.1	0
CFL Total—1 Year	1	0	0	0.0	0
Pro Totals—5 Years	58	9	136	15.1	0

Additional pro statistics: Recovered two fumbles, 1979; recovered one fumble, 1980 and 1983.

ROBERT BRYANT PORTER
(Rob)
Safety—Kansas City Chiefs

Born May 9, 1962, at Mahwah, N.J.
Height, 6.01. Weight, 200.
High School—Mahwah, N.J.
Attended Holy Cross College.
Brother of Steve Porter, outfielder in Kansas City Royals' organization, 1978.

Selected by Philadelphia in 15th round (303rd player selected) of 1984 USFL draft.
Signed as free agent by Kansas City Chiefs, May 4, 1984.
On injured reserve with knee injury, July 31 through entire 1984 season.

TRACY R. PORTER
Wide Receiver—Indianapolis Colts

Born June 1, 1959, at Baton Rouge, La.
Height, 6.02. Weight, 202.
High School—Baton Rouge, La., Southern University Laboratory.
Received bachelor of science degree in finance from Louisiana State University.

Selected by Detroit in 4th round (99th player selected) of 1981 NFL draft.
Traded by Detroit Lions to Baltimore Colts for 10th round pick in 1984 draft, August 29, 1983.
Franchise transferred to Indianapolis, March 31, 1984.

Year Club	G.	P.C.	Yds.	Avg.	TD.
		PASS RECEIVING			
1981—Detroit NFL	12	3	63	21.0	1
1982—Detroit NFL	8	9	124	13.8	0
1983—Baltimore NFL	16	28	384	13.7	0
1984—Indianapolis NFL	16	39	590	15.1	2
Pro Totals—4 Years	52	79	1161	14.7	3

Additional pro statistics: Attempted one pass with no completions, 1982; recovered one fumble and fumbled twice, 1984.

STEPHEN JOHN POTTER
(Steve)
Linebacker—Buffalo Bills

Born November 6, 1957, at Bradford, Pa.
Height, 6.03. Weight, 235.
High School—Erie, Pa., Fairview.
Received bachelor of business administration degree in marketing
from University of Virginia in 1980.

Signed as free agent by Oakland Raiders, May 9, 1980.

Released by Oakland Raiders, August 21, 1980; re-signed by Raiders, August 25, 1980.
Released by Oakland Raiders, September 1, 1980; signed as free agent by Miami Dolphins, May 1, 1981.
Released by Miami Dolphins, August 29, 1983; awarded on waivers to Kansas City Chiefs, August 30, 1983.
Released by Kansas City Chiefs, August 8, 1984; signed as free agent by Buffalo Bills, September 12, 1984.
On non-football injury list with hepatitis, December 11 through remainder of 1984 season.
Miami NFL, 1981 and 1982; Kansas City NFL, 1983; Buffalo NFL, 1984.
Games: 1981 (16), 1982 (9), 1983 (16), 1984 (10). Total—51.
Pro statistics: Intercepted one pass for no yards, 1983.
Played in AFC Championship Game following 1982 season.
Played in NFL Championship Game following 1982 season.

MARVIN POWELL
Offensive Tackle—New York Jets
Born August 30, 1955, at Fort Bragg, N. C.
Height, 6.05. Weight, 270.
High School—Fayetteville, N. C., 71st.
Received bachelor of arts degree in speech and political science from
University of Southern California in 1977 and attending New York Law School.

Named as offensive tackle on THE SPORTING NEWS College All-America Team, 1976.
Named to THE SPORTING NEWS AFC All-Star Team, 1979.
Named to THE SPORTING NEWS NFL All-Star Team, 1981.
Selected by New York Jets in 1st round (4th player selected) of 1977 NFL draft.
New York Jets NFL, 1977 through 1984.
Games: 1977 (11), 1978 (14), 1979 (16), 1980 (15), 1981 (14), 1982 (8), 1983 (16), 1984 (16). Total—110.
Pro statistics: Recovered one fumble, 1978 and 1980.
Played in AFC Championship Game following 1982 season.
Played in Pro Bowl (NFL All-Star Game) following 1979 through 1982 seasons.
Named to Pro Bowl following 1983 season; replaced due to law school by Henry Lawrence.

PHILIP MAURICE POZDERAC
(Phil)
Offensive Tackle—Dallas Cowboys
Born December 19, 1959, at Cleveland, O.
Height, 6.09. Weight, 274.
High School—Garfield Heights, O.
Received bachelor of business administration degree in finance
from University of Notre Dame in 1982.

Selected by Dallas in 5th round (137th player selected) of 1982 NFL draft.
Dallas NFL, 1982 through 1984.
Games: 1982 (7), 1983 (16), 1984 (15). Total—38.
Pro statistics: Caught one pass for one yard, 1984.
Member of Dallas Cowboys for NFC Championship Game following 1982 season; did not play.

DEAN PRATER
Defensive End—Buffalo Bills
Born September 28, 1958, at Altus, Okla.
Height, 6.04. Weight, 245.
High School—Wichita Falls, Tex., Rider.
Attended Oklahoma State University.

Selected by Cleveland in 10th round (271st player selected) of 1981 NFL draft.
Released by Cleveland Browns, August 24, 1981; signed as free agent by Kansas City Chiefs, May 10, 1982.
On commissioner's exempt list, November 20 through November 23, 1982.
On non-football injury list with knee injury, November 24 through remainder of 1982 season.
USFL rights traded with running back Darrell Smith, defensive tackle Mike Perko and placekicker Rex Robinson by Chicago Blitz to Boston Breakers for rights to quarterback Greg Landry, August 11, 1982.
USFL rights traded by New Orleans Breakers to Chicago Blitz for future draft pick, January 26, 1984.
Released by Kansas City Chiefs, August 27, 1984; signed as free agent by Buffalo Bills, September 12, 1984.
Kansas City NFL, 1982 and 1983; Buffalo NFL, 1984.
Games: 1982 (2), 1983 (16), 1984 (13). Total—31.
Pro statistics: Recovered one fumble, 1983.

GUY TYRONE PRATHER
Name pronounced PRAY-ther.
Linebacker—Green Bay Packers
Born March 28, 1958, at Gaithersburg, Md.
Height, 6.02. Weight, 230.
High School—Gaithersburg, Md.
Received bachelor of science degree in accounting from Grambling State University in 1980.

Signed as free agent by Dallas Cowboys, May, 1980.
Released by Dallas Cowboys, August 19, 1980; signed as free agent by Green Bay Packers, January 16, 1981.
Green Bay NFL, 1981 through 1984.
Games: 1981 (16), 1982 (9), 1983 (16), 1984 (16). Total—57.
Pro statistics: Recovered one fumble, 1982 and 1984; returned one kickoff for seven yards, 1984.

ROBERT HENRY PRATT JR.
Guard—Seattle Seahawks
Born May 25, 1951, at Richmond, Va.
Height, 6.04. Weight, 250.
High School—Richmond, Va., St. Christopher's.
Received bachelor of science degree in business administration from
University of North Carolina in 1974.

Selected by Baltimore in 3rd round (67th player selected) of 1974 NFL draft.
Traded by Baltimore Colts to Seattle Seahawks for 5th round pick in 1984 draft, July 12, 1982.
Baltimore NFL, 1974 through 1981; Seattle NFL, 1982 through 1984.
Games: 1974 (13), 1975 (14), 1976 (14), 1977 (14), 1978 (16), 1979 (16), 1980 (16), 1981 (15), 1982 (9), 1983 (15), 1984 (16). Total—158.
Pro statistics: Returned four kickoffs for 64 yards, 1975; returned one kickoff for 21 yards, 1976; recovered one fumble for 21 yards and one touchdown, 1977; recovered one fumble, 1981 through 1983; fumbled once, 1981; caught one pass for 30 yards, 1984.
Played in AFC Championship Game following 1983 season.

RAYMOND NEWTON PRESTON JR.
(Ray)
Linebacker—San Diego Chargers
Born January 25, 1954, at Lawrence, Mass.
Height, 6.00. Weight, 220.
High School—Lawrence, Mass.
Received bachelor of science degree in marketing from Syracuse University.

Selected by San Diego in 11th round (295th player selected) of 1976 NFL draft.
On injured reserve with knee injury, November 7 through remainder of 1984 season.
San Diego NFL, 1976 through 1984.
Games: 1976 (14), 1977 (11), 1978 (16), 1979 (16), 1980 (14), 1981 (16), 1982 (9), 1983 (16), 1984 (10). Total—122.
Pro statistics: Recovered one fumble, 1976 and 1980; returned one kickoff for 16 yards, 1976; returned one kickoff for 15 yards, 1978; intercepted five passes for 121 yards, 1979; recovered two fumbles, 1982; intercepted one pass for 13 yards, 1983.
Played in AFC Championship Game following 1980 and 1981 seasons.

LUKE EARL PRESTRIDGE
Punter—Seattle Seahawks
Born September 17, 1956, at Houston, Tex.
Height, 6.04. Weight, 235.
High School—Houston, Tex., Sharpstown.
Received bachelor of business administration degree in management from Baylor University in 1979.

Led NFL in net punting average with 37.8 in 1982.
Selected by Denver in 7th round (188th player selected) of 1979 NFL draft.
Traded by Denver Broncos to New England Patriots for 10th round pick in 1985 draft, August 20, 1984.
Released by New England Patriots, November 3, 1984; signed as free agent by Seattle Seahawks, February 25, 1985.

		——PUNTING——		
Year Club	G.	No.	Avg.	Blk.
1979—Denver NFL	16	89	39.9	0
1980—Denver NFL	16	70	43.9	0
1981—Denver NFL	16	86	40.4	0
1982—Denver NFL	9	45	*45.0	0
1983—Denver NFL	16	87	41.6	0
1984—New England NFL	9	44	42.8	0
Pro Totals—6 Years	82	421	41.9	0

Additional pro statistics: Rushed once for 29 yards and attempted one pass with no completions, 1979; fumbled once, 1981; rushed once for seven yards, 1983.
Played in Pro Bowl (NFL All-Star Game) following 1982 season.

LARRY THOMAS PRIDEMORE JR.
(Tom)
Safety—Atlanta Falcons
Born April 29, 1956, at Oak Hill, W. Va.
Height, 5.11. Weight, 186.
High School—Ansted, W. Va.
Received bachelor of science degree in business management from
West Virginia University.

Member of West Virginia House of Delegates.
Selected by Atlanta in 9th round (236th player selected) of 1978 NFL draft.
Released by Atlanta Falcons, August 22, 1978; re-signed by Falcons, August 30, 1978.

		-INTERCEPTIONS-				—KICKOFF RET.—				—TOTAL—		
Year Club	G.	No.	Yds.	Avg.	TD.	No.	Yds.	Avg.	TD.	TD.	Pts.	F.
1978—Atlanta NFL	16	1	0	0.0	0	4	71	17.8	0	0	0	0
1979—Atlanta NFL	16	2	20	10.0	0	9	111	12.3	0	0	0	0
1980—Atlanta NFL	16	2	2	1.0	0	3	39	13.0	0	0	0	0
1981—Atlanta NFL	16	2	221	31.6	1	None				1	6	0
1982—Atlanta NFL	9	1	28	28.0	0	None				0	0	0

Year Club	G.	No.	Yds.	Avg.TD.	No.	Yds.	Avg.	TD.	TD.	Pts.	F.
		—INTERCEPTIONS—			—KICKOFF RET.—				—TOTAL—		
1983—Atlanta NFL	16	4	56	14.0 0	None				0	0	0
1984—Atlanta NFL	16	2	0	0.0 0	None				0	0	0
Pro Totals—7 Years	105	19	327	17.2 1	16	221	13.8	0	1	6	0

Additional pro statistics: Recovered three fumbles for minus seven yards, 1978; recovered one fumble for 33 yards, 1979; recovered two fumbles, 1980, 1982 and 1984; recovered three fumbles for 24 yards and returned one punt for no yards, 1981; rushed once for seven yards, 1984.

ANDREW PROVENCE
Nose Tackle—Atlanta Falcons
Born March 8, 1961, at Savannah, Ga.
Height, 6.03. Weight, 260.
High School—Savannah, Ga., Benedictine.
Attended University of South Carolina.

Selected by Washington in 1983 USFL territorial draft.
Selected by Atlanta in 3rd round (75th player selected) of 1983 NFL draft.
Signed by Atlanta Falcons, May 30, 1983.
Atlanta NFL, 1983 and 1984.
Games: 1983 (16), 1984 (16). Total—32.
Pro statistics: Recovered one fumble for 26 yards, 1983; recovered one fumble, 1984.

GREGORY DONALD PRUITT
(Greg)
Running Back—Los Angeles Raiders
Born August 18, 1951, at Houston, Tex.
Height, 5.10. Weight, 190.
High School—Houston, Tex., Elmore.
Received bachelor of arts degree in journalism from University of Oklahoma.
Cousin of Brig Owens, defensive back with Washington Redskins, 1966 through 1977;
Marv Owens, wide receiver with Minnesota Vikings, St. Louis Cardinals and New York Jets,
1972 through 1974; Bob Love, forward with Cincinnati Royals, Milwaukee Bucks,
Chicago Bulls, New York Nets and Seattle SuperSonics, 1966 through 1977;
Beasley Reece, safety with Tampa Bay Buccaneers; and Bo Metcalf, defensive back with Indianapolis Colts.

Established NFL record for most punt return yards, season (666), 1983.
Named as running back on THE SPORTING NEWS College All-America Team, 1972.
Selected by Cleveland in 2nd round (30th player selected) of 1973 NFL draft.
On injured reserve with knee injury, November 1 through remainder of 1979 season.
Traded by Cleveland Browns to Oakland Raiders for 11th round pick in 1983 draft, April 28, 1982.
Franchise transferred to Los Angeles, May 7, 1982.

Year Club	G.	Att.	Yds.	Avg.	TD.	P.C.	Yds.	Avg.	TD.	TD.	Pts.	F.
		—RUSHING—				PASS RECEIVING				—TOTAL—		
1973—Cleveland NFL	13	61	369	6.0	4	9	110	12.2	1	5	30	7
1974—Cleveland NFL	14	126	540	4.3	3	21	274	13.0	1	5	30	10
1975—Cleveland NFL	14	217	1067	4.9	8	44	299	6.8	1	9	54	10
1976—Cleveland NFL	14	209	1000	4.8	4	45	341	7.6	1	5	30	7
1977—Cleveland NFL	14	236	1086	4.6	3	37	471	12.7	1	4	24	8
1978—Cleveland NFL	12	176	960	5.5	3	38	292	7.7	2	5	30	12
1979—Cleveland NFL	6	62	233	3.8	0	14	155	11.1	1	1	6	1
1980—Cleveland NFL	16	40	117	2.9	0	50	444	8.9	5	5	30	1
1981—Cleveland NFL	15	31	124	4.0	0	65	636	9.8	4	4	24	3
1982—Los Angeles Raiders NFL	9	4	22	5.5	0	2	29	14.5	1	1	6	5
1983—Los Angeles Raiders NFL	16	26	154	5.9	2	1	6	6.0	0	3	18	10
1984—Los Angeles Raiders NFL	15	8	0	0.0	0	2	12	6.0	0	0	0	9
Pro Totals—12 Years	158	1196	5672	4.7	27	328	3069	9.4	18	47	282	83

Year Club	G.	Att.	Cmp.	Pct.	Gain	T.P.	P.I.	Avg.	No.	Yds.	Avg.	TD.	No.	Yds.	Avg.	TD.
		—PASSING—							—PUNT RET.—				—KICKOFF RET.—			
1973—Cleveland NFL	13	1	0	00.0	0	0	0	0.00	16	180	11.3	0	16	453	28.3	0
1974—Cleveland NFL	14	2	2	100.0	115	2	0	57.50	27	349	12.9	0	22	606	27.5	*1
1975—Cleveland NFL	14			None					13	130	10.0	0	14	302	21.6	0
1976—Cleveland NFL	14	3	2	66.7	39	1	0	13.00		None			1	27	27.0	0
1977—Cleveland NFL	14	9	4	44.4	28	3	0	3.11		None				None		
1978—Cleveland NFL	12	3	0	00.0	0	0	2	0.00		None			1	31	31.0	0
1979—Cleveland NFL	6			None						None			1	22	22.0	0
1980—Cleveland NFL	16			None						None				None		
1981—Cleveland NFL	15			None						None			3	82	27.3	0
1982—L.A. Raiders NFL	9			None					27	209	7.7	0	14	371	26.5	0
1983—L.A. Raiders NFL	16	1	0	00.0	0	0	0	0.00	*58	*666	11.5	*1	31	604	19.5	0
1984—L.A. Raiders NFL	15			None					53	473	8.9	0	3	16	5.3	0
Pro Totals—12 Years	158	19	8	42.1	182	6	2	9.58	194	2007	10.3	1	106	2514	23.7	1

Additional pro statistics: Recovered two fumbles, 1973 through 1975 and 1984; recovered three fumbles, 1977; recovered one fumble, 1978 and 1979; recovered four fumbles, 1982; recovered seven fumbles, 1983.
Played in AFC Championship Game following 1983 season.
Played in NFL Championship Game following 1983 season.
Played in Pro Bowl (NFL All-Star Game) following 1973, 1974, 1976, 1977 and 1983 seasons.

MICHAEL PRUITT
(Mike)
Fullback—Cleveland Browns
Born April 3, 1954, at Chicago, Ill.
Height, 6.00. Weight, 225.
High School—Chicago, Ill., Wendell Phillips.
Attended Purdue University.

Named to THE SPORTING NEWS AFC All-Star Team, 1979.
Selected by Cleveland in 1st round (7th player selected) of 1976 NFL draft.
On injured reserve with knee injury, November 2 through November 29, 1984; activated, November 30, 1984.

Year Club	G.	—RUSHING—				PASS RECEIVING				—TOTAL—		
		Att.	Yds.	Avg.	TD.	P.C.	Yds.	Avg.	TD.	TD.	Pts.	F.
1976—Cleveland NFL	13	52	138	2.7	0	8	26	3.3	0	0	0	4
1977—Cleveland NFL	13	47	205	4.4	1	3	12	4.0	0	1	6	1
1978—Cleveland NFL	16	135	560	4.1	5	20	112	5.6	0	5	30	3
1979—Cleveland NFL	16	264	1294	4.9	9	41	372	9.1	2	11	66	6
1980—Cleveland NFL	16	249	1034	4.2	6	63	471	7.5	0	6	36	9
1981—Cleveland NFL	16	247	1103	4.5	7	63	442	7.0	1	8	48	5
1982—Cleveland NFL	9	143	516	3.6	3	22	140	6.4	0	3	18	4
1983—Cleveland NFL	15	293	1184	4.0	10	30	157	5.2	2	12	72	4
1984—Cleveland NFL	10	163	506	3.1	6	5	29	5.8	0	6	36	1
Pro Totals—9 Years	124	1595	6540	4.1	47	255	1761	6.9	5	52	312	37

Additional pro statistics: Returned six kickoffs for 106 yards, 1976; returned six kickoffs for 131 yards, 1977; recovered two fumbles, 1978 and 1981 through 1983; recovered one fumble, 1984.
Played in Pro Bowl (NFL All-Star Game) following 1979 and 1980 seasons.

PHILLIP DAVID PUZZUOLI
Name pronounced Pa-ZOOL-ee.
(Dave)
Nose Tackle—Cleveland Browns
Born January 12, 1961, at Greenwich, Conn.
Height, 6.03. Weight, 260.
High School—Stamford, Conn., Catholic.
Attended University of Pittsburgh.

Selected by Tampa Bay in 8th round (85th player selected) of 1983 USFL draft.
Selected by Cleveland in 6th round (149th player selected) of 1983 NFL draft.
Signed by Cleveland Browns, May 31, 1983.
Cleveland NFL, 1983 and 1984.
Games: 1983 (16), 1984 (16). Total—32.
Pro statistics: Recovered one fumble for two yards, 1983; recovered one fumble, 1984.

MICHAEL ANTHONY QUICK
(Mike)
Wide Receiver—Philadelphia Eagles
Born May 14, 1959, at Hamlet, N.C.
Height, 6.02. Weight, 190.
High School—Rockingham, N.C., Richmond.
Attended Fork Union Military Academy and North Carolina State University.

Selected by Philadelphia in 1st round (20th player selected) of 1982 NFL draft.

Year Club	—PASS RECEIVING—				
	G.	P.C.	Yds.	Avg.	TD.
1982—Philadelphia NFL	9	10	156	15.6	1
1983—Philadelphia NFL	16	69	*1409	20.4	13
1984—Philadelphia NFL	14	61	1052	17.2	9
Pro Totals—3 Years	39	140	2617	18.7	23

Additional pro statistics: Recovered one fumble, 1982; fumbled once, 1983; rushed once for minus five yards, 1984.
Played in Pro Bowl (NFL All-Star Game) following 1983 and 1984 seasons.

FRED QUILLAN
Center—San Francisco 49ers
Born January 27, 1956, at Portland, Ore.
Height, 6.05. Weight, 266.
High School—Portland, Ore., Central Catholic.
Attended University of Oregon.

Selected by San Francisco in 7th round (175th player selected) of 1978 NFL draft.
San Francisco NFL, 1978 through 1984.
Games: 1978 (14), 1979 (16), 1980 (16), 1981 (16), 1982 (9), 1983 (14), 1984 (16). Total—101.
Pro statistics: Returned one kickoff for eight yards, 1978; fumbled twice for minus 34 yards, 1979; fumbled once for minus 42 yards, 1980; fumbled once, 1981; recovered one fumble, 1983.
Played in NFC Championship Game following 1981, 1983 and 1984 seasons.
Played in NFL Championship Game following 1981 and 1984 seasons.
Played in Pro Bowl (NFL All-Star Game) following 1984 season.

GEORGE JOSEPH RADACHOWSKY JR.
Defensive Back—Indianapolis Colts
Born September 7, 1962, at Danbury, Conn.
Height, 5.11. Weight, 178.
High School—Danbury, Conn.
Attended Boston College

Selected by Philadelphia in 5th round (84th player selected) of 1984 USFL draft.
Selected by Los Angeles Rams in 7th round (188th player selected) of 1984 NFL draft.
Signed by Los Angeles Rams, July 9, 1984.
Traded by Los Angeles Rams to Indianapolis Colts for 11th round pick in 1985 draft, August 27, 1984.
Indianapolis NFL, 1984.
Games: 1984 (16).
Pro statistics: Returned one kickoff for no yards and fumbled once, 1984.

JOHN RADE
Name pronounced RAY-dee.
Linebacker—Atlanta Falcons
Born August 31, 1960, at Ceres, Calif.
Height, 6.01. Weight, 225.
High School—Sierra Vista, Ariz., Buena.
Attended Boise State University.

Signed as free agent by Boston Breakers, February 10, 1983.
Released by Boston Breakers, February 12, 1983.
Selected by Atlanta in 8th round (215th player selected) of 1983 NFL draft.
Signed by Atlanta Falcons, May 16, 1983.
On injured reserve with pinched nerve in neck, October 24 through remainder of 1984 season.
Atlanta NFL, 1983 and 1984.
Games: 1983 (16), 1984 (7). Total—23.
Pro statistics: Recovered two fumbles for 16 yards and a touchdown, 1983; recovered one fumble, 1984.

J. SCOTT RADECIC
Name pronounced RADD-ah-seck.

(Known by middle name.)
Linebacker—Kansas City Chiefs
Born June 14, 1962, at Pittsburgh, Pa.
Height, 6.03. Weight, 240.
High School—Pittsburgh, Pa., Brentwood.
Attended Penn State University.

Selected by Philadelphia in 1984 USFL territorial draft.
Selected by Kansas City in 2nd round (34th player selected) of 1984 NFL draft.
Signed by Kansas City Chiefs, July 12, 1984.

		——INTERCEPTIONS——			
Year Club	G.	No.	Yds.	Avg.	TD.
1984—Kansas City NFL..........	16	2	54	27.0	1

WAYNE R. RADLOFF
Center—Atlanta Falcons
Born May 17, 1961, at London, England.
Height, 6.05. Weight, 265.
High School—Winter Haven, Fla.
Attended University of Georgia.

Named center on THE SPORTING NEWS USFL All-Star Team, 1984.
Selected by Michigan in 2nd round (15th player selected) of 1983 USFL draft.
Signed by Michigan Panthers, January 22, 1983.
On developmental squad, April 4 through April 9, 1983; activated, April 10, 1983.
Not protected in merger of Michigan Panthers and Oakland Invaders; not selected in USFL dispersal draft, December 6, 1984.
Signed as free agent by Atlanta Falcons, March 1, 1985.
On developmental squad for 1 game with Michigan Panthers in 1983.
Michigan USFL, 1983 and 1984.
Games: 1983 (17), 1984 (18). Total—35.
Pro statistics: Recovered one fumble, 1983.
Played in USFL Championship Game following 1983 season.

THOMAS MICHAEL RAFFERTY
(Tom)
Center—Dallas Cowboys
Born August 2, 1954, at Syracuse, N. Y.
Height, 6.03. Weight, 254.
High School—Manlius, N. Y.
Received bachelor of science degree in physical education from Penn State University;
attending University of Dallas for master's degree.

Selected by Dallas in 4th round (119th player selected) of 1976 NFL draft.

Dallas NFL, 1976 through 1984.
Games: 1976 (13), 1977 (14), 1978 (16), 1979 (16), 1980 (16), 1981 (16), 1982 (9), 1983 (16), 1984 (16). Total—132.
Pro statistics: Fumbled once, 1977; recovered one fumble, 1979 and 1981; recovered one fumble for six yards, 1980;
fumbled twice for minus 30 yards, 1981; recovered two fumbles, 1982 and 1984; caught one pass for eight yards, 1983.
Played in NFC Championship Game following 1977, 1978 and 1980 through 1982 seasons.
Played in NFL Championship Game following 1977 and 1978 seasons.

DAN RAINS
Linebacker—Chicago Bears
Born April 26, 1956, at Rochester, Pa.
Height, 6.01. Weight, 220.
High School—Hopewell, Pa.
Attended University of Cincinnati

Signed as free agent by Philadelphia Eagles, May 10, 1978.
Released by Philadelphia Eagles, July 15, 1978; signed as free agent by Chicago Bears, May 14, 1982.
On injured reserve with hernia, July 29 through December 23, 1982; re-signed after clearing procedural waivers,
December 25, 1982.
Chicago NFL, 1982 through 1984.
Games: 1982 (1), 1983 (15), 1984 (16). Total—32.
Pro statistics: Returned two kickoffs for 11 yards and recovered one fumble, 1983.
Played in NFC Championship Game following 1984 season.

DANIEL RAY RALPH
(Dan)
Defensive Tackle—St. Louis Cardinals
Born March 9, 1961, at Denver, Colo.
Height, 6.04. Weight, 260.
High School—Northglenn, Colo.
Attended University of Colorado and University of Oregon.

Selected by Arizona in 7th round (129th player selected) of 1984 USFL draft.
Selected by Atlanta in 6th round (163rd player selected) of 1984 NFL draft.
Signed by Atlanta Falcons, June 23, 1984.
Released by Atlanta Falcons, August 24, 1984; signed as free agent by St. Louis Cardinals, November 6, 1984.
St. Louis NFL, 1984.
Games: 1984 (6).

DERRICK KENT RAMSEY
Tight End—New England Patriots
Born December 23, 1956, at Hastings, Fla.
Height, 6.05. Weight, 235.
High Schools—Hastings, Fla. and Camden, N.J.
Attended University of Kentucky.

Selected by Oakland in 5th round (136th player selected) of 1978 NFL draft.
Franchise transferred to Los Angeles, May 7, 1982.
Traded by Los Angeles Raiders to New England Patriots for tight end Don Hasselbeck, September 13, 1983.

Year Club	G.	PASS RECEIVING				—KICKOFF RET.—				—TOTAL—		
		P.C.	Yds.	Avg.	TD.	No.	Yds.	Avg.	TD.	TD.	Pts.	F.
1978—Oakland NFL	16		None			7	125	17.9	0	0	0	0
1979—Oakland NFL	16	13	161	12.4	3		None			3	18	0
1980—Oakland NFL	16	5	117	23.4	0	1	10	10.0	0	0	0	0
1981—Oakland NFL	16	52	674	13.0	4		None			4	24	2
1982—Los Angeles Raiders NFL	9		None				None			0	0	0
1983—L. A. Raid. (2)—N. E. (14) NFL	16	24	335	14.0	6		None			6	36	0
1984—New England NFL	16	66	792	12.0	7		None			7	42	0
Pro Totals—7 Years	105	160	2079	13.0	20	8	135	16.9	0	20	120	2

Additional pro statistics: Recovered one fumble, 1980 and 1981.
Played in AFC Championship Game following 1980 season.
Played in NFL Championship Game following 1980 season.

LOWELL WALLACE RAMSEY JR.
(Chuck)
Punter—New York Jets
Born February 24, 1952, at Rock Hill, S. C.
Height, 6.02. Weight, 194.
High School—Knoxville, Tenn., West.
Attended Wake Forest University.

Named as punter on THE SPORTING NEWS College All-America Team, 1973.
Selected by New England in 6th round (141st player selected) of 1974 NFL draft.
Selected by Chicago in 24th round of 1974 WFL draft.
Contract breached by Chicago Fire (WFL) and signed by New England Patriots, June 1975.
Released by New England Patriots, September 1975.
Did not play, 1975 and 1976.
Signed as free agent by Detroit Lions, 1977.
Released by Detroit Lions, August 15, 1977; signed as free agent by New York Jets, September 27, 1977.

Year Club	G.	—PUNTING— No.	Avg.	Blk.
1974—Chicago WFL	...	71	39.9	
1977—New York Jets NFL	12	62	37.1	0
1978—New York Jets NFL	16	74	40.1	0
1979—New York Jets NFL	16	73	40.8	0
1980—New York Jets NFL	16	73	42.4	1
1981—New York Jets NFL	16	81	40.6	0
1982—New York Jets NFL	9	35	38.5	1
1983—New York Jets NFL	16	81	39.7	1
1984—New York Jets NFL	16	74	39.7	1
WFL Totals—1 Year	...	71	39.9	...
NFL Totals—8 Years	117	553	40.0	4
Pro Totals—9 Years	...	624	40.0	...

Additional WFL statistics: Rushed once for minus ten yards, completed one of two passes for 22 yards and kicked three field goals, 1974.

Additional NFL statistics: Recovered one fumble, 1979 and 1981; rushed twice for no yards and fumbled twice for minus 34 yards, 1979; attempted two passes with one completion for six yards and rushed once for minus 15 yards, 1980; rushed three times for no yards and fumbled twice for minus 39 yards, 1981.

Played in AFC Championship Game following 1982 season.

THOMAS LLOYD RAMSEY
(Tom)
Quarterback—New England Patriots
Born July 9, 1961, at Encino, Calif.
Height, 6.00. Weight, 188.
High School—Granada Hills, Calif., Kennedy.
Attended University of California at Los Angeles.

Selected by Los Angeles in 5th round (49th player selected) of 1983 USFL draft.
Signed by Los Angeles Express, February 10, 1983.
Selected by New England in 10th round (267th player selected) of 1983 NFL draft.
On developmental squad, July 2 through remainder of 1983 season.
Traded by Los Angeles Express to Oakland Invaders for 3rd round pick in 1985 draft, March 29, 1984.
On developmental squad, March 30 through April 28, 1984; activated, April 29, 1984.
Released by Oakland Invaders, July 17, 1984; signed by New England Patriots, July 25, 1984.
On injured reserve with thumb injury, August 21 through entire 1984 season.
On developmental squad for 1 game with Los Angeles Express in 1983.
On developmental squad for 4 games with Oakland Invaders in 1984.

Year Club	G.	Att.	Cmp.	—PASSING— Pct.	Gain	T.P.	P.I.	Avg.	Att.	—RUSHING— Yds.	Avg.	TD.	—TOTAL— TD.	Pts.	F.
1983—Los Angeles USFL	17	307	160	52.1	1975	13	14	6.43	28	80	2.9	1	1	6	4
1984—L.A. (5)-Oak. (5) USFL	10	91	54	59.3	512	2	7	5.63	8	38	4.8	0	0	0	1
Pro Totals—2 Years	27	398	214	53.8	2487	15	21	6.25	36	118	3.3	1	1	6	5

USFL Quarterback Rating Points: 1983 (67.1), 1984 (50.3). Total—63.6.

ERNEST TATE RANDLE
(Known by middle name.)
Safety—Indianapolis Colts
Born August 15, 1959, at Fredricksburg, Tex.
Height, 6.00. Weight, 196.
High School—Fort Stockton, Tex.,
Received bachelor of science degree in physical education and health from Texas Tech University.

Selected by Miami in 8th round (220th player selected) of 1982 NFL draft.
Released by Miami Dolphins, September 6, 1982; re-signed by Dolphins, September 7, 1982.
Released by Miami Dolphins, September 8, 1982; claimed on waivers by Houston Oilers, September 10, 1982.
On inactive list, September 12 and September 19, 1982.
Released by Houston Oilers, September 20, 1983; signed as free agent by Baltimore Colts, October 11, 1983.
Franchise transferred to Indianapolis, March 31, 1984.

Year Club	G.	—INTERCEPTIONS— No.	Yds.	Avg.	TD.
1982—Houston NFL	7			None	
1983—Hou.(2)-Bal.(10) NFL	12	1	41	41.0	0
1984—Indianapolis NFL	16	3	66	22.0	0
Pro Totals—3 Years	35	4	107	26.8	0

Additional pro statistics: Recovered two fumbles, 1984.

BRIAN ANTHONY RANSOM
Quarterback—Houston Oilers
Born July 9, 1960, at Nashville, Tenn.
Height, 6.03. Weight, 205.
High School—Nashville, Tenn., North.
Received bachelor of business administration degree in accounting
from Tennessee State University in 1983.

Signed as free agent by Dallas Cowboys, April 28, 1983.
Released by Dallas Cowboys, August 29, 1983; signed as free agent by Houston Oilers, September 29, 1983.

Active for 12 games with Houston Oilers in 1983; did not play.
Active for 16 games with Houston Oilers in 1984; did not play.

SCOTT DAVID RARIDON
Offensive Tackle—Denver Broncos
Born February 22, 1961, at Newton, Iowa.
Height, 6.04. Weight, 266.
High School—Mason City, Iowa.
Attended University of Nebraska.

Selected by Philadelphia in 1st round (16th player selected) of 1984 USFL draft.
Selected by Philadelphia in 6th round (145th player selected) of 1984 NFL draft.
Signed by Philadelphia Eagles, May 22, 1984.
Left Philadelphia Eagles camp voluntarily, July 19, 1984; returned, August 7, 1984.
Left Philadelphia Eagles camp voluntarily, August 13, 1984; placed on reserve/left camp, August 21 through entire 1984 season.
Traded by Philadelphia Eagles to Denver Broncos for draft choice, May 8, 1985.

RANDY ROBERT RASMUSSEN
Center-Guard—Pittsburgh Steelers
Born September 27, 1960, at Minneapolis, Minn.
Height, 6.01. Weight, 253.
High School—St. Paul, Minn., Irondale.
Received bachelor of applied studies degree in business and marketing from
University of Minnesota in 1984.

Selected by Chicago in 12th round (241st player selected) of 1984 USFL draft.
Selected by Pittsburgh in 8th round (220th player selected) of 1984 NFL draft.
Signed by Pittsburgh Steelers, June 18, 1984.
Pittsburgh NFL, 1984.
Games: 1984 (16).
Played in AFC Championship Game following 1984 season.

DARROL ANTHONY RAY
Safety—New York Jets
Born June 25, 1958, at San Francisco, Calif.
Height, 6.01. Weight, 198.
High School—Killeen, Tex.
Attended University of Oklahoma.

Selected by New York Jets in 2nd round (40th player selected) of 1980 NFL draft.

		——INTERCEPTIONS——			
Year Club	G.	No.	Yds.	Avg.	TD.
1980—N.Y. Jets NFL	16	6	132	22.0	1
1981—N.Y. Jets NFL	16	7	227	32.4	2
1982—N.Y. Jets NFL	9	3	91	30.3	0
1983—N.Y. Jets NFL	16	3	77	25.7	0
1984—N.Y. Jets NFL	15	2	54	27.0	0
Pro Totals—5 Years	72	21	581	27.7	3

Additional pro statistics: Recovered one fumble for 75 yards and a touchdown, 1980; fumbled once, 1980, 1981 and 1982; recovered two fumbles for four yards, 1981; recovered one fumble, 1982 and 1983; ran 52 yards on lateral from interception, 1984.

RICK ANTHONY RAZZANO
Linebacker
Born November 15, 1955, at New Castle, Pa.
Height, 5.11. Weight, 227.
High School—New Castle, Pa.
Attended Virginia Tech.

Signed as free agent by Toronto Argonauts, April, 1978.
On injured list, September 28 through remainder of 1978 season.
On injured list, November 1 through remainder of 1979 season.
Granted free agency, May 15, 1980; signed as free agent by Cincinnati Bengals, July 3, 1980.
Released by Cincinnati Bengals, May 17, 1985.

		——INTERCEPTIONS——						——INTERCEPTIONS——			
Year Club	G.	No.	Yds.	Avg.	TD.	Year Club	G.	No.	Yds.	Avg.	TD.
1978—Toronto CFL	8	1	0	0.0	0	1983—Cincinnati NFL	16		None		
1979—Toronto CFL	15	3	49	16.3	0	1984—Cincinnati NFL	10		None		
1980—Cincinnati NFL	14		None			CFL Totals—2 Years	23	4	49	12.3	0
1981—Cincinnati NFL	16	1	11	11.0	0	NFL Totals—5 Years	65	1	11	11.0	0
1982—Cincinnati NFL	9		None			Pro Totals—7 Years	88	5	60	12.0	0

Additional CFL statistics: Recovered one fumble, 1978; recovered one fumble for three yards, 1979.
Additional NFL statistics: Recovered two fumbles, 1980; recovered one fumble, 1983 and 1984.
Played in AFC Championship Game following 1981 season.
Played in NFL Championship Game following 1981 season.

GARY REASONS
Linebacker—New York Giants
Born February 18, 1962, at Crowley, Tex.
Height, 6.04. Weight, 234.
High School—Crowley, Tex.
Attended Northwestern State University.

Selected by New Jersey in 2nd round (26th player selected) of 1984 USFL draft.
USFL rights traded by New Jersey Generals to Tampa Bay Bandits for rights to linebacker Jim LeClair, January 30, 1984.
Selected by New York Giants in 4th round (105th player selected) of 1984 NFL draft.
Signed by New York Giants, July 12, 1984.

| | | —INTERCEPTIONS— | | | |
Year Club	G.	No.	Yds.	Avg.	TD.
1984—N.Y. Giants NFL	16	2	26	13.0	0

Additional pro statistics: Recovered three fumbles, 1984.

LOUIS ANTHONY REDA
Safety—New York Jets
Born October 10, 1961, at Bronx, N.Y.
Height, 6.00. Weight, 192.
High School—Yonkers, N.Y., Roosevelt.
Received bachelor of science degree in criminal justice from University of Delaware in 1984.

Signed as free agent by New York Jets, May 4, 1984.
On injured reserve with knee injury, July 27 through entire 1984 season.

GLEN HERRSCHER REDD
Linebacker—New Orleans Saints
Born June 17, 1958, at Ogden, Utah.
Height, 6.01. Weight, 233.
High School—Ogden, Utah.
Attended Brigham Young University.

Selected by New Orleans in 6th round (166th player selected) of 1981 NFL draft.
On physically unable to perform/active with eye injury, July 27 through August 17, 1982; activated, August 18, 1982.
On injured reserve with broken arm, August 31 through entire 1982 season.
New Orleans NFL, 1981, 1983 and 1984.
Games: 1981 (16), 1983 (16), 1984 (16). Total—48.
Pro statistics: Intercepted one pass for seven yards, 1984.

BARRY REDDEN
Fullback—Los Angeles Rams
Born July 21, 1960, at Sarasota, Fla.
Height, 5.10. Weight, 205.
High School—Sarasota, Fla.
Received degree in psychology from University of Richmond in 1982.

Selected by Los Angeles Rams in 1st round (14th player selected) of 1982 NFL draft.

| | | —RUSHING— | | | | PASS RECEIVING | | | | —TOTAL— | | |
Year Club	G.	Att.	Yds.	Avg.	TD.	P.C.	Yds.	Avg.	TD.	TD.	Pts.	F.
1982—Los Angeles Rams NFL	9	8	24	3.0	0	4	16	4.0	0	0	0	2
1983—Los Angeles Rams NFL	15	75	372	5.0	2	4	30	7.5	0	2	12	2
1984—Los Angeles Rams NFL	14	45	247	5.5	0	4	39	9.8	0	0	0	0
Pro Totals—3 Years.................	38	128	643	5.0	2	12	85	7.1	0	2	12	4

| | | KICKOFF RETURNS | | | |
Year Club	G.	No.	Yds.	Avg.	TD.
1982—L.A. Rams NFL.............	9	22	502	22.8	0
1983—L.A. Rams NFL.............	15	19	358	18.8	0
1984—L.A. Rams NFL.............	14	23	530	23.0	0
Pro Totals—3 Years............	38	64	1390	21.7	0

Additional pro statistics: Recovered one fumble, 1982.

BEASLEY REECE
Safety—Tampa Bay Buccaneers
Born March 18, 1954, at Waco, Tex.
Height, 6.01. Weight, 195.
High School—Waco, Tex.
Attended North Texas State University.
Cousin of Greg Pruitt, running back with Los Angeles Raiders;
and Randy Logan, safety with Philadelphia Eagles, 1973 through 1983.

Selected by Dallas in 9th round (264th player selected) of 1976 NFL draft.
Claimed on waivers from Dallas Cowboys by New York Giants, September 14, 1977.
On injured reserve, with knee injury, November 22 through remainder of 1977 season.
On injured reserve with broken hand, October 30 through remainder of 1978 season.
Released by New York Giants, October 17, 1983; awarded on waivers to Tampa Bay Buccaneers, October 18, 1983.

Year Club		G.	No.	Yds.	Avg.	TD.
1976—Dallas NFL		10	1	6	6.0	0
1977—N.Y. Giants NFL		10		None		
1978—N.Y. Giants NFL		8		None		
1979—N.Y. Giants NFL		16	1	3	3.0	0
1980—N.Y. Giants NFL		16	3	24	8.0	0
1981—N.Y. Giants NFL		16	4	84	21.0	0
1982—N.Y. Giants NFL		9	1	0	0.0	0
1983—N.Y.G.(7)-T.B.(9) NFL		16	8	103	12.9	0
1984—Tampa Bay NFL		16	1	12	12.0	0
Pro Totals—9 Years		117	19	232	12.2	0

Additional pro statistics: Fumbled once, 1976, 1980, 1981 and 1983; caught one pass for six yards, 1976; returned seven kickoffs for 159 yards and returned one punt for minus five yards, 1977; returned two punts for 40 yards, 1978; returned six kickoffs for 81 yards and recovered three fumbles for 11 yards, 1979; returned one punt for eight yards, 1979 and 1982; returned 24 kickoffs for 471 yards, returned two punts for 15 yards and recovered two fumbles for 14 yards, 1980; recovered five fumbles for seven yards and a touchdown, returned one kickoff for 24 yards and returned one punt for no yards, 1981; recovered two fumbles for 13 yards, 1982; returned nine punts for 26 yards and recovered four fumbles, 1983.

DOUG REED
Defensive End—Los Angeles Rams
Born July 16, 1960, at San Diego, Calif.
Height, 6.03. Weight, 250.
High School—San Diego, Calif., Abraham Lincoln.
Attended San Diego City College and San Diego State University.

Selected by Los Angeles in 17th round (193rd player selected) of 1983 USFL draft.
Selected by Los Angeles Rams in 4th round (111th player selected) of 1983 NFL draft.
Signed by Los Angeles Rams, June 3, 1983.
On injured reserve with leg injury, August 29 through entire 1983 season.
Los Angeles Rams NFL, 1984.
Games: 1984 (9).
Pro statistics: Recovered one fumble for two yards, 1984.

BOOKER TED REESE
Defensive End—Los Angeles Rams
Born September 20, 1959, at Jacksonville, Fla.
Height, 6.06. Weight, 260.
High School—Jacksonville, Fla., Ribault.
Attended Bethune-Cookman College.

Selected by Tampa Bay in 2nd round (32nd player selected) of 1982 NFL draft.
On inactive list, September 12, 1982.
Traded by Tampa Bay Buccaneers to Los Angeles Rams for 12th round pick in 1985 draft, September 4, 1984.
On non-football injury list with drug problem, September 29 through November 1, 1984; activated, November 2, 1984.
Tampa Bay NFL, 1982 and 1983; Tampa Bay (1)-Los Angeles Rams (9) NFL, 1984.
Games: 1982 (7), 1983 (16), 1984 (10). Total—33.
Pro statistics: Intercepted two passes for 11 yards, 1983.

MIKE REICHENBACH
Linebacker—Philadelphia Eagles
Born September 14, 1961, at Fort Meade, Md.
Height, 6.02. Weight, 235.
High School—Bethlehem, Pa., Liberty.
Attended East Stroudsburg University.

Signed as free agent by Philadelphia Eagles, June 18, 1984.
Released by Philadelphia Eagles, August 27, 1984; re-signed by Eagles, September 25, 1984.
Philadelphia NFL, 1984.
Games: 1984 (12).
Pro statistics: Recovered two fumbles, 1984.

BRUCE MICHAEL REIMERS
Offensive Tackle—Cincinnati Bengals
Born September 18, 1960, at Algona, Ia.
Height, 6.07. Weight, 280.
High School—Humboldt, Ia.
Attended Iowa State University.

Selected by Los Angeles in 7th round (136th player selected) of 1984 USFL draft.
Selected by Cincinnati in 8th round (204th player selected) of 1984 NFL draft.
Signed by Cincinnati Bengals, June 20, 1984.
Cincinnati NFL, 1984.
Games: 1984 (15).

—DID YOU KNOW—
That the University of Texas had 17 players selected in the 1984 draft?

JOHNNY REMBERT
Linebacker—New England Patriots
Born January 19, 1961, at Hollandale, Miss.
Height, 6.03. Weight, 234.
High School—Arcadia, Fla., DeSoto.
Attended Cowley County Community College and Clemson University.

Selected by Washington in 1983 USFL territorial draft.
Selected by New England in 4th round (101st player selected) of 1983 NFL draft.
Signed by New England Patriots, May 16, 1983.
On injured reserve with knee injury, August 28 through November 2, 1984; activated, November 3, 1984.
New England NFL, 1983 and 1984.
Games: 1983 (15), 1984 (7). Total—22.
Pro statistics: Recovered one fumble, 1983.

MIKE RAY RENFRO
Wide Receiver—Dallas Cowboys
Born June 19, 1955, at Fort Worth, Tex.
Height, 6.00. Weight, 188.
High School—Fort Worth, Tex., Arlington Heights.
Attending Texas Christian University.
Son of Ray Renfro, back with Cleveland Browns, 1952 through 1963 and
assistant coach with Detroit Lions and Dallas Cowboys, 1965 and 1968 through 1972.

Selected by Houston in 4th round (98th player selected) of 1978 NFL draft.
On injured reserve with knee injury, December 5 through remainder of 1978 season.
On injured reserve with pulled hamstring, November 27 through remainder of 1981 season.
On injured reserve with hepatitis, August 30 through September 29, 1983; activated, September 30, 1983.
On injured reserve with knee injury, November 28 through remainder of 1983 season.
Traded with 2nd round pick in 1984 draft and 5th round pick in 1985 draft by Houston Oilers to Dallas Cowboys for wide receiver Butch Johnson and 2nd round pick in 1984 draft, April 13, 1984.

		—PASS RECEIVING—			
Year Club	G.	P.C.	Yds.	Avg.	TD.
1978—Houston NFL	14	26	339	13.0	2
1979—Houston NFL	15	16	323	20.2	2
1980—Houston NFL	16	35	459	13.1	1
1981—Houston NFL	12	39	451	11.6	1
1982—Houston NFL	9	21	295	14.0	3
1983—Houston NFL	9	23	316	13.7	2
1984—Dallas NFL	16	35	583	16.7	2
Pro Totals—7 Years	91	195	2766	14.2	13

Additional pro statistics: Rushed once for nine yards, 1978; fumbled once, 1978, 1979 and 1983; rushed once for 12 yards, 1980; recovered two fumbles for 12 yards and fumbled twice, 1981; rushed once for three yards, 1983; attempted two passes with one completion for 49 yards and a touchdown, 1984.
Played in AFC Championship Game following 1979 season.

EDWARD RANNELL REYNOLDS
(Ed)
Linebacker—New England Patriots
Born September 23, 1961, at Stuttgart, West Germany.
Height, 6.05. Weight, 230.
High School—Ridgeway, Va., Drewry Mason.
Received bachelor of science degree in education from University of Virginia in 1983.

Signed as free agent by New England Patriots, May 10, 1983.
Released by New England Patriots, August 29, 1983; re-signed by Patriots, September 28, 1983.
Released by New England Patriots, August 27, 1984; re-signed by Patriots, August 28, 1984.
New England NFL, 1983 and 1984.
Games: 1983 (12), 1984 (16). Total—28.
Pro statistics: Recovered two fumbles, 1983.

JOHN SUMNER REYNOLDS
(Jack)
Linebacker
Born November 22, 1947, at Cincinnati, O.
Height, 6.01. Weight, 232.
High School—Cincinnati, O., Western Hills.
Attended University of Tennessee.
Brother of Art Reynolds, linebacker with New York Stars (WFL)
and Charlotte Hornets (WFL), 1974 and 1975.

Named to THE SPORTING NEWS NFC All-Star Team, 1979.
Selected by Los Angeles in 1st round (22nd player selected) of 1970 NFL draft.
Released by Los Angeles Rams, May 6, 1981; signed as free agent by San Francisco 49ers, June 20, 1981.
Not invited to San Francisco 49ers camp but not officially released, May, 1985.

Year Club	G.	No.	Yds.	Avg.	TD.	Year Club	G.	No.	Yds.	Avg.	TD.
		—INTERCEPTIONS—						—INTERCEPTIONS—			
1970—Los Angeles NFL	14			None		1978—Los Angeles NFL	16			None	
1971—Los Angeles NFL	4			None		1979—Los Angeles NFL	16			None	
1972—Los Angeles NFL	14			None		1980—Los Angeles NFL	16	1	20	20.0	0
1973—Los Angeles NFL	14	2	52	26.0	0	1981—San Francisco NFL	16	1	0	0.0	0
1974—Los Angeles NFL	14			None		1982—San Francisco NFL	9	1	0	0.0	0
1975—Los Angeles NFL	14	1	15	15.0	0	1983—San Francisco NFL	13			None	
1976—Los Angeles NFL	14			None		1984—San Francisco NFL	15			None	
1977—Los Angeles NFL	9			None		Pro Totals—15 Years	198	6	87	14.5	0

Additional pro statistics: Recovered four fumbles, 1973; recovered one fumble, 1974; recovered two fumbles for 14 yards, 1975; recovered one fumble, 1976 and 1977; recovered two fumbles for four yards and one touchdown, 1979; recovered two fumbles, 1980 and 1983.

Played in NFC Championship Game following 1974 through 1976, 1978, 1979, 1981, 1983 and 1984 seasons.

Played in NFL Championship Game following 1979, 1981 and 1984 seasons.

Played in Pro Bowl (NFL All-Star Game) following 1975 and 1980 seasons.

EARNEST CALVIN RHONE
(Earnie)
Linebacker—Miami Dolphins

Born August 20, 1953, at Ashdown, Ark.
Height, 6.02. Weight, 224.
High School—Ashdown, Ark.
Received bachelor of science degree in education from Henderson State College.

Signed as free agent by Miami Dolphins, 1975.
Missed entire 1976 season due to injury.
On injured reserve with knee injury, October 10 through remainder of 1977 season.

Year Club	G.	No.	Yds.	Avg.	TD.	Year Club	G.	No.	Yds.	Avg.	TD.
		—INTERCEPTIONS—						—INTERCEPTIONS—			
1975—Miami NFL	14	2	2	1.0	0	1981—Miami NFL	16	3	35	11.7	0
1977—Miami NFL	4			None		1982—Miami NFL	9	1	4	4.0	0
1978—Miami NFL	16	2	4	2.0	0	1983—Miami NFL	12	1	15	15.0	0
1979—Miami NFL	16	2	17	8.5	0	1984—Miami NFL	15			None	
1980—Miami NFL	14	3	33	11.0	0	Pro Totals—9 Years	116	14	110	7.9	0

Additional pro statistics: Recovered one fumble, 1979 and 1981; recovered two fumbles for nine yards, 1983.

Played in AFC Championship Game following 1982 and 1984 seasons.

Played in NFL Championship Game following 1982 and 1984 seasons.

BENITO CONCEPCION RICARDO
(Benny)
Placekicker—San Diego Chargers

Born January 4, 1954, at Asuncion, Paraguay.
Height, 5.10. Weight, 170.
High School—Costa Mesa, Calif.
Attended Orange Coast College and received bachelor of science degree
in journalism and business administration from San Diego State University in 1976.

Signed as free agent by San Diego Chargers, 1975.
Released by San Diego Chargers, August 14, 1975; signed as free agent by Southern California Sun (WFL), September 17, 1975.
Signed as free agent by Detroit Lions after World Football League folded, 1976.
Claimed on waivers by Buffalo Bills from Detroit Lions, September 16, 1976.
Released by Buffalo Bills, September 27, 1976; signed as free agent by Detroit Lions, October 19, 1976.
On injured reserve entire 1977 season.
On did not report list, August 19 through September 3, 1980.
Released by Detroit Lions, September 4, 1980; signed as free agent by New Orleans Saints, September 15, 1980.
Released by New Orleans Saints, August 31, 1982; signed as free agent by Los Angeles Raiders, July 1, 1983.
Released by Los Angeles Raiders, August 23, 1983; signed as free agent by Minnesota Vikings, August 30, 1983.
On injured reserve with pulled hamstring, August 21 through September 4, 1984.
Released by Minnesota Vikings, September 5, 1984; signed as free agent by San Diego Chargers, October 12, 1984.
Released by San Diego Chargers, October 29, 1984; re-signed by Chargers, April 23, 1985.

Year Club	G.	XP	XPM	FG	FGA	Pts.	Year Club	G.	XP	XPM	FG	FGA	Pts.
		—PLACE KICKING—							—PLACE KICKING—				
1975—So. Calif. WFL	5	0	0	8	11	24	1983—Minnesota NFL	16	33	1	25	33	108
1976—Buf.(2)-Det.(8)NFL	10	21	2	11	18	54	1984—San Diego NFL	2	5	1	3	3	14
1978—Detroit NFL	16	32	1	20	28	92	WFL Totals—1 Year	5	0	0	8	11	24
1979—Detroit NFL	16	25	1	10	18	55	NFL Totals—7 Years	90	171	9	92	142	447
1980—New Orleans NFL	14	31	3	10	17	61	Pro Totals—8 Years	95	171	9	100	153	471
1981—New Orleans NFL	16	24	0	13	25	63							

Additional pro statistics: Recovered one fumble and punted once for 16 yards, 1976.

ALLEN TROY RICE
Running Back-Safety—Minnesota Vikings

Born April 5, 1962, at Houston, Tex.
Height, 5.10. Weight, 198.
High School—Houston, Tex., Klein.
Attended Wharton County Junior College, Ranger Junior College and Baylor University.

Selected by Houston in 1984 USFL territorial draft.
Selected by Minnesota in 5th round (140th player selected) of 1984 NFL draft.
Signed by Minnesota Vikings, July 20, 1984.

Year Club	G.	Att.	RUSHING Yds.	Avg.	TD.	PASS RECEIVING P.C.	Yds.	Avg.	TD.	TOTAL TD.	Pts.	F.
1984—Minnesota NFL	14	14	58	4.1	1	4	59	14.8	1	2	12	1

Additional pro statistics: Returned three kickoffs for 34 yards and recovered two fumbles, 1984.

HOWARD GLENN RICHARDS
Offensive Tackle—Dallas Cowboys
Born August 7, 1959, at St. Louis, Mo.
Height, 6.06. Weight, 260.
High School—St. Louis, Mo., Southwest.
Attended University of Missouri.
Nephew of Ernie McMillan, offensive line coach with St. Louis Cardinals.

Selected by Dallas in 1st round (26th player selected) of 1981 NFL draft.
On injured reserve with torn tendon in thigh, November 17 through remainder of 1984 season.
Dallas NFL, 1981 through 1984.
Games: 1981 (16), 1982 (8), 1983 (16), 1984 (11). Total—51.
Pro statistics: Recovered one fumble, 1984.
Played in NFC Championship Game following 1981 and 1982 seasons.

ALPETTE RICHARDSON
(Al)
Linebacker—Atlanta Falcons
Born September 23, 1957, at Abbeville, Ala.
Height, 6.03. Weight, 222.
High School—Miami, Fla., Central.
Attended Georgia Tech.

Selected by Atlanta in 8th round (201st player selected) of 1980 NFL draft.
On injured reserve with broken shoulder blade, October 6 through remainder of 1983 season.

Year Club	G.	No.	INTERCEPTIONS Yds.	Avg.	TD.
1980—Atlanta NFL	16	7	139	19.9	0
1981—Atlanta NFL	16	1	9	9.0	0
1982—Atlanta NFL	8		None		
1983—Atlanta NFL	5	1	38	38.0	0
1984—Atlanta NFL	16		None		
Pro Totals—5 Years	61	9	186	20.7	0

Additional pro statistics: Recovered three fumbles (one in end zone for a touchdown), 1980; recovered three fumbles, 1984.

ERIC RICHARDSON
Wide Receiver—Buffalo Bills
Born April 18, 1962, at San Francisco, Calif.
Height, 6.01. Weight, 183.
High School—Novato, Calif.
Attended Monterey Peninsula College and San Jose State University.

Selected by Oakland in 1984 USFL territorial draft.
Selected by Buffalo in 2nd round (41st player selected) of 1984 NFL draft.
Signed by Buffalo Bills, May 17, 1984.
On injured reserve with knee injury, August 28 through entire 1984 season.

MICHAEL CALVIN RICHARDSON
(Mike)
Cornerback—Chicago Bears
Born May 23, 1961, at Compton, Calif.
Height, 6.00. Weight, 188.
High School—Compton, Calif.
Attended Arizona State University.

Named as defensive back on THE SPORTING NEWS College All-America Team, 1981 and 1982.
Selected by Arizona in 1983 USFL territorial draft.
Selected by Chicago in 2nd round (33rd player selected) of 1983 NFL draft.
Signed by Chicago Bears, July 20, 1983.

Year Club	G.	No.	INTERCEPTIONS Yds.	Avg.	TD.
1983—Chicago NFL	16	5	9	1.8	0
1984—Chicago NFL	15	2	7	3.5	0
Pro Totals—2 Years	31	7	16	2.3	0

Additional pro statistics: Returned one kickoff for 17 yards and recovered two fumbles for seven yards, 1983; recovered one fumble, 1984.
Played in NFC Championship Game following 1984 season.

ROBBERT LEE RIDDICK
(Robb)
Running Back—Buffalo Bills

Born April 26, 1957, at Quakertown, Pa.
Height, 6.00. Weight, 195.
High School—Perkasie, Pa., Pennridge.
Attended Millersville State College.
Cousin of Will Lewis, cornerback with Houston Gamblers; and
Tim Lewis, defensive back with Green Bay Packers.

Selected by Buffalo in 9th round (241st player selected) of 1981 NFL draft.
On injured reserve with ankle injury, September 3 through October 16, 1981; activated, October 17, 1981.
On injured reserve with knee injury, September 7 through entire 1982 season.

Year Club	G.	Att.	Yds.	Avg.	TD.	P.C.	Yds.	Avg.	TD.	TD.	Pts.	F.
			—RUSHING—				PASS RECEIVING				—TOTAL—	
1981—Buffalo NFL	10	3	29	9.7	0		None			0	0	1
1983—Buffalo NFL	16	4	18	4.5	0	3	43	14.3	0	0	0	7
1984—Buffalo NFL	16	3	3	1.0	0	23	276	12.0	0	0	0	1
Pro Totals—3 Years	42	10	50	5.0	0	26	319	12.3	0	0	0	9

Year Club	G.	No.	Yds.	Avg.	TD.	No.	Yds.	Avg.	TD.
		—PUNT RETURNS—				—KICKOFF RET.—			
1981—Buffalo NFL	10	4	48	12.0	0	14	257	18.4	0
1983—Buffalo NFL	16	42	241	5.7	0	28	568	20.3	0
1984—Buffalo NFL	16		None				None		
Pro Totals—3 Years	42	46	289	6.3	0	42	825	19.6	0

Additional pro statistics: Recovered one fumble, 1983.

JOHN RIGGINS
Running Back—Washington Redskins

Born August 4, 1949, at Centralia, Kan.
Height, 6.02. Weight, 240.
High School—Centralia, Kan.
Attended University of Kansas.
Brother of Frank Riggins, outfielder in California Angels' organization, 1969 through 1972.

Established NFL records for most touchdowns and most rushing touchdowns, season (24), 1983.
Selected by New York Jets in 1st round (6th player selected) of 1971 NFL draft.
Played out option with New York Jets in 1975 and signed as free agent by Washington Redskins, June 10, 1976.
On injured reserve, December 6 through remainder of 1977 season.
Left Washington Redskins camp voluntarily and placed on left camp-retired list, July 31, 1980; reinstated, May 25, 1981.

Year Club	G.	Att.	Yds.	Avg.	TD.	P.C.	Yds.	Avg.	TD.	TD.	Pts.	F.
			—RUSHING—				PASS RECEIVING				—TOTAL—	
1971—New York Jets NFL	14	180	769	4.3	1	36	231	6.4	2	3	18	6
1972—New York Jets NFL	12	207	944	4.6	7	21	230	11.0	1	8	48	2
1973—New York Jets NFL	11	134	482	3.6	4	23	158	6.9	0	4	24	6
1974—New York Jets NFL	10	169	680	4.0	5	19	180	9.5	2	7	42	3
1975—New York Jets NFL	14	238	1005	4.2	8	30	363	12.1	1	9	54	5
1976—Washington NFL	14	162	572	3.5	3	21	172	8.3	1	4	24	6
1977—Washington NFL	5	68	203	3.0	0	7	95	13.6	2	2	12	0
1978—Washington NFL	15	248	1014	4.1	5	31	299	9.6	0	5	30	7
1979—Washington NFL	16	260	1153	4.4	9	28	163	5.8	3	12	72	5
1981—Washington NFL	15	195	714	3.7	13	6	59	9.8	0	13	78	1
1982—Washington NFL	8	*177	553	3.1	3	10	50	5.0	0	3	18	2
1983—Washington NFL	15	375	1347	3.6	*24	5	29	5.8	0	*24	144	5
1984—Washington NFL	14	327	1239	3.8	*14	7	43	6.1	0	14	84	7
Pro Totals—13 Years	163	2740	10675	3.9	96	244	2072	8.5	12	108	648	55

Additional pro statistics: Recovered two fumbles for minus seven yards, 1971; recovered one fumble, 1973, 1975, 1976 and 1978; recovered two fumbles, 1974; attempted one pass with no completions, 1983.
Played in NFC Championship Game following 1982 and 1983 seasons.
Played in NFL Championship Game following 1982 and 1983 seasons.
Played in Pro Bowl (NFL All-Star Game) following 1975 season.

GERALD ANTONIO RIGGS
Running Back—Atlanta Falcons

Born November 6, 1960, at Tullos, La.
Height, 6.01. Weight, 230.
High School—Las Vegas, Nev., Bonanza.
Attended Arizona State University.

Selected by Atlanta in 1st round (9th player selected) of 1982 NFL draft.

Year Club	G.	Att.	Yds.	Avg.	TD.	P.C.	Yds.	Avg.	TD.	TD.	Pts.	F.
			—RUSHING—				PASS RECEIVING				—TOTAL—	
1982—Atlanta NFL	9	78	299	3.8	5	23	185	8.0	0	5	30	1
1983—Atlanta NFL	14	100	437	4.4	8	17	149	8.8	0	8	48	7
1984—Atlanta NFL	15	353	1486	4.2	13	42	277	6.6	0	13	78	11
Pro Totals—3 Years	38	531	2222	4.2	26	82	611	7.5	0	26	156	19

Year Club	G.	No.	Yds.	Avg.	TD.
1982—Atlanta NFL	9		None		
1983—Atlanta NFL	14	17	330	19.4	0
1984—Atlanta NFL	15		None		
Pro Totals—3 Years	38	17	330	19.4	0

Additional pro statistics: Recovered one fumble, 1983; recovered two fumbles, 1984.

AVON RILEY
Linebacker—Houston Oilers
Born February 10, 1958, at Savannah, Ga.
Height, 6.03. Weight, 236.
High School—Savannah, Ga.
Attended College of the Canyons and University of California at Los Angeles.

Selected by Houston in 9th round (243rd player selected) of 1981 NFL draft.
Houston NFL, 1981 through 1984.
Games: 1981 (16), 1982 (9), 1983 (16), 1984 (16). Total—57.
Pro statistics: Returned one kickoff for 51 yards and recovered one fumble for six yards, 1981; returned one kickoff for 27 yards, 1982; intercepted one pass for no yards, ran 26 yards with lateral on kickoff return and recovered three fumbles for four yards, 1983.

STEVE BRUCE RILEY
Offensive Tackle—Minnesota Vikings
Born November 23, 1952, at Chula Vista, Calif.
Height, 6.06. Weight, 265.
High School—Chula Vista, Calif., Castle Park.
Attended University of Southern California.

Named as offensive tackle on THE SPORTING NEWS College All-America Team, 1973.
Selected by Minnesota in 1st round (25th player selected) of 1974 NFL draft.
On injured reserve with neck injury, October 21 through remainder of 1978 season.
Traded by Minnesota Vikings to New Orleans Saints for 3rd and 5th round picks in 1980 draft, April 18, 1980.
Returned to Vikings, June 1, 1980, after failing physical; Saints received Vikings' 3rd and 5th round picks in 1981 draft.
Minnesota NFL, 1974 through 1984.
Games: 1974 (2), 1975 (14), 1976 (14), 1977 (14), 1978 (5), 1979 (16), 1980 (16), 1981 (16), 1982 (9), 1983 (16), 1984 (16). Total—138.
Pro statistics: Recovered one fumble, 1977, 1979 and 1983.
Played in NFC Championship Game following 1976 and 1977 seasons.
Played in NFL Championship Game following 1976 season.
Member of Minnesota Vikings for NFC and NFL Championship Games following 1974 season; did not play.

DAVE BRIAN RIMINGTON
Center—Cincinnati Bengals
Born May 22, 1960, at Omaha, Neb.
Height, 6.03. Weight, 288.
High School—Omaha, Neb., South.
Received degree from University of Nebraska.

Outland Trophy winner, 1981 and 1982.
Named as center on THE SPORTING NEWS College All-America Team, 1982.
Selected by Boston in 1983 USFL territorial draft.
Selected by Cincinnati in 1st round (25th player selected) of 1983 NFL draft.
Signed by Cincinnati Bengals, June 6, 1983.
Cincinnati NFL, 1983 and 1984.
Games: 1983 (12), 1984 (16). Total—28.
Pro statistics: Recovered one fumble and fumbled once, 1983.

BILL RING
Running Back—San Francisco 49ers
Born December 13, 1956, at Des Moines, Iowa.
Height, 5.10. Weight, 205.
High School—Belmont, Calif., Carlmont.
Attended College of San Mateo and Brigham Young University.

Signed as free agent by Pittsburgh Steelers, May 7, 1980.
Released by Pittsburgh Steelers, August 25, 1980; signed as free agent by San Francisco 49ers, April 14, 1981.
On injured reserve with lacerated finger, August 17 through September 17, 1981; activated after clearing procedural waivers, September 19, 1981.
Released by San Francisco 49ers, September 22, 1981; re-signed by 49ers, October 7, 1981.

		RUSHING				PASS RECEIVING				TOTAL		
Year Club	G.	Att.	Yds.	Avg.	TD.	P.C.	Yds.	Avg.	TD.	TD.	Pts.	F.
1981—San Francisco NFL	12	22	106	4.8	0	3	28	9.3	1	1	6	1
1982—San Francisco NFL	8	48	183	3.8	0	13	94	7.2	0	1	6	1
1983—San Francisco NFL	16	64	254	4.0	2	23	182	7.9	0	2	12	1
1984—San Francisco NFL	16	38	162	4.3	3	3	10	3.3	0	3	18	0
Pro Totals—4 Years	52	172	705	4.1	6	42	314	7.5	1	7	42	3

		KICKOFF RETURNS			
Year Club	G.	No.	Yds.	Avg.	TD.
1981—San Francisco NFL	12	10	217	21.7	0
1982—San Francisco NFL	8	6	145	24.2	0
1983—San Francisco NFL	16	4	68	17.0	0
1984—San Francisco NFL	16	1	27	27.0	0
Pro Totals—4 Years............	52	21	457	21.8	0

Additional pro statistics: Recovered one fumble, 1981 and 1982; recovered two fumbles, 1983.
Played in NFC Championship Game following 1981, 1983 and 1984 seasons.
Played in NFL Championship Game following 1981 and 1984 seasons.

ALAN RISHER
Quarterback—Tampa Bay Buccaneers
Born May 6, 1961, at New Orleans, La.
Height, 6.02. Weight, 190.
High School—Slidell, La., Salem.
Attended Louisiana State University.

Selected by Arizona in 15th round (170th player selected) of 1983 USFL draft.
Signed by Arizona Wranglers, February 2, 1983.
Protected in merger of Arizona Wranglers and Oklahoma Outlaws, December 6, 1984.
On developmental squad, March 3 and March 4, 1985.
Released by Arizona Outlaws, March 5, 1985; signed as free agent by Tampa Bay Buccaneers, May 9, 1985.
On developmental squad for 1 game with Arizona Outlaws in 1985.
Active for 1 game with Arizona Outlaws in 1985; did not play.

		PASSING						RUSHING				TOTAL		
Year Club	G.	Att.	Cmp.	Pct.	Gain	T.P.	P.I.	Avg.	Att.	Yds.	Avg.	TD.	TD.	Pts.	F.
1983—Arizona USFL...................	16	424	236	55.7	2672	20	16	6.30	57	231	4.1	0	0	0	11
1984—Arizona USFL...................	18	103	63	61.2	722	3	7	7.01	6	45	7.5	0	0	0	2
Pro Totals—3 Years...........	34	527	299	56.7	3394	23	23	6.44	63	276	4.4	0	0	0	13

Quarterback Rating Points: 1983 (74.6), 1984 (63.7). Total—72.5.
Additional pro statistics: Recovered seven fumbles and caught one pass for nine yards, 1983; recovered one fumble, 1984.
Played in USFL Championship Game following 1984 season.

CODY LEWIS RISIEN
Name pronounced Rise-un.
Offensive Tackle—Cleveland Browns
Born March 22, 1957, at Bryan, Tex.
Height, 6.07. Weight, 270.
High School—Houston, Tex., Cypress Fairbanks.
Attended Texas A&M University.

Selected by Cleveland in 7th round (183rd player selected) of 1979 NFL draft.
On injured reserve with knee injury, August 27 through entire 1984 season.
Cleveland NFL, 1979 through 1983.
Games: 1979 (15), 1980 (16), 1981 (16), 1982 (9), 1983 (16). Total—72.

JAMES ALEXANDER RITCHER
(Jim)
Guard—Buffalo Bills
Born May 21, 1958, at Berea, O.
Height, 6.03. Weight, 251.
High School—Granger, O., Highland.
Attended North Carolina State University.

Named as center on THE SPORTING NEWS College All-America Team, 1979.
Outland Trophy winner, 1979.
Selected by Buffalo in 1st round of (16th player selected) 1980 NFL draft.
Buffalo NFL, 1980 through 1984.
Games: 1980, (14), 1981 (14), 1982 (9), 1983 (16), 1984 (14). Total—67.

RONALD EUGENE RIVERA
(Ron)
Linebacker—Chicago Bears
Born January 7, 1962, at Fort Ord, Calif.
Height, 6.03. Weight, 244.
High School—Seaside, Calif.
Attended University of California at Berkeley.

Named as linebacker on THE SPORTING NEWS College All-America Team, 1983.
Selected by Oakland in 1984 USFL territorial draft.
Selected by Chicago in 2nd round (44th player selected) of 1984 NFL draft.
Signed by Chicago Bears, July 2, 1984.
Chicago NFL, 1984.
Games: 1984 (15).
Played in NFC Championship Game following 1984 season.

CARL ROACHES
Kick Returner-Wide Receiver—Houston Oilers

Born October 2, 1953, at Houston, Tex.
Height, 5.08. Weight, 170.
High School—Houston, Tex., Smiley.
Received bachelor of science degree in industrial education from Texas A&M University.

Selected by Tampa Bay in 14th round (377th player selected) of 1976 NFL draft.
Released by Tampa Bay Buccaneers, September, 1976; signed as free agent by Saskatchewan Roughriders, March, 1977.
Released by Saskatchewan Roughriders, August, 1977; signed as free agent by Houston Oilers, June 12, 1980.

Year Club	G.	—PUNT RETURNS—				—KICKOFF RET.—				—TOTAL—		
		No.	Yds.	Avg.	TD.	No.	Yds.	Avg.	TD.	TD.	Pts.	F.
1977—Saskatchewan CFL	3	2	12	6.0	0		None			0	0	0
1980—Houston NFL	16	47	384	8.2	0	37	746	20.2	0	0	0	6
1981—Houston NFL	16	39	296	7.6	0	28	769	27.5	*1	1	6	0
1982—Houston NFL	9	19	104	5.5	0	21	441	21.0	0	0	0	1
1983—Houston NFL	16	20	159	8.0	0	34	641	18.9	*1	1	6	3
1984—Houston NFL	16	26	152	5.8	0	30	679	22.6	0	0	0	1
CFL Totals—1 Year	3	2	12	6.0	0	0	0	0.0	0	0	0	0
NFL Totals—5 Years	73	151	1095	7.3	0	150	3276	21.8	2	2	12	11
Pro Totals—6 Years	76	153	1107	7.2	0	150	3276	21.8	2	2	12	11

Additional pro statistics: Recovered three fumbles, 1980; recovered one fumble, 1982 through 1984; caught four passes for 69 yards, 1984.
Played in Pro Bowl (NFL All-Star Game) following 1981 season.

JAMES ELBERT ROBBINS
(Tootie)
Offensive Tackle—St. Louis Cardinals

Born June 2, 1958, at Windsor, N.C.
Height, 6.04. Weight, 278.
High School—Bertie County, N.C.
Attended East Carolina University.

Selected by St. Louis in 4th round (90th player selected) of 1982 NFL draft.
St. Louis NFL, 1982 through 1984.
Games: 1982 (9), 1983 (13), 1984 (16). Total—38.
Pro statistics: Recovered one fumble, 1983.

RANDY ROBBINS
Cornerback—Denver Broncos

Born September 14, 1962, at Casa Grande, Ariz.
Height, 6.02. Weight, 189.
High School—Casa Grande, Ariz., Union.
Attended University of Arizona.

Selected by Arizona in 1984 USFL territorial draft.
Selected by Denver in 4th round (89th player selected) of 1984 NFL draft.
Signed by Denver Broncos, July 6, 1984.

Year Club	G.	—INTERCEPTIONS—			
		No.	Yds.	Avg.	TD.
1984—Denver NFL	16	2	62	31.0	1

Additional pro statistics: Recovered one fumble, 1984.

WILLIAM ROBERTS
Offensive Tackle—New York Giants

Born August 5, 1962, at Miami, Fla.
Height, 6.05. Weight, 280.
High School—Miami, Fla., Carol City.
Attended Ohio State University.

Selected by New Jersey in 1984 USFL territorial draft.
Selected by New York Giants in 1st round (27th player selected) of 1984 NFL draft.
Signed by New York Giants, June 4, 1984.
New York Giants NFL, 1984.
Games: 1984 (11).
Pro statistics: Recovered one fumble, 1984.

FRED LEE ROBINSON
Defensive End—San Diego Chargers

Born October 22, 1961, at Miami, Fla.
Height, 6.04. Weight, 240.
High School—Miami, Fla., Jackson.
Attended Navarro College and University of Miami (Fla.).

Selected by Washington in 2nd round (24th player selected) of 1984 USFL draft.
Selected by Tampa Bay in 8th round (198th player selected) of 1984 NFL draft.
Released by Tampa Bay Buccaneers, August 20, 1984; signed as free agent by San Diego Chargers, August 22, 1984.

Released by San Diego Chargers, August 27, 1984; re-signed by Chargers, August 28, 1984.
San Diego NFL, 1984.
Games: 1984 (16).

JERRY DEWAYNE ROBINSON
Linebacker—Philadelphia Eagles
Born December 18, 1956, at San Francisco, Calif.
Height, 6.02. Weight, 225.
High School—Santa Rosa, Calif., Cardinal Newman.
Attended University of California at Los Angeles.

Named as linebacker on THE SPORTING NEWS College All-America Team, 1978.
Selected by Philadelphia in 1st round (21st player selected) of 1979 NFL draft.

			—INTERCEPTIONS—		
Year Club	G.	No.	Yds.	Avg.	TD.
1979—Philadelphia NFL	16		None		
1980—Philadelphia NFL	16	2	13	6.5	0
1981—Philadelphia NFL	15	1	3	3.0	0
1982—Philadelphia NFL	9	3	19	6.3	0
1983—Philadelphia NFL	16		None		
1984—Philadelphia NFL	15		None		
Pro Totals—6 Years............	87	6	35	5.8	0

Pro statistics: Recovered two fumbles, 1979, 1981 and 1983; recovered four fumbles for 59 yards and one touchdown and fumbled once, 1980; recovered one fumble, 1984.
Played in NFC Championship Game following 1980 season.
Played in NFL Championship Game following 1980 season.
Played in Pro Bowl (NFL All-Star Game) following 1981 season.

MARK LEON ROBINSON
Safety—Kansas City Chiefs
Born September 13, 1962, at Washington, D.C.
Height, 5.10. Weight, 206.
High School—Silver Spring, Md., John F. Kennedy.
Attended Penn State University.
Brother of Eric Robinson, running back with Kansas City Chiefs.

Selected by Philadelphia in 1984 USFL territorial draft.
Selected by Kansas City in 4th round (90th player selected) of 1984 NFL draft.
Signed by Kansas City Chiefs, July 12, 1984.
Kansas City NFL, 1984.
Games: 1984 (16).

MELVIN DELL ROBINSON
(Bo)
Tight End—New England Patriots
Born May 27, 1956, at LaMesa, Tex.
Height, 6.02. Weight, 235.
High School—LaMesa, Tex.
Attended West Texas State University.

Selected by Detroit in 3rd round (67th player selected) of 1979 NFL draft.
Released by Detroit Lions, August 31, 1981; signed as free agent by Atlanta Falcons, September 9, 1981.
On injured reserve with broken arm, September 1 through September 30, 1983; activated, October 1, 1983.
Released by Atlanta Falcons, August 27, 1984; awarded on waivers to New England Patriots, August 28, 1984.

		—RUSHING—				PASS RECEIVING				—TOTAL—		
Year Club	G.	Att.	Yds.	Avg.	TD.	P.C.	Yds.	Avg.	TD.	TD.	Pts.	F.
1979—Detroit NFL...............	14	87	302	3.5	2	14	118	8.4	0	2	12	3
1980—Detroit NFL...............	14	3	2	0.7	0		None			0	0	0
1981—Atlanta NFL...............	15	9	24	2.7	0		None			0	0	0
1982—Atlanta NFL...............	9	19	108	5.7	0	7	55	7.9	2	2	12	0
1983—Atlanta NFL...............	12	3	9	3.0	0	12	100	8.3	0	0	0	1
1984—New England NFL...............	16		None			4	32	8.0	1	1	6	0
Pro Totals—6 Years...................	80	121	445	3.7	2	37	305	8.2	3	5	30	4

Additional pro statistics: Returned one punt for eight yards, 1979; recovered one fumble, 1979 and 1984; returned three kickoffs for 38 yards, 1984.

SHELTON ROBINSON
Linebacker—Seattle Seahawks
Born September 14, 1960, at Goldsboro, N.C.
Height, 6.02. Weight, 233.
High School—Pikeville, N.C., Aycock.
Received bachelor of science degree in industrial relations from
University of North Carolina in 1982.

Signed as free agent by Seattle Seahawks, April 30, 1982.
Seattle NFL, 1982 through 1984.
Games: 1982 (9), 1983 (16), 1984 (16). Total—41.
Pro statistics: Intercepted one pass for 18 yards and recovered four fumbles for 21 yards and two touchdowns, 1983; recovered four fumbles for three yards, 1984.
Played in AFC Championship Game following 1983 season.

REGGIE ROBY
Punter—Miami Dolphins

Born July 30, 1960, at Waterloo, Iowa.
Height, 6.02. Weight, 243.
High School—Waterloo, Iowa, East.
Attended University of Iowa.

Named to THE SPORTING NEWS NFL All-Star Team, 1984.
Led NFL in net punting average with 38.1 in 1984.
Selected by Chicago in 16th round (187th player selected) of 1983 USFL draft.
Selected by Miami in 6th round (167th player selected) of 1983 NFL draft.
Signed by Miami Dolphins, July 9, 1983.

Year Club	G.	No.	—PUNTING— Avg.	Blk.
1983—Miami NFL	16	74	43.1	1
1984—Miami NFL	16	51	44.7	0
Pro Totals—2 Years	32	125	43.8	1

Played in AFC Championship Game following 1984 season.
Played in NFL Championship Game following 1984 season.
Played in Pro Bowl (NFL All-Star Game) following 1984 season.

CHRIS ROCKINS
Safety—Cleveland Browns

Born May 18, 1962, at Sherman, Tex.
Height, 6.00. Weight, 195.
High School—Sherman, Tex.
Attended Oklahoma State University.

Selected by Oklahoma in 1984 USFL territorial draft.
Selected by Cleveland in 2nd round (48th player selected) of 1984 NFL draft.
Signed by Cleveland Browns, May 17, 1984.
Cleveland NFL, 1984.
Games: 1984 (16).
Pro statistics: Intercepted one pass for no yards, 1984.

DEL RODGERS
Running Back—Green Bay Packers

Born June 22, 1960, at Tacoma, Wash.
Height, 5.11. Weight, 202.
High School—Salinas, Calif., North.
Attended University of Utah.

Selected by Green Bay in 3rd round (71st player selected) of 1982 NFL draft.
On injured reserve with neck injury, August 29 through entire 1983 season.

Year Club	G.	——RUSHING—— Att.	Yds.	Avg.	TD.	PASS RECEIVING P.C.	Yds.	Avg.	TD.	—TOTAL— TD.	Pts.	F.
1982—Green Bay NFL	9	46	175	3.8	1	3	23	7.7	0	3	18	2
1984—Green Bay NFL	14	25	94	3.8	0	5	56	11.2	0	1	6	1
Pro Totals—2 Years	23	71	269	3.8	1	8	79	9.9	0	4	24	3

Year Club	G.	KICKOFF RETURNS No.	Yds.	Avg.TD.
1982—Green Bay NFL	9	20	436	21.8 0
1984—Green Bay NFL	14	39	843	21.6 *1
Pro Totals—2 Years	23	59	1279	21.7 1

Additional pro statistics: Recovered two fumbles in end zone for two touchdowns, 1982.

JOHN DARREN RODGERS
Tight End—Pittsburgh Steelers

Born February 7, 1960, at Omaha, Tex.
Height, 6.02. Weight, 238.
High School—Daingerfield, Tex.
Received bachelor of science degree in business technology from
Louisiana Tech University in 1982.

Signed as free agent by Pittsburgh Steelers, May 22, 1982.
Released by Pittsburgh Steelers, August 21, 1984; re-signed by Steelers, October 15, 1984.
On injured reserve with hand injury, December 1 through remainder of 1984 season.

Year Club	G.	—PASS RECEIVING— P.C.	Yds.	Avg.	TD.
1982—Pittsburgh NFL	7	None			
1983—Pittsburgh NFL	15	2	36	18.0	0
1984—Pittsburgh NFL	6	None			
Pro Totals—3 Years	28	2	36	18.0	0

Additional pro statistics: Ran 18 yards with blocked punt for a touchdown, 1982.

DONALD LAVERT ROGERS
(Don)
Safety—Cleveland Browns
Born September 17, 1962, at Texarkana, Ark.
Height, 6.01. Weight, 206.
High School—Sacramento, Calif., Norte del Rio.
Attended University of California at Los Angeles.
Brother of Reggie Rogers, linebacker at University of Washington.

Named as defensive back on THE SPORTING NEWS College All-America Team, 1983.
Selected by San Antonio in 1st round (21st player selected) of 1984 USFL draft.
Selected by Cleveland in 1st round (18th player selected) of 1984 NFL draft.
USFL rights traded by San Antonio Gunslingers to Arizona Wranglers for draft pick, May 2, 1984.
Signed by Cleveland Browns, May 24, 1984.

Year Club		—INTERCEPTIONS—			
Year Club	G.	No.	Yds.	Avg.	TD.
1984—Cleveland NFL	15	1	39	39.0	0

DOUGLAS KEITH ROGERS
(Doug)
Defensive End—New England Patriots
Born June 23, 1960, at Chico, Calif.
Height 6.05. Weight, 270.
High School—Bakersfield, Calif., Highland.
Received bachelor of arts degree in communications and sociology from
Stanford University in 1982.

Selected by Atlanta in 2nd round (36th player selected) of 1982 NFL draft.
Released by Atlanta Falcons, September 13, 1983; awarded on waivers to New England Patriots, September 14, 1983.
Atlanta NFL, 1982; Atlanta (2)-New England (10) NFL, 1983; New England NFL, 1984.
Games: 1982 (9), 1983 (12), 1984 (12). Total—33.

GEORGE WASHINGTON ROGERS
Running Back—Washington Redskins
Born December 8, 1958, at Duluth, Ga.
Height, 6.02. Weight, 224.
High School—Duluth, Ga.
Attended University of South Carolina.

Heisman Trophy winner, 1980.
Named as running back on THE SPORTING NEWS College All-America Team, 1980.
Tied NFL record for most 100-yard games, rushing by rookie (9), 1981.
Named THE SPORTING NEWS NFL Rookie of the Year, 1981.
Named to THE SPORTING NEWS NFL All-Star Team, 1981.
Selected by New Orleans in 1st round (1st player selected) of 1981 NFL draft.
On inactive list, September 19, 1982.
Traded with 5th, 10th and 11th round picks in 1985 draft by New Orleans Saints to Washington Redskins for 1st round pick in 1985 draft, April 26, 1985.

Year Club		—RUSHING—				PASS RECEIVING				—TOTAL—		
Year Club	G.	Att.	Yds.	Avg.	TD.	P.C.	Yds.	Avg.	TD.	TD.	Pts.	F.
1981—New Orleans NFL	16	*378	*1674	4.4	13	16	126	7.9	0	13	78	13
1982—New Orleans NFL	6	122	535	4.4	3	4	21	5.3	0	3	18	4
1983—New Orleans NFL	13	256	1144	4.5	5	12	69	5.8	0	5	30	8
1984—New Orleans NFL	16	239	914	3.8	2	12	76	6.3	0	2	12	2
Pro Totals—4 Years	51	995	4267	4.3	23	44	292	6.6	0	23	138	27

Additional pro statistics: Recovered one fumble, 1981 and 1984; recovered two fumbles, 1983.
Played in Pro Bowl (NFL All-Star Game) following 1981 and 1982 seasons.

JAMES ROGERS
(Jimmy)
Running Back—New Orleans Saints
Born June 29, 1955, at Forrest City, Ark.
Height, 5.10. Weight, 194.
High School—Forrest City, Ark.
Attended University of Oklahoma.

Signed as free agent by Chicago Bears, July 19, 1979.
Released by Chicago Bears, August 13, 1979; signed as free agent by Edmonton Eskimos, March, 1980.
Released by Edmonton Eskimos, July 2, 1980; signed as free agent by New Orleans Saints, July 10, 1980.

Year Club		—RUSHING—				PASS RECEIVING				—TOTAL—		
Year Club	G.	Att.	Yds.	Avg.	TD.	P.C.	Yds.	Avg.	TD.	TD.	Pts.	F.
1980—New Orleans NFL	16	80	366	4.6	1	27	267	9.9	2	3	18	6
1981—New Orleans NFL	15	9	37	4.1	0	2	12	6.0	0	0	0	3
1982—New Orleans NFL	9	60	178	3.0	2	4	17	4.3	0	2	12	0
1983—New Orleans NFL	16	26	80	3.1	0		None			0	0	2
1984—New Orleans NFL	16		None				None			0	0	0
Pro Totals—5 Years	72	175	661	3.8	3	33	296	9.0	2	5	30	11

— 349 —

| | | KICKOFF RETURNS | | | |
Year Club	G.	No.	Yds.	Avg.	TD.
1980—New Orleans NFL	16	41	930	22.7	0
1981—New Orleans NFL	15	28	621	22.2	0
1982—New Orleans NFL	9	1	24	24.0	0
1983—New Orleans NFL	16	7	103	14.7	0
1984—New Orleans NFL	16		None		
Pro Totals—5 Years	72	77	1678	21.8	0

Additional pro statistics: Recovered two fumbles, 1980; recovered one fumble, 1981 and 1983.

JEFFREY CHARLES ROHRER
(Jeff)
Linebacker—Dallas Cowboys
Born December 25, 1958, at Inglewood, Calif.
Height, 6.03. Weight, 225.
High School—Manhattan Beach, Calif., Mira Costa.
Received bachelor of science degree in administrative sciences from
Yale University in 1982.

Selected by Dallas in 2nd round (53rd player selected) of 1982 NFL draft.
Dallas NFL, 1982 through 1984.
Games: 1982 (8), 1983 (16), 1984 (16). Total—40.
Pro statistics: Recovered one fumble for five yards and fumbled once, 1984.
Played in NFC Championship Game following 1982 season.

JAMES JOHN ROMANO
(Jim)
Center—Houston Oilers
Born September 7, 1959, at Glen Cove, N.Y.
Height, 6.03. Weight, 255.
High School—Glen Head, N.Y., North Shore.
Received bachelor of arts degree in commercial recreation from
Penn State University in 1982.

Selected by Los Angeles Raiders in 2nd round (37th player selected) of 1982 NFL draft.
On injured reserve with pulled hamstring, September 20 through remainder of 1983 season.
Traded by Los Angeles Raiders to Houston Oilers for 3rd and 6th round draft picks in 1985 draft, October 9, 1984.
Los Angeles Raiders NFL, 1982 and 1983; Los Angeles Raiders (6)-Houston (8) NFL, 1984.
Games: 1982 (5), 1983 (1), 1984 (14). Total—20.
Pro statistics: Fumbled once for minus 11 yards, 1984.

CHARLES MICHAEL ROMES
Cornerback—Buffalo Bills
Born December 16, 1953, at Verdun, France.
Height, 6.01. Weight, 190.
High School—Durham, N. C., Hillside.
Attended Lake City Junior College and North Carolina Central University.

Selected by Buffalo in 12th round (309th player selected) of 1977 NFL draft.

| | | INTERCEPTIONS | | | |
Year Club	G.	No.	Yds.	Avg.	TD.
1977—Buffalo NFL	14		None		
1978—Buffalo NFL	16	2	95	47.5	1
1979—Buffalo NFL	16	1	0	0.0	0
1980—Buffalo NFL	16	2	41	20.5	0
1981—Buffalo NFL	16	4	113	28.3	0
1982—Buffalo NFL	9	1	8	8.0	0
1983—Buffalo NFL	16	2	27	13.5	0
1984—Buffalo NFL	16	5	130	26.0	0
Pro Totals—8 Years	119	17	414	24.4	1

Additional pro statistics: Returned one kickoff for 18 yards, 1977; fumbled once, 1977, 1978 and 1981; recovered two fumbles, 1978; ran 76 yards with blocked field goal for a touchdown and recovered one fumble for minus 10 yards, 1979; recovered two fumbles for 11 yards, 1981; recovered one fumble, 1984.

JOSEPH HAROLD ROSE
(Joe)
Tight End—Miami Dolphins
Born June 24, 1957, at Marysville, Calif.
Height, 6.03. Weight, 230.
High School—Marysville, Calif.
Received bachelor of arts degree in social science from University of California in 1980.

Selected by Miami in 7th round (185th player selected) of 1980 NFL draft.
On injured reserve with separated shoulder, October 12 through November 16, 1984; activated, November 17, 1984.

Year Club	G.	P.C.	Yds.	Avg.	TD.
1980—Miami NFL	16	13	149	11.5	0
1981—Miami NFL	16	23	316	13.7	2
1982—Miami NFL	9	16	182	11.4	2
1983—Miami NFL	16	29	345	11.9	3
1984—Miami NFL	9	12	195	16.3	2
Pro Totals—5 Years	66	93	1187	12.8	9

Additional pro statistics: Recovered one fumble and returned one kickoff for five yards, 1981.
Played in AFC Championship Game following 1982 and 1984 seasons.
Played in NFL Championship Game following 1982 and 1984 seasons.

KEVIN LESLEY ROSS
Wide Receiver—Kansas City Chiefs
Born January 16, 1962, at Camden, N.J.
Height, 5.09. Weight, 180.
High School—Paulsboro, N.J.
Attended Temple University.

Selected by Philadelphia in 1984 USFL territorial draft.
Selected by Kansas City in 7th round (173rd player selected) of 1984 NFL draft.
Signed by Kansas City Chiefs, June 21, 1984.

Year Club	G.	No.	Yds.	Avg.	TD.
1984—Kansas City NFL	16	6	124	20.7	1

Additional pro statistics: Recovered one fumble, 1984.

PETE ROSTOSKY
Offensive Tackle—Pittsburgh Steelers
Born July 29, 1961, at Monongahela, Pa.
Height, 6.04. Weight, 255.
High School—Elizabeth, Pa., Forward.
Attended University of Connecticut.

Signed as free agent by Pittsburgh Steelers, May 10, 1983.
On injured reserve with knee injury, August 16 through entire 1983 season.
On injured reserve with knee injury, August 14 through October 22, 1984; activated after clearing procedural waivers, October 24, 1984.
Pittsburgh NFL, 1984.
Games: 1984 (8).
Played in AFC Championship Game following 1984 season.

JAMES PETER ROURKE
(Jim)
Offensive Tackle-Guard—Kansas City Chiefs
Born February 10, 1957, at Weymouth, Mass.
Height, 6.05. Weight, 263.
High School—Dorchester, Mass., Boston College High.
Received bachelor of arts degree in sociology from Boston College in 1979.

Selected by Oakland in 9th round (238th player selected) of 1979 NFL draft.
Released by Oakland Raiders, August 27, 1979; signed as free agent by Kansas City Chiefs, February 16, 1980.
Released by Kansas City Chiefs, August 24, 1981; re-signed by Chiefs, September 29, 1981.
Kansas City NFL, 1980 through 1984.
Games: 1980 (15), 1981 (12), 1982 (9), 1983 (11), 1984 (13). Total—60.
Pro statistics: Returned two kickoffs for no yards, 1981.

CURTIS LAMAR ROUSE
Guard—Minnesota Vikings
Born July 13, 1960, at Augusta, Ga.
Height, 6.03. Weight, 318.
High School—Augusta, Ga., Lucy C. Laney.
Attended University of Tennessee at Chattanooga.

Selected by Minnesota in 11th round (286th player selected) of 1982 NFL draft.
Minnesota NFL, 1982 through 1984.
Games: 1982 (5), 1983 (16), 1984 (16). Total—37.
Pro statistics: Recovered two fumbles, 1983; returned two kickoffs for 22 yards and recovered one fumble, 1984.

ROBIN JAMES RUBICK
(Rob)
Tight End—Detroit Lions
Born September 27, 1960, at Newberry, Mich.
Height, 6.02. Weight, 234.
High School—Newberry, Mich.
Attended Grand Valley State College.

Selected by Detroit in 12th round (326th player selected) of 1982 NFL draft.

					PASS RECEIVING			
Year	Club	G.	P.C.	Yds.	Avg.	TD.		
1982—Detroit NFL		7			None			
1983—Detroit NFL		16	10	81	8.1	1		
1984—Detroit NFL		16	14	188	13.4	1		
Pro Totals—3 Years		39	24	269	11.2	2		

Additional pro statistics: Rushed once for one yard and a touchdown, 1982.

MAX CULP RUNAGER
Punter—San Francisco 49ers
Born March 24, 1956, at Greenwood, S.C.
Height, 6.01. Weight, 189.
High School—Orangeburg, S.C., Wilkinson.
Received bachelor of science degree in health and physical education from University of South Carolina.
Selected by Philadelphia in 8th round (211th player selected) of 1979 NFL draft.
Released by Philadelphia Eagles, September 28, 1983; re-signed by Eagles, October 26, 1983.
Released by Philadelphia Eagles, August 27, 1984; signed as free agent by San Francisco 49ers, September 12, 1984.

		PUNTING			
Year	Club	G.	No.	Avg.	Blk.
1979—Philadelphia NFL	16	74	39.6	1	
1980—Philadelphia NFL	16	75	39.3	1	
1981—Philadelphia NFL	15	63	40.7	0	
1982—Philadelphia NFL	9	44	40.5	0	
1983—Philadelphia NFL	12	59	41.7	0	
1984—San Francisco NFL	14	56	41.8	1	
Pro Totals—6 Years	82	371	40.5	3	

Additional pro statistics: Recovered one fumble and fumbled once, 1979; rushed once for six yards, 1983; rushed once for minus five yards, 1984.
Played in NFC Championship Game following 1980 and 1984 seasons.
Played in NFL Championship Game following 1980 and 1984 seasons.

MARK RUSH
Tight End—Minnesota Vikings
Born March 31, 1959, at Fort Lauderdale, Fla.
Height, 6.02. Weight, 230.
High School—Fort Lauderdale, Fla., Stranahan.
Attended University of Miami (Fla.).
Selected by Chicago in 22nd round (259th player selected) of 1983 USFL draft.
Selected by Minnesota in 4th round (100th player selected) of 1983 NFL draft.
USFL rights traded with rights to quarterback Jim Kelly by Chicago Blitz to Houston Gamblers for 1st, 3rd, 8th and 10th round picks in 1984 draft, June 9, 1983.
Signed by Houston Gamblers, June 9, 1983.
On developmental squad, March 9 through March 17, 1984; activated, March 18, 1984.
Released by Houston Gamblers, April 4, 1984; awarded on waivers to Michigan Panthers, April 5, 1984.
On developmental squad, April 7 through April 26, 1984.
Released by Michigan Panthers, April 27, 1984; signed as free agent by San Antonio Gunslingers, May 8, 1984.
Released by San Antonio Gunslingers, March 20, 1985; signed by Minnesota Vikings, April 17, 1985.
On developmental squad for 1 game with Houston Gamblers and 3 games with Michigan Panthers in 1984.

			RUSHING				PASS RECEIVING				TOTAL		
Year	Club	G.	Att.	Yds.	Avg.	TD.	P.C.	Yds.	Avg.	TD.	TD.	Pts.	F.
1984—Hou. (5)-S.A. (7) USFL	12	18	34	1.9	1	9	67	7.4	1	2	12	1
1985—San Antonio USFL	2		None			1	7	7.0	0	0	0	0
Pro Totals—2 Years	14	18	34	1.9	1	10	74	7.4	1	2	12	1

			KICKOFF RETURNS			
Year	Club	G.	No.	Yds.	Avg.	TD.
1984—Hou.(5)-S.A. (7) USFL	12	4	113	28.3	0	
1985—San Antonio USFL	2	1	25	25.0	0	
Pro Totals—2 Years	14	5	138	27.6	0	

Additional pro statistics: Recovered one fumble, 1984.

ROBERT JEFFREY RUSH
(Bob)
Center-Offensive Tackle—Kansas City Chiefs
Born February 27, 1955, at Santa Monica, Calif.
Height, 6.05. Weight, 264.
High School—Clarksville, Tenn., Northwest.
Received bachelor of arts degree in sociology from Memphis State University.
Named center on THE SPORTING NEWS College All-America Team, 1976.
Selected by San Diego in 1st round (24th player selected) of 1977 NFL draft.
On injured reserve with knee injury, July 19 through entire 1978 season.
Traded by San Diego Chargers to Kansas City Chiefs for 3rd round pick in 1985 draft, July 11, 1983.
San Diego NFL, 1977 and 1979 through 1982; Kansas City NFL, 1983 and 1984.
Games: 1977 (14), 1979 (16), 1980 (15), 1981 (16), 1982 (9), 1983 (15), 1984 (16). Total—101.
Pro statistics: Fumbled twice for minus 35 yards, 1980; fumbled twice and recovered one fumble, 1983.
Played in AFC Championship Game following 1980 and 1981 seasons.

RUSTY RUSSELL
Offensive Tackle—Philadelphia Eagles

Born August 16, 1963, at Orangeburg, S.C.
Height, 6.05. Weight, 295.
High School—Orangeburg, S.C., Wilkinson.
Attended University of South Carolina.
Cousin of Rufus Bess, cornerback with Minnesota Vikings.

Selected by Washington in 1984 USFL territorial draft.
Selected by Philadelphia in 3rd round (60th player selected) of 1984 NFL draft.
Signed by Philadelphia Eagles, June 19, 1984.
On injured reserve with broken foot, August 28 through October 17, 1984; activated, October 18, 1984.
Philadelphia NFL, 1984.
Games: 1984 (1).

JEFFREY RONALD RUTLEDGE
(Jeff)
Quarterback—New York Giants

Born January 22, 1957, at Birmingham, Ala.
Height, 6.01. Weight, 195.
High School—Birmingham, Ala., Banks.
Received degree in business education from University of Alabama.
Son of Paul E. (Jack) Rutledge, minor league infielder, 1950 through 1952.

Selected by Los Angeles in 9th round (246th player selected) of 1979 NFL draft.
On injured reserve with mononucleosis, October 22 through remainder of 1980 season.
On injured reserve with broken thumb, November 2 through remainder of 1981 season.
Traded by Los Angeles Rams to New York Giants for 4th round pick in 1983 draft, September 5, 1982.
Active for 9 games with New York Giants in 1982; did not play.

					PASSING						RUSHING				TOTAL	
Year Club	G.	Att.	Cmp.	Pct.	Gain	T.P.	P.I.	Avg.	Att.	Yds.	Avg.	TD.	TD.	Pts.	F.
1979—Los Angeles NFL	3	32	13	40.6	125	1	4	3.91	5	27	5.4	0	0	0	0
1980—Los Angeles NFL	1	4	1	25.0	26	0	0	6.50		None			0	0	0
1981—Los Angeles NFL	4	50	30	60.0	442	3	4	8.84	5	—3	—0.6	0	0	0	0
1983—New York Giants NFL	4	174	87	50.0	1208	3	8	6.94	7	27	3.9	0	0	0	6
1984—New York Giants NFL	16	1	1	100.0	9	0	0	9.00		None			0	0	0
Pro Totals—6 Years	28	261	132	50.6	1810	7	16	6.93	17	51	3.0	0	0	0	6

Quarterback Rating Points: 1979 (23.0), 1980 (54.2), 1981 (75.6), 1983 (59.3), 1984 (104.2). Total—56.7.
Member of Los Angeles Rams for NFC and NFL Championship Game following 1979 season; did not play.

JAMES JOSEPH RYAN
(Jim)
Linebacker—Denver Broncos

Born May 18, 1957, at Camden, N.J.
Height, 6.02. Weight, 215.
High School—Pennsauken, N.J., Bishop Eustace.
Received bachelor of administration degree from College of William & Mary in 1979
and attending University of Denver for master's degree in business administration.

Signed as free agent by Denver Broncos, May 12, 1979.
Denver NFL, 1979 through 1984.
Games: 1979 (16), 1980 (16), 1981 (16), 1982 (9), 1983 (15), 1984 (16). Total—88.
Pro statistics: Recovered one fumble, 1979, 1983 and 1984; intercepted one pass for 21 yards and returned one kickoff for no yards, 1980; returned one kickoff for two yards, 1981; intercepted one pass for 13 yards, 1984.

PATRICK LEE RYAN
(Pat)
Quarterback—New York Jets

Born September 16, 1955, at Hutchinson, Kan.
Height, 6.03. Weight, 210.
High School—Oklahoma City, Okla., Putnam.
Received degree in transportation from University of Tennessee in 1978.

Selected by New York Jets in 11th round (281st player selected) of 1978 NFL draft.

					PASSING						RUSHING				TOTAL	
Year Club	G.	Att.	Cmp.	Pct.	Gain	T.P.	P.I.	Avg.	Att.	Yds.	Avg.	TD.	TD.	Pts.	F.
1978—New York Jets NFL	2	14	9	64.3	106	0	2	7.57		None			0	0	0
1979—New York Jets NFL	1	4	2	50.0	13	0	1	3.25		None			0	0	1
1980—New York Jets NFL	14				None					None			0	0	0
1981—New York Jets NFL	15	10	4	40.0	48	1	1	4.80	3	—5	—1.7	0	0	0	0
1982—New York Jets NFL	9	18	12	66.7	146	2	1	8.11	1	—1	—1.0	0	0	0	0
1983—New York Jets NFL	16	40	21	52.5	259	2	2	6.48	4	23	5.8	0	0	†1	2
1984—New York Jets NFL	16	285	156	54.7	1939	14	14	6.80	23	92	4.0	0	0	†1	4
Pro Totals—7 Years	73	371	204	55.0	2511	19	21	6.77	31	109	3.5	0	0	2	7

†Scored one extra point.
Quarterback Rating Points: 1978 (47.6), 1979 (17.7), 1981 (49.2), 1982 (105.1), 1983 (68.6), 1984 (72.0). Total—69.4.
Additional pro statistics: Recovered one fumble, 1983 and 1984.
Member of New York Jets for AFC Championship Game following 1982 season; did not play.

JOHN JAY SALDI IV
(Known by middle name.)

Name pronounced SAL-dee.

Tight End—Chicago Bears

Born October 8, 1954, at White Plains, N. Y.
Height, 6.03. Weight, 230.
High School—White Plains, N. Y.
Attended University of South Carolina.

Signed as free agent by Dallas Cowboys, 1976.
On injured reserve with broken forearm, September 27 through remainder of 1978 season.
On inactive list, September 13 and September 19, 1982.
Traded by Dallas Cowboys to Chicago Bears for 6th round pick in 1984 draft, May 11, 1983.

Year Club	G.	Att.	RUSHING Yds.	Avg.	TD.	P.C.	PASS RECEIVING Yds.	Avg.	TD.	TD.	TOTAL Pts.	F.
1976—Dallas NFL	14	1	19	19.0	0	1	6	6.0	0	0	0	0
1977—Dallas NFL	14		None			11	108	9.8	2	3	18	0
1978—Dallas NFL	4		None			3	8	2.7	2	2	12	0
1979—Dallas NFL	16	1	—1	—1.0	0	14	181	12.9	1	1	6	0
1980—Dallas NFL	16		None			25	311	12.4	1	1	6	0
1981—Dallas NFL	16		None			8	82	10.3	1	1	6	0
1982—Dallas NFL	5		None			1	8	8.0	0	0	0	0
1983—Chicago NFL	13		None			12	119	9.9	0	0	0	0
1984—Chicago NFL	15		None			9	90	10.0	0	0	0	2
Pro Totals—9 Years	113	2	18	9.0	0	84	913	10.9	7	8	48	2

Year Club	G.	KICKOFF RETURNS No.	Yds.	Avg.TD.	Year Club	G.	KICKOFF RETURNS No.	Yds.	Avg.TD.
1976—Dallas NFL	14	1	9	9.0 0	1981—Dallas NFL	16		None	
1977—Dallas NFL	14		None		1982—Dallas NFL	5		None	
1978—Dallas NFL	4	1	0	0.0 0	1983—Chicago NFL	13		None	
1979—Dallas NFL	16		None		1984—Chicago NFL	15		None	
1980—Dallas NFL	16	1	23	23.0 0	Pro Totals—9 Years	113	3	32	10.7 0

Additional pro statistics: Recovered one fumble for eight yards and one touchdown, 1977; recovered one fumble for eight yards, 1980; recovered two fumbles, 1981.
Played in NFC Championship Game following 1977, 1980 through 1982 and 1984 seasons.
Member of Dallas Cowboys for NFL Championship Game following 1977 season; did not play.

HARVEY SALEM
Offensive Tackle—Houston Oilers

Born January 15, 1961, at Berkeley, Calif.
Height, 6.06. Weight, 285.
High School—El Cerrito, Calif.
Attended University of California at Berkeley.

Named as offensive tackle on THE SPORTING NEWS College All-America Team, 1982.
Selected by Oakland in 1983 USFL territorial draft.
Selected by Houston in 2nd round (30th player selected) of 1983 NFL draft.
Signed by Houston Oilers, July 14, 1983.
Houston NFL, 1983 and 1984.
Games: 1983 (16), 1984 (16). Total—32.

JEROME ELI SALLY
Nose Tackle—New York Giants

Born February 24, 1959, at Chicago, Ill.
Height, 6.03. Weight, 270.
High School—Maywood, Ill., Proviso East.
Attended University of Missouri.

Signed as free agent by New Orleans Saints, May 27, 1982.
Released by New Orleans Saints, August 31, 1982; signed as free agent by New York Giants, December 1, 1982.
New York Giants NFL, 1982 through 1984.
Games: 1982 (4), 1983 (16), 1984 (16). Total—36.
Pro statistics: Recovered one fumble, 1983.

BRIAN SCOTT SALONEN
Tight End—Dallas Cowboys

Born July 29, 1961, at Glasgow, Mont.
Height, 6.02. Weight, 227.
High School—Great Falls, Mont.
Attended University of Montana.

Selected by Houston in 9th round (188th player selected) of 1984 USFL draft.
Selected by Dallas in 10th round (278th player selected) of 1984 NFL draft.
Signed by Dallas Cowboys, June 7, 1984.
Dallas NFL, 1984.
Games: 1984 (16).
Pro statistics: Returned two kickoffs for 30 yards and recovered one fumble, 1984.

LAWRENCE SAMPLETON
Tight End—Philadelphia Eagles

Born September 25, 1959, at Waelder, Tex.
Height, 6.05. Weight, 233.
High School—Seguin, Tex.
Attended University of Texas.

Selected by Philadelphia in 2nd round (47th player selected) of 1982 NFL draft.

		—PASS RECEIVING—			
Year Club	G.	P.C.	Yds.	Avg.	TD.
1982—Philadelphia NFL	9	1	24	24.0	0
1983—Philadelphia NFL	7	2	28	14.0	0
1984—Philadelphia NFL	16		None		
Pro Totals—3 Years............	32	3	52	17.3	0

CLINTON BERNARD SAMPSON
(Clint)
Wide Receiver—Denver Broncos

Born January 4, 1961, at Los Angeles, Calif.
Height, 5.11. Weight, 183.
High School—Los Angeles, Calif., Crenshaw.
Attended Mt. San Antonio College and received degree in public administration
and business management from San Diego State University in 1983.

Selected by Boston in 3rd round (35th player selected) of 1983 USFL draft.
Selected by Denver in 3rd round (60th player selected) of 1983 NFL draft.
Signed by Denver Broncos, July 13, 1983.
On injured reserve with concussion, October 26 through November 19, 1984; activated, November 20, 1984.

		—PASS RECEIVING—			
Year Club	G.	P.C.	Yds.	Avg.	TD.
1983—Denver NFL	16	10	200	20.0	3
1984—Denver NFL	12	9	123	13.7	1
Pro Totals—2 Years............	28	19	323	17.0	4

Additional pro statistics: Fumbled once, 1984.

RON SAMS
Guard—Minnesota Vikings

Born April 12, 1961, at Bridgeville, Pa.
Height, 6.03. Weight, 255.
High School—McDonald, Pa., South Fayette.
Attended University of Pittsburgh.

Selected by Green Bay in 6th round (160th player selected) of 1983 NFL draft.
On injured reserve with torn hamstring, August 29 through October 15, 1983; activated by Green Bay Packers after clearing procedural waivers, October 17, 1983.
On injured reserve with neck injury, November 18 through remainder of 1983 season.
Released by Green Bay Packers, August 27, 1984; awarded on waivers to Minnesota Vikings, August 28, 1984.
Green Bay NFL, 1983; Minnesota NFL, 1984.
Games: 1983 (3), 1984 (12). Total—15.
Pro statistics: Fumbled once for minus 17 yards, 1984.

ERIC DOWNER SANDERS
Offensive Tackle—Atlanta Falcons

Born October 22, 1958, at Reno, Nev.
Height, 6.07. Weight, 280.
High School—Reno, Nev., Wooster.
Attended University of Nevada at Reno.

Selected by Atlanta in 5th round (136th player selected) of 1981 NFL draft.
On injured reserve with knee injury, November 10 through remainder of 1984 season.
Atlanta NFL, 1981 through 1984.
Games: 1981 (16), 1982 (9), 1983 (15), 1984 (10). Total—50.
Pro statistics: Recovered one fumble, 1982.

EUGENE SANDERS
(Gene)
Offensive Tackle—Tampa Bay Buccaneers

Born November 10, 1956, at New Orleans, La.
Height, 6.03. Weight, 275.
High School—Harvey, La., West Jefferson.
Attended University of Washington and received degree in educational curriculum
and instructions from Texas A&M University.

Selected by Tampa Bay in 8th round (217th player selected) of 1979 NFL draft.
On injured reserve with wrist injury, October 11 through November 7, 1980; activated, November 8, 1980.
Tampa Bay NFL, 1979 through 1984.
Games: 1979 (16), 1980 (11), 1981 (16), 1982 (4), 1983 (12), 1984 (16). Total—75.
Pro statistics: Recovered one fumble, 1983.
Played in NFC Championship Game following 1979 season.

LUCIUS M. SANFORD
Linebacker—Buffalo Bills

Born February 13, 1956, at Milledgville, Ga.
Height, 6.02. Weight, 216.
High School—Atlanta, Ga., West Fulton.
Received bachelor of science degree in industrial management from
Georgia Tech in 1978.

Named as linebacker on THE SPORTING NEWS College All-America Team, 1977.
Selected by Buffalo in 4th round (89th player selected) of 1978 NFL draft.
On injured reserve with knee injury, October 31 through remainder of 1984 season.

		—INTERCEPTIONS—			
Year	Club	G.	No.	Yds.	Avg. TD.
1978—Buffalo NFL		16	1	41	41.0 0
1979—Buffalo NFL		16	2	44	22.0 0
1980—Buffalo NFL		16		None	
1981—Buffalo NFL		16		None	
1982—Buffalo NFL		9		None	
1983—Buffalo NFL		16	2	39	19.5 0
1984—Buffalo NFL		8		None	
Pro Totals—7 Years		97	5	124	24.8 0

Additional pro statistics: Recovered one fumble, 1978, 1981 and 1983; ran 25 yards with blocked punt for a touchdown, 1979; recovered blocked punt in end zone for a touchdown and recovered two fumbles for minus one yard, 1980; recovered two fumbles for 46 yards and a touchdown, 1984.

RICHARD FRANCIS SANFORD
(Rick)
Safety—New England Patriots

Born January 9, 1957, at Rock Hill, S.C.
Height, 6.01. Weight, 192.
High School—Rock Hill, S.C., Northwestern.
Received bachelor of science degree in physical education from University of South Carolina
in 1980 and attending South Carolina for master's degree in education.

Named as cornerback on THE SPORTING NEWS College All-America Team, 1978.
Selected by New England in 1st round (25th player selected) of 1979 NFL draft.

		—INTERCEPTIONS—				—KICKOFF RET.—				—TOTAL—		
Year	Club	G.	No.	Yds.	Avg.	TD.	No.	Yds.	Avg.	TD.	TD. Pts. F.
1979—New England NFL		16	1	39	39.0	0	10	179	17.9	0	1 6 0
1980—New England NFL		16	1	0	0.0	0		None			1 6 0
1981—New England NFL		16	3	28	9.3	0	4	82	20.5	0	0 0 0
1982—New England NFL		9	2	105	52.5	*1		None			1 6 0
1983—New England NFL		16	7	24	3.4	0		None			0 0 1
1984—New England NFL		16	2	2	1.0	0		None			0 0 0
Pro Totals—6 Years		89	16	198	12.4	1	14	261	18.6	0	3 18 1

Additional pro statistics: Ran eight yards with blocked punt for a touchdown, recovered two fumbles for 10 yards and returned one punt for one yard, 1979; recovered two fumbles for 22 yards and a touchdown, 1980; recovered three fumbles for two yards, 1981; recovered one fumble, 1982; recovered one fumble for 26 yards and returned one punt for no yards, 1983.

JESSE SAPOLU
Guard—San Francisco 49ers

Born March 10, 1961, at Laie, Western Samoa.
Height, 6.04. Weight, 260.
High School—Honolulu, Haw., Farrington.
Attended University of Hawaii.

Selected by Oakland in 17th round (199th player selected) of 1983 USFL draft.
Selected by San Francisco in 11th round (289th player selected) of 1983 NFL draft.
Signed by San Francisco 49ers, July 10, 1983.
On physically unable to perform/active with fractured foot, July 19 through August 12, 1984.
On physically unable to perform/reserve with fractured foot, August 13 through November 7, 1984; activated, November 8, 1984.
On injured reserve with fractured foot, November 16 through remainder of 1984 season.
San Francisco NFL, 1983 and 1984.
Games: 1983 (16), 1984 (1). Total—17.
Played in NFC Championship Game following 1983 season.

JOHN WESLEY SAWYER
Tight End—Denver Broncos

Born July 26, 1953, at Brookhaven, Miss.
Height, 6.02. Weight, 230.
High School—Baker, La.
Attended University of Southern Mississippi.

Selected by Houston in 11th round (271st player selected) of 1975 NFL draft.
Claimed on waivers from Houston Oilers by Seattle Seahawks, September 14, 1977.
Released by Seattle Seahawks, October 28, 1978; re-signed by Seahawks, November 8, 1978.
On injured reserve with hamstring injury, August 21 through entire 1979 season.

Released by Seattle Seahawks, July 23, 1983; signed as free agent by Washington Redskins, July 28, 1983.

Released by Washington Redskins, October 27, 1983; signed as free agent by Denver Broncos, November 3, 1983.

USFL rights traded by New Orleans Breakers to Los Angeles Express for rights to defensive back Jeff Orlando, January 13, 1984.

On injured reserve with knee injury, November 10 through remainder of 1984 season.

Year Club	G.	P.C.	Yds.	Avg.	TD.	Year Club	G.	P.C.	Yds.	Avg.	TD.
			—PASS RECEIVING—						—PASS RECEIVING—		
1975—Houston NFL	8	7	144	20.6	1	1981—Seattle NFL	16	21	272	13.0	0
1976—Houston NFL	14	18	208	11.5	1	1982—Seattle NFL	7	8	92	11.5	0
1977—Seattle NFL	14	10	105	10.5	0	1983—Wash(7)-Den(7) NFL...	14	3	42	14.0	0
1978—Seattle NFL	11	9	101	11.2	0	1984—Denver NFL	10	17	122	7.2	0
1980—Seattle NFL	16	36	410	11.4	0	Pro Totals—9 Years	110	129	1496	11.6	2

Additional pro statistics: Fumbled once, 1975, 1977, 1978, 1980 and 1983; recovered one fumble and punted once for 32 yards, 1976; returned one kickoff for eight yards, 1981; returned one kickoff for 15 yards, 1983; recovered two fumbles, 1984.

ARTHUR E. SCHLICHTER
(Art)
Quarterback—Indianapolis Colts

Born April 25, 1960, at Washington Court House, O.
Height, 6.03. Weight, 210.
High School—Washington Court House, O., Miami Trace.
Attended Ohio State University.

Selected by Baltimore in 1st round (4th player selected) of 1982 NFL draft.
Suspended by NFL for gambling activities, May 20, 1983; reinstated, June 22, 1984.
Franchise transferred to Indianapolis, March 31, 1984.

Year Club	G.	Att.	Cmp.	Pct.	Gain	T.P.	P.I.	Avg.	Att.	Yds.	Avg.	TD.	TD.	Pts.	F.
				—PASSING—						—RUSHING—				—TOTAL—	
1982—Baltimore NFL	3	37	17	45.9	197	0	2	5.32	1	3	3.0	0	0	0	3
1984—Indianapolis NFL	9	140	62	44.3	702	3	7	5.01	19	145	7.6	1	1	6	4
Pro Totals—2 Years	12	177	79	44.6	899	3	9	5.08	20	148	7.4	1	1	6	7

Quarterback Rating Points: 1982 (40.0), 1984 (46.2). Total—44.8.
Additional pro statistics: Recovered three fumbles for one yard, 1984.

GEORGE PAUL SCHMITT
Safety—St. Louis Cardinals

Born March 6, 1961, at Bryn Mawr, Pa.
Height, 5.11. Weight, 193.
High School—Newtown Square, Pa., Marple.
Received degree in agricultural business management from University of Delaware in 1983.

Selected by Philadelphia in 1983 USFL territorial draft.
Selected by St. Louis in 6th round (157th player selected) of 1983 NFL draft.
Signed by St. Louis Cardinals, June 27, 1983.
On injured reserve with back injury, August 12 through entire 1984 season.
St. Louis NFL, 1983.
Games: 1983 (16).
Pro statistics: Returned four kickoffs for 41 yards, recovered one fumble and fumbled once, 1983.

BRUCE DANIEL SCHOLTZ
Linebacker—Seattle Seahawks

Born September 26, 1958, at La Grange, Tex.
Height, 6.06. Weight, 240.
High School—Austin, Tex., Crockett.
Attended University of Texas.

Selected by Seattle in 2nd round (33rd player selected) of 1982 NFL draft.

Year Club	G.	No.	Yds.	Avg.	TD.
			—INTERCEPTIONS—		
1982—Seattle NFL	9	1	31	31.0	1
1983—Seattle NFL	16	1	8	8.0	0
1984—Seattle NFL	16	1	15	15.0	0
Pro Totals—3 Years	41	3	54	18.0	1

Additional pro statistics: Recovered one fumble, 1982 through 1984.
Played in AFC Championship Game following 1983 season.

TURK LEROY SCHONERT
Quarterback—Cincinnati Bengals

Born January 15, 1957, at Torrance, Calif.
Height, 6.01. Weight, 190.
High School—Anaheim, Calif., Servite.
Attended Stanford University.
Cousin of Steve Schonert, rookie placekicker with Denver Broncos.

Selected by Chicago in 9th round (242nd player selected) of 1980 NFL draft.
Released by Chicago Bears, August 25, 1980; claimed on waivers by Cincinnati Bengals, August 26, 1980.

USFL rights traded by Oakland Invaders to Jacksonville Bulls for rights to running back Ted McKnight, linebacker Mark Jerue and 1st and 5th round picks in 1984 draft, October 24, 1983.
On injured reserve with separated shoulder, December 5 through remainder of 1984 season.
Active for 16 games with Cincinnati Bengals in 1980; did not play.

Year Club	G.	Att.	Cmp.	Pct.	Gain	T.P.	P.I.	Avg.	Att.	Yds.	Avg.	TD.	TD.	Pts.	F.
				—PASSING—						—RUSHING—			—TOTAL—		
1981—Cincinnati NFL	4	19	10	52.6	166	0	0	8.74	7	41	5.9	0	0	0	1
1982—Cincinnati NFL	2	1	1	100.0	6	0	0	6.00	3	—8	—2.7	0	0	0	1
1983—Cincinnati NFL	9	156	92	59.0	1159	2	5	7.43	29	117	4.0	2	2	12	6
1984—Cincinnati NFL	8	117	78	66.7	945	4	7	8.08	13	77	5.9	1	1	6	2
Pro Totals—5 Years	23	293	181	61.8	2276	6	12	7.77	52	227	4.4	3	3	18	10

Quarterback Rating Points: 1981 (82.3), 1982 (91.7), 1983 (73.1), 1984 (77.8). Total—75.6.
Additional pro statistics: Recovered one fumble, 1982; recovered four fumbles, 1983.
Member of Cincinnati Bengals for AFC and NFL Championship Game following 1981 season; did not play.

ADAM SCHREIBER
Guard—Seattle Seahawks
Born February 20, 1962, at Galveston, Tex.
Height, 6.04. Weight, 284.
High School—Huntsville, Ala., Butler.
Attended University of Texas.

Selected by Houston in 1984 USFL territorial draft.
Selected by Seattle in 9th round (243rd player selected) of 1984 NFL draft.
Signed by Seattle Seahawks, June 20, 1984.
Released by Seattle Seahawks, August 27, 1984; re-signed by Seahawks, October 10, 1984.
Seattle NFL, 1984.
Games: 1984 (6).

JAY BRIAN SCHROEDER
Name pronounced SCHRAY-der.
Quarterback—Washington Redskins
Born June 28, 1961, at Milwaukee, Wis.
Height, 6.04. Weight, 215.
High School—Pacific Palisades, Calif.
Attended University of California at Los Angeles.

Selected by Washington in 3rd round (83rd player selected) of 1984 NFL draft.
Active for 16 games with Washington Redskins in 1984; did not play.

RECORD AS BASEBALL PLAYER
Led Carolina League batters in strikeouts with 172 in 1982.
Led South Atlantic League batters in strikeouts with 142 in 1981.
Received reported $100,000 bonus to sign with Toronto Blue Jays, 1979.

Year Club	League	Pos.	G.	AB.	R.	H.	2B.	3B.	HR.	RBI.	B.A.	PO.	A.	E.	F.A.
1979—Utica†	NYP					(Did not play)									
1980—Medicine Hat‡	Pion.	OF	52	171	27	40	6	2	2	21	.234	93	6	5	.952
1981—Florence	S. Atl.	3B-OF	131	417	51	85	17	1	10	47	.204	112	101	28	.884
1982—Kinston	Carol.	OF	132	435	59	95	17	1	15	55	.218	178	17	15	.929
1983—Kinston§	Carol.	C-OF-1B	92	281	30	58	9	2	9	43	.206	519	53	20	.966

Selected by Toronto Blue Jays' organization in 1st round (third player selected) of free-agent draft, June 5, 1979.
†On temporary inactive list, June 30, 1979 through remainder of season.
‡On temporary inactive list, August 14 to September 3, 1980.
§Released, February 28, 1984.

KENNETH MICHAEL SCHROY
(Ken)
Safety—New York Jets
Born September 22, 1952, at Valley Forge, Pa.
Height, 6.02. Weight, 198.
High School—Quakertown, Pa.
Received bachelor of science degree in recreation from University of Maryland in 1975.

Selected by Philadelphia in 10th round (248th player selected) of 1975 NFL draft.
Released by Philadelphia Eagles, August, 1975; signed as free agent by New York Jets, April, 1976.
On injured reserve with broken ankle entire 1976 season.
On injured reserve with rotator cuff injury, November 23 through remainder of 1984 season.

Year Club	G.	No.	Yds.	Avg.	TD.	No.	Yds.	Avg.	TD.	TD.	Pts.	F.
			—INTERCEPTIONS—				—PUNT RETURNS—				—TOTAL—	
1977—New York Jets NFL	14		None			3	38	12.7	0	0	0	0
1978—New York Jets NFL	16		None			3	35	11.7	0	0	0	1
1979—New York Jets NFL	16	1	4	4.0	0	2	12	12.0	0	0	0	0
1980—New York Jets NFL	14	8	91	11.4	1	4	27	6.8	0	1	6	0
1981—New York Jets NFL	16	2	58	29.0	0	1	5	5.0	0	0	0	0
1982—New York Jets NFL	9	1	34	34.0	0		None			0	0	0
1983—New York Jets NFL	16	2	6	3.0	0		None			0	0	0
1984—New York Jets NFL	12	2	13	6.5	0		None			0	0	0
Pro Totals—8 Years	113	16	206	12.9	1	13	117	9.0	0	1	6	1

Additional pro statistics: Recovered two fumbles for 11 yards, 1977; ran 26 yards with lateral on kickoff return,

1978; recovered two fumbles, 1978, 1980 and 1984; returned six kickoffs for 179 yards, 1979; returned one kickoff for 17 yards, 1980; recovered two fumbles for four yards, 1982; recovered one fumble for 24 yards and returned one kickoff for 11 yards, 1983.

Played in AFC Championship Game following 1982 season.

JEFF JOHN SCHUH
Linebacker—Cincinnati Bengals
Born May 22, 1958, at Crystal, Minn.
Height, 6.02. Weight, 228.
High School—Plymouth, Minn., Armstrong.
Attended North Hennepin Junior College and University of Minnesota.

Selected by Cincinnati in 7th round (176th player selected) of 1981 NFL draft.
Left Cincinnati Bengals camp voluntarily, July 22, 1981; returned, July 29, 1981.
Released by Cincinnati Bengals, August 31, 1981; re-signed by Bengals, September 1, 1981.
On injured reserve with toe injury, January 9 through remainder of 1981 season playoffs.
Cincinnati NFL, 1981 through 1984.
Games: 1981 (16), 1982 (9), 1983 (16), 1984 (16). Total—57.
Pro statistics: Recovered one fumble, 1981; intercepted one pass for no yards, 1984.

JOHN SCHUHMACHER
Guard—Houston Oilers
Born September 23, 1955, at Salem, Ore.
Height, 6.03. Weight, 277.
High School—Arcadia, Calif.
Attended University of Southern California.

Selected by Houston in 12th round (322nd player selected) of 1978 NFL draft.
On injured reserve with back injury, August 27 through entire 1979 season.
On injured reserve with back injury, August 26 through entire 1980 season.
On injured reserve with knee injury, September 6 through remainder of 1983 season.
Houston NFL, 1978 and 1981 through 1984.
Games: 1978 (11), 1981 (16), 1982 (9), 1983 (1), 1984 (16). Total—53.
Pro statistics: Recovered one fumble, 1981.
Played in AFC Championship Game following 1978 season.

CHRIS SCHULTZ
Offensive Tackle—Dallas Cowboys
Born February 16, 1960, at Burlington, Ont., Can.
Height, 6.08. Weight, 265.
High School—Burlington, Ont., Can., Aldershot.
Attended University of Arizona.

Selected by Arizona in 1983 USFL territorial draft.
Selected by Dallas in 7th round (189th player selected) of 1983 NFL draft.
Signed by Dallas Cowboys, May 26, 1983.
On injured reserve with knee injury, August 21 through entire 1984 season.
Dallas NFL, 1983.
Games: 1983 (5).

JODY SCHULZ
Linebacker—Philadelphia Eagles
Born August 17, 1960, at Easton, Md.
Height, 6.04. Weight, 235.
High School—Upper Marlboro, Md., Queen Anne.
Attended Chowan College and East Carolina University.

Selected by Washington in 14th round (165th player selected) of 1983 USFL draft.
Selected by Philadelphia in 2nd round (46th player selected) of 1983 NFL draft.
Signed by Philadelphia Eagles, May 24, 1983.
On injured reserve with knee injury, November 23 through remainder of 1983 season.
Expected to miss 1985 season due to knee injury.
Philadelphia NFL, 1983 and 1984.
Games: 1983 (6), 1984 (15). Total—21.

ERIC THOMAS SCOGGINS
Linebacker—Denver Broncos
Born January 23, 1959, at Inglewood, Calif.
Height, 6.02. Weight, 235.
High School—Inglewood, Calif.
Received bachelor of science degree in public administration.
from University of Southern California in 1981.

Selected by Baltimore in 12th round (315th player selected) of 1981 NFL draft.
Released by Baltimore Colts, August 25, 1981; signed as free agent by Oakland Raiders, May 1, 1982.
Released by Los Angeles Raiders, August 10, 1982; signed as free agent by San Francisco 49ers, August 17, 1982.
Released by San Francisco 49ers, September 6, 1982; re-signed by 49ers, September 7, 1982.
Released by San Francisco 49ers, November 23, 1982; signed by Los Angeles Express, January 10, 1983.
Traded by Los Angeles Express to Houston Gamblers for future draft pick, February 20, 1984.
On developmental squad, March 9 through March 30, 1984; activated, March 31, 1984.

On developmental squad, May 24 through remainder of 1984 season.
Released by Houston Gamblers, October 31, 1984; awarded on waivers to Oakland Invaders, November 7, 1984.
Not protected in merger of Oakland Invaders and Michigan Panthers, December 6, 1984.
Signed as free agent by Denver Broncos, March 15, 1985.
On developmental squad for 8 games with Houston Gamblers in 1984.
San Francisco NFL, 1982; Los Angeles USFL, 1983; Houston USFL, 1984.
Games: 1982 (3), 1983 (18), 1984 (9). Total USFL—27. Total Pro—30.
Pro statistics: Intercepted three passes for seven yards and credited with 12½ sacks for 114 yards, 1983.

CARLOS B. SCOTT
Center—St. Louis Cardinals
Born July 2, 1960, at Hempstead, Tex.
Height, 6.04. Weight, 300.
High School—Waller, Tex.
Attended University of Texas at El Paso.

Selected by Arizona in 18th round (215th player selected) of 1983 USFL draft.
Selected by St. Louis in 7th round (184th player selected) of 1983 NFL draft.
Signed by St. Louis Cardinals, July 13, 1983.
St. Louis NFL, 1983 and 1984.
Games: 1983 (13), 1984 (16). Total—29.

LINDSAY EUGENE SCOTT
Wide Receiver—New Orleans Saints
Born December 6, 1960, at Jesup, Ga.
Height, 6.01. Weight, 197.
High School—Jesup, Ga., Wayne County.
Attended University of Georgia.

Selected by New Orleans in 1st round (13th player selected) of 1982 NFL draft.

| | | —PASS RECEIVING— | | | |
Year Club	G.	P.C.	Yds.	Avg.	TD.
1982—New Orleans NFL........	8	17	251	14.8	0
1983—New Orleans NFL........	16	24	274	11.4	0
1984—New Orleans NFL........	16	21	278	13.2	1
Pro Totals—3 Years............	40	62	803	13.0	1

Additional pro statistics: Rushed once for minus four yards, 1982; fumbled once, 1983 and 1984.

RANDOLPH CHARLES SCOTT
(Randy)
Linebacker—Green Bay Packers
Born January 31, 1959, at Decatur, Ga.
Height, 6.01. Weight, 220.
High School—Decatur, Ga., Columbia.
Attended University of Alabama.

Signed as free agent by Green Bay Packers, May 19, 1981.
On injured reserve with knee injury, September 6 through November 17, 1983; activated; November 18, 1983.
Green Bay NFL, 1981 through 1984.
Games: 1981 (16), 1982 (9), 1983 (6), 1984 (16). Total—47.
Pro statistics: Intercepted one pass for 12 yards, 1983.

VICTOR R. SCOTT
Cornerback—Dallas Cowboys
Born June 1, 1962, at East St. Louis, Ill.
Height, 5.11. Weight, 196.
High School—East St. Louis, Ill.
Attended University of Colorado.

Selected by Denver in 1984 USFL territorial draft.
Selected by Dallas in 2nd round (40th player selected) of 1984 NFL draft.
Signed by Dallas Cowboys, June 27, 1984.

| | | —INTERCEPTIONS— | | | |
Year Club	G.	No.	Yds.	Avg.	TD.
1984—Dallas NFL	16	1	5	5.0	0

Additional pro statistics: Recovered two fumbles, 1984.

WILLIE LOUIS SCOTT JR.
Tight End—Kansas City Chiefs
Born February 13, 1959, at Newberry, S.C.
Height, 6.04. Weight, 245.
High School—Newberry, S.C.
Received bachelor of science degree in health education
from University of South Carolina in 1981.

Selected by Kansas City in 1st round (14th player selected) of 1981 NFL draft.

Year Club	—PASS RECEIVING—				
	G.	P.C.	Yds.	Avg.	TD.
1981—Kansas City NFL..........	16	5	72	14.4	1
1982—Kansas City NFL..........	9	8	49	6.1	1
1983—Kansas City NFL..........	16	29	247	8.5	6
1984—Kansas City NFL..........	15	28	253	9.0	3
Pro Totals—4 Years............	56	70	621	8.9	11

Additional pro statistics: Recovered one fumble, 1982; rushed once for one yard, 1983; returned one kickoff for nine yards, 1984.

BUCKY SCRIBNER
Punter—Green Bay Packers
Born July 11, 1960, at Lawrence, Kan.
Height, 6.00. Weight, 202.
High School—Lawrence, Kan.
Attended Pratt Community College and Kansas University.

Selected by Green Bay in 11th round (299th player selected) of 1983 NFL draft.

Year Club	—PUNTING—			
	G.	No.	Avg.	Blk.
1983—Green Bay NFL.....................	16	69	41.6	1
1984—Green Bay NFL.....................	16	85	42.3	0
Pro Totals—2 Years.....................	32	154	42.0	1

Additional pro statistics: Attempted one pass with no completions, 1984.

JOHN SCULLY
Guard—Atlanta Falcons
Born August 2, 1958, at Huntington, N.Y.
Height, 6.06. Weight, 255.
High School—Huntington, N.Y., Holy Family.
Received bachelor of arts degree in sociology from University of Notre Dame in 1980.
Brother-in-law of Tom Thayer, guard with Arizona Outlaws.

Named as center on THE SPORTING NEWS College All-America Team, 1980.
Selected by Atlanta in 4th round (109th player selected) of 1981 NFL draft.
Atlanta NFL, 1981 through 1984.
Games: 1981 (16), 1982 (9), 1983 (16), 1984 (16). Total—57.
Pro statistics: Returned one kickoff for no yards, 1982; recovered one fumble, 1984.

RAYMOND TODD SEABAUGH
(Known by middle name.)
Linebacker—Pittsburgh Steelers
Born March 16, 1961, at Encino, Calif.
Height, 6.04. Weight, 225.
High School—Santa Paula, Calif., Union.
Attended Ventura College and San Diego State University.

Selected by Boston in 8th round (86th player selected) of 1983 USFL draft.
Selected by Pittsburgh in 3rd round (79th player selected) of 1983 NFL draft.
Signed by Pittsburgh Steelers, May 26, 1983.
On injured reserve with back injury, August 16 through entire 1983 season.
Pittsburgh NFL, 1984.
Games: 1984 (16).
Played in AFC Championship Game following 1984 season.

SAMUEL RICARDO SEALE
(Sam)
Wide Receiver—Los Angeles Raiders
Born October 6, 1962, at Barbados, West Indies.
Height, 5.09. Weight, 175.
High School—Orange, N.J.
Attended Western State College.

Selected by Memphis in 15th round (309th player selected) of 1984 USFL draft.
Selected by Los Angeles Raiders in 8th round (224th player selected) of 1984 NFL draft.
Signed by Los Angeles Raiders, June 6, 1984.
Los Angeles Raiders NFL, 1984.
Games: 1984 (12).

VIRGIL LeVAN SEAY
Name pronounced See.
Wide Receiver—Atlanta Falcons
Born January 1, 1958, at Moultrie, Ga.
Height, 5.08. Weight, 180.
High School—Moultrie, Ga.
Attended East Mississippi Junior College and Troy State University.

Selected by Denver in 10th round (270th player selected) of 1980 NFL draft.

Released by Denver Broncos, August 11, 1980; signed as free agent by Washington Redskins, April 6, 1981.
Released by Washington Redskins, November 24, 1984; signed as free agent by Atlanta Falcons, November 29, 1984.

			PASS RECEIVING				—KICKOFF RET.—				—TOTAL—		
Year	Club	G.	P.C.	Yds.	Avg.	TD.	No.	Yds.	Avg.	TD.	TD.	Pts.	F.
1981—Washington NFL		16	26	472	18.2	3	2	36	18.0	0	3	18	0
1982—Washington NFL		8	6	154	25.7	0			None		0	0	0
1983—Washington NFL		14	2	55	27.5	1	9	218	24.2	0	1	6	0
1984—Washington (11)-Atlanta (3) NFL		14	9	111	12.3	1	5	108	21.6	0	1	6	0
Pro Totals—4 Years		52	43	792	18.4	5	16	362	22.6	0	5	30	0

Additional pro statistics: Returned five punts for 57 yards, 1983; returned eight punts for 10 yards, 1984.
Member of Washington Redskins for NFC Championship Game following 1982 and 1983 seasons; did not play.
Played in NFL Championship Game following 1982 season.
Member of Washington Redskins for NFL Championship Game following 1983 season; did not play.

LEE ROY SELMON
Defensive End—Tampa Bay Buccaneers
Born October 20, 1954, at Eufaula, Okla.
Height, 6.03. Weight, 250.
High School—Eufaula, Okla.
Received degree in special education from University of Oklahoma.
Brother of Dewey Selmon, linebacker with Tampa Bay Buccaneers and
San Diego Chargers, 1976 through 1982.

Named as defensive end on THE SPORTING NEWS College All-America Team, 1975.
Outland Trophy winner, 1975.
Named to THE SPORTING NEWS NFC All-Star Team, 1978 and 1979.
Named to THE SPORTING NEWS NFL All-Star Team, 1980.
Selected by Tampa Bay in 1st round (1st player selected) of 1976 NFL draft.
On injured reserve with knee injury, December 5 through remainder of 1978 season.
Tampa Bay NFL, 1976 through 1984.
Games: 1976 (8), 1977 (14), 1978 (14), 1979 (16), 1980 (16), 1981 (14), 1982 (9), 1983 (14), 1984 (16). Total—121.
Pro statistics: Recovered two fumbles, 1977, 1980 and 1984; recovered two fumbles for 29 yards and one touchdown, 1979; recovered one fumble, 1982; recovered one fumble for four yards, 1983.
Played in NFC Championship Game following 1979 season.
Named to played in Pro Bowl (NFL All-Star Game) following 1979 season; replaced due to injury by Al Baker.
Played in Pro Bowl (NFL All-Star Game) following 1980 through 1984 seasons.

ROBIN BRUNO SENDLEIN
Linebacker—Minnesota Vikings
Born December 1, 1958, at Las Vegas, Nev.
Height, 6.03. Weight, 225.
High School—Las Vegas, Nev., Western.
Attended University of Texas.

Selected by Minnesota in 2nd round (45th player selected) of 1981 NFL draft.
Minnesota NFL, 1981 through 1984.
Games: 1981 (16), 1982 (9), 1983 (16), 1984 (15). Total—56.
Pro statistics: Recovered one fumble, 1981.

JOSEPH SPENCE SENSER
(Joe)
Tight End—Minnesota Vikings
Born August 18, 1956, at Philadelphia, Pa.
Height, 6.04. Weight, 240.
High School—Hershey, Pa., Milton Hershey.
Attended West Chester State College.

Selected by Minnesota in 6th round (152nd player selected) of 1979 NFL draft.
On injured reserve with ankle injury, August 21 through entire 1979 season.
On injured reserve with knee injury, August 30 through December 4, 1983; activated, December 5, 1983.
On injured reserve with foot injury, September 1 through October 11, 1984; activated, October 12, 1984.
Active for 3 games with Minnesota Vikings in 1983; did not play.

			—PASS RECEIVING—			
Year	Club	G.	P.C.	Yds.	Avg.	TD.
1980—Minnesota NFL		16	42	447	10.6	7
1981—Minnesota NFL		16	79	1004	12.7	8
1982—Minnesota NFL		9	29	261	9.0	1
1984—Minnesota NFL		8	15	110	7.3	0
Pro Totals—5 Years		49	165	1822	11.0	16

Additional pro statistics: Rushed once for minus one yard and attempted one pass with no completions, 1980; rushed once for two yards, recovered two fumbles and fumbled three times, 1981.
Named to Pro Bowl (NFL All-Star Game) following 1981 season; replaced due to injury by Junior Miller.

—DID YOU KNOW—
That the same five AFC teams made the playoffs in both 1983 and 1984? Those teams were Miami, Pittsburgh, Denver, Seattle and the Raiders.

JOSE RAFAEL SEPTIEN (MICHEL)
(Known by middle name.)

Name pronounced Rah-fay-EL Sep-tee-EN.
Placekicker—Dallas Cowboys
Born December 12, 1953, at Mexico City, Mex.
Height, 5.10. Weight, 180.
High School—Mexico City, Mex., Colegio Vista Hernosa.
Received degree from University of Southwestern Louisiana.
Son of Carlos Septien, member of two Mexican World Cup Soccer teams.

Named to THE SPORTING NEWS NFL All-Star Team, 1981.
Selected by New Orleans in 10th round (258th player selected) of 1977 NFL draft.
Released by New Orleans Saints, August 31, 1977; signed as free agent by Los Angeles Rams, September 14, 1977.
Released by Los Angeles Rams, August 26, 1978; signed as free agent by Dallas Cowboys, August 30, 1978.

		—PLACE KICKING—					
Year	Club	G.	XP.	XPM.	FG.	FGA.	Pts.
1977—Los Angeles NFL....		14	32	3	18	30	86
1978—Dallas NFL		16	*46	1	16	26	94
1979—Dallas NFL		16	40	4	19	29	97
1980—Dallas NFL		16	*59	1	11	17	92
1981—Dallas NFL		16	40	0	*27	35	*121
1982—Dallas NFL		9	28	0	10	14	58
1983—Dallas NFL		16	57	2	22	27	123
1984—Dallas NFL		16	33	1	23	29	102
Pro Totals—8 Years		119	335	12	146	207	773

Additional pro statistics: Recovered two fumbles for 18 yards, 1980; punted two times for 31.0 average 1981.
Played in NFC Championship Game following 1978 and 1980 through 1982 seasons.
Played in NFL Championship Game following 1978 season.
Played in Pro Bowl (NFL All-Star Game) following 1981 season.

CRAIG ALAN SHAFFER
Linebacker—Denver Broncos
Born March 31, 1959, at Terre Haute, Ind.
Height, 6.00. Weight, 230.
High School—Terre Haute, Ind., Schulte.
Received bachelor of science degree in physical education
from Indiana State University in 1982.

Selected by St. Louis in 6th round (150th player selected) of 1982 NFL draft.
On injured reserve with broken ankle, December 8 through remainder of 1982 season.
On injured reserve with broken ankle, November 3 through remainder of 1983 season.
Released by St. Louis Cardinals, September 26, 1984; signed as free agent by Denver Broncos for 1985, November 19, 1984.
St. Louis NFL, 1982 through 1984.
Games: 1982 (5), 1983 (9), 1984 (4). Total—18.

JOSEPH LESLIE SHEARIN
(Joe)
Guard—Los Angeles Rams
Born April 16, 1960, at Dallas, Tex.
Height, 6.04. Weight, 250.
High School—Dallas, Tex., Woodrow Wilson.
Attended University of Texas.

Selected by Los Angeles Rams in 7th round (181st player selected) of 1982 NFL draft.
On injured reserve with neck injury, September 7 through entire 1982 season.
Los Angeles Rams NFL, 1983 and 1984.
Games: 1983 (16), 1984 (15). Total—31.

DONNIE SHELL
Safety—Pittsburgh Steelers
Born August 26, 1952, at Whitmire, S. C.
Height, 5.11. Weight, 190.
High School—Whitmire, S. C.
Received bachelor of science degree in health and physical education from South Carolina State
in 1974 and received master's degree in guidance and counseling from South Carolina State.

Named to THE SPORTING NEWS AFC All-Star Team, 1979.
Named to THE SPORTING NEWS NFL All-Star Team, 1980.
Signed as free agent by Pittsburgh Steelers, 1974.

	—INTERCEPTIONS—						—INTERCEPTIONS—				
Year Club	G.	No.	Yds.	Avg.	TD.	Year Club	G.	No.	Yds.	Avg.	TD.
1974—Pittsburgh NFL	14	1	0	0.0	0	1980—Pittsburgh NFL	16	7	135	19.3	0
1975—Pittsburgh NFL	14	1	29	29.0	0	1981—Pittsburgh NFL	14	5	52	10.4	0
1976—Pittsburgh NFL	14	1	4	4.0	0	1982—Pittsburgh NFL	9	5	27	5.4	0
1977—Pittsburgh NFL	12	3	14	4.7	0	1983—Pittsburgh NFL	16	5	18	3.6	0
1978—Pittsburgh NFL	16	3	21	7.0	0	1984—Pittsburgh NFL	16	7	61	8.7	1
1979—Pittsburgh NFL	16	5	10	2.0	0	Pro Totals—11 Years	157	43	371	8.6	1

Additional pro statistics: Recovered one fumble, 1974, 1975, 1976, 1982 and 1983; caught two passes for 39 yards, 1975; recovered five fumbles for 21 yards and one touchdown and returned one punt for six yards, 1978; recovered two fumbles, 1979 and 1981; recovered one fumble for seven yards, 1980.

Played in NFL Championship Game following 1974, 1975, 1978 and 1979 seasons.
Played in AFC Championship Game following 1974 through 1976, 1978, 1979 and 1984 seasons.
Played in Pro Bowl (NFL All-Star Game) following 1978 through 1982 seasons.

TODD ANDREW SHELL
Linebacker—San Francisco 49ers
Born June 24, 1962, at Mesa, Ariz.
Height, 6.04. Weight, 225.
High School—Mesa, Ariz., Mountain View.
Attended Brigham Young University.

Selected by Denver in 3rd round (51st player selected) of 1984 USFL draft.
Selected by San Francisco in 1st round (24th player selected) of 1984 NFL draft.
Signed by San Francisco 49ers, June 12, 1984.

		——INTERCEPTIONS——			
Year Club	G.	No.	Yds.	Avg.	TD.
1984—San Francisco NFL	16	3	81	27.0	1

Additional pro statistics: Recovered one fumble, 1984.
Played in NFC Championship Game following 1984 season.
Played in NFL Championship Game following 1984 season.

TIMOTHY T. SHERWIN
(Tim)
Tight End—Indianapolis Colts
Born May 4, 1958, at Troy, N.Y.
Height, 6.06. Weight, 245.
High School—Watervliet, N.Y.
Received bachelor of arts degree in sociology from Boston College in 1981.

Selected by Baltimore in 4th round (94th player selected) of 1981 NFL draft.
Franchise transferred to Indianapolis, March 31, 1984.

		——PASS RECEIVING——			
Year Club	G.	P.C.	Yds.	Avg.	TD.
1981—Baltimore NFL	16	2	19	9.5	0
1982—Baltimore NFL	9	21	280	13.3	0
1983—Baltimore NFL	15	25	358	14.3	0
1984—Indianapolis NFL	16	11	169	15.4	0
Pro Totals—4 Years............	56	59	826	14.0	0

Additional pro statistics: Recovered one fumble for a touchdown, 1982; returned one kickoff for two yards, 1984.

WILLIAM DEAN SHIELDS
(Billy)
Offensive Tackle—San Francisco 49ers
Born August 23, 1953, at Vicksburg, Miss.
Height, 6.08. Weight, 284.
High School—Birmingham, Ala., Banks.
Attended Georgia Tech.

Selected by San Diego in 6th round (136th player selected) of 1975 NFL draft.
Traded by San Diego Chargers to Minnesota Vikings for safety John Turner, August 10, 1984.
Placed on did not report list, August 10 through September 2, 1984.
Returned to San Diego Chargers in exchange for 3rd round pick in 1985 draft, September 3, 1984.
Granted roster exemption, September 3 through September 18, 1984.
Released by San Diego Chargers, September 19, 1984; signed as free agent by San Francisco 49ers, September 27, 1984.
San Diego NFL, 1975 through 1983; San Francisco NFL, 1984.
Games: 1975 (11), 1976 (14), 1977 (13), 1978 (16), 1979 (16), 1980 (16), 1981 (16), 1982 (9), 1983 (16), 1984 (10). Total—137.

Pro statistics: Recovered one fumble, 1978 and 1979; recovered two fumbles, 1980.
Played in AFC Championship Game following 1980 and 1981 seasons.
Played in NFC Championship Game following 1984 season.
Played in NFL Championship Game following 1984 season.

JACKIE RENARDO SHIPP
Linebacker—Miami Dolphins
Born March 19, 1962, at Muskogee, Okla.
Height, 6.02. Weight, 236.
High School—Stillwater, Okla., C.E. Donart.
Attended Oklahoma University.

Selected by Oklahoma in 1984 USFL territorial draft.
Selected by Miami in 1st round (14th player selected) of 1984 NFL draft.
Signed by Miami Dolphins, July 14, 1984.
Miami NFL, 1984.
Games: 1984 (16).
Played in AFC Championship Game following 1984 season.
Played in NFL Championship Game following 1984 season.

MICKEY CHARLES SHULER
Tight End—New York Jets

Born August 21, 1956, at Harrisburg, Pa.
Height, 6.03. Weight, 231.
High School—Enola, Pa., East Pennsboro.
Received degree in health and physical education from Pennsylvania State University.

Selected by New York Jets in 3rd round (61st player selected) of 1978 NFL draft.
On injured reserve with shoulder separation, September 1 through November 13, 1981; activated, November 14, 1981.

			—PASS RECEIVING—		
Year	Club	G.	P.C.	Yds.	Avg. TD.
1978—N.Y. Jets NFL		16	11	67	6.1 3
1979—N.Y. Jets NFL		16	16	225	14.1 3
1980—N.Y. Jets NFL		16	22	226	10.3 2
1981—N.Y. Jets NFL		6		None	
1982—N.Y. Jets NFL		9	8	132	16.5 3
1983—N.Y. Jets NFL		16	26	272	10.5 1
1984—N.Y. Jets NFL		16	68	782	11.5 6
Pro Totals—7 Years		95	151	1704	11.3 18

Additional pro statistics: Fumbled once, 1978 through 1980 and 1984; returned one kickoff for 12 yards, 1978; returned one kickoff for 15 yards, 1979; returned two kickoffs for 25 yards, 1980; returned one kickoff for three yards, 1983; returned one kickoff for no yards, 1984.
Played in AFC Championship Game following 1982 season.

ERIC SCOTT SIEVERS
Tight End—San Diego Chargers

Born November 19, 1957, at Urbana, Ill.
Height, 6.03. Weight, 235.
High School—Arlington, Va., Washington & Lee.
Attended University of Maryland.

Selected by San Diego in 4th round (107th player selected) of 1981 NFL draft.

			—PASS RECEIVING—		
Year	Club	G.	P.C.	Yds.	Avg. TD.
1981—San Diego NFL		16	22	276	12.5 3
1982—San Diego NFL		9	12	173	14.4 1
1983—San Diego NFL		16	33	452	13.7 3
1984—San Diego NFL		14	41	438	10.7 3
Pro Totals—4 Years		55	108	1339	12.4 10

Additional pro statistics: Returned two kickoffs for four yards, 1981; recovered one fumble and fumbled once, 1981 and 1984; returned one kickoff for 17 yards, 1982; returned one kickoff for six yards and rushed once for minus seven yards, 1983.
Played in AFC Championship Game following 1981 season.

ROBERT SIKORA JR.
Offensive Tackle—Cleveland Browns

Born June 14, 1962, at Youngstown, O.
Height, 6.08. Weight, 285.
High School—Youngstown, O., Woodrow Wilson.
Attended Hutchinson Community College and Indiana University.

Signed as free agent by Cleveland Browns, June 17, 1984.
Released by Cleveland Browns, August 27, 1984; re-signed by Browns, December 12, 1984.
Active for 1 game with Cleveland Browns in 1984; did not play.

CLEO SIMMONS
Tight End—Indianapolis Colts

Born October 21, 1960, at Mobile, Ala.
Height, 6.02. Weight, 225.
High School—Mobile, Ala., Murphy.
Attended Jackson State University.

Signed as free agent by Dallas Cowboys, April 28, 1983.
Released by Dallas Cowboys, August 29, 1983; re-signed by Cowboys, August 30, 1983.
Released by Dallas Cowboys, August 14, 1984; signed as free agent by Indianapolis Colts, March 20, 1985.
Dallas NFL, 1983.
Games: 1983 (11).

JEFFERY THOMAS SIMMONS
(Jeff)
Wide Receiver—Los Angeles Raiders

Born July 6, 1960, at Stockton, Calif.
Height, 6.02. Weight, 197.
High School—Stockton, Calif., Edison.
Received degree in business from University of Southern California.

Selected by Los Angeles in 1983 USFL territorial draft.
Selected by Los Angeles Rams in 7th round (171st player selected) of 1983 NFL draft.

Signed by Los Angeles Rams, July 8, 1983.
Released by Los Angeles Rams, August 29, 1983; re-signed by Rams, September 6, 1983.
Released by Los Angeles Rams, September 30, 1983; signed by Los Angeles Express, October 17, 1983.
Released by Los Angeles Express, February 6, 1984; signed as free agent by Los Angeles Raiders, May 20, 1984.
On injured reserve with knee injury, August 21 through entire 1984 season.
Los Angeles Rams NFL, 1983.
Games: 1983 (3).
Pro statistics: Returned one kickoff for no yards, 1983.

JOHN CHRISTOPHER SIMMONS
Cornerback—Cincinnati Bengals
Born December 1, 1958, at Little Rock, Ark.
Height, 5.11. Weight, 192.
High School—Little Rock, Ark., Parkview.
Attended Southern Methodist University.

Selected by Cincinnati in 3rd round (64th player selected) of 1981 NFL draft.
On injured reserve with shoulder injury, September 1 through October 8, 1981; activated, October 9, 1981.
On injured reserve with dislocated shoulder, September 7 through December 24, 1982; activated, December 25, 1982.
Released by Cincinnati Bengals, August 29, 1983; re-signed by Bengals, August 31, 1983.

Year Club	G.	No.	Yds.	Avg.	TD.	No.	Yds.	Avg.	TD.	TD.	Pts.	F.
		-PUNT RETURNS-				—KICKOFF RET.—				—TOTAL—		
1981—Cincinnati NFL	11	5	24	4.8	0	1	10	10.0	0	0	0	1
1982—Cincinnati NFL	2	None				None				0	0	0
1983—Cincinnati NFL	16	25	173	6.9	0	14	317	22.6	0	0	0	4
1984—Cincinnati NFL	16	12	98	8.2	0	1	15	15.0	0	1	6	0
Pro Totals—4 Years	45	42	295	7.0	0	16	342	21.4	0	1	6	5

Additional pro statistics: Recovered one fumble, 1981; recovered three fumbles, 1983; intercepted two passes for 43 yards and a touchdown, 1984.
Played in AFC Championship Game following 1981 season.
Played in NFL Championship Game following 1981 season.

PHILIP SIMMS
(Phil)
Quarterback—New York Giants
Born November 3, 1955, at Lebanon, Ky.
Height, 6.03. Weight, 216.
High School—Louisville, Ky., Southern.
Attended Morehead State University.

Selected by New York Giants in 1st round (7th player selected) of 1979 NFL draft.
On injured reserve with separated shoulder, November 18 through December 25, 1981; activated, December 26, 1981.
On injured reserve with knee injury, August 30 through entire 1982 season.
On injured reserve with dislocated thumb, October 13 through remainder of 1983 season.

Year Club	G.	Att.	Cmp.	Pct.	Gain	T.P.	P.I.	Avg.	Att.	Yds.	Avg.	TD.	TD.	Pts.	F.
		————PASSING————							RUSHING				—TOTAL—		
1979—N.Y. Giants NFL	12	265	134	50.6	1743	13	14	6.58	29	166	5.7	1	1	6	9
1980—N.Y. Giants NFL	13	402	193	48.0	2321	15	19	5.77	36	190	5.3	1	1	6	6
1981—N.Y. Giants NFL	10	316	172	54.4	2031	11	9	6.43	19	42	2.2	0	0	0	7
1983—N.Y. Giants NFL	2	13	7	53.8	130	0	1	10.00	None				0	0	0
1984—N.Y. Giants NFL	16	533	286	53.7	4044	22	18	7.59	42	162	3.9	0	0	0	8
Pro Totals—5 Years	53	1529	792	51.8	10269	61	61	6.72	126	560	4.4	2	2	12	30

Quarterback Rating Points: 1979 (65.9), 1980 (58.9), 1981 (74.2), 1983 (56.6), 1984 (78.1). Total—69.9.
Additional pro statistics: Fumbled nine times for minus two yards, 1979; recovered two fumbles, 1980 and 1981; fumbled six times for minus five yards, 1980; fumbled seven times for minus 15 yards, 1981; caught one pass for 13 yards, recovered four fumbles and fumbled eight times for minus five yards, 1984.

RONALD BERNARD SIMPKINS
(Ron)
Linebacker—Cincinnati Bengals
Born April 2, 1958, at Detroit, Mich.
Height, 6.01. Weight, 235.
High School—Detroit, Mich., Western.
Received bachelor of general studies degree from University of Michigan in 1980.

Selected by Cincinnati in 7th round (167th player selected) of 1980 NFL draft.
On injured reserve with pulled hamstring, August 31 through entire 1981 season.
Released by Cincinnati Bengals, September 6, 1982; re-signed by Bengals, September 14, 1982.
On inactive list, September 19, 1982.
Cincinnati NFL, 1980 and 1982 through 1984.
Games: 1980 (16), 1982 (5), 1983 (15), 1984 (16). Total—52.
Pro statistics: Returned three kickoffs for eight yards and fumbled once, 1980; recovered one fumble, 1980, 1983 and 1984.

KEITH EDWARD SIMPSON
Cornerback—Seattle Seahawks
Born March 9, 1956, at Memphis, Tenn.
Height, 6.01. Weight, 195.
High School—Memphis, Tenn., Hamilton.
Attended Memphis State University.

Named as cornerback on THE SPORTING NEWS College All-America Team, 1977.
Selected by Seattle in 1st round (9th player selected) of 1978 NFL draft.

		——INTERCEPTIONS——			
Year Club	G.	No.	Yds.	Avg.TD.	
1978—Seattle NFL	13	2	40	20.0	1
1979—Seattle NFL	15	4	72	18.0	0
1980—Seattle NFL	16	3	15	5.0	0
1981—Seattle NFL	12	2	34	17.0	0
1982—Seattle NFL	8		None		
1983—Seattle NFL	14	4	39	9.8	0
1984—Seattle NFL	15	4	138	34.5	★2
Pro Totals—7 Years	93	19	338	17.8	3

Additional pro statistics: Recovered one fumble, 1978 and 1981; recovered one fumble for three yards, 1980; recovered two fumbles, 1983 and 1984; fumbled once, 1983.

Played in AFC Championship Game following 1983 season.

BILLY RAY SIMS
Running Back—Detroit Lions
Born September 18, 1955, at St. Louis, Mo.
Height, 6.00. Weight, 212.
High School—Hooks, Tex.
Received bachelor of arts degree in recreational therapy from University of Oklahoma in 1980.

Heisman Trophy winner, 1978.
Named THE SPORTING NEWS College Player of the Year, 1978.
Named as running back on THE SPORTING NEWS College All-America Team, 1978 and 1979.
Named THE SPORTING NEWS NFL Rookie of the Year, 1980.
Selected by Detroit in 1st round (1st player selected) of 1980 NFL draft.
On did not report list, September 6 through September 9, 1982; activated, September 10, 1982.
Signed by Houston Gamblers, July 1, 1983, for contract to take effect after being granted free agency, February 1, 1984.
USFL rights subsequently traded by New Jersey Generals to Houston Gamblers for 1st round pick in 1984 draft and future draft picks, October 7, 1983.
Signed by Detroit Lions, December 16, 1983, and Gamblers contract was subsequently voided in court, February 10, 1984.
On injured reserve with knee injury, October 24 through remainder of 1984 season.

		——RUSHING——				PASS RECEIVING				—TOTAL—		
Year Club	G.	Att.	Yds.	Avg.	TD.	P.C.	Yds.	Avg.	TD.	TD.	Pts.	F.
1980—Detroit NFL	16	313	1303	4.2	★13	51	621	12.2	3	★16	96	12
1981—Detroit NFL	14	296	1437	4.9	13	28	451	16.1	2	15	90	9
1982—Detroit NFL	9	172	639	3.7	4	34	342	10.1	0	4	24	7
1983—Detroit NFL	13	220	1040	4.7	7	42	419	10.0	0	7	42	6
1984—Detroit NFL	8	130	687	5.3	5	31	239	7.7	0	5	30	6
Pro Totals—5 Years	60	1131	5106	4.5	42	186	2072	11.1	5	47	282	40

Additional pro statistics: Recovered one fumble, 1980 and 1982; recovered three fumbles, 1981; recovered four fumbles, 1983; recovered two fumbles, 1984.

Played in Pro Bowl (NFL All-Star Game) following 1980 through 1982 seasons.

KENNETH W. SIMS
(Ken)
Defensive End—New England Patriots
Born October 31, 1959, at Kosse, Tex.
Height, 6.05. Weight, 271.
High School—Groesbeck, Tex.
Attended University of Texas.

Named as defensive end on THE SPORTING NEWS College All-America Team, 1981.
Selected by New England in 1st round (1st player selected) of 1982 NFL draft.
New England NFL, 1982 through 1984.
Games: 1982 (9), 1983 (5), 1984 (16). Total—30.

CURT EDWARD SINGER
Offensive Tackle—Washington Redskins
Born November 4, 1961, at Aliquippa, Pa.
Height, 6.05. Weight, 264.
High School—Aliquippa, Pa., Hopewell.
Attended University of Tennessee.

Selected by Memphis in 1984 USFL territorial draft.
Selected by Washington in 6th round (167th player selected) of 1984 NFL draft.
Signed by Washington Redskins, June 26, 1984.
Released by Washington Redskins, August 27, 1984; re-signed by Redskins, August 28, 1984.
On injured reserve with back injury, August 30 through entire 1984 season.

MICHAEL SINGLETARY
(Mike)
Linebacker—Chicago Bears

Born October 9, 1958, at Houston, Tex.
Height, 5.11. Weight, 230.
High School—Houston, Tex., Worthing.
Attended Baylor University.

Named to THE SPORTING NEWS NFL All-Star Team, 1984.
Named as linebacker on THE SPORTING NEWS College All-America Team, 1980.
Selected by Chicago in 2nd round (38th player selected) of 1981 NFL draft.
Chicago NFL, 1981 through 1984.
Games: 1981 (16), 1982 (9), 1983 (16), 1984 (16). Total—57.
Pro statistics: Intercepted one pass for minus three yards, 1981; recovered one fumble, 1982 and 1984; intercepted one pass for no yards and recovered four fumbles for 15 yards, 1983; intercepted one pass for four yards, 1984.
Played in NFC Championship Game following 1984 season.
Played in Pro Bowl (NFL All-Star Game) following 1983 and 1984 seasons.

JERALD GRANT SISEMORE
(Jerry)
Offensive Tackle

Born July 16, 1951, at Olton, Tex.
Height, 6.04. Weight, 265.
High School—Plainview, Tex.
Attended University of Texas.

Named as offensive tackle on THE SPORTING NEWS College All-America Team, 1972.
Selected by Philadelphia in 1st round (3rd player selected) of 1973 NFL draft.
On injured reserve with knee injury, December 24 through remainder of 1982 season.
On injured reserve with tendinitis in shoulder, October 18 through remainder of 1984 season.
Released by Philadelphia Eagles, May 7, 1985.
Philadelphia NFL, 1973 through 1984.
Games: 1973 (13), 1974 (14), 1975 (14), 1976 (14), 1977 (14), 1978 (16), 1979 (16), 1980 (16), 1981 (16), 1982 (7), 1983 (14), 1984 (2). Total—156.
Pro statistics: Recovered one fumble, 1973 through 1975, 1978 and 1982; returned one kickoff for 15 yards, 1975; recovered three fumbles, 1976; recovered two fumbles for minus two yards, 1979.
Played in NFC Championship Game following 1980 season.
Played in NFL Championship Game following 1980 season.
Played in Pro Bowl (NFL All-Star Game) following 1979 and 1981 seasons.

PAUL ANTHONY SKANSI
Wide Receiver—Seattle Seahawks

Born January 11, 1961, at Tacoma, Wash.
Height, 5.11. Weight, 190.
High School—Gig Harbor, Wash., Peninsula.
Attended University of Washington.

Selected by Michigan in 4th round (39th player selected) of 1983 USFL draft.
Selected by Pittsburgh in 5th round (133rd player selected) of 1983 NFL draft.
Signed by Pittsburgh Steelers, June 5, 1983.
Released by Pittsburgh Steelers, August 27, 1984; signed as free agent by Seattle Seahawks, October 25, 1984.

Year Club		—PASS RECEIVING—				-PUNT RETURNS-				—TOTAL—		
	G.	P.C.	Yds.	Avg.	TD.	No.	Yds.	Avg.	TD.	TD.	Pts.	F.
1983—Pittsburgh NFL	15	3	39	13.0	0	43	363	8.4	0	0	0	5
1984—Seattle NFL	7	7	85	12.1	0	16	145	9.1	0	0	0	0
Pro Totals—2 Years	22	10	124	12.4	0	59	508	8.6	0	0	0	5

Additional pro statistics: Recovered two fumbles, 1983.

BOB SLATER
Defensive Tackle—Washington Redskins

Born November 14, 1960, at Pawhuska, Okla.
Height, 6.04. Weight, 265.
High School—Mason, Okla.
Attended University of Oklahoma.

Selected by Oklahoma in 1984 USFL territorial draft.
Selected by Washington in 2nd round (31st player selected) of 1984 NFL draft.
Signed by Washington Redskins, July 16, 1984.
On injured reserve with knee injury, August 28 through entire 1984 season.

JACKIE RAY SLATER
Offensive Tackle—Los Angeles Rams

Born May 27, 1954, at Jackson, Miss.
Height, 6.04. Weight, 271.
High School—Jackson, Miss., Wingfield.
Received bachelor of arts degree from Jackson State University;
attending Livingston University for master's degree in physical education.

Selected by Los Angeles in 3rd round (86th player selected) of 1976 NFL draft.
On injured reserve with knee injury, October 17 through remainder of 1984 season.
Los Angeles Rams NFL, 1976 through 1984.
Games: 1976 (14), 1977 (14), 1978 (16), 1979 (16), 1980 (15), 1981 (11), 1982 (9), 1983 (16), 1984 (7). Total—118.
Pro statistics: Recovered one fumble, 1978 and 1980; recovered one fumble for 13 yards, 1983.
Played in NFC Championship Game following 1976, 1978 and 1979 seasons.
Played in NFL Championship Game following 1979 season.
Played in Pro Bowl (NFL All-Star Game) following 1983 season.

SAM SLATER
Offensive Tackle—Philadelphia Eagles
Born June 8, 1962, at Bronxville, N.Y.
Height, 6.09. Weight, 290.
High School—Van Nuys, Calif.
Attended Weber State College.

Selected by Pittsburgh in 5th round (108th player selected) of 1984 USFL draft.
Selected by Seattle in 7th round (189th player selected) of 1984 NFL draft.
NFL rights released by Seattle Seahawks after failing physical, June 15, 1984; signed as free agent by Philadelphia Eagles, July 11, 1984.
On injured reserve with separated shoulder, August 14 through entire 1984 season.

TONY TYRONE SLATON
Center—Los Angeles Rams
Born April 12, 1961, at Merced, Calif.
Height, 6.03. Weight, 269.
High School—Merced, Calif.
Received bachelor of science degree from University of Southern California in 1984.

Selected by Los Angeles in 1984 USFL territorial draft.
Selected by Buffalo in 6th round (155th player selected) of 1984 NFL draft.
Signed by Buffalo Bills, June 1, 1984.
Released by Buffalo Bills, August 20, 1984; signed as free agent by Los Angeles Rams, August 23, 1984.
On injured reserve with strained abdominal muscles, September 21 through remainder of 1984 season.
Active for 3 games with Los Angeles Rams in 1984; did not play.

GERALD DAVID SMALL
Cornerback—Atlanta Falcons
Born August 10, 1956, at Washington, N. C.
Height, 5.11. Weight, 192.
High School—Edwards Air Force Base, Calif., Desert.
Attended San Jose State University.

Selected by Miami in 4th round (93rd player selected) of 1978 NFL draft.
On physically unable to perform/active with shoulder injury, July 22 through August 9, 1982; activated, August 10, 1982.
Traded by Miami Dolphins to Atlanta Falcons for offensive lineman Ron Lee and 6th round pick in 1985 draft, August 26, 1984.

Year Club	G.	No.	Yds.	Avg.	TD.
1978—Miami NFL	16	4	157	*39.3	1
1979—Miami NFL	16	5	74	14.8	0
1980—Miami NFL	16	7	46	6.6	0
1981—Miami NFL	16			None	
1982—Miami NFL	9	2	41	20.5	0
1983—Miami NFL	15	5	60	12.0	0
1984—Atlanta NFL	16	1	2	2.0	0
Pro Totals—7 Years	104	24	380	15.8	1

Additional pro statistics: Recovered three fumbles, 1978; recovered one fumble, 1980; recovered two fumbles, 1981.
Played in AFC Championship Game following 1982 season.
Played in NFL Championship Game following 1982 season.

DONALD FRED SMEREK
(Don)
Defensive Tackle—Dallas Cowboys
Born December 20, 1957, at Waterford, Mich.
Height, 6.07. Weight, 257.
High School—Henderson, Nev., Basic.
Attended University of Nevada at Reno.

Signed as free agent by Dallas Cowboys, May, 1980.
On injured reserve with rib injury entire 1980 season.
On injured reserve with knee injury, September 19 through remainder of 1981 season.
USFL rights traded by San Antonio Gunslingers to Michigan Panthers for rights to wide receiver Stanley Washington, October 13, 1983.
Dallas NFL, 1981 through 1984.
Games: 1981 (2), 1982 (7), 1983 (15), 1984 (16). Total—40.
Played in NFC Championship Game following 1982 season.

FREDERICK C. SMERLAS
(Fred)
Nose Tackle—Buffalo Bills
Born April 8, 1957, at Waltham, Mass.
Height, 6.03. Weight, 270.
High School—Waltham, Mass.
Attended Boston College.

Selected by Buffalo in 2nd round (32nd player selected) of 1979 NFL draft.
On injured reserve with knee injury, November 29 through remainder of 1979 season.
Buffalo NFL, 1979 through 1984.
Games: 1979 (13), 1980 (16), 1981 (16), 1982 (9), 1983 (16), 1984 (16). Total—86.
Pro statistics: Recovered three fumbles for 23 yards and one touchdown, 1979; recovered one fumble for 17 yards, 1981; recovered two fumbles, 1982 and 1984; intercepted one pass for 25 yards, 1984.
Played in Pro Bowl (NFL All-Star Game) following 1980 through 1983 seasons.

AARON CLAYTON SMITH
Linebacker—Denver Broncos
Born August 10, 1962, at Los Angeles, Calif.
Height, 6.02. Weight, 223.
High School—Playa Del Rey, Calif., St. Bernard.
Received bachelor of science degree in health education
and sociology from Utah State University in 1984.

Selected by Jacksonville in 9th round (187th player selected) of 1984 USFL draft.
Selected by Denver in 6th round (159th player selected) of 1984 NFL draft.
Signed by Denver Broncos, June 7, 1984.
On injured reserve with knee injury, November 5 through remainder of 1984 season.
Denver NFL, 1984.
Games: 1984 (10).
Pro statistics: Returned one kickoff for two yards and fumbled once, 1984.

BILLY RAY SMITH JR.
Linebacker—San Diego Chargers
Born August 10, 1961, at Fayetteville, Ark.
Height, 6.03. Weight, 231.
High School—Plano, Tex.
Attended University of Arkansas.
Son of Billy Ray Smith, Sr., defensive tackle with Los Angeles Rams, Pittsburgh
Steelers and Baltimore Colts, 1957 through 1962 and 1964 through 1970.

Named as defensive end on THE SPORTING NEWS College All-America Team, 1981 and 1982.
Selected by Oakland in 1st round (7th player selected) of 1983 USFL draft.
Selected by San Diego in 1st round (5th player selected) of 1983 NFL draft.
Signed by San Diego Chargers, May 19, 1983.

Year Club	G.	No.	Yds.	Avg.	TD.
1983—San Diego NFL	16	None			
1984—San Diego NFL	16	3	41	13.7	0
Pro Totals—2 Years	32	3	41	13.7	0

Additional pro statistics: Returned one kickoff for 10 yards and recovered one fumble, 1983; recovered three fumbles, 1984.

BYRON SMITH
Defensive End—Indianapolis Colts
Born December 21, 1962, at Los Angeles, Calif.
Height, 6.05. Weight, 264.
High School—Canoga Park, Calif.
Attended University of California.

Selected by Oakland in 1984 USFL territorial draft.
Signed by Oakland Invaders, January 10, 1984.
Released by Oakland Invaders, February 20, 1984; signed as free agent by Saskatchewan Roughriders, March 19, 1984.
Selected by Indianapolis in 3rd round (66th player selected) of 1984 NFL supplemental draft.
On retired list with torn thigh muscle, June 3 through August 28, 1984.
Released by Saskatchewan Roughriders, August 29, 1984; signed by Indianapolis Colts, October 3, 1984.
Granted roster exemption, October 3 through October 14, 1984.
Released by Indianapolis Colts, October 15, 1984; re-signed by Colts, November 28, 1984.
Indianapolis NFL, 1984.
Games: 1984 (3).

CARL DOUGLAS SMITH
(Doug)
Center—Los Angeles Rams
Born November 25, 1956, at Columbus, O.
Height, 6.03. Weight, 253.
High School—Columbus, O., Northland.
Received bachelor of science degree in education from Bowling Green State University in 1978
and attending California State University at Fullerton for master's degree in exercise physiology.

Signed as free agent by Los Angeles Rams, May 16, 1978.
On injured reserve with knee injury, September 28 through remainder of 1979 season.
On injured reserve with knee injury, October 30 through remainder of 1980 season.
Los Angeles Rams NFL, 1978 through 1984.
Games: 1978 (16), 1979 (4), 1980 (8), 1981 (16), 1982 (9), 1983 (14), 1984 (16). Total—83.
Pro statistics: Recovered one fumble and returned one kickoff for eight yards, 1978; fumbled once, 1981 and 1983; recovered two fumbles, 1982.
Played in NFC Championship Game following 1978 season.
Played in Pro Bowl (NFL All-Star Game) following 1984 season.

DENNIS SMITH
Safety—Denver Broncos
Born February 3, 1959, at Santa Monica, Calif.
Height, 6.03. Weight, 200.
High School—Santa Monica, Calif.
Attended University of Southern California.

Selected by Denver in 1st round (15th player selected) of 1981 NFL draft.

Year Club	G.	—INTERCEPTIONS— No.	Yds.	Avg.TD.	
1981—Denver NFL	16	1	65	65.0	0
1982—Denver NFL	8	1	29	29.0	0
1983—Denver NFL	14	4	39	9.8	0
1984—Denver NFL	15	3	13	4.3	0
Pro Totals—4 Years	53	9	146	16.2	0

Additional pro statistics: Recovered two fumbles, 1981; recovered one fumble for 64 yards and a touchdown, 1984.

DONALD LOREN SMITH
(Don)
Defensive End—Atlanta Falcons
Born May 9, 1957, at Oakland, Calif.
Height, 6.05. Weight, 270.
High School—Tarpon Springs, Fla.
Received bachelor of science degree in education from University of Miami in 1979.

Named as defensive lineman on THE SPORTING NEWS College All-America Team, 1978.
Selected by Atlanta in 1st round (17th player selected) of 1979 NFL draft.
Atlanta NFL, 1979 through 1984.
Games: 1979 (16), 1980 (16), 1981 (16), 1982 (9), 1983 (15), 1984 (16). Total—88.
Pro statistics: Recovered one fumble for five yards, 1979; recovered three fumbles for two yards, 1981; recovered three fumbles, 1982; recovered two fumbles, 1984.

GARY LOVELL SMITH
Guard—Cincinnati Bengals
Born January 27, 1960, at Bitburg Air Force Base, Germany.
Height, 6.02. Weight, 265.
High School—Hampton, Va., Kecoughtan.
Attended Virginia Polytechnic Institute and State University.

Signed as free agent by Pittsburgh Steelers, May 13, 1982.
Released by Pittsburgh Steelers, September 6, 1982; signed as free agent by Philadelphia Stars, October 5, 1982.
Released by Philadelphia Stars, February 27, 1983; awarded on procedural waivers to Baltimore Colts, May 5, 1983.
Released by Baltimore Colts, August 29, 1983; signed as free agent by Pittsburgh Maulers, October 7, 1983.
Released by Pittsburgh Maulers, February 20, 1984; signed as free agent by Cincinnati Bengals, May 20, 1984.
Cincinnati NFL, 1984.
Games: 1984 (8).

JOHN THOMAS SMITH
(J. T.)
Wide Receiver-Kick Returner—Kansas City Chiefs
Born October 29, 1955, at Leonard, Tex.
Height, 6.02. Weight, 185.
High School—Leonard, Tex., Big Spring.
Attended North Texas State University.

Named to THE SPORTING NEWS NFL All-Star Team, 1980.
Signed as free agent by Washington Redskins, May, 1978.
Released by Washington Redskins, September 21, 1978; signed as free agent by Kansas City Chiefs, November 7, 1978.
On inactive list, September 19, 1982.
On injured reserve with knee injury, August 30 through October 13, 1983; activated, October 14, 1983.
On injured reserve with separated shoulder, December 10 through remainder of 1984 season.

Year Club	G.	PASS RECEIVING P.C.	Yds.	Avg.	TD.	-PUNT RETURNS- No.	Yds.	Avg.	TD.	—KICKOFF RET.— No.	Yds.	Avg.	TD.	—TOTAL— TD.	Pts.	F.
1978—Wash(6)-KC(6) NFL	12	None				4	33	8.3	0	1	18	18.0	0	0	0	0
1979—Kansas City NFL	16	33	444	13.5	3	58	*612	10.6	2	None				5	30	3
1980—Kansas City NFL	16	46	655	14.2	2	40	*581	*14.5	*2	None				4	24	1

Year—Club	G.	PASS RECEIVING P.C.	Yds.	Avg.	TD.	-PUNT RETURNS- No.	Yds.	Avg.	TD.	—KICKOFF RET.— No.	Yds.	Avg.	TD.	—TOTAL— TD.	Pts.	F.
1981—Kansas City NFL	16	63	852	13.5	2	50	528	10.6	0	None				2	12	2
1982—Kansas City NFL	5	10	168	16.8	1	3	26	8.7	0	None				1	6	0
1983—Kansas City NFL	9	7	85	12.1	0	26	210	8.1	0	1	5	5.0	0	0	0	0
1984—Kansas City NFL	15	8	69	8.6	0	39	332	8.5	0	19	391	20.6	0	0	0	1
Pro Totals—7 Years	89	167	2273	13.6	8	220	2322	10.6	4	21	414	19.7	0	12	72	7

Additional pro statistics: Recovered one fumble for one yard, 1979; recovered two fumbles, 1980; recovered one fumble for 19 yards, 1981.

Played in Pro Bowl (NFL All-Star Game) following 1980 season.

JOHNNY RAY SMITH
Cornerback—San Diego Chargers
Born September 7, 1957, at Crockett, Tex.
Height, 5.09. Weight, 190.
High School—Cleveland, Tex.
Attended Lamar University.

Selected by Tampa Bay in 11th round (283rd player selected) of 1981 NFL draft.
On injured reserve with thigh injury, August 31 through entire 1981 season.
On injured reserve with knee injury, August 21 through October 31, 1984.
Released by Tampa Bay Buccaneers, November 1, 1984; awarded on waivers to San Diego Chargers, November 2, 1984.
On injured reserve with cracked bone in leg, November 9 through remainder of 1984 season.

Year—Club	G.	KICKOFF RETURNS No.	Yds.	Avg.	TD.
1982—Tampa Bay NFL	9	3	47	15.7	0
1983—Tampa Bay NFL	16	8	136	17.0	0
1984—San Diego NFL	1		None		
Pro Totals—3 Years	26	11	183	16.6	0

Additional pro statistics: Recovered three fumbles for six yards 1982; fumbled twice, 1982 and 1983; recovered three fumbles, 1983.

LEONARD PHILLIP SMITH
Safety—St. Louis Cardinals
Born September 2, 1960, at New Orleans, La.
Height, 5.11. Weight, 190.
High School—Baton Rouge, La., Robert E. Lee.
Attended McNeese State University.

Selected by Boston in 2nd round (14th player selected) of 1983 USFL draft.
Selected by St. Louis in 1st round (17th player selected) of 1983 NFL draft.
Signed by St. Louis Cardinals, May 3, 1983.

Year—Club	G.	INTERCEPTIONS No.	Yds.	Avg.	TD.
1983—St. Louis NFL	16		None		
1984—St. Louis NFL	12	2	31	15.5	1
Pro Totals—2 Years	28	2	31	15.5	1

Additional pro statistics: Returned one kickoff for 19 yards, 1983; recovered one fumble, 1984.

LUCIOUS IRVIN SMITH
Cornerback—San Diego Chargers
Born January 17, 1957, at Columbus, Ga.
Height, 5.10. Weight, 190.
High School—San Diego, Calif., Kearny.
Attended San Diego State University and California State University at Fullerton.

Signed as free agent by Los Angeles Rams, May 5, 1980.
Traded with 5th round pick in 1985 draft by Los Angeles Rams to Kansas City Chiefs for quarterback Steve Fuller, August 19, 1983.
Released by Kansas City Chiefs, August 27, 1984; signed as free agent by Buffalo Bills, September 14, 1984.
Released by Buffalo Bills, October 9, 1984; signed as free agent by San Diego Chargers, October 17, 1984.
Los Angeles Rams NFL, 1980 through 1982; Kansas City NFL, 1983; Buffalo (4)-San Diego (9) NFL, 1984.
Games: 1980 (16), 1981 (16), 1982 (8), 1983 (16), 1984 (13). Total—69.
Pro statistics: Recovered two fumbles, 1980; recovered one fumble, 1981 and 1983; intercepted three passes for 99 yards and a touchdown, 1983; intercepted one pass for seven yards, returned one punt for no yards and fumbled once, 1984.

PHILLIP KEITH SMITH
(Phil)
Wide Receiver—Indianapolis Colts
Born April 28, 1961, at Los Angeles, Calif.
Height, 6.03. Weight, 190.
High School—Gardena, Calif., Junipero Serra.
Received degree in public administration from San Diego State University.

Selected by Arizona in 11th round (122nd player selected) of 1983 USFL draft.
Selected by Baltimore in 4th round (85th player selected) of 1983 NFL draft.

Signed by Baltimore Colts, May 19, 1983.
On non-football injury list with sinus condition, November 1 through remainder of 1983 season.
Franchise transferred to Indianapolis, March 31, 1984.

			KICKOFF RETURNS			
Year	Club	G.	No.	Yds.	Avg.	TD.
1983—Baltimore NFL		1		None		
1984—Indianapolis NFL		16	32	651	20.3	*1
Pro Totals—2 Years		17	32	651	20.3	1

Additional pro statistics: Rushed twice for minus 10 yards and fumbled once, 1984.

RICKY SMITH
Cornerback—Washington Redskins
Born July 20, 1960, at Quincy, Fla.
Height, 6.00. Weight, 182.
High School—Quincy, Fla., James A. Shanks.
Received bachelor of science degree in human services from
Alabama State University in 1982.

Selected by New England in 6th round (141st player selected) on 1982 NFL draft.
Traded by New England Patriots to Washington Redskins for 7th round pick in 1985 draft, September 11, 1984.

			—PUNT RETURNS—				—KICKOFF RET.—				—TOTAL—		
Year	Club	G.	No.	Yds.	Avg.	TD.	No.	Yds.	Avg.	TD.	TD.	Pts.	F.
1982—New England NFL		9	16	139	8.7	0	24	567	23.6	*1	1	6	3
1983—New England NFL		16	38	398	10.5	0	42	916	21.8	0	0	0	11
1984—N.E. (1)-Wash. (11) NFL		12		None			1	22	22.0	0	0	0	0
Pro Totals—3 Years		37	54	537	9.9	0	67	1505	22.5	1	1	6	14

Additional pro statistics: Recovered two fumbles, 1982; recovered six fumbles, 1983; intercepted one pass for 37 yards, 1984.

ROBERT BENJAMIN SMITH
Defensive End—Minnesota Vikings
Born December 3, 1962, at Bogalusa, La.
Height, 6.05. Weight, 245.
High School—Bogalusa, La.
Attended Grambling State University.

Selected by New Orleans in 1984 USFL territorial draft.
USFL rights traded by New Orleans Breakers to Arizona Wranglers for defensive end Junior Ah You and past considerations, January 9, 1984.
Signed by Arizona Wranglers, January 9, 1984.
On developmental squad, February 24 through April 20, 1984.
On injured reserve with knee injury, April 21 through June 25, 1984; activated, June 26, 1984.
Selected by Minnesota in 2nd round (40th player selected) of 1984 NFL supplemental draft.
Not protected in merger of Arizona Wranglers and Oklahoma Outlaws, December 6, 1984; signed by Minnesota Vikings, March 21, 1985.
On developmental squad for 8 games with Arizona Wranglers in 1984.
On developmental squad for USFL Championship Game following 1984 season.

TIM SMITH
Wide Receiver—Houston Oilers
Born March 20, 1957, at Tucson, Ariz.
Height, 6.02. Weight, 202.
High School—San Diego, Calif., St. Augustine.
Attended University of Nebraska.

Selected by Houston in 3rd round (79th player selected) of 1980 NFL draft.
On injured reserve with broken finger, September 1 through November 26, 1981; activated, November 27, 1981.

			PASS RECEIVING		
Year	Club	G.	P.C.	Yds.	Avg.	TD.
1980—Houston NFL		16	2	21	10.5	0
1981—Houston NFL		4	2	37	18.5	0
1982—Houston NFL		9		None		
1983—Houston NFL		16	83	1176	14.2	6
1984—Houston NFL		16	69	1141	16.5	4
Pro Totals—5 Years		61	156	2375	15.2	10

Additional pro statistics: Returned one kickoff for no yards, 1980; fumbled once, 1980 and 1983; ran seven yards with lateral on kickoff return, 1982; rushed twice for 16 yards, 1983; recovered one fumble, 1984.

WAYNE LESTER SMITH
Cornerback—St. Louis Cardinals
Born May 9, 1957, at Chicago, Ill.
Height, 6.00. Weight, 170.
High School—Chicago, Ill., Harper.
Attended University of Wisconsin at LaCrosse, Loop Junior College and received bachelor
of arts degree in sociology from Purdue University in 1980.

Selected by Detroit in 11th round (278th player selected) of 1980 NFL draft.
Released by Detroit Lions, December 7, 1982; claimed on waivers by St. Louis Cardinals, December 8, 1982.

On injured reserve with knee injury, December 16 through remainder of 1982 season.

Year Club	G.	No.	Yds.	Avg.	TD.
		—INTERCEPTIONS—			
1980—Detroit NFL..................	16	1	23	23.0	0
1981—Detroit NFL..................	16		None		
1982—Det. (5)-St.L. (1) NFL ..	6	1	10	10.0	0
1983—St. Louis NFL................	16	2	3	1.5	0
1984—St. Louis NFL................	16	4	35	8.8	0
Pro Totals—5 Years............	70	8	71	8.9	0

Additional pro statistics: Recovered two fumbles, 1980; recovered one fumble for four yards, 1981; recovered one fumble, 1983; recovered three fumbles for 12 yards, 1984.

RAY MICHAEL SNELL
Guard-Offensive Tackle—Pittsburgh Steelers
Born February 24, 1958, at Baltimore, Md.
Height, 6.04. Weight, 265.
High School—Hyattsville, Md., Northwestern.
Attended University of Wisconsin.

Named as guard on THE SPORTING NEWS College All-America Team, 1979.
Selected by Tampa Bay in 1st round (22nd player selected) of 1980 NFL draft.
On injured reserve with knee injury, September 13 through November 18, 1982; activated, November 19, 1982.
Traded by Tampa Bay Buccaneers to Pittsburgh Steelers for guard Steve Courson, July 30, 1984.
On injured reserve with knee injury, January 4, 1985 through remainder of 1984 season playoffs.
Tampa Bay NFL, 1980 through 1983; Pittsburgh NFL, 1984.
Games: 1980 (13), 1981 (16), 1982 (7), 1983 (9), 1984 (13). Total—58.
Pro statistics: Recovered one fumble, 1984.

BRYAN SOCHIA
Nose Tackle—Houston Oilers
Born July 21, 1961, at Massena, N.Y.
Height, 6.03. Weight, 250.
High School—Brasher Falls, N.Y., St. Lawrence Central.
Attended Northwestern Oklahoma State University.

Signed as free agent by Houston Oilers, June 2, 1983.
On injured reserve with knee and ankle injuries, August 29 through September 26, 1983; activated after clearing procedural waivers, September 27, 1983.
Houston NFL, 1983 and 1984.
Games: 1983 (12), 1984 (16). Total—28.

KURT SOHN
Name pronounced Sewn.
Wide Receiver—New York Jets
Born June 26, 1957, at Ithaca, N.Y.
Height, 5.11. Weight, 176.
High School—Huntington, N.Y.
Attended Nassau Community College and Fordham University.

Signed as free agent by Los Angeles Rams, May 29, 1980.
Released by Los Angeles Rams, August 18, 1980; signed as free agent by New York Jets, June 16, 1981.
On injured reserve with knee injury, August 19 through remainder of 1983 season.
On physically unable to perform/active with knee injury, July 14 through August 12, 1984; activated, August 13, 1984.
On injured reserve with knee injury, October 26 through November 29, 1984; activated, November 30, 1984.

Year Club	G.	—PUNT RETURNS—				—KICKOFF RET.—				—TOTAL—		
		No.	Yds.	Avg.	TD.	No.	Yds.	Avg.	TD.	TD.	Pts.	F.
1981—New York Jets NFL	16	13	66	5.1	0	26	528	20.3	0	0	0	5
1982—New York Jets NFL	9		None			15	299	19.9	0	0	0	0
1984—New York Jets NFL	5		None				None			0	0	0
Pro Totals—3 Years....................................	30	13	66	5.1	0	41	827	20.2	0	0	0	5

Additional pro statistics: Recovered two fumbles, 1981; caught two passes for 28 yards, 1984.
Played in AFC Championship Game following 1982 season.

FREDDIE SOLOMON
Wide Receiver—San Francisco 49ers
Born January 11, 1953, at Sumter, S. C.
Height, 5.11. Weight, 185.
High School—Sumter, S. C.
Attended University of Tampa.
Related to Roland Solomon, defensive back with Dallas Cowboys,
Buffalo Bills and Denver Broncos, 1980 and 1981.

Selected by Miami in 2nd round (36th player selected) of 1975 NFL draft.
Traded with defensive back Vern Roberson and a 1st and 5th round pick in 1978 draft from Miami Dolphins to San Francisco 49ers for running back Delvin Williams, April 17, 1978.

Year Club	G.	Att.	Yds.	Avg.	TD.	P.C.	Yds.	Avg.	TD.	TD.	Pts.	F.
		RUSHING				PASS RECEIVING				TOTAL		
1975—Miami NFL	14	4	87	21.8	0	22	339	15.4	2	3	18	2
1976—Miami NFL	10	4	60	15.0	1	27	453	16.8	2	4	24	0
1977—Miami NFL	13	6	43	7.2	0	12	181	15.1	1	2	12	2
1978—San Francisco NFL	16	14	70	5.0	1	31	458	14.8	2	3	18	5
1979—San Francisco NFL	15	6	85	14.2	1	57	807	14.2	7	8	48	3
1980—San Francisco NFL	16	8	56	7.0	0	48	658	13.7	8	10	60	5
1981—San Francisco NFL	15	9	43	4.8	0	59	969	16.4	8	8	48	3
1982—San Francisco NFL	9	1	-4	-4.0	0	19	323	17.0	3	3	18	2
1983—San Francisco NFL	13	1	3	3.0	0	31	662	21.4	4	4	24	1
1984—San Francisco NFL	14	6	72	12.0	1	40	737	18.4	10	11	66	0
Pro Totals—10 Years	135	59	515	8.7	4	346	5587	16.1	47	56	336	23

Year Club	G.	No.	Yds.	Avg.	TD.	No.	Yds.	Avg.	TD.
		PUNT RETURNS				KICKOFF RET.			
1975—Miami NFL	14	26	320	12.3	1	17	348	20.5	0
1976—Miami NFL	10	13	205	15.8	1	1	12	12.0	0
1977—Miami NFL	13	32	285	8.9	0	10	273	27.3	1
1978—San Francisco NFL	16	9	35	3.9	0	None			
1979—San Francisco NFL	15	23	142	6.2	0	None			
1980—San Francisco NFL	16	27	298	11.0	*2	4	61	15.3	0
1981—San Francisco NFL	15	29	173	6.0	0	None			
1982—San Francisco NFL	9	13	122	9.4	0	None			
1983—San Francisco NFL	13	5	34	6.8	0	None			
1984—San Francisco NFL	14	None				None			
Pro Totals—10 Years	135	177	1614	9.1	4	32	694	21.7	1

Additional pro statistics: Recovered two fumbles for two yards, 1975; threw one incomplete pass, 1976 and 1980; attempted 10 passes with five completions for 85 yards and one interception, recovered four fumbles and fumbled five times for minus two yards, 1978; attempted one pass with one completion for 12 yards, 1979; recovered two fumbles, 1979 and 1981; recovered five fumbles, 1980; attempted one pass with one completion for 25 yards, 1981; recovered one fumble, 1982 and 1983.

Played in NFC Championship Game following 1981, 1983 and 1984 seasons.

Played in NFL Championship Game following 1981 and 1984 seasons.

RONALD MATHEW SOLT
(Ron)
Guard—Indianapolis Colts
Born May 19, 1962, at Bainebridge, Md.
Height, 6.03. Weight, 275.
High School—Wilkes-Barre, Pa., James M. Coughlin.
Attended University of Maryland.

Selected by Washington in 1984 USFL territorial draft.
Selected by Indianapolis in 1st round (19th player selected) of 1984 NFL draft.
Signed by Indianapolis Colts, August 11, 1984.
Indianapolis NFL, 1984.
Games: 1984 (16).
Pro statistics: Recovered one fumble, 1984.

ROBERT SOWELL
Cornerback—Miami Dolphins
Born June 23, 1961, at Columbus, O.
Height, 5.11. Weight, 175.
High School—Columbus, O., Mifflin.
Attended Howard University.

Signed as free agent by Miami Dolphins, July 3, 1983.
Played semi-pro football with Twin Cities Cougars in 1982.
Miami NFL, 1983 and 1984.
Games: 1983 (16), 1984 (16). Total—32.
Pro statistics: Returned one punt for no yards, 1983; recovered one fumble, 1983 and 1984; intercepted one pass for seven yards, 1984.
Played in AFC Championship Game following 1984 season.
Played in NFL Championship Game following 1984 season.

JOHN STEPHEN SPAGNOLA
Tight End—Philadelphia Eagles
Born August 1, 1957, at Bethlehem, Pa.
Height, 6.04. Weight, 240.
High School—Bethlehem, Pa., Catholic.
Received bachelor of arts degree in political science from Yale University in 1980.

Selected by New England in 9th round (245th player selected) of 1979 NFL draft.
Released by New England Patriots, August 20, 1979; signed as free agent by Philadelphia Eagles, August 27, 1979.
On injured reserve with back injury, August 30 through entire 1983 season.

Year Club	G.	P.C.	Yds.	Avg.	TD.
	PASS RECEIVING				
1979—Philadelphia NFL	16	2	24	12.0	0
1980—Philadelphia NFL	16	18	193	10.7	3
1981—Philadelphia NFL	11	6	83	13.8	0
1982—Philadelphia NFL	9	26	313	12.0	2
1984—Philadelphia NFL	16	65	701	10.8	1
Pro Totals—5 Years	68	117	1314	11.2	6

Additional pro statistics: Recovered one fumble, 1979 through 1981; returned one kickoff for no yards, 1980; fumbled twice, 1980 and 1984.
Played in NFC Championship Game following 1980 season.
Played in NFL Championship Game following 1980 season.

GARY L. SPANI
Name pronounced SPAIN-ee.
Linebacker—Kansas City Chiefs
Born January 9, 1956, at Satanta, Kan.
Height, 6.02. Weight, 228.
High School—Manhattan, Kan.
Attended Kansas State University.

Selected by Kansas City in 3rd round (58th player selected) of 1978 NFL draft.
On injured reserve with knee injury, August 30 through October 13, 1983; activated, October 14, 1983.
Kansas City NFL, 1978 through 1984.
Games: 1978 (14), 1979 (16), 1980 (16), 1981 (16), 1982 (8), 1983 (10), 1984 (14). Total—94.
Pro statistics: Recovered one fumble for six yards, 1978; recovered one fumble, 1979 and 1982; intercepted one pass for 47 yards and a touchdown and recovered four fumbles for 16 yards and one touchdown, 1980; recovered two fumbles for 91 yards and one touchdown, 1981; recovered one fumble for five yards, 1983.

JAMES SPENCER
Linebacker—Minnesota Vikings
Born November 22, 1961, at Dallas, Tex.
Height, 6.02. Weight, 237.
High School—Garland, Tex., Lakeview Centennial.
Attended Oklahoma State University.

Selected by Oklahoma in 1984 USFL territorial draft.
Selected by Minnesota in 10th round (268th player selected) of 1984 NFL draft.
Signed by Minnesota Vikings, June 14, 1984.
On physically unable to perform/reserve with knee injury, August 8 through entire 1984 season.

TODD SPENCER
Running Back—Pittsburgh Steelers
Born July 26, 1962, at Portland, Ore.
Height, 6.00. Weight, 200.
High School—El Cerrito, Calif.
Attended University of Southern California.

Selected by Los Angeles in 1984 USFL territorial draft.
Signed as free agent by Pittsburgh Steelers, June 15, 1984.
On injured reserve with knee injury, October 19 through remainder of 1984 season.

		KICKOFF RETURNS				
Year	Club	G.	No.	Yds.	Avg.	TD.
1984—Pittsburgh NFL		7	18	373	20.7	0

Additional pro statistics: Rushed once for no yards, recovered two fumbles and fumbled five times, 1984.

DANNY RAY SPRADLIN
Linebacker—Tampa Bay Buccaneers
Born March 3, 1959, at Detroit, Mich.
Height, 6.01. Weight, 241.
High School—Maryville, Tenn.
Attended University of Tennessee.

Selected by Dallas in 5th round (137th player selected) of 1981 NFL draft.
Traded by Dallas Cowboys to Tampa Bay Buccaneers for 5th round pick in 1984 draft, August 24, 1983.
Dallas NFL, 1981 and 1982; Tampa Bay NFL, 1983 and 1984.
Games: 1981 (16), 1982 (9), 1983 (16), 1984 (15). Total—56.
Pro statistics: Returned three kickoffs for 35 yards and recovered one fumble, 1983; returned one kickoff for five yards, 1984.
Played in NFC Championship Game following 1981 and 1982 seasons.

KIRK EDWARD SPRINGS
Defensive Back—New York Jets
Born August 16, 1958, at Cincinnati, O.
Height, 6.00. Weight, 192.
High School—Cincinnati, O., Woodward.
Attended Miami (O.) University.

Signed as free agent by Seattle Seahawks, May 7, 1980.
Released by Seattle Seahawks, August 2, 1980; signed as free agent by New York Jets, February 11, 1981.
Released by New York Jets, August 31, 1981; re-signed by Jets, October 13, 1981.

		INTERCEPTIONS				–PUNT RETURNS–				—KICKOFF RET.—				—TOTAL—		
Year	Club	G.	No.	Yds.	Avg.	TD.	No.	Yds.	Avg.	TD.	No.	Yds.	Avg.	TD.	TD.	Pts.	F.
1981—N.Y. Jets NFL		10	2	5	2.5	0	None				None				0	0	1
1982—N.Y. Jets NFL		9	1	0	0.0	0	None				None				0	0	0

Year Club	G.	INTERCEPTIONS				–PUNT RETURNS–				–KICKOFF RET.–				–TOTAL–		
		No.	Yds.	Avg.	TD.	No.	Yds.	Avg.	TD.	No.	Yds.	Avg.	TD.	TD.	Pts.	F.
1983—N.Y. Jets NFL	16		None			23	287	12.5	*1	16	364	22.8	0	1	6	2
1984—N.Y. Jets NFL	16	1	13	13.0	0	28	247	8.8	0	23	521	22.7	0	0	0	3
Pro Totals—4 Years	51	4	18	4.5	0	51	534	10.5	1	39	885	22.7	0	1	6	6

Additional pro statistics: Recovered two fumbles, 1981; recovered one fumble, 1983; recovered two fumbles for four yards, 1984.

Played in AFC Championship Game following 1982 season.

RONALD EDWARD SPRINGS
(Ron)
Fullback—Dallas Cowboys
Born November 4, 1956, at Williamsburg, Va.
Height, 6.01. Weight, 224.
High School—Williamsburg, Val., Lafayette.
Attended Coffeyville Junior College and Ohio State University.

Selected by Dallas in 5th round (136th player selected) of 1979 NFL draft.

Year Club	G.	RUSHING				PASS RECEIVING				—TOTAL—		
		Att.	Yds.	Avg.	TD.	P.C.	Yds.	Avg.	TD.	TD.	Pts.	F.
1979—Dallas NFL	16	67	248	3.7	2	25	251	10.0	1	3	18	2
1980—Dallas NFL	15	89	326	3.7	6	15	212	14.1	1	7	42	1
1981—Dallas NFL	16	172	625	3.6	10	46	359	7.8	2	12	72	3
1982—Dallas NFL	9	59	243	4.1	2	17	163	9.6	2	4	24	3
1983—Dallas NFL	16	149	541	3.6	7	73	589	8.1	1	8	48	3
1984—Dallas NFL	16	68	197	2.9	1	46	454	9.9	3	4	24	1
Pro Totals—6 Years	88	604	2180	3.6	28	222	2028	9.1	10	38	228	13

Year Club	G.	KICKOFF RETURNS			
		No.	Yds.	Avg.	TD.
1979—Dallas NFL	16	38	780	20.5	0
1980—Dallas NFL	15		None		
1981—Dallas NFL	16		None		
1982—Dallas NFL	9		None		
1983—Dallas NFL	16	1	13	13.0	0
1984—Dallas NFL	16		None		
Pro Totals—6 Years	88	39	793	20.3	0

Additional pro statistics: Attempted three passes with one completion for 30 yards and one touchdown and recovered two fumbles, 1979; recovered four fumbles for 11 yards and attempted one pass with one interception, 1981; recovered one fumble, 1982; attempted two passes with one completion for 15 yards and a touchdown and recovered three fumbles, 1983; attempted one pass with no completions, 1984.

Played in NFC Championship Game following 1980 through 1982 seasons.

JACK STEVE SQUIREK
Linebacker—Los Angeles Raiders
Born February 16, 1959, at Cleveland, O.
Height, 6.04. Weight, 230.
High School—Cleveland, O., Cuyahoga Heights.
Attended University of Illinois.

Selected by Los Angeles Raiders in 2nd round (35th player selected) of 1982 NFL draft.
On injured reserve with broken jaw, August 28 through September 28, 1984; activated, September 29, 1984.
Los Angeles Raiders NFL, 1982 through 1984.
Games: 1982 (9), 1983 (16), 1984 (12). Total—37.
Pro statistics: Recovered one fumble, 1982 and 1984.
Played in AFC Championship Game following 1983 season.
Played in NFL Championship Game following 1983 season.

RAY STACHOWICZ
Punter—Detroit Lions
Born March 6, 1959, at Cleveland, O.
Height, 5.11. Weight, 185.
High School—Broadview, O., Brecksville.
Attended Michigan State University.

Selected by Green Bay in 3rd round (62nd player selected) of 1981 NFL draft.
Released by Green Bay Packers, August 23, 1983; awarded on waivers to Detroit Lions, August 25, 1983.
Released by Detroit Lions, August 29, 1983; signed as free agent by Chicago Bears, December 7, 1983.
Released by Chicago Bears, August 27, 1984; signed as free agent by Detroit Lions, May 14, 1985.

Year Club	G.	PUNTING		
		No.	Avg.	Blk.
1981—Green Bay NFL	16	82	40.6	*2
1982—Green Bay NFL	9	42	40.2	0
1983—Chicago NFL	2	12	37.3	*2
Pro Totals—3 Years	27	136	40.2	4

Additional pro statistics. Rushed twice for no yards and fumbled once for minus 10 yards, 1982.

JOHNNY LEE STALLWORTH
(John)
Wide Receiver—Pittsburgh Steelers

Born July 15, 1952, at Tuscaloosa, Ala.
Height, 6.02. Weight, 191.
High School—Tuscaloosa, Ala.
Received bachelor of science degree in business from Alabama A&M University in 1974.

Named to THE SPORTING NEWS AFC All-Star Team, 1979.
Selected by Pittsburgh in 4th round (82nd player selected) of 1974 NFL draft.
On injured reserve with cracked fibula, September 17 through October 31, 1980; activated, November 1, 1980.
On injured reserve with broken foot, November 13 through remainder of 1980 season.
On injured reserve with pulled hamstring, October 7 through November 3, 1983; activated, November 4, 1983.

| | | —RUSHING— | | | | PASS RECEIVING | | | | —TOTAL— | |
Year Club	G.	Att.	Yds.	Avg.	TD.	P.C.	Yds.	Avg.	TD.	TD.	Pts.	F.
1974—Pittsburgh NFL	13	1	—9	—9.0	0	16	269	16.8	1	1	6	0
1975—Pittsburgh NFL	11		None			20	423	21.2	4	4	24	0
1976—Pittsburgh NFL	8		None			9	111	12.3	2	3	18	0
1977—Pittsburgh NFL	14	6	47	7.8	0	44	784	17.8	7	7	42	1
1978—Pittsburgh NFL	16		None			41	798	19.5	9	9	54	2
1979—Pittsburgh NFL	16		None			70	*1183	16.9	8	8	48	4
1980—Pittsburgh NFL	3		None			9	197	21.9	1	1	6	0
1981—Pittsburgh NFL	16	1	17	17.0	0	63	1098	17.4	5	5	30	4
1982—Pittsburgh NFL	9	1	9	9.0	0	27	441	16.3	7	7	42	2
1983—Pittsburgh NFL	4		None			8	100	12.5	0	0	0	0
1984—Pittsburgh NFL	16		None			80	1395	17.4	11	11	66	1
Pro Totals—11 Years	126	9	64	7.1	0	387	6799	17.6	55	56	336	14

Additional pro statistics: Recovered one fumble, 1975 and 1978; advanced one lateral for 47 yards and a touchdown, 1976; recovered three fumbles, 1979.
Played in AFC Championship Game following 1974 through 1976, 1978, 1979 and 1984 seasons.
Played in NFL Championship Game following 1974, 1975, 1978 and 1979 seasons.
Played in Pro Bowl (NFL All-Star Game) following 1979, 1982 and 1984 seasons.

SYLVESTER STAMPS
Wide Receiver—Atlanta Falcons

Born February 24, 1961, at Vicksburg, Miss.
Height, 5.07. Weight, 166.
High School—Vicksburg, Miss.
Attended Jackson State University.

Selected by Birmingham in 18th round (370th player selected) of 1984 USFL draft.
Signed by Birmingham Stallions, January 12, 1984.
Released by Birmingham Stallions, February 8, 1984; signed as free agent by Atlanta Falcons, May 2, 1984.
On injured reserve with hamstring injury, November 29 through remainder of 1984 season.

| | | —RUSHING— | | | | PASS RECEIVING | | | | —TOTAL— | |
Year Club	G.	Att.	Yds.	Avg.	TD.	P.C.	Yds.	Avg.	TD.	TD.	Pts.	F.
1984—Atlanta NFL	10	3	15	5.0	0	4	48	12.0	0	0	0	2

| | | KICKOFF RETURNS | | | |
Year Club	G.	No.	Yds.	Avg.	TD.
1984—Atlanta NFL	10	19	452	23.8	0

L. SCOTT STANKAVAGE
(Known by middle name.)
Quarterback—Denver Broncos

Born July 5, 1962, at Philadelphia, Pa.
Height, 6.01. Weight, 192.
High School—Buckingham, Pa., Central Bucks East.
Received bachelor of science degree in business administration
from University of North Carolina in 1984.

Selected by Philadelphia in 1984 USFL territorial draft.
Signed as free agent by Denver Broncos, May 2, 1984.
Released by Denver Broncos, August 20, 1984; re-signed by Broncos, September 5, 1984.
Released by Denver Broncos, November 13, 1984; re-signed by Broncos, December 27, 1984.

| | | ——PASSING—— | | | | | | ——RUSHING—— | | | —TOTAL— | |
Year Club	G.	Att.	Cmp.	Pct.	Gain	T.P.	P.I.	Avg.	Att.	Yds.	Avg.	TD.	TD.	Pts.	F.
1984—Denver NFL	1	18	4	22.2	58	0	1	3.22		None			0	0	0

Quarterback Rating Points: 1984 (17.4).
Additional pro statistics: Recovered one fumble, 1984.

ROHN T. STARK
(First name pronounced Ron).
Punter—Indianapolis Colts

Born May 4, 1959, at Minneapolis, Minn.
Height, 6.03. Weight, 199.
High School—Pine River, Minn.
Attended United States Air Force Academy Prep School and Florida State University.

Named as punter on THE SPORTING NEWS College All-America Team, 1981.
Led NFL in punting yards with 4,124 in 1983.
Selected by Baltimore in 2nd round (34th player selected) of 1982 NFL draft.
Franchise transferred to Indianapolis, March 31, 1984.

		——PUNTING——		
Year Club	G.	No.	Avg.	Blk.
1982—Baltimore NFL	9	46	44.4	0
1983—Baltimore NFL	16	91	*45.3	0
1984—Indianapolis NFL	16	*98	44.7	0
Pro Totals—3 Years	41	235	44.9	0

Additional pro statistics: Rushed once for eight yards, 1982 and 1983; attempted one pass with no completions, 1982 and 1983; fumbled once, 1982; rushed twice for no yards, attempted one pass with one interception and recovered one fumble, 1984.

GEORGE LAWRENCE STARKE
Offensive Tackle—Washington Redskins
Born July 18, 1948, at New York, N. Y.
Height, 6.05. Weight, 260.
High School—New Rochelle, N. Y.
Received bachelor or arts degree from Columbia University.

Selected by Washington in 11th round (272nd player selected) of 1971 NFL draft.
Traded by Washington Redskins to Kansas City Chiefs for a draft choice, July 24, 1971.
Released by Kansas City Chiefs, 1971; signed as free agent by Dallas Cowboys, 1972.
Claimed on waivers from Dallas Cowboys by Washington Redskins, August 2, 1972.
On injured reserve with knee injury, November 6 through remainder of 1978 season.
Member of Washington Redskins' taxi squad, 1972.
Washington NFL, 1973 through 1984.
Games: 1973 (14), 1974 (14), 1975 (14), 1976 (14), 1977 (14), 1978 (9), 1979 (16), 1980 (13), 1981 (14), 1982 (9), 1983 (16), 1984 (9). Total—156.
Pro statistics: Recovered one fumble, 1973, 1975 and 1979; recovered two fumbles, 1977.
Played in NFC Championship Game following 1982 and 1983 seasons.
Played in NFL Championship Game following 1982 and 1983 seasons.

STEPHEN DALE STARRING
Wide Receiver—New England Patriots
Born July 30, 1961, at Baton Rouge, La.
Height, 5.10. Weight, 172.
High School—Vinton, La.
Attended McNeese State University.

Selected by Washington in 3rd round (28th player selected) of 1983 USFL draft.
Selected by New England in 3rd round (74th player selected) of 1983 NFL draft.
Signed by New England Patriots, May 16, 1983.

		–PASS RECEIVING–				–PUNT RETURNS–				—TOTAL—		
Year Club	G.	P.C.	Yds.	Avg.	TD.	No.	Yds.	Avg.	TD.	TD.	Pts.	F.
1983—New England NFL	15	17	389	22.9	2		None			2	12	1
1984—New England NFL	16	46	657	14.3	4	10	73	7.3	0	4	24	1
Pro Totals—2 Years	31	63	1046	16.6	6	10	73	7.3	0	6	36	2

Additional pro statistics: Recovered one fumble for eight yards and rushed twice for minus 16 yards, 1984.

DEAN STEINKUHLER
Name pronounced Stine-cooler.
Offensive Tackle-Guard—Houston Oilers
Born January 27, 1961, at Burr, Neb.
Height, 6.03. Weight, 273.
High School—Sterling, Neb.
Attended University of Nebraska.

Outland Trophy winner, 1984.
Named as guard on THE SPORTING NEWS College All-America Team, 1983.
Selected by Arizona in 6th round (116th player selected) of 1984 USFL draft.
Signed by Houston Oilers, April 30, 1984.
Selected officially by Houston in 1st round (2nd player selected) of 1984 NFL draft.
On injured reserve with knee injury, November 5 through remainder of 1984 season.
Houston NFL, 1984.
Games: 1984 (10).

JAN STENERUD
Name pronounced Yon STEN-uh-rood.
Placekicker—Minnesota Vikings
Born November 26, 1942, at Fetsund, Norway.
Height, 6.02. Weight, 190.
High School—Lillestrom, Norway.
Received bachelor of science degree in commerce from Montana State University.

Established NFL records for most 100-point seasons, career (7); most field goals made, career (358); highest field goal percentage, game, five attempts (1.000), November 2, 1969 and December 7, 1969, against Buffalo Bills.

Established AFL career record for highest field goal percentage, 70.3.
Named as placekicker on THE SPORTING NEWS College All-America Team, 1966.
Named to THE SPORTING NEWS AFL All-Star Team, 1968 and 1969.
Named to THE SPORTING NEWS AFC All-Star Team, 1970 and 1975.
Selected by Kansas City in 3rd round of 1966 AFL Red Shirt draft.
Released by Kansas City Chiefs, August 26, 1980; signed as free agent by Green Bay Packers, November 25, 1980.
Granted free agency, February 1, 1984; re-signed by Packers and traded to Minnesota Vikings for 7th round pick in 1985 draft, July 17, 1984.

Year Club	G.	XP.	XPM.	FG.	FGA.	Pts.
1967—Kansas City AFL	14	45	0	*21	*36	108
1968—Kansas City AFL	14	39	1	30	40	129
1969—Kansas City AFL	14	38	0	27	35	119
1970—Kansas City NFL	14	26	0	*30	42	116
1971—Kansas City NFL	14	32	0	26	44	110
1972—Kansas City NFL	14	32	0	21	36	95
1973—Kansas City NFL	14	21	2	24	38	93
1974—Kansas City NFL	14	24	2	17	24	75
1975—Kansas City NFL	14	30	1	*22	32	96
1976—Kansas City NFL	14	27	6	21	38	90
1977—Kansas City NFL	14	27	1	8	18	51
1978—Kansas City NFL	16	25	1	20	30	85
1979—Kansas City NFL	16	28	1	12	23	64
1980—Green Bay NFL	4	3	0	3	5	12
1981—Green Bay NFL	16	35	1	22	24	101
1982—Green Bay NFL	9	25	2	13	18	64
1983—Green Bay NFL	16	52	0	21	26	115
1984—Minnesota NFL	16	30	1	20	23	90
Pro Totals—18 Years	247	539	19	358	532	1613

Additional pro statistics: Fumbled once, recovered two fumbles and punted once for 28 yards, 1976.
Played in AFL Championship Game following 1969 season.
Played in AFL-NFL Championship Game following 1969 season.
Played in AFL All-Star Game following 1968 and 1969 seasons.
Played in Pro Bowl (NFL All-Star Game) following 1970, 1971, 1975 and 1984 seasons.

MICHAEL IVER STENSRUD
(Mike)
Nose Tackle—Houston Oilers

Born February 19, 1956, at Forest City, Iowa.
Height, 6.05. Weight, 280.
High School—Lake Mills, Iowa.
Received degree in agricultural administration from Iowa State University.

Selected by Houston in 2nd round (31st player selected) of 1979 NFL draft.
On injured reserve with knee injury, September 21 through November 16, 1979; activated, November 17, 1979.
Houston NFL, 1979 through 1984.
Games: 1979 (6), 1980 (16), 1981 (16), 1982 (9), 1983 (16), 1984 (16). Total—79.
Pro statistics: Recovered one fumble, 1981 through 1984.
Played in AFC Championship Game following 1979 season.

HAL FRANKLIN STEPHENS
Offensive Tackle—Los Angeles Rams

Born April 14, 1961, at Whiteville, N.C.
Height, 6.04. Weight, 252.
High School—Whiteville, N.C.
Attended East Carolina University.

Selected by Memphis in 4th round (80th player selected) of 1984 USFL draft.
USFL rights traded by Memphis Showboats to Oakland Invaders for running back Jack Holmes, January 30, 1984.
Selected by Los Angeles Rams in 5th round (133rd player selected) of 1984 NFL draft.
Signed by Los Angeles Rams, July 9, 1984.
On injured reserve with ankle injury, August 21 through entire 1984 season.

DWIGHT EUGENE STEPHENSON
Center—Miami Dolphins

Born November 20, 1957, at Murfreesboro, N.C.
Height, 6.02. Weight, 255.
High School—Hampton, Va.
Attended University of Alabama.

Named to THE SPORTING NEWS NFL All-Star Team, 1984.
Selected by Miami in 2nd round (48th player selected) of 1980 NFL draft.
Miami NFL, 1980 through 1984.
Games: 1980 (16), 1981 (16), 1982 (9), 1983 (16), 1984 (16). Total—73.
Pro statistics: Recovered one fumble, 1980 and 1984.
Played in AFC Championship Game following 1982 and 1984 seasons.
Played in NFL Championship Game following 1982 and 1984 seasons.
Played in Pro Bowl (NFL All-Star Game) following 1983 and 1984 seasons.

RUFUS STEVENS
Wide Receiver—Kansas City Chiefs

Born January 13, 1961, at Monroe, La.
Height, 6.03. Weight, 182.
High School—Monroe, La., Richwood.
Attended Grambling State University.

Selected by Oklahoma in 5th round (106th player selected) of 1984 USFL draft.
Selected by Kansas City in 6th round (146th player selected) of 1984 NFL draft.
Signed by Kansas City Chiefs, July 12, 1984.
On injured reserve with thigh injury, August 21 through entire 1984 season.

TERRY ALLAN STIEVE

Name pronounced Steve.

Guard—St. Louis Cardinals

Born March 10, 1954, at Baraboo, Wis.
Height, 6.02. Weight, 265.
High School—Baraboo, Wis.
Attended University of Wisconsin.

Selected by New Orleans in 6th round (160th player selected) of 1976 NFL draft.

Traded with defensive end Bob Pollard from New Orleans Saints to St. Louis Cardinals for wide receiver Ike Harris and guard Conrad Dobler, January 31, 1978.

On injured reserve with knee injury, August 26 through entire 1980 season.

New Orleans NFL, 1976 and 1977; St. Louis NFL, 1978, 1979 and 1981 through 1984.

Games: 1976 (14), 1977 (14), 1978 (16), 1979 (14), 1981 (16), 1982 (9), 1983 (16), 1984 (14). Total—113.

Pro statistics: Recovered one fumble, 1977; recovered one fumble for two yards, 1984.

ARTHUR BARRY STILL

(Art)

Defensive End—Kansas City Chiefs

Born December 5, 1955, at Camden, N.J.
Height, 6.07. Weight, 257.
High School—Camden, N.J.
Received bachelor of arts degree in general studies from University of Kentucky in 1978.

Named as defensive end on The Sporting News College All-America Team, 1977.

Named to The Sporting News NFL All-Star Team, 1980.

Selected by Kansas City in 1st round (2nd player selected) of 1978 NFL draft.

On injured reserve with knee injury, September 23 through October 30, 1981; activated, October 31, 1981.

Kansas City NFL, 1978 through 1984.

Games: 1978 (16), 1979 (16), 1980 (16), 1981 (11), 1982 (9), 1983 (15), 1984 (16). Total—99.

Pro statistics: Recovered one fumble, 1978, 1980, 1981 and 1983; recovered one fumble for 13 yards, 1979; recovered one fumble for four yards, 1982; recovered one fumble for three yards, 1984.

Played in Pro Bowl (NFL All-Star Game) following 1980 through 1982 and 1984 seasons.

JEFF OWEN STOVER

Nose Tackle—San Francisco 49ers

Born May 22, 1958, at Corning, Calif.
Height, 6.05. Weight, 275.
High School—Corning, Calif., Union.
Attended University of Oregon.

Signed as free agent by San Francisco 49ers, April 20, 1982.

On injured reserve with knee injury, September 4 through November 15, 1984; activated, November 16, 1984.

San Francisco NFL, 1982 through 1984.

Games: 1982 (9), 1983 (16), 1984 (6). Total—31.

Pro statistics: Recovered one fumble, 1982 and 1983.

Played in NFC Championship Game following 1983 and 1984 seasons.

Played in NFL Championship Game following 1984 season.

TIMOTHY STRACKA

(Tim)

Tight End—Cleveland Browns

Born September 27, 1959, at Madison, Wis.
Height, 6.03. Weight, 225.
High School—Madison, Wis., West.
Received bachelor of science degree in finance and risk management from University of Wisconsin in 1983.

Selected by Cleveland in 6th round (145th player selected) of 1983 NFL draft.

On injured reserve with neck injury, August 29 through October 5, 1984; activated, October 6, 1984.

On injured reserve with broken ankle, November 14 through remainder of 1984 season.

	—PASS RECEIVING—				
Year Club	G.	P.C.	Yds.	Avg.	TD.
1983—Cleveland NFL	13	1	12	12.0	0
1984—Cleveland NFL	6	1	15	15.0	0
Pro Totals—2 Years	19	2	27	13.5	0

THOMAS STRAUTHERS

(Tom)

Defensive End—Philadelphia Eagles

Born April 6, 1961, at Wesson, Miss.
Height, 6.04. Weight, 265.
High School—Brookhaven, Miss.
Attended Jackson State University.

Selected by Oakland in 21st round (247th player selected) of 1983 USFL draft.

Selected by Philadelphia in 10th round (258th player selected) of 1983 NFL draft.

Signed by Philadelphia Eagles, June 15, 1983.

On injured reserve with broken hand, August 16 through November 23, 1983; activated by Philadelphia Eagles after clearing procedural waivers, November 25, 1983.
Philadelphia NFL, 1983 and 1984.
Games: 1983 (4), 1984 (16). Total—20.
Pro statistics: Returned one kickoff for 12 yards, 1984.

RICHARD GENE STRENGER
(Rich)
Offensive Tackle—Detroit Lions
Born March 10, 1960, at Port Washington, Wis.
Height, 6.07. Weight, 269.
High School—Grafton, Wis.
Received bachelor of science degree from University of Michigan in 1983.

Selected by Michigan in 1983 USFL territorial draft.
Selected by Detroit in 2nd round (40th player selected) of 1983 NFL draft.
Signed by Detroit Lions, July 4, 1983.
On injured reserve with knee injury, September 4 through remainder of 1984 season.
Detroit NFL, 1983 and 1984.
Games: 1983 (16), 1984 (1). Total—17.

DONALD JOSEPH STROCK
(Don)
Quarterback—Miami Dolphins
Born November 27, 1950, at Pottstown, Pa.
Height, 6.05. Weight, 220.
High School—Pottstown, Pa., Owen J. Roberts.
Received bachelor of science degree in distributive direction from
Virginia Technical University in 1973.
Brother of Dave Strock, former kicker with Houston Oilers, Miami Dolphins,
Florida Blazers, Shreveport Steamer and Washington Redskins.

Selected by Miami in 5th round (111th player selected) of 1973 NFL draft.
On did not report list, August 16 through September 4, 1983.
Reported and granted roster exemption, September 5, 1983; activated, September 9, 1983.
Member of Miami Dolphins' taxi squad, 1973.

Year Club	G.	Att.	Cmp.	Pct.	Gain	T.P.	P.I.	Avg.	Att.	Yds.	Avg.	TD.	TD.	Pts.	F.
					PASSING						RUSHING			TOTAL	
1974—Miami NFL	1				None				1	—7	—7.0	0	0	0	0
1975—Miami NFL	6	45	26	57.8	230	2	2	5.11	6	38	6.3	1	1	6	1
1976—Miami NFL	4	47	21	44.7	359	3	2	7.64	2	13	6.5	1	1	6	1
1977—Miami NFL	4	4	2	50.0	12	0	1	3.00		None			0	0	0
1978—Miami NFL	16	135	72	53.3	825	12	6	6.11	10	23	2.3	0	0	0	4
1979—Miami NFL	16	100	56	56.0	830	6	6	8.30	3	18	6.0	0	0	0	3
1980—Miami NFL	16	62	30	48.4	313	1	5	5.05	1	—3	—3.0	0	0	0	1
1981—Miami NFL	16	130	79	60.8	901	6	8	6.93	14	—26	—1.9	0	0	0	0
1982—Miami NFL	9	55	30	54.5	306	2	5	5.56	3	—9	—3.0	0	0	0	1
1983—Miami NFL	15	52	34	65.4	403	4	1	7.75	6	—16	—2.7	0	0	0	0
1984—Miami NFL	16	6	4	66.7	27	0	0	4.50	2	—5	—2.5	0	0	0	1
Pro Totals—11 Years	119	636	354	55.7	4206	36	36	6.61	48	26	0.5	2	2	12	12

Quarterback Rating Points: 1975 (67.9), 1976 (74.6), 1977 (16.7), 1978 (83.3), 1979 (78.3), 1980 (35.1), 1981 (71.1), 1982 (44.8), 1983 (106.5), 1984 (76.4). Total—71.3.
Additional pro statistics: Recovered one fumble, 1975, 1978 and 1983; fumbled four times for minus five yards, 1978; fumbled once for minus three yards, 1982; fumbled once for minus two yards, 1984.
Played in AFC Championship Game following 1982 and 1984 seasons.
Played in NFL Championship Game following 1982 and 1984 seasons.

JAMES STUCKEY
(Jim)
Defensive End—San Francisco 49ers
Born June 21, 1958, at Cayce, S.C.
Height, 6.04. Weight, 251.
High School—Columbia, S.C., Airport.
Attended Clemson University.

Named as defensive end on THE SPORTING NEWS College All-America Team, 1979.
Selected by San Francisco in 1st round (20th player selected) of 1980 NFL draft.
San Francisco NFL, 1980 through 1984.
Games: 1980 (16), 1981 (15), 1982 (9), 1983 (16), 1984 (16). Total—72.
Pro statistics: Credited with one safety, 1980; recovered one fumble, 1981 and 1982.
Played in NFC Championship Game following 1981, 1983 and 1984 seasons.
Played in NFL Championship Game following 1981 and 1984 seasons.

MARK WAYNE STUDAWAY
Defensive End—Houston Oilers
Born September 20, 1960, at Memphis, Tenn.
Height, 6.03. Weight, 269.
High School—Memphis, Tenn., South Side.
Attended University of Tennessee.

Selected by Memphis in 1984 USFL territorial draft.
Selected by Houston in 4th round (85th player selected) of 1984 NFL draft.
Signed by Houston Oilers, July 7, 1984.
On injured reserve with knee injury, October 12 through remainder of 1984 season.
Houston NFL, 1984.
Games: 1984 (6).

DAVID DERALD STUDDARD
(Dave)
Offensive Tackle—Denver Broncos
Born November 22, 1955, at San Antonio, Tex.
Height, 6.04. Weight, 260.
High School—Pearsall, Tex.
Received degree in physical education from University of Texas.
Brother of Les Studdard, center with Kansas City Chiefs and Houston Oilers, 1982 and 1983;
nephew of Howard Fest, guard with Cincinnati Bengals and Tampa Bay Buccaneers, 1968 through 1976.
Selected by Baltimore in 9th round (245th player selected) of 1978 NFL draft.
Released by Baltimore Colts, August 30, 1978; signed as free agent by Denver Broncos, January 31, 1979.
Denver NFL, 1979 through 1984.
Games: 1979 (16), 1980 (16), 1981 (16), 1982 (9), 1983 (16), 1984 (16). Total—89.
Pro statistics: Caught one pass for two yards and a touchdown, 1979; recovered one fumble, 1980 and 1983; caught one pass for 10 yards, 1981; returned two kickoffs for eight yards, 1983; caught one pass for minus four yards, 1984.

SCOTT STUDWELL
Linebacker—Minnesota Vikings
Born August 27, 1954, at Evansville, Ind.
Height, 6.02. Weight, 230.
High School—Evansville, Ind., Harrison.
Attended University of Illinois.
Selected by Minnesota in 9th round (250th player selected) of 1977 NFL draft.

			—INTERCEPTIONS—		
Year Club	G.	No.	Yds.	Avg.	TD.
1977—Minnesota NFL............	14	1	4	4.0	0
1978—Minnesota NFL............	13		None		
1979—Minnesota NFL............	14	1	18	18.0	0
1980—Minnesota NFL............	16	1	4	4.0	0
1981—Minnesota NFL............	16		None		
1982—Minnesota NFL............	8	1	3	3.0	0
1983—Minnesota NFL............	16		None		
1984—Minnesota NFL............	16	1	20	20.0	0
Pro Totals—8 Years............	113	5	49	9.8	0

Additional pro statistics: Recovered one fumble for six yards and returned one kickoff for no yards, 1979; recovered one fumble, 1980, 1982 and 1983; recovered three fumbles, 1981.
Played in NFC Championship Game following 1977 season.

MATTHEW JEROME SUHEY
(Matt)
Running Back—Chicago Bears
Born July 7, 1958, at Bellefonte, Pa.
Height, 5.11. Weight, 217.
High School—State College, Pa.
Received bachelor of science degree in marketing from Penn State University in 1980.
Grandson of Bob Higgins, end with Canton Bulldogs, 1920 and 1921, and son of Steve Suhey,
guard with Pittsburgh Steelers, 1948 and 1949.
Selected by Chicago in 2nd round (46th player selected) of 1980 NFL draft.

		—RUSHING—				PASS RECEIVING				—TOTAL—		
Year Club	G.	Att.	Yds.	Avg.	TD.	P.C.	Yds.	Avg.	TD.	TD.	Pts.	F.
1980—Chicago NFL	16	22	45	2.0	0	7	60	8.6	0	0	0	1
1981—Chicago NFL	15	150	521	3.5	3	33	168	5.1	0	3	18	3
1982—Chicago NFL	9	70	206	2.9	3	36	333	9.3	0	3	18	2
1983—Chicago NFL	16	149	681	4.6	4	49	429	8.8	1	5	30	5
1984—Chicago NFL	16	124	424	3.4	4	42	312	7.4	2	6	36	6
Pro Totals—5 Years................	72	515	1877	3.6	14	167	1302	7.8	3	17	102	17

		KICKOFF RETURNS			
Year Club	G.	No.	Yds.	Avg.	TD.
1980—Chicago NFL	16	19	406	21.4	0
1981—Chicago NFL	15		None		
1982—Chicago NFL	9		None		
1983—Chicago NFL	16		None		
1984—Chicago NFL	16		None		
Pro Totals—5 Years............	72	19	406	21.4	0

Additional pro statistics: Returned one punt for four yards, 1980; recovered three fumbles, 1981; recovered one fumble, 1982; attempted one pass with one completion for 74 yards and a touchdown, 1983; attempted one pass with no completions and recovered two fumbles, 1984.
Played in NFC Championship Game following 1984 season.

IVORY ULYSSES SULLY
Safety—Los Angeles Rams
Born June 20, 1957, at Salisbury, Md.
Height, 6.00. Weight, 201.
High School—Leonia, N.J.
Received degree in physical education from University of Delaware.

Signed as free agent by Los Angeles Rams, June, 1979.
On injured reserve with ankle injury, August 14 through October 18, 1979; re-signed after clearing procedural waivers, October 20, 1979.
Released by Los Angeles Rams, October 31, 1979; re-signed by Rams, November 7, 1979.
Los Angeles Rams NFL, 1979 through 1984.
Games: 1979 (6), 1980 (16), 1981 (16), 1982 (9), 1983 (16), 1984 (16). Total—79.
Played in NFC Championship Game following 1979 season.
Played in NFL Championship Game following 1979 season.
Pro statistics: Returned four kickoffs for 36 yards, recovered two fumbles and fumbled once, 1980 and 1981; returned three kickoffs for 31 yards, 1981; returned five kickoffs for 84 yards, 1982; recovered one fumble, 1983 and 1984; credited with one safety and returned one kickoff for three yards, 1984.

DONALD O. SUMMERS
(Don)
Tight End—Denver Broncos
Born February 22, 1961, at Grants Pass, Ore.
Height, 6.04. Weight, 230.
High Schools—Eagle Point, Ore., and Medford, Ore.
Attended Oregon Tech and Boise State University.

Signed as free agent by Oakland Invaders, January 8, 1984.
Released by Oakland Invaders, January 30, 1984; signed as free agent by Denver Broncos, May 2, 1984.

		——PASS RECEIVING——			
Year Club	G.	P.C.	Yds.	Avg.	TD.
1984—Denver NFL	16	3	32	10.7	0

Additional pro statistics: Recovered one fumble, 1984.

DON SWAFFORD
Offensive Tackle—Cincinnati Bengals
Born March 22, 1957, at Dayton, O.
Height, 6.07. Weight, 258.
High School—Canton, O., Northmont.
Attended University of Florida.

Selected by Philadelphia in 7th round (178th player selected) of 1979 NFL draft.
Released by Philadelphia Eagles, August 13, 1979; signed by Hamilton Tiger-Cats, March 12, 1980.
Traded by Hamilton Tiger-Cats to Saskatchewan Roughriders for running back Mike Strickland, June 17, 1980.
Released by Saskatchewan Roughriders, July 20, 1983; signed as free agent by British Columbia Lions, September 18, 1983.
Granted free agency, January 15, 1984; signed as free agent by Cincinnati Bengals, January 26, 1984.
Traded by Cincinnati Bengals to Tampa Bay Buccaneers for 6th round pick in 1985 draft, July 24, 1984.
On injured reserve with back injury, August 27 through entire 1984 season.
Saskatchewan CFL, 1980 through 1982; Saskatchewan (2)-British Columbia (6) CFL, 1983.
Games: 1980 (13), 1981 (16), 1982 (16), 1983 (8). Total—53.
CFL statistics: Recovered one fumble, 1981 and 1982.

JOHN WESLEY SWAIN
Cornerback—Minnesota Vikings
Born September 4, 1959, at Miami, Fla.
Height, 6.01. Weight, 190.
High School—Miami, Fla., Carol City.
Attended University of Miami (Fla.).

Selected by Minnesota in 4th round (101st player selected) of 1981 NFL draft.

		——INTERCEPTIONS——			
Year Club	G.	No.	Yds.	Avg.	TD.
1981—Minnesota NFL.............	12	2	18	9.0	0
1982—Minnesota NFL.............	9	2	20	10.0	0
1983—Minnesota NFL.............	14	6	12	2.0	0
1984—Minnesota NFL.............	15	2	20	10.0	0
Pro Totals—4 Years............	50	12	70	5.8	0

Additional pro statistics: Recovered one fumble, 1981 and 1984.

KARL V. SWANKE
Offensive Tackle-Center—Green Bay Packers
Born December 29, 1957, at Elmhurst, Ill.
Height, 6.06. Weight, 262.
High School—Newington, Conn.
Attended Boston College.
Brother of Rob Swanke, nose tackle with Denver Broncos.

Selected by Green Bay in 6th round (143rd player selected) of 1980 NFL draft.

On injured reserve with knee injury, September 29 through remainder of 1981 season.
On injured reserve with knee injury, December 29 through remainder of 1982 season.
Green Bay NFL, 1980 through 1984.
Games: 1980 (16), 1981 (4), 1982 (8), 1983 (16), 1984 (15). Total—59.
Pro statistics: Caught one pass for two yards and a touchdown 1981; recovered one fumble, 1982; recovered two fumbles, 1983.

ROBERT SCOTT SWANKE
(Rob)
Nose Tackle—Denver Broncos
Born November 17, 1961, at Hartford, Ct.
Height, 6.02. Weight, 252.
High School—Newington, Ct.
Attended Boston College.
Brother of Karl Swanke, offensive tackle-center with Green Bay Packers.
Selected by Pittsburgh in 9th round (168th player selected) of 1984 USFL draft.
Signed as free agent by Denver Broncos, May 2, 1984.
On injured reserve with knee injury, August 21 through entire 1984 season.
USFL rights traded by Pittsburgh Panthers to Denver Gold for rights to tight end Andy Gibler, August 28, 1984.

CALVIN EUGENE SWEENEY
Wide Receiver—Pittsburgh Steelers
Born January 12, 1955, at Riverside, Calif.
Height, 6.02. Weight, 190.
High School—Riverside, Calif., Perris Union.
Attended Riverside Junior College and received business degree from University of Southern California.
Selected by Pittsburgh in 4th round (110th player selected) of 1979 NFL draft.
On injured reserve with foot injury, August 13 through entire 1979 season.
Released by Pittsburgh Steelers, September 1, 1980; re-signed by Steelers, September 8, 1980.
On injured reserve with pulled hamstring, September 4 through October 18, 1984; activated, October 19, 1984.

Year Club	G.	P.C.	Yds.	Avg.	TD.
1980—Pittsburgh NFL............	15	12	282	23.5	1
1981—Pittsburgh NFL............	14	2	53	26.5	0
1982—Pittsburgh NFL............	7	5	50	10.0	0
1983—Pittsburgh NFL............	16	39	577	14.8	5
1984—Pittsburgh NFL............	9	2	25	12.5	0
Pro Totals—5 Years............	61	60	987	16.5	6

Additional pro statistics: Returned three kickoffs for 42 yards, 1980; fumbled once, 1981; rushed once for minus two yards, 1983.
Played in AFC Championship Game following 1984 season.

JAMES JOSEPH SWEENEY
(Jim)
Guard-Center—New York Jets
Born August 8, 1962, at Pittsburgh, Pa.
Height, 6.04. Weight, 260.
High School—Pittsburgh, Pa., Seton LaSalle.
Attended University of Pittsburgh.
Selected by Pittsburgh in 1984 USFL territorial draft.
Selected by New York Jets in 2nd round (37th player selected) of 1984 NFL draft.
Signed by New York Jets, July 12, 1984.
New York Jets NFL, 1984.
Games: 1984 (10).

DENNIS NEAL SWILLEY
Center—Minnesota Vikings
Born June 28, 1955, at Bossier City, La.
Height, 6.03. Weight, 241.
High School—Pine Bluff, Ark.
Attended Texas A&M University and received degree in interior
design/architectural design from North Texas State University.
Selected by Minnesota in 2nd round (55th player selected) of 1977 NFL draft.
On reserve/retired list entire 1984 season.
Minnesota NFL, 1977 through 1983.
Games: 1977 (14), 1978 (14), 1979 (16), 1980 (16), 1981 (16), 1982 (9), 1983 (16). Total—101.
Pro statistics: Returned one kickoff for no yards and fumbled once, 1977; recovered one fumble, 1979 and 1982.
Played in NFC Championship Game following 1977 season.

DARRYL TALLEY
Linebacker—Buffalo Bills
Born November 12, 1960, at Cleveland, O.
Height, 6.04. Weight, 231.
High School—East Cleveland, O., Shaw.
Received degree in physical education from West Virginia University.
Brother of John Talley, quarterback/tight end at West Virginia University.

Named as linebacker on THE SPORTING NEWS College All-America Team, 1982.
Selected by New Jersey in 2nd round (24th player selected) of 1983 USFL draft.
Selected by Buffalo in 2nd round (39th player selected) of 1983 NFL draft.
Signed by Buffalo Bills, June 14, 1983.
Buffalo NFL, 1983 and 1984.
Games: 1983 (16), 1984 (16). Total—32.
Pro statistics: Returned two kickoffs for nine yards and recovered two fumbles for six yards, 1983; recovered one fumble and intercepted one pass for no yards, 1984.

RODNEY DANE TATE
Running Back—Atlanta Falcons
Born February 14, 1959, at Okmulgee, Okla.
Height, 5.11. Weight, 190.
High School—Beggs, Okla.
Attended University of Texas.

Selected by Cincinnati in 4th round (110th player selected) of 1982 NFL draft.
On injured reserve with thigh injury, October 25 through November 27, 1983; activated, November 28, 1983.
Released by Cincinnati Bengals, August 27, 1984; signed as free agent by Atlanta Falcons, September 4, 1984.
On injured reserve with fractured wrist, October 24 through remainder of 1984 season.

		—RUSHING—				PASS RECEIVING				—TOTAL—		
Year Club	G.	Att.	Yds.	Avg.	TD.	P.C.	Yds.	Avg.	TD.	TD.	Pts.	F.
1982—Cincinnati NFL	9	2	2	1.0	0		None		0	0	0	2
1983—Cincinnati NFL	12	25	77	3.1	0	18	142	7.9	0	0	0	3
1984—Atlanta NFL	7		None				None			0	0	1
Pro Totals—3 Years	28	27	79	2.9	0	18	142	7.9	0	0	0	6

		KICKOFF RETURNS			
Year Club	G.	No.	Yds.	Avg.	TD.
1982—Cincinnati NFL	9	14	314	22.4	0
1983—Cincinnati NFL	12	13	218	16.8	0
1984—Atlanta NFL	7	9	148	16.4	0
Pro Totals—3 Years	28	36	680	18.9	0

Additional pro statistics: Recovered two fumbles, 1982; recovered one fumble, 1984.

MOSIULA TATUPU
(Mosi)
Fullback—New England Patriots
Born April 26, 1955, at Pago Pago, American Samoa
Height, 6.00. Weight, 227.
High School—Honolulu, Haw., Punahou.
Attended University of Southern California.
Cousin of Terry Tautolo, linebacker with Detroit Lions; and John Tautolo,
guard with Portland Breakers.

Selected by New England in 8th round (215th player selected) of 1978 NFL draft.

		—RUSHING—				PASS RECEIVING				—TOTAL—		
Year Club	G.	Att.	Yds.	Avg.	TD.	P.C.	Yds.	Avg.	TD.	TD.	Pts.	F.
1978—New England NFL	16	3	6	2.0	0		None			0	0	0
1979—New England NFL	16	23	71	3.1	0	2	9	4.5	0	0	0	0
1980—New England NFL	16	33	97	2.9	3	4	27	6.8	0	3	18	0
1981—New England NFL	16	38	201	5.3	2	12	132	11.0	1	3	18	2
1982—New England NFL	9	30	168	5.6	0		None			0	0	0
1983—New England NFL	16	106	578	5.5	4	10	97	9.7	1	5	30	1
1984—New England NFL	16	133	553	4.2	4	16	159	9.9	0	4	24	4
Pro Totals—7 Years	105	366	1674	4.6	13	44	424	9.6	2	15	90	7

Additional pro statistics: Returned one kickoff for 17 yards, 1978; returned three kickoffs for 15 yards, 1979; recovered three fumbles, 1981; recovered one fumble, 1983 and 1984; returned one kickoff for nine yards, 1984.

TERRY WAYNE TAUSCH
Offensive Tackle-Guard—Minnesota Vikings
Born February 5, 1959, at New Braunfels, Tex.
Height, 6.05. Weight, 270.
High School—New Braunfels, Tex.
Received bachelor of business administration degree in marketing from
University of Texas in 1981.

Named as offensive tackle on THE SPORTING NEWS College All-America Team, 1981.
Selected by Minnesota in 2nd round (39th player selected) of 1982 NFL draft.
Minnesota NFL, 1982 through 1984.
Games: 1982 (2), 1983 (10), 1984 (16). Total—28.

—DID YOU KNOW—

That Detroit's Billy Sims, who sat out the final eight games of the 1984 season because of injury, is the Lions' career rushing leader with 5,106 yards? The former record holder, Dexter Bussey, rushed for 91 yards last season to finish one yard shy of Sims' new mark.

TERRY L. TAUTOLO

Name pronounced Ta-TOE-low.

Linebacker—Detroit Lions

Born August 30, 1954, at Corona, Calif.
Height, 6.02. Weight, 227.
High School—Long Beach, Calif., Millikan.
Attended Long Beach Junior College and University of California at Los Angeles.
Brother of John Tautolo, guard with Portland Breakers; cousin of Manu Tuiasosopo, defensive tackle with San Francisco 49ers; Wilson Faumuina, defensive end with Atlanta Falcons, 1977 through 1981; Mosi Tatupu, running back with New England Patriots; Frank Manumaleuga, linebacker with Kansas City Chiefs and Oakland Invaders, 1979 through 1981, 1983 and 1984; and Jack Thompson, quarterback with Tampa Bay Buccaneers.

Selected by Philadelphia in 13th round (353rd player selected) of 1976 NFL draft.
Traded by Philadelphia Eagles to Chicago Bears for conditional 7th round pick in 1981 draft, August 19, 1980.
Released by Chicago Bears, September 1, 1980; signed as free agent by San Francisco 49ers, September 20, 1980.
Released by San Francisco 49ers, October 7, 1981; signed as free agent by Detroit Lions, October 10, 1981.
Released by Detroit Lions, September 6, 1982; re-signed by Lions after clearing procedural waivers, December 22, 1982.
Released by Detroit Lions, August 23, 1983; signed as free agent by Miami Dolphins, October 18, 1983.
Traded by Miami Dolphins to Detroit Lions for past considerations, August 20, 1984.
On injured reserve with back injury, October 2 through remainder of 1984 season.
Philadelphia NFL, 1976 through 1979; San Francisco NFL, 1980; San Francisco (5)-Detroit (11) NFL, 1981; Detroit NFL, 1982 and 1984; Miami NFL, 1983.
Games: 1976 (13), 1977 (14), 1978 (16), 1979 (16), 1980 (14), 1981 (16), 1982 (2), 1983 (9), 1984 (4). Total—104.
Pro statistics: Returned three kickoffs for 45 yards, 1978; intercepted one pass for no yards, returned one kickoff for 16 yards and recovered two fumbles for six yards, 1980.

JOHNNY TAYLOR

Linebacker—Atlanta Falcons

Born June 21, 1960, at Seattle, Wash.
Height, 6.04. Weight, 240.
High School—Garfield, Wash.
Attended Wenatchee Valley Junior College and University of Hawaii.

Signed as free agent by Atlanta Falcons, May 2, 1984.
Released by Atlanta Falcons, August 21, 1984; re-signed by Falcons after clearing procedural waivers, December 6, 1984.
Atlanta NFL, 1984.
Games: 1984 (2).

LAWRENCE TAYLOR

Linebacker—New York Giants

Born February 4, 1959, at Williamsburg, Va.
Height, 6.03. Weight, 243.
High School—Williamsburg, Va., Lafayette.
Attended University of North Carolina.

Named to THE SPORTING NEWS NFL All-Star Team, 1981, 1983 and 1984.
Named as linebacker on THE SPORTING NEWS College All-America Team, 1980.
Selected by New York Giants in 1st round (2nd player selected) of 1981 NFL draft.

Year Club	G.	No.	Yds.	Avg.	TD.
1981—N.Y. Giants NFL	16	1	1	1.0	0
1982—N.Y. Giants NFL	9	1	97	97.0	*1
1983—N.Y. Giants NFL	16	2	10	5.0	0
1984—N.Y. Giants NFL	16	1	—1	—1.0	0
Pro Totals—4 Years...........	57	5	107	21.4	1

Additional pro statistics: Recovered one fumble for four yards, 1981; fumbled once, 1981 and 1983; recovered two fumbles for three yards, 1983.
Played in Pro Bowl (NFL All-Star Game) following 1981 through 1984 seasons.

LENNY MOORE TAYLOR

Wide Receiver—Green Bay Packers

Born February 15, 1961, at Miami, Fla.
Height, 5.10. Weight, 179.
High School—Miami, Fla., Southridge.
Attended University of Tennessee.

Selected by Memphis in 1984 USFL territorial draft.
Selected by Green Bay in 12th round (313th player selected) of 1984 NFL draft.
Signed by Green Bay Packers, June 29, 1984.
On injured reserve with neck injury, August 21 through November 19, 1984; activated after clearing procedural waivers, November 21, 1984.
Green Bay NFL, 1984.
Games: 1984 (2).
Pro statistics: Caught one pass for eight yards, 1984.

TERRY TAYLOR
Cornerback—Seattle Seahawks
Born July 18, 1961, at Warren, O.
Height, 5.10. Weight, 175.
High School—Youngstown, O., Rayen.
Attended Southern Illinois University.
Cousin of Walter Poole, running back with Chicago Blitz
and Houston Gamblers, 1983 and 1984.

Selected by Chicago in 2nd round (25th player selected) of 1984 USFL draft.
Selected by Seattle in 1st round (22nd player selected) of 1984 NFL draft.
Signed by Seattle Seahawks, July 10, 1984.

		—INTERCEPTIONS—			
Year	Club	G.	No.	Yds.	Avg.TD.
1984—Seattle NFL		16	3	63	21.0 0

WILLIE TEAL
Cornerback—Minnesota Vikings
Born December 20, 1957, at Texarkana, Tex.
Height, 5.10. Weight, 195.
High School—Texarkana, Tex., Liberty Eylau.
Attended Louisiana State University.

Selected by Minnesota in 2nd round (30th player selected) of 1980 NFL draft.
On injured reserve with knee injury, September 12 through December 19, 1980; activated, December 20, 1980.

		—INTERCEPTIONS—				
Year	Club	G.	No.	Yds.	Avg.	TD.
1980—Minnesota NFL		1			None	
1981—Minnesota NFL		16	4	23	5.8	0
1982—Minnesota NFL		9	4	15	3.8	0
1983—Minnesota NFL		16	3	26	8.7	0
1984—Minnesota NFL		11	1	53	53.0	1
Pro Totals—5 Years		53	12	117	9.8	1

Additional pro statistics: Recovered three fumbles for five yards, 1983; returned one punt for no yards and fumbled once, 1984.

JOSEPH ROBERT THEISMANN
(Joe)
Quarterback—Washington Redskins
Born September 9, 1949, at New Brunswick, N. J.
Height, 6.00. Weight, 198.
High School—South River, N. J.
Received bachelor of arts degree in sociology from University of Notre Dame in 1971.

Named to THE SPORTING NEWS NFL All-Star Team, 1983.
Selected by Miami in 4th round (99th player selected) of 1971 NFL draft.
Traded by Miami Dolphins to Washington Redskins for the Redskins' 1st round draft choice in 1976, January 25, 1974.

			—PASSING—							—RUSHING—				—TOTAL—		
Year	Club	G.	Att.	Cmp.	Pct.	Gain	T.P.	P.I.	Avg.	Att.	Yds.	Avg.	TD.	TD.	Pts.	F.
1971—Toronto CFL		14	278	148	53.2	2440	17	21	8.78	81	564	7.0	1	1	8	5
1972—Toronto CFL		6	127	77	60.6	1157	10	13	9.11	21	147	7.0	1	1	6	0
1973—Toronto CFL		14	274	157	57.3	2496	13	13	9.11	70	343	4.9	1	1	6	9
1974—Washington NFL		9	11	9	81.8	145	1	0	13.18	3	12	4.0	1	1	6	0
1975—Washington NFL		14	22	10	45.5	96	1	3	4.36	3	34	11.3	0	0	0	0
1976—Washington NFL		14	163	79	48.5	1036	8	10	6.36	17	97	5.7	1	1	6	2
1977—Washington NFL		14	182	84	46.2	1097	7	9	6.03	29	149	5.1	1	1	6	0
1978—Washington NFL		16	390	187	47.9	2593	13	18	6.65	37	177	4.8	1	1	6	8
1979—Washington NFL		16	395	233	59.0	2797	20	13	7.08	46	181	3.9	4	4	24	3
1980—Washington NFL		16	454	262	57.7	2962	17	16	6.52	29	175	6.0	3	3	18	6
1981—Washington NFL		16	496	293	59.1	3568	19	20	7.19	36	177	4.9	2	2	12	7
1982—Washington NFL		9	252	161	63.9	2033	13	9	8.07	31	150	4.8	0	0	0	4
1983—Washington NFL		16	459	276	60.1	3714	29	11	8.09	37	234	6.3	1	1	6	1
1984—Washington NFL		16	477	283	59.3	3391	24	13	7.11	62	314	5.1	1	1	6	7
NFL Totals—11 Years		156	3301	1877	56.9	23432	152	122	7.10	330	1700	5.2	15	15	90	38
CFL Totals—3 Years		34	679	382	56.3	6093	40	47	8.97	172	1054	6.1	3	3	20	14
Pro Totals—14 Years		190	3980	2259	56.8	29525	192	169	7.42	502	2754	5.5	18	18	110	52

NFL Quarterback Rating Points: 1974 (149.1), 1975 (33.6), 1976 (59.9), 1977 (58.0), 1978 (61.6), 1979 (84.0), 1980 (75.1), 1981 (77.3), 1982 (91.3), 1983 (97.0), 1984 (86.6). Total—79.0.

Additional CFL statistics: Scored one single, kicked one conversion, punted three times for 182 yards and returned one punt for seven yards, 1971; recovered three fumbles, 1973.

Additional NFL statistics: Returned 15 punts for 157 yards, 1974; returned two punts for five yards, 1975; recovered one fumble, 1976 and 1981; recovered three fumbles and fumbled eight times for minus 26 yards, 1978; recovered two fumbles and fumbled three times for minus four yards, 1979; fumbled six times for minus two yards, 1980; recovered one fumble and fumbled four times for minus 21 yards, 1982; recovered six fumbles and fumbled seven times for five yards, 1984.

Played in CFL Championship Game following 1971 season.
Played in NFC Championship Game following 1982 and 1983 seasons.
Played in NFL Championship Game following 1982 and 1983 seasons.
Played in Pro Bowl (NFL All-Star Game) following 1982 and 1983 seasons.

RAY CHARLES THIELEMANN
(R. C.)
Guard—Atlanta Falcons
Born August 12, 1955, at Houston, Tex.
Height, 6.04. Weight, 262.
High School—Houston, Tex., Spring Woods.
Attended University of Arkansas.

Selected by Atlanta in 2nd round (36th player selected) of 1977 NFL draft.
On injured reserve with shoulder separation, September 13 through October 12, 1979; activated, October 13, 1979.
On injured reserve with shoulder injury, December 13 through remainder of 1979 season.
On did not report list, August 16 through August 24, 1983.
Reported and granted exemption, August 25, 1983; activated, September 1, 1983.
Atlanta NFL, 1977 through 1984.
Games: 1977 (14), 1978 (16), 1979 (11), 1980 (16), 1981 (16), 1982 (9), 1983 (16), 1984 (16). Total—114.
Pro statistics: Recovered one fumble, 1977, 1983 and 1984; recovered two fumbles, 1978 through 1981.
Played in Pro Bowl (NFL All-Star Game) following 1981 through 1983 seasons.

CALVIN THOMAS
Running Back—Chicago Bears
Born January 7, 1960, at St. Louis, Mo.
Height, 5.11. Weight, 235.
High School—St. Louis, Mo., McKinley.
Attended University of Illinois.

Signed as free agent by Chicago Bears, May 21, 1982.
On inactive list, September 12, 1982.

Year Club		RUSHING				PASS RECEIVING				TOTAL		
	G.	Att.	Yds.	Avg.	TD.	P.C.	Yds.	Avg.	TD.	TD.	Pts.	F.
1982—Chicago NFL	6	5	4	0.8	0	None				0	0	1
1983—Chicago NFL	13	8	25	3.1	0	2	13	6.5	0	0	0	0
1984—Chicago NFL	16	40	186	4.7	1	9	39	4.3	0	1	6	1
Pro Totals—3 Years	35	53	215	4.1	1	11	52	4.7	0	1	6	2

Additional pro statistics: Recovered one fumble, 1984.
Played in NFC Championship Game following 1984 season.

JEWERL THOMAS JR.
First name pronounced Jerrel.
Running Back—San Diego Chargers
Born September 10, 1957, at Hanford, Calif.
Height, 5.10. Weight, 228.
High School—Hanford, Calif.
Attended University of California at Los Angeles and San Jose State University.
Brother of Ken Thomas, running back with Kansas City Chiefs.

Selected by Los Angeles in 3rd round (58th player selected) of 1980 NFL draft.
Traded by Los Angeles Rams to Kansas City Chiefs for cornerback Eric Harris, August 19, 1983.
Traded by Kansas City Chiefs to San Diego Chargers for 7th round pick in 1985 draft, May 1, 1984.

Year Club		RUSHING				PASS RECEIVING				TOTAL		
	G.	Att.	Yds.	Avg.	TD.	P.C.	Yds.	Avg.	TD.	TD.	Pts.	F.
1980—Los Angeles Rams NFL	16	65	427	6.6	2	5	30	6.0	0	3	18	1
1981—Los Angeles Rams NFL	15	34	118	3.5	0	5	37	7.4	0	0	0	1
1982—Los Angeles Rams NFL	8	16	80	5.0	0	8	49	6.1	0	0	0	0
1983—Kansas City NFL	10	44	115	2.6	0	10	51	5.1	0	0	0	4
1984—San Diego NFL	7	14	43	3.1	2	None				2	12	1
Pro Totals—5 Years	56	173	783	4.5	4	28	167	6.0	0	5	30	7

Additional pro statistics: Recovered blocked punt in end zone for a touchdown, returned two kickoffs for 21 yards, 1980; recovered one fumble, 1980, 1981, 1983 and 1984; returned one kickoff for 15 yards, 1981; attempted two passes with one completion for 18 yards, one touchdown and one interception, 1983.

KELLY SCOTT THOMAS
Offensive Tackle—Tampa Bay Buccaneers
Born September 9, 1960, at Lynwood, Calif.
Height, 6.06. Weight, 270.
High School—La Mirada, Calif.
Attended University of Southern California.

Selected by Los Angeles in 1983 USFL territorial draft.
Selected by Tampa Bay in 4th round (99th player selected) of 1983 NFL draft.
Signed by Tampa Bay Buccaneers, May 20, 1983.
Tampa Bay NFL, 1983 and 1984.
Games: 1983 (14), 1984 (10). Total—24.

KENNETH RAY THOMAS
(Ken)
Running Back—Kansas City Chiefs

Born December 21, 1959, at Hanford, Calif.
Height, 5.09. Weight, 211.
High School—Hanford, Calif.
Attended San Jose State University.
Brother of Jewerl Thomas, running back with San Diego Chargers.

Selected by Oakland in 1983 USFL territorial draft.
Selected by Kansas City in 7th round (173rd player selected) of 1983 NFL draft.
Signed by Kansas City Chiefs, June 1, 1983.
On injured reserve with broken ribs, December 16 through remainder of 1983 season.
On injured reserve with knee injury, August 21 through entire 1984 season.

		—————RUSHING—————				PASS RECEIVING				—TOTAL—		
Year Club	G.	Att.	Yds.	Avg.	TD.	P.C.	Yds.	Avg.	TD.	TD.	Pts.	F.
1983—Kansas City NFL	14	15	55	3.7	0	28	236	8.4	1	1	6	2

Additional pro statistics: Returned one kickoff for six yards and recovered one fumble, 1983.

ROBERT RANDALL THOMAS
(Bob)
Placekicker—Chicago Bears

Born August 7, 1952, at Rochester, N.Y.
Height, 5.10. Weight, 175.
High School—Rochester, N. Y., McQuaid Jesuit.
Received bachelor of arts degree in government from
University of Notre Dame in 1974; attends Loyola University Law School.

Selected by Los Angeles in 15th round (388th player selected) of 1974 NFL draft.
Released by Los Angeles Rams, September, 1974; signed by Jacksonville Sharks (WFL), 1974.
Released by Jacksonville Sharks (WFL), 1974.
Claimed on waivers from Los Angeles Rams by Chicago Bears, February 26, 1975.
On injured reserve with pulled hamstring, September 16 through remainder of 1981 season.
Released by Chicago Bears, September 6, 1982; signed as free agent by Detroit Lions, September 10, 1982.
Released by Detroit Lions, November 20, 1982; signed as free agent by Chicago Bears, December 20, 1982.

	——PLACE KICKING——						——PLACE KICKING——				
Year Club	G.	XP.	XPM.	FG.	FGA.	Pts.	Year Club	G.	XP.	XPM.	FG.	FGA.	Pts.
1975—Chicago NFL	14	18	4	13	23	57	1981—Chicago NFL	2	2	1	2	3	8
1976—Chicago NFL	14	27	3	12	25	63	1982—Det (2)-Chi (2) NFL	4	9	0	10	12	39
1977—Chicago NFL	14	27	3	14	27	69	1983—Chicago NFL	16	35	3	14	25	77
1978—Chicago NFL	16	26	2	17	22	77	1984—Chicago NFL	16	35	2	22	28	101
1979—Chicago NFL	16	34	3	16	27	82	Pro Totals—10 Years	128	248	23	133	210	647
1980—Chicago NFL	16	35	2	13	18	74							

Played in NFC Championship Game following 1984 season.

ZACHARY DWAYNE THOMAS
(Zack)
Wide Receiver—Tampa Bay Buccaneers

Born September 8, 1960, at Cocoa, Fla.
Height, 6.00. Weight, 182.
High School—Cocoa, Fla.
Attended South Carolina State College.

Signed as free agent by Denver Broncos, May 1, 1983.
Released by Denver Broncos, November 20, 1984; signed as free agent by Tampa Bay Buccaneers, December 5, 1984.

		PASS RECEIVING				-PUNT RETURNS-				—KICKOFF RET.—				—TOTAL—		
Year Club	G.	P.C.	Yds.	Avg.	TD.	No.	Yds.	Avg.	TD.	No.	Yds.	Avg.	TD.	TD.	Pts.	F.
1983—Denver NFL	16	12	182	15.2	0	33	368	11.2	*1	28	573	20.5	0	1	6	4
1984—Den. (12)-T.B. (2) NFL	14		None			21	125	6.0	0	18	351	19.5	0	0	0	3
Pro Totals—2 Years	30	12	182	15.2	0	54	493	9.1	1	46	924	20.1	0	1	6	7

Additional pro statistics: Recovered three fumbles, 1983; recovered two fumbles, 1984.

GARY THOMPSON
Cornerback—San Francisco 49ers

Born February 23, 1959, at Castro Valley, Calif.
Height, 6.00. Weight, 180.
High School—Eureka, Calif.
Attended College of the Redwoods and San Jose State University.

Signed as free agent by San Francisco 49ers, May 4, 1982.
Released by San Francisco 49ers, August 21, 1982; signed as free agent by Winnipeg Blue Bombers, April, 1983.
Released by Winnipeg Blue Bombers, July 3, 1983; signed as free agent by Buffalo Bills, July 14, 1983.
Released by Buffalo Bills, October 24, 1984; signed as free agent by San Francisco 49ers, April 16, 1985.
Buffalo NFL, 1983 and 1984.
Games: 1983 (16), 1984 (8). Total—24.

JACK THOMPSON
Quarterback—Tampa Bay Buccaneers

Born May 19, 1956, at Tutuwila, American Samoa.
Height, 6.03. Weight, 217.
High School—Seattle, Wash., Evergreen.
Attended Washington State University.
Cousin of Frank Manumaleuga, linebacker with Kansas City Chiefs and Oakland Invaders,
1979 through 1981, 1983 and 1984; Manu Tuiasosopo, defensive tackle with San Francisco 49ers;
Terry Tautolo, linebacker with Detroit Lions; and John Tautolo, guard with Portland Breakers;
related to Matt Elisara, nose tackle with Denver Gold and Oakland Invaders, 1983.

Named as quarterback on THE SPORTING NEWS College All-America Team, 1978.
Selected by Cincinnati in 1st round (3rd player selected) of 1979 NFL draft.
On suspended list, November 20 through remainder of 1982 season.
Traded by Cincinnati Bengals to Tampa Bay Buccaneers for 1st round pick in 1984 draft, June 2, 1983.
Selected by Seattle Mariners' organization in 34th round of free-agent draft, June 5, 1979.

						—PASSING—						—RUSHING—				—TOTAL—	
Year	Club	G.	Att.	Cmp.	Pct.	Gain	T.P.	P.I.	Avg.	Att.	Yds.	Avg.	TD.	TD.	Pts.	F.
1979—Cincinnati NFL		9	87	39	44.8	481	1	5	5.53	21	116	5.5	5	5	30	3
1980—Cincinnati NFL		14	234	115	49.1	1324	11	12	5.66	18	84	4.7	1	1	6	5
1981—Cincinnati NFL		8	49	21	42.9	267	1	2	5.45		None			0	0	0
1982—Cincinnati NFL		1			None						None			0	0	0
1983—Tampa Bay NFL		14	423	249	58.9	2906	18	21	6.87	26	27	1.0	0	0	0	10
1984—Tampa Bay NFL		5	52	25	48.1	337	2	5	6.48	5	35	7.0	0	0	0	1
Pro Totals—6 Years		51	845	449	53.1	5315	33	45	6.29	70	262	3.7	6	6	36	19

Quarterback Rating Points: 1979 (42.4), 1980 (61.0), 1981 (50.1), 1983 (73.3), 1984 (42.4). Total—63.5.
Additional pro statistics: Recovered one fumble, 1979 and 1984; recovered three fumbles and fumbled five times for minus one yard, 1980; recovered five fumbles, 1983.
Played in AFC Championship Game following 1981 season.
Member of Cincinnati Bengals for NFL Championship Game following 1981 season; did not play.

L. DONNELL THOMPSON
(Known by middle name.)
Defensive End—Indianapolis Colts

Born October 27, 1958, at Lumberton, N.C.
Height, 6.05. Weight, 263.
High School—Lumberton, N.C.
Attended University of North Carolina.

Selected by Baltimore in 1st round (18th player selected) of 1981 NFL draft.
On physically unable to perform/active with shoulder injury, July 24 through August 22, 1982; activated, August 23, 1982.
Franchise transferred to Indianapolis, March 31, 1984.
Placed on suspended list, August 12 through September 11, 1984.
On non-football injury list with shoulder and back injuries, September 12 through October 11, 1984; activated, October 12, 1984.
Baltimore NFL, 1981 through 1983; Indianapolis NFL, 1984.
Games: 1981 (13), 1982 (9), 1983 (14), 1984 (10). Total—46.
Pro statistics: Recovered one fumble, 1981; credited with one safety, 1983.

LEONARD IRWIN THOMPSON
Wide Receiver—Detroit Lions

Born July 28, 1952, at Oklahoma City, Okla.
Height, 5.11. Weight, 192.
High School—Tucson, Ariz., Pueblo.
Attended Arizona Western College and Oklahoma State University.

Selected by Detroit in 8th round (194th player selected) of 1975 NFL draft.
On physically unable to perform/active with foot injury, July 29 through August 30, 1982; activated, August 31, 1982.
Placed on did not report list, August 20 through August 27, 1984.
Reported and granted roster exemption, August 28 through August 31, 1984; activated, September 1, 1984.

			—RUSHING—				PASS RECEIVING				—TOTAL—	
Year	Club	G.	Att.	Yds.	Avg.	TD.	P.C.	Yds.	Avg.	TD.	TD.	Pts.	F.
1975—Detroit NFL		14	1	−12	−12.0	0		None			0	0	2
1976—Detroit NFL		14	1	0	0.0	0	3	52	17.3	0	0	0	0
1977—Detroit NFL		14	31	91	2.9	1	7	42	6.0	0	2	12	0
1978—Detroit NFL		16	1	7	7.0	0	10	167	16.7	4	4	24	2
1979—Detroit NFL		15	5	24	4.8	0	24	451	18.8	2	2	12	3
1980—Detroit NFL		16	6	61	10.2	0	19	511	26.9	3	3	18	1
1981—Detroit NFL		16	10	75	7.5	0	30	550	18.3	3	4	24	1
1982—Detroit NFL		9	2	16	8.0	0	17	328	19.3	4	4	24	0
1983—Detroit NFL		13	4	72	18.0	1	41	752	18.3	3	4	24	2
1984—Detroit NFL		16	3	−7	−2.3	0	50	773	15.5	6	6	36	1
Pro Totals—10 Years		143	64	327	5.1	3	201	3626	18.0	25	29	174	12

Year Club	KICKOFF RETURNS					Year Club	KICKOFF RETURNS			
	G.	No.	Yds.	Avg.	TD.		G.	No.	Yds.	Avg.	TD.
1975—Detroit NFL	14	12	271	22.6	0	1981—Detroit NFL	16	None		
1976—Detroit NFL	14	5	86	17.2	0	1982—Detroit NFL	9	None		
1977—Detroit NFL	14	5	84	16.8	0	1983—Detroit NFL	13	None		
1978—Detroit NFL	16	8	207	25.9	0	1984—Detroit NFL	16	None		
1979—Detroit NFL	15	6	151	25.2	0	Pro Totals—10 Years	143	36	799	22.2	0
1980—Detroit NFL	16	None								

Additional pro statistics: Recovered one fumble, 1976, 1981, 1983 and 1984; ran two yards with blocked punt for a touchdown and attempted one pass with no completions, 1977; returned three punts for 19 yards and recovered four fumbles, 1978; returned nine punts for 117 yards, 1979; recovered two fumbles, 1980.

ROBERT THOMPSON
Linebacker—Tampa Bay Buccaneers
Born February 4, 1960, at Chicago, Ill.
Height, 6.03. Weight, 221.
High School—Blue Island, Ill., Eisenhower.
Attended University of Michigan.

Selected by Michigan in 1983 USFL territorial draft.
Selected by Houston in 8th round (198th player selected) of 1983 NFL draft.
Signed by Houston Oilers, June 25, 1983.
Released by Houston Oilers, August 29, 1983; signed as free agent by Tampa Bay Buccaneers, October 12, 1983.
On injured reserve with broken toes, August 27 through October 17, 1984; activated after clearing procedural waivers, October 19, 1984.
Tampa Bay NFL, 1983 and 1984.
Games: 1983 (10), 1984 (9). Total—19.
Pro statistics: Recovered two fumbles, 1983.

TED CLARENCE THOMPSON
Linebacker—Houston Oilers
Born January 17, 1953, at Atlanta, Tex.
Height, 6.01. Weight, 219.
High School—Atlanta, Tex.
Received bachelor of business administration degree from Southern Methodist University.

Signed as free agent by Houston Oilers, 1975.
Houston NFL, 1975 through 1984.
Games: 1975 (14), 1976 (14), 1977 (14), 1978 (16), 1979 (16), 1980 (15), 1981 (16), 1982 (9), 1983 (16), 1984 (16). Total—146.
Pro statistics: Returned one kickoff for minus five yards and fumbled once, 1975; recovered one fumble, 1975, 1979 and 1982; returned one kickoff for nine yards and recovered three fumbles, 1977; recovered two fumbles, 1978; scored four points on four extra point kicks on four attempts, 1980; ran five yards with lateral from interception and returned one kickoff for 16 yards, 1984.
Played in AFC Championship Game following 1978 and 1979 seasons.

VINCE THOMPSON
Fullback—Detroit Lions
Born February 21, 1957, at Trenton, N.J.
Height, 6.00. Weight, 225.
High School—Levittown, Pa., Woodrow Wilson.
Attended Villanova University.

Signed as free agent by Denver Broncos, May 10, 1979.
Released by Denver Broncos, August 14, 1979; signed as free agent by Philadelphia Eagles, February 1, 1980.
Released by Philadelphia Eagles, August 18, 1980; signed as free agent by Detroit Lions, May 8, 1981.
On inactive list, September 12, 1982.
On injured reserve with abdominal strain, November 20 through remainder of 1982 season.
On injured reserve with pulled hamstring, September 2 through October 7, 1983; activated, October 8, 1983.
On non-football injury list with torn Achilles tendon, July 22 through entire 1984 season.
Active for 1 game with Detroit Lions in 1982; did not play.

Year Club		RUSHING				PASS RECEIVING				—TOTAL—		
	G.	Att.	Yds.	Avg.	TD.	P.C.	Yds.	Avg.	TD.	TD.	Pts.	F.
1981—Detroit NFL	13	35	211	6.0	1	4	40	10.0	0	1	6	1
1983—Detroit NFL	10	40	138	3.5	1	4	16	4.0	0	1	6	1
Pro Totals—3 Years	23	75	349	4.7	2	8	56	7.0	0	2	12	2

WILLIS HOPE THOMPSON
(Weegie)
Wide Receiver—Pittsburgh Steelers
Born March 21, 1961, at Pensacola, Fla.
Height, 6.06. Weight, 210.
High School—Midlothian, Va.
Received bachelor of science degree in management from Florida State University in 1984.

Selected by Tampa Bay in 1984 USFL territorial draft.
USFL rights traded with rights to quarterback Kelly Lowrey by Tampa Bay Bandits to Jacksonville Bulls for rights to wide receiver Mark Militello and running back Mike Grayson, January 4, 1984.
Selected by Pittsburgh in 4th round (108th player selected) of 1984 NFL draft.

Signed by Pittsburgh Steelers, July 22, 1984.

			—PASS RECEIVING—			
Year Club	G.	P.C.	Yds.	Avg.	TD.	
1984—Pittsburgh NFL	16	17	291	17.1	3	

Additional pro statistics: Fumbled once, 1984.
Played in AFC Championship Game following 1984 season.

DON THORP
Nose Tackle—New Orleans Saints
Born July 10, 1962, at Chicago, Ill.
Height, 6.04. Weight, 260.
High School—Buffalo Grove, Ill.
Attended University of Illinois.

Named as defensive lineman on THE SPORTING NEWS College All-America Team, 1983.
Selected by Chicago in 1984 USFL territorial draft.
Selected by New Orleans in 6th round (156th player selected) of 1984 NFL draft.
Signed by New Orleans Saints, June 21, 1984.
On injured reserve with neck injury, October 9 through remainder of 1984 season.
New Orleans NFL, 1984.
Games: 1984 (5).

CLIFFORD RAY THRIFT
(Cliff)
Linebacker—San Diego Chargers
Born May 3, 1956, at Dallas, Tex.
Height, 6.01. Weight, 237.
High School—Purcell, Okla.
Attended East Central (Okla.) University.

Selected by San Diego in 3rd round (73rd player selected) of 1979 NFL draft.
On injured reserve with ruptured tricep, October 28 through December 30, 1981; activated, December 31, 1981.
On injured reserve with pulled hamstring, September 5 through November 11, 1983; activated, November 12, 1983.

		—INTERCEPTIONS—			
Year Club	G.	No.	Yds.	Avg.	TD.
1979—San Diego NFL	16		None		
1980—San Diego NFL	15	1	0	0.0	0
1981—San Diego NFL	7		None		
1982—San Diego NFL	9	2	16	8.0	0
1983—San Diego NFL	6		None		
1984—San Diego NFL	16		None		
Pro Totals—6 Years	69	3	16	5.3	0

Additional pro statistics: Returned one kickoff for 11 yards, 1979; recovered two fumbles, 1979 and 1982; recovered one fumble, 1980.
Played in AFC Championship Game following 1980 and 1981 seasons.

DENNIS LEE THURMAN
Cornerback—Dallas Cowboys
Born April 13, 1956, at Los Angeles, Calif.
Height, 5.11. Weight, 175.
High School—Santa Monica, Calif.
Received degree in journalism from University of Southern California.

Selected by Dallas in 11th round (306th player selected) of 1978 NFL draft.

		—INTERCEPTIONS—			
Year Club	G.	No.	Yds.	Avg.	TD.
1978—Dallas NFL	16	2	35	17.5	0
1979—Dallas NFL	16	1	0	0.0	0
1980—Dallas NFL	16	5	114	22.8	1
1981—Dallas NFL	16	9	187	20.8	0
1982—Dallas NFL	9	3	75	25.0	★1
1983—Dallas NFL	16	6	49	8.2	0
1984—Dallas NFL	16	5	81	16.2	1
Pro Totals—7 Years	105	31	541	17.5	3

Additional pro statistics: Returned three kickoffs for 42 yards, returned one punt for no yards and fumbled twice, 1978; recovered two fumbles, 1978 and 1983; recovered one fumble, 1979, 1981, 1982 and 1984; recovered two fumbles for 14 yards, 1980; returned one kickoff for 17 yards, 1982; recovered fumble in end zone for a touchdown, 1983.
Played in NFC Championship Game following 1978 and 1980 through 1982 seasons.
Played in NFL Championship Game following 1978 season.

JOHN TICE
Tight End—New Orleans Saints
Born June 22, 1960, at Bayshore, N.Y.
Height, 6.05. Weight, 243.
High School—Central Islip, N.Y.
Attended University of Maryland.
Brother of Mike Tice, tight end with Seattle Seahawks.

Selected by Washington in 1983 USFL territorial draft.
Selected by New Orleans in 3rd round (65th player selected) of 1983 NFL draft.
Signed by New Orleans Saints, July 6, 1983.
On injured reserve with ankle injury, November 19 through remainder of 1984 season.

		—PASS RECEIVING—			
Year Club	G.	P.C.	Yds.	Avg.	TD.
1983—New Orleans NFL........	16	7	33	4.7	1
1984—New Orleans NFL........	10	6	55	9.2	1
Pro Totals—2 Years...........	26	13	88	6.8	2

Additional pro statistics: Recovered two fumbles, 1983.

MICHAEL PETER TICE
(Mike)
Tight End—Seattle Seahawks
Born February 2, 1959, at Bayshore, N.Y.
Height, 6.07. Weight, 250.
High School—Central Islip, N.Y.
Attended University of Maryland.
Brother of John Tice, tight end with New Orleans Saints.

Signed as free agent by Seattle Seahawks, April 30, 1981.

		—PASS RECEIVING—			
Year Club	G.	P.C.	Yds.	Avg.	TD.
1981—Seattle NFL....................	16	5	47	9.4	0
1982—Seattle NFL....................	9	9	46	5.1	0
1983—Seattle NFL....................	15		None		
1984—Seattle NFL....................	16	8	90	11.3	3
Pro Totals—4 Years...........	56	22	183	8.3	3

Additional pro statistics: Recovered one fumble, 1982 and 1983; returned two kickoffs for 28 yards, 1983.
Played in AFC Championship Game following 1983 season.

PATRICK LEE TILLEY
(Pat)
Wide Receiver—St. Louis Cardinals
Born February 15, 1953, at Shreveport, La.
Height, 5.10. Weight, 178.
High School—Shreveport, La., Fair Park.
Received bachelor of arts degree in sociology from Louisiana Tech University.

Selected by St. Louis in 4th round (114th player selected) of 1976 NFL draft.
On injured reserve with groin injury, December 17 through remainder of 1980 season.

		-PASS RECEIVING-				-PUNT RETURNS-				—TOTAL—		
Year Club	G.	P.C.	Yds.	Avg.	TD.	No.	Yds.	Avg.	TD.	TD.	Pts.	F.
1976—St. Louis NFL................................	13	26	407	15.7	1	15	146	9.7	0	1	6	2
1977—St. Louis NFL................................	14	5	64	12.8	0	13	111	8.5	0	0	0	1
1978—St. Louis NFL................................	16	62	900	14.5	3	2	8	4.0	0	3	18	1
1979—St. Louis NFL................................	16	57	938	16.5	6		None			6	36	0
1980—St. Louis NFL................................	14	68	966	14.2	6		None			6	36	0
1981—St. Louis NFL................................	16	66	1040	15.8	3		None			3	18	1
1982—St. Louis NFL................................	9	36	465	12.9	2		None			2	12	0
1983—St. Louis NFL................................	16	44	690	15.7	5		None			5	30	1
1984—St. Louis NFL................................	16	52	758	14.6	5		None			5	30	1
Pro Totals—9 Years...................	130	416	6228	15.0	31	30	265	8.8	0	31	186	7

Additional pro statistics: Recovered one fumble, 1977, 1980 and 1983; rushed once for 32 yards, 1978.
Named to play in Pro Bowl (NFL All-Star Game) following 1980 season; replaced due to injury by Wallace Francis.

SCOTT TINSLEY
Quarterback—Los Angeles Rams
Born November 14, 1959, at Oklahoma City, Okla.
Height, 6.02. Weight, 195.
High School—Oklahoma City, Okla., Putnam City.
Attended University of Southern California.

Signed as free agent by Los Angeles Rams, May 12, 1983.
Released by Los Angeles Rams, August 22, 1983; re-signed by Rams after clearing procedural waivers, April 20, 1984.
On injured reserve with Achilles tendon injury, August 21 through entire 1984 season.

ANDRE BERNARD TIPPETT
Linebacker—New England Patriots
Born December 27, 1959, at Birmingham, Ala.
Height, 6.03. Weight, 241.
High School—Newark, N.J., Barringer.
Attended Ellsworth Community College and received bachelor of liberal arts degree from
University of Iowa in 1983.
Cousin of Andre Williams, linebacker at Delaware State College.

Selected by New England in 2nd round (41st player selected) of 1982 NFL draft.
New England NFL, 1982 through 1984.
Games: 1982 (9), 1983 (15), 1984 (16). Total—40.
Pro statistics: Recovered one fumble, 1982 and 1983.
Played in Pro Bowl (NFL All-Star Game) following 1984 season.

GLEN W. TITENSOR
Name pronounced TIGHT-en-sir.
Guard—Dallas Cowboys
Born February 21, 1958, at Bellflower, Calif.
Height, 6.04. Weight, 264.
High School—Garden Grove, Calif., Bolsa Grande.
Attended University of California at Los Angeles and Brigham Young University.

Selected by Dallas in 3rd round (81st player selected) of 1981 NFL draft.
Dallas NFL, 1981 through 1984.
Games: 1981 (16), 1982 (4), 1983 (15), 1984 (15). Total—50.
Pro statistics: Recovered one fumble, 1981.
Played in NFC Championship Game following 1981 season.
Member of Dallas Cowboys for NFC Championship Game following 1982 season; did not play.

RICHARD TODD
Quarterback—New Orleans Saints
Born November 19, 1953, at Birmingham, Ala.
Height, 6.02. Weight, 212.
High School—Mobile, Ala., Davidson
Received bachelor of science degree in physical education from University of Alabama.

Established NFL record for most completions, game (42), September 21, 1980, vs. San Francisco 49ers.
Selected by New York Jets in 1st round (6th player selected) of 1976 NFL draft.
On injured reserve with broken collarbone, November 21 through remainder of 1978 season.
Traded by New York Jets to New Orleans Saints for 1st round pick in 1984 draft, February 18, 1984.

					PASSING						RUSHING				TOTAL	
Year	Club	G.	Att.	Cmp.	Pct.	Gain	T.P.	P.I.	Avg.	Att.	Yds.	Avg.	TD.	TD.	Pts.	F.
1976—N.Y. Jets NFL		13	162	65	40.1	870	3	12	5.37	28	107	3.8	1	1	6	5
1977—N.Y. Jets NFL		12	265	133	50.2	1863	11	17	7.03	24	46	1.9	2	2	12	4
1978—N.Y. Jets NFL		5	107	60	56.1	849	6	10	7.93	14	18	1.3	0	0	0	1
1979—N.Y. Jets NFL		15	334	171	51.2	2660	16	22	7.96	36	93	2.6	5	5	30	7
1980—N.Y. Jets NFL		16	479	264	55.1	3329	17	*30	6.95	49	330	6.7	5	5	30	10
1981—N.Y. Jets NFL		16	497	279	56.1	3231	25	13	6.50	32	131	4.1	0	0	0	5
1982—N.Y. Jets NFL		9	261	153	58.6	1961	14	8	7.51	13	—5	—0.4	1	1	6	4
1983—N.Y. Jets NFL		16	518	308	59.5	3478	18	26	6.71	35	101	2.9	0	0	0	5
1984—New Orleans NFL		15	312	161	51.6	2178	11	19	6.98	28	111	4.0	0	0	0	9
Pro Totals—9 Years		117	2935	1594	54.3	20419	121	157	6.96	259	932	3.6	14	14	84	50

Quarterback Rating Points: 1976 (33.4), 1977 (60.6), 1978 (61.8), 1979 (66.4), 1980 (62.4), 1981 (81.8), 1982 (87.3), 1983 (70.3), 1984 (60.6). Total—67.9.
Additional pro statistics: Recovered two fumbles, 1976 and 1981; fumbled once for minus three yards, 1978; recovered four fumbles and fumbled seven times for minus 10 yards, 1979; recovered three fumbles and fumbled 10 times for minus three yards, 1980; caught one pass for one yard, 1981; fumbled four times for minus six yards, 1982; recovered one fumble, 1983; recovered three fumbles and fumbled nine times for minus 16 yards, 1984.
Played in AFC Championship Game following 1982 season.

JEFFREY MARK TOEWS
Name pronounced Taves.
(Jeff)
Guard-Center—Miami Dolphins
Born November 4, 1957, at San Jose, Calif.
Height, 6.03. Weight, 255.
High School—San Jose, Calif., Del Mar.
Attended University of Washington.
Brother of Loren Toews, linebacker with Pittsburgh Steelers, 1973 through 1983.

Named as offensive tackle on THE SPORTING NEWS College All-America Team, 1978.
Selected by Miami in 2nd round (53rd player selected) of 1979 NFL draft.
On injured reserve, December 7 through remainder of 1980 season.
Miami NFL, 1979 through 1984.
Games: 1979 (11), 1980 (7), 1981 (9), 1982 (9), 1983 (8), 1984 (16). Total—60.
Played in AFC Championship Game following 1982 and 1984 seasons.
Played in NFL Championship Game following 1982 and 1984 seasons.

STACEY J. TORAN
Safety—Los Angeles Raiders
Born November 10, 1961, at Indianapolis, Ind.
Height, 6.02. Weight, 200.
High School—Indianapolis, Ind., Broad Ripple.
Received degree from University of Notre Dame in 1984.

Selected by Chicago in 1984 USFL territorial draft.

Selected by Los Angeles Raiders in 6th round (168th player selected) of 1984 NFL draft.
Signed by Los Angeles Raiders, June 2, 1984.
Los Angeles Raiders NFL, 1984.
Games: 1984 (16).

MORRIS TOWNS
Offensive Tackle—Washington Redskins
Born January 10, 1954, at St. Louis, Mo.
Height, 6.04. Weight, 261.
High School—St. Louis, Mo., Vashon.
Attended University of Missouri and attending University of Houston.

Selected by Houston in 1st round (11th player selected) of 1977 NFL draft.
On injured reserve, October 17 through remainder of 1977 season.
Released by Houston Oilers, August 27, 1984; awarded on waivers to Los Angeles Raiders, August 28, 1984.
Traded by Los Angeles Raiders to Washington Redskins for 10th round pick in 1985 draft, August 30, 1984.
On injured reserve with ankle injury, September 29 through December 28, 1984; activated, December 29, 1984.
Houston NFL, 1977 through 1983; Washington NFL, 1984.
Games: 1977 (1), 1978 (16), 1979 (16), 1980 (16), 1981 (16), 1982 (9), 1983 (14), 1984 (4). Total—92.
Pro statistics: Recovered one fumble, 1979.
Played in AFC Championship Game following 1978 season.
Member of Houston Oilers for AFC Championship Game following 1979 season; did not play.

ANDRE TOWNSEND
Defensive End-Nose Tackle—Denver Broncos
Born October 8, 1962, at Chicago, Ill.
Height, 6.03. Weight, 265.
High School—Aberdeen, Miss.
Attended University of Mississippi.

Selected by Birmingham in 1984 USFL territorial draft.
Selected by Denver in 2nd round (46th player selected) of 1984 NFL draft.
Signed by Denver Broncos, June 18, 1984.
Denver NFL, 1984.
Games: 1984 (16).
Pro statistics: Recovered one fumble, 1984.

GREG TOWNSEND
Defensive End—Los Angeles Raiders
Born November 3, 1961, at Los Angeles, Calif.
Height, 6.03. Weight, 240.
High School—Compton, Calif., Dominguez.
Attended Long Beach City College and Texas Christian University.

Selected by Oakland in 7th round (79th player selected) of 1983 USFL draft.
Selected by Los Angeles Raiders in 4th round (110th player selected) of 1983 NFL draft.
Signed by Los Angeles Raiders, July 7, 1983.
Los Angeles Raiders NFL, 1983 and 1984.
Games: 1983 (16), 1984 (16). Total—32.
Pro statistics: Recovered one fumble for 66 yards and a touchdown, 1983.
Played in AFC Championship Game following 1983 season.
Played in NFL Championship Game following 1983 season.

JOHN TUGGLE
Running Back—New York Giants
Born January 31, 1961, at Honolulu, Haw.
Height, 6.01. Weight, 210.
High School—San Jose, Calif., Independence.
Attended University of California at Berkeley.

Selected by Boston in 5th round (59th player selected) of 1983 USFL draft.
Selected by New York Giants in 12th round (335th player selected) of 1983 NFL draft.
Signed by New York Giants, June 13, 1983.
On physically unable to perform/reserve with knee injury, July 18 through entire 1984 season.

| | | —————RUSHING————— | | | | PASS RECEIVING | | | | —TOTAL— | | |
Year Club	G.	Att.	Yds.	Avg.	TD.	P.C.	Yds.	Avg.	TD.	TD.	Pts.	F.
1983—New York Giants NFL	16	17	49	2.9	1	3	50	16.7	0	1	6	0

| | | KICKOFF RETURNS | | | |
Year Club	G.	No.	Yds.	Avg.	TD.
1983—New York Giants NFL	16	9	156	17.3	0

—DID YOU KNOW—

That the 1984 NFL draft was the first since 1974 in which a quarterback was not selected on the first round? The first quarterback selected in 1974, Danny White by the Cowboys, was picked as the first player in the third round. In 1984, Cincinnati selected Boomer Esiason as the 10th player in the second round.

MANU'ULA ASOVALU TUIASOSOPO

Name pronounced Tooey-ahso-sopo.

In Samoan, first name means, "Happy Bird".

(Manu)
Defensive Tackle—San Francisco 49ers

Born August 30, 1957, at Los Angeles, Calif.
Height, 6.03. Weight, 252.
High School—Long Beach, Calif., St. Anthony.
Attended University of California at Los Angeles.
Cousin of Terry Tautolo, linebacker with Detroit Lions; John Tautolo, guard with Portland Breakers;
Frank Manumaleuga, linebacker with Kansas City Chiefs and Oakland Invaders, 1979 through 1981, 1983 and 1984;
and Jack Thompson, quarterback with Tampa Bay Buccaneers; related to Matt Elisara,
nose tackle with Denver Gold and Oakland Invaders, 1983.

Selected by Seattle in 1st round (18th player selected) of 1979 NFL draft.
On physically unable to perform/active with knee injury, July 30 through August 15, 1982; activated, August 16, 1982.
Traded by Seattle Seahawks to San Francisco 49ers for 4th round pick in 1984 draft and 10th round pick in 1985 draft, April 4, 1984.
Seattle NFL, 1979 through 1983; San Francisco NFL, 1984.
Games: 1979 (16), 1980 (16), 1981 (16), 1982 (9), 1983 (16), 1984 (16). Total—89.
Pro statistics: Recovered one fumble, 1980 and 1982; recovered three fumbles, 1981; recovered two fumbles for six yards, 1984.
Played in AFC Championship Game following 1983 season.
Played in NFC Championship Game following 1984 season.
Played in NFL Championship Game following 1984 season.

MARK PULEMAU TUINEI

Name pronounced TWO-e-nay.

Defensive Tackle—Dallas Cowboys

Born March 31, 1960, at Nanakuli, Oahu, Haw.
Height, 6.05. Weight, 270.
High School—Honolulu, Haw., Punahou.
Attended University of California at Los Angeles and University of Hawaii.
Brother of Tom Tuinei, defensive tackle with Edmonton Eskimos.

Selected by Boston in 19th round (227th player selected) of 1983 USFL draft.
Signed as free agent by Dallas Cowboys, April 28, 1983.
Dallas NFL, 1983 and 1984.
Games: 1983 (10), 1984 (16). Total—26.

WILLIE TULLIS
Cornerback—Houston Oilers

Born April 5, 1958, at Newville, Ala.
Height, 6.00. Weight, 195.
High School—Headland, Ala.
Attended University of Southern Mississippi and Troy State University.

Selected by Houston in 8th round (217th player selected) of 1981 NFL draft.

Year Club	G.	INTERCEPTIONS No.	Yds.	Avg.	TD.	-PUNT RETURNS- No.	Yds.	Avg.	TD.	—KICKOFF RET.— No.	Yds.	Avg.	TD.	—TOTAL— TD.	Pts.	F.
1981—Houston NFL	16	None				2	29	14.5	0	32	779	24.3	*1	1	6	0
1982—Houston NFL	9	None					None			5	91	18.2	0	0	0	0
1983—Houston NFL	16	5	65	13.0	0		None			1	16	16.0	0	0	0	0
1984—Houston NFL	16	4	48	12.0	0		None				None			0	0	1
Pro Totals—4 Years	57	9	113	12.6	0	2	29	14.5	0	38	886	23.3	1	1	6	1

Additional pro statistics: Recovered one fumble, 1984.

DARRYL TURNER
Wide Receiver—Seattle Seahawks

Born December 15, 1961, at Wadley, Ga.
Height, 6.03. Weight, 198.
High School—Flint, Mich., Southwestern.
Attended Michigan State University.

Selected by Michigan in 1984 USFL territorial draft.
Selected by Seattle in 2nd round (49th player selected) of 1984 NFL draft.
Signed by Seattle Seahawks, May 16, 1984.

Year Club	G.	——PASS RECEIVING—— P.C.	Yds.	Avg.	TD.
1984—Seattle NFL	16	35	715	20.4	10

JIMMIE TURNER
Linebacker—Dallas Cowboys

Born February 16, 1962, at Vienna, Ga.
Height, 6.02. Weight, 220.
High School—Vienna, Ga.
Received bachelor of science degree in business administration
from Presbyterian College in 1984.

Signed as free agent by Dallas Cowboys, May 3, 1984.
Released by Dallas Cowboys, August 27, 1984; re-signed by Cowboys, November 14, 1984.
Dallas NFL, 1984.
Games: 1984 (5).

JIMMY LEE TURNER
Cornerback—Cincinnati Bengals

Born June 15, 1959, at Sherman, Tex.
Height, 6.00. Weight, 187.
High School—Sherman, Tex.
Attended University of California at Los Angeles.

Selected by Philadelphia in 7th round (80th player selected) of 1983 USFL draft.
Selected by Cincinnati in 3rd round (81st player selected) of 1983 NFL draft.
Signed by Cincinnati Bengals, May 31, 1983.
Cincinnati NFL, 1983 and 1984.
Games: 1983 (16), 1984 (16). Total—32.
Pro statistics: Intercepted one pass for four yards and recovered one fumble, 1984.

JOHN TURNER
Cornerback-Safety—San Diego Chargers

Born February 22, 1956, at Miami, Fla.
Height, 6.00. Weight, 193.
High School—Miami, Fla., Norland.
Received bachelor of science degree in physical education from University of Miami (Fla.) in 1978.

Selected by Minnesota in 2nd round (48th player selected) of 1978 NFL draft.
Traded by Minnesota Vikings to San Diego Chargers for offensive tackle Billy Shields, August 10, 1984. (Shields did not report and was returned in exchange for 3rd round pick in 1985 draft, September 3, 1984.)
Left San Diego Chargers camp voluntarily, August 13 through August 20, 1984.
Returned and granted roster exemption, August 21 and August 22, 1984; activated, August 23, 1984.

		—INTERCEPTIONS—			
Year Club	G.	No.	Yds.	Avg.	TD.
1978—Minnesota NFL.............	14	1	15	15.0	0
1979—Minnesota NFL.............	16	2	48	24.0	0
1980—Minnesota NFL.............	16	6	22	3.7	0
1981—Minnesota NFL.............	13		None		
1982—Minnesota NFL.............	9	2	43	21.5	*1
1983—Minnesota NFL.............	16	6	37	6.2	0
1984—San Diego NFL	15	2	43	21.5	0
Pro Totals—7 Years............	99	19	208	10.9	1

Additional pro statistics: Returned one punt for no yards and fumbled once, 1979; recovered one fumble, 1980 and 1984; recovered one fumble for 35 yards, 1982; recovered two fumbles for 24 yards, 1983.

KEENA TURNER
Linebacker—San Francisco 49ers

Born October 22, 1958, at Chicago, Ill.
Height, 6.02. Weight, 219.
High School—Chicago, Ill., Vocational.
Attended Purdue University.

Selected by San Francisco in 2nd round (39th player selected) of 1980 NFL draft.

		—INTERCEPTIONS—			
Year Club	G.	No.	Yds.	Avg.	TD.
1980—San Francisco NFL	16	2	15	7.5	0
1981—San Francisco NFL	16	1	0	0.0	0
1982—San Francisco NFL	9		None		
1983—San Francisco NFL	15		None		
1984—San Francisco NFL	16	4	51	12.8	0
Pro Totals—5 Years............	72	7	66	9.4	0

Additional pro statistics: Recovered three fumbles, 1981; recovered one fumble, 1983.
Played in NFC Championship Game following 1981, 1983 and 1984 seasons.
Played in NFL Championship Game following 1981 and 1984 seasons.
Played in Pro Bowl (NFL All-Star Game) following 1984 season.

MAURICE ANTOINE TURNER
Running Back—Minnesota Vikings

Born September 10, 1960, at Salt Lake City, Utah.
Height, 5.11. Weight, 200.
High School—Layton, Utah.
Attended Utah State University.

Selected by Minnesota in 12th round (325th player selected) of 1983 NFL draft.
Released by Minnesota Vikings, August 29, 1983.
USFL rights traded by Houston Gamblers to Oakland Invaders for rights to wide receiver Perry Parmelee, October 28, 1983.
Signed by Oakland Invaders, November 20, 1983.
Released by Oakland Invaders, February 9, 1984; re-signed by Minnesota Vikings after clearing procedural waivers, May 10, 1984.
Released by Minnesota Vikings, August 29, 1984; re-signed by Vikings, September 12, 1984.
Minnesota NFL, 1984.
Games: 1984 (13).
Pro statistics: Returned two kickoffs for 21 yards, 1984.

PERRY WARREN TUTTLE
Wide Receiver—Atlanta Falcons
Born August 2, 1959, at Lexington, N.C.
Height, 6.00. Weight, 178.
High School—Winston-Salem, N.C., North Davidson.
Attended Clemson University.

Named as wide receiver on THE SPORTING NEWS College All-America Team, 1981.
Selected by Buffalo in 1st round (19th player selected) of 1982 NFL draft.
On injured reserve with separated shoulder, August 30 through October 6, 1983; activated, October 7, 1983.
Traded by Buffalo Bills to Tampa Bay Buccaneers for draft choice, August 21, 1984.
Released by Tampa Bay Buccaneers, October 8, 1984; awarded on waivers to Atlanta Falcons, October 9, 1984.

		—PASS RECEIVING—			
Year Club	G.	P.C.	Yds.	Avg.	TD.
1982—Buffalo NFL...................	7	7	107	15.3	0
1983—Buffalo NFL...................	9	17	261	15.4	3
1984—T.B. (3)-Atl. (5) NFL	8	1	7	7.0	0
Pro Totals—3 Years............	24	25	375	15.0	3

Additional pro statistics: Fumbled once, 1983.

ANDRE MIGUEL TYLER
Wide Receiver—Tampa Bay Buccaneers
Born July 17, 1959, at Tucson, Ariz.
Height, 6.00. Weight, 180.
High School—Long Beach, Calif., Polytechnic.
Received bachelor of science degree in communications from Stanford University in 1981.

Selected by Tampa Bay in 6th round (158th player selected) of 1982 NFL draft.
On inactive list, September 12 and September 19, 1982.
On injured reserve with shoulder injury, August 13 through entire 1984 season.
Active for 7 games with Tampa Bay Buccaneers in 1982; did not play.

		—PASS RECEIVING-				–PUNT RETURNS–				—TOTAL—		
Year Club	G.	P.C.	Yds.	Avg.	TD.	No.	Yds.	Avg.	TD.	TD.	Pts.	F.
1983—Tampa Bay NFL	14	6	77	12.8	0	27	208	7.7	0	0	0	1

WENDELL AVERY TYLER
Running Back—San Francisco 49ers
Born May 20, 1955, at Shreveport, La.
Height, 5.10. Weight, 198.
High School—Los Angeles, Calif., Crenshaw.
Attended University of California at Los Angeles.

Selected by Los Angeles in 3rd round (79th player selected) of 1977 NFL draft.
On injured reserve with knee injury, September 12 through remainder of 1978 season.
On non-football injury list with hip injury, September 3 through October 23, 1980; activated, October 24, 1980.
On injured reserve with dislocated elbow, December 6 through remainder of 1980 season.
Traded with defensive tackle Cody Jones and 3rd round pick in 1983 draft by Los Angeles Rams to San Francisco 49ers for 2nd and 4th round picks in 1983 draft, April 25, 1983.

		—RUSHING—				PASS RECEIVING				—TOTAL—		
Year Club	G.	Att.	Yds.	Avg.	TD.	P.C.	Yds.	Avg.	TD.	TD.	Pts.	F.
1977—Los Angeles Rams NFL	14	61	317	5.2	3	1	3	3.0	0	3	18	0
1978—Los Angeles Rams NFL	2	14	45	3.2	0	2	17	8.5	0	0	0	2
1979—Los Angeles Rams NFL	16	218	1109	*5.1	9	32	308	9.6	1	10	60	9
1980—Los Angeles Rams NFL	4	30	157	5.2	0	2	8	4.0	0	0	0	1
1981—Los Angeles Rams NFL	15	260	1074	4.1	12	45	436	9.7	5	17	102	11
1982—Los Angeles Rams NFL	9	137	564	4.1	9	38	375	9.9	4	13	78	*10
1983—San Francisco NFL	14	176	856	4.9	4	34	285	8.4	2	6	36	7
1984—San Francisco NFL	16	246	1262	5.1	7	28	230	8.2	2	9	54	13
Pro Totals—8 Years..................................	90	1142	5384	4.7	44	182	1662	9.1	14	58	348	53

KICKOFF RETURNS						KICKOFF RETURNS				
Year Club	G.	No.	Yds.	Avg.TD.		Year Club	G.	No.	Yds.	Avg.TD.
1977—L.A. Rams NFL.............	14	24	523	21.8	0	1982—L.A. Rams NFL.............	9		None	
1978—L.A. Rams NFL.............	2	2	31	15.5	0	1983—San Francisco NFL	14		None	
1979—L.A. Rams NFL.............	16	1	16	16.0	0	1984—San Francisco NFL	16		None	
1980—L.A. Rams NFL.............	4		None			Pro Totals—8 Years............	90	27	570	21.1	0
1981—L.A. Rams NFL.............	15		None							

Additional pro statistics: Recovered one fumble, 1978, 1979 and 1982; recovered two fumbles, 1984.
Played in NFC Championship Game following 1979, 1983 and 1984 seasons.
Played in NFL Championship Game following 1979 and 1984 seasons.
Played in Pro Bowl (NFL All-Star Game) following 1984 season.

TIMOTHY G. TYRRELL
(Tim)
Running Back—Atlanta Falcons
Born February 19, 1961, at Chicago, Ill.
Height, 6.01. Weight, 201.
High School—Hoffman Estates, Ill., James B. Conant.
Attended William Rainey Harper College and Northern Illinois University.

Selected by Chicago in 1984 USFL territorial draft.
Signed as free agent by Atlanta Falcons, May 2, 1984.
Released by Atlanta Falcons, August 27, 1984; re-signed by Falcons, October 3, 1984.
Atlanta NFL, 1984.
Games: 1984 (11).
Pro statistics: Returned one kickoff for no yards and recovered three fumbles, 1984.

RICHARD KEITH UECKER
(Known by middle name.)
Guard-Offensive Tackle—Green Bay Packers
Born June 29, 1960, at Hollywood, Fla.
Height, 6.05. Weight, 270.
High School—Hollywood, Fla., Hollywood Hills.
Attended Auburn University.

Selected by Denver in 9th round (243rd player selected) of 1982 NFL draft.
On injured reserve with Achilles tendon injury, August 14 through October 21, 1984.
Awarded on procedural waivers to Green Bay Packers, October 23, 1984.
Denver NFL, 1982 and 1983; Green Bay NFL, 1984.
Games: 1982 (5), 1983 (16), 1984 (6). Total—27.
Pro statistics: Returned one kickoff for 12 yards and fumbled once, 1982.

RICHARD VERN UMPHREY III
(Rich)
Center—New York Giants
Born December 13, 1958, at Garden Grove, Calif.
Height, 6.03. Weight, 270.
High School—Tustin, Calif.
Attended University of Utah and University of Colorado.

Selected by New York Giants in 5th round (129th player selected) of 1982 NFL draft.
On non-football injury list with appendectomy, November 10 through remainder of 1983 season.
New York Giants NFL, 1982 through 1984.
Games: 1982 (9), 1983 (10), 1984 (15). Total—34.
Pro statistics: Fumbled once for minus 24 yards, 1982; recovered one fumble, 1983.

BENJAMIN MICHAEL UTT
(Ben)
Guard—Indianapolis Colts
Born June 13, 1959, at Richmond, Calif.
Height, 6.05. Weight, 280.
High School—Vidalia, Ga.
Received bachelor of science degree in industrial management from Georgia Tech in 1982.

Signed as free agent by Dallas Cowboys, May, 1981.
Released by Dallas Cowboys, August 14, 1981; signed as free agent by Baltimore Colts, January 18, 1982.
Franchise transferred to Indianapolis, March 31, 1984.
Baltimore NFL, 1982 and 1983; Indianapolis NFL, 1984.
Games: 1982 (9), 1983 (16), 1984 (16). Total—41.
Pro statistics: Recovered one fumble, 1984.

KEITH VAN HORNE
Offensive Tackle—Chicago Bears
Born November 6, 1957, at Mt. Lebanon, Pa.
Height, 6.07. Weight, 276.
High School—Fullerton, Calif.
Attended University of Southern California.
Brother of Pete Van Horne, first baseman in Chicago Cubs' organization, 1977.

Named as offensive tackle on THE SPORTING NEWS College All-America Team, 1980.
Selected by Chicago in 1st round (11th player selected) of 1981 NFL draft.
Chicago NFL, 1981 through 1984.
Games: 1981 (14), 1982 (9), 1983 (14), 1984 (14). Total—51.
Pro statistics: Recovered one fumble, 1981 and 1982.
Played in NFC Championship Game following 1984 season.

NORWOOD JACOB VANN JR.
Linebacker—Los Angeles Rams
Born February 18, 1962, at Philadelphia, Pa.
Height, 6.01. Weight, 225.
High School—Warsaw, N.C., James Kenan.
Attended East Carolina University.

Selected by Los Angeles Rams in 10th round (253rd player selected) of 1984 NFL draft.
Los Angeles Rams NFL, 1984.
Games: 1984 (16).
Pro statistics: Credited with one safety and recovered two fumbles, 1984.

JEFFREY ALOYSIUS VAN NOTE
(Jeff)
Center—Atlanta Falcons
Born February 7, 1946, at South Orange, N. J.
Height, 6.02. Weight, 250.
High School—Bardstown, Ky., St. Joseph Prep.
Received bachelor of arts degree in history and political science from
University of Kentucky in 1969.

Selected by Atlanta NFL in 11th round (262nd player selected) of 1969 AFL-NFL draft.
Played in Continental Football League with Huntsville, 1969.
Atlanta NFL, 1969 through 1984.
Games: 1969 (1), 1970 (14), 1971 (14), 1972 (14), 1973 (14), 1974 (14), 1975 (14), 1976 (10), 1977 (14), 1978 (16), 1979 (16), 1980 (16), 1981 (16), 1982 (9), 1983 (16), 1984 (16). Total—214.
Pro statistics: Recovered one fumble, 1970, 1972 and 1981; fumbled once, 1971 and 1975; recovered one fumble for 16 yards, 1979; fumbled once for minus 20 yards, 1981.
Played in Pro Bowl (NFL All-Star Game) following 1974, 1975 and 1979 through 1982 seasons.

BRAD ALAN VAN PELT
Linebacker—Los Angeles Raiders
Born April 5, 1951, at Owosso, Mich.
Height, 6.05. Weight, 235.
High School—Owosso, Mich.
Attended Michigan State University.

Named to THE SPORTING NEWS NFC All-Star Team, 1978 and 1979.
Named as safety on THE SPORTING NEWS College All-America Team, 1972.
Selected by New York Giants in 2nd round (40th player selected) of 1973 NFL draft.
Traded by New York Giants to Minnesota Vikings for running back Tony Galbreath, July 12, 1984.
Placed on did not report list, August 21 through October 2, 1984.
Granted roster exemption, October 3 through October 8, 1984.
Traded by Minnesota Vikings to Los Angeles Raiders for 6th round pick in 1985 draft and 2nd round pick in 1986 draft, October 9, 1984.
Granted roster exemption, October 9 through October 14, 1984; activated, October 15, 1984.
Selected by Detroit Tigers' organization in 10th round of free-agent draft, June 5, 1969.
Selected by California Angels' organization in 13th round of free-agent draft, June 6, 1972.
Selected by St. Louis Cardinals' organization in secondary phase of free-agent draft, January 10, 1973.
Selected by Cleveland Indians' organization in secondary phase of free-agent draft, January 9, 1974.

	—INTERCEPTIONS—						—INTERCEPTIONS—			
Year Club	G.	No.	Yds.	Avg.TD.		Year Club	G.	No.	Yds.	Avg.TD.
1973—N.Y. Giants NFL	5		None			1980—N.Y. Giants NFL	15	3	3	1.0 0
1974—N.Y. Giants NFL	12	2	22	11.0 0		1981—N.Y. Giants NFL	14	1	10	10.0 0
1975—N.Y. Giants NFL	14	3	8	2.7 0		1982—N.Y. Giants NFL	9		None	
1976—N.Y. Giants NFL	14	2	13	6.5 0		1983—N.Y. Giants NFL	16	2	7	3.5 0
1977—N.Y. Giants NFL	14	2	9	4.5 0		1984—L.A. Raiders NFL	9	1	9	9.0 0
1978—N.Y. Giants NFL	14	3	32	10.7 0		Pro Totals—12 Years	152	19	113	5.9 0
1979—N.Y. Giants NFL	16		None							

Additional pro statistics: Recovered two fumbles, 1974, 1981 and 1982; recovered one fumble, 1977; recovered one fumble for 42 yards and caught one pass for 20 yards, 1979; recovered three fumbles for 46 yards, 1980.
Played in Pro Bowl (NFL All-Star Game) following 1976 through 1980 seasons.

ELTON VEALS
Running Back—Pittsburgh Steelers
Born March 26, 1961, at Baton Rouge, La.
Height, 5.11. Weight, 230.
High School—Baton Rouge, La., Istrouma.
Attended Merritt College and Tulane University.

Selected by New Orleans in 1984 USFL territorial draft.
Selected by Pittsburgh in 11th round (303rd player selected) of 1984 NFL draft.
Signed by Pittsburgh Steelers, May 19, 1984.

		—RUSHING—				PASS RECEIVING			—TOTAL—		
Year Club	G.	Att.	Yds.	Avg.	TD.	P.C. Yds.	Avg.	TD.	TD.	Pts.	F.
1984—Pittsburgh NFL	15	31	87	2.8	0	None			0	0	0

Additional pro statistics: Returned four kickoffs for 40 yards and recovered one fumble, 1984.
Played in AFC Championship Game following 1984 season.

DAVID VERSER
Wide Receiver—Cincinnati Bengals

Born March 1, 1958, at Kansas City, Kan.
Height, 6.01. Weight, 200.
High School—Kansas City, Kan., Sumner.
Attended University of Kansas.

Selected by Cincinnati in 1st round (10th player selected) of 1981 NFL draft.

		—RUSHING—				PASS RECEIVING				—TOTAL—		
Year Club	G.	Att.	Yds.	Avg.	TD.	P.C.	Yds.	Avg.	TD.	TD.	Pts.	F.
1981—Cincinnati NFL	16	2	11	5.5	0	6	161	26.8	2	2	12	2
1982—Cincinnati NFL	9	1	1	1.0	0	4	98	24.5	1	1	6	0
1983—Cincinnati NFL	13	2	31	15.5	0	7	82	11.7	0	0	0	0
1984—Cincinnati NFL	11	2	5	2.5	0	6	113	18.8	0	0	0	0
Pro Totals—4 Years	49	7	48	6.9	0	23	454	19.7	3	3	18	2

		KICKOFF RETURNS			
Year Club	G.	No.	Yds.	Avg.	TD.
1981—Cincinnati NFL	16	29	691	23.8	0
1982—Cincinnati NFL	9	16	320	20.0	0
1983—Cincinnati NFL	13	13	253	19.5	0
1984—Cincinnati NFL	11	3	46	15.3	0
Pro Totals—4 Years	49	61	1310	21.5	0

Played in AFC Championship Game following 1981 season.
Played in NFL Championship Game following 1981 season.

THOMAS VIGORITO
(Tom)
Running Back-Wide Receiver—Miami Dolphins

Born October 23, 1959, at Passaic, N.J.
Height, 5.10. Weight, 197.
High School—Wayne, N.J., DePaul.
Attended University of Virginia.

Selected by Miami in 5th round (138th player selected) of 1981 NFL draft.
On injured reserve with knee injury, September 6 through remainder of 1983 season.
On physically unable to perform/active with knee injury, July 19 through August 20, 1984.
On physically unable to perform/reserve with knee injury, August 21 through entire 1984 season.

		—RUSHING—				PASS RECEIVING				—TOTAL—		
Year Club	G.	Att.	Yds.	Avg.	TD.	P.C.	Yds.	Avg.	TD.	TD.	Pts.	F.
1981—Miami NFL	16	35	116	3.3	1	33	237	7.2	2	4	24	1
1982—Miami NFL	9	19	99	5.2	1	24	186	7.8	0	2	12	2
1983—Miami NFL	1		None			1	7	7.0	0	0	0	0
Pro Totals—3 Years	26	54	215	4.0	2	58	430	7.4	2	6	36	3

		—PUNT RETURNS—				—KICKOFF RET.—			
Year Club	G.	No.	Yds.	Avg.	TD.	No.	Yds.	Avg.	TD.
1981—Miami NFL	16	36	379	10.5	1	4	84	21.0	0
1982—Miami NFL	9	20	192	9.6	1		None		
1983—Miami NFL	1	1	62	62.0	0		None		
Pro Totals—3 Years	26	57	633	11.1	2	4	84	21.0	0

Additional pro statistics: Recovered one fumble, 1982.
Played in AFC Championship Game following 1982 season.
Played in NFC Championship Game following 1982 season.

SCOTT VIRKUS
Defensive End—Indianapolis Colts

Born September 7, 1959, at Palo Alto, Calif.
Height, 6.05. Weight, 248.
High School—Rochester, N.Y., Greece Olympia.
Attended City College of San Francisco and Purdue University.

Signed as free agent by Buffalo Bills, May 12, 1983.
Released by Buffalo Bills, September 12, 1984; awarded on waivers to New England Patriots, September 13, 1984.
Released by New England Patriots, November 7, 1984; signed as free agent by Pittsburgh Steelers, December 6, 1984.
Released by Pittsburgh Steelers after failing physical, December 7, 1984; signed as free agent by Indianapolis Colts, December 11, 1984.
Played semi-pro football with North Tonawanda Cougars in 1982.
Buffalo NFL, 1983; Buffalo (2)-New England (5)-Indianapolis (1) NFL, 1984.
Games: 1983 (15), 1984 (8). Total—23.

—DID YOU KNOW—

That during the 1984 season, the Minnesota Vikings had a player older than the head coach? Jan Stenerud, who was 41, handled placekicking duties for 38-year-old Coach Les Steckel.

TIMOTHY VOGLER
(Tim)
Center—Buffalo Bills
Born October 20, 1956, at Troy, O.
Height, 6.03. Weight, 245.
High School—Covington, O.
Attended Ohio State University.

Signed as free agent by Buffalo Bills, May 5, 1979.
On injured reserve with broken hand, August 28 through October 5, 1979; activated, October 6, 1979.
On injured reserve with hamstring injury, November 29 through remainder of 1980 season.
Buffalo NFL, 1979 through 1984.
Games: 1979 (10), 1980 (10), 1981 (14), 1982 (6), 1983 (16), 1984 (16). Total—72.
Pro statistics: Returned one kickoff for no yards, 1980.

UWE DETLEF WALTER von SCHAMANN
Name pronounced OO-va Von-SHAH-mun.
Placekicker—Miami Dolphins
Born April 23, 1956, at West Berlin, Germany.
Height, 6.01. Weight, 188.
High School—Fort Worth, Tex., Eastern Hills.
Attended University of Oklahoma.

Established NFL records for most extra points, season (66), 1984; most extra point attempts, season (70), 1984.
Selected by Dallas Tornado in North American Soccer League draft, 1977.
Selected by Miami in 7th round (189th player selected) of 1979 NFL draft.

		——PLACE KICKING——					
Year	Club	G.	XP.	XPM.	FG.	FGA.	Pts.
1979—Miami NFL		16	36	4	21	29	99
1980—Miami NFL		16	32	0	14	23	74
1981—Miami NFL		16	37	1	24	31	109
1982—Miami NFL		9	21	1	15	20	66
1983—Miami NFL		16	45	3	18	27	99
1984—Miami NFL		16	*66	*4	9	19	93
Pro Totals—6 Years		89	237	13	101	149	540

Additional pro statistics: Punted once for 31 yards, 1979.
Played in AFC Championship Game Following 1982 and 1984 seasons.
Played in NFL Championship Game Following 1982 and 1984 seasons.

HENRY CARL WAECHTER
Defensive End—Chicago Bears
Born February 13, 1959, at Epworth, Ia.
Height, 6.05. Weight, 270.
High School—Epworth, Ia., Western Dubuque.
Attended Waldorf Junior College and University of Nebraska.

Selected by Chicago in 7th round (173rd player selected) of 1982 NFL draft.
Released by Chicago Bears, August 29, 1983; signed as free agent by Baltimore Colts, September 28, 1983.
Franchise transferred to Indianapolis, March 31, 1984.
Released by Indianapolis Colts, September 19, 1984; signed as free agent by Chicago Bears, December 5, 1984.
Chicago NFL, 1982; Baltimore NFL, 1983; Indianapolis (1)-Chicago (2) NFL, 1984.
Games: 1982 (9), 1983 (11), 1984 (3). Total—23.
Played in NFC Championship Game following 1984 season.

DANIEL WRIGHT WAGONER
(Dan)
Defensive Back—Minnesota Vikings
Born December 12, 1959, at High Point, N.C.
Height, 5.10. Weight, 180.
High School—High Point, N.C., T. Wingate Andrews.
Attended University of Kansas.

Selected by Detroit in 9th round (231st player selected) of 1982 NFL draft.
On injured reserve with pulled hamstring, August 30 through December 23, 1982; re-signed after clearing procedural waivers, December 25, 1982.
Released by Detroit Lions, September 8, 1984.
USFL rights traded by Chicago Blitz to Orlando Renegades for rights to running back Reggie Evans, October 12, 1984.
Signed as free agent by Minnesota Vikings, October 31, 1984.
Detroit NFL, 1982 and 1983; Detroit (1)-Minnesota (4) NFL, 1984.
Games: 1982 (1), 1983 (14), 1984 (5). Total—20.

STAN WALDEMORE
Guard-Offensive Tackle—New York Jets
Born February 20, 1955, at Newark, N. J.
Height, 6.04. Weight, 269.
High School—Newark, N. J., Essex Catholic.
Received degree in construction management from University of Nebraska in 1978.

Selected by Atlanta in 3rd round (70th player selected) of 1978 NFL draft.
Released by Atlanta Falcons, September 1, 1978; signed as free agent by New York Jets, October 10, 1978.
Released by New York Jets, August 21, 1979; re-signed by Jets, August 28, 1979.
On injured reserve with knee injury, September 29 through remainder of 1983 season.
New York Jets NFL, 1978 through 1984.
Games: 1978 (4), 1979 (16), 1980 (16), 1981 (16), 1982 (9), 1983 (4), 1984 (14). Total—79.
Pro statistics: Fumbled once for minus three yards, 1980; recovered one fumble, 1982 and 1984.
Played in AFC Championship Game following 1982 season.

BYRON BURNEIL WALKER
Wide Receiver—Seattle Seahawks
Born July 28, 1960, at Scott Air Force Base, Ill.
Height, 6.04. Weight, 190.
High School—Warner Robins, Ga.
Attended The Citadel.

Signed as free agent by Seattle Seahawks, April 30, 1982.

| | | —PASS RECEIVING— | | | |
Year Club	G.	P.C.	Yds.	Avg.	TD.
1982—Seattle NFL	9	10	156	15.6	2
1983—Seattle NFL	16	12	248	20.7	2
1984—Seattle NFL	16	13	236	18.2	1
Pro Totals—3 Years	41	35	640	18.3	5

Played in AFC Championship Game following 1983 season.

DWIGHT GERARD WALKER
Wide Receiver—Cleveland Browns
Born January 10, 1959, at Metairie, La.
Height, 5.10. Weight, 185.
High School—Metairie, La., East Jefferson.
Attended Nicholls State University.

Selected by Cleveland in 4th round (87th player selected) of 1982 NFL draft.
On non-football injury list with bruised heart muscle, September 2 through September 27, 1984; activated, September 28, 1984.

| | | —RUSHING— | | | | PASS RECEIVING | | | | —TOTAL— | | |
Year Club	G.	Att.	Yds.	Avg.	TD.	P.C.	Yds.	Avg.	TD.	TD.	Pts.	F.
1982—Cleveland NFL	9		None			8	136	17.0	0	0	0	2
1983—Cleveland NFL	16	19	100	5.3	0	29	273	9.4	1	1	6	1
1984—Cleveland NFL	11	1	—8	—8.0	0	10	122	12.2	0	0	0	1
Pro Totals—3 Years	36	20	92	4.6	0	47	531	11.3	1	1	6	4

| | | —PUNT RETURNS— | | | | —KICKOFF RET.— | | |
Year Club	G.	No.	Yds.	Avg.	TD.	No.	Yds.	Avg.TD.
1982—Cleveland NFL	9	19	101	5.3	0	13	295	22.7 0
1983—Cleveland NFL	16	3	26	8.7	0	29	627	21.6 0
1984—Cleveland NFL	11	6	50	8.3	0		None	
Pro Totals—3 Years	36	28	177	6.3	0	42	922	22.0 0

Additional pro statistics: Recovered two fumbles, 1982; attempted three passes with one completion for 25 yards, intercepted once and recovered three fumbles, 1983.

FULTON LUTHER WALKER JR.
Cornerback—Miami Dolphins
Born April 30, 1958, at Martinsburg, W. Va.
Height, 5.11. Weight, 196.
High School—Martinsburg, W. Va.
Received bachelor of science degree in physical
education from University of West Virginia in 1981.

Named to THE SPORTING NEWS NFL All-Star Team, 1983.
Selected by Miami in 6th round (154th player selected) of 1981 NFL draft.
On injured reserve with broken thumb, August 28 through September 27, 1984; activated, September 28, 1984.

| | | INTERCEPTIONS | | | | -PUNT RETURNS- | | | | —KICKOFF RET.— | | | | —TOTAL— | | |
Year Club	G.	No.	Yds.	Avg.	TD.	No.	Yds.	Avg.	TD.	No.	Yds.	Avg.	TD.	TD.	Pts.	F.
1981—Miami NFL	16	1	0	0.0	0	5	50	10.0	0	38	932	24.5	*1	1	6	4
1982—Miami NFL	9	3	54	18.0	0		None			20	433	21.7	0	0	0	0
1983—Miami NFL	15	1	7	7.0	0	8	86	10.8	0	36	962	*26.7	0	0	0	1
1984—Miami NFL	12		None			21	169	8.0	0	29	617	21.3	0	0	0	2
Pro Totals—4 Years	52	5	61	12.2	0	34	305	9.0	0	123	2944	23.9	1	1	6	7

Additional pro statistics: Recovered two fumbles, 1981; recovered one fumble, 1983.
Played in AFC Championship Game following 1982 and 1984 seasons.
Played in NFL Championship Game following 1982 and 1984 seasons.

JOHN WALKER
Running Back—St. Louis Cardinals
Born August 31, 1961, at Killeen, Tex.
Height, 6.00. Weight, 205.
High School—Killeen, Tex.
Attended University of Texas.

Selected by Houston in 1984 USFL territorial draft.
Selected by St. Louis in 9th round (241st player selected) of 1984 NFL draft.
Signed by St. Louis Cardinals, July 7, 1984.
On injured reserve with eye injury, August 21 through entire 1984 season.

LaQUENTIN ANTONIO WALKER
(Quentin)
Wide Receiver—St. Louis Cardinals
Born August 27, 1961, at Teaneck, N.J.
Height, 6.01. Weight, 200.
High School—Teaneck, N.J.
Attended University of Virginia.

Selected by Washington in 1984 USFL territorial draft.
Selected by St. Louis in 7th round (185th player selected) of 1984 NFL draft.
Signed by St. Louis Cardinals, July 16, 1984.
On injured reserve with leg injury, August 28 through September 27, 1984; activated, September 28, 1984.
On injured reserve with broken ankle, October 26 through remainder of 1984 season.
St. Louis NFL, 1984.
Games: 1984 (3).

RICHARD WALKER
(Rick)
Tight End—Washington Redskins
Born May 28, 1955, at Santa Ana, Calif.
Height, 6.04. Weight, 235.
High School—Santa Ana, Calif., Valley.
Attended Santa Ana Junior College and University of California at Los Angeles.

Selected by Cincinnati in 4th round (85th player selected) of 1977 NFL draft.
Released by Cincinnati Bengals, August 27, 1979; re-signed by Bengals, October 9, 1979.
Released by Cincinnati Bengals, August 26, 1980; signed as free agent by Washington Redskins, September 12, 1980.

	—PASS RECEIVING—				
Year Club	G.	P.C.	Yds.	Avg.	TD.
1977—Cincinnati NFL	6	1	13	13.0	0
1978—Cincinnati NFL	15	12	126	10.5	2
1979—Cincinnati NFL	10	1	14	14.0	1
1980—Washington NFL	15	10	88	8.8	1
1981—Washington NFL	16	11	112	10.2	1
1982—Washington NFL	9	12	92	7.7	1
1983—Washington NFL	16	17	168	9.9	2
1984—Washington NFL	16	5	52	10.4	1
Pro Totals—8 Years	103	69	665	9.6	9

Additional pro statistics: Fumbled once, 1978 and 1980; recovered two fumbles and rushed once for minus eight yards, 1980; rushed once for five yards, 1981; recovered one fumble, 1981 and 1984; rushed twice for 11 yards, 1982; rushed twice for 10 yards, 1983; rushed once for two yards, 1984.
Played in NFC Championship Game following 1982 and 1983 seasons.
Played in NFL Championship Game following 1982 and 1983 seasons.

WESLEY DARCEL WALKER
Wide Receiver—New York Jets
Born May 26, 1955, at San Bernardino, Calif.
Height, 6.00. Weight, 179.
High School—Carson, Calif.
Attended University of California.

Selected by New York Jets in 2nd round (33rd player selected) of 1977 NFL draft.
On injured reserve with knee injury, October 31 through remainder of 1979 season.
On injured reserve with thigh injury, October 11 through November 14, 1980; activated, November 15, 1980.
Placed on did not report list, August 20 through August 26, 1984.
Reported and granted roster exemption, August 27 through August 31, 1984; activated, September 1, 1984.

		—RUSHING—				PASS RECEIVING				—TOTAL—		
Year Club	G.	Att.	Yds.	Avg.	TD.	P.C.	Yds.	Avg.	TD.	TD.	Pts.	F.
1977—New York Jets NFL	14	3	25	8.3	0	35	740	★21.1	3	3	18	2
1978—New York Jets NFL	16	1	—3	—3.0	0	48	★1169	★24.4	8	8	48	2
1979—New York Jets NFL	9		None			23	569	24.7	5	5	30	0
1980—New York Jets NFL	11		None			18	376	20.9	1	1	6	0
1981—New York Jets NFL	13		None			47	770	16.4	9	9	54	0
1982—New York Jets NFL	9		None			39	620	15.9	6	6	36	0
1983—New York Jets NFL	16		None			61	868	14.2	7	7	42	0
1984—New York Jets NFL	12	1	1	1.0	0	41	623	15.2	7	7	42	0
Pro Totals—8 Years	100	5	23	4.6	0	312	5735	18.4	46	46	276	4

Additional pro statistics: Recovered one fumble, 1978.
Played in AFC Championship Game following 1982 season.
Played in Pro Bowl (NFL All-Star Game) following 1978 and 1982 seasons.

EVERSON COLLINS WALLS
Cornerback—Dallas Cowboys

Born December 28, 1959, at Dallas, Tex.
Height, 6.01. Weight, 194.
High School—Dallas, Tex., L.V. Berkner.
Received bachelor of arts degree in business from Grambling State University in 1981.
Cousin of Ralph Anderson, back with Pittsburgh Steelers and New England Patriots,
1971 through 1973; and Herkie Walls, kick returner-wide receiver with Houston Oilers.
Signed as free agent by Dallas Cowboys, May, 1981.

| | | | —INTERCEPTIONS— | | | |
Year	Club	G.	No.	Yds.	Avg.	TD.
1981—Dallas NFL		16	*11	133	12.1	0
1982—Dallas NFL		9	*7	61	8.7	0
1983—Dallas NFL		16	4	70	17.5	0
1984—Dallas NFL		16	3	12	4.0	0
Pro Totals—4 Years		57	25	276	11.0	0

Additional pro statistics: Recovered one fumble, 1981; fumbled once, 1982.
Played in NFC Championship Game following 1981 and 1982 seasons.
Played in Pro Bowl (NFL All-Star Game) following 1981 through 1983 seasons.

McCUREY HERCULES WALLS
(Herkie)
Kick Returner-Wide Receiver—Houston Oilers

Born July 18, 1961, at Garland, Tex.
Height, 5.08. Weight, 160.
High School—Garland, Tex.
Attended University of Texas.
Cousin of Everson Walls, cornerback with Dallas Cowboys.
Selected by Boston in 12th round (134th player selected) of 1983 USFL draft.
Selected by Houston in 7th round (170th player selected) of 1983 NFL draft.
Signed by Houston Oilers, July 6, 1983.

| | | | —RUSHING— | | | | PASS RECEIVING | | | | —TOTAL— | | |
Year	Club	G.	Att.	Yds.	Avg.	TD.	P.C.	Yds.	Avg.	TD.	TD.	Pts.	F.
1983—Houston NFL		16	5	44	8.8	0	12	276	23.0	1	1	6	0
1984—Houston NFL		14	4	20	5.0	0	18	291	16.2	1	1	6	0
Pro Totals—2 Years		30	9	64	7.1	0	30	567	18.9	2	2	12	0

| | | | KICKOFF RETURNS | | | |
Year	Club	G.	No.	Yds.	Avg.	TD.
1983—Houston NFL		16	9	110	12.2	0
1984—Houston NFL		14	15	289	19.3	0
Pro Totals—2 Years		30	24	399	16.6	0

KEN WALTER
Center-Guard—Green Bay Packers

Born March 2, 1958, at Corsicana, Tex.
Height, 6.04. Weight, 260.
High School—Corsicana, Tex.
Attended Texas Tech University.
Selected by Baltimore in 8th round (195th player selected) of 1980 NFL draft.
Released by Baltimore Colts, August 26, 1980; signed as free agent by Edmonton Eskimos, November 19, 1980.
On injured list entire 1981 season.
Traded by Edmonton Eskimos to Calgary Stampeders, July 11, 1983.
Traded by Calgary Stampeders to Edmonton Eskimos, July 18, 1983.
Traded by Edmonton Eskimos to Winnipeg Blue Bombers, September 13, 1983.
Traded by Winnipeg Blue Bombers to Montreal Concordes, September 15, 1983.
Traded by Montreal Concordes to Winnipeg Blue Bombers, September 19, 1983.
Released by Winnipeg Blue Bombers, September 29, 1983; signed as free agent by Green Bay Packers, March 10, 1984.
On injured reserve with ankle injury, August 13 through entire 1984 season.
Edmonton CFL, 1982; Edmonton (1)-Winnipeg (1) CFL, 1983.
Games: 1982 (1), 1983 (2). Total CFL—3.

MICHAEL DAVID WALTER
(Mike)
Linebacker—San Francisco 49ers

Born November 30, 1960, at Salem, Ore.
Height, 6.03. Weight, 238.
High School—Eugene, Ore., Sheldon.
Attended University of Oregon.
Selected by Los Angeles in 20th round (240th player selected) of 1983 USFL draft.
Selected by Dallas in 2nd round (50th player selected) of 1983 NFL draft.
Signed by Dallas Cowboys, July 7, 1983.
Released by Dallas Cowboys, August 27, 1984; awarded on waivers to San Francisco 49ers, August 28, 1984.

Dallas NFL, 1983; San Francisco NFL, 1984.
Games: 1983 (15), 1984 (16). Total—31.
Played in NFC Championship Game following 1984 season.
Played in NFL Championship Game following 1984 season.

DANNY EUGENE WALTERS
Cornerback—San Diego Chargers
Born November 4, 1960, at Prescott, Ark.
Height, 6.01. Weight, 180.
High School—Chicago, Ill., Percy L. Julian.
Attended University of Arkansas.

Selected by New Jersey in 11th round (123rd player selected) of 1983 USFL draft.
Selected by San Diego in 4th round (95th player selected) of 1983 NFL draft.
Signed by San Diego Chargers, July 9, 1983.
On injured reserve with knee injury, November 15 through remainder of 1984 season.

Year Club	G.	No.	Yds.	Avg.	TD.
1983—San Diego NFL	16	7	55	7.9	0
1984—San Diego NFL	8		None		
Pro Totals—2 Years	24	7	55	7.9	0

Header row spans —INTERCEPTIONS—

CHRISTOPHER LAMAR WARD
(Chris)
Offensive Tackle—New Orleans Saints
Born December 16, 1955, at Cleveland, O.
Height, 6.03. Weight, 267.
High School—Dayton, O., Patterson Cooperative.
Attended Ohio State University.

Named as offensive tackle on THE SPORTING NEWS College All-America Team, 1977.
Selected by New York Jets in 1st round (4th player selected) of 1978 NFL draft.
Released by New York Jets, August 29, 1984; signed as free agent by New Orleans Saints, September 3, 1984.
New York Jets NFL, 1978 through 1983; New Orleans NFL, 1984.
Games: 1978 (16), 1979 (16), 1980 (14), 1981 (16), 1982 (9), 1983 (16), 1984 (13). Total—100.
Played in AFC Championship Game following 1982 season.

CURT WARNER
Running Back—Seattle Seahawks
Born March 18, 1961, at Wyoming, W. Va.
Height, 5.11. Weight, 205.
High School—Pineville, W. Va.
Attended Penn State University.

Selected by Philadelphia in 1983 USFL territorial draft.
Selected by Seattle in 1st round (3rd player selected) of 1983 NFL draft.
Signed by Seattle Seahawks, June 29, 1983.
On injured reserve with knee injury, September 5 through remainder of 1984 season.
Selected by Philadelphia Phillies' organization in 32nd round of free-agent draft, June 5, 1979.

Year Club	G.	Att.	Yds.	Avg.	TD.	P.C.	Yds.	Avg.	TD.	TD.	Pts.	F.
1983—Seattle NFL	16	335	1449	4.3	13	42	325	7.7	1	14	84	6
1984—Seattle NFL	1	10	40	4.0	0	1	19	19.0	0	0	0	0
Pro Totals—2 Years	17	345	1489	4.3	13	43	344	8.0	1	14	84	6

Headers span: —RUSHING— / PASS RECEIVING / —TOTAL—

Additional pro statistics: Recovered two fumbles, 1983.
Played in AFC Championship Game following 1983 season.
Played in Pro Bowl (NFL All-Star Game) following 1983 season.

DON WARREN
Tight End—Washington Redskins
Born May 5, 1956, at Bellingham, Wash.
Height, 6.04. Weight, 242.
High School—Covina, Calif., Royal Oak.
Attended Mt. San Antonio Junior College and San Diego State University.

Selected by Washington in 4th round (103rd player selected) of 1979 NFL draft.

Year Club	G.	P.C.	Yds.	Avg.	TD.
1979—Washington NFL	16	26	303	11.7	0
1980—Washington NFL	13	31	323	10.4	0
1981—Washington NFL	16	29	335	11.6	1
1982—Washington NFL	9	27	310	11.5	0
1983—Washington NFL	13	20	225	11.3	2
1984—Washington NFL	16	18	192	10.7	0
Pro Totals—6 Years	83	151	1688	11.2	3

Header row spans —PASS RECEIVING—

Additional pro statistics: Recovered one fumble, 1979; fumbled once, 1980.
Played in NFC Championship Game following 1982 and 1983 seasons.
Played in NFL Championship Game following 1982 and 1983 seasons.

FRANK WILLIAM WARREN III
Defensive End—New Orleans Saints
Born September 14, 1959, at Birmingham, Ala.
Height, 6.04. Weight, 278.
High School—Birmingham, Ala., Phillips.
Attended Auburn University.

Selected by New Orleans in 3rd round (57th player selected) of 1981 NFL draft.
New Orleans NFL, 1981 through 1984.
Games: 1981 (16), 1982 (9), 1983 (16), 1984 (16). Total—57.
Pro statistics: Recovered one fumble, 1981 and 1983; intercepted one pass for six yards, 1983.

JOHN SHEPPARD WARREN
Punter—Dallas Cowboys
Born November 8, 1960, at Jesup, Ga.
Height, 6.00. Weight, 207.
High School—Jesup, Ga., Wayne.
Attended University of Tennessee.

Signed as free agent by Dallas Cowboys, April 28, 1983.
On injured reserve with knee injury, November 18 through remainder of 1983 season.
Released by Dallas Cowboys, August 21, 1984; re-signed by Cowboys after clearing procedural waivers, October 27, 1984.
Released by Dallas Cowboys, November 13, 1984; re-signed by Cowboys, November 20, 1984.

| | | ——PUNTING—— | | |
Year Club	G.	No.	Avg.	Blk.
1983—Dallas NFL	9	39	39.8	0
1984—Dallas NFL	3	21	38.0	0
Pro Totals—2 Years	12	60	39.2	0

ANTHONY WAYNE WASHINGTON
Cornerback—Washington Redskins
Born February 4, 1958, at San Francisco, Calif.
Height, 6.01. Weight, 204.
High School—Fresno, Calif.
Attended Fresno City Junior College, University of California and Fresno State University.
Brother of Tim Washington, cornerback with Indianapolis Colts.

Selected by Pittsburgh in 2nd round (44th player selected) of 1981 NFL draft.
Traded by Pittsburgh Steelers to Washington Redskins for 4th round pick in 1984 draft, August 17, 1983.

| | | ——INTERCEPTIONS—— | | | |
Year Club	G.	No.	Yds.	Avg.	TD.
1981—Pittsburgh NFL	16	3	46	15.3	0
1982—Pittsburgh NFL	9		None		
1983—Washington NFL	16	4	12	3.0	0
1984—Washington NFL	16	1	25	25.0	0
Pro Totals—4 Years	57	8	83	10.4	0

Additional pro statistics: Recovered one fumble, 1983 and 1984; fumbled once, 1983.
Played in NFC Championship Game following 1983 season.
Played in NFL Championship Game following 1983 season.

CHRIS WASHINGTON
Linebacker—Tampa Bay Buccaneers
Born March 6, 1962, at Jackson, Miss.
Height, 6.04. Weight, 225.
High School—Chicago, Ill., Percy L. Julian.
Attended Iowa State University

Selected by Washington in 3rd round (49th player selected) of 1984 USFL draft.
Selected by Tampa Bay in 6th round (142nd player selected) of 1984 NFL draft.
Signed by Tampa Bay Buccaneers, June 5, 1984.
Tampa Bay NFL, 1984.
Games: 1984 (16).

JOE DAN WASHINGTON
Running Back—Atlanta Falcons
Born September 24, 1953, at Crockett, Tex.
Height, 5.10. Weight, 179.
High School—Port Arthur, Tex., Lincoln.
Received bachelor of arts degree in public relations from University of Oklahoma.

Named as running back on THE SPORTING NEWS College All-America Team, 1974.
Selected by San Diego in 1st round (4th player selected) of 1976 NFL draft.
Missed entire 1976 season due to injury.
Traded with 5th round pick in 1979 draft by San Diego Chargers to Baltimore Colts for running back Lydell Mitchell, August 23, 1978.
Traded by Baltimore Colts to Washington Redskins for 2nd round pick in 1981 draft, April 28, 1981.
On injured reserve with knee injury, September 7 through November 19, 1982; activated, November 20, 1982.

On injured reserve with knee injury, September 29 through November 27, 1984; activated, November 28, 1984.

Traded with 2nd round pick in 1985 draft and 1st round pick in 1986 draft by Washington Redskins to Atlanta Falcons for 2nd round pick in 1985 draft and 2nd and 6th round picks in 1986 draft, April 30, 1985.

| Year Club | G. | —RUSHING— | | | | PASS RECEIVING | | | | —TOTAL— | | |
		Att.	Yds.	Avg.	TD.	P.C.	Yds.	Avg.	TD.	TD.	Pts.	F.
1977—San Diego NFL	13	62	217	3.5	0	31	244	7.9	0	0	0	1
1978—Baltimore NFL	16	240	956	4.0	0	45	377	8.4	1	2	12	12
1979—Baltimore NFL	15	242	884	3.7	4	*82	750	9.1	3	7	42	8
1980—Baltimore NFL	16	144	502	3.5	1	51	494	9.7	3	4	24	5
1981—Washington NFL	14	210	916	4.4	4	70	558	8.0	3	7	42	8
1982—Washington NFL	7	44	190	4.3	1	19	134	7.1	1	2	12	2
1983—Washington NFL	15	145	772	5.3	0	47	454	9.7	6	6	36	2
1984—Washington NFL	7	56	192	3.4	1	13	74	5.7	0	1	6	3
Pro Totals—8 Years	103	1143	4629	4.0	11	358	3085	8.6	17	29	174	41

| Year Club | G. | —PUNT RETURNS— | | | | —KICKOFF RET.— | | | |
		No.	Yds.	Avg.	TD.	No.	Yds.	Avg.	TD.
1977—San Diego NFL	13		None				None		
1978—Baltimore NFL	16	7	37	5.3	0	19	499	26.3	*1
1979—Baltimore NFL	15		None			1	1	1.0	0
1980—Baltimore NFL	16		None				None		
1981—Washington NFL	14		None				None		
1982—Washington NFL	7		None				None		
1983—Washington NFL	15		None			1	16	16.0	0
1984—Washington NFL	7		None				None		
Pro Totals—8 Years	103	7	37	5.3	0	21	516	24.6	0

Additional pro statistics: Attempted one pass with one completion for 32 yards and one touchdown, 1977; attempted four passes with two completions for 80 yards and two touchdowns and recovered two fumbles, 1978; attempted one pass with one interception and recovered two fumbles for four yards, 1979; attempted two passes with one completion for 32 yards, 1981; attempted one pass with one completion for 35 yards, 1982; attempted one pass with no completions, 1983 and 1984.

Played in NFC Championship Game following 1982 and 1983 seasons.

Played in NFL Championship Game following 1983 season.

Member of Washington Redskins for NFL Championship Game following 1982 season; did not play.

Played in Pro Bowl (NFL All-Star Game) following 1979 season.

LIONEL WASHINGTON
Cornerback—St. Louis Cardinals
Born October 21, 1960, at New Orleans, La.
Height, 6.00. Weight, 184.
High School—Lutcher, La.
Attended Tulane University.

Selected by Tampa Bay in 20th round (229th player selected) of 1983 USFL draft.
Selected by St. Louis in 4th round (103rd player selected) of 1983 NFL draft.
Signed by St. Louis Cardinals, May 6, 1983.

| Year Club | G. | —INTERCEPTIONS— | | |
		No.	Yds.	Avg.	TD.
1983—St. Louis NFL	16	8	92	11.5	0
1984—St. Louis NFL	15	5	42	8.4	0
Pro Totals—2 Years	31	13	134	10.3	0

Additional pro statistics: Recovered one fumble, 1983 and 1984.

SAMUEL LEE WASHINGTON JR.
(Sam)
Cornerback—Pittsburgh Steelers
Born March 7, 1960, at Tampa, Fla.
Height, 5.08. Weight, 180.
High School—Tampa, Fla., Tampa Bay Tech.
Received bachelor of science degree in health, physical education and recreation from Mississippi Valley State University in 1982.

Signed as free agent by Pittsburgh Steelers, May 5, 1982.
On injured reserve with knee injury, August 31 through December 7, 1982; re-signed after clearing procedural waivers, December 9, 1982.

| Year Club | G. | —INTERCEPTIONS— | | |
		No.	Yds.	Avg.	TD.
1982—Pittsburgh NFL	4		None		
1983—Pittsburgh NFL	16	1	25	25.0	0
1984—Pittsburgh NFL	14	6	138	23.0	*2
Pro Totals—3 Years	34	7	163	23.3	2

Played in AFC Championship Game following 1984 season.

—DID YOU KNOW—

That the 1985 draft was the first since 1968 in which four offensive linemen were taken in the first 10 choices?

ANDRE WATERS
Cornerback—Philadelphia Eagles
Born March 10, 1962, at Belle Glade, Fla.
Height, 5.11. Weight, 182.
High School—Pahokee, Fla.
Attended Cheyney State College.
Signed as free agent by Philadelphia Eagles, June 20, 1984.

Year Club	G.	No.	KICKOFF RETURNS Yds.	Avg.	TD.
1984—Philadelphia NFL........	16	13	319	24.5	*1

Additional pro statistics: Recovered one fumble and fumbled once, 1984.

BOBBY LAWRENCE WATKINS
Cornerback—Detroit Lions
Born May 31, 1960, at Cottonwood, Ida.
Height, 5.10. Weight, 184.
High School—Dallas, Tex., Bishop Dunne.
Attended Southwest Texas State University.
Selected by Detroit in 2nd round (42nd player selected) of 1982 NFL draft.

Year Club	G.	No.	——INTERCEPTIONS—— Yds.	Avg.	TD.
1982—Detroit NFL..................	9	5	22	4.4	0
1983—Detroit NFL..................	16	4	48	12.0	0
1984—Detroit NFL..................	16	6	0	0.0	0
Pro Totals—3 Years............	41	15	70	4.7	0

Additional pro statistics: Recovered one fumble, 1982; recovered three fumbles for six yards and fumbled once, 1983.

STEPHEN ROSS WATSON
(Steve)
Wide Receiver—Denver Broncos
Born May 28, 1957, at Baltimore, Md.
Height, 6.04. Weight, 195.
High School—Wilmington, Del., St. Mark's.
Received degree in parks administration from Temple University.
Signed as free agent by Denver Broncos, May 12, 1979.

Year Club	G.	P.C.	——PASS RECEIVING—— Yds.	Avg.	TD.
1979—Denver NFL	16	6	83	13.8	0
1980—Denver NFL	16	6	146	24.3	0
1981—Denver NFL	16	60	1244	20.7	*13
1982—Denver NFL	9	36	555	15.4	2
1983—Denver NFL	16	59	1133	19.2	5
1984—Denver NFL	16	69	1170	17.0	7
Pro Totals—6 Years	89	236	4331	18.4	27

Additional pro statistics: Returned one kickoff for five yards and recovered one fumble, 1980; rushed twice for six yards and recovered two fumbles, 1981; rushed once for minus four yards, 1982; fumbled once, 1982 and 1983; rushed three times for 17 yards, 1983.
Played in Pro Bowl (NFL All-Star Game) following 1981 season.

FRANK WATTELET
Safety—New Orleans Saints
Born October 25, 1958, at Paola, Kan.
Height, 6.00. Weight, 181.
High School—Abilene, Kan.
Attended University of Kansas.
Signed as free agent by New Orleans Saints, May 27, 1981.
Released by New Orleans Saints after failing physical, July 15, 1981; re-signed by Saints, July 17, 1981.

Year Club	G.	No.	——INTERCEPTIONS—— Yds.	Avg.	TD.
1981—New Orleans NFL........	16	3	16	5.3	0
1982—New Orleans NFL........	9		None		
1983—New Orleans NFL........	16	2	33	16.5	0
1984—New Orleans NFL........	16	2	52	26.0	1
Pro Totals—4 Years............	57	7	101	14.4	1

Additional pro statistics: Recovered one fumble, 1981 and 1982; returned one kickoff for four yards and recovered three fumbles for six yards, 1983; recovered two fumbles for 22 yards and a touchdown, 1984.

RICKEY RICARDO WATTS
Wide Receiver—Cleveland Browns
Born May 16, 1957, at Longview, Tex.
Height, 6.01. Weight, 203.
High School—Longview, Tex.
Received bachelor of arts degree in physical education from University of Tulsa.
Related to Hosea Taylor, defensive end with Houston Gamblers.

Selected by Chicago in 2nd round (39th player selected) of 1979 NFL draft.
On injured reserve with broken foot, August 30 through October 7, 1983; activated, October 8, 1983.
On injured reserve with foot injury, December 9 through remainder of 1983 season.
On injured reserve with broken foot, August 14 through entire 1984 season.
Granted free agency after not receiving qualifying offer, February 1, 1985; signed by Cleveland Browns, May 6, 1985.

		PASS RECEIVING				—KICKOFF RET.—				—TOTAL—		
Year Club	G.	P.C.	Yds.	Avg.	TD.	No.	Yds.	Avg.	TD.	TD.	Pts.	F.
1979—Chicago NFL	16	24	421	17.5	3	14	289	20.6	1	4	24	1
1980—Chicago NFL	15	22	444	20.2	2	1	12	12.0	0	2	12	1
1981—Chicago NFL	12	27	465	17.2	3		None			3	18	3
1982—Chicago NFL	9	8	217	27.1	0	14	330	23.6	0	0	0	1
1983—Chicago NFL	4			None		5	79	15.8	0	0	0	0
Pro Totals—5 Years	56	81	1547	19.1	8	34	710	20.9	1	9	54	6

Additional pro statistics: Rushed once for minus six yards, 1979; returned two punts for 20 yards and rushed once for minus 16 yards, 1980; recovered two fumbles, 1981; rushed once for minus one yard and recovered one fumble, 1982.

TED WATTS
Cornerback—Los Angeles Raiders
Born May 29, 1958, at Tarpon Springs, Fla.
Height, 6.00. Weight, 195.
High School—Tarpon Springs, Fla., Tarpon.
Attended Texas Tech University.

Named as defensive back on THE SPORTING NEWS College All-America Team. 1980.
Selected by Oakland in 1st round (21st player selected) of 1981 NFL draft.
Franchise transferred to Los Angeles, May 7, 1982.

		-INTERCEPTIONS-				–PUNT RETURNS–				—TOTAL—		
Year Club	G.	No.	Yds.	Avg.	TD.	No.	Yds.	Avg.	TD.	TD.	Pts.	F.
1981—Oakland NFL	16	1	12	12.0	0	35	284	8.1	1	1	6	3
1982—Los Angeles Raiders NFL	9	1	0	0.0	0		None			0	0	0
1983—Los Angeles Raiders NFL	16	1	13	13.0	0		None			0	0	0
1984—Los Angeles Raiders NFL	16	1	0	0.0	0		None			0	0	0
Pro Totals—4 Years	57	4	25	6.3	0	35	284	8.1	1	1	6	3

Additional pro statistics: Recovered two fumbles for one yard, 1981; recovered one fumble, 1983.
Played in AFC Championship Game following 1983 season.
Played in NFL Championship Game following 1983 season.

DAVID BENJAMIN WAYMER JR.
(Dave)
Cornerback—New Orleans Saints
Born July 1, 1958, at Brooklyn, N.Y.
Height, 6.01. Weight, 188.
High School—Charlotte, N.C., West.
Received bachelor of arts degree in economics from University of Notre Dame in 1980.

Selected by New Orleans in 2nd round (41st player selected) of 1980 NFL draft.

		—INTERCEPTIONS—			
Year Club	G.	No.	Yds.	Avg.	TD.
1980—New Orleans NFL	16		None		
1981—New Orleans NFL	16	4	54	13.5	0
1982—New Orleans NFL	9		None		
1983—New Orleans NFL	16		None		
1984—New Orleans NFL	16	4	9	2.3	0
Pro Totals—5 Years	73	8	63	7.9	0

Additional pro statistics: Returned three punts for 29 yards and fumbled once, 1980; recovered two fumbles, 1980, 1981 and 1982; recovered three fumbles, 1983.

CLARENCE WEATHERS
Wide Receiver—New England Patriots
Born January 10, 1962, at Green's Pond, S.C.
Height, 5.09. Weight, 170.
High School—Ft. Pierce, Fla.
Attended Delaware State College.
Brother of Robert Weathers, fullback with New England Patriots.

Signed as free agent by New England Patriots, July 20, 1983.
On injured reserve with broken foot, August 28 through October 19, 1984; activated, October 20, 1984.

		—PASS RECEIVING—			
Year Club	G.	P.C.	Yds.	Avg.	TD.
1983—New England NFL.......	16	19	379	19.9	3
1984—New England NFL.......	9	8	115	14.4	2
Pro Totals—2 Years...........	25	27	494	18.3	5

Additional pro statistics: Returned three kickoffs for 58 yards, rushed once for 28 yards, returned four punts for one yard, recovered one fumble and fumbled twice, 1983; returned one punt for seven yards, 1984.

CURTIS WEATHERS
Linebacker—Cleveland Browns
Born September 16, 1956, at Memphis, Tenn.
Height, 6.05. Weight, 230.
High School—Memphis, Tenn., Bishop Byrne.
Attended University of Mississippi.

Selected by Cleveland in 9th round (241st player selected) of 1979 NFL draft.
On injured reserve with knee and hamstring injuries, September 26 through November 2, 1980; activated, November 3, 1980.
On injured reserve with dislocated thumb, December 9 through remainder of 1981 season.
On injured reserve with knee injury, September 7 through November 18, 1982; activated, November 19, 1982.
Cleveland NFL, 1979 through 1984.
Games: 1979 (16), 1980 (10), 1981 (13), 1982 (7), 1983 (16), 1984 (16). Total—78.
Pro statistics: Caught one pass for 14 yards, fumbled once and returned one kickoff for no yards, 1979.

ROBERT JAMES WEATHERS
Fullback—New England Patriots
Born September 13, 1960, at Westfield, N.Y.
Height, 6.02. Weight, 222.
High School—Ft. Pierce, Fla.
Attended Arizona State University.
Brother of Clarence Weathers, wide receiver with New England Patriots.

Selected by New England in 2nd round (40th player selected) of 1982 NFL draft.
On injured reserve with knee injury, September 13 through December 7, 1984; activated, December 8, 1984.

		—RUSHING—				PASS RECEIVING				—TOTAL—		
Year Club	G.	Att.	Yds.	Avg.	TD.	P.C.	Yds.	Avg.	TD.	TD.	Pts.	F.
1982—New England NFL....................	6	24	83	3.5	1	3	24	8.0	0	1	6	1
1983—New England NFL....................	15	73	418	5.7	1	23	212	9.2	0	1	6	4
1984—New England NFL....................	2		None				None			0	0	0
Pro Totals—3 Years...................	23	97	501	5.2	2	26	236	9.1	0	2	12	5

Additional pro statistics: Returned three kickoffs for 68 yards, 1983.

MICHAEL LEWIS WEBSTER
(Mike)
Center—Pittsburgh Steelers
Born March 18, 1952, at Tomahawk, Wis.
Height, 6.01. Weight, 250.
High School—Rhinelander, Wis.
Attended University of Wisconsin.

Named to THE SPORTING NEWS NFL All-Star Team, 1980, 1981 and 1983.
Named to THE SPORTING NEWS AFC All-Star Team, 1978 and 1979.
Selected by Pittsburgh in 5th round (125th player selected) of 1974 NFL draft.
Pittsburgh NFL, 1974 through 1984.
Games: 1974 (14), 1975 (14), 1976 (14), 1977 (14), 1977 (14), 1978 (16), 1980 (16), 1981 (16), 1982 (9), 1983 (16), 1984 (16). Total—161.
Pro statistics: Fumbled twice, 1976; recovered two fumbles for two yards, 1979; recovered two fumbles, 1983.
Played in AFC Championship Game following 1974 through 1976, 1978, 1979 and 1984 seasons.
Played in NFL Championship Game following 1974, 1975, 1978 and 1979 seasons.
Played in Pro Bowl (NFL All-Star Game) following 1978 through 1984 seasons.

CLAYTON CHARLES WEISHUHN
Name pronounced Why-SOON.
Linebacker—New England Patriots
Born October 7, 1959, at San Angelo, Tex.
Height, 6.02. Weight, 220.
High School—Wall, Tex.
Received bachelor of science degree in physical education from
Angelo State University in 1982.

Selected by New England in 3rd round (60th player selected) of 1982 NFL draft.
On injured reserve with knee injury, September 5 through remainder of 1984 season.
New England NFL, 1982 through 1984.
Games: 1982 (9), 1983 (16), 1984 (1). Total—26.
Pro statistics: Recovered one fumble, 1982; ran 27 yards with lateral on interception for a touchdown and recovered three fumbles, 1983.

JOSEPH FREDRICK WELLS
(Joe)
Linebacker—Los Angeles Raiders
Born April 26, 1959, at Phoenix, Ariz.
Height, 6.02. Weight, 230.
High School—Cedar City, Utah.
Received bachelor of science degree in business and marketing from Southern Utah State.

Signed as free agent by Seattle Seahawks, May 19, 1981.
Released by Seattle Seahawks, August 17, 1981; claimed on procedural waivers by New Orleans Saints, March 11, 1982.
Released by New Orleans Saints, September 6, 1982; signed as free agent by Oakland Invaders, January 1, 1983.
Released by Oakland Invaders, February 20, 1983; signed as free agent by Philadelphia Eagles, May 12, 1983.
Released by Philadelphia Eagles, August 23, 1983; signed as free agent by Los Angeles Raiders, May 20, 1984.
On injured reserve with knee injury, August 14 through entire 1984 season.

ALAN LEE WENGLIKOWSKI
(Al)
Linebacker—Buffalo Bills
Born August 3, 1960, at Franklin, O.
Height, 6.01. Weight, 220.
High School—Franklin, O.
Attended University of Pittsburgh.

Selected by Pittsburgh in 1984 USFL territorial draft.
Selected by Kansas City in 10th round (258th player selected) of 1984 NFL draft.
Signed by Kansas City Chiefs, May 29, 1984.
Released by Kansas City Chiefs, August 27, 1984; signed as free agent by Buffalo Bills, October 31, 1984.
Buffalo NFL, 1984.
Games: 1984 (5).

RAIMUND WERSCHING
Name pronounced WERE-shing.
(Ray)
Placekicker—San Francisco 49ers
Born August 21, 1950, at Mondsee, Austria.
Height, 5.11. Weight, 210.
High School—Downey, Calif., Earl Warren.
Attended Cerritos College and received bachelor of science degree in
accounting from University of California at Berkeley.

Tied NFL records for most field goals, game, no misses (6) vs. New Orleans Saints, October 16, 1983; most extra points, no misses, season (56), 1984.
Signed as free agent by Atlanta Falcons, 1971.
Released by Atlanta Falcons, 1971; signed as free agent by San Diego Chargers, 1973.
Released by San Diego Chargers, September 6, 1976; re-signed by Chargers, October 16, 1976.
Released by San Diego Chargers, August, 1977; signed as free agent by San Francisco 49ers, October 11, 1977.
On injured reserve with hip injury, September 12 through October 9, 1981; activated, October 10, 1981.

Year Club	G.	XP.	XPM.	FG.	FGA.	Pts.
1973—San Diego NFL	14	13	2	11	25	46
1974—San Diego NFL	14	0	0	5	11	15
1975—San Diego NFL	14	20	1	12	24	56
1976—San Diego NFL	9	14	2	4	8	26
1977—San Fran. NFL	10	23	0	10	17	53
1978—San Fran. NFL	16	24	1	15	23	69
1979—San Fran. NFL	16	32	3	20	24	92
1980—San Fran. NFL	16	33	*6	15	19	78
1981—San Fran. NFL	12	30	0	17	23	81
1982—San Fran. NFL	9	23	2	12	17	59
1983—San Fran. NFL	16	51	0	25	30	126
1984—San Fran. NFL	16	56	0	25	35	*131
Pro Totals—12 Years	162	319	17	171	256	832

Played in NFC Championship Game following 1981, 1983 and 1984 seasons.
Played in NFL Championship Game following 1981 and 1984 seasons.

EDWARD LEE WEST III
(Ed)
Tight End—Green Bay Packers
Born August 2, 1961, at Colbert County, Ala.
Height, 6.01. Weight, 242.
High School—Leighton, Ala., Colbert County.
Attended Auburn University.

Selected by Birmingham in 1984 USFL territorial draft.
Signed as free agent by Green Bay Packers, May 3, 1984.
Released by Green Bay Packers, August 27, 1984; re-signed by Packers, August 30, 1984.

	—PASS RECEIVING—				
Year Club	G.	P.C.	Yds.	Avg.	TD.
1984—Green Bay NFL	16	6	54	9.0	4

Additional pro statistics: Rushed once for two yards and a touchdown and recovered one fumble, 1984.

JAMES NEWCOMBE WEST
Linebacker—St. Louis Cardinals

Born December 19, 1957, at Fort Worth, Tex.
Height, 6.02. Weight, 220.
High School—Houston, Tex., Ross Sterling.
Received degree in dietetics from Texas Southern University in 1979.

Signed as free agent by Oakland Raiders, May 9, 1980.
Released by Oakland Raiders, August 18, 1980; signed as free agent by Calgary Stampeders, March 21, 1982.
Granted free agency, March 1, 1985; signed by St. Louis Cardinals, April 29, 1985.
Played with Houston Texans of Dixie Football League, 1981.

			—INTERCEPTIONS—		
Year	Club	G.	No.	Yds.	Avg.TD.
1982—Calgary CFL		9		None	
1983—Calgary CFL		15	2	61	30.5	0
1984—Calgary CFL		13	2	31	15.5	1
CFL Totals—3 Years		37	4	92	23.0	1

Additional CFL statistics: Recovered two fumbles, 1982; recovered three fumbles, 1983; recovered one fumble for five yards, 1984.

JEFFREY HAROLD WEST
(Jeff)
Punter—Seattle Seahawks

Born April 6, 1953, at Wheeling, Va.
Height, 6.02. Weight, 205.
High School—Ravenna, O.
Received bachelor of science degree in education from University of Cincinnati.

Selected by Cincinnati in 5th round (122nd player selected) of 1975 NFL draft.
Claimed on waivers from Cincinnati Bengals by St. Louis Cardinals, September 9, 1975.
Released by St. Louis Cardinals, August 24, 1976; signed as free agent by San Diego Chargers, November 3, 1976.
Released by San Diego Chargers, July 28, 1980; signed as free agent by Seattle Seahawks, May 12, 1981.
On injured reserve with broken ankle, December 16 through remainder of 1981 season.

			—PUNTING—		
Year	Club	G.	No.	Avg.	Blk.
1975—St. Louis NFL		14	64	37.7	1
1976—San Diego NFL		6	38	40.7	0
1977—San Diego NFL		14	72	37.6	1
1978—San Diego NFL		16	73	37.3	*2
1979—San Diego NFL		16	75	36.5	0
1981—Seattle NFL		15	66	39.1	0
1982—Seattle NFL		9	48	38.2	0
1983—Seattle NFL		16	79	39.5	0
1984—Seattle NFL		16	95	37.5	0
Pro Totals—9 Years		122	610	38.1	4

Additional pro statistics: Caught one pass for three yards, 1977; rushed once for no yards and fumbled once, 1978; rushed once for minus two yards, 1979; rushed three times for 25 yards, attempted one pass with no completions and fumbled once for minus 13 yards, 1981.
Played in AFC Championship Game following 1983 season.

DWIGHT WHEELER
Center-Offensive Tackle—Los Angeles Raiders

Born January 13, 1955, at Memphis, Tenn.
Height, 6.03. Weight, 274.
High School—Memphis, Tenn., Manassas.
Attended Tennessee State University.

Selected by New England in 4th round (102nd player selected) of 1978 NFL draft.
On injured reserve with broken leg, September 13 through remainder of 1978 season.
On injured reserve with ankle injury, December 12 through remainder of 1979 season.
Released by New England Patriots, August 27, 1984; signed as free agent by Los Angeles Raiders, November 8, 1984.
Released by Los Angeles Raiders, November 12, 1984; re-signed by Raiders, November 15, 1984.
New England NFL, 1978 through 1983; Los Angeles Raiders NFL, 1984.
Games: 1978 (2), 1979 (13), 1980 (16), 1981 (16), 1982 (9), 1983 (16), 1984 (4). Total—76.
Pro statistics: Returned one kickoff for no yards, 1978; fumbled once for minus 14 yards, 1979; fumbled once for minus 41 yards, 1980.

WILLIAM ANDREW WHITAKER
(Bill)
Safety—St. Louis Cardinals

Born January 18, 1959, at Kansas City, Mo.
Height, 6.00. Weight, 182.
High School—Kansas City, Mo., Rockhurst.
Attended University of Missouri.

Selected by Green Bay in 7th round (172nd player selected) of 1981 NFL draft.
Released by Green Bay Packers, August 29, 1983; signed as free agent by St. Louis Cardinals, November 3, 1983.

On injured reserve with abdominal strain, August 21 through September 26, 1984; activated after clearing procedural waivers, September 28, 1984.

On injured reserve with ankle injury, November 23 through remainder of 1984 season.

Green Bay NFL, 1981 and 1982; St. Louis NFL, 1983 and 1984.

Games: 1981 (16), 1982 (9), 1983 (7), 1984 (7). Total—39.

Pro statistics: Returned two punts for one yard and recovered one fumble, 1981.

BRAD DEE WHITE
Defensive Tackle—Indianapolis Colts
Born August 18, 1958, at Rexburg, Idaho.
Height, 6.02. Weight, 260.
High School—Idaho Falls, Idaho, Skyline.
Attended University of Tennessee.

Selected by Tampa Bay in 12th round (310th player selected) of 1981 NFL draft.

Released by Tampa Bay Buccaneers, August 27, 1984; signed as free agent by Indianapolis Colts, August 31, 1984.

Tampa Bay NFL, 1981 through 1983; Indianapolis NFL, 1984.

Games: 1981 (16), 1982 (9), 1983 (16), 1984 (15). Total—56.

CHARLES RAYMOND WHITE
Running Back—Cleveland Browns
Born January 22, 1958, at Los Angeles, Calif.
Height, 5.10. Weight, 190.
High School—San Fernando, Calif.
Attended University of Southern California.

Heisman Trophy winner, 1979.

Named as running back on THE SPORTING NEWS College All-America Team, 1979.

Named THE SPORTING NEWS College Player of the Year, 1979.

Selected by Cleveland in 1st round (27th player selected) of 1980 NFL draft.

On injured reserve with broken ankle, August 16 through entire 1983 season.

On physically unable to perform/active with ankle injury, July 19 through August 11, 1984; activated, August 12, 1984.

On injured reserve with ankle and back injuries, November 30 through remainder of 1984 season.

| | | —RUSHING— | | | | PASS RECEIVING | | | | —TOTAL— | | |
Year Club	G.	Att.	Yds.	Avg.	TD.	P.C.	Yds.	Avg.	TD.	TD.	Pts.	F.
1980—Cleveland NFL	14	86	279	3.2	5	17	153	9.0	1	6	36	1
1981—Cleveland NFL	16	97	342	3.5	1	27	219	8.1	0	1	6	8
1982—Cleveland NFL	9	69	259	3.8	3	34	283	8.3	0	3	18	2
1984—Cleveland NFL	10	24	62	2.6	0	5	29	5.8	0	0	0	0
Pro Totals—4 Years	49	276	942	3.4	9	83	684	8.2	1	10	60	11

Additional pro statistics: Returned one kickoff for 20 yards and recovered one fumble, 1980; returned 12 kickoffs for 243 yards and recovered three fumbles, 1981; returned five kickoffs for 80 yards, 1984.

CRAIG C. WHITE
Wide Receiver—Buffalo Bills
Born October 8, 1961, at St. Joseph, Mo.
Height, 6.01. Weight, 194.
High Schools—Decatur, Ill., Stephen; and Lawrence, Kan.
Attended University of Missouri.

Selected by Houston in 7th round (148th player selected) of 1984 USFL draft.

Selected by Buffalo in 11th round (299th player selected) of 1984 NFL draft.

Signed by Buffalo Bills, July 9, 1984.

Released by Buffalo Bills, August 27, 1984; re-signed by Bills, August 28, 1984.

| | | —PASS RECEIVING— | | | |
Year Club	G.	P.C.	Yds.	Avg.	TD.
1984—Buffalo NFL	14	4	28	7.0	0

Additional pro statistics: Returned one kickoff for five yards, 1984.

EDWARD ALVIN WHITE
(Ed)
Offensive Tackle—San Diego Chargers
Born April 4, 1947, at La Mesa, Calif.
Height, 6.02. Weight, 284.
High Schools—La Mesa, Calif., Helix and Indio, Calif.
Received degree in landscape architecture from University of California at Berkeley.

Named to THE SPORTING NEWS NFC All-Star Team, 1975 and 1976.

Selected by Minnesota NFL in 2nd round (39th player selected) of 1969 AFL-NFL draft.

Traded by Minnesota Vikings to San Diego Chargers for past considerations, July 29, 1978 (past considerations were awarding of White's rights to Chargers for running back Rickey Young).

Minnesota NFL, 1969 through 1977; San Diego NFL, 1978 through 1984.

Games: 1969 (14), 1970 (14), 1971 (14), 1972 (14), 1973 (14), 1974 (13), 1975 (13), 1976 (13), 1977 (13), 1978 (15), 1979 (16), 1980 (16), 1981 (16), 1982 (9), 1983 (16), 1984 (15). Total—225.

Pro statistics: Ran three yards with a lateral from a rushing play, 1972; recovered one fumble, 1973, 1976, 1980 and 1983.

Played in NFC Championship Game following 1973, 1974, 1976 and 1977 seasons.

Played in AFC Championship Game following 1980 and 1981 seasons.

Played in NFL Championship Game following 1969, 1973, 1974 and 1976 seasons.
Played in AFL-NFL Championship Game following 1969 season.
Played in Pro Bowl (NFL All-Star Game) following 1975 through 1977 and 1979 seasons.

RANDY LEE WHITE
Defensive Tackle—Dallas Cowboys
Born January 15, 1953, at Wilmington, Del.
Height, 6.04. Weight, 263.
High School—Wilmington, Del., Thomas McKean.
Attended University of Maryland.

Outland Trophy winner, 1974.
Named as defensive end on THE SPORTING NEWS College All-America Team, 1974.
Named to THE SPORTING NEWS NFC All-Star Team, 1978 and 1979.
Named to THE SPORTING NEWS NFL All-Star Team, 1980, 1981 and 1983.
Selected by Dallas in 1st round (2nd player selected) of 1975 NFL draft.
Placed on did not report list, August 21 through August 26, 1984.
Reported and granted roster exemption, August 27 through September 2, 1984; activated, September 3, 1984.
Dallas NFL, 1975 through 1984.
Games: 1975 (14), 1976 (14), 1977 (14), 1978 (16), 1979 (15), 1980 (16), 1981 (16), 1982 (9), 1983 (16), 1984 (16).
Total—146.
Pro statistics: Recovered two fumbles, 1975 and 1977; recovered one fumble, 1976, 1979, 1982 and 1983; returned one kickoff for 15 yards, 1978.
Played in NFC Championship Game following 1975, 1977, 1978 and 1980 through 1982 seasons.
Played in NFL Championship Game following 1975, 1977 and 1978 seasons.
Played in Pro Bowl (NFL All-Star Game) following 1977 and 1979 through 1984 seasons.
Named to play in Pro Bowl following 1978 season; replaced due to injury by Doug English.

SAMMY WHITE
Wide Receiver—Minnesota Vikings
Born March 16, 1954, at Winnsboro, La.
Height, 5.11. Weight, 200.
High School—Monroe, La., Richwood.
Received degree in education from Grambling State University.
Related to Jimmie Giles, tight end with Tampa Bay Buccaneers.

Named THE SPORTING NEWS NFC Rookie of the Year, 1976.
Selected by Minnesota in 2nd round (54th player selected) of 1976 NFL draft.

Year Club	G.	RUSHING				PASS RECEIVING				TOTAL		
		Att.	Yds.	Avg.	TD.	P.C.	Yds.	Avg.	TD.	TD.	Pts.	F.
1976—Minnesota NFL	14	5	−10	−2.0	0	51	906	17.8	10	10	60	3
1977—Minnesota NFL	14		None			41	760	18.5	*9	9	54	2
1978—Minnesota NFL	16	5	30	6.0	0	53	741	14.0	9	9	54	1
1979—Minnesota NFL	15	1	6	6.0	0	42	715	17.0	4	4	24	1
1980—Minnesota NFL	16	4	65	16.3	0	53	887	16.7	5	5	30	0
1981—Minnesota NFL	16	2	−1	−0.5	0	66	1001	15.2	3	3	18	1
1982—Minnesota NFL	7		None			29	503	17.3	5	5	30	0
1983—Minnesota NFL	11	1	7	7.0	0	29	412	14.2	4	4	24	0
1984—Minnesota NFL	13		None			21	399	19.0	1	1	6	1
Pro Totals—9 Years	122	18	97	5.4	0	385	6324	16.4	50	50	300	9

Year Club	G.	PUNT RETURNS				KICKOFF RET.			
		No.	Yds.	Avg.	TD.	No.	Yds.	Avg.	TD.
1976—Minnesota NFL	14	3	45	15.0	0	9	173	19.2	0
1977—Minnesota NFL	14		None			7	113	16.1	0
1978—Minnesota NFL	16	1	0	0.0	0	3	50	16.7	0
1979—Minnesota NFL	15		None				None		
1980—Minnesota NFL	16		None				None		
1981—Minnesota NFL	16	1	0	0.0	0		None		
1982—Minnesota NFL	7		None				None		
1983—Minnesota NFL	11		None				None		
1984—Minnesota NFL	13		None				None		
Pro Totals—9 Years	122	5	45	9.0	0	19	336	17.7	0

Additional pro statistics: Recovered two fumbles, 1976; recovered one fumble, 1977 and 1980.
Played in NFC Championship Game following 1976 and 1977 seasons.
Played in NFL Championship Game following 1976 season.
Played in Pro Bowl (NFL All-Star Game) following 1976 and 1977 seasons.

WILFORD DANIEL WHITE
(Danny)
Quarterback-Punter—Dallas Cowboys
Born February 9, 1952, at Mesa, Ariz.
Height, 6.02. Weight, 193.
High School—Mesa, Ariz., Westwood.
Attended Arizona State University.
Son of Wilford White, halfback with Chicago Bears, 1951 and 1952.

Selected by Dallas in 3rd round (53rd player selected) of 1974 NFL draft.
Played in World Football League with Memphis Southmen, 1974 and 1975.
Signed by Dallas Cowboys after World Football League folded, April 15, 1976.

Selected by Cleveland Indians' organization in 39th round of free-agent draft, June 5, 1973.
Selected by Houston Astros' organization in secondary phase of free-agent draft, January 9, 1974.
Selected by Cleveland Indians' organization in secondary phase of free-agent draft, June 5, 1974.
Selected by Cleveland Indians' organization in secondary phase of free-agent draft, January 9, 1975.

Year Club	G.	—————PASSING—————							—RUSHING—				—TOTAL—		
		Att.	Cmp.	Pct.	Gain	T.P.	P.I.	Avg.	Att.	Yds.	Avg.	TD.	TD.	Pts.	F.
1974—Memphis WFL	....	155	79	51.0	1190	11	9	7.68	24	103	4.3	0	0	0	....
1975—Memphis WFL	....	195	104	53.3	1445	10	8	7.41	23	116	5.0	0	0	1	....
1976—Dallas NFL	14	20	13	65.0	213	2	2	10.65	6	17	2.8	0	0	0	0
1977—Dallas NFL	14	10	4	40.0	35	0	1	3.50	1	—2	—2.0	0	0	0	0
1978—Dallas NFL	16	34	20	58.8	215	0	1	6.32	5	7	1.4	0	0	0	2
1979—Dallas NFL	16	39	19	48.7	267	1	2	6.85	1	25	25.0	0	0	0	1
1980—Dallas NFL	16	436	260	59.6	3287	28	25	7.54	27	114	4.2	1	1	6	8
1981—Dallas NFL	16	391	223	57.0	3098	22	13	7.92	38	104	2.7	0	0	0	*14
1982—Dallas NFL	9	247	156	63.2	2079	16	12	8.42	17	91	5.4	0	0	0	*10
1983—Dallas NFL	16	533	334	62.7	3980	29	23	7.47	18	31	1.7	4	5	30	10
1984—Dallas NFL	14	233	126	54.1	1580	11	11	6.78	6	21	3.5	0	0	0	2
WFL Totals—2 Years	....	350	183	52.3	2635	21	17	7.53	47	219	4.7	0	0	0	....
NFL Totals—9 Years	131	1943	1155	59.4	14754	109	90	7.59	119	408	3.4	5	6	36	47
Pro Totals—11 Years	....	2293	1338	58.4	17389	130	107	7.58	166	627	3.8	5	6	36	....

NFL Quarterback Rating Points: 1976 (94.4), 1977 (10.4), 1978 (65.3), 1979 (58.6), 1980 (80.8), 1981 (87.5), 1982 (91.1), 1983 (85.6), 1984 (71.5). Total—81.8.

Year Club	G.	——PUNTING——			Year Club	G.	——PUNTING——		
		No.	Avg.	Blk.			No.	Avg.	Blk.
1974—Memphis WFL	....	80	40.9	0	1981—Dallas NFL	16	79	40.8	0
1975—Memphis WFL	....	41	*45.1	0	1982—Dallas NFL	9	37	41.7	0
1976—Dallas NFL	14	70	38.4	2	1983—Dallas NFL	16	38	40.6	1
1977—Dallas NFL	14	80	39.6	1	1984—Dallas NFL	14	82	38.4	0
1978—Dallas NFL	16	76	40.5	1	WFL Totals—2 Years	....	121	42.3	0
1979—Dallas NFL	16	76	41.7	0	NFL Totals—9 Years	131	609	40.3	5
1980—Dallas NFL	16	71	40.9	0	Pro Totals—11 Years	....	730	40.6	5

Additional pro statistics: Scored one action point, 1975; recovered one fumble, 1977; recovered two fumbles and fumbled twice for minus eight yards, 1978; recovered one fumble for 15 yards and caught one pass for minus nine yards, 1980; recovered eight fumbles and fumbled 14 times for minus 34 yards, 1981; recovered two fumbles, 1982; caught one pass for 15 yards and a touchdown and recovered four fumbles, 1983; recovered one fumble and fumbled twice for minus three yards, 1984.
Played in NFC Championship Game following 1977, 1978 and 1980 through 1982 seasons.
Played in NFL Championship Game following 1977 and 1978 seasons.
Played in Pro Bowl (NFL All-Star Game) following 1982 season.

MICHAEL CARROLL WHITWELL
(Mike)
Safety—Cleveland Browns
Born November 14, 1958, at Kenedy, Tex.
Height, 6.00. Weight, 175.
High School—Cotulla, Tex.
Received bachelor of arts degree in business agriculture
from Texas A&M University in 1982.

Selected by Cleveland in 6th round (162nd player selected) of 1982 NFL draft.
On injured reserve with knee injury, August 21 through entire 1984 season.

Year Club	G.	—INTERCEPTIONS—			
		No.	Yds.	Avg.	TD.
1982—Cleveland NFL	9		None		
1983—Cleveland NFL	16	3	67	22.3	0
Pro Totals—2 Years	25	3	67	22.3	0

MIKE WILCHER
Linebacker—Los Angeles Rams
Born March 20, 1960, at Washington, D.C.
Height, 6.03. Weight, 240.
High School—Washington, D.C., Eastern.
Attended University of North Carolina.

Selected by Philadelphia in 1983 USFL territorial draft.
Selected by Los Angeles Rams in 2nd round (36th player selected) of 1983 NFL draft.
Signed by Los Angeles Rams NFL, June 16, 1983.
Los Angeles Rams NFL, 1983 and 1984.
Games: 1983 (15), 1984 (15). Total—30.

JAMES CURTIS WILDER
Running Back—Tampa Bay Buccaneers
Born May 12, 1958, at Sikeston, Mo.
Height, 6.03. Weight, 225.
High School—Sikeston, Mo.
Attended Northeastern Oklahoma A&M and University of Missouri.

Established NFL records for most rushing attempts, season (407), 1984; most combined attempts, season (496), 1984.

Tied NFL record for most rushing attempts, game (43) vs. Green Bay Packers, September 30, 1984.

Selected by Tampa Bay in 2nd round (34th player selected) of 1981 NFL draft.

On injured reserve with broken ribs, November 15 through remainder of 1983 season.

Year Club	G.	Att.	RUSHING Yds.	Avg.	TD.	PASS RECEIVING P.C.	Yds.	Avg.	TD.	TOTAL TD.	Pts.	F.
1981—Tampa Bay NFL	16	107	370	3.5	4	48	507	10.6	1	5	30	3
1982—Tampa Bay NFL	9	83	324	3.9	3	53	466	8.8	1	4	24	5
1983—Tampa Bay NFL	10	161	640	4.0	4	57	380	6.7	2	6	36	1
1984—Tampa Bay NFL	16	*407	1544	3.8	13	85	685	8.1	0	13	78	10
Pro Totals—4 Years	51	758	2878	3.8	24	243	2038	8.4	4	28	168	19

Additional pro statistics: Returned one kickoff for 19 yards and recovered one fumble, 1981; recovered one fumble for three yards, 1982; attempted one pass with one completion for 16 yards and a touchdown and recovered four fumbles, 1984.

Played in Pro Bowl (NFL All-Star Game) following 1984 season.

DOUGLAS WILKERSON
(Doug)
Guard—San Diego Chargers
Born March 27, 1947, at Fayetteville, N. C.
Height, 6.03. Weight, 253.
High School—Fayetteville, N. C., E. E. Smith.
Received bachelor of science degree in elementary and physical education from
North Carolina Central University.

Selected by Houston in 1st round (14th player selected) of 1970 NFL draft.

Traded by Houston Oilers to San Diego Chargers for tight end Willie Frazier, December 18, 1970.

On injured reserve with knee injury, August 28 through September 27, 1979; activated, September 28, 1979.

On injured reserve with broken arm, August 30 through September 30, 1983; activated, October 1, 1983.

Houston NFL, 1970; San Diego NFL, 1971 through 1984.

Games: 1970 (9), 1971 (14), 1972 (14), 1973 (14), 1974 (14), 1975 (14), 1976 (14), 1977 (14), 1978 (16), 1979 (12), 1980 (16), 1981 (16), 1982 (9), 1983 (12), 1984 (16). Total—204.

Pro statistics: Returned one kickoff for no yards, 1971; recovered four fumbles, 1975; recovered two fumbles, 1977; recovered one fumble, 1979, 1981 and 1984.

Played in AFC Championship Game following 1980 and 1981 seasons.

Played in Pro Bowl (NFL All-Star Game) following 1980 through 1982 seasons.

REGGIE WAYMAN WILKES
Linebacker—Philadelphia Eagles
Born May 27, 1956, at Pine Bluff, Ark.
Height, 6.04. Weight, 235.
High School—Atlanta, Ga., Southwest.
Received bachelor of science degree in biology from Georgia Tech in 1978;
attending Morehouse School of Medicine and University of Pennsylvania Medical School (exchange program).
Cousin of Jamaal Wilkes, forward with Los Angeles Lakers.

Selected by Philadelphia in 3rd round (66th player selected) of 1978 NFL draft.

Philadelphia NFL, 1978 through 1984.

Games: 1978 (16), 1979 (16), 1980 (16), 1981 (14), 1982 (9), 1983 (14), 1984 (14). Total—99.

Pro statistics: Recovered six fumbles, 1978; intercepted two passes for no yards and recovered two fumbles, 1979; intercepted one pass for no yards, 1980; intercepted two passes for 18 yards and scored extra point on pass reception, 1981; recovered one fumble, 1982; intercepted one pass for six yards, 1984.

Played in NFC Championship Game following 1980 season.

Played in NFL Championship Game following 1980 season.

JIMMY RAY WILKS
Defensive End—New Orleans Saints
Born March 12, 1958, at Los Angeles, Calif.
Height, 6.05. Weight, 265.
High School—Pasadena, Calif.
Attended University of California and
San Diego State University.

Selected by New Orleans in 12th round (305th player selected) of 1981 NFL draft.

On inactive list, September 19, 1982.

New Orleans NFL, 1981 through 1984.

Games: 1981 (16), 1982 (8), 1983 (16), 1984 (16). Total—56.

Pro statistics: Recovered two fumbles, 1981; recovered one fumble, 1983 and 1984.

GERALD WILLIAM WILLHITE
Running Back—Denver Broncos
Born May 30, 1959, at Sacramento, Calif.
Height, 5.10. Weight, 200.
High School—Rancho Cordova, Calif., Cordova.
Attended American River Junior College and San Jose State University.
Brother of Kevin Willhite, running back at University of Oregon; and
Randy Willhite, defensive back at University of Oregon.

Selected by Denver in 1st round (21st player selected) of 1982 NFL draft.

On injured reserve with pulled hamstring, August 30 through October 27, 1983; activated, October 28, 1983.

			—RUSHING—			PASS RECEIVING				—TOTAL—		
Year Club	G.	Att.	Yds.	Avg.	TD.	P.C.	Yds.	Avg.	TD.	TD.	Pts.	F.
1982—Denver NFL	9	70	347	5.0	2	26	227	8.7	0	2	12	5
1983—Denver NFL	8	43	188	4.4	3	14	153	10.9	1	4	24	0
1984—Denver NFL	16	77	371	4.8	2	27	298	11.0	0	2	12	3
Pro Totals—3 Years	33	190	906	4.8	7	67	678	10.1	1	8	48	8

		—PUNT RETURNS—				—KICKOFF RET.—			
Year Club	G.	No.	Yds.	Avg.	TD.	No.	Yds.	Avg.	TD.
1982—Denver NFL	9	6	63	10.5	0	17	337	19.8	0
1983—Denver NFL	8		None				None		
1984—Denver NFL	16	20	200	10.0	0	4	109	27.3	0
Pro Totals—3 Years	33	26	263	10.1	0	21	446	21.2	0

Additional pro statistics: Attempted two passes with no completions and one interception, 1982; attempted one pass with no completions, 1983; attempted two passes with one completion for 20 yards and recovered two fumbles, 1984.

BYRON WILLIAMS
Wide Receiver—New York Giants
Born October 31, 1960, at Texarkana, Tex.
Height, 6.02. Weight, 180.
High School—Texarkana, Tex., Liberty Eylau.
Attended University of Texas at Arlington.

Selected by Denver in 21st round (249th player selected) of 1983 USFL draft.
Selected by Green Bay in 10th round (253rd player selected) of 1983 NFL draft.
Signed by Green Bay Packers, May 25, 1983.
Released by Green Bay Packers, August 29, 1983; signed as free agent by Philadelphia Eagles, September 13, 1983.
Released by Philadelphia Eagles, September 29, 1983; signed as free agent by New York Giants, October 27, 1983.
Active for 2 games with Philadelphia Eagles in 1983; did not play.

		—PASS RECEIVING—			
Year Club	G.	P.C.	Yds.	Avg.	TD.
1983—Phi (0)-NYG (5) NFL	5	20	346	17.3	1
1984—New York Giants NFL	16	24	471	19.6	2
Pro Totals—2 Years	21	44	817	18.6	3

Additional pro statistics: Fumbled once, 1983.

CRAIG ANTHONY WILLIAMS
Running Back—New England Patriots
Born April 4, 1962, at Jamaica, N.Y.
Height, 6.01. Weight, 225.
High School—Amityville, N.Y., Memorial.
Received bachelor of arts degree in economics and business from Lafayette College in 1984.

Signed as free agent by New York Jets, May 20, 1984.
Released by New York Jets after failing physical, May 30, 1984; signed as free agent by New England Patriots, June 18, 1984.
On injured reserve with knee injury, August 14 through entire 1984 season.

DARRYL EUGENE WILLIAMS
(Dokie)
Wide Receiver—Los Angeles Raiders
Born August 25, 1960, at Oceanside, Calif.
Height, 5.11. Weight, 180.
High School—Oceanside, Calif., El Camino.
Received degree in political science from University of California at Los Angeles.

Selected by Oakland in 8th round (90th player selected) of 1983 USFL draft.
Selected by Los Angeles Raiders in 5th round (138th player selected) of 1983 NFL draft.
Signed by Los Angeles Raiders, July 6, 1983.

		PASS RECEIVING				—KICKOFF RET.—				—TOTAL—		
Year Club	G.	P.C.	Yds.	Avg.	TD.	No.	Yds.	Avg.	TD.	TD.	Pts.	F.
1983—Los Angeles Raiders NFL	16	14	259	18.5	3	5	88	17.6	0	3	18	2
1984—Los Angeles Raiders NFL	16	22	509	23.1	4	24	621	25.9	0	4	24	0
Pro Totals—2 Years	32	36	768	21.3	7	29	709	24.4	0	7	42	2

Member of Los Angeles Raiders for AFC Championship Game following 1983 season; did not play.
Played in NFL Championship Game following 1983 season.

DERWIN DAWAYNE WILLIAMS
Wide Receiver—New England Patriots
Born May 6, 1961, at Brownwood, Tex.
Height, 6.00. Weight, 170.
High School—Brownwood, Tex.
Attended University of New Mexico.

Selected by New England in 7th round (192nd player selected) of 1984 NFL draft.
On injured reserve with concussion, August 27 through entire 1984 season.

EDWARD EUGENE WILLIAMS
(Ed)
Linebacker—New England Patriots

Born September 8, 1961, at Odessa, Tex.
Height, 6.04. Weight, 244.
High School—Odessa, Tex., Ector.
Attended University of Texas.

Selected by San Antonio in 1984 USFL territorial draft.
Selected by New England in 2nd round (43rd player selected) of 1984 NFL draft.
Signed by New England Patriots, July 13, 1984.
New England NFL, 1984.
Games: 1984 (14).
Pro statistics: Recovered one fumble, 1984.

ERIC MICHAEL WILLIAMS
Defensive Tackle—Detroit Lions

Born February 24, 1962, at Stockton, Calif.
Height, 6.04. Weight, 260.
High School—Stockton, Calif., St. Mary's.
Attended Washington State University.
Son of Roy Williams, 2nd round selection of Detroit Lions in 1962 NFL draft.

Selected by New Jersey in 1st round (19th player selected) of 1984 USFL draft.
Selected by Detroit in 3rd round (62nd player selected) of 1984 NFL draft.
Signed by Detroit Lions, July 21, 1984.
Detroit NFL, 1984.
Games: 1984 (12).

ERIC THOMAS WILLIAMS
Safety—Pittsburgh Steelers

Born February 21, 1960, at Raleigh, N.C.
Height, 6.01. Weight, 183.
High School—Garner, N.C.
Attended North Carolina State University.

Selected by Philadelphia in 21st round (248th player selected) of 1983 USFL season.
Selected by Pittsburgh in 6th round (164th player selected) of 1983 NFL season.
Signed by Pittsburgh Steelers, June 1, 1983.
On injured reserve with sprained ankle, September 20 through remainder of 1983 season.

| | | —INTERCEPTIONS— | | | |
Year Club	G.	No.	Yds.	Avg.	TD.
1983—Pittsburgh NFL............	3		None		
1984—Pittsburgh NFL............	16	3	49	16.3	0
Pro Totals—2 Years............	19	3	49	16.3	0

Additional pro statistics: Recovered one fumble for six yards, 1984.
Played in AFC Championship Game following 1984 season.

EUGENE WILLIAMS
Linebacker—Seattle Seahawks

Born June 15, 1960, at Longview, Tex.
Height, 6.01. Weight, 220.
High School—Longview, Tex.
Attended The University of Tulsa.

Selected by Seattle in 7th round (174th player selected) of 1982 NFL draft.
On injured reserve with stress fracture of leg, October 7 through remainder of 1983 season.
On physically unable to perform/active with stress fracture, July 14 through August 13, 1984.
On physically unable to perform/reserve with stress fracture, August 14 through entire 1984 season.
Seattle NFL, 1982 and 1983.
Games: 1982 (9), 1983 (4). Total—13.
Pro statistics: Intercepted one pass for no yards, 1983.

GARDNER WILLIAMS
Defensive Back—San Francisco 49ers

Born December 11, 1961, at Washington, D.C.
Height, 6.02. Weight, 199.
High School—Oakland, Calif., Bishop O'Dowd.
Received bachelor of arts degree in business administration from St. Mary's (Calif.) College in 1984.
Son of Howie Williams, defensive back with Oakland Raiders, 1964 through 1969.

Selected by Michigan in 18th round (369th player selected) of 1984 USFL draft.
Selected by Los Angeles Raiders in 11th round (282nd player selected) of 1984 NFL draft.
Signed by Los Angeles Raiders, June 13, 1984.
Released by Los Angeles Raiders, August 27, 1984; signed as free agent by Detroit Lions, October 18, 1984.
Released by Detroit Lions, November 9, 1984; signed as free agent by San Francisco 49ers, April 16, 1985.
Detroit NFL, 1984.
Games: 1984 (3).

GARY LEON WILLIAMS
Wide Receiver—Cincinnati Bengals
Born September 4, 1959, at Wilmington, O.
Height, 6.02. Weight, 215.
High School—Wilmington, O.
Received degree in recreation education from Ohio State University in 1982.

Selected by Arizona in 2nd round (23rd player selected) of 1983 USFL draft.
Selected by Cincinnati in 11th round (304th player selected) of 1983 NFL draft.
Signed by Cincinnati Bengals, June, 1983.
On non-football injury list with knee injury, July 17 through August 14, 1983.
On physically unable to perform/reserve with knee injury, August 15 through entire 1983 season.
On injured reserve with pulled hamstring, August 27 through September 26, 1984; activated after clearing procedural waivers, September 28, 1984.
Cincinnati NFL, 1984.
Games: 1984 (8).
Pro statistics: Returned one kickoff for no yards, 1984.

GEORGE VAN WILLIAMS
(Known by middle name.)
Running Back—Buffalo Bills
Born March 15, 1959, at Johnson City, Tenn.
Height, 6.00. Weight, 210.
High School—Johnson City, Tenn., All-Science.
Attended East Tennessee State University and Carson-Newman College.

Selected by Buffalo in 4th round (93rd player selected) of 1982 NFL draft.
On injured reserve with knee injury, September 7 through entire 1982 season.

		———RUSHING———				PASS RECEIVING				—TOTAL—		
Year Club	G.	Att.	Yds.	Avg.	TD.	P.C.	Yds.	Avg.	TD.	TD.	Pts.	F.
1983—Buffalo NFL	16	3	11	3.7	0	None				0	0	2
1984—Buffalo NFL	16	18	51	2.8	0	5	46	9.2	1	1	6	1
Pro Totals—2 Years	32	21	62	3.0	0	5	46	9.2	1	1	6	3

		KICKOFF RETURNS			
Year Club	G.	No.	Yds.	Avg.	TD.
1983—Buffalo NFL	16	22	494	22.5	0
1984—Buffalo NFL	16	39	820	21.0	0
Pro Totals—2 Years	32	61	1314	21.5	0

Additional pro statistics: Returned one punt for no yards, 1983; recovered one fumble, 1983 and 1984.

GREG WILLIAMS
Safety—Washington Redskins
Born August 1, 1959, at Greenville, Miss.
Height, 5.11. Weight, 185.
High School—Greenville, Miss., Christian Academy.
Attended Mississippi Delta Junior College and Mississippi State University.

Signed as free agent by Washington Redskins, May 12, 1982.
Washington NFL, 1982 through 1984.
Games: 1982 (9), 1983 (16), 1984 (16). Total—41.
Pro statistics: Returned one punt for nine yards and one kickoff for two yards, 1982; intercepted two passes for 25 yards, returned one kickoff for six yards and recovered four fumbles for four yards, 1983; recovered one fumble and returned one punt for no yards, 1984.
Played in NFC Championship Game following 1982 and 1983 seasons.
Played in NFL Championship Game following 1982 and 1983 seasons.

JAMES HENRY WILLIAMS
(Jimmy)
Linebacker—Detroit Lions
Born November 15, 1960, at Washington, D.C.
Height, 6.02. Weight, 230.
High School—Washington, D.C., Woodrow Wilson.
Attended University of Nebraska.
Brother of Toby Williams, defensive end with New England Patriots.

Selected by Detroit in 1st round (15th player selected) of 1982 NFL draft.
On injured reserve with broken foot, December 20 through remainder of 1982 season.
Detroit NFL, 1982 through 1984.
Games: 1982 (6), 1983 (16), 1984 (16). Total—38.
Pro statistics: Intercepted one pass for four yards, 1982; recovered one fumble, 1983 and 1984.

JAMIE WILLIAMS
Tight End—Houston Oilers
Born February 25, 1960, at Vero Beach, Fla.
Height, 6.04. Weight, 244.
High School—Davenport, Ia., Central.
Attended University of Nebraska.

Selected by Boston in 1983 USFL territorial draft.
Selected by New York Giants in 3rd round (63rd player selected) of 1983 NFL draft.
Signed by New York Giants, June 30, 1983.
Released by New York Giants, August 29, 1983; signed as free agent by St. Louis Cardinals, September 13, 1983.
Released by St. Louis Cardinals, October 5, 1983; signed as free agent by Tampa Bay Buccaneers, January 25, 1984.
USFL rights traded by New Orleans Breakers to New Jersey Generals for past consideration, March 26, 1984.
Released by Tampa Bay Buccaneers, May 8, 1984; awarded on waivers to Houston Oilers, May 21, 1984.

		—PASS RECEIVING—				
Year	Club	G.	P.C.	Yds.	Avg.	TD.
1983—St. Louis NFL		1		None		
1984—Houston NFL		16	41	545	13.3	3
Pro Totals—2 Years		17	41	545	13.3	3

Additional pro statistics: Returned one kickoff for no yards, recovered one fumble and fumbled twice, 1984.

JOEL WILLIAMS
First name pronounced Jo-EL.
Linebacker—Philadelphia Eagles
Born December 13, 1956, at Miami, Fla.
Height, 6.01. Weight, 225.
High School—Miami, Fla., North.
Attended Peru College and received bachelor of business administration degree
from University of Wisconsin at LaCrosse in 1979.
Cousin of Bobby Rusely, linebacker at University of Louisville.

Signed as free agent by Miami Dolphins, July 12, 1979.
Released by Miami Dolphins, August 27, 1979; claimed on waivers by Atlanta Falcons, August 28, 1979.
On injured reserve with knee injury, December 19 through remainder of 1981 season.
USFL rights released by Birmingham Stallions, August 16, 1983; rights awarded on waivers to Pittsburgh Maulers, August 17, 1983.
Traded by Atlanta Falcons to Philadelphia Eagles for 2nd round pick in 1984 draft, August 21, 1983.
Atlanta NFL, 1979 through 1982; Philadelphia NFL, 1983 and 1984.
Games: 1979 (16), 1980 (16), 1981 (10), 1982 (9), 1983 (16), 1984 (16). Total—83.
Pro statistics: Intercepted two passes for 55 yards, recovered three fumbles for 42 yards and one touchdown and credited with one safety, 1980; intercepted one pass for 25 yards and recovered two fumbles for 57 yards and a touchdown, 1981; recovered one fumble, 1982 and 1983; recovered two fumbles, 1984.

JONATHAN WILLIAMS
(Jon)
Running Back—New England Patriots
Born June 1, 1961, at Somerville, N.J.
Height, 5.09. Weight, 209.
High School—Somerville, N.J.
Attended Penn State University.

Selected by Philadelphia in 1984 USFL territorial draft.
Selected by New England in 3rd round (70th player selected) of 1984 NFL draft.
Signed by New England Patriots, July 13, 1984.
On injured reserve with knee injury, November 3 through remainder of 1984 season.

		KICKOFF RETURNS				
Year	Club	G.	No.	Yds.	Avg.	TD.
1984—New England NFL		9	23	461	20.0	0

LEE WILLIAMS
Defensive End—San Diego Chargers
Born October 15, 1962, at Fort Lauderdale, Fla.
Height, 6.06. Weight, 270.
High School—Fort Lauderdale, Fla., Stranahan.
Attended Bethune-Cookman College.

Selected by Tampa Bay in 1984 USFL territorial draft.
USFL rights traded with rights to defensive tackle Dewey Forte by Tampa Bay Bandits to Los Angeles Express for draft choice, March 2, 1984.
Signed by Los Angeles Express, March 6, 1984.
Granted roster exemption, March 6 through March 15, 1984; activated, March 16, 1984.
Selected by San Diego in 1st round (6th player selected) of 1984 NFL supplemental draft.
Released by Los Angeles Express, October 20, 1984; signed by San Diego Chargers, October 22, 1984.
Granted roster exemption, October 22 through October 28, 1984; activated, October 29, 1984.
Los Angeles USFL, 1984; San Diego NFL, 1984.
Games: 1984 USFL (14), 1984 NFL (8). Total Pro—22.
USFL statistics: Credited with 13 sacks for 92 yards, 1984.
NFL statistics: Intercepted one pass for 66 yards and a touchdown, 1984.

LESTER WILLIAMS
Nose Tackle—New England Patriots
Born January 19, 1959, at Miami, Fla.
Height, 6.03. Weight, 272.
High School—Miami, Fla., Carol City.
Attended University of Miami (Fla.).

Named as defensive end on THE SPORTING NEWS College All-America Team, 1981.
Selected by New England in 1st round (27th player selected) of 1982 NFL draft.
On injured reserve with broken arm, October 17 through remainder of 1984 season.
New England NFL, 1982 through 1984.
Games: 1982 (9), 1983 (15), 1984 (7). Total—31.
Pro statistics: Recovered one fumble, 1982 and 1984.

MICHAEL WILLIAMS
(Mike)
Tight End—Washington Redskins
Born August 27, 1959, at Lafayette, Ala.
Height, 6.04. Weight, 251.
High School—Lafayette, Ala.
Attended Alabama A&M University.

Selected by Washington in 5th round (133rd player selected) of 1982 NFL draft.
On injured reserve with knee injury, December 20 through remainder of 1982 season.
On physically unable to perform/active with knee injury, July 23 through August 14, 1984.
On physically unable to perform/reserve, August 15 through Ocober 26, 1983; activated, October 27, 1983.
On injured reserve with hairline fracture in vertebra, September 4 through remainder of 1984 season.

		PASS RECEIVING			
Year Club	G.	P.C.	Yds.	Avg.	TD.
1982—Washington NFL.........	6	3	14	4.7	0
1983—Washington NFL.........	7		None		
1984—Washington NFL.........	1		None		
Pro Totals—3 Years............	14	3	14	4.7	0

Member of Washington Redskins for NFC Championship Game following 1983 season; did not play.
Played in NFL Championship Game following 1983 season.

MICHAEL WILLIAMS
(Mike)
Running Back—Philadelphia Eagles
Born July 16, 1961, at Atmore, Ala.
Height, 6.02. Weight, 225.
High School—Atmore, Ala., Escambia County.
Attended Northeast Mississippi Junior College and Mississippi College.

Selected by Birmingham in 7th round (77th player selected) of 1983 USFL draft.
Selected by Philadelphia in 4th round (89th player selected) of 1983 NFL draft.
Signed by Philadelphia Eagles, May 26, 1983.

		RUSHING				PASS RECEIVING				—TOTAL—		
Year Club	G.	Att.	Yds.	Avg.	TD.	P.C.	Yds.	Avg.	TD.	TD.	Pts.	F.
1983—Philadelphia NFL	15	103	385	3.7	0	17	142	8.4	0	0	0	1
1984—Philadelphia NFL	16	33	83	2.5	0	7	47	6.7	0	0	0	1
Pro Totals—2 Years....................	31	136	468	3.4	0	24	189	7.9	0	0	0	2

Additional pro statistics: Returned three kickoffs for 59 yards, 1983.

NEWTON DENNIS WILLIAMS
Running Back—Indianapolis Colts
Born May 10, 1959, at Charlotte, N.C.
Height, 5.10. Weight, 204.
High School—Charlotte, N.C., North Mecklenburg.
Received bachelor of science degree in telecommunications from Arizona State University.

Selected by San Francisco in 5th round (139th player selected) of 1982 NFL draft.
Released by San Francisco 49ers, September 6, 1982; re-signed by 49ers, September 9, 1982.
On injured reserve with shoulder injury, December 16 through remainder of 1982 season.
Released by San Francisco 49ers, August 16, 1983; awarded on waivers to Baltimore Colts, August 18, 1983.
Franchise transferred to Indianapolis, March 31, 1984.
On injured reserve with ankle injury, August 22 through entire 1984 season.

		RUSHING				PASS RECEIVING				—TOTAL—		
Year Club	G.	Att.	Yds.	Avg.	TD.	P.C.	Yds.	Avg.	TD.	TD.	Pts.	F.
1982—San Francisco NFL	6		None				None			0	0	0
1983—Baltimore NFL	16	28	77	2.8	0	4	46	11.5	0	0	0	0
Pro Totals—2 Years....................	22	28	77	2.8	0	4	46	11.5	0	0	0	0

PERRY LAMAR WILLIAMS
Cornerback—New York Giants
Born May 12, 1961, at Hamlet, N.C.
Height, 6.02. Weight, 203.
High School—Hamlet, N.C., Richmond County.
Attended North Carolina State University.

Selected by Washington in 7th round (76th player selected) of 1983 USFL draft.
Selected by New York Giants in 7th round (178th player selected) of 1983 NFL draft.
Signed by New York Giants, June 13, 1983.
On injured reserve with foot injury, August 17 through entire 1983 season.

Year Club	G.	No.	Yds.	Avg.TD.	
1984—N.Y. Giants NFL	16	3	7	2.3	0

Additional pro statistics: Recovered one fumble, 1984.

QUENCY L. WILLIAMS
Linebacker—Los Angeles Raiders

Born April 10, 1961, at Douglasville, Ga.
Height, 6.02. Weight, 218.
High School—Douglasville, Ga., Douglas County.
Attended Auburn University.

Selected by Birmingham in 1984 USFL territorial draft.
Signed by Birmingham Stallions, January 10, 1984.
Released by Birmingham Stallions, February 13, 1984; signed as free agent by Los Angeles Raiders, May 20, 1984.
On injured reserve with broken hand, August 14 through entire 1984 season.

REGINALD WILLIAMS
(Reggie)
Linebacker—Cincinnati Bengals

Born September 19, 1954, at Flint, Mich.
Height, 6.00. Weight, 228.
High School—Flint, Mich., Southwestern.
Received bachelor of arts degree in psychology from Dartmouth College.

Selected by Cincinnati in 3rd round (82nd player selected) of 1976 NFL draft.

		———INTERCEPTIONS———			
Year Club	G.	No.	Yds.	Avg.TD.	
1976—Cincinnati NFL............	14	1	17	17.0	0
1977—Cincinnati NFL............	14	3	67	22.3	1
1978—Cincinnati NFL............	16	1	11	11.0	0
1979—Cincinnati NFL............	12	2	5	2.5	0
1980—Cincinnati NFL............	14	2	8	4.0	0
1981—Cincinnati NFL............	16	4	33	8.3	0
1982—Cincinnati NFL............	9	1	20	20.0	0
1983—Cincinnati NFL............	16		None		
1984—Cincinnati NFL............	16	2	33	16.5	0
Pro Totals—9 Years............	127	16	194	12.1	1

Additional pro statistics: Recovered blocked punt in end zone for a touchdown, recovered two fumbles and returned one punt for no yards, 1977 and 1980; fumbled once, 1977 and 1980; recovered one fumble for 30 yards, 1978; recovered one fumble, 1979 and 1980; recovered three fumbles, 1981, recovered four fumbles and credited with one safety, 1982; recovered four fumbles for 59 yards and a touchdown, 1983.
Played in AFC Championship Game following 1981 season.
Played in NFL Championship Game following 1981 season.

RICKY C. WILLIAMS
Cornerback—Los Angeles Raiders

Born April 27, 1960, at Santa Monica, Calif.
Height, 6.01. Weight, 195.
High School—Santa Monica, Calif., Samo.
Attended Santa Monica Junior College and Langston College.

Selected by New England in 9th round (233rd player selected) of 1983 NFL draft.
Released by New England Patriots, August 2, 1983; signed as free agent by Oklahoma Outlaws, December 5, 1983.
Released by Oklahoma Outlaws, February 13, 1984; signed as free agent by Los Angeles Raiders, May 20, 1984.
On injured reserve with knee injury, August 27 through entire 1984 season.

ROBERT WILLIAMS
Safety—Pittsburgh Steelers

Born September 26, 1962, at Chicago, Ill.
Height, 5.11. Weight, 202.
High School—Chicago, Ill., Dunbar Vocational.
Attended Eastern Illinois University.

Signed as free agent by Pittsburgh Steelers, June 10, 1984.
On injured reserve with knee injury, August 14 through December 6, 1984; activated after clearing procedural waivers, December 7, 1984.
Pittsburgh NFL, 1984.
Games: 1984 (2).
Played in AFC Championship Game following 1984 season.

ROBERT JERRY WILLIAMS
(Ben)
Defensive End—Buffalo Bills

Born September 1, 1954, at Yazoo City, Miss.
Height, 6.03. Weight, 260.
High School—Yazoo City, Miss.
Attended University of Mississippi.

Selected by Buffalo in 3rd round (78th player selected) of 1976 NFL draft.
Buffalo NFL, 1976 through 1984.
Games: 1976 (13), 1977 (14), 1978 (16), 1979 (16), 1980 (16), 1981 (16), 1982 (9), 1983 (16), 1984 (15). Total—131.
Pro statistics: Recovered one fumble, 1976, 1977, 1980, 1981 and 1982; intercepted one pass for no yards and credited with one safety, 1981; intercepted one pass for 20 yards, 1982; returned three kickoffs for 56 yards and recovered two fumbles, 1983.
Played in Pro Bowl (NFL All-Star Game) following 1982 season.

TOBIAS WILLIAMS
(Toby)
Defensive End—New England Patriots
Born November 19, 1959, at Washington, D.C.
Height, 6.03. Weight, 265.
High School—Washington, D.C., Woodrow Wilson.
Received bachelor of arts degree in criminal justice from University of Nebraska in 1983.
Brother of Jimmy Williams, linebacker with Detroit Lions.

Selected by Boston in 1983 USFL territorial draft.
Selected by New England in 10th round (265th player selected) of 1983 NFL draft.
Signed by New England Patriots, May 25, 1983.
New England NFL, 1983 and 1984.
Games: 1983 (16), 1984 (16). Total—32.
Pro statistics: Recovered one fumble, 1984.

VAUGHN AARON WILLIAMS
Defensive Back—Indianapolis Colts
Born December 14, 1961, at Denver, Colo.
Height, 6.02. Weight, 193.
High School—Denver, Colo., George Washington.
Attended Stanford University.

Selected by Oakland in 1984 USFL territorial draft.
Signed as free agent by San Francisco 49ers, May 10, 1984.
On injured reserve with pulled hamstring, August 27 through September 27, 1984.
Released by San Francisco 49ers, September 28, 1984; signed as free agent by Indianapolis Colts, October 10, 1984.
Indianapolis NFL, 1984.
Games: 1984 (10).

CARLTON WILLIAMSON
Safety—San Francisco 49ers
Born June 12, 1958, at Atlanta, Ga.
Height, 6.00. Weight, 204.
High School—Atlanta, Ga., Brown.
Attended University of Pittsburgh.

Selected by San Francisco in 3rd round (65th player selected) of 1981 NFL draft.
On injured reserve with fractured fibula, August 30 through October 21, 1983; activated, October 22, 1983.

| | | —INTERCEPTIONS— | | | |
Year Club	G.	No.	Yds.	Avg.TD.	
1981—San Francisco NFL	16	4	44	11.0	0
1982—San Francisco NFL	8		None		
1983—San Francisco NFL	9	4	51	12.8	0
1984—San Francisco NFL	15	2	42	21.0	0
Pro Totals—4 Years............	48	10	137	13.7	0

Additional pro statistics: Recovered two fumbles for three yards, 1981.
Played in NFC Championship Game following 1981, 1983 and 1984 seasons.
Played in NFL Championship Game following 1981 and 1984 seasons.
Played in Pro Bowl (NFL All-Star Game) following 1984 season.

CHESTER WILLIS
Running Back—Los Angeles Raiders
Born May 2, 1958, at Eleberton, Ga.
Height, 5.11. Weight, 200.
High School—Gainesville, Ga., Johnson.
Attended Auburn University.

Selected by Oakland in 11th round (304th player selected) of 1981 NFL draft.
On injured reserve with groin injury, December 16 through remainder of 1981 season.
Franchise transferred to Los Angeles, May 7, 1982.
On inactive list, September 19, 1982.
On injured reserve with shoulder injury, December 1, 1983, through January 6, 1984; activated, January 7, 1984.
Released by Los Angeles Raiders, August 27, 1984; re-signed by Raiders, August 28, 1984.

| | | —RUSHING— | | | | PASS RECEIVING | | | | —TOTAL— | | |
Year Club	G.	Att.	Yds.	Avg.	TD.	P.C.	Yds.	Avg.	TD.	TD.	Pts.	F.
1981—Oakland NFL............	15	16	54	3.4	1	1	24	24.0	0	1	6	1
1982—Los Angeles Raiders NFL	8	6	15	2.5	0		None			0	0	2
1983—Los Angeles Raiders NFL	13	5	0	0.0	0		None			0	0	1
1984—Los Angeles Raiders NFL	16	5	4	0.8	0		None			0	0	0
Pro Totals—4 Years..............	52	32	73	2.3	1	1	24	24.0	0	1	6	4

Year Club	G.	No.	Yds.	Avg.	TD.
1981—Oakland NFL	15	15	309	20.6	0
1982—L.A. Raiders NFL	8	1	11	11.0	0
1983—L.A. Raiders NFL	13		None		
1984—L.A. Raiders NFL	16	1	13	13.0	0
Pro Totals—4 Years	52	17	333	19.6	0

Additional pro statistics: Recovered one fumble, 1981 and 1982.
Played in AFC Championship Game following 1983 season.
Played in NFL Championship Game following 1983 season.

KEITH WILLIS
Defensive End—Pittsburgh Steelers
Born July 29, 1959, at Newark, N.J.
Height, 6.01. Weight, 261.
High School—Newark, N.J., Malcolm X. Shabazz.
Attended Northwestern University.

Signed as free agent by Pittsburgh Steelers, April 30, 1982.
Pittsburgh NFL, 1982 through 1984.
Games: 1982 (9), 1983 (14), 1984 (12). Total—35.
Pro statistics: Recovered one fumble, 1983 and 1984.
Played in AFC Championship Game following 1984 season.

OTIS MITCHELL WILLIS
Defensive End—Los Angeles Raiders
Born March 16, 1962, at Dallas, Tex.
Height, 6.07. Weight, 265.
High School—Arlington, Tex., Lamar.
Received bachelor of business administration degree from Southern Methodist University in 1984.

Selected by San Antonio in 4th round (68th player selected) of 1984 USFL draft.
Selected by Los Angeles Raiders in 7th round (183rd player selected) of 1984 NFL draft.
Signed by Los Angeles Raiders, June 15, 1984.
On injured reserve with shoulder injury, August 27 through entire 1984 season.

BRENARD KENRIC WILSON
Defensive Back—Philadelphia Eagles
Born August 15, 1955, at Daytona Beach, Fla.
Height, 6.00. Weight, 180.
High School—Daytona Beach, Fla., Father Lopez.
Received bachelor of science degree in economics from Vanderbilt University.

Signed as free agent by Philadelphia Eagles, May, 1978.
Released by Philadelphia Eagles, August 28, 1978; re-signed by Eagles, December 28, 1978.
On injured reserve with broken foot, December 4 through remainder of 1979 season

		—INTERCEPTIONS—			
Year Club	G.	No.	Yds.	Avg.	TD.
1979—Philadelphia NFL	14	4	70	17.5	0
1980—Philadelphia NFL	16	6	79	13.2	0
1981—Philadelphia NFL	15	5	73	14.6	0
1982—Philadelphia NFL	8	1	0	0.0	0
1983—Philadelphia NFL	16		None		
1984—Philadelphia NFL	16	1	28	28.0	0
Pro Totals—6 Years	85	17	250	14.7	0

Additional pro statistics: Recovered one fumble, 1979 and 1982; returned two kickoffs for no yards, 1979.
Played in NFC Championship Game following 1980 season.
Played in NFL Championship Game following 1980 season.

CHARLES WADE WILSON
(Known by middle name.)
Quarterback—Minnesota Vikings
Born February 1, 1959, at Greenville, Tex.
Height, 6.03. Weight, 210.
High School—Commerce, Tex.
Attended East Texas State University.

Selected by Minnesota in 8th round (210th player selected) of 1981 NFL draft.
On inactive list, September 12, 1982.
On commissioner's exempt list, November 20 through December 7, 1982; activated, December 8, 1982.
Active for 4 games with Minnesota Vikings in 1982; did not play.

		—————PASSING—————							—RUSHING—				—TOTAL—		
Year Club	G.	Att.	Cmp.	Pct.	Gain	T.P.	P.I.	Avg.	Att.	Yds.	Avg.	TD.	TD.	Pts.	F.
1981—Minnesota NFL	3	13	6	46.2	48	0	2	3.69		None			0	0	2
1983—Minnesota NFL	1	28	16	57.1	124	1	2	4.43	3	−3	−1.0	0	0	0	1
1984—Minnesota NFL	8	195	102	52.3	1019	5	11	5.23	9	30	3.3	0	0	0	2
Pro Totals—4 Years	12	236	124	52.5	1191	6	15	5.05	12	27	2.3	0	0	0	5

Quarterback Rating Points: 1981 (16.4), 1983 (50.3), 1984 (52.5). Total—48.6.
Additional pro statistics: Recovered one fumble, 1981.

DARRYAL E. WILSON
Wide Receiver—New England Patriots
Born September 19, 1960, at Florence, Ala.
Height, 6.00. Weight, 182.
High School—Bristol, Va., Virginia.
Attended University of Tennessee.

Selected by New Jersey in 1983 USFL territorial draft.
Selected by New England in 2nd round (47th player selected) of 1983 NFL draft.
Signed by New England Patriots, June 3, 1983.
On injured reserve with knee injury, November 4 through remainder of 1983 season.
On physically unable to perform/reserve with knee injury, August 14 through entire 1984 season.
New England NFL, 1983.
Games: 1983 (9).

DAVID CARLTON WILSON
(Dave)
Quarterback—New Orleans Saints
Born April 27, 1959, at Anaheim, Calif.
Height, 6.03. Weight, 210.
High School—Anaheim, Calif., Katella.
Attended Fullerton Junior College and University of Illinois.

Selected by New Orleans in NFL supplementary draft, July 7, 1981; Saints forfeited 1st round pick in 1982 draft.
On injured reserve with knee injury, August 15 through entire 1982 season.

Year	Club	G.	Att.	Cmp.	Pct.	Gain	T.P.	P.I.	Avg.	Att.	Yds.	Avg.	TD.	TD.	Pts.	F.
					PASSING						RUSHING				TOTAL	
1981—New Orleans NFL		11	159	82	51.6	1058	1	11	6.65	5	1	0.2	0	0	0	4
1983—New Orleans NFL		8	112	66	58.9	770	5	7	6.88	5	3	0.6	1	1	6	5
1984—New Orleans NFL		5	93	51	54.8	647	7	4	6.96	3	—7	—2.3	0	0	0	2
Pro Totals—3 Years		24	364	199	54.7	2475	13	22	6.80	13	—3	—0.2	1	1	6	11

Quarterback Rating Points: 1981 (46.1), 1983 (68.7), 1984 (83.9). Total—63.0.
Additional pro statistics: Recovered three fumbles and fumbled four times for minus eight yards, 1981.

DONALD ALLEN WILSON
Safety—Buffalo Bills
Born July 21, 1961, at Washington, D.C.
Height, 6.02. Weight, 190.
High School—Washington, D.C., Cardoza.
Attended Ellsworth Junior College and North Carolina State University.

Signed as free agent by Buffalo Bills, May 16, 1984.

Year	Club	G.	No.	Yds.	Avg.	TD.	No.	Yds.	Avg.	TD.	TD.	Pts.	F.
				PUNT RETURNS				KICKOFF RET.				TOTAL	
1984—Buffalo NFL		16	33	297	9.0	1	34	576	16.9	0	1	6	3

Additional pro statistics: Recovered one fumble for 40 yards, 1984.

EARL WILSON
Defensive End—San Diego Chargers
Born September 13, 1958, at Long Branch, N.J.
Height, 6.04. Weight, 268.
High School—Atlantic City, N.J.
Attended University of Kentucky.

Signed as free agent by Toronto Argonauts, August 1, 1982.
Granted free agency, March 1, 1985; signed by San Diego Chargers, April 10, 1985.
Toronto CFL, 1982 through 1984.
Games: 1982 (11), 1983 (16), 1984 (14). Total—41.
CFL statistics: Intercepted three passes for eight yards, 1982; recovered two fumbles, 1984.

MARC DOUGLAS WILSON
Quarterback—Los Angeles Raiders
Born February 15, 1957, at Bremerton, Wash.
Height, 6.06. Weight, 205.
High School—Seattle, Wash., Shorecrest.
Received bachelor of arts degree in economics from Brigham Young University in 1980.

Selected by Oakland in 1st round (15th player selected) of 1980 NFL draft.
Franchise transferred to Los Angeles, May 7, 1982.
On injured reserve with dislocated shoulder, November 7 through December 30, 1983; activated, December 31, 1983.

Year	Club	G.	Att.	Cmp.	Pct.	Gain	T.P.	P.I.	Avg.	Att.	Yds.	Avg.	TD.	TD.	Pts.	F.
					PASSING						RUSHING				TOTAL	
1980—Oakland NFL		2	5	3	60.0	31	0	0	6.20	1	3	3.0	0	0	0	0
1981—Oakland NFL		13	366	173	47.3	2311	14	19	6.31	30	147	4.9	2	2	12	8
1982—L.A. Raiders NFL		8	2	1	50.0	4	0	0	2.00		None			0	0	0
1983—L.A. Raiders NFL		10	117	67	57.3	864	8	6	7.38	13	122	9.4	0	0	0	4
1984—L.A. Raiders NFL		16	282	153	54.3	2151	15	17	7.63	30	56	1.9	1	1	6	11
Pro Totals—5 Years		49	772	397	51.4	5361	37	42	6.94	74	328	4.4	3	3	18	23

Quarterback Rating Points: 1980 (77.9), 1981 (58.8), 1982 (56.3), 1983 (82.0), 1984 (71.7). Total—67.3.
Additional pro statistics: Recovered two fumbles and fumbled eight times for minus three yards, 1981; recovered one fumble, 1983; recovered three fumbles and fumbled 11 times for minus 11 yards, 1984.
Played in AFC Championship Game following 1983 season.
Member of Oakland Raiders for AFC Championship Game following 1980 season; did not play.
Played in NFL Championship Game following 1983 season.
Member of Oakland Raiders for NFL Championship Game following 1980 season; did not play.

MICHAEL RUBEN WILSON
(Mike)
Wide Receiver—San Francisco 49ers
Born December 19, 1958, at Los Angeles, Calif.
Height, 6.03. Weight, 210.
High School—Carson, Calif.
Attended Washington State University.

Selected by Dallas in 9th round (246th player selected) of 1981 NFL draft.
Released by Dallas Cowboys, August 24, 1981; signed as free agent by San Francisco 49ers, August 27, 1981.
On injured reserve with broken finger, September 9 through November 19, 1982; activated, November 20, 1982.

| | | | —PASS RECEIVING— | | |
Year Club	G.	P.C.	Yds.	Avg.	TD.
1981—San Francisco NFL	16	9	125	13.9	1
1982—San Francisco NFL	6	6	80	13.3	1
1983—San Francisco NFL	15	30	433	14.4	0
1984—San Francisco NFL	13	17	245	14.4	1
Pro Totals—4 Years............	50	62	883	14.2	3

Additional pro statistics: Returned four kickoffs for 67 yards and recovered one fumble, 1981; fumbled once, 1983; returned one kickoff for 14 yards, 1984.
Played in NFC Championship Game following 1981, 1983 and 1984 seasons.
Played in NFL Championship Game following 1981 and 1984 seasons.

OTIS RAY WILSON
Linebacker—Chicago Bears
Born September 15, 1957, at New York, N.Y.
Height, 6.02. Weight, 231.
High School—Brooklyn, N.Y., Thomas Jefferson.
Attended Syracuse University and University of Louisville.

Named as linebacker on THE SPORTING NEWS College All-America Team, 1979.
Selected by Chicago in 1st round (19th player selected) of 1980 NFL draft.

| | | —INTERCEPTIONS— | | | |
Year Club	G.	No.	Yds.	Avg.	TD.
1980—Chicago NFL	16	2	4	2.0	0
1981—Chicago NFL	15		None		
1982—Chicago NFL	9	2	39	19.5	*1
1983—Chicago NFL	16	1	6	6.0	0
1984—Chicago NFL	15		None		
Pro Totals—5 Years............	71	5	49	9.8	1

Additional pro statistics: Fumbled once, 1980; recovered three fumbles for 31 yards, 1981.
Played in NFC Championship Game following 1984 season.

STANLEY T. WILSON
Running Back—Cincinnati Bengals
Born August 23, 1961, at Los Angeles, Calif.
Height, 5.10. Weight, 210.
High School—Banning, Calif.
Attended University of Oklahoma.

Selected by New Jersey in 1983 USFL territorial draft.
Selected by Cincinnati in 9th round (248th player selected) of 1983 NFL draft.
Signed by Cincinnati Bengals, May 19, 1983.
On non-football injury list with drug problem, August 23 through September 20, 1984; activated, September 21, 1984.
On injured reserve with dislocated shoulder, October 1 through October 31, 1984.
On non-football injury list with drug problem, November 1 through remainder of 1984 season.

| | | —RUSHING— | | | | PASS RECEIVING | | | | —TOTAL— | | |
Year Club	G.	Att.	Yds.	Avg.	TD.	P.C.	Yds.	Avg.	TD.	TD.	Pts.	F.
1983—Cincinnati NFL..........................	10	56	267	4.8	1	12	107	8.9	1	2	12	4
1984—Cincinnati NFL..........................	1	17	74	4.4	0	2	15	7.5	0	0	0	0
Pro Totals—2 Years....................	11	73	341	4.7	1	14	122	8.7	1	2	12	4

| | | KICKOFF RETURNS | | | |
Year Club	G.	No.	Yds.	Avg.	TD.
1983—Cincinnati NFL.............	10	7	161	23.0	0
1984—Cincinnati NFL.............	1		None		
Pro Totals—2 Years............	11	7	161	23.0	0

Additional pro statistics: Recovered two fumbles, 1983.

STEVE ALAN WILSON
Center—Tampa Bay Buccaneers
Born May 19, 1954, at Fort Sill, Okla.
Height, 6.04. Weight, 265.
High School—Macon, Ga., Southwest.
Received degree in business management from University of Georgia.

Selected by Tampa Bay in 5th round (154th player selected) of 1976 NFL draft.
On injured reserve with hand injury, December 9 through remainder of 1983 season.
Tampa Bay NFL, 1976 through 1984.
Games: 1976 (12), 1977 (14), 1978 (16), 1979 (16), 1980 (15), 1981 (15), 1982 (8), 1983 (10), 1984 (16). Total—122.
Pro statistics: Recovered two fumbles, 1978; recovered one fumble, 1980, 1982 and 1983; fumbled once, 1983 and 1984.
Played in NFC Championship Game following 1979 season.

STEVEN ANTHONY WILSON
(Steve)
Cornerback—Denver Broncos
Born August 24, 1957, at Los Angeles, Calif.
Height, 5.10. Weight, 195.
High School—Durham, N.C., Northern.
Received bachelor of business administration degree from Howard University in 1979.
Son of (Touchdown) Tommy Wilson, halfback with Los Angeles Rams, Cleveland Browns
and Minnesota Vikings, 1956 through 1963.

Signed as free agent by Dallas Cowboys, May 6, 1979.
Released by Dallas Cowboys, August 14, 1979; re-signed by Cowboys, August 29, 1979.
Released by Dallas Cowboys, September 6, 1982; signed as free agent by Denver Broncos, September 14, 1982.

		INTERCEPTIONS				–PUNT RETURNS–				—KICKOFF RET.—				—TOTAL—		
Year Club	G.	No.	Yds.	Avg.	TD.	No.	Yds.	Avg.	TD.	No.	Yds.	Avg.	TD.	TD.	Pts.	F.
1979—Dallas NFL	16		None			35	236	6.7	0	19	328	17.3	0	0	0	1
1980—Dallas NFL	16	4	82	20.5	0		None			7	139	19.9	0	0	0	0
1981—Dallas NFL	16	2	0	0.0	0		None			2	32	16.0	0	0	0	0
1982—Denver NFL	8	2	22	11.0	0		None			6	123	20.5	0	0	0	0
1983—Denver NFL	16	5	91	18.2	0		None			24	485	20.2	0	0	0	0
1984—Denver NFL	15	4	59	14.8	0	1	0	0.0	0		None			0	0	1
Pro Totals—6 Years	87	17	254	14.9	0	36	236	6.6	0	58	1107	19.1	0	0	0	2

Additional pro statistics: Recovered one fumble, 1979, 1981 and 1984; caught three passes for 76 yards, 1979.
Played in NFC Championship Game following 1980 and 1981 seasons.

TIM WILSON
Fullback—New Orleans Saints
Born January 14, 1954, at New Castle, Del.
Height, 6.03. Weight, 235.
High School—New Castle, Del., DeLaWarr.
Attended University of Maryland and received degree from University of Houston.

Selected by Houston in 3rd round (66th player selected) of 1977 NFL draft.
Traded with 11th round pick in 1984 draft by Houston Oilers to Los Angeles Raiders for 9th round pick in 1984 draft, June 13, 1983.
Released by Los Angeles Raiders, July 27, 1983; awarded on waivers to New Orleans Saints, July 28, 1983 (Raiders received 7th round pick in 1984 draft from Saints as past consideration for waiving Wilson).
On injured reserve with pulled hamstring, October 8 through December 16, 1983; activated, December 17, 1983.
On injured reserve with knee injury, November 24 through remainder of 1984 season.

		—RUSHING—				PASS RECEIVING				—TOTAL—		
Year Club	G.	Att.	Yds.	Avg.	TD.	P.C.	Yds.	Avg.	TD.	TD.	Pts.	F.
1977—Houston NFL	10	99	343	3.5	3	20	107	5.4	0	3	18	1
1978—Houston NFL	16	126	431	3.4	0	15	91	6.1	1	1	6	5
1979—Houston NFL	16	84	319	3.8	2	29	208	7.2	1	3	18	2
1980—Houston NFL	16	66	257	3.9	1	30	170	5.7	1	2	12	2
1981—Houston NFL	16	13	35	2.7	0	5	33	6.6	0	0	0	2
1982—Houston NFL	9		None				None			0	0	0
1983—New Orleans NFL	6	8	21	2.6	0		None			0	0	0
1984—New Orleans NFL	12	2	8	4.0	0		None			0	0	0
Pro Totals—8 Years	101	398	1414	3.6	6	99	609	6.2	3	9	54	12

		KICKOFF RETURNS			
Year Club	G.	No.	Yds.	Avg.	TD.
1977—Houston NFL	10	2	33	16.5	0
1978—Houston NFL	16	2	29	14.5	0
1979—Houston NFL	16	2	30	15.0	0
1980—Houston NFL	16		None		
1981—Houston NFL	16	3	41	13.7	0
1982—Houston NFL	9	2	40	20.0	0
1983—New Orleans NFL	6		None		
1984—New Orleans NFL	12	1	16	16.0	0
Pro Totals—8 Years	101	12	189	15.8	0

Additional pro statistics: Recovered one fumble, 1977 and 1978; recovered two fumbles, 1979.
Played in AFC Championship Game following 1978 season.

WAYNE MacARTHUR WILSON
Fullback—New Orleans Saints
Born September 4, 1957, at Montgomery County, Md.
Height, 6.03. Weight, 218.
High School—Ellicott, Md., Howard.
Received degree in recreation from Shepherd College.

Selected by Houston in 12th round (324th player selected) of 1979 NFL draft.
Released by Houston Oilers, August 29, 1979; signed as free agent by New Orleans Saints, September 11, 1979.

Year Club	G.	Att.	Yds.	Avg.	TD.	P.C.	Yds.	Avg.	TD.	TD.	Pts.	F.
		—RUSHING—				PASS RECEIVING				—TOTAL—		
1979—New Orleans NFL	14	5	26	5.2	0		None			0	0	1
1980—New Orleans NFL	15	63	188	3.0	1	31	241	7.8	1	2	12	3
1981—New Orleans NFL	16	44	137	3.1	1	31	384	12.4	4	5	30	1
1982—New Orleans NFL	8	103	413	4.0	3	25	175	7.0	2	5	30	4
1983—New Orleans NFL	14	199	787	4.0	9	20	178	8.9	2	11	66	6
1984—New Orleans NFL	14	74	261	3.5	1	33	314	9.5	3	4	24	2
Pro Totals—6 Years	81	488	1812	3.7	15	140	1292	9.2	12	27	162	17

		KICKOFF RETURNS			
Year Club	G.	No.	Yds.	Avg.	TD.
1979—New Orleans NFL	14	11	230	20.9	0
1980—New Orleans NFL	15	9	159	17.7	0
1981—New Orleans NFL	16	31	722	23.3	0
1982—New Orleans NFL	8	7	192	27.4	0
1983—New Orleans NFL	14	9	239	26.6	0
1984—New Orleans NFL	14	1	23	23.0	0
Pro Totals—6 Years	81	68	1565	23.0	0

Additional pro statistics: Recovered one fumble, 1979, 1981 and 1982; recovered two fumbles, 1980.

WILLIAM MIKE WILSON
(Known by middle name.)
Offensive Tackle—Cincinnati Bengals
Born May 28, 1955, at Norfolk, Va.
Height, 6.05. Weight, 271.
High School—Gainesville, Ga., Johnson.
Attended University of Georgia.

Selected by Cincinnati in 4th round (103rd player selected) of 1977 NFL draft.
Signed by Toronto Argonauts, May, 1977.
Released by Toronto Argonauts, July 6, 1978; signed by Cincinnati Bengals, July 6, 1978; activated, October 13, 1978.
Placed on physically unable to perform list with knee injury, July 6, 1978.
Toronto CFL, 1977; Cincinnati NFL, 1978 through 1984.
Games: 1977 (16), 1978 (9), 1979 (16), 1980 (16), 1981 (16), 1982 (9), 1983 (16), 1984 (16). Total NFL—98. Total Pro—114.
Played in AFC Championship Game following 1981 season.
Played in NFL Championship Game following 1981 season.

SAMMY WINDER
Running Back—Denver Broncos
Born July 15, 1959, at Madison, Miss.
Height, 5.11. Weight, 203.
High School—Madison, Miss., Ridgeland.
Attended University of Southern Mississippi.

Selected by Denver in 5th round (131st player selected) of 1982 NFL draft.

Year Club	G.	Att.	Yds.	Avg.	TD.	P.C.	Yds.	Avg.	TD.	TD.	Pts.	F.
		—RUSHING—				PASS RECEIVING				—TOTAL—		
1982—Denver NFL	8	67	259	3.9	1	11	83	7.5	0	1	6	1
1983—Denver NFL	14	196	757	3.9	3	23	150	6.5	0	3	18	7
1984—Denver NFL	16	296	1153	3.9	4	44	288	6.5	2	6	36	5
Pro Totals—3 Years	38	559	2169	3.9	8	78	521	6.7	2	10	60	13

Additional pro statistics: Recovered one fumble, 1982; recovered two fumbles, 1984.
Played in Pro Bowl (NFL All-Star Game) following 1984 season.

DAVID ROGERS WINDHAM
Linebacker—New England Patriots
Born March 14, 1961, at Mobile, Ala.
Height, 6.02. Weight, 240.
High School—Prichard, Ala., C.F. Vigor.
Attended Jackson State University.

Selected by Denver in 13th round (259th player selected) of 1984 USFL draft.
Signed by Denver Gold, January 12, 1984.
Released by Denver Gold, February 13, 1984.
Selected by New England in 9th round (251st player selected) of 1984 NFL draft.
On injured reserve with knee injury, August 8 through entire 1984 season.

BLAKE LEO WINGLE
Guard—Pittsburgh Steelers
Born April 17, 1960, at Pottsville, Calif.
Height, 6.02. Weight, 267.
High School—Oxnard, Calif., Rio Mesa.
Attended Ventura College, California Poly State University at San Luis Obispo and
received degree in College of letters and sciences from University of California at Los Angeles.

Selected by Pittsburgh in 9th round (244th player selected) of 1983 NFL draft.
Pittsburgh NFL, 1983 and 1984.
Games: 1983 (16), 1984 (15). Total—31.
Member of Pittsburgh Steelers for AFC Championship Game following 1984 season; did not play.

RICHARD ALLEN WINGO
(Rich)
Linebacker—Green Bay Packers
Born July 16, 1956, at Elkhart, Ind.
Height, 6.01. Weight, 230.
High School—Elkhart, Ind., Central.
Received bachelor of science degree in education from University of Alabama in 1979.

Selected by Green Bay in 7th round (184th player selected) of 1979 NFL draft.
On injured reserve with back injury, September 2 through remainder of 1980 season.
On injured reserve with knee injury, December 9, 1982 through January 4, 1983; activated, January 5, 1983.

| | | | —INTERCEPTIONS— | | | |
Year	Club	G.	No.	Yds.	Avg.	TD.
1979—Green Bay NFL		16	2	13	6.5	0
1981—Green Bay NFL		16	1	38	38.0	0
1982—Green Bay NFL		5	1	0	0.0	0
1983—Green Bay NFL		16		None		
1984—Green Bay NFL		16		None		
Pro Totals—5 Years		69	4	51	12.8	0

Additional pro statistics: Recovered one fumble, 1979; scored extra point on pass reception, 1981.

KELLEN BOSWELL WINSLOW
Tight End—San Diego Chargers
Born November 5, 1957, at St. Louis, Mo.
Height, 6.05. Weight, 242.
High School—East St. Louis, Ill.
Attended University of Missouri.

Tied NFL record for most touchdowns, pass receptions, game (5), November 22, 1981, against Oakland Raiders.
Named as tight end on THE SPORTING NEWS College All-America Team, 1978.
Named to THE SPORTING NEWS NFL All-Star Team, 1980 and 1981.
Selected by San Diego in 1st round (13th player selected) of 1979 NFL draft.
On injured reserve with broken leg, October 19 through remainder of 1979 season.
Left San Diego Chargers voluntarily and granted roster exemption, September 3 through September 9, 1984;
activated, September 10, 1984.
On injured reserve with knee injury, October 23 through remainder of 1984 season.

| | | | —PASS RECEIVING— | | | |
Year	Club	G.	P.C.	Yds.	Avg.	TD.
1979—San Diego NFL		7	25	255	10.2	2
1980—San Diego NFL		16	*89	1290	14.5	9
1981—San Diego NFL		16	*88	1075	12.2	10
1982—San Diego NFL		9	54	721	13.4	6
1983—San Diego NFL		16	88	1172	13.3	8
1984—San Diego NFL		7	55	663	12.1	2
Pro Totals—6 Years		71	399	5176	13.0	37

Additional pro statistics: Fumbled once, 1979, 1982 and 1984; fumbled twice, 1980 and 1981; attempted two passes with no completions, 1981; recovered two fumbles, 1981 and 1983; attempted one pass with no completions, 1982; fumbled three times, 1983.
Played in AFC Championship Game following 1980 and 1981 seasons.
Played in Pro Bowl (NFL All-Star Game) following 1980 through 1983 seasons.

DENNIS EDWARD WINSTON
Linebacker—New Orleans Saints
Born October 25, 1955, at Forrest City, Ark.
Height, 6.00. Weight, 241.
High School—Marianna, Ark., Robert E. Lee.
Attended University of Arkansas.
Cousin of Clifford Brooks, back with Cleveland Browns, Philadelphia Eagles,
New York Jets and Buffalo Bills, 1972 through 1976.

Selected by Pittsburgh in 5th round (132nd player selected) of 1977 NFL draft.
Traded by Pittsburgh Steelers to New Orleans Saints for 6th round pick in 1982 draft, April 27, 1982.

			—INTERCEPTIONS—			
Year Club	G.	No.	Yds.	Avg.	TD.	
1977—Pittsburgh NFL	13	2	7	3.5	0	
1978—Pittsburgh NFL............	16		None			
1979—Pittsburgh NFL............	16	3	48	16.0	1	
1980—Pittsburgh NFL............	14		None			
1981—Pittsburgh NFL............	14	1	1	1.0	0	
1982—New Orleans NFL.......	9	2	—2	—1.0	0	
1983—New Orleans NFL........	16	3	21	7.0	0	
1984—New Orleans NFL.......	16	2	90	45.0	*2	
Pro Totals—8 Years............	114	13	165	12.7	3	

Additional pro statistics: Recovered one fumble, 1978, 1983 and 1984; recovered three fumbles, 1979; recovered blocked punt in end zone for a touchdown, recovered four fumbles and returned one kickoff for 13 yards, 1980; recovered two fumbles, 1982; fumbled once, 1983.

Played in AFC Championship Game following 1978 and 1979 seasons.

Played in NFL Championship Game following 1978 and 1979 seasons.

BLAISE WINTER
Defensive End—Indianapolis Colts
Born January 31, 1962, at Blauvelt, N.Y.
Height, 6.03. Weight, 262.
High School—Orangeburg, N.Y., Tappan Zee.
Attended Syracuse University.

Selected by New Jersey in 1984 USFL territorial draft.
Selected by Indianapolis in 2nd round (35th player selected) of 1984 NFL draft.
Signed by Indianapolis Colts, July 27, 1984.
Indianapolis NFL, 1984.
Games: 1984 (16).
Pro statistics: Recovered one fumble, 1984.

LEO JOSEPH WISNIEWSKI
Nose Tackle—Indianapolis Colts
Born November 6, 1959, at Hancock, Mich.
Height, 6.01. Weight, 263.
High School—Pittsburgh, Pa., Fox Chapel.
Received bachelor of arts degree in speech communications from Penn State University.

Selected by Baltimore in 2nd round (28th player selected) of 1982 NFL draft.
On injured reserve with knee injury, September 7 through November 18, 1982; activated, November 19, 1982.
Franchise transferred to Indianapolis, March 31, 1984.
On injured reserve with knee injury, December 4 through remainder of 1984 season.
Baltimore NFL, 1982 and 1983; Indianapolis NFL, 1984.
Games: 1982 (7), 1983 (15), 1984 (14). Totals—36.
Pro statistics: Recovered two fumbles, 1983; recovered one fumble, 1984.

JOHN JOSEPH WITKOWSKI
Quarterback—Detroit Lions
Born June 18, 1962, at Flushing, N.Y.
Height, 6.01. Weight, 205.
High School—Lindenhurst, N.Y.
Received bachelor of arts degree in economics from Columbia University in 1984.

Selected by Philadelphia in 7th round (138th player selected) of 1984 USFL draft.
Selected by Detroit in 6th round (160th player selected) of 1984 NFL draft.
Signed by Detroit Lions, June 10, 1984.

		—PASSING—							—RUSHING—			—TOTAL—		
Year Club	G.	Att.	Cmp.	Pct.	Gain	T.P.	P.I.	Avg.	Att.	Yds.	Avg.	TD.	TD.	Pts. F.
1984—Detroit NFL......................	3	34	13	38.2	210	0	0	6.18	7	33	4.7	0	0	0 1

Quarterback Raiting Points: 1984 (59.7).

MARK STEVEN WITTE
Tight End—Tampa Bay Buccaneers
Born December 3, 1959, at Corpus Christi, Tex.
Height, 6.03. Weight, 230.
High School—San Marcos, Tex.
Attended North Texas State University.

Selected by Denver in 7th round (81st player selected) of 1983 USFL draft.
Selected by Tampa Bay in 11th round (297th player selected) of 1983 NFL draft.
Signed by Tampa Bay Buccaneers, June 1, 1983.

		—PASS RECEIVING—			
Year Club	G.	P.C.	Yds.	Avg.	TD.
1983—Tampa Bay NFL	16	2	15	7.5	0
1984—Tampa Bay NFL	16		None		
Pro Totals—2 Years............	32	2	15	7.5	0

Additional pro statistics: Recovered one fumble, 1984.

CRAIG ALAN WOLFLEY
Guard—Pittsburgh Steelers
Born May 19, 1958, at Buffalo, N.Y.
Height, 6.01. Weight, 255.
High School—Orchard Park, N.Y.
Received bachelor of science degree in communication from Syracuse University in 1980.
Brother of Ronnie Wolfley, rookie running back with St. Louis Cardinals.

Selected by Pittsburgh in 5th round (138th player selected) of 1980 NFL draft.
On injured reserve with pulled hamstring, October 5 through November 18, 1984; activated, November 19, 1984.
Pittsburgh NFL, 1980 through 1984.
Games: 1980 (16), 1981 (16), 1982 (9), 1983 (14), 1984 (9). Total—64.
Pro statistics: Recovered two fumbles, 1982; recovered one fumble, 1983.
Played in AFC Championship Game following 1984 season.

GEORGE WONSLEY
Running Back—Indianapolis Colts
Born November 23, 1960, at Moss Point, Miss.
Height, 6.00. Weight, 212.
High School—Moss Point, Miss.
Attened Mississippi State University.
Brother of Otis Wonsley, running back with Washington Redskins.

Selected by New Jersey in 1984 USFL territorial draft.
Selected by Indianapolis in 4th round (103rd player selected) of 1984 NFL draft.
Signed by Indianapolis Colts, May 24, 1984.

		—RUSHING—				PASS RECEIVING				—TOTAL—		
Year Club	G.	Att.	Yds.	Avg.	TD.	P.C.	Yds.	Avg.	TD.	TD.	Pts.	F.
1984—Indianapolis NFL	14	37	111	3.0	0	9	47	5.2	0	0	0	0

Additional pro statistics: Returned four kickoffs for 52 yards, 1984.

OTIS WONSLEY
Running Back—Washington Redskins
Born August 13, 1957, at Pascagoula, Miss.
Height, 5.10. Weight, 214.
High School—Moss Point, Miss.
Attended Alcorn State University.
Brother of George Wonsley, running back with Indianapolis Colts.

Selected by New York Giants in 9th round (229th player selected) of 1980 NFL draft.
Released by New York Giants, September 1, 1980; signed as free agent by Washington Redskins, April 6, 1981.
On injured reserve with knee injury, December 18 through remainder of 1981 season.

		—RUSHING—				PASS RECEIVING				—TOTAL—		
Year Club	G.	Att.	Yds.	Avg.	TD.	P.C.	Yds.	Avg.	TD.	TD.	Pts.	F.
1981—Washington NFL	15	3	11	3.7	0	1	5	5.0	0	0	0	1
1982—Washington NFL	9	11	36	3.3	0	1	1	1.0	1	1	6	0
1983—Washington NFL	16	25	88	3.5	0		None			0	0	0
1984—Washington NFL	16	18	38	2.1	4		None			4	24	0
Pro Totals—4 Years	56	57	173	3.0	4	2	6	3.0	1	5	30	1

		KICKOFF RETURNS			
Year Club	G.	No.	Yds.	Avg.	TD.
1981—Washington NFL	15	6	124	20.7	0
1982—Washington NFL	9	1	14	14.0	0
1983—Washington NFL	16	2	36	18.0	0
1984—Washington NFL	16		None		
Pro Totals—4 Years	56	9	174	19.3	0

Additional pro statistics: Recovered one fumble, 1982 and 1983.
Played in NFC Championship Game following 1982 and 1983 seasons.
Played in NFL Championship Game following 1982 and 1983 seasons.

KENNETH EMIL WOODARD
(Ken)
Linebacker—Denver Broncos
Born January 22, 1960, at Detroit, Mich.
Height, 6.01. Weight, 218.
High School—Detroit, Mich., Martin Luther King.
Attended Tuskegee Institute.

Selected by Denver in 10th round (274th player selected) of 1982 NFL draft.
Denver NFL, 1982 through 1984.
Games: 1982 (9), 1983 (16), 1984 (16). Total—41.
Pro statistics: Recovered one fumble, 1983; intercepted one pass for 27 yards and a touchdown, 1984.

—DID YOU KNOW—

That since 1967, only one player from Virginia Tech has been picked on the first round of the NFL draft? Bruce Smith was the No. 1 overall pick in 1985 by Buffalo.

DAVID EUGENE WOODLEY
Quarterback—Pittsburgh Steelers

Born October 25, 1958, at Shreveport, La.
Height, 6.02. Weight, 204.
High School—Shreveport, La., Byrd.
Attended Louisiana State University.

Selected by Miami in 8th round (214th player selected) of 1980 NFL draft.
Granted free agency, February 1, 1984; re-signed by Dolphins and traded to Pittsburgh Steelers for 3rd round pick in 1984 draft and conditional 3rd round pick in 1985 draft, February 21, 1984.

| | | | —PASSING— | | | | | | | —RUSHING— | | | | —TOTAL— | |
Year	Club	G.	Att.	Cmp.	Pct.	Gain	T.P.	P.I.	Avg.	Att.	Yds.	Avg.	TD.	TD.	Pts.	F.
1980—Miami NFL		13	327	176	53.8	1850	14	17	5.66	55	214	3.9	3	3	18	3
1981—Miami NFL		15	366	191	52.2	2470	12	13	6.75	63	272	4.3	4	4	24	9
1982—Miami NFL		9	179	98	54.7	1080	5	8	6.03	36	207	5.8	2	3	18	2
1983—Miami NFL		5	89	43	48.3	528	3	4	5.93	19	78	4.1	0	0	0	4
1984—Pittsburgh NFL		7	156	85	54.5	1273	8	7	8.16	11	14	1.3	0	0	0	5
Pro Totals—5 Years		49	1117	593	53.1	7201	42	49	6.45	184	785	4.3	9	10	60	23

Quarterback Rating Points: 1980 (63.2), 1981 (69.7), 1982 (63.4), 1983 (59.6), 1984 (79.9). Total—67.6.
Additional pro statistics: Recovered two fumbles and fumbled nine times for minus 21 yards, 1981; caught one pass for 15 yards and a touchdown and recovered three fumbles, 1982; caught one pass for six yards, 1983; recovered two fumbles and fumbled five times for minus four yards, 1984.
Played in AFC Championship Game following 1982 season.
Member of Pittsburgh Steelers for AFC Championship Game following 1984 season; did not play.
Played in NFL Championship Game following 1982 season.

JOHN WOODRING
Linebacker—New York Jets

Born April 4, 1959, at Philadelphia, Pa.
Height, 6.02. Weight, 232.
High School—Erdenheim, Pa., Springfield.
Received degree in applied math and economics from Brown University in 1981.

Selected by New York Jets in 6th round (142nd player selected) of 1981 NFL draft.
On injured reserve with knee injury, November 14 through December 10, 1981; activated, December 11, 1981.
New York Jets NFL, 1981 through 1984.
Games: 1981 (12), 1982 (9), 1983 (14), 1984 (15). Total—50.
Pro statistics: Recovered two fumbles, 1981; recovered four fumbles, 1983; recovered one fumble, 1984.
Played in AFC Championship Game following 1982 season.

DWAYNE DONZELL WOODRUFF
Cornerback—Pittsburgh Steelers

Born February 18, 1957, at Bowling Green, Ky.
Height, 6.00. Weight, 198.
High School—New Richmond, O.
Received bachelor of science degree in commerce from University of Louisville in 1979.

Selected by Pittsburgh in 6th round (161st player selected) of 1979 NFL draft.
USFL rights traded with rights to quarterback Jeff Hostetler by Pittsburgh Maulers to Arizona Wranglers for a draft pick, May 2, 1984.

| | | | —INTERCEPTIONS— | | | |
Year	Club	G.	No.	Yds.	Avg.	TD.
1979—Pittsburgh NFL		16	1	31	31.0	0
1980—Pittsburgh NFL		16	1	0	0.0	0
1981—Pittsburgh NFL		16	1	17	17.0	0
1982—Pittsburgh NFL		9	5	53	10.6	0
1983—Pittsburgh NFL		15	3	85	28.3	0
1984—Pittsburgh NFL		16	5	56	11.2	1
Pro Totals—6 Years		88	16	242	15.1	1

Additional pro statistics: Recovered one fumble and fumbled once, 1981; recovered one fumble for 65 yards and a touchdown, 1984.
Played in AFC Championship Game following 1979 and 1984 seasons.
Played in NFL Championship Game following 1979 season.

TONY DEWAYNE WOODRUFF
Wide Receiver—Philadelphia Eagles

Born November 12, 1958, at Hazen, Ark.
Height, 6.00. Weight, 185.
High School—Fresno, Calif., Roosevelt.
Attended King's River Community College, Los Angeles Harbor College
and Fresno State University.

Selected by Philadelphia in 9th round (244th player selected) of 1982 NFL draft.
On inactive list, September 12 and September 19, 1982.
On injured reserve with broken collarbone, August 16 through November 9, 1983; activated after clearing procedural waivers, November 11, 1983.

Year Club			—PASS RECEIVING—			
	G.	P.C.	Yds.	Avg.	TD.	
1982—Philadelphia NFL	1		None			
1983—Philadelphia NFL	6	6	70	11.7	2	
1984—Philadelphia NFL	16	30	484	16.1	3	
Pro Totals—3 Years............	23	36	554	15.4	5	

Additional pro statistics: Recovered one fumble and fumbled once, 1983.

RICK L. WOODS
Safety—Pittsburgh Steelers
Born November 16, 1959, at Boise, Ida.
Height, 6.00. Weight, 191.
High School—Boise, Ida.
Attended Boise State University.

Selected by Pittsburgh in 4th round (97th player selected) of 1982 NFL draft.
On injured reserve with elbow injury, December 9, 1982 through January 6, 1983; activated, January 7, 1983.

Year Club		–INTERCEPTIONS–				–PUNT RETURNS–				—TOTAL—		
	G.	No.	Yds.	Avg.	TD.	No.	Yds.	Avg.	TD.	TD.	Pts.	F.
1982—Pittsburgh NFL..............................	5	1	12	12.0	0	13	142	10.9	0	0	0	2
1983—Pittsburgh NFL..............................	15	5	53	10.6	0	5	46	9.2	0	1	6	0
1984—Pittsburgh NFL..............................	15	2	0	0.0	0	6	40	6.7	0	0	0	0
Pro Totals—3 Years.................................	35	8	65	8.1	0	24	228	9.5	0	1	6	2

Additional pro statistics: Recovered two fumbles, 1982; recovered two fumbles for 38 yards and a touchdown, 1983.
Played in AFC Championship Game following 1984 season.

RAYMOND LEE WOODWARD
(Ray)
Defensive End—San Diego Chargers
Born August 20, 1961, at Corrigan, Tex.
Height, 6.06. Weight, 267.
High School—Corrigan, Tex., Corrigan-Camden.
Attended University of Texas.

Selected by Houston in 1984 USFL territorial draft.
Selected by San Diego in 8th round (199th player selected) of 1984 NFL draft.
Signed by San Diego Chargers, June 27, 1984.
On injured reserve with dislocated shoulder, August 13 through entire 1984 season.

HAROLD WOOLFOLK
(Butch)
Running Back—Houston Oilers
Born March 1, 1960, at Milwaukee, Wis.
Height, 6.01. Weight, 212.
High School—Westfield, N.J.
Received bachelor of science degree in physical therapy
from University of Michigan in 1982.

Tied NFL record for most rushing attempts, game (43) vs. Philadelphia Eagles, November 20, 1983.
Selected by New York Giants in 1st round (18th player selected) of 1982 NFL draft.
Traded by New York Giants to Houston Oilers for 3rd round pick in 1985 draft, March 21, 1985.

Year Club		——RUSHING——				PASS RECEIVING				—TOTAL—		
	G.	Att.	Yds.	Avg.	TD.	P.C.	Yds.	Avg.	TD.	TD.	Pts.	F.
1982—New York Giants NFL	9	112	439	3.9	2	23	224	9.7	2	4	24	5
1983—New York Giants NFL	16	246	857	3.5	4	28	368	13.1	0	4	24	8
1984—New York Giants NFL	15	40	92	2.3	1	9	53	5.9	0	1	6	1
Pro Totals—3 Years....................................	40	398	1388	3.5	7	60	645	10.8	2	9	54	14

Year Club		KICKOFF RETURNS			
	G.	No.	Yds.	Avg.	TD.
1982—N.Y. Giants NFL	9	20	428	21.4	0
1983—N.Y. Giants NFL	16	2	13	6.5	0
1984—N.Y. Giants NFL	15	14	232	16.6	0
Pro Totals—3 Years............	40	36	673	18.7	0

Additional pro statistics: Recovered one fumble, 1982 through 1984.

RONALD J. WOOTEN
(Ron)
Guard—New England Patriots
Born June 28, 1959, at Cape Cod, Mass.
Height, 6.04. Weight, 273.
High School—Kinston, N.C.
Received bachelor of science degree in chemistry
from University of North Carolina in 1981.

Selected by New England in 6th round (157th player selected) of 1981 NFL draft.
On injured reserve with back injury, August 31 through entire 1981 season.
New England NFL, 1982 through 1984.
Games: 1982 (9), 1983 (16), 1984 (16). Total—41.

BRET JOSEPH WRIGHT
Punter—New York Jets
Born January 5, 1962, at Hammond, La.
Height, 6.03. Weight, 210.
High School—Ponchatoula, La.
Received degree in constructional drafting from Southeastern Louisiana University.

Selected by New York Jets in 8th round (217th player selected) of 1984 NFL draft.
Released by New York Jets, August 21, 1984; re-signed by Jets, May 7, 1985.

ERIC WRIGHT
Cornerback—San Francisco 49ers
Born April 18, 1959, at St. Louis, Mo.
Height, 6.01. Weight, 180.
High School—East St. Louis, Ill., Assumption.
Attended University of Missouri.

Selected by San Francisco in 2nd round (40th player selected) of 1981 NFL draft.
On inactive list, September 19, 1982.

		—INTERCEPTIONS—			
Year Club	G.	No.	Yds.	Avg.	TD.
1981—San Francisco NFL	16	3	26	8.7	0
1982—San Francisco NFL	7	1	31	31.0	0
1983—San Francisco NFL	16	7	*164	23.4	*2
1984—San Francisco NFL	16	2	0	0.0	0
Pro Totals—4 Years...........	55	13	221	17.0	2

Additional pro statistics: Recovered two fumbles, 1981; recovered one fumble, 1983.
Played in NFC Championship Game following 1981, 1983 and 1984 seasons.
Played in NFL Championship Game following 1981 and 1984 seasons.
Played in Pro Bowl (NFL All-Star Game) following 1984 season.

JAMES WILLIE WRIGHT
(Jim)
Tight End—Denver Broncos
Born September 1, 1956, at Fort Hood, Tex.
Height, 6.03. Weight, 240.
High School—Brenham, Tex.
Attended Blinn Junior College and received bachelor of science
degree in psychology from Texas Christian University in 1978.

Selected by Atlanta in 7th round (179th player selected) of 1978 NFL draft.
On injured reserve with knee injury, August 13 through remainder of 1979 season.
Released by Atlanta Falcons, August 26, 1980; signed as free agent by Denver Broncos, December 15, 1980.
On injured reserve with shoulder and neck injuries, October 21 through remainder of 1983 season.

		—PASS RECEIVING—			
Year Club	G.	P.C.	Yds.	Avg.	TD.
1978—Atlanta NFL	15	2	26	13.0	0
1980—Denver NFL	1		None		
1981—Denver NFL	16	3	22	7.3	1
1982—Denver NFL	9	9	120	13.3	1
1983—Denver NFL	6	13	134	10.3	0
1984—Denver NFL	16	11	118	10.7	1
Pro Totals—6 Years...........	63	38	420	11.1	3

Additional pro statistics: Returned two kickoffs for 31 yards, 1978; rushed once for 11 yards and recovered one fumble for one yard, 1981; rushed once for minus four yards, 1982; rushed once for minus 11 yards and fumbled twice, 1983.

LOUIS DONNEL WRIGHT
Cornerback—Denver Broncos
Born January 31, 1953, at Gilmer, Tex.
Height, 6.02. Weight, 200.
High School—Bakersfield, Calif.
Attended Arizona State University, Bakersfield College and San Jose State University.

Named to The Sporting News NFL All-Star Team, 1984.
Named to The Sporting News AFC All-Star Team, 1977 through 1979.
Selected by Denver in 1st round (17th player selected) of 1975 NFL draft.
On injured reserve with calf injury, November 28 through remainder of 1981 season.

	—INTERCEPTIONS—						—INTERCEPTIONS—			
Year Club	G.	No.	Yds.	Avg.	TD.	Year Club	G.	No.	Yds.	Avg. TD.
1975—Denver NFL	11	2	9	4.5	0	1981—Denver NFL	8		None	
1976—Denver NFL	14		None			1982—Denver NFL	9	2	18	9.0 0
1977—Denver NFL	14	3	128	*42.7	*1	1983—Denver NFL	16	6	50	8.3 0
1978—Denver NFL	16	2	2	1.0	0	1984—Denver NFL	16	1	1	1.0 0
1979—Denver NFL	16	2	20	10.0	0	Pro Totals—10 Years.........	135	18	228	12.7 1
1980—Denver NFL	15		None							

Additional pro statistics: Recovered one fumble for four yards, 1975; fumbled once, 1975, 1978 and 1983; recovered one fumble, 1976 and 1982; ran one lateral 32 yards, 1976; recovered two fumbles, 1978; recovered one fumble for 78 yards and a touchdown, 1979; recovered one fumble for minus five yards, 1981; returned one punt for no yards and recovered one fumble for 40 yards, 1983; recovered two fumbles for 27 yards and a touchdown, 1984.

Played in AFC Championship Game following 1977 season.
Played in NFL Championship Game following 1977 season.
Played in Pro Bowl (NFL All-Star Game) following 1977 through 1979 and 1983 seasons.

RANDY WRIGHT
Quarterback—Green Bay Packers
Born January 12, 1961, at St. Charles, Ill.
Height, 6.02. Weight, 194.
High School—St. Charles, Ill.
Attended University of Wisconsin.

Selected by Memphis in 9th round (188th player selected) of 1984 USFL draft.
USFL rights released by Memphis Showboats, February 7, 1984.
Selected by Green Bay in 6th round (153rd player selected) of 1984 NFL draft.
Signed by Green Bay Packers, June 30, 1984.
On injured reserve with knee injury, December 12 through remainder of 1984 season.

					—PASSING—						—RUSHING—			—TOTAL—	
Year	Club	G.	Att.	Cmp.	Pct.	Gain	T.P.	P.I.	Avg.	Att.	Yds.	Avg.	TD.	TD.	Pts.	F.
1984—Green Bay NFL		8	62	27	43.5	310	2	6	5.00	8	11	1.4	0	0	0	1

Quarterback Rating Points: 1984 (30.4).
Additional pro statistics: Recovered one fumble, 1984.

TIMOTHY JON WRIGHTMAN
(Tim)
Tight End—Chicago Bears
Born March 27, 1960, at Harbor City, Calif.
Height, 6.03. Weight, 236.
High School—San Pedro, Calif., Mary Star of the Sea.
Attended University of California at Los Angeles.

Selected by Chicago in 3rd round (62nd player selected) of 1982 NFL draft.
Signed by Chicago Blitz, August 5, 1982.
USFL rights subsequently traded by Arizona Wranglers to Chicago Blitz for rights to quarterback Dan Manucci, October 22, 1982.
On injured reserve with knee injury, March 3 through May 5, 1983; activated, May 6, 1983.
Franchise transferred to Arizona, September 30, 1983.
On reserve/non-football injury with knee injury, February 20 through April 20, 1984; activated, April 21, 1984.
On developmental squad, April 21 through remainder of 1984 season.
Granted free agency, November 30, 1984; signed by Chicago Bears, March 21, 1985.
On developmental squad for 10 games with Arizona Wranglers in 1984.

		—PASS RECEIVING—				
Year	Club	G.	P.C.	Yds.	Avg.	TD.
1983—Chicago USFL		9	6	86	14.3	0

On developmental squad for USFL Championship Game following 1984 season.

JEFFREY LEE YEATES
(Jeff)
Defensive End—Atlanta Falcons
Born August 3, 1951, at Buffalo, N. Y.
Height, 6.03. Weight, 257.
High School—Tonawanda, N. Y., Cardinal O'Hara.
Received bachelor of science degree in business management from Boston College in 1973.

Selected by Buffalo in 4th round (103rd player selected) of 1973 NFL draft.
Missed entire 1973 season because of knee injury.
Released by Buffalo Bills, September 28, 1976; signed as free agent by Atlanta Falcons, December 1, 1976.
Released by Atlanta Falcons, August 27, 1984; re-signed by Falcons, September 19, 1984.
Buffalo NFL, 1974 and 1975; Buffalo (2)-Atlanta (3) NFL, 1976; Atlanta NFL, 1977 through 1984.
Games: 1974 (10), 1975 (13), 1976 (5), 1977 (13), 1978 (16), 1979 (16), 1980 (16), 1981 (16), 1982 (9), 1983 (16), 1984 (8). Total—138.
Pro statistics: Recovered five fumbles, 1979; intercepted one pass for five yards and recovered one fumble for four yards, 1980; recovered one fumble, 1981 and 1983.

ANDRE BENOISE YOUNG
Safety—San Diego Chargers
Born November 22, 1960, at West Monroe, La.
Height, 6.00. Weight, 190.
High School—West Monroe, La.
Attended Louisiana Tech University.

Selected by San Diego in 10th round (273rd player selected) of 1982 NFL draft.

			-INTERCEPTIONS-				—KICKOFF RET.—				—TOTAL—		
Year	Club	G.	No.	Yds.	Avg.	TD.	No.	Yds.	Avg.	TD.	TD.	Pts.	F.
1982—San Diego NFL		8	2	9	4.5	0	4	45	11.3	0	0	0	1
1983—San Diego NFL		15	2	49	24.5	1	3	41	13.7	0	1	6	0
1984—San Diego NFL		13	2	31	15.5	0		None			0	0	1
Pro Totals—3 Years		36	6	89	14.8	1	7	86	12.3	0	1	6	2

Additional pro statistics: Recovered two fumbles, 1982; recovered one fumble, 1983 and 1984.

CHARLE EDWARD YOUNG
Tight End—Seattle Seahawks

Born February 5, 1951, at Fresno, Calif.
Height, 6.04. Weight, 234.
High School—Fresno, Calif., Edison.
Received bachelor of arts degree from University of Southern California.

Named to THE SPORTING NEWS NFC All-Star Team, 1974 and 1975.
Named as tight end on THE SPORTING NEWS College All-America Team, 1972.
Selected by Philadelphia in 1st round (6th player selected) of 1973 NFL draft.
Traded by Philadelphia Eagles to Los Angeles Rams for quarterback Ron Jaworski, March 10, 1977.
Traded with 3rd and 4th round picks in 1980 draft by Los Angeles Rams to San Francisco 49ers for 3rd round pick in 1980 draft and 3rd round pick in 1983 draft, April 28, 1980.
Released by San Francisco 49ers, July 21, 1983; signed as free agent by Seattle Seahawks, July 27, 1983.

Year Club	G.	Att.	Yds.	Avg.	TD.	P.C.	Yds.	Avg.	TD.	TD.	Pts.	F.
		—RUSHING—				PASS RECEIVING				—TOTAL—		
1973—Philadelphia NFL	14	4	24	6.0	1	55	854	15.5	6	7	42	0
1974—Philadelphia NFL	14	6	38	6.3	0	63	696	11.0	3	3	18	4
1975—Philadelphia NFL	14	2	1	0.5	0	49	659	13.4	3	3	18	0
1976—Philadelphia NFL	14	1	6	6.0	0	30	374	12.5	0	0	0	1
1977—Los Angeles NFL	14			None		5	35	7.0	1	1	6	0
1978—Los Angeles NFL	16	2	6	3.0	0	18	213	11.8	0	0	0	1
1979—Los Angeles NFL	15			None		13	144	11.1	2	2	12	2
1980—San Francisco NFL	16			None		29	325	11.2	2	2	12	0
1981—San Francisco NFL	16			None		37	400	10.8	5	5	30	0
1982—San Francisco NFL	9			None		22	189	8.6	0	0	0	1
1983—Seattle NFL	16			None		36	529	14.7	2	2	12	1
1984—Seattle NFL	15	1	5	5.0	0	33	337	10.2	1	1	6	1
Pro Totals—12 Years	173	16	80	5.0	1	390	4755	12.2	25	26	156	11

Additional pro statistics: Recovered one fumble, 1973, 1975, 1979 and 1983; returned one kickoff for 14 yards, 1980.
Played in NFC Championship Game following 1979 and 1981 seasons.
Played in AFC Championship Game following 1983 season.
Member of Los Angeles Rams for NFC Championship Game following 1978 season; did not play.
Played in NFL Championship Game following 1981 season.
Member of Los Angeles Rams for NFL Championship Game following 1979 season; did not play.
Played in Pro Bowl (NFL All-Star Game) following 1973 through 1975 seasons.

DAVID J. YOUNG
(Dave)
Tight End—Indianapolis Colts

Born February 9, 1959, at Akron, O.
Height, 6.05. Weight, 242.
High School—Akron, O., East.
Attended Purdue University.
Cousin of Levert Carr, offensive lineman with San Diego Chargers,
Buffalo Bills and Houston Oilers, 1969 through 1973.

Named as tight end on THE SPORTING NEWS College All-America Team, 1980.
Selected by New York Giants in 2nd round (32nd player selected) of 1981 NFL draft.
On injured reserve with broken thumb, September 1 through October 8, 1981; activated, October 9, 1981.
On non-football injury list due to being overweight, July 30 through August 15, 1982; activated, August 16, 1982.
Released by New York Giants, August 26, 1982; claimed on waivers by New England Patriots, August 27, 1982.
Released by New England Patriots, September 6, 1982.
USFL rights traded with guard Calvin Close by Oakland Invaders to Arizona Wranglers for rights to defensive back Frank Duncan and defensive tackle Scott Setterlund, January 4, 1983.
Signed as free agent by Buffalo Bills, April 10, 1983.
Released by Buffalo Bills, August 29, 1983; re-signed by Bills, August 30, 1983.
Released by Buffalo Bills, October 4, 1983; signed as free agent by Baltimore Colts, November 23, 1983.
Franchise transferred to Indianapolis, March 31, 1984.
Active for 5 games with Buffalo Bills in 1983; did not play.

Year Club	G.	P.C.	Yds.	Avg.	TD.
		—PASS RECEIVING—			
1981—N.Y. Giants NFL	11	5	49	9.8	1
1983—Buf. (0)-Balt. (1) NFL	1		None		
1984—Indianapolis NFL	13	14	164	11.7	2
Pro Totals—3 Years	25	19	213	11.2	3

FREDD YOUNG
Linebacker—Seattle Seahawks

Born November 14, 1961, at Dallas, Tex.
Height, 6.01. Weight, 220.
High School—Dallas, Tex., Woodrow Wilson.
Attended New Mexico State University.

Selected by Arizona in 1984 USFL territorial draft.
Selected by Seattle in 3rd round (76th player selected) of 1984 NFL draft.
Signed by Seattle Seahawks, May 17, 1984.
Seattle NFL, 1984.
Games: 1984 (16).
Played in Pro Bowl (NFL All-Star Game) following 1984 season.

GLEN YOUNG
Wide Receiver—Cleveland Browns
Born October 11, 1960, at Greenwood, Miss.
Height, 6.02. Weight, 205.
High School—Greenwood, Miss.
Attended Mississippi State University.

Selected by Oakland in 2nd round (18th player selected) of 1983 USFL draft.
Selected by Philadelphia in 3rd round (62nd player selected) of 1983 NFL draft.
Signed by Philadelphia Eagles, May 13, 1983.
Released by Philadelphia Eagles, August 27, 1984; awarded on waivers to St. Louis Cardinals, August 28, 1984.
Released by St. Louis Cardinals, September 5, 1984; signed as free agent by Cleveland Browns, November 14, 1984.
Active for 1 game with St. Louis Cardinals in 1984; did not play.

Year Club		PASS RECEIVING				-PUNT RETURNS-				—KICKOFF RET.—				—TOTAL—		
	G.	P.C.	Yds.	Avg.	TD.	No.	Yds.	Avg.	TD.	No.	Yds.	Avg.	TD.	TD.	Pts.	F.
1983—Philadelphia NFL	16	3	125	41.7	1	14	93	6.6	0	26	547	21.0	0	1	6	2
1984—St.L. (0)-Cle. (2) NFL ...	2	1	47	47.0	0			None		5	134	26.8	0	0	0	0
Pro Totals—2 Years.......	18	4	172	43.0	1	14	93	6.6	0	31	681	22.0	0	1	6	2

Additional pro statistics: Recovered one fumble, 1983.

RICKEY DARNELL YOUNG
Running Back—Minnesota Vikings
Born December 7, 1953, at Mobile, Ala.
Height, 6.02. Weight, 200.
High School—Prichard, Ala., C. F. Vigor.
Received degree in recreation from Jackson State University.
Cousin of Robert Brazile, linebacker with Houston Oilers; uncle of Walter Payton, running back with
Chicago Bears; and Eddie Payton, kick returner with Cleveland Browns, Detroit Lions,
Kansas City Chiefs, Toronto Argonauts and Minnesota Vikings, 1977 through 1982.

Selected by San Diego Chargers in 7th round (164th player selected) of 1975 NFL draft.
Traded by San Diego Chargers to Minnesota Vikings for rights to guard Ed White, July 28, 1978.
Released by Minnesota Vikings, August 27, 1984; signed as free agent by Miami Dolphins, September 15, 1984.
Released by Miami Dolphins after failing physical, September 15, 1984; signed as free agent by Minnesota Vikings, May 13, 1985.

Year Club		——RUSHING——				PASS RECEIVING				—TOTAL—		
	G.	Att.	Yds.	Avg.	TD.	P.C.	Yds.	Avg.	TD.	TD.	Pts.	F.
1975—San Diego NFL	14	138	577	4.2	5	21	166	7.9	1	6	36	5
1976—San Diego NFL	14	162	802	5.0	4	47	441	9.4	1	5	30	2
1977—San Diego NFL	14	157	543	3.5	4	48	423	8.8	0	4	24	4
1978—Minnesota NFL	16	134	417	3.1	1	*88	704	8.0	5	6	36	6
1979—Minnesota NFL	16	188	708	3.8	3	72	519	7.2	4	7	42	2
1980—Minnesota NFL	16	130	351	2.7	3	64	499	7.8	2	5	30	2
1981—Minnesota NFL	16	47	129	2.7	0	43	296	6.9	2	2	12	4
1982—Minnesota NFL	9	16	49	3.1	1	4	44	11.0	1	2	12	0
1983—Minnesota NFL	16	39	90	2.3	2	21	193	9.2	0	2	12	0
Pro Totals—9 Years..................	131	1011	3666	3.6	23	408	3285	8.1	16	39	234	25

Year Club		KICKOFF RETURNS				Year Club		KICKOFF RETURNS			
	G.	No.	Yds.	Avg.	TD.		G.	No.	Yds.	Avg.	TD.
1975—San Diego NFL	14	15	323	21.5	0	1980—Minnesota NFL.............	16			None	
1976—San Diego NFL	14			None		1981—Minnesota NFL.............	16	1	15	15.0	0
1977—San Diego NFL	14			None		1982—Minnesota NFL.............	9			None	
1978—Minnesota NFL.............	16	1	8	8.0	0	1983—Minnesota NFL.............	16	3	27	9.0	0
1979—Minnesota NFL.............	16			None		Pro Totals—9 Years...........	131	20	373	18.7	0

Additional pro statistics: Recovered two fumbles, 1975 and 1978; recovered one fumble, 1977 and 1982.

ROYNELL YOUNG
Cornerback—Philadelphia Eagles
Born December 1, 1957, at New Orleans, La.
Height, 6.01. Weight, 181.
High School—New Orleans, La., Cohen.
Attended Alcorn State University.

Selected by Philadelphia in 1st round (23rd player selected) of 1980 NFL draft.
On injured reserve with strained abdominal muscles, October 12 through November 15, 1984; activated, November 16, 1984.

Year Club		—INTERCEPTIONS—			
	G.	No.	Yds.	Avg.	TD.
1980—Philadelphia NFL	16	4	27	6.8	0
1981—Philadelphia NFL	13	4	35	8.8	0
1982—Philadelphia NFL	9	4	0	0.0	0
1983—Philadelphia NFL	16	1	0	0.0	0
1984—Philadelphia NFL	7			None	
Pro Totals—5 Years...........	61	13	62	4.8	0

Additional pro statistics: Returned one kickoff for 18 yards and recovered two fumbles, 1983.
Played in NFC Championship Game following 1980 season.
Played in NFL Championship Game following 1980 season.
Played in Pro Bowl (NFL All-Star Game) following 1981 season.

TYRONE DONNIVE YOUNG
Wide Receiver—New Orleans Saints
Born April 29, 1960, at Ocala, Fla.
Height, 6.06. Weight, 192.
High School—Ocala, Fla., Forest.
Attended University of Florida.

Selected by Tampa Bay in 1983 USFL territorial draft.
Signed as free agent by New Orleans Saints, May 20, 1983.

		—PASS RECEIVING—			
Year	Club	G.	P.C.	Yds.	Avg.	TD.
1983—New Orleans NFL........		16	7	85	12.1	3
1984—New Orleans NFL........		16	29	597	20.6	3
Pro Totals—2 Years............		32	36	682	18.9	6

Additional pro statistics: Fumbled once, 1984.

HERBERT JACKSON YOUNGBLOOD III
(Jack)
Defensive End—Los Angeles Rams
Born January 26, 1950, at Monticello, Fla.
Height, 6.04. Weight, 242.
High School—Monticello, Fla., Jefferson County.
Attended University of Florida.

Named to THE SPORTING NEWS NFC All-Star Team, 1974 through 1979.
Named as defensive end on THE SPORTING NEWS College All-America Team, 1970.
Selected by Los Angeles in 1st round (20th player selected) of 1971 NFL draft.
On did not report list, August 19 through September 3, 1980; activated, September 4, 1980.
Los Angeles Rams NFL, 1971 through 1984.
Games: 1971 (14), 1972 (14), 1973 (14), 1974 (14), 1975 (14), 1976 (14), 1977 (14), 1978 (16), 1979 (16), 1980 (16), 1981 (16), 1982 (9), 1983 (16), 1984 (15). Total—202.
Pro statistics: Returned two kickoffs for 36 yards, 1971; recovered one fumble for three yards, 1972; recovered one fumble, 1973; credited with one safety, 1975 and 1983; recovered two fumbles for nine yards, 1975; recovered one fumble for one yard, 1976; recovered one fumble, 1977 and 1978; recovered two fumbles, 1983; recovered one fumble for nine yards, 1984.
Played in NFC Championship Game following 1974 through 1976, 1978 and 1979 seasons.
Played in NFL Championship Game following 1979 season.
Played in Pro Bowl (NFL All-Star Game) following 1973 through 1979 seasons.

JIMMY LEE YOUNGBLOOD
(Jim)
Linebacker—Los Angeles Rams
Born February 23, 1950, at Union, S. C.
Height, 6.03. Weight, 231.
High School—Jonesville, S. C.
Attended Tennessee Tech University.

Named to THE SPORTING NEWS NFC All-Star Team, 1979.
Selected by Los Angeles in 2nd round (42nd player selected) of 1973 NFL draft.
On did not report list, August 19 through September 3, 1980; activated, September 4, 1980.
On injured reserve with knee injury, December 23 through remainder of 1982 season.
Granted free agency when option not renewed, February 1, 1984.
USFL rights traded by Memphis Showboats to Arizona Wranglers for rights to center Art Kuehn, February 3, 1984.
Signed by Seattle Seahawks, March 6, 1984.
Released by Seattle Seahawks, August 21, 1984; signed as free agent by Washington Redskins, September 12, 1984.
Released by Washington Redskins, October 17, 1984; signed as free agent by Los Angeles Rams, November 13, 1984.

		—INTERCEPTIONS—			
Year	Club	G.	No.	Yds.	Avg.	TD.
1973—Los Angeles NFL.........		14	1	15	15.0	1
1974—Los Angeles NFL.........		14		None		
1975—Los Angeles NFL.........		14		None		
1976—Los Angeles NFL.........		14	2	28	14.0	0
1977—Los Angeles NFL.........		14	2	27	13.5	*1
1978—Los Angeles NFL..........		16	2	50	25.0	0
1979—Los Angeles NFL.........		16	5	89	17.8	*2
1980—Los Angeles NFL..........		15	1	33	33.0	1
1981—Los Angeles NFL..........		16	1	20	20.0	0
1982—L.A. Rams NFL............		7		None		
1983—L.A. Rams NFL............		7		None		
1984—Wa. (4)-Rams (5) NFL		9		None		
Pro Totals—12 Years........		156	14	262	18.7	5

Additional pro statistics: Returned one kickoff for no yards, 1974; recovered one fumble for two yards, 1976; recovered three fumbles for two yards, 1978.
Played in NFC Championship Game following 1974 through 1976, 1978 and 1979 seasons.
Played in NFL Championship Game following 1979 season.
Played in Pro Bowl (NFL All-Star Game) following 1979 season.

JOHN ZAMBERLIN
Linebacker—Kansas City Chiefs
Born February 13, 1956, at Tacoma, Wash.
Height, 6.02. Weight, 226.
Attended Pacific Lutheran University.

Selected by New England in 5th round (135th player selected) of 1979 NFL draft.
Left New England Patriots camp voluntarily, August 1, 1979; returned, August 7, 1979.
Released by New England Patriots, August 27, 1979; re-signed by Patriots, August 28, 1979.
Released by New England Patriots, August 29, 1983; awarded on waivers to Kansas City Chiefs, August 31, 1983.
On injured reserve with pinched nerve in neck, October 18 through December 12, 1984; activated, December 13, 1984.
New England NFL, 1979 through 1982; Kansas City NFL, 1983 and 1984.
Games: 1979 (16), 1980 (16), 1981 (16), 1982 (8), 1983 (14), 1984 (8). Total—78.
Pro statistics: Intercepted one pass for 11 yards and recovered one fumble, 1981.

JAMES ARTHUR ZORN
(Jim)
Quarterback—Seattle Seahawks
Born May 10, 1953, at Whittier, Calif.
Height, 6.02. Weight, 200.
High School—Cerritos, Calif., Gahr.
Attended Cerritos College and California Poly State University—Pomona.

Signed as free agent by Dallas Cowboys, 1975.
Released by Dallas Cowboys, September 19, 1975; signed as free agent by Seattle Seahawks, January 8, 1976.

Year Club	G.	Att.	Cmp.	Pct.	Gain	T.P.	P.I.	Avg.	Att.	Yds.	Avg.	TD.	TD.	Pts.	F.
				PASSING						RUSHING			TOTAL		
1976—Seattle NFL	14	*439	208	47.4	2571	12	*27	5.86	52	246	4.7	4	4	24	7
1977—Seattle NFL	10	251	104	41.4	1687	16	19	6.72	25	141	5.6	1	1	6	1
1978—Seattle NFL	16	443	248	56.0	3283	15	20	7.41	59	290	4.9	6	6	36	11
1979—Seattle NFL	16	505	285	56.4	3661	20	18	7.25	46	279	6.1	2	2	12	6
1980—Seattle NFL	16	488	276	56.6	3346	17	20	6.86	44	214	4.9	1	1	6	12
1981—Seattle NFL	13	397	236	59.4	2788	13	9	7.02	30	140	4.7	1	1	6	2
1982—Seattle NFL	9	245	126	51.4	1540	7	11	6.29	15	113	7.5	1	1	6	5
1983—Seattle NFL	16	205	103	50.2	1166	7	7	5.69	30	71	2.4	1	1	6	4
1984—Seattle NFL	16	17	7	41.2	80	0	2	4.71	7	—3	—0.4	0	0	0	0
Pro Totals—9 Years	126	2990	1593	53.3	20122	107	133	6.73	308	1491	4.8	17	17	102	48

Quarterback Rating Points: 1976 (49.2), 1977 (54.3), 1978 (72.2), 1979 (77.6), 1980 (72.4), 1981 (82.3), 1982 (62.1), 1983 (64.8), 1984 (16.4). Total—68.2.
Additional pro statistics: Recovered three fumbles, 1976 and 1978; recovered one fumble, 1977; fumbled 11 times for minus 18 yards, 1978; recovered four fumbles and fumbled 12 times for minus 13 yards, 1980; caught one pass for 27 yards, recovered one fumble and fumbled five times for minus three yards, 1982.
Played in AFC Championship Game following 1983 season.

ADDITIONAL PLAYER TRANSACTIONS

The following player transactions involve players in the Register occurring after May 28, 1985.

BRYANT, CULLEN—Released by Seattle Seahawks, June 5, 1985.

BURGESS, FERNANZA—Released by New York Jets, May 29, 1985.

CAMPBELL, RICH—Released by Green Bay Packers, May 30, 1985.

DUFEK, DON—Released by Seattle Seahawks, June 5, 1985.

GRIFFIN, RAY—Signed as free agent by Seattle Seahawks, June 5, 1985.

KANE, RICK—Signed as free agent by Detroit Lions, May 29, 1985.

RAMSEY, CHUCK—Released by New York Jets, May 29, 1985.

WHITE, CHARLES—Released by Cleveland Browns, June 4, 1985.

Additional Active Players

REX ALAN BURNINGHAM
Offensive Tackle—Los Angeles Raiders
Born September 1, 1959, at Springfield, Mass.
Height, 6.04. Weight, 265.
High School—Bountiful, Utah.
Attended Ricks Junior College and Brigham Young University.

Selected by New Orleans in 16th round (319th player selected) of 1984 USFL draft.
Signed by New Orleans Breakers, January 14, 1984.
On developmental squad, February 24 through March 22, 1984; activated, March 23, 1984.
On developmental squad, April 6 through May 28, 1984; activated, May 29, 1984.
Franchise transferred to Portland, November 13, 1984.
Released by Portland Breakers, February 2, 1985; signed as free agent by Los Angeles Raiders, May 10, 1985.
On developmental squad for 12 games with New Orleans Breakers in 1984.
New Orleans USFL, 1984.
Games: 1984 (6).

STUART R. CRUM
(Stu)
Placekicker—New York Jets
Born November 4, 1959, at San Jose, Calif.
Height, 5.07. Weight, 165.
High School—Ballwin, Mo., Parkway West.
Received bachelor of science degree in business administration from University of Tulsa.

Selected by New York Jets in 12th round (328th player selected) of 1983 NFL draft.
Signed by Oklahoma Outlaws, July 12, 1983.
On reserve/retired list, March 15 through June 19, 1984.
Released by Oklahoma Outlaws, June 20, 1984; awarded on waivers to Chicago Blitz, July 17, 1984.
NFL rights traded by New York Jets to Kansas City Chiefs for 10th round pick in 1985 draft, July 17, 1984 (deal voided when Blitz awarded USFL rights).
Chicago Blitz franchise disbanded, November 20, 1984.
Signed by New York Jets, May 17, 1985.

		——PLACE KICKING——					
Year	Club	G.	XP.	XPM.	FG.	FGA.	Pts.
1984—Oklahoma USFL	......	3	5	0	0	4	5

CHUCKY ALAN DAVIS
Running Back—Atlanta Falcons
Born April 21, 1961, at Macon, Ga.
Height, 6.00. Weight, 213.
High School—Mason, Ga., Southwest.
Attended University of Wisconsin.

Signed as free agent by Ottawa Rough Riders, May 10, 1984.
Released by Ottawa Rough Riders, August 5, 1984; signed as free agent by Atlanta Falcons, May 14, 1985.

		——RUSHING——				PASS RECEIVING				—TOTAL—		
Year	Club	G.	Att.	Yds.	Avg.	TD.	P.C.	Yds.	Avg.	TD.	TD. Pts. F.
1984—Ottawa CFL	......	3	26	135	5.2	0	7	54	7.7	1	1 6 2

Additional CFL statistics: Returned two kickoffs for 39 yards, 1984.

MYRON RAY DUPREE
Cornerback—Philadelphia Eagles
Born October 15, 1961, at New York, N.Y.
Height, 5.11. Weight, 180.
High School—Rocky Mount, N.C.
Attended North Carolina Central University.

Selected by Denver in 7th round (172nd player selected) of 1983 NFL draft.
Released by Denver Broncos, August 29, 1983; re-signed by Broncos, August 30, 1983.
Released by Denver Broncos, August 6, 1984; signed as free agent by Philadelphia Eagles, May 29, 1985.
Denver NFL, 1983.
Games: 1983 (16).

EARNEL MICHAEL DURDEN
(Mike)
Safety—New York Jets
Born May 4, 1959, at Los Angeles, Calif.
Height, 6.01. Weight, 185.
High School—La Mesa, Calif., Helix.
Attended University of California at Los Angeles.
Son of Earnel Durden, assistant coach with San Diego Chargers.

Selected by Arizona in 14th round (167th player selected) of 1983 USFL draft.
Signed as free agent by San Francisco 49ers, May 6, 1983.

Released by San Francisco 49ers, August 29, 1983; signed as free agent by Edmonton Eskimos, October 4, 1983.
Released by Edmonton Eskimos, October 21, 1984; signed as free agent by New York Jets, May 10, 1985.
Edmonton CFL, 1983 and 1984.
Games: 1983 (1), 1984 (6). Total—7.
CFL statistics: Récovered one fumble, 1984.

DAN CLEMENT FIKE JR.
Offensive Tackle—Cleveland Browns
Born June 16, 1961, at Mobile, Ala.
Height, 6.06. Weight, 275.
High School—Pensacola, Fla., Pine Forest.
Attended University of Florida.

Selected by Tampa Bay in 1984 USFL territorial draft.
Selected by New York Jets in 10th round (274th player selected) of 1983 NFL draft.
Signed by New York Jets, June 10, 1983.
Released by New York Jets, August 29, 1983; signed by Tampa Bay Bandits, November 13, 1983.
Signed by Cleveland Browns, January 20, 1985, to take affect after being granted free agency following 1985 USFL season.
Tampa Bay USFL, 1984.
Games: 1984 (18).

MICHAEL DEWAYNE FURNAS
(Mike)
Running Back—New York Jets
Born April 18, 1961, at Miami, Okla.
Height, 6.00. Weight, 235.
High School—Commerce, Okla.
Attended Northeastern Oklahoma A & M and University of Tennessee.

Selected by Memphis in 1984 USFL territorial draft.
Signed by Memphis Showboats, January 19, 1984.
Released by Memphis Showboats, February 20, 1984; signed as free agent by Washington Redskins, June 20, 1984.
Released by Washington Redskins, July 23, 1984; signed as free agent by New York Jets, May 10, 1985.
Played guard and fullback for Milan in Italian Football League, 1984.

ERIC HALSTER KAIFES
Punter—New York Jets
Born July 16, 1960, at Kansas City, Kan.
Height, 6.04. Weight, 215.
High School—Kansas City, Mo., Bishop Ward.
Attended Coffeyville Community College and received bachelor of science degree
from Southern Methodist University.

Signed as free agent by Buffalo Bills, May 1, 1982.
Released by Buffalo Bills, August 23, 1982; signed as free agent by Oklahoma Outlaws, August 10, 1983.
Released by Oklahoma Outlaws, January 24, 1984; signed as free agent by Chicago Bears, May 4, 1984.
Released by Chicago Bears, August 21, 1984; signed as free agent by New York Jets, May 10, 1985.

DOUGLAS ARTHUR KELLERMEYER
(Doug)
Offensive Lineman—Houston Oilers
Born June 1, 1961, at Bucyrus, O.
Height, 6.02. Weight, 275.
High School—Scottsdale, Ariz., Coronado.
Attended Brigham Young University.

Signed as free agent by Arizona Wranglers, January 10, 1984.
Released injured by Arizona Wranglers, February 13, 1984; signed as free agent by Los Angeles Raiders, May 20, 1984.
Released by Los Angeles Raiders, August 1, 1984; signed as free agent by Houston Oilers, August 4, 1984.
Released by Houston Oilers, August 27, 1984; signed as free agent by Orlando Renegades, January 23, 1985.
Released by Orlando Renegades, February 11, 1985; signed as free agent by Houston Oilers, May 6, 1985.

ROBERT KENT KNAPTON
(Bob)
Linebacker—Washington Redskins
Born May 22, 1960, at Bitburg Air Force Base, West Germany.
Height, 6.02. Weight, 225.
High School—Yuma, Colo.
Received bachelor of science degree in earth science and geology
from University of Northern Colorado in 1982.

Signed as free agent by Seattle Seahawks, April 30, 1982.
Released by Seattle Seahawks, July 30, 1982.
USFL rights traded by Oakland Invaders to Denver Gold for past consideration, November 18, 1982.
Signed by Denver Gold, December 17, 1982.
Released by Denver Gold, February 8, 1983; re-signed by Gold, February 11, 1983.
Released by Denver Gold, February 27, 1983; re-signed by Gold, May 5, 1983.

Selected by Memphis Showboats in 21st round (126th player selected) of USFL expansion draft, September 7, 1983.
Released by Memphis Showboats, February 6, 1984; signed as free agent by Denver Gold, March 24, 1984.
Traded with draft choice by Denver Gold to Chicago Blitz for defensive end Bruce Thornton, March 29, 1984.
Franchise disbanded, November 20, 1984.
Selected by New Jersey Generals in USFL dispersal draft, December 6, 1984.
Released by New Jersey Generals, February 1, 1985; signed as free agent by Washington Redskins, May 13, 1985.
Denver USFL, 1983; Denver (1)-Chicago (13) USFL, 1984.
Games: 1983 (8), 1984 (14). Total—22.
Pro statistics: Intercepted one pass for four yards and recovered one fumble, 1984.

JOHN JOSEPH KRIMM JR.
Safety—Los Angeles Raiders
Born May 30, 1960, at Philadelphia, Pa.
Height, 6.02. Weight, 190.
High School—Columbus, O., Bishop Watterson.
Attended University of Notre Dame.

Named as defensive back on THE SPORTING NEWS College All-America Team, 1981.
Selected by New Orleans in 3rd round (76th player selected) of 1982 NFL draft.
On injured reserve with knee injury, August 15 through entire 1983 season.
Released by New Orleans Saints, August 23, 1984; signed as free agent by Los Angeles Raiders, March 20, 1985.
New Orleans NFL, 1982.
Games: 1982 (9).

MATTHEW SCOTT LONG
(Matt)
Center—Chicago Bears
Born March 16, 1961, at Glendale, Calif.
Height, 6.02. Weight, 260.
High School—Ventura, Calif., Bueno.
Attended San Diego State University.

Selected by New Jersey in 12th round (237th player selected) of 1984 USFL draft.
Signed as free agent by Chicago Bears, May 22, 1984.
On injured reserve with knee injury, August 14 through October 2, 1984.
Released by Chicago Bears, October 3, 1984; re-signed by Bears, May 8, 1985.

JOEY LYNN LUMPKIN
Linebacker—San Francisco 49ers
Born February 19, 1960, at Ardmore, Okla.
Height, 6.02. Weight, 230.
High School—Scottsdale, Ariz.
Attended Arizona State University.

Signed as free agent by Buffalo Bills, May 1, 1982.
On inactive list, September 12 and September 19, 1982.
Released by Buffalo Bills, August 29, 1983; re-signed by Bills, September 13, 1983.
Released by Buffalo Bills, August 27, 1984; signed as free agent by San Francisco 49ers, April 16, 1985.
Buffalo NFL, 1982 and 1983.
Games: 1982 (6), 1983 (14). Total—20.
Pro statistics: Recovered one fumble, 1983.

JOHN DOUGLAS MEYER
Defensive End—Los Angeles Rams
Born May 28, 1959, at Phoenix, Ariz.
Height, 6.06. Weight, 256.
High School—Phoenix, Ariz., Alhambra.
Attended Scottsdale Community College, Glendale Community College
and Arizona State University.

Selected by Pittsburgh in 2nd round (43rd player selected) of 1982 NFL draft.
On injured reserve with knee injury, September 7 through entire 1982 season.
On physically unable to perform/active with knee injury, July 15 through August 15, 1983.
On physically unable to perform/reserve with knee injury, August 16 through entire 1983 season.
Released by Pittsburgh Steelers after failing physical, July 15, 1984; signed as free agent by Los Angeles Rams,
May 20, 1985.

THOMAS LEWIS MORRIS
Safety—Detroit Lions
Born April 2, 1960, at Anniston, Ala.
Height, 5.11. Weight, 175.
High School—Long Beach, Calif., Millikan.
Attended Cypress College, Golden West College and received bachelor of science degree
in urban development from Michigan State University in 1982.
Brother of Randall Morris, running back with Seattle Seahawks.

Selected by Tampa Bay in 7th round (185th player selected) of 1982 NFL draft.
On inactive list, September 19, 1982.
On injured reserve with pulled hamstring, October 14 through November 10, 1983; activated, November 11, 1983.
Released by Tampa Bay Buccaneers, August 20, 1984; awarded on waivers to Indianapolis Colts, August 21, 1984.
Released by Indianapolis Colts, August 27, 1984; re-signed by Colts, August 28, 1984.

Released by Indianapolis Colts, August 31, 1984; signed by Michigan Panthers, September 5, 1984.
Franchise merged with Oakland Invaders, November 20, 1984.
Released injured by Oakland Invaders, February 18, 1985; signed as free agent by Detroit Lions, May 9, 1985.
Tampa Bay NFL, 1982 and 1983.
Games: 1982 (8), 1983 (12). Total—20.
Pro statistics: Recovered one fumble, 1983.

SHAWN NEWELL
Defensive Tackle—Chicago Bears
Born February 26, 1962, at Riverside, Calif.
Height, 6.03. Weight, 257.
High School—Riverside, Calif., Polytechnic.
Attended University of Utah.

Signed as free agent by Chicago Bears, June 21, 1984.
On injured reserve with knee injury, July 24 through entire 1984 season.

KELVIN RAY NEWTON
Linebacker—Tampa Bay Buccaneers
Born April 20, 1959, at Beaumont, Tex.
Height, 6.01. Weight, 235.
High School—Beaumont, Tex., French.
Received bachelor of arts degree in communications from Texas Christian University.

Signed as free agent by Dallas Cowboys, May 4, 1981.
Released by Dallas Cowboys, July 20, 1981; signed by Denver Gold, February 1, 1983.
Released by Denver Gold, June 20, 1984; awarded on waivers to Oakland Invaders, July 17, 1984.
Granted free agency, November 30, 1984; signed by Tampa Bay Buccaneers, February 28, 1985.
Denver USFL, 1983 and 1984.
Games: 1983 (18), 1984 (17). Total—35.
Pro statistics: Recovered one fumble, 1983; intercepted one pass for 14 yards, 1984.

MAOMAO NIKO
Guard—Denver Broncos
Born March 31, 1960, at San Francisco, Calif.
Height, 6.03. Weight, 290.
High School—Hayward, Calif., Mount Eden.
Attended San Jose State University.

Selected by Oakland in 1983 USFL territorial draft.
Signed as free agent by Denver Broncos, April 29, 1983.
On injured reserve with knee injury, August 23 through entire 1983 season.
Released by Denver Broncos, August 27, 1984; re-signed by Broncos for 1985, October 9, 1984.

SCOTT EDWARD NIZOLEK
Tight End—New York Jets
Born February 23, 1961, at Red Bank, N.J.
Height, 6.02. Weight, 225.
High School—West Haven, Conn., Notre Dame.
Received bachelor of science degree in marketing from Boston College.

Selected by Boston in 1983 USFL territorial draft.
Signed as free agent by Philadelphia Eagles, May 12, 1983.
Released by Philadelphia Eagles, August 29, 1983.
USFL rights traded by New Orleans Breakers (franchise transferred from Boston, October 18, 1983) to Philadelphia Stars for rights to guard Norm Hopely, November 29, 1983.
Signed by Philadelphia Stars, November 29, 1983.
On developmental squad, February 24 through April 19, 1984; activated, June 21, 1984.
Franchise transferred to Baltimore, November 1, 1984.
On developmental squad, April 6 through April 23, 1985.
Released by Baltimore Stars, April 24, 1985; signed as free agent by New York Jets, May 15, 1985.
On developmental squad for 15 games with Philadelphia Stars in 1984.
On developmental squad for 3 games with Baltimore Stars in 1985.
Philadelphia USFL, 1984; Baltimore USFL, 1985.
Games: 1984 (3), 1985 (6). Total—9.
Pro statistics: Returned one kickoff for 23 yards, 1985.
Played in USFL Championship Game following 1984 season.

CHET PARLAVECCHIO
Linebacker—New York Jets
Born February 14, 1960, at Newark, N.J.
Height, 6.02. Weight, 225.
High School—Seton Hall, N.J., Seton Hall Prep.
Attended Penn State University.

Selected by Green Bay in 6th round (152nd player selected) of 1982 NFL draft.
On injured reserve with knee injury, September 6 through entire 1982 season.
Released by Green Bay Packers, September 20, 1983; signed as free agent by St. Louis Cardinals, October 6, 1983.
Released by St. Louis Cardinals, August 6, 1984; awarded on waivers to Indianapolis Colts, August 7, 1984.
Released by Indianapolis Colts, August 20, 1984; signed by Baltimore Stars, January 3, 1985.
On reserve/retired, January 22 through January 29, 1985.
Released by Baltimore Stars, January 30, 1985; signed as free agent by New York Jets, May 7, 1985.
Green Bay (3)-St. Louis (9) NFL, 1983.
Games: 1983 (12).

JAY CHARLES PELUSI
(J.C.)
Nose Tackle—Cleveland Browns
Born December 16, 1960, at Youngstown, O.
Height, 6.01. Weight, 242.
High School—Youngstown, O., Chaney.
Attended University of Pittsburgh.

Selected by Philadelphia in 16th round (185th player selected) of 1983 USFL draft.
Signed as free agent by Saskatchewan Rough Riders, April 18, 1983.
Traded by Saskatchewan Roughriders to Ottawa Rough Riders for running back John Park, October 3, 1983.
Released by Ottawa Rough Riders, June 27, 1984; signed as free agent by Pittsburgh Steelers, July 27, 1984.
Released by Pittsburgh Steelers, August 20, 1984; signed as free agent by Cleveland Browns, May 24, 1985.
Saskatchewan CFL, 1983.
Games: 1984 (8).

RUDY PHILLIPS
Guard—Buffalo Bills
Born February 25, 1958, at Dallas, Tex.
Height, 6.02. Weight, 250.
High School—Dallas, Tex., Lincoln.
Received degree from North Texas State University.

Signed as free agent by Pittsburgh Steelers, May 15, 1981.
Released by Pittsburgh Steelers, August 24, 1981; signed as free agent by Ottawa Rough Riders, September 13, 1981.
Granted free agency, March 1, 1985; signed by Buffalo Bills, May 16, 1985.
Ottawa CFL, 1981 through 1984.
Games: 1981 (6), 1982 (13), 1983 (16), 1984 (13). Total—48.
CFL statistics: Recovered one fumble, 1981.
Played in CFL Championship Game following 1981 season.

DAVID PONDER
Defensive Lineman—Dallas Cowboys
Born June 27, 1962, at Cairo, Ga.
Height, 6.03. Weight, 250.
High School—Cairo, Ga.
Attended Florida State University.

Signed as free agent by Dallas Cowboys, May 3, 1984.
Released by Dallas Cowboys, August 27, 1984; re-signed by Cowboys, March 21, 1985.

KEVIN CRAIG POTTER
Safety—Chicago Bears
Born December 19, 1959, at St. Louis, Mo.
Height, 5.10. Weight, 188.
High School—St. Louis, Mo., DeSmet and Soldan.
Received bachelor of educational studies in psychology from University of Missouri.

Selected by Denver in 8th round (88th player selected) of 1983 USFL draft.
Selected by Houston in 9th round (226th player selected) of 1983 NFL draft.
Signed by Houston Oilers, June 22, 1983.
On injured reserve with hamstring injury, August 22 through September 12, 1983.
Released by Houston Oilers, September 13, 1983; signed as free agent by Chicago Bears, October 25, 1983.
Released by Chicago Bears, August 27, 1984.
USFL rights traded by Denver Gold to Chicago Blitz (franchise disbanded November 20, 1984) for draft pick, October 8, 1984.
Re-signed by Chicago Bears, December 12, 1984.
Granted free agency, February 1, 1985; signed by Memphis Showboats, February 3, 1985.
Released by Memphis Showboats, February 18, 1985; re-signed by Chicago Bears, May 9, 1985.
Chicago NFL, 1983 and 1984.
Games: 1983 (8), 1984 (1). Total—9.
Played in NFC Championship Game following 1984 season.

JOHN WILLIAM PUZAR
Center—Dallas Cowboys
Born June 27, 1962, at Los Angeles, Calif.
Height, 6.06. Weight, 255.
High School—Cupertino, Calif.
Attended De Anza College and California State University at Long Beach.

Selected by Los Angeles in 1984 USFL territorial draft.
Selected by Seattle in 8th round (216th player selected) of 1984 NFL draft.
Signed by Seattle Seahawks, May 19, 1984.
Released by Seattle Seahawks, August 21, 1984; signed as free agent by Dallas Cowboys for 1985, December 5, 1984.

DAVID RACKLEY
Cornerback—San Diego Chargers
Born February 2, 1961, at Miami, Fla.
Height, 5.09. Weight, 170.
High School—Miami, Fla., Jackson.
Attended Miami Dade Junior College and Texas Southern University.

Signed by Los Angeles Express, March 30, 1984.
On developmental squad, March 30 through remainder of 1984 season.
Released by Los Angeles Express, February 4, 1985; signed as free agent by San Diego Chargers, April 12, 1985.
On developmental squad for 13 games with Los Angeles Express in 1984.

MICHAEL ANTHONY REVELL
(Mike)
Running Back—Dallas Cowboys
Born January 23, 1962, at Brooksville, Fla.
Height, 5.11. Weight, 198.
High School—Brooksville, Fla., Hernando.
Received bachelor of arts degree in speech communications from Bethune-Cookman College.
Selected by Dallas in 8th round (222nd player selected) of 1984 NFL draft.
Released by Dallas Cowboys, August 21, 1984; re-signed by Cowboys, March 20, 1985.

JOHN TERAN ROBERTSON
Offensive Tackle—Philadelphia Eagles
Born September 26, 1961, at Eden, N.C.
Height, 6.05. Weight, 270.
High School—Eden, N.C., Morehead.
Received bachelor of science degree in industrial technology from
East Carolina University in 1984.
Selected by Memphis in 10th round (205th player selected) of 1984 USFL draft.
Selected by Philadelphia in 11th round (284th player selected) of 1984 NFL draft.
Signed by Philadelphia Eagles, May 25, 1984.
On injured reserve with back injury, August 27 through September 19, 1984.
Released by Philadelphia Eagles, September 20, 1984; re-signed by Eagles for 1985, October 22, 1984.

ERIC PARKER ROBINSON
Running Back—Kansas City Chiefs
Born December 12, 1960, at Washington, D.C.
Height, 5.08. Weight, 188.
High School—Wheaton, Md., John F. Kennedy.
Received bachelor of science degree in environmental health science
from Indiana State University.
Brother of Mark Robinson, safety with Kansas City Chiefs.
Named as kickoff returner on THE SPORTING NEWS USFL All-Star Team, 1983.
Signed by Washington Federals, January 26, 1983.
On developmental squad, May 26 through May 31, 1983; activated, June 1, 1983.
On developmental squad, June 8 through June 17, 1983; activated, June 18, 1983.
Franchise transferred to Orlando, October 12, 1984.
Released by Orlando Renegades, January 18, 1985; signed as free agent by Kansas City Chiefs, May 15, 1985.
On developmental squad for 2 games with Washington Federals in 1983.

Year Club	G.	Att.	Yds.	Avg.	TD.	P.C.	Yds.	Avg.	TD.	TD.	Pts.	F.
			RUSHING			PASS RECEIVING				—TOTAL—		
1983—Washington USFL	16	49	97	2.0	0	18	172	9.6	0	1	6	4
1984—Washington USFL	18		None			9	58	6.4	0	0	0	7
Pro Totals—2 Years	34	49	97	2.0	0	27	230	8.5	0	1	6	11

Year Club	G.	No.	Yds.	Avg.	TD.	No.	Yds.	Avg.TD.	
		—PUNT RETURNS—				—KICKOFF RET.—			
1983—Washington USFL	16	24	171	7.1	0	21	609	★29.0	★1
1984—Washington USFL	18	28	215	7.7	0	45	1073	23.8	0
Pro Totals—2 Years	34	52	386	7.4	0	66	1682	25.5	1

Additional pro statistics: Recovered one fumble, 1983; recovered four fumbles, 1984.

STEVEN C. ROGERS
(Steve)
Offensive Tackle—Philadelphia Eagles
Born January 9, 1959, at Escondido, Calif.
Height, 6.04. Weight, 265.
High School—Escondido, Calif., Orange Glen.
Attended Oregon State University, Palomar Junior College and Brigham Young University.
Signed as free agent by Kansas City Chiefs, May 17, 1982.
Released by Kansas City Chiefs, August 23, 1982; signed by Denver Gold, January 10, 1983.
Granted free agency, November 30, 1984; signed as free agent by Philadelphia Eagles, May 24, 1985.
Denver USFL, 1983 and 1984.
Games: 1983 (18), 1984 (18). Total—36.
Pro statistics: Recovered one fumble, 1983.

WILLIE DEAN ROSBOROUGH
Defensive End—Washington Redskins
Born January 9, 1961, at Los Angeles, Calif.
Height, 6.04. Weight, 243.
High School—Simi Valley, Calif.
Attended University of Washington.

Signed as free agent by Philadelphia Stars, January 25, 1983.
On developmental squad, July 1 through July 4, 1983; activated, July 5, 1983.
On developmental squad, February 24 through March 1, 1984; activated, March 2, 1984.
On developmental squad, March 10 through March 16, 1984; activated, March 17, 1984.
On developmental squad, April 7 through May 11, 1984; activated, May 12, 1984.
Franchise transferred to Baltimore, November 1, 1984.
Released by Baltimore Stars, February 18, 1985; awarded on waivers to Portland Breakers, February 19, 1985.
On developmental squad, March 22 through March 31, 1984; activated, April 1, 1985.
Released by Portland Breakers, April 10, 1985; signed as free agent by Washington Redskins, May 16, 1985.
On developmental squad for 1 game with Philadelphia Stars in 1983.
On developmental squad for 7 games with Philadelphia Stars in 1984.
On developmental squad for 1 game with Portland Breakers in 1985.
Philadelphia USFL, 1983 and 1984; Portland USFL, 1985.
Games: 1983 (17), 1984 (10), 1985 (5). Total—32.
Pro statistics: Recovered two fumbles, intercepted one pass for one yard and credited with five sacks for 19 yards, 1983; recovered one fumble, 1984; credited with one sack for 10 yards, 1985.
Played in USFL Championship Game following 1983 and 1984 seasons.

TODD CHRISTIAN ST. LOUIS
(Formerly known as Todd Hernandez.)
Running Back—Cleveland Browns
Born July 18, 1962, at Milwaukee, Wis.
Height, 5.10. Weight, 190.
High School—Germantown, Wis., Washington.
Received bachelor of arts degree in physical education from
Augustana College (S.D.) in 1984.

Signed as free agent by Atlanta Falcons, June 20, 1984.
Released by Atlanta Falcons, August 21, 1984; signed as free agent by Cleveland Browns, April 25, 1985.

MARK SHUMATE
Defensive Tackle—New York Jets
Born March 30, 1960, at Poynette, Wis.
Height, 6.05. Weight, 265.
High School—Poynette, Wis.
Attended University of Wisconsin.

Selected by Kansas City in 10th round (257th player selected) of 1983 NFL draft.
Released by Kansas City Chiefs, August 22, 1983; signed as free agent by Edmonton Eskimos, May 3, 1984.
Released by Edmonton Eskimos, August 28, 1984; signed as free agent by New York Jets, May 10, 1985.
Edmonton CFL, 1984.
Games: 1984 (8).

RICKY CLYDE SIMMONS
Wide Receiver—Atlanta Falcons
Born January 29, 1961, at Tyler, Tex.
Height, 5.10. Weight, 174.
High School—Greenville, Tex.
Attended University of Nebraska.

Selected by Washington in 4th round (69th player selected) of 1984 USFL draft.
Signed by Washington Federals, January 13, 1984.
Franchise transferred to Orlando, October 12, 1984.
Released by Orlando Renegades, March 7, 1985; signed as free agent by Atlanta Falcons, April 6, 1985.

		—PASS RECEIVING—			
Year Club	G.	P.C.	Yds.	Avg.	TD.
1984—Washington USFL	18	33	455	13.8	4
1985—Orlando USFL	2	2	37	18.5	0
Pro Totals—2 Years	20	35	492	14.1	4

Additional pro statistics: Ran 26 yards with lateral on kickoff return, recovered one fumble and fumbled once, 1984; rushed once for minus 10 yards, 1985.

ALLANDA SMITH
Safety—Minnesota Vikings
Born March 7, 1962, at Houston, Tex.
Height, 6.02. Weight, 190.
High School—Houston, Tex., Booker T. Washington.
Attended Texas Christian University.

Selected by Washington in 1st round (8th player selected) of the 1984 USFL draft.
Rights traded by Washington Federals to Los Angeles Express for draft choice, February 29, 1984.
Signed by Los Angeles Express, March 2, 1984.
Granted roster exemption, March 2, 1984; activated, March 30, 1984.

Selected by Minnesota in 1st round (13th player selected) of 1984 NFL supplemental draft.
Released by Los Angeles Express, May 30, 1985; signed by Minnesota Vikings, May 31, 1985.
Los Angeles USFL, 1984 and 1985.
Games: 1984 (13), 1985 (15). Total—28.
Additional pro statistics: Returned lateral on interception for 19 yards, 1985.

GENE SMITH
Cornerback—Los Angeles Raiders
Born August 20, 1962, at Washington, D.C.
Height, 6.01. Weight, 200.
High School—Washington, D.C., McKinley Technical.
Attended Georgetown University (did not play college football).

Selected by Indiana in 5th round (94th player selected) of 1984 NBA draft.
Released by Indiana Pacers, October 24, 1984; signed as free agent by Los Angeles Raiders, March 21, 1985.

MARK STEVENSON
Center-Guard—San Diego Chargers
Born February 24, 1956, at Waukegan, Ill.
Height, 6.03. Weight, 266.
High School—Rock Island, Ill.
Attended University of Missouri and Western Illinois University.

Signed as free agent by Seattle Seahawks, May 15, 1979.
Released by Seattle Seahawks after failing physical, July 15, 1979; signed as free agent by Chicago Bears, May 7, 1982.
Released by Chicago Bears, July 27, 1982; signed by Chicago Blitz, January 26, 1983.
On injured reserve with knee injury, April 13 through remainder of 1983 season.
Franchise transferred to Arizona, September 30, 1983.
Played with Chicago Fire of American Football Association, 1981.
On reserve/non-football injury with knee injury, February 20 through April 19, 1984; activated, April 20, 1984.
On developmental squad, April 20 through May 11, 1984.
On injured reserve with knee injury, May 12 through remainder of 1984 season.
Protected in merger of Arizona Wranglers and Oklahoma Outlaws, December 6, 1984.
Traded by Arizona Outlaws to Memphis Showboats for defensive back Bryan Howard, January 21, 1985.
Released injured by Memphis Showboats, February 18, 1985; signed as free agent by San Diego Chargers, April 26, 1985.
On developmental squad for 3 games with Arizona Wranglers in 1984.
Chicago USFL, 1983.
Games: 1983 (6).

ROWLAND TATUM
Linebacker—Philadelphia Eagles
Born November 20, 1962, at Inglewood, Calif.
Height, 6.01. Weight, 218.
High School—Inglewood, Calif., Morningside.
Attended Ohio State University.

Selected by New Jersey in 1984 USFL territorial draft.
Selected by Miami in 6th round (165th player selected) of 1984 NFL draft.
Signed by Miami Dolphins, July 13, 1984.
Released by Miami Dolphins, August 27, 1984; signed as free agent by Philadelphia Eagles, May 3, 1985.

MATTHEW NATHANIEL TEAGUE
Defensive End-Linebacker—Los Angeles Raiders
Born October 22, 1958, at Cincinnati, O.
Height, 6.04. Weight, 233.
High School—New Orleans, La., Alcee Fortier.
Attended Prairie View A&M University.

Selected by Dallas in 10th round (273rd player selected) of 1980 NFL draft (choice forfeited because of eligibility question).
Selected by Atlanta in 7th round of supplemental draft, June, 1980.
On injured reserve with knee injury, September 2 through entire 1980 season.
Released by Atlanta Falcons, August 30, 1982; signed as free agent by Ottawa Rough Riders, September 5, 1982.
Released by Ottawa Rough Riders, June 26, 1983; signed as free agent by Toronto Argonauts, August 25, 1983.
Released by Toronto Argonauts, July 1, 1984; awarded on waivers to Saskatchewan Roughriders, July 2, 1984.
Released by Saskatchewan Roughriders, August 5, 1984; signed as free agent by Los Angeles Raiders, April 21, 1985.
Atlanta NFL, 1981; Ottawa CFL, 1982; Toronto CFL, 1983; Sasktachewan CFL, 1984.
Games: 1981 (11), 1982 (2), 1983 (8), 1984 (4). Total CFL—14. Total Pro—25.
CFL statistics: Recovered one fumble, 1983.

KEITH ANTON WASHINGTON
Wide Receiver—Miami Dolphins
Born October 8, 1959, at Albany, N.Y.
Height, 5.10. Weight, 170.
High School—Delray Beach, Fla., Atlantic.
Did not attend college.

Signed as free agent by Miami Dolphins, March 29, 1985.

RECORD AS OUTFIELDER

Tied for Western Carolina League lead in caught stealing with 15 in 1979.
Tied for Eastern League lead in double plays by outfielders with 4 in 1983.

Year Club	League	Pos.	G.	AB.	R.	H.	2B.	3B.	HR.	RBI.	B.A.	PO.	A.	E.	F.A.
1977—Auburn	NYP	OF	53	175	22	37	4	2	0	8	.211	86	7	6	.939
1978—Spartanburg†	W. Car.	OF	38	141	19	35	4	1	0	9	.248	68	6	3	.961
1979—Spartanburg	W. Car.	OF	121	423	49	106	6	2	0	30	.251	226	19	7	.972
1980—Peninsula	Carol.	OF	123	447	87	120	11	3	0	31	.268	217	12	⋆13	.946
1981—Reading	East.	OF	61	146	26	38	1	0	0	14	.260	91	3	0	1.000
1981—Peninsula	Carol.	OF	53	202	39	56	3	2	0	14	.277	112	2	4	.966
1982—Reading	East.	OF	136	503	78	145	11	7	1	40	.288	⋆295	17	14	.957
1983—Reading‡§	East.	⋆OF-P	132	468	73	114	11	2	0	33	.244	⋆308	⋆23	6	.982

Selected by Philadelphia Phillies' organization in 5th round of free-agent draft, June 7, 1977.
†On Helena suspended list, June 23, 1978 through remainder of season.
‡Granted free agency, October 20, 1983; signed by California Angels' organization, December 6, 1983.
§Released, March 30, 1984.

PITCHING RECORD

Year Club	League	G.	IP.	W.	L.	Pct.	H.	R.	ER.	SO.	BB.	ERA.
1983—Reading	Eastern	3	4⅓	0	0	.000	4	1	1	0	3	2.08

TIMOTHY BERNARD WASHINGTON
(Tim)
Cornerback—Indianapolis Colts
Born November 7, 1959, at Fresno, Calif.
Height, 5.09. Weight, 184.
High School—Fresno, Calif.
Attended Fresno City College, University of California and Fresno State University.
Brother of Anthony Washington, cornerback with Washington Redskins.
Selected by San Francisco in 12th round (334th player selected) of 1982 NFL draft.
Released by San Francisco 49ers, September 6, 1982; re-signed by 49ers, September 16, 1982.
On commissioner's exempt list, November 20 through November 23, 1982.
Released by San Francisco 49ers, November 24, 1982; signed as free agent by Kansas City Chiefs, December 30, 1982.
Released by Kansas City Chiefs, August 1, 1983; signed as free agent by Oakland Invaders, October 12, 1983.
Released by Oakland Invaders, January 30, 1984; awarded on waivers to Oklahoma Outlaws, January 31, 1984.
Released by Oklahoma Outlaws, February 1, 1984; signed as free agent by Pittsburgh Maulers, February 4, 1984.
Released by Pittsburgh Maulers, February 13, 1984; signed as free agent by Indianapolis Colts, December 27, 1984.
San Francisco (1)-Kansas City (1) NFL, 1982.
Games: 1982 (2).

ARTHUR LEE WHITTINGTON
(Art)
Running Back—Houston Oilers
Born September 4, 1955, at Cuero, Tex.
Height, 5.11. Weight, 1985.
Hight School—Cuero, Tex.
Attended Southern Methodist University.
Selected by Oakland in 7th round (176th players selected) of 1978 NFL draft.
On injured reserve with knee injury, October 8 through November 16, 1979; activated, November 17, 1979.
Franchise transferred to Los Angeles, May 7, 1982.
Released by Los Angeles Raiders, August 4, 1982; claimed on waivers by Buffalo Bills, August 6, 1982.
On commissioner's exempt list, November 20 through November 23, 1982.
Released by Buffalo Bills, November 24, 1982.
USFL rights traded by Philadelphia Stars to Oakland Invaders for rights to wide receiver Curt Grieve and a 9th round pick in 1984 draft, February 18, 1983.
Signed by Oakland Invaders, February 18, 1983.
On developmental squad, June 24 through July 8, 1983; activated, July 9, 1983.
On developmental squad, February 24 through March 2, 1984; activated, March 3, 1984.
On developmental squad, April 6 through April 15, 1984; activated, April 16, 1984.
Not protected in merger of Oakland Invaders and Michigan Panthers, December 6, 1984; signed as free agent by Houston Oilers, May 6, 1985.
On developmental squad for 2 games with Oakland Invaders in 1983 and 1984.

Year Club		G.	Att.	RUSHING Yds.	Avg.	TD.	PASS RECEIVING P.C.	Yds.	Avg.	TD.	TOTAL TD.	Pts.	F.
1978—Oakland NFL.............		16	172	661	3.8	7	23	106	4.6	0	7	42	2
1979—Oakland NFL.............		9	109	397	3.6	2	19	240	12.6	0	2	12	3
1980—Oakland NFL.............		15	91	299	3.3	3	19	205	10.8	0	4	24	3
1981—Oakland NFL.............		16	69	220	3.2	1	23	213	9.3	2	3	18	4
1982—Buffalo NFL.............		2	7	15	2.1	0	None				0	0	2
1983—Oakland USFL...........		16	282	1043	3.7	6	66	584	8.8	2	8	48	14
1984—Oakland USFL...........		15	115	419	3.6	0	28	219	7.8	0	0	0	0
NFL Totals—5 Years...................		58	448	1592	3.6	13	84	764	9.1	2	16	96	14
USFL Totals—2 Years................		31	397	1462	3.7	6	94	803	8.5	2	8	48	14
Pro Totals—7 Years...................		89	845	3054	3.6	19	178	1567	8.8	4	24	144	28

Year Club	G.	KICKOFF RETURNS		
		No.	Yds.	Avg.TD.
1978—Oakland NFL..................	16	23	473	20.6 0
1979—Oakland NFL..................	9	5	46	9.2 0
1980—Oakland NFL..................	15	21	392	18.7 *1
1981—Oakland NFL..................	16	25	563	22.5 0
1982—Buffalo NFL....................	2	2	39	19.5 0
1983—Oakland USFL.............	16		None	
1984—Oakland USFL.............	15		None	
NFL Totals—5 Years.............	58	76	1513	19.9 1
USFL Totals—2 Years...........	31	0	0	0.0 0
Pro Totals—7 Years................	89	76	1513	19.9 1

Additional NFL statistics: Recovered one fumble, 1978 and 1979; recovered three fumbles, 1980; returned two punts for four yards, 1981.

Additional USFL statistics: Recovered two fumbles, 1983.

Played in AFC Championship Game following 1980 season.

Played in NFL Championship Game following 1980 season.

OLIVER LAVELL WILLIAMS JR.
Wide Receiver—Indianapolis Colts
Born October 17, 1960, at Chicago, Ill.
Height, 6.02. Weight, 178.
High School—Gardena, Calif., Serra.
Attended Los Angeles Harbor Junior College and University of Illinois.
Brother of David and Steven Williams, wide receivers at University of Illinois.

Selected by Chicago in 1983 USFL territorial draft.
Selected by Chicago in 12th round (313th player selected) of 1983 NFL draft.
Signed by Chicago Bears, May 12, 1983.
On injured reserve with back injury, August 16 through September 19, 1983.
Released by Chicago Bears, September 20, 1983; signed by Chicago Blitz, November 21, 1983.
Released by Chicago Blitz, February 14, 1984; re-signed by Blitz, February 17, 1984.
On developmental squad, February 24 through March 13, 1984.
Released by Chicago Blitz, March 14, 1984; signed as free agent by St. Louis Cardinals, July 17, 1984.
Released by St. Louis Cardinals, August 27, 1984; signed as free agent by Arizona Outlaws, January 6, 1985.
Released by Arizona Outlaws, February 11, 1985; signed as free agent by San Antonio Gunslingers, February 19, 1985.
Released by San Antonio Gunslingers, March 20, 1985; signed as free agent by Indianapolis Colts, March 29, 1985.
On developmental squad for 3 games with Chicago Blitz in 1984.

Year Club	PASS RECEIVING				
	G.	P.C.	Yds.	Avg.	TD.
1985—San Antonio USFL........	2	1	16	16.0	0

Additional pro statistics: Returned five punts for five yards, 1985.

STEVE WRAY
Quarterback—Indianapolis Colts
Born January 29, 1960, at Nuremburg, West Germany.
Height, 6.02. Weight, 215.
High School—Plainfield, Ind.
Attended Franklin College.

Signed as free agent by Seattle Seahawks, April 28, 1983.
On injured reserve with ankle injury, August 29 through entire 1983 season.
Released by Seattle Seahawks, August 27, 1984.
USFL rights traded with rights to kicker Marco Morales by Memphis Showboats to Denver Gold for rights to linebacker John Harper and defensive back Rod Perry, January 3, 1985.
USFL rights traded by Denver Gold to Birmingham Stallions for future considerations, January 25, 1985.
Signed by Birmingham Stallions, January 29, 1985.
Released by Birmingham Stallions, February 18, 1985; signed as free agent by Indianapolis Colts, March 28, 1985.

FELIX CARL WRIGHT
Safety—Cleveland Browns
Born June 22, 1959, at Carthage, Mo.
Height, 6.02. Weight, 190.
High School—Carthage, Mo.
Received bachelor of science degree in physical education and history
from Drake University in 1981.

Signed as free agent by Houston Oilers, May 17, 1982.
Released by Houston Oilers, August 23, 1982; signed as free agent by Hamilton Tiger-Cats, October 24, 1982.
Granted free agency, March 1, 1985; signed by Cleveland Browns, May 6, 1985.

Year Club	INTERCEPTIONS				
	G.	No.	Yds.	Avg.TD.	
1982—Hamilton CFL..............	2	2	32	16.0	0
1983—Hamilton CFL..............	12	6	140	23.3	1
1984—Hamilton CFL..............	16	7	100	14.3	1
CFL Totals—3 Years..........	30	15	272	18.1	2

Additional CFL statistics: Returned one punt for three yards, 1982; returned seven punts for 36 yards, recovered three fumbles for 10 yards and fumbled twice, 1983; recovered two fumbles, 1984.

CHARLES WILLIAM YANCY
(Billy)
Cornerback—San Diego Chargers

Born June 16, 1958, at Limestone, Me.
Height, 5.10. Weight, 175.
High School—Los Angeles, Calif., Alexander Hamilton.
Attended Saddleback Community College, California State
University at Los Angeles and Fresno State University.

Signed as free agent by Los Angeles Rams, May 6, 1981.
Released by Los Angeles Rams, August 18, 1981; signed as free agent by Calgary Stampeders, October 18, 1981.
On reserve list, October 18 through remainder of 1981 season.
Released by Calgary Stampeders, July 4, 1982; awarded on procedural waivers from Los Angeles Rams to Detroit Lions, July 15, 1982.
Released by Detroit Lions, September 6, 1982; signed by Oakland Invaders, January 11, 1983.
On developmental squad, May 14 through May 19, 1983; activated, May 20, 1983.
On developmental squad, May 29 through June 3, 1983; activated, June 4, 1983.
On developmental squad, June 13, through June 19, 1983; activated, June 20, 1983.
Traded by Oakland Invaders to Pittsburgh Maulers for draft choice, February 10, 1984.
On injured reserve with pulled hamstring, May 10 through May 15, 1984.
Traded by Pittsburgh Maulers to Oklahoma Outlaws for draft choice, May 16, 1984.
On injured reserve, May 16 through June 3, 1984; activated, June 4, 1984.
On developmental squad, June 4 through remainder of 1984 season.
Not protected in merger of Oklahoma Outlaws and Arizona Wranglers; selected by Arizona Outlaws in USFL dispersal draft, December 6, 1984.
Released by Arizona Wranglers, January 19, 1985; signed as free agent by Orlando Renegades, January 28, 1985.
Released by Orlando Renegades, January 28, 1985; signed as free agent by San Diego Chargers, April 12, 1985.
On developmental squad for 3 games with Oakland Invaders in 1983.

Year Club		G.	No.	Yds.	Avg.	TD.	No.	Yds.	Avg.	TD.	TD.	Pts.	F.
			—PUNT RETURNS—				—KICKOFF RET.—				—TOTAL—		
1983—Oakland USFL		14	12	59	4.9	0	2	30	15.0	0	0	0	1
1984—Pittsburgh USFL		12			None				None		0	0	0
Pro Totals—2 Years		26	12	59	4.9	0	2	30	15.0	0	0	0	1

Additional pro statistics: Recovered two fumbles for 15 yards, 1984.

ANDRE CURTIS YOUNG
Linebacker—Green Bay Packers

Born April 16, 1960, at Akron, O.
Height, 6.01. Weight, 210.
High School—Akron, O., Garfield.
Attended Bowling Green State University.

Selected by Denver in 24th round (280th player selected) of 1983 USFL draft.
Selected by Cincinnati in 12th round (332nd player selected) of 1983 NFL draft.
Signed by Cincinnati Bengals, June 29, 1983.
Released by Cincinnati Bengals, August 29, 1983; signed as free agent by Calgary Stampeders, October 24, 1983.
Released by Calgary Stampeders, June 18, 1984; signed as free agent by Green Bay Packers, February 15, 1985.
Calgary CFL, 1983.
Games: 1983 (1).

RENARD F. YOUNG
Cornerback—Kansas City Chiefs

Born July 31, 1961, at Los Angeles, Calif.
Height, 5.10. Weight, 178.
High School—Los Angeles, Calif., Verbum Dei.
Attended Los Angeles Southwest Community College, University of
Nevada at Las Vegas and San Diego State University.

Signed as free agent by Seattle Seahawks, June 29, 1984.
Released by Seattle Seahawks, August 27, 1984.
USFL rights traded by Memphis Showboats to Tampa Bay Bandits for rights to center Larry Rubens, November 26, 1984.
Signed as free agent by Tampa Bay Bandits, December 14, 1984.
Released by Tampa Bay Bandits, February 18, 1985; signed as free agent by Kansas City Chiefs, May 9, 1985.

RONALD CHARLES ZIOLKOWSKI
(Ron)
Linebacker—Indianapolis Colts

Born April 5, 1962, at Pittsburgh, Pa.
Height, 6.01. Weight, 230.
High School—Carnegie, Pa., Carlynton.
Attended James Madison University.

Signed as free agent by Detroit Lions, June 20, 1984.
Released by Detroit Lions, August 27, 1984; signed by Indianapolis Colts, May 6, 1985.

NFL Veterans In USFL

ROSS BROWNER
Defensive End—Houston Gamblers
Born March 22, 1954, at Warren, O.
Height, 6.03. Weight, 261.
High School—Warren, O., Western Reserve.
Received bachelor of arts degree in economics from University of Notre Dame in 1978.
Brother of Jim Browner, defensive back with Cincinnati Bengals, 1979 and 1980; Keith Browner, linebacker with Tampa Bay Buccaneers; and Joey Browner, defensive back with Minnesota Vikings.

Outland Trophy winner, 1976.
Named as defensive end on THE SPORTING NEWS College All-America Team, 1976 and 1977.
Selected by Cincinnati in 1st round (8th player selected) of 1978 NFL draft.
On suspended list for violating league drug policy, July 25 through September 25, 1983; reinstated, September 26, 1983.
Granted roster exemption, September 26, 1983; activated September 27, 1983.
Granted free agency, February 1, 1985; signed by Houston Gamblers, May 17, 1985.
Cincinnati NFL, 1978 through 1984.
Games: 1978 (11), 1979 (16), 1980 (15), 1981 (16), 1982 (9), 1983 (12), 1984 (16). Total—95.
Pro statistics: Recovered three fumbles for 21 yards, 1978; returned two kickoffs for 29 yards, 1979; recovered one fumble, 1979 through 1981 and 1984; intercepted one pass for 29 yards, 1982; credited with one extra point, 1983.
Played in AFC Championship Game following 1981 season.
Played in NFL Championship Game following 1981 season.

EDWARD AUGUSTINE LUTHER
(Ed)
Quarterback—Jacksonville Bulls
Born January 2, 1957, at Gardena, Calif.
Height, 6.03. Weight, 210.
High School—Santa Fe Springs, Calif., St. Paul.
Received bachelor of arts degree in political science
from San Jose State University in 1980.

Selected by San Diego in 4th round (101st player selected) of 1980 NFL draft.
Granted free agency, February 1, 1985.
USFL rights traded by Oakland Invaders to Jacksonville Bulls for draft pick, March 4, 1985.
Signed by Jacksonville Bulls, March 4, 1985.

				PASSING						RUSHING				TOTAL	
Year Club	G.	Att.	Cmp.	Pct.	Gain	T.P.	P.I.	Avg.	Att.	Yds.	Avg.	TD.	TD.	Pts.	F.
1980—San Diego NFL	5	3	2	66.7	26	0	1	8.67	3	5	1.7	0	0	0	0
1981—San Diego NFL	16	15	7	46.7	68	0	1	4.53	3	—8	—2.7	0	0	0	0
1982—San Diego NFL	9	4	2	50.0	55	0	1	13.75	1	—13	—13.0	0	0	0	1
1983—San Diego NFL	16	287	151	52.6	1875	7	17	6.53	9	—14	—1.6	0	0	0	6
1984—San Diego NFL	15	151	83	55.0	1163	5	3	7.70	4	11	2.8	0	0	0	2
Pro Totals—5 Years	61	460	245	53.3	3187	12	23	6.93	20	—19	—1.0	0	0	0	9

Quarterback Rating Points: 1980 (54.2), 1981 (32.0), 1982 (56.3), 1983 (56.6), 1984 (82.7). Total—63.2.
Additional pro statistics: Recovered one fumble, 1982; recovered two fumbles, 1984.
Member of San Diego Chargers for AFC Championship Game following 1980 season; did not play.
Played in AFC Championship Game following 1981 season.

LUIS ERNESTO SHARPE JR.
Offensive Tackle—Memphis Showboats
Born June 16, 1960, at Havana, Cuba.
Height, 6.04. Weight, 260.
High School—Detroit, Mich., Southwestern.
Attended University of California at Los Angeles.

Named as offensive tackle on THE SPORTING NEWS College All-America Team, 1981.
Selected by St. Louis in 1st round (16th player selected) of 1982 NFL draft.
Granted free agency, February 1, 1985.
USFL rights traded by Houston Gamblers to Memphis Showboats for draft picks, April 18, 1985.
Signed by Memphis Showboats, April 18, 1985.
St. Louis NFL, 1982 through 1984.
Games: 1982 (9), 1983 (16), 1984 (16). Total—41.
Pro statistics: Recovered one fumble, 1982 and 1984; rushed once for 11 yards and recovered two fumbles, 1983.

—DID YOU KNOW—

That the New York Jets' second-round selection in the 1984 NFL draft, tight end Glenn Dennison, attended the same high school as Jets Coach Joe Walton and former Jets quarterback Joe Namath? That high school was in Beaver Falls, Pa.

NFL Head Coaches

LEEMAN BENNETT
Tampa Bay Buccaneers
Born June 20, 1938, at Paducah, Ky.
High School—Paducah, Ky., Tilghman.
Received bachelor of science degree from University of Kentucky in 1961.

COACHING RECORD

Assistant coach at University of Kentucky, 1961, 1962 and 1965.
In Military Service, 1963 and 1964.
Assistant coach at University of Pittsburgh, 1966.
Assistant coach at University of Cincinnati, 1967 and 1968.
Assistant coach at United States Naval Academy, 1969.
Assistant coach, St. Louis Cardinals NFL, 1970 and 1971.
Assistant coach, Detroit Lions NFL, 1972.
Assistant coach, Los Angeles Rams NFL, 1973 through 1976.

Year Club	Pos.	W.	L.	T.
1977—Atlanta NFL	†Second	7	7	0
1978—Atlanta NFL	†Second	9	7	0
1979—Atlanta NFL	†Third	6	10	0
1980—Atlanta NFL	†First	12	4	0
1981—Atlanta NFL	†Second	7	9	0
1982—Atlanta NFL	‡§Fourth	5	4	0
Pro Totals—6 Years		46	41	0

†Western Division (National Conference).
‡Tied for position.
§National Conference.

PLAYOFF RECORD

Year Club	W.	L.
1978—Atlanta NFL	1	1
1980—Atlanta NFL	0	1
1982—Atlanta NFL	0	1
Pro Totals—3 Years	1	3

1978—Won conference playoff game from Philadelphia, 14-13; lost conference playoff game to Dallas, 27-20.
1980—Lost conference playoff game to Dallas, 30-27.
1982—Lost conference playoff game to Minnesota, 30-24.

RAYMOND EMMETT BERRY
New England Patriots
Born February 27, 1933, at Corpus Christi, Tex.
High School—Paris, Tex.
Attended Schreiner Institute and received bachelor of arts degree from
Southern Methodist University in 1955.

Played wide receiver.
Inducted into Pro Football Hall of Fame, 1973.
Named to THE SPORTING NEWS NFL Western Conference All-Star Team, 1957 through 1960.
Selected (as future choice) by Baltimore in 20th round of 1954 NFL draft.

Year Club	G.	P.C.	Yds.	Avg.	TD.	Year Club	G.	P.C.	Yds.	Avg.	TD.
1955—Baltimore NFL	12	13	205	15.8	0	1962—Baltimore NFL	14	51	687	13.5	3
1956—Baltimore NFL	12	37	601	16.2	2	1963—Baltimore NFL	9	44	703	16.0	3
1957—Baltimore NFL	12	47	*800	17.0	6	1964—Baltimore NFL	12	43	663	15.4	6
1958—Baltimore NFL	12	*56	794	14.2	*9	1965—Baltimore NFL	14	58	739	12.7	7
1959—Baltimore NFL	12	*66	*959	14.5	*14	1966—Baltimore NFL	14	56	786	14.0	7
1960—Baltimore NFL	12	*74	*1298	17.5	10	1967—Baltimore NFL	7	11	167	15.2	1
1961—Baltimore NFL	12	75	873	11.6	0	Pro Totals—13 Years	154	631	9275	14.7	68

Additional pro statistics: Returned two kickoffs for 27 yards, 1955; fumbled once, 1962.
Played in NFL Championship Game following 1958, 1959 and 1964 seasons.
Played in Pro Bowl (NFL All-Star Game) following 1958, 1959, 1961, 1963 and 1964 seasons.

COACHING RECORD

Assistant coach, Dallas Cowboys NFL, 1968.
Assistant coach at University of Arkansas, 1970 through 1972.
Assistant coach, Detroit Lions NFL, 1973 through 1975.
Assistant coach, Cleveland Browns NFL, 1976 and 1977.
Assistant coach, New England Patriots NFL, 1978 through 1981.
Training camp assistant coach, Minnesota Vikings NFL, 1984.

Year Club	Pos.	W.	L.	T.
1984—New England NFL†	‡Second	4	4	0

†Replaced Ron Meyer, October 25, 1984 with 5-3 record and in third place.
‡Eastern Division (American Conference).

FRANCIS MARION CAMPBELL

(Known by middle name.)
Philadelphia Eagles

Born May 25, 1929, at Chester, S. C.
High School—Chester, S. C.
Received bachelor of science degree in education from University of Georgia.

Played defensive lineman.
Name to THE SPORTING NEWS NFL East Division All-Star Team, 1960.
Selected by San Francisco in 4th round of 1952 NFL draft.
Military service, 1952 and 1953.
Traded by San Francisco 49ers to Philadelphia Eagles for 6th round draft choice, September 20, 1956.
San Francisco NFL, 1954 and 1955; Philadelphia NFL, 1956 through 1961.
Games: 1954 (12), 1955 (11), 1956 (12), 1957 (10), 1958 (11), 1959 (12), 1960 (12), 1961 (14). Total—94.
Pro statistics: Recovered two fumbles, 1954; recovered one fumble, 1955, 1958 and 1960; intercepted one pass for no yards, 1955 and 1959; intercepted one pass for one yard and fumbled once, 1956; recovered three fumbles, 1959.
Played in NFL Championship Game following 1960 season.
Played in Playoff Bowl Game following 1961 season.
Played in Pro Bowl (NFL All-Star Game) following 1960 and 1961 seasons.

COACHING RECORD

Assistant coach, Boston Patriots AFL, 1962 and 1963.
Assistant coach, Minnesota Vikings NFL, 1964 through 1966.
Assistant coach, Los Angeles Rams NFL, 1967 and 1968.
Assistant coach, Atlanta Falcons NFL, 1969 through part of 1974.
Assistant coach, Philadelphia Eagles NFL, 1977 through 1982.

Year Club	Pos.	W.	L.	T.
1974—Atlanta NFL†	‡Fourth	1	5	0
1975—Atlanta NFL	‡Third	4	10	0
1976—Atlanta NFL§	‡Fourth	1	4	0
1983—Philadelphia NFL	xFifth	5	11	0
1984—Philadelphia NFL	xFifth	6	9	1
Pro Totals—5 Years..................................		17	39	1

†Replaced Norm Van Brocklin, November 5, 1974 with 2-6 record and tied for third place.
‡Western Division (National Conference).
§Replaced by General Manager Pat Peppler, October 11, 1976.
xEastern Division (National Conference).

HUGH THOMAS CAMPBELL
Houston Oilers

Born May 21, 1941, at San Jose, Calif.
High School—Los Gatos, Calif.
Received bachelor of science degree in education from Washington
State University in 1963; received master's degree
in teaching from Washington State in 1965.

Played wide receiver.
Selected by San Francisco in 4th round of 1963 NFL draft.
Signed by Saskatchewan Roughriders, 1963.
Missed 1968 season due to injury.
Released by Saskatchewan Roughriders, 1970.

Year Club	G.	P.C.	Yds.	Avg.	TD.
1963—Saskatchewan CFL......	16	30	426	14.2	3
1964—Saskatchewan CFL......	16	65	1000	15.4	11
1965—Saskatchewan CFL......	16	73	1329	18.2	10
1966—Saskatchewan CFL......	16	66	1109	16.8	17
1967—Saskatchewan CFL......	16	42	710	16.9	8
1969—Saskatchewan CFL......	16	45	851	18.9	11
Pro Totals—6 Years............	96	321	5425	16.9	60

Additional pro statistics: Fumbled once, 1964; rushed 16 yards on lateral, recovered two fumbles and fumbled four times, 1965.
Played in CFL Championship Game (Grey Cup) following 1966, 1967 and 1969 seasons.

COACHING RECORD

Year Club	Pos.	W.	L.	T.	Year Club	Pos.	W.	L.	T.
1970—Whitworth	†‡......	2	7	0	1981—Edmonton CFL	yFirst	14	1	1
1971—Whitworth	†‡......	2	7	0	1982—Edmonton CFL	yxFirst	11	5	0
1972—Whitworth	†‡......	7	2	0	1983—Los Angeles USFL	zSecond	8	10	0
1973—Whitworth	†Third	4	5	0	1984—Houston NFL	aFourth	3	13	0
1974—Whitworth	†Fourth	6	3	0	College Totals—7 Years............		35	30	0
1975—Whitworth	§xFirst	7	3	0	CFL Totals—6 Years		70	21	5
1976—Whitworth	§Fifth	6	3	0	USFL Totals—1 Year............		8	10	0
1977—Edmonton CFL	yxFirst	10	6	0	NFL Totals—1 Year................		3	13	0
1978—Edmonton CFL	yFirst	10	4	2	Pro Totals—8 Years................		81	44	5
1979—Edmonton CFL	yFirst	12	2	2					
1980—Edmonton CFL	yFirst	13	3	0					

†Pacific Northwest Conference.
‡Ineligible for conference title.
§Northwest Conference.
xTied for position.
yWestern Conference.
zPacific Division.
aCentral Division (American Conference).

PLAYOFF RECORD

Year Club	W.	L.
1977—Edmonton CFL	1	1
1978—Edmonton CFL	2	0
1979—Edmonton CFL	2	0
1980—Edmonton CFL	2	0
1981—Edmonton CFL	2	0
1982—Edmonton CFL	2	0
Pro Totals—6 Years	11	1

1977—Won conference playoff from British Columbia, 38-1; lost CFL Championship Game (Grey Cup) to Montreal, 41-6.
1978—Won conference playoff game from Calgary, 26-13; won CFL Championship Game (Grey Cup) from Montreal, 20-13.
1979—Won conference playoff game from Calgary, 19-7; won CFL Championship Game (Grey Cup) from Montreal, 17-9.
1980—Won conference playoff game from Winnipeg, 34-24; won CFL Championship Game (Grey Cup) from Hamilton, 48-10.
1981—Won conference playoff game from British Columbia, 22-16; won CFL Championship Game (Grey Cup) from Ottawa, 26-23.
1982—Won conference playoff game from Winnipeg, 24-21; won CFL Championship Game (Grey Cup) from Toronto, 32-16.

DONALD DAVID CORYELL
(Don)
San Diego Chargers
Born October 17, 1924, at Seattle, Wash.
High School—Seattle, Wash., Lincoln.
Received bachelor of arts degree in 1950 and master of arts degree in 1951 from
University of Washington.

COACHING RECORD

Named NFL Coach of the Year by THE SPORTING NEWS, 1974.
Assistant coach at Punahou Academy, Honolulu, 1951.
Head coach at Farrington High School, Honolulu, 1952.
Assistant coach at University of Washington, 1953 and 1954.
Head coach and athletic director at Fort Ord, Calif., 1956.
Assistant coach at University of Southern California, 1960.

Year Club	Pos.	W.	L.	T.	Year Club	Pos.	W.	L.	T.
1955—Wenatchee Valley JC	†First	7	0	1	1972—San Diego State	yFirst	10	1	0
1957—Whittier	‡First	6	2	1	1973—St. Louis NFL	zFourth	4	9	1
1958—Whittier	‡First	9	1	0	1974—St. Louis NFL	zxFirst	10	4	0
1959—Whittier	‡First	8	2	0	1975—St. Louis NFL	zFirst	11	3	0
1961—San Diego State	§xThird	7	2	1	1976—St. Louis NFL	zxSecond	10	4	0
1962—San Diego State	§First	8	2	0	1977—St. Louis NFL	zThird	7	7	0
1963—San Diego State	§xFirst	7	2	0	1978—San Diego NFLa	bxSecond	8	4	0
1964—San Diego State	§Second	8	2	0	1979—San Diego NFL	bFirst	12	4	0
1965—San Diego State	§Third	8	2	0	1980—San Diego NFL	bxFirst	11	5	0
1966—San Diego State	§First	11	0	0	1981—San Diego NFL	bxFirst	10	6	0
1967—San Diego State	§First	10	1	0	1982—San Diego NFL	cxFourth	6	3	0
1968—San Diego State	......	9	0	1	1983—San Diego NFL	bxFourth	6	10	0
1969—San Diego State	yFirst	11	0	0	1984—San Diego NFL	bFifth	7	9	0
1970—San Diego State	yxFirst	9	2	0	College Totals—16 Years		134	24	4
1971—San Diego State	yxFourth	6	5	0	Pro Totals—12 Years		102	68	1

†Washington State Junior College Conference
‡Southern California Intercollegiate Athletic Conference.
§California Collegiate Athletic Association.
xTied for postion.
yPacific Coast Athletic Association.
zEastern Division (National Conference.).
aReplaced Tommy Prothro, September 25, 1978 with 1-3 record and tied for fourth place; St. Louis received third-round pick in 1980 draft from San Diego as compensation.
bWestern Division (American Conference.).
cAmerican Conference.

PLAYOFF RECORD

Year Club	W.	L.
1974—St. Louis NFL	0	1
1975—St. Louis NFL	0	1
1979—San Diego NFL	0	1
1980—San Diego NFL	1	1
1981—San Diego NFL	1	1
1982—San Diego NFL	1	1
Pro Totals—6 Years	3	6

1974—Lost conference playoff game to Minnesota, 30-14.
1975—Lost conference playoff game to Los Angeles, 35-23.
1979—Lost conference playoff game to Houston, 17-14.
1980—Won conference playoff game from Buffalo, 20-14; lost conference championship game to Oakland, 34-27.
1981—Won conference playoff game in overtime from Miami, 41-38; lost conference championship game to Cincinnati, 27-7.
1982—Won conference playoff game from Pittsburgh, 31-28; lost conference playoff game to Miami, 34-13.

COLLEGIATE BOWL GAME RECORD

Year Club	W.	L.
1966—San Diego State	1	0
1967—San Diego State	1	0
1969—San Diego State	1	0
Totals—3 Years	3	0

1966—Won Camellia Bowl from Montana State, 28-7.
1967—Won Camellia Bowl from San Francisco State, 27-6.
1969—Won Pasadena Bowl from Boston University, 28-7.

MICHAEL KELLER DITKA
(Mike)
Chicago Bears

Born October 18, 1939, at Carnegie, Pa.
High School—Aliquippa, Pa.
Attended University of Pittsburgh.

Played tight end.
Named as end on THE SPORTING NEWS College All-America Team, 1960.
Named NFL Rookie of the Year by THE SPORTING NEWS, 1961.
Named to THE SPORTING NEWS NFL Western Conference All-Star Team, 1961 through 1965.
Selected by Chicago in 1st round of 1961 NFL draft.
Traded by Chicago Bears to Philadelphia Eagles for quarterback Jack Concannon and a 1968 draft choice, April 26, 1967.
Traded by Philadelphia Eagles to Dallas Cowboys for receiver Dave McDaniels, January 18, 1969.

Year Club	—PASS RECEIVING— G.	P.C.	Yds.	Avg.	TD.	Year Club	—PASS RECEIVING— G.	P.C.	Yds.	Avg.	TD.
1961—Chicago NFL	14	56	1076	19.2	12	1968—Philadelphia NFL	11	13	111	8.5	2
1962—Chicago NFL	14	58	904	15.6	5	1969—Dallas NFL	12	17	268	15.8	3
1963—Chicago NFL	14	59	794	13.5	8	1970—Dallas NFL	14	8	98	12.3	0
1964—Chicago NFL	14	75	897	12.0	5	1971—Dallas NFL	14	30	360	12.0	1
1965—Chicago NFL	14	36	454	12.6	2	1972—Dallas NFL	14	17	198	11.6	1
1966—Chicago NFL	14	32	378	11.8	2	Pro Totals—12 Years	158	427	5812	13.6	43
1967—Philadelphia NFL	9	26	274	10.5	2						

Additional pro statistics: Recovered one fumble for a touchdown, 1962 and 1964; fumbled once, 1969; rushed twice for two yards, returned three kickoffs for 30 yards and recovered one fumble, 1971.
Played in NFC Championship Game following 1970 through 1972 seasons.
Played in NFL Championship Game following 1963, 1970 and 1971 seasons.
Played in Pro Bowl (NFL All-Star Game) following 1961 through 1965 seasons.

COACHING RECORD

Assistant coach, Dallas Cowboys NFL, 1973 through 1981.

Year Club	Pos.	W.	L.	T.
1982—Chicago NFL	††Eleventh	3	6	0
1983—Chicago NFL	‡§Second	8	8	0
1984—Chicago NFL	§First	10	6	0
Pro Totals—3 Years		21	20	0

†National Conference.
‡Tied for position.
§Central Division (National Conference).

PLAYOFF RECORD

Year Club	W.	L.
1984—Chicago NFL	1	1

1984—Won conference playoff game from Washington, 23-19; lost conference championship game to San Francisco, 23-0.

RODNEY DOUGLAS DOWHOWER
(Rod)
Indianapolis Colts

Born April 15, 1943, at Ord, Neb.
High School—Santa Barbara, Calif.
Attended Santa Barbara City Junior College, received bachelor of arts degree in
social science from San Diego State University and master's degree in
history from U.S. International University, both in 1971.

Signed as free agent by San Francisco 49ers, 1965.
On taxi squad during entire 1965 season.
Released by San Francisco 49ers, August, 1966.

Graduate assistant at San Diego State University, 1966 and 1967.
Assistant coach at San Diego State University, 1968 through 1972.
Assistant coach, St. Louis Cardinals NFL, 1973, 1983 and 1984.
Assistant coach at University of California at Los Angeles, 1974 and 1975.
Assistant coach at Boise State University, 1976.
Assistant coach at Stanford University, 1977 and 1978.
Assistant coach, Denver Broncos NFL, 1980 through 1982.

Year	Club	Pos.	W.	L.	T.
1979—Stanford		†Sixth	5	5	1

†Pacific 10.

THOMAS RAYMOND FLORES
(Tom)
Los Angeles Raiders

Born March 21, 1937, at Fresno, Calif.
High School—Sanger, Calif.
Attended Fresno City College and received bachelor of arts degree in education
from University of the Pacific in 1958.

Played quarterback.
Threw six touchdown passes in a game, December 22, 1963.
Drafted by Calgary Stampeders, 1958.
Released by Calgary Stampeders, 1958; signed as free agent by Washington Redskins, 1959.
Released by Washington Redskins, 1959; signed as free agent by Oakland Raiders, 1959.
Traded with offensive end Art Powell and 2nd round draft choice by Oakland AFL to Buffalo AFL for quarterback
Daryle Lamonica, offensive end Glenn Bass and 3rd and 5th round draft choices, 1967.
Released by Buffalo, signed by Kansas City, 1969.
On Kansas City Chiefs' taxi squad entire 1970 season.

Year Club	G.	Att.	Cmp.	Pct.	Gain	T.P.	P.I.	Avg.	Att.	Yds.	Avg.	TD.	TD.	Pts.	F.
				PASSING						RUSHING			TOTAL		
1960—Oakland AFL	14	252	136	*54.0	1738	12	12	6.90	19	123	6.5	3	3	18	..
1961—Oakland AFL	14	366	190	51.9	2176	15	19	5.95	23	36	1.6	1	1	6	..
1962—Oakland AFL					Missed entire season because of illness.										
1963—Oakland AFL	14	247	113	45.7	2101	20	13	8.51	12	2	0.2	0	0	0	..
1964—Oakland AFL	14	200	98	49.0	1389	7	14	6.95	11	64	5.8	0	0	0	3
1965—Oakland AFL	14	269	122	45.3	1593	14	11	5.92	11	32	2.9	0	0	0	0
1966—Oakland AFL	14	306	151	49.4	2638	24	14	8.62	5	50	10.0	1	1	6	2
1967—Buffalo AFL	13	64	22	34.4	260	0	8	4.06	None				0	0	0
1968—Buffalo AFL	1	5	3	60.0	15	0	1	3.00	None				0	0	0
1969—Buf.-K. C. AFL	13	6	3	50.0	49	0	0	8.17	1	0	0.0	0	0	0	0
Pro Totals—10 Years	111	1715	838	48.9	11959	92	92	6.97	82	307	3.7	5	5	30	....

Played in AFL All-Star Game following 1966 season.

Freshman coach at University of the Pacific, 1959.
Assistant coach, Buffalo Bills NFL, 1971.
Assistant coach, Oakland Raiders NFL, 1972 through 1978.

Year Club	Pos.	W.	L.	T.	Year Club	Pos.	W.	L.	T.
1979—Oakland NFL	†‡Third	9	7	0	1983—L.A. Raiders NFL	†First	12	4	0
1980—Oakland NFL	†‡First	11	5	0	1984—L.A. Raiders NFL	†Third	11	5	0
1981—Oakland NFL	†Fourth	7	9	0	Pro Totals—6 Years		58	31	0
1982—L.A. Raiders NFL	§First	8	1	0					

†Western Division (American Conference).
‡Tied for position.
§American Conference.

Year Club	W.	L.
1980—Oakland NFL	4	0
1982—Los Angeles Raiders NFL	1	1
1983—Los Angeles Raiders NFL	3	0
1984—Los Angeles Raiders NFL	0	1
Pro Totals—4 Years	8	2

1980—Won conference playoff game from Houston, 27-7; won conference playoff game from Cleveland, 14-12; won
conference championship game from San Diego, 34-27; won NFL championship game (Super Bowl XV) from
Philadelphia, 27-10.
1982—Won conference playoff game from Cleveland, 27-10; lost conference playoff game to New York Jets, 17-14.
1983—Won conference playoff game from Pittsburgh, 38-10; won conference championship game from Seattle, 30-14;
won NFL championship game (Super Bowl XVIII) from Washington, 38-9.
1984—Lost wild-card playoff game to Seattle, 13-7.

JOE JACKSON GIBBS
Washington Redskins

Born November 25, 1940, at Mocksville, N. C.
High School—Sante Fe, Calif., Spring.
Attended Cerritos Junior College, received bachelor of science degree in physical education from
San Diego State University in 1964 and received master's degree from San Diego State in 1966.

Named NFL Coach of the Year by THE SPORTING NEWS, 1982 and 1983.
Graduate assistant at San Diego State University, 1964 and 1965.
Assistant coach at San Diego State University, 1966.
Assistant coach at Florida State University, 1967 and 1968.
Assistant coach at University of Southern California, 1969 and 1970.
Assistant coach at University of Arkansas, 1971 and 1972.
Assistant coach, St. Louis Cardinals NFL, 1973 through 1977.
Assistant coach, Tampa Bay Buccaneers NFL, 1978.
Assistant coach, San Diego Chargers NFL, 1979 and 1980.

Year Club	Pos.	W.	L.	T.
1981— Washington NFL	†Fourth	8	8	0
1982— Washington NFL	‡First	8	1	0
1983— Washington NFL	†First	14	2	0
1984— Washington NFL	†First	11	5	0
Pro Totals—4 Years..................		41	16	0

†Eastern Division (National Conference).
‡National Conference.

PLAYOFF RECORD

Year Club	W.	L.
1982—Washington NFL..	4	0
1983—Washington NFL..	2	1
1984—Washington NFL..	0	1
Pro Totals—3 Years................................	6	2

1982—Won conference playoff game from Detroit, 31-7; won conference playoff game from Minnesota, 21-7; won conference championship game from Dallas, 31-17; won NFL championship game (Super Bowl XVII) from Miami, 27-17.
1983—Won conference playoff game from Los Angeles Rams, 51-7; won conference championship game from San Francisco, 24-21; lost NFL championship game (Super Bowl XVIII) to Los Angeles Raiders, 38-9.
1984—Lost conference playoff game to Chicago, 23-19.

HAROLD PETER GRANT
(Bud)
Minnesota Vikings

Born May 20, 1927, at Superior, Wis.
High School—Superior, Wis., Central.
Attended University of Minnesota.

Played offensive end.
Selected by Philadelphia in 1st round of 1950 NFL draft.

Year Club	G.	P.C.	PASS RECEIVING Yds.	Avg.	TD.
1951—Philadelphia NFL........	12		None		
1952—Philadelphia NFL........	12	56	997	17.8	7
1953—Winnipeg CFL..............	16	★68	922	13.5	5
1954—Winnipeg CFL..............	16	★49	752	15.3	5
1955—Winnipeg CFL..............	16	36	556	15.4	2
1956—Winnipeg CFL..............	16	★63	★970	15.3	1
NFL Totals—2 Years..........	24	56	997	17.8	7
CFL Totals—4 Years	64	216	3200	14.8	13
Pro Totals—6 Years............	88	272	4197	15.4	20

Additional NFL statistics: Returned one punt for nine yards, 1951; fumbled four times, 1952.
Additional CFL statistics: Intercepted four passes, rushed once for nine yards and returned two punts for four yards, 1953; intercepted one pass for five yards and fumbled three times, 1954; fumbled once, 1955 and 1956; intercepted two passes for six yards, returned one punt for five yards and returned one kickoff for 29 yards, 1956.

COACHING RECORD

Named NFL Coach of the Year by THE SPORTING NEWS, 1969.

Year Club	Pos.	W.	L.	T.	Year Club	Pos.	W.	L.	T.
1957— Winnipeg CFL	†Second	12	4	0	1975— Minnesota NFL	§First	12	2	0
1958— Winnipeg CFL	†First	13	3	0	1976— Minnesota NFL	§First	11	2	1
1959— Winnipeg CFL	†First	12	4	0	1977— Minnesota NFL	§xFirst	9	5	0
1960— Winnipeg CFL	†First	14	2	0	1978— Minnesota NFL	§xFirst	8	7	1
1961— Winnipeg CFL	†First	13	3	0	1979— Minnesota NFL	§Third	7	9	0
1962— Winnipeg CFL	†First	11	5	0	1980— Minnesota NFL	§xFirst	9	7	0
1963— Winnipeg CFL	†Fourth	7	9	0	1981— Minnesota NFL	§Fourth	7	9	0
1964— Winnipeg CFL	†Fifth	1	14	1	1982— Minnesota NFL	yxFourth	5	4	0
1965— Winnipeg CFL	†Second	11	5	0	1983— Minnesota NFL	§xSecond	8	8	0
1966— Winnipeg CFL	†Second	8	7	1	CFL Totals—10 Years		102	56	2
1967— Minnesota NFL	‡Fourth	3	8	3	NFL Totals—17 Years..............................		151	87	5
1968— Minnesota NFL	‡First	8	6	0	Pro Totals—27 Years................................		253	143	7
1969— Minnesota NFL	‡First	12	2	0					
1970— Minnesota NFL	§First	12	2	0					
1971— Minnesota NFL	§First	11	3	0					
1972— Minnesota NFL	§Third	7	7	0					
1973— Minnesota NFL	§First	12	2	0					
1974— Minnesota NFL	§First	10	4	0					

PLAYOFF RECORD

Year Club	W.	L.	Year Club	W.	L.
1957—Winnipeg CFL	3	2	1973—Minnesota NFL	2	1
1958—Winnipeg CFL	3	1	1974—Minnesota NFL	2	1
1959—Winnipeg CFL	3	0	1975—Minnesota NFL	0	1
1960—Winnipeg CFL	1	2	1976—Minnesota NFL	2	1
1961—Winnipeg CFL	3	0	1977—Minnesota NFL	1	1
1962—Winnipeg CFL	3	1	1978—Minnesota NFL	0	1
1965—Winnipeg CFL	3	2	1980—Minnesota NFL	0	1
1966—Winnipeg CFL	1	2	1982—Minnesota NFL	1	1
1968—Minnesota NFL	0	2			
1969—Minnesota NFL	2	1	NFL Totals—12 Years	10	13
1970—Minnesota NFL	0	1	CFL Totals—8 Years	20	10
1971—Minnesota NFL	0	1	Pro Totals—20 Years	30	23

1957—Won conference playoff game from Calgary, 15-3 (after 13-13 tie); won conference championship series from Edmonton, two games to one (19-7, 4-5, 17-2); lost CFL championship game to Hamilton, 32-7.

1958—Won conference championship series from Edmonton, two games to one (30-7, 7-30, 23-7); won CFL championship game from Hamilton, 35-28.

1959—Won conference championship series from Edmonton, two games to none (19-11, 16-8); won CFL championship game from Hamilton, 21-7.

1960—Lost conference championship series to Edmonton, two games to one (22-16, 5-10, 2-4).

1961—Won conference championship series from Calgary, two games to none (14-1, 43-14); won CFL championship game from Hamilton, 21-14.

1962—Won conference championship series from Calgary, two games to one (14-20, 19-11, 12-7); won CFL championship game from Hamilton, 28-27.

1965—Won conference playoff game from Saskatchewan, 15-9; won conference championship series from Calgary, two games to one (9-27, 15-11, 19-2); lost CFL championship game to Hamilton, 22-16.

1966—Won conference playoff game from Edmonton, 16-8; lost conference championship series to Saskatchewan, two games to none (7-14, 19-21).

1968—Lost conference playoff game to Baltimore, 24-14; lost Playoff Bowl to Dallas, 17-13.

1969—Won conference playoff game from Los Angeles, 23-20; won NFL championship game from Cleveland, 27-7; lost AFL-NFL playoff game (Super Bowl IV) to Kansas City, 23-7.

1970—Lost conference playoff game to San Francisco, 17-14.

1971—Lost conference playoff game to Dallas, 20-12.

1973—Won conference playoff game from Washington, 27-20; won conference championship game from Dallas, 27-10; lost NFL championship game (Super Bowl VIII) to Miami, 24-7.

1974—Won conference playoff game from St. Louis, 30-14; won NFL championship game from Los Angeles, 14-10; lost NFL championship game (Super Bowl IX) to Pittsburgh, 16-6.

1975—Lost conference playoff game to Dallas, 17-14.

1976—Won conference playoff game from Washington, 35-20; won conference championship game from Los Angeles, 24-13; lost NFL championship game (Super Bowl XI) to Oakland, 32-14.

1977—Won conference playoff game from Los Angeles, 14-7; lost conference championship game to Dallas, 23-6.

1978—Lost conference playoff game to Los Angeles, 34-10.

1980—Lost conference playoff game to Philadelphia, 31-16.

1982—Won conference playoff game from Atlanta, 30-24; lost conference playoff game to Washington, 21-7.

NBA RECORD

Sea.—Team	G.	Min.	FGA	FGM	Pct.	FTA	FTM	Pct.	Reb.	Ast.	PF	Disq.	Pts.	Avg.
1949-50—Minneapolis	35	....	115	42	.365	17	1	.412	....	19	36	....	91	2.6
1950-51—Minneapolis	61	....	184	53	.288	83	52	.627	115	71	106	0	159	2.6
Totals	96	....	299	95	.318	100	53	.530	....	90	142	....	250	2.6

Member of NBA championship team, 1949-50.

ALVIS FORREST GREGG

(Known by middle name.)

Green Bay Packers

Born October 18, 1933, at Birthright, Tex.
High School—Sulphur Springs, Tex.
Received bachelor of science degree in physical education from
Southern Methodist University in 1959.

Played offensive tackle.
Inducted into Pro Football Hall of Fame, 1977.
Named to THE SPORTING NEWS NFL Western Conference All-Star Teams, 1959, 1962, 1963, 1965 and 1967.
Selected by Green Bay in 2nd round of 1956 NFL draft.
Military service, 1957.
Released by Green Bay Packers and signed as free agent by Dallas Cowboys, 1971.
Green Bay NFL, 1956 and 1958 through 1970; Dallas NFL, 1971.
Games: 1956 (11), 1958 (12), 1959 (12), 1960 (12), 1961 (14), 1962 (14), 1963 (14), 1964 (14), 1965 (14), 1966 (14), 1967 (14), 1968 (14), 1969 (14), 1970 (14), 1971 (6). Total—193.
Pro statistics: Recovered one fumble, 1958, 1965 and 1967; recovered two fumbles, 1963 and 1968; returned two kickoffs for 21 yards, 1970.
Played in NFL Championship Game following 1960 through 1962 and 1965 through 1967 seasons.
Played in AFL-NFL Championship Games following 1966 and 1967 seasons.
Played in Pro Bowl (NFL All-Star Game) following 1960 through 1964 and 1966 through 1968 seasons.

COACHING RECORD

Assistant coach, Green Bay Packers NFL, 1969 and 1970.
Assistant coach, San Diego Chargers NFL, 1972 and 1973.
Assistant coach, Cleveland Browns NFL, 1974.

Year	Club	Pos.	W.	L.	T.
1975—Cleveland NFL	†Fourth	3	11	0	
1976—Cleveland NFL	†Third	9	5	0	
1977—Cleveland NFL‡	†Fourth	6	7	0	
1979—Toronto CFL	§Fourth	5	11	0	
1980—Cincinnati NFL	†Fourth	6	10	0	
1981—Cincinnati NFL	First	12	4	0	

Year	Club	Pos.	W.	L.	T.
1982—Cincinnati NFL	xySecond	7	2	0
1983—Cincinnati NFL	†Third	7	9	0
1984—Green Bay NFL	zSecond	8	8	0
NFL Totals—8 Years		58	56	0
CFL Totals—1 Year		5	11	0
Pro Totals—9 Years		63	67	0

†Central Division (American Conference).
‡Replaced by interim coach Dick Modzelewski, December 12, 1977.
§Eastern Conference.
xAmerican Conference.
yTied for position.
zCentral Division (National Conference).

PLAYOFF RECORD

Year	Club	W.	L.
1981—Cincinnati NFL	2	1
1982—Cincinnati NFL	0	1
Pro Totals—2 Years	2	2

1981—Won conference playoff game from Buffalo, 28-21; won conference championship game from San Diego, 27-7; lost NFL championship game (Super Bowl XVI) to San Francisco, 26-21.
1982—Lost conference playoff game to New York Jets, 44-17.

JAMES MARTIN MICHAEL HANIFAN
(Jim)
St. Louis Cardinals

Born September 21, 1933, at Compton, Calif.
High School—Covina, Calif.
Received bachelor of arts degree in history and political science
from University of California in 1955.

Played offensive end.
Played while in service at Fort Ord, Calif., 1956.
In military service in Germany, 1957 and 1958.

Year	Club	—PASS RECEIVING—				
		G.	P.C.	Yds.	Avg.	TD.
1955—Toronto CFL	10	25	325	13.0	0

COACHING RECORD

Assistant coach at Yuba Junior College, 1959 through 1961.
Head coach at Charter Oak High School (Covina, Calif.), 1962 and 1963 (Won 12, Lost 6).
Assistant coach at Glendale City College, 1964 and 1965.
Assistant coach at University of Utah, 1966 through 1969.
Assistant coach at University of California, 1970 and 1971.
Assistant coach at San Diego State University, 1972.
Assistant coach, St. Louis Cardinals NFL, 1973 through 1978.
Assistant coach, San Diego Chargers NFL, 1979.

Year	Club	Pos.	W.	L.	T.
1980—St. Louis NFL	†Fourth	5	11	0
1981—St. Louis NFL	†Fifth	7	9	0
1982—St. Louis NFL	‡§Fourth	5	4	0
1983—St. Louis NFL	†Third	8	7	1
1984—St. Louis NFL	†§Second	9	7	0
Pro Totals—5 Years		34	38	1

†Eastern Division (National Conference).
‡National Conference.
§Tied for position.

PLAYOFF RECORD

Year	Club	W.	L.
1982—St. Louis NFL	0	1

1982—Lost conference playoff game to Green Bay, 41-16.

DANIEL E. HENNING
(Dan)
Atlanta Falcons

Born June 21, 1942, at Bronx, N.Y.
High School—Fresh Meadows, N.Y., St. Francis Prep.
Attended College of William & Mary.
Father of Dan Henning, Jr., quarterback at University of Maryland.

Played quarterback.
Signed as free agent by San Diego Chargers, February 19, 1964.
Released by San Diego Chargers, September 1, 1964; re-signed by Chargers, December 2, 1964.
Released by San Diego Chargers, August 2, 1965; re-signed by Chargers, July 2, 1966.
Released by San Diego Chargers, August 25, 1966; re-signed and placed on taxi squad for 1966 season.
Released by San Diego Chargers, August 29, 1967.
Active for 1 game with San Diego Chargers in 1966; did not play.
Played with Springfield, Mass., of Atlantic Coast Football League, 1964.
Played with Norfolk Neptunes of Continental Football League, 1965 and 1967.

COACHING RECORD

Assistant coach at Homer L. Ferguson High School, Newport News, Va., 1967.
Assistant coach at Florida State University, 1968 through 1970 and 1974.
Assistant coach at Virginia Tech, 1971 and 1973.
Assistant coach, Houston Oilers NFL, 1972.
Assistant coach, New York Jets NFL, 1976 through 1978.
Assistant coach, Miami Dolphins NFL, 1979 and 1980.
Assistant coach, Washington Redskins NFL, 1981 and 1982.

Year Club	Pos.	W.	L.	T.
1983— Atlanta NFL	†Fourth	7	9	0
1984— Atlanta NFL	†Fourth	4	12	0
Pro Totals—2 Years		11	21	0

†Western Division (National Conference).

CHARLES ROBERT KNOX SR.
(Chuck)
Seattle Seahawks

Born April 27, 1932, at Sewickley, Pa.
High School—Sewickley, Pa.
Received bachelor of arts degree in history from Juniata College in 1954.
Father of Chuck Knox Jr., running back at University of Arizona.

COACHING RECORD

Named NFL Coach of the Year by THE SPORTING NEWS, 1973 and 1980.
Assistant coach at Juniata College, 1954.
Assistant coach at Tyrone (Pa.) High School, 1955.
Head coach at Ellwood City (Pa.) High School, 1956 through 1958 (Won 10, Lost 16, Tied 2).
Assistant coach at Wake Forest University, 1959 and 1960.
Assistant coach at University of Kentucky, 1961 and 1962.
Assistant coach, New York Jets AFL, 1963 through 1966.
Assistant coach, Detroit Lions NFL, 1967 through 1972.

Year Club	Pos.	W.	L.	T.	Year Club	Pos.	W.	L.	T.
1973— Los Angeles NFL	†First	12	2	0	1980— Buffalo NFL	‡First	11	5	0
1974— Los Angeles NFL	†First	10	4	0	1981— Buffalo NFL	‡Third	10	6	0
1975— Los Angeles NFL	†First	12	2	0	1982— Buffalo NFL	x§Eighth	4	5	0
1976— Los Angeles NFL	†First	10	3	1	1983— Seattle NFL	ySecond	9	7	0
1977— Los Angeles NFL	†First	10	4	0	1984— Seattle NFL	ySecond	12	4	0
1978— Buffalo NFL	‡§Fourth	5	11	0	Pro Totals—12 Years		112	62	1
1979— Buffalo NFL	‡Fourth	7	9	0					

†Western Division (National Conference).
‡Eastern Division (American Conference).
§Tied for position.
xAmerican Conference.
yWestern Division (American Conference).

PLAYOFF RECORD

Year Club	W.	L.
1973—Los Angeles NFL	0	1
1974—Los Angeles NFL	1	1
1975—Los Angeles NFL	1	1
1976—Los Angeles NFL	1	1
1977—Los Angeles NFL	0	1
1980—Buffalo NFL	0	1
1981—Buffalo NFL	1	1
1983—Seattle NFL	2	1
1984—Seattle NFL	1	1
Pro Totals—9 Years	7	9

1973—Lost conference playoff game to Dallas, 27-16.
1974—Won conference playoff game from Washington, 19-10; lost conference championship game to Minnesota, 14-10.
1975—Won conference playoff game from St. Louis, 35-23; lost conference championship game to Dallas, 37-7.
1976—Won conference playoff game from Dallas, 14-12; lost conference championship game to Minnesota, 24-13.
1977—Lost conference playoff game to Minnesota, 14-7.
1980—Lost conference playoff game to San Diego, 20-14.
1981—Won conference playoff game from New York Jets, 31-27; lost conference playoff game to Cincinnati, 28-21.
1983—Won wild-card playoff game from Denver, 31-7; won conference playoff game from Miami, 27-20; lost conference championship game to Los Angeles Raiders, 30-14.
1984—Won wild-card playoff game from Los Angeles Raiders, 13-7; lost conference playoff game to Miami, 31-10.

THOMAS WADE LANDRY
(Tom)
Dallas Cowboys

Born September 11, 1924, at Mission, Tex.
High School—Mission, Tex.
Received bachelor of business administration degree from University of Texas in 1949
and bachelor of science degree in industrial engineering from University of Houston.

Played defensive back.
Selected in 4th round from New York AAFC by New York Giants NFL in AAFC-NFL merger, 1950.

Year Club	G.	—INTERCEPTIONS—				—PUNTING—			—TOTAL—		
		No.	Yds.	Avg.	TD.	No.	Avg.	Blk.	TD.	Pts.	F.
1949—New York AAFC	13	1	44	44.0	0	51	44.1	★2	0	0	..
1950—New York Giants NFL	12	2	0	0.0	0	58	36.8	1	1	6	0
1951—New York Giants NFL	10	8	121	15.1	★2	15	42.5	0	3	18	0
1952—New York NFL	12	8	99	12.4	1	82	41.0	1	2	12	5
1953—New York NFL	12	3	55	18.3	0	44	40.3	0	0	0	1
1954—New York NFL	12	8	71	8.9	0	64	42.5	0	0	0	1
1955—New York NFL	12	2	14	7.0	0	★75	40.3	1	0	0	0
AAFC Totals—1 Year	13	1	44	44.0	0	51	44.1	2	0	0	..
NFL Totals—6 Years	70	31	360	11.6	3	338	40.4	3	6	36	7
Pro Totals—7 Years	83	32	404	12.6	3	389	40.9	5	6	36	..

Year Club	G.	—PUNT RETURNS—				—KICKOFF RET.—			
		No.	Yds.	Avg.	TD.	No.	Yds.	Avg.	TD.
1949—New York AAFC	13	3	52	17.3	0	2	39	19.5	0
1950—New York Giants NFL	12		None				None		
1951—New York Giants NFL	10	1	0	0.0	0	1	0	0.0	0
1952—New York NFL	12	10	88	8.8	0	1	20	20.0	0
1953—New York NFL	12	1	5	5.0	0	2	38	19.0	0
1954—New York NFL	12		None				None		
1955—New York NFL	12		None				None		
AAFC Totals—1 Year	13	3	52	17.3	0	2	39	19.5	0
NFL Totals—6 Years	70	12	93	7.8	0	4	58	14.5	0
Pro Totals—7 Years	83	15	145	9.7	0	6	97	16.2	0

Additional AAFC statistics: Rushed 29 times for 91 yards and caught six passes for 109 yards, 1949.
Additional NFL statistics: Rushed seven times for 40 yards and a touchdown, 1952; attempted 47 passes with 11 completions for 172 yards, one touchdown and seven interceptions, 1952; recovered two fumbles for 41 yards and one touchdown, 1950; recovered one fumble for nine yards and a touchdown, 1951; recovered two fumbles, 1952; recovered one fumble, 1953 and 1955; recovered two fumbles for 14 yards, 1954.
Played in Pro Bowl (NFL All-Star Game) following 1954 season.

COACHING RECORD

Named NFL Coach of the Year by THE SPORTING NEWS, 1966.
Player-coach for New York Giants NFL, 1954 and 1955.
Assistant coach for New York Giants NFL, 1956 through 1959.

Year Club	Pos.	W.	L.	T.	Year Club	Pos.	W.	L.	T.
1960—Dallas NFL	†Seventh	0	11	1	1974—Dallas NFL	yThird	8	6	0
1961—Dallas NFL	‡Sixth	4	9	1	1975—Dallas NFL	ySecond	10	4	0
1962—Dallas NFL	‡Fifth	5	8	1	1976—Dallas NFL	yFirst	11	3	0
1963—Dallas NFL	‡Fifth	4	10	0	1977—Dallas NFL	yFirst	12	2	0
1964—Dallas NFL	‡Fifth	5	8	1	1978—Dallas NFL	yFirst	12	4	0
1965—Dallas NFL	§‡Second	7	7	0	1979—Dallas NFL	y§First	11	5	0
1966—Dallas NFL	‡First	10	3	1	1980—Dallas NFL	y§First	12	4	0
1967—Dallas NFL	xFirst	9	5	0	1981—Dallas NFL	yFirst	12	4	0
1968—Dallas NFL	xFirst	12	2	0	1982—Dallas NFL	zSecond	6	3	0
1969—Dallas NFL	xFirst	11	2	1	1983—Dallas NFL	ySecond	12	4	0
1970—Dallas NFL	yFirst	10	4	0	1984—Dallas NFL	y§Second	9	7	0
1971—Dallas NFL	yFirst	11	3	0	Pro Totals—25 Years		223	126	6
1972—Dallas NFL	ySecond	10	4	0					
1973—Dallas NFL	§yFirst	10	4	0					

†Western Conference.
‡Eastern Conference.
§Tied for position.
xCapitol Division (Eastern Conference).
yEastern Division (National Conference).
zNational Conference.

PLAYOFF RECORD

Year Club	W.	L.	Year Club	W.	L.
1965—Dallas NFL	0	1	1976—Dallas NFL	0	1
1966—Dallas NFL	0	1	1977—Dallas NFL	3	0
1967—Dallas NFL	1	1	1978—Dallas NFL	2	1
1968—Dallas NFL	1	1	1979—Dallas NFL	0	1
1969—Dallas NFL	0	2	1980—Dallas NFL	2	1
1970—Dallas NFL	2	1	1981—Dallas NFL	1	1
1971—Dallas NFL	3	0	1982—Dallas NFL	2	1
1972—Dallas NFL	1	1	1983—Dallas NFL	0	1
1973—Dallas NFL	1	1	Pro Totals—18 Years	21	17
1975—Dallas NFL	2	1			

1965—Lost Playoff Bowl to Baltimore, 35-3.
1966—Lost NFL championship game to Green Bay, 34-27.
1967—Won conference playoff game from Cleveland, 52-14; lost NFL championship game to Green Bay, 21-17.
1968—Lost conference playoff game to Cleveland, 31-20; won Playoff Bowl from Minnesota, 17-13.
1969—Lost conference playoff game to Cleveland, 38-14; lost Playoff Bowl to Los Angeles, 31-0.
1970—Won conference playoff game from Detroit, 5-0; won conference championship game from San Francisco, 17-10; lost NFL championship game (Super Bowl V) to Baltimore, 16-13.
1971—Won conference playoff game from Minnesota, 20-12; won conference championship game from San Francisco, 14-3; won NFL championship game (Super Bowl VI) from Miami, 24-3.
1972—Won conference playoff game from San Francisco, 30-28; lost conference championship game to Washington, 26-3.
1973—Won conference playoff game from Los Angeles, 27-16; lost conference championship game to Minnesota, 27-10.
1975—Won conference playoff game from Minnesota, 17-14; won conference championship game from Los Angeles, 37-7; lost NFL championship game (Super Bowl X) to Pittsburgh, 21-17.
1976—Lost conference playoff game to Los Angeles, 14-12.
1977—Won conference playoff game from Chicago, 37-7; won conference championship game from Minnesota, 23-6; won NFL championship game (Super Bowl XII) from Denver, 27-10.
1978—Won conference playoff game from Atlanta, 27-20; won conference championship game from Los Angeles, 28-0; lost NFL championship game (Super Bowl XIII) to Pittsburgh, 35-31.
1979—Lost conference playoff game to Los Angeles, 21-19.
1980—Won conference playoff game from Los Angeles, 34-13; won conference playoff game from Atlanta, 30-27; lost conference championship game to Philadelphia, 20-7.
1981—Won conference playoff game from Tampa Bay, 38-0; lost conference championship game to San Francisco, 28-27.
1982—Won conference playoff game from Tampa Bay, 30-17; won conference playoff game from Green Bay, 37-26; lost conference championship game to Washington, 31-17.
1983—Lost wild-card playoff game to Los Angeles Rams, 24-17.

JOHN MACKOVIC
Kansas City Chiefs
Born October 1, 1943, at Barberton, O.
High School—Barberton, O.
Received bachelor of arts degree in Spanish from Wake Forest University in 1964.

COACHING RECORD
Graduate assistant at Miami University (Ohio), 1965.
Assistant coach at Barberton High School, Barberton, O., 1966.
Freshman coach at Army, 1967 and 1968.
Assistant coach at San Jose State University, 1969 and 1970.
Assistant coach at Army, 1971 and 1972.
Assistant coach at University of Arizona, 1973 through 1976.
Assistant coach at Purdue University, 1977.
Assistant coach, Dallas Cowboys NFL, 1981 and 1982.

Year	Club	Pos.	W.	L.	T.
1978—Wake Forest		†Sixth	1	10	0
1979—Wake Forest		†‡Second	8	4	0
1980—Wake Forest		†‡Fourth	5	6	0
1983—Kansas City NFL		‡§Fourth	6	10	0
1984—Kansas City NFL		§Fourth	8	8	0
College Totals—3 Years			14	20	0
Pro Totals—2 Years			14	18	0

†Atlantic Coast Conference.
‡Tied for position.
§Western Division (American Conference).

COLLEGIATE BOWL GAME RECORD

Year	Club		W.	L.
1979—Wake Forest			0	1

1979—Lost Tangerine Bowl to Louisiana State, 34-10.

CHARLES HENRY NOLL
(Chuck)
Pittsburgh Steelers
Born January 5, 1932, at Cleveland, O.
High School—Cleveland, O., Benedictine.
Received bachelor of science degree in education from University of Dayton in 1953.
Played linebacker and offensive guard.
Selected by Cleveland in 21st round of 1953 NFL draft.

Year Club	G.	INTERCEPTIONS No.	Yds.	Avg.	TD.	—KICKOFF RET.— No.	Yds.	Avg.	TD.	—TOTAL— TD.	Pts.	F.
1953—Cleveland NFL	12	None				1	2	2.0	0	0	0	0
1954—Cleveland NFL	12	None						None		0	0	0
1955—Cleveland NFL	12	5	74	14.8	1			None		1	8	0
1956—Cleveland NFL	12	1	13	13.0	0			None		1	6	0
1957—Cleveland NFL	5	None						None		0	0	0
1958—Cleveland NFL	12	None						None		0	0	0
1959—Cleveland NFL	12	2	5	2.5	0	1	20	20.0	0	0	0	0
Pro Totals—7 Years	77	8	92	11.5	1	2	22	11.0	0	2	14	0

Additional pro statistics: Recovered two fumbles for 10 yards, 1954; credited with one safety, 1955; recovered one fumble for 39 yards and a touchdown, 1956.

Played in NFL Championship Game following 1953 through 1955 seasons.

COACHING RECORD

Assistant coach, Los Angeles Chargers AFL, 1960.
Assistant coach, San Diego Chargers AFL, 1961 through 1965.
Assistant coach, Baltimore Colts NFL, 1966 through 1968.

Year Club	Pos.	W.	L.	T.	Year Club	Pos.	W.	L.	T.
1969—Pittsburgh NFL	†Fourth	1	13	0	1978—Pittsburgh NFL	‡First	14	2	0
1970—Pittsburgh NFL	‡Third	5	9	0	1979—Pittsburgh NFL	‡First	12	4	0
1971—Pittsburgh NFL	‡Second	6	8	0	1980—Pittsburgh NFL	‡Third	9	7	0
1972—Pittsburgh NFL	‡First	11	3	0	1981—Pittsburgh NFL	‡Second	8	8	0
1973—Pittsburgh NFL	†§First	10	4	0	1982—Pittsburgh NFL	x§Fourth	6	3	0
1974—Pittsburgh NFL	‡First	10	3	1	1983—Pittsburgh NFL	‡First	10	6	0
1975—Pittsburgh NFL	‡First	12	2	0	1984—Pittsburgh NFL	‡First	9	7	0
1976—Pittsburgh NFL	‡§First	10	4	0	Pro Totals—16 Years		142	88	1
1977—Pittsburgh NFL	‡First	9	5	0					

†Century Division (Eastern Conference).
‡Central Division (American Conference).
§Tied for position.
xAmerican Conference.

PLAYOFF RECORD

Year Club	W.	L.	Year Club	W.	L.
1972—Pittsburgh NFL	1	1	1979—Pittsburgh NFL	3	0
1973—Pittsburgh NFL	0	1	1982—Pittsburgh NFL	0	1
1974—Pittsburgh NFL	3	0	1983—Pittsburgh NFL	0	1
1975—Pittsburgh NFL	3	0	1984—Pittsburgh NFL	1	1
1976—Pittsburgh NFL	1	1	Pro Totals—11 Years	15	7
1977—Pittsburgh NFL	0	1			
1978—Pittsburgh NFL	3	0			

1972—Won conference playoff game from Oakland, 13-7; lost conference championship game to Miami, 21-17.
1973—Lost conference playoff game to Oakland, 33-14.
1974—Won conference playoff game from Buffalo, 32-14; won conference championship game from Oakland, 24-13; won NFL championship game (Super Bowl IX) from Minnesota, 16-6.
1975—Won conference playoff game from Baltimore, 28-10; won conference championship game from Oakland, 16-10; won NFL championship game (Super Bowl X) from Dallas, 21-17.
1976—Won conference playoff game from Baltimore, 40-14; lost conference championship game to Oakland, 24-7.
1977—Lost conference playoff game to Denver, 34-21.
1978—Won conference playoff game from Denver, 33-10; won conference championship game from Houston, 34-5; won NFL championship game (Super Bowl XIII) from Dallas, 35-31.
1979—Won conference playoff game from Miami, 34-14; won conference championship game from Houston, 27-13; won NFL championship game (Super Bowl XIV) from Los Angeles, 31-19.
1982—Lost conference playoff game to San Diego, 31-28.
1983—Lost conference playoff game to Los Angeles Raiders, 38-10.
1984—Won conference playoff game from Denver, 24-17; lost conference championship game to Miami, 45-28.

DUANE CHARLES PARCELLS
(Bill)
New York Giants

Born August 22, 1941, at Englewood, N.J.
High School—Oradell, N.J., River Dell.
Received bachelor of arts degree in education from Wichita State University in 1964.

COACHING RECORD

Assistant coach at Hastings College, 1964.
Assistant coach at Wichita State University, 1965.
Assistant coach at West Point, 1966 through 1969.
Assistant coach at Florida State University, 1970 through 1972.
Assistant coach at Vanderbilt University, 1973 and 1974.
Asstant coach at Texas Tech University, 1975 through 1977.
Assistant coach, New England Patriots, NFL, 1980.
Assistant coach, New York Giants NFL, 1981 and 1982.

Year Club	Pos.	W.	L.	T.
1978—Air Force	....	3	8	0
1983—New York Giants NFL	†Fifth	3	12	1
1984—New York Giants NFL	†‡Second	9	7	0
College Totals—1 Year		3	8	0
Pro Totals—2 Years		12	19	1

†Eastern Division (National Conference).

PLAYOFF RECORD

Year Club	W.	L.
1984—New York Giants NFL	1	1

1984—Won wild-card playoff game from Los Angeles Rams, 16-10; lost conference playoff game to San Francisco, 21-10.

OAIL ANDREW PHILLIPS
(Bum)
(Nicknamed by sister, who could not pronounce "brother.")
New Orleans Saints
Born September 29, 1923, at Orange, Tex.
High School—Beaumont, Tex., French.
Attended Lamar Junior College and received bachelor of science degree in
education from Stephen F. Austin State in 1949.
Father of Wade Phillips, defensive coordinator with New Orleans Saints.

COACHING RECORD
Assistant coach at Nederland (Tex.) High School, 1950.
Head coach at Nederland (Tex.) High School, 1951 through 1956 (Won 56, Lost 13, Tied 1).
Head coach at Jacksonville (Tex.) High School, 1958 (Won 5, Lost 5).
Head coach at Amarillo (Tex.) High School, 1959 through 1961 (Won 18, Lost 12, Tied 1).
Head coach at Port Neches (Tex.) High School, 1963 and 1964 (Won 12, Lost 6, Tied 2).
Assistant coach at Texas A&M University, 1957.
Assistant coach at University of Houston, 1965 and 1966.
Assistant coach, San Diego Chargers AFL, 1967 through 1969.
Assistant coach, San Diego Chargers NFL, 1970 and 1971.
Assistant coach at Southern Methodist University, 1972.
Assistant coach at Oklahoma State University, 1973.
Assistant coach, Houston Oilers NFL, 1974.

Year Club	Pos.	W.	L.	T.
1962—Texas Western	....	4	5	0
1975—Houston NFL	†Third	10	4	0
1976—Houston NFL	†Fourth	5	9	0
1977—Houston NFL	†‡Second	8	6	0
1978—Houston NFL	†Second	10	6	0
1979—Houston NFL	†Second	11	5	0
1980—Houston NFL	†‡First	11	5	0
1981—New Orleans NFL	§Fourth	4	12	0
1982—New Orleans NFL	x‡Eighth	4	5	0
1983—New Orleans NFL	§Third	8	8	0
1984—New Orleans NFL	§Third	7	9	0
Pro Totals—10 Years		78	69	0

†Central Division (American Conference).
‡Tied for position.
§Western Division (National Conference).
xNational Conference.

PLAYOFF RECORD
Year Club	W.	L.
1978—Houston NFL..............................	2	1
1979—Houston NFL..............................	2	1
1980—Houston NFL..............................	0	1
Pro Totals—3 Years.................................	4	3

1978—Won conference playoff game from Miami, 17-9; won conference playoff game from New England, 31-14; lost
conference championship game to Pittsburgh, 34-5.
1979—Won conference playoff game from Denver, 13-7; won conference playoff game from San Diego, 17-14; lost
conference championship game to Pittsburgh, 27-13.
1980—Lost conference playoff game to Oakland, 27-7.

DANIEL EDWARD REEVES
(Dan)
Denver Broncos
Born January 19, 1944, at Rome, Ga.
High School—Americus, Ga.
Attended University of South Carolina.

Played running back.
Named to THE SPORTING NEWS NFL Eastern Conference All-Star Team, 1966.
Signed as free agent by Dallas NFL, 1965.

Year Club	G.	RUSHING Att.	Yds.	Avg.	TD.	PASS RECEIVING P.C.	Yds.	Avg.	TD.	TOTAL TD.	Pts.	F.
1965—Dallas NFL	13	33	102	3.1	2	9	210	23.3	1	3	18	0
1966—Dallas NFL	14	175	757	4.3	8	41	557	13.6	8	*16	96	6
1967—Dallas NFL	14	173	603	3.5	5	39	490	12.6	6	11	66	7
1968—Dallas NFL	4	40	178	4.5	4	7	84	12.0	1	5	30	0
1969—Dallas NFL	13	59	173	2.9	4	18	187	10.4	1	5	30	2
1970—Dallas NFL	14	35	84	2.4	2	12	140	11.7	0	2	12	4
1971—Dallas NFL	14	17	79	4.6	0	3	25	8.3	0	0	0	1
1972—Dallas NFL	14	3	14	4.7	0		None			0	0	0
Pro Totals—8 Years.................	100	535	1990	3.7	25	129	1693	13.1	17	42	252	20

Year	Club		G.	Att.	Cmp.	Pct.	Gain	T.P.	P.I.	Avg.	No.	Yds.	Avg.	TD.
						PASSING						KICKOFF RET.		
1965—Dallas NFL			13	2	1	50.0	11	0	0	5.50	2	45	22.5	0
1966—Dallas NFL			14	6	3	50.0	48	0	0	8.00	3	56	18.7	0
1967—Dallas NFL			14	7	4	57.1	195	2	1	27.86			None	
1968—Dallas NFL			4	4	2	50.0	43	0	0	10.75			None	
1969—Dallas NFL			13	3	1	33.3	35	0	1	11.67			None	
1970—Dallas NFL			14	3	1	33.3	14	0	1	4.67			None	
1971—Dallas NFL			14	5	2	40.0	24	0	1	4.80			None	
1972—Dallas NFL			14	2	0	00.0	0	0	0	0.00			None	
Pro Totals—8 Years			100	32	14	43.8	370	2	4	11.56	5	101	20.2	0

Additional pro statistics: Returned two punts for minus one yard, 1966.
Played in NFC Championship Game following 1970 and 1971 seasons.
Played in NFL Championship Game following 1966, 1967, 1970 and 1971 seasons.

COACHING RECORD

Player-coach, Dallas Cowboys NFL, 1970 and 1971.
Assistant coach, Dallas Cowboys NFL, 1972 and 1974 through 1980.

Year	Club	Pos.	W.	L.	T.
1981—Denver NFL		†‡First	10	6	0
1982—Denver NFL		§12th	2	7	0
1983—Denver NFL		†‡Second	9	7	0
1984—Denver NFL		†First	13	3	0
Pro Totals—4 Years			34	23	0

†Western Division (American Conference).
‡Tied for position.
§American Conference.

PLAYOFF RECORD

Year	Club	W.	L.
1983—Denver NFL		0	1
1984—Denver NFL		0	1
Pro Totals—2 Years		0	2

1983—Lost wild-card playoff game to Seattle, 31-7.
1984—Lost conference playoff game to Pittsburgh, 24-17.

JOHN ALEXANDER ROBINSON
Los Angeles Rams
Born July 25, 1935, at Chicago, Ill.
High School—San Mateo, Calif.
Received bachelor of science degree in education from University of Oregon in 1958.
COACHING RECORD
Assistant coach at University of Oregon, 1960 through 1971.
Assistant coach at University of Southern California, 1972 through 1974.
Assistant coach, Oakland Raiders NFL, 1975.

Year	Club	Pos.	W.	L.	T.	Year	Club	Pos.	W.	L.	T.
1976—Southern California		†First	11	1	0	1982—Southern California		§x	8	3	0
1977—Southern California		†‡Second	8	4	0	1983—Los Angeles Rams NFL		ySecond	9	7	0
1978—Southern California		§First	12	1	0	1984—Los Angeles Rams NFL		ySecond	10	6	0
1979—Southern California		§First	11	0	1	College Totals—7 Years			67	14	2
1980—Southern California		§Third	8	2	1	Pro Totals—2 Years			19	13	0
1981—Southern California		‡§Second	9	3	0						

†Pacific-8 Conference.
‡Tied for position.
§Pacific-10 Conference.
xIneligible for conference title.
yWestern Division (National Conference).

PLAYOFF RECORD

Year	Club	W.	L.
1983—Los Angeles Rams NFL		1	1
1984—Los Angeles Rams NFL		0	1
Pro Totals—2 Years		1	2

1983—Won wild-card playoff game from Dallas, 24-17; lost conference playoff game to Washington, 51-7.
1984—Lost wild-card game to New York Giants, 16-13.

COLLEGIATE BOWL GAME RECORD

Year	Club	W.	L.
1976—Southern California		1	0
1977—Southern California		1	0
1978—Southern California		1	0
1979—Southern California		1	0
1981—Southern California		0	1
Totals—5 Years		4	1

1976—Won Rose Bowl from Michigan, 14-6.
1977—Won Bluebonnet Bowl from Texas A&M, 47-28.
1978—Won Rose Bowl from Michigan, 17-10.
1979—Won Rose Bowl from Ohio State, 17-16.
1981—Lost Fiesta Bowl to Penn State, 26-10.

DARRYL D. ROGERS
Detroit Lions

Born May 28, 1935, at Los Angeles, Calif.
High School—Long Beach, Calif., Jordan.
Attended Long Beach City College and received bachelor of arts degree
in 1957 and master's degree in physical education in
1964, both from Fresno State University.

Signed as free agent by Los Angeles Rams, April, 1959.
Released by Los Angeles Rams, August, 1959.
In U.S. Marine Corps, 1958 and 1959.

COACHING RECORD

Named College Coach of the Year by THE SPORTING NEWS, 1978.
Assistant coach at Fresno City College, 1961 through 1964.

Year	Club	Pos.	W.	L.	T.	Year	Club	Pos.	W.	L.	T.
1965—	Hayward State	†§.....	3	7	0	1976—	Michigan State	‡zSeventh	4	6	1
1966—	Fresno State	‡xSecond	7	3	0	1977—	Michigan State	zThird	7	3	1
1967—	Fresno State	‡xSecond	3	8	0	1978—	Michigan State	‡zFirst	8	3	0
1968—	Fresno State	xFirst	7	4	0	1979—	Michigan State	‡zSeventh	5	6	0
1969—	Fresno State	‡yFifth	6	4	0	1980—	Arizona State	aFourth	7	4	0
1970—	Fresno State	yThird	8	4	0	1981—	Arizona State	‡aSecond	9	2	0
1971—	Fresno State	yThird	6	5	0	1982—	Arizona State	‡aThird	10	2	0
1972—	Fresno State	‡yThird	6	4	1	1983—	Arizona State	‡aSixth	6	4	1
1973—	San Jose State	ySecond	5	4	2	1984—	Arizona State	aSixth	5	6	0
1974—	San Jose State	‡ySecond	8	3	1		College Totals—20 Years.........................		129	84	7
1975—	San Jose State	yFirst	9	2	0						

†Ineligible for conference title.
‡Tied for position.
§Far Western Conference.
xCalifornia Collegiate Athletic Association.
yPacific Coast Athletic Association.
zBig 10 Conference.
aPacific-10 Conference.

COLLEGIATE BOWL GAME RECORD

Year	Club	W.	L.
1968—	Fresno State	0	1
1971—	Fresno State	0	1
1982—	Arizona State	1	0
	Totals—3 Years..	1	2

1968—Lost Camelia Bowl to Humboldt State, 29-14.
1971—Lost Mercy Bowl to California State-Fullerton, 17-14.
1982—Won Fiesta Bowl from Oklahoma, 32-21.

MARTIN EDWARD SCHOTTENHEIMER
(Marty)
Cleveland Browns

Born September 23, 1943, at Canonsburg, Pa.
High School—McDonald, Pa.
Received bachelor of arts degree in English from University of Pittsburgh in 1964.

Played linebacker.
Selected by Buffalo in 7th round of 1965 AFL draft.
Released by Buffalo Bills and signed with Boston Patriots, 1969.
Traded by New England Patriots to Pittsburgh Steelers for offensive tackle Mike Haggerty and a draft choice,
July 10, 1971.
Released by Pittsburgh Steelers, 1971.

		—INTERCEPTIONS—						—INTERCEPTIONS—			
Year	Club	G.	No.	Yds.	Avg.TD.	Year	Club	G.	No.	Yds.	Avg.TD.
1965—	Buffalo AFL..................	14			None	1970—	Boston NFL....................	12			None
1966—	Buffalo AFL..................	14	1	20	20.0 0		AFL Totals—5 Years.........	67	6	133	22.2 1
1967—	Buffalo AFL..................	14	3	88	29.3 1		NFL Totals—1 Year..........	12	0	0	0.0 0
1968—	Buffalo AFL..................	14	1	22	22.0 0		Pro Totals—6 Years...........	79	6	133	22.2 1
1969—	Boston AFL..................	11	1	3	3.0 0						

Additional pro statistics: Returned one kickoff for 13 yards, 1969; returned one kickoff for eight yards, 1970.
Played in AFL Championship Game following 1965 and 1966 seasons.
Played in AFL All-Star Game following 1965 season.

Assistant coach, Portland WFL, 1974.
Assistant coach, New York Giants NFL, 1975 through 1977.
Assistant coach, Detroit Lions NFL, 1978 and 1979.
Assistant coach, Cleveland Browns NFL, 1980 through 1984.

Year	Club	Pos.	W.	L.	T.
1984—Cleveland NFL†		‡Third	4	4	0

†Replaced Sam Rutigliano, October 22, 1984 with 1-7 record and in third place.
‡Central Division (American Conference).

DONALD FRANCIS SHULA
(Don)
Miami Dolphins

Born January 4, 1930, at Painesville, O.
High School—Painesville, O., Harvey.
Attended John Carroll University.
Father of David Shula, assistant coach with Miami Dolphins,
and Mike Shula, quarterback at University of Alabama.

Played defensive back.
Selected by Cleveland in 9th round of 1951 NFL draft.
Traded with quarterback Harry Agganis, defensive backs Bert Rechichar and Carl Taseff, end Gern Nagler, guards Elmer Willhoite, Ed Sharkey and Art Spinney and tackles Dick Batten and Stu Sheetz by Cleveland NFL to Baltimore NFL for linebacker Tom Catlin, guard Herschel Forester, halfback John Petitbon and tackles Don Colo and Mike McCormack, March 25, 1953.
Sold by Baltimore NFL to Washington NFL, 1957.

Year	Club	G.	No.	Yds.	Avg.	TD.	Year	Club	G.	No.	Yds.	Avg.	TD.
			INTERCEPTIONS							INTERCEPTIONS			
1951—Cleveland NFL		12	4	23	5.8	0	1955—Baltimore NFL		9	5	64	12.8	0
1952—Cleveland NFL		5		None			1956—Baltimore NFL		12	1	2	2.0	0
1953—Baltimore NFL		12	3	46	15.3	0	1957—Washington NFL		11	3	48	16.0	0
1954—Baltimore NFL		12	5	84	16.8	0	Pro Totals—7 Years		73	21	267	12.7	0

Additional pro statistics: Returned one kickoff for six yards, 1951; caught one pass for six yards, 1953; rushed twice for three yards, 1954; recovered one fumble, 1953; recovered two fumbles for 26 yards, 1955; recovered one fumble for six yards and returned one kickoff for no yards, 1956.
Played in NFL Championship Game following 1951 and 1952 seasons.

COACHING RECORD

Named NFL Coach of the Year by THE SPORTING NEWS, 1964, 1968, 1970 and 1972.
Assistant coach at University of Virginia, 1958.
Assistant coach at University of Kentucky, 1959.
Assistant coach, Detroit Lions NFL, 1960 through 1962.

Year	Club	Pos.	W.	L.	T.	Year	Club	Pos.	W.	L.	T.
1963—Baltimore NFL		†Third	8	6	0	1974—Miami NFL		§First	11	3	0
1964—Baltimore NFL		†First	12	2	0	1975—Miami NFL		§xFirst	10	4	0
1965—Baltimore NFL		†Second	10	3	1	1976—Miami NFL		§Third	6	8	0
1966—Baltimore NFL		†Second	9	5	0	1977—Miami NFL		§xFirst	10	4	0
1967—Baltimore NFL		†Second	11	1	2	1978—Miami NFL		§xFirst	11	5	0
1968—Baltimore NFL		‡First	13	1	0	1979—Miami NFL		§First	10	6	0
1969—Baltimore NFL		‡Second	8	5	1	1980—Miami NFL		§Third	8	8	0
1970—Miami NFL		§Second	10	4	0	1981—Miami NFL		§First	11	4	1
1971—Miami NFL		§First	10	3	1	1982—Miami NFL		yxSecond	7	2	0
1972—Miami NFL		§First	14	0	0	1983—Miami NFL		§First	12	4	0
1973—Miami NFL		§First	12	2	0	1984—Miami NFL		§First	14	2	0
						Pro Totals—22 Years			227	82	6

†Western Conference.
‡Coastal Division (Western Conference).
§Eastern Division (American Conference).
xTied for position.
yAmerican Conference.

PLAYOFF RECORD

Year	Club	W.	L.	Year	Club	W.	L.
1964—Baltimore NFL	0	1	1978—Miami NFL	0	1
1965—Baltimore NFL	1	1	1979—Miami NFL	0	1
1966—Baltimore NFL	1	0	1981—Miami NFL	0	1
1968—Baltimore NFL	2	1	1982—Miami NFL	3	1
1970—Miami NFL	0	1	1983—Miami NFL	0	1
1971—Miami NFL	2	1	1984—Miami NFL	2	1
1972—Miami NFL	3	0	Pro Totals—15 Years	17	12
1973—Miami NFL	3	0			
1974—Miami NFL	0	1			

1964—Lost NFL championship game to Cleveland, 27-0.
1965—Lost conference playoff game to Green Bay, 13-10; won Playoff Bowl from Dallas, 35-3.
1966—Won Playoff Bowl from Philadelphia, 20-14.
1968—Won conference playoff game from Minnesota, 24-14; won NFL championship game from Cleveland, 34-0; lost AFL-NFL playoff game (Super Bowl III) to New York Jets, 16-7.

1970—Lost conference playoff game to Oakland, 21-14.
1971—Won conference playoff game from Kansas City, 27-24; won conference playoff game from Baltimore, 21-0; lost NFL championship game (Super Bowl VI) to Dallas, 24-3.
1972—Won conference playoff game from Cleveland, 20-14; won conference championship game from Pittsburgh, 21-17; won NFL championship game (Super Bowl VII) from Washington, 14-7.
1973—Won conference playoff game from Cincinnati, 34-16; won conference championship game from Oakland, 27-10; won NFL championship game (Super Bowl VIII) from Minnesota, 24-7.
1974—Lost conference playoff game to Oakland, 28-26.
1978—Lost conference playoff game to Houston, 17-9.
1979—Lost conference playoff game to Pittsburgh, 34-14.
1981—Lost conference playoff game in overtime to San Diego, 41-38.
1982—Won conference playoff game from New England, 28-13; won conference playoff game from San Diego, 34-13; won conference championship game from New York Jets, 14-0; lost NFL championship game (Super Bowl XVII) to Washington, 27-17.
1983—Lost conference playoff game to Seattle, 27-20.
1984—Won conference playoff game from Seattle, 31-10; won conference championship game from Pittsburgh, 45-28; lost NFL championship game (Super Bowl XIX) to San Francisco, 38-16.

GEORGE KAY STEPHENSON
(Known by middle name.)
Buffalo Bills
Born December 17, 1944, at DeFuniak Springs, Fla.
High School—Pensacola, Fla.
Received bachelor of arts degree in physical education from University of Florida in 1967.

Played quarterback.
Signed as free agent by San Diego Chargers, 1967.
Traded by San Diego Chargers to Buffalo Bills for 5th round draft choice, August 29, 1968.
On injured reserve entire 1969 season.
Released by Buffalo Bills, 1970; signed as free agent by Atlanta Falcons, May, 1970.
Released by Atlanta Falcons, August, 1970; signed by Jacksonville Sharks, 1974.

Year Club	G.	Att.	Cmp.	Pct.	Gain	T.P.	P.I.	Avg.	Att.	Yds.	Avg.	TD.	TD.	Pts.	F.
1967—San Diego AFL	7	26	11	42.3	117	2	2	4.50	2	11	5.5	0	0	0	0
1968—Buffalo AFL	7	79	29	36.7	364	4	7	4.61	4	30	7.5	0	0	0	0
1974—Jacksonville WFL	....	149	68	45.6	815	4	11	5.47	14	3	0.2	0	0	0	0
AFL Totals—2 Years	14	105	40	38.1	481	6	9	4.58	6	41	6.8	0	0	0	0
WFL Totals—1 Year	....	149	68	45.6	815	4	11	5.47	14	3	0.2	0	0	0	0
Pro Totals—3 Years	....	254	108	42.5	1296	10	20	5.10	20	44	2.2	0	0	0	0

COACHING RECORD
Assistant coach at Rice University, 1971.
Head coach and athletic director at Baker County High School, Baker, Fla., 1973.
Assistant coach and Director of Player Personnel, Jacksonville Sharks WFL, 1975.
Assistant coach, Los Angeles Rams NFL, 1977.
Assistant coach, Buffalo Bills NFL, 1978 through 1982.

Year Club	Pos.	W.	L.	T.
1983— Buffalo NFL	†‡Second	8	8	0
1984— Buffalo NFL	†Fifth	2	14	0
Pro Totals—2 Years		10	22	0

†Eastern Division (American Conference).
‡Tied for position.

WILLIAM ERNEST WALSH
(Bill)
San Francisco 49ers
Born November 30, 1931, at Los Angeles, Calif.
High School—Los Angeles, Calif., Hayward.
Attended San Mateo Junior College and received bachelor of arts degree and master's degree in education from San Jose State in 1959.

COACHING RECORD
Named THE SPORTING NEWS NFL Coach of the Year, 1981.
Assistant coach at Monterey Peninsula College, 1955.
Assistant coach at San Jose State University, 1956.
Head coach at Washington Union High, Fremont, Calif., 1957 through 1959.
Assistant coach at University of California, 1960 through 1962.
Assistant coach at Stanford University, 1963 through 1965.
Assistant coach, Oakland Raiders AFL, 1966.
Assistant coach, Cincinnati Bengals AFL, 1968 and 1969.
Assistant coach, Cincinnati Bengals NFL, 1970 through 1975.
Assistant coach, San Diego Chargers NFL, 1976.

Year Club	Pos.	W.	L.	T.	Year Club	Pos.	W.	L.	T.
1967—San Jose CoFL	†Second	7	5	0	1982—San Francisco NFL	z§11th	3	6	0
1977—Stanford	‡§Second	9	3	0	1983—San Francisco NFL	yFirst	10	6	0
1978—Stanford	xFourth	8	4	0	1984—San Francisco NFL	yFirst	15	1	0
1979—San Francisco NFL	yFourth	2	14	0	College Totals—2 Years		17	7	0
1980—San Francisco NFL	yThird	6	10	0	Pro Totals—6 Years		49	40	0
1981—San Francisco NFL	yFirst	13	3	0					

†Continental League.
‡Pacific Eight Conference.
§Tied for position.
xPacific Ten Conference.
yWestern Division (National Conference).
zNational Conference.

PLAYOFF RECORD

Year Club	W.	L.
1981—San Francisco NFL	3	0
1983—San Francisco NFL	1	1
1984—San Francisco NFL	3	0
Pro Totals—3 Years	7	1

1981—Won conference playoff game from New York Giants, 38-34; won conference championship game from Dallas, 28-27; won NFL championship game (Super Bowl XVI) from Cincinnati, 26-21.
1983—Won conference playoff game from Detroit, 24-23; lost conference championship game to Washington, 24-21.
1984—Won conference playoff game from New York Giants, 21-10; won conference championship game from Chicago, 23-0; won NFL championship game (Super Bowl XIX) from Miami, 38-16.

COLLEGIATE BOWL GAME RECORD

Year Club	W.	L.
1977—Stanford	1	0
1978—Stanford	1	0
Totals—2 Years	2	0

1977—Won Sun Bowl from Louisiana State, 24-14.
1978—Won Bluebonnet Bowl from Georgia, 25-22.

JOSEPH FRANK WALTON
(Joe)
New York Jets

Born December 15, 1935, at Beaver Falls, Pa.
High School—Beaver Falls, Pa.
Received bachelor of arts degree in history from University of Pittsburgh in 1957.
Son of Frank Walton, guard with Boston Redskins, 1934 and 1935;
and Washington Redskins, 1944 and 1945; assistant coach, Pittsburgh Steelers, 1946.

Played tight end.
Named end on THE SPORTING NEWS College All-America Team, 1956.
Selected by Washington in 2nd round of 1957 NFL draft.

			——PASS RECEIVING——			
Year Club	G.	P.C.	Yds.	Avg.	TD.	
1957—Washington NFL	12	3	57	19.0	0	
1958—Washington NFL	12	32	532	16.6	5	
1959—Washington NFL	9	21	317	15.1	3	
1960—Washington NFL	12	27	401	14.9	3	
1961—N.Y. Giants NFL	12	36	544	15.1	2	
1962—N.Y. Giants NFL	14	33	406	12.3	9	
1963—N.Y. Giants NFL	12	26	371	14.3	6	
Pro Totals—7 Years	83	178	2628	14.8	28	

Additional pro statistics: Intercepted one pass for 55 yards, 1957; fumbled once, 1958, 1959, 1961 and 1962; recovered one fumble for four yards, 1960.

COACHING RECORD

Scout for New York Giants NFL, 1967 and 1968.
Assistant coach, New York Giants NFL, 1969 through 1973.
Assistant coach, Washington Redskins NFL, 1974 through 1980.
Assistant coach, New York Jets NFL, 1981 and 1982.

Year Club	Pos.	W.	L.	T.
1983—New York Jets NFL	†‡Fourth	7	9	0
1984—New York Jets NFL	†Third	7	9	0
Pro Totals—2 Years		14	18	0

†Eastern Division (American Conference).
‡Tied for position.

SAMUEL DAVID WYCHE
(Sam)
Cincinnati Bengals

Born January 5, 1945, at Atlanta, Ga.
High School—Atlanta, Ga., North Fulton.
Received bachelor of arts degree in business administration from Furman University
in 1966 and received master's degree from University of South Carolina.
Brother of Joseph (Bubba) Wyche, former quarterback with Saskatchewan Roughriders,
Detroit Wheels, Chicago Fire and Shreveport Steamer.

Played quarterback.
Played in Continental Football League with Wheeling Ironmen, 1966.

Signed as free agent by Cincinnati AFL, 1968.
Traded by Cincinnati Bengals to Washington Redskins for running back Henry Dyer, May 5, 1971.
Traded by Washington Redskins to Detroit Lions for quarterback Bill Cappelman, August 17, 1974.
Released by Detroit Lions, September 2, 1975; signed as free agent by St. Louis Cardinals, 1976.
Released by St. Louis Cardinals, September 23, 1976; signed as free agent by Buffalo Bills, October 26, 1976.
Member of Washington Redskins' taxi squad, 1973.
Active for 7 games with Buffalo Bills in 1976; did not play.

Year Club	G.	Att.	Cmp.	Pct.	Gain	T.P.	P.I.	Avg.	Att.	Yds.	Avg.	TD.	TD.	Pts.	F.
				PASSING						RUSHING			TOTAL		
1966—Wheeling CoFL	....	18	9	50.0	101	0	1	5.61	5	—11	—2.2	0	0	0	0
1968—Cincinnati AFL	3	55	35	63.6	494	2	2	8.98	12	74	6.2	0	0	0	2
1969—Cincinnati AFL	7	108	54	50.0	838	7	4	7.76	12	107	8.9	1	1	6	1
1970—Cincinnati NFL	13	57	26	45.6	411	3	2	7.21	19	118	6.2	2	2	12	3
1971—Washington NFL	1				None				1	4	4.0	0	0	0	0
1972—Washington NFL	7				None						None		0	0	0
1974—Detroit NFL	14	1	0	00.0	0	0	1	0.00	1	0	0.0	0	0	0	0
1976—St. Louis NFL	1	1	1	100.0	5	0	0	5.00			None		0	0	0
AFL Totals—2 Years	10	163	89	54.9	1332	9	6	8.17	24	181	7.5	1	1	6	3
NFL Totals—5 Years	36	59	27	45.8	416	3	3	7.05	21	122	5.8	2	2	12	3
Pro Totals—7 Years	46	222	116	52.3	1748	12	9	7.87	45	303	6.7	3	3	18	6

Additional CoFL statistics: Intercepted three passes for nine yards, 1966.
Additional AFL statistics: Caught one pass for five yards, 1968.
Additional NFL statistics: Recovered one fumble for minus one yard, 1970.
Played in NFL Championship Game following 1972 season.

COACHING RECORD

Graduate assistant at University of South Carolina, 1967.
Assistant coach, San Francisco 49ers NFL, 1979 through 1982.

Year Club	Pos.	W.	L.	T.
1983—Indiana	†‡Eighth	3	8	0
1984—Cincinnati NFL	§Second	8	8	0
College Totals—1 Year		3	8	0
Pro Totals—1 Year		8	8	0

†Big Ten Conference.
‡Tied for position.
§Central Division (American Conference).

Recently Retired Coach

JOHN HARVEY McKAY

Born July 5, 1923, at Everettsville, W. Va.
High School—Shinnston, W. Va.
Attended Purdue University and received bachelor of science degree
in physical education from University of Oregon.
Father of J. K. McKay, wide receiver with Tampa Bay Buccaneers, 1976 through 1978.

COACHING RECORD

Assistant coach at University of Oregon, 1950 through 1958.
Assistant coach at University of Southern California, 1959.

Year Club	Pos.	W.	L.	T.	Year Club	Pos.	W.	L.	T.
1960—Southern California	†Second	4	6	0	1973—Southern California	yFirst	9	2	1
1961—Southern California	†‡Second	4	5	1	1974—Southern California	yFirst	10	1	1
1962—Southern California	§First	11	0	0	1975—Southern California	yFifth	8	4	0
1963—Southern California	§Second	7	3	0	1976—Tampa Bay NFL	zFifth	0	14	0
1964—Southern California	‡xFirst	7	3	0	1977—Tampa Bay NFL	aFifth	2	12	0
1965—Southern California	xSecond	7	2	1	1978—Tampa Bay NFL	aFifth	5	11	0
1966—Southern California	xFirst	7	4	0	1979—Tampa Bay NFL	a‡First	10	6	0
1967—Southern California	yFirst	10	1	0	1980—Tampa Bay NFL	a‡Fourth	5	10	1
1968—Southern California	yFirst	9	1	1	1981—Tampa Bay NFL	aFirst	9	7	0
1969—Southern California	yFirst	10	0	1	1982—Tampa Bay NFL	b‡Fourth	5	4	0
1970—Southern California	‡ySixth	6	4	1	1983—Tampa Bay NFL	aFifth	2	14	0
1971—Southern California	‡yThird	6	4	1	1984—Tampa Bay NFL	aThird	6	10	0
1972—Southern California	yFirst	12	0	0	College Totals—16 Years		127	40	8
					Pro Totals—9 Years		44	88	1

†Big Five Conference.
‡Tied for position.
§Big Six Conference.
xPacific Athletic Conference.
yPacific Eight Conference.
zWestern Division (American Conference).
aCentral Division (National Conference).
bNational Conference.

PLAYOFF RECORD

Year Club	W.	L.
1979—Tampa Bay NFL	1	1
1981—Tampa Bay NFL	0	1
1982—Tampa Bay NFL	0	1
Pro Totals—3 Years	1	3

1979—Won conference playoff game from Philadelphia, 24-17; lost conference championship game to Los Angeles, 9-0.
1981—Lost conference playoff game to Dallas, 38-0.
1982—Lost conference playoff game to Dallas, 30-17.

COLLEGIATE BOWL GAME RECORD

Year Club	W.	L.
1962—Southern California	1	0
1966—Southern California	0	1
1967—Southern California	1	0
1968—Southern California	0	1
1969—Southern California	1	0
1972—Southern California	1	0
1973—Southern California	0	1
1974—Southern California	1	0
1975—Southern California	1	0
Totals—9 Years	6	3

1962—Won Rose Bowl from Wisconsin, 42-37.
1966—Lost Rose Bowl to Purdue, 14-13.
1967—Won Rose Bowl from Indiana, 14-3.
1968—Lost Rose Bowl to Ohio State, 27-16.
1969—Won Rose Bowl from Michigan, 10-3.
1972—Won Rose Bowl from Ohio State, 42-17.
1973—Lost Rose Bowl to Ohio State, 42-21.
1974—Won Rose Bowl from Ohio State, 18-17.
1975—Won Liberty Bowl from Texas A&M, 20-0.

—DID YOU KNOW—

That since 1967, Southern California leads all colleges with 34 selections in the first round of the NFL draft?

Recently Retired Players

ROBERT PAUL BREUNIG
Name pronounced BREW-nig.

(Bob)

Born July 4, 1953, at Inglewood, Calif.
Height, 6.02. Weight, 227.
High School—Phoenix, Ariz., Alhambra.
Received bachelor's degree in business from Arizona State University.

Named as linebacker on THE SPORTING NEWS College All-America Team, 1974.
Selected by Dallas in 3rd round (70th player selected) of 1975 NFL draft.
On injured reserve with back injury, November 28 through remainder of 1984 season.

			INTERCEPTIONS			
Year Club	G.	No.	Yds.	Avg.	TD.	
1975—Dallas NFL	10		None			
1976—Dallas NFL	14		None			
1977—Dallas NFL	14	1	15	15.0	0	
1978—Dallas NFL	16	1	2	2.0	0	
1979—Dallas NFL	16		None			
1980—Dallas NFL	16	3	34	11.3	0	
1981—Dallas NFL	16	2	8	4.0	0	
1982—Dallas NFL	9	1	1	1.0	0	
1983—Dallas NFL	16	1	0	0.0	0	
1984—Dallas NFL	8		None			
Pro Totals—10 Years	135	9	60	6.7	0	

Additional pro statistics: Caught one pass for 21 yards, returned two kickoffs for 13 yards, 1975; recovered one fumble, 1975, 1977, 1978, 1982 and 1983; recovered three fumbles, 1976.
Played in NFC Championship Game following 1975, 1977, 1978 and 1980 through 1982 seasons.
Played in NFL Championship Game following 1975, 1977 and 1978 seasons.
Played in Pro Bowl (NFL All-Star Game) following 1979, 1980 and 1982 seasons.

DEXTER MANLEY BUSSEY

Born March 11, 1952, at Dallas, Tex.
Height, 5.11. Weight, 210.
High School—Dallas, Tex., John F. Kennedy.
Attended University of Oklahoma and University of Texas at Arlington.

Selected by Detroit in 3rd round (65th player selected) of 1974 NFL draft.

		RUSHING				PASS RECEIVING				TOTAL		
Year Club	G.	Att.	Yds.	Avg.	TD.	P.C.	Yds.	Avg.	TD.	TD.	Pts.	F.
1974—Detroit NFL	11	9	22	2.4	0	4	24	6.0	0	0	0	1
1975—Detroit NFL	13	157	696	4.4	2	14	175	12.5	2	4	24	7
1976—Detroit NFL	14	196	858	4.4	3	28	218	7.8	0	3	18	6
1977—Detroit NFL	8	85	338	4.0	4	11	116	10.5	1	5	30	2
1978—Detroit NFL	16	225	924	4.1	5	31	275	8.9	1	6	36	9
1979—Detroit NFL	16	144	625	4.3	1	15	102	6.8	0	1	6	3
1980—Detroit NFL	16	145	720	5.0	3	39	364	9.3	0	3	18	2
1981—Detroit NFL	16	105	446	4.2	0	18	92	5.1	0	0	0	3
1982—Detroit NFL	9	48	136	2.8	0	16	138	8.6	0	0	0	2
1983—Detroit NFL	15	57	249	4.4	0	8	49	6.1	1	1	6	1
1984—Detroit NFL	16	32	91	2.8	0	9	63	7.0	0	0	0	0
Pro Totals—11 Years	150	1203	5105	4.2	18	193	1616	8.4	5	23	138	36

Additional pro statistics: Returned five kickoffs for 59 yards and recovered one fumble, 1974; returned two kickoffs for 38 yards and recovered three fumbles, 1975; recovered two fumbles, 1976, 1978 and 1982; returned one kickoff for 14 yards, 1976.

LEE HAROLD CARMICHAEL

(Known by middle name.)

Born September 22, 1949, at Jacksonville, Fla.
Height, 6.08. Weight, 225.
High School—Jacksonville, Fla., William M. Raines.
Attended Southern University.

Established NFL record for most consecutive games, receptions (127)—streak stopped December 21, 1980, vs. Dallas Cowboys.
Named to THE SPORTING NEWS NFC All-Star Team, 1978 and 1979.
Selected by Philadelphia in 7th round (161st player selected) of 1971 NFL draft.
Released by Philadelphia Eagles, April 30, 1984; signed as free agent by New York Jets, August 9, 1984.
Released by New York Jets, August 27, 1984; signed as free agent by Dallas Cowboys, September 6, 1984.
Released by Dallas Cowboys, November 14, 1984.

		RUSHING				PASS RECEIVING				TOTAL		
Year Club	G.	Att.	Yds.	Avg.	TD.	P.C.	Yds.	Avg.	TD.	TD.	Pts.	F.
1971—Philadelphia NFL	9		None			20	288	14.4	0	0	0	2
1972—Philadelphia NFL	·13		None			20	276	13.8	2	2	12	1
1973—Philadelphia NFL	14	3	42	14.0	0	*67	*1116	16.7	9	9	54	3
1974—Philadelphia NFL	14	2	−6	−3.0	0	56	649	11.6	8	8	48	1

Year Club	G.	Att.	RUSHING Yds.	Avg.	TD.	PASS RECEIVING P.C.	Yds.	Avg.	TD.	TOTAL TD.	Pts.	F.
1975—Philadelphia NFL	14	1	6	6.0	0	49	639	13.0	7	7	42	2
1976—Philadelphia NFL	14			None		42	503	12.0	5	5	30	0
1977—Philadelphia NFL	14			None		46	665	14.5	7	7	42	0
1978—Philadelphia NFL	16	1	21	21.0	0	55	1072	19.5	8	8	48	1
1979—Philadelphia NFL	16	1	0	0.0	0	52	872	16.8	11	11	66	0
1980—Philadelphia NFL	16			None		48	815	17.0	9	9	54	4
1981—Philadelphia NFL	16	1	1	1.0	0	61	1028	16.9	6	6	36	3
1982—Philadelphia NFL	9			None		35	540	15.4	4	4	24	3
1983—Philadelphia NFL	15			None		38	515	13.6	3	3	18	0
1984—Dallas NFL	2			None		1	7	7.0	0	0	0	0
Pro Totals—14 Years	182	9	64	7.1	0	590	8985	15.2	79	79	474	20

Additional pro statistics: Recovered one fumble, 1973, 1974, 1977, 1981 and 1982; attempted one pass with no completions, 1974; recovered three fumbles, 1976; recovered three fumbles for 33 yards, 1979; attempted one pass with one completion for 45 yards and a touchdown, 1983.

Played in NFC Championship Game following 1980 season.

Played in NFL Championship Game following 1980 season.

Played in Pro Bowl (NFL All-Star Game) following 1973 and 1978 through 1980 seasons.

JAMES CARMEN CEFALO
(Jimmy)

Born October 6, 1956, at Pittston, Pa.
Height, 5.11. Weight, 188.
High School—Pittston, Pa., Area.
Received bachelor of science degree in journalism from
Penn State University in 1978.

Selected by Miami in 3rd round (81st player selected) of 1978 NFL draft.
On injured reserve with knee injury, September 6 through remainder of 1983 season.

Year Club	G.	PASS RECEIVING P.C.	Yds.	Avg.	TD.	PUNT RETURNS No.	Yds.	Avg.	TD.	TOTAL TD.	Pts.	F.
1978—Miami NFL	16	6	145	24.2	3	28	232	8.3	0	3	18	3
1979—Miami NFL	16	12	223	18.6	3	2	10	5.0	0	3	18	0
1980—Miami NFL	16	11	199	18.1	1		None			1	6	0
1981—Miami NFL	16	29	631	21.8	3		None			3	18	0
1982—Miami NFL	9	17	356	20.9	1		None			1	6	1
1983—Miami NFL	1		None				None			0	0	0
1984—Miami NFL	16	18	185	10.3	2		None			2	12	1
Pro Totals—7 Years	90	93	1739	18.7	13	30	242	8.1	0	13	78	5

Additional pro statistics: Returned two kickoffs for 40 yards and recovered one fumble, 1978.

Played in AFC Championship Game following 1982 and 1984 seasons.

Played in NFL Championship Game following 1982 and 1984 seasons.

DOUG H. DIEKEN

Born February 12, 1949, at Streator, Ill.
Height, 6.05. Weight, 252.
High School—Streator, Ill.
Attended University of Illinois.

Selected by Cleveland in 6th round (142nd player selected) of 1971 NFL draft.
Cleveland NFL, 1971 through 1984.
Games: 1971 (14), 1972 (14), 1973 (14), 1974 (14), 1975 (14), 1976 (14), 1977 (14), 1978 (16), 1979 (16), 1980 (16), 1981 (16), 1982 (9), 1983 (16), 1984 (16). Total—203.
Pro statistics: Returned one kickoff for 16 yards and scored one safety, 1971; recovered one fumble, 1973, 1974, 1977, 1980 and 1984; returned two kickoffs for 14 yards, 1973; recovered one fumble, 1974 and 1977; recovered four fumbles, 1975; recovered two fumbles, 1976 and 1978; caught one pass for 14 yards and a touchdown, 1983.

Played in Pro Bowl (NFL All-Star Game) following 1980 season.

FRANCO HARRIS

Born March 7, 1950, at Fort Dix, N. J.
Height, 6.02. Weight, 225.
High School—Mt. Holly, N. J., Rancocas Valley Regional.
Received bachelor of science degree in hotel and food service administration from
Penn State University in 1972.

Tied NFL record for most seasons, 1,000 yards rushing (8).
Named by THE SPORTING NEWS as AFC Rookie of the Year, 1972.
Named to THE SPORTING NEWS AFC All-Star Team, 1972, 1975 and 1977.
Selected by Pittsburgh in 1st round (13th player selected) of 1972 NFL draft.
Placed on did not report list, August 14 through August 19, 1984.
Released by Pittsburgh Steelers, August 20, 1984; signed as free agent by Seattle Seahawks, September 5, 1984.
Released by Seattle Seahawks, October 30, 1984.

Year Club	G.	Att.	RUSHING Yds.	Avg.	TD.	PASS RECEIVING P.C.	Yds.	Avg.	TD.	TOTAL TD.	Pts.	F.
1972—Pittsburgh NFL	14	188	1055	5.6	10	21	180	8.6	1	11	66	7
1973—Pittsburgh NFL	12	188	698	3.7	3	10	69	6.9	0	3	18	8
1974—Pittsburgh NFL	12	208	1006	4.8	5	23	200	8.7	1	6	36	9
1975—Pittsburgh NFL	14	262	1246	4.8	10	28	214	7.6	1	11	66	9
1976—Pittsburgh NFL	14	289	1128	3.9	*14	23	151	6.6	0	14	84	8

Year	Club	G.	Att.	Yds.	RUSHING Avg.	TD.	PASS RECEIVING P.C.	Yds.	Avg.	TD.	TD.	TOTAL Pts.	F.
1977—Pittsburgh NFL		14	300	1162	3.9	11	11	62	5.6	0	11	66	10
1978—Pittsburgh NFL		16	310	1082	3.5	8	22	144	6.5	0	8	48	4
1979—Pittsburgh NFL		15	267	1186	4.4	11	36	291	8.1	1	12	72	11
1980—Pittsburgh NFL		13	208	789	3.8	4	30	196	6.5	2	6	36	7
1981—Pittsburgh NFL		16	242	987	4.1	8	37	250	6.8	1	9	54	6
1982—Pittsburgh NFL		9	140	604	4.3	2	31	249	8.0	0	2	12	1
1983—Pittsburgh NFL		16	279	1007	3.6	5	34	278	8.2	2	7	42	10
1984—Seattle NFL		8	68	170	2.5	0	1	3	3.0	0	0	0	0
Pro Totals—13 Years		173	2949	12120	4.1	91	307	2287	7.4	9	100	600	90

Year	Club	KICKOFF RETURNS G.	No.	Yds.	Avg.	TD.	Year	Club	KICKOFF RETURNS G.	No.	Yds.	Avg.	TD.
1972—Pittsburgh NFL		14	8	183	22.9	0	1979—Pittsburgh NFL		15		None		
1973—Pittsburgh NFL		12	1	23	23.0	0	1980—Pittsburgh NFL		13		None		
1974—Pittsburgh NFL		12		None			1981—Pittsburgh NFL		16		None		
1975—Pittsburgh NFL		14	1	27	27.0	0	1982—Pittsburgh NFL		9		None		
1976—Pittsburgh NFL		14		None			1983—Pittsburgh NFL		16		None		
1977—Pittsburgh NFL		14		None			1984—Seattle NFL		8		None		
1978—Pittsburgh NFL		16		None			Pro Totals—13 Years		173	10	233	23.3	0

Additional pro statistics: Recovered one fumble for minus five yards, 1972; recovered two fumbles, 1973, 1974 and 1976; recovered three fumbles, 1975; recovered one fumble and attempted one pass with no completions, 1978; recovered four fumbles, 1980.

Played in AFC Championship Game following 1972, 1974, 1975, 1978 and 1979 seasons.

Member of Pittsburgh Steelers for AFC Championship Game following 1976 season; did not play.

Played in NFL Championship Game following 1974, 1975, 1978 and 1979 seasons.

Played in Pro Bowl (NFL All-Star Game) following 1972 through 1975 and 1977 through 1980 seasons.

Named to Pro Bowl following 1976 season; replaced due to injury.

JAMES WARREN HART
(Jim)

Born April 29, 1944, at Evanston, Ill.

Height, 6.01. Weight, 210.

High School—Skokie, Ill., Niles West.

Received bachelor of science degree in education from Southern Illinois University in 1967.

Named to THE SPORTING NEWS NFC All-Star Team, 1974.

Established NFL record for longest non-scoring pass, 98 yards to Bobby Moore (Ahmad Rashad) vs. Los Angeles Rams, December 10, 1972.

Signed as free agent by St. Louis Cardinals, 1966.

Released by St. Louis Cardinals, February 1, 1984.

USFL rights traded by Oklahoma Outlaws to Denver Gold for 4th round pick in 1985 draft, February 2, 1984.

Signed by Washington Redskins, February 14, 1984.

Year	Club	G.	Att.	Cmp.	PASSING Pct.	Gain	T.P.	P.I.	Avg.	Att.	Yds.	RUSHING Avg.	TD.	TD.	TOTAL Pts.	F.
1966—St. Louis NFL		1	11	4	36.4	29	0	0	2.64			None		0	0	0
1967—St. Louis NFL		14	397	192	48.4	3008	19	*30	7.58	13	36	2.8	3	3	18	5
1968—St. Louis NFL		13	316	140	44.3	2059	15	18	6.52	19	20	1.1	6	6	36	3
1969—St. Louis NFL		9	169	84	49.7	1086	6	12	6.43	7	16	2.3	2	2	12	1
1970—St. Louis NFL		14	373	171	45.8	2575	14	18	6.90	18	18	1.0	0	0	0	6
1971—St. Louis NFL		11	243	110	45.3	1626	8	14	6.69	13	9	0.7	0	0	0	2
1972—St. Louis NFL		6	119	60	50.4	857	5	5	7.20	9	17	1.9	0	0	0	3
1973—St. Louis NFL		12	320	178	55.6	2223	15	10	6.95	3	—3	—1.0	0	0	0	2
1974—St. Louis NFL		14	*388	200	51.5	2411	20	8	6.21	10	21	2.1	2	2	12	5
1975—St. Louis NFL		14	345	182	52.8	2507	19	19	7.27	11	7	0.6	1	1	6	7
1976—St. Louis NFL		14	388	218	56.2	2946	18	13	7.59	8	7	0.9	0	0	0	4
1977—St. Louis NFL		14	355	186	52.4	2542	13	20	7.16	11	18	1.6	0	0	0	5
1978—St. Louis NFL		15	477	240	50.3	3121	16	18	6.54	11	11	1.0	2	2	12	5
1979—St. Louis NFL		14	378	194	51.3	2218	9	20	5.87	6	11	1.8	0	0	0	5
1980—St. Louis NFL		15	425	228	53.6	2946	16	20	6.93	9	11	1.2	0	0	0	4
1981—St. Louis NFL		10	241	134	55.6	1694	11	14	7.03	3	2	0.7	0	0	0	4
1982—St. Louis NFL		4	33	19	57.6	199	1	0	6.03			None		0	0	5
1983—St. Louis NFL		5	91	50	54.9	592	4	8	6.51	5	12	2.4	0	0	0	5
1984—Washington NFL		2	7	3	42.9	26	0	0	3.71	3	—6	—2.0	0	0	0	0
Pro Totals—19 Years		201	5076	2593	51.1	34665	209	247	6.83	159	207	1.3	16	16	96	66

Quarterback Rating Points: 1966 (44.9), 1967 (58.3), 1968 (58.1), 1969 (52.7), 1970 (61.7), 1971 (54.6), 1972 (70.6), 1973 (80.1), 1974 (79.5), 1975 (71.8), 1976 (81.7), 1977 (64.6), 1978 (66.8), 1979 (55.2), 1980 (68.7), 1981 (68.9), 1982 (85.2), 1983 (53.0), 1984 (53.3). Total—66.4.

Additional pro statistics: Recovered one fumble, 1971 and 1976; recovered two fumbles and fumbled three times for minus five yards, 1972; recovered one fumble and fumbled five times for minus three yards, 1974; recovered two fumbles and fumbled seven times for minus 11 yards, 1975; recovered three fumbles and fumbled five times for minus 12 yards, 1977; recovered two fumbles and fumbled five times for minus six yards, 1978; recovered one fumble, fumbled five times for minus seven yards and caught one pass for minus four yards, 1979; fumbled four times for minus five yards, 1980; fumbled four times for minus nine yards, 1981; recovered two fumbles, 1983.

Played in Pro Bowl (NFL All-Star Game) following 1974 through 1977 seasons.

LOUIE JAMES KELCHER

Born August 23, 1953, at Beaumont, Tex.
Height, 6.05. Weight, 310.
High School—Beaumont, Tex., French.
Attended Southern Methodist University.

Named to THE SPORTING NEWS AFC All-Star Team, 1977 and 1978.
Selected by San Diego in 2nd round (30th player selected) of 1975 NFL draft.
On injured reserve with knee injury, August 28 through December 6, 1979; activated, December 7, 1979.
Announced retirement, August 1, 1982; returned, August 19, 1982.
Released by San Diego Chargers, August 29, 1983; re-signed by Chargers, August 30, 1983.
On reserve/retired, November 17, 1983.
Traded from San Diego Chargers reserve list to San Francisco 49ers for 8th and 12th round picks in 1984 draft and 9th round pick in 1985 draft, March 28, 1984.
San Diego NFL, 1975 through 1983; San Francisco NFL, 1984.
Games: 1975 (13), 1976 (14), 1977 (12), 1978 (15), 1979 (1), 1980 (15), 1981 (14), 1982 (8), 1983 (8), 1984 (16). Total—116.
Pro statistics: Recovered one fumble, 1976, 1978, 1981 and 1982; recovered two fumbles, 1977 and 1980; intercepted one pass for no yards, 1978; intercepted one pass for two yards, 1980.
Played in NFC Championship Game following 1984 season.
Played in AFC Championship Game following 1980 and 1981 seasons.
Played in NFL Championship Game following 1984 season.
Played in Pro Bowl (NFL All-Star Game) following 1977, 1978 and 1980 seasons.

GREGORY PAUL LANDRY
(Greg)

Born December 18, 1946, at Nashua, N. H.
Height, 6.04. Weight, 210.
High School—Nashua, N. H.
Received bachelor of science degree in physical education from University of Massachusetts
and received master's degree in sports administration from Loyola University.

Selected by Detroit NFL in 1st round (11th player selected) of 1968 AFL-NFL draft.
Traded by Detroit Lions to Baltimore Colts for 4th and 5th round picks in 1979 draft and 3rd round pick in 1980 draft, April 29, 1979.
On injured reserve with back injury, November 25 through remainder of 1981 season.
Released by Baltimore Colts, July 23, 1982.
USFL rights traded by Boston Breakers to Chicago Blitz for rights to defensive tackles Mike Perko and Dean Prater, placekicker Rex Robinson and running back Darrell Smith, August 11, 1982.
Signed by Chicago Blitz, August 12, 1982.
On injured reserve with broken ankle, May 26 through remainder of 1983 season.
Franchise transferred to Arizona, September 30, 1983.
Granted free agency, November 30, 1984; signed by Chicago Bears, December 5, 1984.

Year Club	G.	Att.	Cmp.	Pct.	Gain	T.P.	P.I.	Avg.	Att.	Yds.	Avg.	TD.	TD.	Pts.	F.
1968—Detroit NFL	5	48	23	47.9	338	2	7	7.04	7	39	5.6	1	1	6	0
1969—Detroit NFL	10	160	80	50.0	853	4	10	5.33	33	243	7.4	1	1	6	2
1970—Detroit NFL	12	136	83	61.0	1072	9	5	7.88	35	350	10.0	1	1	6	3
1971—Detroit NFL	14	261	136	52.1	2237	16	13	8.57	76	530	7.0	3	3	18	5
1972—Detroit NFL	14	268	134	50.0	2066	18	17	7.71	81	524	6.5	9	9	54	3
1973—Detroit NFL	7	128	70	54.7	908	3	10	7.09	42	267	6.4	2	2	12	2
1974—Detroit NFL	5	82	49	59.8	572	3	3	6.98	22	95	4.3	1	1	6	2
1975—Detroit NFL	6	56	31	55.4	403	1	0	7.20	20	92	4.6	0	0	0	4
1976—Detroit NFL	14	291	168	57.7	2191	17	8	7.53	43	234	5.4	1	1	6	5
1977—Detroit NFL	11	240	135	56.3	1359	6	7	5.66	25	99	4.0	0	0	0	2
1978—Detroit NFL	5	77	48	62.3	452	1	1	5.87	5	29	5.8	0	0	0	3
1979—Baltimore NFL	16	457	270	59.1	2932	15	15	6.42	31	115	3.7	0	0	0	8
1980—Baltimore NFL	16	47	24	51.1	275	2	3	5.85	7	26	3.7	1	1	6	0
1981—Baltimore NFL	11	29	14	48.3	195	0	1	6.72	1	11	11.0	0	1	6	2
1983—Chicago USFL	12	344	188	56.3	2383	16	9	7.13	21	67	3.2	1	1	6	9
1984—Arizona USFL	16	449	283	63.0	3534	26	15	7.87	18	25	1.4	1	1	6	6
1984—Chicago NFL	1	20	11	55.0	199	1	3	9.95	2	1	0.5	1	1	6	0
NFL Totals—15 Years	147	2300	1276	55.5	16052	98	103	6.98	430	2655	6.2	21	22	132	41
USFL Totals—2 Years	28	793	471	59.4	5917	42	24	7.46	39	92	2.4	2	2	12	15
Pro Totals—17 Years	175	3093	1747	56.5	21969	140	127	7.10	469	2747	5.9	23	24	144	56

NFL Quarterback Rating Points: 1968 (45.8), 1969 (48.1), 1970 (92.3), 1971 (80.7), 1972 (72.0), 1973 (52.4), 1974 (77.9), 1975 (84.3), 1976 (89.6), 1977 (68.8), 1978 (77.4), 1979 (75.3), 1980 (56.7), 1981 (56.2), 1984 (66.5). Total—73.0.
USFL Quarterback Rating Points: 1984 (92.8).
Additional NFL statistics: Recovered four fumbles and fumbled five times for minus two yards, 1971; recovered one fumble, 1974; recovered two fumbles and fumbled four times for minus nine yards, 1975; recovered two fumbles and fumbled five times for minus 12 yards, 1976; recovered two fumbles, 1978; recovered three fumbles and fumbled eight times for minus 13 yards, 1979; recovered one fumble for 11 yards and a touchdown and fumbled twice, 1981.
Additional USFL statistics: Recovered five fumbles, 1983; recovered three fumbles, 1984.
Played in USFL Championship Game following 1984 season.
Member of Chicago Bears for NFC Championship Game following 1984 season; did not play.
Played in Pro Bowl (NFL All-Star Game) following 1971 season.

—DID YOU KNOW—

That 11 University of Wisconsin players were selected in the 1985 NFL draft?

RODNEY CORNELL PERRY
(Rod)
Born September 11, 1953, at Fresno, Calif.
Height, 5.09. Weight, 185.
High School—Fresno, Calif., Hoover.
Attended Fresno City College and University of Colorado.

Named to THE SPORTING NEWS NFC All-Star Team, 1978.
Selected by Los Angeles in 4th round (98th player selected) of 1975 NFL draft.
On injured reserve with knee injury, October 25 through November 23, 1979; activated, November 24, 1979.
Traded with 3rd round pick in 1984 draft by Los Angeles Rams to Detroit Lions for tight end David Hill, August 19, 1983.
Returned to Rams, August 22, 1983, after failing physical due to knee injury.
Released by Los Angeles Rams, August 26, 1983; signed as free agent by Cleveland Browns, August 30, 1983.
On injured reserve with dislocated shoulder, September 19 through October 18, 1984; activated, October 19, 1984.
USFL rights traded with rights to linebacker John Harper by Denver Gold to Memphis Showboats for rights to kicker Marco Morales and quarterback Steve Wray, January 3, 1985.

Year Club	G.	No.	Yds.	Avg.	TD.
1975—Los Angeles NFL	9		None		
1976—Los Angeles NFL	14	8	79	9.9	0
1977—Los Angeles NFL	5	1	0	0.0	0
1978—Los Angeles NFL	16	8	117	14.6	•3
1979—Los Angeles NFL	9		None		
1980—Los Angeles NFL	16	5	115	23.0	1
1981—Los Angeles NFL	16	3	18	6.0	0
1982—L.A. Rams NFL	9	3	57	19.0	0
1983—Cleveland NFL	16	1	21	21.0	0
1984—Cleveland NFL	8	1	17	17.0	0
Pro Totals—10 Years	118	30	424	14.1	4

Additional pro statistics: Recovered two fumbles for 25 yards, 1976; recovered one fumble, 1978 and 1983; recovered two fumbles for 41 yards, 1982.
Played in NFC Championship Game following 1975, 1976, 1978 and 1979 seasons.
Played in NFL Championship Game following 1979 season.
Played in Pro Bowl (NFL All-Star Game) following 1978 and 1980 seasons.

TERRY RICHARD SCHMIDT
Born May 28, 1952, at Columbus, Ind.
Height, 6.00. Weight, 185.
High School—Columbus, Ind., North.
Received bachelor of science degree in biology and pre-dental preparation
from Ball State University in 1974; attending dental school at Loyola (Ill.).

Selected by New Orleans in 5th round (121st player selected) of 1974 NFL draft.
Claimed on waivers by Chicago Bears from New Orleans Saints, September 7, 1976.

Year Club	G.	No.	Yds.	Avg.	TD.
1974—New Orleans NFL	9	4	27	6.8	1
1975—New Orleans NFL	13	1	37	37.0	0
1976—Chicago NFL	9		None		
1977—Chicago NFL	10		None		
1978—Chicago NFL	16	2	23	11.5	0
1979—Chicago NFL	16	6	44	7.3	1
1980—Chicago NFL	16	1	0	0.0	0
1981—Chicago NFL	16	2	4	2.0	0
1982—Chicago NFL	9	4	39	9.8	0
1983—Chicago NFL	13	5	31	6.2	1
1984—Chicago NFL	15	1	0	0.0	0
Pro Totals—11 Years	142	26	205	7.9	3

Additional pro statistics: Recovered one fumble, 1974, 1978, 1980 and 1981; returned one kickoff for 23 yards, 1974; returned 11 punts for 76 yards, returned two kickoffs for 54 yards, fumbled three times and recovered three fumbles, 1975.
Played in NFC Championship Game following 1984 season.

HERBERT CARNELL SCOTT JR.
Born January 18, 1953, at Virginia Beach, Va.
Height, 6.02. Weight, 263.
High School—Virginia Beach, Va., Kellam.
Attended Virginia Union University.

Named to THE SPORTING NEWS NFC All-Star Team, 1979.
Named to THE SPORTING NEWS NFL All-Star Team, 1981.
Selected by Dallas in 13th round (330th player selected) of 1975 NFL draft.
On inactive list, September 13 and September 19, 1982.
Dallas NFL, 1975 through 1984.
Games: 1975 (14), 1976 (14), 1977 (11), 1978 (16), 1979 (16), 1980 (16), 1981 (16), 1982 (6), 1983 (16), 1984 (15).
Total—140.
Pro statistics: Recovered one fumble, 1982 and 1983.
Played in NFC Championship Game following 1975, 1977, 1978 and 1980 through 1982 seasons.
Played in NFL Championship Game following 1975, 1977 and 1978 seasons.
Played in Pro Bowl (NFL All-Star Game) following 1979 through 1981 seasons.

SHERMAN SMITH

Born November 1, 1954, at Youngstown, O.
Height, 6.04. Weight, 225.
High School—Youngstown, O., North.
Received degree in education from Miami (Ohio) University.
Cousin of Mike Cobb, tight end with Birmingham Stallions.

Selected by Seattle in 2nd round (58th player selected) of 1976 NFL draft.
On injured reserve with knee injury, October 25 through remainder of 1980 season.
Traded by Seattle Seahawks to Kansas City Chiefs for conditional draft pick, August 8, 1983; deal voided August 12, 1983, after failing physical with neck injury.
On non-football injury list with neck injury, August 18 through August 26, 1983.
Traded by Seattle Seahawks to San Diego Chargers, August 27, 1983, as part of deal that sent wide receiver Roger Carr to Chargers for 5th round pick in 1984 draft, August 24, 1983.
On physically unable to perform/reserve with knee injury, July 21 through entire 1984 season.
Granted free agency after not receiving qualifying offer, February 1, 1985.

			——RUSHING——				PASS RECEIVING				—TOTAL—		
Year	Club	G.	Att.	Yds.	Avg.	TD.	P.C.	Yds.	Avg.	TD.	TD.	Pts.	F.
1976—Seattle NFL		12	119	537	4.5	4	36	384	10.7	1	5	30	8
1977—Seattle NFL		14	163	763	4.7	4	30	419	14.0	2	6	36	6
1978—Seattle NFL		12	165	805	4.9	6	28	366	13.1	1	7	42	3
1979—Seattle NFL		16	194	775	4.0	11	48	499	10.4	4	15	90	1
1980—Seattle NFL		3	23	94	4.1	0	6	72	12.0	1	1	6	0
1981—Seattle NFL		16	83	253	3.0	3	44	406	9.2	1	4	24	3
1982—Seattle NFL		9	63	202	3.2	0	19	196	10.3	0	0	0	1
1983—San Diego NFL		13	24	91	3.8	0	6	51	8.5	0	0	0	2
Pro Totals—8 Years		95	834	3520	4.2	28	217	2393	11.0	10	38	228	24

			KICKOFF RETURNS			
Year	Club	G.	No.	Yds.	Avg.	TD.
1976—Seattle NFL		12	5	78	15.6	0
1977—Seattle NFL		14	3	56	18.7	0
1978—Seattle NFL		12		None		
1979—Seattle NFL		16		None		
1980—Seattle NFL		3		None		
1981—Seattle NFL		16		None		
1982—Seattle NFL		9		None		
1983—San Diego NFL		13	2	32	16.0	0
Pro Totals—8 Years		95	10	166	16.6	0

Additional pro statistics: Recovered one fumble, 1976 through 1980, 1982 and 1983; attempted two passes with no completions, 1976; attempted one pass with no completions, 1977, 1982 and 1983; attempted one pass with one completion for 11 yards, 1979; recovered two fumbles, 1981.

KEN MICHAEL STABLER

Born December 25, 1945, at Foley, Ala.
Height, 6.03. Weight, 210.
High School—Foley, Ala.
Received degree in physical education from University of Alabama.

Named AFC Player of the Year by THE SPORTING NEWS, 1974 and 1976.
Named to THE SPORTING NEWS AFC All-Star Team, 1974 and 1976.
Led NFL in passing with 103.7 points in 1976.
Selected by Oakland AFL in 2nd round (52nd player selected) of 1968 AFL-NFL draft.
Member of Oakland Raiders' taxi squad, 1968.
Did not play in 1969.
Traded by Oakland Raiders to Houston Oilers for quarterback Dan Pastorini, March 17, 1980.
Released by Houston Oilers, July 15, 1982; signed as free agent by New Orleans Saints, August 24, 1982.
Retired, October 26, 1984.
Played in Continental Football League with Spokane Shockers, 1968.
Selected by New York Yankees' organization in 10th round of free-agent draft, June 13, 1966.

			——————PASSING——————							——RUSHING——				—TOTAL—		
Year	Club	G.	Att.	Cmp.	Pct.	Gain	T.P.	P.I.	Avg.	Att.	Yds.	Avg.	TD.	TD.	Pts.	F.
1968—Spokane CoFL		1	41	17	34.1	125	0	3	3.05			None		0	0	....
1970—Oakland NFL		3	7	2	28.6	52	0	1	7.43	1	—4	—4.0	0	0	0	1
1971—Oakland NFL		14	48	24	50.0	268	1	4	5.58	4	29	7.3	2	2	12	1
1972—Oakland NFL		14	74	44	59.5	524	4	3	7.08	6	27	4.5	0	0	0	2
1973—Oakland NFL		14	260	163	*62.7	1997	14	10	7.68	21	101	4.8	0	0	0	5
1974—Oakland NFL		14	310	178	57.4	2469	*26	12	7.96	12	—2	—0.2	1	1	6	3
1975—Oakland NFL		14	293	171	58.4	2296	16	24	7.84	6	—5	—0.8	0	0	0	4
1976—Oakland NFL		12	291	194	*66.7	2737	27	17	*9.41	7	—2	—0.3	1	1	6	5
1977—Oakland NFL		13	294	169	57.5	2176	20	20	7.40	3	—3	—1.0	0	0	0	3
1978—Oakland NFL		16	406	237	58.4	2944	16	30	7.25	4	0	0.0	0	0	0	9
1979—Oakland NFL		16	498	304	61.0	3615	26	22	7.26	16	—4	—0.3	0	0	0	10
1980—Houston NFL		16	457	293	64.1	3202	13	28	7.01	15	—22	—1.5	0	0	0	7
1981—Houston NFL		13	285	165	57.9	1988	14	18	6.98	10	—3	—0.3	0	0	0	7
1982—New Orleans NFL		8	189	117	61.9	1343	6	10	7.11	3	—4	—1.3	0	0	0	4
1983—New Orleans NFL		14	311	176	56.6	1988	9	18	6.39	9	—14	—1.6	0	0	0	4
1984—New Orleans NFL		3	70	33	47.1	339	2	5	4.84	1	—1	—1.0	0	0	0	1
Pro Totals—15 Years		184	3793	2270	59.8	27938	194	222	7.37	118	93	0.8	4	4	24	66

Quarterback Rating Points: 1970 (18.5), 1971 (39.4), 1972 (95.8), 1973 (88.5), 1974 (94.8), 1975 (67.6), 1976 (103.7), 1977 (75.2), 1978 (63.1), 1979 (82.2), 1980 (68.6), 1981 (69.5), 1982 (71.9), 1983 (61.4), 1984 (41.3). Total—75.1.

Additional pro statistics: Recovered one fumble and fumbled once for minus ten yards, 1971; recovered two fumbles, 1972, 1975, 1980 and 1981; recovered one fumble and fumbled five times for minus one yard, 1973; recovered one fumble and fumbled three times for minus 11 yards, 1974; fumbled four times for minus two yards, 1975; recovered one fumble, 1976; fumbled three times for minus three yards, 1977; recovered one fumble and fumbled nine times for minus four yards, 1978; recovered five fumbles and fumbled 10 times for minus 30 yards, 1979; fumbled seven times for minus 16 yards, 1980; fumbled seven times for minus 13 yards, 1981.

Played in AFC Championship Game following 1973 through 1977 seasons.
Played in NFL Championship Game following 1976 season.
Played in Pro Bowl (NFL All-Star Game) following 1973, 1974 and 1977 seasons.

ROBERT CHARLES SWENSON
(Bob)
Born July 1, 1953, at Stockton, Calif.
Height, 6.03. Weight, 225.
High School—Tracy, Calif.
Received degree in marketing from University of California at Berkeley.

Named to THE SPORTING NEWS NFL All-Star Team, 1981.
Signed as free agent by Denver Broncos, 1975.
On injured reserve with broken arm, September 2, through entire 1980 season.
Granted free agency, February 1, 1982.
On did not report list, August 21 through November 22, 1982.
Signed by Denver Broncos, November 23, 1982 and granted two-game exemption; activated, December 7, 1982.
On injured reserve with knee injury, September 13 through remainder of 1983 season.
On injured reserve with knee injury, August 28 through entire 1984 season.

Year Club	G.	No.	Yds.	Avg.	TD.
1975—Denver NFL	14	1	4	4.0	0
1976—Denver NFL	14	2	31	15.5	0
1977—Denver NFL	14	1	0	0.0	0
1978—Denver NFL	16	1	0	0.0	0
1979—Denver NFL	16	3	0	0.0	0
1981—Denver NFL	16	3	53	17.7	0
1982—Denver NFL	4		None		
1983—Denver NFL	2		None		
Pro Totals—8 Years	96	11	88	8.0	0

Additional pro statistics: Recovered one fumble for five yards, 1976; recovered one fumble for four yards, 1978; recovered four fumbles for 93 yards and one touchdown and fumbled once, 1979; recovered three fumbles, 1981.
Played in AFC Championship Game following 1977 season.
Played in NFL Championship Game following 1977 season.
Played in Pro Bowl (NFL All-Star Game) following 1981 season.

MICHAEL LEE WASHINGTON
(Mike)
Born July 1, 1953, at Montgomery, Ala.
Height, 6.02. Weight, 200.
High Schools—Montgomery, Ala., Robert E. Lee and Booker T. Washington.
Received degree in education from University of Alabama.

Selected by Baltimore in 3rd round (53rd player selected) of 1975 NFL draft.
Missed entire 1975 season due to knee injury.
Traded by Baltimore Colts to Tampa Bay Buccaneers for 3rd round pick in 1976 draft, April 2, 1976.
On injured reserve with knee injury, October 12 through remainder of 1976 season.
On injured reserve with broken ribs, November 11 through December 11, 1983; activated, December 12, 1983.
On injured reserve with neck injury, September 4 through remainder of 1984 season.
Released injured by Tampa Bay Buccaneers, May 8, 1985.

Year Club	G.	No.	Yds.	Avg.	TD.
1976—Tampa Bay NFL	5		None		
1977—Tampa Bay NFL	14	5	71	14.2	1
1978—Tampa Bay NFL	16	5	43	8.6	0
1979—Tampa Bay NFL	15	3	64	21.3	1
1980—Tampa Bay NFL	16	4	30	7.5	0
1981—Tampa Bay NFL	14	6	156	26.0	1
1982—Tampa Bay NFL	8	3	13	4.3	0
1983—Tampa Bay NFL	10	2	41	20.5	0
1984—Tampa Bay NFL	1		None		
Pro Totals—9 Years	99	28	418	14.9	3

Additional pro statistics: Recovered one fumble, 1977 and 1981; returned one missed field goal for 79 yards and a touchdown, 1978.
Played in NFC Championship Game following 1979 season.

—DID YOU KNOW—
That Southern California had three players picked on the first round of the NFL draft in three consecutive years (1980-83)?